Collins LONDON

D0505637

CONTENTS

Key to Map Pages 2-3

Key to Map Symbols 4-5

Central London Maps 6-37

Main London Maps 38-207

Theatres and Cinemas Map 208

Shopping Map 209

Index to Places of Interest 210-211

Index to Place Names 212-213

Index to Street Names 214-376

Published by Collins
An imprint of HarperCollins*Publishers*
77-85 Fulham Palace Road, Hammersmith, London
W6 8JB

The HarperCollins website address is:
www.**fire**and**water**.com

Copyright © HarperCollins*Publishers* Ltd 2001
Mapping © Bartholomew Ltd 1998, 2000, 2001

Collins® is a registered trademark of
HarperCollins*Publishers* Limited

Mapping generated from Bartholomew digital databases

Bartholomew website address is:
www.bartholomewmaps.com

London Underground Map by permission of London
Regional Transport LRT Registered User No. 00/3264

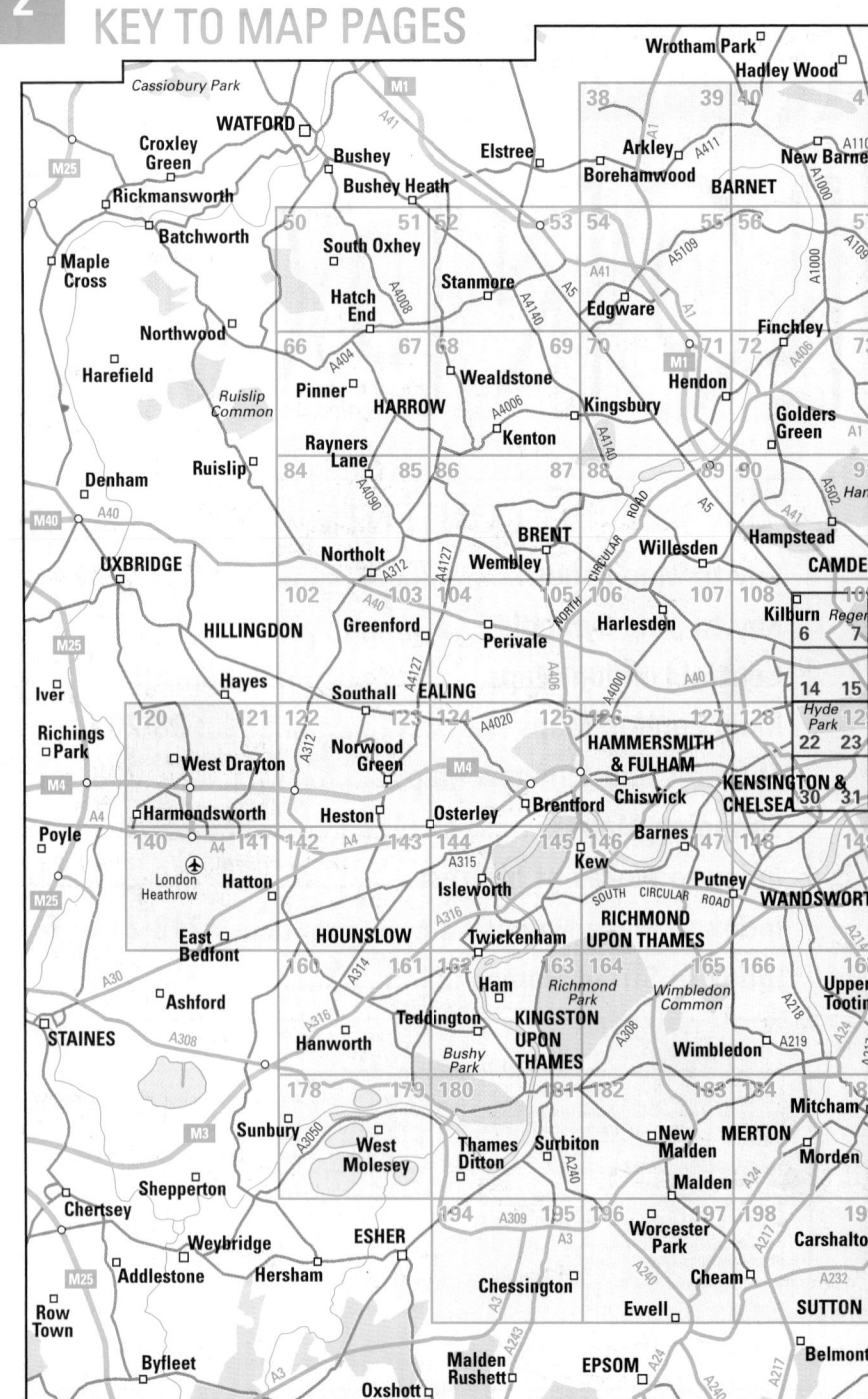

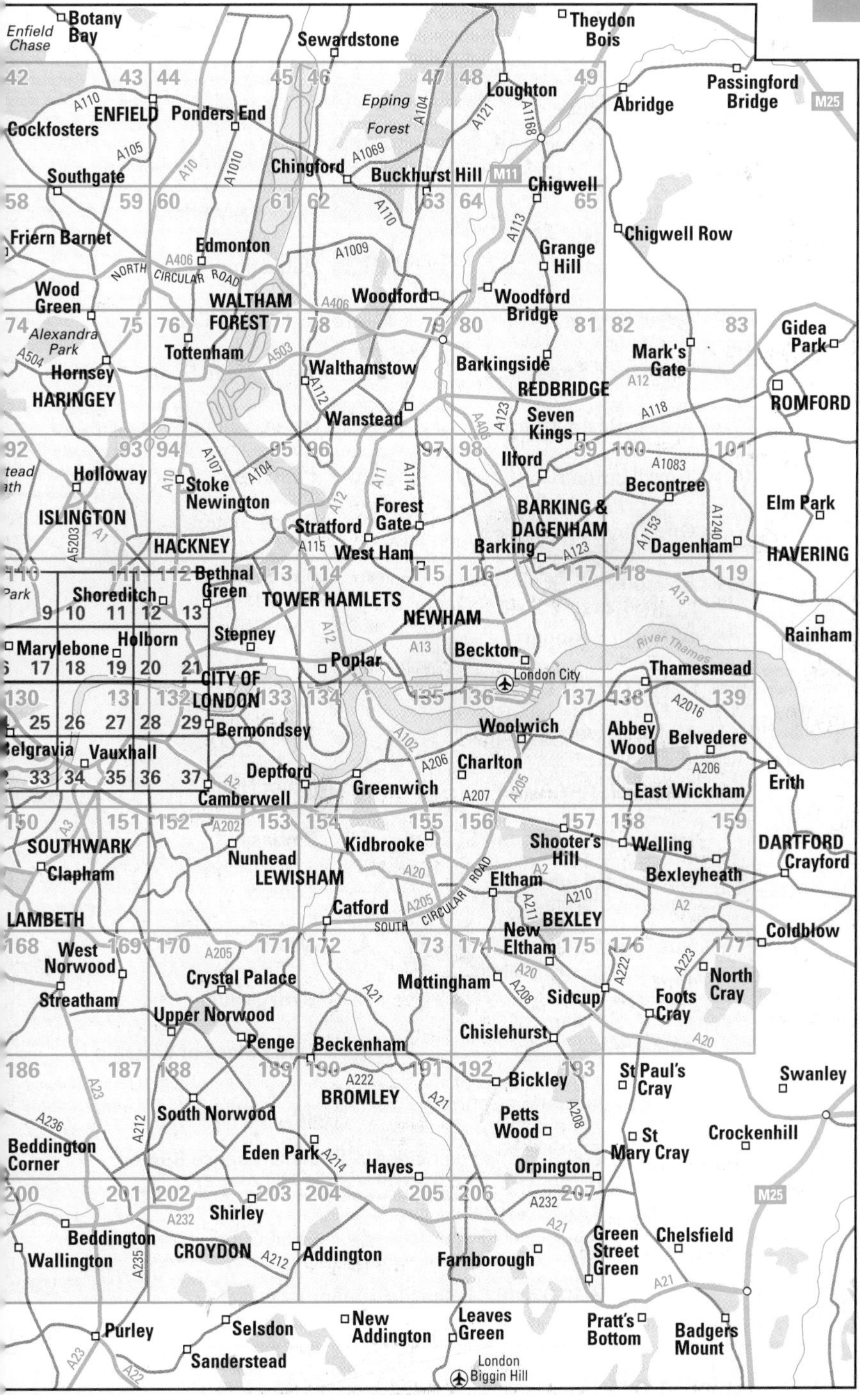

Enfield Chase
Botany Bay
Sewardstone
Theydon Bois

42 43 44 45 46 47 48 49
Epping Forest
Loughton
Passingford Bridge
M25
A110 ENFIELD Ponders End A104 A121 A1168 Abridge
Cockfosters A1069
A105 Chingford A1069 Buckhurst Hill M11 Chigwell
Southgate A10 A1010 A110 A113 Chigwell Row

58 59 60 61 62 63 64 65
Friern Barnet Edmonton A1009 Grange Hill
Wood Green NORTH CIRCULAR ROAD A406 Woodford Woodford Bridge
WALTHAM FOREST A406

74 75 76 77 78 79 80 81 82 83
Alexandra Park Tottenham A503 Walthamstow Barkingside Mark's Gate Gidea Park
A504 Hornsey A112 REDBRIDGE A12 ROMFORD
HARINGEY Wanstead A123 Seven Kings A118

92 93 94 95 96 97 98 99 100 101
tead th Holloway Stoke Newington A10 A107 A104 A11 A114 Ilford A1083 Becontree Elm Park
ISLINGTON A5203 A1 HACKNEY A12 Forest Gate A1153 Dagenham A1240 HAVERING
Stratford A115 West Ham BARKING & DAGENHAM
Barking A123

110 111 112 113 114 115 116 117 118 119
Park Shoreditch Bethnal Green TOWER HAMLETS River Thames Rainham
9 10 11 12 13 Stepney NEWHAM
Marylebone Holborn Poplar A12 A13 Beckton
17 18 19 20 21 CITY OF LONDON Thamesmead
130 131 132 133 134 135 136 137 138 139
25 26 27 28 29 Bermondsey London City
Belgravia Vauxhall A102 Woolwich Abbey Wood Belvedere A2016
33 34 35 36 37 Deptford A206 Charlton East Wickham Erith
Camberwell Greenwich A205 A207 A206

150 151 152 153 154 155 156 157 158 159
SOUTHWARK A202 Kidbrooke Shooter's Hill Welling DARTFORD
Clapham Nunhead LEWISHAM A20 Eltham CIRCULAR ROAD Bexleyheath Crayford
LAMBETH Catford A205 SOUTH A211 BEXLEY A2 Coldblow
A210

168 169 170 171 172 173 174 175 176 177
West Norwood A205 New Eltham North Cray
Streatham Crystal Palace A21 Mottingham A208 Sidcup A222 A223 Foots Cray
Upper Norwood Penge Beckenham Chislehurst A20

186 187 188 189 190 191 192 193
BROMLEY A222 Bickley St Paul's Cray Swanley
South Norwood A212 Petts Wood St Mary Cray Crockenhill
Beddington Corner Eden Park A214 Hayes A21 Orpington M25
A236 A23

200 201 202 203 204 205 206 207
Shirley A232 Green Street Green Chelsfield
Beddington CROYDON A212 Addington Farnborough A232 A21
Wallington A235

Purley Selsdon New Addington Leaves Green Pratt's Bottom Badgers Mount
Sanderstead A22 A23 London Biggin Hill

4

KEY TO CENTRAL MAP SYMBOLS

M4	Motorway		Leisure & Tourism
Dual **A4**	Primary Route		Shopping
Dual **A40**	'A' Road		Administration
B504	'B' Road		Health & Welfare
	Other Road		Education
	Street Market		Industry & Commerce
	Pedestrian Street		Public Open Space
•————————•	Access Restriction		Park/Garden/Sports Ground
======= -------	Track/Footpath		Cemetery
→	One Way Street	▪ *POL*	Police Station
– – – – – –	Riverbus	▪ Fire Sta	Fire Station
CITY	Borough Boundary	▪ *PO*	Post Office
EC2	Postal District Boundary	▦	Cinema
—▦—	Main Railway Station	▢	Theatre
—▧—	Other Railway Station	⊠	Major Hotel
⬤	London Underground Station	⊐	Embassy
-DLR-	Docklands Light Railway Station	+	Church
➤	Bus/Coach Station	☾	Mosque
P	Car Park	✡	Synagogue
WC	Public Toilet	Mormon ▪	Other Place of Worship
i	Tourist Information Centre		

The reference grid on this atlas coincides with the Ordnance Survey
National Grid System. The grid interval is 250 metres.

A	Grid Reference	**8**	Page Continuation Number

Scale 1:10,000 (6.3 inches to 1 mile)

0   0.25   0.50   0.75   1 kilometre

0   ¼   ½ mile

KEY TO MAIN MAP SYMBOLS

M4	Motorway		Leisure & Tourism
Dual A4	Primary Route	USA	Administration & Law Embassy
Dual A40	'A' Road		Health & Welfare
B504	'B' Road		Education
	Other Road		Industry & Commerce
	Toll		Cemetery
	Street Market		Golf Course
	Pedestrian Street		Public Open Space/ Allotments
	Cycle Path		Park/Garden/Sports Ground
-------	Track/Footpath		Wood/Forest
→	One Way Street	Pol	Police Station
_P_	Pedestrian Ferry	Fire Sta	Fire Station
_V_	Vehicle Ferry	PO	Post Office
	County/Borough Boundary	Lib	Library
	Postal District Boundary	▲	Youth Hostel
	Main Railway Station	□	Tower Block
	Other Railway Station	i	Tourist Information Centre
	London Underground Station	Ⓗ	Heliport
DLR	Docklands Light Railway Station	wc	Public Toilet
	Tramway Station	+	Church
	Bus/Coach Station	☾	Mosque
P	Car Park	✡	Synagogue

The reference grid on this atlas coincides with the Ordnance Survey
National Grid System. The grid interval is 500 metres.

A	Grid Reference	24	Page Continuation Number

Scale 1:20,000 (3.2 inches to 1 mile)

25	OS National Grid Kilometre Square

0	0.25	0.50	0.75	1 kilometre
0		¼		½ mile

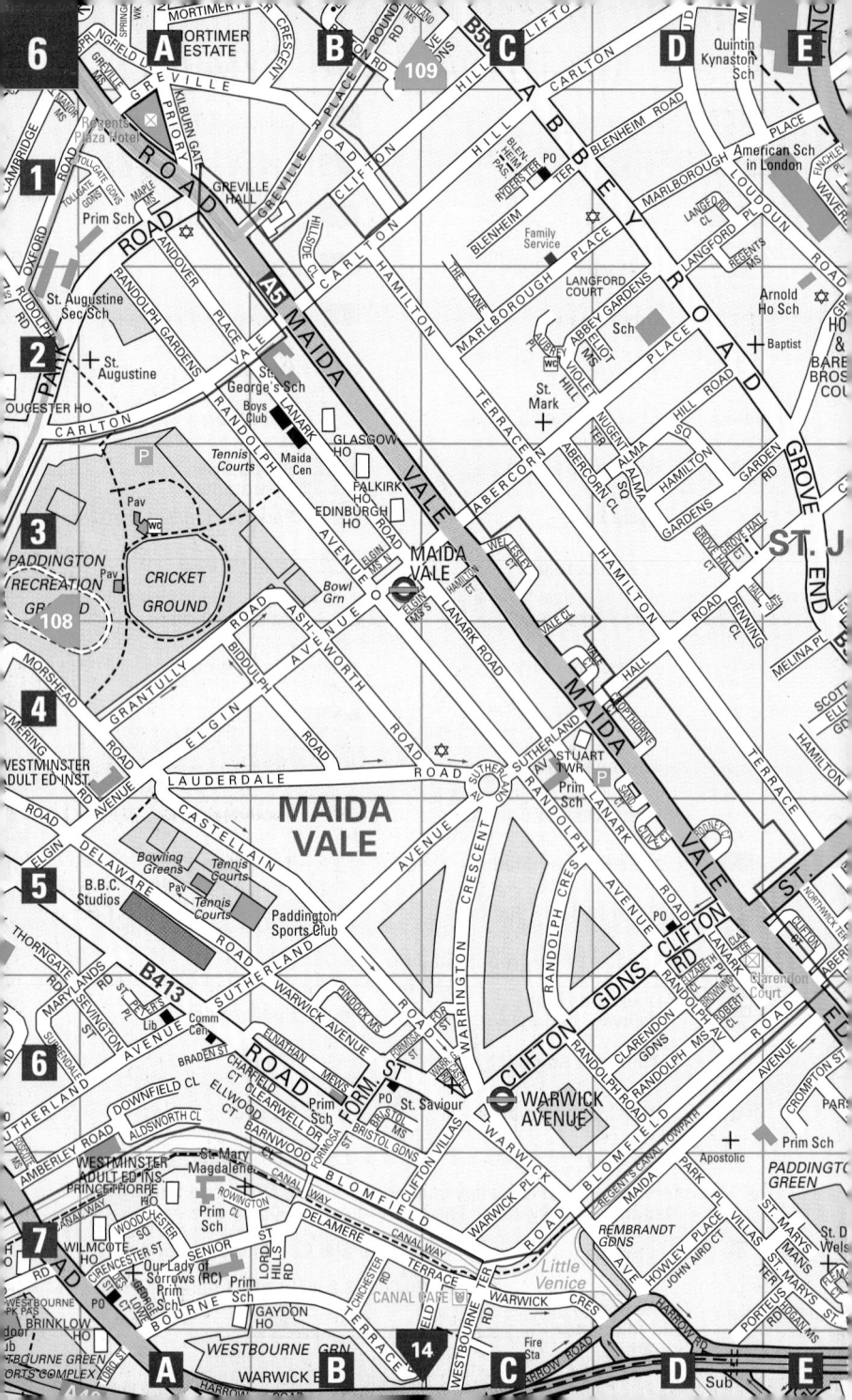

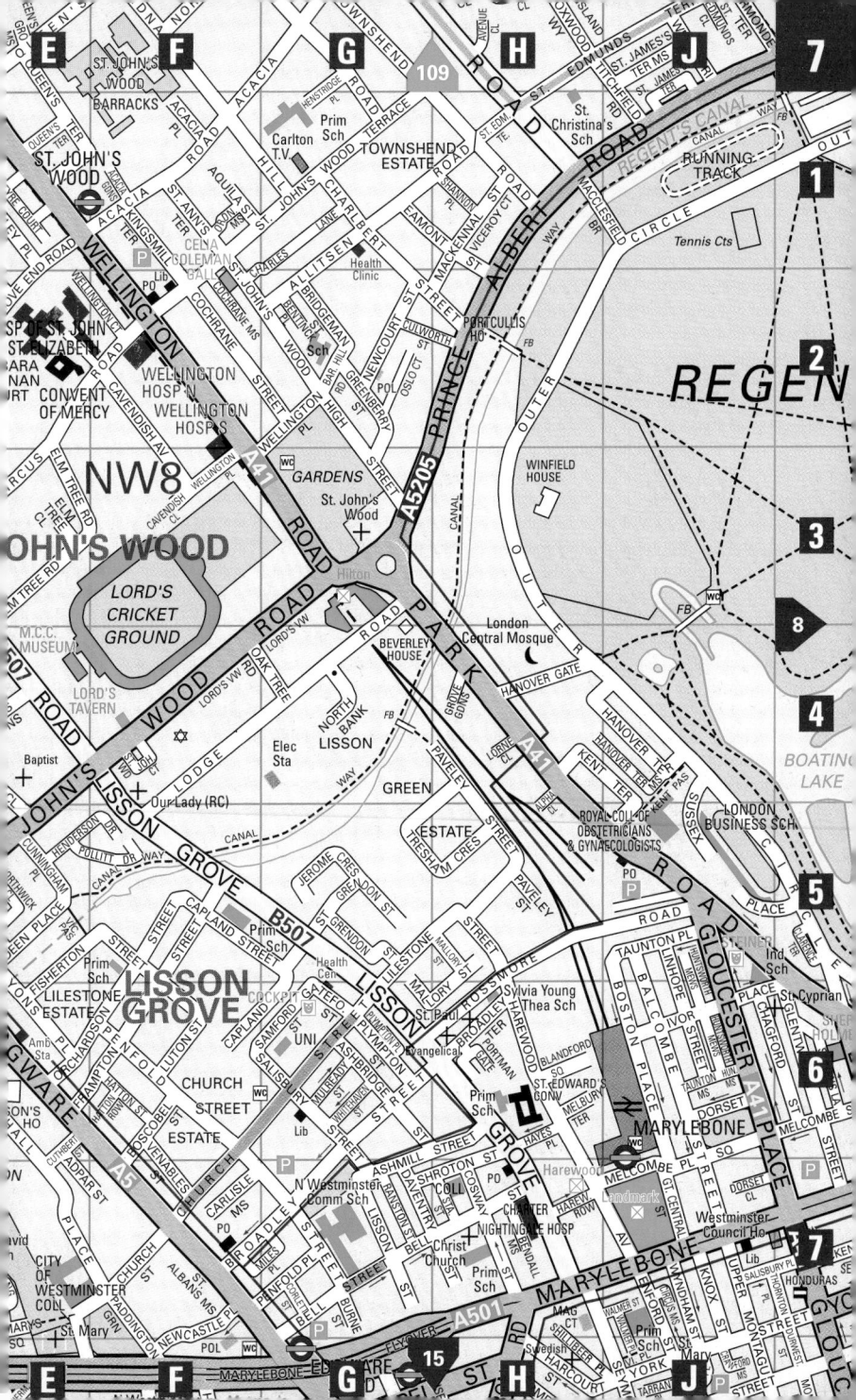

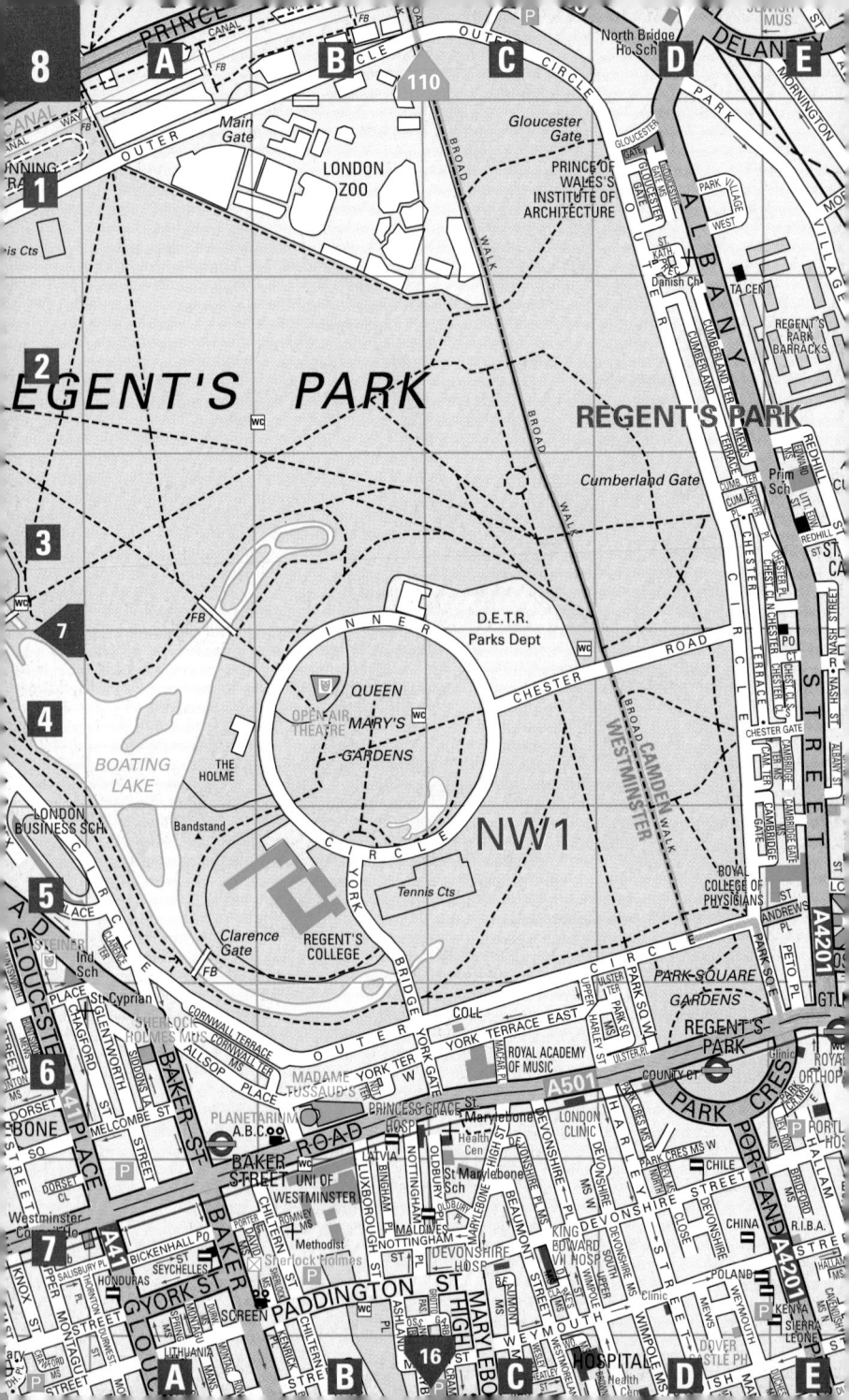

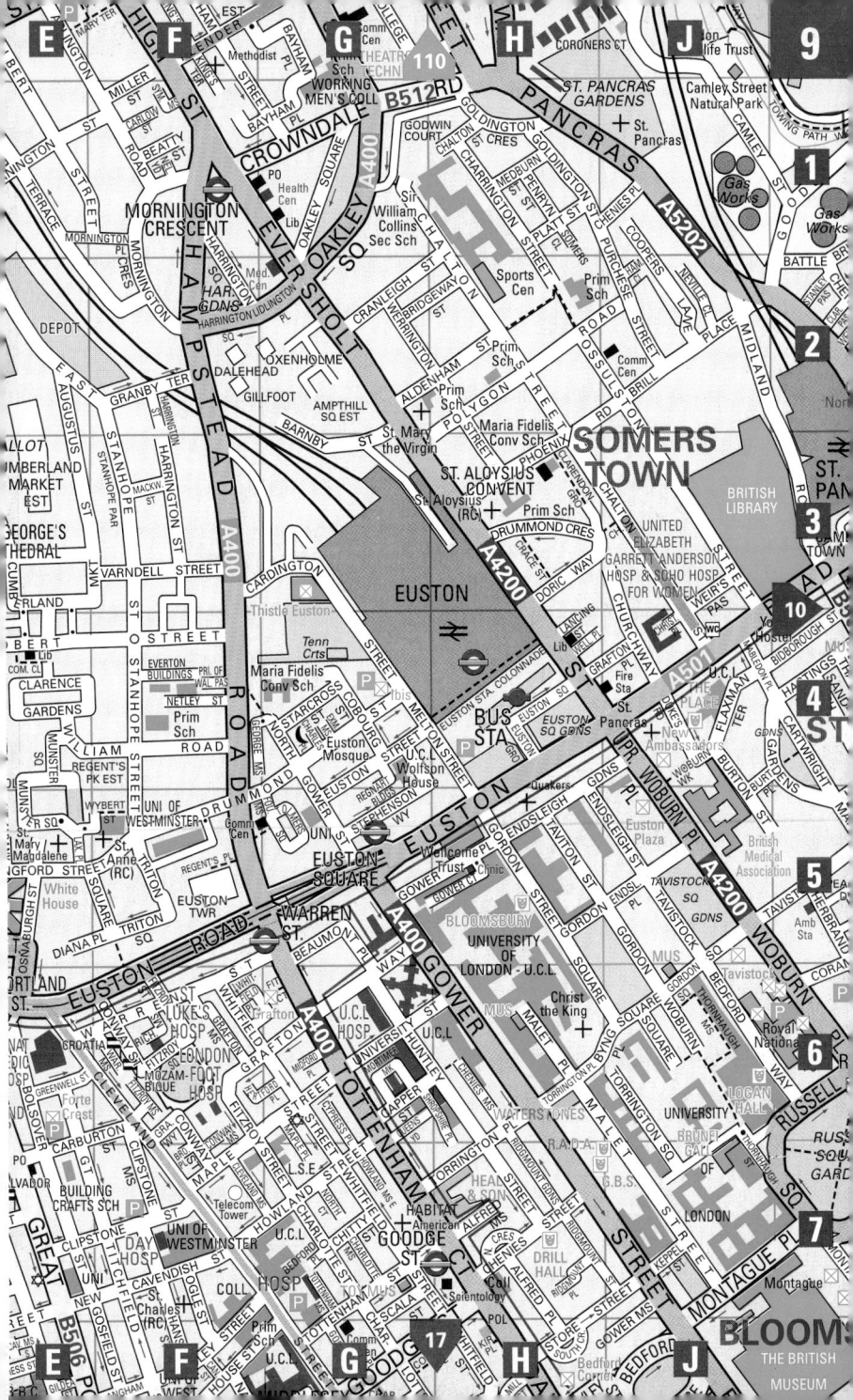

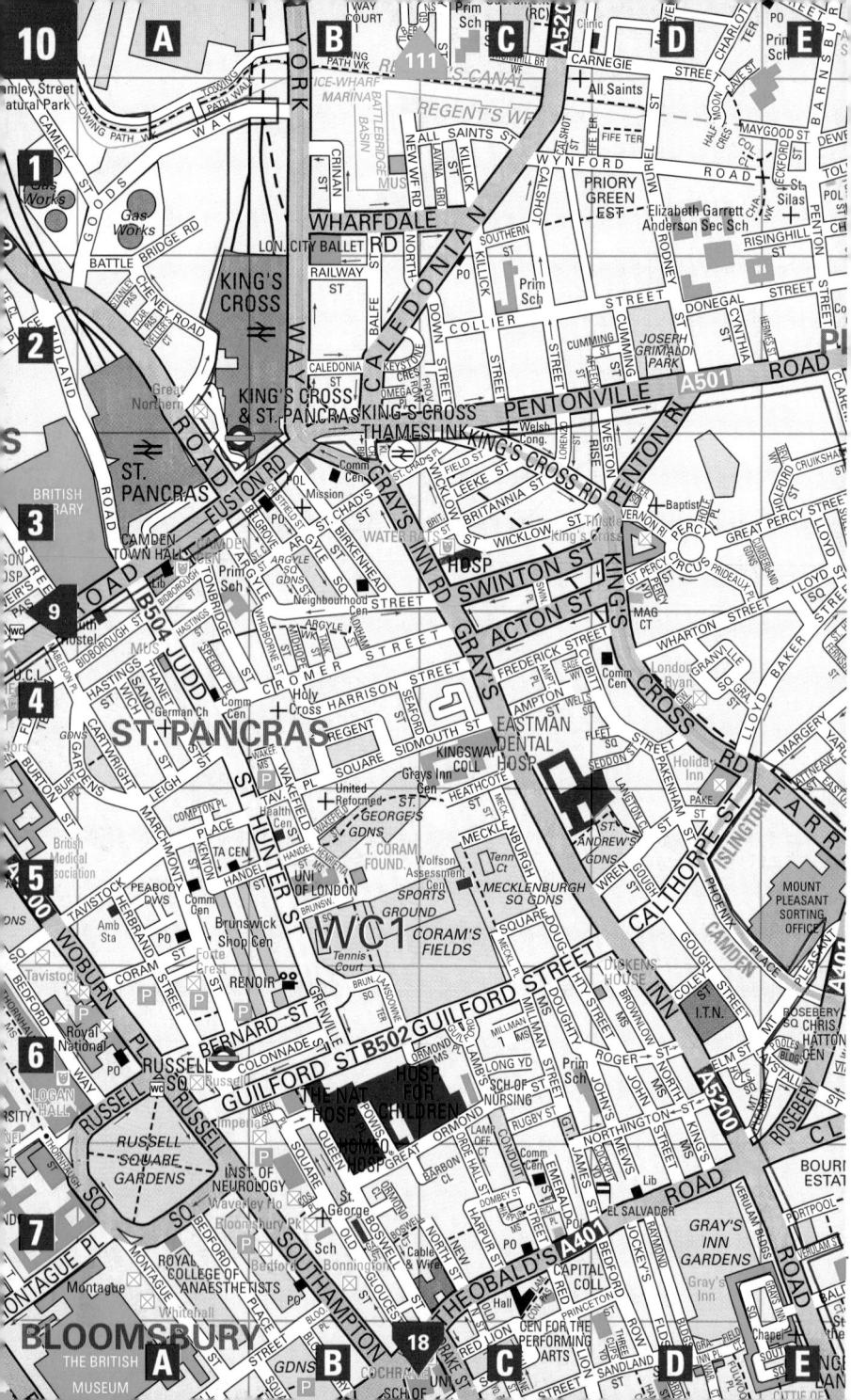

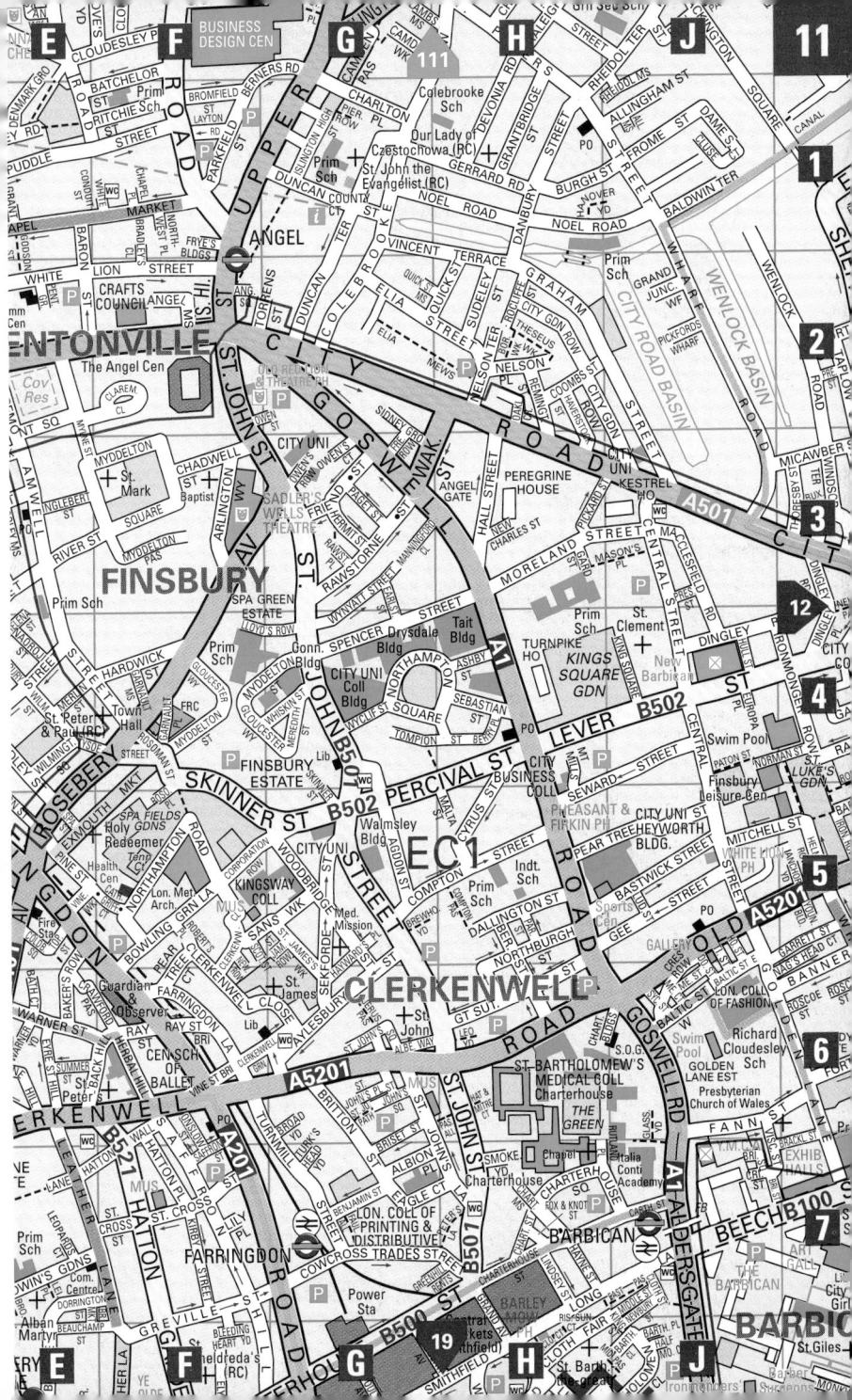

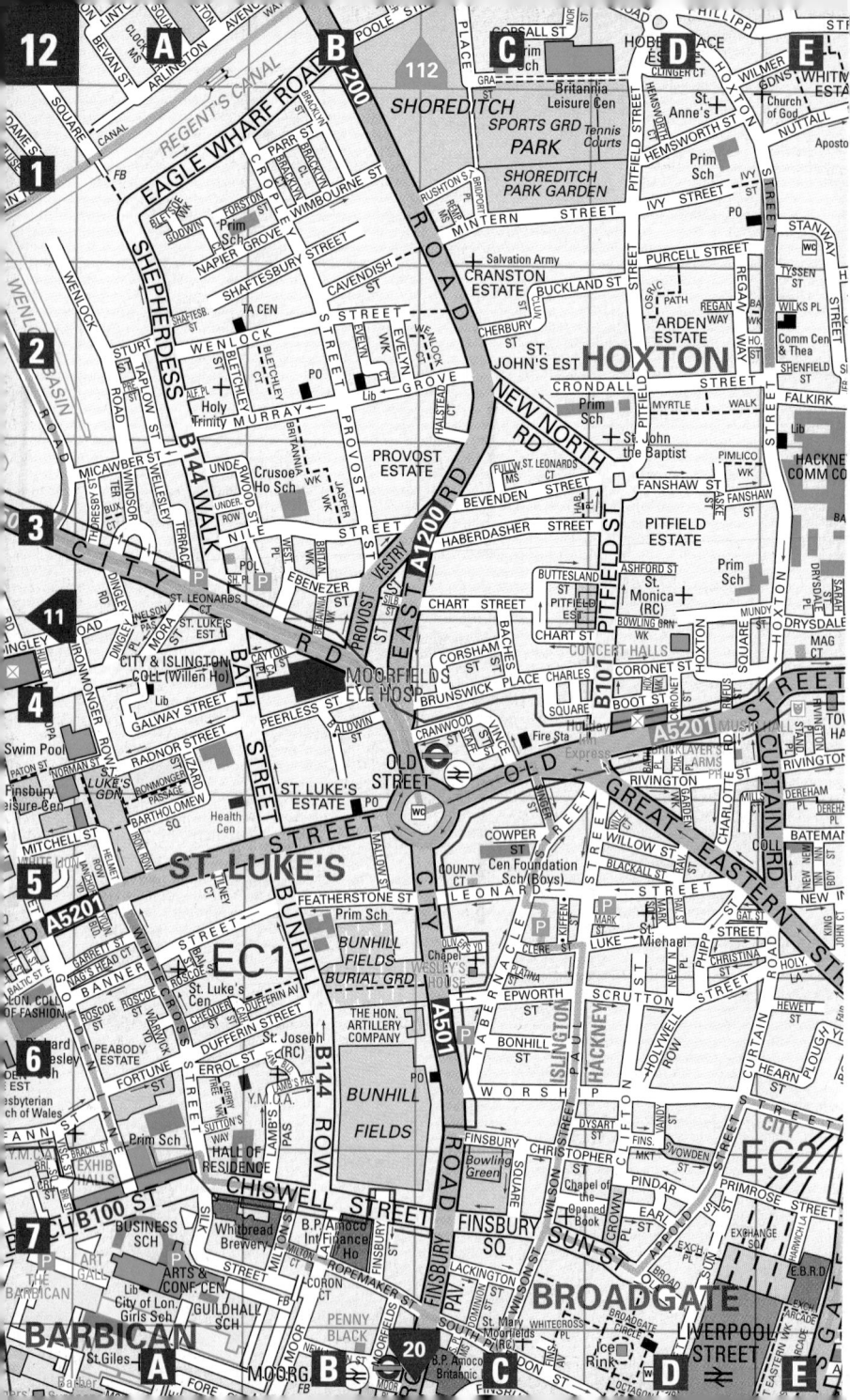

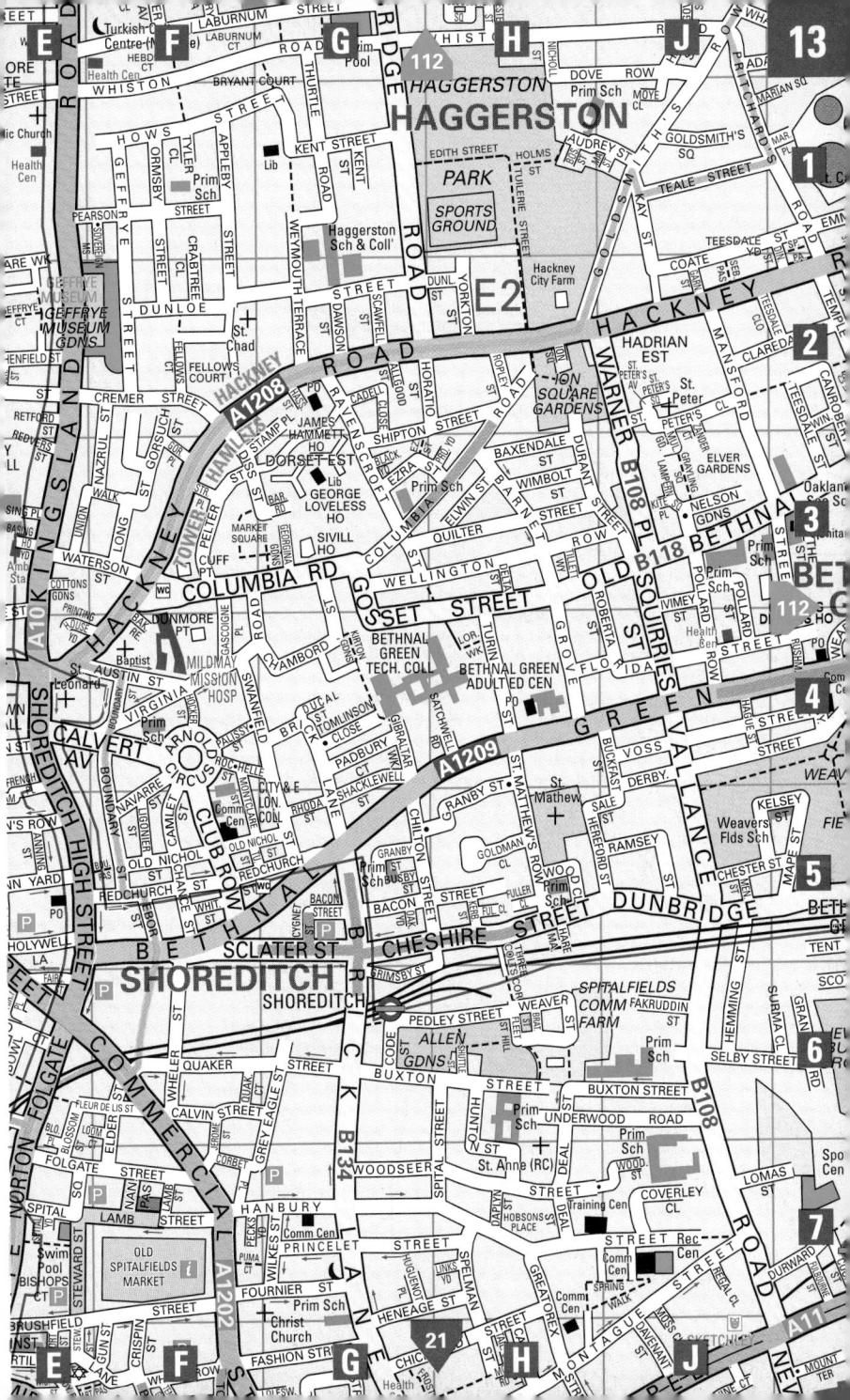

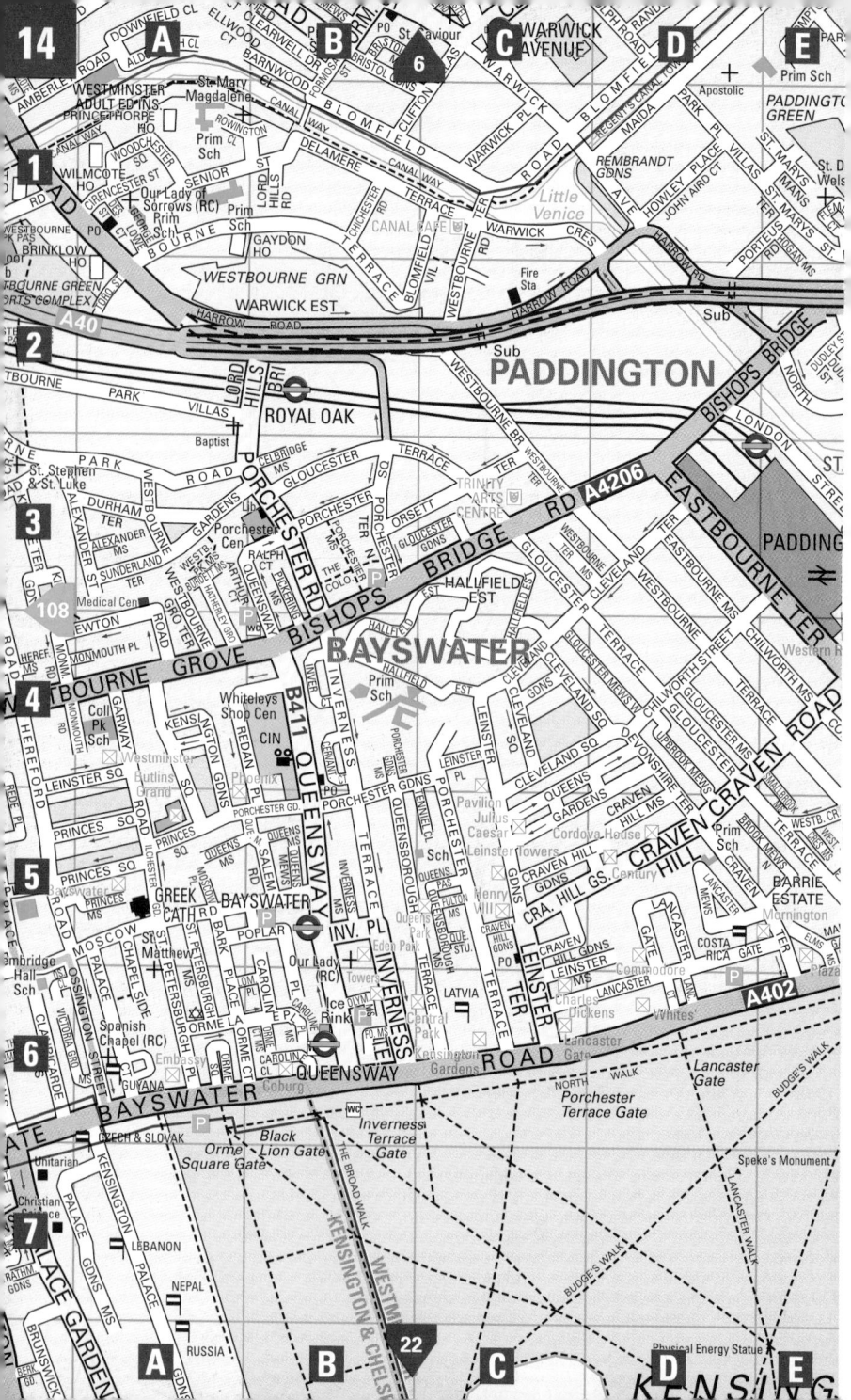

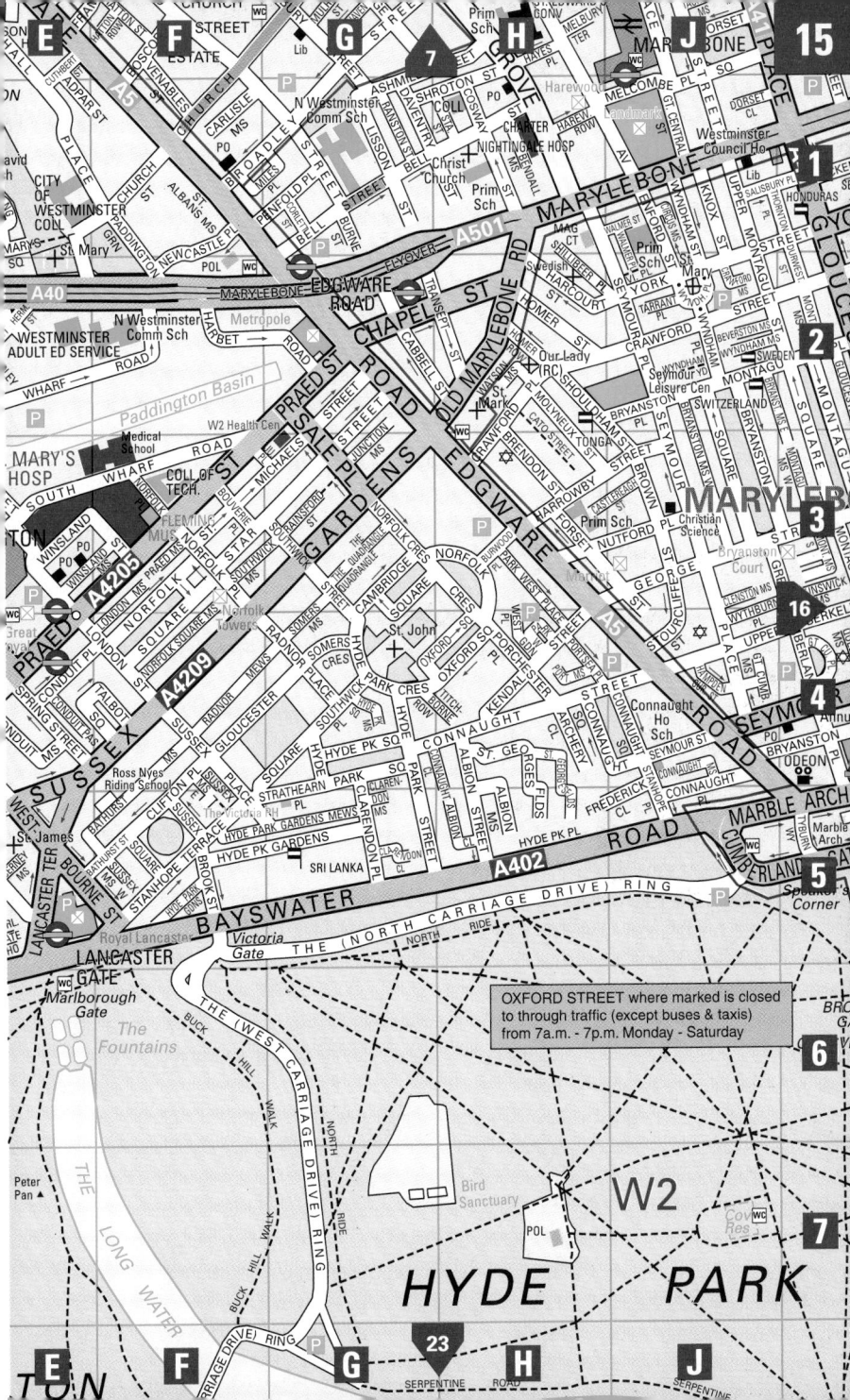

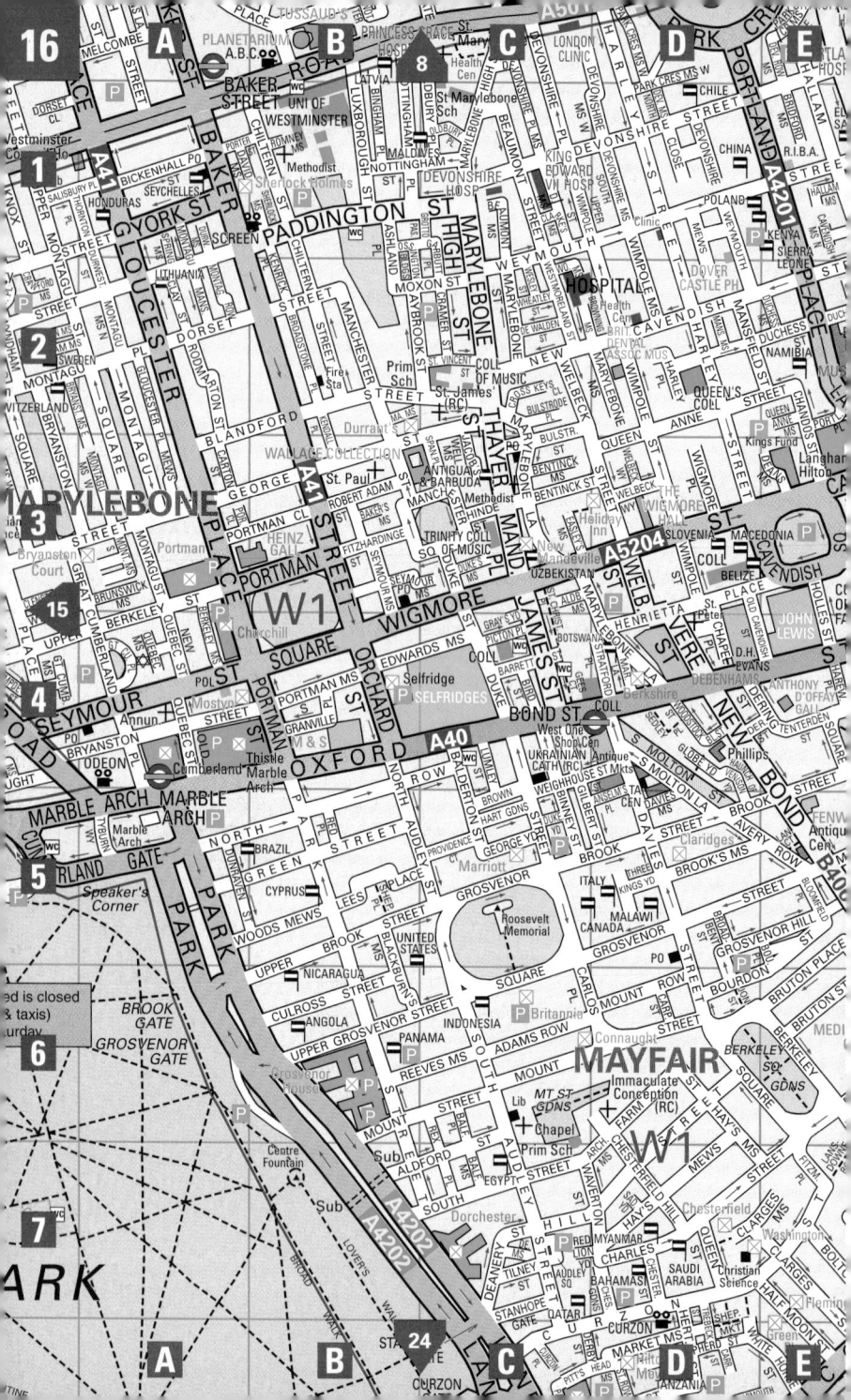

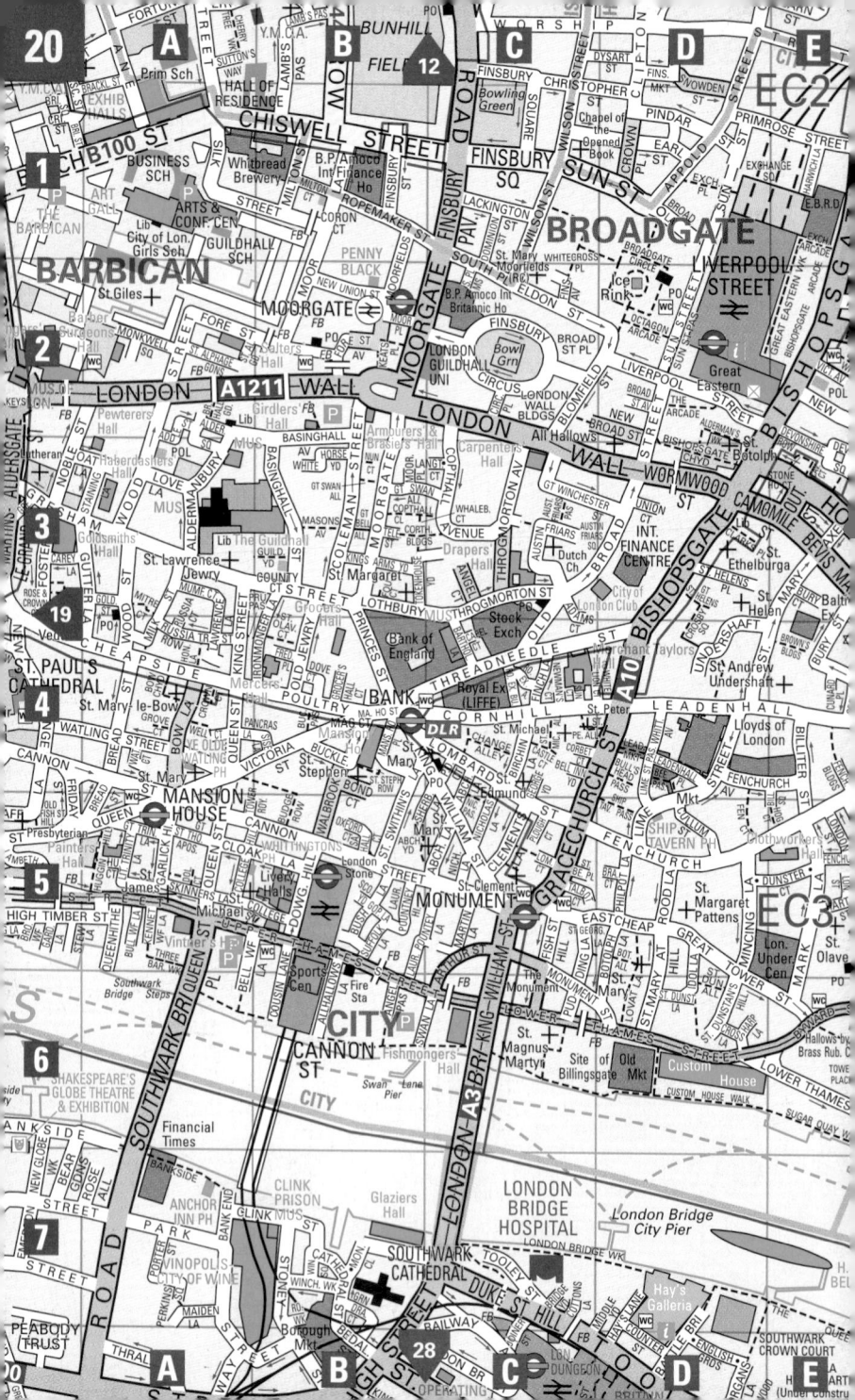

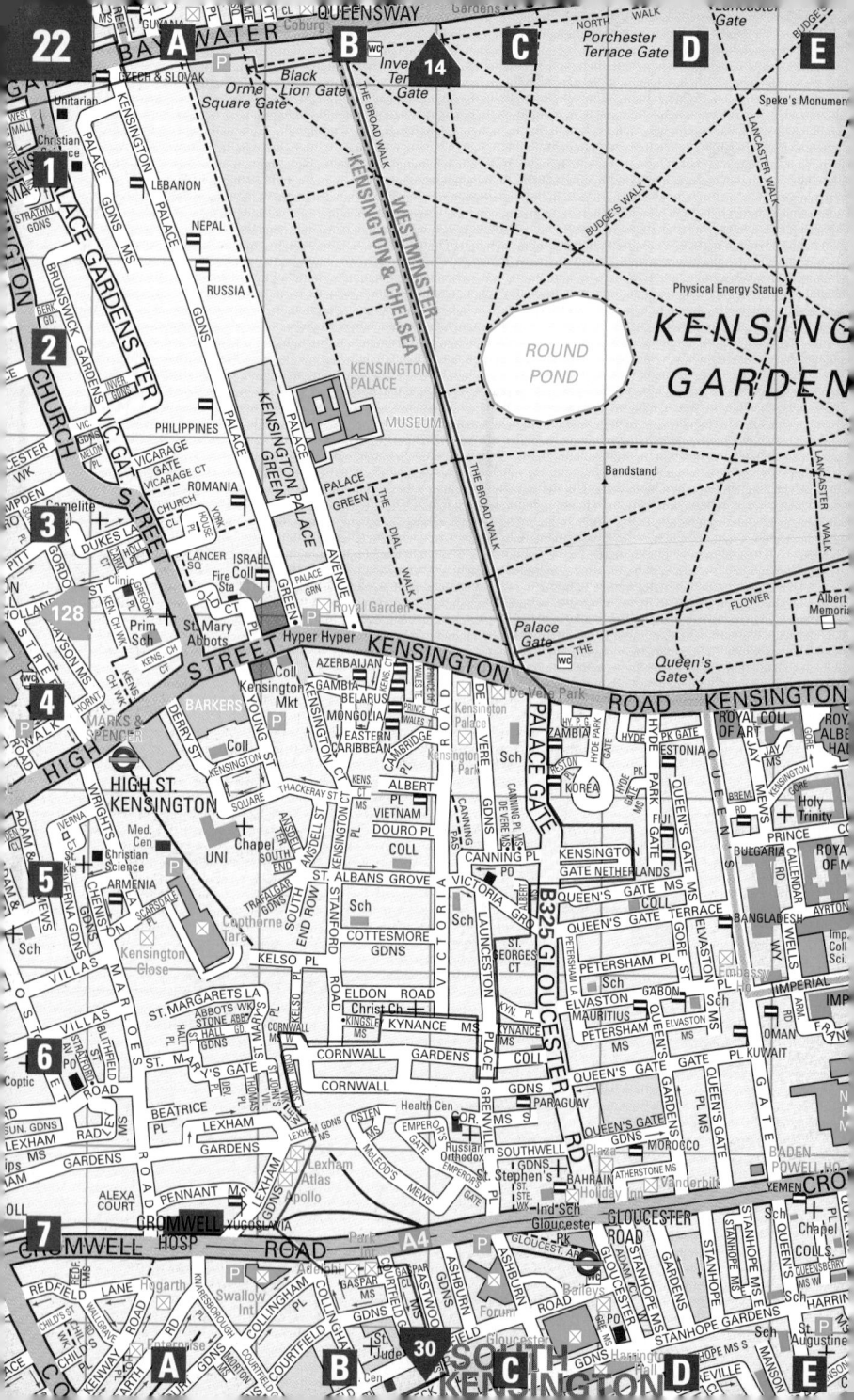

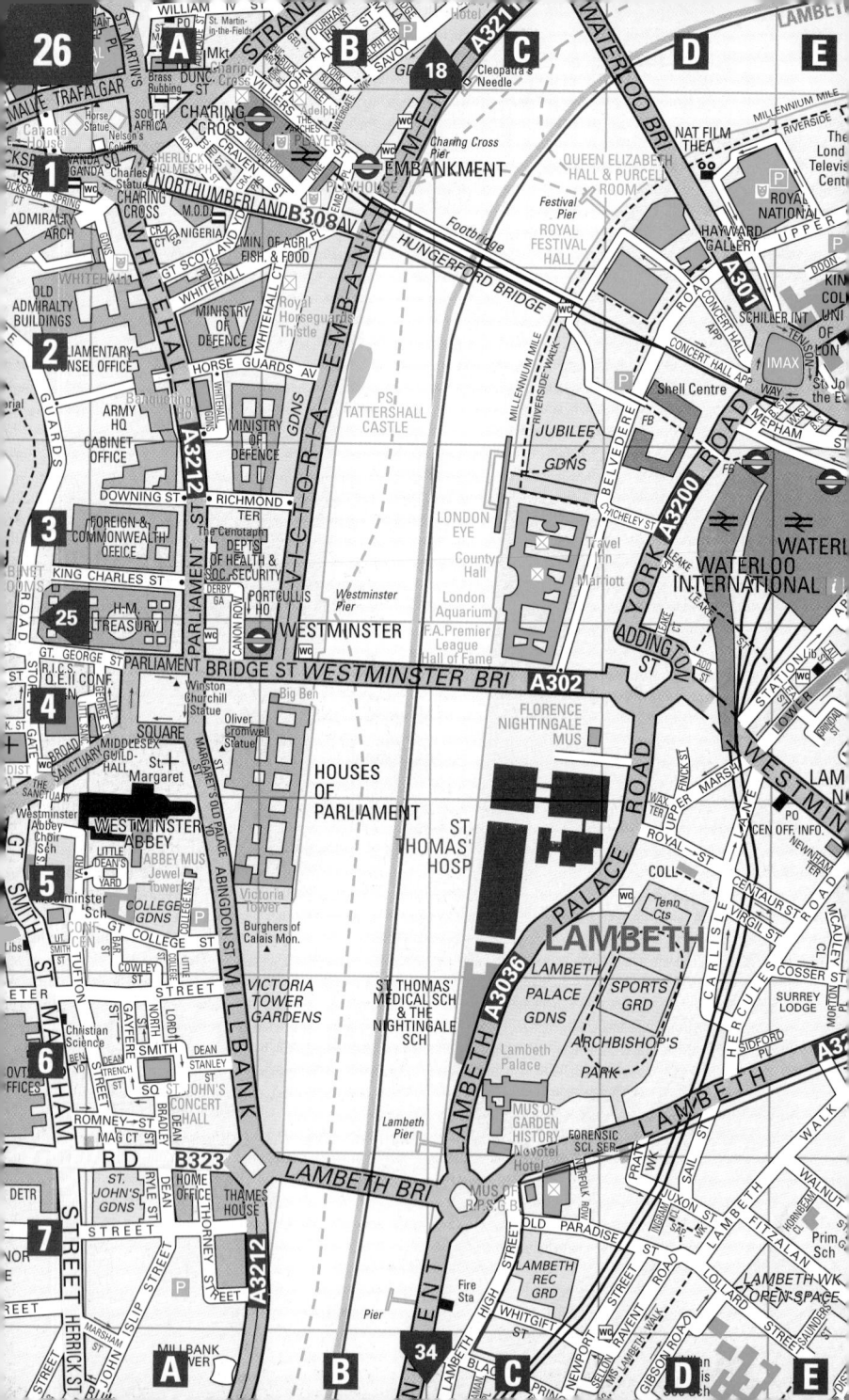

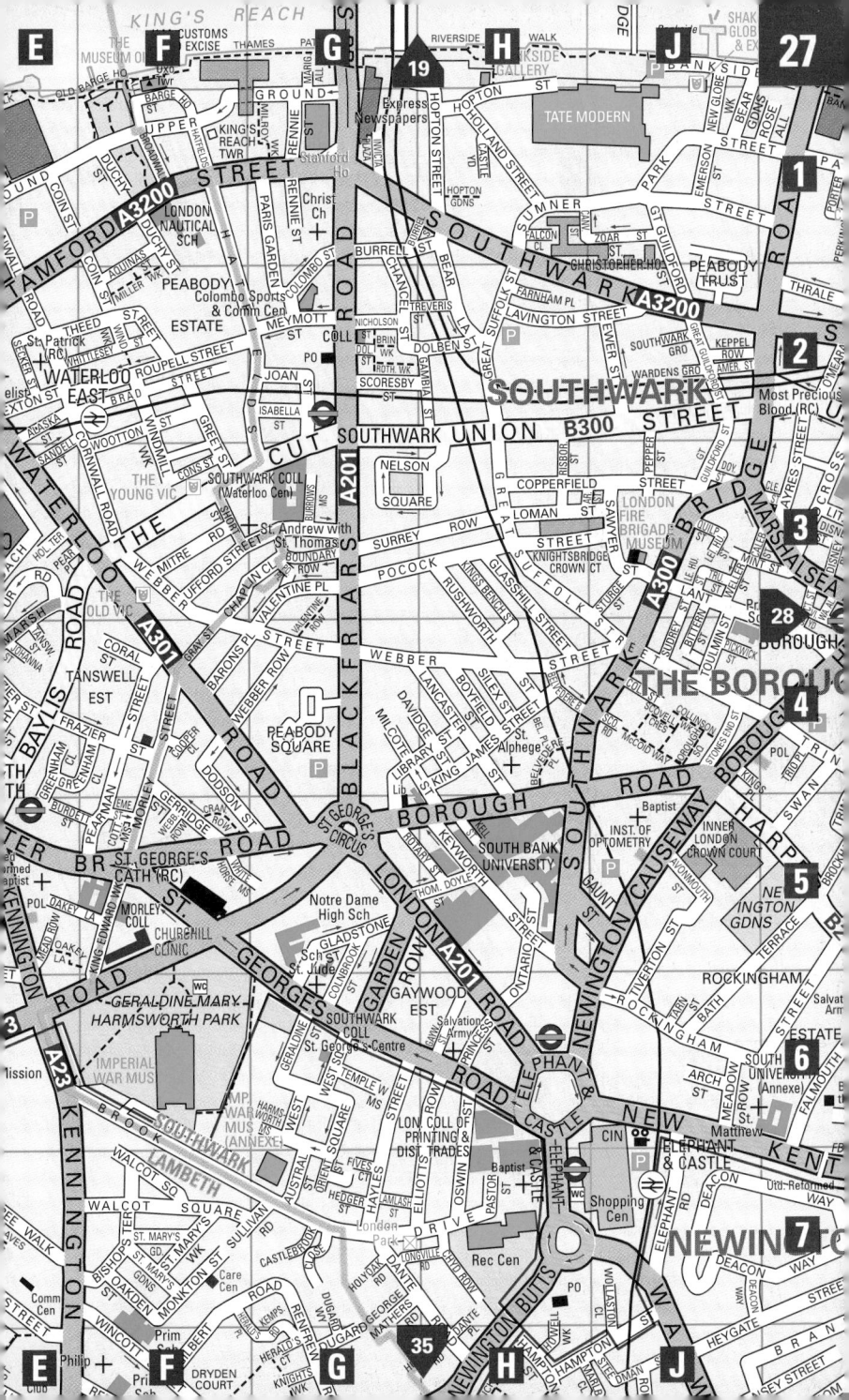

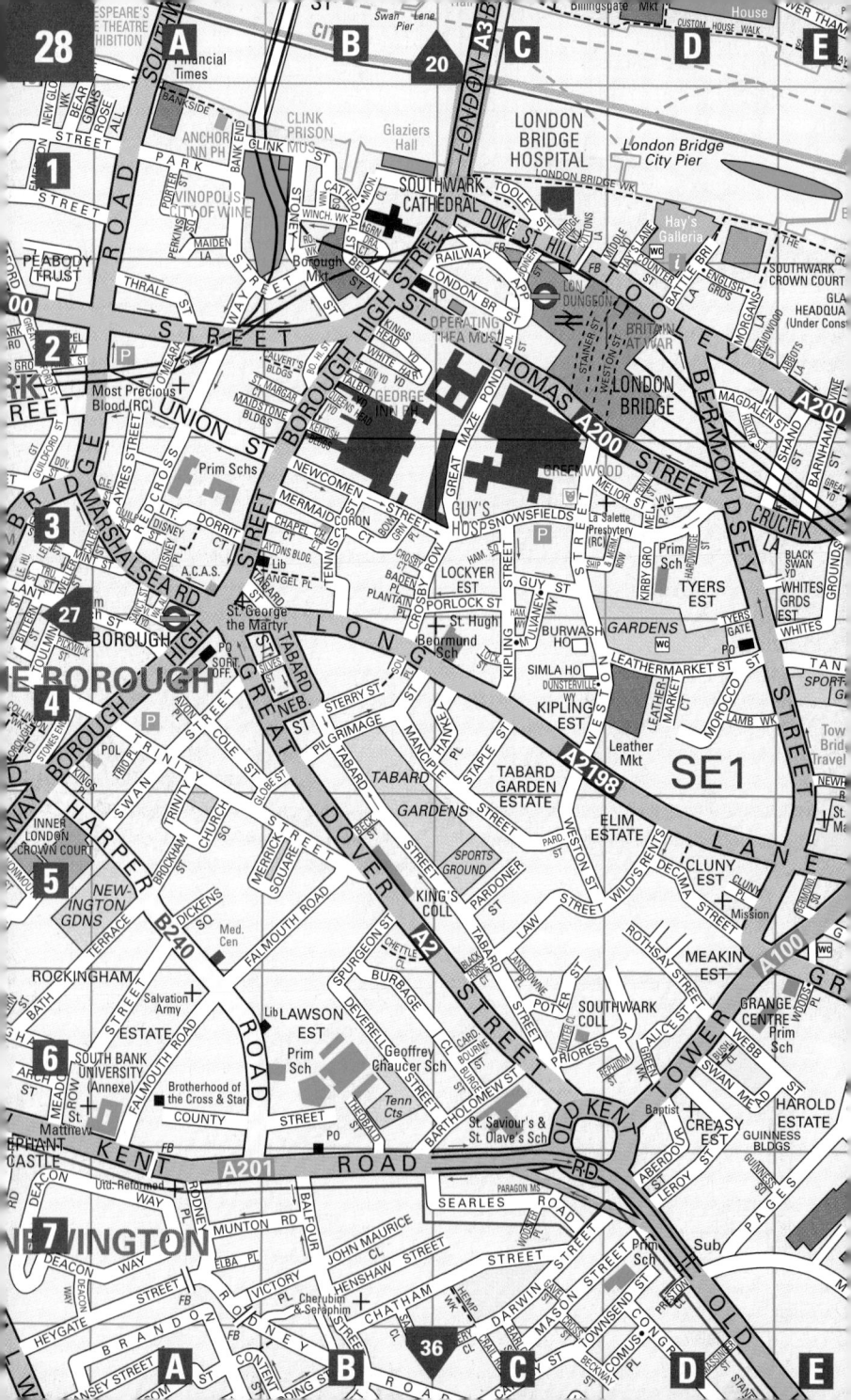

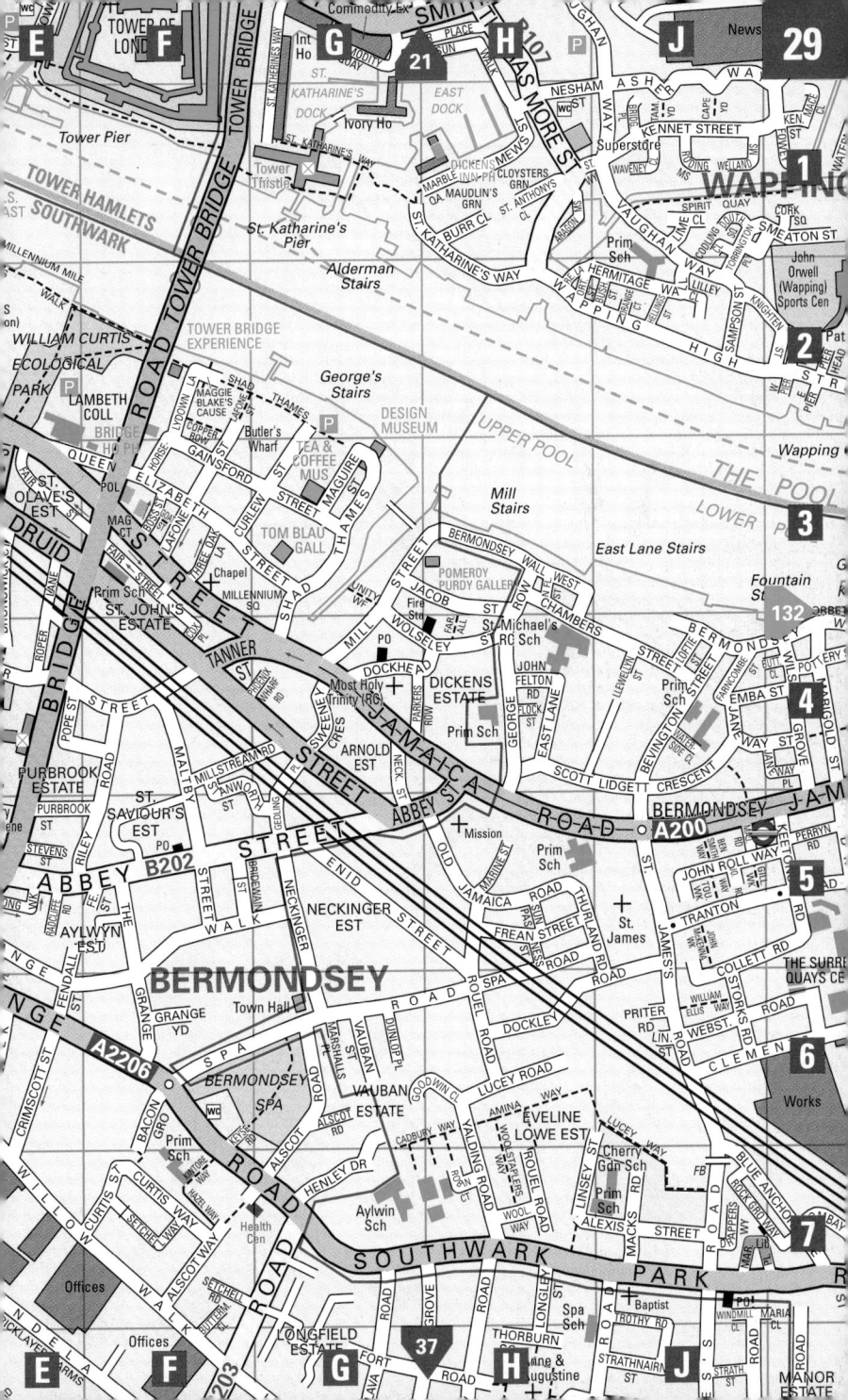

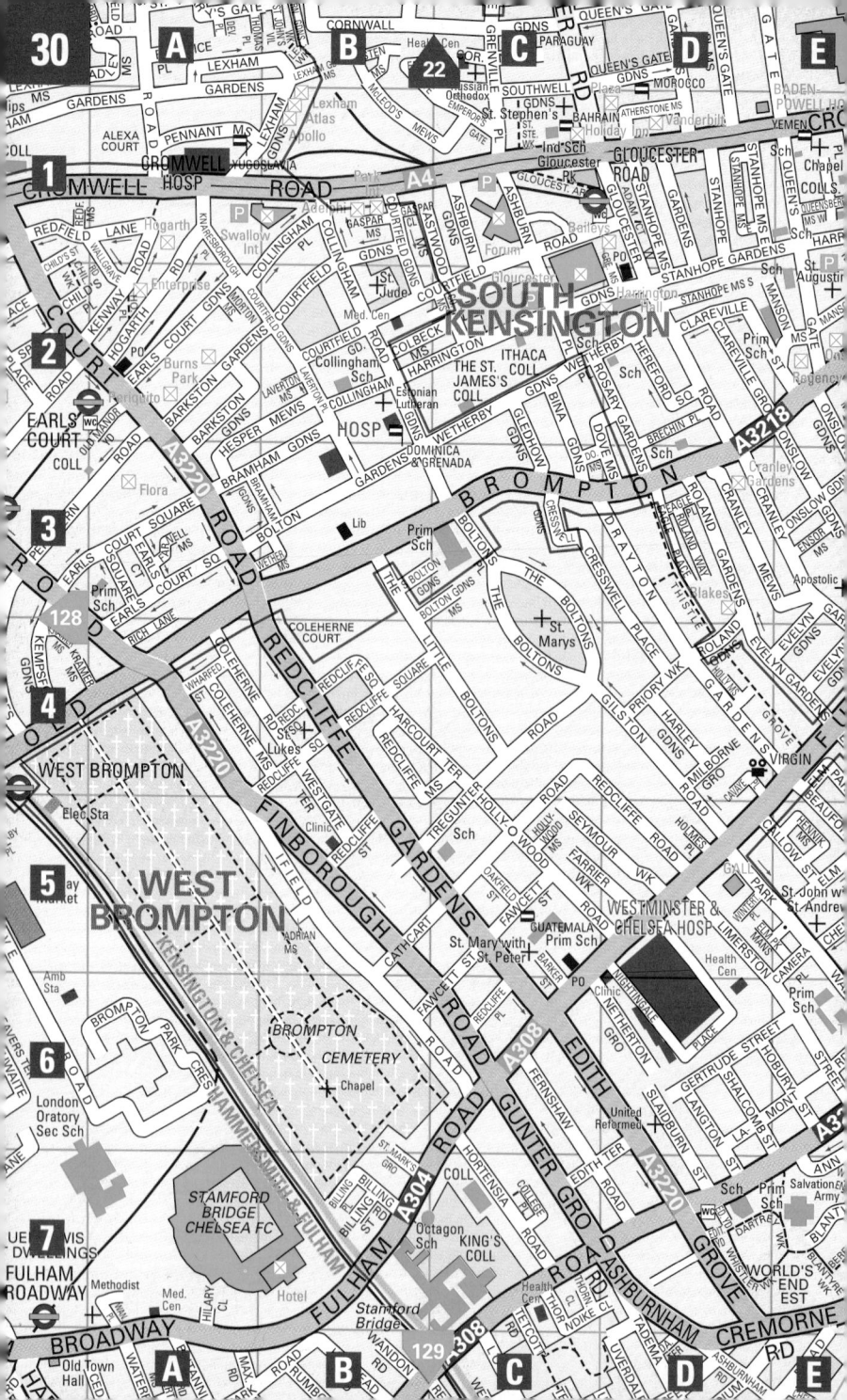

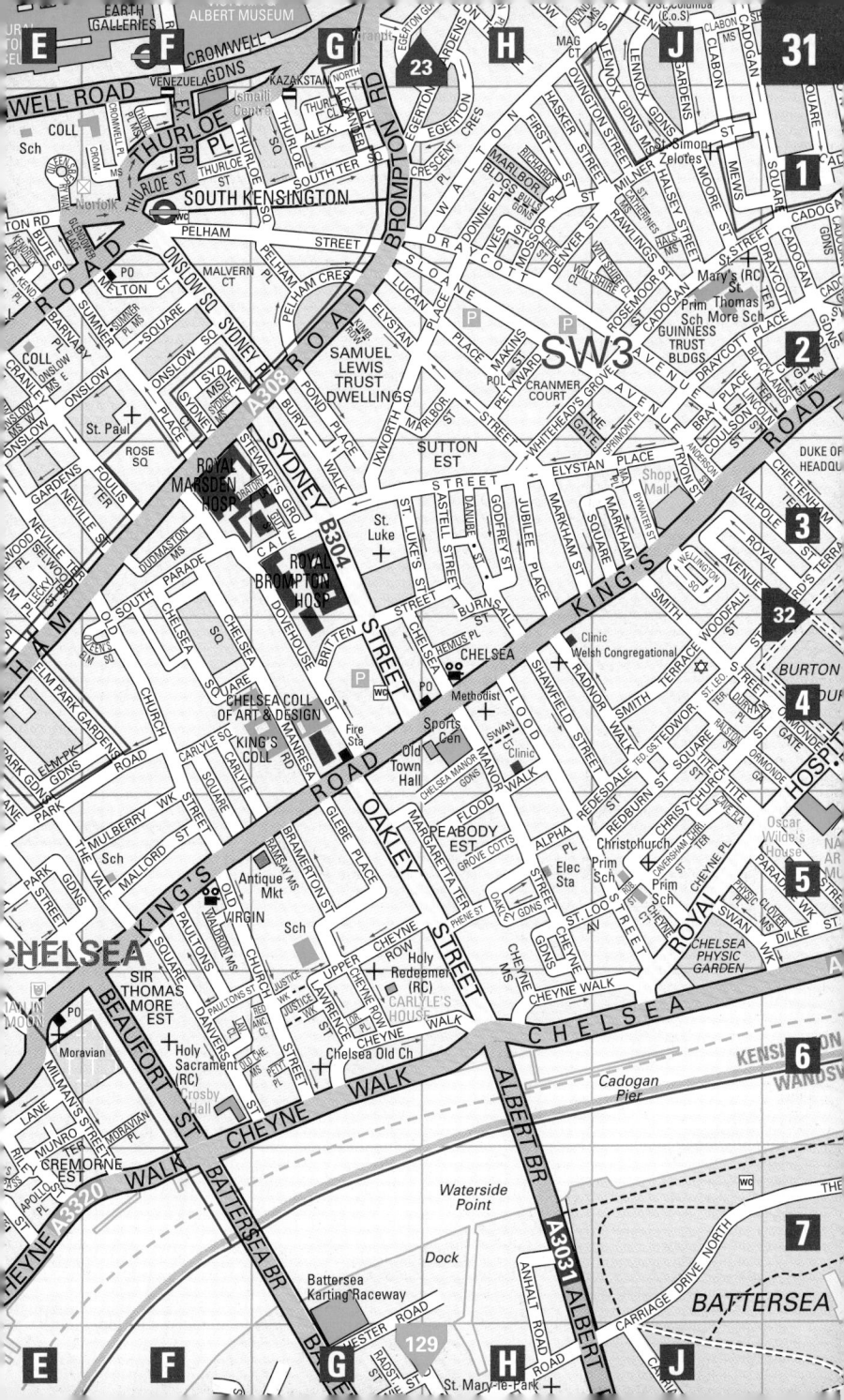

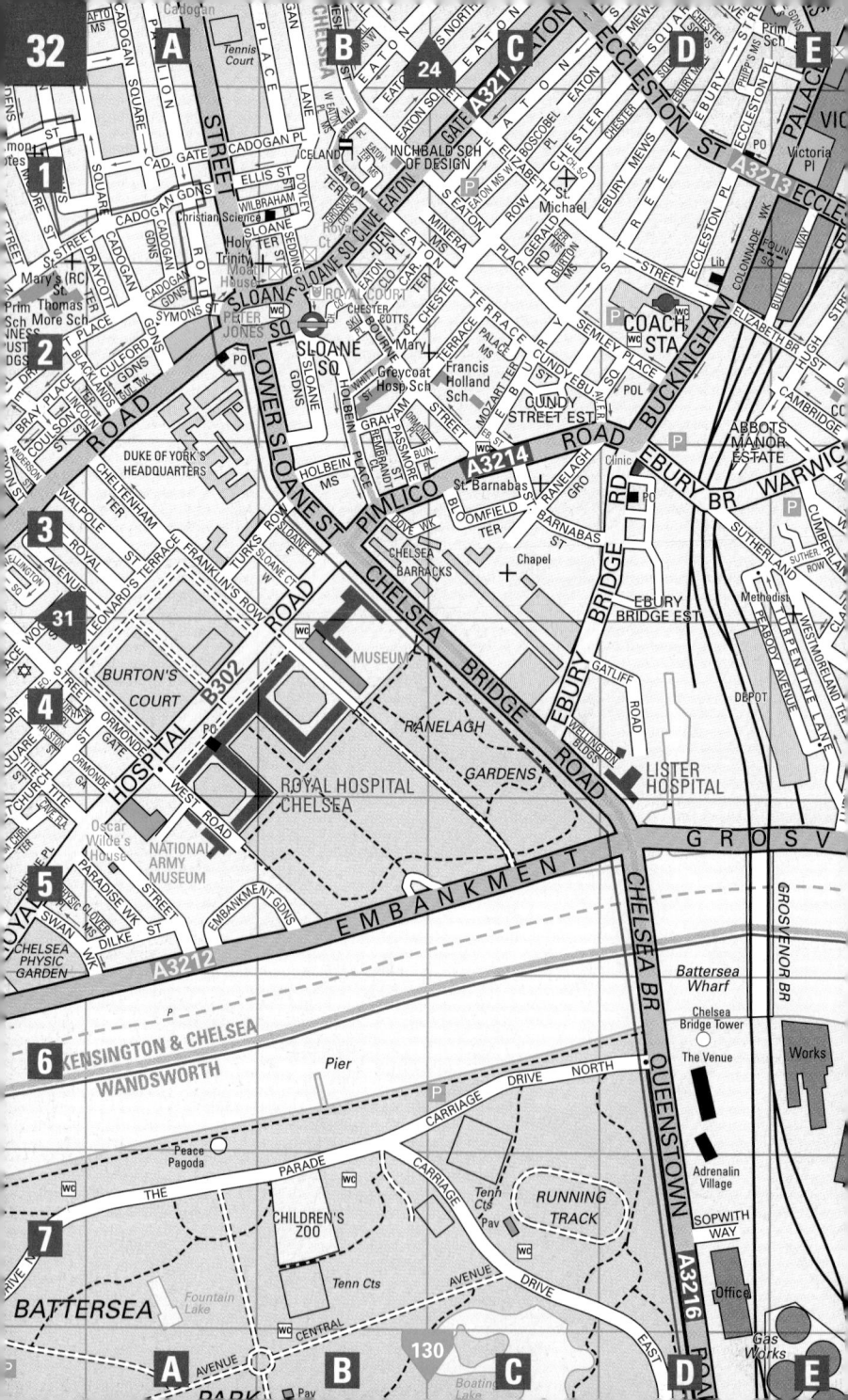

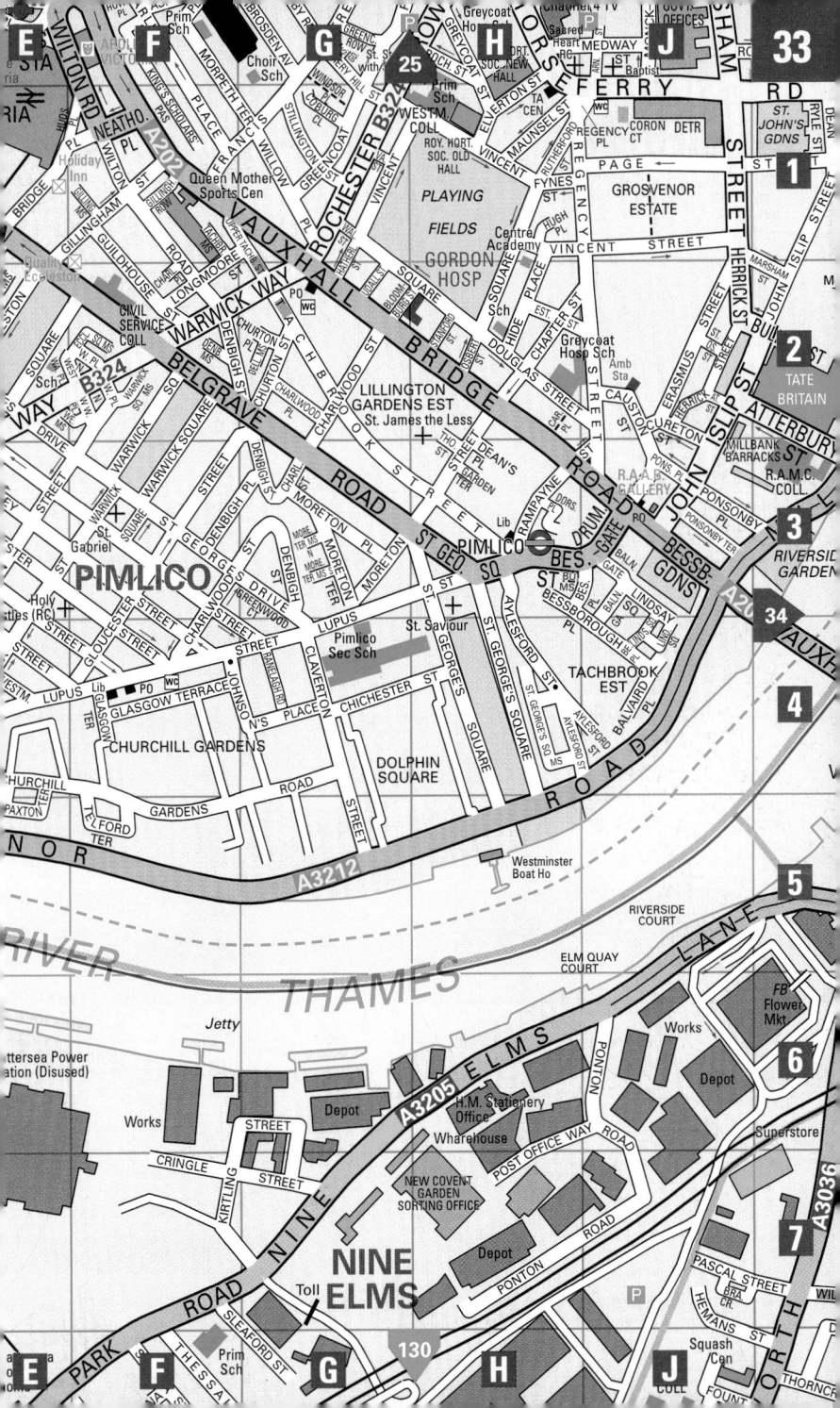

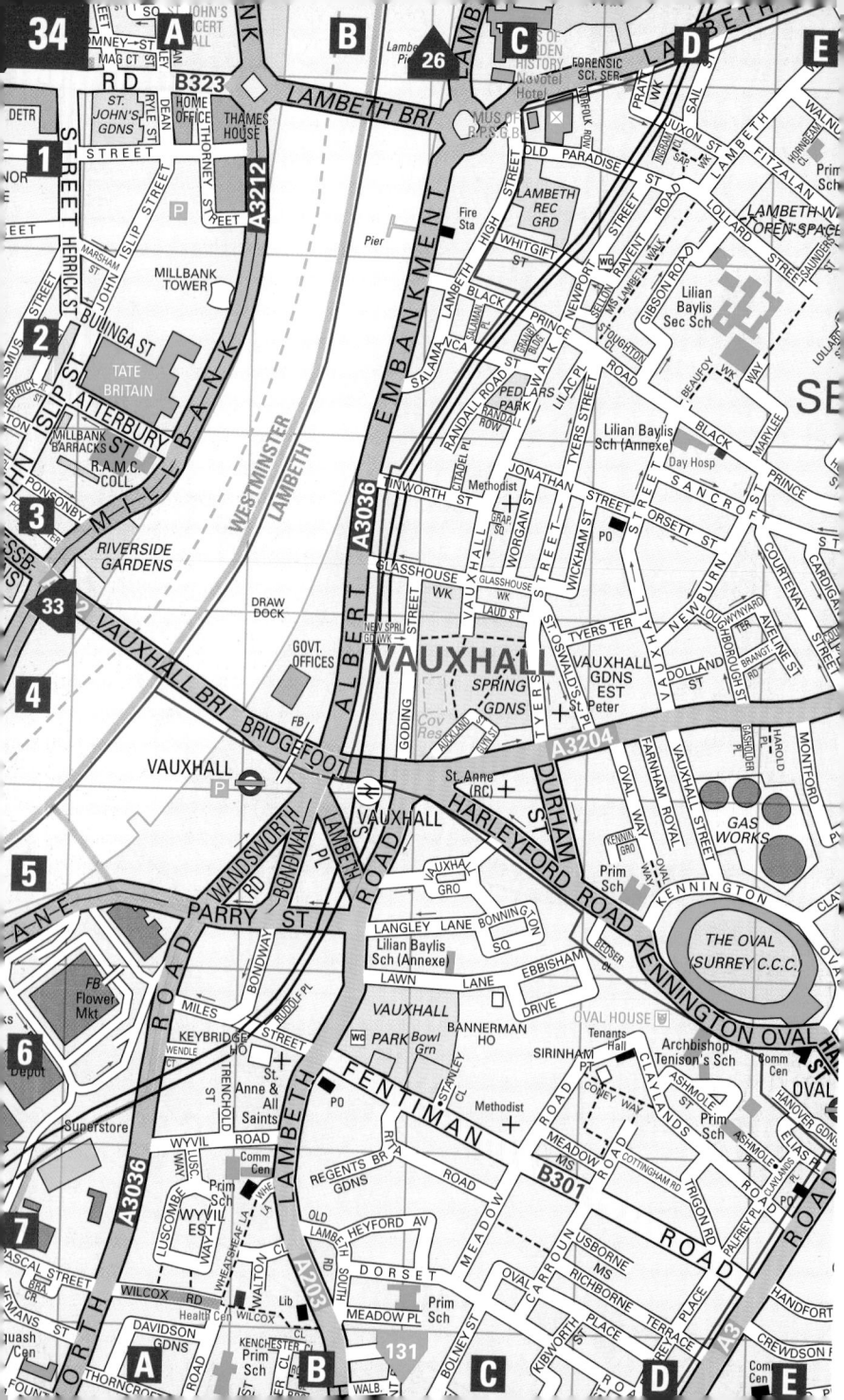

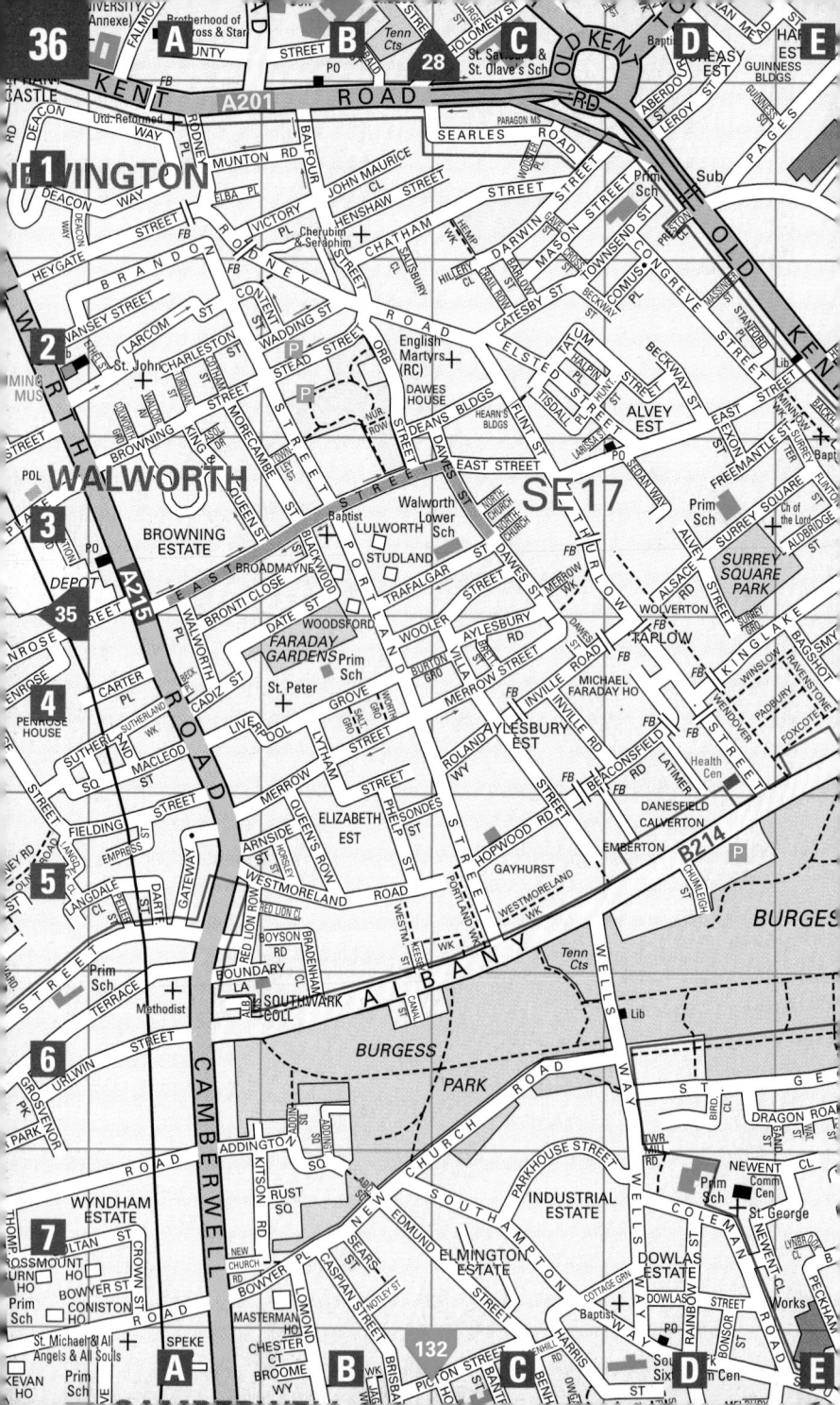

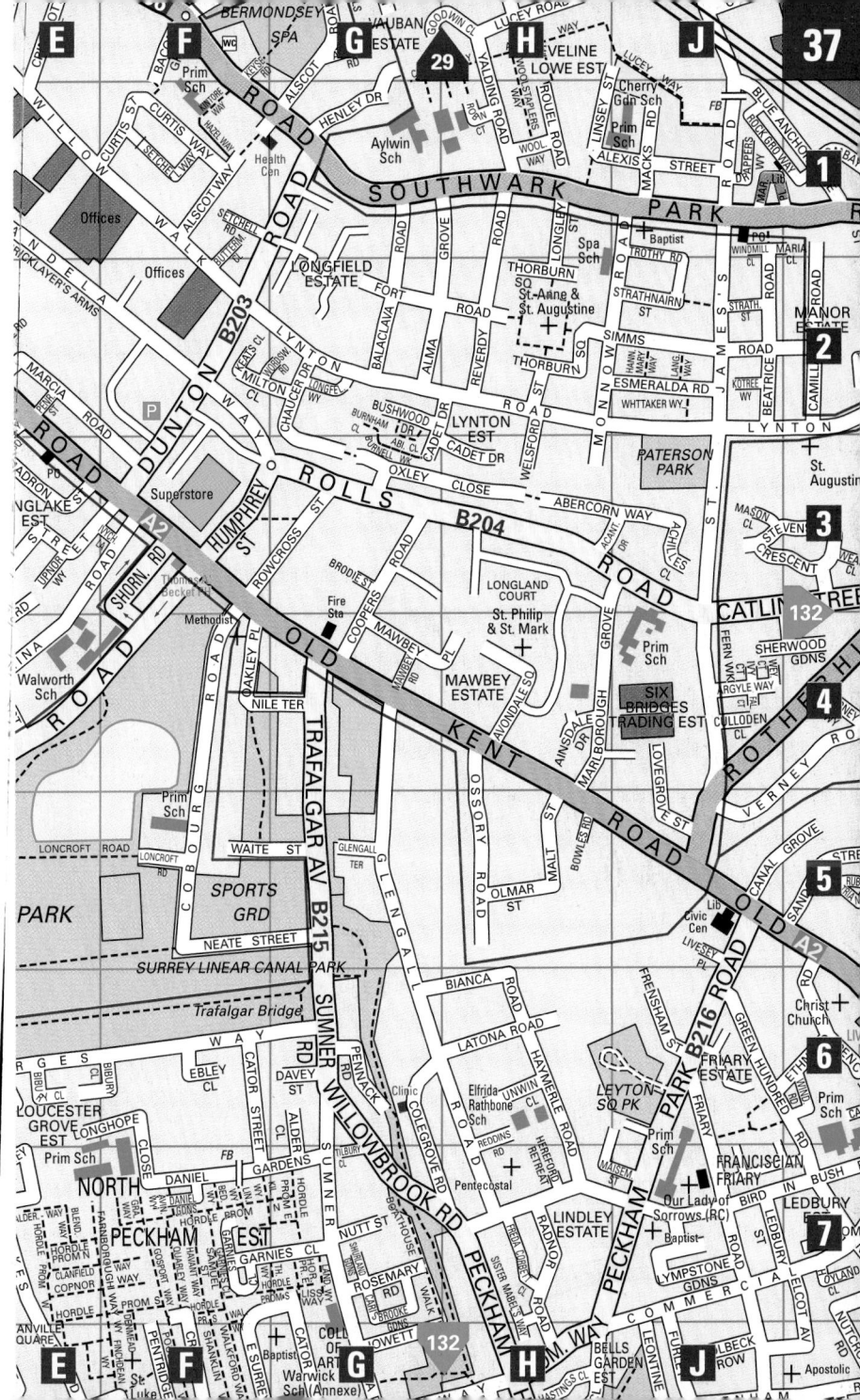

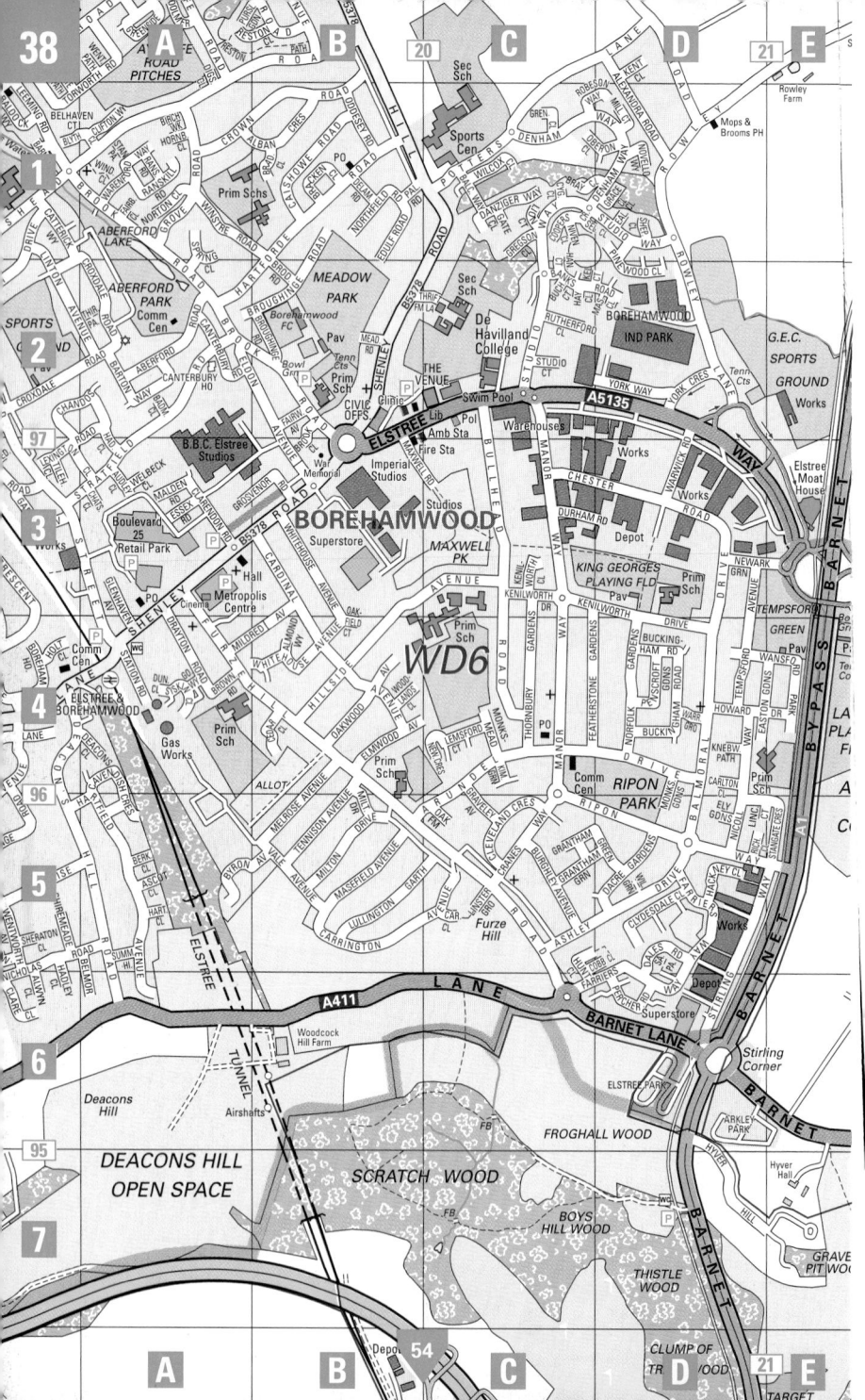

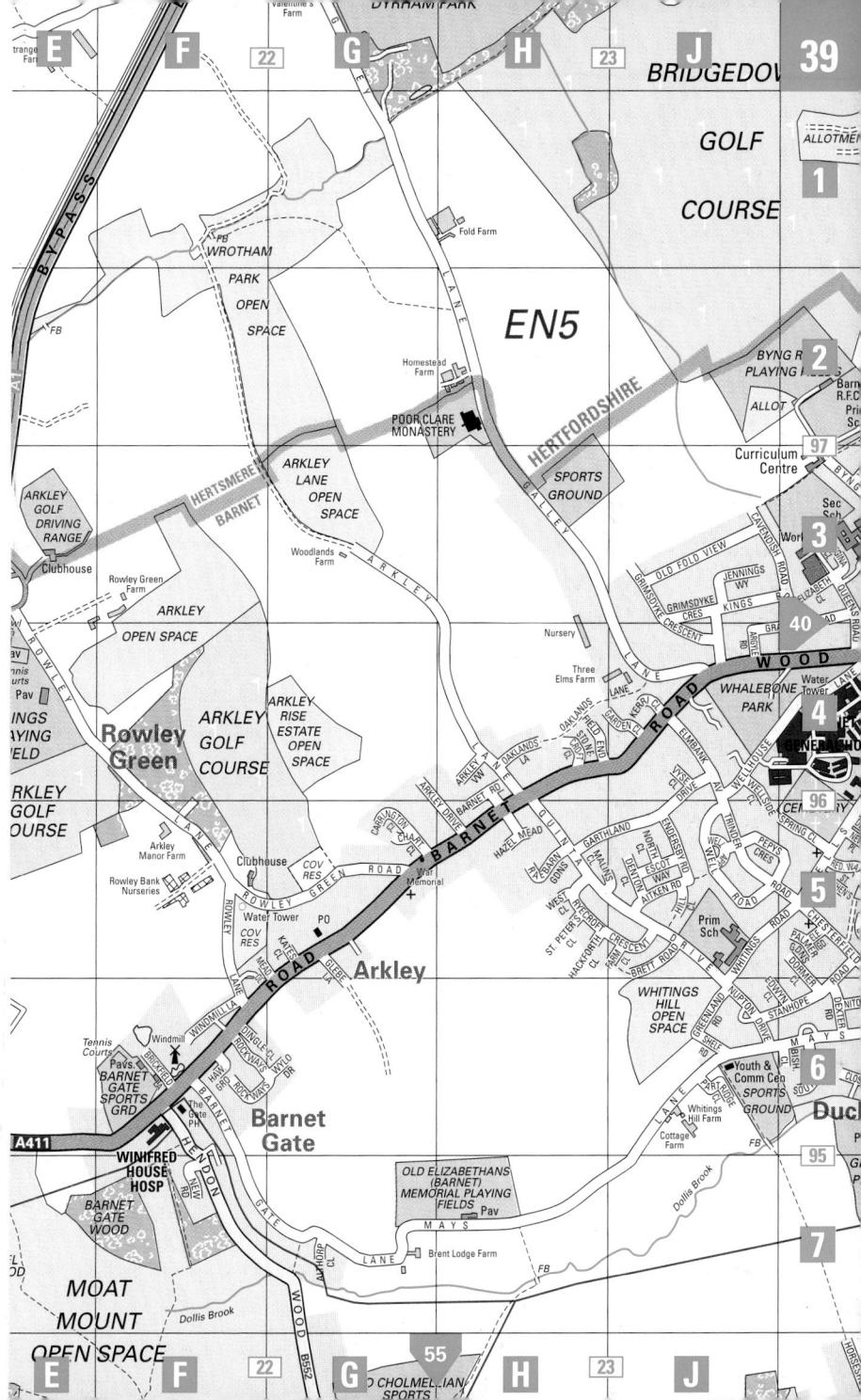

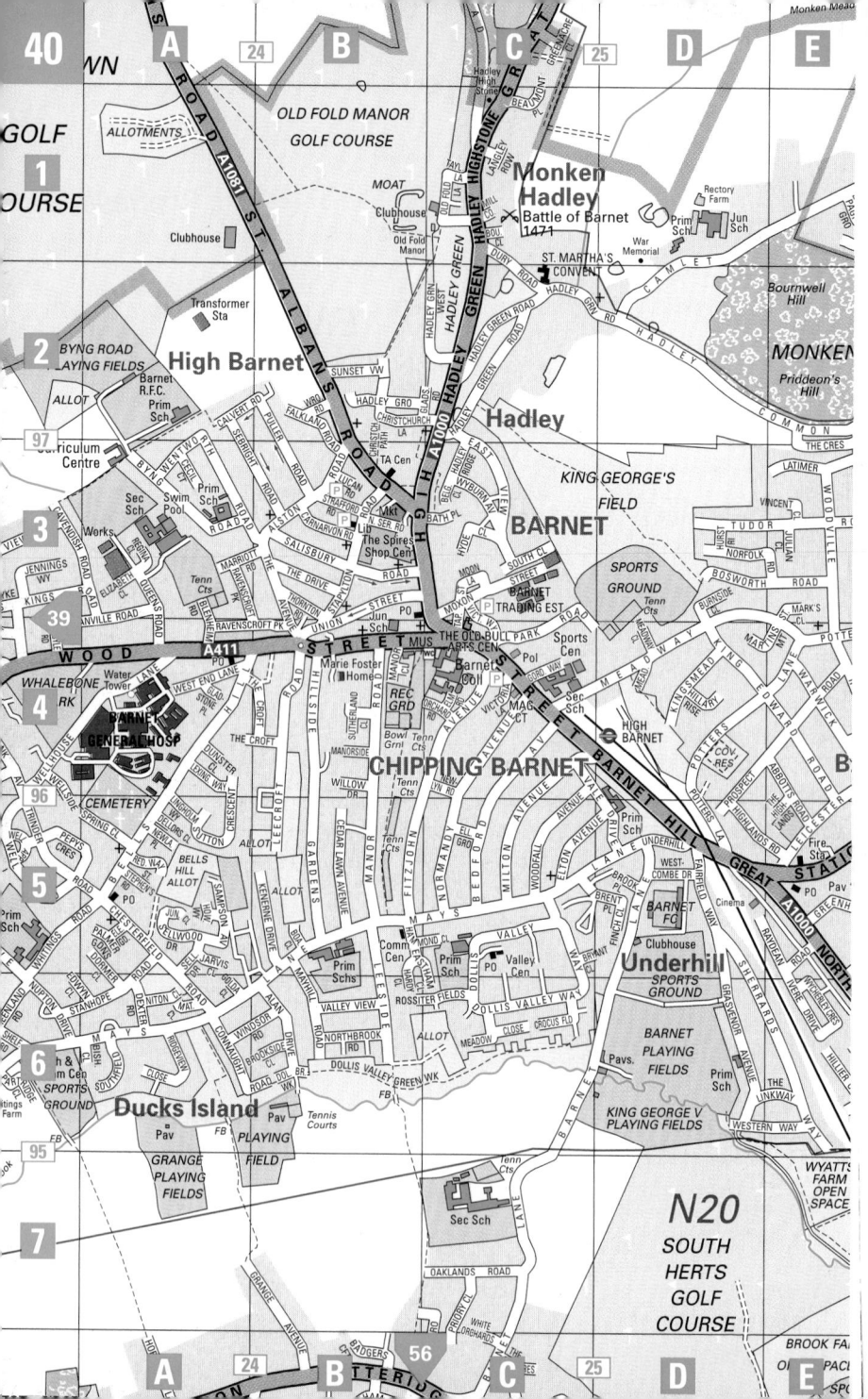

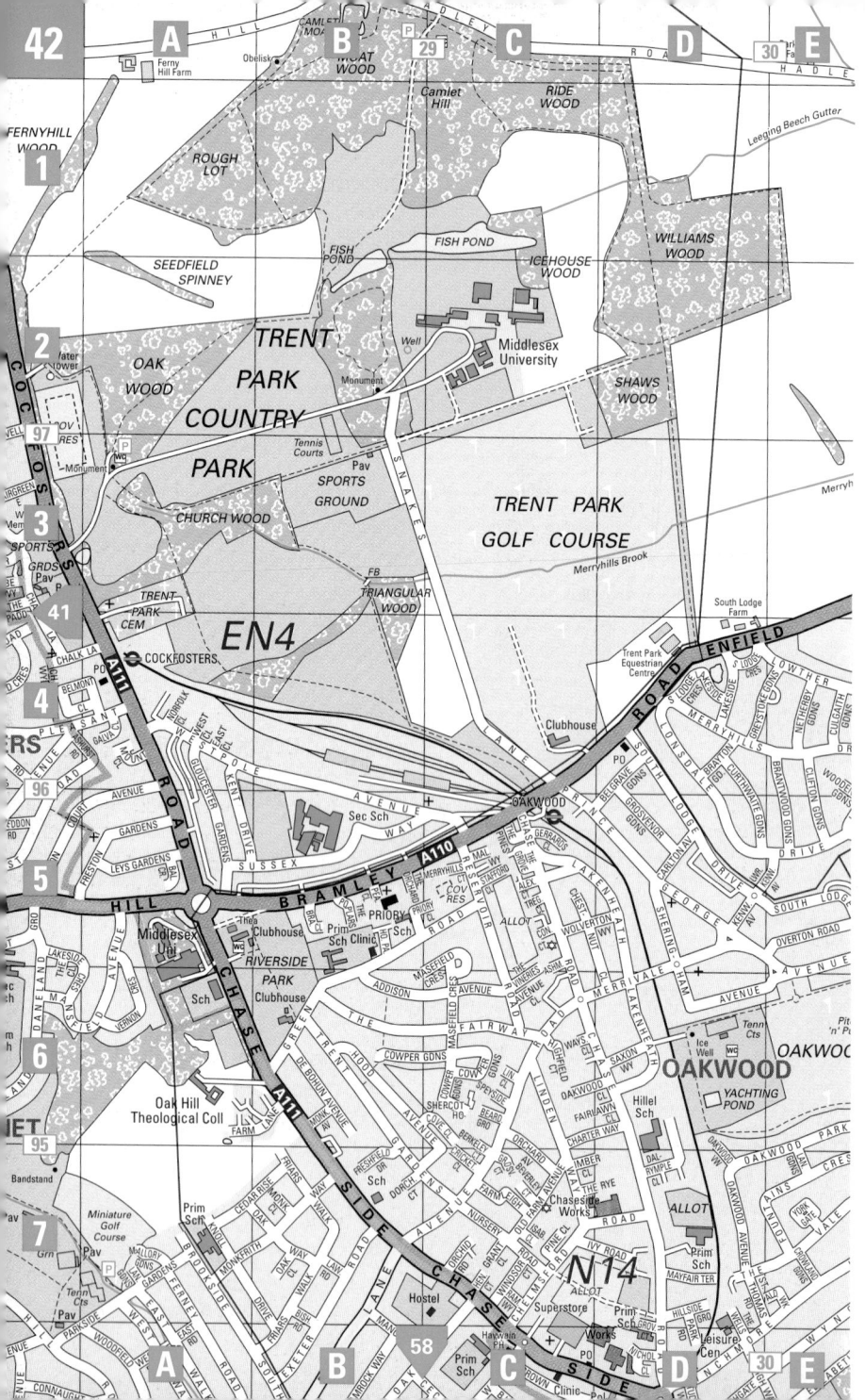

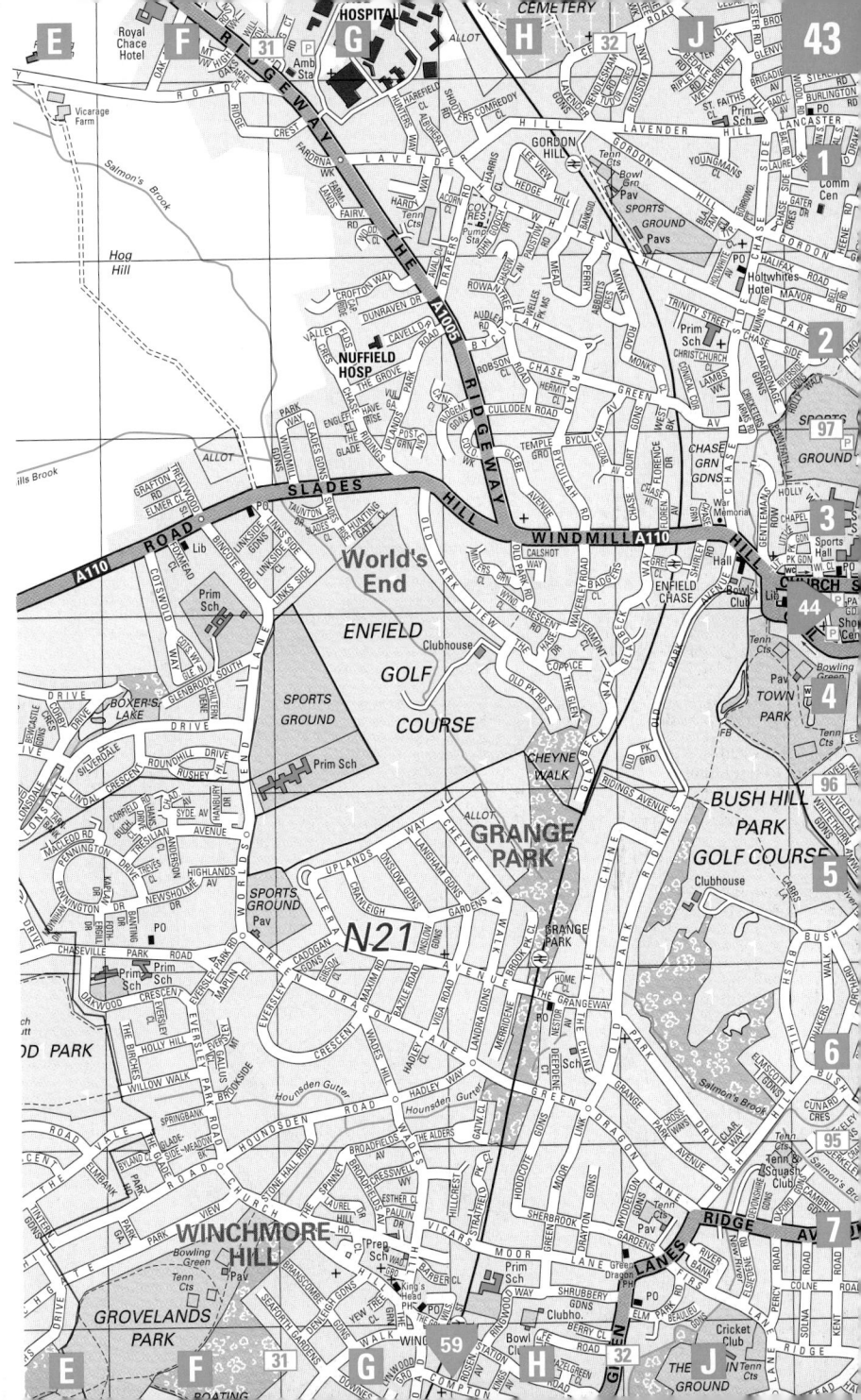

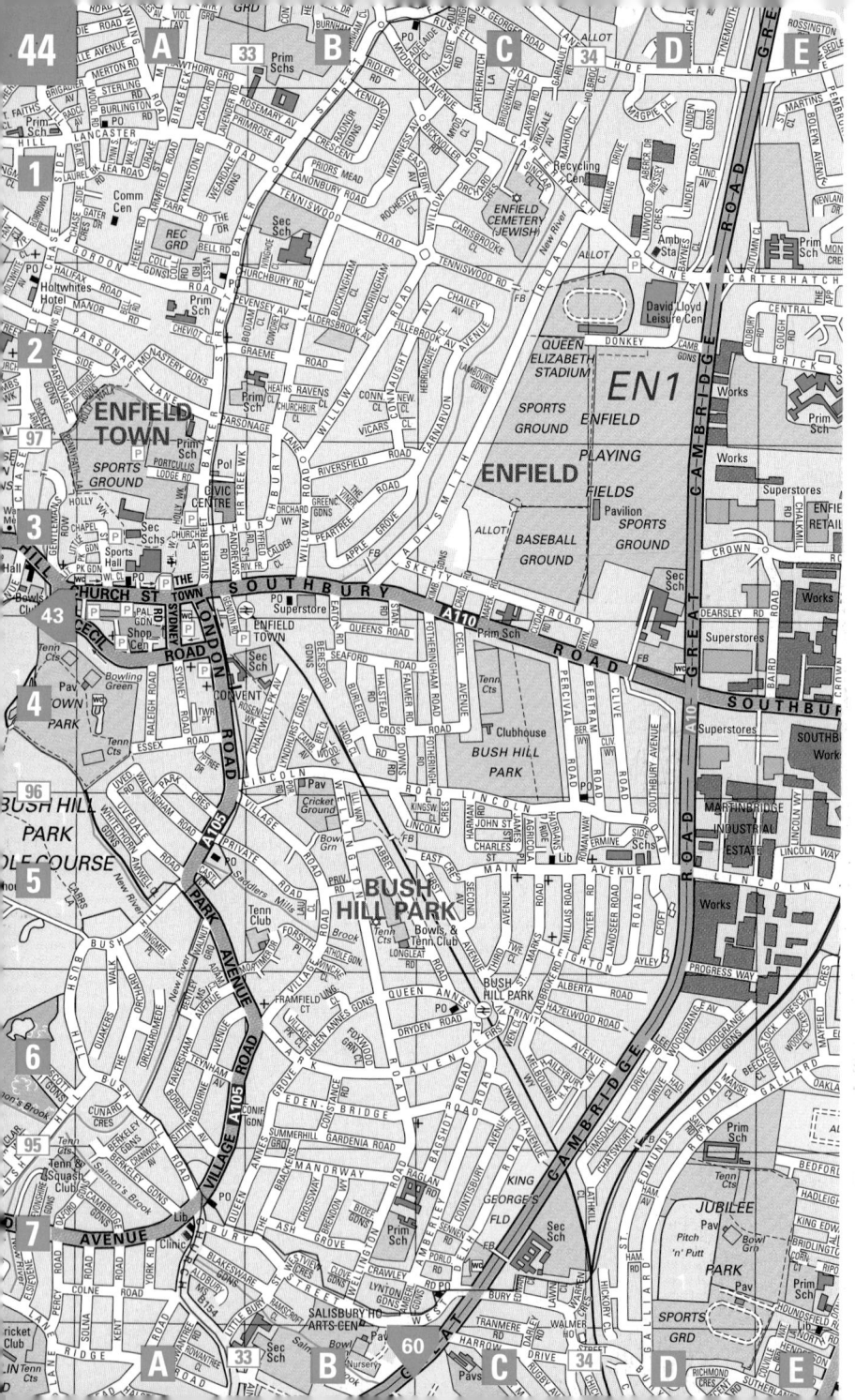

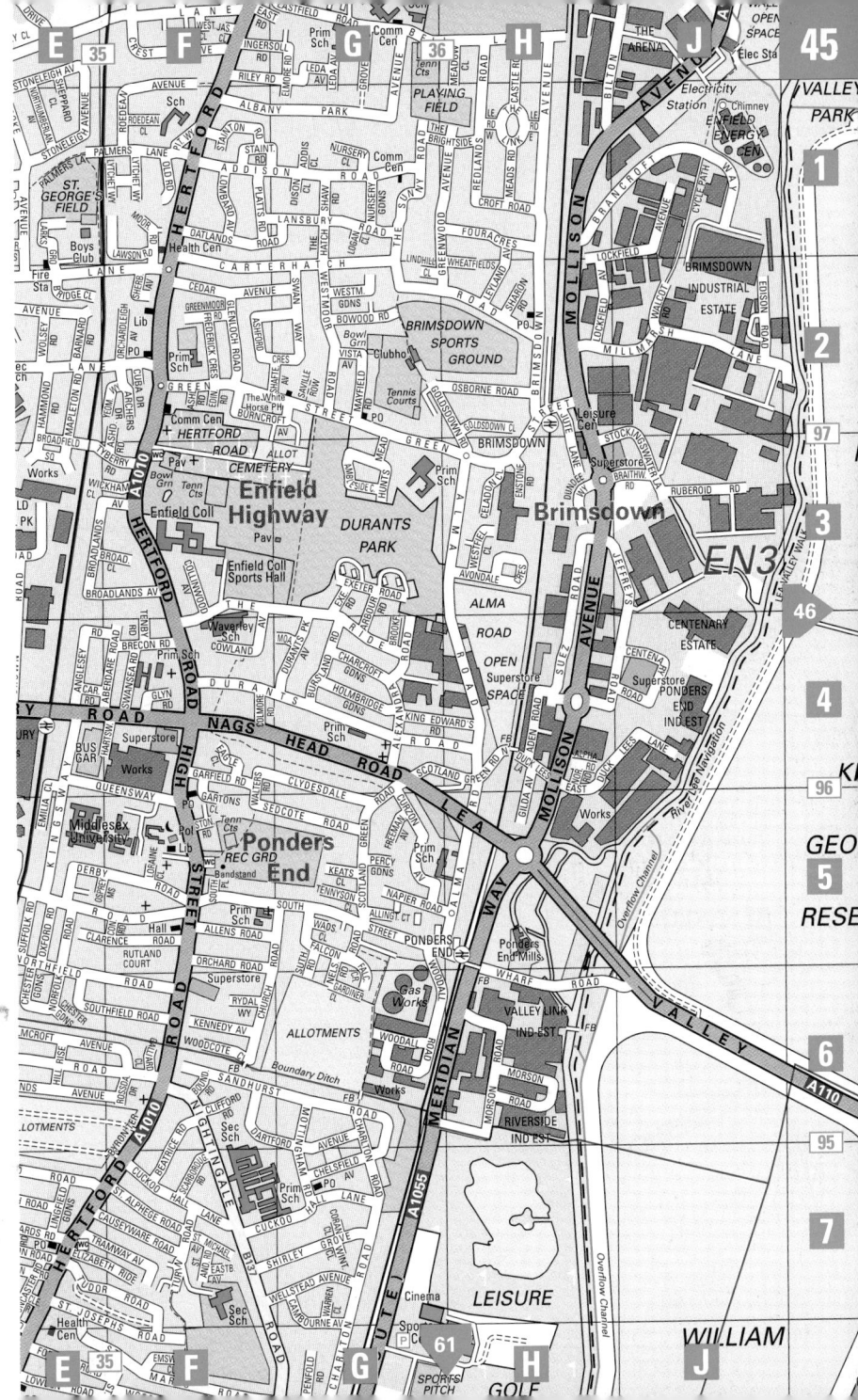

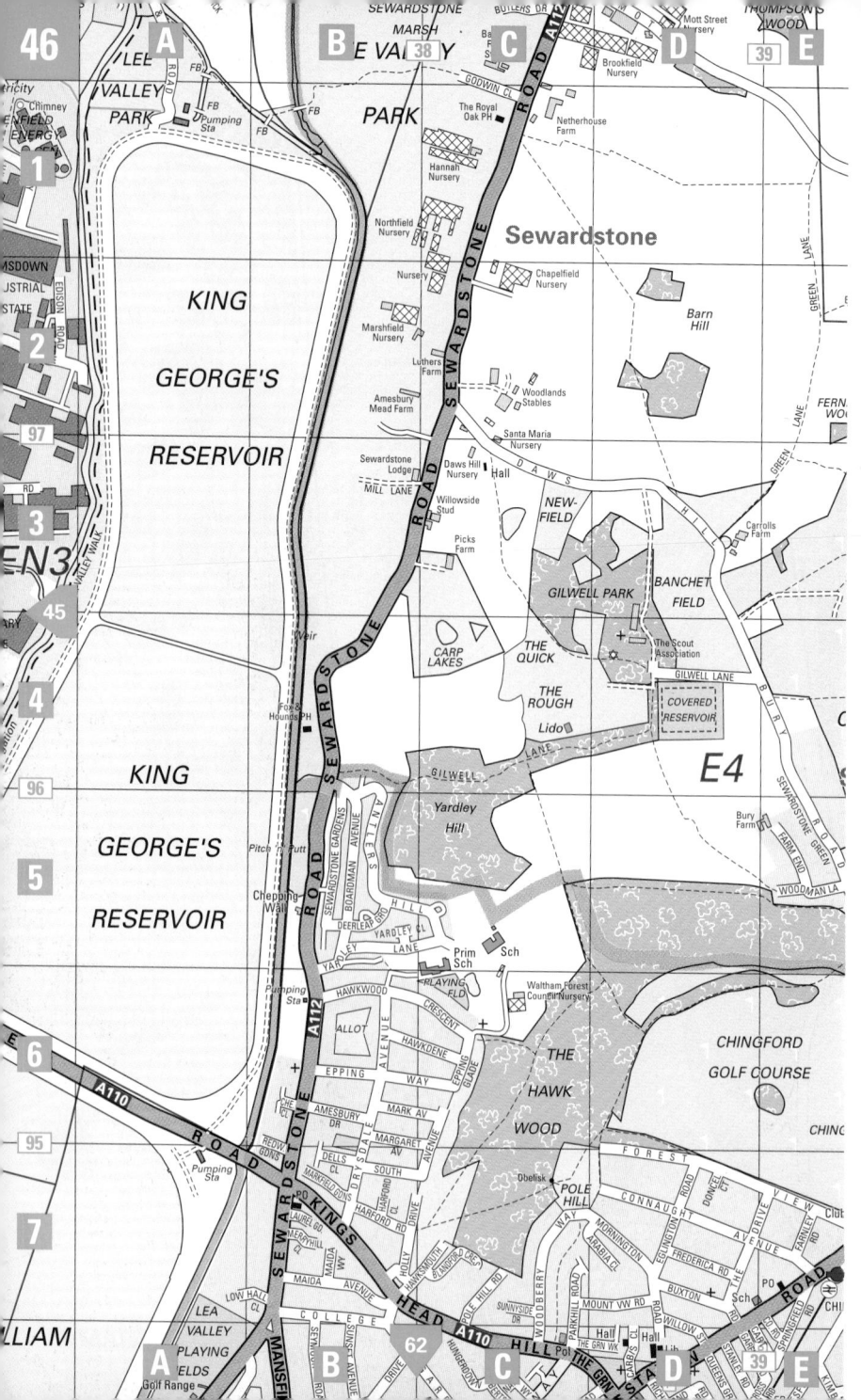

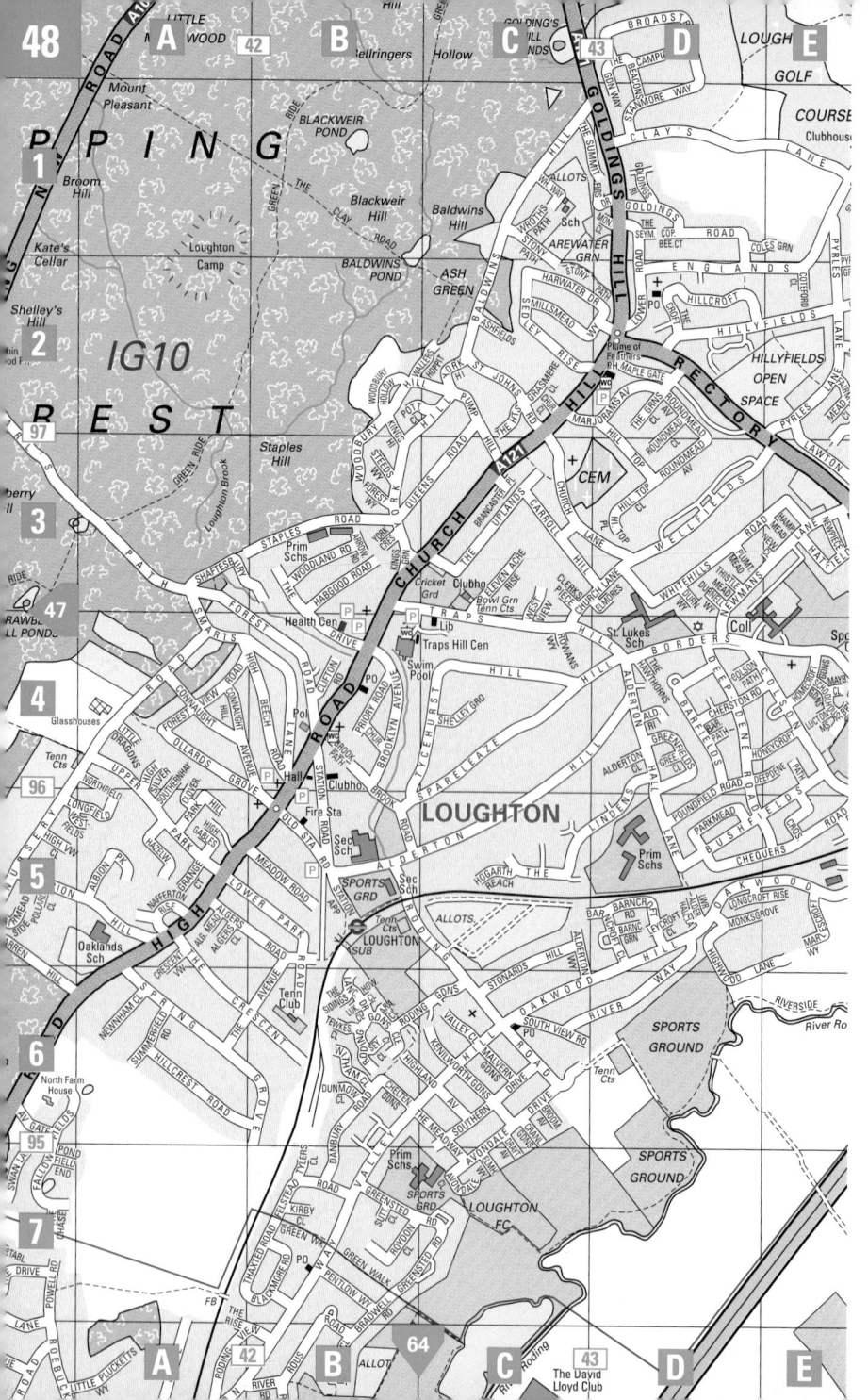

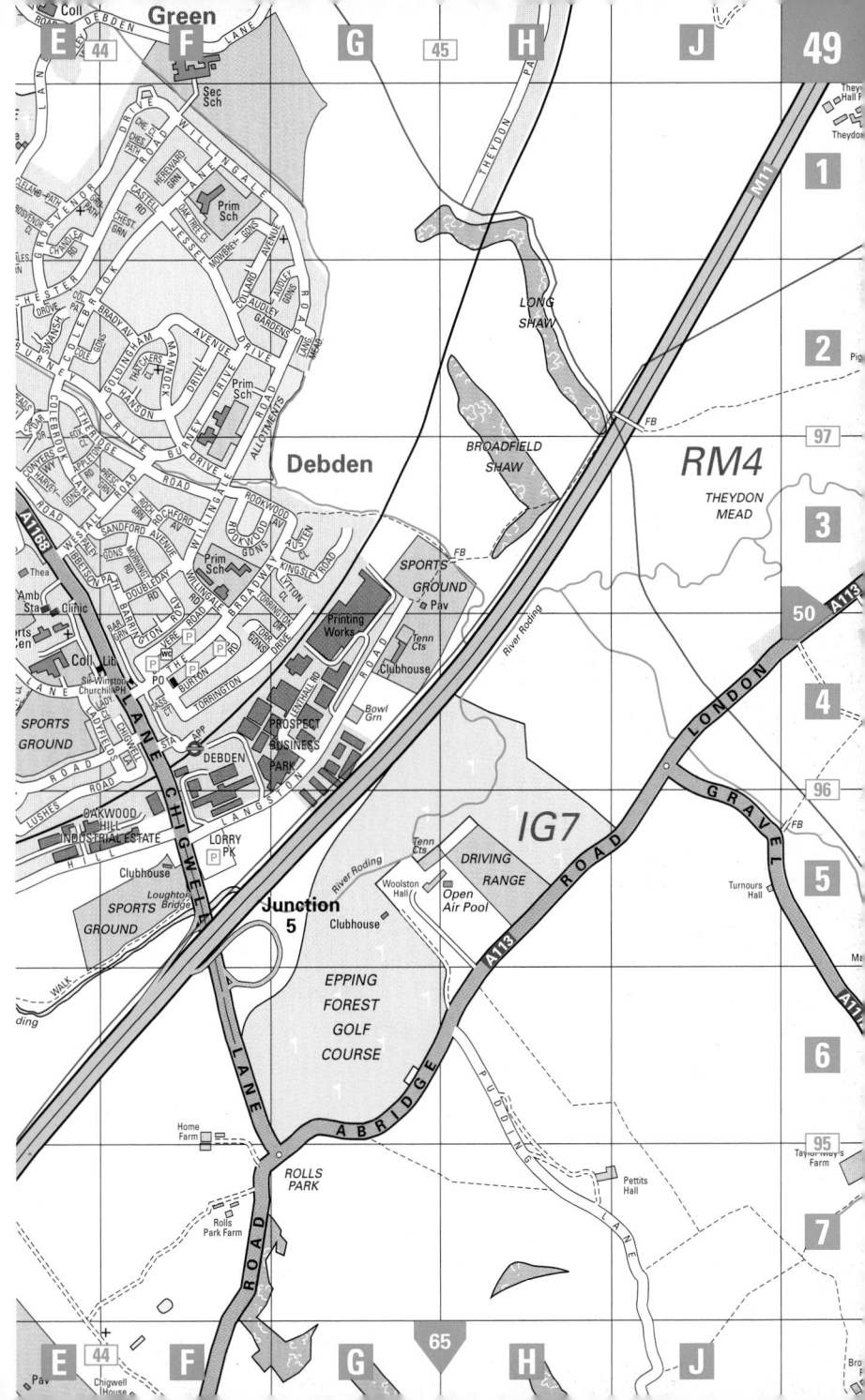

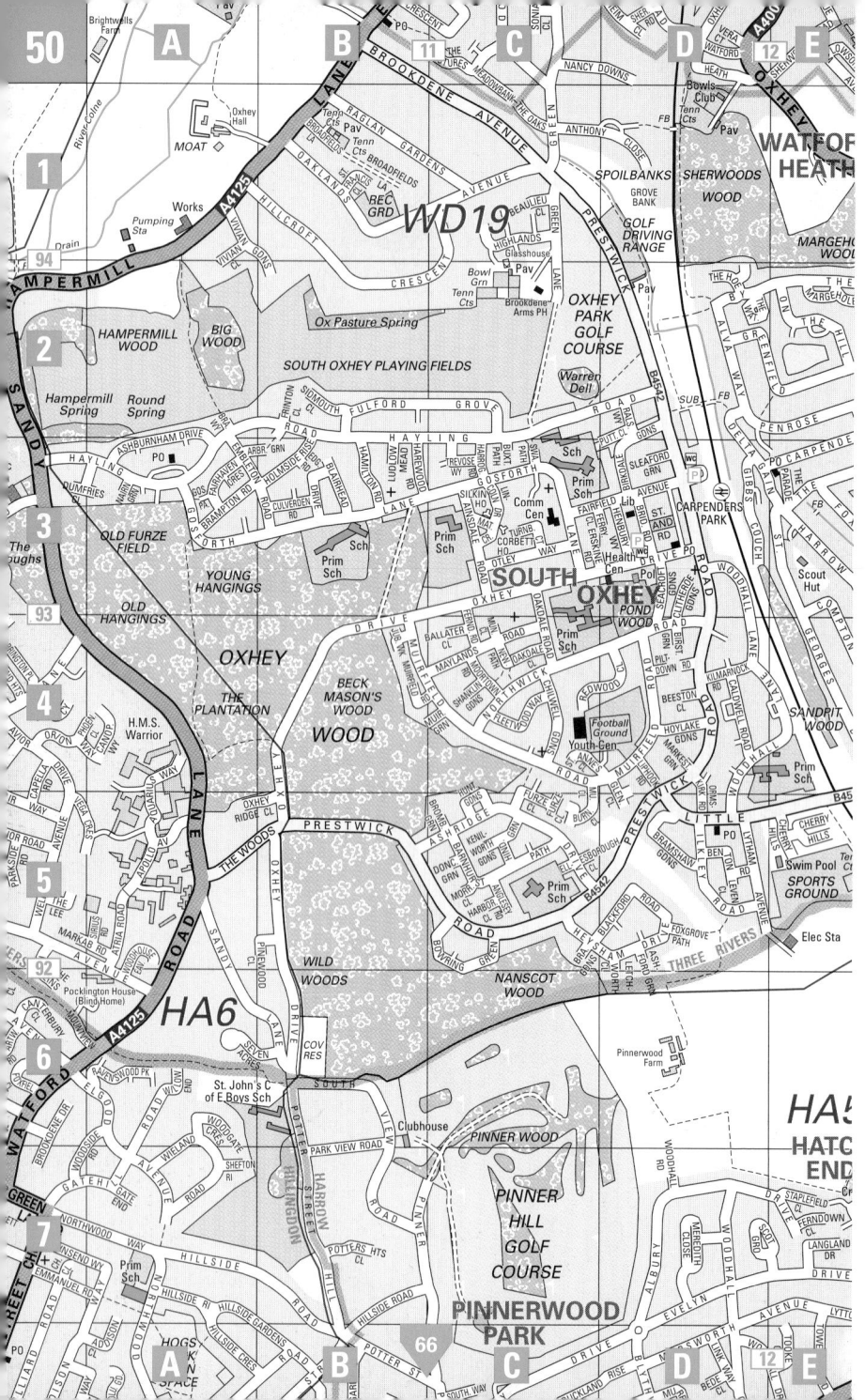

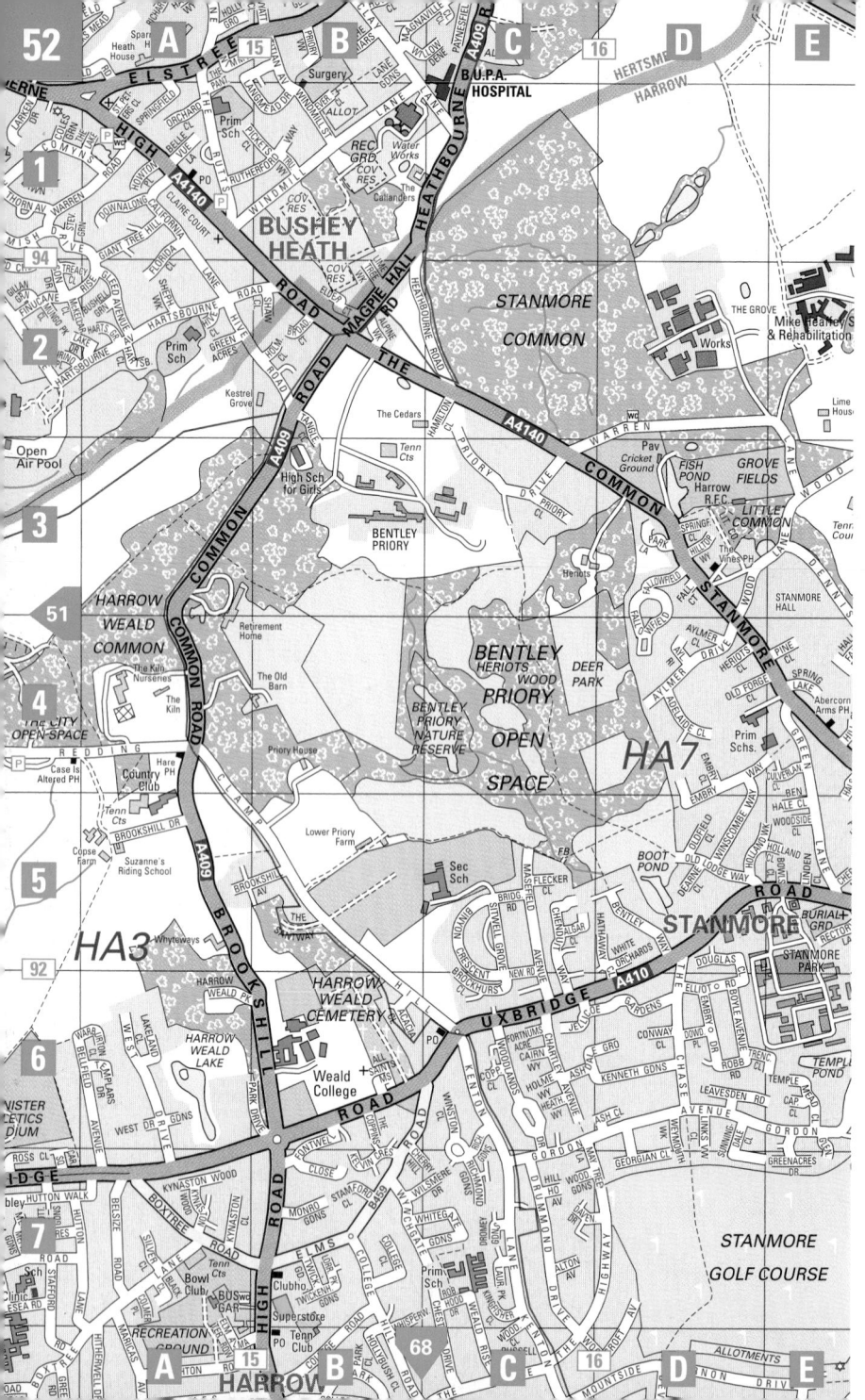

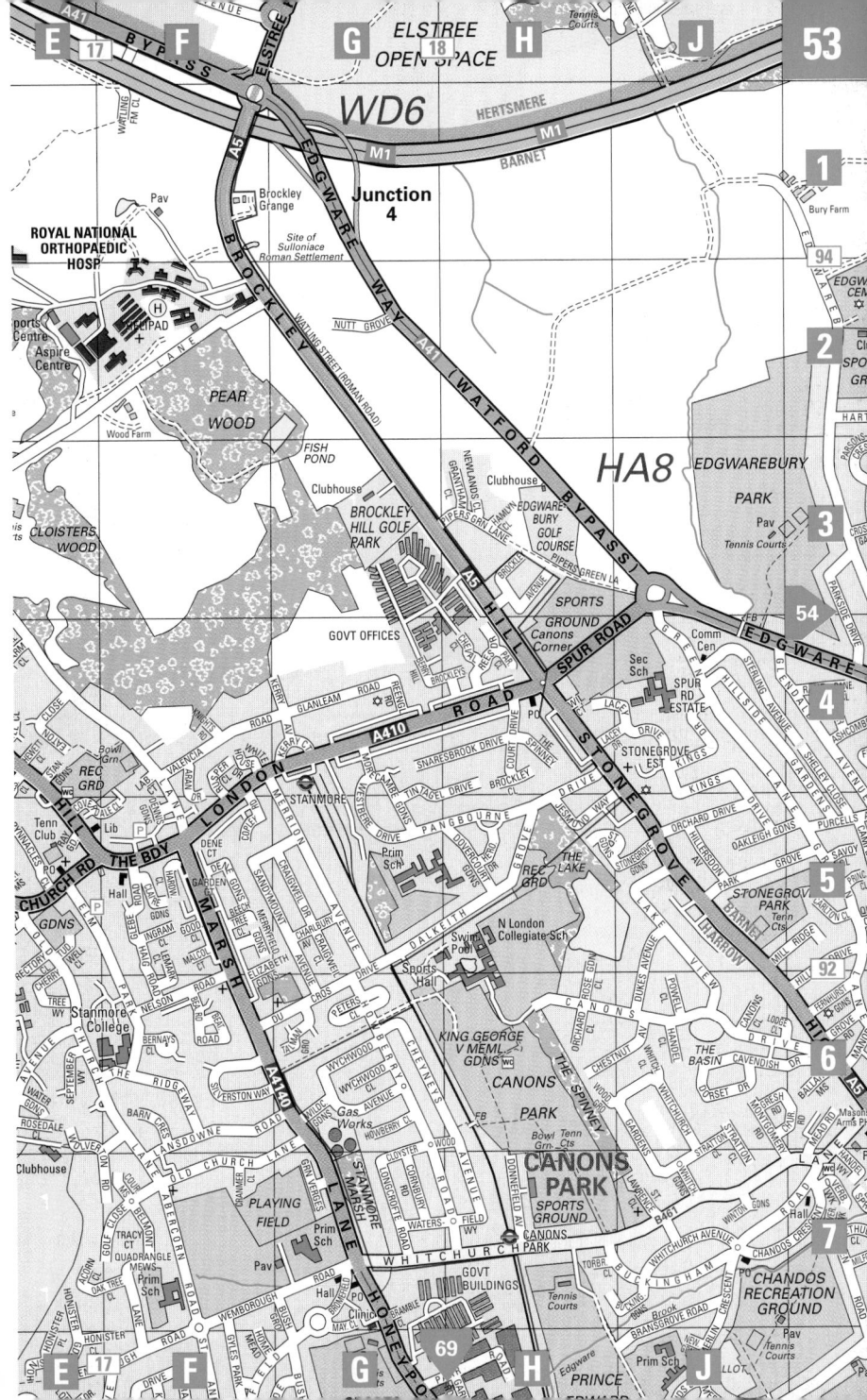

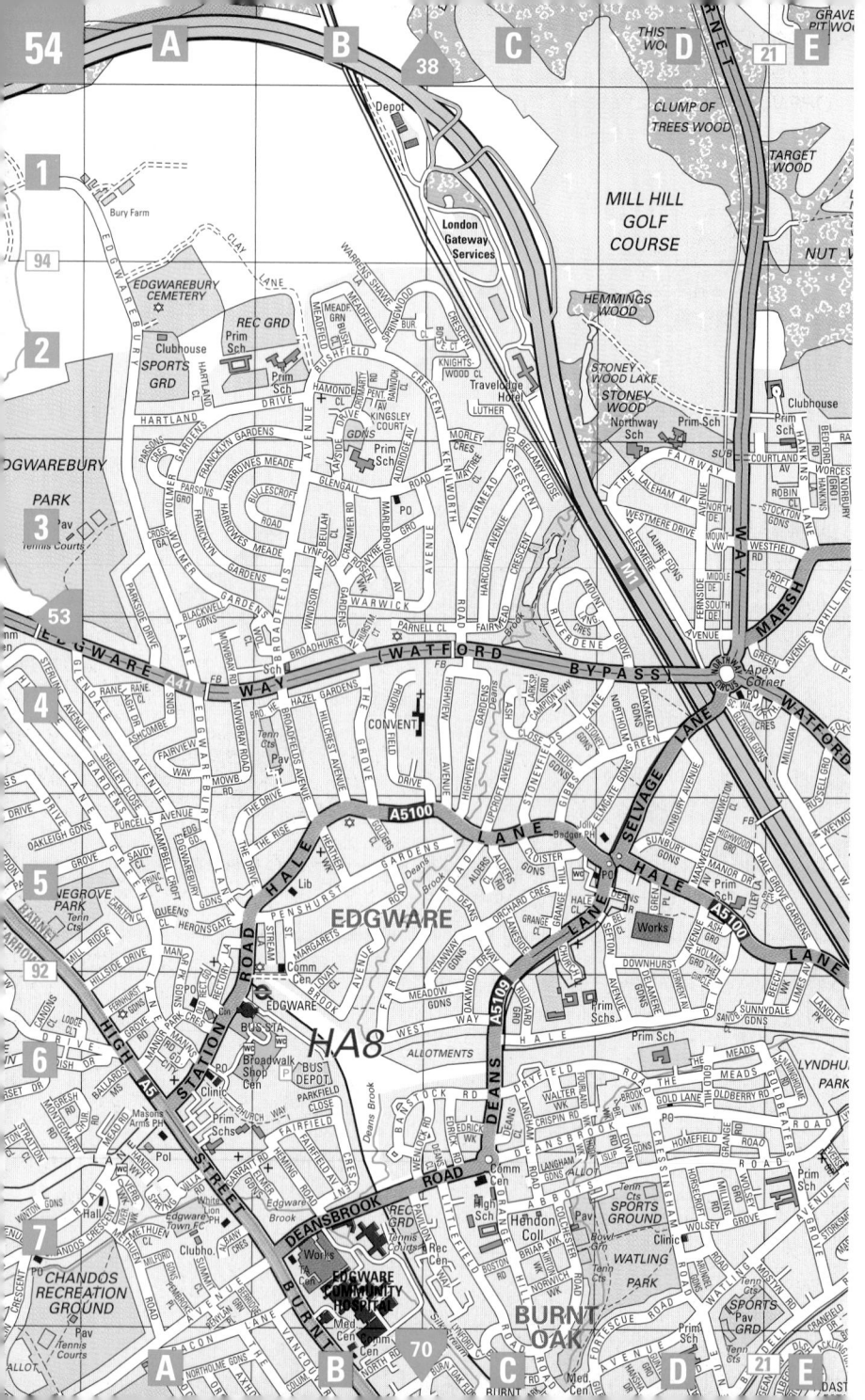

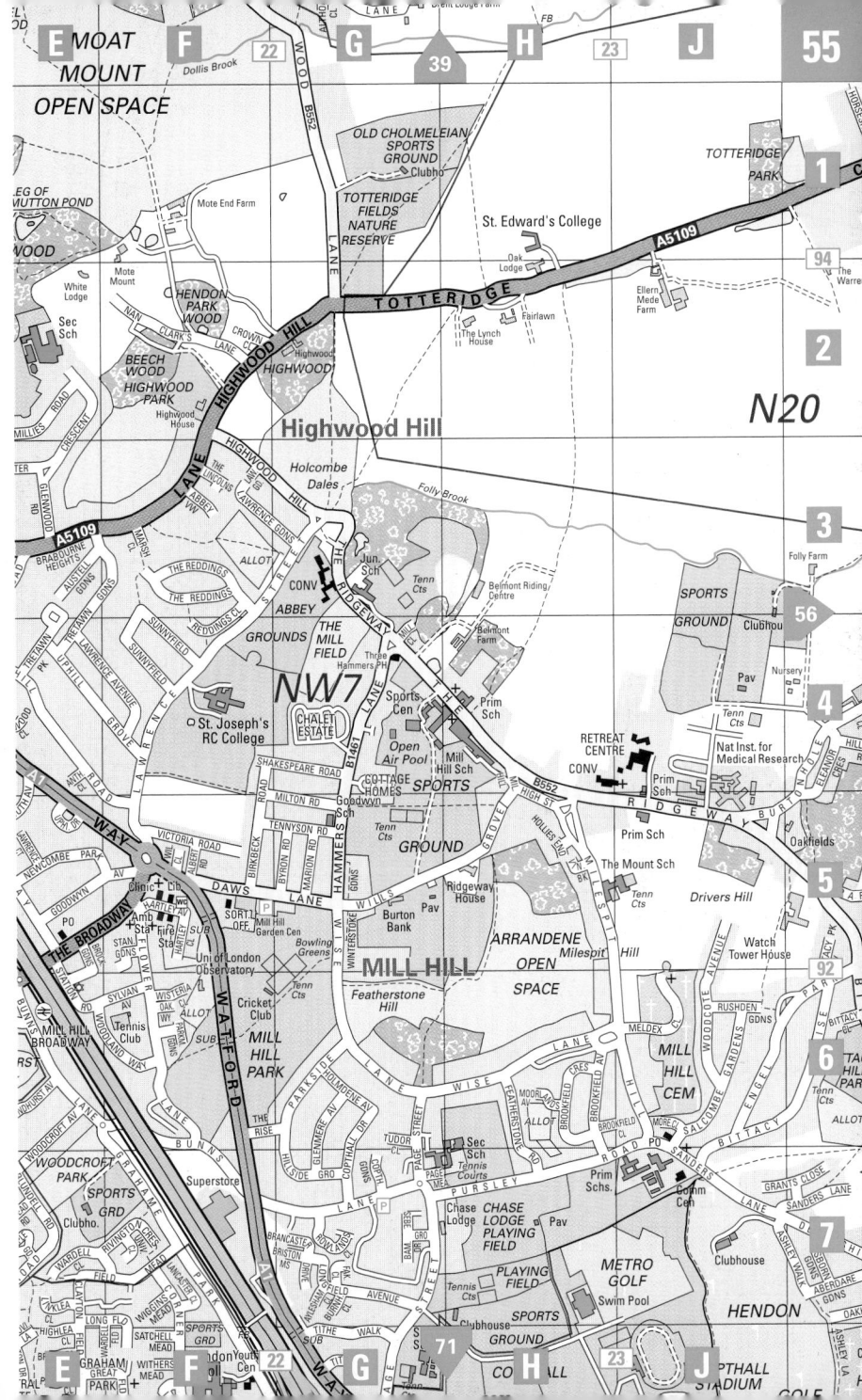

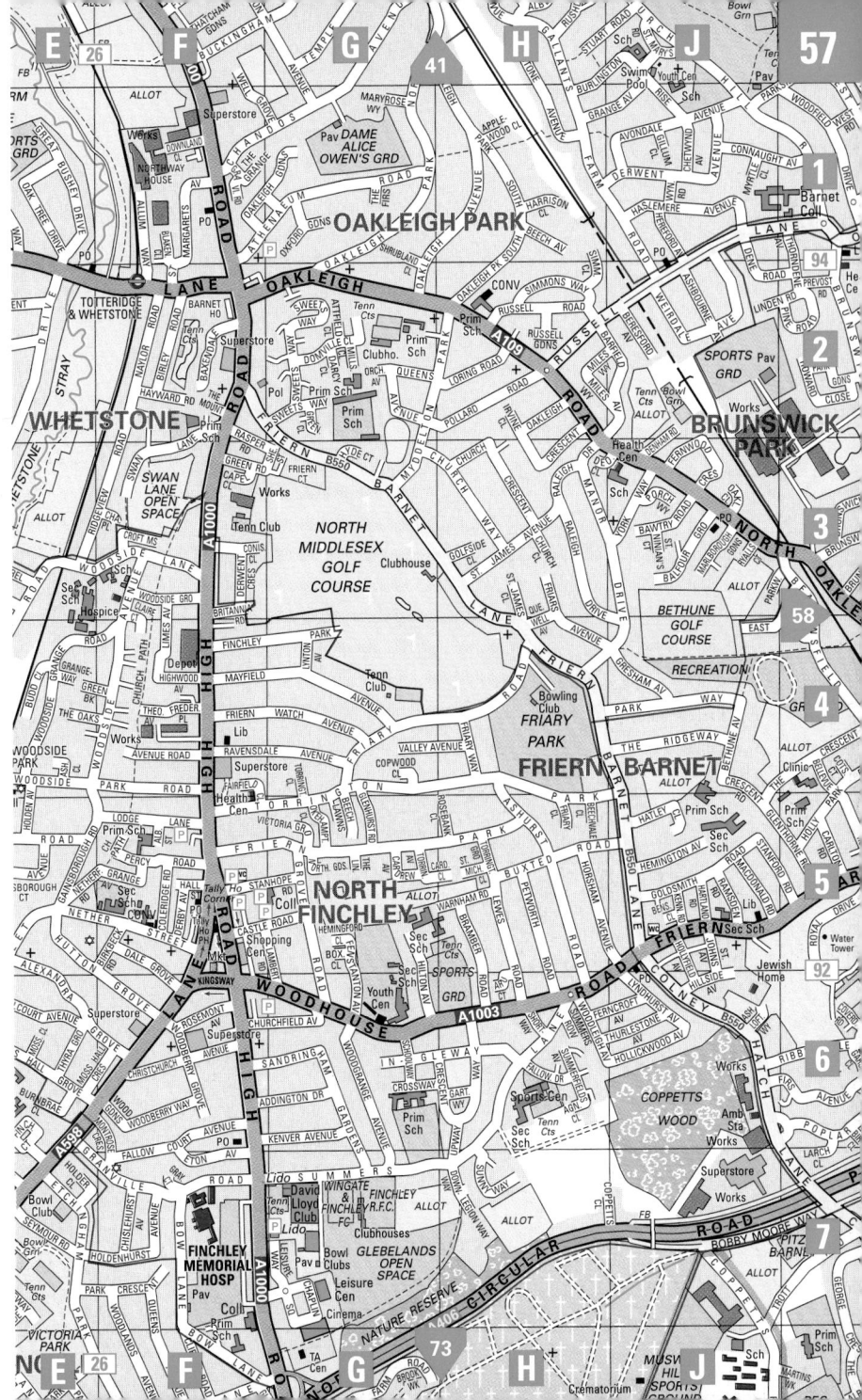

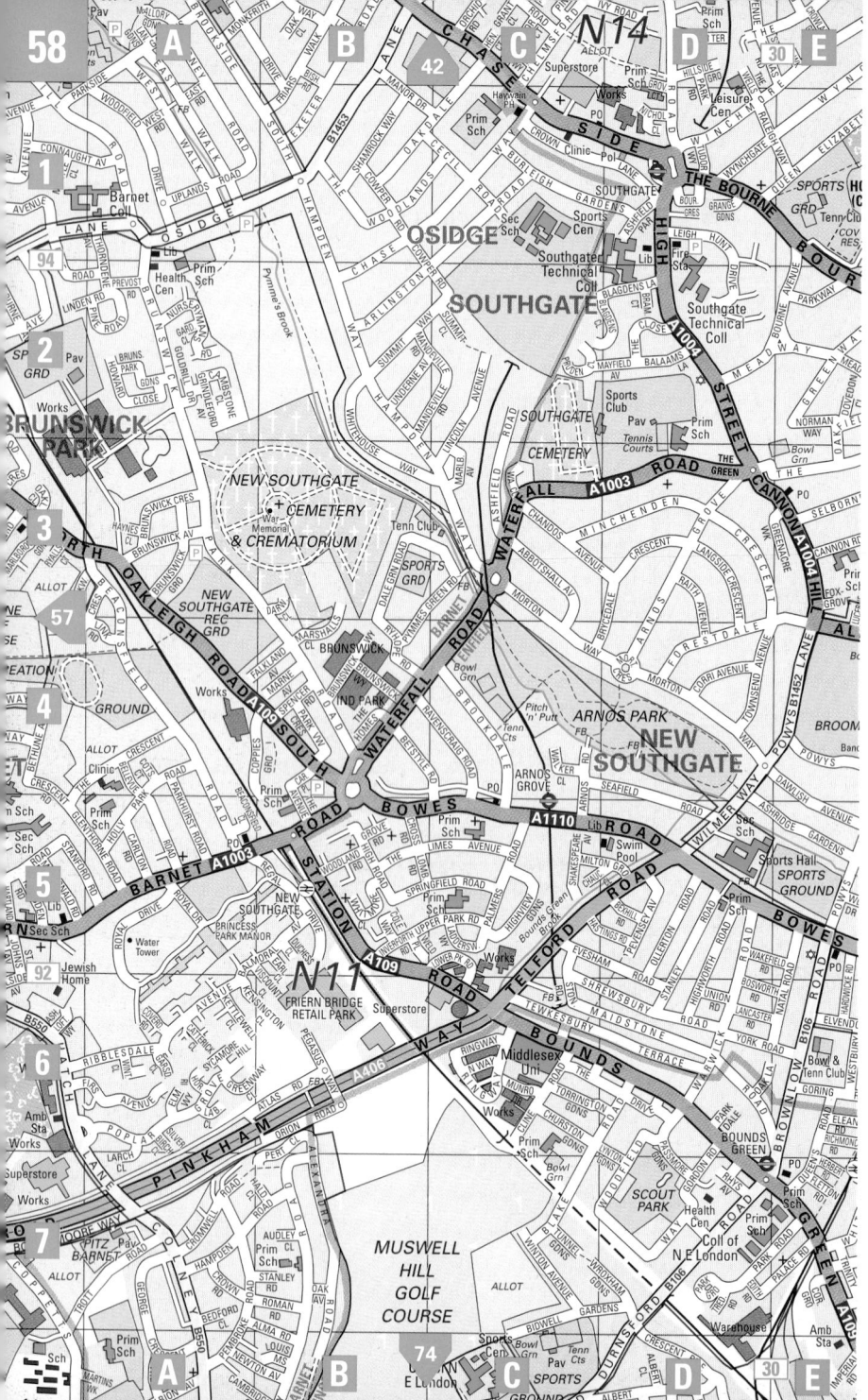

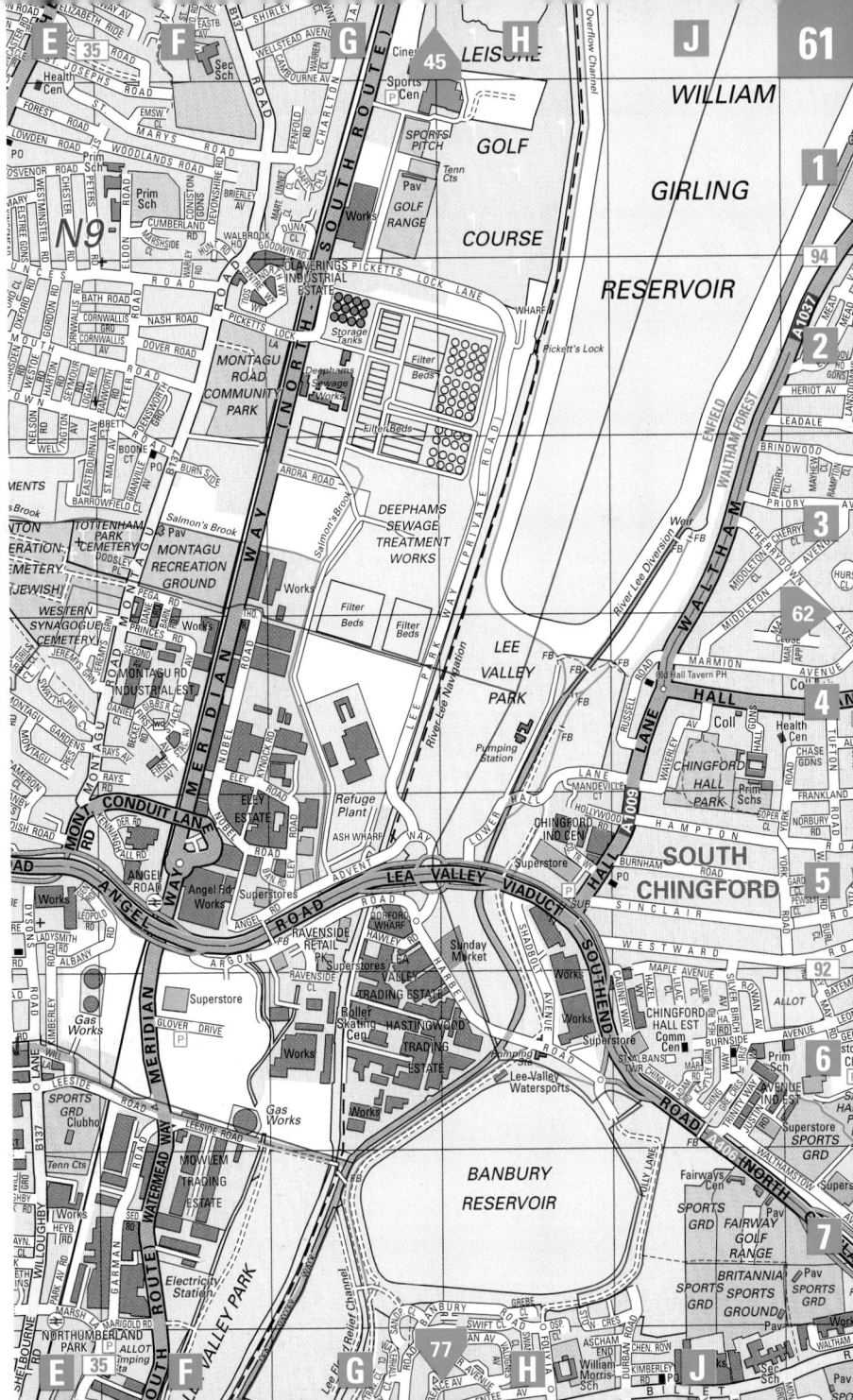

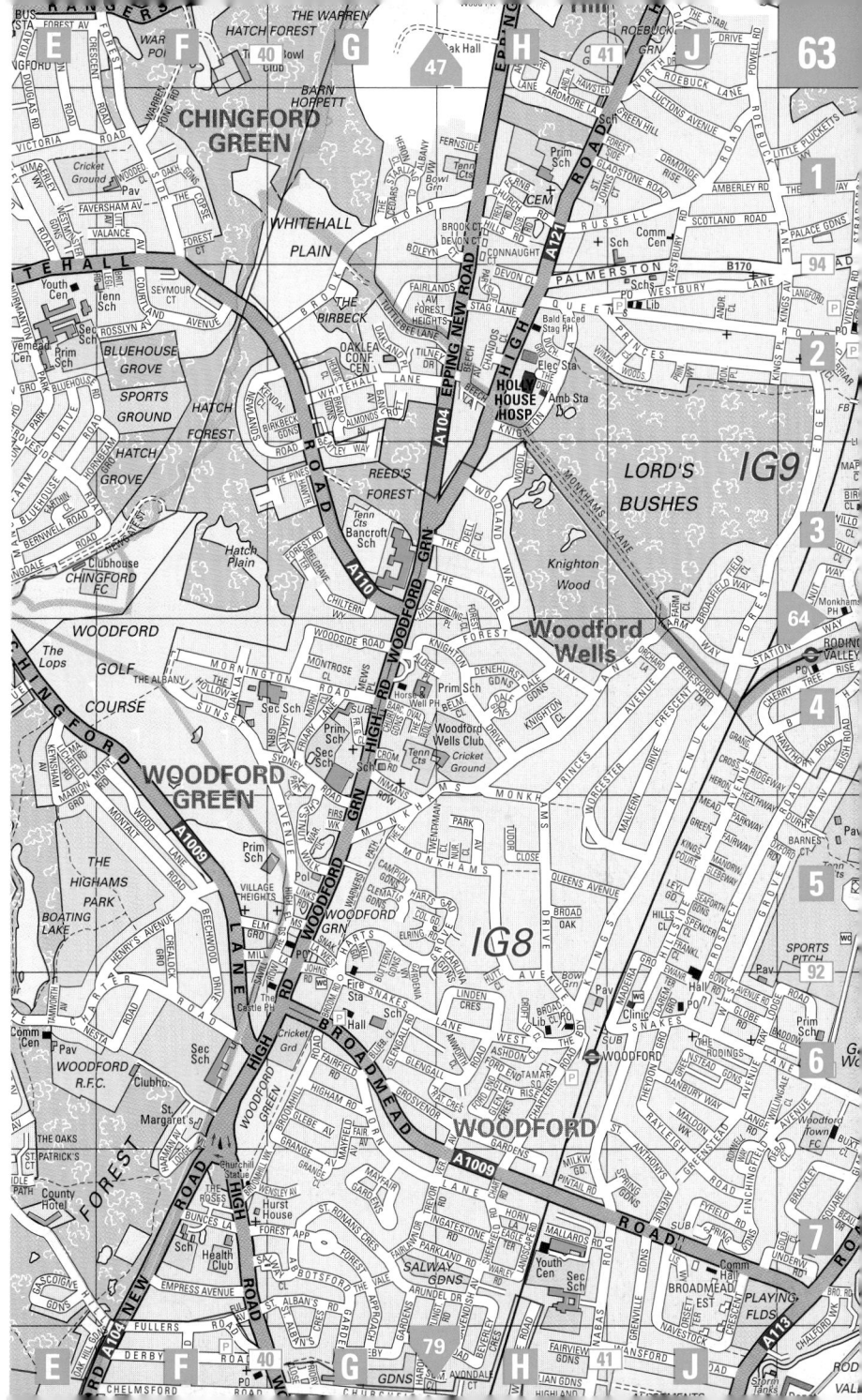

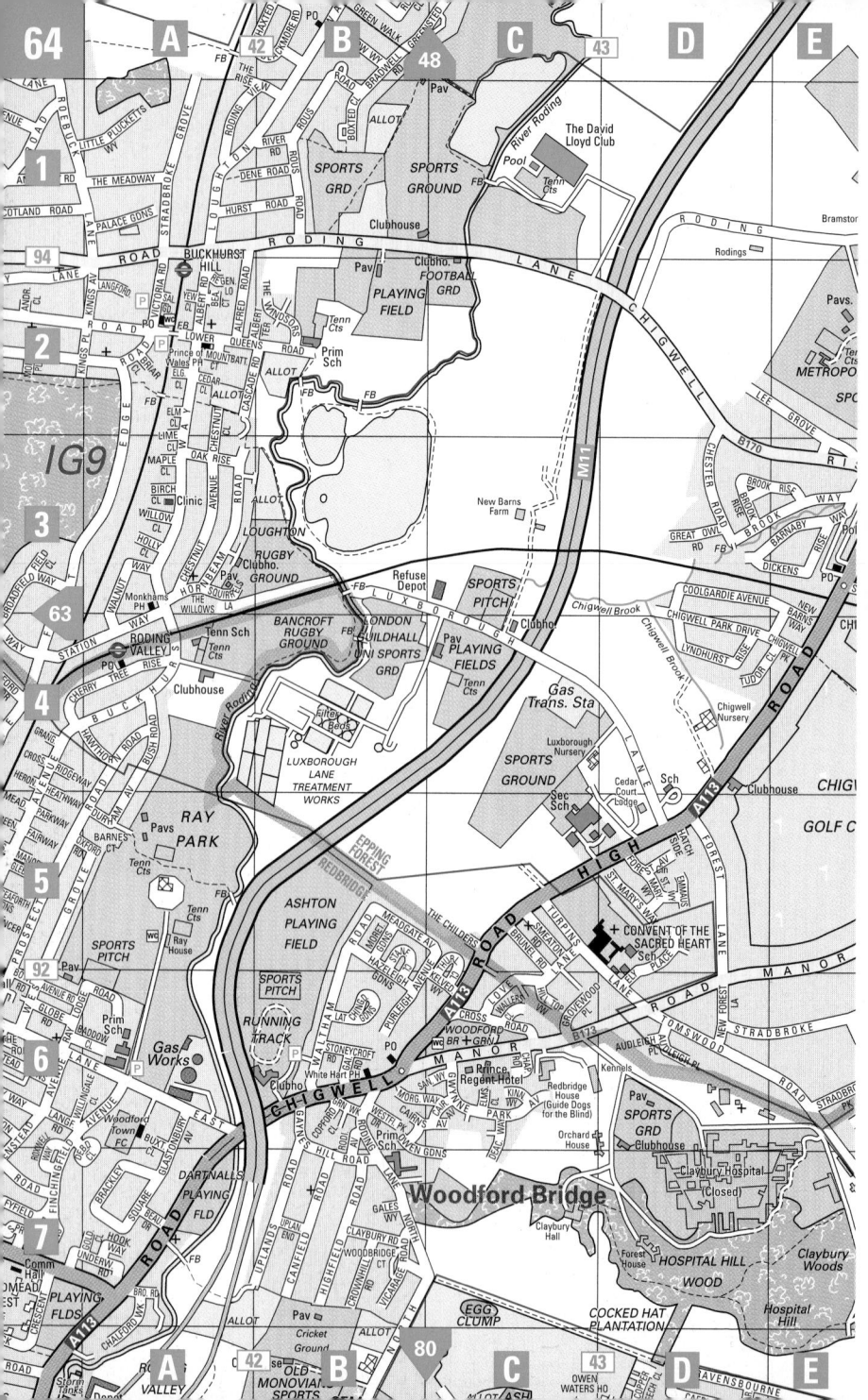

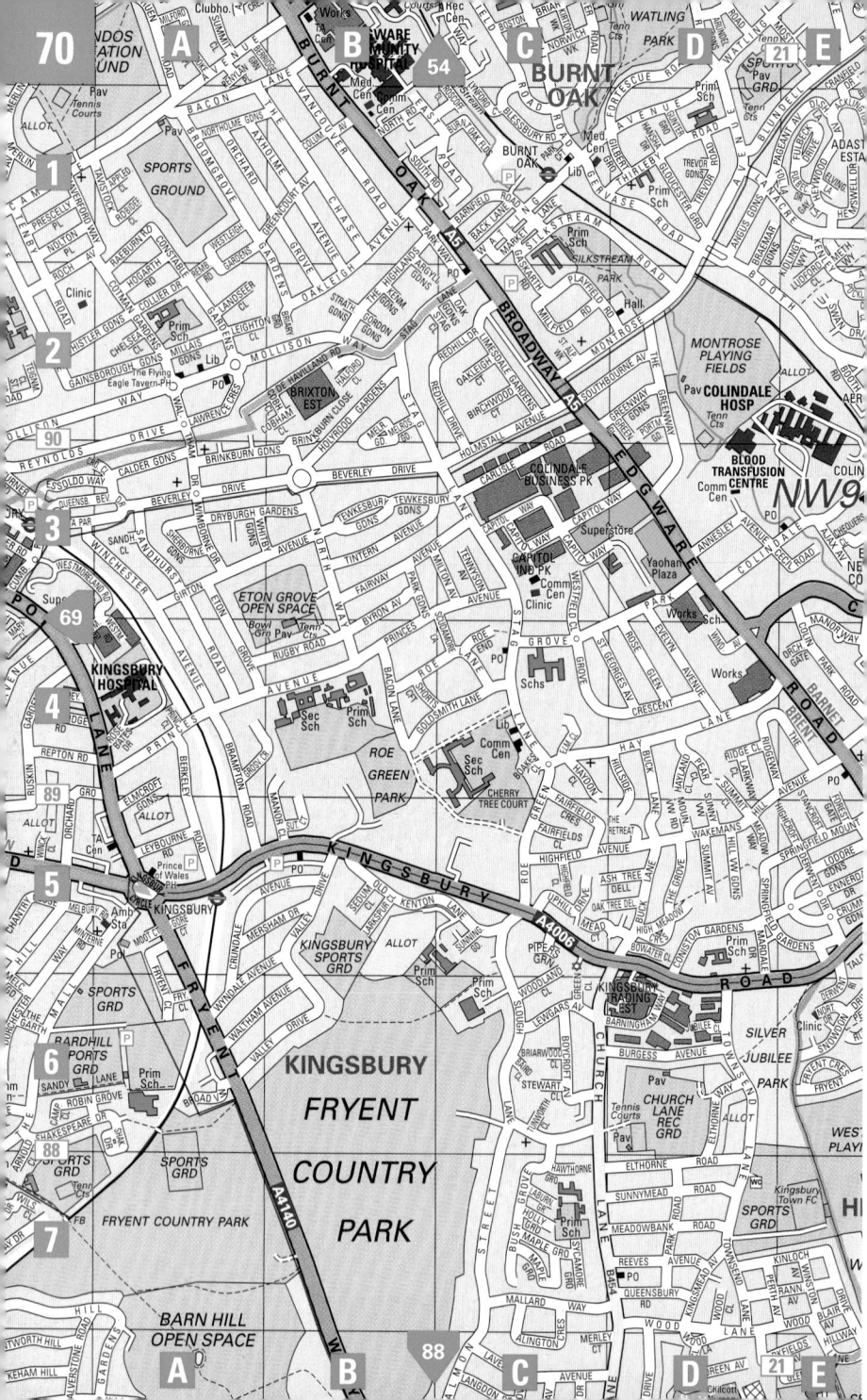

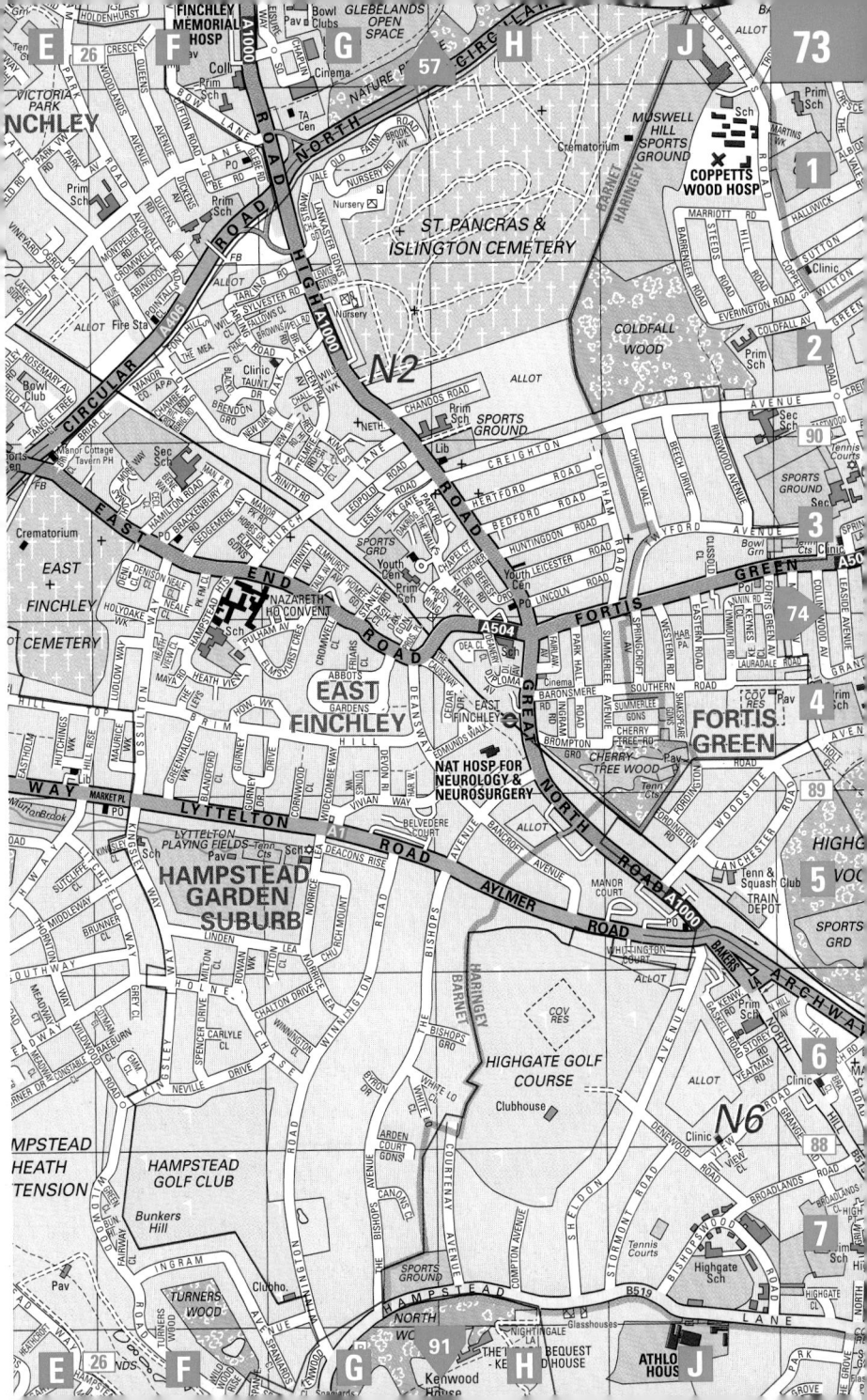

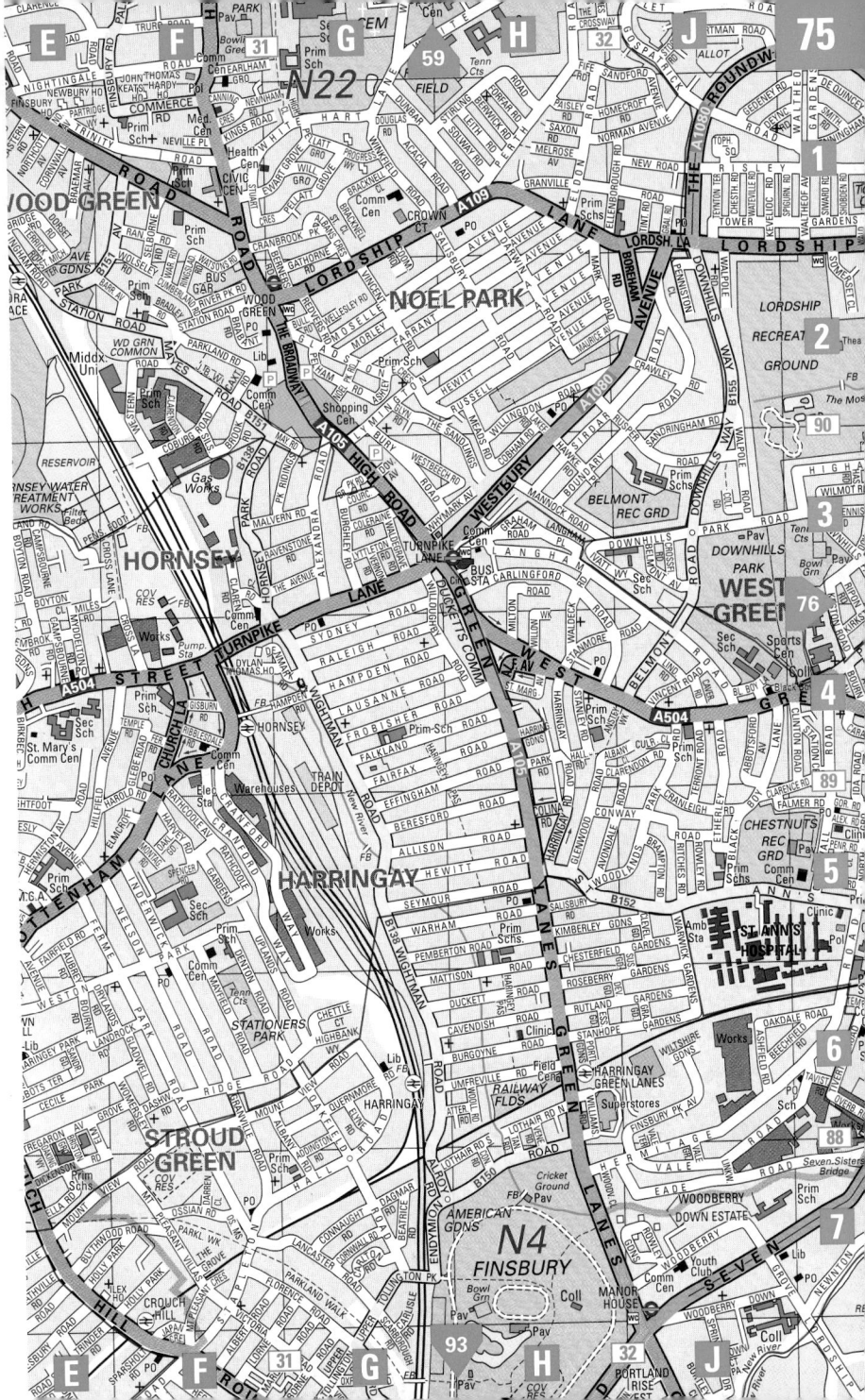

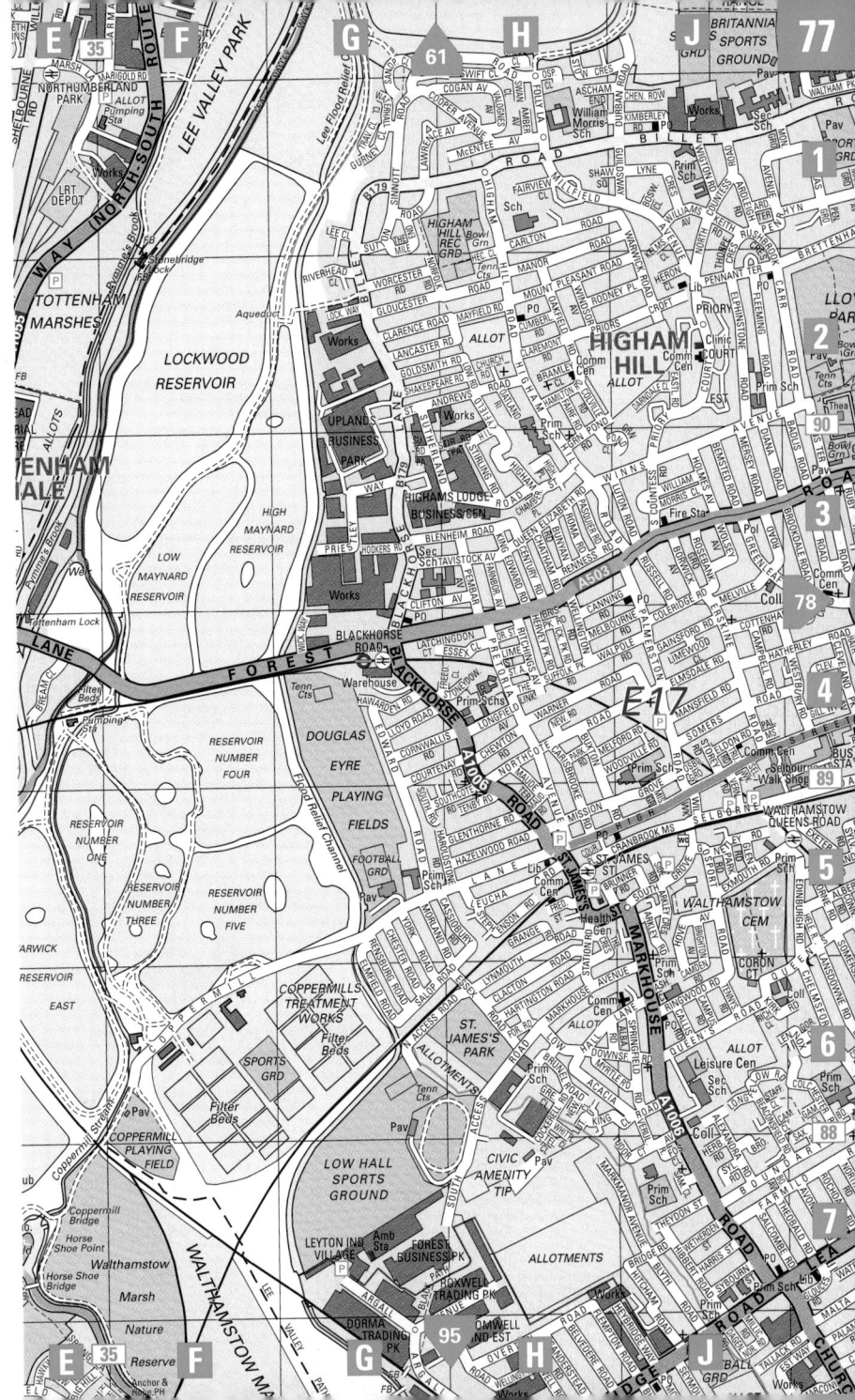

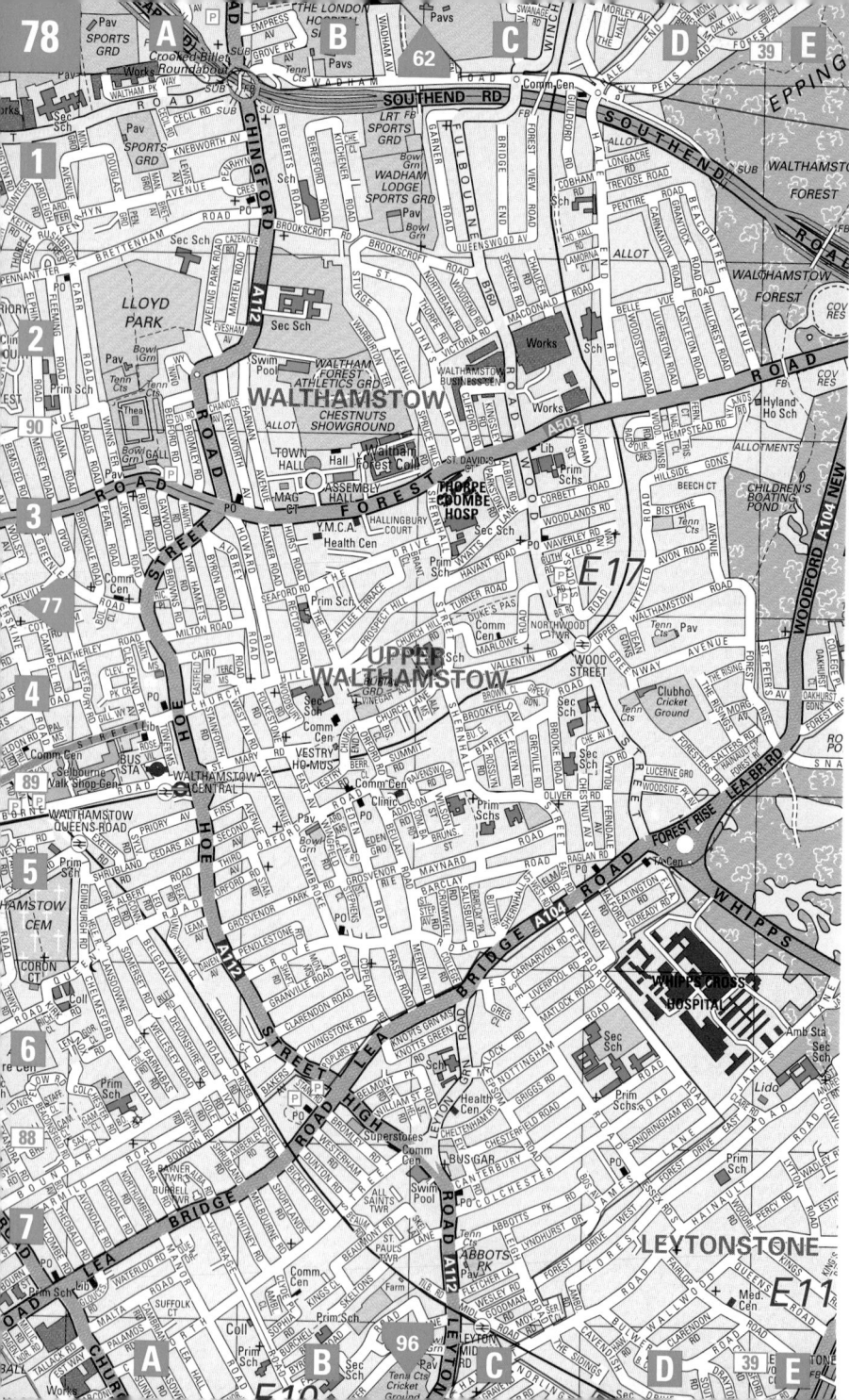

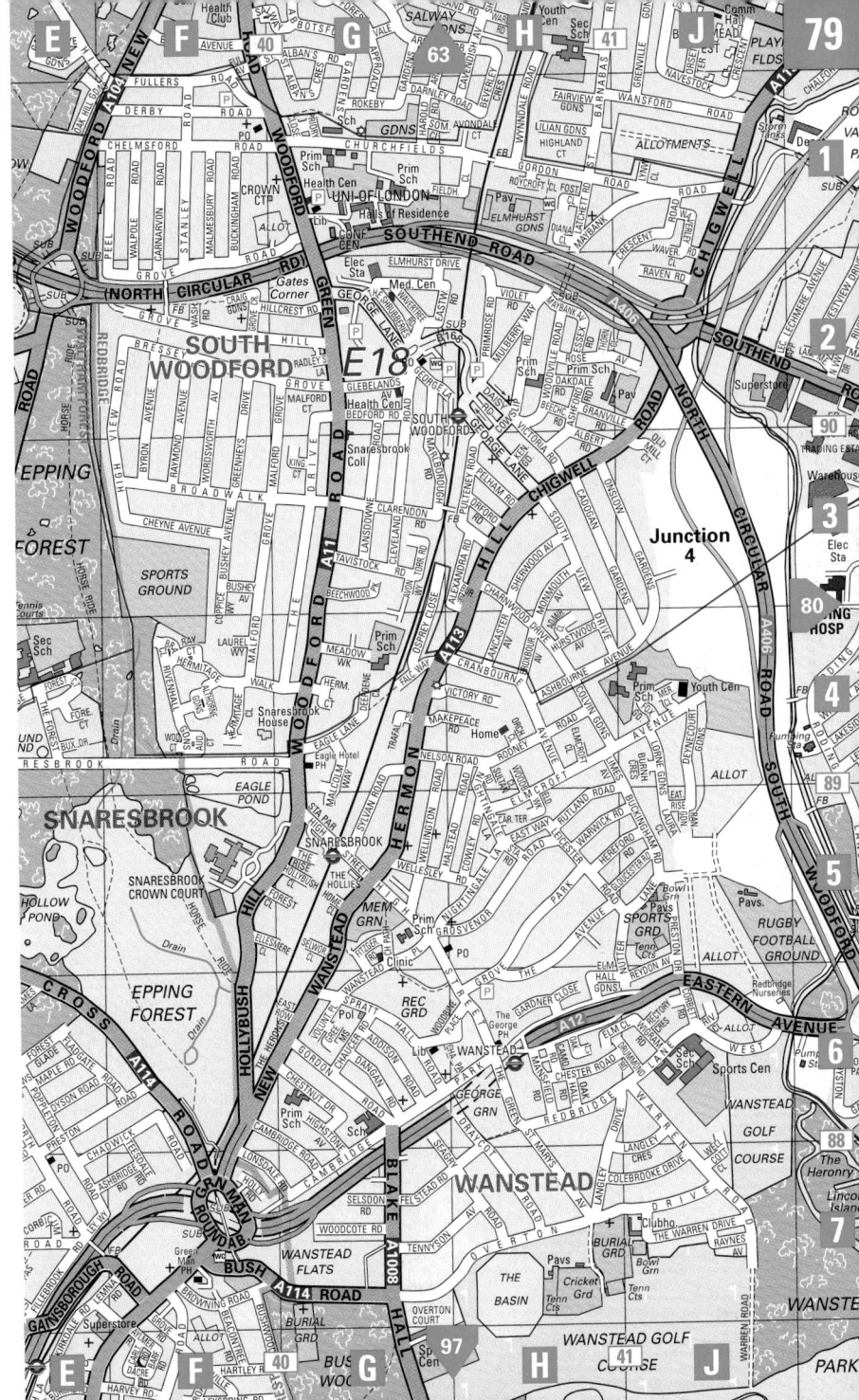

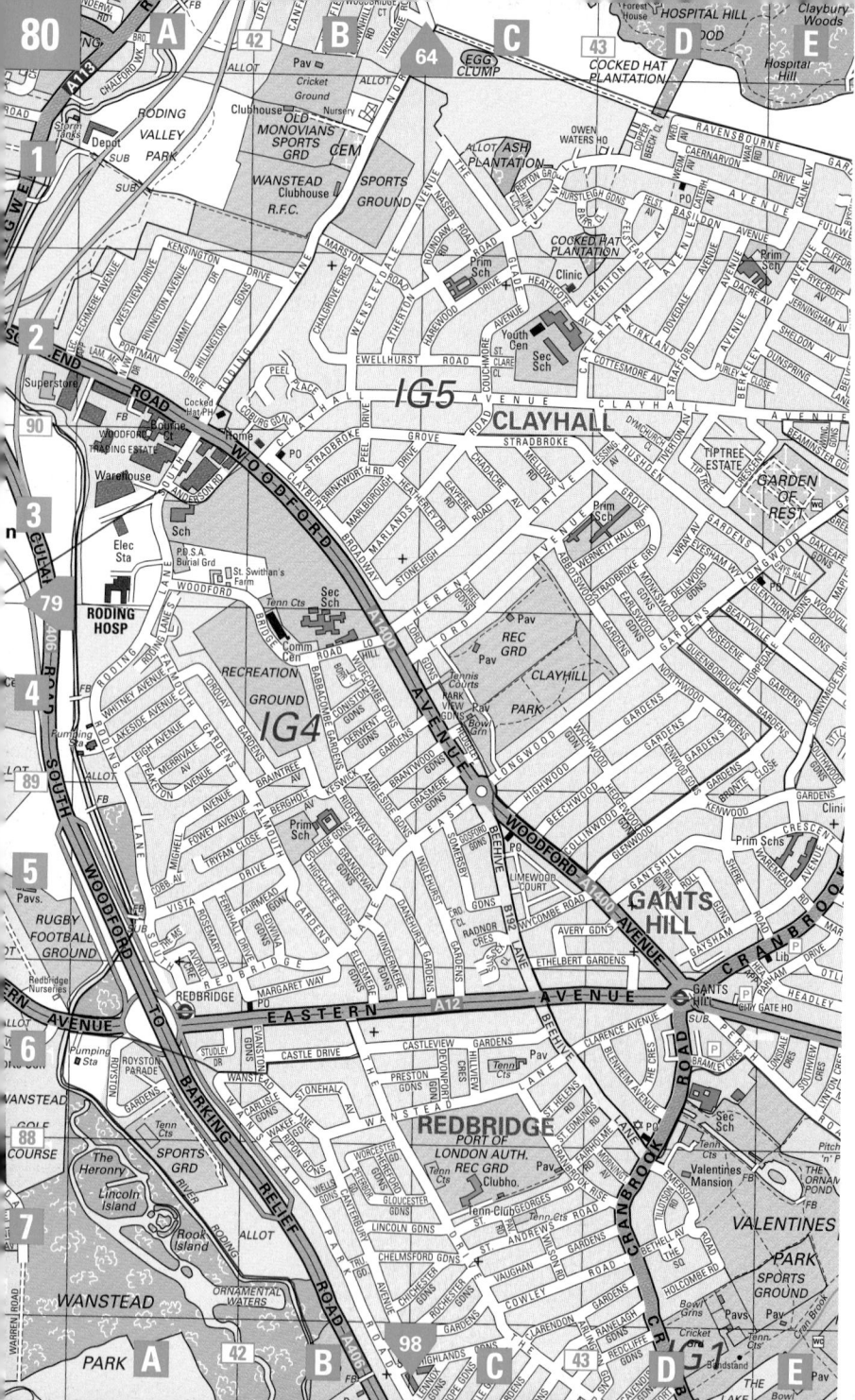

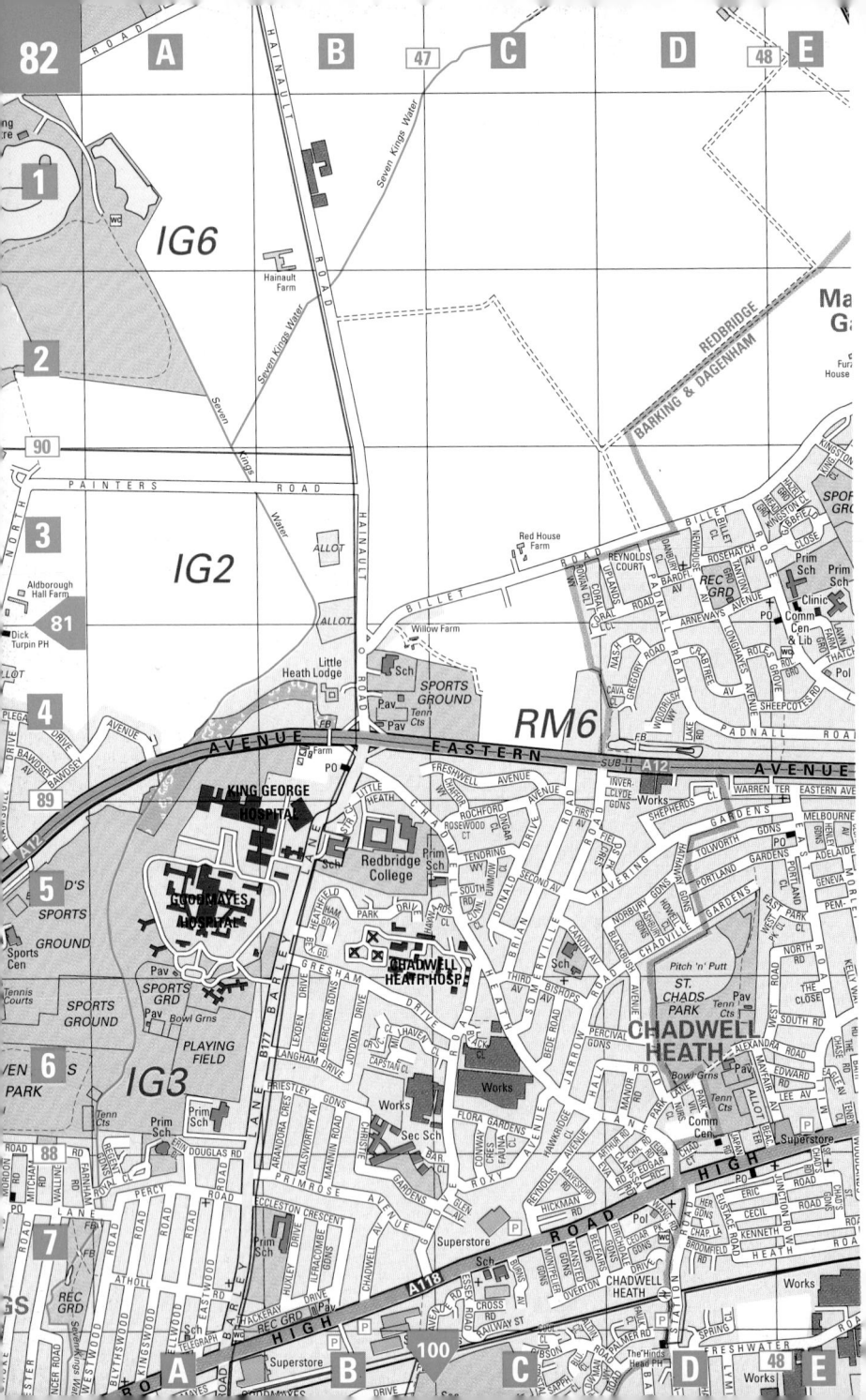

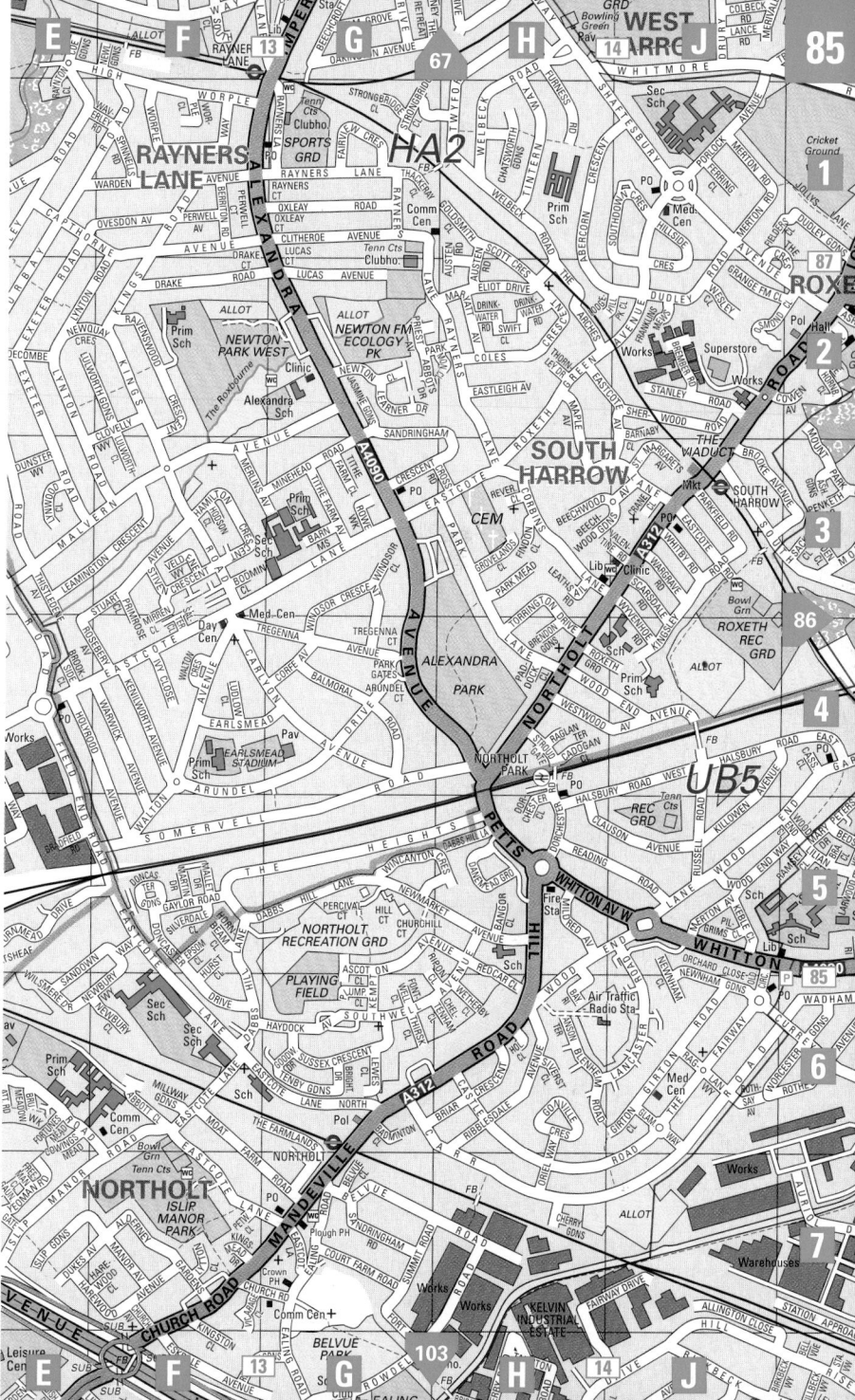

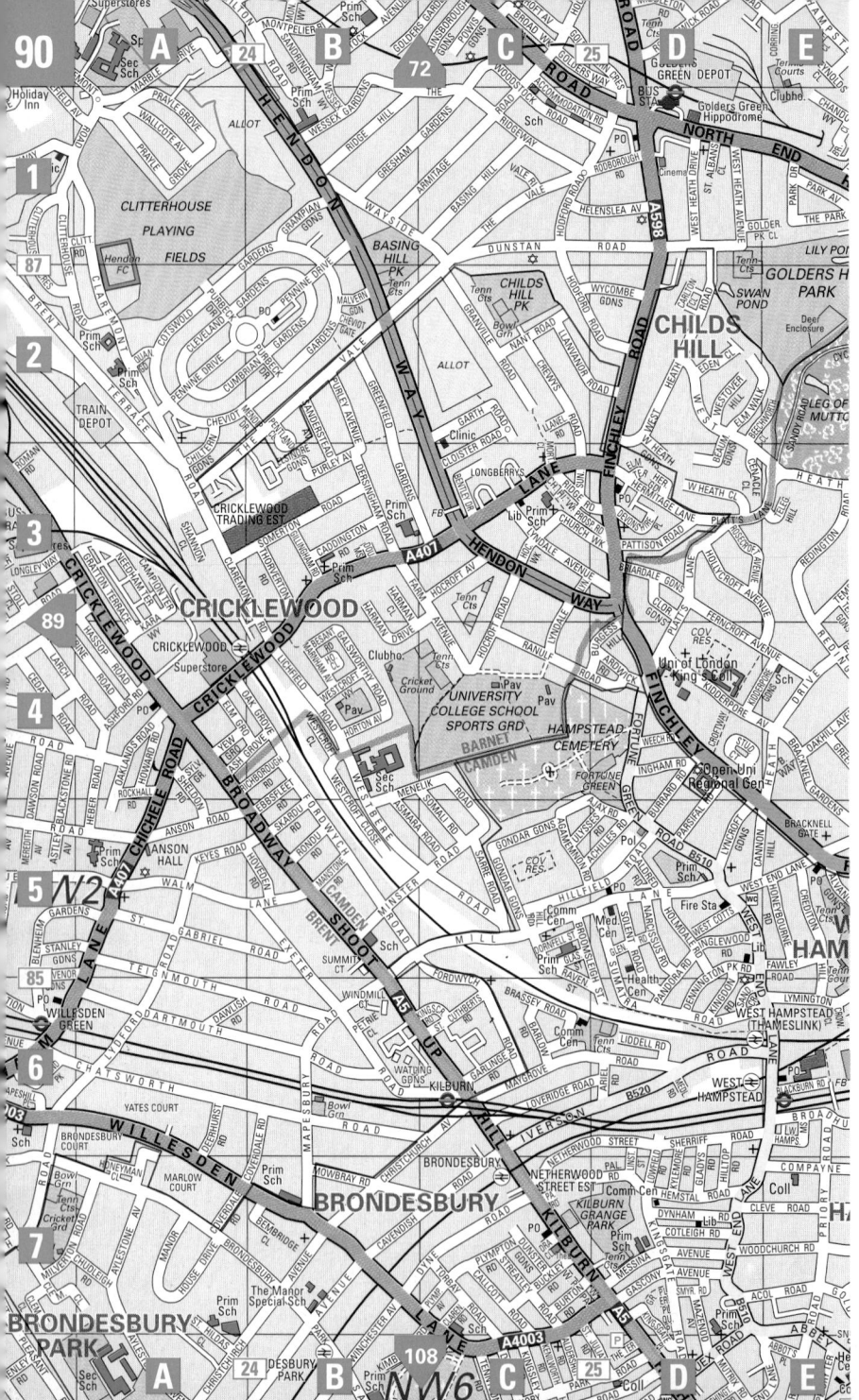

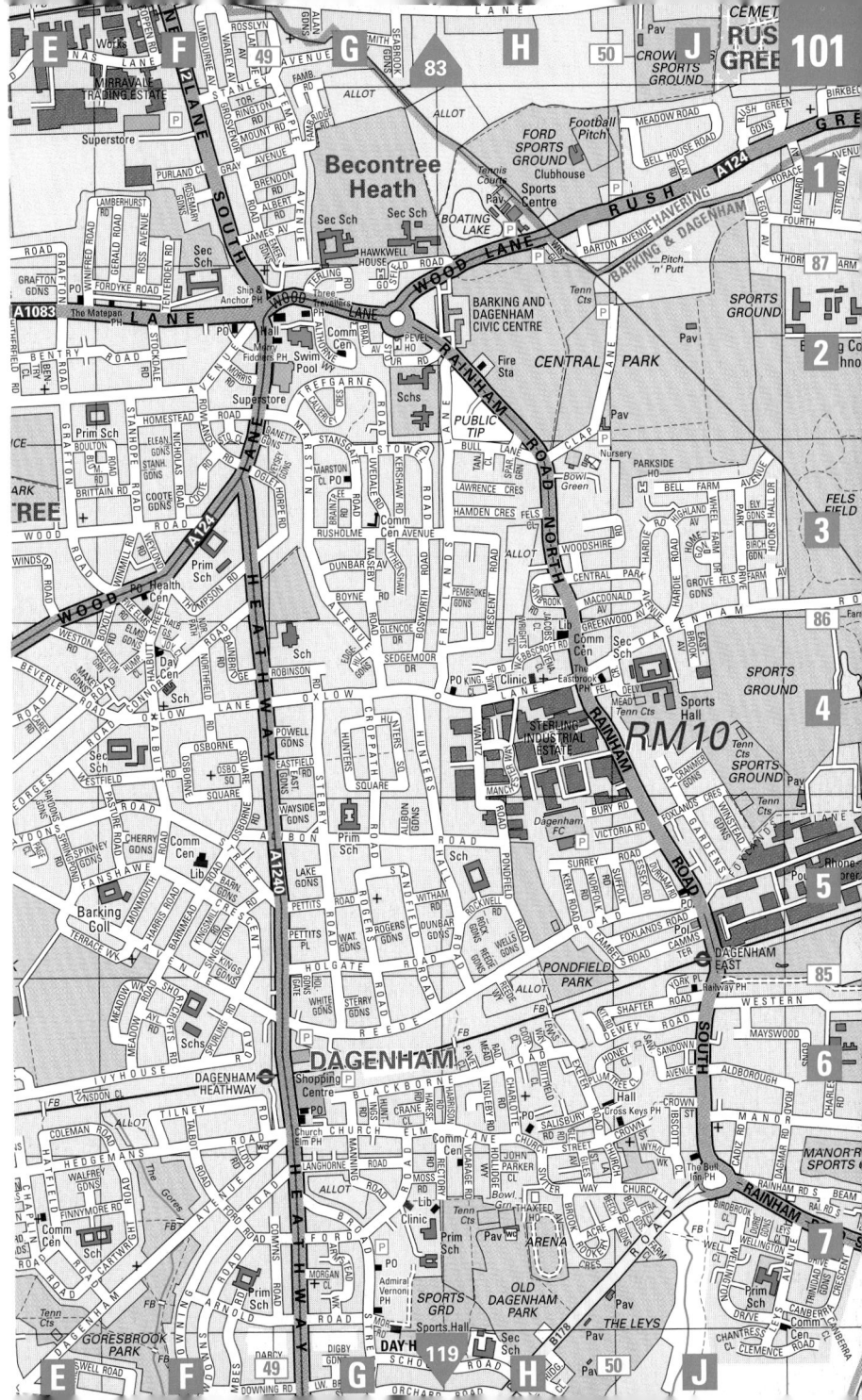

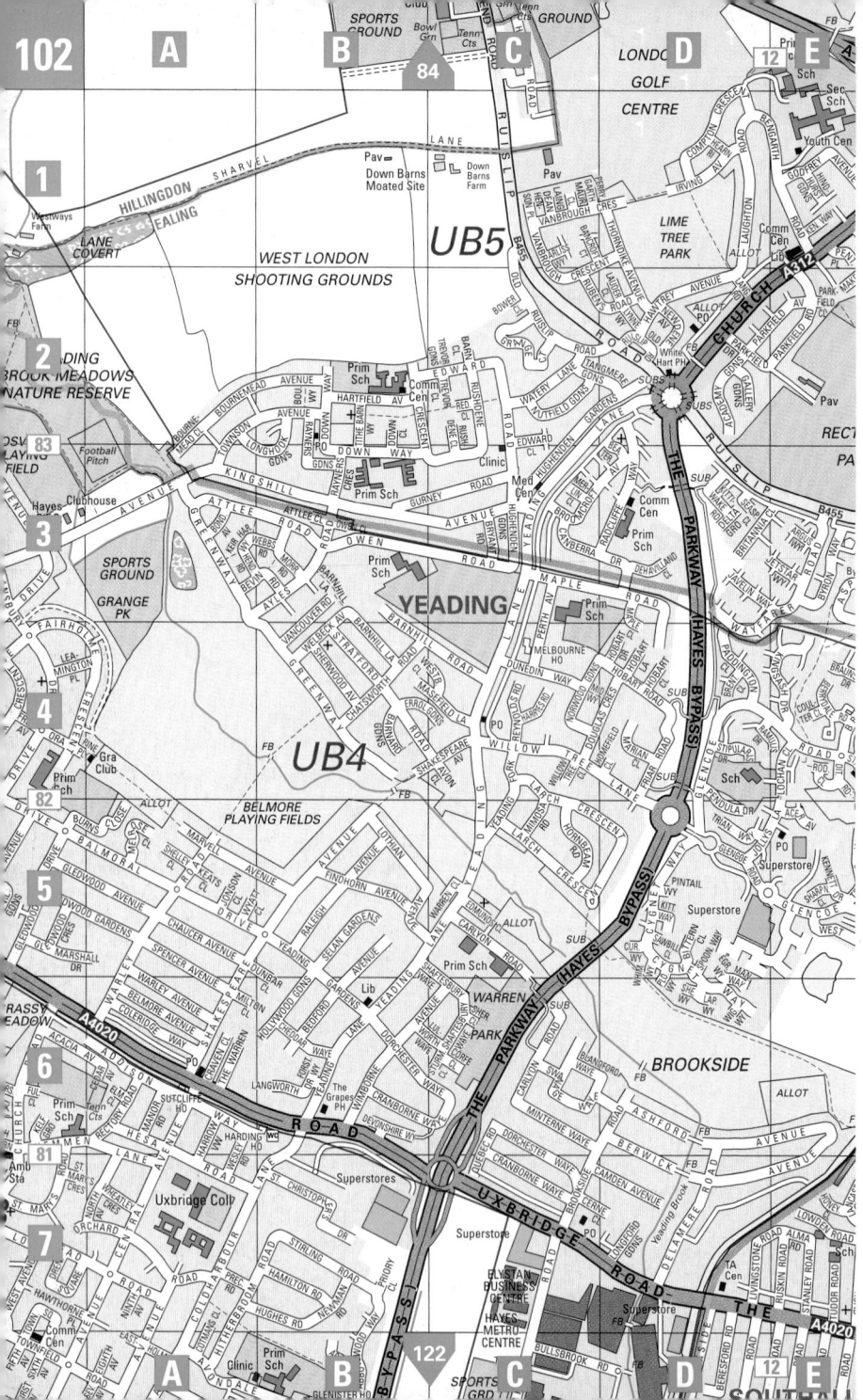

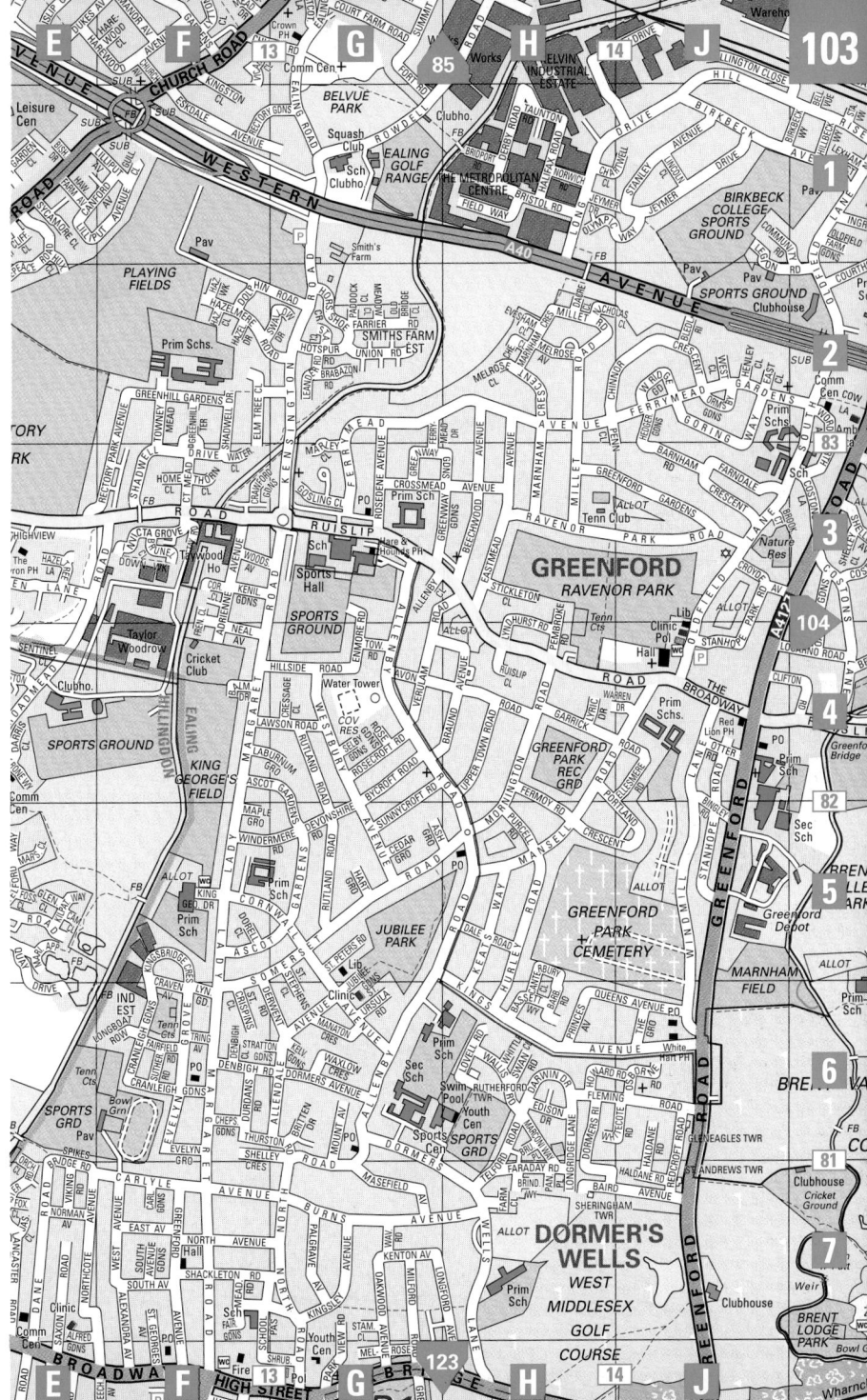

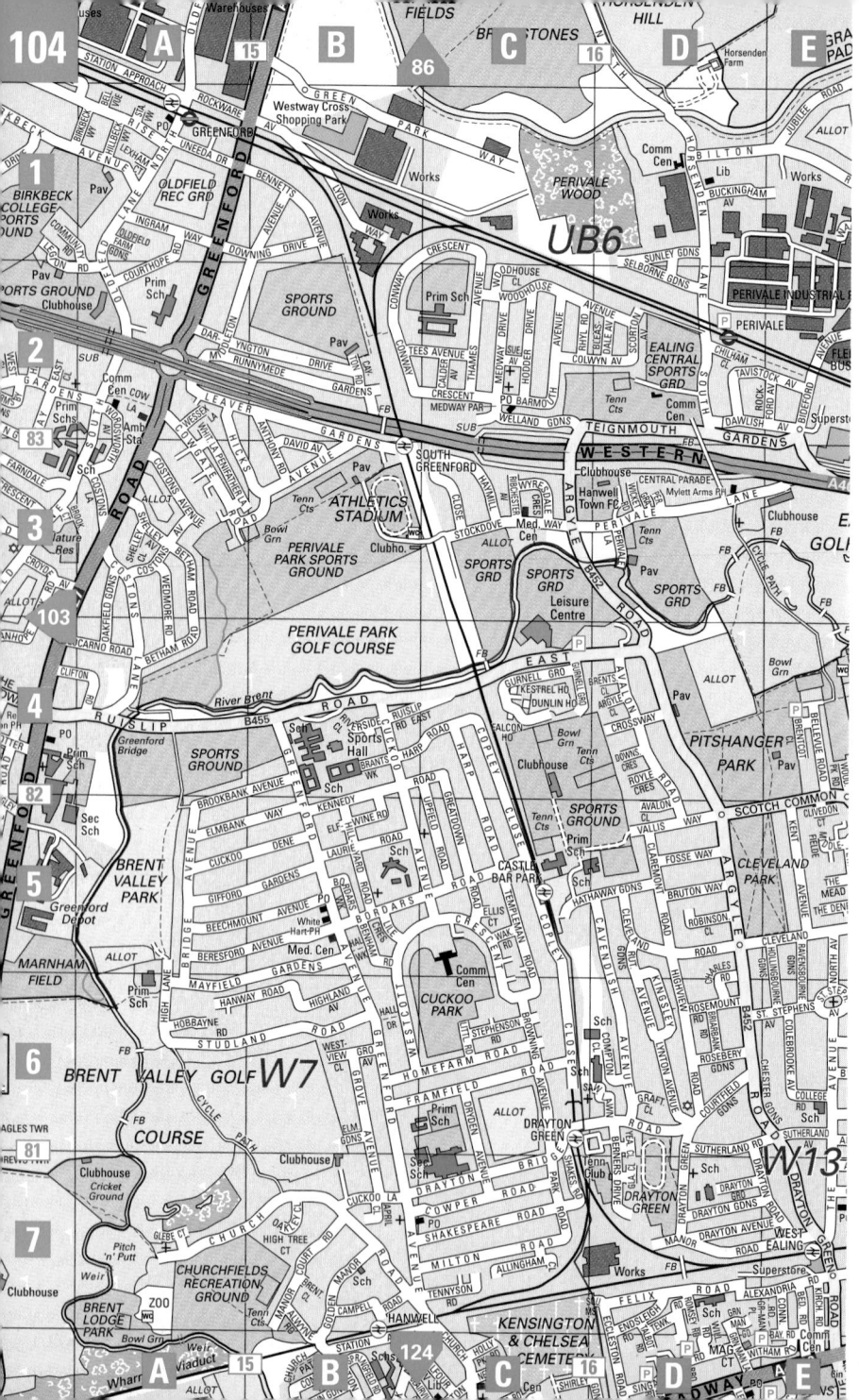

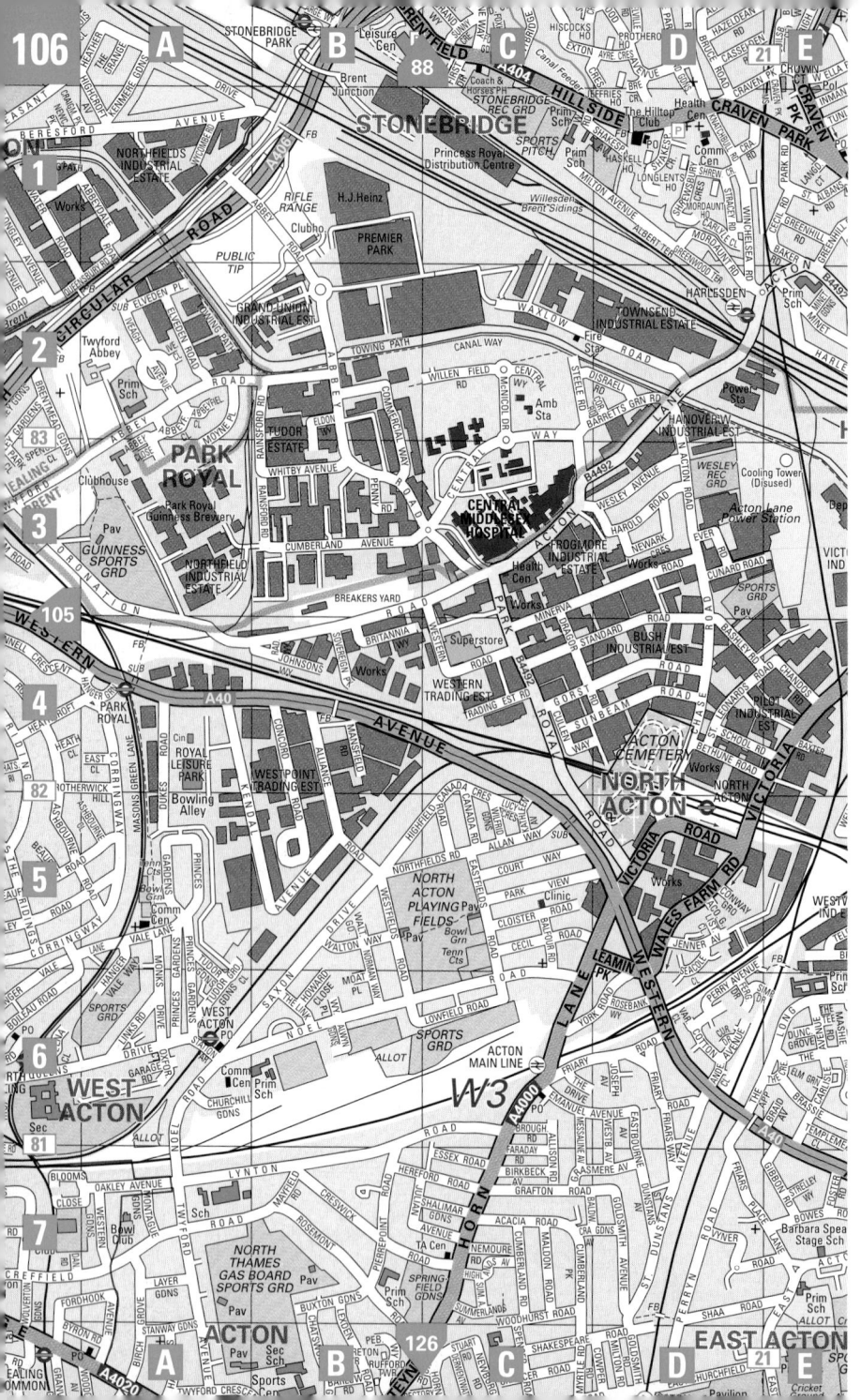

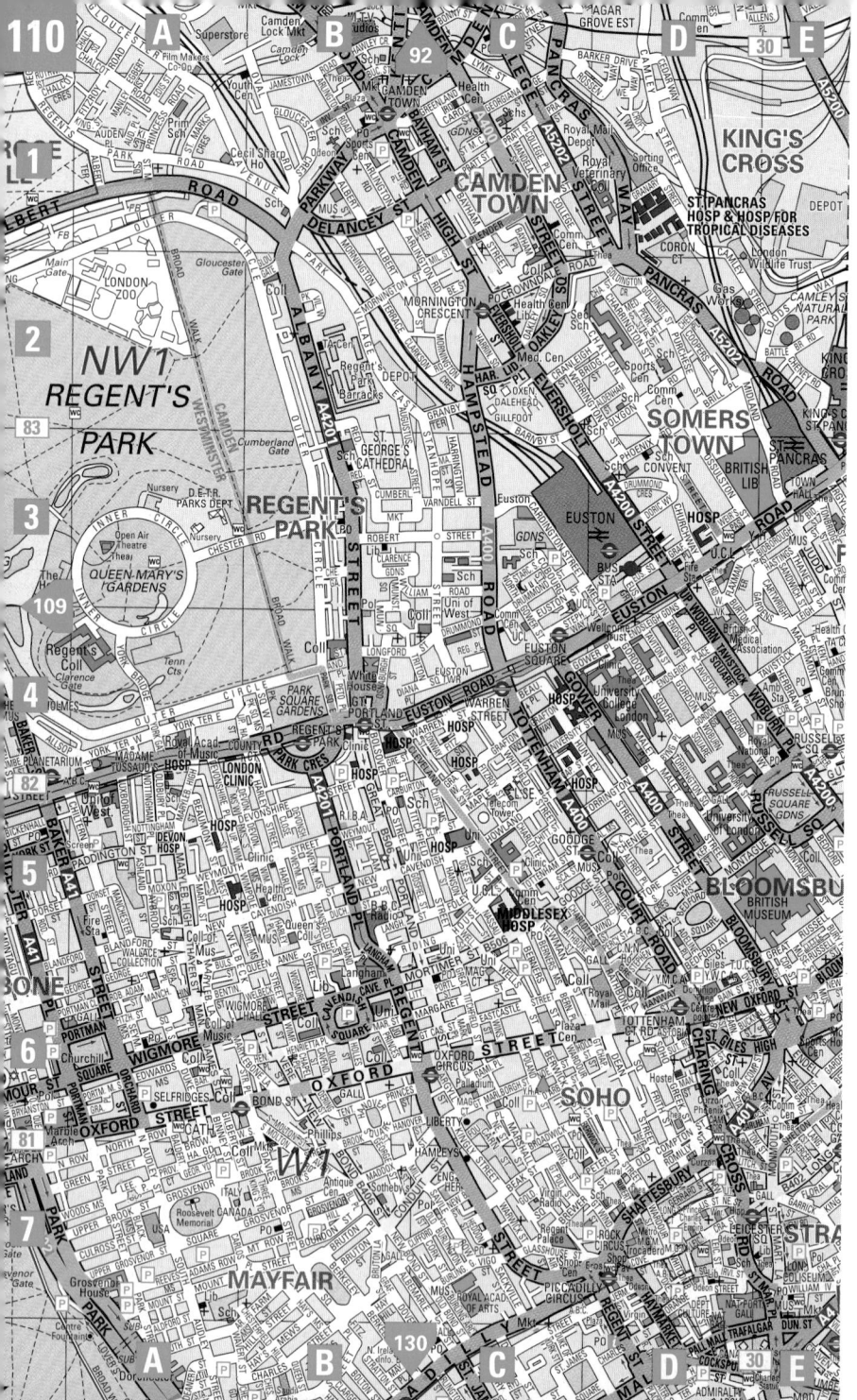

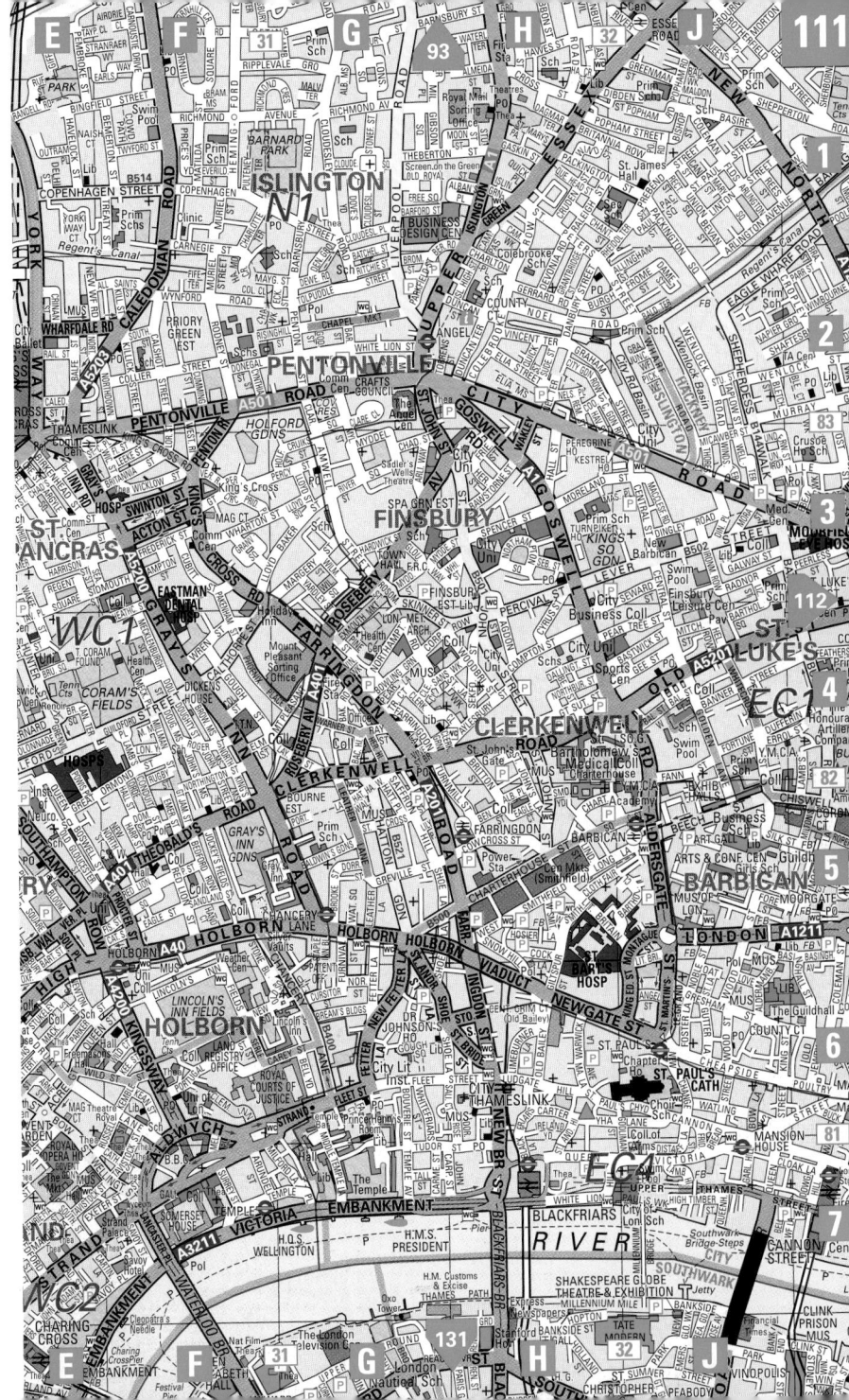

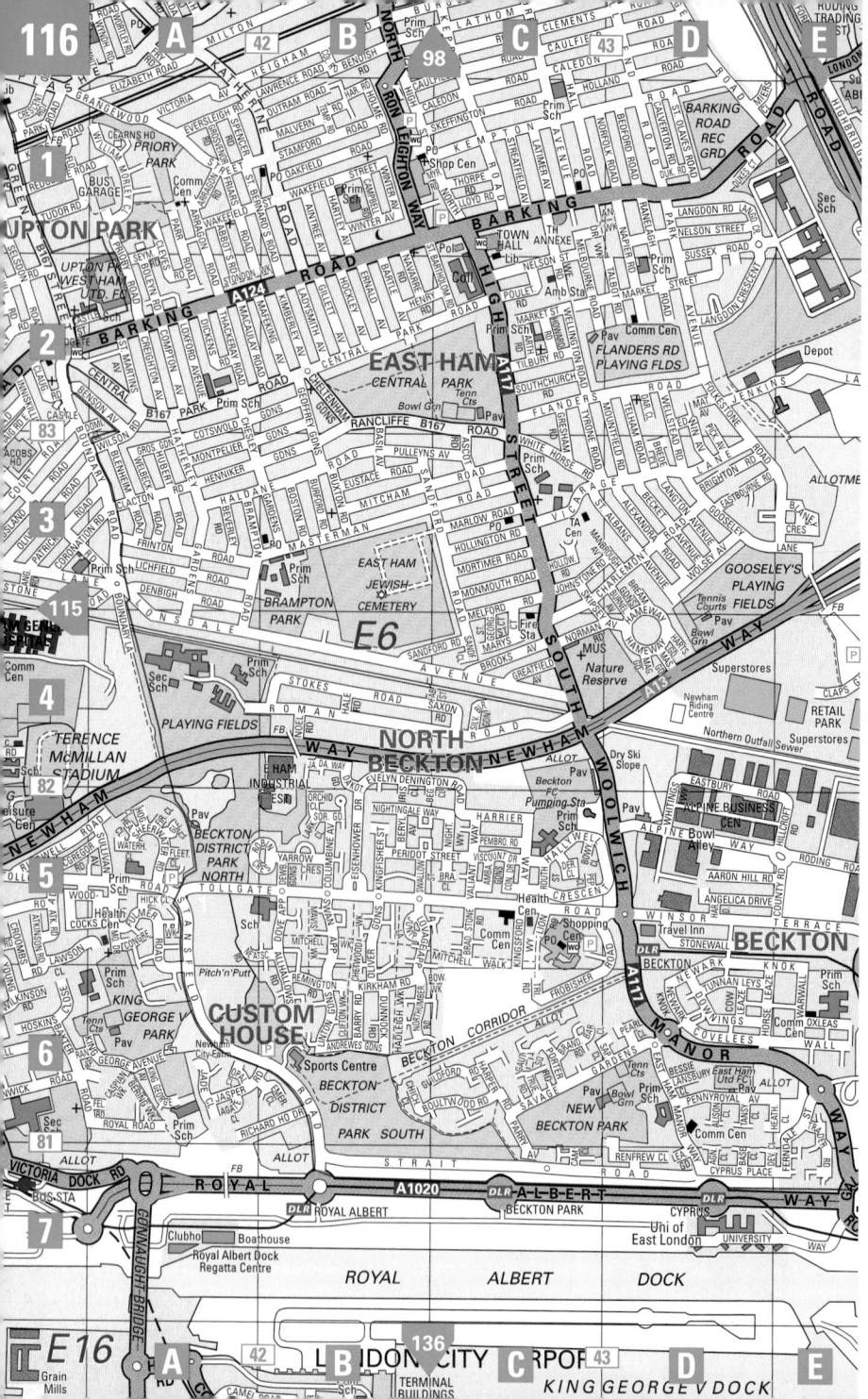

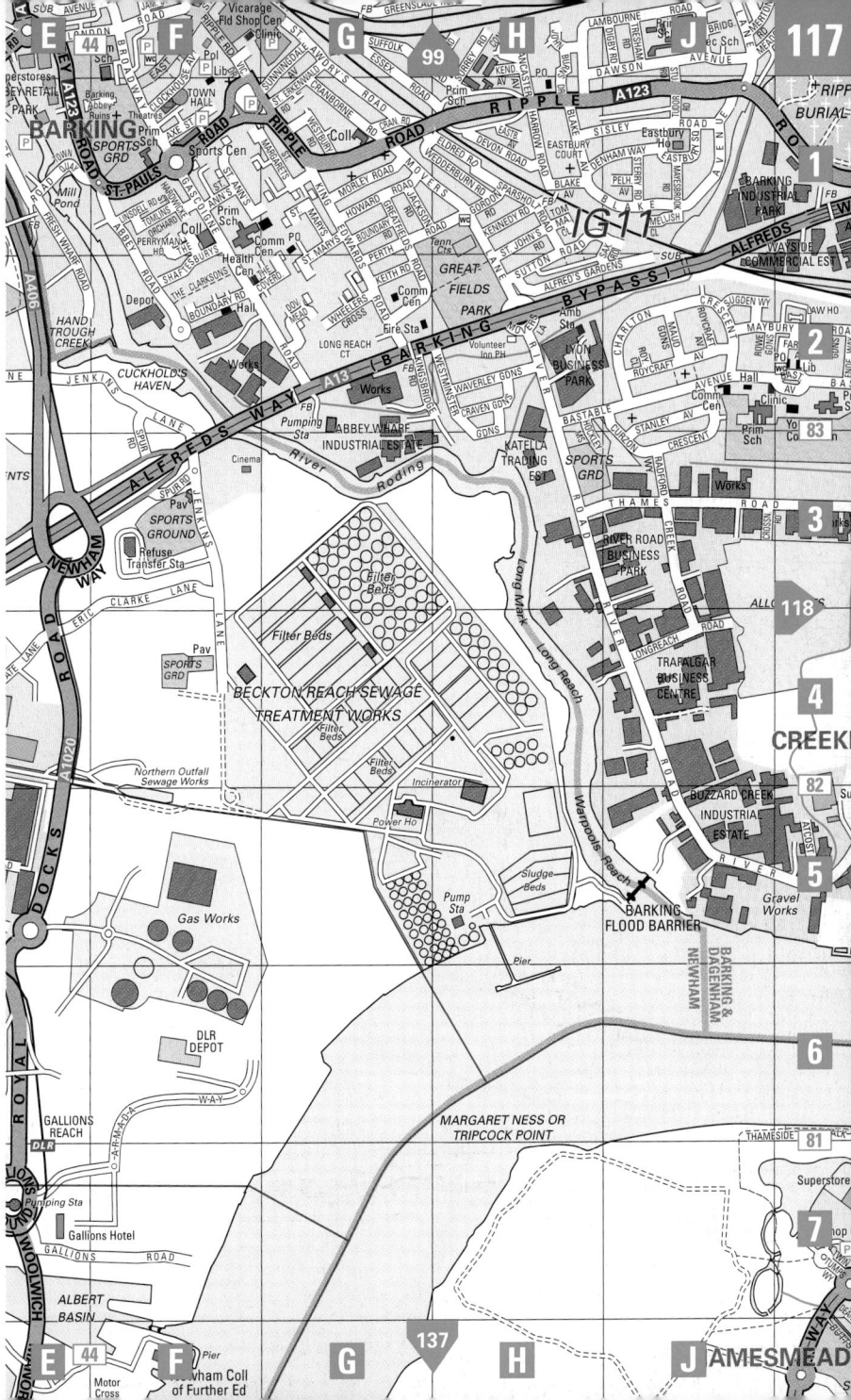

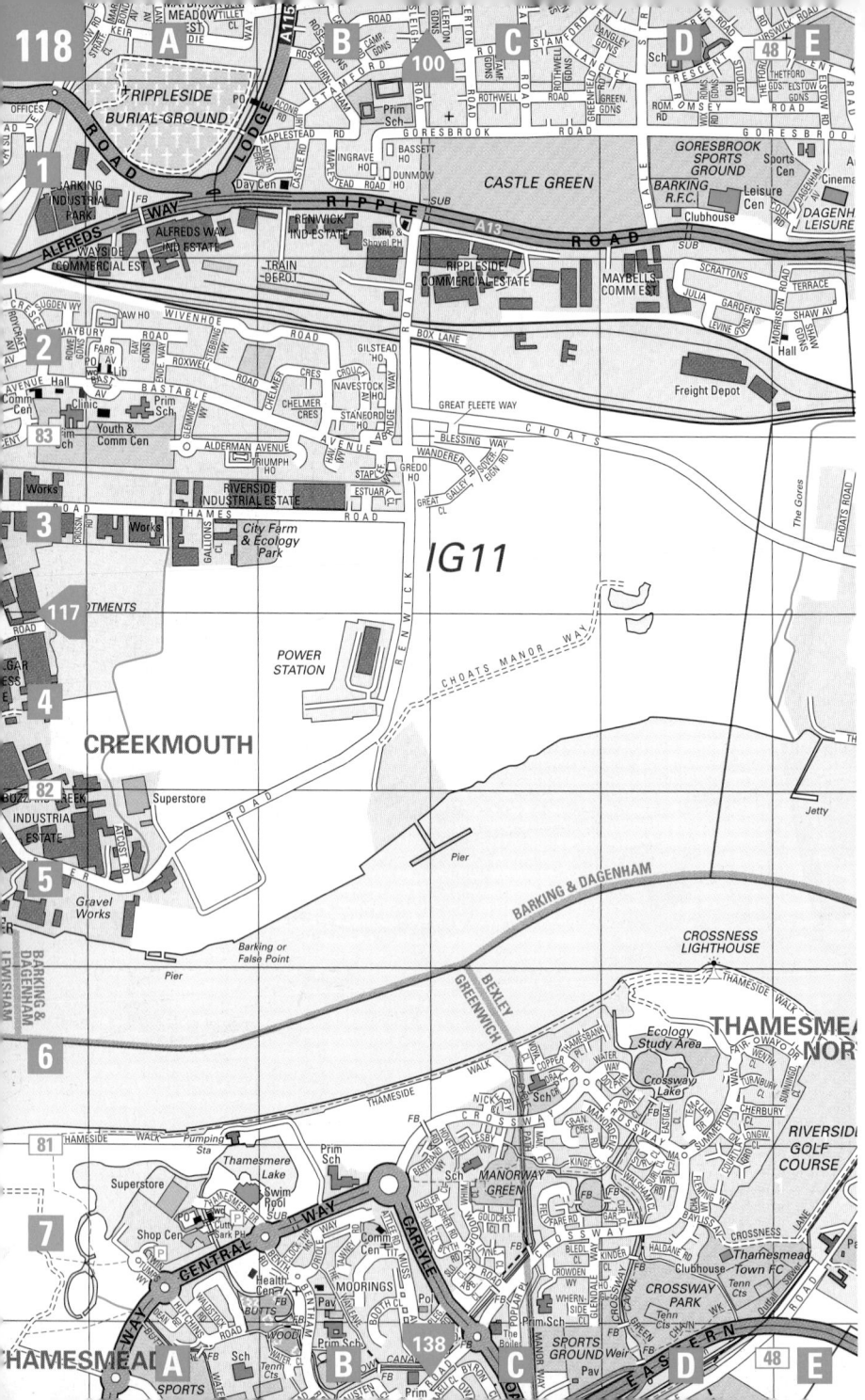

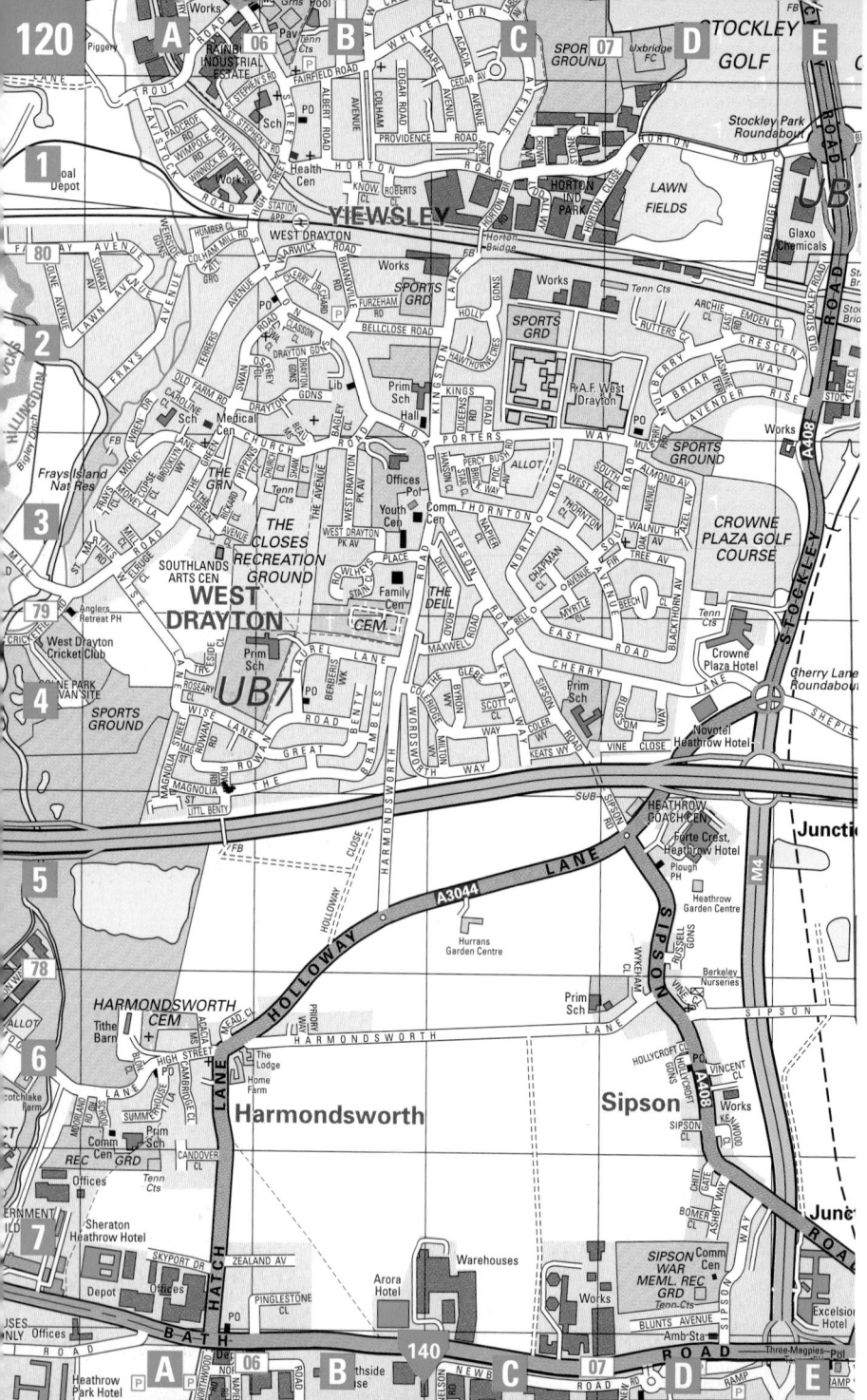

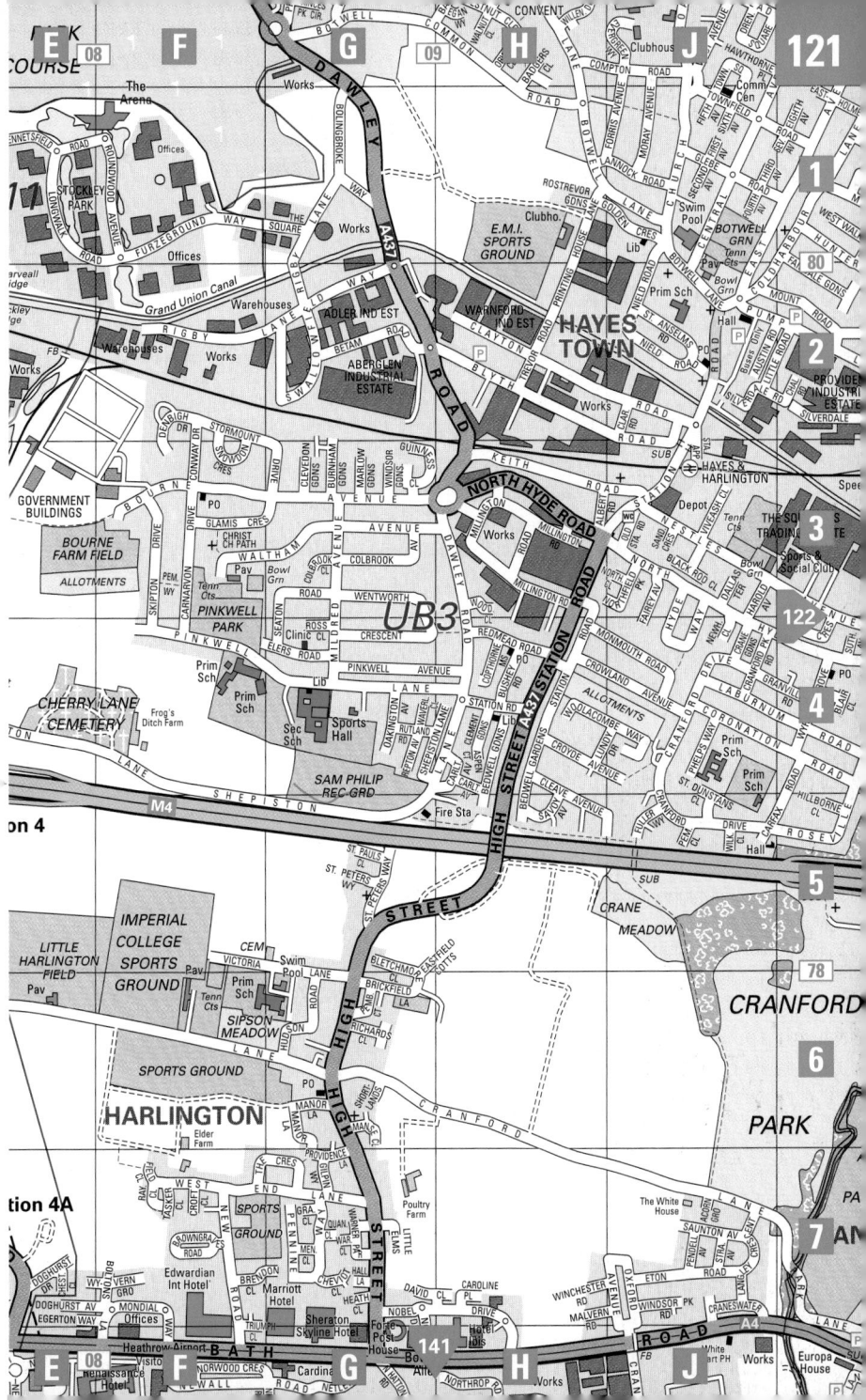

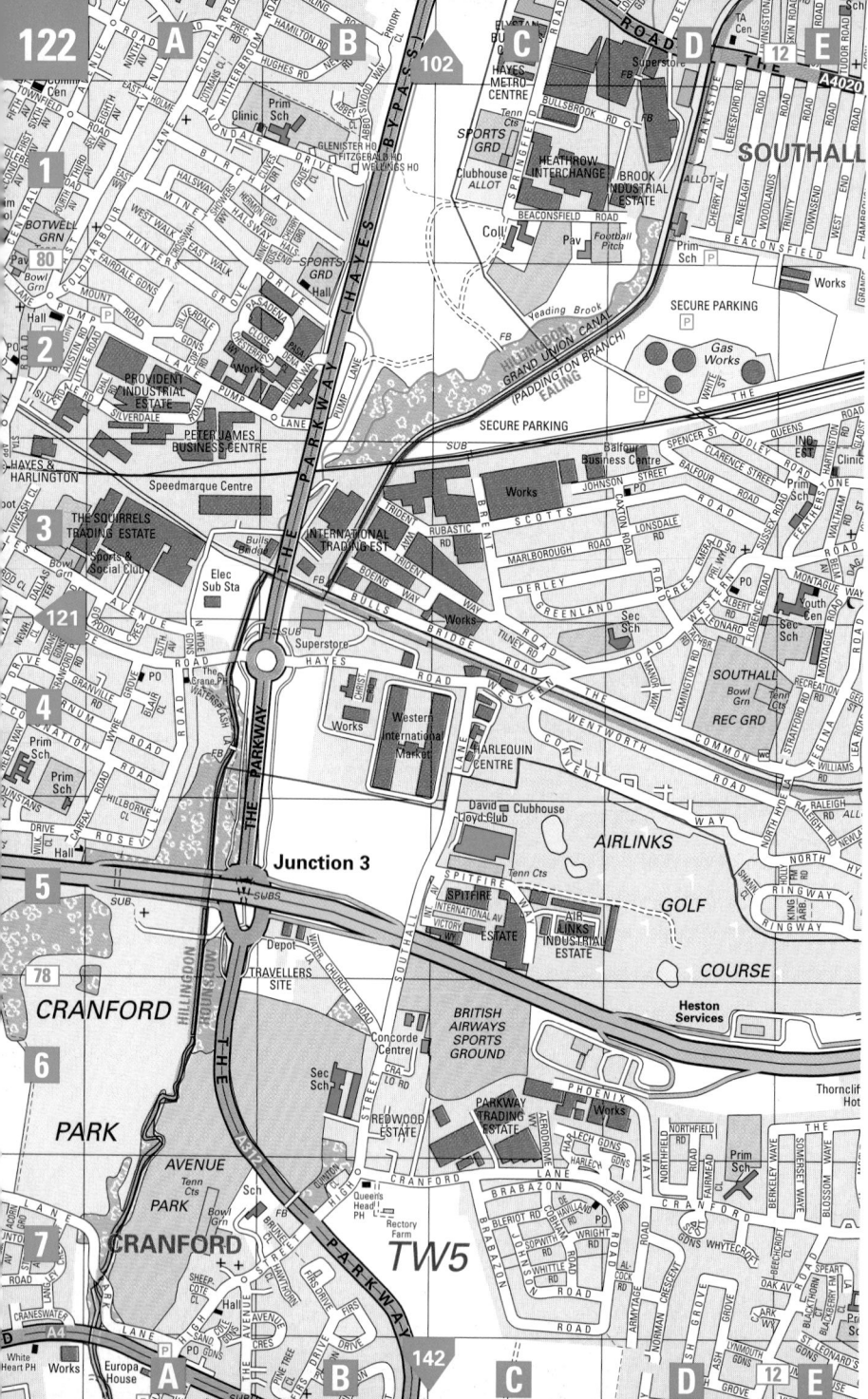

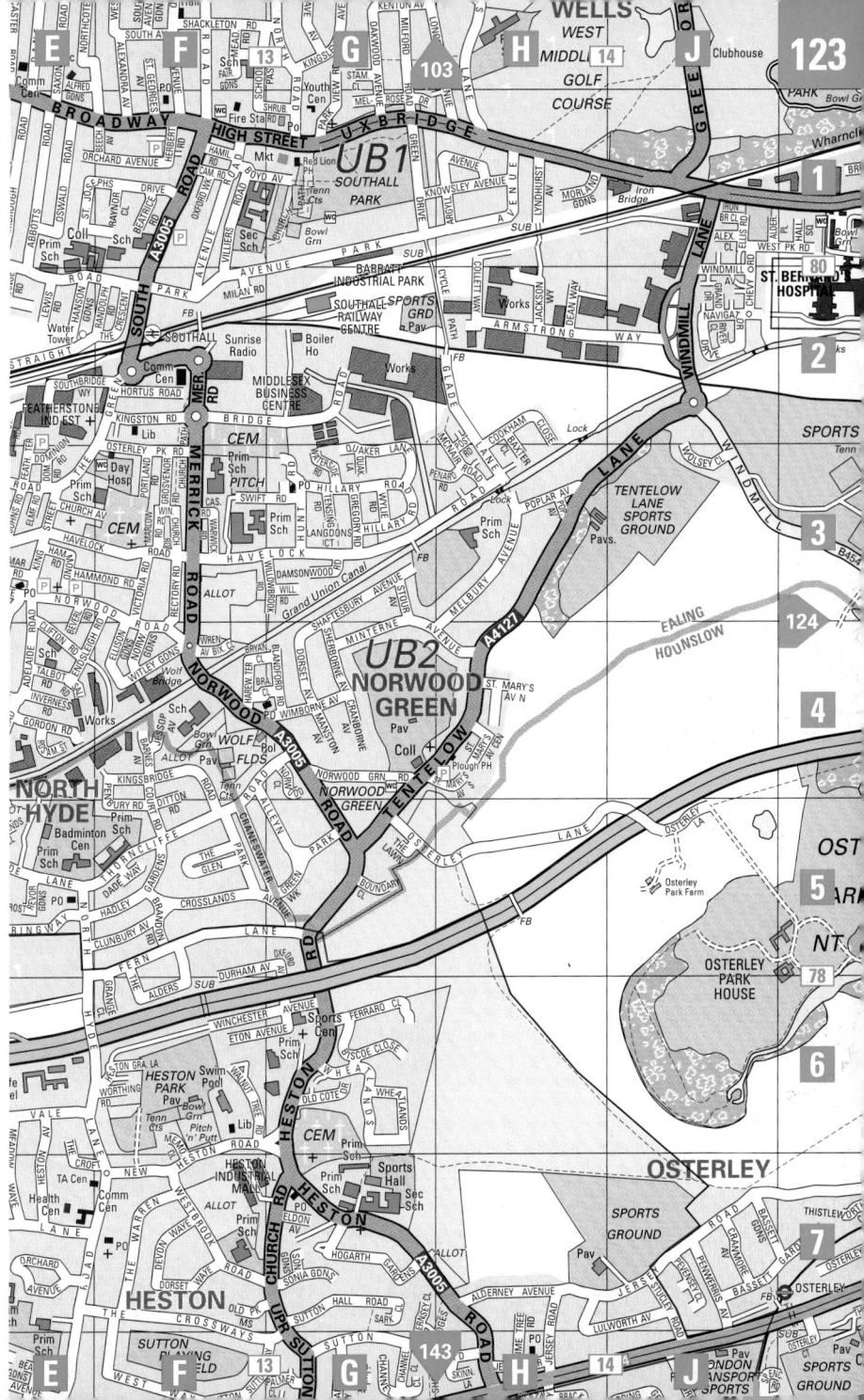

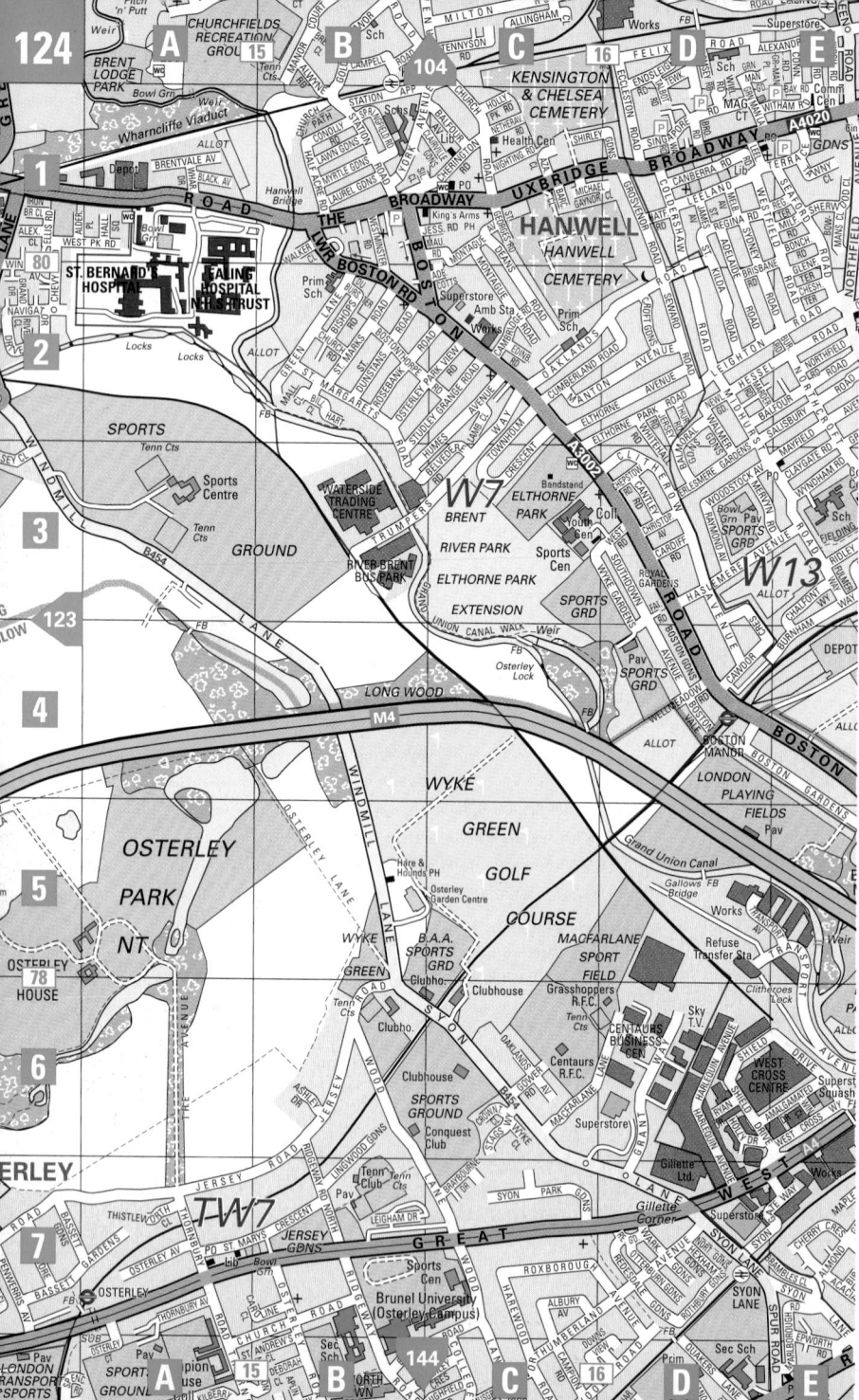

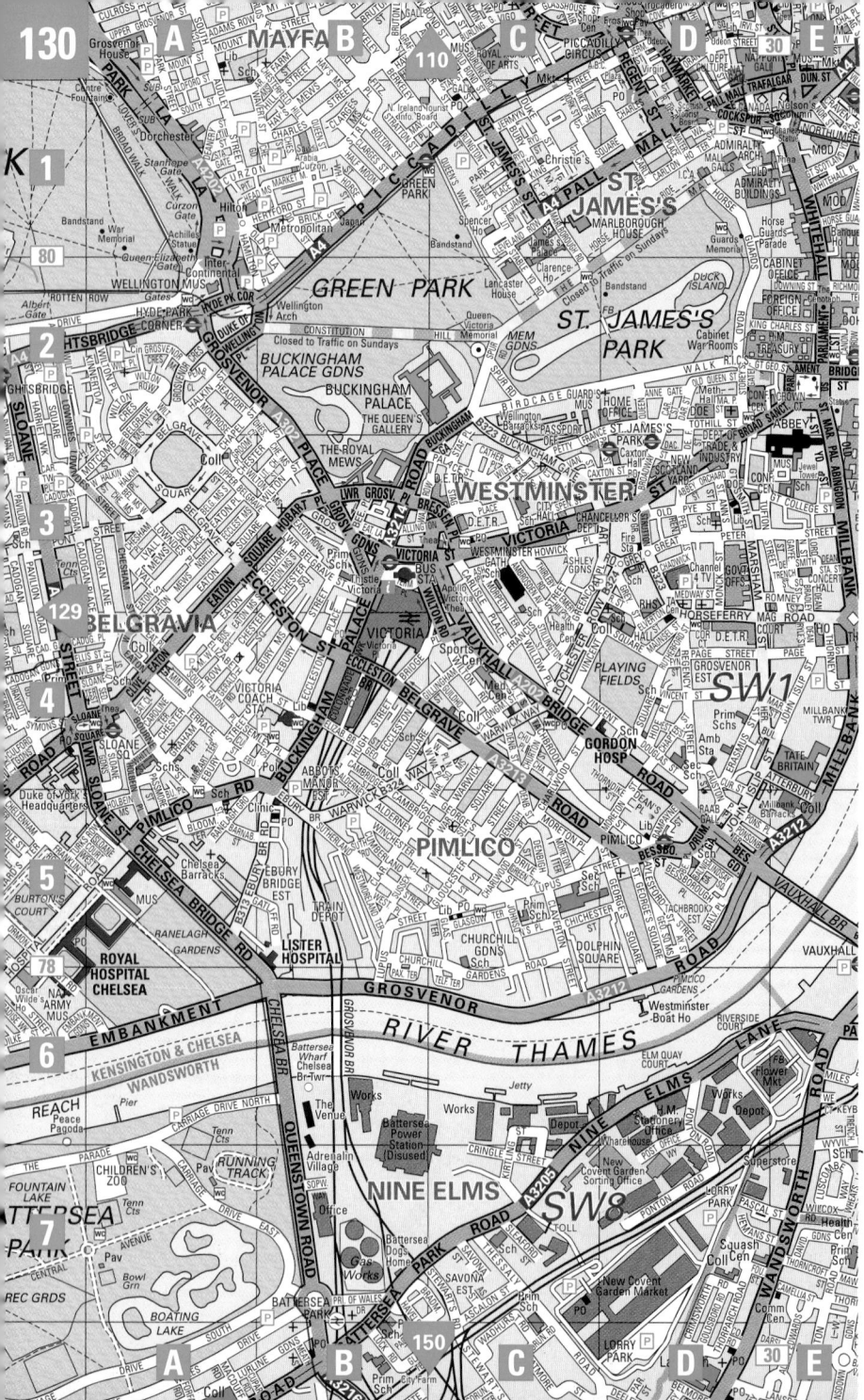

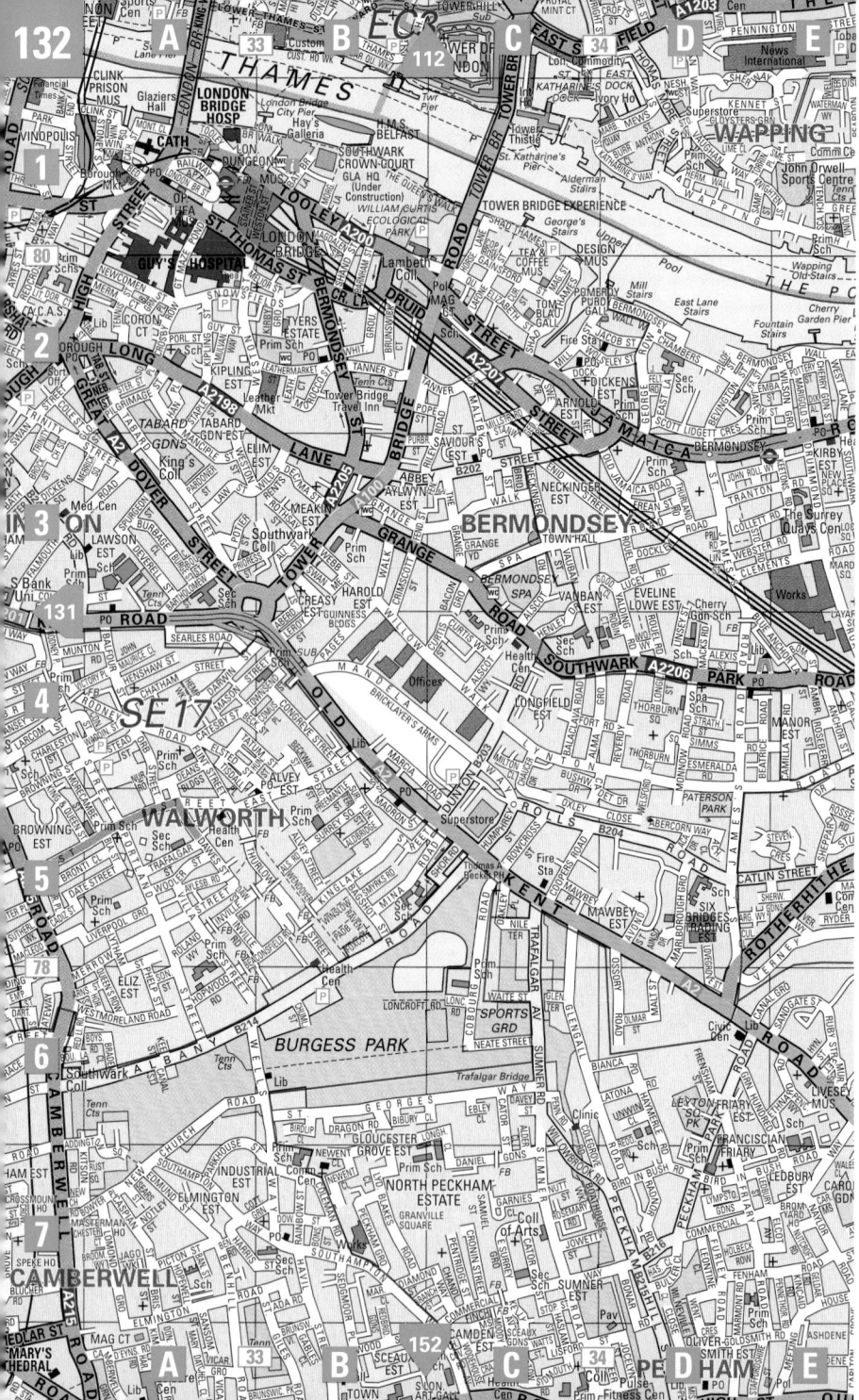

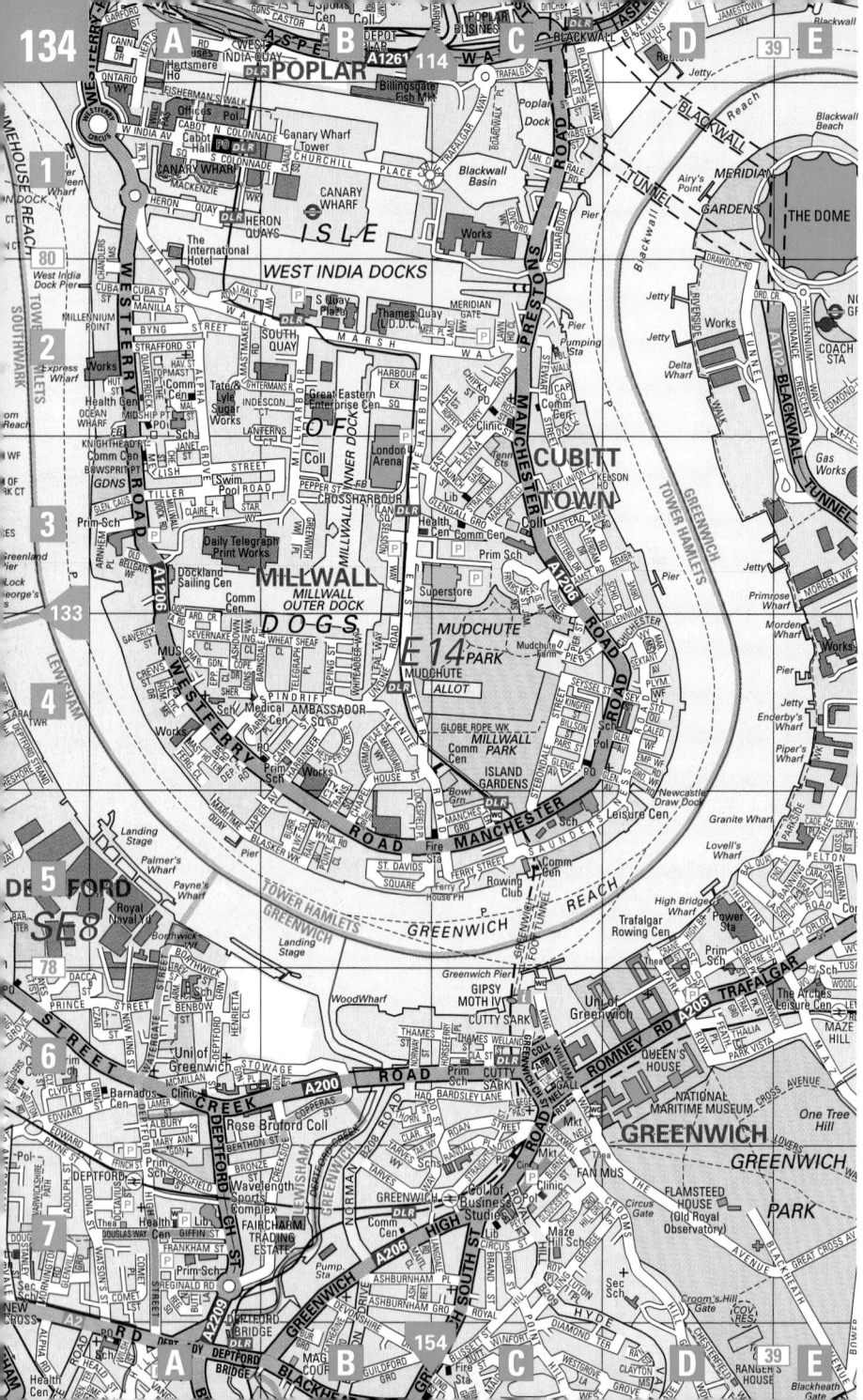

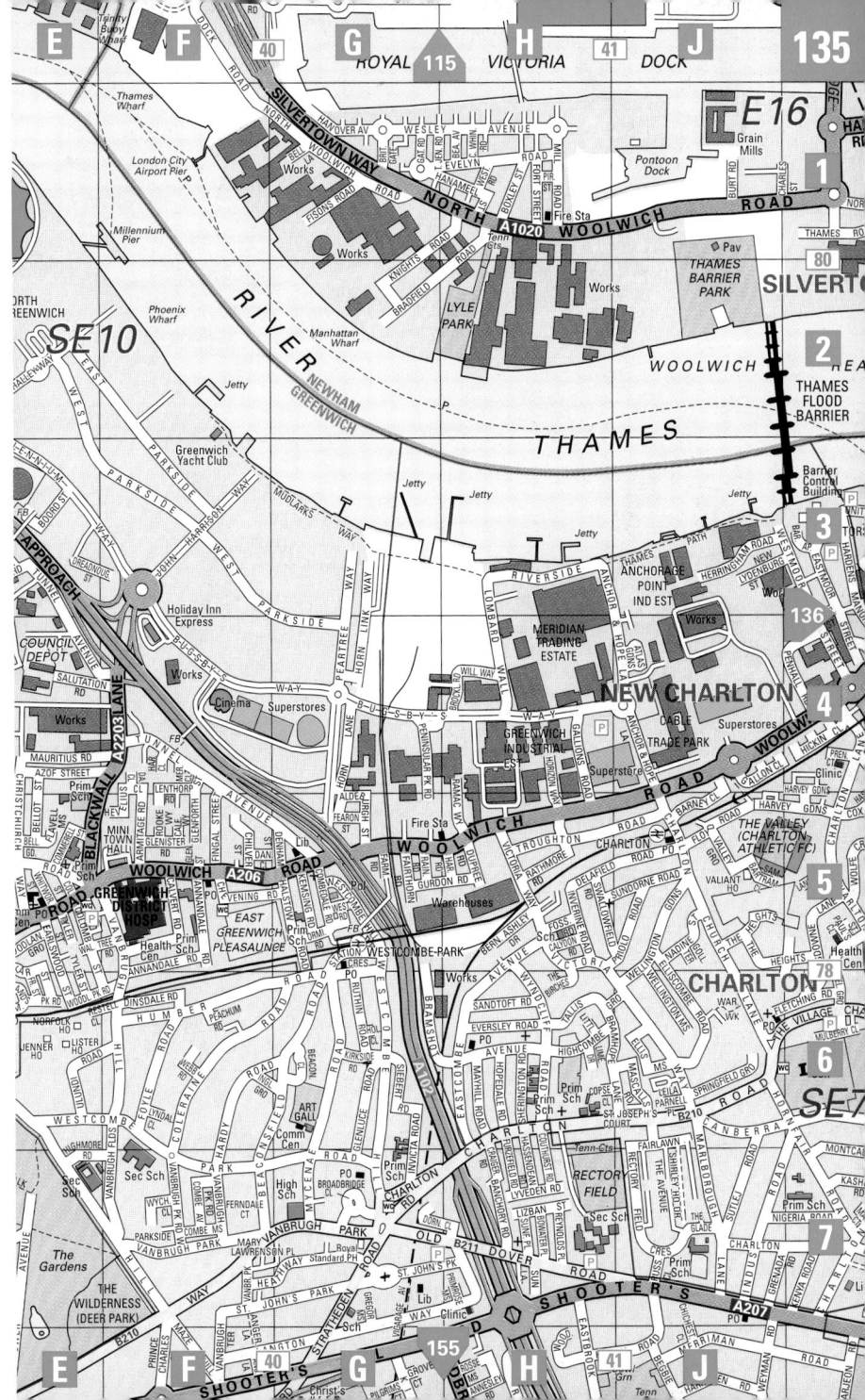

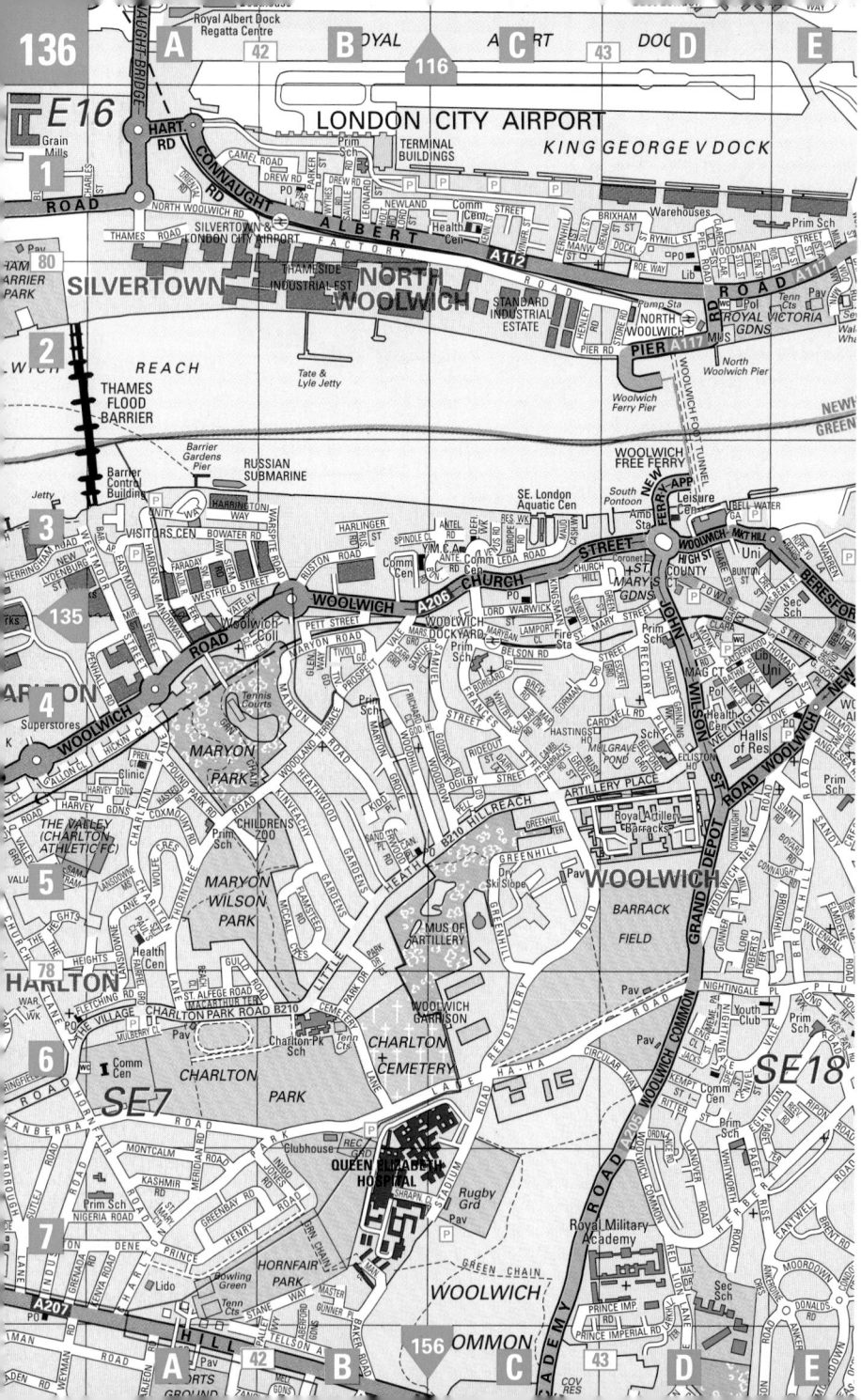

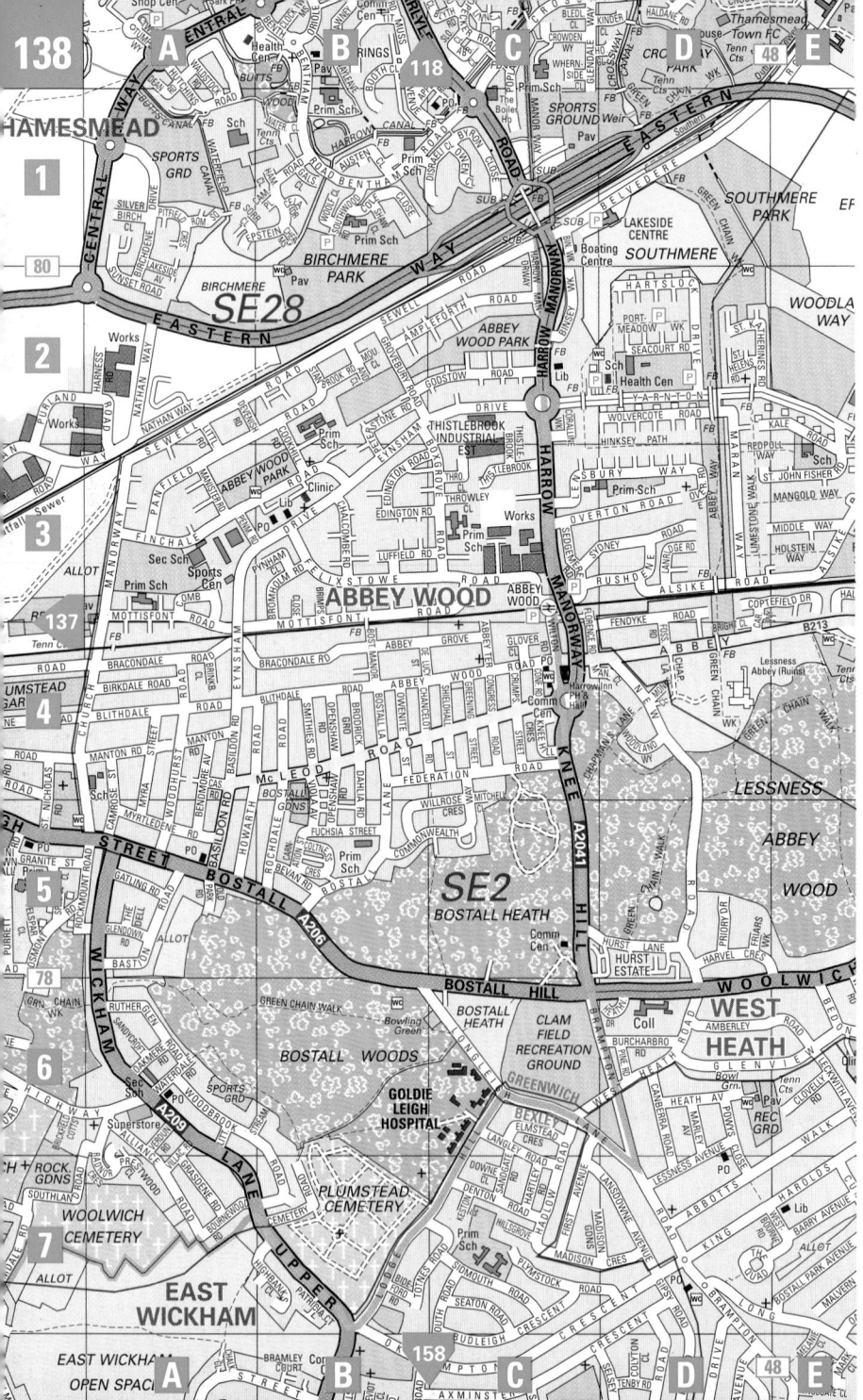

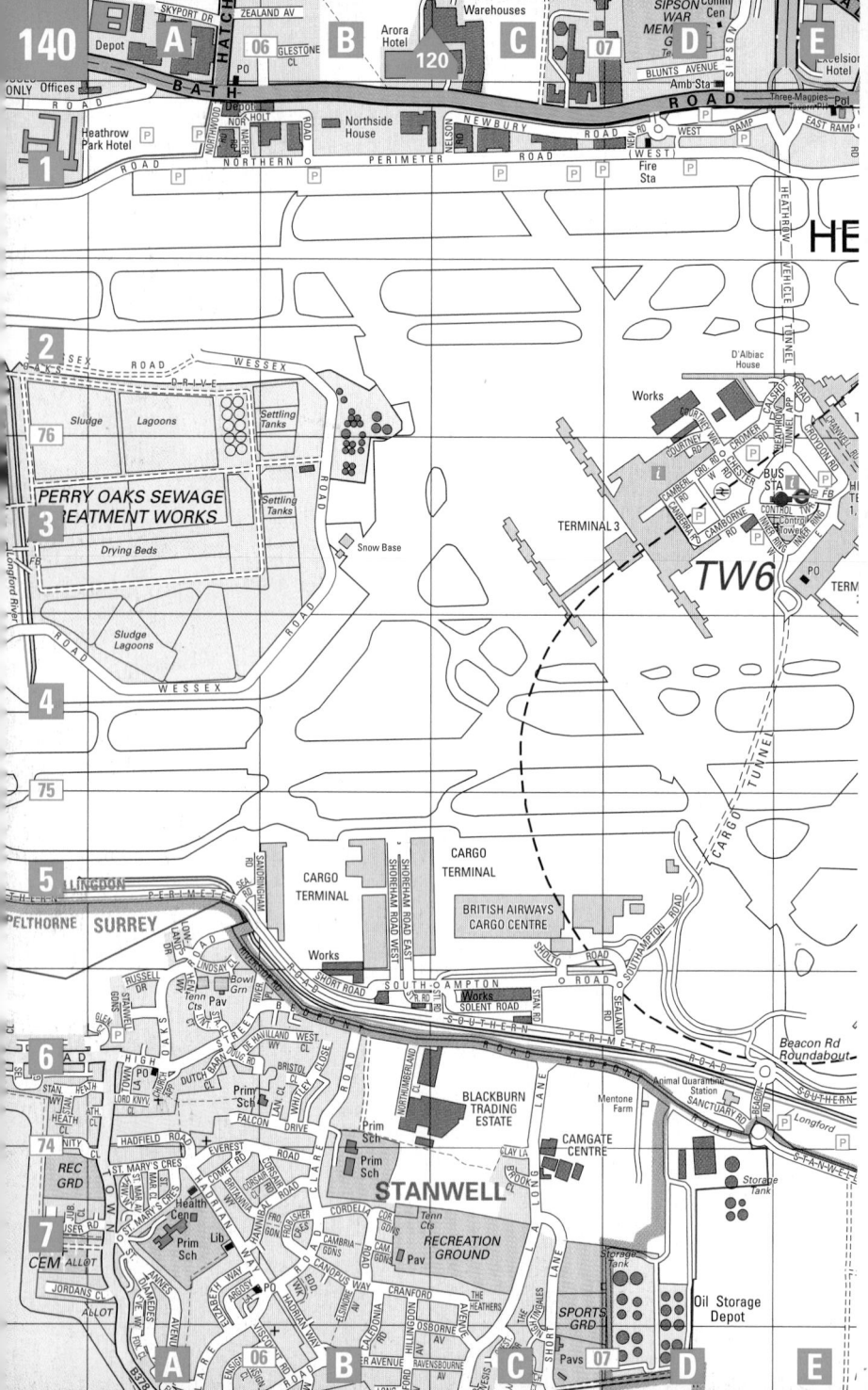

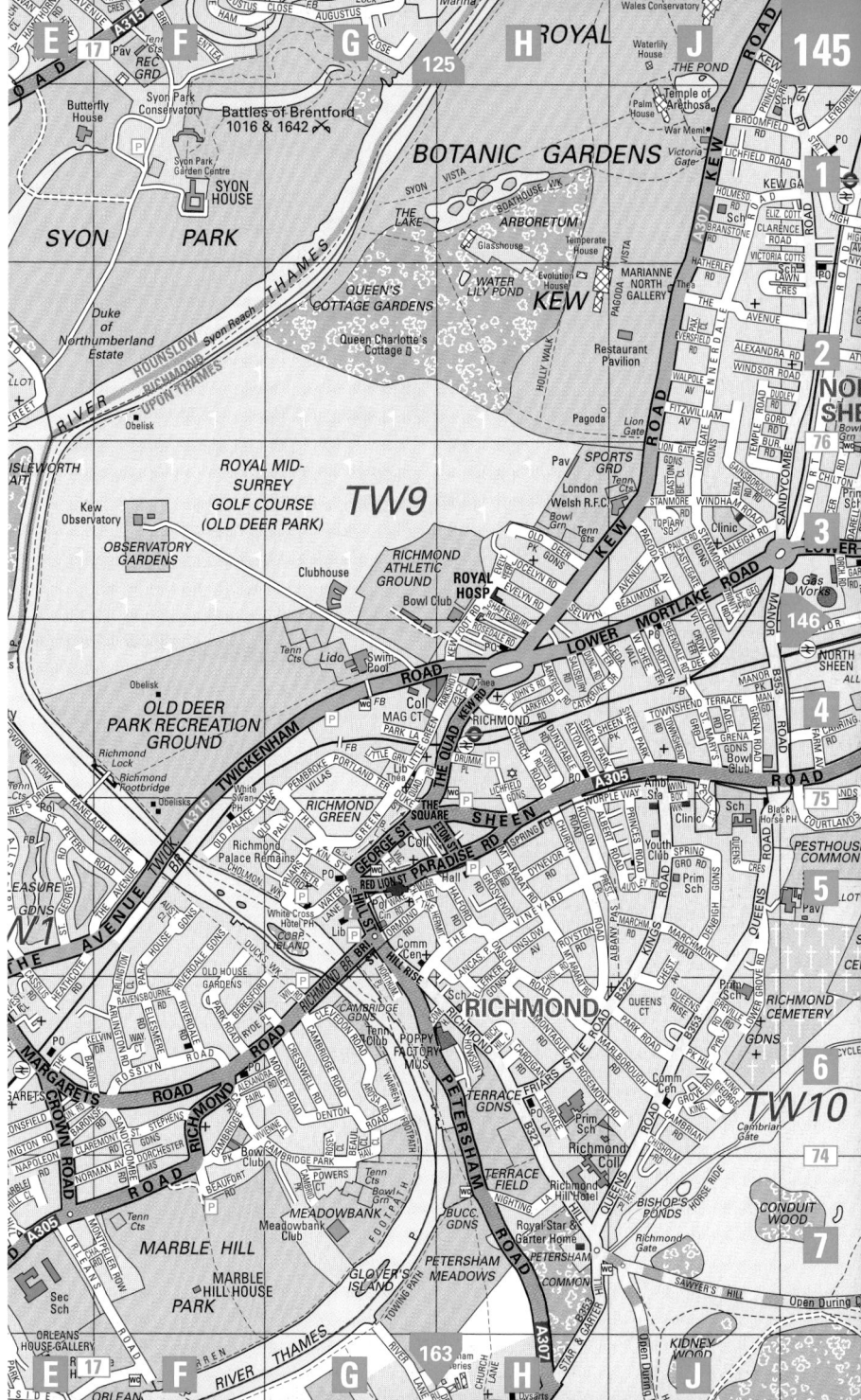

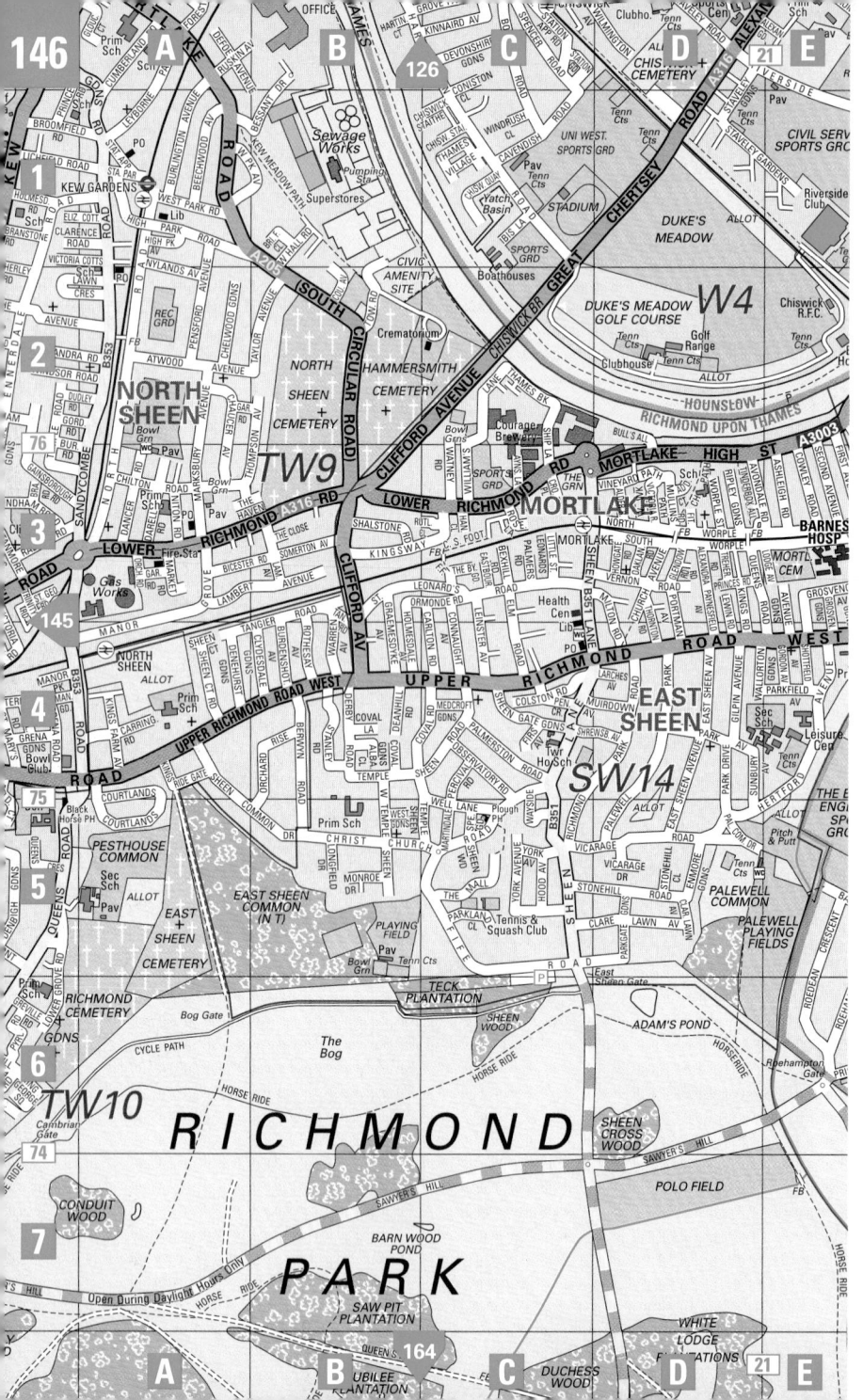

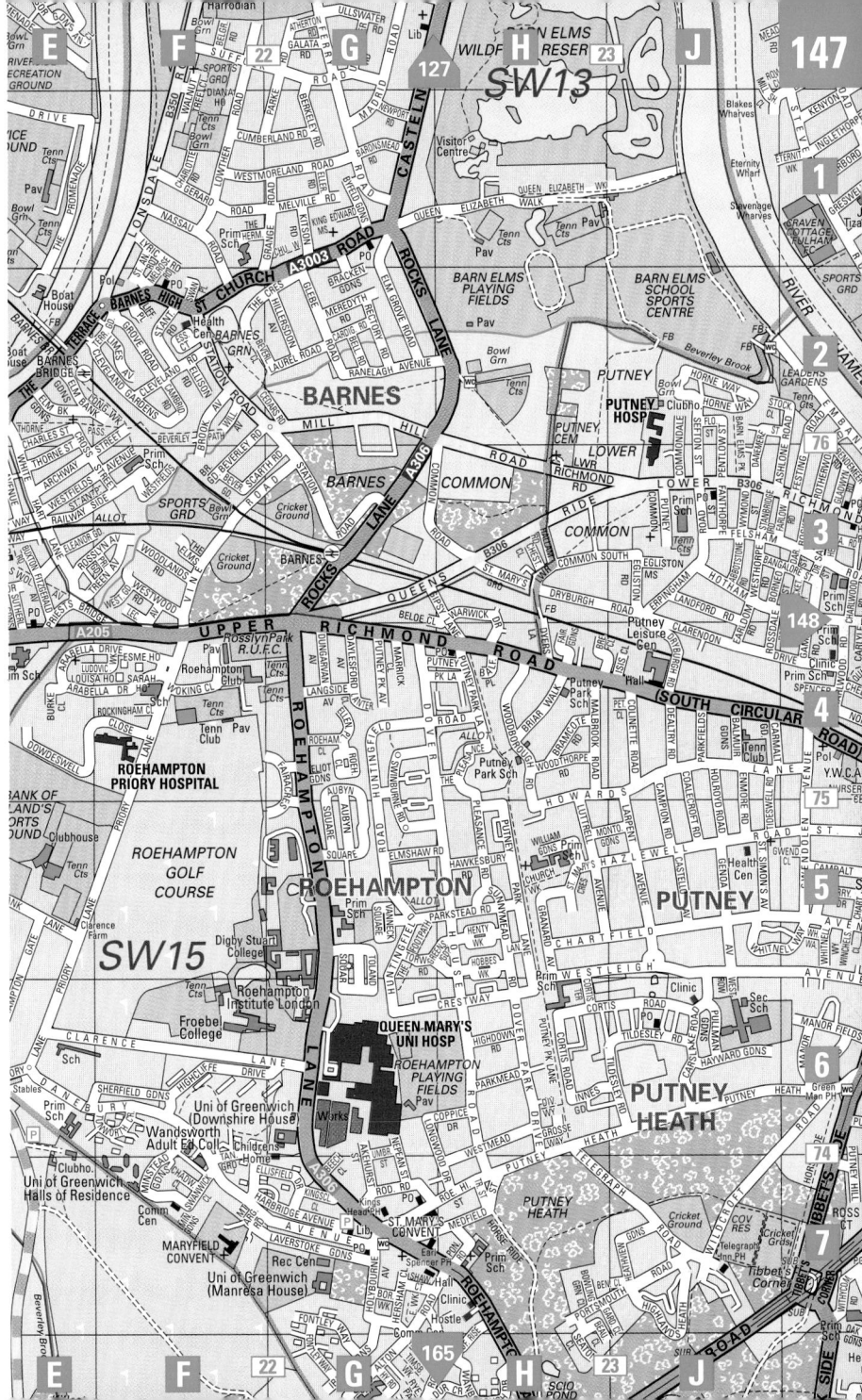

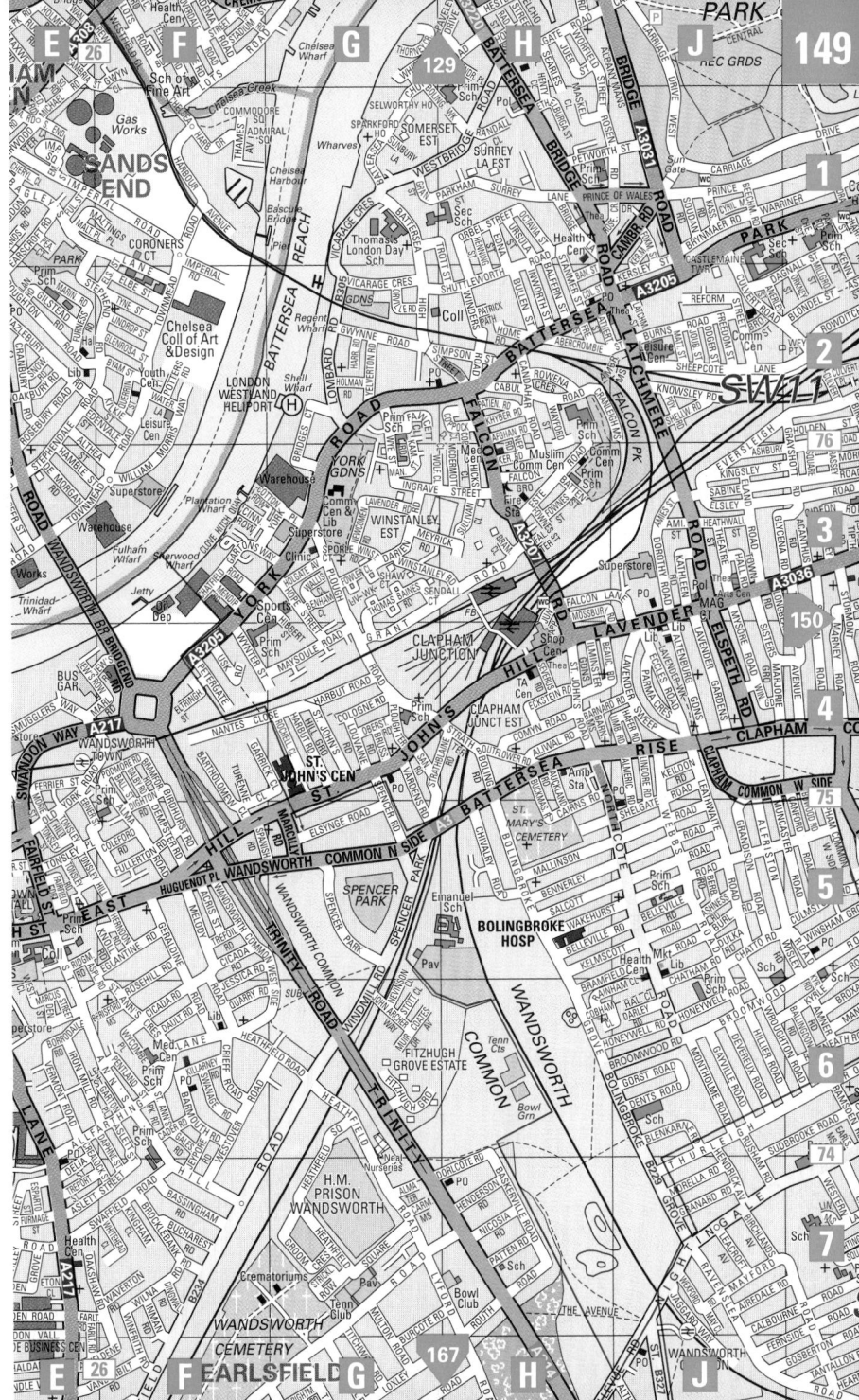

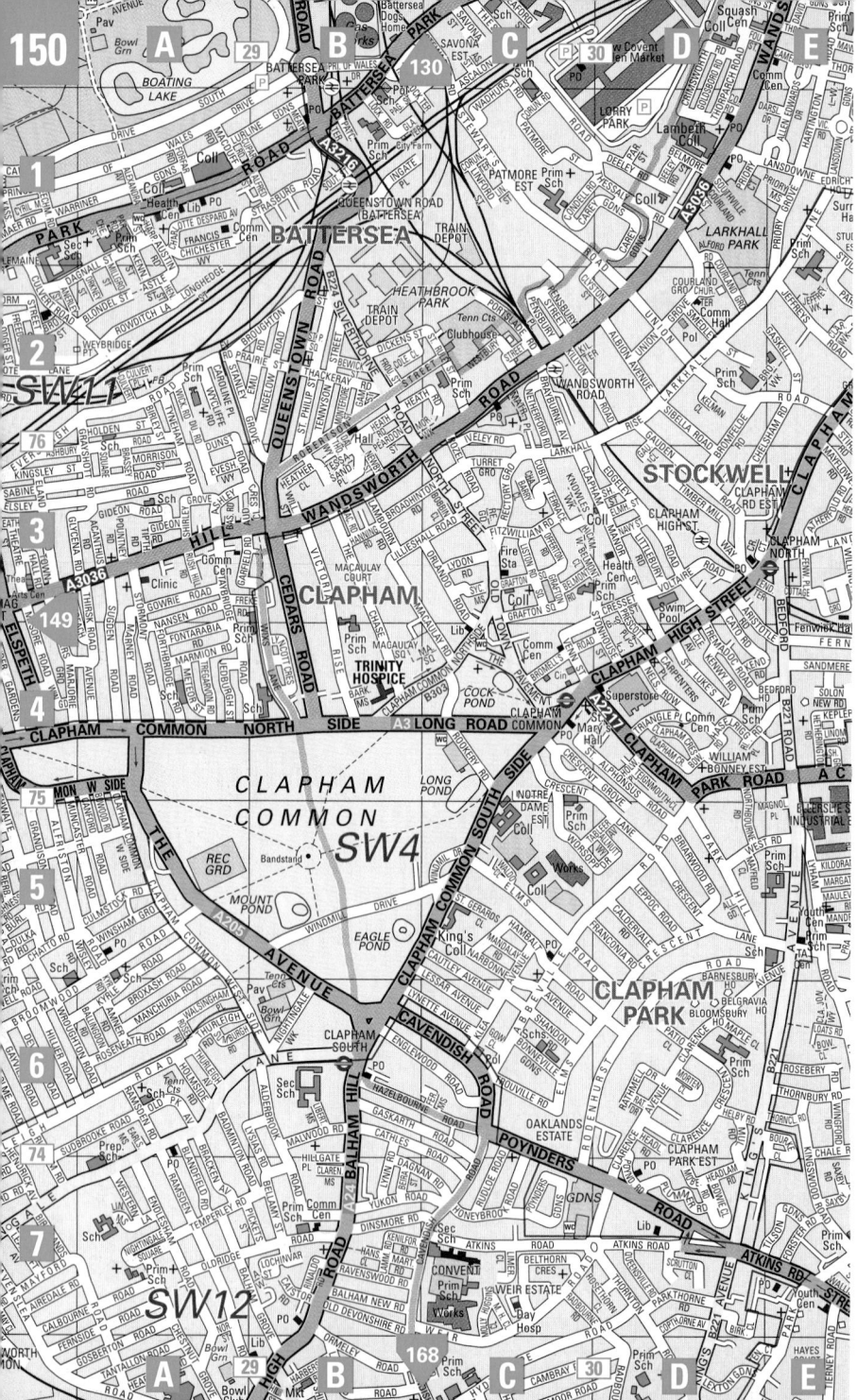

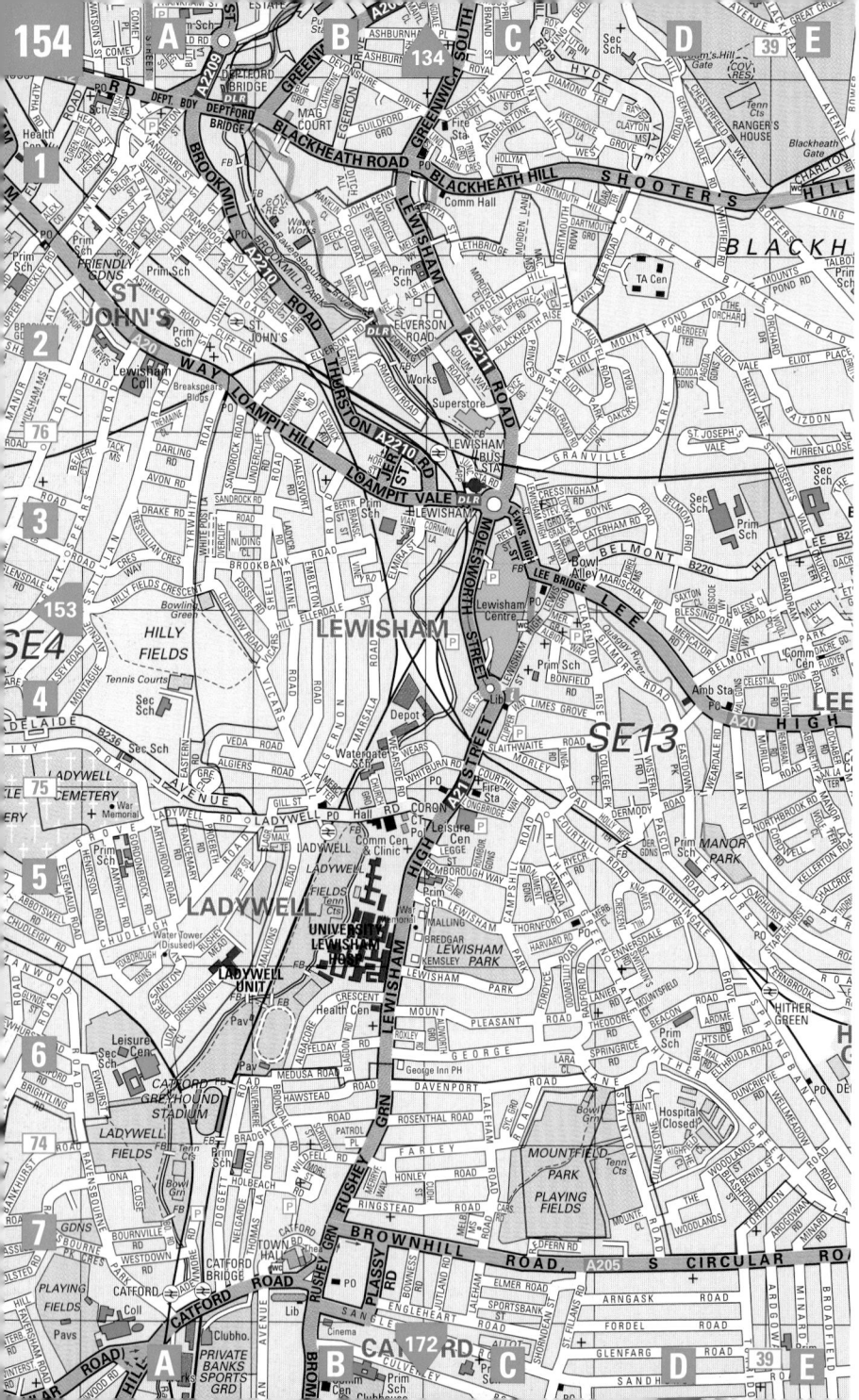

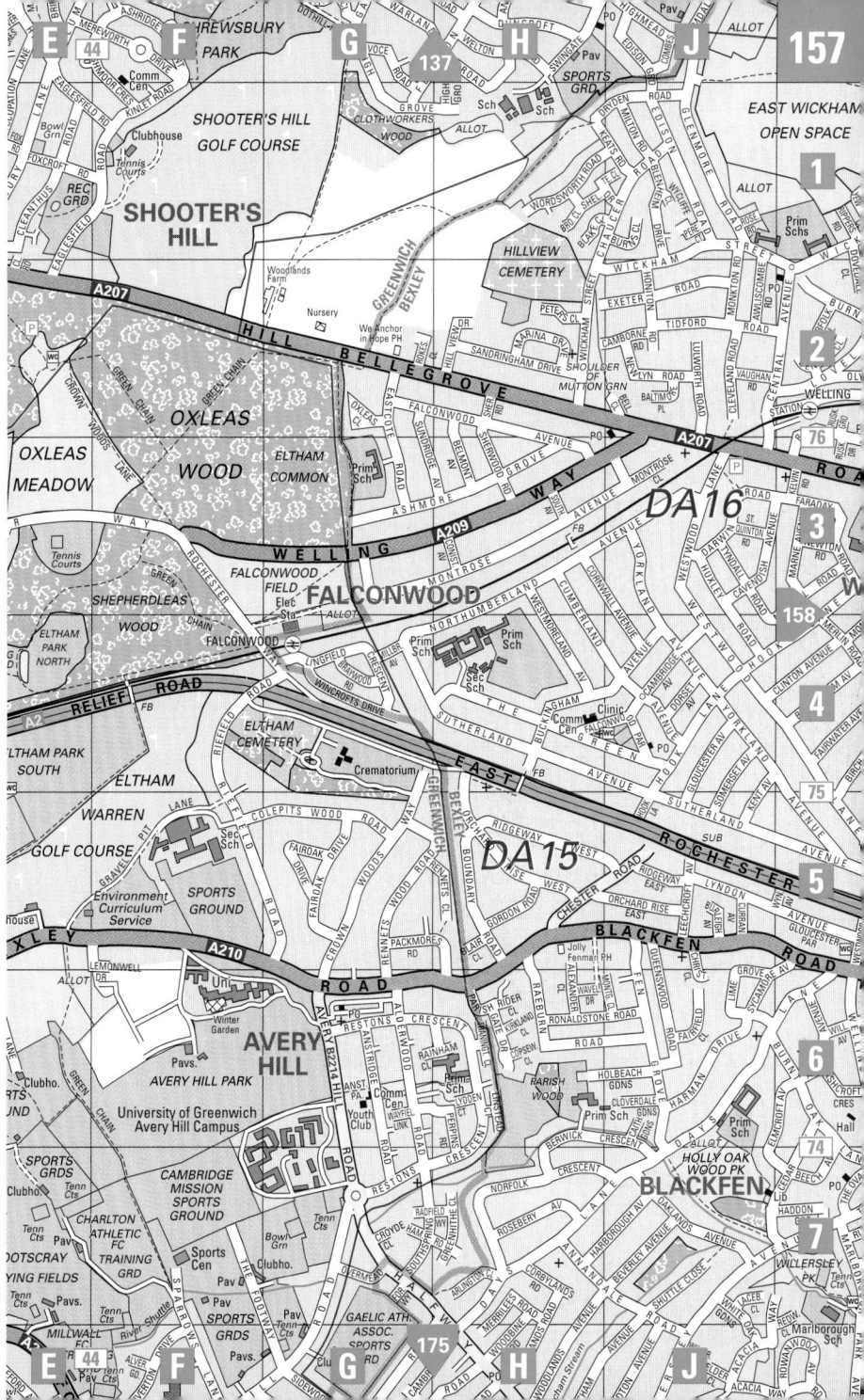

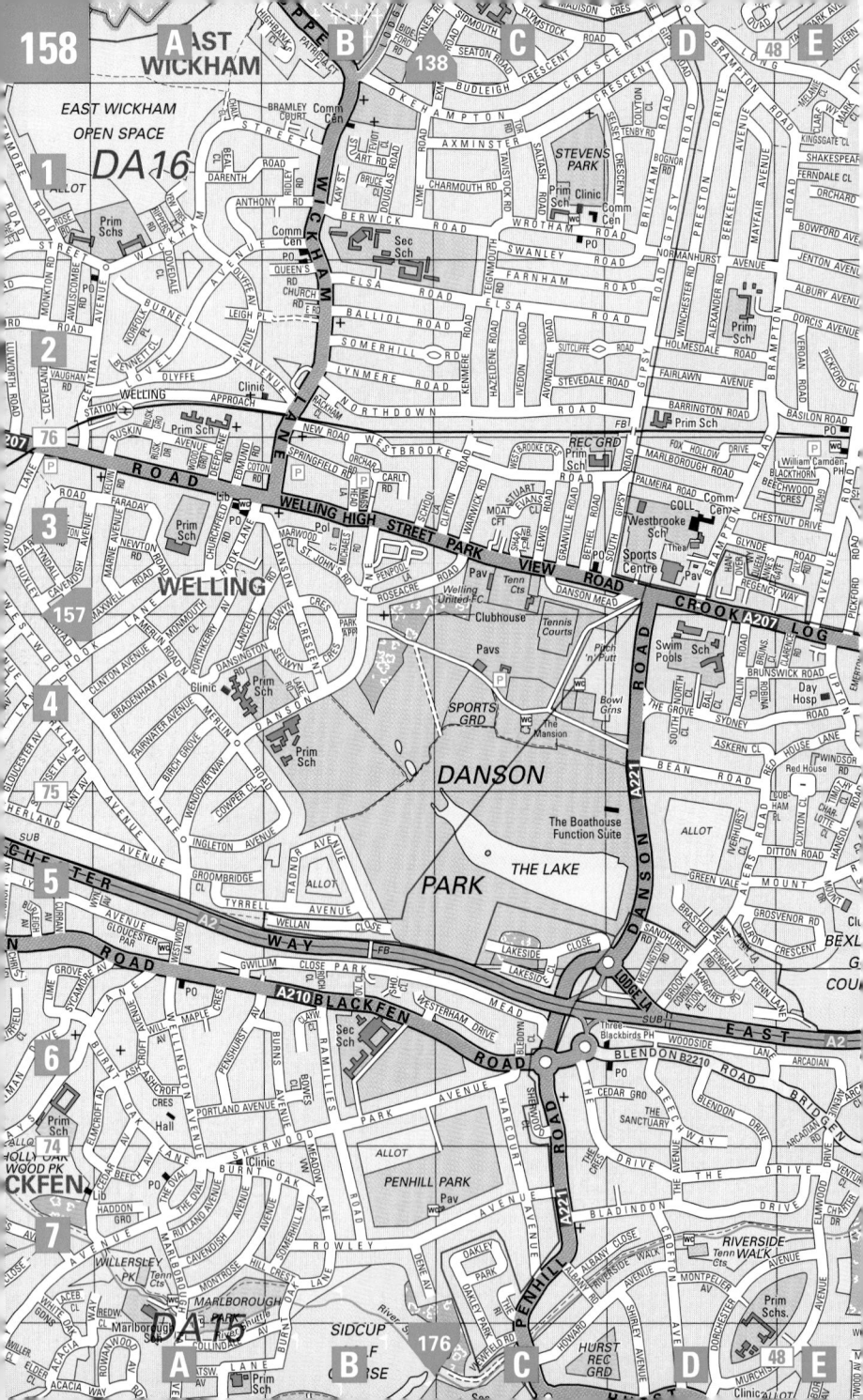

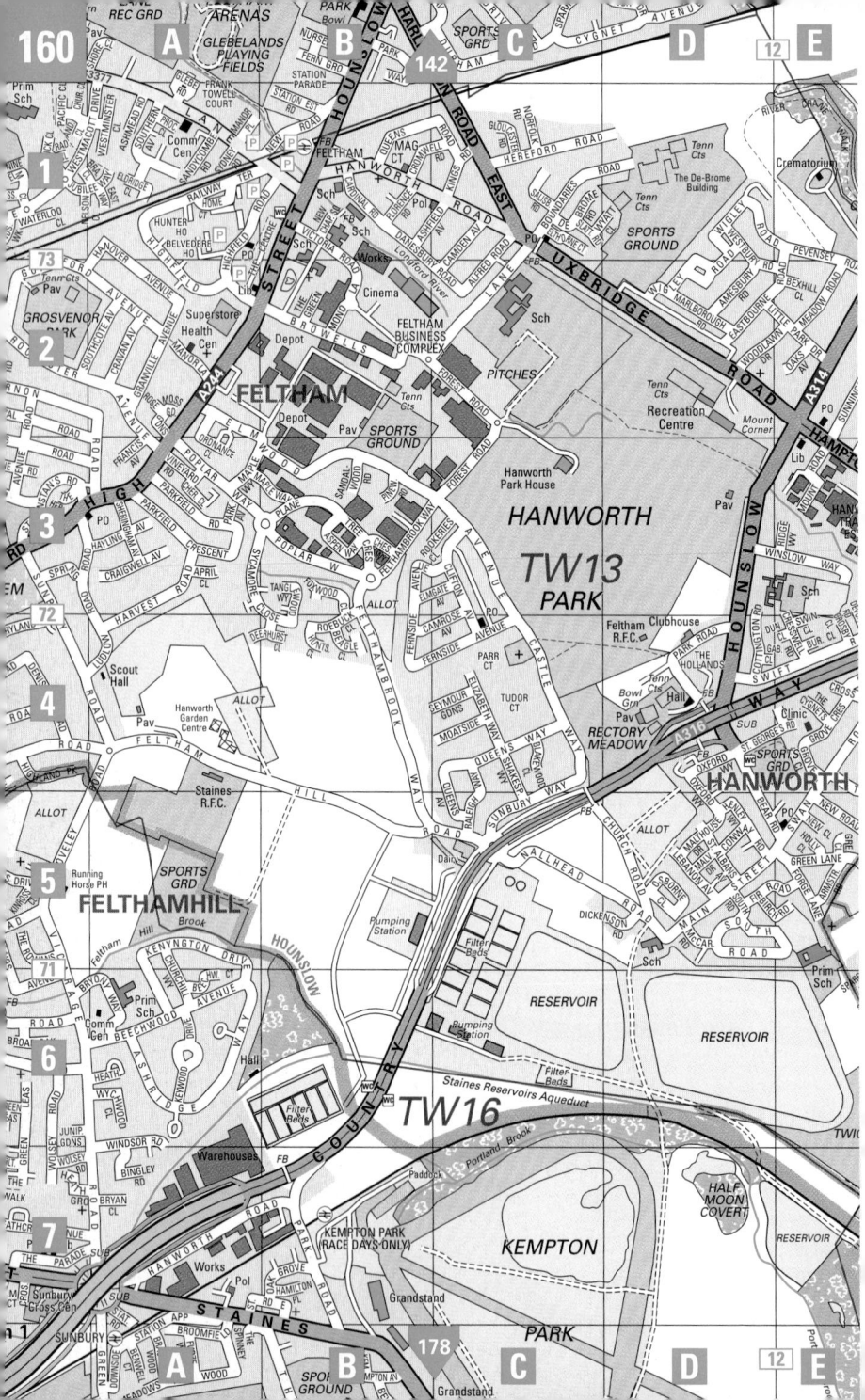

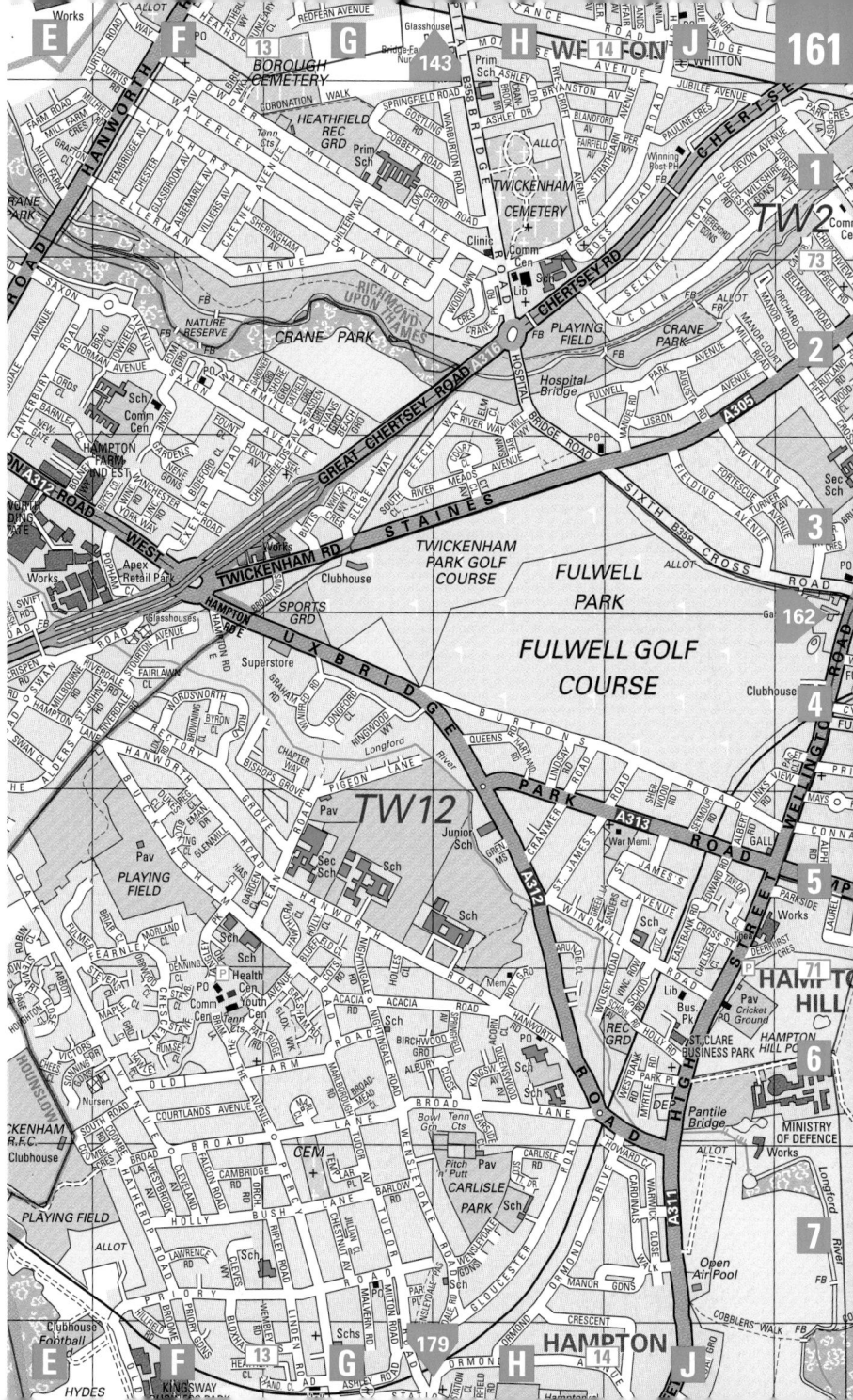

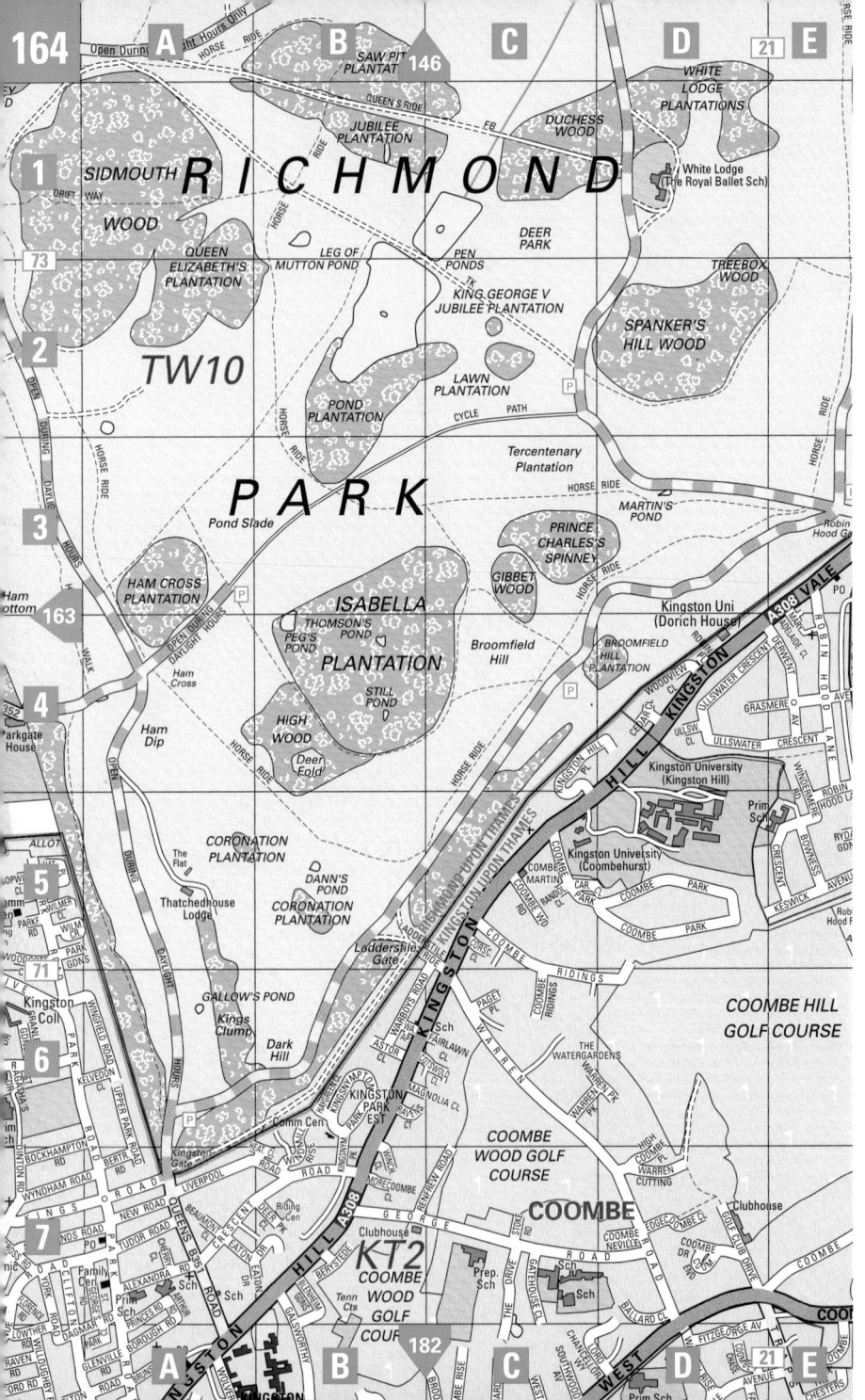

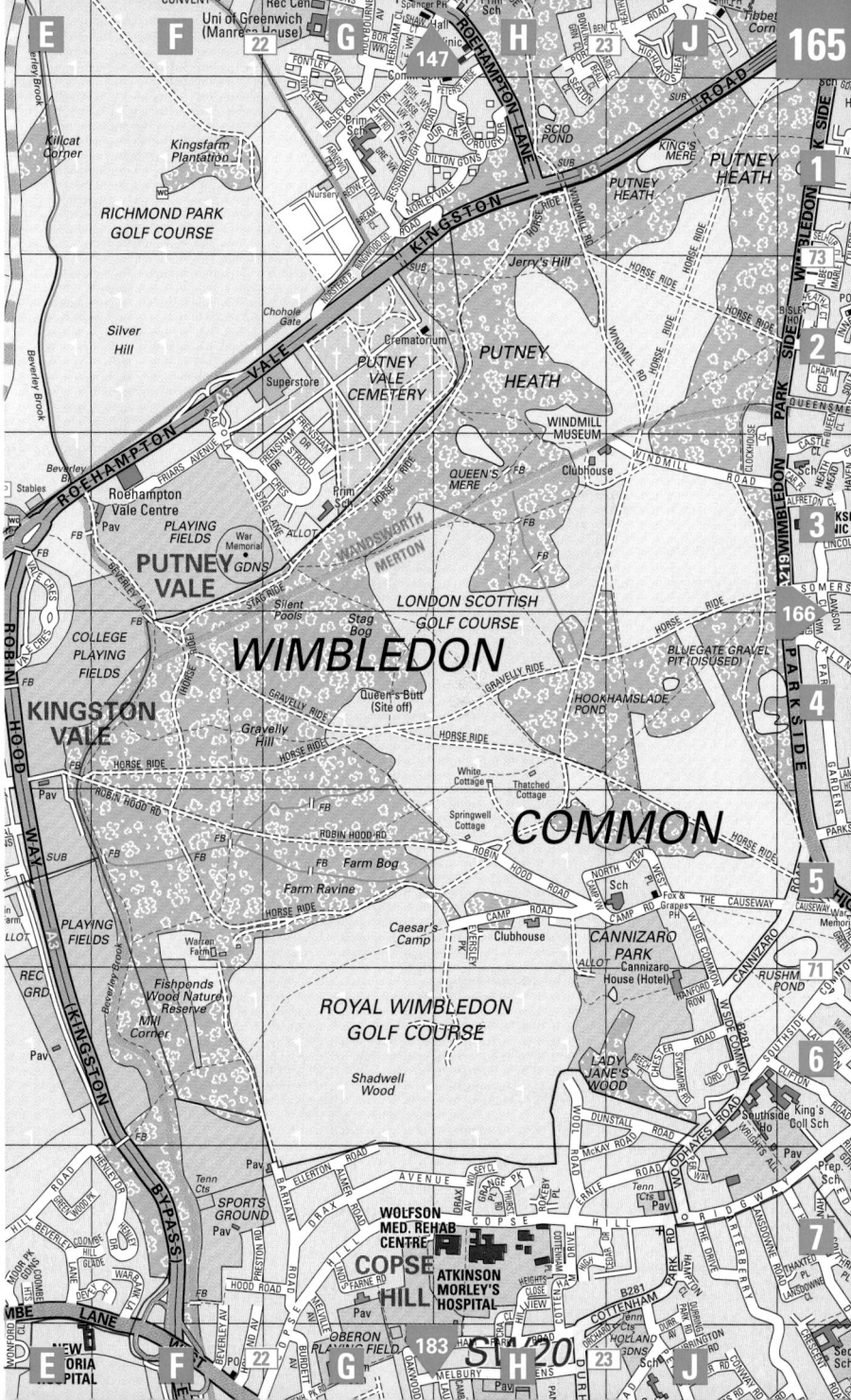

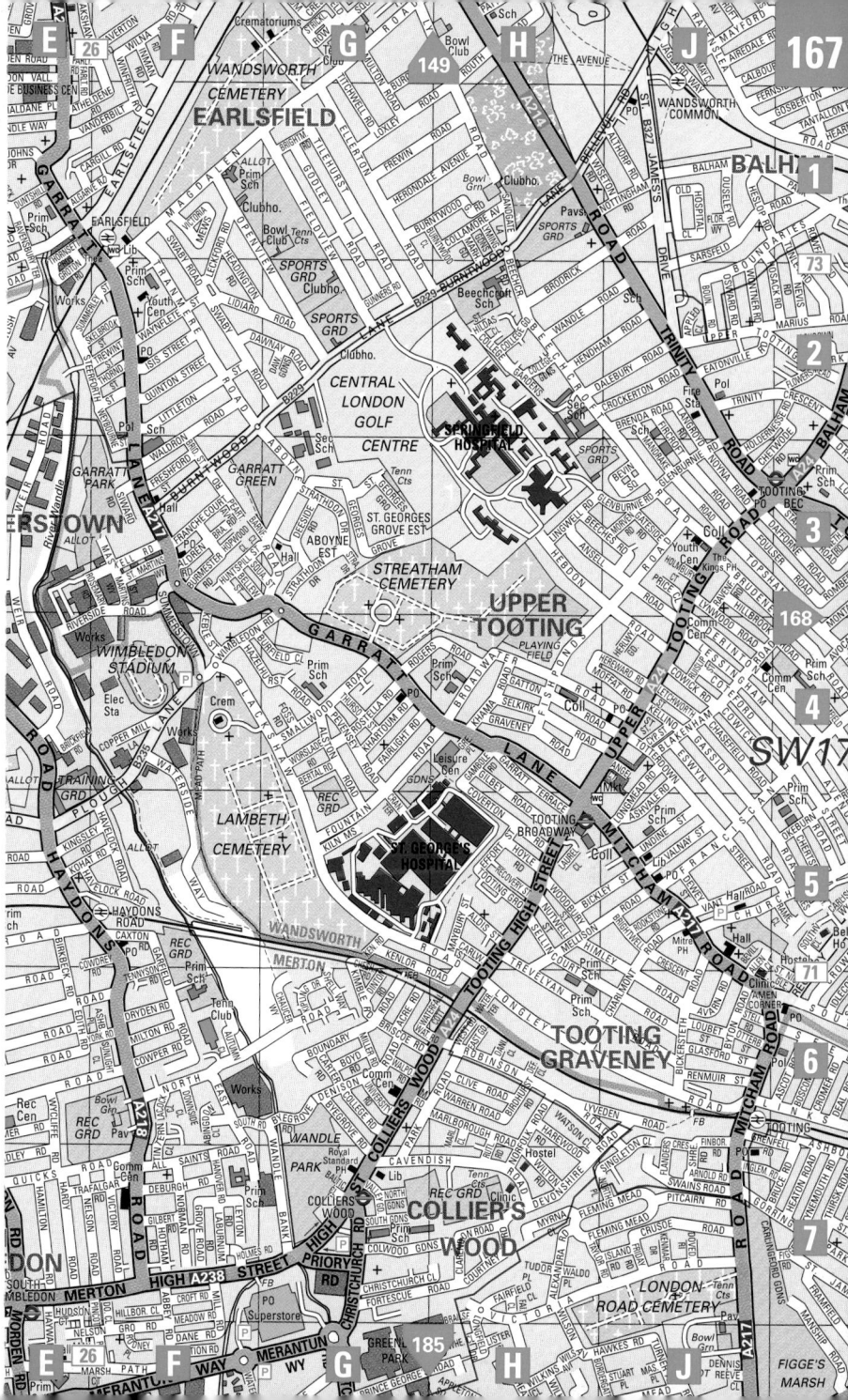

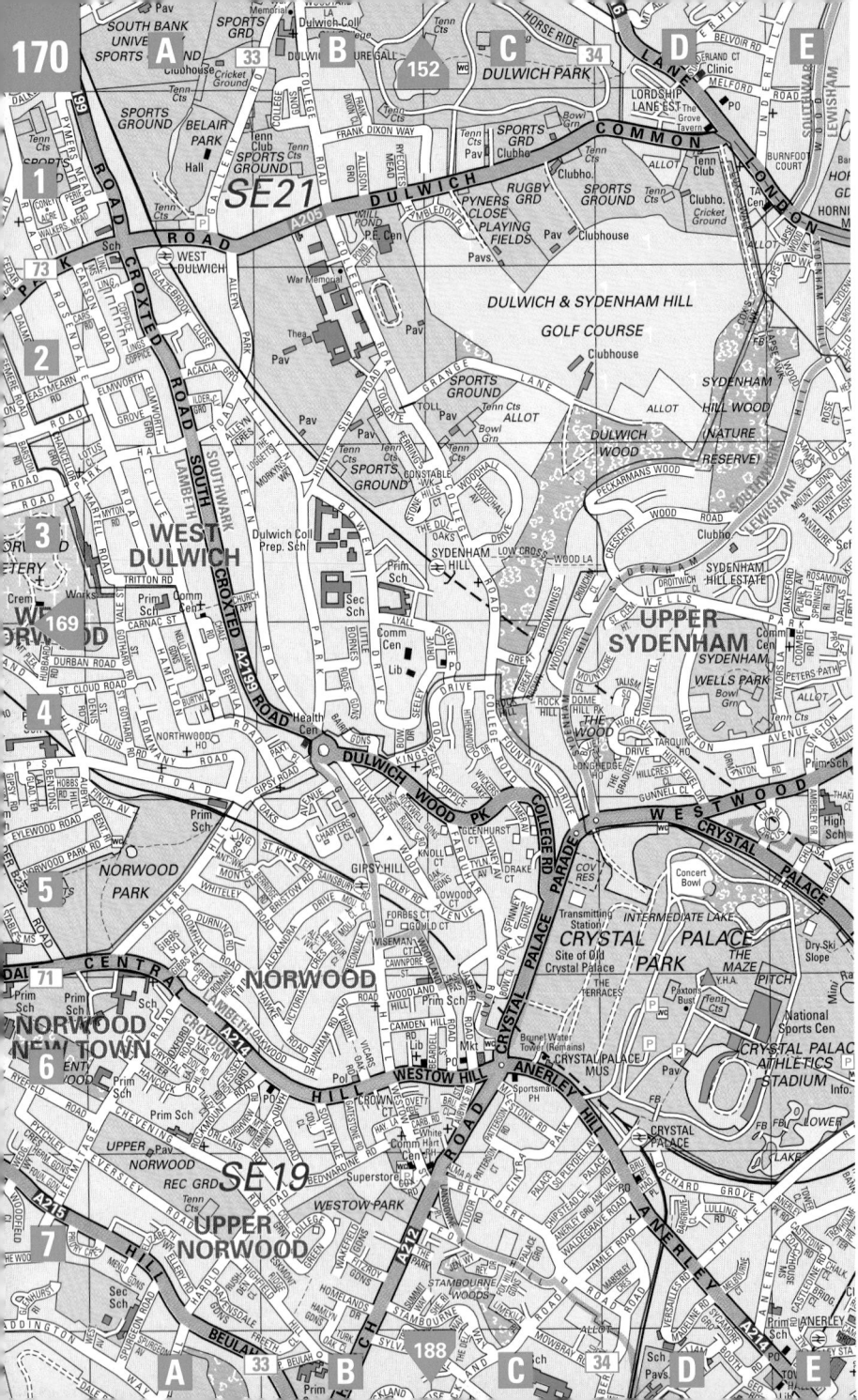

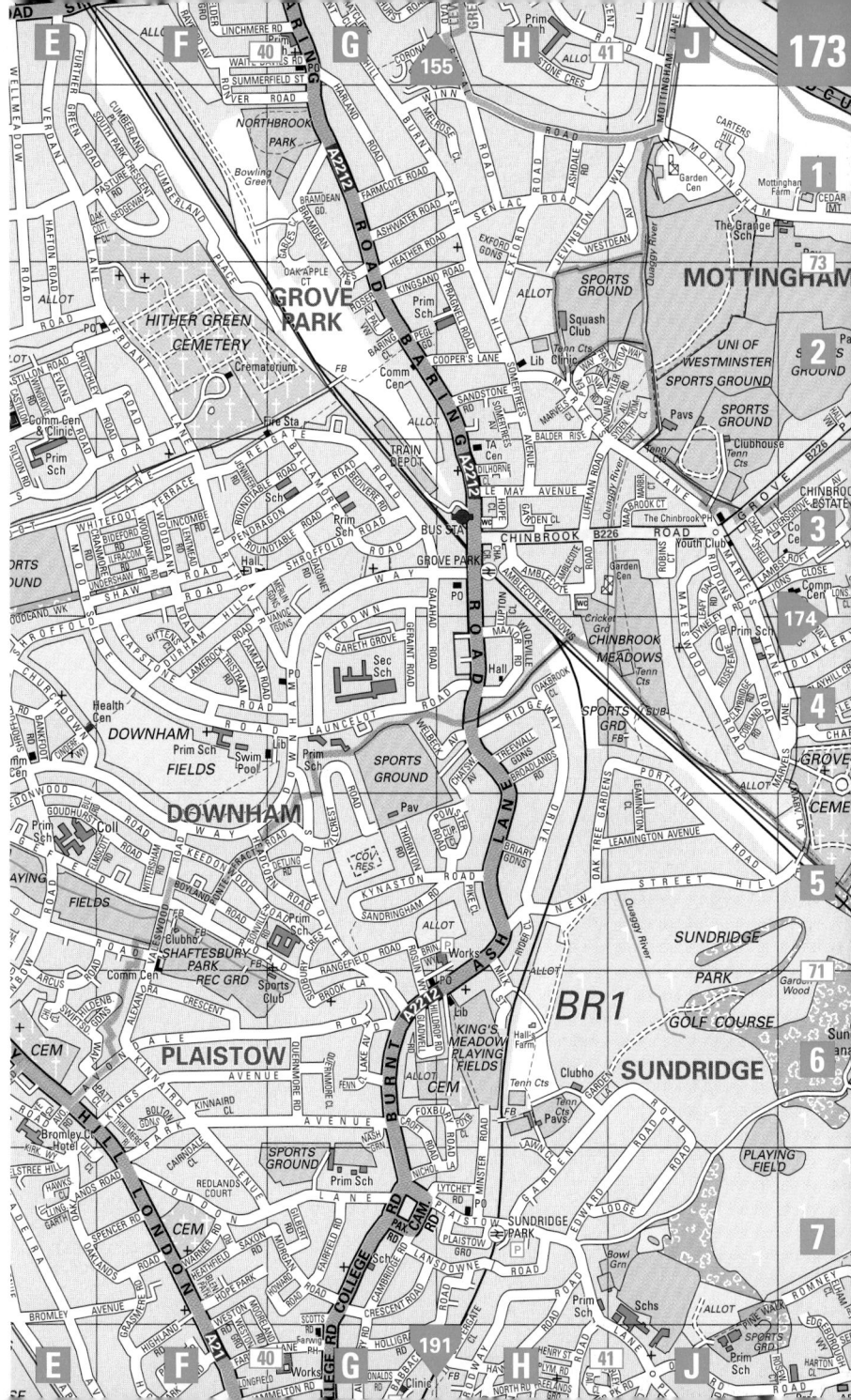

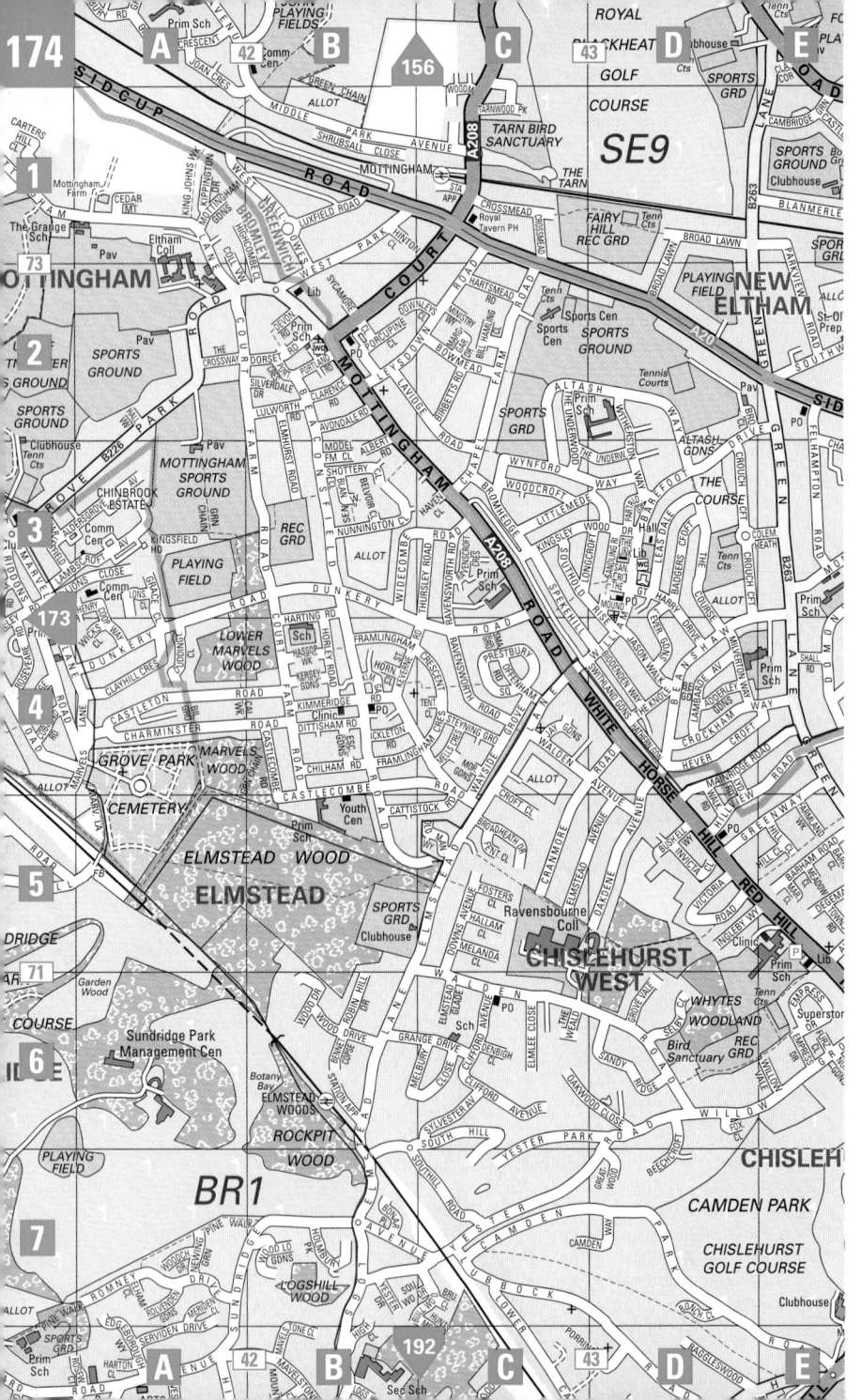

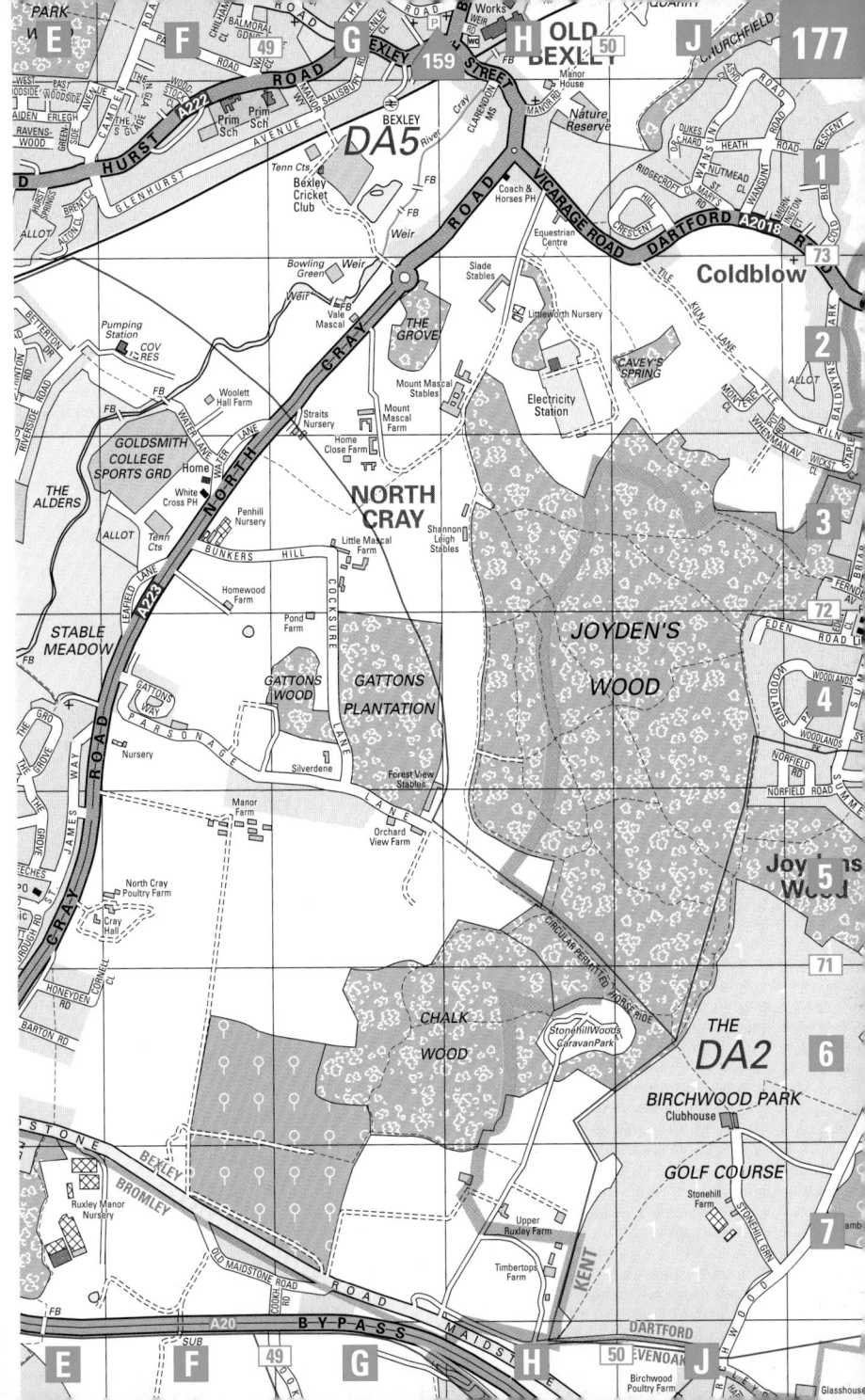

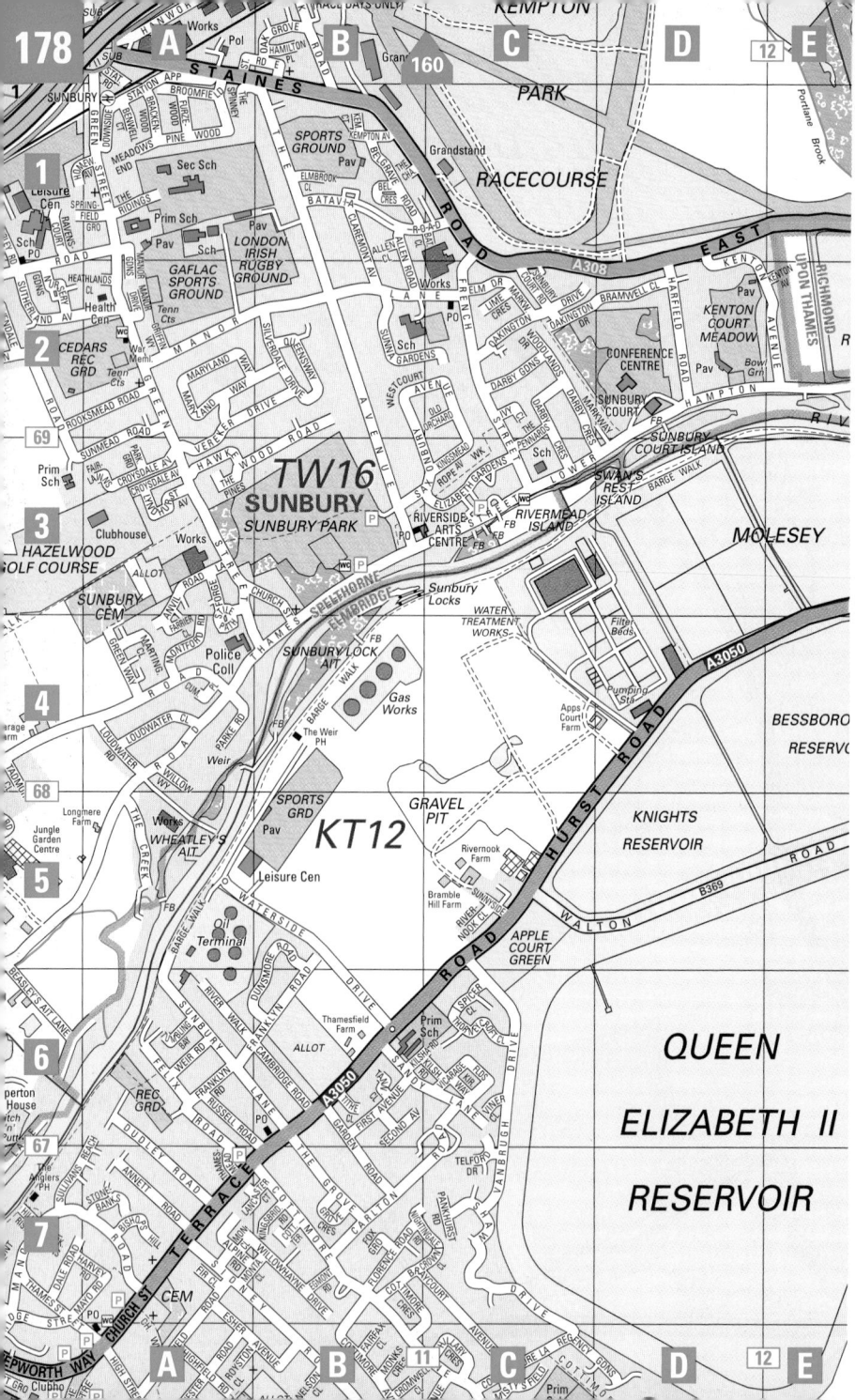

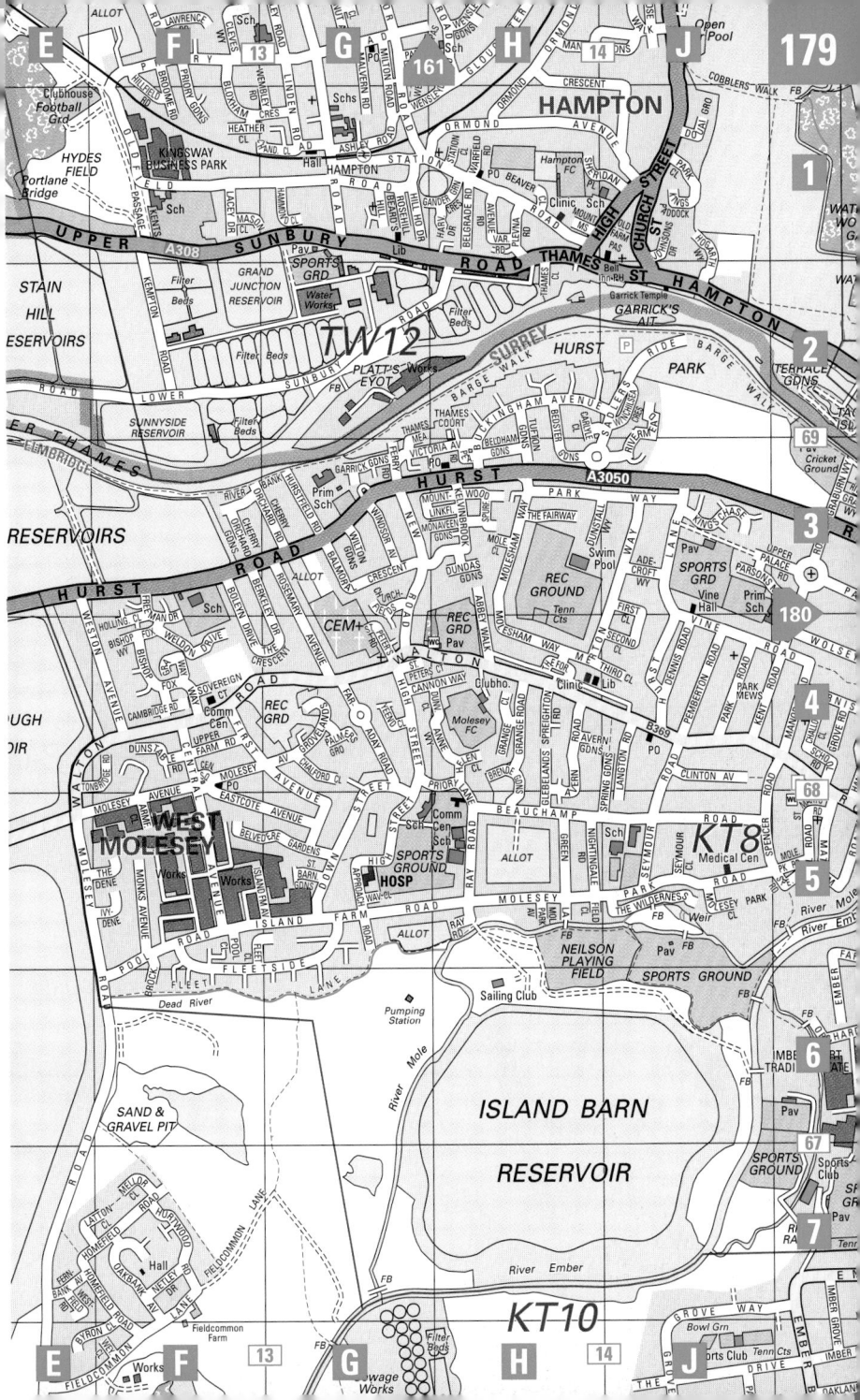

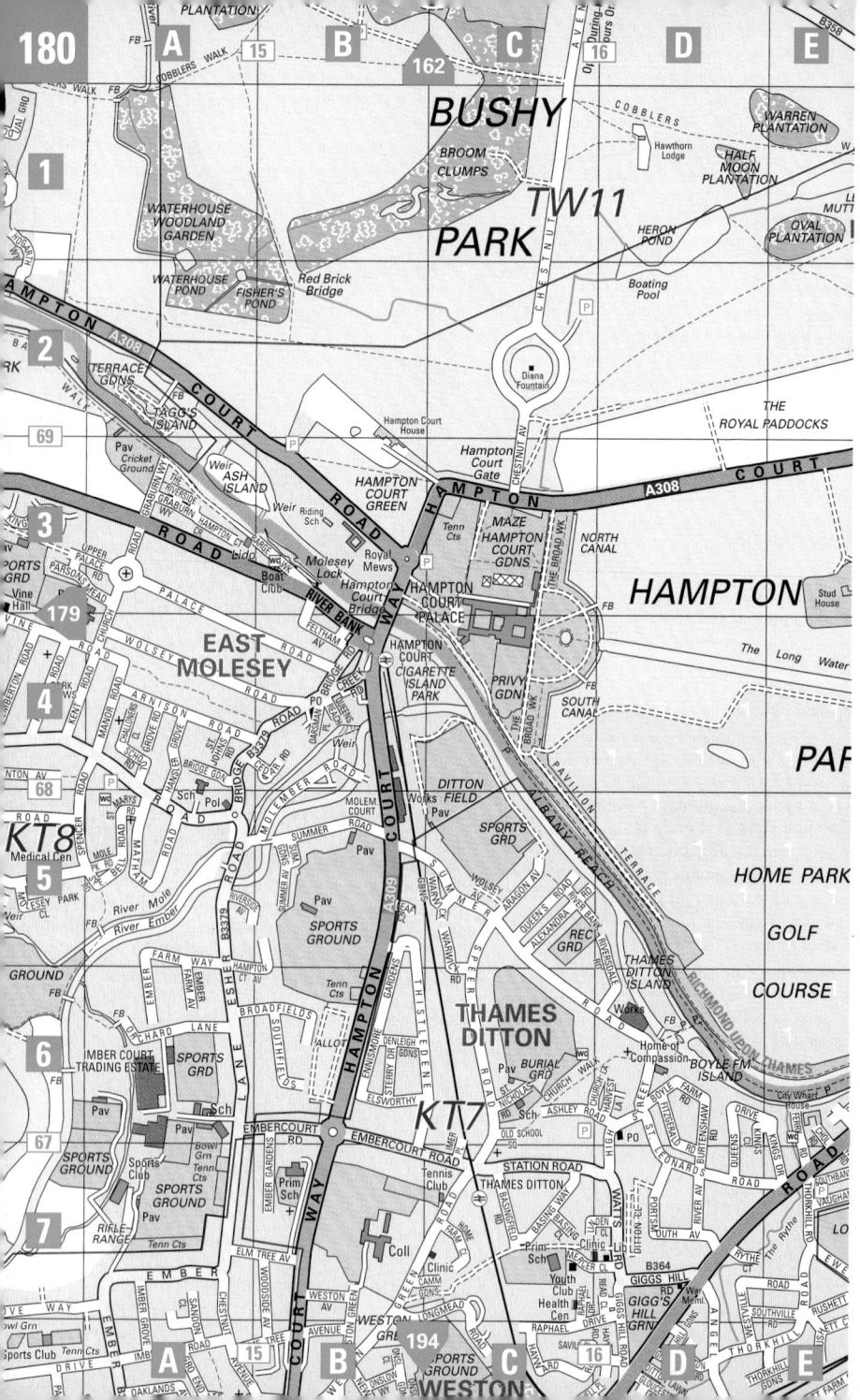

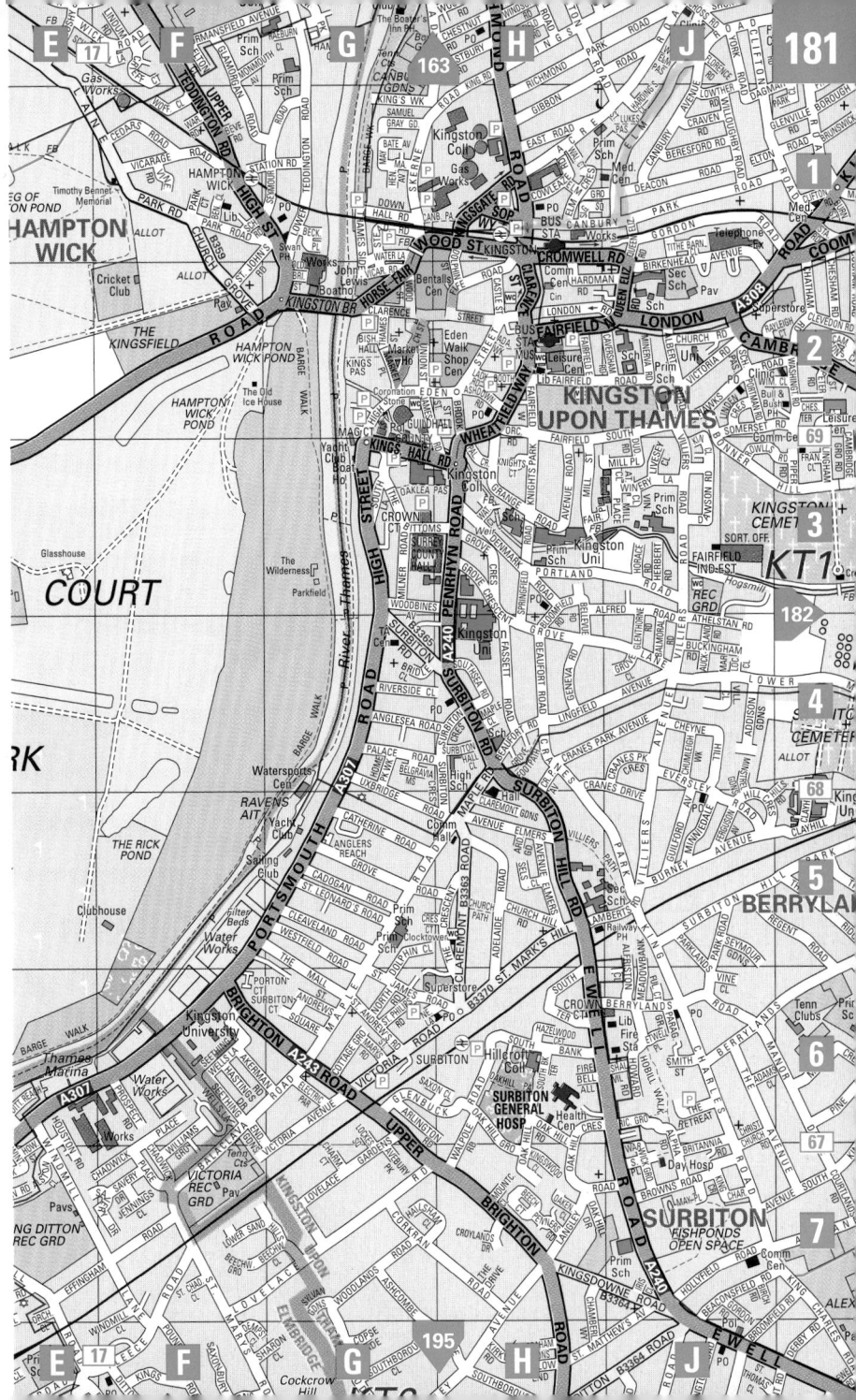

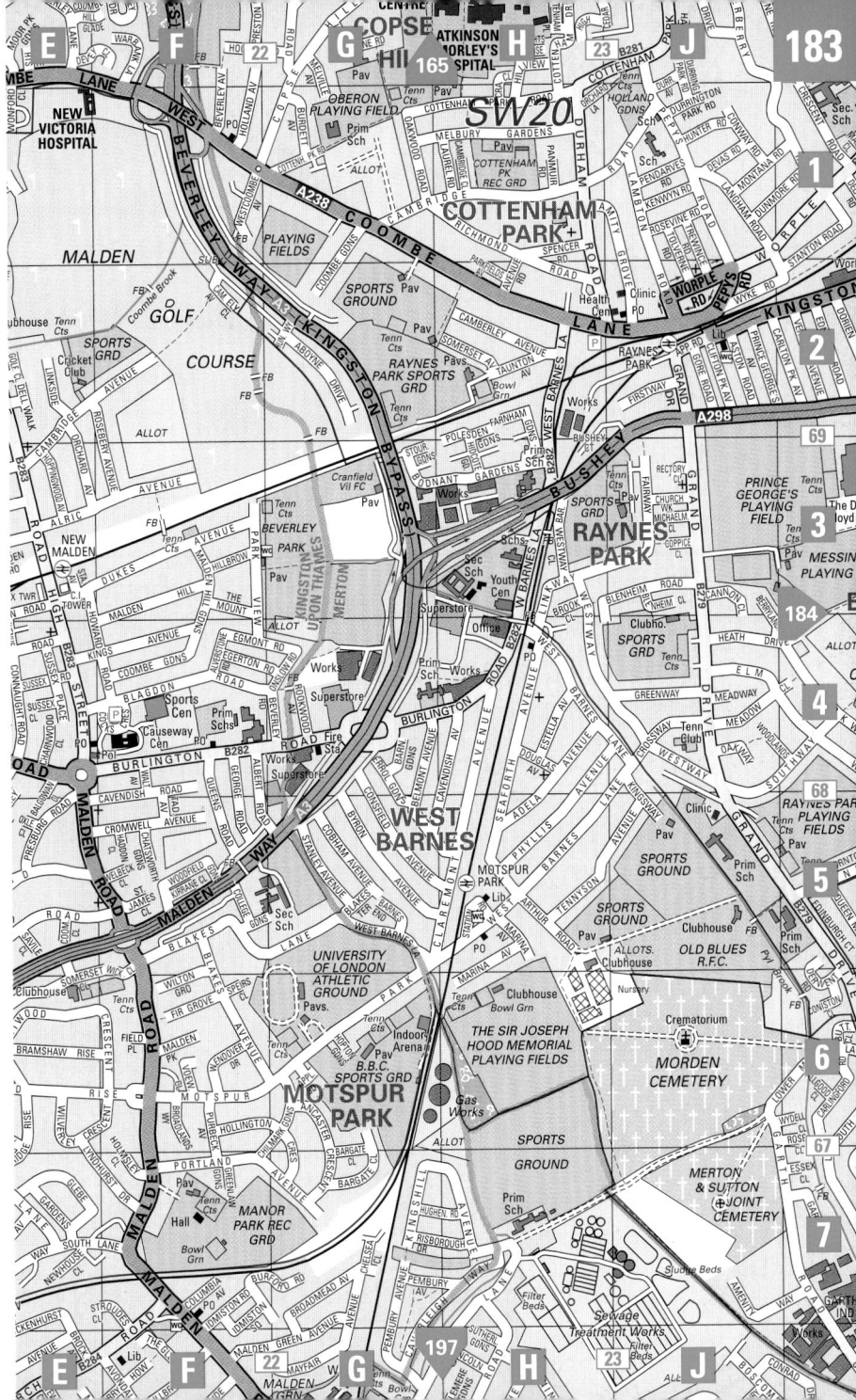

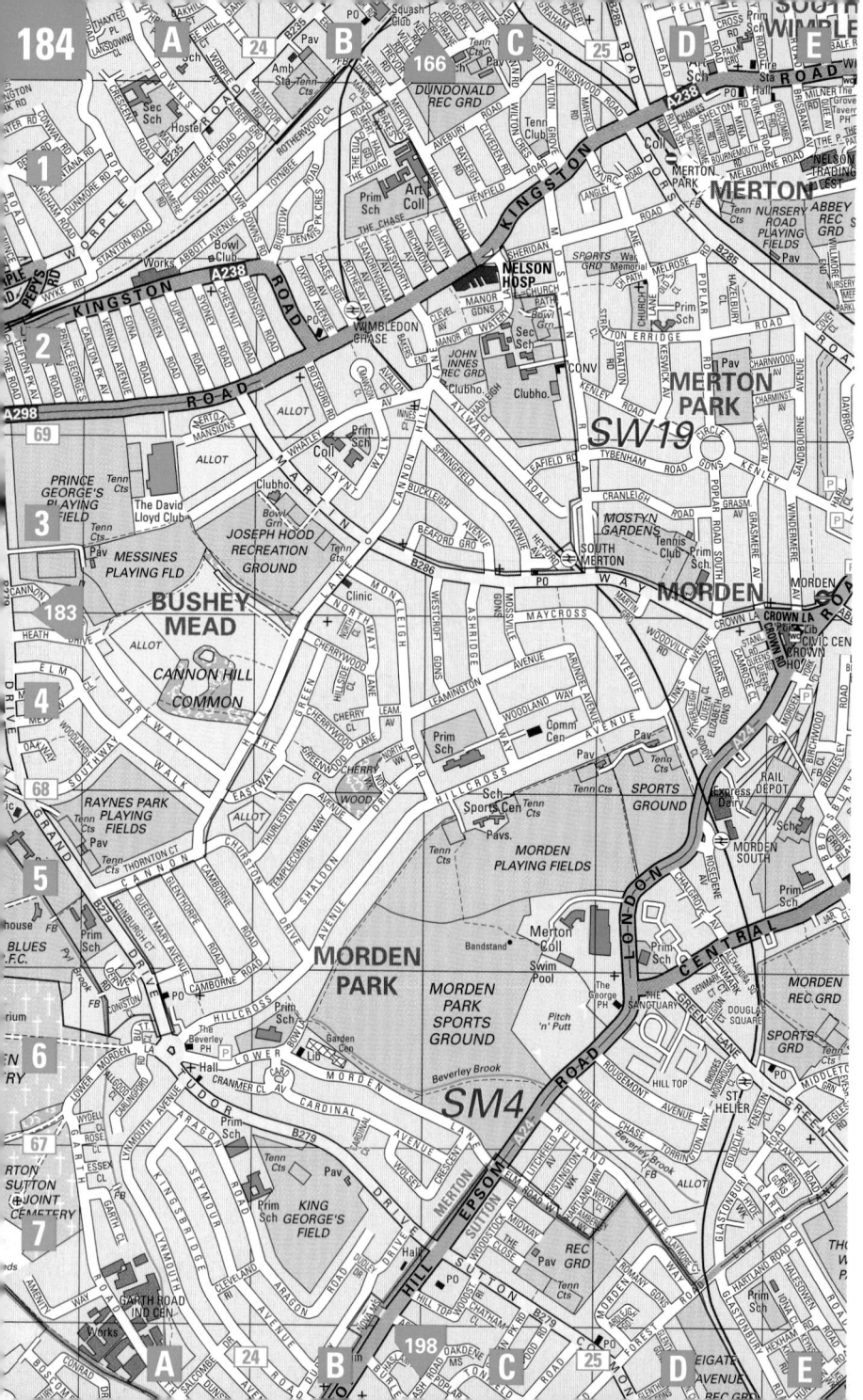

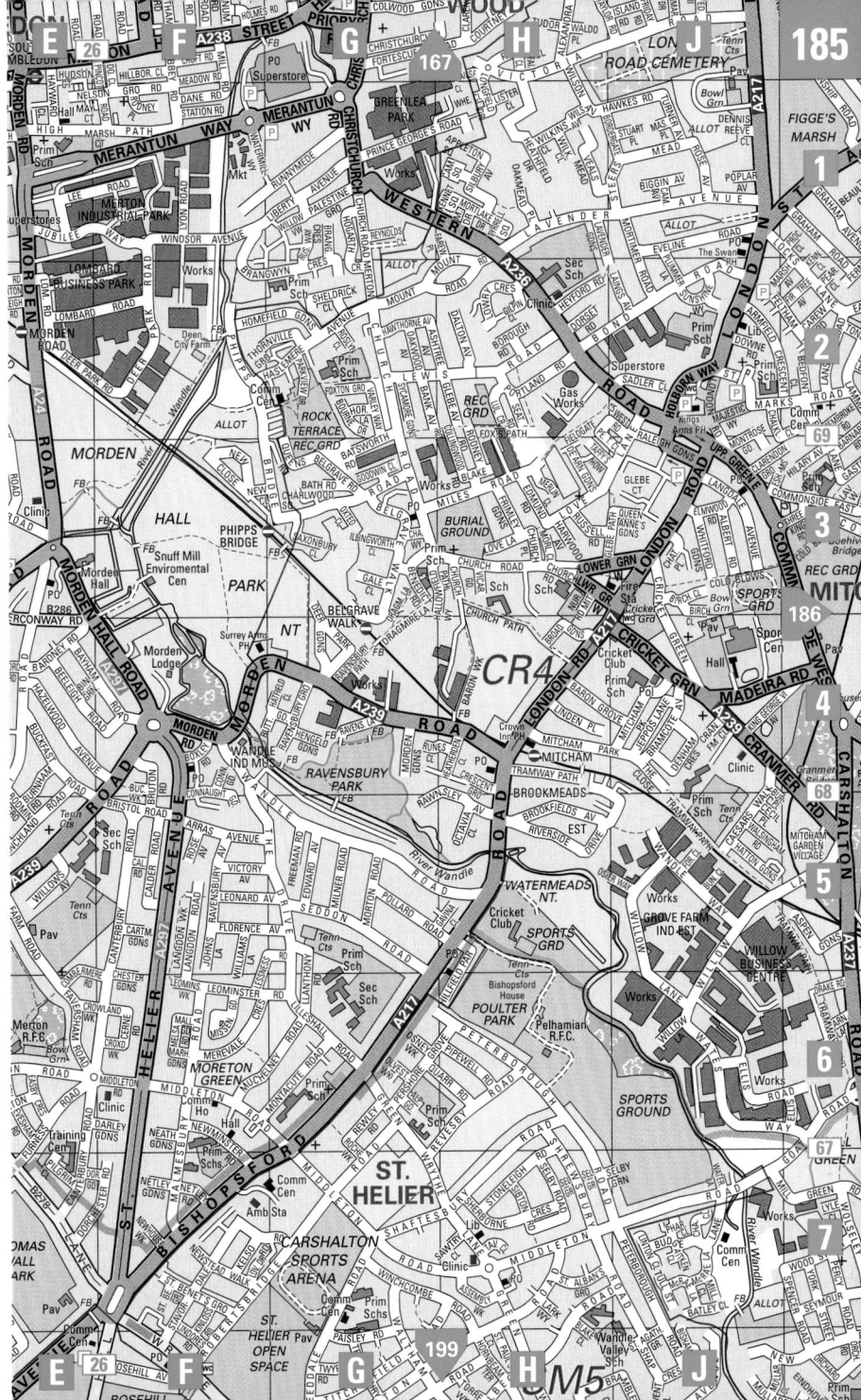

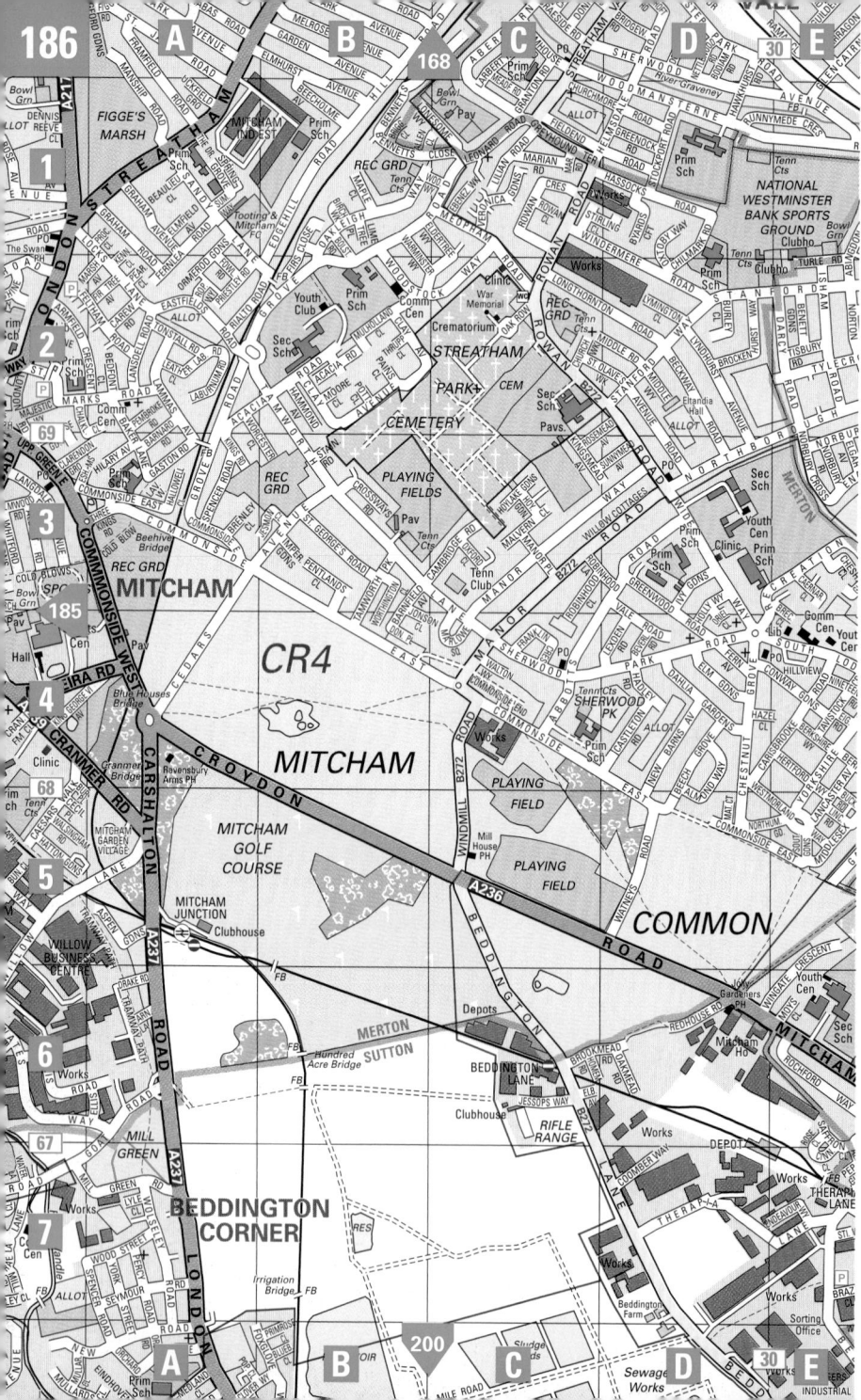

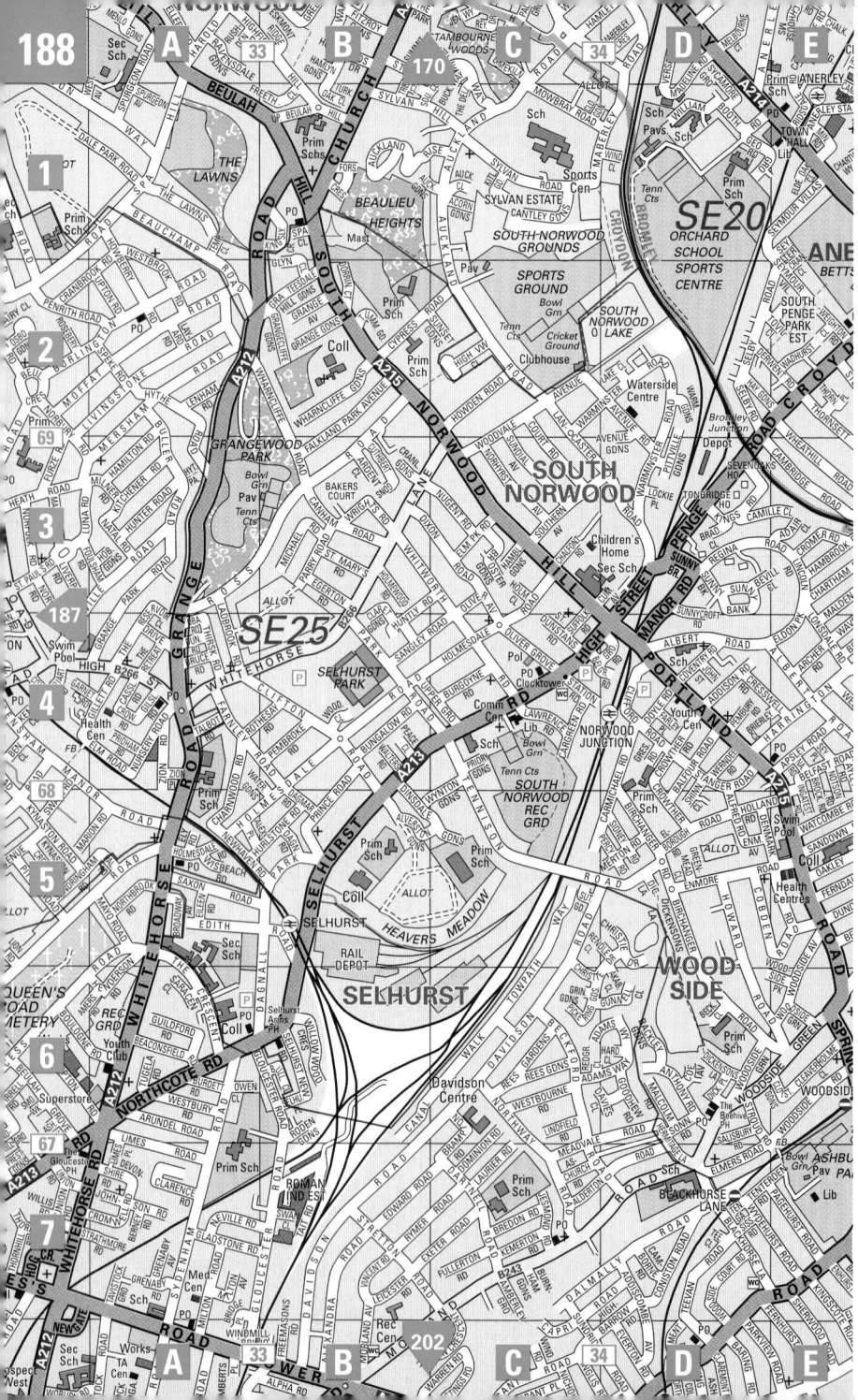

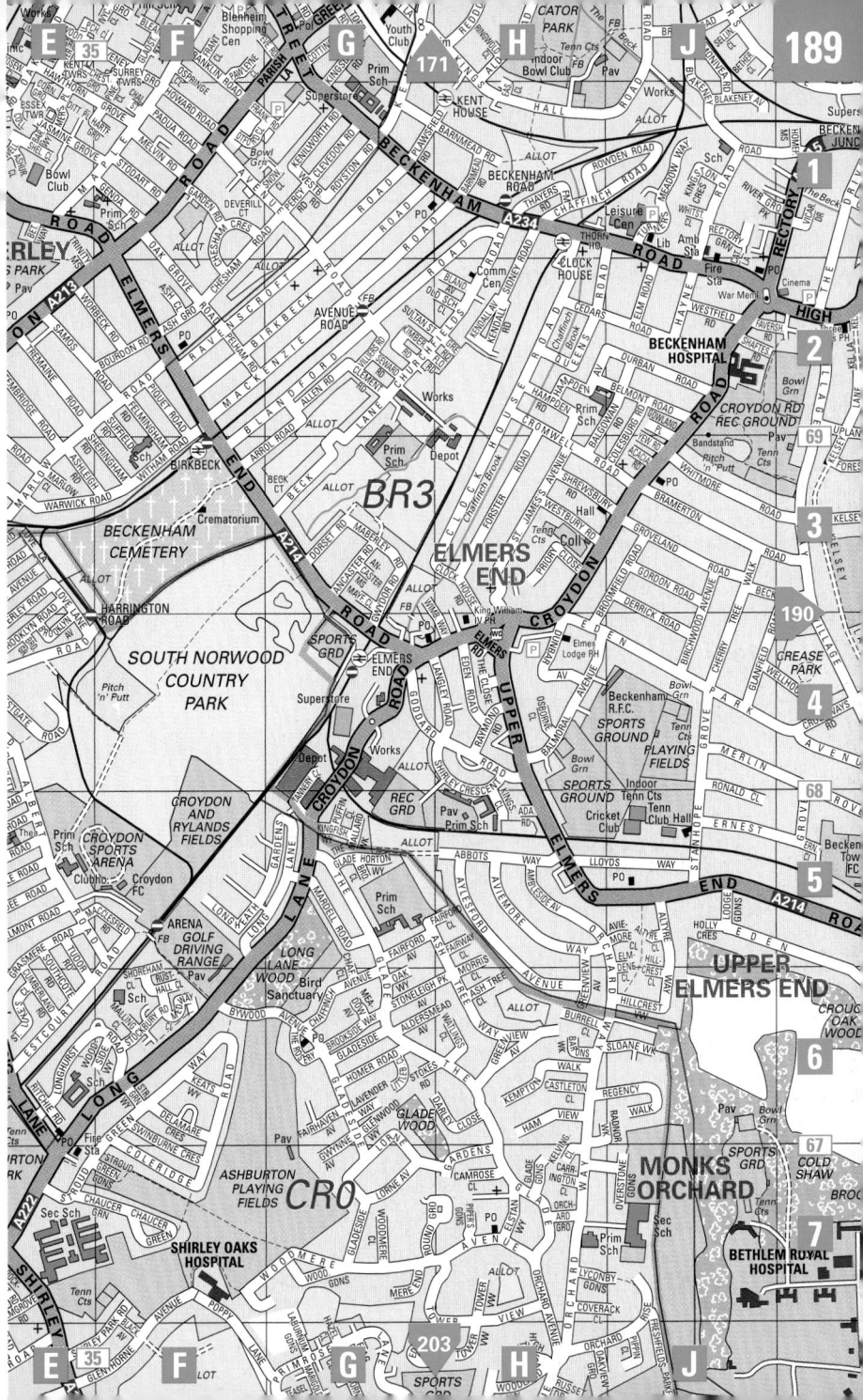

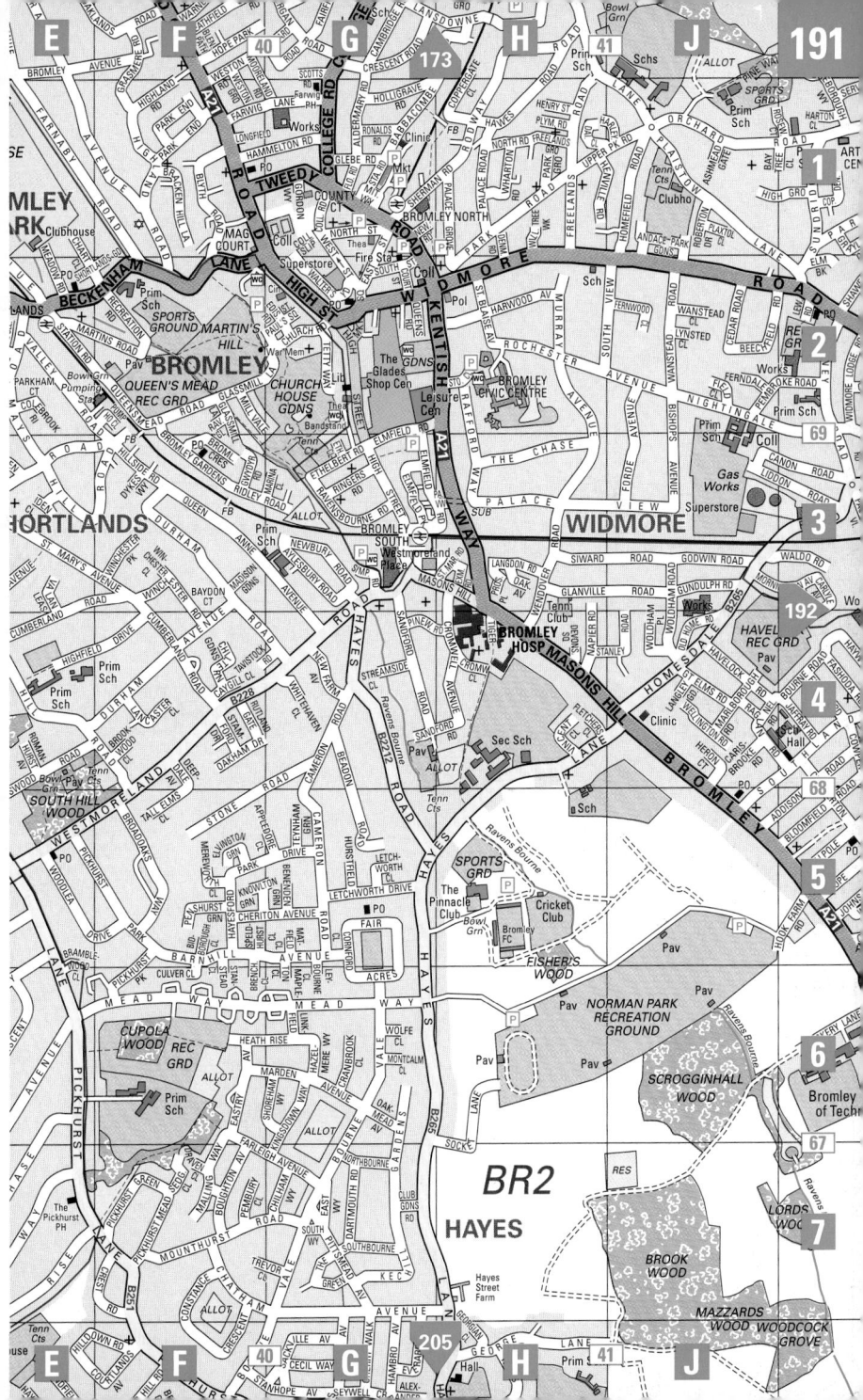

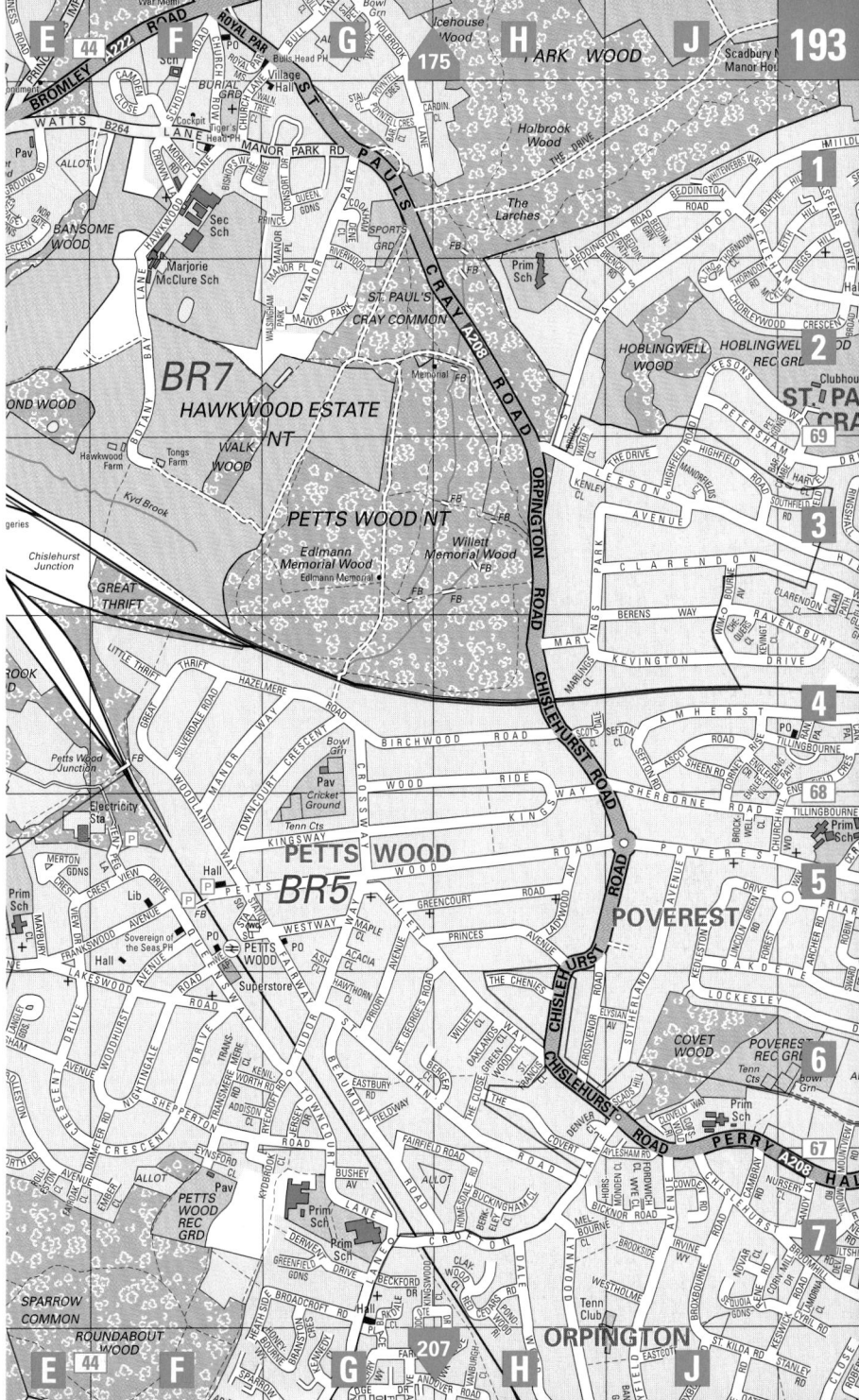

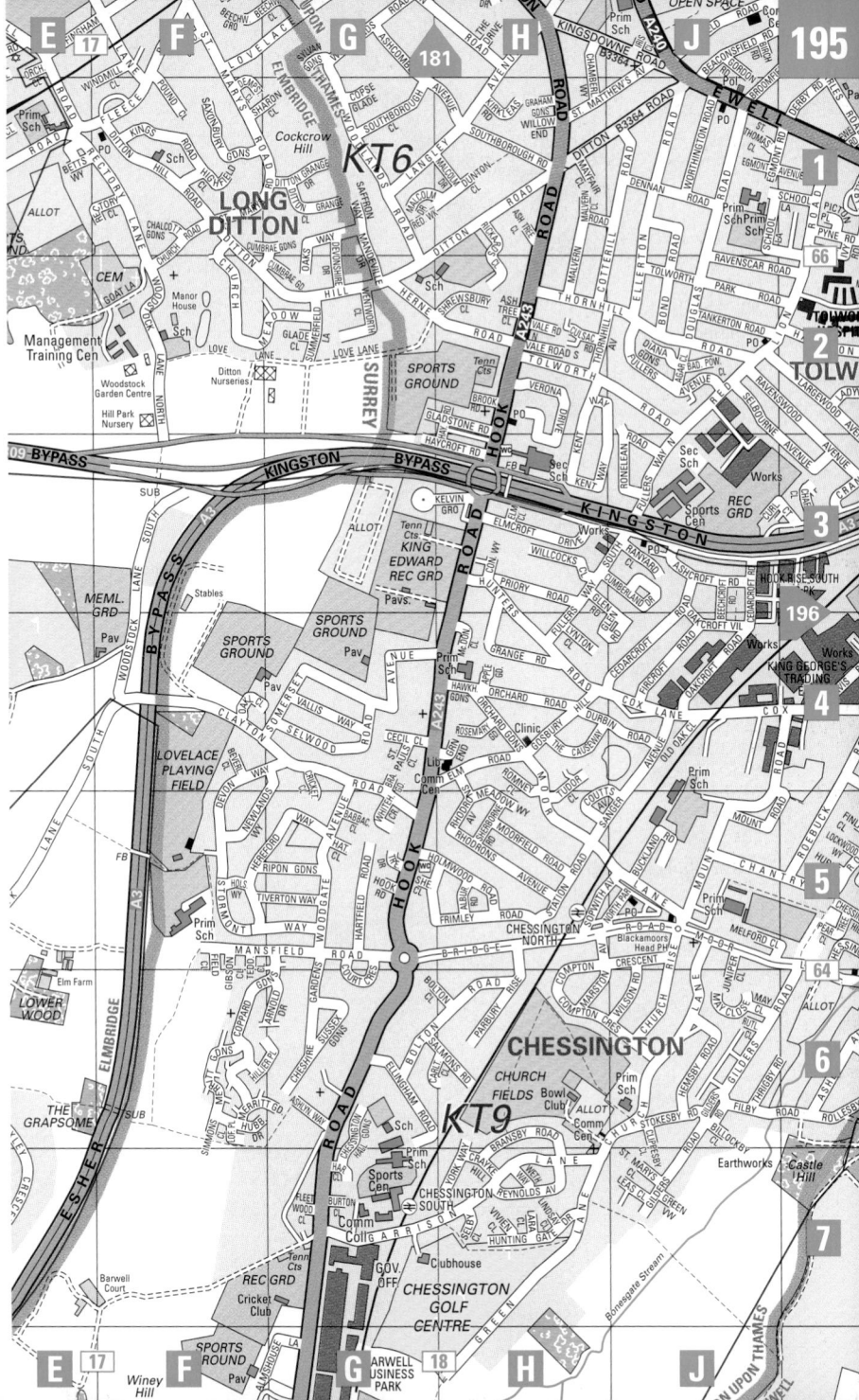

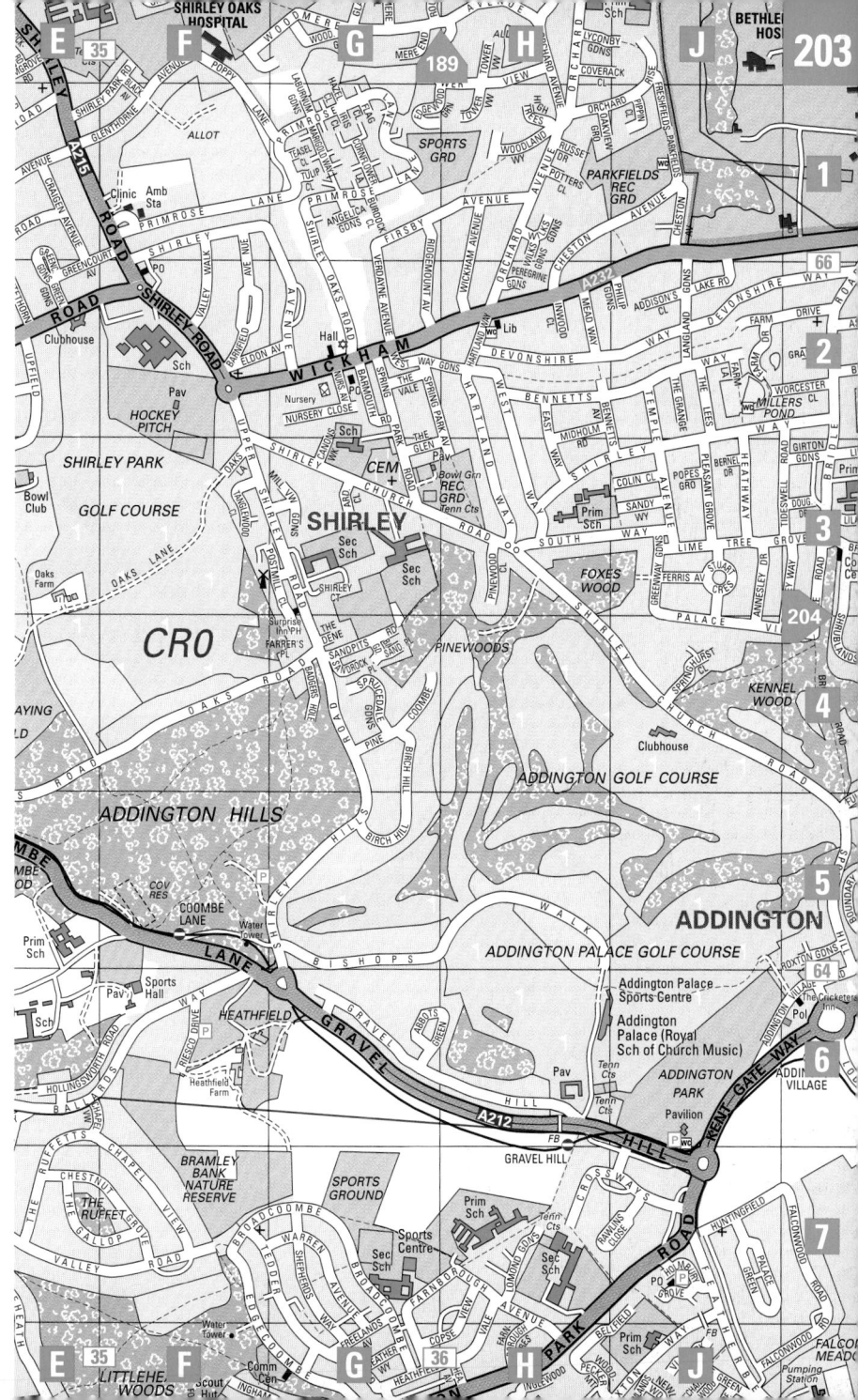

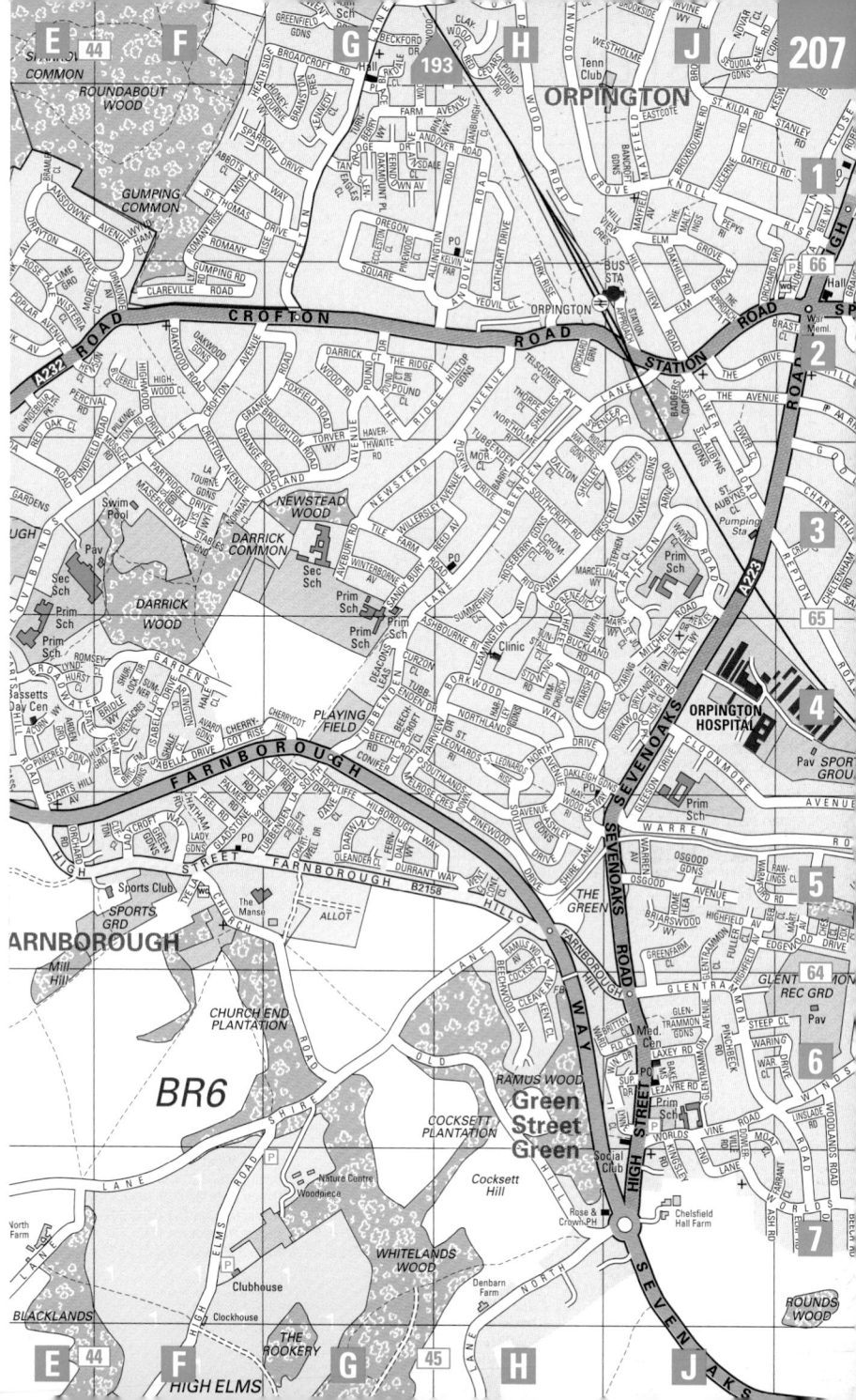

WEST END THEATRES & CINEMAS

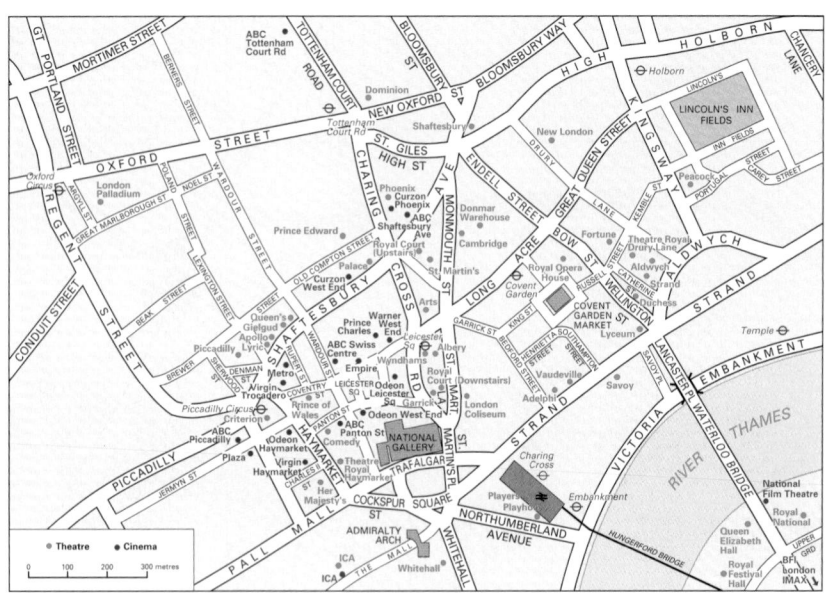

THEATRES

Adelphi *020 7344 0055*
Albery *020 7369 1730*
Aldwych *020 7416 6003*
Apollo *020 7416 6022*
Arts *020 7836 2132*
Cambridge *020 7494 5054*
Comedy *020 7369 1731*
Criterion *020 7369 1747*
Dominion *020 7656 1888*
Donmar Warehouse
 020 7369 1732
Duchess *020 7494 5075*
Fortune *020 7836 2238*
Garrick *020 7494 5085*
Gielgud *020 7494 5065*
Her Majesty's *020 7494 5400*
ICA *020 7930 3647*

London Coliseum *020 7632 8300*
London Palladium *020 7494 5020*
Lyceum *020 7420 8191*
Lyric *020 7494 5045*
New London *020 7405 0072*
Palace *020 7434 0909*
Peacock *020 7314 8800*
Phoenix *020 7369 1733*
Piccadilly *020 7369 1734*
Players *020 7839 1134*
Playhouse *020 7839 4401*
Prince Edward *020 7734 8951*
Prince of Wales *020 7839 5987*
Queen Elizabeth Hall
 020 7960 4242
Queen's *020 7494 5041*
Royal Court Theatre Downstairs
 020 7565 5000

Royal Court Theatre Upstairs
 020 7565 5000
Royal Festival Hall *020 7960 4242*
Royal National *020 7452 3000*
Royal Opera House
 020 7304 4000
St. Martin's *020 7836 1443*
Savoy *020 7836 8888*
Shaftesbury *020 7379 5399*
Strand *020 7930 8800*
Theatre Royal, Drury Lane
 020 7494 5550
Theatre Royal, Haymarket
 020 7930 8800
Vaudeville *020 7836 9987*
Whitehall *020 7369 1735*
Wyndhams *020 7369 1736*

CINEMAS

ABC Panton St *020 7930 0631*
ABC Piccadilly *020 7437 3561*
ABC ShaftesburyAvenue
 020 7836 6279
ABC Swiss Centre *020 7439 4470*
ABC Tottenham Court Rd
 020 7636 6148
BFI London IMAX *020 7902 1200*
Curzon Phoenix *020 7369 1721*
Curzon West End *020 7369 1722*

Empire *020 7437 1234*
ICA *020 7930 3647*
Metro *020 7437 0757*
National Film Theatre
 020 7928 3232
Odeon Haymarket *0426 915353*
Odeon Leicester Sq
 020 8315 4215
Odeon Mezzanine
(Odeon Leicester Sq)
 020 8315 4215

Odeon West End *020 8315 4221*
Plaza *020 7437 1234*
Prince Charles *020 7437 8181*
Virgin Haymarket *0870 907 0712*
Virgin Trocadero *0870 907 0716*
Warner West End *020 7437 4347*

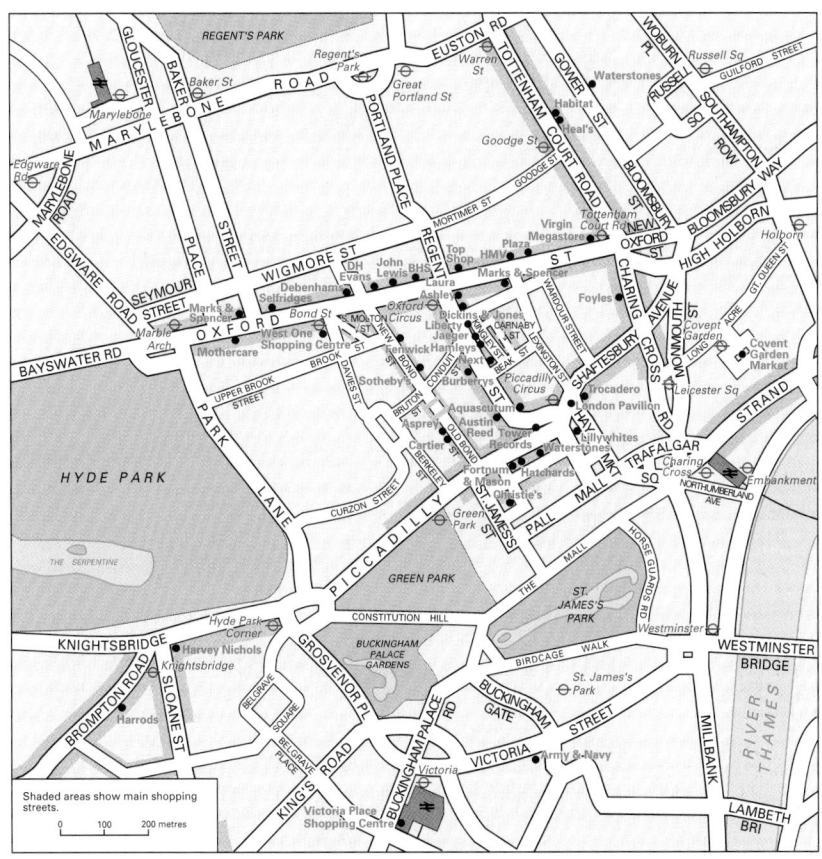

SHOPS

Aquascutum *020 7734 6090*
Army & Navy *020 7834 1234*
Asprey *020 7493 6767*
Austin Reed *020 7734 6789*
BHS (Oxford St) *020 7629 2011*
Cartier *020 7493 6962*
Christie's *020 7839 9060*
Covent Garden Market
020 7836 9137
DH Evans *020 7629 8800*
Debenhams *020 7580 3000*
Dickins & Jones *020 7734 7070*
Fenwick *020 7629 9161*
Fortnum & Mason *020 7734 8040*
Foyles *020 7437 5660*
Habitat (Tottenham Court Rd)
020 7631 3880
Hamleys *020 7734 3161*
Harrods *020 7730 1234*

Harvey Nichols *020 7235 5000*
Hatchards *020 7439 9921*
Heal's *020 7636 1666*
HMV *020 7631 3423*
Jaeger *020 7200 4000*
John Lewis *020 7629 7711*
Laura Ashley (Regent St)
020 7355 1363
Liberty *020 7734 1234*
Lillywhites *020 7930 3181*
London Pavilion *020 7437 1838*
Marks & Spencer (Marble Arch)
020 7935 7954
Marks & Spencer (Oxford St)
020 7437 7722
Mothercare *020 7580 1688*
Next (Regent St) *020 7434 2515*
Plaza on Oxford St
020 7637 8811

Selfridges *020 7629 1234*
Sotheby's *020 7493 8080*
Top Shop & Top Man
020 7636 7700
Tower Records *020 7439 2500*
Trocadero *020 7439 1791*
Victoria Place Shopping Centre
020 7931 8811
Virgin Megastore *020 7580 5822*
Waterstones (Gower St)
020 7636 1577
Waterstones (Piccadilly)
020 7851 2400

INDEX TO PLACES OF INTEREST

Admiralty Arch	**25**	**J1**
Africa Centre, King St. WC2	**18**	**A5**
Agnew Galleries	**25**	**F1**
Albert Memorial	**22**	**E3**
Alexander Fleming Laboratory	**15**	**F3**
Museum, Praed St. W2		
Alexandra Palace	**74**	**D2**
Anthony d'Offay Gallery	**16**	**E4**
Apollo Labatts (Hammersmith)	**127**	**J5**
Apollo Victoria Theatre	**25**	**F6**
Apsley House, Wellington	**24**	**B3**
Museum		
Arsenal Football Club	**93**	**H3**
Association Gallery, The	**11**	**J5**
Avery Hill Park, Eltham	**157**	**F6**
B.B.C. Experience,	**16**	**E2**
Portland Pl. W1		
Baden-Powell House	**30**	**D1**
Baker Street	**8**	**A6**
Bank of England	**20**	**B4**
Bank of England Museum	**20**	**C4**
Bankside Gallery	**19**	**H6**
Banqueting House	**26**	**A2**
Barbican Arts	**20**	**A1**
and Conference Centre		
Barn Elms Wildfowl Reserve	**127**	**H7**
Barnes Common	**147**	**G3**
Barnet Football Club	**40**	**D5**
Barnet Museum, Wood St.	**40**	**B4**
Battersea Dogs Home	**130**	**B7**
Battersea Park	**31**	**J7**
Bedford Hill Gallery	**168**	**B1**
Bentley Priory, Stanmore	**52**	**B3**
Bermondsey Leather Market	**28**	**D4**
Bethnal Green	**113**	**E3**
Museum of Childhood		
Big Ben	**26**	**B4**
Billingsgate Fish Market	**134**	**B1**
Blackheath	**154**	**D1**
Bloomsbury Square	**18**	**B2**
Borough Market	**28**	**B2**
Boston Manor, Brentford	**124**	**E5**
Bramah Tea	**29**	**G3**
and Coffee Museum		
Brentford Football Club	**125**	**G6**
Britain at War Experience	**28**	**D2**
British Airways London Eye	**26**	**C3**
British Dental Association	**16**	**D2**
Museum, Wimpole St.		
British Library	**9**	**J3**
British Library	**70**	**E3**
Newspaper Collection		
British Medical Association	**9**	**J5**
British Museum	**18**	**A2**
Brixton Academy, The	**151**	**F3**
Broadgate Ice and Arena	**20**	**D2**
Brockwell Park SE24	**151**	**H6**
Brompton Oratory,	**23**	**G6**
Brompton Rd.		
Bruce Castle Museum,	**76**	**B1**
Tottenham		
Brunei Gallery,	**9**	**J6**
Thornhaugh St. WC1		
Brunel Engine House	**133**	**F2**
Buckingham Palace	**24**	**E4**
Burgh House	**91**	**G4**
(Hampstead Museum)		
Burlington Arcade	**17**	**F6**
Bushy Park	**180**	**C1**
Business Design Centre	**111**	**G1**
Cabaret Mechanical Theatre,	**18**	**B5**
Covent Garden		
Cabinet War Rooms	**25**	**J3**
Camden Arts Centre	**91**	**F5**
Camden Lock Market	**92**	**B7**
and Waterbuses		
Camley Street Natural Park	**9**	**J1**
Canary Wharf Tower,	**134**	**B1**
Isle of Dogs		
Carlyle's House	**31**	**G6**
Carnaby Street	**17**	**F4**
Caxton Hall	**25**	**G5**
Cecil Sharp House	**110**	**A1**
Celia Coleman Gallery,	**7**	**F1**
St. John's Wood High St. NW8		
Cenotaph, The	**26**	**A3**
Central Criminal Court	**19**	**H3**
(Old Bailey)		
Centrepoint	**17**	**J3**
Charlton Athletic Football Club	**135**	**J5**
Chartered Insurance Institutes	**20**	**A3**
Museum, Aldermanbury EC2		
Charterhouse	**19**	**H1**
Chelsea Antique Market	**31**	**F5**
Chelsea Football Club	**30**	**A7**
Chelsea Physic Garden	**31**	**J5**
Chinatown, Gerrard St. W1	**17**	**H5**
Chislehurst Caves,	**192**	**D1**
Caveside Clo.		
Chiswick House	**126**	**E6**
Christie's	**25**	**G1**
Church Farm House Museum,	**71**	**H3**
Hendon		
City University	**11**	**G4**
City of Westminster Archives	**25**	**J5**
Centre, The, St. Ann's St. SW1		
Clapham Common	**150**	**A4**
Clarence House	**25**	**G3**
Cleopatra's Needle	**18**	**C6**
Clink Prison Museum,	**28**	**B1**
Southwark		
Clockmakers Company	**20**	**A3**
Collection, The, Guildhall Library		
Coliseum, The	**18**	**A6**
College of Arms	**19**	**H5**
Commonwealth Institute	**128**	**C3**
Conference Forum, The	**21**	**H3**
County Hall	**26**	**C3**
Court Dress Collection,	**22**	**B2**
Kensington Palace		
Courtauld Gallery	**18**	**C5**
Covent Garden	**18**	**B5**
Crafts Council	**11**	**F2**
Croydon Museum	**201**	**J3**
Crystal Palace Football Club	**188**	**B4**
Crystal Palace	**170**	**D6**
National Sport Centre		
Crystal Palace Park	**170**	**C5**
Cuming Museum	**35**	**J2**
Custom House	**20**	**D6**
Cutty Sark	**134**	**C6**
Danson Park, Welling	**158**	**C4**
Department of the	**25**	**F5**
Environment, Transport and Regions		
Departments of Health	**26**	**A3**
and Social Security		
Design Museum	**29**	**G2**
Dickens House	**10**	**D6**
Doctor Johnson's House	**19**	**F4**
Dome, The	**134**	**E1**
Dominion Theatre	**17**	**J3**
Downing Street	**26**	**A3**
Dulwich College Picture	**152**	**B7**
Gallery		
Ealing Common	**125**	**H1**
Earls Court Exhibition Centre	**128**	**D5**
Earth Galleries	**23**	**F6**
Eastbury Manor House,	**117**	**J1**
Barking		
Eltham Palace	**156**	**B7**
Epping Forest	**47**	**J1**
Eros	**17**	**H6**
Estorick Collection of	**93**	**H6**
Modern Italian Art		
F.A. Premier League	**26**	**C4**
Hall of Fame		
Fairfield Halls, Croydon	**202**	**A3**
Family Records Centre,	**11**	**F4**
Public Record Office		
Fan Museum	**134**	**C7**
Faraday Museum	**17**	**F6**
Fenton House, Hampstead	**91**	**F3**
Finsbury Park N4	**75**	**H7**
Flamsteed House Museum	**134**	**D7**
Fleet Street	**19**	**F4**
Florence Nightingale Museum	**26**	**C4**
Flower Market,	**34**	**A6**
New Covent Garden Market		
Foreign and Commonwealth	**26**	**A3**
Office		
Fortnum and Mason	**25**	**F1**
Forum Club	**92**	**B5**
Freemason's Hall	**18**	**B3**
(United Grand Lodge of England)		
Freightliners City Farm	**93**	**F6**
Freud Museum	**91**	**G6**
Fulham Football Club	**148**	**A1**
Fulham Palace Museum	**148**	**B2**
Geffrye Museum	**13**	**E2**
George Inn,	**28**	**B2**
Borough High St. SE1		
Gipsy Moth IV	**134**	**C6**
Goldsmiths' Hall	**20**	**A3**
Grange Museum of Community	**89**	**E4**
History, Neasden La. NW10		
Gray's Inn	**18**	**D1**
Green Park	**24**	**E3**
Greenwich Borough Museum	**137**	**J5**
Greenwich Park	**134**	**D7**
Greenwich Pier	**134**	**C6**
Guards Museum	**25**	**G4**
Guildhall Art Gallery,	**20**	**A3**
Guildhall Library		
Guildhall, The	**20**	**A3**
Gunnersbury Park	**126**	**A3**
Museum and Art Centre		
Gunnersbury Park, Ealing	**125**	**J4**
H.M. Treasury	**26**	**A3**
H.M.S. Belfast	**28**	**E1**
H.M.S. President	**19**	**F5**
H.Q.S. Wellington,	**19**	**E5**
Master Mariners' Hall		
Hackney City Farm	**13**	**H2**
Hackney Marsh	**95**	**H3**
Hackney Museum,	**95**	**E6**
Hackney Central Hall		
Hall Place, Bexley	**159**	**J6**
Ham House	**163**	**F1**
Hamleys	**17**	**F5**
Hampstead Heath	**91**	**G2**
Hampton Court Palace and Park	**180**	**B3**
Harlequins F.C. (Rugby)	**144**	**B7**
Harrods	**23**	**J5**
Harrow Arts Centre	**51**	**H7**
Harrow Museum	**67**	**J3**
and Heritage Centre		
Harrow School	**86**	**B1**
Hay's Galleria	**28**	**D1**
Hayward Gallery	**26**	**D1**
Heathrow Airport (London)	**140**	**E1**
Heinz Gallery, R.I.B.A.	**16**	**B3**
Highgate Cemetery	**92**	**A1**
Hogarth's House,	**127**	**E6**
Hogarth La. W4		
Holland House and Park	**128**	**C2**
Home Office	**25**	**H4**
Horniman Museum	**170**	**E1**
Horse Guards Parade	**25**	**J2**
Hounslow Heath	**142**	**E6**
House of Detention,	**11**	**F5**
Clerkenwell Cl. EC1		
Houses of Parliament	**26**	**B4**
Hurlingham House	**148**	**D3**
Hurlingham Park	**148**	**C2**
Hyde Park	**23**	**G1**
Hyde Park Corner	**24**	**C3**
Imperial College,	**23**	**E5**
University of London		
Imperial War Museum	**27**	**F6**
Institute of Contemporary Arts	**25**	**J1**
(I.C.A.)		
International Finance Centre	**20**	**D3**
Ismaili Centre	**31**	**F1**
and Zamana Gallery		
Jewel Tower,	**26**	**A5**
Houses of Parliament		
Jewish Museum	**110**	**B1**
Jubilee Gardens	**26**	**C2**
Keats House	**91**	**H4**
Kempton Park Racecourse	**160**	**C7**
Kensal Green Cemetery	**107**	**J3**
Kensington Gardens	**22**	**D2**
Kensington Palace	**22**	**B2**
Kenwood House	**91**	**H1**
(The Iveagh Bequest)		
Kew Bridge Steam Museum	**125**	**J5**
Kew Observatory	**145**	**E3**
Kew Palace,	**125**	**H7**
Royal Botanic Gardens		
Kings Road	**31**	**F5**
Kingston Museum	**181**	**H2**
and Heritage Centre		
Lambeth Palace	**26**	**C6**
Lancaster House	**25**	**F3**
Le Palais	**127**	**J4**
Leadenhall Market	**20**	**D4**
Leicester Square	**17**	**J5**
Leighton House Museum	**128**	**C3**
Lessnes Abbey (ruins)	**138**	**D4**
Leyton Orient Football Club	**96**	**B3**
Liberty	**17**	**F4**
Lifetimes Museum, Croydon	**201**	**J3**
Lincoln's Inn	**18**	**D3**
Linley Sambourne House	**128**	**D2**
Little Holland House, Carshalton	**199**	**H7**
Little Venice (Waterbuses)	**14**	**C1**
Livesey Museum	**132**	**E6**
Lloyds of London	**20**	**D4**
London Aquarium	**26**	**C3**
London Arena	**134**	**B3**
London Brass Rubbing Centre,	**18**	**A6**
St. Martin-in-the-Fields Church		
London Bridge	**28**	**C1**
London Canal Museum, The	**10**	**B1**
London Central Mosque	**7**	**H4**

London City Airport	136	B1
London Commodity Exchange	21	G6
London Dungeon	28	C2
London Fire Brigade Museum	27	J3
London Gas Museum, The	114	C4
London Metropolitan Archives	11	F5
London Palladium	17	F4
London Peace Pagoda	32	A6
London Silver Vaults	18	E2
London Stone	20	B5
London Transport Museum, Covent Gdn. WC2	18	B5
London Wildlife Trust	110	D1
London Zoo	8	B1
Lord's, Middlesex County Cricket Club and Museum	7	F3
Lyric Art Gallery	127	J4
Madame Tussaud's	8	B6
Mall Galleries	25	J1
Mansion House	20	B4
Marble Arch	16	A5
Marble Hill House, Twickenham	145	F7
Marlborough House	25	G2
Medici Galleries, Grafton St. W1	16	E6
Methodist Central Hall	25	J4
Middlesex Guildhall	26	A4
Millwall Football Club	133	F5
Ministry of Agriculture, Fisheries and Food	26	A1
Ministry of Defence	26	A2
Monument, The	20	C5
Morden Hall Park N.T.	185	E3
Museum Interpretative Centre, Norman Rd. E6	116	C4
Museum of Artillery, The Rotunda	136	C5
Museum of Garden History	26	C6
Museum of Instruments, Royal College of Music	23	E5
Museum of London	19	J2
Museum of Richmond	145	G5
Museum of the Royal Pharmaceutical Society of Great Britain (R.P.S.G.B.)	34	C1
Musical Museum, High St., Brentford	125	H6
National Army Museum	32	A5
National Gallery	17	J6
National Maritime Museum	134	D6
National Museum of Cartoon Art	19	F1
National Portrait Gallery	17	J6
Natural History Museum	22	E6
Nelson's Column	26	A1
New Covent Garden Market	130	D7
New Scotland Yard	25	H5
Nonsuch Mansion House, Sutton	197	J6
North Woolwich Old Station Museum	136	D2
Old Admiralty Buildings (M.o.D.)	25	J2
Old Curiosity Shop	18	C3
Old Spitalfields Market	21	F1
Olympia	128	B3
Operating Theatre Museum and Herb Garret	28	C2
Orleans House Gallery, Twickenham	163	E1
Oscar Wilde's House	32	A5
Osterley Park House	123	J5
Oval, The, Surrey County Cricket Club	34	D5
Oxford Circus	17	F3
Oxford Street	17	G3
P.S. Tattershall Castle	26	B2
Pall Mall	25	G2
Passport Office	25	G5
Patent Office	18	E2
Percival David Foundation of Chinese Art, Gordon Sq. WC1	9	J6
Peter Pan Statue	23	E1
Petrie Museum of Egyptian Archaeology, Malet Pl. WC1	9	H6
Petticoat Lane (Market)	21	E2
Photographers' Gallery, Great Newport St. WC2	17	J5
Physical Energy Statue	22	D2
Piccadilly Circus	17	G6
Pitshanger Manor Museum, Ealing	125	F1
Planetarium	8	A6
Polish Institute and Sikorski Museum, Princes Gate SW7	23	F4
Pollock's Toy Museum	17	G1
Pomeroy Purdy Gallery	29	H3
Poppy Factory Museum, The, Richmond	145	G6
Portcullis House - New Parliamentary Building	26	A3
Prince Henry's Room	19	E4
Public Record Office	126	B7
Queen Elizabeth Hall and Purcell Room	26	C1
Queen Elizabeth II Conference Centre	25	J4
Queen Elizabeth's Hunting Lodge, Epping Forest	47	F7
Queen Mary's Gardens, Regent's Pk. NW1	8	B4
Queen Victoria Memorial	25	F3
Queen's Gallery, The	24	E4
Queen's Ice Rink	14	B6
Queen's Tower	23	E5
Queens Club (Tennis Centre)	128	B5
Queens Park Rangers Football Club	127	H1
R.A.A.B. Gallery	33	J3
Ragged School Museum, Copperfield Rd. E3	113	H5
Ranelagh Gardens	32	B4
Regent Street	17	E3
Regent's Park	7	J2
Richmond Palace (remains)	145	F5
Richmond Park	146	A6
Rock Circus	17	H6
Roman Bath, Strand La. WC2	18	D5
Roosevelt Memorial, W1 Grosvenor Sq.	16	C5
Rotherhithe Heritage Museum	133	H1
Royal Academy of Arts	17	F6
Royal Academy of Dramatic Art (R.A.D.A.)	17	H1
Royal Academy of Music	8	C6
Royal Air Force Museums, Hendon	71	G2
Royal Albert Dock Regatta Centre	116	A7
Royal Albert Hall	22	E4
Royal Botanic Gardens, Kew	125	H7
Royal College of Art	22	D4
Royal College of Music	23	E5
Royal College of Surgeons	18	D3
Royal Courts of Justice	18	D4
Royal Exchange (L.I.F.F.E.)	20	C4
Royal Festival Hall	26	C1
Royal Geographical Society	23	E4
Royal Horticultural Society (New Hall)	25	H6
Royal Horticultural Society (Old Hall)	33	H1
Royal Hospital Chelsea and Museum	32	B4
Royal Mews, The	24	E5
Royal Military Academy	136	C7
Royal National Theatre	26	D1
Royal Naval College	134	D6
Royal Opera House	18	B4
Rugby Football Union Twickenham	144	B6
Russian Submarine, Unity Way SE18	136	A3
Sadler's Wells Theatre	11	F3
St. Bartholomew-the-Great Church, Cloth Fair EC1	19	H2
St. Bride's Church and Crypt Museum	19	G4
St. Bride's Printing Library, Bride La. EC4	19	G4
St. Clement Danes Church, Strand WC2	18	D4
St. James's Palace	25	G3
St. James's Park	25	H3
St. John's Gate and Museum of the Order of St. John	11	G6
St. Katharine's Dock	29	H1
St. Lawrence Jewry Church, Gresham St. EC2	20	A3
St. Martin-in-the-Fields Church, Trafalgar Sq. WC2	18	A6
St. Mary at Hill Church, Lovat La. EC3	20	D6
St. Mary-le-Bow Church	20	A4
St. Paul's Cathedral	19	J4
Salvation Army International Heritage Centre, Judd St. WC1	10	A4
Science Museum	23	F6
Selfridges	16	B4
Serpentine Gallery	23	F2
Serpentine, The	23	G2
Shakespeare's Globe Theatre and Exhibition	19	J6
Shell Centre	26	D2
Sherlock Holmes Museum	8	A6
Sir John Soane's Museum, Lincoln's Inn Fields WC2	18	C3
Skinners' Hall, Dowgate Hill EC4	20	B5
Smithfield Central Market	19	H2
Soho	17	H5
Somerset House	18	C5
Sotheby's	17	E5
South London Art Gallery	152	B1
Southwark Cathedral	28	B1
Speaker's Corner	16	A5
Spencer House	25	F2
Spitalfields Community Farm	13	H6
Sternberg Centre, Finchley	72	E2
Stock Exchange	20	C4
Strand	18	A6
Surrey Docks Farm	133	J2
Sutton Heritage Centre, Carshalton	199	J4
Sutton House	95	F5
Syon House and Park, Brentford	145	F1
Tate Britain	34	A2
Tate Modern	27	H1
Telecom Tower	17	F1
Temple Bar	18	E4
Temple of Mithras, Queen Victoria St. EC4	20	A4
Temple, The	19	E5
Thames Flood Barrier and Visitors Centre	136	A3
Thames House	34	A1
Theatre Museum, Russell St. WC2	18	B5
Theatre Royal	18	B4
Tottenham Hotspur Football Club	60	C7
Tower Bridge Experience	29	F2
Tower Pier	29	E1
Tower of London	21	F6
Toynbee Hall	21	G3
Trafalgar Square	25	J1
Trent Park Country Park, Enfield	42	B2
Trinity House	21	E5
Trocadero Centre	17	H6
University College London	9	H5
University of London	9	J6
Valence House Museum, Dagenham	100	D2
Victoria Coach Station	32	D2
Victoria Embankment Gardens	18	B6
Victoria Park E9	95	H7
Victoria Tower	26	A5
Victoria and Albert Museum	23	F6
Vinopolis - City of Wine	28	A1
Wallace Collection	16	B3
Walworth City Farm	35	H4
Wandsworth Museum, Garratt La. SW18	148	E5
Watermans Art Centre, Brentford	125	H6
Wellcome Trust	9	H5
Wellington Arch	24	C3
Wembley Conference Centre	87	J4
Wembley Stadium	88	A4
Wesley's House	12	C5
West Ham United Football Club	115	J2
Westminster Abbey	26	A5
Westminster Abbey Museum	26	A5
Westminster Cathedral	25	F6
Westminster City Hall	25	G5
Westminster Pier	26	B3
Whitbread Shire Horse Stables, Garratt St. EC1	12	A5
Whitechapel Art Gallery	21	G3
Whitehall	26	A1
William Morris Gallery, Lloyd Park E17	78	A3
Wimbledon (All England Tennis and Croquet Club)	166	B4
Wimbledon Common	165	F4
Wimbledon Football Club (share Selhurst Park with Crystal Palace F.C.)	188	B4
Wimbledon Windmill Museum	165	H2
Woolwich Common	136	C7
Y.H.A., Carter La. EC4	19	H4
Y.H.A., Earl's Ct. SW5	30	A3
Y.H.A., Holland Ho. W8	128	C2
Y.M.C.A.	17	H3
Y.W.C.A.	17	J2

INDEX TO PLACE NAMES

A

Abbey Wood SE2	138	B3
Acton W3	126	A1
Addington, Croy.	203	J5
Addiscombe, Croy.	202	C1
Aldborough Hatch, Ilf.	81	H3
Aldersbrook E12	97	H2
Alperton, Wem.	105	J1
Anerley SE20	188	E1
Arkley, Barn.	39	G5
Avery Hill SE9	157	F6

B

Balham SW12	167	J1
Barking, Bark.	117	E1
Barkingside, Ilf.	81	E3
Barnes SW13	147	G2
Barnet, Barn.	40	C3
Barnet Gate, Barn.	39	F6
Barnsbury N1	93	F7
Battersea SW11	150	B1
Bayswater W2	**14**	**B4**
Beckenham, Beck.	190	B1
Beckton E6	116	D5
Becontree, Dag.	100	D3
Becontree Heath, Dag.	101	G1
Beddington, Wall.	200	D2
Beddington Corner, Mitch.	186	A7
Bedford Park W4	126	D3
Belgravia SW1	**24**	**B6**
Bell Green SE6	171	J3
Bellingham SE6	172	B3
Belmont, Har.	68	D2
Belsize Park NW3	91	H6
Belvedere, Belv.	139	H4
Benhilton, Sutt.	199	E2
Bermondsey SE1	**29**	**F6**
Berrylands, Surb.	181	J5
Bexley, Bex.	159	G6
Bexleyheath, Bexh.	159	F5
Bickley, Brom.	192	C3
Blackfen, Sid.	157	J7
Blackheath SE3	155	E1
Blackheath Park SE3	155	G4
Bloomsbury WC1	**17**	**J2**
Borehamwood, Borwd.	38	B3
Borough, The SE1	**27**	**J4**
Bow E3	113	J2
Bowes Park N22	59	E6
Brentford, Brent.	125	G6
Brimsdown, Enf.	45	H3
Brixton SW2	150	E4
Broad Green, Croy.	187	G6
Broadgate EC2	**20**	**C1**
Brondesbury NW2	90	B7
Brondesbury Park NW6	89	J7
Brunswick Park N11	57	J2
Buckhurst Hill, Buck.H.	47	H7
Burnt Oak, Edg.	54	C7
Bush Hill Park, Enf.	44	B5
Bushey, Wat.	52	B1
Bushey Mead SW20	184	A3

C

Camberwell SE5	131	J7
Camden Town NW1	110	C1
Canning Town E16	115	G6
Canonbury N1	93	J6
Canons Park, Edg.	53	H7
Carpenters Park, Wat.	51	F2
Carshalton, Cars.	199	H5
Castelnau SW13	127	G6
Catford SE6	172	B1
Chadwell Heath, Rom.	82	D6
Charlton SE7	135	J6
Cheam, Sutt.	198	A6
Chelsea SW3	**31**	**E5**
Chessington, Chess.	195	H6
Chigwell, Chig.	65	E3
Childs Hill NW2	90	D2
Chingford E4	62	B1
Chingford Green E4	63	F1
Chingford Hatch E4	62	C4
Chipping Barnet, Barn.	40	B4
Chislehurst, Chis.	174	D7
Chislehurst West, Chis.	174	C5
Chiswick W4	126	D6
Church End N3	72	C1
Church End NW10	88	E6
Clapham SW4	150	B3
Clapham Park SW4	150	D6
Clapton Park E5	95	H4
Claygate, Esher	194	B7
Clayhall, Ilf.	80	C2
Clerkenwell EC1	**11**	**G6**
Cockfosters, Barn.	41	H4
Coldblow, Bex.	177	J2
Collier Row, Rom.	83	G1
Collier's Wood SW19	167	G7
Coombe, Kings.T.	164	C7
Copse Hill SW20	165	G7
Cottenham Park SW20	183	H1
Cranbrook, Ilf.	98	C1
Cranford, Houns.	122	A7
Creekmouth, Bark.	118	A4
Cricklewood NW2	90	A3
Crouch End N8	74	C6
Croydon, Croy.	202	A2
Cubitt Town E14	134	C3
Custom House E16	116	A6

D

Dagenham, Dag.	101	G6
Dalston E8	94	D7
Dartmouth Park NW5	92	B3
De Beauvoir Town N1	112	A1
Debden, Loug.	49	G3
Deptford SE8	133	J5
Dollis Hill NW2	89	H3
Dormer's Wells, Sthl.	103	H7
Downham, Brom.	173	F5
Ducks Island, Barn.	40	A6
Dulwich SE21	152	B7

E

Ealing W5	105	F7
Earls Court SW5	128	C5
Earlsfield SW18	167	F1
East Acton W3	126	D1
East Barnet, Barn.	41	H6
East Dulwich SE22	152	D6
East Finchley N2	73	G4
East Ham E6	116	B2
East Molesey, E.Mol.	180	A4
East Sheen SW14	146	D4
East Wickham, Well.	138	A7
Eastcote, Pnr.	66	C6
Eastcote Village, Pnr.	66	B5
Eden Park, Beck.	190	A5
Edgware, Edg.	54	B5
Edmonton N9	60	D4
Elmers End, Beck.	189	H3
Elmstead, Chis.	174	A5
Eltham SE9	156	A6
Enfield, Enf.	44	C3
Enfield Highway, Enf.	45	F3
Enfield Town, Enf.	44	A2

F

Falconwood, Well.	157	G3
Farnborough, Orp.	206	E5
Feltham, Felt.	160	A2
Finchley N3	72	E1
Finsbury EC1	**11**	**F3**
Finsbury Park N4	93	G1
Foots Cray, Sid.	176	B6
Forest Gate E7	97	G5
Forest Hill SE23	171	G1
Fortis Green N2	73	J4
Friday Hill E4	62	D2
Friern Barnet N11	57	H4
Fulham SW6	148	B2
Fullwell Cross, Ilf.	81	G1
Furzedown SW17	168	A5

G

Gants Hill, Ilf.	80	D5
Golders Green NW11	72	D7
Goodmayes, Ilf.	100	B2
Gospel Oak NW5	92	A4
Grange Hill, Chig.	65	F6
Grange Park N21	43	H5
Green Street Green, Orp.	207	H6
Greenford, Grnf.	103	H3
Greenwich SE10	134	D6
Grove Park SE12	173	G3
Grove Park W4	126	B7
Gunnersbury W4	126	A4

H

Hackbridge, Wall.	200	B2
Hackney E8	94	E6
Hackney Wick E9	96	A5
Hadley, Barn.	40	C2
Haggerston E2	**13**	**G1**
Hainault, Ilf.	65	H7
Hale End E4	62	D6
Ham, Rich.	163	F3
Hammersmith W6	127	J5
Hampstead NW3	91	G4
Hampstead Garden Suburb N2	73	F5
Hampton, Hmptn.	179	H1
Hampton Hill, Hmptn.	161	J6
Hampton Wick, Kings.T.	181	E1
Hanwell W7	124	C1
Hanworth, Felt.	160	D4
Harlesden NW10	106	E2
Harlington, Hayes	121	F6
Harmondsworth, West Dr.	120	A5
Harringay N8	75	G4
Harrow, Har.	68	A7
Harrow on the Hill, Har.	86	B7
Harrow Weald, Har.	68	A1
Hatch End, Pnr.	50	E7
Hatton, Felt.	141	J4
Hayes, Brom.	191	H7
Hayes Town, Hayes	121	H2
Headstone, Har.	67	J4
Hendon NW4	71	H4
Herne Hill SE24	151	J5
Heston, Houns.	123	F7
High Barnet, Barn.	40	A2
High Beach, Loug.	47	G1
Higham Hill E17	77	H2
Highams Park E4	62	D5
Highbury N5	93	H5
Highgate N6	92	A2
Highwood Hill NW7	55	G2
Hinchley Wood, Esher	194	C3
Hither Green SE13	154	E6
Holborn WC2	**18**	**C3**
Holders Hill NW4	72	A2
Holloway N7	92	E4
Homerton E9	95	H5
Honor Oak SE23	153	F6
Honor Oak Park SE4	153	H6
Hornsey N8	75	F3
Hounslow, Houns.	143	F4
Hounslow West, Houns.	142	D3
Hoxton N1	**12**	**D2**
Hyde, The NW9	71	F4

I

Ilford, Ilf.	99	F3
Isleworth, Islw.	144	C3
Islington N1	111	F1

J

Joydens Wood, Bex.	177	J5

K

Kennington SE11	**35**	**E5**
Kensal Green NW10	107	J3
Kensal Rise NW6	108	A2
Kensal Town W10	108	A4
Kensington W8	128	C2
Kentish Town NW5	92	C6
Kenton, Har.	68	E5
Keston, Brom.	205	J5
Kew, Rich.	126	A6
Kidbrooke SE3	155	H3
Kilburn NW6	108	C2
King's Cross N1	110	D1
Kingsbury NW9	70	B6
Kingsland N1	94	B6
Kingston upon Thames, Kings.T.	181	H2
Kingston Vale SW15	165	E4

L

Ladywell SE13	154	A5
Lambeth SE1	**26**	**C5**
Lamorbey, Sid.	175	J1
Lampton, Houns.	143	H1
Lea Bridge E5	95	G3
Lee SE12	154	E4
Lessness Heath, Belv.	139	H5
Lewisham SE13	154	B4
Leyton E11	96	B1
Leytonstone E11	78	D7
Limehouse E14	113	H7
Lisson Grove NW8	**7**	**F6**
Little Ealing W5	125	F4
Little Ilford E12	98	B5
Long Ditton, Surb.	195	F1
Longlands, Chis.	175	F3
Loughton, Loug.	48	C5
Lower Clapton E5	95	G4

Lower Edmonton N9 60 C1
Lower Holloway N7 93 F5
Lower Sydenham SE26 171 G4
Loxford, Ilf. 99 F5

M

Maida Hill W9 108 C4
Maida Vale W9 **6** **B5**
Manor Park E12 98 B4
Mark's Gate, Rom. 82 E2
Marylebone NW1 **15** **J3**
Mayfair W1 **16** **D6**
Merry Hill, Wat. 51 G1
Merton SW19 184 D1
Merton Park SW19 184 D2
Mile End E1 113 G3
Mill Hill NW7 55 G5
Millwall E14 134 B3
Mitcham, Mitch. 186 A3
Monken Hadley, Barn. 40 C1
Monks Orchard, Croy. 189 J7
Morden, Mord. 184 D3
Morden Park, Mord. 184 B5
Mortlake SW14 146 C3
Motspur Park, N.Mal. 183 G6
Mottingham SE9 173 J2
Muswell Hill N10 74 B3

N

Neasden NW2 89 E3
New Barnet, Barn. 41 E4
New Beckenham, Beck. 171 J6
New Charlton SE7 135 J4
New Cross SE14 153 H1
New Cross Gate SE14 153 G1
New Eltham SE9 174 D2
New Malden, N.Mal. 182 D3
New Southgate N11 58 D4
Newbury Park, Ilf. 81 G5
Newington SE1 **35** **J1**
Nine Elms SW8 **33** **G7**
Noel Park N22 75 G2
Norbiton, Kings.T. 182 B2
Norbury SW16 187 G1
North Acton W3 106 D4
North Beckton E6 116 B4
North Cheam, Sutt. 197 J3
North Cray, Sid. 177 G3
North Finchley N12 57 G5
North Harrow, Har. 67 G6
North Hyde, Sthl. 123 E4
North Kensington W10 107 J6
North Sheen, Rich. 146 A2
North Wembley, Wem. 87 E2
North Woolwich E16 136 B2
Northolt, Nthlt. 85 F7
Northumberland Heath, Erith 139 J7
Norwood SE19 170 A6
Norwood Green, Sthl. 123 G4
Norwood New Town SE19 169 J6
Notting Hill W11 108 B7
Nunhead SE15 153 F3

O

Oakleigh Park N20 57 G1
Oakwood N14 42 D6
Old Bexley, Bex. 159 H7
Old Ford E3 113 J1
Old Malden, Wor.Pk. 196 D1
Old Oak Common NW10 107 F5
Orpington, Orp. 207 H1
Osidge N14 58 B1
Osterley, Islw. 123 J7

P

Paddington W2 **14** **C2**
Palmers Green N13 59 F3
Park Langley, Beck. 190 C5
Park Royal NW10 106 A3
Parsons Green SW6 148 D1
Peckham SE15 152 D1
Penge SE20 171 F7
Pentonville N1 **10** **E2**
Perivale, Grnf. 105 F1
Petersham, Rich. 163 H1
Petts Wood, Orp. 193 G5
Pimlico SW1 **33** **F3**
Pinner, Pnr. 67 E4
Pinner Green, Pnr. 66 C2
Pinnerwood Park, Pnr. 50 C7
Plaistow E13 115 F3
Plaistow, Brom. 173 F6
Plumstead SE18 137 H5
Ponders End, Enf. 45 F5

Poplar E14 114 B7
Poverest, Orp. 193 J5
Preston, Wem. 69 H7
Primrose Hill NW8 109 J1
Putney SW15 148 B4
Putney Heath SW15 147 J6
Putney Vale SW15 165 F3

Q

Queensbury, Har. 69 G3

R

Rayners Lane, Har. 85 F1
Raynes Park SW20 183 H3
Redbridge, Ilf. 80 C6
Regent's Park NW1 **8** **C2**
Richmond, Rich. 145 H6
Roehampton SW15 147 G5
Rosehill, Sutt. 198 E1
Rotherhithe SE16 133 G3
Rowley Green, Barn. 39 F4
Roxeth, Har. 86 A2
Ruislip Manor, Ruis. 84 A2
Rush Green, Rom. 83 J7

S

Saint Helier, Cars. 185 G7
Saint James's SW1 **25** **G2**
Saint John's SE8 154 A2
Saint John's Wood NW8 **6** **E3**
Saint Luke's EC1 **12** **A5**
Saint Margarets, Twick. 144 D5
Saint Pancras WC1 **10** **A4**
Sands End SW6 149 F1
Selhurst SE25 188 B6
Seven Kings, Ilf. 81 H7
Sewardstone E4 46 C1
Sewardstonebury E4 47 E4
Shacklewell N16 94 C4
Shadwell E1 113 F7
Shepherd's Bush W12 127 J1
Shirley, Croy. 203 G3
Shooter's Hill SE18 157 F1
Shoreditch E1 **13** **F6**
Shortlands, Brom. 190 E3
Sidcup, Sid. 175 J4
Silvertown E16 135 J2
Sipson, West Dr. 120 D6
Snaresbrook E11 79 E5
Soho W1 **17** **H5**
Somers Town NW1 **9** **H3**
South Acton W3 126 A3
South Beddington, Wall. 200 D6
South Chingford E4 61 J5
South Croydon, S.Croy. 201 J6
South Hackney E9 95 F7
South Hampstead NW6 91 E7
South Harrow, Har. 85 H3
South Kensington SW7 **30** **C2**
South Lambeth SW8 150 E1
South Norwood SE25 188 C3
South Oxhey, Wat. 50 C3
South Tottenham N15 76 B5
South Wimbledon SW19 166 E7
South Woodford E18 79 F2
Southall, Sthl. 122 D1
Southborough, Brom. 192 C6
Southend SE6 172 B4
Southfields SW18 166 D1
Southgate N14 58 C2
Southwark SE1 **27** **H2**
Spring Grove, Islw. 144 B1
Stamford Hill N16 94 B1
Stanmore, Stan. 52 D5
Stanwell, Stai. 140 B7
Stepney E1 113 F5
Stockwell SW9 150 D3
Stoke Newington N16 94 B2
Stonebridge NW10 106 B1
Stoneleigh, Epsom 197 G5
Strand WC2 **18** **A5**
Stratford E15 96 C6
Strawberry Hill, Twick. 162 B3
Streatham SW16 169 E4
Streatham Hill SW2 151 F7
Streatham Park SW16 168 C4
Streatham Vale SW16 168 D7
Stroud Green N4 75 H6
Sudbury, Wem. 86 D5
Summerstown SW17 166 B3
Sunbury, Sun. 178 A3
Sundridge, Brom. 173 J6
Surbiton, Surb. 181 J7
Sutton, Sutt. 198 E6

Sydenham SE26 171 F5

T

Teddington, Tedd. 162 D6
Thames Ditton, T.Ditt. 180 C6
Thamesmead SE28 137 J1
Thamesmead North SE28 118 D6
Thamesmead West SE18 137 F3
Thornton Heath, Th.Hth. 187 H4
Tokyngton, Wem. 88 B6
Tolworth, Surb. 196 A2
Tooting Graveney SW17 167 H6
Tottenham N17 76 B1
Tottenham Hale N17 76 E3
Totteridge N20 56 B1
Tufnell Park N7 92 D4
Tulse Hill SE21 169 J1
Twickenham, Twick. 162 D2

U

Underhill, Barn. 40 D5
Upper Clapton E5 94 E1
Upper Edmonton N18 60 D6
Upper Elmers End, Beck. 189 J5
Upper Holloway N19 92 C3
Upper Norwood SE19 170 A7
Upper Sydenham SE26 170 D4
Upper Tooting SW17 167 H3
Upper Walthamstow E17 78 B4
Upton E7 97 H7
Upton Park E6 115 J1

V

Vauxhall SE11 **34** **B4**

W

Waddon, Croy. 201 G2
Walham Green SW6 128 E7
Wallington, Wall. 200 C5
Walthamstow E17 78 B2
Walworth SE17 **35** **J3**
Wandsworth SW18 148 C5
Wanstead E11 79 H7
Wapping E1 **29** **J1**
Watford Heath, Wat. 50 E1
Wealdstone, Har. 68 C3
Welling, Well. 158 A3
Wembley, Wem. 87 H4
Wembley Park, Wem. 87 J2
West Acton W3 106 A6
West Barnes, N.Mal. 183 G5
West Brompton SW10 **30** **A5**
West Drayton, West Dr. 120 A3
West Dulwich SE21 170 A3
West Ewell, Epsom 196 E7
West Green N15 75 J3
West Ham E15 97 F7
West Hampstead NW6 90 E5
West Harrow, Har. 67 J7
West Heath SE2 138 D6
West Hendon NW9 71 E7
West Kilburn W9 108 C3
West Molesey, W.Mol. 179 F5
West Norwood SE27 169 J3
West Wickham, W.Wick. 204 C2
Westbourne Green W2 108 D5
Westminster SW1 **25** **F5**
Weston Green, T.Ditt. 194 C1
Whetstone N20 57 E2
Whitechapel E1 **21** **H4**
Whitton, Twick. 143 H7
Widmore, Brom. 191 H3
Willesden NW10 89 F6
Willesden Green NW10 89 H7
Wimbledon SW19 166 B6
Wimbledon Park SW19 166 C3
Winchmore Hill N21 43 F7
Wood Green N22 74 E1
Woodford, Wdf.Grn. 63 H6
Woodford Bridge, Wdf.Grn. 64 B7
Woodford Green, Wdf.Grn. 63 F4
Woodford Wells, Wdf.Grn. 63 H4
Woodlands, Islw. 144 B2
Woodside, Croy. 188 D5
Woolwich SE18 136 D5
Worcester Park, Wor.Pk. 197 F2
World's End, Enf. 43 G3
Wrythe, The, Cars. 199 H2

Y

Yeading, Hayes 102 B3
Yiewsley, West Dr. 120 B1

INDEX TO STREET NAMES

General Abbreviations

All.	Alley	Embk.	Embankment	Pav.	Pavilion
Allot.	Allotments	Est.	Estate	Pk.	Park
Amb.	Ambulance	Ex.	Exchange	Pl.	Place
App.	Approach	Exhib.	Exhibition	Pol.	Police
Arc.	Arcade	F.B.	Footbridge	Prec.	Precinct
Av./Ave.	Avenue	F.C.	Football Club	Prim.	Primary
Bdy.	Broadway	Fld./Flds.	Field/Fields	Prom.	Promenade
Bk.	Bank	Fm.	Farm	Pt.	Point
Bldgs.	Buildings	Gall.	Gallery	Quad.	Quadrant
Boul.	Boulevard	Gar.	Garage	R.C.	Roman Catholic
Bowl.	Bowling	Gdn./Gdns.	Garden/Gardens	Rd./Rds	Road/Roads
Br./Bri.	Bridge	Govt.	Government	Rec.	Recreation
C. of E.	Church of England	Gra.	Grange	Res.	Reservoir
Cath.	Cathedral	Grd./Grds.	Ground/Grounds	Ri.	Rise
Cem.	Cemetery	Grn./Grns.	Green/Greens	S.	South
Cen.	Central, Centre	Gro./Gros.	Grove/Groves	Sch.	School
Cft./Cfts.	Croft/Crofts	Gt.	Great	Sec.	Secondary
Ch.	Church	Ho./Hos.	House/Houses	Shop.	Shopping
Chyd.	Churchyard	Hosp.	Hospital	Sq.	Square
Cin.	Cinema	Hts.	Heights	St.	Saint
Circ.	Circus	Ind.	Industrial	St./Sts.	Street/Streets
Cl./Clo.	Close	Int.	International	Sta.	Station
Co.	County	Junct.	Junction	Sub.	Subway
Coll.	College	La./Las.	Lane/Lanes	Swim.	Swimming
Comm.	Community	Lib.	Library	T.A.	Territorial Army
Conv.	Convent	Lo.	Lodge	T.H.	Town Hall
Cor./Cors.	Corner/Corners	Lwr.	Lower	Tenn.	Tennis
Coron.	Coroners	Mag.	Magistrates	Ter.	Terrace
Cotts.	Cottages	Mans.	Mansions	Thea.	Theatre
Cov.	Covered	Mem.	Memorial	Trd.	Trading
Crem.	Crematorium	Mkt./Mkts	Market/Markets	Twr./Twrs.	Tower/Towers
Cres.	Crescent	Ms.	Mews	Uni.	University
Ct./Cts.	Court/Courts	Mt.	Mount	Vil.	Villa, Villas
Ctyd.	Courtyard	Mus.	Museum	Vw.	View
Dep.	Depot	N.	North	W.	West
Dev.	Development	N.T.	National Trust	Wd.	Wood
Dr.	Drive	Nat.	National	Wds.	Woods
Dws.	Dwellings	P.H.	Public House	Wf.	Wharf
E.	East	P.O.	Post Office	Wk.	Walk
Ed.	Education	Par.	Parade	Wks.	Works
Elec.	Electricity	Pas.	Passage	Yd.	Yard

Post Town Abbreviations

Bark.	Barking	Har.	Harrow	Stai.	Staines
Barn.	Barnet	Hmptn.	Hampton	Stan.	Stanmore
Beck.	Beckenham	Houns.	Hounslow	Sthl.	Southall
Belv.	Belvedere	Ilf.	Ilford	Sun.	Sunbury-on-
Bex.	Bexley	Islw.	Isleworth		Thames
Bexh.	Bexleyheath	Kes.	Keston	Surb.	Surbiton
Borwd.	Borehamwood	Kings.T.	Kingston upon	Sutt.	Sutton
Brent.	Brentford		Thames	T.Ditt.	Thames Ditton
Brom.	Bromley	Loug.	Loughton	Tedd.	Teddington
Buck.H.	Buckhurst Hill	Mitch.	Mitcham	Th.Hth.	Thornton Heath
Cars.	Carshalton	Mord.	Morden	Twick.	Twickenham
Chess.	Chessington	N.Mal.	New Malden	Uxb.	Uxbridge
Chig.	Chigwell	Nthlt.	Northolt	W.Mol.	West Molesey
Chis.	Chislehurst	Nthwd.	Northwood	W.Wick.	West Wickham
Cob.	Cobham	Orp.	Orpington	Wall.	Wallington
Croy.	Croydon	Pnr.	Pinner	Walt.	Walton-on-Thames
Dag.	Dagenham	Pot.B.	Potters Bar	Wat.	Watford
Dart.	Dartford	Pur.	Purley	Wdf.Grn.	Woodford Green
E.Mol.	East Molesey	Rain.	Rainham	Well.	Welling
Edg.	Edgware	Rich.	Richmond	Wem.	Wembley
Enf.	Enfield	Rom.	Romford	West Dr.	West Drayton
Epp.	Epping	Ruis.	Ruislip	Wor.Pk.	Worcester Park
Felt.	Feltham	S.Croy.	South Croydon		
Grnf.	Greenford	Sid.	Sidcup		

The street name and postal district or post town of an entry is followed by the page number and grid reference on which the name will be found, e.g. Abbey Road SW19 will be found on page 167 and in square F7.

All streets within the Central London enlarged scale section (pages 6-37) are shown in bold type when named in the index, e.g. **Abbey St. SE1** will be found on page **29** and in square **E5.**

This index contains some street names in standard text which are followed by another street named in italics. In these cases the street in standard text does not actually appear on the map due to insufficient space but can be located close to the street named in italics.

A

A.C. Ct., T.Ditt. 180 D6
Harvest La.
Aaron Hill Rd. E6 116 D5
Abberley Ms. SW4 150 B3
Cedars Rd.
Abbess Cl. E6 116 B5
Oliver Gdns.
Abbess Cl. SW2 169 H1
Abbeville Rd. N8 74 D4
Barrington Rd.
Abbeville Rd. SW4 150 C6
Abbey Av., Wem. 105 H2
Abbey Cl., Hayes 122 B1
Abbey Cl., Nthlt. 103 F3
Invicta Gro.
Abbey Cl., Pnr. 66 B3
Abbey Cres., Belv. 139 G4
Abbey Dr. SW17 168 A5
Church La.
Abbey Gdns. NW8 6 C2
Abbey Gdns. NW8 109 F2
Abbey Gdns. SE16 132 D4
Monnow Rd.
Abbey Gdns. W6 128 B6
Abbey Gro. SE2 138 B4
Abbey Ind. Est., Wem. 105 J1
Abbey La. E15 114 C2
Abbey La., Beck. 172 A7
Abbey Ms. E17 78 A5
Leamington Av.
Abbey Orchard St. SW1 25 J5
Abbey Orchard St. SW1 130 D3
Abbey Par. SW19 167 F7
Merton High St.
Abbey Par. W5 105 J3
Hanger La.
Abbey Pk., Beck. 172 A7
Abbey Retail Pk., Bark. 117 E1
Abbey Rd. E15 114 E2
Abbey Rd. NW6 6 C1
Abbey Rd. NW6 90 E7
Abbey Rd. NW8 109 F2
Abbey Rd. NW10 106 B2
Abbey Rd. SE2 138 D4
Abbey Rd. SW19 167 F7
Abbey Rd., Bark. 117 F1
Abbey Rd., Belv. 138 D4
Abbey Rd., Bexh. 159 E4
Abbey Rd., Croy. 201 H3
Abbey Rd., Enf. 44 B5
Abbey Rd., Ilf. 81 G5
Abbey Rd. Est. NW8 109 E1
Abbey St. E13 115 G4
Abbey St. SE1 29 E5
Abbey St. SE1 132 B3
Abbey Ter. SE2 138 C4
Abbey Vw. NW7 55 F3
Abbey Wk., W.Mol. 179 H3
Abbey Way SE2 138 D3
Abbey Wf. Ind. Est., Bark. 117 G2
Abbey Wd. Rd. SE2 138 B4
Abbeydale Rd., Wem. 106 A1
Abbeyfield Est. SE16 133 F4
Abbeyfield Rd. SE16 133 F4
Abbeyfields Cl. NW10 106 A2
Abbeyhill Rd., Sid. 176 C2
Abbot St. E8 94 C6
Abbots Cl. N1 93 J6
Alwyne Rd.
Abbots Cl., Orp. 207 F1
Abbots Cl., Ruis. 84 D3
Abbots Dr., Har. 85 G2
Abbots Gdns. N2 73 G4
Abbots Gdns. W8 22 A6
Abbots Grn., Croy. 203 G6
Abbots La. SE1 28 E2
Abbots Manor Est. SW1 32 D2
Abbots Manor Est. SW1 130 B4
Abbots Pk. SW2 169 G1
Abbot's Pl. NW6 108 E1
Abbot's Rd. E6 116 A1
Abbots Rd., Edg. 54 C7
Abbots Ter. N8 74 E6
Abbots Wk. W8 22 A6
Abbots Way, Beck. 189 H5
Abbotsbury Cl. E15 114 C2
Abbotsbury Cl. W14 128 C2
Abbotsbury Rd.
Abbotsbury Gdns., Pnr. 66 C6
Abbotsbury Ms. SE15 153 F3
Abbotsbury Rd. W14 128 B2
Abbotsbury Rd., Brom. 205 F2
Abbotsbury Rd., Mord. 184 E5
Abbotsford Av. N15 75 J4
Abbotsford Gdns., Wdf.Grn. 63 G7
Abbotsford Rd., Ilf. 100 A2
Abbotshade Rd. SE16 133 G1
Abbotshall Av. N14 58 C3
Abbotshall Rd. SE6 172 D1
Abbotsleigh Cl., Sutt. 198 E7
Abbotsleigh Rd. SW16 168 C4
Abbotsmede Cl., Twick. 162 C2
Abbotstone Rd. SW15 147 J3
Abbotswell Rd. SE4 153 J5
Abbotswood Cl., Belv. 138/139 E3
Coptefield Dr.
Abbotswood Gdns., Ilf. 80 C3
Abbotswood Rd. SE22 152 B4
Abbotswood Rd. SW16 168 D3
Abbotswood Way, Hayes 122 B1
Abbott Av. SW20 184 A2
Abbott Cl., Hmptn. 161 E6
Abbott Cl., Nthlt. 85 F6
Abbott Rd. E14 114 C5
Abbotts Cl. SE28 118 C7
Abbotts Cl., Rom. 83 H3
Abbotts Cres. E4 62 D4
Abbotts Cres., Enf. 43 H2
Abbotts Dr., Wem. 86 E2
Abbotts Pk. Rd. E10 78 C7
Abbotts Rd., Barn. 40 E4
Abbotts Rd., Mitch. 186 C4
Abbotts Rd., Sthl. 123 E1
Abbotts Rd., Sutt. 198 C3
Abbotts Wk., Bexh. 138 D7
Abchurch La. EC4 20 C5
Abchurch La. EC4 112 A7
Abchurch Yd. EC4 20 B5
Abdale Rd. W12 127 H1
Aberavon Rd. E3 113 H3
Abercairn Rd. SW16 168 C7
Aberconway Rd., Mord. 184 E3
Abercorn Cl. NW7 56 B7
Abercorn Cl. NW8 6 C3
Abercorn Cl. NW8 109 F3
Abercorn Cres., Har. 85 H1
Abercorn Gdns., Har. 69 G7
Abercorn Gdns., Rom. 82 B6
Abercorn Pl. NW8 6 C3
Abercorn Pl. NW8 109 F3
Abercorn Rd. NW7 56 B7
Abercorn Rd., Stan. 53 F7
Abercorn Way SE1 37 H3
Abercorn Way SE1 132 D5
Abercrombie Dr., Enf. 44 D1
Abercrombie St. SW11 149 H2
Aberdare Cl., W.Wick. 204 C2
Aberdare Gdns. NW6 91 E7
Aberdare Gdns. NW7 56 A7
Aberdare Rd., Enf. 45 F4
Aberdeen La. N5 93 H5
Aberdeen Par. N18 60/61 E5
Angel Rd.
Aberdeen Pk. N5 93 J5
Aberdeen Pk. Ms. N5 93 J4
Aberdeen Pl. NW8 6 E5
Aberdeen Pl. NW8 109 G4
Aberdeen Rd. N5 93 J4
Aberdeen Rd. N18 60 E5
Aberdeen Rd. NW10 89 F5
Aberdeen Rd., Croy. 201 J4
Aberdeen Rd., Har. 68 C2
Aberdeen Sq. E14 133 J1
Westferry Circ.
Aberdeen Ter. SE3 154 D2
Aberdour Rd., Ilf. 100 B3
Aberdour St. SE1 36 D1
Aberdour St. SE1 132 B4
Aberfeldy St. E14 114 C6
Aberford Gdns. SE18 156 B1
Aberford Rd., Borwd. 38 A2
Aberfoyle Rd. SW16 168 D6
Abergeldie Rd. SE12 155 H6
Aberglen Ind. Est., Hayes 121 G2
Abernethy Rd. SE13 154 E4
Abersham Rd. E8 94 C5
Abery St. SE18 137 H4
Abingdon Cl. NW1 92 D6
Camden Sq.
Abingdon Cl. SE1 37 G3
Abingdon Cl. SW19 167 F6
Abingdon Rd. N3 73 F2
Abingdon Rd. SW16 186 E2
Abingdon Rd. W8 128 D3
Abingdon St. SW1 26 A5
Abingdon St. SW1 130 E3
Abingdon Vil. W8 128 D3
Abinger Cl., Bark. 100 A4
Abinger Cl., Brom. 192 B3
Abinger Cl., Wall. 200/201 E5
Garden Cl.
Abinger Gdns., Islw. 144 B3
Abinger Gro. SE8 133 J6
Abinger Ms. W9 108 D4
Warlock Rd.
Abinger Rd. W4 127 E3
Ablett St. SE16 133 F5
Abney Gdns. N16 94 C2
Stoke Newington High St.
Aboyne Dr. SW20 183 G2
Aboyne Est. SW17 167 G3
Aboyne Rd. NW10 88 E3
Aboyne Rd. SW17 167 G3
Abridge Rd., Chig. 49 G6
Abridge Way, Bark. 118 B3
Abyssinia Cl. SW11 149 H4
Cairns Rd.
Acacia Av. N17 60 A7
Acacia Av., Brent. 124 E7
Acacia Av., Mitch. 186 B2
Acacia Rd.
Acacia Av., Ruis. 84 A1
Acacia Av., Wem. 87 H5
Acacia Cl. SE8 133 H4
Acacia Cl. SE20 188 D2
Selby Rd.
Acacia Cl., Orp. 193 G5
Acacia Cl., Stan. 52 B6
Acacia Dr., Sutt. 198 C1
Acacia Gdns. NW8 7 F1
Acacia Gdns., W.Wick. 204 C2
Acacia Gro. SE21 170 A2
Acacia Gro., N.Mal. 182 D3
Acacia Ms., West Dr. 120 A6
Acacia Pl. NW8 7 F1
Acacia Pl. NW8 109 G2
Acacia Rd. E11 97 E2
Acacia Rd. E17 77 H6
Acacia Rd. N22 75 G1
Acacia Rd. NW8 7 F1
Acacia Rd. NW8 109 G2
Acacia Rd. SW16 187 E1
Acacia Rd. W3 106 C7
Acacia Rd., Beck. 189 J3
Acacia Rd., Enf. 44 A1
Acacia Rd., Hmptn. 161 G6
Acacia Rd., Mitch. 186 B2
Acacia Way, Sid. 175 J1
Academy Gdns., Croy. 202 C1
Academy Gdns., Nthlt. 102 D2
Academy Pl. SE18 156 C1
Academy Rd. SE18 156 C1
Acanthus Dr. SE1 37 H3
Acanthus Dr. SE1 132 D5
Acanthus Rd. SW11 150 A3
Accommodation Rd. NW11 72 C7
Acer Av., Hayes 102 E5
Acfold Rd. SW6 148 E1
Achilles Cl. SE1 37 J3
Achilles Cl. SE1 132 D5
Achilles Rd. NW6 90 D5
Achilles St. SE14 133 H7
Achilles Way W1 24 C2
Acklam Rd. W10 108 C5
Acklington Dr. NW9 70 E1
Ackmar Rd. SW6 148 D1
Ackroyd Dr. E3 113 J5
Ackroyd Rd. SE23 153 G7
Ackworth Cl. N9 45 F7
Turin Rd.
Acland Cl. SE18 137 G7
Clothworkers Rd.
Acland Cres. SE5 152 A4
Acland Rd. NW2 89 H6
Acock Gro., Nthlt. 85 H5
Dorchester Rd.
Acol Cres., Ruis. 84 B5
Acol Rd. NW6 90 D7
Aconbury Rd., Dag. 118 B1
Acorn Cl. E4 62 B5
The Lawns
Acorn Cl., Chis. 175 F5
Acorn Cl., Enf. 43 H1
Acorn Cl., Hmptn. 161 H6
Acorn Cl., Stan. 53 E7
Acorn Ct., Ilf. 81 H6
Acorn Gdns. SE19 188 C1
Acorn Gdns. W3 106 D5
Acorn Gro., Hayes 121 J7
Acorn Par. SE15 132/133 E7
Carlton Gro.
Acorn Wk. SE16 133 H1
Acorn Way SE23 171 G3
Acorn Way, Orp. 207 E4
Acorns, The, Chig. 65 H4
Acre Dr. SE22 152 D4
Acre La. SW2 150 E4
Acre La., Cars. 200 A4
Acre La., Wall. 200 A4
Acre Path, Nthlt. 84/85 E6
Arnold Rd.
Acre Rd. SW19 167 G6
Acre Rd., Dag. 101 H7
Acre Rd., Kings.T. 181 H1
Acris St. SW18 149 F5
Acton Cl. N9 60 D2
Acton Hill Ms. W3 126 B1
Uxbridge Rd.
Acton La. NW10 106 E2
Acton La. W3 126 C2
Acton La. W4 126 D3
Acton Ms. E8 112 C1
Acton Pk. Ind. Est. W3 126 D2
Acton St. WC1 10 C4
Acton St. WC1 111 F3
Acuba Rd. SW18 166 E2
Acworth Cl. N9 45 F7
Turin Rd.
Ada Gdns. E14 114 D6
Ada Gdns. E15 115 F1
Ada Pl. E2 112 D1
Ada Rd. SE5 132 B7
Ada Rd., Wem. 87 G3
Ada St. E8 112 E1
Adair Cl. SE25 188 E3
Adair Rd. W10 108 B4
Adair Twr. W10 108 B4
Appleford Rd.
Adam & Eve Ct. W1 17 G3
Adam & Eve Ms. W8 128 D3
Adam Ct. SW7 30 D1
Adam Pl. N16 94 C2
Stoke Newington High St.
Adam Rd. E4 61 J6
Adam St. WC2 18 B6
Adam St. WC2 111 E7
Adam Wk. SW6 127 J7
Adams Cl. N3 56 D7
Falkland Av.
Adams Cl. NW9 88 B2
Adams Cl., Surb. 181 J6
Adams Ct. EC2 20 C3
Adams Gdns. Est. SE16 133 F2
St. Marychurch St.
Adams Pl. E14 134 B1
North Colonnade
Adams Pl. N7 93 F5
George's Rd.
Adams Rd. N17 76 B2
Adams Rd., Beck. 189 H5
Adams Row W1 16 C6
Adams Row W1 110 A7
Adams Sq., Bexh. 158/159 E3
Regency Way
Adams Wk., Kings.T. 181 H2
Adams Way, Croy. 188 C6
Adamson Rd. E16 115 G6
Adamson Rd. NW3 91 G7
Adamsrill Cl., Enf. 44 A6
Adamsrill Rd. SE26 171 H4
Adare Wk. SW16 169 F3
Adastral Est. NW9 70 E1
Adcock Wk., Orp. 207 J4
Borkwood Pk.
Adderley Gdns. SE9 174 D4
Adderley Gro. SW11 150 A5
Culmstock Rd.
Adderley Rd., Har. 68 C1
Adderley St. E14 114 C6
Addington Ct. SW14 146 D3
Addington Dr. N12 57 F6
Addington Gro. SE26 171 H4
Addington Rd. E3 114 A3
Addington Rd. E16 115 E4
Addington Rd. N4 75 G6
Addington Rd., Croy. 201 G1
Addington Rd., W.Wick. 205 E2
Addington Sq. SE5 36 A6
Addington Sq. SE5 131 J6
Addington St. SE1 26 D4
Addington Village Rd., Croy. 204 A5
Addis Cl., Enf. 45 G1
Addiscombe Av., Croy. 188 D7
Addiscombe Cl., Har. 69 F5
Addiscombe Ct. Rd., Croy. 202 B1
Addiscombe Gro., Croy. 202 A2
Addiscombe Rd., Croy. 202 B2
Addison Av. N14 42 B6
Addison Av. W11 128 B1
Addison Av., Houns. 143 J1
Addison Br. Pl. W14 128 C4

Addison Cl., Nthwd. 66 A1
Addison Cl., Orp. 193 F6
Addison Cres. W14 128 B3
Addison Dr. SE12 155 H5
Eltham Rd.
Addison Gdns. W14 128 A3
Addison Gdns., Surb. 181 J4
Addison Gro. W4 127 E3
Addison Pl. W11 128 B1
Addison Pl., Sthl. 103 G7
Longford Av.
Addison Rd. E11 79 G6
Addison Rd. E17 78 B5
Addison Rd. SE25 188 D4
Addison Rd. W14 128 C3
Addison Rd., Brom. 191 J5
Addison Rd., Enf. 45 F1
Addison Rd., Ilf. 81 F1
Addison Rd., Tedd. 162 E6
Addison Way NW11 72 C4
Addison Way, Hayes 102 A6
Addison's Cl., Croy. 203 J2
Addle Hill EC4 19 H5
Addle St. EC2 20 A2
Adecroft Way, W.Mol. 179 J3
Adela Av., N.Mal. 183 H5
Adela St. W10 108 B4
Kensal Rd.
Adelaide Av. SE4 153 J4
Adelaide Cl., Stan. 52 D4
Adelaide Cotts. W7 124 C2
Adelaide Gdns., Rom. 82 E5
Adelaide Gro. W12 127 G1
Adelaide Rd. E10 96 C3
Adelaide Rd. NW3 91 G7
Adelaide Rd. SW18 148 D5
Putney Br. Rd.
Adelaide Rd. W13 124 D1
Adelaide Rd., Chis. 175 E5
Adelaide Rd., Houns. 142 E1
Adelaide Rd., Ilf. 99 E2
Adelaide Rd., Rich. 145 J4
Adelaide Rd., Sthl. 123 E4
Adelaide Rd., Surb. 181 H5
Adelaide Rd., Tedd. 162 C6
Adelaide St. WC2 18 A6
Adelaide Ter., Brent. 125 G5
Adelaide Wk. SW9 151 G4
Sussex Wk.
Adelina Gro. E1 113 F5
Adelina Ms. SW12 168 D1
King's Av.
Adeline Pl. WC1 17 J2
Adeline Pl. WC1 110 D5
Adeliza Cl., Bark. 98/99 E7
North St.
Adelphi Ter. WC2 18 B6
Aden Gro. N16 94 A4
Aden Rd., Enf. 45 H4
Aden Rd., Ilf. 81 E7
Aden Ter. N16 94 A4
Adeney Cl. W6 128 A6
Adenmore Rd. SE6 154 A7
Adie Rd. W6 127 J3
Adine Rd. E13 115 H4
Adler Ind. Est., Hayes 121 G2
Adler St. E1 21 H3
Adler St. E1 112 D6
Adley St. E5 95 H5
Adlington Cl. N18 60 B5
Admaston Rd. SE18 137 F7
Admiral Ct. NW4 71 G5
Barton Cl.
Admiral Pl. SE16 133 H1
Admiral Seymour Rd. SE9 156 C4
Admiral Sq. SW10 149 G1
Admiral St. SE8 154 A1
Admiral Wk. W9 108 D5
Admirals Cl. E18 79 H4
Admirals Wk. NW3 91 F3
Admirals Way E14 134 A2
Admiralty Cl. SE8 134 A7
Reginald Sq.
Admiralty Rd., Tedd. 162 C6
Adolf St. SE6 172 B4
Adolphus Rd. N4 93 H2
Adolphus St. SE8 133 J7
Adomar Rd., Dag. 100 D3
Adpar St. W2 7 E6
Adpar St. W2 109 G4
Adrian Av. NW2 89 H1
North Circular Rd.
Adrian Ms. SW10 30 B5
Adrian Ms. SW10 129 E6
Adrienne Av., Sthl. 103 F4
Advance Rd. SE27 169 J4
Advent Ct., Wdf.Grn. 63 F4
Wood La.
Advent Way N18 61 G5
Adys Rd. SE15 152 C3
Aerodrome Rd. NW4 71 F3
Aerodrome Rd. NW9 71 F2
Aerodrome Way, Houns. 122 C6
Aeroville NW9 71 E2
Affleck St. N1 10 D2
Afghan Rd. SW11 149 H2
Agamemnon Rd. NW6 90 C5
Agar Cl., Surb. 195 J2
Agar Gro. NW1 92 C7
Agar Gro. Est. NW1 92 D7
Agar Pl. NW1 92 C7
Agar St. WC2 18 A6
Agar St. WC2 110 E7
Agate Cl. E16 116 A6
Agate Rd. W6 127 J3
Agatha Cl. E1 132/133 E1
Prusom St.
Agaton Rd. SE9 175 F2
Agave Rd. NW2 89 J4
Agdon St. EC1 11 G5
Agdon St. EC1 111 H4
Agincourt Rd. NW3 91 J4
Agnes Av., Ilf. 98 E4
Agnes Cl. E6 116 D7
Agnes Gdns., Dag. 100 D4
Agnes Rd. W3 127 F1
Agnes St. E14 113 J6
Agnesfield Cl. N12 57 H6
Agnew Rd. SE23 153 G7
Agricola Ct. E3 113 J1
Parnell Rd.
Agricola Pl., Enf. 44 C5
Aidan Cl., Dag. 100 E4
Aileen Wk. E15 97 F7
Ailsa Av., Twick. 144 D5
Ailsa Rd., Twick. 145 E5
Ailsa St. E14 114 C5
Ainger Ms. NW3 91 J7
Ainger Rd.
Ainger Rd. NW3 91 J7
Ainsdale Cl., Orp. 207 G1
Ainsdale Cres., Pnr. 67 G3
Ainsdale Dr. SE1 37 H4
Ainsdale Dr. SE1 132 D5
Ainsdale Rd. W5 105 G4
Ainsdale Rd., Wat. 50 C3
Ainsley Av., Rom. 83 H6
Ainsley Cl. N9 60 B1
Ainsley St. E2 113 E3
Ainslie Wk. SW12 150 B7
Ainslie Wd. Cres. E4 62 B5
Ainslie Wd. Gdns. E4 62 B4
Ainslie Wd. Rd. E4 62 A5
Ainsty Est. SE16 133 G2
Ainsworth Cl. NW2 89 G3
Ainsworth Cl. SE15 152 B2
Lyndhurst Gro.
Ainsworth Rd. E9 95 F7
Ainsworth Rd., Croy. 201 H2
Ainsworth Way NW8 109 F1
Aintree Av. E6 116 B1
Aintree Cres., Ilf. 81 F2
Aintree Est. SW6 128 B7
Dawes Rd.
Aintree Rd., Grnf. 105 E2
Aintree St. SW6 128 B7
Air Links Ind. Est., Houns. 122 C5
Air St. W1 17 G6
Air St. W1 110 C7
Aird Ct., Hmptn. 179 F1
Oldfield Rd.
Airdrie Cl. N1 93 F7
Airdrie Cl., Hayes 102/103 E5
Glencoe Rd.
Airedale Av. W4 127 F4
Airedale Av. S. W4 127 F5
Netheravon Rd. S.
Airedale Rd. SW12 149 J7
Airedale Rd. W5 125 F3
Airlie Gdns. W8 128 D1
Campden Hill Rd.
Airlie Gdns., Ilf. 99 E1
Airport Roundabout E16 136 A1
Connaught Br.
Airthrie Rd., Ilf. 100 B2
Aisgill Av. W14 128 C5
Aisher Rd. SE28 118 C7
Aislibie Rd. SE12 155 E4
Aitken Cl. E8 112 D1
Pownall Rd.
Aitken Cl., Mitch. 185 J7
Aitken Rd. SE6 172 B2
Aitken Rd., Barn. 39 J5
Ajax Av. NW9 70 E3
Ajax Rd. NW6 90 D5
Akabusi Cl., Croy. 188 D6
Akehurst St. SW15 147 G6
Akenside Rd. NW3 91 G5
Akerman Rd. SW9 151 H2
Akerman Rd., Surb. 181 F6
Alabama St. SE18 137 G7
Alacross Rd. W5 125 F2
Alan Dr., Barn. 40 B6
Alan Gdns., Rom. 83 G7
Alan Hocken Way E15 114 E2
Alan Rd. SW19 166 B5
Alandale Dr., Pnr. 66 B2
Alander Ms. E17 78 C4
Alanthus Cl. SE12 155 F6
Alaska St. SE1 27 E2
Alba Cl., Hayes 102 D4
Ramulis Dr.
Alba Gdns. NW11 72 B6
Alba Pl. W11 108 C6
Portobello Rd.
Albacore Cres. SE13 154 B6
Alban Cres., Borwd. 38 B1
Alban Highwalk EC2 111 J5
London Wall
Albany W1 17 F6
Albany, The, Wdf.Grn. 63 F4
Albany Cl. N15 75 H4
Albany Cl. SW14 146 B4
Albany Cl., Bex. 158 C7
Albany Ct. E4 46 B6
Chelwood Cl.
Albany Ctyd. W1 17 G6
Albany Cres., Edg. 54 A7
Albany Cres., Esher 194 B6
Albany Mans. SW11 129 H7
Albany Ms. N1 93 G7
Barnsbury Pk.
Albany Ms. SE5 36 A6
Albany Ms., Brom. 173 G6
Avondale Rd.
Albany Ms., Kings.T. 163 G6
Albany Pk. Rd.
Albany Ms., Sutt. 198/199 E5
Camden Rd.
Albany Pk. Av., Enf. 45 F1
Albany Pk. Rd., Kings.T. 163 H6
Albany Pas., Rich. 145 J5
Albany Pl. N7 93 G4
Benwell Rd.
Albany Pl., Brent. 125 H6
Albany Rd.
Albany Rd. E10 78 A7
Albany Rd. E12 98 A4
Albany Rd. E17 77 J6
Albany Rd. N4 75 F6
Albany Rd. N18 61 E5
Albany Rd. SE5 36 B6
Albany Rd. SE5 132 A6
Albany Rd. SW19 166 E5
Albany Rd. W13 104 E7
Albany Rd., Belv. 139 F6
Albany Rd., Bex. 158 C7
Albany Rd., Brent. 125 G6
Albany Rd., Chis. 175 E5
Albany Rd., N.Mal. 182 D4
Albany Rd., Rich. 145 J5
Albert Rd.
Albany Rd., Rom. 83 F6
Albany St. NW1 8 D1
Albany St. NW1 110 B2
Albany Ter. NW1 110 B4
Marylebone Rd.
Albany Vw., Buck.H. 63 G1
Albatross St. SE18 137 H7
Albatross Way SE16 133 G2
Albemarle SW19 166 A2
Albemarle App., Ilf. 81 E6
Albemarle Av., Twick. 161 F1
Albemarle Gdns., Ilf. 81 E6
Albemarle Gdns., N.Mal. 182 D4
Albemarle Pk., Stan. 53 F5
Marsh La.
Albemarle Rd., Barn. 41 H7
Albemarle Rd., Beck. 190 B1
Albemarle St. W1 17 E6
Albemarle St. W1 110 B7
Albemarle Way EC1 11 G6
Alberon Gdns. NW11 72 C4
Albert Av. E4 62 A4
Albert Av. SW8 131 F7
Albert Br. SW3 31 H6
Albert Br. SW3 129 H6
Albert Br. SW11 31 H6
Albert Br. SW11 129 H6
Albert Br. Rd. SW11 31 H7
Albert Br. Rd. SW11 129 H7
Albert Carr Gdns. SW16 168 E5
Albert Cl. E9 112/113 E1
Northiam St.
Albert Cl. N22 74 D1
Albert Ct. SW7 23 E4
Albert Ct. SW7 129 G2
Albert Cres. E4 62 A4
Albert Dr. SW19 166 B2
Albert Embk. SE1 34 B4
Albert Embk. SE1 131 E5
Albert Gdns. E1 113 G6
Albert Gate SW1 24 A3
Albert Gate SW1 129 J2
Albert Gro. SW20 184 A1
Albert Hall Mans. SW7 23 E4
Albert Mans. SW11 149 J1
Albert Br. Rd.
Albert Ms. E14 113 H7
Narrow St.
Albert Ms. W8 22 C5
Albert Pl. N3 72 D1
Albert Pl. N17 76 C3
High Rd.
Albert Pl. W8 22 B4
Albert Pl. W8 129 E2
Albert Rd. E10 96 C2
Albert Rd. E16 136 B1
Albert Rd. E17 78 A5
Albert Rd. E18 79 H3
Albert Rd. N4 93 F1
Albert Rd. N15 76 B6
Albert Rd. N22 74 C1
Albert Rd. NW4 72 A4
Albert Rd. NW6 108 C2
Albert Rd. NW7 55 F5
Albert Rd. SE9 174 B3
Albert Rd. SE20 171 G7
Albert Rd. SE25 188 D4
Albert Rd. W5 105 E4
Albert Rd., Barn. 41 F4
Albert Rd., Belv. 139 F5
Albert Rd., Bex. 159 G6
Albert Rd., Brom. 192 A5
Albert Rd., Buck.H. 64 A2
Albert Rd., Dag. 101 G1
Albert Rd., Hmptn. 161 J5
Albert Rd., Har. 67 J3
Albert Rd., Hayes 121 H3
Albert Rd., Houns. 143 G4
Albert Rd., Ilf. 99 E3
Albert Rd., Kings.T. 181 J2
Albert Rd., Mitch. 185 J3
Albert Rd., N.Mal. 183 F4
Albert Rd., Rich. 145 H5
Albert Rd., Sthl. 122 D3
Albert Rd., Sutt. 199 G5
Albert Rd., Tedd. 162 C6
Albert Rd., Twick. 162 C1
Albert Rd., West Dr. 120 B1
Albert Rd. Est., Belv. 139 F5
Albert Sq. E15 97 E5
Albert Sq. SW8 131 F7
Albert St. N12 57 F5
Albert St. NW1 110 B1
Albert Ter. NW1 110 A1
Albert Ter. NW10 106 D1
Albert Ter., Buck.H. 64 A2
Albert Ter. Ms. NW1 110 A1
Regents Pk. Rd.
Albert Way SE15 132 E7
Alberta Av., Sutt. 198 B4
Alberta Est. SE17 35 H3
Alberta Est. SE17 131 H5
Alberta Rd., Enf. 44 C6
Alberta Rd., Erith 159 J1
Alberta St. SE17 35 G3
Alberta St. SE17 131 H5
Albion Av. N10 74 A1
Albion Av. SW8 150 D2
Albion Bldgs. EC1 111 J5
Bartholomew Cl.
Albion Cl. W2 15 H5
Albion Dr. E8 94 C7
Albion Est. SE16 133 G2
Albion Gdns. W6 127 H4
Albion Gro. N16 94 B4
Albion Hill SE13 154 B2
Albion Hill, Loug. 47 J5
Albion Ms. N1 111 G1
Albion Ms. NW6 90 C7
Kilburn High Rd.
Albion Ms. W2 15 H4
Albion Ms. W2 109 H6
Albion Ms. W6 127 H4
Galena Rd.
Albion Par. N16 94 A4
Albion Rd.
Albion Pk., Loug. 48 A5
Albion Pl. EC1 19 G1
Albion Pl. EC1 111 H5
Albion Pl. SE25 188 D3
High St.
Albion Pl. W6 127 H4
Albion Rd. E17 78 C3
Albion Rd. N16 94 A4
Albion Rd. N17 76 C2
Albion Rd., Bexh. 159 F4
Albion Rd., Houns. 143 G4
Albion Rd., Kings.T. 182 C1
Albion Rd., Sutt. 199 G6
Albion Rd., Twick. 162 B1
Albion Sq. E8 94 C7
Albion St. SE16 133 F2

Name	Page	Grid
Albion St. W2	15	H4
Albion St. W2	109	H6
Albion St., Croy.	201	H1
Albion Ter. E8	94	C7
Albion Vil. Rd. SE26	171	F3
Albion Way EC1	19	J2
Albion Way SE13	154	C4
Albion Way, Wem.	88	B3
North End Rd.		
Albion Yd. E1	113	E5
Albrighton Rd. SE22	152	B3
Albuhera Cl., Enf.	43	G1
Albury Av., Bexh.	158	E2
Albury Av., Islw.	124	C7
Albury Cl., Hmptn.	161	G6
Albury Dr., Pnr.	50	D7
Albury Ms. E12	97	J1
Albury Rd., Chess.	195	H5
Albury St. SE8	134	A6
Albyfield, Brom.	192	C3
Albyn Rd. SE8	154	A1
Alcester Cres. E5	95	E2
Alcester Rd., Wall.	200	B4
Alcock Cl., Wall.	200	D7
Alcock Rd., Houns.	122	D7
Alconbury Rd. E5	94	D2
Alcorn Cl., Sutt.	198	D2
Alcott Cl. W7	104	C5
Westcott Cres.		
Alcuin Ct., Stan.	53	F7
Old Ch. La.		
Aldborough Rd., Dag.	101	J6
Aldborough Rd. N.,	81	J5
Ilf.		
Aldborough Rd. S.,	99	H1
Ilf.		
Aldbourne Rd. W12	127	F1
Aldbridge St. SE17	36	E3
Aldbridge St. SE17	132	B5
Aldburgh Ms. W1	16	C3
Aldbury Av., Wem.	88	B7
Aldbury Ms. N9	44	A7
Aldebert Ter. SW8	131	E7
Aldeburgh Cl. E5	94/95	E2
Southwold Rd.		
Aldeburgh Pl.,	63	G4
Wdf.Grn.		
Aldeburgh St. SE10	135	G5
Alden Av. E15	115	F3
Aldenham St. NW1	9	G2
Aldenham Rd. NW1	110	D2
Aldensley Rd. W6	127	H3
Alder Cl. SE15	37	G6
Alder Cl. SE15	132	C6
Alder Gro. NW2	89	H2
Alder Ms. N19	92	C2
Bredgar Rd.		
Alder Rd. SW14	146	D3
Alder Rd., Sid.	175	J3
Alder Wk., Ilf.	99	F5
Alderbrook Rd.	150	B6
SW12		
Alderbury Rd.	127	G6
SW13		
Aldergrove	142/143	E2
Gdns., Houns.		
Bath Rd.		
Alderholt Way SE15	36	E7
Alderman Av., Bark.	118	A3
Alderman Judge	181	H2
Mall, Kings.T.		
Eden St.		
Aldermanbury EC2	20	A3
Aldermanbury EC2	111	J6
Aldermanbury Sq.	20	A2
EC2		
Aldermans Hill N13	58	E4
Alderman's Wk. EC2	20	D2
Aldermary Rd., Brom.	191	G1
Aldermoor Rd. SE6	171	J3
Alderney Av., Houns.	123	H7
Alderney Gdns.,	85	F7
Nthlt.		
Alderney Rd. E1	113	G4
Alderney St. SW1	32	E3
Alderney St. SW1	130	B4
Alders, The N21	43	G6
Alders, The, Felt.	161	E4
Alders, The, Houns.	123	F6
Alders, The, W.Wick.	204	B1
Alders Av., Wdf.Grn.	62	E6
Alders Cl. E11	97	H2
Aldersbrook Rd.		
Alders Cl. W5	125	G3
Alders Cl., Edg.	54	C5
Alders Gro., E.Mol.	180	A5
Esher Rd.		
Alders Rd., Edg.	54	C5
Aldersbrook Av., Enf.	44	B2
Aldersbrook Dr.,	163	J6
Kings.T.		
Aldersbrook La. E12	98	C3
Aldersbrook Rd. E11	97	H2
Aldersbrook Rd. E12	98	A3
Aldersey Gdns., Bark.	99	G6
Aldersford Cl. SE4	153	G5
Aldersgate St. EC1	19	J3
Aldersgate St. EC1	111	J5
Aldersgrove Av. SE9	173	J3
Aldershot Rd. NW6	108	C1
Aldersmead Av.,	189	G6
Croy.		
Aldersmead Rd.,	171	H7
Beck.		
Alderson Pl., Sthl.	123	J1
Alderson St. W10	108	B4
Kensal Rd.		
Alderton Cl. NW10	88	D3
Alderton Cl., Loug.	48	D4
Alderton Cres. NW4	71	H5
Alderton Hall La.,	48	D4
Loug.		
Alderton Hill, Loug.	48	B5
Alderton Ms., Loug.	48	D4
Alderton Hall La.		
Alderton Ri., Loug.	48	D4
Alderton Rd. SE24	151	J3
Alderton Rd., Croy.	188	C7
Alderton Way NW4	71	H5
Alderton Way, Loug.	48	C5
Alderville Rd. SW6	148	C2
Alderwick Dr., Houns.	144	A3
Alderwood Rd. SE9	157	G6
Aldford St. W1	24	B1
Aldford St. W1	130	A1
Aldgate EC3	21	F4
Aldgate EC3	112	C6
Aldgate Av. E1	21	F3
Aldgate High St.	21	F4
EC3		
Aldgate High St. EC3	112	C6
Aldine Ct. W12	127	J1
Aldine St.		
Aldine Pl. W12	127	J1
Uxbridge Rd.		
Aldine St. W12	127	J2
Aldington Cl., Dag.	82	C7
Aldington Rd. SE18	136	A3
Aldis Ms. SW17	167	H5
Aldis St.		
Aldis St. SW17	167	H5
Aldred Rd. NW6	90	D5
Aldren Rd. SW17	167	F3
Aldrich Gdns., Sutt.	198	C3
Aldrich Ter. SW18	167	F2
Lidiard Rd.		
Aldriche Way E4	62	C6
Aldridge Av., Edg.	54	B3
Aldridge Av., Ruis.	84	D2
Aldridge Av., Stan.	69	H1
Aldridge Ri., N.Mal.	182	E7
Aldridge Rd. Vil.	108	C5
W11		
Aldridge Wk. N14	42	E7
Aldrington Rd.	168	C5
SW16		
Aldsworth Cl. W9	6	A6
Aldsworth Cl. W9	108	E4
Aldwick Cl. SE9	175	G3
Aldwick Rd., Croy.	201	F3
Aldworth Gro. SE13	154	C6
Aldworth Rd. E15	96	E7
Aldwych WC2	18	C5
Aldwych WC2	111	F7
Aldwych Av., Ilf.	81	F4
Alers Rd., Bexh.	158	D5
Alesia Cl. N22	58/59	E7
Nightingale Rd.		
Alestan Beck Rd. E16	116	A6
Fulmer Rd.		
Alexa Ct. W8	30	A1
Alexander Av. NW10	89	H7
Alexander Cl., Barn.	41	G4
Alexander Cl., Sid.	157	H5
Alexander Cl., Sthl.	123	J1
Alexander Cl.,	162	C2
Twick.		
Alexander Evans Ms.	171	G1
SE23		
Sunderland Rd.		
Alexander Pl. SW7	31	G1
Alexander Pl. SW7	129	H4
Alexander Rd. N19	92	E3
Alexander Rd., Bexh.	158	D2
Alexander Rd., Chis.	175	E5
Alexander Sq. SW3	31	G1
Alexander Sq. SW3	129	H4
Alexander St. W2	108	D6
Alexandra Av. N22	74	D1
Alexandra Av. SW11	150	A1
Alexandra Av. W4	126	D7
Alexandra Av., Har.	85	F1
Alexandra Av., Sthl.	123	F1
Alexandra Av., Sutt.	198	D3
Alexandra Cl., Har.	85	G3
Alexandra Av.		
Alexandra Cotts.	153	J1
SE14		
Alexandra Ct. N14	42	C5
Alexandra Ct., Wem.	87	J4
Alexandra Cres.,	173	F6
Brom.		
Alexandra Dr. SE19	170	B5
Alexandra Dr., Surb.	182	A7
Alexandra Gdns. N10	74	B4
Alexandra Gdns. W4	126	D7
Alexandra Gdns.,	143	H2
Houns.		
Alexandra Gro. N4	93	H1
Alexandra Gro. N12	57	E5
Alexandra Ms. N2	73	J3
Fortis Grn.		
Alexandra Ms. SW19	166	D6
Alexandra Rd.		
Alexandra Palace N22	74	D2
Alexandra Palace	74	C3
Way N22		
Alexandra Pk. Rd.	74	B2
N10		
Alexandra Pk. Rd.	74	D2
N22		
Alexandra Pl. NW8	109	F1
Alexandra Pl. SE25	188	A5
Alexandra Pl., Croy.	202	B1
Alexandra Rd.		
Alexandra Rd. E6	116	D3
Alexandra Rd. E10	96	C3
Alexandra Rd. E17	77	J6
Alexandra Rd. E18	79	H3
Alexandra Rd. N8	55	G3
Alexandra Rd. N9	44	E7
Alexandra Rd. N10	58	B7
Alexandra Rd. N15	76	A5
Alexandra Rd. NW4	72	A4
Alexandra Rd. NW8	91	F7
Alexandra Rd. SE26	171	G6
Alexandra Rd. SW14	146	D3
Alexandra Rd. SW19	166	C6
Alexandra Rd. W4	126	D2
Alexandra Rd., Brent.	125	G6
Alexandra Rd., Croy.	202	B1
Alexandra Rd., Enf.	45	G4
Alexandra Rd.,	143	H2
Houns.		
Alexandra Rd.,	164	A7
Kings.T.		
Alexandra Rd., Mitch.	167	H7
Alexandra Rd., Rich.	145	J2
Alexandra Rd.,	82	D6
(Chadwell Heath), Rom.		
Alexandra Rd., T.Ditt.	180	C5
Alexandra Rd.,	145	F6
Twick.		
Alexandra Sq., Mord.	184	D5
Alexandra St. E16	115	G5
Alexandra St. SE14	133	H7
Alexandra Wk. SE19	170	B5
Alexandria Rd. W13	104	D7
Alexis St. SE16	37	H1
Alexis St. SE16	132	D4
Alfearn Rd. E5	95	F4
Alford Grn., Croy.	204	D6
Alford Pl. N1	12	A2
Alford Rd. SW8	150	D1
Alfoxton Av. N15	75	H4
Alfred Cl. W4	126	D4
Belmont Rd.		
Alfred Gdns., Sthl.	103	E7
Alfred Ms. W1	17	H1
Alfred Ms. W1	110	D5
Alfred Pl. WC1	17	H1
Alfred Pl. WC1	110	D5
Alfred Prior Ho. E12	98	D4
Alfred Rd. E15	79	F5
Alfred Rd. SE25	188	D5
Alfred Rd. W2	108	D5
Alfred Rd. W3	126	C1
Alfred Rd., Belv.	139	F5
Alfred Rd., Buck.H.	64	A2
Alfred Rd., Felt.	160	C2
Alfred Rd., Kings.T.	181	H3
Alfred Rd., Sutt.	199	F5
Alfred St. E3	113	J3
Alfreda St. SW11	150	B1
Alfred's Gdns., Bark.	117	H2
Alfreds Way, Bark.	117	E3
Alfreds Way Ind. Est.,	118	A1
Bark.		
Alfriston Cl. SW19	166	A3
Alfriston Av., Croy.	187	E7
Alfriston Av., Har.	67	G6
Alfriston Rd. SW11	149	J5
Alfriston Rd., Surb.	181	J5
Algar Cl., Islw.	144	D3
Algar Rd.		
Algar Cl., Stan.	52	C5
Algar Rd., Islw.	144	D3
Algarve Rd. SW18	167	E1
Algernon Rd. NW4	71	G6
Algernon Rd. NW6	108	D1
Algernon Rd. SE13	154	B4
Algers Cl., Loug.	48	A5
Algers Mead, Loug.	48	A5
Algers Rd., Loug.	48	A5
Algiers Rd. SE13	154	A4
Alibon Gdns., Dag.	101	G5
Alibon Rd., Dag.	101	G5
Alice Ct. SW15	148	C4
Deodar Rd.		
Alice Gilliatt Ct. W14	128	C6
Alice La. E3	113	J1
Alice Ms., Tedd.	162	C5
Luther Rd.		
Alice St. SE1	28	D6
Alice St. SE1	132	B3
Alice Thompson Cl.	173	J2
SE12		
Alice Walker Cl. SE24	151	H4
Shakespeare Rd.		
Alice Way, Houns.	143	H4
Alicia Av., Har.	69	E4
Alicia Cl., Har.	69	F4
Alicia Gdns., Har.	69	E4
Alie St. E1	21	G4
Alie St. E1	112	C6
Alington Cres. NW9	88	C1
Alison Cl. E6	116	D6
Alison Cl., Croy.	203	G1
Shirley Oaks Rd.		
Aliwal Rd. SW11	149	H4
Alkerden Rd. W4	127	E5
Alkham Rd. N16	94	C2
All Hallows Rd. N17	76	B1
All Saints Cl. N9	60	C2
All Saints Dr. SE3	155	E2
All Saints Ms., Har.	52	B6
All Saints Pas.	148/149	E5
SW18		
Wandsworth High St.		
All Saints Rd. SW19	167	F7
All Saints Rd. W3	126	C3
All Saints Rd. W11	108	C5
All Saints Rd., Sutt.	199	E3
All Saints St. N1	10	C1
All Saints St. N1	111	F2
All Saints Ter. E10	78	B7
All Souls Av. NW10	107	H2
All Souls Pl. W1	17	E2
High Rd.		
Allan Cl., N.Mal.	182	D5
Allan Way W3	106	C5
Allandale Av. N3	72	B3
Allard Cres., Bushey	51	J1
Allard Gdns. SW4	150	D5
Allardyce St. SW4	151	F4
Allbrook Cl., Tedd.	162	B5
Allcroft Rd. NW5	92	A5
Allen Cl., Mitch.	186	B1
Allen Cl., Sun.	178	B1
Allen Ct., Grnf.	86	C5
Allen Edwards Dr.	150	E1
SW8		
Allen Pl., Twick.	162	D1
Church St.		
Allen Rd. E3	113	J2
Allen Rd. N16	94	B4
Allen Rd., Beck.	189	G2
Allen Rd., Croy.	187	F7
Allen Rd., Sun.	178	B1
Allen St. W8	128	D3
Allenby Cl., Grnf.	103	G3
Allenby Rd. SE23	171	H3
Allenby Rd., Sthl.	103	G6
Allendale Av., Sthl.	103	G6
Allendale Cl. SE5	152	A1
Daneville Rd.		
Allendale Cl. SE26	171	G5
Allendale Rd., Grnf.	86	E6
Allens Rd., Enf.	45	F5
Allensbury Pl. NW1	92	D7
Allenswood Rd. SE9	156	B3
Allerford Ct., Har.	67	H5
Allerford Rd. SE6	172	B4
Allerton Ct. NW4	72	A2
Holders Hill Rd.		
Allerton Rd. N16	93	J2
Allerton Wk. N7	93	F2
Durham Rd.		
Allestree Rd. SW6	128	B7
Alleyn Cres. SE21	170	A2
Alleyn Pk. SE21	170	A2
Alleyn Pk., Sthl.	123	F4
Alleyn Rd. SE21	170	A3
Alleyndale Rd., Dag.	100	C2
Allfarthing La. SW18	149	E6
Allgood Cl., Mord.	184	A6
Allgood St. E2	13	G2
Allhallows La. EC4	20	B6
Allhallows Rd. E6	116	B5
Alliance Cl., Wem.	87	G4
Alliance Rd. E13	115	J4
Alliance Rd. SE18	138	A6
Alliance Rd. W3	106	B4

Allied Way W3 126/127 E2
Larden Rd.
Allingham Cl. W7 104 C7
Allingham Ms. N1 11 J1
Allingham St. N1 11 J1
Allingham St. N1 111 J2
Allington Av. N17 60 B6
Allington Cl. SW19 166 A5
High St. Wimbledon
Allington Cl., Grnf. 85 J7
Allington Ct. SW19 166 A5
High St. Wimbledon
Allington Ct., Enf. 45 G5
Allington Rd. NW4 71 H5
Allington Rd. W10 108 B2
Allington Rd., Har. 67 J5
Allington Rd., Orp. 207 G2
Allington St. SW1 25 F6
Allington St. SW1 130 B3
Allison Cl. SE10 154 C1
Dartmouth Hill
Allison Gro. SE21 170 B1
Allison Rd. N8 75 G5
Allison Rd. W3 106 C6
Allitsen Rd. NW8 7 G2
Allitsen Rd. NW8 109 H2
Allnutt Way SW4 150 D5
Alloa Rd. SE8 133 G5
Alloa Rd., Ilf. 100 A2
Allonby Gdns., Wem. 87 F1
Alloway Rd. E3 113 H3
Allsop Pl. NW1 8 A6
Allsop Pl. NW1 109 J4
Allum Way N20 57 F1
Allwood Cl. SE26 171 G4
Alma Av. E4 62 C7
Alma Cres., Sutt. 198 B5
Alma Gro. SE1 37 G2
Alma Gro. SE1 132 C4
Alma Pl. NW10 107 H3
Harrow Rd.
Alma Pl. SE19 170 C7
Alma Pl., Th.Hth. 187 G5
Alma Rd. N10 58 A7
Alma Rd. SW18 149 F5
Alma Rd., Cars. 199 H5
Alma Rd., Enf. 45 H5
Alma Rd., Esher 194 B1
Alma Rd., Sid. 176 A3
Alma Rd., Sthl. 102 E7
Alma Row, Har. 68 A1
Alma Sq. NW8 6 D3
Alma Sq. NW8 109 F3
Alma St. E15 96 D6
Alma St. NW5 92 B6
Alma Ter. SW18 149 G7
Alma Ter. W8 128 D3
Allen St.
Almack Rd. E5 95 F4
Almeida St. N1 93 H7
Almer Rd. SW20 165 G7
Almeric Rd. SW11 149 J4
Almington St. N4 93 F1
Almond Av. W5 125 H3
Almond Av., Cars. 199 J2
Almond Av., West Dr. 120 D3
Almond Cl. SE15 152 D2
Almond Cl., Brom. 192 D7
Almond Cl., Felt. 160 A1
Highfield Rd.
Almond Gro., Brent. 124 E7
Almond Rd. N17 60 D7
Almond Rd. SE16 133 E4
Almond Way, Borwd. 38 B4
Almond Way, Brom. 192 D7
Almond Way, Har. 67 H2
Almond Way, Mitch. 186 D5
Almonds Av., Buck.H. 63 G2
Almorah Rd. N1 94 A7
Almorah Rd., Houns. 142 D1
Alnwick Gro., Mord. 184/185 E4
Bordesley Rd.
Alnwick Rd. E16 115 J6
Alnwick Rd. SE12 155 H7
Alperton La., Grnf. 105 G3
Alperton La., Wem. 105 G3
Alperton St. W10 108 B4
Alpha Cl. NW1 7 H4
Alpha Gro. E14 134 A2
Alpha Pl. NW6 108 D2
Alpha Pl. SW3 31 H5
Alpha Pl. SW3 129 H6
Alpha Rd. E4 62 B3
Alpha Rd. N18 60 D6
Alpha Rd. SE14 153 J1
Alpha Rd., Croy. 202 B1
Alpha Rd., Enf. 45 H4
Alpha Rd., Surb. 181 J6
Alpha Rd., Tedd. 162 A5
Alpha St. SE15 152 D2
Alphabet Gdns., Cars. 185 G6
Alphabet Sq. E3 114 A5
Hawgood St.
Alphea Cl. SW19 167 H7
Courtney Rd.
Alpine Av., Surb. 196 C2
Alpine Cl., Croy. 202 B3
Alpine Copse, Brom. 192 D2
Alpine Gro. E9 95 F7
Alpine Rd. SE16 133 F4
Alpine Rd., Walt. 178 A7
Alpine Vw., Cars. 199 H5
Alpine Wk., Stan. 52 B2
Alpine Way E6 116 D5
Alric Av. NW10 88 D7
Alric Av., N.Mal. 183 E3
Alroy Rd. N4 75 G7
Alsace Rd. SE17 36 D3
Alsace Rd. SE17 132 B5
Alscot Rd. SE1 37 G1
Alscot Rd. SE1 132 C4
Alscot Way SE1 37 F1
Alscot Way SE1 132 C4
Alsike Rd. SE2 138 D3
Alsike Rd., Erith 138 E3
Alsom Av., Wor.Pk. 197 G4
Alston Cl., Surb. 181 E7
Alston Rd. N18 60 E5
Alston Rd. SW17 167 G4
Alston Rd., Barn. 40 B3
Alt Gro. SW19 166 C7
St. George's Rd.
Altair Cl. N17 60 C6
Altash Way SE9 174 C2
Altenburg Av. W13 125 E3
Altenburg Gdns. SW11 149 J4
Altham Rd., Pnr. 51 E7
Althea St. SW6 149 E3
Althorne Gdns. E18 79 F4
Althorne Way, Dag. 101 G2
Althorp Cl., Barn. 39 G7
Althorp Rd. SW17 167 J1
Althorpe Gro. SW11 149 G1
Westbridge Rd.
Althorpe Ms. SW11 149 G1
Westbridge Rd.
Althorpe Rd., Har. 67 J5
Altmore Av. E6 98 C7
Alton Av., Stan. 52 C7
Alton Cl., Bex. 177 E1
Alton Cl., Islw. 144 C2
Alton Gdns., Beck. 172 A7
Alton Gdns., Twick. 144 A7
Alton Rd. N17 76 A3
Alton Rd. SW15 165 G1
Alton Rd., Croy. 201 G3
Alton Rd., Rich. 145 H4
Alton St. E14 114 B5
Altyre Cl., Beck. 189 J5
Altyre Rd., Croy. 202 A2
Altyre Way, Beck. 189 J5
Alva Way, Wat. 50 D2
Alvanley Gdns. NW6 90 E5
Alverston Gdns. SE25 188 B5
Alverstone Av. SW19 166 D2
Alverstone Av., Barn. 41 H7
Alverstone Gdns. SE9 175 F1
Alverstone Rd. E12 98 D4
Alverstone Rd. NW2 89 J7
Alverstone Rd., N.Mal. 183 F4
Alverstone Rd., Wem. 87 J1
Alverton St. SE8 133 J5
Alveston Av., Har. 69 E3
Alvey Est. SE17 36 D2
Alvey Est. SE17 132 B4
Alvey St. SE17 36 D3
Alvey St. SE17 132 B5
Alvia Gdns., Sutt. 199 F4
Alvington Cres. E8 94 C5
Alway Av., Epsom 196 C5
Alwold Cres. SE12 155 H6
Alwyn Av. W4 126 D5
Alwyn Cl., Croy. 204 B7
Alwyn Gdns. NW4 71 G4
Alwyn Gdns. W3 106 B6
Alwyne La. N1 93 H7
Alwyne Vil.
Alwyne Pl. N1 93 J6
Alwyne Rd. N1 93 J7
Alwyne Rd. SW19 166 C6
Alwyne Rd. W7 104 B7
Alwyne Sq. N1 93 J6
Alwyne Vil. N1 93 H7
Alyth Gdns. NW11 72 D6
Alzette Ho. E2 113 G3
Amalgamated Dr., Brent. 124 D6
Amanda Cl., Chig. 65 G6
Amanda Ms., Rom. 83 J5
Amazon St. E1 112/113 E6
Hessel St.
Ambassador Cl., Houns. 142 E2
Ambassador Gdns. E6 116 C5
Ambassador Sq. E14 134 B4
Ambassador's Ct. SW1 25 G2
Amber Av. E17 77 H1
Amber Ct. SW17 168 A4
Brudenell Rd.
Amber Gro. NW2 90 A1
Prayle Gro.
Amber St. E15 96 D6
Salway Rd.
Amberden Av. N3 72 D3
Ambergate St. SE17 35 H3
Ambergate St. SE17 131 H5
Amberley Cl., Orp. 207 J5
Warnford Rd.
Amberley Cl., Pnr. 67 F3
Amberley Ct., Sid. 176 C5
Amberley Gdns., Enf. 44 B7
Amberley Gdns., Epsom 197 F4
Amberley Gro. SE26 170 E4
Amberley Gro., Croy. 188 C7
Amberley Rd. E10 78 B7
Amberley Rd. N13 59 F2
Amberley Rd. SE2 138 D6
Amberley Rd. W9 108 D5
Amberley Rd., Buck.H. 63 J1
Amberley Rd., Enf. 44 C7
Amberley Way, Houns. 142 C5
Amberley Way, Mord. 184 C7
Amberley Way, Rom. 83 H4
Amberside Cl., Islw. 144 A6
Amberwood Ri., N.Mal. 182 E6
Amblecote Cl. SE12 173 H3
Amblecote Meadows SE12 173 H3
Amblecote Rd. SE12 173 H3
Ambler Rd. N4 93 H3
Ambleside, Brom. 172 D6
Ambleside Av. SW16 168 D4
Ambleside Av., Beck. 189 H5
Ambleside Cl. E9 95 F5
Churchill Wk.
Ambleside Cl. E10 78 B7
Ambleside Cres., Enf. 45 G3
Ambleside Gdns. SW16 168 D5
Ambleside Gdns., Ilf. 80 B4
Ambleside Gdns., Sutt. 199 F6
Ambleside Gdns., Wem. 87 G1
Ambleside Rd. NW10 89 F7
Ambleside Rd., Bexh. 159 G2
Ambrooke Rd., Belv. 139 G3
Ambrosden Av. SW1 25 G6
Ambrosden Av. SW1 130 C3
Ambrose Av. NW11 72 B7
Ambrose Cl. E6 116 B5
Lovage App.
Ambrose Cl., Orp. 207 J3
Stapleton Rd.
Ambrose Ms. SW11 149 H2
Ambrose St. SE16 132 E4
Ambrose Wk. E3 114 A2
Malmesbury Rd.
Amelia St. SE17 35 H3
Amelia St. SE17 131 H5
Amen Cor. EC4 19 H4
Amen Cor. SW17 167 J6
Amen Ct. EC4 19 H3
Amenity Way, Mord. 183 J7
America Sq. EC3 21 F5
America St. SE1 27 J2
Amerland Rd. SW18 148 C6
Amersham Av. N18 60 A6
Amersham Gro. SE14 133 J7
Amersham Rd. SE14 153 J1
Amersham Rd., Croy. 187 J6
Amersham Vale SE14 133 J7
Amery Gdns. NW10 107 H1
Amery Rd., Har. 86 D2
Amesbury Av. SW2 169 E2
Amesbury Cl., Wor.Pk. 197 J1
Amesbury Dr. E4 46 B6
Amesbury Rd., Brom. 192 A3
Amesbury Rd., Dag. 100 D7
Amesbury Rd., Felt. 160 D2
Amethyst Rd. E15 96 D4
Amherst Av. W13 105 F6
Amherst Dr., Orp. 193 J4
Amherst Rd. W13 105 F6
Amhurst Gdns., Islw. 144 C1
Amhurst Par. N16 76 C7
Amhurst Pk.
Amhurst Pk. N16 76 A7
Amhurst Pas. E8 94 D5
Amhurst Rd. E8 94 E5
Amhurst Rd. N16 94 C4
Amhurst Ter. E8 94 D4
Amhurst Wk. SE28 138 A1
Pitfield Cres.
Amidas Gdns., Dag. 100 B4
Amiel St. E1 113 F4
Amies St. SW11 149 J3
Amina Way SE16 29 H6
Amis Av., Epsom 196 B6
Amity Gro. SW20 183 J1
Amity Rd. E15 115 F1
Ammanford Gdn. NW9 70/71 E6
Ruthin Cl.
Amner Rd. SW11 150 A6
Amor Rd. W6 127 J3
Amott Rd. SE15 152 D3
Amoy Pl. E14 114 A6
Ampere Way, Croy. 187 E7
Ampleforth Rd. SE2 138 B2
Ampthill Sq. Est. NW1 9 G2
Ampton Pl. WC1 10 C4
Ampton St. WC1 10 C4
Ampton St. WC1 111 F3
Amroth Cl. SE23 171 E1
Amsterdam Rd. E14 134 C3
Amundsen Ct. E14 134 A5
Napier Av.
Amwell Cl., Enf. 44 A5
Amwell Ct. Est. N4 93 J1
Amwell St. EC1 11 E3
Amwell St. EC1 111 G3
Amy Cl., Wall. 200/201 E7
Mollison Dr.
Amy Warne Cl. E6 116 B4
Evelyn Denington Rd.
Amyand Cotts., Twick. 144/145 E6
Amyand Pk. Rd.
Amyand La., Twick. 144/145 E7
Marble Hill Gdns.
Amyand Pk. Gdns., Twick. 144/145 E7
Amyand Pk. Rd.
Amyand Pk. Rd., Twick. 144 D7
Amyruth Rd. SE4 154 A5
Anatola Rd. N19 92 B2
Dartmouth Pk. Hill
Ancaster Cres., N.Mal. 183 G6
Ancaster Ms., Beck. 189 G3
Ancaster Rd., Beck. 189 G3
Ancaster St. SE18 137 H7
Anchor & Hope La. SE7 135 H3
Anchor Cl., Bark. 117 H3
Thames Rd.
Anchor Ms. SW12 150 B6
Hazelbourne Rd.
Anchor St. SE16 132 E4
Anchor Wf. E3 114 B5
Watts Gro.
Anchor Yd. EC1 12 A5
Anchorage Cl. SW19 166 D5
Anchorage Pt. Ind. Est. SE7 135 J3
Ancill Cl. W6 128 B6
Ancona Rd. NW10 107 G2
Ancona Rd. SE18 137 G5
Andace Pk. Gdns., Brom. 191 J1
Andalus Rd. SW9 151 E3
Ander Cl., Wem. 87 G4
Anderson Cl. N21 43 F5
Anderson Cl. W3 106 D6
Anderson Cl., Sutt. 198 D1
Anderson Ho., Bark. 117 G2
The Coverdales
Anderson Pl., Houns. 143 H4
Anderson Rd. E9 95 G6
Anderson Rd., Wdf.Grn. 80 A3
Anderson St. SW3 31 J3
Anderson St. SW3 129 J5
Anderson Way, Belv. 139 H2
Anderton Cl. SE5 152 A3
Andmark Ct., Sthl. 123 F1
Herbert Rd.
Andover Av. E16 116 A6
King George Av.
Andover Cl., Grnf. 103 H4
Ruislip Rd.
Andover Pl. NW6 6 A1
Andover Pl. NW6 108 E2
Andover Rd. N7 93 F2

Andover Rd., Orp. 207 G1
Andover Rd., Twick. 162 A1
Andre St. E8 94 D5
Andrew Borde St. 17 J3
WC2
Andrew Cl., Ilf. 65 G6
Andrew Pl. SW8 150 D1
Cowthorpe Rd.
Andrew St. E14 114 C6
Andrewes Gdns. E6 116 B6
Andrews Cl. E6 116 B6
Linton Gdns.
Andrews Cl., Buck.H. 63 J2
Andrews Cl., Har. 68 A7
Bessborough Rd.
Andrews Cl., 198 A2
Wor.Pk.
Andrews Crosse 18 E4
WC2
Andrews Pl. SE9 156 E6
Andrew's Rd. E8 112 E1
Andrews Rd., N.Mal. 157 H7
Andwell Cl. SE2 138 B2
Anerley Gro. SE19 170 C7
Anerley Hill SE19 170 C6
Anerley Pk. SE20 170 E7
Anerley Pk. Rd. SE20 170 E7
Anerley Rd. SE19 170 D7
Anerley Rd. SE20 170 D7
Anerley Sta. Rd. 188 E1
SE20
Anerley St. SW11 149 J2
Anerley Vale SE19 170 C7
Anfield Cl. SW12 150 C7
Angel All. E1 21 G3
Angel Cl. N18 60 C4
Angel Cor. Par. N18 60 D5
Fore St.
Angel Ct. EC2 20 C3
Angel Ct. EC2 112 A6
Angel Ct. SW1 25 G2
Angel Ct. SW17 167 J4
Angel Gate EC1 11 H3
Angel Hill, Sutt. 198/199 E3
Sutton Common Rd.
Angel Hill Dr., Sutt. 199 E3
Angel La. E15 96 D6
Angel Ms. N1 11 F2
Angel Ms. N1 111 G2
Angel Ms. SW15 147 G7
Roehampton High St.
Angel Pas. EC4 20 B6
Angel Pl. N18 60 D5
Angel Pl. SE1 28 B3
Angel Rd. N18 60 E5
Angel Rd., Har. 68 B6
Angel Rd., T.Ditt. 180 D7
Angel Rd. Wks. N18 61 F5
Angel Sq. EC1 11 F2
Angel St. EC1 19 J3
Angel St. EC1 111 J6
Angel Wk. W6 127 J4
Angelfield, Houns. 143 H4
Angelica Dr. E6 116 D5
Angelica Gdns., Croy. 203 G1
Angell Pk. Gdns. 151 G3
SW9
Angell Rd. SW9 151 G3
Angerstein La. SE3 135 F7
Angle Grn., Dag. 100 C1
Anglers, Rich. 163 F4
Lockesmeade Rd.
Angler's La. NW5 92 B6
Anglers Reach, Surb. 181 G5
Angles Rd. SW16 169 E4
Anglesea Av. SE18 136 E4
Anglesea Rd. SE18 136 E4
Anglesea Rd., 181 G4
Kings.T.
Anglesea Ter. W6 127 H3
Wellesley Av.
Anglesey Ct. Rd., 200 A6
Cars.
Anglesey Gdns., 200 A6
Cars.
Anglesey Rd., Enf. 45 E4
Anglesey Rd., Wat. 50 C5
Anglesmede Cres., 67 G3
Pnr.
Anglesmede Way, 67 F3
Pnr.
Anglia Cl. N17 60/61 E7
Park La.
Anglia Ho. E14 113 H6
Anglia Wk. E6 116 C1
Anglian Rd. E11 96 D3
Anglo Rd. E3 113 J2
Angrave Ct. E8 112 C1
Angrave Pas. E8 112 C1
Haggerston Rd.
Angus Cl., Chess. 196 A5
Angus Dr., Ruis. 84 C4
Angus Gdns. NW9 70 D1

Angus Rd. E13 115 J3
Angus St. SE14 133 H7
Anhalt Rd. SW11 31 H7
Anhalt Rd. SW11 129 H7
Ankerdine Cres. 136 D7
SE18
Anlaby Rd., Tedd. 162 B5
Anley Rd. W14 128 A2
Anmersh Gro., Stan. 69 G1
Ann La. SW10 30 E7
Ann La. SW10 129 G7
Ann Moss Way SE16 133 F3
Ann St. SE18 137 G4
Anna Cl. E8 112 C1
Anna Neagle Cl. E7 97 G4
Dames Rd.
Annabel Cl. E14 114 B6
Annandale Rd. SE10 135 F6
Annandale Rd. W4 126 E4
Annandale Rd., Croy. 202 D2
Annandale Rd., Sid. 157 H7
Anne Boleyn's Wk., 163 H5
Kings.T.
Anne Boleyn's Wk., 198 A7
Sutt.
Anne Case Ms., 182 D3
N.Mal.
Sycamore Gro.
Anne St. E13 115 G4
Anne Way, W.Mol. 179 H4
Anne Way, Ilf. 65 F6
Annesley Av. NW9 70 D3
Annesley Cl. NW10 88 E3
Annesley Dr., Croy. 203 J3
Annesley Rd. SE3 155 H1
Annesley Wk. N19 92 C2
Annett Rd., Walt. 178 A7
Annette Cl., Har. 68 B2
Spencer Rd.
Annette Cres. N1 93 J7
Essex Rd.
Annette Rd. N7 93 F4
Annie Besant Cl. E3 113 J1
Anning St. EC2 13 E5
Annington Rd. N2 73 J3
Annis Rd. E9 95 H6
Ann's Cl. SW1 24 A4
Ann's Pl. E1 21 F2
Annsworthy Av., 188 A3
Th.Hth.
Grange Pk. Rd.
Annsworthy Cres. 188 A2
SE25
Grange Rd.
Ansdell Rd. SE15 153 F2
Ansdell St. W8 22 B5
Ansdell St. W8 129 E3
Ansdell Ter. W8 22 B5
Ansell Gro., Cars. 200 A1
Ansell Rd. SW17 167 H3
Anselm Cl., Croy. 202 C3
Park Hill Ri.
Anselm Rd. SW6 128 D6
Anselm Rd., Pnr. 51 F7
Ansford Rd., Brom. 172 C5
Ansleigh Pl. W11 108 A7
Anson Cl., Rom. 83 H2
Anson Rd. N7 92 D4
Anson Rd. NW2 90 A5
Anson Ter., Nthlt. 85 H6
Anstey Rd. SE15 152 D3
Anstey Wk. N15 75 H4
Anstice Cl. W4 127 E7
Anstridge Path SE9 157 G6
Anstridge Rd. SE9 157 G6
Antelope Rd. SE18 136 C3
Anthony Cl. NW7 55 E4
Anthony Cl., Wat. 50 C1
Anthony Rd. SE25 188 D6
Anthony Rd., Grnf. 104 B2
Anthony Rd., Well. 158 A1
Anthony St. E1 112/113 E6
Commercial Rd.
Antigua Cl. SE19 170 A5
Salters Hill
Antigua Wk. SE19 170 A5
Antill Rd. E3 113 H3
Antill Rd. N15 76 C4
Antill Ter. E1 113 G6
Antlers Hill E4 46 B5
Anton Cres., Sutt. 198 D3
Anton St. E8 94 D5
Antoneys Cl., Pnr. 66 D2
Antrim Gro. NW3 91 J6
Antrim Mans. NW3 91 H6
Antrim Rd. NW3 91 J6
Antrobus Cl., Sutt. 198 C5
Antrobus Rd. W4 126 C4
Anvil Cl. SW16 168 C7
Anvil Rd., Sun. 178 A3
Anworth Cl., Wdf.Grn. 63 H6
Apex Cl., Beck. 190 B1
Apex Cor. NW7 54 D4
Apex Retail Pk., Felt. 161 F3

Apex Twr., N.Mal. 182 E3
Aplin Way, Islw. 144 B1
Apollo Av., Brom. 191 H1
Rodway Rd.
Apollo Av., Nthwd. 50 A5
Apollo Pl. E11 96 E3
Apollo Pl. SW10 31 E7
Apollo Pl. SW10 129 G7
Apollo Way SE28 137 G3
Broadwater Rd.
Apostle Way, Th.Hth. 187 H2
Apothecary St. EC4 19 G4
High St.
Appach Rd. SW2 151 G6
Apple Garth, Brent. 125 G4
Apple Gro., Chess. 195 H4
Apple Gro., Enf. 44 B3
Apple Mkt., Kings.T. 181 G2
Eden St.
Apple Tree Yd. SW1 25 G1
Appleby Cl. E4 62 C6
Appleby Cl. N15 76 A5
Appleby Cl., Twick. 162 A2
Appleby Rd. E8 94 D7
Appleby Rd. E16 115 F6
Appleby St. E2 13 F1
Appleby St. E2 112 C2
Appledore Av., Bexh. 159 J1
Appledore Av., Ruis. 84 B3
Appledore Cl. SW17 167 J2
Appledore Cl., Brom. 191 F5
Appledore Cl., Edg. 70 A1
Appledore Cres., Sid. 175 H3
Appleford Rd. W10 108 B4
Applegarth, Croy. 204 B7
Applegarth, Esher 194 C5
Applegarth Dr., Ilf. 81 J4
Applegarth Rd. SE28 138 B1
Applegarth Rd. W14 128 A3
Appleton Gdns., 183 G6
N.Mal.
Appleton Rd. SE9 156 B3
Appleton Rd., Loug. 49 E3
Appleton Sq., Mitch. 185 H1
Appletree Cl. 188/189 E1
SE20
Jasmine Gro.
Appletree Gdns., 41 H4
Barn.
Appold St. EC2 20 D1
Appold St. EC2 112 B5
Apprentice Way E5 94/95 E4
Clarence Rd.
Approach, The NW4 72 A5
Approach, The W3 106 D6
Approach, The, Enf. 44 E2
Approach, The, Orp. 207 J2
Approach Rd. N16 94 B5
Cowper Rd.
Approach Rd. E2 113 F2
Approach Rd. SW20 183 J2
Approach Rd., Barn. 41 G4
Approach Rd., 179 G5
W.Mol.
Aprey Gdns. NW4 71 J4
April Cl. W7 104 B7
April Cl., Felt. 160 A3
April Cl., Orp. 207 J5
Briarswood Way
April Glen SE23 171 G3
April St. E8 94 C4
Apsley Cl., Har. 67 J5
Apsley Rd. SE25 188 E4
Apsley Rd., N.Mal. 182 C3
Apsley Way NW2 89 G2
Apsley Way W1 24 C3
Aquarius Business 89 G1
Pk. NW2
Aquarius Way, 50 A5
Nthwd.
Aquila St. NW8 7 F1
Aquila St. NW8 109 G2
Aquinas St. SE1 27 F2
Arabella Dr. SW15 147 E4
Arabia Cl. E4 46 D7
Arabin Rd. SE4 153 H4
Aragon Av., T.Ditt. 180 C5
Aragon Cl., Brom. 206 C1
Aragon Cl., Loug. 48 B6
Aragon Dr., Ilf. 65 F7
Aragon Dr., Ruis. 84 D1
Aragon Ms. E1 29 H1
Aragon Rd., Kings.T. 163 H6
Aragon Rd., Mord. 184 A6
Aran Dr., Stan. 53 F4
Arandora Cres., Rom. 82 B7
Arbery Rd. E3 113 H3
Arbor Cl., Beck. 190 B2
Arbor Ct. N16 94 A2
Lordship Rd.
Arbor Rd. E4 62 D3
Arborfield Cl. SW2 169 F1

Arbour Rd., Enf. 45 G4
Arbour Sq. E1 113 G6
Arbroath Grn., Wat. 50 A3
Arbroath Rd. SE9 156 B3
Arbury Ter. SE26 170/171 E3
Oaksford Av.
Arbuthnot La., Bex. 159 E6
Arbuthnot Rd. SE14 153 G2
Arbutus St. E8 112 B1
Arcade, The EC2 20 D2
Arcade, The, Croy. 201 J3
High St.
Arcadia Av. N3 72 D1
Arcadia Cl., Cars. 200 A4
Arcadia St. E14 114 A6
Arcadian Av., Bex. 158 E6
Arcadian Cl., Bex. 158 E6
Arcadian Gdns. N22 59 F7
Arcadian Rd., Bex. 158 E6
Arch St. SE1 27 J6
Arch St. SE1 131 J3
Archangel St. SE16 133 G2
Archbishops Pl. 151 F6
SW2
Archdale Pl., N.Mal. 182 B3
Archdale Rd. SE22 152 C5
Archel Rd. W14 128 C6
Archer Cl., Kings.T. 163 H7
Archer Ho. SW11 149 G1
Vicarage Cres.
Archer Ms., Hmptn. 161 J6
Windmill Rd.
Archer Rd. SE25 188 E4
Archer St. W1 17 H5
Archers Dr., Enf. 45 F2
Archers Wk. SE15 152 C1
Wodehouse Av.
Archery Cl. W2 15 H4
Archery Cl. W2 109 H6
Archery Cl., Har. 68 C3
Archery Rd. SE9 156 C5
Arches, The SW6 148 C2
Munster Rd.
Arches, The WC2 26 B1
Arches, The, Har. 85 H2
Archibald Ms. W1 24 C1
Archibald Ms. W1 130 A1
Archibald Rd. N7 92 D4
Archibald St. E3 114 A3
Archie Cl., West Dr. 120 D2
Archway Cl. N19 92 C2
St. Johns Way
Archway Cl. SW19 166 E4
Archway Cl. W10 108 A5
Archway Cl., Wall. 200 D3
Archway Mall N19 92 C2
Magdala Av.
Archway Rd. N6 74 A6
Archway Rd. N19 92 C1
Archway Rd. SW13 147 E3
Arcola St. E8 94 C5
Arctic St. NW5 92 B5
Gillies St.
Arcus Rd., Brom. 173 E6
Ardbeg Rd. SE24 152 A6
Arden Cl., Har. 86 A3
Arden Ct. Gdns. N2 73 G6
Arden Cres. E14 134 A4
Arden Cres., Dag. 100 C7
Arden Est. N1 12 D2
Arden Est. N1 112 B2
Arden Gro., Orp. 207 E4
Arden Ms. E17 78 B5
Arden Mhor, Pnr. 66 B4
Arden Rd. N3 72 B3
Arden Rd. W13 105 F7
Ardent Cl. SE25 188 B3
Ardfern Av. SW16 187 G3
Ardfillan Rd. SE6 172 D1
Ardgowan Rd. SE6 154 E7
Ardilaun Rd. N5 93 J4
Ardingly Cl., Croy. 203 G3
Ardleigh Gdns., Sutt. 184 D7
Ardleigh Ho., Bark. 117 F1
St. Ann's
Ardleigh Ms., Ilf. 98/99 E3
Bengal Rd.
Ardleigh Rd. E17 77 J1
Ardleigh Rd. N1 94 A6
Ardleigh Ter. E17 77 J1
Ardley Cl. NW10 88 E3
Ardley Cl. SE6 171 H3
Ardlui Rd. SE27 169 J2
Ardmay Gdns., Surb. 181 H5
Ardmere Rd. SE13 154 D6
Ardmore La., Buck.H. 47 H7
Ardmore Pl., Buck.H. 47 H7
Ardoch Rd. SE6 172 D2
Ardra Rd. N9 61 G3
Ardrossan Gdns., 197 G3
Wor.Pk.
Ardshiel Cl. SW15 148 A3
Bemish Rd.
Ardwell Av., Ilf. 81 F5

Ardwell Rd. SW2	169	E2	
Ardwick Rd. NW2	90	D4	
Arewater Grn., Loug.	48	C1	
Argali Ho., Erith	138/139	E3	
Kale Rd.			
Argall Av. E10	77	G7	
Argall Way E10	95	G1	
Argent St. SE1	**27**	**H3**	
Argenta Way NW10	88	B7	
Argon Ms. SW6	128	D7	
Argon Rd. N18	61	F5	
Argosy La., Stai.	140	A7	
Argus Cl., Rom.	83	H1	
Argus Way W3	126	B3	
Argus Way, Nthlt.	102	E3	
Argyle Av., Houns.	143	G6	
Argyle Cl. W13	104	D4	
Argyle Pas. N17	76	C1	
Argyle Pl. W6	127	H4	
Argyle Rd. E1	113	G4	
Argyle Rd. E15	96	E4	
Argyle Rd. E16	115	J6	
Argyle Rd. N12	56	D5	
Argyle Rd. N17	76	D1	
Argyle Rd. N18	60	D4	
Argyle Rd. W13	104	D5	
Argyle Rd., Barn.	39	J4	
Argyle Rd., Grnf.	104	C3	
Argyle Rd., Har.	67	H5	
Argyle Rd., Houns.	143	H5	
Argyle Rd., Ilf.	98	D2	
Argyle Rd., Tedd.	162	B5	
Argyle Sq. WC1	**10**	**B3**	
Argyle Sq. WC1	111	E3	
Argyle St. WC1	**10**	**A3**	
Argyle St. WC1	110	E3	
Argyle Wk. WC1	**10**	**B4**	
Argyle Way SE16	**37**	**J4**	
Argyle Way SE16	132	D5	
Argyll Av., Sthl.	123	H1	
Argyll Cl. SW9	151	F3	
Dalyell Rd.			
Argyll Rd. W8	128	D2	
Argyll St. W1	**17**	**F4**	
Argyll St. W1	110	C6	
Arica Rd. SE4	153	H4	
Ariel Rd. NW6	90	D6	
Ariel Way W12	127	J1	
Ariel Way, Houns.	142	B3	
Aristotle Rd. SW4	150	D3	
Arkell Gro. SE19	169	H7	
Arkindale Rd. SE6	172	C3	
Arkley Cres. E17	77	J5	
Arkley Dr., Barn.	39	G4	
Arkley La., Barn.	39	G3	
Arkley Pk., Barn.	38	D6	
Arkley Rd. E17	77	J5	
Arkley Vw., Barn.	39	H4	
Arklow Ms., Surb.	195	H2	
Vale Rd. S.			
Arklow Rd. SE14	133	J6	
Arkwright Rd. NW3	91	F5	
Arlesey Cl. SW15	148	B6	
Lytton Gro.			
Arlesford Rd. SW9	151	E3	
Arlingford Rd. SW2	151	G5	
Arlington N12	56	D3	
Arlington Av. N1	111	J2	
Arlington Cl., Sid.	157	H7	
Arlington Cl., Sutt.	198	D2	
Arlington Cl., Twick.	145	F6	
Arlington Ct., Hayes	121	G5	
Shepiston La.			
Arlington Dr., Cars.	199	J2	
Arlington Gdns. W4	126	C5	
Arlington Gdns., Ilf.	98	D1	
Arlington Lo. SW2	151	F4	
Arlington Ms.,	144/145	E6	
Twick.			
Arlington Rd.			
Arlington Pl. SE10	134	C7	
Greenwich S. St.			
Arlington Rd. N14	58	B2	
Arlington Rd. NW1	110	B1	
Arlington Rd. W13	104	E6	
Arlington Rd., Rich.	163	G2	
Arlington Rd., Surb.	181	G6	
Arlington Rd., Tedd.	162	C4	
Arlington Rd., Twick.	145	F6	
Arlington Rd.,	79	G1	
Wdf.Grn.			
Arlington Sq. N1	111	J1	
Arlington St. SW1	**25**	**F1**	
Arlington St. SW1	130	C1	
Arlington Way EC1	**11**	**F3**	
Arlington Way EC1	111	G3	
Arliss Way, Nthlt.	102	C1	
Arlow Rd. N21	59	G1	
Armada St. SE8	134	A6	
Watergate St.			
Armada St. SE8	134	A6	
Armada Way E6	117	F7	
Armadale Cl. N17	76	E4	

Armadale Rd. SW6	128	D7	
Armadale Rd., Felt.	142	A5	
Armagh Rd. E3	113	J1	
Armfield Cl., W.Mol.	179	F5	
Armfield Cres.,	185	J2	
Mitch.			
Armfield Rd., Enf.	44	A1	
Arminger Rd. W12	127	H1	
Armistice Gdns.	188	D3	
SE25			
Penge Rd.			
Armitage Rd. NW11	90	C1	
Armitage Rd. SE10	135	F5	
Armour Cl. N7	93	F6	
Roman Way			
Armoury Rd. SE8	154	B2	
Armoury Way SW18	148	D5	
Armstead Wk., Dag.	101	G7	
Armstrong Av.,	62	E6	
Wdf.Grn.			
Armstrong Cl. E6	116	C6	
Porter Rd.			
Armstrong Cl., Dag.	100	D1	
Palmer Rd.			
Armstrong Cl., Pnr.	66	A6	
Armstrong Cl., Walt.	178	A6	
Sunbury La.			
Armstrong Cres.,	41	G3	
Barn.			
Armstrong Rd. SW7	**22**	**E6**	
Armstrong Rd. SW7	129	G3	
Armstrong Rd. W3	127	F1	
Armstrong Rd., Felt.	160	E5	
Armstrong Way,	123	H2	
Sthl.			
Armytage Rd., Houns.	122	D7	
Arnal Cres. SW18	148	B7	
Arncliffe Cl. N11	58	A6	
Kettlewell Cl.			
Arncroft Ct., Bark.	118	B3	
Renwick Rd.			
Arndale Cen. SW18	148	E6	
Arndale Wk.	148/149	E5	
SW18			
Garratt La.			
Arne Gro., Orp.	207	J3	
Arne St. WC2	**18**	**B4**	
Arne St. WC2	111	E6	
Arne Wk. SE3	155	F4	
Arnett Sq. E4	61	J6	
Silver Birch Av.			
Arneway St. SW1	**25**	**J6**	
Arneways Av., Rom.	82	D3	
Arnewood Cl. SW15	165	G1	
Arney's La., Mitch.	186	A6	
Arngask Rd. SE6	154	D7	
Arnham Pl. E14	134	A3	
Arnham Way SE22	152	B5	
East Dulwich Gro.			
Arnham Wf. E14	134	A3	
Arnham Pl.			
Arnison Rd., E.Mol.	180	A4	
Arnold Circ. E2	**13**	**F4**	
Arnold Circ. E2	112	C3	
Arnold Cl., Har.	69	J7	
Arnold Cres., Islw.	144	A5	
Arnold Dr., Chess.	195	G6	
Arnold Est. SE1	**29**	**G4**	
Arnold Est. SE1	132	C2	
Arnold Gdns. N13	59	H5	
Arnold Rd. E3	114	A3	
Arnold Rd. N15	76	C3	
Arnold Rd. SW17	167	J7	
Arnold Rd., Dag.	101	F7	
Arnold Rd., Nthlt.	84	D6	
Arnos Gro. N14	58	D4	
Arnos Rd. N11	58	C5	
Arnott Cl. SE28	118	C7	
Applegarth Rd.			
Arnott Cl. W4	126	D4	
Fishers La.			
Arnould Av. SE5	152	A4	
Arnsberg Way, Bexh.	159	G4	
Arnside Gdns., Wem.	87	G1	
Arnside Rd., Bexh.	159	G1	
Arnside St. SE17	**36**	**A5**	
Arnside St. SE17	131	J6	
Arnulf St. SE6	172	B4	
Arnulls Rd. SW16	169	G6	
Arodene Rd. SW2	151	F6	
Arosa Rd., Twick.	145	G6	
Arragon Gdns. SW16	168	E7	
Arragon Gdns.,	204	B3	
W.Wick.			
Arragon Rd. E6	116	A1	
Arragon Rd. SW18	166	E1	
Arragon Rd., Twick.	144	D7	
Arran Cl., Wall.	200	B4	
Arran Cl., Erith	139	J6	
Arran Grn., Wat.	50	C1	
Prestwick Rd.			
Arran Ms. W5	125	J1	
Arran Rd. SE6	172	B2	
Arran Wk. N1	93	J7	

Arras Av., Mord.	185	F5	
Arrol Rd., Beck.	189	F3	
Arrow Rd. E3	114	B3	
Arrowscout Wk.,	102/103	E3	
Nthlt.			
Argus Way			
Arrowsmith Cl., Chig.	65	J5	
Arrowsmith Path,	65	J5	
Chig.			
Arrowsmith Rd., Chig.	65	H5	
Arrowsmith Rd., Loug.	48	B3	
Arsenal Rd. SE9	156	C2	
Arterberry Rd. SW20	165	J7	
Artesian Cl. NW10	88	D7	
Artesian Gro., Barn.	41	F4	
Artesian Rd. W2	108	D6	
Artesian Wk. E11	96	E3	
Arthur Ct. W2	**14**	**A3**	
Arthur Gro. SE18	137	F4	
Arthur Henderson Ho.	148	C2	
SW6			
Arthur Horsley Wk.	97	F5	
E7			
Magpie Cl.			
Arthur Rd. E6	116	C2	
Arthur Rd. N7	93	F4	
Arthur Rd. N9	60	C2	
Arthur Rd. SW19	166	D3	
Arthur Rd., Kings.T.	164	A7	
Arthur Rd., N.Mal.	183	H5	
Arthur Rd., Rom.	82	C7	
Arthur St. EC4	**20**	**C6**	
Arthurdon Rd. SE4	154	A5	
Artichoke Hill E1	112/113	E7	
Pennington St.			
Artichoke Pl. SE5	152	A1	
Camberwell Ch. St.			
Artillery Cl., Ilf.	81	F6	
Horns Rd.			
Artillery La. E1	**21**	**E2**	
Artillery La. E1	112	B5	
Artillery La. W12	107	G6	
Artillery Pas. E1	**21**	**E2**	
Artillery Pl. SE18	136	C4	
Artillery Pl. SW1	**25**	**H6**	
Artillery Pl., Har.	51	J7	
Chicheley Rd.			
Artillery Row SW1	**25**	**H6**	
Artillery Row SW1	130	D3	
Artington, Orp.	207	F4	
Artisan Cl. E6	116/117	E6	
Ferndale St.			
Artizan St. E1	**21**	**E3**	
Arundel Av., Mord.	184	C4	
Arundel Cl. E15	97	E4	
Arundel Cl. SW11	149	H5	
Chivalry Rd.			
Arundel Cl., Bex.	159	F6	
Arundel Cl., Croy.	201	H3	
Arundel Cl., Hmptn.	161	H5	
Arundel Cl. N12	57	H6	
Arundel Ct., Har.	85	G4	
Arundel Dr., Borwd.	38	C5	
Arundel Dr., Har.	85	F4	
Arundel Dr., Wdf.Grn.	63	G7	
Arundel Gdns. N21	59	G1	
Arundel Gdns. W11	108	C7	
Arundel Gdns., Edg.	54	D7	
Arundel Gdns., Ilf.	100	A2	
Arundel Great Ct.	**18**	**D5**	
WC2			
Arundel Gro. N16	94	B5	
Arundel Pl. N1	93	G6	
Arundel Rd., Barn.	41	H3	
Arundel Rd., Croy.	188	A6	
Arundel Rd., Houns.	142	C3	
Arundel Rd., Kings.T.	182	B2	
Arundel Rd., Sutt.	198	C7	
Arundel Sq. N7	93	G6	
Arundel St. WC2	**18**	**D5**	
Arundel St. WC2	111	F7	
Arundel Ter. SW13	127	H6	
Arvon Rd. N5	93	G5	
Asbaston Ter., Ilf.	99	F5	
Buttsbury Rd.			
Ascalon St. SW8	130	C7	
Ascham Dr. E4	62	B7	
Rushcroft Rd.			
Ascham End E17	77	H1	
Ascham St. NW5	92	C5	
Aschurch Rd., Croy.	188	C7	
Ascot Cl., Borwd.	38	A5	
Ascot Cl., Ilf.	65	H6	
Ascot Cl., Nthlt.	85	G5	
Ascot Gdns., Sthl.	103	F5	
Ascot Rd. E6	116	C3	
Ascot Rd. N15	76	A5	
Ascot Rd. N18	60	D4	
Ascot Rd. SW17	168	A6	
Ascot Rd., Orp.	193	J4	
Ascott Av. W5	125	H2	
Ash Cl. SE20	189	F2	
Ash Cl., Cars.	199	J2	

Ash Cl., Edg.	54	C4	
Ash Cl., N.Mal.	182	D2	
Ash Cl., Orp.	193	G5	
Ash Cl., Sid.	176	B3	
Ash Cl., Stan.	52	D6	
Ash Ct., Epsom	196	C4	
Ash Gro. E8	113	E1	
Ash Gro. N13	59	J3	
Ash Gro. NW2	90	A4	
Ash Gro. SE20	189	F2	
Ash Gro. W5	125	H2	
Ash Gro., Enf.	44	B7	
Ash Gro., Houns.	142	D1	
Ash Gro., Sthl.	103	G5	
Ash Gro., Wem.	86	D4	
Ash Gro., W.Wick.	204	C2	
Ash Hill Cl., Bushey	51	H1	
Ash Hill Dr., Pnr.	66	C3	
Ash Island, E.Mol.	180	A3	
Ash Rd. E15	97	E5	
Ash Rd., Croy.	204	A2	
Ash Rd., Orp.	207	J7	
Ash Rd., Sutt.	184	B7	
Ash Row, Brom.	192	D7	
Ash Tree Cl., Croy.	189	H6	
Ash Tree Cl., Surb.	195	H1	
Ash Tree Dell NW9	70	C5	
Ash Tree Way, Croy.	189	H5	
Ash Wk. SW2	169	F1	
Ash Wk., Wem.	87	F4	
Ashbourne Av. E18	79	H4	
Ashbourne Av. N20	57	J2	
Ashbourne Av.	72	C5	
NW11			
Ashbourne Av., Bexh.	139	E7	
Ashbourne Av., Har.	86	A2	
Ashbourne Cl. N12	57	E4	
Ashbourne Cl. W5	106	A5	
Ashbourne Ct. E5	95	H4	
Daubeney Rd.			
Ashbourne Gro. NW7	54	D5	
Ashbourne Gro.	152	C5	
SE22			
Ashbourne Gro. W4	127	E5	
Ashbourne Par. W5	105	J4	
Ashbourne Rd.			
Ashbourne Ri., Orp.	207	G4	
Ashbourne Rd. W5	105	J5	
Ashbourne Rd.,	168	A6	
Mitch.			
Ashbourne Ter. SW19	166	D7	
Ashbourne Way	72	C5	
NW11			
Ashbourne Av.			
Ashbridge St. NW8	**7**	**G6**	
Ashbridge St. NW8	109	H4	
Ashbrook Rd. N19	92	D1	
Ashbrook Rd., Dag.	101	H3	
Ashburn Gdns. SW7	**30**	**C1**	
Ashburn Gdns. SW7	129	F4	
Ashburn Pl. SW7	**30**	**C1**	
Ashburn Pl. SW7	129	F4	
Ashburnham Av.,	68	C6	
Har.			
Ashburnham Cl. N2	73	G3	
Ashburnham Cl., Wat.	50	A3	
Ashburnham Dr.			
Ashburnham Dr.,	50	A3	
Wat.			
Ashburnham Gdns.,	68	C6	
Har.			
Ashburnham Gro.	134	B7	
SE10			
Ashburnham Pl.	134	B7	
SE10			
Ashburnham Retreat	134	B7	
SE10			
Ashburnham Rd.	107	J3	
NW10			
Ashburnham Rd.	129	F7	
SW10			
Ashburnham Rd.,	139	J4	
Belv.			
Ashburnham Rd.,	163	E3	
Rich.			
Ashburton Av., Croy.	202	E1	
Ashburton Av., Ilf.	99	H4	
Ashburton Cl., Croy.	202	D1	
Ashburton Ct., Pnr.	66	D3	
Ashburton Gdns.,	202	D2	
Croy.			
Ashburton Gro. N7	93	G4	
Ashburton Rd. E16	115	G6	
Ashburton Rd., Croy.	202	D1	
Ashburton Rd., Ruis.	84	A2	
Ashburton Ter. E13	115	G2	
Grasmere Rd.			
Ashbury Gdns., Rom.	82	D5	
Ashbury Pl. SW19	167	F6	
Ashbury Rd. SW11	149	J3	
Ashby Av., Chess.	196	A6	
Ashby Gro. N1	93	J7	
Ashby Ms. SE4	153	J2	

Ashby Rd. N15 76 D5
Ashby Rd. SE4 153 J2
Ashby St. EC1 11 H4
Ashby Wk., Croy. 187 J6
Ashby Way, West Dr. 120 D7
Ashchurch Gro. W12 127 G2
Ashchurch Pk. Vil. W12 127 G3
Ashchurch Ter. W12 127 G3
Ashcombe Av., Surb. 181 G7
Ashcombe Gdns., Edg. 54 A4
Ashcombe Pk. NW2 89 E3
Ashcombe Rd. SW19 166 D5
Ashcombe Rd., Cars. 200 A6
Ashcombe Sq., N.Mal. 182 C3
Ashcombe St. SW6 148 E2
Ashcroft, Pnr. 51 G6
Ashcroft Av., Sid. 158 A6
Ashcroft Cres., Sid. 158 A6
Ashcroft Rd. E3 113 H3
Ashcroft Rd., Chess. 195 J3
Ashcroft Sq. W6 127 J4
King St.
Ashdale Cl., Twick. 143 J7
Ashdale Gro., Stan. 52 C6
Ashdale Rd. SE12 173 H1
Ashdale Way, Twick. 143 J7
Ashdale Cl.
Ashdene SE15 152 E1
Ashdene, Pnr. 66 C3
Ashdon Cl., Wdf.Grn. 63 H6
Ashdon Rd. NW10 107 E1
Ashdown Cl., Beck. 190 B2
Ashdown Cl., Bex. 159 J7
Ashdown Cres. NW5 92 A5
Queens Cres.
Ashdown Est. E11 96/97 E4
High Rd. Leytonstone
Ashdown Rd., Enf. 45 F3
Ashdown Rd., Kings.T. 181 H2
Ashdown Wk. E14 134 A4
Ashdown Wk., Rom. 83 H2
Ashdown Way SW17 168 A2
Ashen E6 116 D6
Downings
Ashen Gro. SW19 166 D3
Ashenden Rd. E5 95 G5
Ashentree Ct. EC4 19 F4
Asher Loftus Way N11 57 J6
Asher Way E1 29 J1
Asher Way E1 112 D7
Ashfield Av., Felt. 160 B1
Ashfield Cl., Beck. 172 A7
Ashfield Cl., Rich. 163 H1
Ashfield La., Chis. 175 F6
Ashfield Par. N14 58 D1
Ashfield Rd. N4 75 J6
Ashfield Rd. N14 58 C3
Ashfield Rd. W3 127 F1
Ashfield St. E1 112 E5
Ashfield Yd. E1 112/113 E5
Ashfield St.
Ashfields, Loug. 48 C2
Ashford Av. N8 74 E4
Ashford Av., Hayes 102 D6
Ashford Cl. E17 77 J6
Ashford Cres., Enf. 45 F2
Ashford Grn., Wat. 50 D5
Ashford Rd. E6 98 D6
Ashford Rd. E18 79 H2
Ashford Rd. NW2 90 A4
Ashford St. N1 12 D3
Ashgrove Rd., Brom. 172 D6
Ashgrove Rd., Ilf. 99 J1
Ashingdon Cl. E4 62 C3
Ashington Rd. SW6 148 C2
Ashlake Rd. SW16 168 E4
Ashland Pl. W1 16 B1
Ashland Pl. W1 110 A5
Ashlar Pl. SE18 136/137 E4
Masons Hill
Ashleigh Gdns., Sutt. 198 E2
Ashleigh Rd. SE20 189 E3
Ashleigh Rd. SW14 146 E3
Ashley Av., Ilf. 81 E2
Ashley Av., Mord. 184 D5
Chalgrove Av.
Ashley Cl. NW4 71 J2
Ashley Cl., Pnr. 66 B2
Ashley Cres. N22 75 G2
Ashley Cres. SW11 150 A3
Ashley Dr., Borwd. 38 C5
Ashley Dr., Islw. 124 B6
Ashley Dr., Twick. 143 H7
Ashley Gdns. N13 59 J4
Ashley Gdns. SW1 25 G6
Ashley Gdns. SW1 130 C3
Ashley Gdns., Orp. 207 H5
Ashley Gdns., Rich. 163 G3
Ashley Gdns., Wem. 87 H2
Ashley Gro., Loug. 48 B3
Staples Rd.
Ashley La. NW4 71 J2
Ashley La., Croy. 201 H4
Ashley Pl. SW1 25 F6
Ashley Pl. SW1 130 C3
Ashley Rd. E4 62 A5
Ashley Rd. E7 97 J7
Ashley Rd. N17 76 D3
Ashley Rd. N19 92 E1
Ashley Rd. SW19 166 E6
Ashley Rd., Enf. 45 F2
Ashley Rd., Hmptn. 179 G1
Ashley Rd., Rich. 145 H3
Jocelyn Rd.
Ashley Rd., T.Ditt. 180 C6
Ashley Rd., Th.Hth. 187 F4
Ashley Wk. NW7 55 J7
Ashlin Rd. E15 96 D4
Ashling Rd., Croy. 202 D1
Ashlone Rd. SW15 147 J3
Ashlyns Way, Chess. 195 G6
Ashmead N14 42 C6
Ashmead Gate, Brom. 191 J1
Ashmead Rd. SE8 154 A2
Ashmead Rd., Felt. 160 A1
Ashmere Av., Beck. 190 D2
Ashmere Cl., Sutt. 197 J5
Ashmere Gro. SW2 150 E4
Ashmill St. NW1 15 G1
Ashmill St. NW1 109 H5
Ashmole Pl. SW8 34 E6
Ashmole Pl. SW8 131 F6
Ashmole St. SW8 34 D6
Ashmole St. SW8 131 F6
Ashmore Ct., Houns. 123 G6
Wheatlands
Ashmore Gro., Well. 157 G3
Ashmore Rd. W9 108 C4
Ashmount Est. N19 74 D7
Ashmount Rd.
Ashmount Rd. N15 76 C5
Ashmount Rd. N19 74 C7
Ashmount Ter. W5 125 G4
Murray Rd.
Ashneal Gdns., Har. 86 A3
Ashness Gdns., Grnf. 86 E6
Ashness Rd. SW11 149 J5
Ashridge Cl., Har. 69 F6
Ashridge Cres. SE18 137 F7
Ashridge Dr., Wat. 50 C5
Ashridge Gdns. N13 58 D5
Ashridge Gdns., Pnr. 66 E4
Ashridge Way, Mord. 184 C3
Ashridge Way, Sun. 160 A6
Ashtead Rd. E5 76 D7
Ashton Cl., Sutt. 198 D4
Ashton Gdns., Houns. 143 F4
Ashton Gdns., Rom. 83 E6
Ashton Rd. E15 96 D5
Ashton St. E14 114 C7
Ashtree Av., Mitch. 185 H2
Ashtree Cl., Orp. 206/207 E4
Broadwater Gdns.
Ashurst Cl. SE20 189 E1
Ashurst Dr., Ilf. 81 E6
Ashurst Rd. N12 57 H5
Ashurst Rd., Barn. 41 J5
Ashurst Wk., Croy. 202 E2
Ashvale Rd. SW17 167 J5
Ashville Rd. E11 96 D2
Ashwater Rd. SE12 173 G1
Ashwell Cl. E6 116 B6
Northumberland Rd.
Ashwin St. E8 94 C6
Ashwood Gdns., Croy. 204 B6
Ashwood Gdns., Hayes 121 J4
Cranford Dr.
Ashwood Rd. E4 62 D3
Ashworth Cl. SE5 152 A2
Hascombe Ter.
Ashworth Rd. W9 6 B3
Ashworth Rd. W9 109 E3
Aske St. N1 12 D3
Askern Cl., Bexh. 158 D4
Askew Cres. W12 127 F2
Askew Rd. W12 127 F1
Askham Ct. W12 127 G1
Askham Rd. W12 127 G1
Askill Dr. SW15 148 B5
Keswick Rd.
Asland Rd. E15 114 E1
Aslett St. SW18 149 E7
Asmara Rd. NW2 90 B5
Asmuns Hill NW11 72 D5
Asmuns Pl. NW11 72 C5
Asolando Dr. SE17 36 A2
Aspen Cl. N19 92 C2
Hargrave Pk.
Aspen Cl. W5 125 J2
Aspen Cl., West Dr. 120 C1
Aspen Copse, Brom. 192 C2
Aspen Ct., Hayes 121 H4
Aspen Dr., Wem. 86 D4
Aspen Gdns. W6 127 H5
Aspen Gdns., Mitch. 186 A5
Aspen Grn., Erith 139 F3
Aspen La., Nthlt. 102 E3
Aspen Way E14 114 B7
Aspen Way, Felt. 160 B3
Aspenlea Rd. W6 128 A6
Aspern Gro. NW3 91 H5
Aspinall Rd. SE4 153 G3
Aspinden Rd. SE16 133 E4
Aspley Rd. SW18 149 E5
Asplins Rd. N17 76 D1
Asquith Cl., Dag. 100 C1
Crystal Way
Ass Ho. La., Har. 51 H4
Assam St. E1 21 H3
Assata Ms. N1 93 H6
St. Paul's Rd.
Assembly Pas. E1 113 F5
Assembly Wk., Cars. 185 H7
Assurance Cotts., Belv. 139 F5
Heron Hill
Astall Cl., Har. 68 B1
Astbury Rd. SE15 153 F1
Aste St. E14 134 C2
Astell St. SW3 31 H3
Astell St. SW3 129 H5
Asteys Row N1 93 H7
River Pl.
Asthall Gdns., Ilf. 81 F4
Astle St. SW11 150 A2
Astley Av. NW2 89 J5
Aston Av., Har. 69 F7
Aston Cl., Sid. 176 A3
Aston Grn., Houns. 142 C2
Aston Ms., Rom. 82 C7
Reynolds Av.
Aston Rd. SW20 183 J2
Aston Rd. W5 105 G6
Aston Rd., Esher 194 B5
Aston St. E14 113 H6
Aston Ter. SW12 150 B6
Cathles Rd.
Astonville St. SW18 166 D1
Astor Av., Rom. 83 J6
Astor Cl., Kings.T. 164 B6
Astoria Wk. SW9 151 G3
Astrop Ms. W6 127 J3
Astrop Ter. W6 127 J3
Astwood Ms. SW7 30 C1
Astwood Ms. SW7 129 E4
Asylum Rd. SE15 133 E7
Atalanta St. SW6 148 A1
Atbara Ct., Tedd. 163 E6
Atbara Rd., Tedd. 163 E6
Atcham Rd., Houns. 143 J4
Atcost Rd., Bark. 118 A5
Atheldene Rd. SW18 167 E1
Athelney St. SE6 172 A3
Athelstan Rd., Kings.T. 181 J4
Athelstane Gro. E3 113 J2
Athelstane Ms. N4 93 G1
Stroud Grn. Rd.
Athelstone Rd., Har. 68 A2
Athena Cl., Har. 86 B2
Byron Hill Rd.
Athena Cl., Kings.T. 181 J3
Athenaeum Pl. N10 74 B3
Fortis Grn. Rd.
Athenaeum Rd. N20 57 F1
Athenlay Rd. SE15 153 G5
Athens Gdns. W9 108 D4
Elgin Av.
Atherden Rd. E5 95 F4
Atherfold Rd. SW9 150 E3
Atherley Way, Houns. 143 F7
Atherstone Ms. SW7 30 D1
Atherstone Ms. SW7 129 F4
Atherton Cl., Stai. 140 A6
Atherton Dr. SW19 166 A4
Atherton Hts., Wem. 87 F6
Atherton Ms. E7 97 F6
Atherton Pl., Har. 68 A3
Atherton Pl., Sthl. 103 H7
Longford Av.
Atherton Rd. E7 97 F5
Atherton Rd. SW13 127 G7
Atherton Rd., Ilf. 80 B2
Atherton St. SW11 149 H2
Athlon Rd., Wem. 105 G2
Athlone, Esher 194 B6
Athlone Cl. E5 94/95 E4
Goulton Rd.
Athlone Rd. SW2 151 F7
Athlone St. NW5 92 A6
Athol Cl., Pnr. 66 B1
Athol Gdns., Pnr. 66 B1
Athol Rd., Erith 139 J5
Athol Sq. E14 114 C6
Athole Gdns., Enf. 44 B5
Atholl Rd., Ilf. 82 A7
Atkins Dr., W.Wick. 204 D2
Atkins Rd. E10 78 B6
Atkins Rd. SW12 150 D7
Atkinson Rd. E16 115 J5
Atlantic Rd. SW9 151 G4
Atlantis Cl., Bark. 117 H3
Thames Rd.
Atlas Gdns. SE7 135 J4
Atlas Ms. E8 94 C6
Tyssen St.
Atlas Ms. N7 93 F6
Atlas Rd. E13 115 G2
Atlas Rd. N11 58 B6
Atlas Rd. NW10 107 E3
Atlas Rd., Wem. 88 C4
Atley Rd. E3 114 A1
Atlip Rd., Wem. 105 H1
Atney Rd. SW15 148 B4
Atria Rd., Nthwd. 50 A5
Attenborough Cl., Wat. 50/51 E3
Harrow Way
Atterbury Rd. N4 75 G6
Atterbury St. SW1 33 J2
Atterbury St. SW1 130 E4
Attewood Av. NW10 88 E3
Attewood Rd., Nthlt. 85 E6
Attfield Cl. N20 57 G2
Attlee Cl., Hayes 102 B3
Attlee Cl., Th.Hth. 187 J6
Attlee Rd. SE28 118 B7
Attlee Rd., Hayes 102 A3
Attlee Ter. E17 78 B4
Attneave St. WC1 10 E4
Atwater Cl. SW2 169 G1
Atwell Cl. E10 78 B6
Belmont Pk. Rd.
Atwell Pl., T.Ditt. 194 C1
Atwell Rd. SE15 152 D2
Rye La.
Atwood Av., Rich. 146 A2
Atwood Rd. W6 127 H4
Atwoods All., Rich. 146 A1
Leyborne Pk.
Aubert Pk. N5 93 H4
Aubert Rd. N5 93 H4
Aubrey Pl. NW8 6 C2
Aubrey Rd. E17 78 A3
Aubrey Rd. N8 75 E5
Aubrey Rd. W8 128 C1
Aubrey Wk. W8 128 C1
Aubyn Hill SE27 169 J4
Aubyn Sq. SW15 147 G4
Auckland Cl. SE19 188 C1
Auckland Gdns. SE19 188 B1
Auckland Hill SE27 169 J4
Auckland Ri. SE19 188 B1
Auckland Rd. E10 96 B3
Auckland Rd. SE19 188 C1
Auckland Rd. SW11 149 H4
Auckland Rd., Ilf. 99 E1
Auckland Rd., Kings.T. 181 J4
Auckland St. SE11 34 C4
Auden Pl. NW1 110 A1
Audleigh Pl., Chig. 64 D6
Audley Cl. N10 58 B7
Audley Cl. SW11 150 A3
Audley Cl., Borwd. 38 A3
Audley Ct. E18 79 F4
Audley Ct., Pnr. 66 C2
Rickmansworth Rd.
Audley Dr. E16 135 H1
Wesley Av.
Audley Gdns., Ilf. 99 J2
Audley Gdns., Loug. 49 F2
Audley Pl., Sutt. 198 D7
Audley Rd. NW4 71 H6
Audley Rd. W5 105 J5
Audley Rd., Enf. 43 H2
Audley Rd., Rich. 145 J5
Audley Sq. W1 24 C1
Audrey Cl., Beck. 190 B6
Audrey Gdns., Wem. 87 E2
Audrey Rd., Ilf. 98 E3
Audrey St. E2 13 H1
Audrey St. E2 112 D2
Audric Cl., Kings.T. 182 A1
Augurs La. E13 115 H3
Augusta Cl., W.Mol. 179 F3
Freeman Dr.
Augusta Rd., Twick. 161 J2
Augusta St. E14 114 B6
Augustine Rd. W14 128 A3
Augustine Rd., Har. 67 H1

Name	Page	Grid
Augustus Cl., Brent.	125	F7
Augustus Rd. SW19	166	B1
Augustus St. NW1	9	E2
Augustus St. NW1	110	B2
Aulton Pl. SE11	35	F4
Aulton Pl. SE11	131	G5
Aultone Way, Cars.	199	J3
Aultone Way, Sutt.	199	E2
Aurelia Gdns., Croy.	187	F5
Aurelia Rd., Croy.	187	E6
Auriga Ms. N16	94	A5
Auriol Cl., Wor.Pk.	196/197	E3
Auriol Pk. Rd.		
Auriol Dr., Grnf.	86	A7
Auriol Pk. Rd., Wor.Pk.	197	E3
Auriol Rd. W14	128	B4
Austell Gdns. NW7	55	E3
Austen Cl. SE28	138	B1
Austen Cl., Loug.	49	G3
Austen Ho. NW6	108	D3
Austen, Erith	139	H7
Austen Rd., Har.	85	H2
Austin Av., Brom.	192	B5
Austin Cl. SE23	153	J7
Austin Cl., Twick.	145	F5
Austin Ct. E6	115	J1
Kings Rd.		
Austin Friars EC2	20	C3
Austin Friars EC2	112	A6
Austin Friars Pas. EC2	20	C3
Austin Friars Sq. EC2	20	C3
Austin Rd. SW11	150	A1
Austin Rd., Hayes	121	J2
Austin St. E2	13	F4
Austin St. E2	112	C3
Austral Cl., Sid.	175	J3
Austral St. SE11	35	G1
Austral St. SE11	131	H4
Australia Rd. W12	107	H7
Austyn Gdns., Surb.	196	B1
Autumn Cl. SW19	167	F6
Autumn Cl., Enf.	44	D1
Autumn St. E3	114	A1
Avalon Cl. SW20	184	B2
Avalon Cl. W13	104	D5
Avalon Cl., Enf.	43	G2
Avalon Rd. SW6	148	E1
Avalon Rd. W13	104	D4
Avard Gdns., Orp.	207	F4
Avarn Rd. SW17	167	J6
Ave Maria La. EC4	19	H4
Ave Maria La. EC4	111	H6
Avebury Ct. N1	112	A1
Poole St.		
Avebury Pk., Surb.	181	G7
Avebury Rd. E11	96	D1
Southwest Rd.		
Avebury Rd. SW19	184	C1
Avebury Rd., Orp.	207	G3
Avebury St. N1	112	A1
Poole St.		
Aveline St. SE11	34	E3
Aveline St. SE11	131	G5
Aveling Pk. Rd. E17	78	A2
Avenell Rd. N5	93	H3
Avening Rd. SW18	148	D7
Brathway Rd.		
Avening Ter. SW18	148	D6
Avenons Rd. E13	115	G4
Avenue, The E4	62	D6
Avenue, The (Leytonstone) E11	97	F2
Avenue, The (Wanstead) E11	97	F2
Avenue, The N3	72	D2
Avenue, The N8	75	G3
Avenue, The N10	74	C2
Avenue, The N11	58	B4
Avenue, The N17	76	B2
Avenue, The NW6	108	A1
Avenue, The SE7	135	J7
Avenue, The SE10	134	D7
Avenue, The SW4	150	A5
Avenue, The SW11	149	J7
Bellevue Rd.		
Avenue, The SW18	149	H7
Avenue, The W4	126	E3
Avenue, The W13	104	E7
Avenue, The, Barn.	40	B3
Avenue, The, Beck.	190	B1
Avenue, The, Bex.	158	D7
Avenue, The, Brom.	192	A3
Avenue, The, Cars.	200	A7
Avenue, The, Croy.	202	B3
Avenue, The, Epsom	197	H7
Avenue, The, Esher	194	B6
Avenue, The, Hmptn.	161	F6
Avenue, The, Har.	68	C1
Avenue, The, Houns.	143	H5
Avenue, The (Cranford), Houns.	142	A1
Avenue, The, Islw.	124	A6
Avenue, The, Kes.	206	A3
Avenue, The, Loug.	48	A6
Avenue, The, Orp.	207	J2
Avenue, The (St. Paul's Cray), Orp.	176	B7
Avenue, The, Pnr.	67	F6
Avenue, The (Hatch End), Pnr.	51	G7
Avenue, The, Rich.	145	J2
Avenue, The, Sun.	178	B1
Avenue, The, Surb.	181	J6
Avenue, The (Cheam), Sutt.	197	J7
Avenue, The, Twick.	145	F5
Avenue, The, Wem.	87	J2
Avenue, The, West Dr.	120	B3
Avenue, The, W.Wick.	190	D7
Avenue, The, Wor.Pk.	197	F2
Avenue Cl. N14	42	C6
Avenue Cl. NW8	109	H1
Avenue Cl., Houns.	142	A1
The Av.		
Avenue Cl., West Dr.	120	A3
Avenue Cres. W3	126	B2
Avenue Cres., Houns.	122	B7
Avenue Elmers, Surb.	181	H5
Avenue Gdns. SE25	188	D3
Avenue Gdns. SW14	146	E3
Avenue Gdns. W3	126	B2
Avenue Gdns., Houns.	122	A7
The Av.		
Avenue Gdns., Tedd.	162	C7
Avenue Gate, Loug.	47	J6
Avenue Ind. Est. E4	61	J6
Avenue Ms. N10	74	B3
Avenue Pk. Rd. SE27	169	H2
Avenue Rd. E7	97	H5
Avenue Rd. N6	74	C7
Avenue Rd. N12	57	F4
Avenue Rd. N14	42	C7
Avenue Rd. N15	76	A5
Avenue Rd. NW3	91	G7
Avenue Rd. NW8	109	G1
Avenue Rd. NW10	107	F2
Avenue Rd. SE20	189	F1
Avenue Rd. SE25	188	D2
Avenue Rd. SW16	186	D2
Avenue Rd. SW20	183	H2
Avenue Rd. W3	126	B2
Avenue Rd., Beck.	189	F1
Avenue Rd., Belv.	139	J4
Avenue Rd., Bexh.	158	E3
Avenue Rd., Brent.	125	F5
Avenue Rd., Erith	139	J7
Avenue Rd., Hmptn.	179	H1
Avenue Rd., Islw.	144	C1
Avenue Rd., Kings.T.	181	H3
Avenue Rd., N.Mal.	182	E4
Avenue Rd., Pnr.	66	E3
Avenue Rd. (Chadwell Heath), Rom.	82	B7
Avenue Rd., Sthl.	123	F2
Avenue Rd., Tedd.	162	D7
Avenue Rd., Wall.	200	C7
Avenue Rd., Wdf.Grn.	63	J6
Avenue S., Surb.	181	J7
Avenue Ter., N.Mal.	182	C3
Kingston Rd.		
Averil Gro. SW16	169	H6
Averill St. W6	128	A6
Avern Gdns., W.Mol.	179	H4
Avern Rd., W.Mol.	179	H5
Avery Fm. Row SW1	32	C2
Avery Gdns., Ilf.	80	C5
Avery Hill Rd. SE9	157	G6
Avery Row W1	16	D5
Avery Row W1	110	B7
Aviary Cl. E16	115	F5
Aviary Rd., Wok.	47	H1
Aviary Sq. E1	113	G6
Avoca Rd. SW17	168	A4
Avocet Ms. SE28	137	G3
Avon Cl., Hayes	102	C4
Avon Cl., Sutt.	199	F4
Avon Cl., Wor.Pk.	197	G2
Avon Ct., Grnf.	103	H4
Braund Av.		
Avon Ms., Pnr.	67	F1
Avon Path, S.Croy.	201	J6
Avon Pl. SE1	28	A4
Avon Rd. E17	78	D3
Avon Rd. SE4	154	A3
Avon Rd., Grnf.	103	G4
Avon Way E18	79	G3
Avondale Av. N12	56	E5
Avondale Av. NW2	89	E3
Avondale Av., Barn.	57	J1
Avondale Av., Esher	194	D3
Avondale Av., Wor.Pk.	197	F1
Avondale Cl., Loug.	48	C7
Avondale Ct. E11	96	E1
Avondale Ct. E16	114/115	E5
Avondale Rd.		
Avondale Ct. E18	79	H1
Avondale Cres., Enf.	45	H3
Avondale Cres., Ilf.	80	A5
Avondale Dr., Hayes	122	A1
Avondale Dr., Loug.	48	C7
Avondale Gdns., Houns.	143	F5
Avondale Ms., Brom.	173	G6
Avondale Rd.		
Avondale Pk. Gdns. W11	108	B7
Avondale Pk. Rd. W11	108	B7
Avondale Pavement SE1	132	D5
Avondale Sq.		
Avondale Ri. SE15	152	C3
Avondale Rd. E16	115	E5
Avondale Rd. E17	78	A7
Avondale Rd. N3	73	F1
Avondale Rd. N13	59	G2
Avondale Rd. N15	75	H5
Avondale Rd. SE9	174	B2
Avondale Rd. SW14	146	D3
Avondale Rd. SW19	166	E5
Avondale Rd., Brom.	173	E6
Avondale Rd., Har.	68	C3
Avondale Rd., S.Croy.	201	J6
Avondale Rd., Well.	158	C2
Avondale Sq. SE1	37	H4
Avonmouth St. SE1	27	J5
Avonmouth St. SE1	131	J3
Avonwick Rd., Houns.	143	H2
Avril Way E4	62	C5
Avro Way, Wall.	201	E7
Awlfield Av. N17	76	A1
Awliscombe Rd., Well.	157	J2
Axe St., Bark.	117	F1
Axholme Av., Edg.	70	A1
Axminster Cres., Well.	158	C1
Axminster Rd. N7	93	E3
Aybrook St. W1	16	B2
Aybrook St. W1	110	A5
Aycliffe Cl., Brom.	192	C2
Aycliffe Rd. W12	127	F1
Aylands Cl., Wem.	87	H2
Preston Rd.		
Ayles Rd., Hayes	102	C4
Aylesbury Cl. E7	97	F6
Atherton Rd.		
Aylesbury Est. SE17	36	C4
Aylesbury Rd. SE17	36	C4
Aylesbury Rd. SE17	132	A5
Aylesbury Rd., Brom.	191	G3
Aylesbury St. EC1	11	G6
Aylesbury St. EC1	111	H4
Aylesbury St. NW10	88	D3
Aylesford Av., Beck.	189	H5
Aylesford St. SW1	33	H3
Aylesford St. SW1	130	D5
Aylesham Cl. NW7	55	G7
Aylesham Rd., Orp.	193	J7
Aylestone Av. NW6	108	A1
Aylett Rd. SE25	188	E4
Aylett Rd., Islw.	144	B2
Ayley Cft., Enf.	44	D5
Ayliffe Cl., Kings.T.	182	A2
Cambridge Gdns.		
Aylmer Cl., Stan.	52	D4
Aylmer Dr., Stan.	52	D4
Aylmer Par. N2	73	J5
Aylmer Rd.		
Aylmer Rd. E11	97	F1
Aylmer Rd. N2	73	H5
Aylmer Rd. W12	128	A2
Aylmer Rd., Dag.	100	E3
Ayloffe Rd., Dag.	101	F6
Aylton Est. SE16	133	F2
Renforth St.		
Aylward Rd. SE23	171	G2
Aylward Rd. SW20	184	C2
Aylward St. E1	113	F6
Aylwards Ri., Stan.	52	D4
Aylwyn Est. SE1	29	F5
Aylwyn Est. SE1	132	B3
Aynhoe Rd. W14	128	A4
Aynscombe La. SW14	146	C3
Aynscombe Path SW14	146	C2
Thames Bank		
Ayr Ct. W3	106	A5
Monks Dr.		
Ayres Cl. E13	115	G3
Ayres Cres. NW10	88	D7
Ayres St. SE1	28	A3
Ayres St. SE1	131	J2
Ayrsome Rd. N16	94	B3
Ayrton Rd. SW7	23	E5
Aysgarth Rd. SE21	152	B6
Aytoun Pl. SW9	151	F2
Aytoun Rd. SW9	151	F2
Azalea Cl. W7	124	C1
Azalea Cl., Ilf.	98	E5
Azalea Ct., Wdf.Grn.	62/63	E7
The Bridle Path		
Azalea Wk., Pnr.	66	B5
Azalea Wk., Sthl.	123	J2
Navigator Dr.		
Azenby Rd. SE15	152	C2
Azile Everitt Ho. SE18	137	F5
Vicarage Pk.		
Azof St. SE10	135	E4

B

Name	Page	Grid
Baalbec Rd. N5	93	H5
Babbacombe Cl., Chess.	195	G5
Babbacombe Gdns., Ilf.	80	B4
Babbacombe Rd., Brom.	191	G1
Baber Dr., Felt.	142	C6
Babington Ri., Wem.	88	A6
Babington Rd. NW4	71	H4
Babington Rd. SW16	168	D5
Babington Rd., Dag.	100	C5
Babmaes St. SW1	17	G6
Bacchus Wk. N1	12	D2
Baches St. N1	12	C3
Baches St. N1	112	A3
Back Ch. La. E1	21	H5
Back Ch. La. E1	112	D7
Back Hill EC1	11	E6
Back Hill EC1	111	G4
Back La. N8	74	E5
Back La. NW3	91	F4
Heath St.		
Back La., Bex.	159	G7
Back La., Brent.	125	G6
Back La., Edg.	70	C1
Back La., Rich.	163	F3
Back La., Rom.	82/83	E7
St. Chad's Rd.		
Back Rd., Sid.	176	A4
Backhouse Pl. SE17	36	E2
Backley Gdns. SE25	188	D6
Bacon Gro. SE1	29	F6
Bacon Gro. SE1	132	C3
Bacon La. NW9	70	B4
Bacon La., Edg.	70	A7
Bacon St. E1	13	G5
Bacon St. E1	112	C4
Bacon St. E2	13	G5
Bacon St. E2	112	C4
Bacon Ter., Dag.	100	B5
Fitzstephen Rd.		
Bacons La. N6	92	A1
Bacton NW5	92	A5
Bacton St. E2	113	F3
Roman Rd.		
Baddow Cl., Dag.	119	G1
Baddow Cl., Wdf.Grn.	64	A6
Baddow Wk. N1	111	J1
Baden Pl. SE1	28	B3
Baden Powell Cl., Dag.	119	E1
Baden Powell Cl., Surb.	195	J2
Baden Rd. N8	74	D4
Baden Rd., Ilf.	98	E5
Badger Cl., Felt.	160	A3
Sycamore Cl.		
Badger Cl., Houns.	142	C3
Badgers Cl., Enf.	43	H3
Badgers Cl., Har.	68	A6
Badgers Copse, Orp.	207	J2
Badgers Copse, Wor.Pk.	197	F2

Badgers Cft. N20 56 B1
Badgers Cft. SE9 174 D3
Badgers Hole, Croy. 203 G4
Badgers Wk., N.Mal. 182 E2
Badlis Rd. E17 78 A3
Badminton Cl., Borwd. 38 A2
Badminton Cl., Har. 68 B4
Badminton Cl., Nthlt. 85 G6
Badminton Ms. E16 135 G1
Hanameel St.
Badminton Rd. SW12 150 A6
Badsworth Rd. SE5 131 J7
Baffin Way E14 114 C7
Prestons Rd.
Bagley Cl., West Dr. 120 B2
Bagley's La. SW6 149 E1
Bagleys Spring, Rom. 83 E4
Bagshot Ct. SE18 156 D1
Prince Imperial Rd.
Bagshot Rd., Enf. 44 C7
Bagshot St. SE17 36 E4
Bagshot St. SE17 132 B5
Baildon St. SE8 134 A7
Watson's St.
Bailey Cl. E4 62 C4
Bailey Cl., Chess. 195 G6
Ashlyns Way
Bailey Pl. SE26 171 G6
Baillies Wk. W5 125 G2
Liverpool Rd.
Bainbridge Rd., Dag. 101 F4
Bainbridge St. WC1 17 J3
Bainbridge St. WC1 110 D6
Baines Cl., S.Croy. 201 J5
Brighton Rd.
Baird Av., Sthl. 103 H7
Baird Cl. E10 96 A1
Church Rd.
Baird Cl. NW9 70 C6
Baird Gdns. SE19 170 B4
Baird Rd., Enf. 44 E4
Baird St. EC1 12 A5
Baizdon Rd. SE3 154 E2
Baker La., Mitch. 186 A2
Baker Pas. NW10 106/107 E1
Acton La.
Baker Rd. NW10 106 E1
Baker Rd. SE18 136 B7
Baker St. NW1 8 A6
Baker St. NW1 109 J4
Baker St. W1 16 A1
Baker St. W1 109 J5
Baker St., Enf. 44 A3
Bakers Av. E17 78 B6
Bakers Ct. SE25 188 B3
Bakers End SW20 184 B2
Bakers Fld. N7 92 D4
Crayford Rd.
Bakers Gdns., Cars. 199 H2
Bakers Hill E5 95 F1
Bakers Hill, Barn. 41 E2
Bakers La. N6 73 J5
Baker's Ms. W1 16 B3
Bakers Ms., Orp. 207 J6
Bakers Pas. NW3 91 F4
Heath St.
Baker's Rents E2 13 F4
Bakers Row E15 114 E2
Baker's Row EC1 11 E6
Baker's Row EC1 111 G4
Baker's Yd. EC1 111 G4
Baker's Row
Bakery Cl. SW9 151 F1
Bakery Path, Edg. 54 B6
Station Rd.
Bakery Pl. SW11 149 J4
Altenburg Gdns.
Bakewell Way, N.Mal. 182 E2
Bala Gdn. NW9 70/71 E6
Snowdon Dr.
Balaam St. E13 115 G3
Balaams La. N14 58 D2
Balaclava Rd. SE1 37 G2
Balaclava Rd. SE1 132 C4
Balaclava Rd., Surb. 181 F7
Balcaskie Rd. SE9 156 C5
Balchen Rd. SE3 156 A2
Balchier Rd. SE22 152 E6
Balcombe Cl., Bexh. 158 D4
Balcombe St. NW1 7 J6
Balcombe St. NW1 109 J4
Balcon Way, Borwd. 38 C1
Balcorne St. E9 95 F7
Balder Ri. SE12 173 H2
Balderton St. W1 16 C4
Balderton St. W1 110 A6
Baldock St. E3 114 B2
Baldry Gdns. SW16 169 E6
Baldwin Cres. SE5 151 J1
Baldwin Gdns., Houns. 143 J1
Gresham Rd.
Baldwin St. EC1 12 B4
Baldwin Ter. N1 11 J1
Baldwin Ter. N1 111 J2
Baldwin's Gdns. EC1 18 E1
Baldwin's Gdns. EC1 111 G5
Baldwins Hill, Loug. 48 C2
Baldwyn Gdns. W3 106 D7
Balfe St. N1 10 B2
Balfe St. N1 111 E2
Balfern Gro. W4 127 E5
Balfern St. SW11 149 H1
Balfour Av. W7 124 C1
Balfour Gro. N20 57 J3
Balfour Ho. W10 108 A5
St. Charles Sq.
Balfour Ms. N9 60 D3
The Bdy.
Balfour Ms. W1 24 C1
Balfour Pl. SW15 147 H4
Balfour Pl. W1 16 C6
Balfour Rd. N5 93 J4
Balfour Rd. SE25 188 D4
Balfour Rd. SW19 166 E7
Balfour Rd. W3 106 C5
Balfour Rd. W13 124 D2
Balfour Rd., Brom. 192 A5
Balfour Rd., Cars. 199 J7
Balfour Rd., Har. 68 A5
Balfour Rd., Houns. 143 H3
Balfour Rd., Ilf. 98 E2
Balfour Rd., Sthl. 122 D3
Balfour St. SE17 36 B1
Balfour St. SE17 132 A4
Balgonie Rd. E4 62 D1
Balgowan Cl., N.Mal. 183 E5
Balgowan Rd., Beck. 189 H3
Balgowan St. SE18 137 J4
Balham Continental Mkt. SW12 168 B1
Balham Gro. SW12 150 A7
Balham High Rd. SW12 168 A1
Balham High Rd. SW17 168 A2
Balham Hill SW12 150 B7
Balham New Rd. SW12 150 B7
Balham Pk. Rd. SW12 167 J1
Balham Rd. N9 60 D2
Balham Sta. Rd. SW12 168 B1
Balkan Wk. E1 112/113 E7
Pennington St.
Balladier Wk. E14 114 B5
Ballamore Rd., Brom. 173 G3
Ballance Rd. E9 95 G6
Ballantine St. SW18 149 F4
Ballard Cl., Kings.T. 164 D7
Ballards Cl., Dag. 119 H1
Ballards Fm. Rd., Croy. 202 D6
Ballards Fm. Rd., S.Croy. 202 D6
Ballards La. N3 72 D1
Ballards La. N12 72 D1
Ballards Ms., Edg. 54 A6
Ballards Ri., S.Croy. 202 D6
Ballards Rd. NW2 89 G2
Ballards Rd., Dag. 119 H1
Ballards Way, Croy. 203 E6
Ballards Way, S.Croy. 202 D6
Ballast Quay SE10 134 D5
Ballater Cl., Wat. 50 C4
Ballater Rd. SW2 151 E4
Ballater Rd., S.Croy. 202 C5
Ballina St. SE23 153 G6
Ballingdon Rd. SW11 150 A6
Ballinger Pt. E3 114 B3
Bromley High St.
Balliol Av. E4 62 D4
Balliol Rd. N17 76 B1
Balliol Rd. W10 107 J6
Balliol Rd., Well. 158 B2
Balloch Rd. SE6 172 D1
Ballogie Av. NW10 89 E4
Ballow Cl. SE5 132 B7
Harris St.
Balls Pond Pl. N1 94 A6
Balls Pond Rd.
Balls Pond Rd. N1 94 A6
Balmain Cl. W5 125 G1
Balmer Rd. E3 113 J2
Balmes Rd. N1 112 A1
Balmoral Av. N11 58 A5
Balmoral Av., Beck. 189 H4
Balmoral Cl. SW15 148 A6
Westleigh Av.
Balmoral Cres., W.Mol. 179 G3
Balmoral Dr., Borwd. 38 D5
Balmoral Dr., Hayes 102 A5
Balmoral Dr., Sthl. 103 F4
Balmoral Gdns. W13 124 D3
Balmoral Gdns., Bex. 159 F7
Balmoral Gdns., Ilf. 99 J1
Balmoral Gro. N7 93 F6
Balmoral Ms. W12 127 F2
Balmoral Rd. E7 97 J4
Balmoral Rd. E10 96 B2
Balmoral Rd. NW2 89 H6
Balmoral Rd., Har. 85 G4
Balmoral Rd., Kings.T. 181 J4
Balmoral Rd., Wor.Pk. 197 H3
Balmore Cres., Barn. 42 A5
Balmore St. N19 92 B2
Balmuir Gdns. SW15 147 J4
Balnacraig Av. NW10 89 E4
Balniel Gate SW1 33 J3
Balniel Gate SW1 130 D5
Baltic Cl. SW19 167 G7
Baltic Ct. SE16 133 G2
Timber Pond Rd.
Baltic Pl. N1 112 B1
Kingsland Rd.
Baltic St. E. EC1 11 J6
Baltic St. E. EC1 111 J4
Baltic St. W. EC1 11 J6
Baltic St. W. EC1 111 J4
Baltimore Pl., Well. 157 J2
Balvaird Pl. SW1 33 J4
Balvaird Pl. SW1 130 D5
Balvernie Gro. SW18 148 C7
Bamber Ho., Bark. 117 F1
St. Margarets
Bamborough Gdns. W12 127 J2
Bamford Av., Wem. 105 J1
Bamford Ct. E15 96 B5
Clays La.
Bamford Rd., Bark. 99 F6
Bamford Rd., Brom. 172 C5
Bampfylde Cl., Wall. 200 C3
Bampton Dr. NW7 55 G7
Bampton Rd. SE23 171 G3
Banavie Gdns., Beck. 190 C1
Banbury Cl., Enf. 43 H1
Holtwhites Hill
Banbury Ct. WC2 18 A5
Banbury Ct., Sutt. 198 D7
Banbury Enterprise Cen., Croy. 201 H2
Factory La.
Banbury Rd. E9 95 G7
Banbury Rd. E17 61 G7
Banbury St. SW11 149 H2
Banbury Wk., Nthlt. 103 G2
Brabazon Rd.
Banchory Rd. SE3 135 H7
Bancroft Av. N2 73 H5
Bancroft Av., Buck.H. 63 G2
Bancroft Ct., Nthlt. 102 C1
Bancroft Gdns., Har. 67 J1
Bancroft Gdns., Orp. 207 J1
Bancroft Rd. E1 113 F3
Bancroft Rd., Har. 67 J2
Bandon Ri., Wall. 200 D5
Bangalore St. SW15 147 J3
Bangor Cl., Nthlt. 85 H5
Banim St. W6 127 H3
Banister Rd. W10 108 A3
Bank, The N6 92 B1
Cholmeley Pk.
Bank Av., Mitch. 185 G2
Bank End SE1 28 A1
Bank End SE1 131 J1
Bank La. SW15 146 E5
Bank La., Kings.T. 163 H7
Bankfoot Rd., Brom. 173 E4
Bankhurst Rd. SE6 153 J7
Banks La., Bexh. 159 F4
Banks Rd., Borwd. 38 C2
Banks Way E12 98 D4
Grantham Rd.
Banksia Rd. N18 61 F5
Banksian Wk., Islw. 144 B1
Bankside SE1 19 J6
Bankside SE1 111 J7
Bankside, Enf. 43 H1
Bankside, S.Croy. 202 C6
Bankside, Sthl. 122 D1
Bankside Av., Nthlt. 102 A2
Townson Av.
Bankside Cl., Cars. 199 H6
Bankside Cl., Islw. 144 C4
Bankside Dr., T.Ditt. 194 E1
Bankside Rd., Ilf. 99 F5
Bankside Way SE19 170 B6
Lunham Rd.
Bankton Rd. SW2 151 G4
Bankwell Rd. SE13 155 E4
Banner St. EC1 12 A6
Banner St. EC1 111 J4
Bannerman Ho. SW8 34 C6
Bannerman Ho. SW8 131 F6
Banning St. SE10 134 E5
Bannister Cl. SW2 169 G1
Ewen Cres.
Bannister Cl., Grnf. 86 A5
Bannister Ho. E9 95 G5
Homerton High St.
Bannockburn Rd. SE18 137 H4
Banstead Gdns. N9 60 B3
Banstead Rd., Cars. 199 H6
Banstead St. SE15 153 F3
Banstead Way, Wall. 201 E5
Banstock Rd., Edg. 54 B6
Banting Dr. N21 43 F5
Banton Cl., Enf. 44/45 E2
Central Av.
Bantry St. SE5 132 A7
Banwell Rd., Bex. 158 D6
Woodside La.
Banyard Rd. SE16 132/133 E3
Southwark Pk. Rd.
Baptist Gdns. NW5 92 A6
Queens Cres.
Barandon Wk. W11 108 A7
Barb Ms. W6 127 J3
Barbara Brosnan Ct. NW8 6 E2
Barbara Hucklesby Cl. N22 75 H2
The Sandlings
Barbauld Rd. N16 94 B3
Barber Cl. N21 43 G7
Barber's All. E13 115 H3
Barbers Rd. E15 114 B2
Barbican, The EC2 19 J1
Barbican, The EC2 111 J5
Barbican Rd., Grnf. 103 H6
Barbon Cl. WC1 18 C1
Barbot Cl. N9 60 D3
Barchard St. SW18 148 E5
Barchester Cl. W7 124 C1
Barchester Rd., Har. 68 A2
Barchester St. E14 114 B5
Barclay Cl. SW6 128 D7
Barclay Oval, Wdf.Grn. 63 G4
Barclay Path E17 78 C5
Barclay Rd. E11 97 E1
Barclay Rd. E13 115 J4
Barclay Rd. E17 78 C5
Barclay Rd. N18 60 A6
Barclay Rd. SW6 128 D7
Barclay Rd., Croy. 202 A3
Barclay Way SE22 152 D7
Lordship La.
Barcombe Av. SW2 169 E2
Barcombe Cl., Orp. 193 J3
Bard Rd. W10 108 A7
Barden St. SE18 137 H7
Bardfield Av., Rom. 82 D3
Bardney Rd., Mord. 185 E4
Bardolph Rd. N7 92 E4
Bardolph Rd., Rich. 145 J3
St. Georges Rd.
Bardsey Pl. E1 113 F5
Mile End Rd.
Bardsey Wk. N1 93 J6
Clephane Rd.
Bardsley Cl., Croy. 202 C3
Bardsley La. SE10 134 C6
Barfett St. W10 108 C4
Barfield Av. N20 57 H2
Barfield Rd. E11 97 F1
Barfield Rd., Brom. 192 D3
Barfields, Loug. 48 D4
Barfields Gdns., Loug. 48 D4
Barfields
Barfields Path, Loug. 48 D4
Barford Cl. NW4 71 G1
Barford St. N1 111 G1
Barforth Rd. SE15 153 E3
Barfreston Way SE20 189 E1
Bargate Cl. SE18 137 J5
Bargate Cl., N.Mal. 183 G6
Barge Ho. Rd. E16 137 E1
Barge Ho. St. SE1 27 F1
Barge Wk., E.Mol. 181 G2
Barge Wk., Kings.T. 181 G1
Barge Wk., Walt. 179 J2
Bargery Rd. SE6 172 B1
Bargrove Cl. SE20 170 D7
Bargrove Cres. SE6 171 J2
Elm La.
Barham Cl., Brom. 206 B1
Barham Cl., Chis. 174 E5
Barham Cl., Rom. 83 H2
Barham Cl., Wem. 87 E6
Barham Rd. SW20 165 G7
Barham Rd., Chis. 174 E5

Barham Rd., S.Croy. 201 J5
Baring Cl. SE12 173 G2
Baring Rd. SE12 155 G7
Baring Rd., Barn. 41 G3
Baring Rd., Croy. 202 D1
Baring St. N1 112 A1
Bark Pl. W2 **14** **A5**
Bark Pl. W2 108 E7
Barkantine 134 A2
Shop. Par., The E14
The Quarterdeck
Barker Cl., N.Mal. 182 C3
California Rd.
Barker Dr. NW1 92 C7
Barker Ms. SW4 150 B4
Barker St. SW10 **30** **C5**
Barker St. SW10 129 F6
Barker Wk. SW16 168 D3
Barker Way SE22 170 D1
Dulwich Common
Barkham Rd. N17 60 A7
Barking Ind. Pk., 117 J1
Bark.
Barking Rd. E6 116 A2
Barking Rd. E13 115 H4
Barking Rd. E16 115 F5
Barkston Gdns. SW5 **30** **A3**
Barkston Gdns. SW5 128 E4
Barkway Ct. N4 93 J3
Queens Dr.
Barkwood Cl., Rom. 83 J5
Barkworth Rd. SE16 133 E5
Barlborough St. 133 F7
SE14
Barlby Gdns. W10 108 A4
Barlby Rd. W10 108 A5
Barley La., Ilf. 82 A7
Barley La., Rom. 82 B6
Barley Mow Pas. **19** **H2**
EC1
Barley Mow Pas. W4 126 D5
Barley Shotts 108 C5
Business Pk. W10
St. Ervans Rd.
Barleycorn Way E14 113 J7
Barleyfields Cl., Rom. 82 B7
Barlow Cl., Wall. 200/201 E6
Cobham Cl.
Barlow Pl. W1 **17** **E6**
Barlow Rd. NW6 90 C6
Barlow Rd. W3 126 B1
Barlow Rd., Hmptn. 161 G7
Barlow St. SE17 **36** **C2**
Barmeston Rd. SE6 172 B2
Barmor Cl., Har. 67 H2
Barmouth Av., Grnf. 104 C2
Barmouth Rd. SW18 149 F6
Barmouth Rd., Croy. 203 G2
Barn Cl., Nthlt. 102 C2
Barn Cres., Stan. 53 F6
Barn Elms Pk. SW15 147 J2
Barn Hill, Wem. 88 B2
Barn Ms., Har. 85 G3
Barn Ri., Wem. 88 A1
Barn St. N16 94 B3
Stoke Newington Ch. St.
Barn Way, Wem. 88 A1
Barnabas Ct. N21 43 G5
Cheyne Wk.
Barnabas Rd. E9 95 G5
Barnaby Cl., Har. 85 J2
Barnaby Pl. SW7 **31** **E2**
Barnaby Pl. SW7 129 G4
Barnaby Way, Chig. 64 E3
Barnard Cl. SE18 136 D4
Barnard Cl., Chis. 193 G1
Barnard Cl., Sun. 160 B7
Oak Gro.
Barnard Cl., Wall. 200 D7
Barnard Gdns., 102 B4
Hayes
Barnard Gdns., 183 G4
N.Mal.
Barnard Gro. E15 97 F7
Vicarage La.
Barnard Hill N10 74 A2
Barnard Ms. SW11 149 H4
Barnard Rd. SW11 149 H4
Barnard Rd., Enf. 45 E2
Barnard Rd., Mitch. 186 A3
Barnardo Dr., Ilf. 81 F4
Barnardo St. E1 113 G6
Devonport St.
Barnardos Village, Ilf. 81 F3
Barnard's Inn EC1 **19** **F3**
Barnby Sq. E15 114/115 E1
Barnby St.
Barnby St. E15 114 E1
Barnby St. NW1 **9** **G2**
Barnby St. NW1 110 C2
Barncroft Cl., Loug. 48 D5
Barncroft Grn., 48 D5
Loug.
Barncroft Rd., Loug. 48 D5

Barnehurst Av., Bexh. 159 J1
Barnehurst Av., Erith 159 J1
Barnehurst Cl., Erith 159 J1
Barnehurst Rd., 159 J2
Bexh.
Barnes All., Hmptn. 179 J2
Hampton Ct. Rd.
Barnes Av. SW13 127 G7
Barnes Av., Sthl. 123 F4
Barnes Br. SW13 147 E2
Barnes Br. W4 147 E2
Barnes Cl. E12 98 A4
Barnes Cl. E16 115 J5
Ridgwell Rd.
Barnes Ct., Wdf.Grn. 64 A5
Barnes End, N.Mal. 183 G5
Barnes High St. 147 F2
SW13
Barnes Ho., Bark. 117 G1
St. Marys
Barnes Pikle W5 105 F7
Barnes Rd. N18 61 F4
Barnes Rd., Ilf. 99 F5
Barnes St. E14 113 H6
Barnes Ter. SE8 133 J5
Barnesbury Ho. 150 D5
SW4
Barnet Bypass, Barn. 38 E3
Barnet Dr., Brom. 206 B2
Barnet Gate La., 39 F6
Barn.
Barnet Gro. E2 **13** **H3**
Barnet Gro. E2 112 D3
Barnet Hill, Barn. 40 D4
Barnet Ho. N20 57 F2
Barnet La. N20 56 C1
Barnet La., Barn. 40 C6
Barnet Rd. (Arkley), 39 H5
Barn.
Barnet Trd. Est., 40 C3
Barn.
Barnet Way NW7 38 D7
Barnet Wd. Rd., 205 J2
Brom.
Barnett St. E1 112/113 E6
Cannon St. Rd.
Barney Cl. SE7 135 J5
Barnfield, N.Mal. 182 E6
Barnfield Av., Croy. 203 F2
Barnfield Av., 163 H5
Kings.T.
Barnfield Av., Mitch. 186 B4
Barnfield Cl. N4 74/75 E7
Crouch Hill
Barnfield Cl. SW17 167 F3
Barnfield Gdns. 136/137 E6
SE18
Plumstead Common Rd.
Barnfield Gdns., 163 H4
Kings.T.
Barnfield Pl. E14 134 A4
Barnfield Rd. SE18 137 E6
Barnfield Rd. W5 105 F4
Barnfield Rd., Belv. 139 F6
Barnfield Rd., Edg. 70 C1
Barnfield Wd. Cl., 190 D6
Beck.
Barnfield Wd. Rd., 190 D6
Beck.
Barnham Rd., Grnf. 103 J3
Barnham St. SE1 **28** **E3**
Barnham St. SE1 132 B2
Barnhill, Pnr. 66 C5
Barnhill Av., Brom. 191 F5
Barnhill La., Hayes 102 B3
Barnhill Rd., Hayes 102 B3
Barnhill Rd., Wem. 88 C3
Barnhurst Path, Wat. 50 C5
Barningham Way 70 D6
NW9
Barnlea Cl., Felt. 161 E2
Barnmead Gdns., 101 F5
Dag.
Barnmead Rd., Beck. 189 H1
Barnmead Rd., Dag. 101 F5
Barnsbury Cl., N.Mal. 182 C5
Barnsbury Cres., 196 C1
Surb.
Barnsbury Est. N1 111 G1
Barnsbury Rd.
Barnsbury Gro. N7 93 F7
Barnsbury La., Surb. 196 B2
Barnsbury Pk. N1 93 G7
Barnsbury Rd. N1 **10** **E1**
Barnsbury Rd. N1 111 G2
Barnsbury Sq. N1 93 G7
Barnsbury St. N1 93 G7
Barnsbury Ter. N1 93 F7
Barnscroft SW20 183 H3
Barnsdale Av. E14 134 A4
Barnsdale Rd. W9 108 C4
Barnsley St. E1 113 E4
Barnstaple Rd., 84 C3
Ruis.

Barnston Wk. N1 111 J1
Popham St.
Barnwell Rd. SW2 151 G5
Barnwood Cl. W9 **6** **A6**
Barnwood Cl. W9 108 E4
Baron Cl. N11 58 A5
Balmoral Av.
Baron Gdns., Ilf. 81 F3
Baron Gro., Mitch. 185 H4
Baron Rd., Dag. 100 D1
Baron St. N1 **11** **E1**
Baron St. N1 111 G2
Baron Wk. E16 115 F5
Baron Wk., Mitch. 185 H4
Baroness Rd. E2 **13** **G3**
Baronet Gro. N17 76 D1
St. Paul's Rd.
Baronet Rd. N17 76 D1
Barons, The, Twick. 145 E6
Barons Ct., Wall. 200 D3
Whelan Way
Barons Ct. Rd. W14 128 B5
Barons Gate, Barn. 41 H6
Barons Keep W14 128 B5
Barons Mead, Har. 68 B4
Barons Pl. SE1 131 G2
Barons Pl. SE1 **27** **F4**
Barons Wk., Croy. 189 H6
Baronsfield Rd., 145 E6
Twick.
Baronsmead Rd. 147 G1
SW13
Baronsmede W5 125 J2
Baronsmere Rd. N2 73 H4
Barque Ms. SE8 134 A6
Watergate St.
Barrack Rd., Houns. 142 D4
Barracks La., Barn. 40 B3
High St.
Barratt Av. N22 75 F2
Barratt Ind. Pk., Sthl. 123 G2
Tudor Rd.
Barrenger Rd. N10 73 J1
Barrett Rd. E17 78 C4
Barrett St. W1 **16** **C4**
Barrett St. W1 110 A6
Barretts Grn. Rd. 107 E2
NW10
Barretts Gro. N16 94 B5
Barrhill Rd. SW2 169 E2
Barrie Est. W2 **14** **E5**
Barrie Ho. W3 126 B2
Barriedale SE14 153 H2
Barrier App. SE7 136 A3
Barrier Pt. Rd. E16 135 G3
North Woolwich Rd.
Barringer Sq. SW17 168 A4
Barrington Cl. NW5 92 A5
Barrington Cl., Ilf. 80 C1
Barrington Cl., Loug. 49 F4
Barrington Rd.
Barrington Grn., 49 F4
Loug.
Barrington Rd. E12 98 D6
Barrington Rd. N8 74 D5
Barrington Rd. SW9 151 H3
Barrington Rd., 158 D2
Bexh.
Barrington Rd., 49 F3
Loug.
Barrington Rd., Sutt. 198 D1
Barrington Vil. SE18 156 D1
Barrow Av., Cars. 199 J7
Barrow Cl. N21 59 H3
Barrow Hedges Cl., 199 H7
Cars.
Barrow Hedges Way, 199 H7
Cars.
Barrow Hill, Wor.Pk. 196 E2
Barrow Hill Cl., 196/197 E2
Wor.Pk.
Barrow Hill
Barrow Hill Rd. NW8 **7** **G2**
Barrow Hill Rd. NW8 109 H2
Barrow Pt. Av., Pnr. 66 E2
Barrow Pt. La., Pnr. 66 E2
Barrow Rd. SW16 168 D6
Barrow Rd., Croy. 201 G5
Barrow Wk., Brent. 125 F5
Glenhurst Rd.
Barrowdene Cl., 66/67 E2
Pnr.
Paines La.
Barrowell Grn. N21 59 H2
Barrowfield Cl. N9 61 E3
Barrowgate Rd. W4 126 C5
Barrs Rd. NW10 88 D7
Barry Av. N15 76 C6
Craven Pk. Rd.
Barry Av., Bexh. 138 E7
Barry Cl., Orp. 207 H3
Barry Rd. E6 116 B6
Barry Rd. NW10 88 C7

Barry Rd. SE22 152 D6
Barset Rd. SE15 153 F3
Barson Cl. SE20 171 F7
Barston Rd. SE27 169 J3
Barstow Cres. SW2 169 F1
Barter St. WC1 **18** **B2**
Barter St. WC1 111 E5
Barters Wk., Pnr. 66/67 E3
High St.
Barth Rd. SE18 137 H4
Bartholomew Cl. **19** **J2**
EC1
Bartholomew Cl. EC1 111 J5
Bartholomew Cl. 149 F4
SW18
Bartholomew La. **20** **C4**
EC2
Bartholomew Pl. EC1 **19** **J2**
Bartholomew Rd. 92 C6
NW5
Bartholomew Sq. 112/113 E4
E1
Coventry Rd.
Bartholomew Sq. **12** **A5**
EC1
Bartholomew Sq. 111 J4
EC1
Bartholomew St. **28** **B6**
SE1
Bartholomew St. SE1 132 A3
Bartholomew Vil. 92 C6
NW5
Bartle Av. E6 116 B2
Bartle Rd. W11 108 B6
Bartlett Cl. E14 114 A6
Bartlett Ct. EC4 **19** **F3**
Bartlett St., S.Croy. 202 A5
Bartletts Pas. EC4 **19** **F3**
Barton Av., Rom. 101 H1
Barton Cl. E6 116 C6
Barton Cl. E9 95 F5
Churchill Wk.
Barton Cl. NW4 71 G4
Barton Cl. SE15 152/153 E3
Kirkwood Rd.
Barton Cl., Bexh. 158 E5
Barton Cl., Chig. 65 F2
Barton Cl., N.Mal. 182 D2
Barton Meadows, Ilf. 81 F4
Barton Rd. W14 128 B5
Barton Rd., Sid. 177 E6
Barton St. SW1 **26** **A5**
Barton Way, Borwd. 38 A2
Bartonway NW8 109 G2
Queen's Ter.
Bartram Rd. SE4 153 H5
Barville Cl. SE4 153 H4
St. Norbert Rd.
Barwick Rd. E7 97 H4
Barwood Av., 204 B1
W.Wick.
Basden Gro., Felt. 161 G2
Basedale Rd., Dag. 100 B7
Baseing Cl. E6 116 D7
Bashley Rd. NW10 106 D4
Basil Av. E6 116 B2
Basil Gdns. SE27 169 J5
Basil Gdns., Croy. 203 G1
Primrose La.
Basil St. SW3 **23** **J5**
Basil St. SW3 129 J3
Basildene Rd., Houns. 142 D2
Basildon Av., Ilf. 80 D1
Basildon Rd. SE2 138 A5
Basilon Rd., Bexh. 158 E2
Basin S. E16 137 E1
Basing Cl., T.Ditt. 180 C7
Basing Ct. SE15 152 C1
Basing Dr., Bex. 159 F6
Basing Hill NW11 90 C1
Basing Hill, Wem. 87 J2
Basing Ho., Bark. 117 G1
St. Margarets
Basing Ho. Yd. E2 **13** **E3**
Basing Pl. E2 **12** **E3**
Basing St. W11 108 C6
Basing Way N3 72 E3
Basing Way, T.Ditt. 180 C7
Basingdon Way SE5 152 A4
Basingfield Rd., 180 C7
T.Ditt.
Basinghall Av. EC2 **20** **B2**
Basinghall Av. EC2 112 A5
Basinghall St. EC2 **20** **B3**
Basinghall St. EC2 111 J5
Basire St. N1 111 J1
Baskerville Rd. SW18 149 H7
Basket Gdns. SE9 156 B5
Baslow Cl., Har. 68 A1
Baslow Wk. E5 95 G4
Overbury St.
Basnett Rd. SW11 150 A3
Basque Ct. SE16 133 G2
Poolmans St.

Bassano St. SE22 152 C5
Bassant Rd. SE18 137 J6
Bassein Pk. Rd. W12 127 F2
Bassett Gdns., Islw. 123 J7
Bassett Ho., Dag. 118 B1
Bassett Rd. W10 108 A6
Bassett St. NW5 92 A6
Bassett Way, Grnf. 103 H6
Bassetts Cl., Orp. 206 E4
Bassetts Way, Orp. 206 E4
Bassingham Rd. 149 F7
 SW18
Bassingham Rd., 87 G6
 Wem.
Bassishaw Highwalk 111 J5
 EC2
 London Wall
Basswood Cl. 152/153 E3
 SE15
 Linden Gro.
Bastable Av., Bark. 117 H2
Bastion Highwalk 111 J5
 EC2
 London Wall
Bastion Rd. SE2 138 A5
Baston Manor Rd., 205 H3
 Brom.
Baston Rd., Brom. 205 H1
Bastwick St. EC1 11 J5
Bastwick St. EC1 111 J4
Basuto Rd. SW6 148 D1
Batavia Cl., Sun. 178 C1
Batavia Ms. SE14 133 H7
 Goodwood Rd.
Batavia Rd. SE14 133 H7
Batavia Rd., Sun. 178 B1
Batchelor St. N1 11 E1
Batchelor St. N1 111 G2
Bate St. E14 113 J7
 Three Colt St.
Bateman Cl., Bark. 99 F6
 Glenny Rd.
Bateman Ho. SE17 35 G6
Bateman Rd. E4 62 A6
Bateman St. W1 17 H4
Bateman's Bldgs. W1 17 H4
Bateman's Row EC2 12 E5
Bateman's Row EC2 112 B4
Bates Cres. SW16 168 C7
Bates Cres., Croy. 201 G5
Bateson St. SE18 137 H4
Bath Cl. SE15 132/133 E7
 Asylum Rd.
Bath Ct. EC1 11 E6
Bath Ho. Rd., Croy. 200 E1
Bath Pas., Kings.T. 181 G2
 St. James Rd.
Bath Pl. EC2 12 D4
Bath Pl., Barn. 40 C3
Bath Rd. E7 98 A6
Bath Rd. N9 61 E2
Bath Rd. W4 127 E4
Bath Rd., Hayes 141 F1
Bath Rd., Houns. 142 C1
Bath Rd., Mitch. 185 G3
Bath Rd., Rom. 82 E6
Bath Rd., West Dr. 140 A1
Bath St. EC1 12 A4
Bath St. EC1 112 A3
Bath Ter. SE1 27 J6
Bath Ter. SE1 131 J3
Bathgate Rd. SW19 166 A3
Baths Rd., Brom. 192 A4
Bathurst Av. 184/185 E1
 SW19
 Brisbane Av.
Bathurst Ms. W2 15 E5
Bathurst Rd., Ilf. 98 E1
Bathurst St. W2 15 E5
Bathurst St. W2 109 G7
Bathway SE18 136 D4
Batley Cl., Mitch. 185 J7
Batley Pl. N16 94 C3
Batley Rd. N16 94 C3
 Stoke Newington High St.
Batley Rd., Enf. 43 J1
Batman Cl. W12 127 H1
Batoum Gdns. W6 127 J3
Batson St. W12 127 G2
Batsworth Rd., Mitch. 185 G3
Batten Cl. E6 116 C6
 Savage Gdns.
Batten St. SW11 149 H3
Battenburg Wk. SE18 170 B5
 Brabourne Cl.
Battersby Rd. SE6 172 D2
Battersea Br. SW3 31 F7
Battersea Br. SW3 129 G7
Battersea Br. SW11 31 F7
Battersea Br. SW11 129 G7
Battersea Br. Rd. 129 H7
 SW11

Battersea Ch. Rd. 149 G1
 SW11
Battersea High St. 149 G1
 SW11
Battersea Pk. SW11 31 J7
Battersea Pk. SW11 129 J7
Battersea Pk. Rd. 150 B1
 SW8
Battersea Pk. Rd. 149 H2
 SW11
Battersea Ri. SW11 149 H5
Battersea Sq. SW11 149 G1
 Battersea High St.
Battersea Rd. SE28 137 H2
 Waterloo Ter.
Battishill Gdns. N1 93 H7
Battishill St. N1 93 H7
 Waterloo Ter.
Battle Br. La. SE1 28 D2
Battle Br. La. SE1 132 B1
Battle Br. Rd. NW1 10 A2
Battle Br. Rd. NW1 110 E2
Battle Cl. SW19 167 F6
 North Rd.
Battle Rd., Belv. 139 J4
Battle Rd., Erith 139 J4
Battledean Rd. N5 93 H5
Batty St. E1 21 J3
Batty St. E1 112 D6
Baudwin Rd. SE6 172 E2
Baugh Rd., Sid. 176 C5
Baulk, The SW18 148 D7
Bavant Rd. SW16 187 E2
Bavaria Rd. N19 92 E2
Bavdene Ms. NW4 71 H4
 The Burroughs
Bavent Rd. SE5 151 J2
Bawdale Rd. SE22 152 C5
Bawdsey Av., Ilf. 81 J4
Bawtree Rd. SE14 133 H7
Bawtry Rd. N20 57 J3
Baxendale N20 57 F2
Baxendale St. E2 13 H3
Baxendale St. E2 112 D3
Baxter Rd. E16 115 J6
Baxter Rd. N1 94 A6
Baxter Rd. N18 60 E4
Baxter Rd. NW10 106 E4
Baxter Rd., Ilf. 98 E5
Bay Ct. W5 125 H3
 Popes La.
Bay Tree Cl., Brom. 191 J1
Baycroft Cl., Pnr. 66 C3
Baydon Ct., Brom. 191 F3
Bayes Cl. SE26 171 F5
Bayfield Rd. SE9 156 A4
Bayford Ms. E8 94/95 E7
 Bayford St.
Bayford Rd. NW10 108 A3
Bayford St. E8 95 E7
Bayham Pl. NW1 9 F1
Bayham Pl. NW1 110 C1
Bayham Rd. W4 126 D3
Bayham Rd. W13 104 E7
Bayham Rd., Mord. 185 E4
Bayham St. NW1 110 C1
Bayley St. WC1 17 H2
Bayley St. WC1 110 D5
Bayley Wk. SE2 138/139 E5
 Woolwich Rd.
Baylin Rd. SW18 148/149 E6
 Garratt La.
Baylis Rd. SE1 27 E4
Baylis Rd. SE1 131 G2
Bayliss Av. SE28 118 D7
Bayliss Cl. N21 42/43 E5
 Macleod Rd.
Bayne Cl. E6 116 C6
 Savage Gdns.
Baynes Cl., Enf. 44 D2
Baynes Ms. NW3 91 G6
 Belsize La.
Baynes St. NW1 92 C7
Baynham Cl., Bex. 159 F6
Bayonne Rd. W6 128 B6
Bayshill Ri., Nthlt. 85 H6
Bayston Rd. N16 94 C3
Bayswater Rd. W2 15 F5
Bayswater Rd. W2 108 E7
Baythorne St. E3 113 J5
Baytree Cl., Sid. 175 J1
Baytree Rd. SW2 151 F4
Bazalgette Cl., N.Mal. 182 D5
Bazalgette Gdns., 182 D5
 N.Mal.
Bazely St. E14 114 C7
Bazile Rd. N21 43 G6
Beach Gro., Felt. 161 G2
Beacham Cl. SE7 136 A5
Beachborough Rd., 172 C4
 Brom.
Beachcroft Rd. E11 97 E3
Beachcroft Way N19 92 D1

Beachy Rd. E3 96 A7
Beacon Gate SE14 153 G3
Beacon Gro., Cars. 200 A4
Beacon Hill N7 92 E5
Beacon Rd. SE13 154 D6
Beacon Rd., Houns. 140 D6
Beacon Rd. 140 E6
 Roundabout, Houns.
Beacons Cl. E6 116 B5
 Oliver Gdns.
Beaconsfield Cl. N11 58 A4
Beaconsfield Cl. SE3 135 G6
Beaconsfield Cl. W4 126 C5
Beaconsfield Par. 174 B4
 SE9
 Beaconsfield Rd.
Beaconsfield Rd. E10 96 C2
Beaconsfield Rd. 115 F4
 E16
Beaconsfield Rd. E17 77 J6
Beaconsfield Rd. N9 60 D4
Beaconsfield Rd. N11 58 A3
Beaconsfield Rd. N15 76 B4
Beaconsfield Rd. 89 F6
 NW10
Beaconsfield Rd. SE3 135 F7
Beaconsfield Rd. SE9 174 B2
Beaconsfield Rd. 36 C4
 SE17
Beaconsfield Rd. 132 A5
 SE17
Beaconsfield Rd. W4 126 D3
Beaconsfield Rd. W5 125 F2
Beaconsfield Rd., 192 A3
 Brom.
Beaconsfield Rd., 188 A6
 Croy.
Beaconsfield Rd., 194 B7
 Esher
Beaconsfield Rd., 122 C1
 Hayes
Beaconsfield Rd. 182 D2
 N.Mal.
Beaconsfield Rd., 122 D1
 Sthl.
Beaconsfield Rd., 181 J7
 Surb.
Beaconsfield Rd., 144 E6
 Twick.
Beaconsfield Ter., 82 D6
 Rom.
Beaconsfield Ter. Rd. 128 B3
 W14
Beaconsfield Wk. E6 116 D6
 East Ham Manor Way
Beaconsfield Wk. 148 C1
 SW6
Beacontree Av. E17 78 D1
Beacontree Rd. E11 79 F7
Beadlow Cl., Cars. 185 G6
 Olveston Wk.
Beadman Pl. SE27 169 H4
 Norwood High St.
Beadman St. SE27 169 H4
Beadnell Rd. SE23 171 G1
Beadon Rd. W6 127 J4
Beadon Rd., Brom. 191 G4
Beaford Gro. SW20 184 B3
Beagle Cl., Felt. 160 B4
Beak St. W1 17 G5
Beak St. W1 110 C7
Beal Cl., Well. 158 A1
Beal Rd., Ilf. 98 D2
Beale Cl. N13 59 H5
Beale Pl. E3 113 J2
Beale Rd. E3 113 J1
Beam Av., Dag. 119 H1
Beaminster Gdns., 80 E2
 Ilf.
Beamish Dr., Bushey 51 J1
Beamish Rd. N9 60 D1
Bean Rd., Bexh. 158 D4
Beanacre Cl. E9 95 J6
Beanshaw SE9 174 D4
Beansland Gro., Rom. 83 E2
Bear All. EC4 19 G3
Bear Cl., Rom. 83 H6
Bear Gdns. SE1 27 J1
Bear Gdns. SE1 131 J1
Bear La. SE1 27 H1
Bear La. SE1 131 H1
Beard Rd., Kings.T. 163 J5
Beardell St. SE19 170 C6
Beardow Gro. N14 42 C6
Beard's Hill, Hmptn. 179 G1
Beard's Hill Cl., 179 G1
 Hmptn.
 Beard's Hill
Beardsfield E13 115 G1
 Valetta Rd.
Beardsley Ter., Dag. 100 B5
 Fitzstephen Rd.

Beardsley Way W3 126 D2
Bearfield Rd., 163 H7
 Kings.T.
Bearstead Ri. SE4 153 J5
Bearstead Ter., Beck. 190 A1
 Copers Cope Rd.
Beatrice Av. SW16 187 F3
Beatrice Av., Wem. 87 H5
Beatrice Cl. E13 115 G4
 Chargeable La.
Beatrice Cl., Pnr. 66 A4
Beatrice Cl., Pnr. 66 A4
 Reid Cl.
Beatrice Ct., Buck.H. 64 A2
Beatrice Pl. W8 22 A6
Beatrice Pl. W8 128 E3
Beatrice Rd. E17 78 A5
Beatrice Rd. N4 75 G7
Beatrice Rd. N9 45 F7
Beatrice Rd. SE1 37 J2
Beatrice Rd. SE1 132 D4
Beatrice Rd., Rich. 145 J5
 Albert Rd.
Beatrice Rd., Sthl. 123 F1
Beatson Wk. SE16 133 H1
Beattock Ri. N10 74 B4
Beatty Rd. N16 94 B4
Beatty Rd., Stan. 53 F6
Beatty St. NW1 9 F1
Beatty St. NW1 110 C2
Beattyville Gdns., Ilf. 80 D3
Beauchamp Cl. W4 126 C3
 Church Path
Beauchamp Ct., Stan. 53 F5
 Hardwick Cl.
Beauchamp Pl. SW3 23 H5
Beauchamp Pl. SW3 129 H3
Beauchamp Rd. E7 97 H7
Beauchamp Rd. SE19 188 A1
Beauchamp Rd. 149 H4
 SW11
Beauchamp Rd. 179 H5
 E.Mol.
Beauchamp Rd., Sutt. 198 D5
Beauchamp Rd. 144 D7
 Twick.
Beauchamp Rd. 179 H5
 W.Mol.
Beauchamp St. EC1 19 E2
Beauchamp Ter. 147 H3
 SW15
 Dryburgh Rd.
Beauclerc Rd. W6 127 H3
Beauclerk Cl., Felt. 160 B1
 Florence Rd.
Beaudesert Ms., 120 B2
 West Dr.
Beaufort E6 116 D5
 Newark Knok
Beaufort Av., Har. 68 D4
Beaufort Cl. E4 62 B6
 Higham Sta. Av.
Beaufort Cl. SW15 147 H7
Beaufort Cl. W5 105 J5
Beaufort Cl., Rom. 83 J4
Beaufort Cl., Rich. 163 F4
 Beaufort Rd.
Beaufort Dr. NW11 72 D4
Beaufort Gdns. NW4 71 J6
Beaufort Gdns. SW3 23 H5
Beaufort Gdns. SW3 129 H3
Beaufort Gdns. SW16 169 F7
Beaufort Gdns., 143 E1
 Houns.
Beaufort Gdns., Ilf. 98 D1
Beaufort Ms. SW6 128 C6
 Lillie Rd.
Beaufort Rd. W5 105 J5
Beaufort Rd., Kings.T. 181 H4
Beaufort Rd., Rich. 163 F4
Beaufort Rd., Twick. 145 F7
Beaufort St. SW3 31 F6
Beaufort St. SW3 129 G6
Beaufort Way, Epsom 197 G7
Beaufoy Rd. N17 60 B7
Beaufoy Wk. SE11 34 D2
Beaufoy Wk. SE11 131 F4
Beaulieu Av. E16 135 H1
Beaulieu Av. SE26 170 E4
Beaulieu Cl. NW9 71 E4
Beaulieu Cl. SE5 152 A3
Beaulieu Cl., Houns. 143 F5
Beaulieu Cl., Mitch. 186 A1
Beaulieu Cl., Twick. 145 G7
Beaulieu Cl., Wat. 50 C1
Beaulieu Dr., Pnr. 66 D6
Beaulieu Gdns. N21 43 J7
Beaulieu Pl. W4 126 C3
 Rothschild Rd.
Beaumanor Gdns. 174 D4
 SE9
Beaumaris Dr., 64 A7
 Wdf.Grn.
Beaumont Av. W14 128 C5

Name	Page	Grid
Beaumont Av., Har.	67	H6
Beaumont Av., Rich.	145	J3
Beaumont Av., Wem.	87	F5
Beaumont Cl., Kings.T.	164	A7
Beaumont Cres. W14	128	C5
Beaumont Gdns. NW3	90	D3
Beaumont Gro. E1	113	G4
Beaumont Ms. W1	**16**	**C1**
Beaumont Pl. W1	**9**	**G5**
Beaumont Pl. W1	110	C4
Beaumont Pl., Barn.	40	C1
Beaumont Pl., Islw.	144	C5
Beaumont Ri. N19	92	D1
Beaumont Rd. E10	78	B7
Beaumont Rd. E13	115	H3
Beaumont Rd. SE19	169	J6
Beaumont Rd. SW19	148	B7
Beaumont Rd. W4	126	C3
Beaumont Rd., Orp.	193	G6
Beaumont Sq. E1	113	G4
Beaumont St. W1	**16**	**C1**
Beaumont St. W1	110	A5
Beaumont Wk. NW3	91	J7
Beauvais Ter., Nthlt.	102	D3
Beauval Rd. SE22	152	C6
Beaver Cl. SE20	170	D7
Lullington Rd.		
Beaver Cl., Hmptn.	179	H1
Beaver Gro., Nthlt.	102/103	E3
Jetstar Way		
Beaverbank Rd. SE9	175	G1
Beavers Cres., Houns.	142	C4
Beavers La., Houns.	142	C3
Beavers La. Camp, Houns.	142	C3
Beavers La.		
Beaverwood Rd., Chis.	175	H6
Beavor Gro. W6	127	G4
Beavor La.		
Beavor La. W6	127	G4
Bebbington Rd. SE18	137	H4
Bebletts Cl., Orp.	207	J5
Bec Cl., Ruis.	84	D3
Beccles Dr., Bark.	99	H6
Beccles St. E14	113	J7
Beck Cl. SE13	154	B1
Beck Ct., Beck.	189	G3
Beck La., Beck.	189	G3
Beck River Pk., Beck.	190	A1
Rectory Rd.		
Beck Rd. E8	112	E1
Beck Way, Beck.	189	J3
Beckenham Business Cen., Beck.	171	H6
Beckenham Gdns. N9	60	B3
Beckenham Gro., Brom.	190	D2
Beckenham Hill Rd. SE6	172	B5
Beckenham Hill Rd., Beck.	172	B5
Beckenham La., Brom.	191	E2
Beckenham Pl. Pk., Beck.	172	B7
Beckenham Rd., Beck.	189	G1
Beckenham Rd., W.Wick.	190	B7
Beckers, The N16	94	D3
Rectory Rd.		
Becket Av. E6	116	D3
Becket Cl. SE25	188	D6
Becket Fold, Har.	68	C5
Courtfield Cres.		
Becket Rd. N18	61	F4
Becket St. SE1	**28**	**B5**
Beckett Cl. NW10	88	D6
Beckett Cl. SW16	168	D2
Beckett Cl., Belv.	138/139	E3
Tunstock Way		
Beckett Wk., Beck.	171	H6
Becketts Cl., Felt.	142	B6
Becketts Cl., Orp.	207	J3
Becketts, Kings.T.	181	G1
Beckford Dr., Orp.	193	G7
Beckford Pl. SE17	**36**	**A4**
Beckford Rd., Croy.	188	C6
Becklow Gdns. W12	127	G2
Becklow Rd.		
Becklow Ms. W12	127	F2
Becklow Rd.		
Becklow Rd. W12	127	G2
Becks Rd., Sid.	176	A3
Beckton Rd. Roundabout E16	116	C7
Royal Albert Way		
Beckton Rd. E16	115	F5
Beckway Rd. SW16	186	D2
Beckway St. SE17	**36**	**C2**
Beckway St. SE17	132	A4
Beckwith Rd. SE24	152	A6
Beclands Rd. SW17	168	A6
Becmead Av. SW16	168	D4
Becmead Av., Har.	68	E5
Becondale Rd. SE19	170	B5
Bective Pl. SW15	148	C4
Bective Rd.		
Bective Rd. E7	97	G4
Bective Rd. SW15	148	C4
Becton Pl., Erith	139	H7
Bedale St. SE1	**28**	**B2**
Bedale St. SE1	132	A1
Beddington Cross, Croy.	186/187	E7
Beddington Fm. Rd.		
Beddington Fm. Rd., Croy.	200	E1
Beddington Gdns., Cars.	200	A6
Beddington Gdns., Wall.	200	B6
Beddington Grn., Orp.	193	J1
Beddington Gro., Wall.	200	D5
Beddington La., Croy.	186	C5
Beddington Path, Orp.	193	J1
Beddington Rd., Ilf.	81	J7
Beddington Rd., Orp.	193	H2
Beddington Trd. Pk. W., Croy.	200	E1
Bede Cl., Pnr.	66	D1
Bede Rd., Rom.	82	C6
Bedenham Way SE15	**37**	**F7**
Bedens Rd., Sid.	176	E6
Bedfont Cl., Felt.	141	F6
Bedfont Cl., Mitch.	186	A2
Bedfont La., Felt.	141	J7
Bedfont Rd., Stai.	140	B6
Bedford Av. WC1	**17**	**J2**
Bedford Av. WC1	110	D5
Bedford Av., Barn.	40	C5
Bedford Av., Hayes	102	B6
Bedford Cl. N10	58	A7
Bedford Cl. W4	127	E6
Bedford Cor. W4	126/127	E4
The Av.		
Bedford Ct. WC2	**18**	**A6**
Bedford Gdns. W8	128	D1
Bedford Hill SW12	168	B1
Bedford Hill SW16	168	B1
Bedford Ho. SW4	150	D4
Bedford Ms. N2	73	H3
Bedford Pk., Croy.	201	J1
Bedford Pk. Cor. W4	126/127	E4
Bath Rd.		
Bedford Pas. SW6	128	B7
Dawes Rd.		
Bedford Pl. W1	**17**	**G1**
Bedford Pl. WC1	**18**	**A1**
Bedford Pl. WC1	110	E5
Bedford Pl., Croy.	202	A1
Bedford Rd. E6	116	D1
Bedford Rd. E17	78	A2
Bedford Rd. E18	79	G2
Bedford Rd. N2	73	H3
Bedford Rd. N8	74	D6
Bedford Rd. N9	44	E7
Bedford Rd. N15	76	B4
Bedford Rd. N22	74	E1
Bedford Rd. NW7	54	E3
Bedford Rd. SW4	150	E3
Bedford Rd. W4	126	D3
Bedford Rd. W13	104	E7
Bedford Rd., Har.	67	J6
Bedford Rd., Ilf.	99	E3
Bedford Rd., Sid.	175	H3
Bedford Rd., Twick.	162	A3
Bedford Rd., Wor.Pk.	197	J2
Bedford Row WC1	**18**	**D1**
Bedford Row WC1	111	F5
Bedford Sq. WC1	**17**	**J2**
Bedford Sq. WC1	110	D5
Bedford St. WC2	**18**	**A5**
Bedford St. WC2	111	E7
Bedford Ter. SW2	150/151	E5
Lyham Rd.		
Bedford Way WC1	**9**	**J6**
Bedford Way WC1	110	D4
Bedfordbury WC2	**18**	**A5**
Bedgebury Gdns. SW19	166	B2
Bedgebury Rd. SE9	156	A4
Bedivere Rd., Brom.	173	G3
Bedlow Way, Croy.	201	F4
Bedonwell Rd. SE2	138	E6
Bedonwell Rd., Belv.	139	G6
Bedonwell Rd., Bexh.	139	G6
Bedser Cl. SE11	**34**	**D5**
Bedser Cl., Th.Hth.	187	J3
Bedser Dr., Grnf.	86	A5
Bedster Gdns., W.Mol.	179	H2
Bedwardine Rd. SE19	170	B7
Bedwell Gdns., Hayes	121	H5
Bedwell Rd. N17	76	B1
Bedwell Rd., Belv.	139	G5
Beeby Rd. E16	115	H5
Beech Av. N20	57	H1
Beech Av. W3	126	E1
Beech Av., Brent.	125	E7
Beech Av., Buck.H.	63	H2
Beech Av., Ruis.	84	B1
Beech Av., Sid.	158	A7
Beech Cl. N9	44	D6
Beech Cl. SE8	133	J6
Clyde St.		
Beech Cl. SW15	147	G7
Beech Cl. SW19	165	A6
Beech Cl., Cars.	199	J2
Beech Cl., Loug.	48/49	E2
Cedar Dr.		
Beech Cl., Stai.	140	A7
St. Mary's Cres.		
Beech Cl., Sun.	178	D2
Harfield Rd.		
Beech Cl., West Dr.	120	D3
Beech Copse, Brom.	192	C2
Beech Copse, S.Croy.	202	B5
Beech Ct. E17	78	D3
Beech Ct. SE9	156	B6
Beech Ct., Ilf.	98	D3
Riverdene Rd.		
Beech Ct., Surb.	181	H7
Beech Dell, Kes.	206	C4
Beech Dr. N2	73	J3
Beech Gdns. EC2	111	J5
Aldersgate St.		
Beech Gdns. W5	125	H2
Beech Gdns., Dag.	101	H7
Beech Gro., Ilf.	65	H6
Beech Gro., Mitch.	186	D4
Beech Gro., N.Mal.	182	D3
Beech Hall Cres. E4	62	D7
Beech Hall Rd. E4	62	C7
Beech Hill Av., Barn.	41	F1
Beech Ho., Croy.	204	B6
Beech Ho. Rd., Croy.	202	A3
Beech La., Buck.H.	63	H2
Beech Lawns N12	57	G5
Beech N11	59	E6
Beech Rd. SW16	187	E2
Beech Rd., Felt.	141	H7
Beech Row, Rich.	163	H4
Beech St. EC2	**19**	**J1**
Beech St. EC2	111	J5
Beech St., Rom.	83	J4
Beech Tree Cl. Stan.	53	F5
Beech Tree Glade E4	63	F1
Forest Side		
Beech Tree Pl., Sutt.	198/199	E5
St. Nicholas Way		
Beech Wk. NW7	54	E6
Beech Way, Twick.	161	G3
Beechcroft Av. NW11	72	C7
Beechcroft Av., Har.	67	G7
Beechcroft Av., N.Mal.	182	C1
Beechcroft Av., Sthl.	123	F1
Beechcroft Cl., Houns.	122	E7
Beechcroft Cl., Orp.	207	G4
Beechcroft Gdns., Wem.	93	J7
Beechcroft Rd. E18	79	H2
Beechcroft Rd. SW14	146	C3
Elm Rd.		
Beechcroft Rd. SW17	167	H2
Beechcroft Rd., Chess.	195	J3
Beechcroft Rd., Orp.	207	G4
Beechdale N21	59	F2
Beechdale Rd. SW2	151	F6
Beechen Cliff Way, Islw.	144	C1
Henley Cl.		
Beechen Gro., Pnr.	67	F3
Beeches, The, Houns.	143	H1
Beeches Av., Cars.	199	H5
Beeches Cl. SE20	189	F1
Genoa Rd.		
Beeches Ct., Brom.	173	G6
Avondale Rd.		
Beeches Rd. SW17	167	H3
Beeches Rd., Sutt.	198	B1
Beechfield Cotts., Brom.	191	J2
Widmore Rd.		
Beechfield Gdns., Rom.	83	J7
Beechfield Rd. N4	75	J6
Beechfield Rd. SE6	171	J1
Beechfield Rd., Brom.	191	J2
Beechhill Rd. SE9	156	D5
Beechmont Cl., Brom.	172	E5
Beechmore Gdns., Sutt.	198	A2
Beechmore Rd. SW11	149	J1
Beechmount Av. W7	104	A5
Beecholme Av., Mitch.	186	B1
Beecholme Est. E5	94/95	E3
Prout Rd.		
Beechvale Cl. N12	57	H5
Beechway, Bex.	158	D6
Beechwood Av. N3	72	C3
Beechwood Av., Grnf.	103	H3
Beechwood Av., Har.	85	H3
Beechwood Av., Orp.	207	H5
Beechwood Av., Rich.	146	A1
Beechwood Av., Sun.	160	A6
Beechwood Av., Th.Hth.	187	H4
Beechwood Circle, Har.	85	H3
Beechwood Gdns.		
Beechwood Cl. NW7	54	D5
Beechwood Cl., Surb.	181	F7
Beechwood Ct., Cars.	199	J4
Beechwood Ct., Sun.	160	A6
Beechwood Cres., Bexh.	158	D3
Beechwood Dr., Kes.	206	A4
Beechwood Dr., Wdf.Grn.	63	F5
Beechwood Gdns. NW10	105	J3
St. Annes Gdns.		
Beechwood Gdns., Ilf.	80	C5
Beechwood Gro. W3	106/107	E7
East Acton La.		
Beechwood Gro., Surb.	181	F7
Beechwood Ms. N9	60	D2
Beechwood Pk. E18	79	G3
Beechwood Ri., Chis.	175	E4
Beechwood Rd. E8	94	C6
Beechwood Rd. N8	74	D4
Beechwoods Ct. SE19	170	C5
Crystal Palace Par.		
Beechworth Cl. NW3	90	D2
Beecroft Rd. SE4	153	H5
Beehive Cl. E8	94	C7
Beehive La., Ilf.	80	C6
Beehive Pas. EC3	**20**	**D4**
Beehive Pl. SW9	151	G3
Beeken Dene, Orp.	207	F4
Isabella Dr.		
Beeleigh Rd., Mord.	185	E4
Beeston Cl. E8	94	D5
Ferncliff Rd.		
Beeston Pl. SW1	**24**	**E6**
Beeston Rd., Barn.	41	G6
Beeston Way, Felt.	142	C6
Beethoven St. W10	108	B3
Beeton Cl., Pnr.	51	G7
Begbie Rd. SE3	155	J1
Beggars Hill, Epsom	197	F7
Beggars Roost La., Sutt.	198	D6
Begonia Cl. E6	116	B5
Begonia Pl., Hmptn.	161	G6
Gresham Rd.		
Begonia Wk. W12	107	F6
Du Cane Rd.		
Beira St. SW12	150	B7
Bekesbourne St. E14	113	H6
Ratcliffe La.		
Belcroft Cl., Brom.	173	F7
Hope Pk.		
Beldham Gdns., W.Mol.	179	H3
Belfairs Dr., Rom.	82	C7
Belfairs Grn., Wat.	50	D5
Heysham Dr.		

Belfast Rd. N16 94 C2
Belfast Rd. SE25 188 E4
Belfont Wk. N7 93 E4
Belford Gro. SE18 136 D4
Belfort Rd. SE15 153 F2
Belfry Cl. SE16 132/133 E5
Masters Dr.
Belgrade Rd. N16 94 B4
Belgrade Rd., Hmptn. 179 H1
Belgrave Cl. N14 42 C5
Prince George Av.
Belgrave Cl. NW7 54 D5
Belgrave Cl. W3 126 C2
Avenue Rd.
Belgrave Cres., Sun. 178 B1
Belgrave Gdns. N14 42 D5
Belgrave Gdns. NW8 109 E1
Belgrave Gdns., Stan. 53 F5
Copley Rd.
Belgrave Ms. N. SW1 24 B4
Belgrave Ms. N. SW1 130 A3
Belgrave Ms. S. SW1 24 C5
Belgrave Ms. S. SW1 130 A3
Belgrave Ms. W. **24 B5**
SW1
Belgrave Ms. W. 130 A3
SW1
Belgrave Pl. SW1 24 C5
Belgrave Pl. SW1 130 A3
Belgrave Rd. E10 96 C1
Belgrave Rd. E11 97 G2
Belgrave Rd. E13 115 J4
Belgrave Rd. E17 78 A5
Belgrave Rd. SE25 188 C4
Belgrave Rd. SW1 33 F2
Belgrave Rd. SW1 130 B4
Belgrave Rd. SW13 127 F7
Belgrave Rd., 143 F3
Houns.
Belgrave Rd., Ilf. 98 C1
Belgrave Rd., Mitch. 185 G3
Belgrave Rd., Sun. 178 B1
Belgrave Sq. SW1 24 B5
Belgrave Sq. SW1 130 A3
Belgrave St. E1 113 G6
Belgrave Ter., 63 G3
Wdf.Grn.
Belgrave Wk., Mitch. 185 G3
Belgrave Yd. SW1 24 D6
Belgravia Cl., Barn. 40 C3
Belgravia Gdns., 172 E6
Brom.
Belgravia Ho. SW4 150 E6
Belgravia Ms., 181 G4
Kings.T.
Belgrove St. WC1 10 A3
Belgrove St. WC1 111 E3
Belham Wk. SE5 152 A1
D'Eynsford Rd.
Belinda Rd. SW9 151 H3
Belitha Vil. N1 93 F7
Bell Av., West Dr. 120 C4
Bell Cl., Pnr. 66 C3
Bell Cl., Surb. 196 B2
Barnsbury La.
Bell Dr. SW18 148 B7
Bell Fm. Av., Dag. 101 J3
Bell Gdns. E10 96 A1
Church Rd.
Bell Gdns. E17 77 J5
Markhouse Rd.
Bell Grn. SE26 171 J3
Bell Grn. La. SE26 171 H5
Bell Hill, Croy. 201 J3
Surrey St.
Bell Ho. Rd., Rom. 101 J1
Bell Inn Yd. EC3 20 C4
Bell La. E1 21 F2
Bell La. E1 112 C5
Bell La. E16 135 G1
Bell La. NW4 72 A4
Bell La., Twick. 162 D1
The Embk.
Bell La., Wem. 87 G2
Magnet Rd.
Bell Meadow SE19 170 B4
Dulwich Wd. Av.
Bell Rd., E.Mol. 180 A5
Bell Rd., Enf. 44 A1
Bell Rd., Houns. 143 H4
Bell St. NW1 15 G1
Bell St. NW1 109 H5
Bell Water Gate SE18 136 D3
Bell Wf. La. EC4 20 A5
Bell Wf. La. EC4 111 J7
Bell Yd. WC2 18 E3
Bell Yd. WC2 111 G6
Bellamy Cl. E14 134 A2
Byng St.
Bellamy Cl. W14 128 C5
Aisgill Av.
Bellamy Dr., Edg. 54 C3
Bellamy Dr., Stan. 68 E1
Bellamy Rd. E4 62 B6

Bellamy Rd., Enf. 44 A2
Bellamy St. SW12 150 B7
Bellasis Av. SW2 168 E2
Bellclose Rd., 120 B2
West Dr.
Belle Vue, Grnf. 104 A1
Belle Vue Est. NW4 71 J4
Bell La.
Belle Vue La., Bushey 52 A1
Belle Vue Pk., Th.Hth. 187 J3
Belle Vue Rd. E17 78 D2
Belle Vue Rd. W13 94 C1
Bell La.
Bellefields Rd. SW9 151 F3
Bellegrove Cl., Well. 157 J2
Bellegrove Par., Well. 157 J3
Bellegrove Rd.
Bellegrove Rd., Well. 157 G2
Bellenden Rd. SE15 152 C2
Bellestaines 62 A2
Pleasaunce E4
Belleville Rd. SW11 149 J5
Bellevue Ms. N11 58 A5
Bellevue Rd.
Bellevue Par. SW17 167 H1
Bellevue Rd.
Bellevue Pl. E1 113 F4
Bellevue Rd. N11 58 A4
Bellevue Rd. SW13 147 G2
Bellevue Rd. SW17 167 H1
Bellevue Rd. W13 104 E4
Bellevue Rd., Bexh. 159 F5
Bellevue Rd., 181 H3
Kings.T.
Bellevue St. SW17 167 F3
Bellfield Av., Har. 52 A6
Bellflower Cl. E6 116 B5
Sorrel Gdns.
Bellgate Ms. NW5 92 B3
York Ri.
Bellingham Ct., Bark. 118 B3
Renwick Rd.
Bellingham Grn. 172 A3
SE6
Bellingham Rd. SE6 172 B3
Bello Cl. SE24 151 H7
Bellot Gdns. SE10 135 E5
Bellot St. SE10 135 E5
Bellring Cl., Belv. 139 G6
Bells All. SW6 148 D2
Bells Gdn. Est. SE15 132 D7
Buller Cl.
Bells Hill, Barn. 40 A5
Belltrees Gro. SW16 169 F5
Bellwood Rd. SE15 153 G4
Belmarsh Rd. SE28 137 H2
Western Way
Belmont Av. N9 60 D1
Belmont Av. N13 59 E5
Belmont Av. N17 75 J3
Belmont Av., Barn. 41 J5
Belmont Av., N.Mal. 183 G5
Belmont Av., Sthl. 122 E3
Belmont Av., Well. 157 H3
Belmont Av., Wem. 105 J1
Belmont Circle, Har. 68 E1
Belmont Cl. E4 62 D5
Belmont Cl. N20 56 E1
Belmont Cl. SW4 150 C3
Belmont Cl., Barn. 41 J4
Belmont Cl., Wdf.Grn. 63 H4
Belmont Cl. NW11 72 C5
Belmont Gro. SE13 154 D3
Belmont Gro. W4 126 D4
Belmont Rd.
Belmont Hall Ct. 154 D3
SE13
Belmont Gro.
Belmont Hill SE13 154 D3
Belmont La., Chis. 175 F5
Belmont La., Stan. 53 F7
Belmont Ms. SW19 166 A2
Chapman Sq.
Belmont Pk. SE13 154 D4
Belmont Pk. Cl. SE13 154 D4
Belmont Pk.
Belmont Pk. Rd. E10 78 B6
Belmont Rd. N15 75 J4
Belmont Rd. N17 75 J4
Belmont Rd. SE25 189 E5
Belmont Rd. SW4 150 C3
Belmont Rd. W4 126 D4
Belmont Rd., Beck. 189 J2
Belmont Rd., Chis. 175 E5
Belmont Rd., Erith 139 G7
Belmont Rd., Har. 68 C3
Belmont Rd., Ilf. 99 F3
Belmont Rd., Twick. 162 A2
Belmont Rd., Wall. 200 B5
Belmont St. NW1 92 A7
Belmont Ter. W4 126 D4
Belmont Rd.
Belmor, Borwd. 38 A5
Belmore Av., Hayes 102 A6

Belmore La. N7 92 D5
Belmore St. SW8 150 D1
Beloe Cl. SW15 147 G3
Belper Ct. E5 95 G4
Pedro St.
Belsham St. E9 95 F6
Belsize Av. N13 59 F6
Belsize Av. NW3 91 H6
Belsize Av. W13 125 E3
Belsize Ct. NW3 91 H5
Belsize La.
Belsize Cres. NW3 91 G5
Belsize Gdns., Sutt. 199 E4
Belsize Gro. NW3 91 H6
Belsize La. NW3 91 G6
Belsize Ms. NW3 91 G6
Belsize La.
Belsize Pk. NW3 91 G6
Belsize Pk. Gdns. 91 H6
NW3
Belsize Pk. Ms. NW3 91 G6
Belsize La.
Belsize Pl. NW3 91 G6
Belsize La.
Belsize Rd. NW6 91 F7
Belsize Rd., Har. 52 A7
Belsize Sq. NW3 91 G6
Belsize Ter. NW3 91 G6
Belson Rd. SE18 136 C4
Beltane Dr. SW19 166 A3
Belthorn Cres. SW12 150 C7
Belton Rd. E7 97 H7
Belton Rd. E11 96 E4
Belton Rd. N17 76 B3
Belton Rd. NW2 89 G6
Belton Rd., Sid. 176 A4
Belton Way E3 114 A5
Beltran Rd. SW6 148 E2
Beltwood Rd., Belv. 139 J4
Belvedere Av. SW19 166 B5
Belvedere Av., Ilf. 80 E2
Belvedere Bldgs. **27 H4**
SE1
Belvedere Cl., Tedd. 162 B5
Belvedere Ct. N2 73 G5
Belvedere Dr. SW19 166 B5
Belvedere Gdns., 179 F5
W.Mol.
Belvedere Gro. SW19 166 B5
Belvedere Ho., Felt. 160 A1
Belvedere Ind. Est., 139 J3
Belv.
Belvedere Ms. SE15 153 E3
Belvedere Pl. SE1 **27 H4**
Belvedere Pl. SE1 131 H2
Belvedere Rd. E10 95 H1
Belvedere Rd. SE1 **26 D3**
Belvedere Rd. SE1 131 F1
Belvedere Rd. SE2 138 D1
Belvedere Rd. SE19 170 C7
Belvedere Rd. W7 124 C3
Belvedere Rd., Bexh. 159 F3
Belvedere Sq. SW19 166 B5
Belvedere Strand 71 F2
NW9
Belvedere Way, Har. 69 H6
Belvoir Cl. SE9 174 B3
Belvoir Rd. SE22 152 D7
Belvue Cl., Nthlt. 85 G7
Belvue Rd., Nthlt. 85 G7
Bembridge Cl. NW6 90 B7
Bemerton Est. N1 93 F7
Bemerton St. N1 111 F1
Bemish Rd. SW15 148 A3
Bempton Dr., Ruis. 84 B2
Bemsted Rd. E17 77 J3
Ben Hale Cl., Stan. 52 E4
Ben Jonson Rd. E1 113 H5
Ben Smith Way **29 J5**
SE16
Ben Tillett Cl., Bark. 100 A7
Ben Tillett Cl. E16 136 C1
Newland St.
Benares Rd. SE18 137 J4
Benbow Rd. W6 127 H3
Benbow St. SE8 134 A6
Benbury Cl., Brom. 172 C5
Bench Fld., S.Croy. 202 C6
Bencroft Rd. SW16 168 C7
Bencurtis Pk., 204 D3
W.Wick.
Bendall Ms. NW1 **15 H1**
Bendemeer Rd. 148 A3
SW15
Bendish Rd. E6 98 B7
Bendmore Av. SE2 138 A5
Bendon Valley SW18 148 E7
Benedict Cl., 138/139 E3
Belv.
Tunstock Way
Benedict Cl., Orp. 207 H3
Benedict Dr., Felt. 141 G7
Benedict Rd. SW9 151 F3
Benedict Rd., Mitch. 185 G3

Benedict Way N2 73 F3
Benenden Grn., 191 G5
Brom.
Benett Gdns. SW16 186 E2
Benfleet Cl., Sutt. 199 F3
Bengal Ct. EC3 112 A6
Birchin La.
Bengal Rd., Ilf. 98 E4
Bengarth Dr., Har. 68 A2
Bengarth Rd., Nthlt. 102 D1
Bengeworth Rd. SE5 151 J3
Bengeworth Rd., 86 D2
Har.
Benham Cl. SW11 149 G3
Benham Cl., Chess. 195 F6
Merritt Gdns.
Benham Gdns., 143 F7
Houns.
Benham Rd. W7 104 B5
Benhams Pl. NW3 91 F4
Holly Wk.
Benhill Av., Sutt. 199 E4
Benhill Rd. SE5 132 A7
Benhill Rd., Sutt. 199 F3
Benhill Wd. Rd., Sutt. 199 F3
Benhilton Gdns., 199 E3
Sutt.
Benhurst Ct. SW16 169 G5
Benhurst La. SW16 169 G5
Benin St. SE13 154 D7
Benjafield Cl. N18 60/61 E4
Brettenham Rd.
Benjamin Cl. E8 112 D1
Benjamin St. EC1 **19 G1**
Benjamin St. EC1 111 H5
Benledi St. E14 114 D6
Benn St. E9 95 H6
Bennerley Rd. SW11 149 H5
Bennet's Hill EC4 **19 H5**
Bennetsfield Rd., 120 E1
Uxb.
Bennett Cl., Kings.T. 181 F1
Bennett Cl., Well. 158 A2
Bennett Gro. SE13 154 B1
Bennett Pk. SE3 155 F3
Bennett Rd. E13 115 J4
Bennett Rd. N16 94 B4
Bennett Rd., Rom. 83 E6
Bennett St. SW1 **25 F1**
Bennett St. W4 127 E6
Bennetts Av., Croy. 203 H2
Bennetts Av., Grnf. 104 B1
Bennetts Castle La., 100 C4
Dag.
Bennetts Cl. N17 60 C6
Bennetts Cl., Mitch. 186 B1
Bennetts Copse, Chis. 174 B6
Bennetts Way, Croy. 203 H2
Bennetts Yd. SW1 **25 J6**
Benningholme Rd., 54 E6
Edg.
Bennington Rd. N17 76 B1
Bennington Rd., 62 E7
Wdf.Grn.
Benn's Wk., Rich. 145 H4
Rosedale Rd.
Benrek Cl., Ilf. 81 F1
Bensbury Cl. SW15 147 H7
Bensham Cl., 187 J4
Th.Hth.
Bensham Gro., 187 J2
Th.Hth.
Bensham La., Croy. 187 H7
Bensham La., Th.Hth. 187 H4
Bensham Manor Rd., 187 J4
Th.Hth.
Bensington Ct., Felt. 141 G6
Bensley Cl. N11 57 J5
Benson Av. E6 115 J2
Benson Cl., Houns. 143 G4
Benson Quay E1 113 F7
Garnet St.
Benson Rd. SE23 171 F1
Benson Rd., Croy. 201 G3
Bentfield Gdns. SE9 173 J3
Aldersgrove Av.
Benthal Rd. N16 94 D2
Bentham Ct. N1 93 J7
Rotherfield St.
Bentham Rd. E9 95 G6
Bentham Rd. SE28 118 B7
Bentham Rd. NW10 88 C5
Bentham Wk. NW10 88 C5
Bentinck Ms. W1 **16 C3**
Bentinck Pl. NW8 **7 G2**
Bentinck Rd., 120 A1
West Dr.
Bentinck St. W1 **16 C3**
Bentinck St. W1 110 A6
Bentley Dr. NW2 90 C3
Bentley Dr., Ilf. 81 F6
Bentley Ms., Enf. 44 A6
Bentley Rd. N1 94 B6
Tottenham Rd.
Bentley Way, Stan. 52 D5

Bentley Way, Wdf.Grn. 63 G2
Benton Rd., Ilf. 99 G1
Benton Rd., Wat. 50 D5
Bentons La. SE27 169 J4
Bentons Ri. SE27 170 A5
Bentry Cl., Dag. 101 E2
Bentry Rd., Dag. 101 E2
Bentworth Rd. W12 107 H6
Benwell Ct., Sun. 178 A1
Benwell Rd. N7 93 G4
Benwick Cl. SE16 133 E3
Benworth St. E3 113 J3
Benyon Rd. N1 112 A1
Southgate Rd.
Berber Rd. SW11 149 J5
Berberis Wk., West Dr. 120 B4
Berberry Cl., Edg. 54 C4
Larkspur Gro.
Bercta Rd. SE9 175 F2
Bere St. E1 113 G7
Cranford St.
Berenger Wk. SW10 30 E7
Berens Rd. NW10 108 A3
Berens Way, Chis. 193 J4
Beresford Av. N20 57 J2
Beresford Av. W7 104 A5
Beresford Av., Surb. 196 B1
Beresford Av., Twick. 145 F6
Beresford Av., Wem. 105 J1
Beresford Dr., Brom. 192 A3
Beresford Dr., Wdf.Grn. 63 J4
Beresford Gdns., Enf. 44 B4
Beresford Gdns., Houns. 143 F5
Beresford Gdns., Rom. 83 E5
Beresford Rd. E4 62 E1
Beresford Rd. E17 78 B1
Beresford Rd. N2 73 H3
Beresford Rd. N5 93 J5
Beresford Rd. N8 75 G5
Beresford Rd., Har. 68 A5
Beresford Rd., Kings.T. 181 J1
Beresford Rd., N.Mal. 182 C4
Beresford Rd., Sthl. 122 D1
Beresford Rd., Sutt. 198 C7
Beresford Sq. SE18 136 E4
Beresford St. SE18 136 E3
Beresford Ter. N5 93 J5
Berestede Rd. W6 127 F5
Bergen Sq. SE16 133 H3
Norway Gate
Berger Cl., Orp. 193 G6
Berger Rd. E9 95 G6
Berghem Ms. W14 128 A3
Blythe Rd.
Bergholt Av., Ilf. 80 B5
Bergholt Cres. N16 76 B7
Bergholt Ms. NW1 92 C7
Rossendale Way
Bering Sq. E14 134 A5
Napier Av.
Bering Wk. E16 116 A6
Berisford Ms. SW18 149 F6
Berkeley Av., Bexh. 158 D1
Berkeley Av., Grnf. 86 B6
Berkeley Av., Houns. 142 A2
Berkeley Av., Ilf. 80 D2
Berkeley Cl., Borwd. 38 A5
Berkeley Cl., Kings.T. 163 H7
Berkeley Cl., Orp. 193 H7
Berkeley Cl., Ruis. 84 A3
Berkeley Ct. N14 42 C6
Berkeley Ct., Wall. 200 C3
Berkeley Cres., Barn. 41 G5
Berkeley Dr., W.Mol. 179 F3
Berkeley Gdns. N21 44 A7
Berkeley Gdns. W8 128 D1
Brunswick Gdns.
Berkeley Gdns., Esher 194 D6
Berkeley Ho. E3 114 A4
Berkeley Ms. W1 16 A3
Berkeley Pl. SW19 166 A6
Berkeley Rd. E12 98 B5
Berkeley Rd. N8 74 D5
Berkeley Rd. N15 76 A6
Berkeley Rd. NW9 70 A4
Berkeley Rd. SW13 147 G1
Berkeley Sq. W1 16 E6
Berkeley Sq. W1 110 B7
Berkeley St. W1 17 E6
Berkeley St. W1 110 B7
Berkeley Wk. N7 93 F2
Durham Rd.
Berkeley Waye, Houns. 122 D7
Berkhampstead Rd., Belv. 139 G5
Berkhamsted Av., Wem. 87 J6
Berkley Gro. NW1 91 J7
Berkley Rd.
Berkley Rd. NW1 91 J7
Berkshire Gdns. N13 59 G6
Berkshire Gdns. N18 60 E5
Berkshire Rd. E9 95 J6
Berkshire Sq., Mitch. 186/187 E4
Berkshire Way
Berkshire Way, Mitch. 186 E4
Bermans Way NW10 89 E4
Bermondsey Sq. SE1 28 E5
Bermondsey St. SE1 28 D2
Bermondsey St. SE1 132 B2
Bermondsey Wall E. SE16 29 J4
Bermondsey Wall E. SE16 132 D2
Bermondsey Wall W. SE16 29 H3
Bermondsey Wall W. SE16 132 D2
Bernal Cl. SE28 118 D7
Haldane Rd.
Bernard Ashley Dr. SE7 135 H5
Bernard Av. W13 125 E3
Bernard Cassidy St. E16 115 F5
Bernard Gdns. SW19 166 C5
Bernard Rd. N15 76 C5
Bernard Rd., Rom. 83 J7
Bernard Rd., Wall. 200 B4
Bernard St. WC1 10 A6
Bernard St. WC1 110 E4
Bernards Cl., Ilf. 65 F6
Bernays Cl., Stan. 53 F6
Bernays Gro. SW9 151 F4
Berne Rd., Th.Hth. 187 J5
Bernel Dr., Croy. 203 J3
Berners Dr. W13 104 D6
Berners Ms. W1 17 G2
Berners Ms. W1 110 C5
Berners Pl. W1 17 G3
Berners Pl. W1 110 C6
Berners Rd. N1 11 F1
Berners Rd. N1 111 G1
Berners Rd. N22 75 G1
Berners St. W1 17 G2
Berners St. W1 110 C5
Bernersmede SE3 155 G3
Blackheath Pk.
Berney Rd., Croy. 188 A7
Bernhart Cl., Edg. 54 C7
Orange Hill Rd.
Bernville Way, Har. 69 J5
Kenton Rd.
Bernwell Rd. E4 63 E3
Berridge Grn., Edg. 54 A7
Berridge Ms. NW6 90 D5
Hillfield Rd.
Berridge Rd. SE19 170 A5
Berriman Rd. N7 93 F3
Berriton Rd., Har. 85 F1
Berry Cl. N21 59 H1
Berry Cl. NW10 88 E7
Berry Ct., Houns. 143 F5
Berry Hill, Stan. 53 G4
Berry La. SE21 170 A4
Berry Pl. EC1 11 H4
Berry St. EC1 11 H5
Berry St. EC1 111 H4
Berry Way W5 125 H3
Berrybank Cl. E4 62 C2
Greenbank Cl.
Berrydale Rd., Hayes 102 E4
Berryfield Cl. E17 78 B4
Berryfield Cl., Brom. 192 B1
Berryfield Rd. SE17 35 H3
Berryfield Rd. SE17 131 H5
Berryhill SE9 156 E4
Berryhill Gdns. SE9 156 E4
Berrylands SW20 183 J3
Berrylands, Surb. 182 A5
Berrylands Rd., Surb. 181 J6
Berryman Cl., Dag. 100 C3
Bennetts Castle La.
Berrymans La. SE26 171 G4
Berrymead Gdns. W3 126 C1
Berrymede Rd. W4 126 D3
Bert Rd., Th.Hth. 187 J5
Bertal Rd. SW17 167 G4
Berthon St. SE8 134 A7
Bertie Rd. NW10 89 G6
Bertie Rd. SE26 171 G6
Bertram Cotts. SW19 166 D7
Hartfield Rd.
Bertram Rd. NW4 71 G6
Bertram Rd., Enf. 44 D4
Bertram Rd., Kings.T. 164 A7
Bertram St. N19 92 B2
Bertram Way, Enf. 44 C4
Bertrand St. SE13 154 B3
Bertrand Way SE28 118 B7
Berwick Av., Hayes 102 D6
Berwick Cl., Stan. 52 C7
Gordon Av.
Berwick Cres., Sid. 157 H6
Berwick Rd. E16 115 H6
Berwick Rd. N22 75 H1
Berwick Rd., Well. 158 B1
Berwick St. W1 17 H4
Berwick St. W1 110 D6
Berwyn Av., Houns. 143 H1
Berwyn Rd. SE24 169 H1
Berwyn Rd., Rich. 146 B4
Beryl Av. E6 116 B5
Beryl Ho. SE18 137 J5
Spinel Cl.
Beryl Rd. W6 128 A5
Berystede, Kings.T. 164 B7
Besant Ct. N1 94 A5
Newington Grn. Rd.
Besant Rd. NW2 90 B4
Besant Wk. N7 93 F2
Newington Barrow Way
Besant Way NW10 88 C5
Besley St. SW16 168 C6
Bessant Dr., Rich. 146 B1
Bessborough Gdns. SW1 33 J3
Bessborough Gdns. SW1 130 D5
Bessborough Pl. SW1 33 J3
Bessborough Pl. SW1 130 D5
Bessborough Rd. SW15 165 G1
Bessborough Rd., Har. 86 A1
Bessborough St. SW1 33 H3
Bessborough St. SW1 130 D5
Bessemer Rd. SE5 151 J2
Bessie Lansbury Cl. E6 116 D6
Bessingby Rd., Ruis. 84 A2
Bessingham Wk. SE4 153 G4
Frendsbury Rd.
Besson St. SE14 153 F1
Bessy St. E2 113 F3
Roman Rd.
Bestwood St. SE8 133 G4
Beswick Ms. NW6 90/91 E6
Lymington Rd.
Betam Rd., Hayes 121 G2
Betchworth Cl., Sutt. 199 G5
Turnpike La.
Betchworth Rd., Ilf. 99 H2
Betham Rd., Grnf. 104 A3
Bethany Waye, Felt. 141 H7
Bethecar Rd., Har. 68 B5
Bethel Rd., Well. 158 C3
Bethell Av. E16 115 F4
Bethell Av., Ilf. 80 D7
Bethersden Cl., Beck. 171 J7
Bethnal Grn. Rd. E1 13 F5
Bethnal Grn. Rd. E1 112 C4
Bethnal Grn. Rd. E2 13 F5
Bethnal Grn. Rd. E2 112 C4
Bethune Av. N11 57 J4
Bethune Rd. N16 76 A7
Bethune Rd. NW10 106 D4
Bethwin Rd. SE5 35 H7
Bethwin Rd. SE5 131 H7
Betjeman Cl., Pnr. 67 G4
Betony Cl., Croy. 203 G1
Primrose La.
Betoyne Av. E4 62 E4
Betstyle Rd. N11 58 B4
Betterton Dr., Sid. 177 E2
Betterton St. WC2 18 A4
Betterton St. WC2 111 E6
Bettons Pk. E15 115 E1
Bettridge Rd. SW6 148 C2
Betts Cl., Beck. 189 H2
Kendall Rd.
Betts Ms. E17 77 J6
Queen's Rd.
Betts Rd. E16 115 H7
Victoria Dock Rd.
Betts St. E1 112/113 E7
The Highway
Betts Way SE20 189 E1
Betts Way, Surb. 195 E1
Beulah Av., Th.Hth. 187 F4
Beulah Rd.
Beulah Cl., Edg. 54 B3
Beulah Cres., Th.Hth. 187 J2
Beulah Gro., Croy. 187 J6
Beulah Hill SE19 169 H6
Beulah Path E17 78 B5
Addison Rd.
Beulah Rd. E17 78 B5
Beulah Rd. SW19 166 C7
Beulah Rd., Sutt. 198 D4
Beulah Rd., Th.Hth. 187 J3
Bev Callender Cl. SW8 150 B3
Daley Thompson Way
Bevan Av., Bark. 100 A7
Bevan Ct., Croy. 201 G5
Bevan Rd. SE2 138 B5
Bevan Rd., Barn. 41 J4
Bevan St. N1 111 J1
Bevenden St. N1 12 C3
Bevenden St. N1 112 A3
Bevercote Wk., Belv. 139 F6
Osborne Rd.
Beveridge Rd. NW10 88/89 E7
Curzon Cres.
Beverley Av. SW20 183 F1
Beverley Av., Houns. 143 F4
Beverley Av., Sid. 157 J7
Beverley Cl. N21 59 J1
Beverley Cl. SW11 149 G4
Maysoule Rd.
Beverley Cl. SW13 147 F2
Beverley Cl., Chess. 195 F4
Beverley Cl., Enf. 44 B4
Beverley Cotts. SW15 164 D4
Kingston Vale
Beverley Ct. N14 42 C7
Beverley Ct. SE4 153 J3
Beverley Cres., Wdf.Grn. 79 H1
Beverley Dr., Edg. 70 B3
Beverley Gdns. NW11 72 B7
Beverley Gdns. SW13 147 F3
Beverley Gdns., Stan. 68 D1
Beverley Gdns., Wem. 87 J1
Beverley Gdns., Wor.Pk. 197 G1
Green La.
Beverley Ho. NW8 7 G4
Beverley La. SW15 165 F3
Beverley La., Kings.T. 165 E7
Beverley Ms. E4 62 D6
Beverley Rd.
Beverley Path SW13 147 F2
Beverley Rd. E4 62 D6
Beverley Rd. E6 116 A3
Beverley Rd. SE20 188/189 E2
Wadhurst Cl.
Beverley Rd. SW13 147 F3
Beverley Rd. W4 127 F5
Beverley Rd., Bexh. 159 J2
Beverley Rd., Brom. 206 B2
Beverley Rd., Dag. 101 E4
Beverley Rd., Kings.T. 181 F1
Beverley Rd., Mitch. 186 D4
Beverley Rd., N.Mal. 183 G4
Beverley Rd., Ruis. 84 A2
Beverley Rd., Sthl. 123 E3
Beverley Rd., Wor.Pk. 197 J2
Beverley Way SW20 183 F1
Beverley Way, N.Mal. 183 F1
Beversbrook Rd. N19 92 D3
Beverston Ms. W1 15 J2
Beverstone Rd. SW2 151 F5
Beverstone Rd., Th.Hth. 187 G4
Bevill Allen Cl. SW17 167 J5
Bevill Cl. SE25 188 D3
Bevin Cl. SE16 133 H1
Stave Yd. Rd.
Bevin Ct. WC1 111 G3
Holford St.
Bevin Rd., Hayes 102 A3
Bevin Sq. SW17 167 J3
Bevin Way WC1 10 E3
Bevington Rd. W10 108 B5
Bevington Rd., Beck. 190 B2
Bevington St. SE16 29 J4
Bevington St. SE16 132 D2
Bevis Marks EC3 20 E3
Bevis Marks EC3 112 B6
Bewcastle Gdns., Enf. 43 E4
Bewdley St. N1 93 G7
Bewick St. SW8 150 B2
Bewley St. E1 112/113 E7
Dellow St.
Bewlys Rd. SE27 169 H5
Bexhill Cl., Felt. 160 E2
Bexhill Rd. N11 58 D5
Bexhill Rd. SE4 153 J6
Bexhill Rd. SW14 146 C3
Bexhill Wk. E15 114/115 E2
Mitre Rd.
Bexley Gdns. N9 60 A3

Bexley Gdns., Rom.	82	B5	Bingham Rd., Croy.	202	D1	Birdhurst Gdns.,	202	A4	Bishops Pk. Rd.	187	E1
Bexley High St., Bex.	159	G7	Bingham St. N1	94	A6	S.Croy.			SW16		
Bexley La., Sid.	176	C3	Bingley Rd. E16	115	J6	Birdhurst Ri., S.Croy.	202	B5	Bishops Pl., Sutt.	199	F5
Bexley Rd. SE9	156	E5	Bingley Rd., Grnf.	103	J5	Birdhurst Rd. SW18	149	F4	Lind Rd.		
Bexley Rd., Erith	139	J7	Bingley Rd., Sun.	160	A7	Birdhurst Rd. SW19	167	H6	Bishops Rd. N6	74	A6
Beynon Rd., Cars.	199	J5	Binney St. W1	16	C5	Birdhurst Rd., S.Croy.	202	B5	Bishops Rd. SW6	148	C1
Bianca Ho. N1	112	B2	Binney St. W1	110	A6	Birdlip Cl. SE15	36	D6	Bishops Rd. W7	124	B2
Crondall St.			Binns Rd. W4	126	E5	Birdlip Cl. SE15	132	B6	Bishops Rd., Croy.	187	H7
Bianca Rd. SE15	37	H6	Binns Ter. W4	126/127	E5	Birds Fm. Av., Rom.	83	H1	Bishops Ter. SE11	35	F1
Bianca Rd. SE15	132	C6	Binns Rd.			Birdsfield La. E3	113	J1	Bishops Ter. SE11	131	G4
Bibsworth Rd. N3	72	C2	Binsey Wk. SE2	138	C1	Birdwood Cl., Tedd.	162	B4	Bishops Wk., Chis.	193	F1
Bibury Cl. SE15	37	E6	Binyon Cres., Stan.	52	C5	Birkbeck Av. W3	106	C7	Bishops Wk., Croy.	203	G5
Bibury Cl. SE15	132	B6	Birbetts Rd. SE9	174	C2	Birkbeck Av., Grnf.	103	J1	Bishop's Wk., Pnr.	66/67	E3
Bicester Rd., Rich.	146	A3	Birch Av. N13	59	J3	Birkbeck Gdns.,	63	F2	High St.		
Bickenhall St. W1	16	A1	Birch Cl. E16	115	E5	Wdf.Grn.			Bishops Way E2	113	E2
Bickenhall St. W1	109	J5	Birch Cl. N19	92	C2	Birkbeck Gro. W3	126	D2	Bishopsford Rd.,	185	F7
Bickersteth Rd.	167	J6	Hargrave Pk.			Birkbeck Hill SE21	169	H2	Mord.		
SW17			Birch Cl. SE15	152	D2	Birkbeck Ms. E8	94	C5	Bishopsgate EC2	20	E2
Bickerton Rd. N19	92	C2	Bournemouth Rd.			Sandringham Rd.			Bishopsgate EC2	112	B6
Bickley Cres., Brom.	192	B4	Birch Cl., Brent.	124	E7	Birkbeck Pl. SE21	169	J1	Bishopsgate Arc.	20	E2
Bickley Pk. Rd.,	192	B3	Birch Cl., Buck.H.	64	A3	Birkbeck Rd. E8	94	C5	EC2		
Brom.			Birch Cl., Houns.	144	A3	Birkbeck Rd. N8	75	E4	Bishopsgate Chyd.	20	D3
Bickley Rd. E10	78	B7	Birch Cl., Rom.	83	H3	Birkbeck Rd. N12	57	F5	EC2		
Bickley Rd., Brom.	192	A2	Birch Cl., Tedd.	162	D5	Birkbeck Rd. N17	76	C1	Bishopsthorpe Rd.	171	G4
Bickley St. SW17	167	H5	Birch Gdns., Dag.	101	J3	Birkbeck Rd. NW7	55	F5	SE26		
Bicknell Rd. SE5	151	J3	Birch Grn. NW9	54/55	E7	Birkbeck Rd. SW19	167	E5	Bishopswood Rd. N6	73	J7
Bicknoller Rd., Enf.	44	C1	Clayton Fld.			Birkbeck Rd. W3	126	D1	Bisley Cl., Wor.Pk.	197	J1
Bicknor Rd., Orp.	193	H7	Birch Gro. E11	96	E3	Birkbeck Rd. W5	125	F4	Bispham Rd. NW10	105	J3
Bidborough Cl.,	191	F5	Birch Gro. SE12	155	F7	Birkbeck Rd., Beck.	189	F2	Bisson Rd. E15	114	C2
Brom.			Birch Gro. W3	126	A1	Birkbeck Rd., Enf.	44	A1	Bisterne Av. E17	78	D3
Bidborough St. WC1	10	A4	Birch Gro., Well.	158	A4	Birkbeck Rd., Ilf.	81	G5	Bittacy Cl. NW7	56	A6
Bidborough St. WC1	110	D3	Birch Hill, Croy.	203	G5	Birkbeck Rd., Sid.	176	A3	Bittacy Hill NW7	56	A6
Biddenden Way SE9	174	D4	Birch Mead, Orp.	206	D2	Birkbeck St. E2	113	E3	Bittacy Pk. Av. NW7	56	A6
Bidder St. E16	114	E5	Birch Pk., Har.	51	J7	Birkbeck Way, Grnf.	103	J1	Bittacy Ri. NW7	55	J6
Biddestone Rd. N7	93	F4	Birch Rd., Felt.	160	D5	Birkdale Av., Pnr.	67	G3	Bittacy Rd. NW7	56	A6
Biddulph Rd. W9	6	A4	Birch Rd., Rom.	83	H3	Birkdale Cl.	132/133	E5	Bittern Cl., Hayes	102	D5
Biddulph Rd. W9	108	E3	Birch Row, Brom.	192	D7	SE16			Bittern St. SE1	27	J4
Bideford Av., Grnf.	104	E2	Birch Tree Av.,	205	F5	Masters Dr.			Bittoms, The,	181	G3
Bideford Cl., Edg.	70	A1	W.Wick.			Birkdale Cl., Orp.	193	G7	Kings.T.		
Bideford Cl., Felt.	161	F3	Birch Tree Way, Croy.	202	E2	Birkdale Gdns., Croy.	203	G4	Bixley Cl., Sthl.	123	F4
Bideford Gdns., Enf.	44	B7	Birch Wk., Borwd.	38	A1	Birkdale Gdns., Wat.	50	D3	Black Boy La. N15	75	J5
Bideford Rd., Brom.	173	F3	Birch Wk., Erith	139	J6	Birkdale Rd. SE2	138	A4	Black Fan Cl., Enf.	43	J1
Bideford Rd., Ruis.	84	B3	Birch Wk., Mitch.	186	B1	Birkdale Rd. W5	105	H5	Black Friars Ct. EC4	19	G5
Bideford Rd., Well.	138	B7	Bircham Path SE4	153	G4	Birkenhead Av.,	181	J2	Black Friars La. EC4	19	G5
Bidwell Gdns. N11	58	C7	St. Norbert Rd.			Kings.T.			Black Friars La. EC4	111	H7
Bidwell St. SE15	153	E1	Birchanger Rd.	188	D5	Birkenhead St. WC1	10	B3	Black Gates, Pnr.	67	F3
Big Hill E5	95	E1	SE25			Birkenhead St. WC1	111	E3	Church La.		
Bigbury Cl. N17	60	A7	Birchdale Gdns.,	82	D7	Birkhall Rd. SE6	172	D1	Black Horse Ct. SE1	28	C5
Weir Hall Rd.			Rom.			Birkwood Cl. SW12	150	D7	Black Lion La. W6	127	G4
Bigbury Rd. N17	60	B7	Birchdale Rd. E7	97	J5	Birley Rd. N20	57	F2	Black Lion Ms. W6	127	G4
Barkham Rd.			Birchdene Dr. SE28	138	A2	Birley St. SW11	150	A2	Black Lion La.		
Biggerstaff Rd. E15	114	C1	Birchen Cl. NW9	88	D2	Birnam Rd. N4	93	F2	Black Path E10	77	G7
Biggerstaff St. N4	93	G2	Birchen Gro. NW9	88	D2	Birse Cres. NW10	89	E4	Black Prince Rd. SE1	34	C2
Biggin Av., Mitch.	185	J1	Birchend Cl., S.Croy.	202	A6	Birstall Grn., Wat.	50	D4	Black Prince Rd. SE1	131	F4
Biggin Hill SE19	169	H7	Birches, The N21	43	F6	Birstall Rd. N15	76	B5	Black Prince Rd. SE11	34	D2
Biggin Hill Cl.,	163	F5	Birches, The E17	135	H6	Biscay Rd. W6	128	A5	Black Prince Rd. SE11	131	F4
Kings.T.			Birches, The, Orp.	206	D4	Biscoe Cl., Houns.	123	G6	Black Rod Cl., Hayes	121	J3
Biggin Way SE19	169	H7	Birches Cl., Mitch.	185	J3	Biscoe Way SE13	154	D3	Black Swan Yd. SE1	28	E3
Bigginwood Rd.	169	H7	Birches Cl., Pnr.	66	E5	Bisenden Rd., Croy.	202	B2	Blackall St. EC2	12	D5
SW16			Birches, The, Orp.	114	A7	Bisham Cl., Cars.	199	J1	Blackberry Fm. Cl.,	122	E7
Biggs Row SW15	148	A3	Birchfield St. E14			Bisham Gdns. N6	92	A1	Houns.		
Felsham Rd.			Birchington Cl.,	159	H1	Bishop Butt Cl., Orp.	207	J3	Blackbird Hill NW9	88	C2
Bigland St. E1	112	E6	Bexh.			Stapleton Rd.			Blackbird Yd. E2	13	G3
Bignell Rd. SE18	136	E5	Birchington Rd. N8	74	D6	Bishop Cl. W4	126	C5	Blackborne Rd., Dag.	101	G6
Bignold Rd. E7	97	G4	Birchington Rd.	108	D1	Bishop Fox Way,	179	F4	Blackbrook La.,	192	D3
Bigwood Rd. NW11	72	E5	NW6			W.Mol.			Brom.		
Bill Hamling Cl. SE9	174	C2	Birchington Rd.,	181	J7	Bishop Ken Rd., Har.	68	C2	Blackburn Rd. NW6	90	E6
Bill Nicholson Way	76	C3	Surb.			Bishop Kings Rd.	128	B4	Blackburn Trd. Est.,	140	E6
N17			Birchlands Av. SW12	149	J7	W14			Stai.		
High Rd.			Birchmead Av., Pnr.	66	C4	Bishop St. N1	111	J1	Blackburne's Ms. W1	16	B5
Billet Cl., Rom.	82	D3	Birchmere Row SE3	155	F2	Bishop Way NW10	88	E7	Blackburne's Ms. W1	110	A7
Billet La. E17	77	G2	Birchmore Wk. N5	93	J3	Bishop Wilfred Wd.	152	D2	Blackbush Av., Rom.	82	D5
Billet Rd., Rom.	82	B3	Birchville Ct., Bushey	52	B1	Cl. SE15			Blackbush Cl., Sutt.	199	E7
Billets Hart Cl. W7	124	B2	Heathbourne Rd.			Moncrieff St.			Blackdown Cl. N2	73	F2
Billing Pl. SW10	30	B7	Birchway, Hayes	122	A1	Bishop's Av. E13	115	H1	Blackdown Ter. SE18	136	D7
Billing Rd. SW10	129	E7	Birchwood Av. N10	74	A3	Bishops Av. SW6	148	A2	Prince Imperial Rd.		
Billing Rd. SW10	30	B7	Birchwood Av., Beck.	189	J4	Bishops Av., Brom.	191	J2	Blackett St. SW15	148	A3
Billing St. SW10	129	E7	Birchwood Av., Sid.	176	B2	Bishops Av., Rom.	82	C6	Blackfen Cl., Sid.	157	H5
Billing St. SW10	30	B7	Birchwood Av., Wall.	200	A3	Bishops Av., The N2	73	G7	Blackfen Rd., Wat.	50	D5
Billingford Cl. SE4	153	G4	Birchwood Cl., Mord.	184	E4	Bishops Br. W2	14	D2	Blackford's Path	147	G7
Billings Cl., Dag.	100	C7	Birchwood Ct. N13	59	H5	Bishops Br. W2	109	F5	SW15		
Ellerton Rd.			Birchwood Ct., Edg.	70	C2	Bishops Br. Rd. W2	14	B4	Roehampton High St.		
Billiter Sq. EC3	20	E5	Birchwood Dr. NW3	91	E3	Bishops Br. Rd. W2	109	H6	Blackfriars Br. EC4	19	G5
Billiter St. EC3	20	E4	Birchwood Gro.,	161	G6	Bishops Cl. E17	78	B4	Blackfriars Br. EC4	111	H7
Billiter St. EC3	112	B6	Hmptn.			Bishops Cl. N19	92	C3	Blackfriars Br. SE1	19	G5
Billockby Cl., Chess.	195	J6	Birchwood Rd. SW17	168	B5	Wyndham Cres.			Blackfriars Br. SE1	111	H7
Billson St. E14	134	C4	Birchwood Rd., Orp.	193	G4	Bishops Cl. SE9	175	F2	Blackfriars Pas. EC4	19	G5
Bilsby Gro. SE9	174	A4	Bird in Bush Rd.	132	D7	Bishops Cl., Barn.	40	A6	Blackfriars Rd. SE1	27	G4
Bilton Rd., Grnf.	105	F1	SE15			Bishops Cl., Enf.	44/45	E2	Blackfriars Rd. SE1	131	H1
Bilton Way, Enf.	45	H1	Bird St. W1	16	C4	Central Av.			Blackheath Av. SE10	134	D7
Bilton Way, Hayes	122	B2	Bird Wk., Twick.	161	F1	Bishops Cl., Rich.	163	G3	Blackheath Gro. SE3	155	F2
Bina Gdns. SW5	30	C2	Bird-in-Hand La.,	192	A2	Bishops Cl., Sutt.	198	D3	Blackheath Hill SE10	154	C1
Bina Gdns. SW5	129	F4	Brom.			Bishop's Ct. EC4	19	G3	Blackheath Pk. SE3	155	F3
Bincote Rd., Enf.	43	F3	Bird-in-Hand Pas.	171	F2	Bishop's Ct. WC2	18	E3	Blackheath Ri. SE13	154	C2
Binden Rd. W12	127	F3	SE23			Bishops Dr., Felt.	141	G6	Blackheath Vale SE3	155	E2
Bindon Grn., Mord.	185	E4	Dartmouth Rd.			Bishops Dr., Nthlt.	103	E1	Blackheath Village	155	F3
Binfield Rd. SW4	151	E1	Birdbrook Cl., Dag.	101	J7	Bishops Gro. N2	73	G6	SE3		
Binfield Rd., S.Croy.	202	C5	Birdbrook Rd. SE3	155	J3	Bishops Gro., Hmptn.	161	F4	Blackhorse La. E17	77	G4
Bingfield St. N1	111	E1	Birdcage Wk. SW1	25	G4	Bishop's Hall,	181	G2	Blackhorse La., Croy.	188	D7
Bingham Ct. N1	93	H7	Birdcage Wk. SW1	130	C2	Kings.T.			Blackhorse Ms. E17	77	G3
Halton Rd.			Birdham Cl., Brom.	192	B5	Bishops Hill, Walt.	178	A7	Blackhorse La.		
Bingham Pl. W1	16	B1	Birdhurst Av.,	202	A4	Bishop's Pk. SW6	148	A7	Blackhorse Rd. E17	77	G4
			S.Croy.			Bishop's Pk. Rd. SW6	148	A2	Blackhorse Rd. SE8	133	H5

Name	Page	Grid
Blackhorse Rd., Sid.	176	A4
Blacklands Rd. SE6	172	C4
Blacklands Ter. SW3	**31**	**J2**
Blacklands Ter. SW3	129	J4
Blackmore Av., Sthl.	124	A1
Blackmore Rd.,	48	B7
Buck.H.		
Blackmores Gro.,	162	D6
Tedd.		
Blackpool Rd. SE15	152	E2
Blacks Rd. W6	127	J4
Queen Caroline St.		
Blackshaw Pl. N1	94	B7
Hertford Rd.		
Blackshaw Rd. SW17	167	F4
Blacksmiths Cl., Rom.	82	C6
Blackstock Ms. N4	93	H2
Blackstock Rd.		
Blackstock Rd. N4	93	H2
Blackstock Rd. N5	93	H2
Blackstone Est. E8	94	E7
Blackstone Rd. NW2	89	J5
Blackthorn Av.,	120	D4
West Dr.		
Blackthorn Ct., Houns.	122	E7
Blackthorn Gro.,	158	E3
Bexh.		
Blackthorn St. E3	114	A4
Blackthorne Av., Croy.	189	F7
Blackthorne Dr. E4	62	D4
Blacktree Ms. SW9	151	G3
Blackwall La. SE10	135	E5
Blackwall Pier E14	114	E7
Blackwall Tunnel E14	134	D1
Blackwall Tunnel	134	E2
App. SE10		
Blackwall Tunnel	114	A2
Northern App. E3		
Blackwall Tunnel	114	A2
Northern App. E14		
Blackwall Way E14	114	C7
Blackwater Cl. E7	97	F4
Blackwater Rd.,	198/199	E4
Sutt.		
High St.		
Blackwater St. SE22	152	C5
Blackwell Cl. E5	95	G4
Blackwell Cl., Har.	52	A7
Blackwell Gdns., Edg.	54	A3
Blackwood St. SE17	**36**	**B3**
Blackwood St. SE17	132	A5
Blade Ms. SW15	148	C4
Deodar Rd.		
Blades Cl. SW15	148	C4
Deodar Rd.		
Bladindon Dr., Bex.	157	C7
Bladon Gdns., Har.	67	H6
Blagdens Cl. N14	58	C2
Blagdens La. N14	58	D2
Blagdon Rd. SE13	154	B6
Blagdon Rd., N.Mal.	183	F4
Blagdon Wk., Tedd.	163	F6
Blagrove Rd. W10	108	B5
Blair Av. NW9	70	E7
Blair Cl. N1	93	J6
Blair Cl., Hayes	122	A4
Blair Cl., Sid.	157	H5
Blair St. E14	114	C6
Blairderry Rd. SW2	169	E2
Blairhead Dr., Wat.	50	B3
Blake Av., Bark.	117	H1
Blake Cl. W10	107	J5
Blake Cl., Cars.	185	H7
Blake Cl., Well.	157	H1
Blake Gdns. SW6	148	E1
Blake Hall Cres. E11	97	G1
Blake Hall Rd. E11	79	G7
Blake Ho., Beck.	172	A6
Blake Rd. E16	115	F4
Blake Rd. N11	58	C7
Blake Rd., Croy.	202	B2
Blake Rd., Mitch.	185	H3
Blake St. SE8	134	A6
Watergate St.		
Blakeden Dr., Esher	194	C6
Blakehall Rd., Cars.	199	J6
Blakeley Cotts. SE10	134	D2
Tunnel Av.		
Blakemore Rd.	168	E3
SW16		
Blakemore Rd.,	187	F5
Th.Hth.		
Blakemore Way, Belv.	139	E3
Blakeney Av., Beck.	189	J1
Blakeney Cl. E8	94	D5
Ferncliff Rd.		
Blakeney Cl. N20	57	F1
Blakeney Cl. NW1	92	D7
Rossendale Way		
Blakeney Rd., Beck.	171	J7
Blakenham Rd.	167	J4
SW17		
Blaker Ct. SE7	135	J7
Fairlawn		
Blaker Rd. E15	114	C1
Blakes Av., N.Mal.	183	F5
Blakes Grn., W.Wick.	204	C1
Blakes La., N.Mal.	183	F5
Blakes Rd. SE15	**36**	**E7**
Blakes Rd. SE15	132	B7
Blakes Ter., N.Mal.	183	G5
Blakesley Av. W5	105	F6
Blakesley Wk. SW20	184	C2
Kingston Rd.		
Blakesware Gdns.	44	A7
N9		
Blakewood Cl., Felt.	160	C4
Blanch Cl. SE15	133	F7
Culmore Rd.		
Blanchard Cl. SE9	174	B3
Blanchard Way E8	94	D6
Blanche St. E16	115	F4
Blanchedowne SE5	152	A4
Blanchland Rd.,	184	E5
Mord.		
Bland St. SE9	156	A4
Blandfield Rd. SW12	150	A6
Blandford Av., Beck.	189	H2
Blandford Av., Twick.	161	H1
Blandford Cl. N2	73	F4
Blandford Cl., Croy.	201	E3
Blandford Cl., Rom.	83	H4
Blandford Cres. E4	46	C7
Blandford Rd. W4	126	E3
Blandford Rd. W5	125	G2
Blandford Rd., Beck.	189	F2
Blandford Rd., Sthl.	123	G4
Blandford Rd., Tedd.	162	A5
Blandford Sq. NW1	**7**	**H6**
Blandford Sq. NW1	109	H4
Blandford St. W1	**16**	**A3**
Blandford St. W1	110	A5
Blandford Waye,	102	C6
Hayes		
Blaney Cres. E6	116	E3
Blanmerle Rd. SE9	174	E1
Blann Cl. SE9	156	A6
Blantyre St. SW10	**30**	**E7**
Blantyre Wk. SW10	129	G7
Blantyre Wk. SW10	**30**	**E7**
Blashford NW3	91	J7
Blashford St. SE13	154	D7
Blasker Wk. E14	134	A5
Blawith Rd., Har.	68	B4
Blaydon Cl. N17	60	E7
Blaydon Wk. N17	60	E7
Bleak Hill La. SE18	137	J6
Blean Gro. SE20	171	F7
Bleasdale Av., Grnf.	104	D2
Blechynden St. W10	108	A7
Bramley Rd.		
Bleddyn Cl., Sid.	158	C6
Bledlow Cl. SE28	118	C7
Bledlow Ri., Grnf.	103	J2
Bleeding Heart Yd.	**19**	**F2**
EC1		
Blegborough Rd.	168	C6
SW16		
Blendon Dr., Bex.	158	D6
Blendon Path, Brom.	173	F7
Blendon Rd., Bex.	158	D6
Blendon Ter. SE18	137	F5
Blendworth Way	**37**	**E7**
SE15		
Blenheim Av., Ilf.	80	D6
Blenheim Cl. N21	59	J1
Elm Pk. Rd.		
Blenheim Cl. SW20	183	J3
Blenheim Cl., Grnf.	104	A2
Leaver Gdns.		
Blenheim Cl., Rom.	83	J4
Blenheim Cl., Wall.	200	C7
Blenheim Ct. N19	92/93	E2
Marlborough Rd.		
Blenheim Ct., Sid.	175	G3
Blenheim Cres. W11	108	B6
Blenheim Cres.	201	J7
S.Croy.		
Blenheim Dr., Well.	157	J1
Blenheim Gdns.	89	J5
NW2		
Blenheim Gdns. SW2	151	F6
Blenheim Gdns.,	164	B7
Kings.T.		
Blenheim Gdns.,	200	C6
Wall.		
Blenheim Gdns.,	87	H3
Wem.		
Blenheim Gro.	152	D2
SE15		
Blenheim Pas. NW8	**6**	**C1**
Blenheim Ri. N15	76	C4
Talbot Rd.		
Blenheim Rd. E6	116	A3
Blenheim Rd. E15	97	E4
Blenheim Rd. E17	77	G3
Blenheim Rd. NW8	**6**	**C1**
Blenheim Rd. NW8	109	F2
Blenheim Rd. SE20	171	F7
Maple Rd.		
Blenheim Rd. W4	126	E3
Blenheim Rd., Barn.	40	A3
Blenheim Rd., Brom.	192	B4
Blenheim Rd., Har.	67	H6
Blenheim Rd., Nthlt.	85	H6
Blenheim Rd., Sid.	176	C1
Blenheim Rd., Sutt.	198	D3
Blenheim St. W1	**16**	**D4**
Blenheim Ter. NW8	**6**	**C1**
Blenheim Ter. NW8	109	F2
Blenheim Way, Islw.	144	D1
Blenkarne Rd. SW11	149	J6
Bleriot Rd., Houns.	122	C7
Blessbury Rd., Edg.	70	C1
Blessing Way, Bark.	118	C3
Blessington Cl.	154	D3
SE13		
Blessington Rd.	154	D3
SE13		
Bletchingley Cl.,	187	H4
Th.Hth.		
Bletchley Ct. N1	**12**	**B2**
Bletchley Ct. N1	112	A2
Bletchley St. N1	**12**	**A2**
Bletchley St. N1	111	J2
Bletchmore Cl.,	121	G5
Hayes		
Bletsoe Wk. N1	**12**	**A1**
Blewbury Ho. SE2	138	D2
Yarnton Way		
Blincoe Cl. SW19	166	A2
Blind La., Loug.	47	E2
Bliss Cres. SE13	154	B2
Coldbath St.		
Blissett St. SE10	154	C1
Blisworth Cl.,	102/103	E4
Hayes		
Braunston Dr.		
Blithbury Rd., Dag.	100	B6
Blithdale Rd. SE2	138	A4
Blithfield St. W8	**22**	**A6**
Blithfield St. W8	128	E3
Blockley Rd., Wem.	86	E2
Bloemfontein Av.	127	H1
W12		
Bloemfontein Rd.	107	H7
W12		
Blomfield Rd. W9	**14**	**D1**
Blomfield Rd. W9	109	F5
Blomfield St. EC2	**20**	**C2**
Blomfield St. EC2	112	A5
Blomfield Vil. W2	**14**	**B2**
Blomfield Vil. W2	109	E5
Blomville Rd., Dag.	101	E3
Blondel St. SW11	150	A2
Blondell Cl., West Dr.	120	A6
Blondin Av. W5	125	F4
Blondin St. E3	114	A2
Bloom Gro. SE27	169	H3
Bloom Pk. Rd. SW6	128	C7
Bloomburg St. SW1	**33**	**G2**
Bloomfield Cres., Ilf.	81	E6
Bloomfield Pl. W1	**16**	**E5**
Bloomfield Rd. N6	74	A6
Bloomfield Rd. SE18	137	E5
Bloomfield Rd.,	192	A5
Brom.		
Bloomfield Rd.,	181	J4
Kings.T.		
Bloomfield Ter. SW1	**32**	**C3**
Bloomfield Ter. SW1	130	A5
Bloomhall Rd. SE19	170	A5
Bloomsbury Cl. W5	105	J7
Bloomsbury Ct.	**18**	**B2**
WC1		
Bloomsbury Ct., Pnr.	67	F3
Bloomsbury Ho.	150	D6
SW4		
Bloomsbury Pl.	149	F5
SW18		
Fullerton Rd.		
Bloomsbury Pl. WC1	**18**	**B1**
Bloomsbury Pl. WC1	111	E5
Bloomsbury Sq.	**18**	**B2**
WC1		
Bloomsbury Sq.	111	E5
WC1		
Bloomsbury St. WC1	**17**	**J2**
Bloomsbury St. WC1	110	D5
Bloomsbury Way	**18**	**A3**
WC1		
Bloomsbury Way	110	E6
WC1		
Blore Cl. SW8	150	D1
Thessaly Rd.		
Blore Ct. W1	**17**	**H4**
Blossom Cl. W5	125	H2
Almond Av.		
Blossom Cl., Dag.	119	F1
Blossom Cl., S.Croy.	202	C5
Blossom La., Enf.	43	J1
Blossom Pl. E1	**13**	**E6**
Blossom St. E1	**21**	**E1**
Blossom St. E1	112	B4
Blossom Way,	120	D4
West Dr.		
Blossom Waye,	122	E7
Houns.		
Blount St. E14	113	H5
Bloxam Gdns. SE9	156	B5
Bloxhall Rd. E10	95	J1
Bloxham Cres.,	179	F1
Hmptn.		
Bloxworth Cl., Wall.	200	C3
Blucher Rd. SE5	131	J7
Blue Anchor All.,	145	H4
Rich.		
Kew Rd.		
Blue Anchor La.	**37**	**J1**
SE16		
Blue Anchor La.	132	D4
SE16		
Blue Anchor Yd. E1	21	H5
Blue Anchor Yd. E1	112	D7
Blue Ball Yd. SW1	**25**	**F2**
Bluebell Av. E12	98	B5
Bluebell Cl. E9	113	F1
Moulins Rd.		
Bluebell Cl. SE26	170	C4
Bluebell Cl., Orp.	207	F2
Bluebell Cl., Wall.	200	B1
Bluebell Way, Ilf.	98	E6
Blueberry Cl.,	63	G6
Wdf.Grn.		
Bluefield Cl., Hmptn.	161	G5
Bluegates, Epsom	197	G7
Bluehouse Rd. E4	63	E3
Blundell Rd., Edg.	70	C1
Blundell St. N7	93	E7
Blunden Cl., Dag.	100	C1
Blunt Rd., S.Croy.	202	A5
Blunts Av., West Dr.	120	D7
Blunts Rd. SE9	156	D5
Blurton Rd. E5	95	F4
Blyth Cl. E14	134	D4
Manchester Rd.		
Blyth Cl., Twick.	144	C6
Grimwood Rd.		
Blyth Rd. E17	77	J7
Blyth Rd. SE28	118	C7
Blyth Rd., Brom.	191	F1
Blyth Rd., Hayes	121	H2
Blythe Cl. SE6	153	J7
Blythe Hill SE6	153	J7
Blythe Hill, Orp.	193	J1
Blythe Hill La. SE6	153	J7
Blythe Rd. W14	128	A3
Blythe St. E2	112	E3
Blythe Vale SE6	171	J1
Blythswood Rd., Ilf.	100	A1
Blythwood Rd. N4	75	E7
Blythwood Rd., Pnr.	66	D1
Boades Ms. NW3	91	G4
New End		
Boadicea St. N1	111	F1
Copenhagen St.		
Boakes Cl. NW9	70	C4
Boardman Av. E4	46	B5
Boardman Cl., Barn.	40	B5
Boardwalk Pl. E14	134	C1
Boar's Head Yd.,	125	G7
Brent.		
Brent Way		
Boat Lifter Way SE16	133	H4
Sweden Gate		
Boathouse Wk. SE15	**37**	**G7**
Boathouse Wk. SE15	132	C7
Boathouse Wk.,	145	H1
Rich.		
Bob Anker Cl. E13	115	G3
Chesterton Rd.		
Bob Marley Way	151	G4
SE24		
Mayall Rd.		
Bobbin Cl. SW4	150	C3
Bobby Moore Way	57	J7
N10		
Bockhampton Rd.,	163	J7
Kings.T.		
Bocking St. E8	112	E1
Boddicott Cl. SW19	166	B2
Bodiam Cl., Enf.	44	A2
Bodiam Rd. SW16	168	D7
Bodley Cl., N.Mal.	182	E5
Bodley Manor Way	151	G7
SW2		
Papworth Way		
Bodley Rd., N.Mal.	182	D6
Bodmin Cl., Har.	85	F3
Bodmin Gro., Mord.	185	E5
Bodmin St. SW18	166	D1
Bodnant Gdns.	183	G3
SW20		

Bodney Rd. E8 94 E5
Boeing Way, Sthl. 122 B3
Boevey Path, Belv. 139 F6
Bogey La., Orp. 206 D7
Bognor Gdns., Wat. 50 C5
Bowring Grn.
Bognor Rd., Well. 158 D1
Bohemia Pl. E8 95 E6
Bohun Gro., Barn. 41 H6
Boileau Par. W5 105 J6
Boileau Rd.
Boileau Rd. SW13 127 G7
Boileau Rd. W5 105 J6
Bolden St. SE8 154 B2
Bolderwood Way, W.Wick. 204 B2
Boldmere Rd., Pnr. 66 C7
Boleyn Av., Enf. 44 E1
Boleyn Cl. E17 78 A4
Boleyn Cl., Loug. 48 B6
Roding Gdns.
Boleyn Ct., Buck.H. 63 G1
Boleyn Dr., Ruis. 84 D2
Boleyn Dr., W.Mol. 179 F3
Boleyn Gdns., Dag. 101 J7
Boleyn Gdns., W.Wick. 204 B2
Boleyn Gro., W.Wick. 204 C2
Boleyn Rd. E6 116 A2
Boleyn Rd. E7 97 G7
Boleyn Rd. N16 94 B5
Boleyn Way, Barn. 41 F3
Boleyn Way, Ilf. 65 F6
Bolina Rd. SE16 133 F5
Bolingbroke Gro. SW11 149 H4
Bolingbroke Rd. W14 128 A3
Bolingbroke Wk. SW11 129 G7
Bolingbroke Way, Hayes 121 G1
Bolliger Ct. NW10 106 C4
Park Royal Rd.
Bollo Br. Rd. W3 126 B3
Bollo La. W3 126 B2
Bollo La. W4 126 C4
Bolney Gate SW7 23 G4
Bolney St. SW8 131 F7
Bolney Way, Felt. 161 E3
Bolsover St. W1 9 E6
Bolsover St. W1 110 B4
Bolstead Rd., Mitch. 186 B1
Bolt Ct. EC4 19 F4
Boltmore Cl. NW4 72 A3
Bolton Cl. SE20 188 D2
Selby Rd.
Bolton Cl., Chess. 195 G6
Bolton Cres. SE5 35 F6
Bolton Cres. SE5 131 H6
Bolton Gdns. NW10 108 A2
Bolton Gdns. SW5 30 B3
Bolton Gdns. SW5 129 E5
Bolton Gdns., Brom. 173 F6
Bolton Gdns., Tedd. 162 D6
Bolton Gdns. Ms. SW10 30 C3
Bolton Gdns. Ms. SW10 129 E5
Bolton Rd. E15 97 F6
Bolton Rd. N18 60 C5
Bolton Rd. NW8 109 E1
Bolton Rd. NW10 107 E1
Bolton Rd. W4 126 C7
Bolton Rd., Chess. 195 G6
Bolton Rd., Har. 67 J4
Bolton St. W1 24 E1
Bolton St. W1 130 B1
Bolton Wk. N7 93 F2
Durham Rd.
Boltons, The SW10 30 C3
Boltons, The SW10 129 F5
Boltons, The, Wem. 86 C4
Boltons, The, Wdf.Grn. 63 G4
Boltons La., Hayes 121 F7
Boltons Pl. SW5 30 C3
Boltons Pl. SW5 129 F5
Bombay St. SE16 132 E4
Bomer Cl., West Dr. 120 D7
Bomore Rd. W11 108 A7
Bon Marche Ter. Ms. SE27 170 B4
Gipsy Rd.
Bonar Pl., Chis. 174 B7
Bonar Rd. SE15 132 D7
Bonchester Cl., Chis. 174 D7
Bonchurch Cl., Sutt. 199 E7
Bonchurch Rd. W10 108 B5
Bonchurch Rd. W13 124 E1
Bond Ct. EC4 20 B4
Bond Ct. EC4 112 A6
Bond Gdns., Wall. 200 C4
Bond Rd., Mitch. 185 H2
Bond Rd., Surb. 195 J2
Bond St. E15 96 E5
Bond St. W4 126 E4
Bond St. W5 105 G7
Bondfield Av., Hayes 102 A3
Bondfield Rd. E6 116 B5
Lovage App.
Bonding Yd. Wk. SE16 133 H3
Finland St.
Bondway SW8 34 B5
Bondway SW8 131 E6
Boneta Rd. SE18 136 C3
Bonfield Rd. SE13 154 C4
Bonham Gdns., Dag. 100 D2
Bonham Rd. SW2 151 F5
Bonham Rd., Dag. 100 D2
Bonheur Rd. W4 126 D2
Bonhill St. EC2 12 C6
Bonhill St. EC2 112 A4
Boniface Gdns., Har. 51 H7
Boniface Wk., Har. 51 H7
Bonner Hill Rd., Kings.T. 181 J3
Bonner Rd. E2 113 F2
Bonner St. E2 113 F2
Bonnersfield Cl., Har. 68 C6
Bonnersfield La., Har. 68 D6
Bonneville Gdns. SW4 150 C6
Bonnington Sq. SW8 34 C5
Bonnington Sq. SW8 131 F6
Bonnington Twr., Brom. 192 B6
Bonny St. NW1 92 C7
Bonser Rd., Twick. 162 C2
Bonsor St. SE5 132 B7
Bonville Gdns. NW4 71 G4
Handowe Cl.
Bonville Rd., Brom. 173 F5
Book Ms. WC2 17 J4
Bookbinders' Cotts. N20 57 J3
Manor Dr.
Booker Cl. E14 113 J5
Wallwood St.
Booker Rd. N18 60 D5
Boone Ct. N9 61 F3
Boone St. SE13 155 E4
Boones Rd. SE13 155 E4
Boord St. SE10 135 E3
Boot St. N1 12 D4
Boot St. N1 112 B3
Booth Cl. E9 112/113 E1
Victoria Pk. Rd.
Booth Cl. SE28 118 B7
Booth Rd. NW9 70 E2
Booth Rd., Croy. 201 H2
Waddon New Rd.
Boothby Rd. N19 92 D2
Booth's Pl. W1 17 G2
Bordars Rd. W7 104 B5
Bordars Wk. W7 104 B5
Borden Av., Enf. 44 A6
Border Cres. SE26 170 E5
Border Gdns., Croy. 204 B4
Border Rd. SE26 171 E5
Bordergate, Mitch. 185 H1
Borders La., Loug. 48 D4
Bordesley Rd., Mord. 185 E4
Bordon Wk. SW15 147 G7
Boreas Wk. N1 11 H2
Boreham Av. E16 115 G6
Boreham Cl. E11 96 C1
Hainault Rd.
Boreham Rd. N22 75 J2
Borehamwood Ind. Pk., Borwd. 38 D2
Borgard Rd. SE18 136 C4
Borkwood Pk., Orp. 207 J4
Borkwood Way, Orp. 207 H4
Borland Rd. SE15 153 F4
Borland Rd., Tedd. 163 E6
Borneo St. SW15 147 J3
Borough High St. SE1 27 J4
Borough High St. SE1 131 J2
Borough Hill, Croy. 201 H3
Borough Rd. SE1 27 G5
Borough Rd. SE1 131 H3
Borough Rd., Islw. 144 B1
Borough Rd., Kings.T. 182 A1
Borough Rd., Mitch. 185 H2
Borough Sq. SE1 27 J4
Borrett Cl. SE17 35 J4
Borrodaile Rd. SW18 149 E6
Borrowdale Av., Har. 68 D2
Borrowdale Cl., Ilf. 80 B4
Borrowdale Ct., Enf. 43 J1
Borthwick Ms. E15 96/97 E4
Borthwick Rd.
Borthwick Rd. E15 96 E4
Borthwick Rd. NW9 71 F6
West Hendon Bdy.
Borthwick St. SE8 134 A5
Borwick Av. E17 77 J3
Bosbury Rd. SE6 172 C3
Boscastle Rd. NW5 92 B3
Bosco Cl., Orp. 207 J4
Strickland Way
Boscobel Pl. SW1 32 C1
Boscobel Pl. SW1 130 A4
Boscobel St. NW8 7 F6
Boscobel St. NW8 109 G4
Boscombe Av. E10 78 D7
Boscombe Cl. E5 95 H5
Boscombe Gdns. SW16 169 E6
Boscombe Rd. SW17 168 A6
Boscombe Rd. SW19 184 E1
Boscombe Rd. W12 127 G1
Boscombe Rd., Wor.Pk. 197 J1
Bosgrove E4 62 C1
Boss St. SE1 29 F3
Bostal Row, Bexh. 159 F3
Harlington Rd.
Bostall Heath SE2 138 C5
Bostall Hill SE2 138 A5
Bostall La. SE2 138 B5
Bostall Manorway SE2 138 B4
Bostall Pk. Av., Bexh. 138 E7
Bostall Rd., Orp. 176 B7
Boston Gdns. W4 127 E6
Boston Gdns. W7 124 D4
Boston Gdns., Brent. 124 D4
Boston Manor Rd., Brent. 124 E4
Boston Pk. Rd., Brent. 125 F5
Boston Pl. NW1 7 J6
Boston Pl. NW1 109 J4
Boston Rd. E6 116 B3
Boston Rd. E17 78 A6
Boston Rd. W7 124 B1
Boston Rd., Croy. 187 F6
Boston Rd., Edg. 54 C7
Boston St. E2 13 H1
Boston Vale W7 124 D4
Bostonthorpe Rd. W7 124 B2
Bosun Cl. E14 134 A2
Byng St.
Boswell Ct. WC1 18 B1
Boswell Path, Hayes 121 J4
Croyde Av.
Boswell Rd., Th.Hth. 187 J4
Boswell St. WC1 18 B1
Boswell St. WC1 111 E5
Bosworth Cl. E17 77 J1
Bosworth Rd. N11 58 D6
Bosworth Rd. W10 108 B4
Bosworth Rd., Barn. 40 D3
Bosworth Rd., Dag. 101 G4
Botany Bay La., Chis. 193 F2
Botany Cl., Barn. 41 H4
Boteley Cl. E4 62 D2
Botha Rd. E13 115 H5
Botham Cl., Edg. 54 C7
Pavilion Way
Bothwell Cl. E16 115 F5
Bothwell St. W6 128 A6
Delorme St.
Botolph All. EC3 20 D5
Botolph La. EC3 20 D5
Botsford Rd. SW20 184 B2
Botts Ms. W2 108 D6
Chepstow Rd.
Botts Pas. W2 108 D6
Chepstow Rd.
Botwell La., Hayes 121 H1
Boucher Cl., Tedd. 162 C5
Boughton Av., Brom. 191 F7
Boughton Rd. SE28 137 H3
Boulcott St. E1 113 G6
Boulevard, The SW17 168 A2
Balham High Rd.
Boulevard, The, Pnr. 67 G4
Pinner Rd.
Boulevard 25 Retail Pk., Borwd. 38 A3
Boulogne Rd., Croy. 187 J6
Boulton Ho., Brent. 125 H5
Green Dragon La.
Boulton Rd., Dag. 101 E3
Boultwood Rd. E6 116 B6
Bounces La. N9 60 E2
Bounces Rd. N9 60 E1
Boundaries Rd. SW12 167 J2
Boundaries Rd., Felt. 160 C1
Boundary Av. E17 77 J7
Boundary Cl. SE20 188 D2
Haysleigh Gdns.
Boundary Cl., Barn. 40 C1
Boundary Cl., Ilf. 99 H4
Loxford La.
Boundary Cl., Kings.T. 182 B3
Boundary Cl., Sthl. 123 G5
Boundary La. E13 116 A3
Boundary La. SE17 36 A6
Boundary La. SE17 131 J6
Boundary Pas. E2 13 F5
Boundary Rd. E13 115 J3
Boundary Rd. E17 77 J7
Boundary Rd. N9 45 F6
Boundary Rd. N22 75 H3
Boundary Rd. NW8 109 E1
Boundary Rd. SW19 167 G6
Boundary Rd., Bark. 117 F2
Boundary Rd., Cars. 200 B6
Boundary Rd., Pnr. 66 D6
Boundary Rd., Sid. 157 H5
Boundary Rd., Wall. 200 B6
Boundary Rd., Wem. 87 H3
Boundary Row SE1 27 G3
Boundary St. E2 13 F4
Boundary St. E2 112 C4
Boundary Way, Croy. 204 A5
Boundfield Rd. SE6 172 E3
Bounds Grn. Rd. N11 58 C6
Bounds Grn. Rd. N22 58 C6
Bourchier St. W1 17 H5
Bourdon Pl. W1 16 E5
Bourdon Rd. SE20 189 F2
Bourdon St. W1 16 D6
Bourdon St. W1 110 B7
Bourke Cl. NW10 88/89 E6
Mayo Rd.
Bourke Cl. SW4 150 E6
Bourlet Cl. W1 17 F2
Bourn Av. N15 76 A4
Bourn Av., Barn. 41 G5
Bournbrook Rd. SE3 156 A3
Bourne, The N14 58 D1
Bourne Av. N14 58 E2
Bourne Av., Hayes 121 F3
Bourne Av., Ruis. 84 C5
Bourne Ct., Ruis. 84 B5
Bourne Dr., Mitch. 185 G2
Bourne Est. EC1 18 E1
Bourne Est. EC1 111 G5
Bourne Gdns. E4 62 B4
Bourne Hill N13 58 E1
Bourne Pl. W4 126 D5
Dukes Av.
Bourne Rd. E7 97 F3
Bourne Rd. N8 75 E6
Bourne Rd., Bex. 159 H6
Bourne Rd., Brom. 192 A4
Bourne Rd., Dart. 159 J6
Bourne St. SW1 32 B2
Bourne St. SW1 130 A4
Bourne St., Croy. 201 H2
Waddon New Rd.
Bourne Ter. W2 14 A1
Bourne Ter. W2 108 E5
Bourne Vale, Brom. 191 G7
Bourne Vw., Grnf. 86 C6
Bourne Way, Brom. 205 F2
Bourne Way, Epsom 196 C4
Bourne Way, Sutt. 198 C5
Bournemead Av., Nthlt. 102 A2
Bournemead Cl., Nthlt. 102 A2
Bournemead Way, Nthlt. 102 B2
Bournemouth Cl. SE15 152 D2
Bournemouth Rd. SE15 152 D2
Bournemouth Rd. SW19 184 D1
Bourneside Cres. N14 58 D1
Bourneside Gdns. SE6 172 C5
Bournevale Rd. SW16 168 E4
Bournewood Rd. SE18 138 A7
Bournville Rd. SE6 154 A7
Bournwell Cl., Barn. 41 J3
Bourton Cl., Hayes 122 A1
Avondale Dr.
Bousfield Rd. SE14 153 G2
Boutflower Rd. SW11 149 H4
Bouverie Gdns., Har. 69 G6
Bouverie Ms. N16 94 B2
Bouverie Rd.
Bouverie Pl. W2 15 F3

Name	Page	Grid
Bouverie Pl. W2	109	G6
Bouverie Rd. N16	94	B2
Bouverie Rd., Har.	67	J6
Bouverie St. EC4	**19**	**F4**
Bouverie St. EC4	111	G6
Boveney Rd. SE23	153	G7
Bovill Rd. SE23	153	G7
Bovingdon Av., Wem.	88	A6
Bovingdon Cl. N19	92	C2
Junction Rd.		
Bovingdon La. NW9	71	E1
Bovingdon Rd. SW6	148	E1
Bovingdon Sq.,	186/187	E4
Mitch.		
Leicester Av.		
Bow Br. Est. E3	114	B3
Bow Chyd. EC4	**20**	**A4**
Bow Common La.	113	H4
E3		
Bow Ind. Pk. E15	96	A7
Bow La. EC4	**20**	**A4**
Bow La. EC4	111	J6
Bow La. N12	73	F1
Bow La., Mord.	184	B6
Bow Rd. E3	113	J3
Bow St. E15	96	E5
Bow St. WC2	**18**	**B4**
Bow St. WC2	111	G6
Bowater Cl. NW9	70	D5
Bowater Cl. SW2	150	E6
Bowater Pl. SE3	135	H7
Bowater Rd. SE18	136	A3
Bowden Cl. SE11	**35**	**F4**
Bowden St. SE11	131	G5
Bowditch SE8	133	J5
Bowdon Rd. E17	78	A7
Bowen Dr. SE21	170	B3
Bowen Rd., Har.	67	J7
Bowen St. E14	114	B6
Bower Av. SE10	154	E1
Bower Cl., Nthlt.	102	C2
Bower St. E1	113	G6
Bowerdean St. SW6	148	E1
Bowerman Av. SE14	133	H6
Bowers Wk. E6	116	C6
Bowes Cl., Sid.	158	B6
Bowes Rd. N11	58	B5
Bowes Rd. N13	58	E5
Bowes Rd. W3	106	E7
Bowes Rd., Dag.	100	C4
Bowfell Rd. W6	127	J6
Bowford Av., Bexh.	158	E1
Bowhill Cl. SW9	131	G7
Bowie Cl. SW4	150	D7
Bowl Ct. EC2	**13**	**E6**
Bowl Ct. EC2	112	B4
Bowland Rd. SW4	150	D4
Bowland Rd.	63	J6
Wdf.Grn.		
Bowland Yd. SW1	**24**	**A4**
Bowles Rd. SE1	**37**	**H5**
Bowley Cl. SE19	170	C6
Bowley La. SE19	170	C5
Bowling Grn. Cl.	147	H7
SW15		
Bowling Grn. La.	**11**	**F5**
EC1		
Bowling Grn. La.	111	G4
EC1		
Bowling Grn. Pl. SE1	**28**	**B3**
Bowling Grn. Pl. SE1	132	A2
Bowling Grn. Row	136	C3
SE18		
Samuel St.		
Bowling Grn. St.	**35**	**E5**
SE11		
Bowling Grn. St.	131	G6
SE11		
Bowling Grn. Wk. N1	**12**	**D3**
Bowls, The, Chig.	65	H4
Bowls Cl., Stan.	52	E5
Bowman Av. E16	115	F7
Bowman Av. SW18	166	C1
Bowmans Cl. W13	124	E1
Bowmans Lea SE23	153	F7
Bowmans Meadow,	200	B3
Wall.		
Bowmans Ms. E1	**21**	**H5**
Bowmans Ms. N7	92/93	E3
Seven Sisters Rd.		
Bowmans Pl. N7	92/93	E3
Holloway Rd.		
Bowman's Trd. Est.	69	J3
NW9		
Westmoreland Rd.		
Bowmead SE9	174	C2
Bowmore Wk. NW1	92	D7
St. Paul's Cres.		
Bowness Cl. E8	94	C6
Beechwood Rd.		
Bowness Cres.	164	E5
SW15		
Bowness Dr., Houns.	143	E4
Bowness Rd. SE6	154	B7
Bowness Rd., Bexh.	159	H2
Bowood Rd. SW11	150	A4
Bowood Rd., Enf.	45	G2
Bowring Grn., Wat.	50	C5
Bowrons Av., Wem.	87	G7
Bowsley Rd., Felt.	160	A1
Highfield Rd.		
Bowyer Cl. E6	116	C5
Bowyer Pl. SE5	**36**	**A7**
Bowyer Pl. SE5	132	A7
Bowyer St. SE5	**36**	**A7**
Bowyer St. SE5	131	J7
Box La., Bark.	118	B2
Boxall Rd. SE21	152	B6
Boxgrove Rd. SE2	138	C3
Boxley Rd., Mord.	185	F4
Boxley St. E16	135	H1
Boxmoor Rd., Har.	68	E4
Boxoll Rd., Dag.	101	F4
Boxted Cl., Buck.H.	64	B1
Boxtree La., Har.	67	J1
Boxtree Rd., Har.	52	A7
Boxwood Cl., West Dr.	120	C2
Hawthorne Cres.		
Boxworth Cl. N12	57	G5
Boxworth Gro. N1	111	F1
Richmond Av.		
Boyard Rd. SE18	136	E5
Boyce St. SE1	**26**	**D2**
Boyce Way E13	115	G4
Boycroft Av. NW9	70	C6
Boyd Av., Sthl.	123	F1
Boyd Cl., Kings.T.	164	A7
Boyd Rd. SW19	167	G6
Boyd St. E1	**21**	**H4**
Boyd St. E1	112	D6
Boydell Ct. NW8	91	G7
St. John's Wd. Pk.		
Boyfield St. SE1	**27**	**H4**
Boyfield St. SE1	131	H2
Boyland Rd., Brom.	173	F5
Boyle Av., Stan.	52	D6
Boyle Fm. Island,	180	D6
T.Ditt.		
Boyle Fm. Rd., T.Ditt.	180	D6
Boyle St. W1	**17**	**F5**
Boyne Av. NW4	72	A4
Boyne Rd. SE13	154	C3
Boyne Rd., Dag.	101	G3
Boyne Ter. Ms. W11	128	C1
Boyseland Ct., Edg.	54	C2
Boyson Rd. SE17	**36**	**B5**
Boyson Rd. SE17	132	A6
Boyton Cl. E1	113	G4
Stayner's Rd.		
Boyton Cl. N8	75	E3
Boyton Rd. N8	75	E3
Brabant Ct. EC3	**20**	**D5**
Brabant Rd. N22	75	F2
Brabazon Av., Wall.	200	E7
Brabazon Rd.,	122	C7
Houns.		
Brabazon Rd., Nthlt.	103	G2
Brabazon St. E14	114	B6
Brabourn Gro. SE15	153	F2
Brabourne Cl. SE19	170	B5
Brabourne Cres.,	139	F6
Bexh.		
Brabourne Hts. NW7	55	E3
Brabourne Ri., Beck.	190	C5
Bracewell Av., Grnf.	86	C5
Bracewell Rd. W10	107	J5
Bracewood Gdns.,	202	C3
Croy.		
Bracey Ms. N4	92/93	E2
Bracey St.		
Bracey St. N4	93	E2
Bracken, The E4	62	C2
Hortus Rd.		
Bracken Av. SW12	150	A6
Bracken Av., Croy.	204	B3
Bracken Cl. E6	116	C5
Bracken Cl., Borwd.	38	B1
Bracken Cl., Twick.	143	G7
Hedley Rd.		
Bracken Dr., Chig.	65	E6
Bracken End, Islw.	144	A5
Bracken Gdns. SW13	147	G2
Bracken Hill Cl.,	191	F1
Brom.		
Bracken Hill La.		
Bracken Hill La.,	191	F1
Brom.		
Bracken Ind. Est., Ilf.	65	J7
Bracken Ms. E4	62	C2
Hortus Rd.		
Bracken Ms., Rom.	83	G6
Brackenbridge Dr.,	84	D3
Ruis.		
Brackenbury Gdns.	127	H3
W6		
Brackenbury Rd. N2	73	F3
Brackenbury Rd. W6	127	H3
Brackendale N21	59	F2
Brackendale Cl.,	143	H1
Houns.		
Brackenfield Cl. E5	94/95	E4
Tiger Way		
Brackenwood, Sun.	178	A1
Brackley Cl., Wall.	201	E7
Brackley Rd. W4	127	E5
Brackley Rd., Beck.	171	J7
Brackley Sq., Wdf.Grn.	64	A7
Brackley St. EC1	**19**	**J1**
Brackley Ter. W4	127	E5
Bracklyn Cl. N1	**12**	**B1**
Bracklyn Ct. N1	**12**	**B1**
Bracklyn St. N1	**12**	**B1**
Bracklyn St. N1	112	A2
Bracknell Cl. N22	75	G1
Bracknell Gdns.	90	E4
NW3		
Bracknell Gate NW3	90	E5
Bracknell Way NW3	90	E4
Bracondale Rd. SE2	138	A4
Brad St. SE1	**27**	**F2**
Bradbourne Rd.,	159	G7
Bex.		
Bradbourne St. SW6	148	D2
Bradbury Cl., Borwd.	38	B1
Bradbury Cl., Sthl.	123	F4
Bradbury Ms. N16	94	B5
Bradbury St.		
Bradbury St. N16	94	B5
Braddock Cl., Islw.	144	C3
Braddon Rd., Rich.	145	J3
Braddyll St. SE10	134	E5
Braden St. W9	**6**	**A6**
Bradenham Av.,	158	A4
Well.		
Bradenham Cl. SE17	**36**	**B5**
Bradenham Rd., Har.	68	E4
Bradfield Dr., Bark.	100	A5
Bradfield Rd. E16	135	G2
Bradfield Rd., Ruis.	85	E5
Bradford Cl. N17	60	B6
Commercial Rd.		
Bradford Cl.	170/171	E4
SE26		
Coombe Rd.		
Bradford Cl., Brom.	206	C1
Bradford Dr., Epsom	197	F6
Bradford Rd. W3	126/127	E2
Warple Way		
Bradford Rd., Ilf.	99	G1
Bradgate Rd. SE6	154	A6
Brading Cres. E11	97	H2
Brading Rd. SW2	151	F7
Brading Rd., Croy.	187	F6
Bradiston Rd. W9	108	C3
Bradley Cl. N7	93	F6
Sutterton St.		
Bradley Gdns. W13	104	E6
Bradley Ms. SW17	167	J1
Bellevue Rd.		
Bradley Rd. N22	75	F2
Bradley Rd. SE19	169	J6
Bradley Stone Rd.	116	C5
E6		
Bradley's Cl. N1	**11**	**F1**
Bradman Row, Edg.	54	C7
Pavilion Way		
Bradmead SW8	130	B7
Bradmore Ho. E1	113	F5
Bradmore Pk. Rd.	127	H3
W6		
Bradshaw Cl. SW19	166	D6
Bradshaws Cl. SE25	188	D3
Bradstock Rd. E9	95	G6
Bradstock Rd.,	197	G5
Epsom		
Bradwell Av., Dag.	101	G2
Bradwell Cl. E18	79	F4
Bradwell Ms. N18	60	D4
Lyndhurst Rd.		
Bradwell Rd., Buck.H.	64	B1
Bradwell St. E1	113	G3
Brady Av., Loug.	49	F2
Brady St. E1	112	E4
Bradymead E6	116/117	E6
Warwall		
Braemar Av. N22	75	E1
Braemar Av. NW10	88	D3
Braemar Av. SW19	166	D2
Braemar Av., Bexh.	159	J4
Braemar Av., Th.Hth.	187	G3
Braemar Av., Wem.	87	G7
Braemar Gdns.	70	D1
NW9		
Braemar Gdns., Sid.	175	G3
Braemar Gdns.,	204	C1
W.Wick.		
Braemar Rd. E13	115	F4
Braemar Rd. N15	76	B5
Braemar Rd., Brent.	125	H6
Braemar Rd., Wor.Pk.	197	H3
Braes St. N1	93	H7
Braeside, Beck.	172	A5
Braeside Av. SW19	184	B1
Braeside Cl., Pnr.	51	G7
The Av.		
Braeside Cres.,	159	J4
Bexh.		
Braeside Rd. SW16	168	C7
Braesyde Cl., Belv.	139	F4
Brafferton Rd.,	201	J4
Croy.		
Braganza St. SE17	**35**	**G3**
Braganza St. SE17	131	H5
Bragg Cl., Dag.	100	B6
Porters Av.		
Braham St. E1	**21**	**G3**
Braham St. E1	112	C6
Braid Av. W3	106	E6
Braid Cl., Felt.	161	F2
Braidwood Rd. SE6	172	D1
Braidwood St. SE1	**28**	**D2**
Brailsford Cl., Mitch.	167	H7
Brailsford Rd. SW2	151	G5
Brainton Av., Felt.	142	B7
Braintree Av., Ilf.	80	B4
Braintree Rd., Dag.	101	G3
Braintree Rd., Ruis.	84	B4
Braintree St. E2	113	F3
Braithwaite Av.,	83	G7
Rom.		
Braithwaite Gdns.,	69	F1
Stan.		
Braithwaite Rd., Enf.	45	J3
Bramah Grn. SW9	151	G1
Bramalea Cl. N6	74	A6
Bramall Cl. E15	97	F5
Idmiston Rd.		
Bramber Ct., Brent.	125	H4
Sterling Pl.		
Bramber Rd. N12	57	H5
Bramber Rd. W14	128	C6
Bramble Cl., Croy.	204	A4
Bramble Cl., Stan.	53	G7
Bramble Cft., Erith	139	J4
Bramble Gdns. W12	107	F7
Wallflower St.		
Bramble La.,	161	F6
Hmptn.		
Brambleacres Cl.,	198	D7
Sutt.		
Bramblebury Rd.	137	F5
SE18		
Brambledown Cl.,	191	E5
W.Wick.		
Brambledown Rd.,	200	A7
Cars.		
Brambledown Rd.,	202	B7
S.Croy.		
Brambledown Rd.,	200	B7
Wall.		
Brambles, The, Chig.	65	F5
Clayside		
Brambles, The,	120	B4
West Dr.		
Brambles Cl., Islw.	124	E7
Bramblewood Cl.,	199	H1
Cars.		
Bramblings, The, E4	62	D4
Bramcote Av.,	185	J4
Mitch.		
Bramcote Ct., Mitch.	185	J4
Bramcote Av.		
Bramcote Gro. SE16	133	F5
Bramcote Rd. SW15	147	H4
Bramdean Cres.	173	G1
SE12		
Bramdean Gdns.	173	G1
SE12		
Bramerton Rd.,	189	J3
Beck.		
Bramerton St. SW3	**31**	**G5**
Bramerton St. SW3	129	H6
Bramfield Ct. N4	93	J2
Queens Dr.		
Bramfield Rd. SW11	149	H6
Bramford Ct. N14	58	D2
Bramford Rd. SW18	149	F4
Bramham Gdns.	**30**	**A3**
SW5		
Bramham Gdns.	129	E5
SW5		
Bramham Gdns.,	195	G4
Chess.		
Bramhope La. SE7	135	H6
Bramlands Cl. SW11	149	H3
Bramley Cl. E17	77	H2
Bramley Cl. N14	42	B5
Bramley Cl., Hayes	102	A7
Orchard Rd.		
Bramley Cl., Orp.	207	E1
Bramley Cl., S.Croy.	201	H5
Bramley Cl., Twick.	143	J6

Name	Page	Grid
Bramley Ct., Well.	158	B1
Bramley Cres. SW8	**33**	**J7**
Bramley Cres., Ilf.	80	D6
Bramley Gdns., Wat.	50	C5
Bramley Hill, S.Croy.	201	H5
Bramley Rd. N14	42	B5
Bramley Rd. N5	125	F3
Bramley Rd. W10	108	A7
Bramley Rd., Sutt.	199	G5
Bramley Way, Houns.	143	F5
Bramley Way, W.Wick.	204	B2
Brampton Cl. E5	95	E2
Brampton Gdns. N15	75	J5
Brampton Rd.		
Brampton Gro. NW4	71	H4
Brampton Gro., Har.	68	D4
Brampton Gro., Wem.	88	A1
Brampton La. NW4	71	J4
Brampton Pk. Rd. N22	75	G3
Brampton Rd. E6	116	A3
Brampton Rd. N15	75	J5
Brampton Rd. NW9	70	A4
Brampton Rd. SE2	138	C6
Brampton Rd., Bexh.	138	D7
Brampton Rd., Croy.	188	C7
Brampton Rd., Wat.	50	A3
Bramshaw Gdns., Wat.	50	D5
Bramshaw Ri., N.Mal.	183	E6
Bramshaw Rd. E9	95	G6
Bramshill Cl., Chig.	65	H5
Tine Rd.		
Bramshill Gdns. NW5	92	B3
Bramshill Rd. NW10	107	F2
Bramshot Av. SE7	135	G6
Bramshot Way, Wat.	50	A2
Bramston Cl., Ilf.	65	J6
Bramston Rd. NW10	107	G2
Bramston Rd. SW17	167	F3
Bramwell Cl., Sun.	178	D2
Bramwell Ms. N1	111	F1
Brancaster Dr. NW7	55	F7
Brancaster Pl., Loug.	48	C3
Brancaster Rd. E12	98	C4
Brancaster Rd. SW16	168	E3
Brancaster Rd., Ilf.	81	G6
Brancepeth Gdns., Buck.H.	63	G2
Branch Hill NW3	91	F3
Branch Pl. N1	112	A1
Branch Rd. E14	113	H7
Branch St. SE15	132	B7
Brancker Cl., Wall.	200/201	E7
Brown Cl.		
Brancker Rd., Har.	69	G3
Brancroft Way, Enf.	45	H1
Brand St. SE10	134	C7
Brandlehow Rd. SW15	148	C4
Brandon Est. SE17	**35**	**H6**
Brandon Est. SE17	131	H6
Brandon Rd. E17	78	C3
Brandon Rd. N7	92	E7
Brandon Rd., Sthl.	123	F5
Brandon Rd., Sutt.	198	E4
Brandon St. SE17	**36**	**A2**
Brandon St. SE17	131	J4
Brandram Rd. SE13	154	E3
Brandreth Rd. E6	116	C6
Brandreth Rd. SW17	168	B2
Brandries, The, Wall.	200	D3
Brandville Gdns., Ilf.	81	E4
Brandville Rd., West Dr.	120	B2
Brandy Way, Sutt.	198	D7
Brangbourne Rd., Brom.	172	C5
Brangton Rd. SE11	**34**	**D4**
Brangton Rd. SE11	131	F5
Brangwyn Cres. SW19	185	G1
Branksea St. SW6	128	B7
Branksome Av. N18	60	C5
Branksome Rd. SW2	151	E5
Branksome Rd. SW19	184	D1
Branksome Way, Har.	69	H6
Branksome Way, N.Mal.	182	C1
Bransby Rd., Chess.	195	H6
Branscombe Gdns. N21	43	G7
Branscombe St. SE13	154	B3
Bransdale Cl. NW6	108/109	E1
West End La.		
Bransgrove Rd., Edg.	69	J1
Branston Cres., Orp.	207	G1
Branstone Rd., Rich.	145	J1
Brants Wk. W7	104	B4
Brantwood Av., Erith	139	J7
Brantwood Av., Islw.	144	D4
Brantwood Cl. E17	78	B3
Brantwood Gdns., Enf.	42	E4
Brantwood Gdns., Ilf.	80	B4
Brantwood Rd. N17	60	D6
Brantwood Rd. SE24	151	J5
Brantwood Rd., Bexh.	159	H2
Brasenose Dr. SW13	127	J6
Brasher Cl., Grnf.	86	A5
Brass Tally All. SE16	133	G2
Middleton Dr.		
Brassey Cl., Felt.	160	A1
Brassey Rd. NW6	90	C6
Brassey Sq. SW11	150	A3
Brassie Av. W3	106	E6
Brasted Cl. SE26	171	F4
Brasted Cl., Bexh.	158	D5
Brathway Rd. SW18	148	D7
Bratley St. E1	**13**	**H6**
Braund Av., Grnf.	103	H4
Braundton Av., Sid.	175	J1
Braunston Dr., Hayes	102	E4
Bravington Pl. W9	108	C4
Bravington Rd.		
Bravington Rd. W9	108	C2
Brawne Ho. SE17	**35**	**G6**
Braxfield Rd. SE4	153	H4
Braxted Pk. SW16	169	F6
Bray NW3	91	H7
Bray Cl., Borwd.	38	C1
Bray Cres. SE16	133	G2
Marlow Way		
Bray Dr. E16	115	F7
Bray Pas. E16	115	G7
Bray Pl. SW3	**31**	**J2**
Bray Pl. SW3	129	J4
Bray Rd. NW7	56	A6
Brayards Rd. SE15	152	E2
Brayards Rd. Est. SE15	152	E2
Braybourne Dr., Islw.	124	C7
Braybrook St. W12	107	F5
Braybrooke Gdns. SE19	170	C7
Fox Hill		
Brayburne Av. SW4	150	C2
Braycourt Av., Walt.	178	B7
Braydon Rd. N16	94	D1
Brayfield Ter. N1	93	G7
Lofting Rd.		
Brayford Sq. E1	113	F6
Summercourt Rd.		
Brayton Gdns., Enf.	42	D4
Braywood Rd. SE9	157	G4
Brazil Cl., Croy.	186	E7
Breach La., Dag.	119	G3
Bread St. EC4	**20**	**A4**
Bread St. EC4	111	J7
Breakspears Ms. SE4	154	A2
Breakspears Rd.		
Breakspears Rd. SE4	153	J4
Bream Cl. N17	77	E4
Bream Gdns. E6	116	D3
Bream St. E3	96	A7
Breamore Cl. SW15	165	G1
Breamore Rd., Ilf.	99	J2
Bream's Bldgs. EC4	**19**	**E3**
Bream's Bldgs. EC4	111	G6
Breamwater Gdns., Rich.	163	E3
Brearley Cl., Edg.	54	C7
Pavilion Way		
Breasley Cl. SW15	147	H4
Brechin Pl. SW7	**30**	**D2**
Brecknock Rd. N7	92	C4
Brecknock Rd. N19	92	C4
Brecknock Rd. Est. N7	92	C4
Breckonmead, Brom.	191	J2
Wanstead Rd.		
Brecon Cl., Mitch.	186	E3
Brecon Cl., Wor.Pk.	197	J2
Brecon Rd. W6	128	B6
Brecon Rd., Enf.	45	F4
Brede Cl. E6	116	D3
Bredgar Rd. N19	92	C2
Bredhurst Cl. SE20	171	F6
Bredon Rd. SE5	151	J3
Bredon Rd., Croy.	188	C7
Breer St. SW6	148	E3
Breezers Hill E1	**21**	**J6**
Brember Rd., Har.	85	J2
Bremer Ms. E17	78	B4
Church La.		
Bremer Rd. SW7	**22**	**D4**
Bremner Rd. SW7	129	F2
Brenchley Cl., Brom.	191	F6
Brenchley Cl., Chis.	192	D1
Brenchley Gdns. SE23	153	F6
Brenchley Rd., Orp.	193	J1
Brenda Rd. SW17	167	J2
Brende Gdns., W.Mol.	179	H4
Brendon Av. NW10	89	E4
Brendon Cl., Hayes	121	F7
Brendon Gdns., Har.	85	H4
Brendon Gdns., Ilf.	81	H5
Brendon Gro. N2	73	F2
Brendon Rd. SE9	175	G2
Brendon Rd., Dag.	101	F1
Brendon St. W1	**15**	**H3**
Brendon St. W1	109	H6
Brendon Way, Enf.	44	B7
Brenley Cl., Mitch.	186	A3
Brenley Gdns. SE9	156	A4
Brent, Bex.	177	E1
Brent Cres. NW10	105	J2
Brent Cross Gdns. NW4	72	A6
Haley Rd.		
Brent Cross Shop. Cen. NW4	71	J7
Brent Grn. NW4	71	J5
Brent Grn. Wk., Wem.	88	C3
Brent Lea, Brent.	125	F7
Brent Pk. NW10	88	D5
Brent Pk. Rd. NW4	71	H7
Brent Pk. Rd. NW9	89	G1
Brent Pl., Barn.	40	D5
Brent Rd. E16	115	G5
Brent Rd. SE18	136	E7
Brent Rd., Brent.	125	F6
Brent Rd., Sthl.	122	C3
Brent Side, Brent.	125	F6
Brent St. NW4	71	J4
Brent Ter. NW2	89	J2
Brent Vw. Rd. NW9	71	G7
Brent Way N3	56	D6
Brent Way, Brent.	125	G7
Brent Way, Wem.	88	B6
Brentcot Cl. W13	104	E4
Brentfield NW10	88	B7
Brentfield Cl. NW10	88	D6
Normans Mead		
Brentfield Gdns. NW2	72	A7
Hendon Way		
Brentfield Rd. NW10	88	D6
Brentford Business Cen., Brent.	125	F7
Brentford Cl., Hayes	102	D4
Brentham Way W5	105	G4
Brenthouse Rd. E9	95	E7
Brenthurst Rd. NW10	89	F6
Brentmead Cl. W7	104	B7
Brentmead Gdns. NW10	105	J2
Brentmead Pl. NW11	72	A6
North Circular Rd.		
Brenton St. E14	113	H6
Brentside Cl. W13	104	D4
Brentside Executive Cen., Brent.	125	E6
Brentvale Av., Sthl.	124	A1
Brentvale Av., Wem.	105	J1
Brentwick Gdns., Brent.	125	H4
Brentwood Cl. SE9	175	F1
Brentwood Ho. SE18	136	A6
Shooter's Hill Rd.		
Brereton Rd. N17	60	C7
Bressenden Pl. SW1	**25**	**E5**
Bressenden Pl. SW1	130	B3
Bressey Av., Enf.	44	D1
Bressey Gro. E18	79	F2
Brett Cl. N16	94	B2
Yoakley Rd.		
Brett Cl., Nthlt.	102	D3
Broomcroft Av.		
Brett Ct. N9	61	F2
Brett Cres. NW10	88	D7
Brett Gdns., Dag.	100	E7
Brett Ho. Cl. SW15	148	A6
Putney Heath La.		
Brett Pas. E8	94/95	E5
Kenmure Rd.		
Brett Rd. E8	95	E5
Brett Rd., Barn.	39	J5
Brettell St. SE17	**36**	**C4**
Brettenham Av. E17	78	A1
Brettenham Rd. E17	78	A2
Brettenham Rd. N18	60	E4
Brewer St. W1	**17**	**G5**
Brewer St. W1	110	C7
Brewer's Grn. SW1	**25**	**H5**
Brewers Hall Gdns. EC2	**20**	**A2**
Brewers La., Rich.	145	G5
Brewery Cl., Wem.	86	D5
Brewery La., Twick.	144	C7
Brewery Rd. N7	92	E7
Brewery Rd. SE18	137	G5
Brewery Rd., Brom.	206	B1
Brewery Sq. SE1	132	C1
Horselydown La.		
Brewhouse La. E1	133	E1
Brewhouse Rd. SE18	136	C4
Brewhouse St. SW15	148	B3
Brewhouse Wk. SE16	133	H1
Brewhouse Yd. EC1	**11**	**G5**
Brewood Rd., Dag.	100	B6
Brewster Gdns. W10	107	J5
Brewster Ho. E14	113	J7
Brewster Rd. E10	96	B1
Brian Rd., Rom.	82	C5
Briant St. SE14	**153**	**G1**
Briants Cl., Pnr.	67	F2
Briar Av. SW16	169	F7
Briar Cl. N2	73	E3
Briar Cl. N13	59	J3
Briar Cl., Buck.H.	64	A2
Briar Cl., Hmptn.	161	F5
Briar Cl., Islw.	144	C5
Briar Cl., Sutt.	197	J4
Briar Cres., Nthlt.	85	H6
Briar Gdns., Brom.	205	F1
Briar La., Croy.	204	B4
Briar Pas. SW16	187	E3
Briar Pl. SW16	187	F3
Briar Rd. NW2	89	J4
Briar Rd. SW16	187	E3
Briar Rd., Har.	69	F5
Briar Rd., Twick.	162	B1
Briar Wk. SW15	147	H4
Briar Wk. W10	108	B4
Droop St.		
Briar Wk., Edg.	54	C7
Briar Way, West Dr.	120	D2
Briarbank Rd. W13	104	D6
Briardale Gdns. NW3	90	D3
Briarfield Av. N3	72	E2
Briaris Cl. N17	60	E7
Briarswood Way, Orp.	207	J5
Briarwood Cl. NW9	70	C6
Briarwood Dr., Nthwd.	66	A2
Briarwood Rd. SW4	150	D5
Briarwood Rd., Epsom	197	G6
Briary Cl. NW3	91	H7
Fellows Rd.		
Briary Ct., Sid.	176	B5
Briary Gdns., Brom.	173	H5
Briary Gro., Edg.	70	B2
Briary La. N9	60	C3
Brick Ct. EC4	**18**	**E4**
Brick Fm. Cl., Rich.	146	B1
Brick La. E1	**13**	**G6**
Brick La. E1	112	C5
Brick La. E2	**13**	**G4**
Brick La. E2	112	C3
Brick La., Enf.	44	E2
Brick La., Stan.	53	G7
Honeypot La.		
Brick St. W1	**24**	**D2**
Brick St. W1	130	B1
Brickfield Cl., Brent.	125	F7
Brickfield Cotts. SE18	137	J6
Brickfield Fm. Gdns., Orp.	207	F4
Brickfield La., Barn.	39	F6
Brickfield La., Hayes	121	G6
Brickfield Rd. SW19	167	E4
Brickfield Rd., Th.Hth.	187	H1
Brickfields, Har.	86	A2
Brickfields Way, West Dr.	120	C3
Bricklayer's Arms SE1	**36**	**E1**
Bricklayer's Arms SE1	**132**	**B4**
Brickwood Cl. SE26	171	E3
Brickwood Rd., Croy.	202	B2
Bride Ct. EC4	**19**	**G4**

Name	Page	Grid
Bride La. EC4	19	G4
Bride St. N7	93	F6
Brideale Cl. SE15	132	C7
Colegrove Rd.		
Bridewain St. SE1	29	G5
Bridewell St. SE1	132	C3
Bridewell Pl. E1	132/133	E1
Brewhouse La.		
Bridewell Pl. EC4	19	G4
Bridford Ms. W1	16	E1
Bridge, The, Har.	68	B3
Bridge App. NW1	92	A7
Bridge Av. W6	127	J5
Bridge Av. W7	104	A5
Bridge Cl. W10	108	A6
Kingsdown Cl.		
Bridge Cl., Enf.	45	E2
Bridge Cl., Tedd.	162	C4
Shacklegate La.		
Bridge Dr. N13	59	F4
Bridge End E17	78	C1
Bridge Gdns., E.Mol.	180	A4
Bridge Gate N21	43	J7
Ridge Av.		
Bridge Ho. Quay E14	134	C1
Prestons Rd.		
Bridge La. NW11	72	B5
Bridge La. SW11	149	H1
Bridge Meadows SE14	133	G6
Bridge Pk. SW18	148	D5
Bridge Pl. SW1	33	E1
Bridge Pl. SW1	130	B4
Bridge Pl., Croy.	188	A7
Bridge Rd. E6	98	C7
Bridge Rd. E15	96	D7
Bridge Rd. E17	77	J7
Bridge Rd. N9	60	D3
The Bdy.		
Bridge Rd. N22	75	E1
Bridge Rd. NW10	88	E6
Bridge Rd., Beck.	171	J7
Bridge Rd., Bexh.	159	E2
Bridge Rd., Chess.	195	H5
Bridge Rd., Croy.	201	J3
Duppas Hill Rd.		
Bridge Rd., E.Mol.	180	A4
Bridge Rd., Houns.	144	A3
Bridge Rd., Islw.	144	A3
Bridge Rd., Sthl.	123	F2
Bridge Rd., Sutt.	199	E6
Bridge Rd., Twick.	144	E6
Bridge Rd., Wall.	200	C5
Bridge Row, Croy.	202	A1
Cross Rd.		
Bridge St. SW1	26	A4
Bridge St. SW1	130	E2
Bridge St. W4	126	D4
Bridge St., Pnr.	66	D3
Bridge St., Rich.	145	G5
Bridge Ter. E15	96	D7
Bridge Vw. W6	127	J5
Bridge Way N11	58	C3
Pymmes Grn. Rd.		
Bridge Way NW11	72	C5
Bridge Way, Twick.	143	J7
Bridge Wf. Rd., Islw.	144/145	D2
Church St.		
Bridge Yd. SE1	28	C1
Bridgefield Rd., Sutt.	198	D6
Bridgefoot SE1	34	A4
Bridgefoot SE1	131	E5
Bridgeland Rd. E16	115	G7
Bridgeman Rd. N1	93	F7
Bridgeman Rd., Tedd.	162	D6
Bridgeman St. NW8	7	G2
Bridgeman St. NW8	109	H2
Bridgend Rd. SW18	149	F4
Bridgenhall Rd., Enf.	44	C1
Bridgeport Pl. E1	29	J1
Bridges Ct. SW11	149	G3
Bridges La., Croy.	200	E4
Bridges Ms. SW19	166/167	E6
Bridges Rd.		
Bridges Pl. SW6	148	C1
Bridges Rd. SW19	166	E6
Bridges Rd., Stan.	52	C5
Bridges Rd. Ms. SW19	166/167	E6
Bridges Rd.		
Bridgetown Cl. SE19	170	B5
St. Kitts Ter.		
Bridgeview St., Ilf.	65	G6
Bridgewater Cl., Chis.	193	H3
Bridgewater Gdns., Edg.	69	J2
Bridgewater Rd., Ruis.	84	A4
Bridgewater Rd., Wem.	87	F7
Bridgewater Sq. EC2	19	J1
Bridgewater St. EC2	19	J1
Bridgeway, Bark.	99	J7
Bridgeway, Wem.	87	H7
Bridgeway St. NW1	9	H2
Bridgeway St. NW1	110	C2
Bridgewood Cl. SE20	170	E7
Bridgewood Rd. SW16	168	D7
Bridgewood Rd., Wor.Pk.	197	G4
Bridgford St. SW18	167	F3
Bridgman Rd. W4	126	C3
Bridgwater Rd. E15	114	C1
Bridle Cl., Epsom	196	D5
Bridle Cl., Kings.T.	181	G4
Bridle Cl., Sun.	178	A3
Forge La.		
Bridle La. W1	17	G5
Bridle La., Twick.	144/145	E6
Crown Rd.		
Bridle Path, Croy.	201	F3
Bridle Path, The, Wdf.Grn.	62	E7
Bridle Rd., Croy.	204	A3
Bridle Rd., Esher	194	E6
Bridle Rd., Pnr.	66	C6
Bridle Way, Croy.	204	A5
Bridle Way, Orp.	207	F4
Bridleway, The, Wall.	200	C4
Bridlington Rd. N9	44	E1
Bridlington Rd., Wat.	50	D3
Bridport Av., Rom.	83	H6
Bridport Pl. N1	12	C1
Bridport Pl. N1	112	A2
Bridport Rd. N18	60	B5
Bridport Rd., Grnf.	103	H1
Bridport Rd., Th.Hth.	187	G3
Bridport Ter. SW8	150	D1
Wandsworth Rd.		
Bridstow Pl. W2	108	D6
Talbot Rd.		
Brief St. SE5	151	H1
Brierley, Croy.	204	B6
Brierley Av. N9	61	F1
Brierley Cl. SE25	188	D4
Brierley Rd. E11	96	D4
Brierley Rd. SW12	168	C2
Brierly Gdns. E2	113	F2
Royston St.		
Brig Ms. SE8	134	A6
Watergate St.		
Brigade Cl., Har.	86	A2
Brigade St. SE3	155	F2
Royal Par.		
Brigadier Av., Enf.	43	J1
Briggeford Cl. E5	94	D2
Geldeston Rd.		
Briggs Cl., Mitch.	186	B1
Bright Cl., Belv.	138	D4
Bright St. E14	114	B6
Brightfield Rd. SE12	155	F5
Brightling Rd. SE4	153	J6
Brightlingsea Pl. E14	113	J7
Brightman Rd. SW18	167	G1
Brighton Av. E17	77	J5
Brighton Dr., Nthlt.	85	G6
Brighton Gro. SE14	153	H1
New Cross Rd.		
Brighton Rd. E6	116	D3
Brighton Rd. N2	73	F2
Brighton Rd. N16	94	B4
Brighton Rd., S.Croy.	201	J5
Brighton Rd., Surb.	181	F6
Brighton Ter. SW9	151	F4
Brightside, The, Enf.	45	G1
Brightside Rd. SE13	154	D6
Brightwell Cl., Croy.	201	G1
Sumner Rd.		
Brightwell Cres. SW17	167	J5
Brigstock Rd., Belv.	139	H4
Brigstock Rd., Th.Hth.	187	G5
Brill Pl. NW1	9	J2
Brill Pl. NW1	110	D2
Brim Hill N2	73	F4
Brimpsfield Cl. SE2	138	B3
Brimsdown Av., Enf.	45	H2
Brimsdown Ind. Est., Enf.	45	J2
Brindle Gate, Sid.	175	H1
Brindley Cl., Bexh.	159	H3
Brindley Cl., Wem.	105	G1
Brindley St. SE14	153	J1
Brindley Way, Brom.	173	G5
Brindley Way, Sthl.	103	H7
Brinkburn Cl. SE2	138	A4
Brinkburn Cl., Edg.	70	B2
Brinkburn Gdns., Edg.	70	A3
Brinkley Rd., Wor.Pk.	197	H2
Brinklow Cres. SE18	137	E7
Brinklow Ho. W2	14	A1
Brinklow Ho. W2	108	E5
Brinkworth Rd., Ilf.	80	B3
Brinkworth Way E9	95	J6
Brinsdale Rd. NW4	72	A4
Brinsley Rd., Har.	68	A2
Brinsley St. E1	112/113	E6
Watney St.		
Brinsworth Cl., Twick.	162	A2
Brinton Wk. SE1	27	G2
Brion Pl. E14	114	C5
Brisbane Av. SW19	184	E1
Brisbane Ct. N10	58	B7
Sydney Rd.		
Brisbane Rd. E10	96	B2
Brisbane Rd. W13	124	D2
Brisbane Rd., Ilf.	81	E7
Brisbane St. SE5	132	A7
Briscoe Cl. E11	97	F2
Briscoe Rd. SW19	167	G6
Briset Rd. SE9	156	A3
Briset St. EC1	19	G1
Briset Way N7	93	F2
Brisett St. W1	16	D5
Bristol Cl., Stai.	140	B6
Portsmouth Rd.		
Bristol Cl., Wall.	200	E7
Bristol Gdns. W9	6	B6
Bristol Gdns. W9	109	E4
Bristol Ms. W9	6	B6
Bristol Ms. W9	109	E4
Bristol Pk. Rd. E17	77	H4
Bristol Rd. E7	97	J6
Bristol Rd., Grnf.	103	H1
Bristol Rd., Mord.	185	F5
Briston Gro. N8	75	E6
Briston Ms. NW7	55	G7
Bristow Rd. SE19	170	B5
Bristow Rd., Bexh.	159	E1
Bristow Rd., Croy.	200	E4
Bristow Rd., Houns.	143	J3
Britannia Cl. SW4	150	D4
Bowland Rd.		
Britannia Cl., Nthlt.	102	D3
Britannia Gate E16	135	G1
Britannia La., Twick.	143	J7
Britannia Rd. E14	134	A4
Britannia Rd. N12	57	F3
Britannia Rd. SW6	128	E7
Britannia Rd., Ilf.	98	E3
Britannia Rd., Surb.	181	J7
Britannia Row N1	111	H1
Britannia St. WC1	10	C3
Britannia St. WC1	111	F3
Britannia Wk. N1	12	B3
Britannia Wk. N1	112	A2
Britannia Way NW10	106	B4
Britannia Way SW6	148/149	E1
Britannia Rd.		
Britannia Way, Stai.	140	A7
British Gro. W4	127	F5
British Gro. Pas. W4	127	F5
British Gro. S. W4	127	F5
British Gro. Pas.		
British Legion Rd. E4	63	F2
Briton Cl., S.Croy.	202	B7
Briton Cres., S.Croy.	202	B7
Briton Hill Rd., S.Croy.	202	B6
Brittain Rd., Dag.	101	E3
Britten Cl. NW11	90	E1
Britten Dr., Sthl.	103	G6
Britten St. SW3	31	G4
Britten St. SW3	129	H5
Britten's Ct. E1	112	E7
Britton Cl. SE6	154	D7
Brownhill Rd.		
Britton St. EC1	11	G6
Britton St. EC1	111	H4
Brixham Cres., Ruis.	84	A1
Brixham Gdns., Ilf.	99	H5
Brixham Rd., Well.	158	D1
Brixham St. E16	136	D1
Brixton Est., Edg.	70	B2
Brixton Hill SW2	151	E7
Brixton Hill Pl. SW2	150/151	E7
Brixton Hill		
Brixton Oval SW2	151	G4
Brixton Rd. SW9	151	G2
Brixton Sta. Rd. SW9	151	G4
Brixton Water La.	151	F5
Broad Ct. WC2	18	B4
Broad Grn. Av., Croy.	187	H7
Broad La. EC2	20	D1
Broad La. EC2	112	B5
Broad La. N8	75	F5
Tottenham La.		
Broad La. N15	76	C4
Broad La., Hmptn.	161	G6
Broad Lawn SE9	174	D2
Broad Oak, Wdf.Grn.	63	H5
Broad Oak Cl. E4	62	A5
Royston Av.		
Broad Sanctuary SW1	25	J4
Broad Sanctuary SW1	130	D2
Broad St., Dag.	101	G7
Broad St., Tedd.	162	C6
Broad St. Av. EC2	20	D2
Broad St. Pl. EC2	20	C2
Broad Vw. NW9	70	A6
Broad Wk. N21	59	F2
Broad Wk. NW1	8	D4
Broad Wk. NW1	110	B3
Broad Wk. SE3	155	J2
Broad Wk. W1	24	B1
Broad Wk. W1	130	A1
Broad Wk., Houns.	142	D1
Broad Wk., Rich.	125	J7
Broad Wk., The W8	22	B1
Broad Wk., The W8	129	E1
Broad Wk., The, E.Mol.	180	C3
Broad Wk. La. NW11	72	C7
Broad Yd. EC1	11	G6
Broadbent Cl. N6	92	B1
Broadbent St. W1	16	D5
Broadberry Ct. N18	60	E5
Broadbridge Cl. SE3	135	G7
Broadcoombe, S.Croy.	203	F7
Broadcroft Av., Stan.	69	G2
Broadcroft Rd., Orp.	193	G7
Broadfield Cl. NW2	89	J3
Broadfield Cl., Croy.	201	F2
Progress Way		
Broadfield Ct., Bushey	52	B2
Broadfield La. NW1	92	E7
Broadfield Rd. SE6	154	E7
Broadfield Sq., Enf.	45	E2
Broadfield Way, Buck.H.	63	J3
Broadfields, E.Mol.	180	A6
Broadfields, Har.	67	H2
Broadfields Av. N21	43	G7
Broadfields Av., Edg.	54	B4
Broadfields Hts., Edg.	54	B4
Broadfields La., Wat.	50	B1
Broadfields Way NW10	89	F5
Broadgate E13	115	J2
Broadgate EC2	112	B5
Liverpool St.		
Broadgate Circle EC2	20	D1
Broadgate Rd. E16	116	A6
Fulmer Rd.		
Broadgates Av., Barn.	41	E1
Broadgates Rd. SW18	167	G1
Ellerton Rd.		
Broadhead Strand NW9	71	F1
Broadheath Dr., Chis.	174	C5
Broadhinton Rd. SW4	150	B3
Broadhurst Av., Edg.	54	B4
Broadhurst Av., Ilf.	99	J4
Broadhurst Cl. NW6	91	F6
Broadhurst Gdns.		
Broadhurst Cl., Rich.	145	J5
Lower Gro. Rd.		
Broadhurst Gdns. NW6	90	E6
Broadhurst Gdns., Chig.	65	F4
Broadhurst Gdns., Ruis.	84	C2
Broadlands, Felt.	161	F3
Broadlands Av. SW16	168	E2
Broadlands Av., Enf.	45	E3
Broadlands Cl. N6	74	A7
Broadlands Cl. SW16	168	E2
Broadlands Cl., Enf.	45	E3
Broadlands Rd. N6	73	J7
Broadlands Rd., Brom.	173	H4
Broadlands Way, N.Mal.	183	F6
Broadlawns Ct., Har.	68	C1
Broadley St. NW8	15	F1
Broadley Ter. NW1	7	H6
Broadley Ter. NW1	109	H4
Broadmayne SE17	36	B3
Broadmead SE6	172	A3
Broadmead Av., Wor.Pk.	183	G7

Name	Page	Grid
Broadmead Cl., Hmptn.	161	G6
Broadmead Cl., Pnr.	51	E7
Broadmead Est., Wdf.Grn.	63	J7
Broadmead Rd., Hayes	102	E4
Broadmead Rd., Nthlt.	102	E4
Broadmead Rd., Wdf.Grn.	63	G6
Broadoaks, Surb.	196	B1
Broadoaks Way, Brom.	191	F5
Broadstone Pl. W1	**16**	**B2**
Broadview Rd. SW16	168	D7
Broadwalk E18	79	F3
Broadwalk, Har.	67	G5
Broadwall SE1	**27**	**F1**
Broadwall SE1	131	G1
Broadwater Gdns., Orp.	207	E4
Broadwater Rd. N17	76	B1
Broadwater Rd. SE28	137	G3
Broadwater Rd. SW17	167	H4
Broadway E15	96	D7
Broadway SW1	**25**	**H5**
Broadway SW1	130	D3
Broadway W13	124	D1
Broadway, Bark.	99	F7
Broadway, Bexh.	159	E4
Broadway, Surb.	196	B1
Broadway, The E4	62	D6
Broadway, The E13	115	H2
Broadway, The N8	74	E6
Broadway, The N9	60	D3
Broadway, The N14	58	D1
Winchmore Hill Rd.		
Broadway, The N22	75	G2
Broadway, The NW7	55	E5
Broadway, The SW13	146/147	E2
The Ter.		
Broadway, The SW19	166	C6
Broadway, The W5	105	G7
Broadway, The W7	124	B1
Broadway, The, Croy.	200/201	E4
Croydon Rd.		
Broadway, The, Dag.	101	F2
Whalebone La. S.		
Broadway, The, Grnf.	103	J4
Broadway, The, Har.	68	B3
Broadway, The, Loug.	49	F4
Broadway, The, Pnr.	51	F7
Broadway, The, Sthl.	102	D7
Broadway, The, Stan.	53	F5
Broadway, The, Sutt.	198	B6
Broadway, The, T.Ditt.	194	B1
Hampton Ct. Way		
Broadway, The, Wem.	87	H3
East La.		
Broadway, The, Wdf.Grn.	63	H6
Broadway Av., Croy.	188	A5
Broadway Av., Twick.	144	E6
Broadway Cl., Wdf.Grn.	63	H6
Broadway Ct. SW19	166	D6
The Bdy.		
Broadway Gdns., Mitch.	185	H4
Broadway Mkt. E8	112	E1
Broadway Mkt. Ms. E8	112	D1
Brougham Rd.		
Broadway Ms. E5	76	C7
Broadway Ms. N13	59	F5
Elmdale Rd.		
Broadway Ms. N21	59	H1
Compton Rd.		
Broadway Par. N8	74	E6
Broadway Pl. SW19	166	C6
Hartfield Rd.		
Broadwick St. W1	**17**	**G5**
Broadwick St. W1	110	C6
Broadwood Ter. W8	128	C4
Pembroke Rd.		
Brocas Cl. NW3	91	H7
Fellows Rd.		
Brock Pl. E3	114	B4
Brock Rd. E13	115	H5
Brock St. SE15	153	F3
Evelina Rd.		
Brockdish Av., Bark.	99	J5
Brockenhurst, W.Mol.	179	F6
Brockenhurst Av., Wor.Pk.	197	E1
Brockenhurst Gdns. NW7	55	E5
Brockenhurst Gdns., Ilf.	99	F5
Brockenhurst Ms. N18	60	D4
Lyndhurst Rd.		
Brockenhurst Rd., Croy.	188	E7
Brockenhurst Way SW16	186	D2
Burrow Rd.		
Brocket Cl., Chig.	65	J5
Brocket Way, Chig.	65	H5
Brockham Cl. SW19	166	C5
Brockham Cres., Croy.	204	D3
Brockham Dr. SW2	151	F7
Fairview Pl.		
Brockham Dr., Ilf.	81	E6
Brockham St. SE1	**28**	**A5**
Brockham St. SE1	131	J3
Brockhurst Cl., Stan.	52	C6
Brockill Cres. SE4	153	H4
Brocklebank Rd. SE7	135	H4
Brocklebank Rd. SW18	149	F7
Brocklehurst St. SE14	133	G7
Brocklesby Rd. SE25	188	E4
Brockley Av., Stan.	53	H3
Brockley Cl., Stan.	53	H4
Brockley Cross SE4	153	H3
Endwell Rd.		
Brockley Footpath SE15	153	F4
Brockley Gdns. SE4	153	J2
Brockley Gro. SE4	153	J3
Brockley Hall Rd. SE4	153	H6
Brockley Hill, Stan.	53	F1
Brockley Ms. SE4	153	H5
Brockley Pk. SE23	153	H7
Brockley Ri. SE23	153	H6
Brockley Rd. SE4	153	J3
Brockley Vw. SE23	153	H7
Brockley Way SE4	153	G5
Brockleyside, Stan.	53	H4
Brockman Ri., Brom.	172	D4
Brocks Dr., Sutt.	198	B3
Brockshot Cl., Brent.	125	G5
Brockway Cl. E11	97	E1
Brockwell Cl., Orp.	193	J5
Brockwell Pk. Gdns. SE24	151	G7
Brodewater Rd., Borwd.	38	B2
Brodia Rd. N16	94	B3
Brodie Rd. E4	62	C1
Brodie St. SE1	**37**	**G3**
Brodlove La. E1	113	G7
Brodrick Gro. SE2	138	B4
Brodrick Rd. SW17	167	H2
Brograve Gdns., Beck.	190	B2
Broke Wk. E8	112	D1
Broken Wf. EC4	**19**	**J5**
Brokesley St. E3	113	J4
Bromar Rd. SE5	152	B3
Bromborough Grn., Wat.	50	C5
Brome Rd. SE9	156	C3
Bromefield, Stan.	69	F1
Bromehead Rd. E1	113	F6
Bromell's Rd. SW4	150	C4
Bromfelde Rd. SW4	150	D2
Bromfelde Wk. SW4	150	D2
Bromfield St. N1	**11**	**F1**
Bromfield St. N1	111	G2
Bromhall Rd., Dag.	100	B6
Bromhedge SE9	174	C3
Bromholm Rd. SE2	138	B3
Bromleigh Ct. SE23	170/171	E2
Lapse Wd. Wk.		
Bromley Av., Brom.	173	E7
Bromley Common, Brom.	191	J4
Bromley Cres., Brom.	191	F3
Bromley Gdns., Brom.	191	F3
Bromley Gro., Brom.	190	D2
Bromley Hall Rd. E14	114	D5
Bromley High St. E3	114	B3
Bromley Hill, Brom.	172	E6
Bromley La., Chis.	175	F7
Bromley Pk., Brom.	191	F1
London Rd.		
Bromley Pl. W1	**17**	**F1**
Bromley Rd. E10	78	B6
Bromley Rd. E17	78	A3
Bromley Rd. N17	60	A3
Bromley Rd. N18	76	C1
Bromley Rd. SE6	172	B1
Bromley Rd., Beck.	190	B1
Bromley Rd., Brom.	190	C2
Bromley Rd. (Downham), Brom.	172	C4
Bromley Rd., Chis.	193	E1
Bromley St. E1	113	G5
Brompton Arc. SW3	**23**	**J4**
Brompton Cl. SE20	188	D2
Selby Rd.		
Brompton Cl., Houns.	143	F5
Brompton Gro. N2	73	H4
Brompton Pk. Cres. SW6	**30**	**A6**
Brompton Pk. Cres. SW6	128	E6
Brompton Pl. SW3	**23**	**H5**
Brompton Rd. SW1	129	H3
Brompton Rd. SW3	**23**	**H5**
Brompton Rd. SW3	129	H3
Brompton Rd. SW7	**23**	**H5**
Brompton Rd. SW7	129	H3
Brompton Sq. SW3	**23**	**G5**
Brompton Sq. SW3	129	H3
Brompton Ter. SE18	156	D1
Prince Imperial Rd.		
Bromwich Av. N6	92	A2
Bromyard Av. W3	127	E1
Bromyard Ho. SE15	**37**	**J7**
Bromyard Ho. SE15	132	E7
Brondesbury Ct. NW2	89	J6
Brondesbury Ms. NW6	90	D7
Willesden La.		
Brondesbury Pk. NW2	89	H6
Brondesbury Pk. NW6	90	A7
Brondesbury Rd. NW6	108	C2
Brondesbury Vil. NW6	108	C2
Bronsart Rd. SW6	128	B7
Bronson Rd. SW20	184	A2
Bronte Cl. E7	97	G4
Bective Rd.		
Bronte Cl., Erith	139	H7
Bronte Cl., Ilf.	80	D5
Bronte Ho. NW6	108	D3
Bronti Cl. SE17	**36**	**A4**
Bronti Cl. SE17	131	J5
Bronze Age Way, Belv.	139	J3
Bronze Age Way, Erith	139	J3
Bronze St. SE8	134	A7
Brook Av., Dag.	101	H7
Brook Av., Edg.	54	B6
Brook Av., Wem.	88	A3
Brook Cl. NW7	56	B7
Frith Ct.		
Brook Cl. SW17	168	A2
Balham High Rd.		
Brook Cl. SW20	183	H3
Brook Cl. W3	126	A1
West Lo. Av.		
Brook Cl., Borwd.	38	B3
Brook Cl., Stai.	140	C7
Brook Cres. E4	62	A4
Brook Cres. N9	60	E4
Brook Dr. SE11	**27**	**F6**
Brook Dr. SE11	131	G4
Brook Dr., Har.	67	J4
Brook Gdns. E4	62	B4
Brook Gdns. SW13	147	F3
Brook Gdns., Kings.T.	182	C1
Brook Gate W1	**16**	**A6**
Brook Gate W1	109	J7
Brook Grn. W6	128	A4
Brook Ind. Est., Hayes	122	D1
Brook La. SE3	155	H2
Brook La., Bex.	158	D6
Brook La., Brom.	173	G6
Brook La. N., Brent.	125	G5
Brook Mead, Epsom	197	E6
Brook Meadow N12	56	E4
Brook Meadow Cl., Wdf.Grn.	62	E6
Brook Ms. N. W2	**14**	**D5**
Brook Par., Chig.	64/65	E3
High Rd.		
Brook Path, Loug.	48	B4
Brook Pl., Barn.	40	D5
Brook Ri., Chig.	64	D3
Brook Rd. N8	74	E4
Brook Rd. N22	75	F3
Brook Rd. NW2	89	G2
Brook Rd., Borwd.	38	A2
Brook Rd., Buck.H.	63	G2
Brook Rd., Ilf.	81	H6
Brook Rd., Loug.	48	B5
Brook Rd., Surb.	195	H2
Brook Rd., Th.Hth.	187	J4
Brook Rd., Twick.	144	D6
Brook Rd. S., Brent.	125	G6
Brook St. N17	76	C2
Brook St. W1	**16**	**C5**
Brook St. W1	110	B6
Brook St. W2	**15**	**F5**
Brook St. W2	109	G7
Brook St., Belv.	139	H5
Brook St., Erith	139	H6
Brook St., Kings.T.	181	H2
Brook Vale, Erith	159	H1
Brook Wk. N2	73	G1
Brook Wk., Edg.	54	D6
Brook Way, Chig.	64	D3
Brookbank Av. W7	104	A5
Brookbank Rd. SE13	154	A3
Brookdale N11	58	C4
Brookdale Rd. E17	78	A3
Brookdale Rd. SE6	154	B6
Brookdale Rd., Bex.	159	E6
Brookdene Rd. SE18	137	J4
Brooke Av., Har.	85	J3
Brooke Rd. E5	94	D3
Brooke Rd. E17	78	C4
Brooke Rd. N16	94	C3
Brooke St. EC1	**19**	**E2**
Brooke St. EC1	111	G5
Brookehowse Rd. SE6	172	B3
Brookend Rd., Sid.	175	H1
Brooke's Ct. EC1	**19**	**E1**
Brookes Mkt. EC1	**19**	**F1**
Brookfield N6	92	A3
Brookfield Av. E17	78	C4
Brookfield Av. NW7	55	H6
Brookfield Av. W5	105	G4
Brookfield Av., Sutt.	199	G4
Brookfield Cl. NW7	55	H6
Brookfield Ct., Grnf.	103	J3
Brookfield Ct., Har.	69	G5
Brookfield Cres. NW7	55	H6
Brookfield Cres., Har.	69	H5
Brookfield Gdns., Esher	194	C6
Brookfield Pk. NW5	92	B3
Brookfield Path, Wdf.Grn.	62	E6
Brookfield Rd. E9	95	H6
Brookfield Rd. N9	60	D3
Brookfield Rd. W4	126	D2
Brookfields, Enf.	45	G4
Brookfields Av., Mitch.	185	H5
Brookhill Cl. SE18	136	E5
Brookhill Cl., Barn.	41	H5
Brookhill Rd. SE18	136	E5
Brookhill Rd., Barn.	41	H5
Brookhouse Gdns. E4	62	E4
Brooking Rd. E7	97	G5
Brookland Cl. NW11	72	D4
Brookland Garth NW11	72	E4
Brookland Hill NW11	72	D4
Brookland Ri. NW11	72	D4
Brooklands Av. SW19	166	E2
Brooklands Av., Sid.	175	G2
Brooklands Dr., Grnf.	105	G1
Brooklands Pk. SE3	155	G3
Brooklands Rd., T.Ditt.	194	C1
Brooklea Cl. NW9	71	E1
Brooklyn Av. SE25	189	E4
Brooklyn Av., Loug.	48	B4
Brooklyn Cl., Cars.	199	H2
Brooklyn Gro. SE25	189	E4
Brooklyn Rd. SE25	188	E4
Brooklyn Rd., Brom.	192	A5
Brooklyn Way, West Dr.	120	A3
Brookmarsh Trd. Est. SE10	134	B7
Norman Rd.		
Brookmead Av., Brom.	192	C5
Brookmead Rd., Croy.	186	C6
Brookmeads Est., Mitch.	185	H5
Brookmill Rd. SE8	154	A1
Brooks Av. E6	116	C4
Brooks Cl. SE9	174	D2
Brooks Ct. E15	96	B5
Clays La.		
Brooks La. W4	126	A6
Brook's Ms. W1	**16**	**D5**

Brook's Ms. W1 110 B7
Brooks Rd. E13 115 G1
Brooks Rd. W4 126 A5
Brooksbank St. E9 95 G6
Brooksby Ms. N1 93 G7
Brooksby St.
Brooksby St. N1 93 G7
Brooksby's Wk. E9 95 G5
Brookscroft Rd. E17 78 B1
Brookshill, Har. 52 A5
Brookshill Av., Har. 52 A5
Brookshill Dr., Har. 52 A5
Brookside N21 43 F6
Brookside, Barn. 41 H6
Brookside, Cars. 200 A5
Brookside, Ilf. 65 F6
Brookside, Orp. 193 J7
Brookside Cl., Barn. 40 B6
Brookside Cl., Felt. 160 A3
Sycamore Cl.
Brookside Cl., Har. 69 G5
Brookside Cl. (Kenton), Har. 85 E4
Brookside Cres., Wor.Pk. 197 G1
Green La.
Brookside Rd. N9 60 E4
Brookside Rd. N19 92 C2
Junction Rd.
Brookside Rd. NW11 72 B6
Brookside Rd., Hayes 102 C7
Brookside S., Barn. 42 A7
Brookside Wk. N3 72 B2
Brookside Wk. N12 56 D6
Brookside Wk. NW4 72 B4
Brookside Wk. NW11 72 B4
Brookside Way, Croy. 189 G6
Brooksville Av. NW6 108 B1
Brookview Rd. SW16 168 C5
Brookville Rd. SW6 128 C7
Brookway SE3 155 G3
Brookwood Av. SW13 147 F2
Brookwood Cl., Brom. 191 F4
Brookwood Rd. SW18 166 C1
Brookwood Rd., Houns. 143 H1
Broom Cl., Brom. 192 B6
Broom Cl., Tedd. 163 G7
Broom Gdns., Croy. 204 A3
Broom Lock, Tedd. 163 F6
Broom Mead, Bexh. 159 G5
Broom Pk., Tedd. 163 G7
Broom Rd., Croy. 204 A3
Broom Rd., Tedd. 163 F6
Broom Water, Tedd. 163 F6
Broom Water W., Tedd. 163 F5
Broomcroft Av., Nthlt. 102 C3
Broome Rd., Hmptn. 161 F7
Broome Way SE5 131 J7
Broomfield E17 77 J7
Broomfield, Sun. 178 A1
Broomfield Av. N13 59 F5
Broomfield Av., Loug. 48 C6
Broomfield La. N13 59 F4
Broomfield Pl. W13 124/125 E1
Broomfield Rd.
Broomfield Rd. N13 59 E5
Broomfield Rd. W13 125 E1
Broomfield Rd., Beck. 189 H3
Broomfield Rd., Bexh. 159 G5
Broomfield Rd., Rich. 145 J1
Broomfield Rd., Rom. 82 D7
Broomfield Rd., Surb. 195 J1
Broomfield Rd., Tedd. 163 F6
Melbourne Rd.
Broomfield St. E14 114 A5
Broomgrove Gdns., Edg. 70 A1
Broomgrove Rd. SW9 151 F2
Broomhill Ri., Bexh. 159 G5
Broomhill Rd. SW18 148 D5
Broomhill Rd., Ilf. 100 A2
Broomhill Rd., Wdf.Grn. 63 G6
Broomhill Wk., Wdf.Grn. 63 F7
Broomhouse La. SW6 148 D2
Broomhouse Rd. SW6 148 D2
Broomloan La., Sutt. 198 D2
Broomsleigh St. NW6 90 C5
Broomwood Cl., Croy. 189 G5
Broomwood Rd. SW11 149 J6
Broseley Gro. SE26 171 H5
Broster Gdns. SE25 188 C3
Brough Cl. SW8 130/131 E7
Kenchester Cl.
Brough Cl., Kings.T. 163 G5
Brougham Rd. E8 112 D1
Brougham Rd. W3 106 C6
Brougham St. SW11 149 J2
Broughinge Rd., Borwd. 38 B2
Broughton Av. N3 72 B3
Broughton Av., Rich. 163 E3
Broughton Dr. SW9 151 G4
Broughton Gdns. N6 74 C6
Broughton Rd. SW6 148 E2
Broughton Rd. W13 105 E7
Broughton Rd., Orp. 207 G2
Broughton Rd., Th.Hth. 187 G6
Broughton Rd. App. SW6 148/149 E2
Wandsworth Br. Rd.
Broughton St. SW8 150 A2
Brouncker Rd. W3 126 C2
Browells La., Felt. 160 B2
Brown Cl., Wall. 200 E7
Brown Hart Gdns. W1 16 C5
Brown Hart Gdns. W1 110 A7
Brown St. W1 15 J3
Brown St. W1 109 J6
Brownfield St. E14 114 B6
Browngraves Rd., Hayes 121 F7
Brownhill Rd. SE6 154 B7
Browning Av. W7 104 C6
Browning Av., Sutt. 199 H4
Browning Av., Wor.Pk. 197 H1
Browning Cl. E17 78 C4
Browning Cl. W9 6 D6
Browning Cl., Hmptn. 161 F4
Browning Cl., Well. 157 H1
Browning Est. SE17 36 A3
Browning Est. SE17 131 J5
Browning Ho. W12 107 J6
Wood La.
Browning Ms. W1 16 D2
Browning Rd. E11 79 F7
Browning Rd. E12 98 C6
Browning St. SE17 36 A3
Browning St. SE17 131 J5
Browning Way, Houns. 142 D1
Brownlea Gdns., Ilf. 100 A2
Brownlow Ms. WC1 10 D6
Brownlow Ms. WC1 111 F4
Brownlow Rd. E7 97 H4
Woodford Rd.
Brownlow Rd. E8 112 C1
Brownlow Rd. N3 56 E7
Brownlow Rd. N11 58 E6
Brownlow Rd. NW10 89 E7
Brownlow Rd. W13 124 D1
Brownlow Rd., Borwd. 38 A4
Brownlow Rd., Croy. 202 B4
Brownlow St. WC1 18 D2
Brown's Bldgs. EC3 20 E4
Brown's Bldgs. EC3 112 B6
Browns La. NW5 92 B5
Browns Rd. E17 78 A3
Browns Rd., Surb. 181 J7
Brownspring Dr. SE9 175 E4
Brownswell Rd. N2 73 G2
Brownswood Rd. N4 93 H3
Broxash Rd. SW11 150 A6
Broxbourne Av. E18 79 H4
Broxbourne Rd. E7 97 G3
Broxbourne Rd., Orp. 193 J7
Broxholm Rd. SE27 169 G3
Broxted Rd. SE6 171 J2
Broxwood Way NW8 109 H1
Bruce Castle Rd. N17 76 C1
Bruce Cl. W10 108 B5
Ladbroke Gro.
Bruce Cl., Well. 158 B1
Bruce Gdns. N20 57 J3
Balfour Gro.
Bruce Gro. N17 76 B1
Bruce Hall Ms. SW17 168 A4
Brudenell Rd.
Bruce Rd. E3 114 B3
Bruce Rd. NW10 88 D7
Bruce Rd. SE25 188 A4
Bruce Rd., Barn. 40 B3
St. Albans Rd.
Bruce Rd., Har. 68 B2
Bruce Rd., Mitch. 168 A7
Bruckner St. W10 108 C3
Brudenell Rd. SW17 167 J3
Bruffs Meadow, Nthlt. 85 E6
Bruges Pl. NW1 92 C7
Randolph St.
Brumfield Rd., Epsom 196 C5
Brummel Cl., Bexh. 159 J3
Brune St. E1 21 F2
Brune St. E1 112 C5
Brunel Cl. SE19 170 C6
Brunel Cl., Houns. 122 B7
Brunel Cl., Nthlt. 103 F3
Brunel Est. W2 108 D5
Brunel Pl., Sthl. 103 H6
Brunel Rd. E17 77 H6
Brunel Rd. SE16 133 F2
Brunel Rd. W3 106 E5
Brunel Rd., Wdf.Grn. 64 C5
Brunel St. E16 115 F6
Victoria Dock Rd.
Brunel Wk. N15 76 B4
Brunel Wk., Twick. 143 G7
Stephenson Rd.
Brunner Cl. NW11 73 F5
Brunner Rd. E17 77 J5
Brunner Rd. W5 105 G4
Bruno Pl. NW9 88 C2
Brunswick Av. N11 58 A3
Brunswick Cen. WC1 10 A5
Brunswick Cl., Bexh. 158 D4
Brunswick Cl., Pnr. 67 E6
Brunswick Cl., T.Ditt. 194 C1
Brunswick Cl., Twick. 162 A3
Brunswick Ct. EC1 111 H3
Northampton Sq.
Brunswick Ct. SE1 29 E4
Brunswick Ct. SE1 132 B2
Brunswick Ct., Barn. 41 G5
Brunswick Cres. N11 58 A3
Brunswick Gdns. W5 105 H3
Brunswick Gdns. W8 128 D1
Brunswick Gdns., Ilf. 65 F7
Brunswick Gro. N11 58 A3
Brunswick Ind. Pk. N11 58 B4
Brunswick Ms. SW16 168 D6
Potters La.
Brunswick Ms. W1 16 A3
Brunswick Pk. SE5 152 A1
Brunswick Pk. Gdns. N11 58 A2
Brunswick Pk. Rd. N11 58 A2
Brunswick Pl. N1 12 C4
Brunswick Pl. N1 112 A3
Brunswick Pl. SE19 170 D7
Brunswick Quay SE16 133 G3
Brunswick Rd. E10 96 C1
Brunswick Rd. E14 114 C6
Blackwall Tunnel Northern App.
Brunswick Rd. N15 76 B5
Brunswick Rd. W5 105 G4
Brunswick Rd., Bexh. 158 D4
Brunswick Rd., Kings.T. 182 A1
Brunswick Rd., Sutt. 199 E4
Brunswick Sq. N17 60 C6
Brunswick Sq. WC1 10 B6
Brunswick Sq. WC1 111 E4
Brunswick St. E17 78 C5
Brunswick Vil. SE5 152 B1
Brunswick Way N11 58 B4
Brunton Pl. E14 113 H6
Brushfield St. E1 21 E2
Brushfield St. E1 112 B5
Brussels Rd. SW11 149 G4
Bruton Cl., Chis. 174 C7
Bruton La. W1 17 E6
Bruton La. W1 110 B7
Bruton Pl. W1 16 E6
Bruton Pl. W1 110 B7
Bruton Rd., Mord. 185 F5
Bruton St. W1 16 E6
Bruton St. W1 110 B7
Bruton Way W13 104 D5
Bryan Av. NW10 89 H7
Bryan Cl., Sun. 160 A7
Bryan Rd. SE16 133 J2
Bryan's All. SW6 148/149 E2
Wandsworth Br. Rd.
Bryanston Av., Twick. 161 H1
Bryanston Cl., Sthl. 123 F4
Bryanston Ms. E. W1 15 J2
Bryanston Ms. W. W1 15 J2
Bryanston Pl. W1 15 J2
Bryanston Pl. W1 109 J5
Bryanston Sq. W1 15 J2
Bryanston Sq. W1 109 J5
Bryanston St. W1 15 J4
Bryanston St. W1 109 J6
Bryanstone Rd. N8 74 D5
Bryant Cl., Barn. 40 C5
Bryant Ct. E2 13 F1
Bryant Ct. E2 112 C2
Bryant Rd., Nthlt. 102 C3
Bryant St. E15 96 D7
Bryantwood Rd. N7 93 G5
Bryce Rd., Dag. 100 C4
Brycedale Cres. N14 58 D4
Bryden Cl. SE26 171 H5
Brydges Pl. WC2 18 A6
Brydges Rd. E15 96 D5
Brydon Wk. N1 110/111 E1
Outram Pl.
Bryer Ct. EC2 111 J5
Aldersgate St.
Bryett Rd. N7 93 E3
Brymay Cl. E3 114 A2
Bryn-y-Mawr Rd., Enf. 44 C4
Brynmaer Rd. SW11 149 J1
Bryony Cl., Loug. 48 E4
Bryony Rd. W12 107 G7
Buchan Rd. SE15 153 F3
Buchanan Cl. N21 43 F5
Buchanan Ct., Borwd. 38 C2
Buchanan Gdns. NW10 107 H2
Bucharest Rd. SW18 149 F7
Buck Hill Wk. W2 15 F6
Buck La. NW9 70 D5
Buck St. NW1 92 B7
Buck Wk. E17 78 D4
Foresters Dr.
Buckden Cl. N2 73 J4
Southern Rd.
Buckden Cl. SE12 155 F6
Upwood Rd.
Buckfast Rd., Mord. 185 E4
Buckfast St. E2 13 J4
Buckfast St. E2 112 D3
Buckhold Rd. SW18 148 D6
Buckhurst Av., Cars. 199 H1
Buckhurst St. E1 113 E4
Buckhurst Way, Buck.H. 64 A4
Buckingham Arc. WC2 18 B6
Buckingham Av. N20 41 F7
Buckingham Av., Felt. 142 B6
Buckingham Av., Grnf. 104 D1
Buckingham Av., Th.Hth. 187 G1
Buckingham Av., Well. 157 H4
Buckingham Av., W.Mol. 179 H3
Buckingham Cl. W5 105 F5
Buckingham Cl., Enf. 44 B2
Buckingham Cl., Hmptn. 161 F5
Buckingham Cl., Orp. 193 H7
Buckingham Ct. NW4 71 G3
Buckingham Dr., Chis. 175 E5
Buckingham Gdns., Edg. 53 J7
Buckingham Gdns., Th.Hth. 187 G2
Buckingham Gdns., W.Mol. 179 H2
Buckingham Av.
Buckingham Gate SW1 25 F4
Buckingham Gate SW1 130 C3
Buckingham La. SE23 153 H7
Buckingham Ms. N1 94 B6
Buckingham Rd.
Buckingham Ms. NW10 107 F2
Buckingham Rd.
Buckingham Ms. SW1 25 F5
Buckingham Palace Rd. SW1 32 D2
Buckingham Palace Rd. SW1 130 B4
Buckingham Pl. SW1 25 F5
Buckingham Rd. E10 96 B3
Buckingham Rd. E11 79 J5
Buckingham Rd. E15 97 F5
Buckingham Rd. E18 79 F1
Buckingham Rd. N1 94 B6
Buckingham Rd. N22 74 E1
Buckingham Rd. NW10 107 F2

Buckingham Rd., Borwd. 38 D4
Buckingham Rd., Edg. 53 J7
Buckingham Rd., Hmptn. 161 F5
Buckingham Rd., Har. 68 A5
Buckingham Rd., Ilf. 99 G2
Buckingham Rd., Kings.T. 181 J4
Buckingham Rd., Mitch. 186 E5
Buckingham Rd., Rich. 163 G2
Buckingham St. WC2 18 B6
Buckland Cres. NW3 91 G7
Buckland Ri., Pnr. 66 C1
Buckland Rd. E10 96 C2
Buckland Rd., Chess. 195 J5
Buckland Rd., Orp. 207 H4
Buckland St. N1 12 C2
Buckland St. N1 112 A2
Buckland Wk. W3 126 C2
Church Rd.
Buckland Wk., Mord. 185 F4
Buckland Way, Wor.Pk. 197 J1
Bucklands Rd., Tedd. 163 F6
Buckle St. E1 21 G3
Buckleigh Av. SW20 184 B3
Buckleigh Rd. SW16 168 D6
Buckleigh Way SE19 188 C1
Buckler Gdns. SE9 174 C3
Southold Ri.
Bucklers All. SW6 128 C6
Bucklers Way, Cars. 199 J3
Bucklersbury EC4 20 B4
Bucklersbury EC4 112 A6
Bucklersbury Pas. EC4 20 B4
Buckles Ct., Belv. 138 D3
Fendyke Rd.
Buckley Rd. NW6 90 C7
Buckley St. SE1 26 E2
Buckmaster Cl. SW9 151 F3
Stockwell Pk. Rd.
Buckmaster Rd. SW11 149 H4
Bucknall St. WC2 17 J3
Bucknall St. WC2 110 D6
Bucknell Cl. SW2 151 F4
Buckner Rd. SW2 151 F4
Buckrell Rd. E4 62 D2
Buckstone Cl. SE23 153 F6
Buckstone Rd. N18 60 D5
Buckters Rents SE16 133 H1
Buckthorne Rd. SE4 153 H6
Budd Cl. N12 57 E4
Buddings Circle, Wem. 88 C3
Budd's All., Twick. 145 F5
Arlington Cl.
Budge La., Mitch. 185 J7
Budge Row EC4 20 B5
Budge's Wk. W2 22 C1
Budge's Wk. W2 109 F7
Budleigh Cres., Well. 158 C1
Budoch Ct., Ilf. 100 A2
Budoch Dr., Ilf. 100 A2
Buer Rd. SW6 148 B2
Bugsby's Way SE7 135 H4
Bugsby's Way SE10 135 F4
Bulganak Rd., Th.Hth. 187 J4
Bulinga St. SW1 34 A2
Bulinga St. SW1 130 D4
Bull All., Well. 158 B3
Welling High St.
Bull Inn Ct. WC2 18 B6
Bull La. N18 60 B5
Bull La., Chis. 175 G7
Bull La., Dag. 101 H3
Bull Rd. E15 115 F2
Bull Wf. La. EC4 20 A5
Bullace Row SE5 151 J1
Camberwell Rd.
Bullards Pl. E2 113 G3
Bullbanks Rd., Belv. 139 J4
Bullen St. SW11 149 H2
Buller Cl. SE15 132 D7
Buller Rd. N17 76 D2
Buller Rd. N22 75 G2
Buller Rd. NW10 108 A3
Chamberlayne Rd.
Buller Rd., Bark. 99 H7
Buller Rd., Th.Hth. 188 A2
Bullers Cl., Sid. 176 E5
Bullers Wd. Dr., Chis. 174 B7
Bullescroft Rd., Edg. 54 A3
Bullhead Rd., Borwd. 38 C3
Bullied Way SW1 32 E2
Bullivant St. E14 114 C7
Bullrush Cl., Croy. 188 B6
Bull's All. SW14 146 D2
Bulls Br. Ind. Est., Sthl. 122 B3
Hayes Rd.
Bulls Br. Rd., Sthl. 122 B3
Bulls Gdns. SW3 31 H1
Bull's Head Pas. EC3 20 D4
Bullsbrook Rd., Hayes 122 C1
Bulmer Gdns., Har. 69 G7
Bulmer Ms. W11 108 D7
Ladbroke Rd.
Bulmer Pl. W11 128 D1
Bulow Est. SW6 148/149 E2
Broughton Rd.
Bulstrode Av., Houns. 143 F2
Bulstrode Gdns., Houns. 143 F3
Bulstrode Pl. W1 16 C2
Bulstrode Rd., Houns. 143 G3
Bulstrode St. W1 16 C3
Bulstrode St. W1 110 A6
Bulwer Ct. Rd. E11 96 D1
Bulwer Gdns., Barn. 41 F4
Bulwer Rd.
Bulwer Rd. E11 78 D7
Bulwer Rd. N18 60 B4
Bulwer Rd., Barn. 41 E4
Bulwer St. W12 127 J1
Bunces La., Wdf.Grn. 63 F7
Bungalow Rd. SE25 188 B4
Bungalows, The SW16 168 B7
Bungalows, The, Wall. 200 B5
Bunhill Row EC1 12 B5
Bunhill Row EC1 112 A4
Bunhouse Pl. SW1 32 B3
Bunhouse Pl. SW1 130 A5
Bunkers Hill NW11 73 F7
Bunkers Hill, Belv. 139 G4
Bunkers Hill, Sid. 177 F3
Bunning Way N7 93 E7
Bunns La. NW7 55 F6
Bunsen St. E3 113 H2
Kenilworth Rd.
Bunting Cl. N9 61 G1
Dunnock Cl.
Bunting Cl., Mitch. 185 J5
Buntingbridge Rd., Ilf. 81 G5
Bunton St. SE18 136 D3
Bunyan Rd. E17 77 H3
Buonaparte Ms. SW1 33 H3
Burbage Cl. SE1 28 B6
Burbage Cl. SE1 132 A3
Burbage Rd. SE21 152 A6
Burbage Rd. SE24 151 J6
Burberry Cl., N.Mal. 182 E2
Burbridge Way N17 76 C2
Burcham St. E14 114 B6
Burcharbro Rd. SE2 138 D6
Burchell Rd. E10 96 B1
Burchell Rd. SE15 153 E1
Burchett Way, Rom. 83 F6
Burcote Rd. SW18 167 G1
Burden Cl., Brent. 125 F5
Burden Way E11 97 H2
Brading Cres.
Burdenshott Av., Rich. 146 B4
Burder Cl. N1 94 B6
Burder Rd. N1 94 B6
Balls Pond Rd.
Burdett Av. SW20 183 G1
Burdett Cl. W7 124 C2
Cherington Rd.
Burdett Cl., Sid. 176 E5
Burdett Ms. NW3 91 G6
Belsize Cres.
Burdett Ms. W2 14 A3
Burdett Rd. E3 113 J4
Burdett Rd. E14 113 J4
Burdett Rd., Croy. 188 A6
Burdett Rd., Rich. 145 J3
Burdett St. SE1 27 E5
Burdetts Rd., Dag. 119 F1
Burdock Cl., Croy. 203 G1
Burdock Rd. N17 76 D3
Burdon La., Sutt. 198 B7
Burfield Cl. SW17 167 G4
Burford Cl., Dag. 100 C3
Burford Cl., Ilf. 81 F4
Burford Gdns. N13 59 F3
Burford Rd. E6 116 B3
Burford Rd. E15 96 D7
Burford Rd. SE6 171 J2
Burford Rd., Brent. 125 H5
Burford Rd., Brom. 192 B4
Burford Rd., Sutt. 198 D2
Burford Rd., Wor.Pk. 183 F7
Burford Wk. SW6 128/129 E7
Cambria St.
Burford Way, Croy. 204 C6
Burge St. SE1 28 C6
Burge St. SE1 132 A3
Burges Ct. E6 98 D7
Burges Gro. SW13 127 H7
Burges Rd. E6 98 B7
Burgess Av. NW9 70 D6
Burgess Cl., Felt. 160 E4
Burgess Hill NW2 90 D4
Burgess Rd. E15 96 E4
Burgess Rd., Sutt. 198 E4
Burgess St. E14 114 A5
Burgh St. N1 11 H1
Burgh St. N1 111 H2
Burghill Rd. SE26 171 H4
Burghley Av., Borwd. 38 C5
Burghley Av., N.Mal. 182 D1
Burghley Hall Cl. SW19 166 B1
Princes Way
Burghley Pl., Mitch. 186 A5
Burghley Rd. E11 97 E1
Burghley Rd. N8 75 G3
Burghley Rd. NW5 92 B5
Burghley Rd. SW19 166 A4
Burghley Twr. W3 107 F7
Burgon St. EC4 19 H4
Burgos Cl., Croy. 201 G6
Burgos Gro. SE10 154 B1
Burgoyne Rd. N4 75 H6
Burgoyne Rd. SE25 188 C4
Burgoyne Rd. SW9 151 F3
Burham Cl. SE20 171 F7
Maple Rd.
Burhill Gro., Pnr. 66 E2
Burke Cl. SW15 147 E4
Burke St. E16 115 F6
Burket Cl., Sthl. 123 F4
Kingsbridge Rd.
Burland Rd. SW11 149 J5
Burleigh Av., Sid. 157 J5
Burleigh Av., Wall. 200 A3
Burleigh Gdns. N14 58 C1
Burleigh Ho. W10 108 A5
St. Charles Sq.
Burleigh Pl. SW15 148 A5
Burleigh Rd., Enf. 44 B4
Burleigh Rd., Sutt. 198 B1
Burleigh St. WC2 18 C5
Burleigh Wk. SE6 172 C1
Muirkirk Rd.
Burleigh Way, Enf. 44 A3
Church St.
Burley Cl. E4 62 A5
Burley Cl. SW16 186 D2
Burley Rd. E16 115 J6
Burlington Arc. W1 17 F6
Burlington Arc. W1 110 C7
Burlington Av., Rich. 146 A1
Burlington Av., Rom. 83 H6
Burlington Cl. E6 116 B6
Northumberland Rd.
Burlington Cl. W9 108 C4
Burlington Cl., Felt. 141 G7
Burlington Cl., Orp. 206 E2
Burlington Cl., Pnr. 66 B3
Burlington Gdns. W1 17 F6
Burlington Gdns. W1 110 C7
Burlington Gdns. W3 126 C1
Burlington Gdns. W4 126 C5
Burlington Gdns., Rom. 83 E7
Burlington La. W4 126 E7
Burlington Ms. SW15 148 C5
Upper Richmond Rd.
Burlington Ms. W3 126 C1
Burlington Pl. SW6 148 B2
Burlington Rd.
Burlington Pl., Wdf.Grn. 63 G3
Burlington Ri., Barn. 57 H1
Burlington Rd. N10 74 A2
Tetherdown
Burlington Rd. N17 76 D1
Burlington Rd. SW6 148 B2
Burlington Rd. W4 126 C5
Burlington Rd., Enf. 44 A1
Burlington Rd., Islw. 144 A1
Burlington Rd., N.Mal. 183 G4
Burlington Rd., Th.Hth. 187 J2
Burma Rd. N16 94 A4
Burmester Rd. SW17 167 F3
Burn Side N9 61 F3
Burnaby Cres. W4 126 B6
Burnaby Gdns. W4 126 C6
Burnaby St. SW10 129 F7
Burnbrae Cl. N12 57 E6
Burnbury Rd. SW12 168 C1
Burncroft Av., Enf. 45 F2
Burne Jones Ho. W14 128 C4
Burne St. NW1 15 G1
Burne St. NW1 109 H5
Burnell Av., Rich. 163 F5
Burnell Av., Well. 158 A2
Burnell Gdns., Stan. 69 G1
Burnell Rd., Sutt. 199 E4
Burnell Wk. SE1 37 G3
Burnels Av. E6 116 D3
Burness Cl. N7 93 F6
Roman Way
Burnett Cl. E9 95 F5
Burney Av., Surb. 181 J5
Burney Dr., Loug. 49 E2
Burney St. SE10 134 C7
Burnfoot Av. SW6 148 B1
Burnfoot Ct. SE22 170 E1
Burnham NW3 91 H7
Burnham Cl. NW7 55 G7
Burnham Cl. SE1 37 G2
Burnham Cl., Har. 68 D4
Burnham Ct. NW4 71 J4
Burnham Cres. E11 79 J4
Burnham Dr., Wor.Pk. 198 A2
Burnham Gdns., Croy. 188 C7
Burnham Gdns., Hayes 121 G3
Burnham Gdns., Houns. 142 B1
Burnham Rd. E4 61 J5
Burnham Rd., Dag. 100 B7
Burnham Rd., Mord. 185 E5
Burnham Rd., Sid. 176 E2
Burnham St. E2 113 F3
Burnham St., Kings.T. 182 A1
Burnham Way SE26 171 J5
Burnham Way W13 124 E4
Burnhill Rd., Beck. 190 A2
Burnley Cl., Wat. 50 C5
Burnley Rd. NW10 89 G5
Burnley Rd. SW9 151 F2
Burns Av., Felt. 142 A6
Burns Av., Rom. 82 C7
Burns Av., Sid. 158 B6
Burns Av., Sthl. 103 G7
Burns Cl. E17 78 C4
Burns Cl. SW19 167 G6
North Rd.
Burns Cl., Well. 157 J1
Burns Rd. NW10 107 F1
Burns Rd. SW11 149 J2
Burns Rd. W13 124 E2
Burns Rd., Wem. 105 G2
Burns Way, Houns. 142 D2
Burnsall St. SW3 31 H3
Burnsall St. SW3 129 H5
Burnside Av. E4 61 J6
Burnside Cl. SE16 133 G1
Burnside Cl., Barn. 40 D3
Burnside Cl., Twick. 144 D6
Burnside Cres., Wem. 105 G1
Burnside Rd., Dag. 100 C2
Burnt Ash Hill SE12 155 F6
Burnt Ash La., Brom. 173 G6
Burnt Ash Rd. SE12 155 F5
Burnt Oak Bdy., Edg. 54 B7
Burnt Oak Flds., Edg. 70 C1
Burnt Oak La., Sid. 158 A6
Burnthwaite Rd. SW6 128 D7
Burntwood Cl. SW18 167 G1
Burntwood Gra. Rd. SW18 167 G1
Burntwood La. SW17 167 H2
Burntwood Vw. SE19 170 C5
Bowley La.
Buross St. E1 112/113 E6
Commercial Rd.
Burr Cl. E1 29 H1
Burr Cl. E1 132 D1
Burr Cl., Bexh. 159 F3
Burr Rd. SW18 148 D7
Burrage Gro. SE18 137 F4
Burrage Pl. SE18 137 E5
Burrage Rd. SE18 137 F5
Burrard Rd. E16 115 H6
Burrard Rd. NW6 90 D4
Burrell Cl., Croy. 189 H6
Burrell Cl., Edg. 54 B2
Burrell Row, Beck. 190 A2
High St.
Burrell St. SE1 27 G1
Burrell St. SE1 131 H1
Burrell Twr. E10 78 A7
Burrells Wf. Sq. E14 134 B5
Burritt Rd., Kings.T. 182 A2
Burroughs, The NW4 71 H5
Burroughs Gdns. NW4 71 H4

Name	Page	Grid
Burroughs Par. NW4	71	H4
The Burroughs		
Burrow Cl., Chig.	65	J5
Burrow Rd.		
Burrow Grn., Chig.	65	J5
Burrow Rd. SE22	152	B4
Burrow Rd., Chig.	65	J5
Burrow Wk. SE21	151	J7
Rosendale Rd.		
Burrows Ms. SE1	**27**	**G3**
Burrows Rd. NW10	107	J3
Bursdon Cl., Sid.	175	J2
Bursland Rd., Enf.	45	G4
Burslem St. E1	**21**	**J4**
Burslem St. E1	112	D6
Burstock Rd. SW15	148	B4
Burston Rd. SW15	148	A5
Burston Vil. SW15	148	A5
St. John's Av.		
Burstow Rd. SW20	184	B1
Burt Rd. E16	135	J1
Burtenshaw Rd., T.Ditt.	180	D7
Burtley Cl. N4	93	J1
Burtley Cl., Chess.	195	G7
Burton Cl. SW3	129	J5
Franklin's Row		
Burton Gdns., Houns.	143	F1
Burton Gro. SE17	**36**	**B4**
Burton La. SW9	151	G2
Burton Ms. SW1	**32**	**C2**
Burton Pl. WC1	**9**	**J4**
Burton Rd. E18	79	H3
Burton Rd. NW6	90	C7
Burton Rd. SW9	151	H2
Burton Rd., Kings.T.	163	H7
Burton Rd., Loug.	49	F4
Burton St. WC1	**9**	**J4**
Burton St. WC1	110	D3
Burtonhole Cl. NW7	56	A4
Burtonhole La. NW7	56	B4
Burtons Rd., Hmptn.	161	H4
Burtwell La. SE27	170	A4
Burwash Ho. SE1	**28**	**C4**
Burwash Rd. SE18	137	G5
Burwell Av., Grnf.	86	B6
Burwell Cl. E1	112/113	E6
Bigland St.		
Burwell Rd. E10	95	H1
Burwell Wk. E3	114	A4
Burwood Av., Brom.	205	H2
Burwood Av., Pnr.	66	C5
Burwood Cl., Surb.	196	A1
Burwood Pl. W2	**15**	**H3**
Burwood Pl. W2	109	H6
Bury Cl. SE16	133	G1
Rotherhithe St.		
Bury Ct. EC3	**20**	**E3**
Bury Gro., Mord.	184	E5
Bury Pl. WC1	**18**	**A2**
Bury Pl. WC1	111	E6
Bury Rd. E4	47	E5
Bury Rd. N22	75	G3
Bury Rd., Dag.	101	H5
Bury St. EC3	**20**	**E4**
Bury St. EC3	112	B6
Bury St. N9	60	D1
Bury St. SW1	**25**	**F1**
Bury St. SW1	130	C1
Bury St. W. N9	44	A7
Bury Wk. SW3	**31**	**G2**
Bury St. SW3	129	H5
Busbridge Ho. E14	114	A5
Brabazon St.		
Busby Ms. NW5	92	D6
Torriano Av.		
Busby Pl. NW5	92	D6
Busby St. E2	**13**	**G5**
Bush Cl., Ilf.	81	G5
Bush Cotts. SW18	148	D5
Putney Br. Rd.		
Bush Ct. W12	128	A2
Bush Gro. NW9	70	C7
Bush Gro., Stan.	69	G1
Bush Hill N21	43	J7
Bush Hill Rd. N21	44	A6
Bush Hill Rd., Har.	69	H3
Bush Ind. Est. NW10	106	D4
Bush La. EC4	**20**	**B5**
Bush Rd. E8	112	E1
Bush Rd. E11	79	F7
Bush Rd. SE8	133	G4
Bush Rd., Buck.H.	64	A4
Bush Rd., Rich.	126	A6
Bushbaby Cl. SE1	**28**	**D6**
Bushberry Rd. E9	95	H6
Bushell Cl. SW2	169	F2
Bushell Grn., Bushey	52	A2
Bushell St. E1	**29**	**J2**
Bushell Way, Chis.	174	D5
Bushey Av. E18	79	F3
Bushey Av., Orp.	193	G7
Bushey Cl. E4	62	C3
Bushey Ct. SW20	183	H2
Bushey Down SW12	168	B2
Bedford Hill		
Bushey Hill Rd. SE5	152	B1
Bushey La., Sutt.	198	D4
Bushey Lees, Sid.	157	J6
Fen Gro.		
Bushey Rd. E13	115	J2
Bushey Rd. N15	76	B6
Bushey Rd. SW20	183	H3
Bushey Rd., Croy.	204	A2
Bushey Rd., Hayes	121	H4
Bushey Rd., Sutt.	198	E4
Bushey Way, Beck.	190	D6
Bushfield Cl., Edg.	54	B2
Bushfield Cres., Edg.	54	B2
Bushfields, Loug.	48	D5
Bushgrove Rd., Dag.	100	D4
Bushmead Cl. N15	76	C4
Copperfield Dr.		
Bushmoor Cres. SE18	137	F7
Bushnell Rd. SW17	168	B2
Bushway, Dag.	100	D4
Bushwood E11	97	F1
Bushwood Dr. SE1	**37**	**G2**
Bushwood Dr. SE1	132	C4
Bushwood Rd., Rich.	126	A6
Bycroft Rd., Sthl.	103	G4
Bycroft St. SE20	171	G7
Parish La.		
Bushy Pk., Tedd.	180	C1
Bushy Pk. Gdns. Tedd.	162	A5
Bushy Pk. Rd., Tedd.	163	E7
Bushy Rd., Tedd.	162	C6
Butcher Row E1	113	G7
Butcher Row E14	113	G7
Butchers Rd. E16	115	G6
Bute Av., Rich.	163	H2
Bute Ct., Wall.	200	C5
Bute Rd.		
Bute Gdns. W6	128	A4
Bute Gdns., Wall.	200	C5
Bute Gdns. W., Wall.	200	C5
Bute Rd., Croy.	201	G1
Bute Rd., Ilf.	81	E5
Bute Rd., Wall.	200	C4
Bute St. SW7	**31**	**E1**
Bute St. SW7	129	G4
Bute Wk. N1	94	A6
Marquess Rd.		
Butler Av., Har.	68	A7
Butler Pl. SW1	**25**	**H5**
Butler Rd. NW10	89	F7
Curzon Cres.		
Butler Rd., Dag.	100	B4
Butler Rd., Har.	67	J7
Butler St. E2	113	F3
Knottisford St.		
Butlers Wf. SE1	132	C2
Lafone St.		
Butter Hill, Cars.	200	A3
Butter Hill, Wall.	200	A3
Butterfield Cl. N17	59	J6
Devonshire Rd.		
Butterfield Cl. SE16	132/133	E2
Wilson Gro.		
Butterfield Cl., Twick.	144	C6
Rugby Rd.		
Butterfield Sq. E6	116	C6
Harper Rd.		
Butterfields E17	78	C5
Butterfly La. SE9	156	E6
Butterfly Wk. SE5	152	A1
Denmark Hill		
Butteridges Cl., Dag.	119	F1
Buttermere Cl. E15	96	D4
Buttermere Cl. SE1	**37**	**F1**
Buttermere Cl., Mord.	184	A6
Buttermere Dr. SW15	148	B5
Buttermere Wk. E8	94	C6
Butterwick W6	127	J4
Butterworth Gdns., Wdf.Grn.	63	G6
Buttesland St. N1	**12**	**C3**
Buttesland St. N1	112	A3
Buttfield Cl., Dag.	101	H6
Buttmarsh Cl. SE18	137	E5
Butts, The, Brent.	125	G6
Butts, The, Sun.	178	C3
Elizabeth Gdns.		
Butts Cotts., Felt.	161	F3
Butts Cres., Felt.	161	G3
Butts Piece, Nthlt.	102	B2
Longhook Gdns.		
Butts Rd., Brom.	173	E5
Buttsbury Rd., Ilf.	99	F5
Buxhall Cres. E9	95	J6
Eastway		
Buxted Rd. E8	94	C7
Buxted Rd. N12	57	H5
Buxted Rd. SE22	152	B4
Buxton Cl., Wdf.Grn.	64	A6
Buxton Ct. N1	**12**	**A3**
Buxton Cres., Sutt.	198	B4
Buxton Dr. E11	79	E4
Buxton Dr., N.Mal.	182	D2
Buxton Gdns. W3	106	B7
Buxton Path, Wat.	50	C3
Buxton Rd. E4	46	D7
Buxton Rd. E6	116	B3
Buxton Rd. E15	96	E5
Buxton Rd. E17	77	H4
Buxton Rd. N19	92	D1
Buxton Rd. NW2	89	H6
Buxton Rd. SW14	147	E3
Buxton Rd., Ilf.	81	H6
Buxton Rd., Th.Hth.	187	H5
Buxton St. E1	**13**	**G6**
Buxton St. E1	112	C4
Buzzard Creek Ind. Est., Bark.	117	J5
By the Wd., Wat.	50	D2
Byam St. SW6	149	F2
Byards Cft. SW16	186	D1
Byatt Wk., Hmptn.	160/161	E6
Victors Dr.		
Bychurch End, Tedd.	162	C5
Church Rd.		
Bycroft Rd., Sthl.	103	G4
Bycroft St. SE20	171	G7
Parr Rd.		
Bycullah Av., Enf.	43	H3
Bycullah Rd., Enf.	43	H3
Bye, The W3	107	E6
Bye Way, The, Har.	68	B1
Byegrove Rd. SW19	167	G6
Byeway, The W14	146	C3
Byeways, Twick.	161	H3
Byeways, The, Surb.	182	A5
Byfeld Gdns. SW13	147	G1
Byfield Cl. SE16	133	H2
Byfield Pas., Islw.	144	D3
Byfield Rd., Islw.	144	D3
Byford Cl. E15	97	E7
Bygrove, Croy.	204	B6
Bygrove St. E14	114	B6
Byland Cl. N21	43	F7
Byland Cl. SE2	138	B3
Finchale Rd.		
Bylands Cl. SE16	133	G1
Rotherhithe St.		
Byne Rd. SE26	171	F6
Byne Rd., Cars.	199	H2
Bynes Rd., S.Croy.	202	A7
Byng Pl. WC1	**9**	**H6**
Byng Pl. WC1	110	D4
Byng Rd., Barn.	40	A3
Byng St. E14	134	A2
Bynon Av., Bexh.	159	E3
Byre, The N14	42	B6
Byre Rd. N14	42	A6
Farm La.		
Byrne Rd. SW12	168	B1
Byron Av. E12	98	B6
Byron Av. E18	79	F3
Byron Av. NW9	70	B4
Byron Av., Borwd.	38	A5
Byron Av., Houns.	142	A2
Byron Av., N.Mal.	183	G5
Byron Av., Sutt.	199	G4
Byron Av. E., Sutt.	199	G4
Byron Cl. E8	112	D1
Byron Cl. SE26	171	H4
Porthcawe Rd.		
Byron Cl. SE28	138	C1
Byron Cl., Hmptn.	161	F4
Byron Cl. W9	108	D4
Lanhill Rd.		
Byron Ct., Enf.	43	H2
Bycullah Rd.		
Byron Ct., Har.	68	B6
Byron Dr. N2	73	G6
Byron Dr., Erith	139	H7
Byron Gdns., Sutt.	199	G4
Byron Hill Rd., Har.	86	A1
Byron Rd., Beck.	172	A6
Byron Ms. NW3	91	H5
Byron Ms. W9	108	D4
Shirland Rd.		
Byron Rd. E10	96	B1
Byron Rd. E17	78	A3
Byron Rd. NW2	89	H2
Byron Rd. NW7	55	G5
Byron Rd. W5	125	J1
Byron Rd., Har.	68	B6
Byron Rd. (Wealdstone), Har.	68	C2
Byron Rd., Wem.	87	F3
Byron St. E14	114	C6
St. Leonards Rd.		
Byron Ter. N9	45	F7
Byron Way, Nthlt.	102	E3
Byron Way, West Dr.	120	C4
Bysouth Cl. N15	76	A4
Bysouth Cl., Ilf.	80	E1
Bythorn St. SW9	151	F3
Byton Rd. SW17	167	J6
Byward Av., Felt.	142	C6
Byward St. EC3	**20**	**E6**
Byward St. EC3	112	B7
Bywater Pl. SE16	133	H1
Bywater St. SW3	**31**	**J3**
Bywater St. SW3	129	J5
Byway, The, Epsom	197	F4
Bywell Pl. W1	**17**	**F2**
Bywood Av., Croy.	189	F6
Byworth Wk. N19	92	D1
Courtauld Rd.		

C

Name	Page	Grid
C.I. Twr., N.Mal.	183	E3
Cabbell St. NW1	**15**	**G2**
Cabbell St. NW1	109	H5
Cabinet Way E4	61	J6
Cable Pl. SE10	154	C1
Diamond Ter.		
Cable St. E1	**21**	**H5**
Cable St. E1	112	D7
Cable Trade Pk. SE7	135	J4
Cabot Sq. E14	134	A1
Cabot Way E6	116	A1
Parr Rd.		
Cabul Rd. SW11	149	H2
Cactus Cl. SE15	152	B2
Lyndhurst Gro.		
Cactus Wk. W12	107	F6
Du Cane Rd.		
Cadbury Cl., Islw.	144	D1
Cadbury Way SE16	**29**	**G6**
Caddington Cl., Barn.	41	H5
Caddington Rd. NW2	90	B3
Caddis Cl., Stan.	52	C7
Daventer Dr.		
Cade Rd. SE10	154	D1
Cadell Cl. E2	**13**	**G2**
Cader Rd. SW18	149	F6
Cadet Dr. SE1	**37**	**G3**
Cadet Dr. SE1	132	C4
Cadet Pl. SE10	134	E5
Cadiz Rd., Dag.	101	J7
Cadiz St. SE17	**36**	**A4**
Cadiz St. SE17	131	J5
Cadley Ter. SE23	171	F2
Cadman Cl. SW9	131	H7
Langton Rd.		
Cadmer Cl., N.Mal.	182	E4
Cadmus Cl. SW4	150	D3
Aristotle Rd.		
Cadogan Cl., Beck.	190	D1
Cadogan Cl., Har.	85	H4
Cadogan Cl., Tedd.	162	B5
Cadogan Cl., Sutt.	199	E6
Cadogan Gdns. E18	79	H3
Cadogan Gdns. N3	72	E1
Cadogan Gdns. N21	43	G5
Cadogan Gdns. SW3	**32**	**A1**
Cadogan Gdns. SW3	129	J4
Cadogan Gate SW1	**32**	**A1**
Cadogan Gate SW1	129	J4
Cadogan La. SW1	**24**	**B6**
Cadogan La. SW1	130	A3
Cadogan Pl. SW1	**24**	**A6**
Cadogan Pl. SW1	129	J3
Cadogan Rd., Surb.	181	G5
Cadogan Sq. SW1	**24**	**A6**
Cadogan Sq. SW1	129	J3
Cadogan St. SW3	**31**	**J2**
Cadogan St. SW3	129	J4
Cadogan Ter. E9	95	J6
Cadoxton Av. N15	76	C6
Cadwallon Rd. SE9	175	E2
Caedmon Rd. N7	93	F4
Caerleon Cl., Sid.	176	C5
Caerleon Ter. SE2	138	B4
Blithdale Rd.		
Caernarvon Cl., Mitch.	186	E3
Caernarvon Dr., Ilf.	80	D1
Caesars Wk., Mitch.	185	J5
Cahill St. EC1	**12**	**A6**
Cahir St. E14	134	B4
Cains La., Felt.	141	H5
Caird St. W10	108	B3
Cairn Av. W5	125	G1
Cairn Way, Stan.	52	C6
Cairndale Cl., Brom.	173	F7
Cairnfield Av. NW2	89	E3
Cairngorm Cl., Tedd.	162	D5
Vicarage Rd.		
Cairns Av., Wdf.Grn.	64	B6
Cairns Rd. SW11	149	H5
Cairo New Rd., Croy.	201	H2
Cairo Rd. E17	78	A4
Caishowe Rd., Borwd.	38	B1

Name	No.	Grid
Caistor Ms. SW12	150	B7
Caistor Rd.		
Caistor Pk. Rd. E15	115	F1
Caistor Rd. SW12	150	B7
Caithness Gdns., Sid.	157	J6
Caithness Rd. W14	128	A4
Caithness Rd., Mitch.	168	B7
Calabria Rd. N5	93	H6
Calais Gate SE5	151	H1
Calais St.		
Calais St. SE5	151	H1
Calbourne Rd. SW12	149	J7
Calcott Wk. SE9	174	A4
Caldbeck Av.	197	G2
Wor.Pk.		
Caldecot Rd. SE5	151	J2
Caldecott Way E5	95	G3
Calder Av., Grnf.	104	C2
Calder Cl., Enf.	44	B3
Calder Gdns., Edg.	70	A3
Calder Rd., Mord.	185	F5
Calderon Pl. W10	107	J5
St. Quintin Gdns.		
Calderon Rd. E11	96	C4
Caldervale Rd. SW4	150	D5
Calderwood St. SE18	136	D4
Caldicot Grn. NW9	70/71	E6
Snowdon Dr.		
Caldwell Rd., Wat.	50	D4
Caldwell St. SW9	131	F7
Caldwell Yd. EC4	111	J7
Upper Thames St.		
Caldy Rd., Belv.	139	H3
Caldy Wk. N1	93	J6
Clephane Rd.		
Cale St. SW3	31	G3
Cale St. SW3	129	H5
Caleb St. SE1	27	J3
Caledon Rd. E6	116	C1
Caledon Rd., Wall.	200	A4
Caledonia St. N1	10	B2
Caledonia St. N1	111	E2
Caledonian Cl., Ilf.	100	B1
Caledonian Rd. N1	10	B2
Caledonian Rd. N1	111	F2
Caledonian Rd. N7	93	F5
Caledonian Wf. E14	134	D4
Caletock Way SE10	135	F5
Calico Row SW11	149	F3
York Pl.		
Calidore Cl. SW2	151	F6
Endymion Rd.		
California La., Bushey	52	A1
California Rd., N.Mal.	182	C4
Callaby Ter. N1	94	A6
Wakeham St.		
Callaghan Cl. SE13	154/155	E4
Glenton Rd.		
Callander Rd. SE6	172	B2
Callard Av. N13	59	H5
Callcott Rd. NW6	90	C7
Callcott St. W8	128	D1
Hillgate Pl.		
Callendar Rd. SW7	22	E5
Callendar Rd. SW7	129	G3
Callingham Cl. E14	113	J5
Wallwood St.		
Callis Fm. Cl., Stai.	140	B6
Bedfont Rd.		
Callis Rd. E17	77	J6
Callow St. SW3	30	D5
Callow St. SW3	129	G6
Calmont Rd., Brom.	172	D6
Calne Av., Ilf.	80	E1
Calonne Rd. SW19	166	A4
Calshot Rd., Houns.	140	D2
Calshot St. N1	10	C1
Calshot St. N1	111	F2
Calshot Way, Enf.	43	H3
Calshot Way, Houns.	140/141	E2
Calshot Rd.		
Calthorpe Gdns., Edg.	53	H5
Jesmond Way		
Calthorpe Rd., Sutt.	199	F3
Calthorpe St. WC1	10	D5
Calthorpe St. WC1	111	F4
Calton Av. SE21	152	B5
Calton Rd., Barn.	41	F6
Calverley Cl., Beck.	172	B6
Calverley Cres., Dag.	101	G2
Calverley Gdns., Har.	69	G7
Calverley Gro. N19	92	D1
Calverley Rd., Epsom	197	G6
Calvert Av. E2	13	E4
Calvert Av. E2	112	B3
Calvert Cl., Belv.	139	G4
Calvert Cl., Sid.	176	E6
Calvert Rd. SE10	135	F5
Calvert Rd., Barn.	40	A2
Calvert St. NW1	110	A1
Chalcot Rd.		
Calverton SE5	36	D5
Calverton Rd. E6	116	D1
Calvert's Bldgs. SE1	28	B2
Calvin St. E1	13	F6
Calvin St. E1	112	C4
Calydon Rd. SE7	135	H5
Calypso Way SE16	133	J3
Cam Rd. E15	114	D1
Camac Rd., Twick.	162	A1
Cambalt Rd. SW15	148	A5
Camberley Av. SW20	183	H2
Camberley Av., Enf.	44	B4
Camberley Cl., Sutt.	198	A3
Camberley Rd., Houns.	140	D3
Cambert Way SE3	155	H4
Camberwell Ch. St. SE5	152	A1
Camberwell Glebe SE5	152	A1
Camberwell Grn. SE5	152	A1
Camberwell Gro. SE5	152	A1
Camberwell New Rd. SE5	35	E6
Camberwell New Rd. SE5	131	G7
Camberwell Pas. SE5	151	J1
Camberwell Grn.		
Camberwell Rd. SE5	36	A6
Camberwell Rd. SE5	131	J6
Camberwell Sta. Rd. SE5	151	J1
Cambeys Rd., Dag.	101	H5
Camborne Av. W13	125	E2
Camborne Ms. W11	108	B6
St. Marks Rd.		
Camborne Rd. SW18	148	D7
Camborne Rd., Croy.	188	C7
Camborne Rd., Houns.	140	D3
Camborne Rd., Mord.	184	A5
Camborne Rd., Sid.	176	C3
Camborne Rd., Sutt.	198	D7
Camborne Rd., Well.	157	J2
Camborne Way, Houns.	143	G1
Cambourne Av. N9	45	G7
Cambray Rd. SW12	168	C1
Cambray Rd., Orp.	193	J7
Cambria Cl., Houns.	143	G4
Cambria Cl., Sid.	175	G1
Cambria Ct., Felt.	142	B7
Hounslow Rd.		
Cambria Gdns., Stai.	140	B7
Cambria Rd. SE5	151	J3
Cambria St. SW6	129	E7
Cambrian Av., Ilf.	81	H5
Cambrian Cl. SE27	169	H3
Cambrian Rd. E10	78	A7
Cambrian Rd., Rich.	145	J6
Cambridge Av. NW6	108	D2
Cambridge Av., Grnf.	86	C5
Cambridge Av., N.Mal.	183	F2
Cambridge Av., Well.	157	J4
Cambridge Barracks Rd. SE18	136	C4
Cambridge Circ. WC2	17	J4
Cambridge Circ. WC2	110	D6
Cambridge Cl. E17	77	J6
Cambridge Cl. N22	75	G1
Pellatt Gro.		
Cambridge Cl. NW10	88	C3
Cambridge Cl. SW20	183	H1
Cambridge Cl., Houns.	143	E4
Cambridge Cl., West Dr.	120	A6
Cambridge Cotts., Rich.	126	A6
Cambridge Cres. E2	112	E2
Cambridge Cres., Tedd.	162	D5
Cambridge Dr. SE12	155	G5
Cambridge Dr., Ruis.	84	C2
Cambridge Gdns. N10	74	B1
Cambridge Gdns. N13	59	G5
Cambridge Gdns. N17	60	A7
Great Cambridge Rd.		
Cambridge Gdns. N21	44	A7
Cambridge Gdns. NW6	108	D2
Cambridge Gdns. W10	108	B6
Cambridge Gdns., Enf.	44	D2
Cambridge Gdns., Kings.T.	182	A2
Cambridge Gate NW1	8	E4
Cambridge Gate Ms. NW1	8	E4
Cambridge Grn. SE9	174	E1
Cambridge Gro. SE20	170	E7
Cambridge Gro. W6	127	H4
Cambridge Gro. Rd., Kings.T.	182	A2
Cambridge Heath Rd. E1	113	E2
Cambridge Heath Rd. E2	113	E2
Cambridge Mans. SW11	149	J1
Cambridge Rd.		
Cambridge Par., Enf.	44	D1
Great Cambridge Rd.		
Cambridge Pk. E11	79	G3
Cambridge Pk., Twick.	145	G2
Cambridge Pk. Rd. E11	79	F7
Cambridge Pk.		
Cambridge Pl. W8	22	B4
Cambridge Pl. W8	129	E2
Cambridge Rd. E4	62	D1
Cambridge Rd. E11	79	F6
Cambridge Rd. NW6	108	D3
Cambridge Rd. SE20	188	E3
Cambridge Rd. SW11	149	J1
Cambridge Rd. SW13	147	F2
Cambridge Rd. SW20	183	G1
Cambridge Rd. W7	124	C2
Cambridge Rd., Bark.	99	F7
Cambridge Rd., Brom.	173	G7
Cambridge Rd., Cars.	199	H6
Cambridge Rd., Hmptn.	161	F7
Cambridge Rd., Har.	67	G5
Cambridge Rd., Houns.	143	E4
Cambridge Rd., Ilf.	99	H1
Cambridge Rd., Kings.T.	181	J2
Cambridge Rd., Mitch.	186	C3
Cambridge Rd., N.Mal.	182	E4
Cambridge Rd., Rich.	126	A7
Cambridge Rd., Sid.	175	H4
Cambridge Rd., Sthl.	123	F1
Cambridge Rd., Tedd.	162	C4
Cambridge Rd., Twick.	145	G6
Cambridge Rd., Walt.	178	B6
Cambridge Rd., W.Mol.	179	F4
Cambridge Rd. N. W4	126	B5
Cambridge Rd. S. W4	126	B5
Oxford Rd. S.		
Cambridge Row SE18	137	E5
Cambridge Sq. W2	15	G3
Cambridge Sq. W2	109	H6
Cambridge Sq. SW1	32	E2
Cambridge Sq. SW1	130	B5
Cambridge Ter. N13	59	G5
Cambridge Ter. NW1	8	E4
Cambridge Ter. Ms. NW1	8	E4
Cambstone Cl. N11	58	A2
Cambus Cl., Hayes	103	E5
Cambus Rd. E16	115	G5
Camdale Rd. SE18	137	J7
Camden Av., Felt.	160	C2
Camden Av., Hayes	102	C7
Camden Cl., Chis.	175	F7
Camden Est. SE15	152	C1
Camden Gdns. NW1	92	B7
Kentish Town Rd.		
Camden Gdns., Sutt.	198	E5
Camden Gdns., Th.Hth.	187	H3
Camden Gro., Chis.	175	E6
Camden High St. NW1	110	B1
Camden Hill Rd. SE19	170	B6
Camden La. N7	92	D6
Rowstock Gdns.		
Camden Lock Pl. NW1	92	B7
Chalk Fm. Rd.		
Camden Ms. NW1	92	D6
Camden Pk. Rd. NW1	92	D6
Camden Pk. Rd., Chis.	174	C7
Camden Pas. N1	111	H1
Camden Rd. E11	79	H6
Camden Rd. E17	77	J6
Camden Rd. N7	92	D5
Camden Rd. NW1	92	C7
Camden Rd., Bex.	177	F1
Camden Rd., Cars.	199	J4
Camden Rd., Sutt.	198	D5
Camden Row SE3	155	E2
Camden Sq. SE15	152	C1
Watts St.		
Camden Sq. NW1	92	D6
Camden St. NW1	92	C7
Camden Ter. NW1	92	D6
North Vil.		
Camden Wk. N1	111	H1
Camden Way, Chis.	174	C7
Camden Way, Th.Hth.	187	H3
Camdenhurst St. E14	113	H6
Camel Gro., Kings.T.	163	G5
Camel Rd. E16	136	A1
Camelford Wk. W11	108	B6
Lancaster Rd.		
Camellia Cl., Wdf.Grn.	62/63	E7
The Bridle Path		
Camellia Pl., Twick.	143	H7
Camellia St. SW8	130	E7
Camelot Cl. SE28	137	G2
Camelot Cl. SW19	166	D4
Camelot St. SE15	132/133	E7
Bird in Bush Rd.		
Camera Pl. SW10	30	E5
Camera Pl. SW10	129	G6
Cameron Cl. N18	61	E4
Cameron Cl. N20	57	H2
Myddelton Pk.		
Cameron Pl. E1	112/113	E6
Varden St.		
Cameron Rd. SE6	171	J2
Cameron Rd., Brom.	191	G4
Cameron Rd., Croy.	187	H6
Cameron Rd., Ilf.	99	H1
Cameron Sq., Mitch.	185	H1
Camerton Cl. E8	94	C6
Buttermere Wk.		
Camgate Cen., Stai.	140	C6
Camilla Rd. SE16	132	E4
Camille Cl. SE25	188	D3
Camlan Rd., Brom.	173	F4
Camlet St. E2	13	F5
Camlet St. E2	112	C4
Camlet Way, Barn.	40	D2
Camley St. NW1	9	J1
Camley St. NW1	92	D7
Camm Gdns., Kings.T.	181	J2
Church Rd.		
Camms Ter., Dag.	101	J5
Camomile Av., Mitch.	185	J1
Camomile St. EC3	20	D3
Camomile St. EC3	112	B6
Camp Rd. SW19	165	J5
Camp Vw. SW19	165	H5
Campana Rd. SW6	148	D1
Campbell Av., Ilf.	81	F4
Campbell Cl. SE18	156	D1
Moordown		
Campbell Cl. SW16	168	D4
Campbell Cl., Ruis.	66	A6
Campbell Cl., Twick.	162	A2
Campbell Cl. N17	76	C1
Campbell Cft., Edg.	54	A5
Campbell Gordon Way NW2	89	H4
Campbell Rd. E3	114	A3
Campbell Rd. E6	116	B1
Campbell Rd. E15	97	F4
Trevelyan Rd.		
Campbell Rd. E17	77	J4
Campbell Rd. N17	76	D1
Campbell Rd. W7	104	B7
Campbell Rd., Croy.	187	H7
Campbell Rd., E.Mol.	180	C3
Hampton Ct. Rd.		
Campbell Rd., Twick.	162	A2
Campbell Wk. N1	110/111	E1
Outram Pl.		
Campdale Rd. N7	92	D3
Campden Cres., Dag.	100	B4
Campden Cres., Wem.	87	E2
Campden Gro. W8	128	D2
Campden Hill W8	128	D2
Campden Hill Gdns. W8	128	D1
Campden Hill Gate W8	128	D2
Duchess of Bedford's Wk.		
Campden Hill Pl. W11	128	C1
Holland Pk. Av.		
Campden Hill Rd. W8	128	D2
Campden Hill Sq. W8	128	C1
Campden Ho. Cl. W8	128	D2
Hornton St.		

Name	Page	Grid
Campden Rd., S.Croy.	202	B5
Campden St. W8	128	D1
Campen Cl. SW19	166	B2
Queensmere Rd.		
Camperdown St. E1	21	G4
Campfield Rd. SE9	156	A7
Campion Cl. E6	116	C7
Campion Cl., Croy.	202	B4
Campion Cl., Har.	69	J6
Campion Gdns., Wdf.Grn.	63	G5
Campion Pl. SE28	138	B1
Campion Rd. SW15	147	J4
Campion Rd., Islw.	144	C1
Campion Ter. NW2	90	A3
Campion Way, Edg.	54	C4
Camplin Rd., Har.	69	H5
Camplin St. SE14	133	G7
Campsbourne, The N8	74/75	E4
Rectory Gdns.		
Campsbourne Rd. N8	75	E3
Campsey Gdns., Dag.	100	B7
Campsey Rd., Dag.	100	B7
Campsfield Rd. N8	74/75	E3
Campsbourne Rd.		
Campshill Pl. SE13	154	C5
Campshill Rd.		
Campshill Rd. SE13	154	C5
Campus Rd. E17	77	J6
Campus Way NW4	71	H3
Greyhound Hill		
Camrose Av., Edg.	69	J1
Camrose Av., Erith	139	H6
Camrose Av., Felt.	160	B4
Camrose Cl., Croy.	189	H7
Camrose Cl., Mord.	184	D4
Camrose St. SE2	138	A5
Canada Av. N18	59	J6
Canada Cres. W3	106	C5
Canada Est. SE16	133	F3
Canada Gdns. SE13	154	C5
Canada Rd. W3	106	C4
Canada Sq. E14	134	B1
Canada St. SE16	133	G2
Canada Way W12	107	H7
Canadian Av. SE6	172	B1
Canal App. SE8	133	H5
Canal Cl. E1	113	H4
Canal Cl. W10	108	A4
Canal Gro. SE15	132	D6
Canal Head SE15	152	D1
Peckham High St.		
Canal Path E2	112	C1
Canal Rd. E3	113	H4
Canal St. SE5	36	B6
Canal St. SE5	132	A6
Canal Wk. N1	112	A1
Canal Wk. SE26	171	F5
Canal Wk., Croy.	188	B6
Canal Way NW1	7	F5
Canal Way NW8	7	F5
Canal Way NW10	107	F4
Canal Way W10	108	A4
Canal Way Wk. W10	108	A4
Canary Wf. Twr. E14	134	A1
Canberra Cl. NW4	71	G3
Canberra Dr., Hayes	102	C3
Canberra Dr., Nthlt.	102	C3
Canberra Rd. E6	116	C1
Barking Rd.		
Canberra Rd. SE7	135	J6
Canberra Rd. W13	124	D1
Canberra Rd., Bexh.	138	D6
Canberra Rd., Houns.	140	D3
Canbury Av., Kings.T.	141	J1
Canbury Ms. SE26	170	D3
Wells Pk. Rd.		
Canbury Pk. Rd., Kings.T.	181	H1
Canbury Pas., Kings.T.	181	G1
Cancell Rd. SW9	151	G1
Candahar Rd. SW11	149	H2
Candler St. N15	76	A6
Candover Cl., West Dr.	120	A7
Candover St. W1	17	F2
Candy St. E3	113	J1
Cane Cl., Wall.	201	E7
Caney Ms. NW2	90	A2
Claremont Rd.		
Canfield Dr., Ruis.	84	B5
Canfield Gdns. NW6	91	F7
Canfield Pl. NW6	91	F6
Canfield Gdns.		
Canfield Rd., Wdf.Grn.	64	B7
Canford Av., Nthlt.	103	E1
Canford Cl., Enf.	43	G2
Canford Gdns., N.Mal.	182	D6
Canford Pl., Tedd.	163	E6
Canford Rd. SW11	150	A5
Canham Rd. SE25	188	B3
Canham Rd. W3	126	E2
Canmore Gdns. SW16	168	C7
Cann Hall Rd. E11	96	E4
Canning Cres. N22	75	F1
Canning Cross SE5	152	B2
Canning Pas. W8	22	C5
Canning Pas. W8	129	F3
Canning Pl. W8	22	C5
Canning Pl. W8	129	F3
Canning Pl. Ms. W8	22	C4
Canning Rd. E15	114	E2
Canning Rd. E17	77	H4
Canning Rd. N5	93	H3
Canning Rd., Croy.	202	C2
Canning Rd., Har.	68	C3
Cannington Rd., Dag.	100	C6
Cannizaro Rd. SW19	165	J6
Cannon Cl. SW20	183	J3
Cannon Cl., Hmptn.	161	H6
Hanworth Rd.		
Cannon Dr. E14	114	A7
Cannon Hill N14	58	D3
Cannon Hill NW6	90	D5
Cannon Hill La. SW20	184	B3
Cannon La. NW3	91	G3
Cannon La., Pnr.	84	E1
Cannon Pl. NW3	91	G3
Cannon Pl. SE7	136	B5
Cannon Rd. N14	58	E3
Cannon Rd., Bexh.	159	E1
Cannon St. EC4	19	J4
Cannon St. EC4	111	J6
Cannon St. Rd. E1	112	E6
Cannon Trd. Est., Wem.	88	B4
Cannon Way, W.Mol.	179	G4
Cannon Wf. Business Cen. SE8	133	H4
Cannonbury Av., Pnr.	66	D6
Canon Av., Rom.	82	C5
Canon Beck Rd. SE16	133	F2
Canon Mohan Cl. N14	42	B6
Farm La.		
Canon Rd., Brom.	191	J3
Canon Row SW1	26	A4
Canon Row SW1	130	E2
Canon St. N1	111	J1
Canonbie Rd. SE23	153	F7
Canonbury Cres. N1	93	J7
Canonbury Gro. N1	93	J7
Canonbury La. N1	93	H7
Canonbury Pk. N. N1	93	J6
Canonbury Pk. S. N1	93	J6
Canonbury Pl. N1	93	H6
Canonbury Rd. N1	93	H6
Canonbury Rd., Enf.	44	B1
Canonbury Sq. N1	93	H7
Canonbury St. N1	93	J7
Canonbury Vil. N1	93	H7
Canonbury Yd. N1	111	J1
New N. Rd.		
Canons Cl. N2	73	G7
Canons Cl., Edg.	53	J6
Canons Cor., Edg.	53	H4
Canons Dr., Edg.	53	H6
Canons Pk. Cl., Edg.	53	H7
Donnefield Av.		
Canons Wk., Croy.	203	G3
Canonsleigh Rd., Dag.	100	B7
Canopus Way, Nthwd.	50	A4
Canopus Way, Stai.	140	B7
Canrobert St. E2	112	E3
Cantelowes Rd. NW1	92	D6
Canterbury Av., Ilf.	80	B7
Canterbury Av., Sid.	176	C2
Canterbury Cl. E6	116	C6
Harper Rd.		
Canterbury Cl., Beck.	190	B1
Canterbury Cl., Chig.	65	J3
Canterbury Cl., Grnf.	103	H6
Canterbury Cres. SW9	151	G3
Canterbury Gro. SE27	169	H3
Canterbury Pl. SE17	35	H2
Canterbury Pl. SE17	131	H4
Canterbury Rd. E10	78	C7
Canterbury Rd. NW6	108	D2
Canterbury Rd., Borwd.	38	A2
Canterbury Rd., Croy.	187	F7
Canterbury Rd., Felt.	161	E2
Canterbury Rd., Har.	67	H5
Canterbury Rd., Mord.	185	F5
Canterbury Ter. NW6	108	D2
Canterbury Gdns. SE19	188	C1
Cantley Rd., Ilf.	81	F6
Cantley Rd. W7	124	D3
Canton St. E14	114	A6
Cantrell Rd. E3	113	J4
Cantwell Rd. SE18	136	E7
Canute Gdns. SE16	133	G4
Canvey St. SE1	27	H1
North St.		
Cape Cl., Bark.	99	F6
Cape Rd. N17	76	D3
High Cross Rd.		
Cape Yd. E1	29	J1
Capel Av., Wall.	201	F5
Capel Cl. N20	57	F3
Capel Cl., Brom.	206	B1
Capel Ct. EC2	20	C4
Capel Ct. SE20	189	F1
Melvin Rd.		
Capel Gdns., Ilf.	99	J4
Capel Gdns., Pnr.	67	F4
Capel Rd. E7	97	H4
Capel Rd. E12	97	J4
Capel Rd., Barn.	41	H6
Capener's Cl. SW1	24	B4
Capern Rd. SW18	167	F1
Cargill Rd.		
Capital Business Cen., Wem.	105	G2
Capital Interchange Way, Brent.	126	A5
Capitol Ind. Pk. NW9	70	C3
Capitol Way NW9	70	C3
Capland St. NW8	7	F5
Capland St. NW8	109	G4
Caple Par. NW10	106/107	E2
Harley Rd.		
Caple Rd. NW10	107	F2
Capper St. WC1	9	G6
Capper St. WC1	110	C4
Capstan Cl., Rom.	82	B5
Capstan Ride, Enf.	43	G2
Capstan Rd. SE8	133	J4
Capstan Sq. E14	134	C2
Capstan Way SE16	133	H1
Capstone Rd., Brom.	173	F4
Capthorne Av., Har.	85	E1
Capuchin Cl., Stan.	52	E6
Capulet Ms. E16	135	G1
Hanover Av.		
Capworth St. E10	96	A1
Caradoc Cl. W2	108	D6
Caradoc St. SE10	134	E5
Caradon Cl. E11	96/97	E2
Brockway Cl.		
Caradon Way N15	76	A4
Caravel Cl. E14	134	A3
Tiller Rd.		
Caravel Ms. SE8	134	A6
Watergate St.		
Caravelle Gdns., Nthlt.	102	D3
Javelin Way		
Caraway Cl. E13	115	H5
Caraway Pl., Wall.	200	B3
Carberry Rd. SE19	170	B6
Carbery Av. W3	125	J2
Carbis Cl. E4	62	D1
Carbis Rd. E14	113	J6
Carbuncle Pas. Way N17	76	D2
Carburton St. W1	17	E1
Carburton St. W1	110	B5
Cardale St. E14	134	C3
Plevna St.		
Carden Rd. SE15	152	E3
Cardiff Rd. W7	124	D3
Cardiff Rd., Enf.	45	E4
Cardiff St. SE18	137	H7
Cardigan Gdns., Ilf.	100	A2
Cardigan Rd. E3	113	J2
Cardigan Rd. SW13	147	G2
Cardigan Rd. SW19	167	F6
Haydons Rd.		
Cardigan Rd., Rich.	145	H6
Cardigan St. SE11	34	E3
Cardigan St. SE11	131	G5
Cardigan Wk. N1	93	J7
Ashby Gro.		
Cardinal Av., Borwd.	38	B3
Cardinal Av., Kings.T.	163	H5
Cardinal Av., Mord.	184	B6
Cardinal Bourne St. SE1	28	C6
Cardinal Bourne St. SE1	132	A3
Cardinal Cl., Chis.	193	G1
Cardinal Cl., Edg.	54	D7
Abbots Rd.		
Cardinal Cl., Mord.	184	B7
Cardinal Cl., Wor.Pk.	197	G4
Cardinal Cres., N.Mal.	182	C2
Cardinal Dr., Ilf.	65	F6
Cardinal Pl. SW15	148	A4
Cardinal Rd., Felt.	160	B1
Cardinal Rd., Ruis.	84	D1
Cardinal Way, Har.	68	B3
Wolseley Rd.		
Cardinals Wk., Hmptn.	161	J7
Cardinals Way N19	92	D1
Cardine Ms. SE15	132	E7
Cardington Sq., Houns.	142	D4
Cardington St. NW1	9	F3
Cardington St. NW1	110	C3
Cardozo Rd. N7	93	E5
Cardrew Av. N12	57	G5
Cardrew Cl. N12	57	H5
Cardross St. W6	127	H3
Cardwell Rd. N7	92	E4
Cardwell Rd. SE18	136	C4
Carew Cl. N7	93	F2
Carew Rd. N17	76	D2
Carew Rd. W13	125	F2
Carew Rd., Mitch.	186	A2
Carew Rd., Th.Hth.	187	H3
Carew Rd., Wall.	200	C6
Carew St. SE5	151	J2
Carew Way, Wat.	51	F3
Carey Ct., Bexh.	159	H5
Carey Gdns. SW8	150	C1
Carey La. EC2	19	J3
Carey Pl. SW1	33	H2
Carey Rd., Dag.	101	E4
Carey St. WC2	18	D4
Carey St. WC2	111	F6
Carey Way, Wem.	88	C4
Carfax Pl. SW4	150	D4
Holwood Pl.		
Carfax Rd., Hayes	121	J5
Carfree Cl. N1	93	G7
Bewdley St.		
Cargill Rd. SW18	167	E1
Cargreen Pl. SE25	188	C4
Cargreen Rd.		
Cargreen Rd. SE25	188	C4
Carholme Rd. SE23	171	J1
Carisbrooke Av., Bex.	176	D1
Carisbrooke Cl., Enf.	44	C1
Carisbrooke Cl., Stan.	69	G2
Carisbrooke Gdns. SE15	37	G7
Carisbrooke Rd. E17	77	H4
Carisbrooke Rd., Brom.	191	J4
Carisbrooke Rd., Mitch.	186	D4
Carker's La. NW5	92	B5
Carleton Cl., Esher	194	A1
Carleton Rd. N7	92	D5
Carleton Vil. NW5	92	C5
Leighton Gro.		
Carlile Cl. E3	113	J2
Carlina Gdns., Wdf.Grn.	63	H5
Carlingford Gdns., Mitch.	167	J7
Carlingford Rd. N15	75	H3
Carlingford Rd. NW3	91	G4
Carlingford Rd., Mord.	184	A6
Carlisle Av. EC3	21	E4
Carlisle Av. W3	106	E6
Carlisle Cl., Kings.T.	182	A1
Carlisle Cl., Pnr.	66	E7
Carlisle Gdns., Har.	69	G7
Carlisle Gdns., Ilf.	80	B6
Carlisle La. SE1	26	D6
Carlisle La. SE1	131	F3
Carlisle Ms. NW8	15	F1
Carlisle Ms. NW8	109	G5
Carlisle Pl. N11	58	B4
Carlisle Pl. SW1	25	F6
Carlisle Rd. E10	96	A1
Carlisle Rd. N4	75	G7
Carlisle Rd. NW6	108	B1
Carlisle Rd. NW9	70	C3
Carlisle Rd., Hmptn.	161	H7
Carlisle Rd., Sutt.	198	C5
Carlisle St. W1	17	H4
Carlisle Wk. E8	94	C6
Laurel St.		
Carlisle Way SW17	168	A5

Carlos Pl. W1 16 C6
Carlos Pl. W1 110 A7
Carlow St. NW1 9 F1
Carlton Av. N14 42 D5
Carlton Av., Felt. 142 C6
Carlton Av., Har. 68 E5
Carlton Av., Hayes 121 H4
Carlton Av., S.Croy. 202 B7
Carlton Av. E., Wem. 87 H1
Carlton Av. W., Wem. 86 E2
Carlton Cl. NW3 90 D2
Carlton Cl., Borwd. 38 D4
Carlton Cl., Chess. 195 G6
Carlton Cl., Edg. 54 A5
Carlton Cl., Nthlt. 85 J5
Whitton Av. W.
Carlton Ct. SW9 151 H1
Carlton Ct., Ilf. 81 G3
Carlton Cres., Sutt. 198 B4
Carlton Dr. SW15 148 B5
Carlton Dr., Ilf. 81 G3
Carlton Gdns. SW1 25 H2
Carlton Gdns. SW1 130 D1
Carlton Gdns. W5 105 F6
Carlton Gro. SE15 152 E1
Carlton Hill NW8 6 B2
Carlton Hill NW8 109 E2
Carlton Ho., Felt. 141 J7
Carlton Ho. Ter. SW1 25 H2
Carlton Ho. Ter. SW1 130 D1
Carlton Pk. Av. SW20 183 J2
Carlton Rd. E11 97 F1
Carlton Rd. E12 98 A4
Carlton Rd. E17 77 H1
Carlton Rd. N4 75 G7
Carlton Rd. N11 58 A5
Carlton Rd. SW14 146 C3
Carlton Rd. W4 126 D2
Carlton Rd. W5 105 F7
Carlton Rd., Erith 139 H6
Carlton Rd., N.Mal. 182 E2
Carlton Rd., Sid. 175 J5
Carlton Rd., S.Croy. 202 A6
Carlton Rd., Walt. 178 B7
Carlton Rd., Well. 158 B3
Carlton Sq. E1 113 G4
Argyle Rd.
Carlton St. SW1 17 H6
Carlton Ter. E11 79 H5
Carlton Ter. N18 60 A3
Carlton Ter. SE26 171 F3
Carlton Twr. Pl. SW1 24 A5
Carlton Twr. Pl. SW1 129 J3
Carlton Vale NW6 108 E2
Carlton Vil. SW15 147 J5
St. John's Av.
Carlwell St. SW17 167 H5
Carlyle Av., Brom. 192 A3
Carlyle Av., Sthl. 103 F7
Carlyle Cl. N2 73 F6
Carlyle Cl. NW10 106 D1
Carlyle Cl., W.Mol. 179 H2
Carlyle Gdns., Sthl. 103 F7
Carlyle Ms. E1 113 G4
Alderney Rd.
Carlyle Pl. SW15 148 A4
Carlyle Rd. E12 98 B4
Carlyle Rd. SE28 118 B7
Carlyle Rd. W5 125 F5
Carlyle Rd., Croy. 202 D2
Carlyle Sq. SW3 31 F4
Carlyle Sq. SW3 129 G5
Carlyon Av., Har. 85 F4
Carlyon Cl., Wem. 105 H1
Carlyon Rd., Hayes 102 C6
Carlyon Rd., Wem. 105 H2
Carmalt Gdns. SW15 147 J4
Carmarthen Gdn. NW9 70/71 E6
Snowdon Dr.
Carmel Ct. W8 22 A3
Carmel Ct., Wem. 88 B2
Carmelite Cl., Har. 67 J1
Carmelite Rd., Har. 67 J1
Carmelite St. EC4 19 F5
Carmelite St. EC4 111 G7
Carmelite Wk., Har. 67 J1
Carmelite Way, Har. 67 J2
Carmen St. E14 114 B6
Carmichael Cl. SW11 149 G3
Darien Rd.
Carmichael Cl., Ruis. 84 A4
Carmichael Ms. SW18 149 G7
Carmichael Rd. SE25 188 D5
Carminia Rd. SW17 168 B2
Carnaby St. W1 17 F4
Carnaby St. W1 110 C6
Carnac St. SE27 170 A4
Carnanton Rd. E17 78 D1
Carnarvon Av., Enf. 44 C3
Carnarvon Dr., Hayes 121 F3
Carnarvon Rd. E10 78 C6
Carnarvon Rd. E15 97 F6
Carnarvon Rd. E18 79 F1
Carnarvon Rd., Barn. 40 B3
Carnation St. SE2 138 B5
Carnbrook Rd. SE3 156 A3
Carnecke Gdns. SE9 156 B5
Carnegie Cl., Surb. 195 J2
Fullers Av.
Carnegie Pl. SW19 166 A3
Carnegie St. N1 111 F1
Carnforth Cl., Epsom 196 B6
Carnforth Rd. SW16 168 D7
Carnie Lo. SW17 168 B3
Manville Rd.
Carnoustie Dr. N1 93 F7
Carnwath Rd. SW6 148 D3
Carol St. NW1 110 C1
Carolina Cl. E15 96 E5
Carolina Rd., Th.Hth. 187 H2
Caroline Cl. N10 74 B2
Alexandra Pk. Rd.
Caroline Cl. SW16 169 F4
Caroline Cl. W2 14 B6
Caroline Cl., Croy. 202 B4
Brownlow Rd.
Caroline Cl., Islw. 124 A7
Caroline Cl., West Dr. 120 A2
Caroline Ct., Stan. 52 D6
The Chase
Caroline Gdns. SE15 132 E7
Caroline Pl. SW11 150 A2
Caroline Pl. W2 14 B5
Caroline Pl. W2 109 E7
Caroline Pl., Hayes 121 H7
Caroline Pl. Ms. W2 14 B6
Caroline Rd. SW19 166 C7
Caroline St. E1 113 G6
Caroline Ter. SW1 32 B2
Caroline Ter. SW1 130 A4
Caroline Wk. W6 128 B6
Carpenders Av., Wat. 50 E3
Carpenders Pk., Wat. 51 E2
Carpenter Gdns. N21 59 H2
Carpenter St. W1 16 D6
Carpenters Ct., Twick. 162 B2
Carpenters Pl. SW4 150 D4
Carpenters Rd. E15 96 B6
Carr Gro. SE18 136 B4
Carr Rd. E17 77 J2
Carr Rd., Nthlt. 85 H6
Carr St. E14 113 H5
Carrara Wk. SW9 151 G4
Somerleyton Rd.
Carriage Dr. E. SW11 32 B7
Carriage Dr. E. SW11 130 A7
Carriage Dr. N. SW11 32 C6
Carriage Dr. N. SW11 130 A6
Carriage Dr. S. SW11 149 J1
Carriage Dr. W. SW11 129 J7
Carriage Ms., Ilf. 99 F2
Carriage Pl. N16 94 A3
Carrick Cl., Islw. 144 D3
Carrick Dr., Ilf. 81 F1
Carrick Gdns. N17 60 B7
Flexmere Rd.
Carrick Ms. SE8 134 A6
Watergate St.
Carrill Way, Belv. 138 D4
Carrington Av., Borwd. 38 B5
Carrington Av., Houns. 143 H5
Carrington Cl., Barn. 39 G5
Carrington Cl., Borwd. 38 C5
Carrington Cl., Croy. 189 H7
Carrington Cl., Kings.T. 164 C5
Carrington Gdns. E7 97 H4
Woodford Rd.
Carrington Rd., Rich. 146 A4
Carrington Sq., Har. 51 J7
Carrington St. W1 24 D2
Carrol Cl. NW5 92 B4
Carroll Cl. E15 97 F5
Carroll Hill, Loug. 48 C3
Carron Cl. E14 114 B6
Carronade Pl. SE28 137 F3
Carroun Rd. SW8 34 C7
Carroun Rd. SW8 131 F7
Carrow Rd., Dag. 100 B7
Carroway La., Grnf. 104 A3
Cowgate Rd.
Carrs La. N21 43 J5
Carshalton Gro., Sutt. 199 G4
Carshalton Pk. Rd., Cars. 199 J5
Carshalton Pl., Cars. 200 A4
Carshalton Rd., Cars. 199 F5
Carshalton Rd., Mitch. 186 A4
Carshalton Rd., Sutt. 199 F5
Carslake Rd. SW15 147 J6
Carson Rd. E16 115 G4
Carson Rd. SE21 170 A2
Carson Rd., Barn. 41 J4
Carstairs Rd. SE6 172 C3
Carston Cl. SE12 155 G5
Carswell Cl., Ilf. 80 A4
Roding La. S.
Carswell Rd. SE6 154 C7
Cart La. E4 46 D7
Carter Cl., Wall. 200 D7
Carter Ct. EC4 111 H6
Carter La.
Carter La. EC4 19 H4
Carter La. EC4 111 H6
Carter Pl. SE17 36 A4
Carter Pl. SE17 131 J5
Carter Rd. E13 115 H1
Carter Rd. SW19 167 G6
Carter St. SE17 35 J5
Carter St. SE17 131 J6
Carteret St. SW1 25 H4
Carteret St. SW1 130 D2
Carteret Way SE8 133 H4
Carterhatch La., Enf. 44 D2
Carterhatch Rd., Enf. 45 F2
Carters Cl., Wor.Pk. 198 A2
Carters Hill Cl. SE9 173 J1
Carters La. SE23 171 H2
Carters Yd. SW18 148 D5
Wandsworth High St.
Carthew Rd. W6 127 H3
Carthew Vil. W6 127 H3
Carthusian St. EC1 19 J1
Carthusian St. EC1 111 J5
Cartier Circle E14 134 B1
Carting La. WC2 18 B6
Carting La. WC2 111 E7
Cartmel Cl. N17 60/61 E7
Heybourne Rd.
Cartmel Gdns., Mord. 185 F5
Cartmel Rd., Bexh. 159 G1
Carton St. W1 16 A3
Cartwright Gdns. WC1 10 A4
Cartwright Gdns. WC1 110 E3
Cartwright Rd., Dag. 101 F7
Cartwright St. E1 21 G5
Cartwright St. E1 112 C7
Cartwright Way SW13 127 H7
Carver Cl. W4 126 C3
Carver Rd. SE24 151 J6
Carville Cres., Brent. 125 H5
Cary Rd. E11 97 E4
Carysfort Rd. N8 74 D5
Carysfort Rd. N16 94 A3
Cascade Av. N10 74 C4
Cascade Cl., Buck.H. 64 A2
Cascade Rd.
Cascade Rd., Buck.H. 64 A2
Casella Rd. SE14 133 G7
Casewick Rd. SE27 169 H4
Casimir Rd. E5 95 E3
Casino Av. SE24 151 J5
Caspian St. SE5 36 B7
Caspian St. SE5 132 A7
Caspian Wk. E16 116 A6
Caspian Wf. E3 114 B5
Violet Rd.
Cassandra Cl., Nthlt. 86 A4
Casselden Rd. NW10 88 D7
Cassidy Rd. SW6 128 D7
Cassilda Rd. SE2 138 A4
Cassilis Rd., Twick. 145 E5
Cassiobury Av., Felt. 141 J6
Cassiobury Rd. E17 77 G5
Cassis Ct., Loug. 49 F4
Cassland Rd. E9 95 F7
Cassland Rd., Th.Hth. 188 A4
Casslee Rd. SE6 153 J7
Casson St. E1 21 H2
Casson St. E1 112 D5
Castalia Sq. E14 134 C2
Roserton St.
Castalia St. E14 134 C2
Plevna St.
Castell Rd., Loug. 49 F1
Castellain Rd. W9 6 C6
Castellain Rd. W9 108 E4
Castellane Cl., Stan. 52 C7
Daventer Dr.
Castello Av. SW15 147 J5
Castelnau SW13 127 H6
Castelnau Gdns. SW13 127 H6
Arundel Ter.
Castelnau Pl. SW13 127 H6
Castelnau
Castelnau Row SW13 127 H6
Lonsdale Rd.
Casterbridge NW6 109 E1
Casterbridge Rd. SE3 155 G3
Casterton St. E8 94/95 E6
Wilton Way
Castile Rd. SE18 136 D4
Castillon Rd. SE6 172 E2
Castlands Rd. SE6 171 J2
Castle Av. E4 62 D5
Castle Baynard St. EC4 19 H5
Castle Cl. E9 95 H5
Swinnerton St.
Castle Cl. SW19 166 A3
Castle Cl. W3 126 B2
Park Rd. E.
Castle Cl., Brom. 190 E3
Castle Ct. EC3 20 C4
Castle Ct. SE26 171 H4
Champion Rd.
Castle Dr., Ilf. 80 B6
Castle La. SW1 25 G5
Castle La. SW1 130 C3
Castle Ms. N12 57 F5
Castle Rd.
Castle Ms. NW1 92 B6
Castle Rd.
Castle Par., Epsom 197 G7
Ewell Bypass
Castle Pl. NW1 92 B6
Castle Pl. W4 126/127 E4
Windmill Rd.
Castle Pt. E13 115 J2
Castle Rd. N12 57 F5
Castle Rd. NW1 92 B6
Castle Rd., Dag. 118 B1
Castle Rd., Enf. 45 H1
Castle Rd., Islw. 144 C2
Castle Rd., Nthlt. 85 H6
Castle Rd., Sthl. 123 F3
Castle St. E6 115 J2
Castle St., Kings.T. 181 H2
Castle Wk., Sun. 178 C3
Elizabeth Gdns.
Castle Way SW19 166 A3
Castle Way, Felt. 160 C4
Castle Yd. N6 74 A7
North Rd.
Castle Yd. SE1 27 H1
Castle Yd., Rich. 145 G5
Hill St.
Castlebar Hill W5 105 E5
Castlebar Ms. W5 105 F5
Castlebar Pk. W5 105 E5
Castlebar Rd. W5 105 F5
Castlebrook Cl. SE11 35 G1
Castlebrook Cl. SE11 131 H4
Castlecombe Dr. SW19 148 A7
Castlecombe Rd. SE9 174 B4
Castledine Rd. SE20 170 E7
Castleford Av. SE9 174 E1
Castleford Cl. N17 60 C6
Castlegate, Rich. 145 J3
Castlehaven Rd. NW1 92 B7
Castleleigh Ct., Enf. 44 A5
Castlemaine Av., S.Croy. 202 C5
Castlemaine Twr. SW11 149 J1
Castlereagh St. W1 15 J3
Castleton Av., Wem. 87 H4
Castleton Cl., Croy. 189 H6
Castleton Gdns., Wem. 87 H3
Castleton Rd. E17 78 D2
Castleton Rd. SE9 174 A4
Castleton Rd., Ilf. 100 A1
Castleton Rd., Mitch. 186 D4
Castleton Rd., Ruis. 84 D1
Castletown Rd. W14 128 B5
Castleview Cl. N4 93 J1
Castleview Gdns., Ilf. 80 B6
Castlewood Dr. SE9 156 C2
Castlewood Rd. N15 76 D6
Castlewood Rd. N16 76 D7
Castlewood Rd., Barn. 41 G3
Castor La. E14 114 B7
Cat Hill, Barn. 41 H6
Caterham Av., Ilf. 80 C2
Caterham Rd. SE13 154 C3
Catesby St. SE17 36 C2
Catesby St. SE17 132 A4
Catford Bdy. SE6 154 B7
Catford Hill SE6 171 J2
Catford Ms. SE6 154 B7
Holbeach Rd.
Catford Rd. SE6 154 A7
Cathall Rd. E11 96 D3
Cathay St. SE16 133 E2
Cathay Wk., Nthlt. 103 G2
Brabazon Rd.

Name	Page	Ref
Cathcart Dr., Orp.	207	H2
Cathcart Hill N19	92	C3
Cathcart Rd. SW10	**30**	**B5**
Cathcart St. SW10	129	F6
Cathcart St. NW5	92	B6
Cathedral Piazza SW1	**25**	**F6**
Cathedral Pl. EC4	**19**	**J3**
Cathedral St. SE1	**28**	**B1**
Cathedral St. SE1	132	A1
Catherall Rd. N5	93	J3
Catherine Cl., Loug.	48	C6
Roding Gdns.		
Catherine Dr., Rich.	145	H4
Catherine Gdns., Houns.	144	A4
Catherine Griffiths Ct. EC1	**11**	**F5**
Catherine Gro. SE10	154	B1
Catherine Pl. SW1	**25**	**F5**
Catherine Pl. SW1	130	C3
Catherine Rd., Surb.	181	G5
Catherine St. WC2	**18**	**C5**
Catherine St. WC2	111	F7
Catherine Wheel All. E1	**20**	**E2**
Catherine Wheel Rd., Brent.	125	G7
Catherine Wheel Yd. SW1	**25**	**F2**
Catherine's Cl., West Dr.	120	A3
Money La.		
Cathles Rd. SW12	150	B6
Cathnor Rd. W12	127	H2
Catlin St. SE16	**37**	**J3**
Catlin St. SE16	132	D5
Catling Cl. SE23	171	F3
Catlins La., Pnr.	66	B3
Cato Rd. SW4	150	D3
Cato St. W1	**15**	**H2**
Cato St. W1	109	H5
Cator La., Beck.	189	J2
Cator Rd. SE26	171	G6
Cator Rd., Cars.	199	J5
Cator St. SE15	**37**	**F6**
Cator St. SE15	132	C6
Catterick Cl. N11	58	A6
Cattistock Rd. SE9	174	B5
Cattley Cl., Barn.	40	B4
Wood St.		
Catton St. WC1	**18**	**C2**
Catton St. WC1	111	F5
Caulfield Rd. E6	98	C7
Caulfield Rd. SE15	153	E2
Causeway, The N2	73	H4
Causeway, The SW18	148	E4
Causeway, The SW19	166	A6
Causeway, The, Cars.	200	A3
Causeway, The, Chess.	195	H4
Causeway, The, Esher	194	C7
Causeway, The, Felt.	142	A4
Causeway, The, Tedd.	162	C6
Broad St.		
Causeyware Rd. N9	45	E7
Causton Rd. N6	74	B7
Cautley Av. SW4	150	C5
Cavalier Cl., Rom.	83	J4
Cavalry Barracks, Houns.	142	D3
Cavalry Cres., Houns.	142	D4
Cavalry Gdns. SW15	148	C5
Upper Richmond Rd.		
Cavaye Pl. SW10	**30**	**D4**
Cave Rd. E13	115	H2
Cave Rd., Rich.	163	F4
Cave St. N1	**10**	**D1**
Cavell Dr., Enf.	43	G2
Cavell Rd. N17	60	A7
Cavell St. E1	113	E5
Cavendish Av. N3	72	D2
Cavendish Av. NW8	**7**	**F2**
Cavendish Av. NW8	109	G2
Cavendish Av. W13	104	D5
Cavendish Av., Erith	139	J6
Cavendish Av., Har.	86	A4
Cavendish Av., N.Mal.	183	H5
Cavendish Av., Ruis.	84	B5
Cavendish Av., Sid.	158	A7
Cavendish Av., Well.	157	J3
Cavendish Av., Wdf.Grn.	79	H1
Cavendish Cl. N18	60/61	E5
Cavendish Rd.		
Cavendish Cl. NW6	90	C7
Cavendish Rd.		
Cavendish Cl. NW8	**7**	**F3**
Cavendish Cl. NW8	109	G3
Cavendish Ct. EC3	**20**	**E3**
Cavendish Cres., Borwd.	38	A4
Cavendish Dr. E11	96	D1
Cavendish Dr., Edg.	53	J6
Cavendish Dr., Esher	194	B5
Cavendish Gdns., Bark.	99	H5
Cavendish Gdns., Ilf.	98	D1
Cavendish Gdns., Rom.	83	E5
Cavendish Ms. N. W1	**16**	**E1**
Cavendish Ms. S. W1	**16**	**E2**
Cavendish Par., Houns.	142/143	E2
Bath Rd.		
Cavendish Pl. W1	**16**	**E3**
Cavendish Pl. W1	110	B6
Cavendish Rd. E4	62	C6
Cavendish Rd. N4	75	G6
Cavendish Rd. N18	60	E5
Cavendish Rd. NW6	90	B7
Cavendish Rd. SW12	150	B6
Cavendish Rd. SW19	167	G7
Cavendish Rd. W4	146	C1
Cavendish Rd., Barn.	39	J3
Cavendish Rd., Croy.	201	H1
Cavendish Rd., N.Mal.	183	F5
Cavendish Rd., Sutt.	199	F7
Cavendish Sq. W1	**16**	**E3**
Cavendish Sq. W1	110	B6
Cavendish St. N1	**12**	**B2**
Cavendish St. N1	112	A2
Cavendish Ter., Felt.	160	A2
High St.		
Cavendish Way, W.Wick.	204	B1
Cavenham Gdns., Ilf.	99	G3
Caverleigh Way, Wor.Pk.	197	G1
Caversham Av. N13	59	G3
Caversham Av., Sutt.	198	B2
Caversham Flats SW3	**31**	**J5**
Caversham Rd. N15	75	J4
Caversham Rd. NW5	92	C6
Caversham Rd., Kings.T.	181	J2
Caversham St. SW3	**31**	**J5**
Caversham St. SW3	129	J6
Caverswall St. W12	107	J6
Caveside Cl., Chis.	192	D1
Cawdor Cres. W7	124	D4
Cawnpore St. SE19	170	B5
Caxton Gro. E3	114	A3
Caxton Ms., Brent.	125	G6
The Butts		
Caxton Rd. N22	75	F2
Caxton Rd. SW19	167	F5
Caxton Rd. W12	128	A2
Caxton Rd., Sthl.	122	D3
Caxton St. SW1	**25**	**G5**
Caxton St. SW1	130	C3
Caxton St. N. E16	115	F7
Victoria Dock Rd.		
Caygill Cl., Brom.	191	F4
Cayley Cl., Wall.	200	E7
Cayley Rd., Sthl.	123	H3
McNair Rd.		
Cayton Pl. EC1	**12**	**B4**
Cayton Rd., Grnf.	104	B2
Cayton St. EC1	**12**	**B4**
Cazenove Rd. E17	78	A1
Cazenove Rd. N16	94	C2
Cearns Ho. E6	116	A1
Cecil Av., Bark.	99	G7
Cecil Av., Enf.	44	C4
Cecil Av., Wem.	87	J5
Cecil Cl. W5	105	G5
Helena Rd.		
Cecil Cl., Chess.	195	G4
Cecil Ct. WC2	**17**	**J6**
Cecil Ct., Barn.	40	A3
Cecil Ct., Pnr.	67	E4
Cecil Pl., Mitch.	185	J5
Cecil Rd. E11	97	E3
Cecil Rd. E13	115	G1
Cecil Rd. E17	78	A1
Cecil Rd. N10	74	B2
Cecil Rd. N14	58	C1
Cecil Rd. NW9	70	E3
Cecil Rd. NW10	106	E1
Cecil Rd. SW19	166	E7
Cecil Rd. W3	106	C5
Cecil Rd., Croy.	187	F6
Cecil Rd., Enf.	44	A4
Cecil Rd., Har.	68	B3
Cecil Rd., Houns.	143	J2
Cecil Rd., Ilf.	98	E4
Cecil Rd., Rom.	82	D7
Cecil Rd., Sutt.	198	C6
Cecil Way, Brom.	205	G1
Cecile Pk. N8	75	E6
Cecilia Cl. N2	73	F3
Cecilia Rd. E8	94	D5
Cedar Av., Barn.	41	H7
Cedar Av., Enf.	45	F2
Cedar Av., Hayes	102	A6
Cedar Av., Rom.	82	E5
Cedar Av., Ruis.	84	C6
Cedar Av., Sid.	158	A7
Cedar Av., Twick.	143	H6
Cedar Av., West Dr.	120	C1
Cedar Cl. SE21	169	J1
Cedar Cl. SW15	164	D4
Cedar Cl., Borwd.	38	B4
Cedar Cl., Brom.	206	B3
Cedar Cl., Buck.H.	64	A2
Cedar Cl., Cars.	199	J6
Cedar Cl., E.Mol.	180	B4
Cedar Rd.		
Cedar Cl., Rom.	83	J4
Cedar Copse, Brom.	192	C2
Cedar Ct. E8	94	C7
Cedar Ct. N1	93	J7
Essex Rd.		
Cedar Ct. SE9	156	B6
Cedar Ct. SW19	166	A3
Cedar Cres., Brom.	206	B3
Cedar Dr. N2	73	H4
Cedar Dr., Loug.	49	E2
Cedar Dr., Pnr.	51	G6
Cedar Gdns., Sutt.	199	F6
Cedar Gro. W5	125	H3
Cedar Gro., Bex.	158	C6
Cedar Gro., Sthl.	103	G5
Cedar Hts., Rich.	163	H1
Cedar Ho., Croy.	204	B6
Cedar Lawn Av., Barn.	40	B5
Cedar Mt. SE9	174	A1
Cedar Pk., Chig.	64/65	E4
High Rd.		
Cedar Pk. Gdns., Rom.	82	D7
Cedar Pl. SE7	135	J5
Floyd Rd.		
Cedar Ri. N14	42	A7
Cedar Rd. N17	76	C1
Cedar Rd. NW2	89	J4
Cedar Rd., Brom.	191	J2
Cedar Rd., Croy.	202	B2
Cedar Rd., E.Mol.	180	B4
Cedar Rd., Houns.	142	C2
Cedar Rd., Rom.	83	J4
Cedar Rd., Sutt.	199	F6
Cedar Rd., Tedd.	162	D5
Cedar Ter., Rich.	145	J4
Cedar Tree Gro. SE27	169	H5
Cedar Vista, Rich.	145	H1
Kew Rd.		
Cedar Wk., Esher	194	C6
Cedar Way NW1	92	D7
Cedarcroft Rd., Chess.	195	J4
Cedarhurst, Brom.	172/173	E7
Elstree Hill		
Cedarhurst Dr. SE9	155	J5
Cedarne Rd. SW6	128	E7
Cedars, The E15	115	F1
Portway		
Cedars, The W13	105	F6
Heronsforde		
Cedars, The, Buck.H.	63	G1
Cedars, The, Tedd.	162	C6
Adelaide Rd.		
Cedars Av. E17	78	A5
Cedars Av., Mitch.	186	A4
Cedars Cl. NW4	72	A3
Church St.		
Cedars Cl. N9	60	B2
Cedars Ms. SW4	150	B4
Cedars Rd.		
Cedars Rd. E15	97	E6
Cedars Rd. N9	60	D2
Cedars Rd. N21	59	H2
Cedars Rd. SW4	150	B3
Cedars Rd. SW13	147	F2
Cedars Rd. W4	126	C5
Cedars Rd., Beck.	189	H2
Cedars Rd., Croy.	201	E3
Cedars Rd., Kings.T.	181	F1
Cedars Rd., Mord.	184	D4
Cedars Rd. SW16	169	F6
Cedra Ct. N16	94	D1
Cedric Rd. SE9	175	F3
Celadon Cl., Enf.	45	H3
Celandine Cl. E14	114	A5
Celandine Dr. E8	94	C7
Richmond Rd.		
Celandine Dr. SE28	138	B1
Celandine Way E15	115	E3
Celbridge Ms. W2	**14**	**B3**
Celestial Gdns. SE13	154	D4
Celia Rd. N19	92	C4
Celtic Av., Brom.	190	E3
Celtic St. E14	114	B5
Cemetery La. SE7	136	B6
Cemetery Rd. E7	97	F4
Cemetery Rd. N17	60	B7
Cemetery Rd. SE2	138	B7
Cenacle Cl. NW3	90	D3
Centaur St. SE1	**26**	**D5**
Centaur St. SE1	131	F3
Centaurs Business Cen., Islw.	124	D6
Centenary Est., Enf.	45	J4
Centenary Rd., Enf.	45	J4
Centenary Wk., Loug.	47	H3
Central Av. E11	96	D2
Central Av. N2	73	G2
Central Av. N9	60	B3
Central Av. SW11	129	J7
Central Av., Enf.	44	E2
Central Av., Hayes	102	A7
Central Av., Houns.	143	J4
Central Av., Pnr.	67	F6
Central Av., Wall.	201	E5
Central Av., Well.	157	J2
Central Av., W.Mol.	179	F4
Central Circ. NW4	71	H5
Hendon Way		
Central Gdns., Central Rd.	184/185	E5
Central Hill SE19	170	A5
Central Mkts. EC1	**19**	**H2**
Central Mkts. EC1	111	H5
Central Par., Felt.	142	C7
Central Par., Grnf.	104	D3
Central Par., Houns.	123	G7
Heston Rd.		
Central Par., Surb.	181	H6
St. Mark's Hill		
Central Pk. Av., Dag.	101	H3
Central Pk. Est., Houns.	142	D5
Central Pk. Rd. E6	116	A2
Central Pl. SE25	188/189	E4
Portland Rd.		
Central Rd., Mord.	184	D5
Central Rd., Wem.	86	E5
Central Rd., Wor.Pk.	197	G2
Central Sch. Footpath SW14	146	C3
Central Sq. NW11	72	E6
Central Sq., Wem.	87	H5
Station Gro.		
Central Sq., W.Mol.	179	F4
Central St. EC1	**11**	**J4**
Central St. EC1	111	J3
Central Way NW10	106	C2
Central Way SE28	118	A7
Central Way, Cars.	199	H7
Central Way, Felt.	142	B5
Centre, The, Felt.	160	A2
Centre Av. W3	126	D1
Centre Av. W10	107	J3
Harrow Rd.		
Centre Common Rd., Chis.	175	F6
Centre Rd. E7	97	G2
Centre Rd. E11	97	G2
Centre Rd., Dag.	119	H2
Centre St. E2	113	E2
Centre Way E17	62	C7
Centre Way N9	61	F2
Centreway, Ilf.	99	F2
Centric Cl. NW1	110	B1
Oval Rd.		
Centurion Cl. N7	93	F7
Centurion Ct., Wall.	200	B2
Wandle Rd.		
Centurion La. E3	113	J2
Libra Rd.		
Centurion Way, Erith	139	G3
Century Cl. NW4	72	A5
Century Ms. E5	95	F4
Lower Clapton Rd.		
Century Rd. E17	77	H3
Cephas Av. E1	113	F4
Cephas St. E1	113	F4
Ceres Rd. SE18	137	J4
Cerise Rd. SE15	152	D1
Cerne Cl., Hayes	102	D7
Cerne Rd., Mord.	185	F6
Cerney Ms. W2	**15**	**E5**
Cervantes Ct. W2	**14**	**B4**
Cester St. E2	112	D1
Whiston Rd.		
Ceylon Rd. W14	128	A3
Chadacre Av., Ilf.	80	C3
Chadacre Rd., Epsom	197	H6
Chadbourn St. E14	114	B5
Chadd Dr., Brom.	192	B3
Chadd Grn. E13	115	G1
Chadview Ct., Rom.	82	D7

Name	Page	Grid
Chadville Gdns., Rom.	82	D5
Chadway, Dag.	100	C1
Chadwell Av., Rom.	82	B7
Chadwell Heath La., Rom.	82	B5
Chadwell St. EC1	**11**	**F3**
Chadwell St. EC1	111	G3
Chadwick Av. E4	62	D4
Chadwick Av. N21	43	F5
Chadwick Av. SW19	166	D6
Chadwick Cl. SW15	147	F7
Chadwick Cl. W7	104	C5
Westcott Cres.		
Chadwick Cl., Tedd.	162	D6
Chadwick Cl., Surb.	181	F7
Chadwick Rd. E11	79	E7
Chadwick Rd. NW10	107	F1
Chadwick Rd. SE15	152	C2
Chadwick Rd., Ilf.	99	E3
Chadwick St. SW1	**25**	**J6**
Chadwick St. SW1	130	D3
Chadwick Way SE28	118	D7
Chadwin Rd. E13	115	H5
Chadworth Way, Esher	194	A5
Chaffinch Av., Croy.	189	G6
Chaffinch Cl. N9	61	G1
Chaffinch Cl., Croy.	189	G6
Chaffinch Cl., Surb.	196	A3
Chaffinch Rd., Beck.	189	H1
Chafford Way, Rom.	82	C4
Chagford St. NW1	**7**	**J6**
Chagford St. NW1	109	J4
Chailey Av., Enf.	44	C2
Chailey Cl., Houns.	142	D1
Springwell Rd.		
Chailey St. E5	95	F3
Chalbury Wk. N1	111	F2
Chalcombe Rd. SE2	138	B3
Chalcot Cl., Sutt.	198	D7
Chalcot Cres. NW1	109	J1
Chalcot Gdns. NW3	91	J6
Chalcot Ms. SW16	168	E3
Chalcot Rd. NW1	92	A7
Chalcot Sq. NW1	92	A7
Chalcott Gdns., Surb.	195	F1
Chalcroft Rd. SE13	154	E5
Chaldon Path, Th.Hth.	187	H4
Chaldon Rd. SW6	128	B7
Chale Rd. SW2	150	E6
Chalet Est. NW7	55	G4
Chalfont Av., Wem.	88	B6
Chalfont Ct. NW9	71	F3
Chalfont Grn. N9	60	B3
Chalfont Rd. N9	60	C3
Chalfont Rd. SE25	188	C3
Chalfont Rd., Hayes	122	A2
Chalfont Wk., Pnr.	66	C2
Willows Cl.		
Chalford Way W13	124	E3
Chalford Cl., W.Mol.	179	G4
Chalford Rd. SE21	170	A4
Chalford Wk., Wdf.Grn.	80	A1
Chalgrove Av., Mord.	184	D5
Chalgrove Cres., Ilf.	80	B2
Chalgrove Gdns. N3	72	B3
Chalgrove Rd. N17	76	E1
Chalgrove Rd., Sutt.	199	G7
Chalice Cl., Wall.	200	D6
Lavender Vale		
Chalk Fm. Rd. NW1	92	A7
Chalk Hill Rd. W6	128	A4
Shortlands		
Chalk La., Barn.	41	J4
Chalk Pit Way, Sutt.	199	F5
Chalk Rd. E13	115	J5
Chalkenden Cl. SE20	170	E7
Chalkhill Rd., Wem.	88	B3
Chalklands, Wem.	88	C3
Chalkley Cl., Mitch.	185	J2
Chalkmill Rd., Enf.	44	E3
Chalkstone Cl., Wall.	158	A1
Chalkwell Pk. Av., Enf.	44	B4
Challice Way SW2	169	F1
Challin St. SE20	189	F1
Challis Rd., Brent.	125	G5
Challoner Cl. N2	73	G2
Challoner Cres. W14	128	C5
Challoner St.		
Challoner St. W14	128	C5
Challoners Cl., E.Mol.	180	A4
Chalmers Wk. SE17	**35**	**H6**
Chalmers Way, Felt.	142	A5
Chaloner Ct. SE1	**28**	**B3**
Chalsey Rd. SE4	153	J4
Chalton Dr. N2	73	F6
Chalton St. NW1	**9**	**J3**
Chalton St. NW1	110	D2
Chamber St. E1	**21**	**G5**
Chamber St. E1	112	C7
Chamberlain Cl. SE28	137	G3
Broadwater Rd.		
Chamberlain Cotts. SE5	152	A1
Camberwell Gro.		
Chamberlain Cres., W.Wick.	204	B1
Chamberlain Gdns., Houns.	143	J1
Gresham Rd.		
Chamberlain La., Pnr.	66	A4
Chamberlain Pl. E17	77	H3
Chamberlain Rd. N2	73	F2
Chamberlain Rd. N9	60	D3
Chamberlain Rd. W13	124	D2
Midhurst Rd.		
Chamberlain St. NW1	91	J7
Regents Pk. Rd.		
Chamberlain Wk., Felt.	160/161	E4
Burgess Cl.		
Chamberlain Way, Pnr.	66	B3
Chamberlain Way, Surb.	181	H7
Chamberlayne Rd. NW10	108	A3
Chambers Gdns. N2	73	G1
Chambers La. NW10	89	H7
Chambers Pl., S.Croy.	202	A7
Rolleston Rd.		
Chambers Rd. N7	92	E4
Chambers St. SE16	**29**	**H3**
Chambers St. SE16	132	D2
Chambord St. E2	**13**	**G4**
Chambord St. E2	112	C3
Champion Cres. SE26	171	H4
Champion Gro. SE5	152	A3
Champion Hill SE5	152	A3
Champion Hill Est. SE5	152	B3
Champion Pk. SE5	152	A2
Champion Pk. Est. SE5	152	A3
Denmark Hill		
Champion Rd. SE26	171	H4
Champness Cl. SE27	170	A4
Rommany Rd.		
Champneys Cl., Sutt.	198	C7
Chance St. E1	**13**	**F5**
Chance St. E1	112	C4
Chance St. E2	**13**	**F5**
Chance St. E2	112	C4
Chancel St. SE1	**27**	**G1**
Chancel St. SE1	131	H1
Chancellor Gro. SE21	169	J2
Chancellor Pl. E14	134	A1
South Colonnade		
Chancellor Pl. NW9	71	F2
Chancellors Rd. W6	127	J5
Chancellors St. W6	127	J5
Chancelot Rd. SE2	138	B4
Chancery La. WC2	**18**	**E3**
Chancery La. WC2	111	G5
Chancery La., Beck.	190	B2
Chancery Ms. SW17	167	H2
Beechcroft Rd.		
Chanctonbury Cl. SE9	175	E3
Chanctonbury Gdns., Sutt.	198	E7
Chanctonbury Way N12	56	C4
Chandler Av. E16	115	G5
Chandler Cl., Hmptn.	179	G1
Chandler Rd., Loug.	49	E1
Chandler St. E1	132/133	E1
Wapping La.		
Chandler Way SE15	132	J7
Chandlers Cl., Felt.	141	J7
Chandlers Ms. E14	134	A2
Chandlers Way SW2	151	G7
Chandos Av. E17	78	A2
Chandos Av. N14	58	C3
Chandos Av. N20	57	F1
Chandos Av. W5	125	F4
Chandos Cl., Buck.H.	83	H2
Chandos Cres., Edg.	53	J7
Chandos Par., Edg.	53	J7
Chandos Cres.		
Chandos Pl. WC2	**18**	**A6**
Chandos Pl. WC2	110	E7
Chandos Rd. E15	96	D5
Chandos Rd. N2	73	G2
Chandos Rd. N17	76	B2
Chandos Rd. NW2	89	J5
Chandos Rd. NW10	106	E4
Chandos Rd., Har.	67	J5
Chandos Rd., Pnr.	66	C7
Chandos St. W1	**16**	**E2**
Chandos St. W1	110	B5
Chandos Way NW11	90	E1
Change All. EC3	**20**	**C4**
Channel Cl., Houns.	143	G1
Channel Gate Rd. NW10	107	F3
Channelsea Rd. E15	114	D1
Chant Sq. E15	96	D7
Chant St. E15	96	D7
Chantress Cl., Dag.	119	J1
Chantrey Rd. SW9	151	F3
Chantry Cl. NW7	39	F6
Hendon Wd. La.		
Chantry Cl., Har.	69	J5
Chantry Cl., Sid.	176/177	E5
Ellenborough Rd.		
Chantry La., Brom.	192	A5
Bromley Common		
Chantry Pl., Har.	67	H1
Chantry Pt. W9	108	C4
Chantry Rd., Chess.	195	J5
Chantry Rd., Har.	67	H1
Chantry St. N1	111	H1
Chantry Way, Mitch.	185	G3
Chapel Cl. SE1	**28**	**B3**
Chapel Cl. N2	73	H3
Chapel Fm. Rd. SE9	174	C3
Chapel Ho. St. E14	134	B5
Chapel La., Chig.	65	J3
Chapel La., Pnr.	66	D3
Chapel La., Rom.	82	D7
Chapel Mkt. N1	**10**	**E1**
Chapel Mkt. N1	111	G2
Chapel Path E11	79	G6
Chapel Pl. EC2	**12**	**D4**
Chapel Pl. N1	**11**	**F1**
Chapel Pl. N17	60	C7
White Hart La.		
Chapel Pl. W1	**16**	**D4**
Chapel Pl. W1	110	B6
Chapel Rd. SE27	169	H4
Chapel Rd. W13	125	E1
Chapel Rd., Bexh.	159	G4
Chapel Rd., Houns.	143	H3
Chapel Rd., Ilf.	98	D3
Chapel Rd., Twick.	145	E7
Chapel Side W2	**14**	**A5**
Chapel Side W2	108	E7
Chapel Stones N17	76	C1
Chapel St. NW1	**15**	**G2**
Chapel St. NW1	109	H5
Chapel St. SW1	**24**	**C5**
Chapel St. SW1	130	A3
Chapel St., Enf.	43	J3
Chapel Ter., Loug.	48	B4
Forest Rd.		
Chapel Vw., S.Croy.	203	E6
Chapel Wk. NW4	71	H4
Chapel Wk., Croy.	201	J2
Wellesley Rd.		
Chapel Way N7	93	F3
Sussex Way		
Chapel Yd. SW18	148	D5
Wandsworth High St.		
Chapelmount Rd., Wdf.Grn.	64	C6
Chaplin Cl. SE1	**27**	**F3**
Chaplin Cl. SE1	131	G2
Chaplin Cl. E15	115	E2
Chaplin Rd. N17	76	C3
Chaplin Rd. NW2	89	G6
Chaplin Rd., Dag.	101	E7
Chaplin Rd., Wem.	87	F6
Chaplin Sq. N12	57	G7
Chapman Cl., West Dr.	120	C3
Chapman Cres., Har.	69	H6
Chapman Pk. Ind. Est. NW10	89	F6
Chapman Rd. E9	95	J6
Chapman Rd., Belv.	139	G5
Chapman Rd., Croy.	201	G1
Chapman Sq. SW19	166	A2
Chapman St. E1	112	E7
Chapman's La. SE2	138	C4
Chapman's La., Belv.	138	D4
Chapone Pl. W1	**17**	**H4**
Chapter Cl. W4	126	C3
Beaumont Rd.		
Chapter Ho. Ct. EC4	**19**	**J4**
Chapter Rd. NW2	89	G5
Chapter Rd. SE17	**35**	**H4**
Chapter Rd. SE17	131	H5
Chapter St. SW1	**33**	**H2**
Chapter St. SW1	130	D4
Chapter Way, Hmptn.	161	G4
Chara Pl. W4	126	D6
Charcroft Gdns., Enf.	45	G4
Chardin Rd. W4	126/127	E4
Elliott Rd.		
Chardmore Rd. N16	94	D1
Chardwell Cl. E6	116	B6
Northumberland Rd.		
Charecroft Way W12	128	A2
Charfield Ct. W9	**6**	**A6**
Charford Rd. E16	115	G6
Chargeable La. E13	115	F4
Chargeable St. E16	115	F4
Chargrove Cl. SE16	133	G2
Marlow Way		
Charing Cl., Orp.	207	J4
Charing Cross SW1	**26**	**A1**
Charing Cross Rd. WC2	**17**	**J3**
Charing Cross Rd. WC2	110	D6
Charlbert St. NW8	**7**	**G1**
Charlbert St. NW8	109	H2
Charlbury Av., Stan.	53	G5
Charlbury Gdns., Ilf.	99	J2
Charlbury Gro. W5	105	F6
Charldane Rd. SE9	174	E3
Charlecote Gro. SE26	171	E3
Charlecote Rd., Dag.	100	E3
Charlemont Rd. E6	116	C3
Charles Babbage Cl., Chess.	195	G6
Ashlyns Rd.		
Charles Barry Cl. SW4	150	C3
Charles Burton Ct. E5	95	H5
Ashenden Rd.		
Charles Cl., Sid.	176	B4
Charles Cobb Gdns., Croy.	201	G5
Charles Coveney Rd. SE15	152	C1
Charles Cres., Har.	68	A7
Charles Dickens Ho. E2	112	E3
Charles Flemwell Ms. E16	135	G1
Hanameel St.		
Charles Grinling Wk. SE18	136	D4
Charles Ho. N17	60	C7
Love La.		
Charles La. NW8	**7**	**F2**
Charles Pl. NW1	**9**	**G4**
Charles Rd. E7	97	J7
Lens Rd.		
Charles Rd. SW19	184	D1
Charles Rd. W13	104	D5
Charles Rd., Rom.	82	D7
Charles II St. SW1	**25**	**H1**
Charles II St. SW1	130	D1
Charles Sevright Dr. NW7	56	A5
Charles Sq. N1	**12**	**C4**
Charles Sq. N1	112	A3
Charles Sq. Est. N1	112	A3
Pitfield St.		
Charles St. E16	136	A1
Charles St. SW13	147	E2
Charles St. W1	**24**	**D1**
Charles St. W1	130	B1
Charles St., Croy.	201	J3
Charles St., Enf.	44	C5
Charles St., Houns.	143	F2
Charles Whincup Rd. E16	135	H1
Charlesfield SE9	173	J3
Charleston Cl., Felt.	160	A3
Vineyard Rd.		
Charleston St. SE17	**36**	**A2**
Charleston St. SE17	131	J4
Charleville Circ. SE26	170	D5
Charleville Rd. W14	128	B5
Charleville Rd., Erith	139	J7
Northumberland Pk.		
Charlmont Rd. SW17	167	J6
Charlotte Cl., Bexh.	158	E5
Charlotte Cl., Ilf.	80	C1
Fullwell Av.		
Charlotte Despard Av. SW11	150	A1
Charlotte Ms. W1	**17**	**G1**
Charlotte Ms. W10	108	A6
Charlotte Ms. W14	128	B4
Munden St.		
Charlotte Pl. NW9	70	C5
Uphill Dr.		
Charlotte Pl. SW1	**33**	**F2**
Charlotte Pl. W1	**17**	**G2**
Charlotte Rd. EC2	**12**	**D5**
Charlotte Rd. EC2	112	B4
Charlotte Rd. SW13	147	F1
Charlotte Rd., Dag.	101	H6
Charlotte Rd., Wall.	200	C6
Charlotte Row SW4	150	C3
North St.		
Charlotte Sq., Rich.	145	J6
Greville Rd.		
Charlotte St. W1	**17**	**G2**

Charlotte St. W1 110 C5
Charlotte Ter. N1 111 F1
Charlow Cl. SW6 149 F2
Townmead Rd.
Charlton Ch. La. SE7 135 J5
Charlton Cres., Bark. 117 J2
Charlton Dene SE7 135 J7
Charlton Kings Rd. NW5 92 D5
Charlton La. SE7 136 A5
Charlton Pk. La. SE7 136 A7
Charlton Pk. Rd. SE7 136 A6
Charlton Pl. N1 11 G1
Charlton Pl. N1 111 H2
Charlton Rd. N9 61 G1
Charlton Rd. NW10 107 E1
Charlton Rd. SE3 135 G7
Charlton Rd. SE7 135 H6
Charlton Rd., Har. 69 G4
Charlton Rd., Wem. 87 J1
Charlton Way SE3 154 E1
Charlwood Cl., Har. 52 B7
Kelvin Cres.
Charlwood Pl. SW1 33 G2
Charlwood Pl. SW1 130 C4
Charlwood Rd. SW15 148 A3
Charlwood Sq., Mitch. 185 G3
Charlwood St. SW1 33 G2
Charlwood St. SW1 130 C5
Charlwood Ter. SW15 148 A4
Cardinal Pl.
Charmian Av., Stan. 69 G3
Charminster Av. SW19 184 E2
Charminster Ct., Surb. 181 G7
Charminster Rd. SE9 174 A4
Charminster Rd., Wor.Pk. 198 A1
Charmouth Rd., Well. 158 C1
Charnock Rd. E5 94 E3
Charnwood Av. SW19 184 D2
Charnwood Cl., N.Mal. 183 E4
Charnwood Dr. E18 79 H3
Charnwood Gdns. E14 134 A4
Charnwood Pl. N20 57 F3
Charnwood Rd. SE25 188 A5
Charnwood St. E5 94 D2
Charrington Rd., Croy. 201 H2
Drayton Rd.
Charrington St. NW1 9 H1
Charrington St. NW1 110 D2
Charsley Rd. SE6 172 B2
Chart Cl., Brom. 191 E1
Chart Cl., Croy. 189 F6
Stockbury Rd.
Chart St. N1 12 C3
Chart St. N1 112 A3
Charter Av., Ilf. 99 G1
Charter Ct., N.Mal. 182 E3
Charter Cres., Houns. 142 E4
Charter Dr., Bex. 158 E7
Charter Rd., Kings.T. 182 B3
Charter Rd., The, Wdf.Grn. 62 E6
Charter Sq., Kings.T. 182 B2
Charter Way N3 72 C4
Charter Way N14 42 C6
Charterhouse Av., Wem. 87 F4
Charterhouse Bldgs. EC1 11 H6
Charterhouse Ms. EC1 19 H1
Charterhouse Sq. EC1 19 H1
Charterhouse Sq. EC1 111 H5
Charterhouse St. EC1 19 F2
Charterhouse St. EC1 111 H5
Charteris Rd. N4 93 G1
Charteris Rd. NW6 108 C1
Charteris Rd., Wdf.Grn. 63 H7
Charters Cl. SE19 170 B5
Chartfield Av. SW15 147 H5
Chartfield Sq. SW15 148 A5
Chartham Gro. SE27 169 G3
Royal Circ.
Chartham Rd. SE25 188 E3
Chartley Av. NW2 88 E3
Chartley Av., Stan. 52 C6
Charton Cl., Belv. 139 F6
Nuxley Rd.
Chartridge Cl., Barn. 39 G5
Chartwell Cl. SE9 175 F2
Chartwell Cl., Croy. 202 A1
Tavistock Rd.
Chartwell Cl., Grnf. 103 H1
Chartwell Dr., Orp. 207 G5
Chartwell Gdns., Sutt. 198 B4
Chartwell Pl., Har. 86 A2
Chartwell Pl., Sutt. 198 C4
Chartwell Way SE20 188 E1
Charwood SW16 169 G4
Chase, The E12 98 A4
Chase, The SW4 150 B3
Chase, The SW16 169 F7
Chase, The SW20 184 B1
Chase, The, Bexh. 159 H3
Chase, The, Brom. 191 H3
Chase, The, Chig. 65 F4
Chase, The, Edg. 70 B1
Chase, The, Loug. 47 J7
Chase, The, Pnr. 67 F4
Chase, The (Eastcote), Pnr. 66 C6
Chase, The (Chadwell Heath), Rom. 82 E6
Chase, The, Stan. 52 D5
Chase, The, Sun. 178 B1
Chase, The, Wall. 200 E5
Chase Ct. Gdns., Enf. 43 J3
Chase Gdns. E4 62 A4
Chase Gdns., Twick. 144 A6
Chase Grn., Enf. 43 J3
Chase Grn. Av., Enf. 43 H2
Chase Hill, Enf. 43 J3
Chase La., Ilf. 81 G5
Chase Ridings, Enf. 43 G2
Chase Rd. N14 42 D6
Chase Rd. NW10 106 D4
Chase Rd. W3 106 D4
Chase Side N14 42 A6
Chase Side, Enf. 43 J3
Chase Side Av. SW20 184 B1
Chase Side Av., Enf. 43 J2
Chase Side Cres., Enf. 43 J1
Chase Side Pl., Enf. 43 J2
Chase Side
Chase Way N14 58 B2
Chasefield Rd. SW17 167 J4
Chaseley Dr. W4 146 B1
Wellesley Rd.
Chaseley St. E14 113 H6
Chasemore Cl., Mitch. 185 J7
Chasemore Gdns., Croy. 201 H5
Thorneloe Gdns.
Chaseville Pk. Rd. N21 43 E5
Chasewood Av., Enf. 43 H2
Chasewood Pk., Har. 86 C3
Chatfield Rd. SW11 149 F3
Chatfield Rd., Croy. 201 H1
Chatham Av., Brom. 191 F7
Chatham Cl. NW11 72 D5
Chatham Cl., Sutt. 184 C7
Chatham Pl. E9 95 F6
Chatham Rd. E17 77 H3
Chatham Rd. E18 79 F2
Grove Hill
Chatham Rd. SW11 149 J6
Chatham Rd., Kings.T. 182 A2
Chatham Rd., Orp. 207 F5
Chatham St. SE17 36 B1
Chatham St. SE17 132 A4
Chatsfield Pl. W5 105 H6
Chatsworth Av. NW4 71 J2
Chatsworth Av. SW20 184 B1
Chatsworth Av., Brom. 173 H4
Chatsworth Av., Sid. 176 A1
Chatsworth Av., Wem. 87 J5
Chatsworth Cl. NW4 71 J2
Chatsworth Cl., Borwd. 38 A3
Chatsworth Cl., W.Wick. 205 F2
Chatsworth Ct. W8 128 D4
Chatsworth Ct., Stan. 53 F5
Marsh La.
Chatsworth Cres., Houns. 144 A4
Chatsworth Dr., Enf. 44 D7
Chatsworth Est. E5 95 G4
Elderfield Rd.
Chatsworth Gdns. W3 106 B7
Chatsworth Gdns., Har. 85 H1
Chatsworth Gdns., N.Mal. 183 F5
Chatsworth Par., Orp. 193 F5
Queensway
Chatsworth Pl., Mitch. 185 J3
Chatsworth Pl., Tedd. 162 D4
Chatsworth Ri. W5 105 J4
Chatsworth Rd. E5 95 F3
Chatsworth Rd. E15 97 F5
Chatsworth Rd. NW2 90 A6
Chatsworth Rd. W4 126 C6
Chatsworth Rd. W5 105 J4
Chatsworth Rd., Croy. 202 A4
Chatsworth Rd., Hayes 102 B4
Chatsworth Rd., Sutt. 198 A5
Chatsworth Way SE27 169 H3
Chatterton Rd. N4 93 H3
Chatterton Rd., Brom. 192 A4
Chatto Rd. SW11 149 J5
Chaucer Av., Hayes 102 A5
Chaucer Av., Houns. 142 B2
Chaucer Av., Rich. 146 A2
Chaucer Cl. N11 58 C5
Chaucer Ct. N16 94 B4
Chaucer Dr. SE1 37 G2
Chaucer Dr. SE1 132 C4
Chaucer Gdns., Sutt. 198 D3
Chaucer Grn., Croy. 189 E7
Chaucer Ho., Sutt. 198 D3
Chaucer Rd. E7 97 G6
Chaucer Rd. E11 79 G6
Chaucer Rd. E17 78 C2
Chaucer Rd. SE24 151 G5
Chaucer Rd. W3 126 C1
Chaucer Rd., Sid. 176 C1
Chaucer Rd., Sutt. 198 D4
Chaucer Rd., Well. 157 H1
Chaucer Way SW19 167 G6
Chauncey Cl. N9 60 D3
Chaundrye Cl. SE9 156 B6
Chauntler Cl. E16 115 H6
Cheam Common Rd., Wor.Pk. 197 H2
Cheam Mans., Sutt. 198 B7
Cheam Pk. Way, Sutt. 198 B6
Cheam Rd., Sutt. 198 C6
Cheam St. SE15 152/153 E3
Evelina Rd.
Cheapside EC2 20 A4
Cheapside EC2 111 J6
Cheapside N13 59 J4
Taplow Rd.
Cheddar Rd., Houns. 140 D2
Cromer Rd.
Cheddar Waye, Hayes 102 B6
Cheddington Rd. N18 60 B3
Chedworth Cl. E16 115 F6
Hallsville Rd.
Cheeseman Cl., Hmptn. 161 E6
Cheesemans Ter. W14 128 C5
Chelford Rd., Brom. 172 D5
Chelmer Cres., Bark. 118 B2
Chelmer Rd. E9 95 G5
Chelmsford Cl. E6 116 C6
Guildford Rd.
Chelmsford Cl. W6 128 A6
Chelmsford Gdns., Ilf. 80 B7
Chelmsford Rd. E11 96 D1
Chelmsford Rd. E17 78 A6
Chelmsford Rd. E18 79 F1
Chelmsford Rd. N14 42 C7
Chelmsford Sq. NW10 107 J1
Chelsea Br. SW1 32 D5
Chelsea Br. SW1 130 B6
Chelsea Br. SW8 32 D5
Chelsea Br. SW8 130 B6
Chelsea Br. Rd. SW1 32 B3
Chelsea Br. Rd. SW1 130 A5
Chelsea Cloisters SW3 129 H4
Lucan Pl.
Chelsea Cl. NW10 106 D1
Winchelsea Rd.
Chelsea Cl., Edg. 70 A2
Chelsea Cl., Hmptn. 161 J5
Chelsea Cl., Wor.Pk. 183 G7
Chelsea Embk. SW3 31 H6
Chelsea Embk. SW3 129 H6
Chelsea Gdns., Sutt. 198 B4
Chelsea Harbour SW10 149 G1
Chelsea Harbour Dr. SW10 149 F1
Chelsea Manor Gdns. SW3 31 G5
Chelsea Manor Gdns. SW3 129 H6
Chelsea Manor St. SW3 31 G4
Chelsea Manor St. SW3 129 H5
Chelsea Pk. Gdns. SW3 31 E5
Chelsea Pk. Gdns. SW3 129 G6
Chelsea Sq. SW3 31 F3
Chelsea Sq. SW3 129 G5
Chelsea Wf. SW10 129 G7
Chelsfield Av. N9 45 G7
Chelsfield Gdns. SE26 171 F3
Chelsfield Grn. N9 45 G7
Chelsfield Av.
Chelsham Rd. SW4 150 D3
Chelsham Rd., S.Croy. 202 A6
Chelston App., Ruis. 84 A2
Chelston Rd., Ruis. 84 A1
Chelsworth Dr. SE18 137 G6
Cheltenham Av., Twick. 144 D7
Cheltenham Cl., N.Mal. 182 C3
Northcote Rd.
Cheltenham Cl., Nthlt. 85 H6
Cheltenham Gdns. E6 116 B2
Cheltenham Gdns., Loug. 48 B6
Cheltenham Pl. W3 126 B1
Cheltenham Pl., Har. 69 H4
Cheltenham Rd. E10 78 C6
Cheltenham Rd. SE15 153 F4
Cheltenham Ter. SW3 32 A3
Cheltenham Ter. SW3 129 J5
Chelverton Rd. SW15 148 A4
Chelwood Cl. E4 46 B6
Chelwood Gdns., Rich. 146 A2
Chelwood Gdns. Pas., Rich. 146 A2
Chelwood Gdns.
Chelwood Wk. SE4 153 H4
Chenappa Cl. E13 115 G3
Chenduit Way, Stan. 52 C5
Cheney Rd. NW1 10 A2
Cheney Rd. NW1 110 E2
Cheney Row E17 77 J1
Cheney St., Pnr. 66 C5
Cheneys Rd. E11 97 E3
Chenies, The, Orp. 193 H6
Chenies Ms. WC1 9 H6
Chenies Pl. NW1 9 J1
Chenies Pl. NW1 110 D2
Chenies St. WC1 17 H1
Chenies St. WC1 110 D5
Cheniston Gdns. W8 22 A5
Cheniston Gdns. W8 128 E3
Chepstow Cl. SW15 148 B6
Lytton Gro.
Chepstow Cres. W11 108 D7
Chepstow Cres., Ilf. 81 H6
Chepstow Gdns., Sthl. 103 F6
Chepstow Pl. W2 108 D6
Chepstow Ri., Croy. 202 B3
Chepstow Rd. W2 108 D6
Chepstow Rd. W7 124 D3
Chepstow Rd., Croy. 202 B3
Chepstow Vil. W11 108 C7
Chepstow Way SE15 152 C1
Chequer St. EC1 12 A6
Chequers Cl. NW9 70 E3
Chequers Cl., Orp. 193 J4
Chequers Gdns. N13 59 H5
Chequers La., Dag. 119 F4
Chequers Par. SE9 156 C6
Eltham High St.
Chequers Rd., Loug. 48 D5
Chequers Way N13 59 J5
Cherbury Cl. SE28 118 D6
Cherbury Ct. N1 112 A2
Cherbury St.
Cherbury St. N1 12 C2
Cherbury St. N1 112 A2
Cherchefelle Ms., Stan. 52 E5
Cherimoya Gdns., W.Mol. 179 H3
Kelvinbrook
Cherington Rd. W7 124 C1
Cheriton Av., Brom. 191 F5
Cheriton Av., Ilf. 80 C2
Cheriton Cl. W5 105 F5
Cheriton Cl., Barn. 41 J3
Cheriton Dr. SE18 137 G7
Cheriton Sq. SW17 168 A2
Cherry Av., Sthl. 122 D1
Cherry Blossom Cl. N13 59 H5
Cherry Cl. E17 78 B5
Eden Rd.
Cherry Cl. SW2 151 G7
Tulse Hill
Cherry Cl. W5 125 G3
Cherry Cl., Cars. 199 J2
Cherry Cl., Mord. 184 B4
Cherry Cres., Brent. 124 E7
Cherry Gdn. St. SE16 132 E2
Cherry Gdns., Dag. 101 F5
Cherry Gdns., Nthlt. 85 H7
Cherry Garth, Brent. 125 G4

Name	Page	Grid
Cherry Gro., Hayes	122	B1
Cherry Hill, Barn.	41	E6
Cherry Hill, Har.	52	B6
Cherry Hill Gdns., Croy.	201	F4
Cherry Hills, Wat.	50	E5
Cherry La., West Dr.	120	C4
Cherry La. Roundabout, West Dr.	120	C4
Cherry Laurel Wk. SW2	151	F6
Beechdale Rd.		
Cherry Orchard, West Dr.	120	B2
Cherry Orchard Gdns., Croy.	202	A2
Oval Rd.		
Cherry Orchard Gdns., W.Mol.	179	F3
Cherry Orchard Rd., Brom.	206	B2
Cherry Orchard Rd., Croy.	202	A2
Cherry Orchard Rd., W.Mol.	179	G3
Cherry Tree Cl. E9	113	F1
Moulins Rd.		
Cherry Tree Cl., Wem.	86	C4
Cherry Tree Dr. SW16	169	E3
Cherry Tree Ri., Buck.H.	63	J4
Cherry Tree Rd. E15	96/97	E4
Wingfield Rd.		
Cherry Tree Rd. N2	73	J4
Cherry Tree Wk. EC1	**12**	**A6**
Cherry Tree Wk., Beck.	189	J4
Cherry Tree Wk., W.Wick.	205	F4
Cherry Tree Way, Stan.	53	E6
Cherry Wk., Brom.	205	G1
Cherry Way, Epsom	196	D6
Cherry Wd. Way W5	106	A5
Hanger Vale La.		
Cherrycot Hill, Orp.	207	G4
Cherrycot Ri., Orp.	207	F4
Cherrycroft Gdns., Pnr.	51	F7
Westfield Pk.		
Cherrydown Av. E4	61	J3
Cherrydown Cl. E4	61	J3
Cherrydown Rd., Sid.	176	D2
Cherrydown Wk., Rom.	83	H2
Cherrywood Cl. E3	113	H3
Cherrywood Cl., Kings.T.	164	A7
Cherrywood Dr. SW15	148	A5
Cherrywood La., Mord.	184	B4
Cherston Gdns., Loug.	48	D4
Cherston Rd.		
Cherston Rd., Loug.	48	D4
Chertsey Dr., Sutt.	198	B2
Chertsey Rd. E11	96	D2
Chertsey Rd., Ilf.	99	G4
Chertsey Rd., Twick.	144	C6
Chertsey St. SW17	168	A5
Chervil Cl., Felt.	160	A3
Chervil Ms. SE28	138	B1
Cherwell Ct., Epsom	196	C4
Cheryls Cl. SW6	149	E1
Cheseman St. SE26	171	E3
Chesfield Rd., Kings.T.	163	H7
Chesham Av., Orp.	192	E6
Chesham Cl. SW1	**24**	**B6**
Chesham Cres. SE20	189	F2
Chesham Ms. SW1	**24**	**B5**
Chesham Ms. SW1	130	A3
Chesham Pl. SW1	**24**	**B6**
Chesham Pl. SW1	130	A3
Chesham Rd. SE20	189	F2
Chesham Rd. SW19	167	G5
Chesham Rd., Kings.T.	182	A1
Chesham St. NW10	88	D3
Chesham St. SW1	**24**	**B6**
Chesham St. SW1	130	A3
Chesham Ter. W13	124	E2
Cheshire Cl. E17	78	E1
Cheshire Cl. SE4	153	J2
Cheshire Cl., Mitch.	186	E3
Cheshire Cl. EC4	**19**	**F4**
Cheshire Gdns., Chess.	195	G6
Cheshire Rd. N22	59	F7
Cheshire St. E2	**13**	**G5**
Cheshire St. E2	112	C4
Chesholm Rd. N16	94	B3
Cheshunt Rd. E7	97	H6
Cheshunt Rd., Belv.	139	G5
Chesil Ct. E2	113	E2
Chesilton Rd. SW6	148	C1
Chesley Gdns. E6	116	A2
Chesney Cres., Croy.	204	C7
Chesney St. SW11	150	A1
Chesnut Est. N17	76	C3
Chesnut Gro. N17	76	C3
Chesnut Rd.		
Chesnut Rd. N17	76	C3
Chessington Av. N3	72	B3
Chessington Av., Bexh.	139	E7
Chessington Cl., Epsom	196	C6
Chessington Ct., Pnr.	67	F4
Chessington Hall Gdns., Chess.	195	G7
Chessington Hill Pk., Chess.	196	A5
Chessington Lo. N3	72	C3
Chessington Way, W.Wick.	204	B2
Chesson Rd. W14	128	C6
Chesswood Way, Pnr.	66	D2
Chester Av., Rich.	145	J5
Chester Av., Twick.	161	F1
Chester Cl. SW1	**24**	**C4**
Chester Cl. SW1	130	A2
Chester Cl. SW13	147	H3
Chester Cl., Loug.	49	F1
Chester Cl., Sutt.	198	D2
Chester Cl. N. NW1	**8**	**E3**
Chester Cl. S. NW1	**8**	**E4**
Chester Cotts. SW1	**32**	**B2**
Chester Ct. NW1	**8**	**E3**
Chester Ct. SE5	132	A7
Chester Cres. E8	94	C6
Ridley Rd.		
Chester Dr., Har.	67	F6
Chester Gdns. W13	104	D6
Chester Gdns., Enf.	45	E6
Chester Gdns., Mord.	185	F6
Chester Gate NW1	**8**	**D4**
Chester Gate NW1	110	B3
Chester Grn., Loug.	49	F1
Chester Ms. SW1	**24**	**D5**
Chester Ms. SW1	130	B3
Chester Path, Loug.	49	F1
Chester Pl. NW1	**8**	**E3**
Chester Rd. E7	98	A7
Chester Rd. E11	79	H6
Chester Rd. E16	115	E4
Chester Rd. E17	77	G5
Chester Rd. N9	61	E1
Chester Rd. N17	76	A3
Chester Rd. N19	92	B2
Chester Rd. NW1	**8**	**C4**
Chester Rd. NW1	110	A3
Chester Rd. SW19	165	J6
Chester Rd., Borwd.	38	C3
Chester Rd., Chig.	64	D3
Chester Rd., Houns.	142	B3
Chester Rd. (Heathrow Airport), Houns.	140	D3
Chester Rd., Ilf.	99	J1
Chester Rd., Loug.	49	E2
Chester Rd., Sid.	157	H5
Chester Row SW1	**32**	**B2**
Chester Row SW1	130	A4
Chester Sq. SW1	**32**	**D1**
Chester Sq. SW1	130	B3
Chester Sq. Ms. SW1	**24**	**D6**
Chester St. E2	**13**	**J5**
Chester St. E2	112	D4
Chester St. SW1	**24**	**C5**
Chester St. SW1	130	A3
Chester Ter. NW1	**8**	**D3**
Chester Way SE11	**35**	**F2**
Chester Way SE11	131	G4
Chesterfield Dr., Esher	194	D2
Chesterfield Gdns. N4	75	H5
Chesterfield Gdns. SE10	134	D7
Crooms Hill		
Chesterfield Gdns. W1	**24**	**D1**
Chesterfield Gdns. W1	130	B1
Chesterfield Gro. SE22	152	C5
Chesterfield Hill W1	**16**	**D6**
Chesterfield Hill W1	110	B7
Chesterfield Ms. N4	75	H5
Chesterfield Gdns.		
Chesterfield Rd. E10	78	C6
Chesterfield Rd. N3	56	D6
Chesterfield Rd. W4	126	C6
Chesterfield Rd., Barn.	40	A5
Chesterfield Rd., Epsom	196	D7
Chesterfield St. W1	**24**	**D1**
Chesterfield St. W1	130	B1
Chesterfield Wk. SE10	154	D1
Chesterfield Way SE15	133	F7
Chesterfield Way, Hayes	122	A2
Chesterford Gdns. NW3	91	E4
Chesterford Ho. SE18	136	A7
Shooter's Hill Rd.		
Chesterford Rd. E12	98	C5
Chesters, The, N.Mal.	182	E1
Chesterton Cl. SW18	148	D5
Ericson Cl.		
Chesterton Cl., Grnf.	103	H2
Chesterton Rd. E13	115	G3
Chesterton Rd. W10	108	A5
Chesterton Sq. W8	128	C4
Pembroke Rd.		
Chesterton Ter. E13	115	G3
Chesterton Ter. Kings.T.	182	A2
Chesthunte Rd. N17	75	J1
Chestnut All. SW6	128	C6
Lillie Rd.		
Chestnut Av. E7	97	H4
Chestnut Av. N8	74	E5
Chestnut Av. SW14	146	D3
Thornton Rd.		
Chestnut Av., Brent.	125	G4
Chestnut Av., Buck.H.	64	A3
Chestnut Av., E.Mol.	180	C3
Chestnut Av., Edg.	53	H6
Chestnut Av., Epsom	196	E4
Chestnut Av., Esher	180	A7
Chestnut Av., Hmptn.	161	G7
Chestnut Av., Tedd.	180	C2
Chestnut Av., Wem.	86	E5
Chestnut Av., W.Wick.	205	E5
Chestnut Av. N. E17	78	C4
Chestnut Av. S. E17	78	C4
Chestnut Cl. N14	42	C5
Chestnut Cl. N16	94	A2
Lordship Gro.		
Chestnut Cl. SE6	172	C5
Chestnut Cl. SE14	153	J3
Shardeloes Rd.		
Chestnut Cl. SW16	169	G4
Chestnut Cl., Buck.H.	64	A2
Chestnut Cl., Cars.	199	J1
Chestnut Cl., Sid.	176	A1
Chestnut Cl., WestDr.	121	E7
Chestnut Cl. SW6	128	C6
North End Rd.		
Chestnut Cl., Surb.	181	H7
Penners Gdns.		
Chestnut Dr. E11	79	G6
Chestnut Dr., Bexh.	158	D3
Chestnut Dr., Har.	52	C7
Chestnut Dr., Pnr.	66	D6
Chestnut Gro. SE20	171	F7
Chestnut Gro. SW12	150	A7
Chestnut Gro. W5	125	G3
Chestnut Gro., Barn.	41	J5
Chestnut Gro., Ilf.	65	H6
Chestnut Gro., Islw.	144	D4
Chestnut Gro., Mitch.	186	D4
Chestnut Gro., N.Mal.	182	D3
Chestnut Gro., S.Croy.	203	E7
Chestnut Gro., Wem.	86	E5
Chestnut La. N20	56	B1
Chestnut Ri. SE18	137	G6
Chestnut Rd. SE27	169	H3
Chestnut Rd. SW20	184	A2
Chestnut Rd., Kings.T.	163	H7
Chestnut Rd., Twick.	162	B2
Chestnut Wk. Wdf.Grn.	63	G5
Chestnut Way, Felt.	160	B3
Chestnuts, The SE14	153	J1
Cheston Av., Croy.	203	H2
Chettle Cl. SE1	**28**	**B5**
Chettle Ct. N8	75	G6
Chetwode Rd. SW17	167	J3
Chetwood Wk. E6	116	B6
Chetwynd Av., Barn.	57	J1
Chetwynd Rd. NW5	92	B4
Cheval Pl. SW7	**23**	**H5**
Cheval Pl. SW7	129	H3
Cheval St. E14	134	A3
Chevalier Cl., Stan.	53	H4
Cheveney Wk., Brom.	191	G3
Marina Cl.		
Chevening Rd. NW6	108	B1
Chevening Rd. SE10	135	F5
Chevening Rd. SE19	170	A6
Chevenings, The, Sid.	176	C3
Cheverton Rd. N19	92	D1
Chevet St. E9	95	H5
Kenworthy Rd.		
Cheviot Cl., Enf.	44	A2
Cheviot Cl., Hayes	121	G7
Cheviot Gdns. NW2	90	A2
Cheviot Gdns. SE27	169	H4
Cheviot Gate NW2	90	B2
Cheviot Rd. SE27	169	G5
Cheviot Way, Ilf.	81	H4
Chevron Cl. E16	115	G6
Chevy Rd., Sthl.	123	J2
Chewton Rd. E17	77	H4
Cheyne Av. E18	79	F3
Cheyne Av., Twick.	161	F1
Cheyne Cl. NW4	71	J5
Cheyne Cl., Brom.	206	B3
Cedar Cres.		
Cheyne Gdns. SW3	**31**	**J5**
Cheyne Gdns. SW3	**31**	**H5**
Cheyne Gdns. SW3	129	H6
Cheyne Hill, Surb.	181	J4
Cheyne Ms. SW3	**31**	**H5**
Cheyne Ms. SW3	129	H6
Cheyne Path W7	104	C6
Copley Cl.		
Cheyne Pl. SW3	**31**	**J6**
Cheyne Pl. SW3	129	J6
Cheyne Row SW3	**31**	**G6**
Cheyne Row SW3	129	H6
Cheyne Wk. N21	43	H5
Cheyne Wk. NW4	71	J6
Cheyne Wk. SW3	**31**	**H6**
Cheyne Wk. SW3	129	H6
Cheyne Wk. SW10	**31**	**E7**
Cheyne Wk. SW10	129	G7
Cheyne Wk., Croy.	202	D2
Cheyneys Av., Edg.	53	G6
Chichele Gdns., Croy.	202	C4
Brownlow Rd.		
Chichele Rd. NW2	90	A5
Chicheley Gdns., Har.	51	J7
Chicheley Rd., Har.	51	J7
Chicheley St. SE1	**26**	**D3**
Chicheley St. SE1	131	F2
Chichester Cl. E6	116	B6
Chichester Cl. SE3	155	J1
Chichester Cl., Hmptn.	161	F6
Maple Cl.		
Chichester Ct., Stan.	69	H3
Chichester Gdns., Ilf.	80	B7
Chichester Ms. SE27	169	G4
Chichester Rents WC2	**18**	**E3**
Chichester Rd. E11	97	E3
Chichester Rd. N9	60	D1
Chichester Rd. NW6	108	D2
Chichester Rd. W2	**14**	**B1**
Chichester Rd. W2	109	E5
Chichester Rd., Croy.	202	B3
Chichester St. SW1	**33**	**G4**
Chichester St. SW1	130	C5
Chichester Way E14	134	D4
Chichester Way, Felt.	142	B7
Chicksand St. E1	**21**	**G2**
Chicksand St. E1	112	C5
Chiddingfold N12	56	D3
Chiddingstone Av., Bexh.	139	F7
Chiddingstone St. SW6	148	D2
Chieveley Rd., Bexh.	159	H4
Chignell Pl. W13	124	D1
Broadway		
Chigwell Hill E1	112/113	E7
Pennington St.		
Chigwell Hurst Ct., Pnr.	66	D3
Chigwell La., Loug.	49	F5
Chigwell Pk., Chig.	64	D3
Chigwell Pk. Dr., Chig.	64	D3
Chigwell Ri., Chig.	64	D2
Chigwell Rd. E18	79	H3
Chigwell Rd. Wdf.Grn.	79	J2
Chilcot Cl. E14	114	B6
Grundy St.		
Childebert Rd. SW17	168	B2
Childeric Rd. SE14	133	H7
Childerley St. SW6	148	A1
Fulham Palace Rd.		
Childers, The, Wdf.Grn.	64	C5
Childers St. SE8	133	H6
Childs Hill Wk. NW2	90	C3
Childs La. SE19	170	B6
Westow St.		

Child's Pl. SW5 128 D4
Child's St. SW5 128 D4
Child's Wk. SW5 128 D4
  Child's Pl.
Childs Way NW11 72 C5
Chilham Cl., Bex. 159 F7
Chilham Cl., Grnf. 104 D2
Chilham Rd. SE9 174 B4
Chilham Way, Brom. 191 G7
Chillerton Rd. SW17 168 A5
Chillingworth Gdns., 162 C3
  Twick.
  Tower Rd.
Chillingworth Rd. N7 93 G5
  Liverpool Rd.
Chilmark Gdns., 183 F7
  N.Mal.
Chilmark Rd. SW16 186 D2
Chiltern Av., Twick. 161 G1
Chiltern Cl., Croy. 202 B3
Chiltern Cl., Wor.Pk. 197 J2
  Cotswold Way
Chiltern Dene, Enf. 43 F4
Chiltern Dr., Surb. 182 B5
Chiltern Gdns. NW2 90 A3
Chiltern Gdns., Brom. 191 F4
Chiltern Rd. E3 114 A4
Chiltern Rd., Ilf. 81 H4
Chiltern Rd., Pnr. 66 C5
Chiltern St. W1 16 B1
Chiltern St. W1 110 A5
Chiltern Way, 63 G3
  Wdf.Grn.
Chilthorne Cl. SE6 153 J7
  Ravensbourne Pk. Cres.
Chilton Av. W5 125 G4
Chilton Gro. SE8 133 G4
Chilton Rd., Edg. 54 A6
  Manor Pk. Cres.
Chilton Rd., Rich. 146 A3
Chilton St. E2 13 G5
Chilton St. E2 112 C4
Chiltonian Ind. Est. 155 F6
  SE12
Chiltons, The E18 79 G2
  Grove Hill
Chilver St. SE10 135 F5
Chilwell Gdns., Wat. 50 C4
Chilworth Ct. SW19 166 A1
  Windlesham Gro.
Chilworth Gdns., 199 F3
  Sutt.
Chilworth Ms. W2 14 D4
Chilworth Ms. W2 109 F6
Chilworth St. W2 14 D4
Chilworth St. W2 109 F6
Chimes Av. N13 59 G5
Chinbrook Cres. SE12 173 H3
Chinbrook Est. SE9 174 A3
Chinbrook Rd. SE12 173 H3
Chinchilla Dr., Houns. 142 C2
Chine, The N10 74 C4
Chine, The N21 43 H6
Chine, The, Wem. 87 E5
Ching Ct. WC2 18 A4
Ching Way E4 61 J6
Chingdale Rd. E4 62 E3
Chingford Av. E4 62 B3
Chingford Hall Est. E4 61 J6
Chingford Ind. Cen. 61 H5
  E4
Chingford La., 63 E4
  Wdf.Grn.
Chingford Mt. Rd. E4 62 A4
Chingford Rd. E4 62 A6
Chingford Rd. E17 78 B1
Chingley Cl., Brom. 173 E6
Chinnor Cres., Grnf. 103 H2
Chip St. SW4 150 D4
Chipka St. E14 134 C2
Chipley St. SE14 133 H6
Chipmunk Gro., 102/103 E3
  Nthlt.
  Argus Way
Chippendale St. E5 95 G3
Chippenham Av., 88 B5
  Wem.
Chippenham Gdns. 108 D3
  NW6
Chippenham Ms. W9 108 D4
Chippenham Rd. W9 108 D4
Chipping Cl., Barn. 40 B3
  St. Albans Rd.
Chipstead Av., 187 H4
  Th.Hth.
Chipstead Cl. SE19 170 C7
Chipstead Gdns. 89 H2
  NW2
Chipstead St. SW6 148 D1
Chirk Cl., Hayes 102/103 E4
  Braunston Dr.
Chisenhale Rd. E3 113 H2
Chisholm Rd., Croy. 202 B2
Chisholm Rd., Rich. 145 J6

Chisledon Wk. E9 95 J6
  Osborne Rd.
Chislehurst Av. N12 57 F7
Chislehurst Rd., 192 A2
  Brom.
Chislehurst Rd., Chis. 192 A2
Chislehurst Rd., Orp. 193 H4
Chislehurst Rd., Rich. 145 H6
Chislehurst Rd., Sid. 176 A5
Chislet Cl., Beck. 172 A7
  Abbey La.
Chisley Rd. N15 76 B6
Chiswell Sq. SE3 155 H2
  Brook La.
Chiswell St. EC1 20 A1
Chiswell St. EC1 111 J5
Chiswick Br. SW14 146 C2
Chiswick Br. W4 146 C2
Chiswick Cl., Croy. 201 F3
Chiswick Common 126 D4
  Rd. W4
Chiswick Ct., Pnr. 67 F3
Chiswick High Rd. W4 126 D4
Chiswick High Rd., 125 J5
  Brent.
Chiswick Ho. Grds. 126 D6
  W4
Chiswick La. W4 127 E5
Chiswick La. S. W4 127 F5
Chiswick Mall W4 127 F6
Chiswick Mall W6 127 F6
Chiswick Quay W4 146 C1
Chiswick Rd. N9 60 D2
Chiswick Rd. W4 126 C4
Chiswick 126 A5
  Roundabout W4
  Chiswick High Rd.
Chiswick Sq. W4 126/127 E6
  Hogarth Roundabout
Chiswick Staithe W4 146 C1
Chiswick Ter. W4 126 C4
  Acton La.
Chiswick Village W4 126 B5
Chiswick Wf. W4 127 F6
Chitterfield Gate, 120 D7
  West Dr.
Chitty St. W1 17 G1
Chitty St. W1 110 C5
Chitty's La., Dag. 100 D2
Chivalry Rd. SW11 149 H5
Chivenor Gro., 163 G5
  Kings.T.
Chivers Rd. E4 62 B3
Choats Manor Way, 118 C4
  Bark.
Choats Rd., Bark. 118 C2
Choats Rd., Dag. 118 E3
Chobham Gdns. 166 A2
  SW19
Chobham Rd. E15 96 D5
Cholmeley Cres. N6 74 B7
Cholmeley Pk. N6 92 B1
Cholmley Gdns. NW6 90 D5
  Fortune Grn. Rd.
Cholmley Rd., T.Ditt. 180 E6
Cholmondeley Av. 107 G2
  NW10
Cholmondeley Wk. 145 F5
  Rich.
Choppins Ct. E1 132/133 E1
  Wapping La.
Chopwell Cl. E15 96 D7
  Bryant St.
Chorleywood Cres., 193 J2
  Orp.
Choumert Gro. SE15 152 D2
Choumert Rd. SE15 152 C3
Choumert Sq. SE15 152 D2
Chow Sq. E8 94 C5
  Arcola St.
Chrislaine Cl. 140 A6
  (Stanwell), Stai.
  High St.
Christ St. E14 114 B5
Christ Ch. Pas. EC1 19 H3
Christ Ch. Path, 121 F3
  Hayes
Christ Ch. Rd., Beck. 190 A2
  Fairfield Rd.
Christ Ch. Rd., Surb. 181 J6
Christchurch Av. N12 57 F6
Christchurch Av., 90 B7
  NW6
Christchurch Av., 69 E4
  Har.
Christchurch Av., 162 D5
  Tedd.
Christchurch Av., 87 H6
  Wem.
Christchurch Cl. 167 G7
  SW19
Christchurch Cl., Enf. 43 J2
Christchurch Gdns., 68 D4
  Har.

Christchurch Grn., 87 H6
  Wem.
Christchurch Hill NW3 91 G3
Christchurch La., 40 B2
  Barn.
Christchurch Pk., 199 F7
  Sutt.
Christchurch Pas. 91 F3
  NW3
Christchurch Pas., 40 B3
  Barn.
Christchurch Rd. N8 74 E6
Christchurch Rd. SW2 169 F1
Christchurch Rd. 146 B5
  SW14
Christchurch Rd. 167 G7
  SW19
Christchurch Rd., 140 D3
  Houns.
  Courtney Rd.
Christchurch Rd., Ilf. 99 E1
Christchurch Rd., Sid. 175 J4
Christchurch Sq. E9 113 F1
  Victoria Pk. Rd.
Christchurch St. SW3 31 J5
Christchurch St. SW3 129 J6
Christchurch Ter. 31 J5
  SW3
Christchurch Way 135 E4
  SE10
Christian Ct. SE16 133 J1
Christian Flds. SW16 169 G7
Christian St. E1 21 J3
Christian St. E1 112 D6
Christie Dr., Croy. 188 D5
Christie Gdns., Rom. 82 B6
Christie Rd. E9 95 H6
Christina Sq. N4 93 H1
  Adolphus Rd.
Christina St. EC2 12 D5
Christine Worsley Cl. 59 H2
  N21
  Highfield Rd.
Christopher Av. W7 124 D3
Christopher Cl. SE16 133 G2
Christopher Cl., Sid. 157 J5
Christopher Gdns., 100 D5
  Dag.
  Wren Rd.
Christopher Pl. NW1 9 J4
Christopher Rd., Sthl. 122 B4
Christopher St. EC2 12 C6
Christopher St. EC2 112 A4
Christopher's Ms. 128 B1
  W11
  Penzance St.
Chryssell Rd. SW9 131 G7
Chubworthy St. SE14 133 H6
Chudleigh Cres., Ilf. 99 H4
Chudleigh Gdns., 199 F3
  Sutt.
Chudleigh Rd. NW6 90 A7
Chudleigh Rd. SE4 153 J5
Chudleigh Rd., Twick. 144 C7
Chudleigh St. E1 113 G6
Chudleigh Way, Ruis. 84 A1
Chulsa Rd. SE26 170 E5
Chumleigh St. SE5 36 D5
Chumleigh St. SE5 132 B6
Chumleigh Wk., 181 J4
  Surb.
Church All., Croy. 201 G1
Church App. SE21 170 A3
Church App., Stai. 140 A6
Church Av. E4 62 D6
Church Av. NW1 92 B6
  Kentish Town Rd.
Church Av. SW14 146 D3
Church Av., Beck. 190 A1
Church Av., Nthlt. 85 F7
Church Av., Pnr. 67 E6
Church Av., Sid. 176 A5
Church Av., Sthl. 123 E3
Church Cl. N20 57 H3
Church Cl. W8 22 A3
Church Cl., Edg. 54 C5
Church Cl., Loug. 48 C2
Church Cl., West Dr. 120 B3
Church Cl., Rich. 145 G5
  George St.
Church Cres. E9 95 G7
Church Cres. N3 72 C1
Church Cres. N10 74 B4
Church Cres. N20 57 H3
Church Dr. NW9 88 D1
Church Dr., Har. 67 F6
Church Dr., W.Wick. 205 E3
Church Elm La., Dag. 101 G6
Church End E17 78 B4
Church End NW4 71 H3
Church Entry EC4 19 H4
Church Fm. La., Sutt. 198 B6
Church Gdns. W5 125 G2
Church Gdns., Wem. 86 D4

Church Gate SW6 148 B3
Church Gro. SE13 154 B4
Church Gro., Kings.T. 181 F1
Church Hill E17 78 A4
Church Hill N21 43 F7
Church Hill SE18 136 C3
Church Hill SW19 166 C5
Church Hill, Cars. 199 J5
Church Hill, Har. 86 B1
Church Hill, Loug. 48 B3
Church Hill Rd. E17 78 B4
Church Hill Rd., Barn. 41 J7
Church Hill Rd., 115 H5
  Surb.
Church Hill Rd., Sutt. 198 A4
Church Hill Wd., Orp. 193 J5
Church Hyde SE18 137 H6
  Old Mill Rd.
Church La. E11 97 E1
Church La. E17 78 B4
Church La. N2 73 G3
Church La. N8 75 F4
Church La. N9 60 D2
Church La. N17 76 B1
Church La. NW9 88 C2
Church La. SW17 168 B4
Church La. SW19 184 C1
Church La. W5 125 F2
Church La., Brom. 206 B1
Church La., Chess. 195 J6
Church La., Chis. 193 F1
Church La., Dag. 101 H6
Church La., Enf. 44 A3
Church La., Har. 68 C1
Church La., Loug. 48 C3
Church La., Pnr. 67 E3
Church La., Rich. 163 H1
Church La., Tedd. 162 C5
Church La., T.Ditt. 180 C6
Church La., Twick. 162 D1
Church La., Wall. 200 D3
Church Manor Est. 131 G7
  SW9
  Vassall Rd.
Church Manorway 137 J4
  SE2
Church Meadow, 195 F2
  Surb.
Church Mt. N2 73 G5
Church Paddock Ct., 200 D3
  Wall.
Church Pas. EC2 111 J6
  Gresham St.
Church Pas., Barn. 40 C4
  Wood St.
Church Pas., Surb. 181 H5
Church Path E11 79 G5
Church Path E17 78 B4
  St. Mary Rd.
Church Path N12 57 F5
Church Path N17 60 B7
  White Hart La.
Church Path N20 57 F4
Church Path NW10 89 E7
Church Path SW14 146 D3
Church Path SW19 184 D2
Church Path W4 126 C3
Church Path W7 123 G1
Church Path, Croy. 201 J2
Church Path, Mitch. 185 H3
Church Path, Sthl. 123 F3
Church Pl. SW1 17 G6
Church Pl. W5 125 G2
  Church Gdns.
Church Pl., Mitch. 185 H3
Church Pl., Twick. 162/163 E1
  Church St.
Church Ri. SE23 171 G1
Church Ri., Chess. 195 J6
Church Rd. E10 96 B2
Church Rd. E12 98 B5
Church Rd. E17 77 H2
Church Rd. N6 74 A6
Church Rd. N17 76 B1
Church Rd. NW4 71 H4
Church Rd. NW10 89 E6
Church Rd. SE19 188 B1
Church Rd. SW13 147 F2
Church Rd. 166 B4
  (Wimbledon) SW19
Church Rd. W3 126 C1
Church Rd. W7 124 C1
Church Rd., Bark. 99 F6
Church Rd., Bexh. 159 F2
Church Rd., Brom. 191 G2
Church Rd. 190 D7
  (Shortlands), Brom.
Church Rd., Buck.H. 63 H1
Church Rd., Croy. 201 H3
Church Rd., E.Mol. 180 A4
Church Rd., Enf. 45 F6
Church Rd. 196 D7
  (West Ewell), Epsom
Church Rd., Esher 194 C6

Name	Page	Grid
Church Rd., Felt.	160	D5
Church Rd., Hayes	121	J1
Church Rd. (Cranford), Houns.	122	B5
Church Rd. (Heston), Houns.	123	G7
Church Rd., Ilf.	81	H6
Church Rd., Islw.	144	A1
Church Rd., Kes.	206	A7
Church Rd., Kings.T.	181	J2
Church Rd., Loug.	47	H2
Church Rd., Mitch.	185	G2
Church Rd., Nthlt.	85	F7
Church Rd. (Farnborough), Orp.	207	F5
Church Rd., Rich.	145	H5
Church Rd. (Ham), Rich.	163	J5
Church Rd., Sid.	176	A4
Church Rd., Sthl.	123	F3
Church Rd., Stan.	53	E5
Church Rd., Surb.	195	F2
Church Rd., Sutt.	198	B6
Church Rd., Tedd.	162	B4
Church Rd., Wall.	200	C3
Church Rd., Well.	158	B2
Church Rd., West Dr.	120	A3
Church Rd., Wor.Pk.	196	E1
Church Rd. Merton SW19	185	G1
Church Row NW3	91	F4
Church Row, Chis.	175	F7
Church St. E15	115	E1
Church St. E16	136	E1
Church St. N9	60	B2
Church St. NW8	15	F1
Church St. W2	15	F1
Church St. W2	109	G5
Church St. W4	127	E6
Church St., Croy.	201	J2
Church St., Dag.	101	H6
Church St., Enf.	44	A3
Church St., Hmptn.	179	J1
Church St., Islw.	144	E3
Church St., Kings.T.	181	G2
Church St., Sun.	178	B3
Church St., Sutt.	198/199	E5
High St.		
Church St., Twick.	162	D1
Church St. Est. NW8	7	F6
Church St. Est. NW8	109	G4
Church St. N. E15	115	E1
Church St. Pas. E15	114/115	E1
Church St.		
Church Stretton Rd., Houns.	143	J5
Church Ter. NW4	71	H3
Church Ter. SE13	154	E4
Church Ter. SW8	150	D2
Church Ter., Rich.	145	G5
Church Vale N2	73	J3
Church Vale SE23	171	F2
Church Wk. N6	92	A3
Swains La.		
Church Wk. N16	94	A4
Church Wk. NW2	90	C3
Church Wk. NW4	71	J3
Church Wk. NW9	88	D2
Church Wk. SW13	147	G1
Church Wk. SW15	147	H5
Church Wk. SW16	186	C2
Church Wk. SW20	183	J3
Church Wk., Brent.	125	F6
Church Wk., Enf.	44	A3
Church La.		
Church Wk., Rich.	145	G5
Red Lion La.		
Church Way, T.Ditt.	180	C6
Church Way N20	57	H3
Church Way, Barn.	41	J4
Church Way, Edg.	54	A6
Churchbury La., Enf.	44	B2
Churchbury La., Enf.	44	A3
Churchbury Rd. SE9	156	A7
Churchbury Rd., Enf.	44	A2
Churchcroft Cl. SW12	150	A7
Endlesham Rd.		
Churchdown, Brom.	173	E4
Churchfield Av. N12	57	F6
Churchfield Cl., Har.	67	J4
Churchfield Rd. W3	126	C1
Churchfield Rd. W7	124	B2
Churchfield Rd. W13	125	E1
Churchfield Rd., Well.	158	A3
Churchfields E18	79	G1
Churchfields SE10	134	C6
Roan St.		
Churchfields, Loug.	48	B4
Churchfields, W.Mol.	179	G3
Churchfields Av., Felt.	161	F3
Churchfields Rd., Beck.	189	G2
Churchill Av., Har.	68	E6
Churchill Ct. W5	105	J4
Churchill Ct., Nthlt.	85	G5
Churchill Gdns. SW1	33	F4
Churchill Gdns. SW1	130	C5
Churchill Gdns. W3	106	A6
Churchill Gdns. Rd. SW1	33	E4
Churchill Gdns. Rd. SW1	130	B5
Churchill Ms., Wdf.Grn.	63	F6
High Rd. Woodford Grn.		
Churchill Pl. E14	134	B1
Churchill Pl., Har.	68	B4
Sandridge Cl.		
Churchill Rd. E16	115	J6
Churchill Rd. NW2	89	H6
Churchill Rd. NW5	92	B4
Churchill Rd., Edg.	53	J6
Churchill Rd., S.Croy.	201	J7
Churchill Ter. E4	62	A4
Churchill Wk. E9	95	F5
Churchill Way, Brom.	191	G3
Ethelbert Rd.		
Churchill Way, Sun.	160	A5
Churchley Rd. SE26	171	E4
Churchmead Cl., Barn.	41	H6
Churchmead Rd. NW10	89	G6
Churchmore Rd. SW16	186	C1
Churchview Rd., Twick.	162	A1
Churchway NW1	9	J3
Churchway NW1	110	D3
Churchwell Path E9	95	F5
Churchwood Gdns., Wdf.Grn.	63	G4
Churchyard Row SE11	35	H1
Churston Av. E13	115	H1
Churston Cl. SW2	169	H1
Tulse Hill		
Churston Dr., Mord.	184	A5
Churston Gdns. N11	58	C6
Churton Pl. SW1	33	G2
Churton Pl. SW1	130	C4
Churton St. SW1	33	G2
Churton St. SW1	130	C4
Chusan Pl. E14	113	J6
Commercial Rd.		
Chyngton Cl., Sid.	175	J3
Cibber Rd. SE23	171	G2
Cicada Rd. SW18	149	F5
Cicely Rd. SE15	152	D1
Cinderford Way, Brom.	173	E4
Cinema Par. W5	105	J4
Ashbourne Rd.		
Cinnamon Cl., Croy.	186	E7
Cinnamon Row SW11	149	F3
Cinnamon St. E1	133	E1
Cintra Pk. SE19	170	C7
Circle, The NW2	89	E3
Circle, The NW7	54	D5
Circle Gdns. SW19	184	D2
Circuits, The, Pnr.	66	C4
Circular Rd. N17	76	C3
Circular Way SE18	136	C6
Circus Ms. W1	15	J1
Circus Pl. EC2	20	C2
Circus Rd. NW8	6	E3
Circus Rd. NW8	109	G3
Circus St. SE10	134	C7
Cirencester St. W2	14	A1
Cirencester St. W2	108	E5
Cissbury Ring N. N12	56	C5
Cissbury Ring S. N12	56	C5
Cissbury Rd. N15	76	A5
Citadel Pl. SE11	34	C3
Citizen Rd. N7	93	G4
Citron Ter. SE15	152/153	E3
Nunhead La.		
City Gdn. Row N1	11	H2
City Gdn. Row N1	111	H2
City Rd. EC1	11	G2
City Rd. EC1	111	H2
Civic Way, Ilf.	81	F4
Civic Way, Ruis.	84	D5
Clabon Ms. SW1	23	J6
Clabon Ms. SW1	129	J3
Clack St. SE16	133	F2
Clacton Rd. E6	116	A3
Clacton Rd. E17	77	H6
Clacton Rd. N17	76	C2
Sperling Rd.		
Claigmar Gdns. N3	72	E1
Claire Ct. N12	57	F3
Claire Ct., Bushey	52	A1
Claire Ct., Pnr.	51	F7
Westfield Pk.		
Claire Gdns., Stan.	53	F5
Claire Pl. E14	134	A3
Clairvale Rd., Houns.	142	D1
Clairvale Rd. SW16	168	B5
Clairville Gdns. W7	124	C1
Clairville Pt. SE23	171	G3
Clamp Hill, Stan.	52	A4
Clancarty Rd. SW6	148	D2
Clandon Cl. W3	126	B2
Avenue Rd.		
Clandon Cl., Epsom	197	F6
Clandon Gdns. N3	72	D3
Clandon Rd., Ilf.	99	H2
Clandon St. SE8	154	A2
Clanfield Way SE15	37	E7
Clanricarde Gdns. W2	108	D7
Clapham Common N. Side SW4	150	B4
Clapham Common S. Side SW4	150	B5
Clapham Common W. Side SW4	150	A4
Clapham Cres. SW4	150	D4
Clapham High St. SW4	150	D4
Clapham Junct. Est. SW11	149	H4
Clapham Manor St. SW4	150	C3
Clapham Pk. Est. SW4	150	D6
Clapham Pk. Rd. SW4	150	D4
Clapham Rd. SW9	150	E3
Clapham Rd. SW9	150	D3
Claps Gate La. E6	116	E4
Clapton Common E5	76	C7
Clapton Pk. Est. E5	95	H4
Blackwell Cl.		
Clapton Pas. E5	95	F5
Clapton Sq. E5	95	E5
Clapton Ter. N16	94	D1
Oldhill St.		
Clapton Way E5	94	D4
Clara Pl. SE18	136	D4
Clare Cl. N2	73	F3
Thomas More Way		
Clare Cor. SE9	156	E7
Clare Gdns. E7	97	G4
Clare Gdns. W11	108	B6
Westbourne Pk. Rd.		
Clare Gdns., Bark.	99	J6
Clare La. N1	93	J7
Clare Lawn Av. SW14	146	D5
Clare Mkt. WC2	18	C4
Clare Ms. SW6	128/129	E7
Waterford Rd.		
Clare Pl. SW15	147	F7
Minstead Gdns.		
Clare Rd. E11	78	D6
Clare Rd. NW10	89	G7
Clare Rd. SE14	153	J1
Clare Rd., Grnf.	86	A6
Clare Rd., Houns.	143	F3
Clare Rd., Stai.	140	B7
Clare St. E2	113	E2
Clare Way, Bexh.	158	E1
Claredale St. E2	13	J2
Claredale St. E2	112	D2
Claremont Av., Har.	69	H5
Claremont Av., N.Mal.	183	G5
Claremont Av., Sun.	178	B1
Claremont Cl. E16	136	D1
Claremont Cl. N1	11	G2
Claremont Cl. SW2	168/169	E1
Streatham Hill		
Claremont Cl., Orp.	206	D4
Claremont Cl., Surb.	181	G6
St. James Rd.		
Claremont Gdns., Ilf.	99	H2
Claremont Gdns., Surb.	181	H5
Claremont Gro. W4	126/127	E7
Edensor Gdns.		
Claremont Gro., Wdf.Grn.	63	J6
Claremont Pk. N3	72	B1
Claremont Rd. E7	97	H5
Claremont Rd. E17	77	H2
Claremont Rd. N6	74	C7
Claremont Rd. NW2	90	A3
Claremont Rd. W9	108	B2
Claremont Rd. W13	104	D6
Claremont Rd., Brom.	192	B4
Claremont Rd., Croy.	202	D1
Claremont Rd., Esher	194	B7
Claremont Rd., Har.	68	B2
Claremont Rd., Surb.	181	H6
Claremont Rd., Tedd.	162	C5
Claremont Rd., Twick.	145	F6
Claremont Sq. N1	10	E2
Claremont Sq. N1	111	G2
Claremont St. E16	136	D1
Claremont St. N18	60	D6
Claremont St. SE10	134	B6
Claremont Way NW2	89	J1
Clarence Av. SW4	150	D6
Clarence Av., Brom.	192	B4
Clarence Av., Ilf.	80	D6
Clarence Av., N.Mal.	182	C2
Clarence Cres. SW4	150	D6
Clarence Cres., Sid.	176	B3
Clarence Gdns. NW1	9	E4
Clarence Gdns. NW1	110	B3
Clarence La. SW15	147	E6
Clarence Ms. E5	95	E5
Clarence Ms. SE16	133	G1
Clarence Ms. SW12	150	B7
Clarence Pas. NW1	10	A2
Clarence Pl. E5	95	E5
Clarence Rd. E5	95	E4
Clarence Rd. E12	98	A5
Clarence Rd. E16	115	E4
Clarence Rd. E17	77	G2
Clarence Rd. N15	75	J5
Clarence Rd. N22	59	E7
Clarence Rd. NW6	90	C7
Clarence Rd. SE9	174	B2
Clarence Rd. SE19	166	E6
Clarence Rd. W4	126	A5
Clarence Rd., Bexh.	158	E4
Clarence Rd., Brom.	192	A3
Clarence Rd., Croy.	188	A7
Clarence Rd., Enf.	45	E5
Clarence Rd., Rich.	176	B3
Clarence Rd., Sid.	176	B3
Clarence Rd., Sutt.	198	E4
Clarence Rd., Tedd.	162	C6
Clarence Rd., Wall.	200	B5
Clarence St., Kings.T.	181	H2
Clarence St., Rich.	145	H4
Clarence St., Sthl.	122	D3
Clarence Ter. NW1	8	A5
Clarence Ter., Houns.	143	H4
Clarence Wk. SW4	150	E2
Clarence Way NW1	92	B7
Clarence Way Est. NW1	92	B7
Clarendon Cl. E9	95	F7
Clarendon Cl. W2	15	G5
Clarendon Cres., Twick.	162	A3
Clarendon Cross W11	108	B7
Portland Rd.		
Clarendon Dr. SW15	147	J4
Clarendon Gdns. NW4	71	H3
Clarendon Gdns. W9	6	D6
Clarendon Gdns. W9	109	F4
Clarendon Gdns., Ilf.	98	C1
Clarendon Gdns., Wem.	87	G3
Clarendon Gro. NW1	9	H3
Clarendon Gro., Mitch.	185	J3
Clarendon Ms. W2	15	G4
Clarendon Ms., Bex.	177	H1
Clarendon Ms., Borwd.	38	A3
Clarendon Rd.		
Clarendon Pl. W2	15	G5
Clarendon Pl. W2	109	H7
Clarendon Ri. SE13	154	C3
Clarendon Rd. E11	96	D1
Clarendon Rd. E17	78	B6
Clarendon Rd. E18	79	G3
Clarendon Rd. N8	75	F3
Clarendon Rd. N15	75	H4
Clarendon Rd. N18	60	D6
Clarendon Rd. N22	75	F2
Clarendon Rd. SW19	167	H7
Clarendon Rd. W5	105	H4
Clarendon Rd. W11	108	B7
Clarendon Rd., Borwd.	38	A3
Clarendon Rd., Croy.	201	H2
Clarendon Rd., Har.	68	B6
Clarendon Rd., Hayes	121	J2
Clarendon Rd., Wall.	200	C6
Clarendon St. SW1	32	E4
Clarendon St. SW1	130	B5
Clarendon Ter. W9	6	D5
Clarendon Wk. W11	108	B6
Clarendon Way N21	43	J6
Clarendon Way, Chis.	193	J3
Clarendon Way, Orp.	193	J3
Clarens St. SE6	171	J2
Claret Gdns. SE25	188	B4

Name	Page	Grid
Clareville Gro. SW7	30	D2
Clareville Gro. SW7	129	F4
Clareville Rd., Orp.	207	F2
Clareville St. SW7	30	D2
Clareville St. SW7	129	F4
Clarewood Wk. SW9	151	G4
Somerleyton Rd.		
Clarges Ms. W1	24	D1
Clarges Ms. W1	130	B1
Clarges St. W1	24	E1
Clarges St. W1	130	B1
Claribel Rd. SW9	151	H2
Claridge Rd., Dag.	100	D1
Clarina Rd. SE20	171	G7
Evelina Rd.		
Clarissa Rd., Rom.	82	D7
Clarissa St. E8	112	C1
Clark St. E1	113	E5
Clark Way, Houns.	122	D7
Clarke Path N16	94	D1
Braydon Rd.		
Clarkes Av., Wor.Pk.	198	A1
Clarke's Ms. W1	16	C1
Clarks Pl. EC2	20	D3
Clarks Rd., Ilf.	99	G2
Clarkson Rd. E16	115	F6
Clarkson Row NW1	110	B2
Clarkson St. E2	112	E3
Clarksons, The, Bark.	117	F2
Classon Cl.,	120	B2
West Dr.		
Claude Rd. E10	96	C2
Claude Rd. E13	115	H1
Claude Rd. SE15	152	E2
Claude St. E14	134	A4
Claudia Jones Way	150	E6
SW2		
Claudia Pl. SW19	166	B1
Claughton Rd. E13	115	J2
Clauson Av., Nthlt.	85	H5
Clave St. E1	132/133	E1
Cinnamon St.		
Clavell St. SE10	134	C6
Claverdale Rd. SW2	151	F7
Clavering Av. SW13	127	H6
Clavering Cl., Twick.	162	D4
Clavering Rd. E12	98	A1
Claverings Ind. Est.	61	G2
N9		
Claverley Gro. N3	56	D7
Claverley Vil. N3	56/57	E7
Claverley Gro.		
Claverton St. SW1	33	G4
Claverton St. SW1	130	C5
Claxton Gro. W6	128	A5
Clay Av., Mitch.	186	B2
Clay La., Edg.	54	A1
Clay La., Stai.	140	C7
Clay Rd., The, Loug.	48	B1
Clay St. W1	16	A2
Claybank Gro. SE13	154	B3
Algernon Rd.		
Claybourne Ms. SE19	170	B7
Church Rd.		
Claybridge Rd. SE12	173	J4
Claybrook Cl. N2	73	G3
Claybrook Rd. W6	128	A6
Claybury Bdy., Ilf.	80	B3
Claybury Rd.,	64	B7
Wdf.Grn.		
Claydon Dr., Croy.	201	E4
Claydown Ms. SE18	136	D5
Woolwich New Rd.		
Clayfarm Rd. SE9	175	F2
Claygate Cres., Croy.	204	C6
Claygate La., Esher	194	D2
Claygate La., T.Ditt.	194	D1
Claygate Lo. Cl.,	194	B7
Esher		
Claygate Rd. W13	124	E3
Clayhall Av., Ilf.	80	B3
Clayhill, Surb.	182	A5
Clayhill Cres. SE9	174	A4
Claylands Pl. SW8	34	E7
Claylands Pl. SW8	131	G7
Claylands Rd. SW8	34	D6
Claylands Rd. SW8	131	F6
Claymill Ho. SE18	137	F5
Claymore Cl., Mord.	184	D7
Claymore Ct. E17	77	G1
Billet Rd.		
Claypole Dr., Houns.	143	E1
Claypole Rd. E15	114	C2
Clayponds Av.,	125	H4
Brent.		
Clayponds Gdns. W5	125	G4
Clayponds La., Brent.	125	H5
Clays La. E15	96	B5
Clay's La., Loug.	48	D1
Clays La. Cl. E15	96	B5
Clayside, Chig.	65	F6
Clayton Av., Wem.	87	H7
Clayton Cl. E6	116	C6
Brandreth Rd.		
Clayton Cres., Brent.	125	G5
Clayton Fld. NW9	55	E7
Clayton Ms. SE10	154	D1
Clayton Rd. SE15	152	D1
Clayton Rd., Chess.	195	H4
Clayton Rd., Hayes	121	H2
Clayton Rd., Islw.	144	B3
Clayton Rd., Rom.	101	J1
Clayton St. SE11	34	E5
Clayton St. SE11	131	G6
Clayton Ter., Hayes	102	D5
Jollys La.		
Claywood Cl., Orp.	193	J6
Clayworth Cl., Sid.	158	B6
Cleanthus Cl.	156/157	E1
SE18		
Cleanthus Rd. SE18	157	E1
Clearbrook Way E1	113	G6
West Arbour St.		
Clearwater Ter. W11	128	A2
Lorne Gdns.		
Clearwell Dr. W9	6	A6
Clearwell Dr. W9	108	C4
Cleave Av., Hayes	121	H4
Cleave Av., Orp.	207	H6
Cleaveland Rd., Surb.	181	G5
Cleaver Sq. SE11	35	F3
Cleaver Sq. SE11	131	G5
Cleaver St. SE11	35	F3
Cleaver St. SE11	131	G5
Cleaverholme Cl.	188	E6
SE25		
Cleeve Hill SE23	171	E1
Cleeve Pk. Gdns., Sid.	176	B2
Cleeve Way SW15	147	F7
Danebury Av.		
Clegg St. E1	132/133	E1
Prusom St.		
Clegg St. E13	115	G2
Cleland Path, Loug.	49	E1
Clem Attlee Ct. SW6	128	C6
Clem Attlee Est. SW6	128	C6
Lillie Rd.		
Clem Attlee Par. SW6	128	C6
Clem Attlee Ct.		
Clematis Gdns.,	63	G5
Wdf.Grn.		
Clematis St. W12	107	F7
Clemence Rd., Dag.	119	J1
Clemence St. E14	113	J5
Clement Av. SW4	150	D4
Clement Cl. NW6	89	J7
Clement Cl. W4	126	D4
Acton La.		
Clement Gdns.,	121	H4
Hayes		
Clement Rd. SW19	166	B5
Clement Rd., Beck.	189	G2
Clementhorpe Rd.	100	C6
Dag.		
Clementina Rd. E10	95	J1
Clementine Cl.	124/125	E2
W13		
Balfour Rd.		
Clements Av. E16	115	G7
Clements Ct., Houns.	142	D4
Clements Ct., Ilf.	98/99	E3
Clements La.		
Clement's Inn WC2	18	D4
Clement's Inn WC2	111	F6
Clement's Inn Pas.	18	D4
WC2		
Clements La. EC4	20	C5
Clements La. EC4	112	A7
Clements La., Ilf.	98	E3
Clements Pl., Brent.	125	G5
Clements Rd. E6	98	C7
Clements Rd. SE16	29	J6
Clements Rd. SE16	132	D3
Clements Rd., Ilf.	98	E3
Clendon Way SE18	137	G4
Polthorne Gro.		
Clennam St. SE1	28	A3
Clensham La., Sutt.	198	D2
Clenston Ms. W1	15	J3
Clephane Rd. N1	94	A6
Clere St. EC2	12	C5
Clerkenwell Cl. EC1	11	F5
Clerkenwell Grn. EC1	11	G4
Clerkenwell Grn. EC1	111	H4
Clerkenwell Rd. EC1	10	E6
Clerkenwell Rd. EC1	111	G4
Clerks Piece, Loug.	48	C3
Clermont Rd. E9	113	F1
Cleve Rd. NW6	90	D7
Cleve Rd., Sid.	176	D3
Clevedon Cl. N16	94	C3
Smalley Cl.		
Clevedon Gdns.,	121	G3
Hayes		
Clevedon Gdns.,	142	B1
Houns.		
Clevedon Rd. SE20	189	G1
Clevedon Rd.,	182	A2
Kings.T.		
Clevedon Rd., Twick.	145	G6
Cleveland Av. SW20	184	C2
Cleveland Av. W4	127	F4
Cleveland Av., Hmptn.	161	F7
Cleveland Cres.,	38	C5
Borwd.		
Cleveland Gdns. N4	75	J5
Cleveland Gdns. NW2	90	A2
Cleveland Gdns.	147	F2
SW13		
Cleveland Gdns. W2	14	C4
Cleveland Gdns. W2	109	F6
Cleveland Gdns.,	197	E2
Wor.Pk.		
Cleveland Gro. E1	113	F4
Cleveland Way		
Cleveland Ms. W1	17	F1
Cleveland Pk., Stai.	140	B6
Northumberland Cl.		
Cleveland Pk. Av. E17	78	A4
Cleveland Pk. Cres.	78	A4
E17		
Cleveland Pl. SW1	25	G1
Cleveland Rd., Mord.	184	A7
Cleveland Rd. E18	79	G3
Cleveland Rd. N1	94	A7
Cleveland Rd. N9	45	E7
Cleveland Rd. SW13	147	F2
Cleveland Rd. W4	126	C3
Antrobus Rd.		
Cleveland Rd. W13	104	E5
Cleveland Rd., Ilf.	99	E3
Cleveland Rd., Islw.	144	D4
Cleveland Rd., N.Mal.	182	E4
Cleveland Rd., Well.	157	J2
Cleveland Rd.,	197	E2
Wor.Pk.		
Cleveland Row	25	F2
SW1		
Cleveland Row SW1	130	C1
Cleveland Sq. W2	14	C4
Cleveland Sq. W2	109	F6
Cleveland St. W1	9	F6
Cleveland St. W1	110	B4
Cleveland Ter. W2	14	D3
Cleveland Ter. W2	109	F6
Cleveland Way E1	113	F4
Cleveley Cl. SE7	136	A4
Cleveley Cres. W5	105	H2
Cleveleys Rd. E5	95	E3
Cleverly Est. W12	127	G1
Cleves Cl., Loug.	48	B6
Cleves Rd. E6	116	A1
Cleves Rd., Rich.	163	F3
Cleves Wk., Ilf.	65	F7
Cleves Way, Hmptn.	161	F7
Cleves Way, Ruis.	84	D1
Clewer Cres., Har.	68	A1
Clewer Ho. SE2	138	D2
Wolvercote Rd.		
Clichy Est. E1	113	F5
Clifden Rd. E5	95	F5
Clifden Rd., Brent.	125	G6
Clifden Rd., Twick.	162	C1
Cliff Rd. NW1	92	D6
Cliff Ter. SE8	154	A2
Cliff Vil. NW1	92	D6
Cliff Wk. E16	115	F5
Cliffe Rd., S.Croy.	202	A5
Cliffe Wk., Sutt.	199	F5
Turnpike La.		
Clifford Av. SW14	146	B3
Clifford Av., Chis.	174	C6
Clifford Av., Ilf.	80	E1
Clifford Av., Wall.	200	C4
Clifford Cl., Nthlt.	103	E1
Clifford Dr. SW9	151	H4
Clifford Gdns. NW10	107	J2
Clifford Rd. E16	115	F4
Clifford Rd. E17	78	C2
Clifford Rd. N9	45	F6
Clifford Rd. SE25	188	D4
Clifford Rd., Barn.	41	E3
Clifford Rd., Hours.	142	D3
Clifford Rd., Rich.	163	G2
Clifford Rd., Wem.	105	G1
Clifford St. W1	17	F6
Clifford St. W1	110	C7
Clifford Way NW10	89	F4
Clifford's Inn Pas.	19	E4
EC4		
Cliffview Rd. SE13	154	A3
Clifton Av. E17	77	G3
Clifton Av. N3	72	C1
Clifton Av. W12	127	F1
Clifton Av., Felt.	160	C3
Clifton Av., Stan.	69	E2
Clifton Av., Wem.	87	J6
Clifton Cl., Orp.	207	F5
Clifton Ct. N4	93	G2
Playford Rd.		
Clifton Ct. NW8	6	E5
Clifton Cres. SE15	133	E7
Clifton Est. SE15	152/153	E1
Consort Rd.		
Clifton Gdns. N15	76	C6
Clifton Gdns. NW11	72	C6
Clifton Gdns. W4	126	D4
Dolman Rd.		
Clifton Gdns. W9	6	C6
Clifton Gdns. W9	109	F4
Clifton Gdns., Enf.	42	E4
Clifton Gro. E8	94	D6
Clifton Hill NW8	6	B1
Clifton Hill NW8	109	E2
Clifton Pk. Av. SW20	183	J2
Clifton Pl. SE16	133	F2
Canon Beck Rd.		
Clifton Pl. W2	15	F5
Clifton Pl. W2	109	G7
Clifton Ri. SE14	133	H7
Clifton Rd. E7	98	A6
Clifton Rd. E16	115	E5
Clifton Rd. N3	73	F1
Clifton Rd. N8	74	D6
Clifton Rd. N22	74	C1
Clifton Rd. NW10	107	G2
Clifton Rd. SE25	188	B4
Clifton Rd. SW19	166	A6
Clifton Rd. W9	6	D5
Clifton Rd. W9	109	F4
Clifton Rd., Grnf.	103	J4
Clifton Rd., Har.	69	J5
Clifton Rd., Ilf.	81	G6
Clifton Rd., Islw.	144	B2
Clifton Rd., Kings.T.	163	J7
Clifton Rd., Loug.	48	B4
Clifton Rd., Sid.	175	H4
Clifton Rd., Sthl.	123	E4
Clifton Rd., Tedd.	162	B4
Clifton Rd., Wall.	200	B5
Clifton Rd., Well.	158	C3
Clifton St. EC2	12	D6
Clifton St. EC2	112	B4
Clifton Ter. N4	93	G2
Clifton Vil. W9	14	B1
Clifton Vil. W9	109	E5
Clifton Wk. E6	116	B6
King St.		
Clifton Wk. W6	127	H4
Clifton Way SE15	133	F7
Clifton Way, Borwd.	38	A1
Clifton Way, Wem.	105	H1
Clinch Ct. E16	115	G5
Cline Rd. N11	58	C6
Clinger Ct. N1	112	B1
Pitfield St.		
Clink St. SE1	28	A1
Clink St. SE1	132	A1
Clinton Av., E.Mol.	179	J4
Clinton Av., Well.	157	J4
Clinton Cres., Ilf.	65	H6
Clinton Rd. E3	113	H3
Clinton Rd. E7	97	G4
Clinton Rd. N15	76	A4
Clipper Cl. SE16	133	G2
Kinburn St.		
Clipper Way SE13	154	C4
Clippesby Cl.,	195	J6
Chess.		
Clipstone Ms. W1	9	F6
Clipstone Ms. W1	110	C4
Clipstone Rd., Houns.	143	G3
Clipstone St. W1	17	E1
Clipstone St. W1	110	C5
Clissold Cl. N2	73	J3
Clissold Ct. N4	93	J2
Clissold Cres. N16	94	A3
Clissold Rd. N16	94	A3
Clitherow Av., Har.	85	G1
Clitherow Gdns., Har.	50	D3
Clitheroe Rd. SW9	151	E2
Clitherow Av. W7	124	D3
Clitherow Pas., Brent.	125	F5
Clitherow Rd., Brent.	125	F5
Clitterhouse Cres.	89	J1
NW2		
Clitterhouse Rd. NW2	89	J1
Clive Av. N18	60	D6
Claremont St.		
Clive Ct. W9	6	D5
Clive Pas. SE21	170	A3
Clive Rd.		
Clive Rd. SE21	170	A3
Clive Rd. SW19	167	H6
Clive Rd., Belv.	139	G4
Clive Rd., Enf.	44	D4
Clive Rd., Felt.	142	A6
Clive Rd., Twick.	162	C4
Clive Way, Enf.	44	D4
Cliveden Cl. N12	57	F4
Woodside Av.		
Cliveden Pl. SW1	32	B1
Cliveden Pl. SW1	130	A4
Cliveden Rd. SW19	184	C1

Name	Page	Grid
Clivedon Ct. W13	104	E5
Clivedon Rd. E4	62	C5
Clivesdale Dr., Hayes	122	B1
Cloak La. EC4	**20**	**A5**
Cloak La. EC4	111	J7
Clock Ho. Rd., Beck.	189	H3
Clock Twr. Ms. N1	111	J1
Arlington Av.		
Clock Twr. Ms. SE28	118	B7
Clock Twr. Pl. N7	92	E6
Clock Twr. Rd., Islw.	144	C3
Clockhouse Av.,	117	F1
Bark.		
Clockhouse Cl. SW19	165	J3
Clockhouse Pl. SW15	148	B5
Cloister Cl., Tedd.	162	E5
Cloister Gdns. SE25	188	E6
Cloister Gdns., Edg.	54	C5
Cloister Rd. NW2	90	C3
Cloister Rd. W3	106	C5
Cloisters Av., Brom.	192	C5
Cloisters Mall,	181	G2
Kings.T.		
Union St.		
Clonard Way, Pnr.	51	G6
Clonbrock Rd. N16	94	B4
Cloncurry St. SW6	148	A2
Clonmel Cl., Har.	86	A1
Clonmel Rd. SW6	128	C7
Clonmel Rd., Tedd.	162	A4
Clonmell Rd. N17	76	A3
Clonmore St. SW18	166	C1
Cloonmore Av., Orp.	207	J4
Clorane Gdns. NW3	90	D3
Close, The E4	62	C7
Beech Hall Rd.		
Close, The N14	58	D2
Close, The N20	56	C2
Close, The SE3	154	D2
Heath La.		
Close, The, Barn.	41	J6
Close, The, Beck.	189	H4
Close, The, Bex.	159	G6
Close, The, Har.	67	J2
Close, The, Islw.	144	A2
Close, The, Mitch.	185	J4
Close, The, N.Mal.	182	C2
Close, The, Orp.	193	H6
Close, The	66	C7
(Eastcote), Pnr.		
Close, The	67	F7
(Rayners La.), Pnr.		
Close, The, Rich.	146	B3
Close, The, Rom.	82	E6
Close, The, Sid.	176	B5
Close, The, Sutt.	184	C7
Close, The	88	C3
(Barnhill Rd.), Wem.		
Close, The	87	H6
(Lyon Pk. Av.), Wem.		
Cloth Ct. EC1	**19**	**H2**
Cloth Fair EC1	**19**	**H2**
Cloth Fair EC1	111	H5
Cloth St. EC1	**19**	**J1**
Clothier St. E1	**21**	**E3**
Clothworkers Rd.	137	G7
SE18		
Cloudesdale Rd.	168	B2
SW17		
Cloudesley Pl. N1	111	G1
Cloudesley Rd. N1	111	G1
Cloudesley Rd.,	159	F1
Bexh.		
Cloudesley Sq. N1	111	G1
Cloudesley St. N1	111	G1
Clouston Cl., Wall.	200	E5
Clova Rd. E7	97	F6
Clove Cres. E14	114	D7
Clove Hitch Quay	149	F3
SW11		
Clove St. E13	115	G4
Barking Rd.		
Clovelly Av. NW9	71	F4
Clovelly Cl., Pnr.	66	B3
Clovelly Gdns. SE19	188	C1
Clovelly Gdns., Enf.	44	B7
Clovelly Gdns., Rom.	83	H1
Clovelly Rd. N8	74	D4
Clovelly Rd. W4	126	C2
Clovelly Rd. W5	125	F2
Clovelly Rd., Bexh.	138	E6
Clovelly Rd., Houns.	143	G2
Clovelly Way E1	113	F6
Jamaica St.		
Clovelly Way, Har.	85	F2
Clovelly Way, Orp.	193	J6
Clover Cl. E11	96	D2
Norman Rd.		
Clover Ms. SW3	**31**	**J5**
Clover Way, Wall.	200	A1
Cloverdale Gdns.,	157	J6
Sid.		
Cloverleys, Loug.	48	A5
Clowders Rd. SE6	171	J3
Clowser Cl., Sutt.	199	F5
Turnpike La.		
Cloyster Wd., Edg.	53	G7
Cloysters Grn. E1	**29**	**H1**
Cloysters Grn. E1	132	D1
Club Gdns. Rd.,	191	G7
Brom.		
Club Row E1	**13**	**F5**
Club Row E1	112	C4
Club Row E2	**13**	**F5**
Club Row E2	112	C4
Clunbury Av., Sthl.	123	F5
Clunbury St. N1	**12**	**C2**
Cluny Est. SE1	**28**	**D5**
Cluny Ms. SW5	128	D4
Cluny Pl. SE1	**28**	**D5**
Cluse Ct. N1	**11**	**J1**
Clutton St. E14	114	B5
Clydach Rd., Enf.	44	C4
Clyde Circ. N15	76	B4
Clyde Pl. E10	78	B7
Clyde Rd. N15	76	B4
Clyde Rd. N22	74	D1
Clyde Rd., Croy.	202	C1
Clyde Rd., Sutt.	198	D5
Clyde Rd., Wall.	200	C5
Clyde St. SE8	133	J6
Clyde Ter. SE23	171	F2
Clyde Vale SE23	171	F2
Clydesdale, Enf.	45	G4
Clydesdale Av.,	69	G3
Stan.		
Clydesdale Cl.,	38	D5
Borwd.		
Clydesdale Cl., Islw.	144	C3
Clydesdale Gdns.,	146	B4
Rich.		
Clydesdale Ho.,	138/139	E4
Erith		
Kale Rd.		
Clydesdale Rd. W11	108	C6
Clymping Dene, Felt.	142	B7
Clyston St. SW8	150	C2
Coach & Horses Yd.	**17**	**E5**
W1		
Coach Ho. La. N5	93	H4
Highbury Hill		
Coach Ho. La. SW19	166	A4
Coach Ho. Ms. SE23	153	G6
Coach Ho. Yd.	148/149	A4
SW18		
Ebner St.		
Coach Yd. Ms. N19	92/93	E1
Trinder Rd.		
Coachhouse Ms.	170	E7
SE20		
Coal Wf. Rd. W12	128	A2
Shepherds Bush Pl.		
Coaldale Wk. SE21	151	J7
Lairdale Cl.		
Coalecroft Rd. SW15	147	J4
Coate St. E2	**13**	**J2**
Coate St. E2	112	D2
Coates Av. SW18	149	G6
Coates Hill Rd.,	192	D2
Brom.		
Coates Wk., Brent.	125	H5
Cobb Cl., Borwd.	38	C5
Cobb St. E1	**21**	**F2**
Cobb St. E1	112	C5
Cobbett Rd. SE9	156	B3
Cobbett Rd., Twick.	161	G1
Cobbett St. SW8	131	F7
Cobbetts Av., Ilf.	80	A5
Cobblers Wk., E.Mol.	180	D1
Cobblers Wk.,	161	J7
Hmptn.		
Cobblers Wk.,	180	D1
Kings.T.		
Cobblers Wk., Tedd.	162	A7
Cobblestone Pl.,	201	J1
Croy.		
Oakfield Rd.		
Cobbold Est. NW10	89	F6
Cobbold Ms. W12	127	F2
Cobbold Rd.		
Cobbold Rd. E11	97	F3
Cobbold Rd. NW10	89	F6
Cobbold Rd. W12	127	F2
Cobb's Ct. EC4	111	H6
Carter La.		
Cobb's Rd., Houns.	143	F4
Cobden Rd. E11	97	E3
Cobden Rd. SE25	188	D5
Cobden Rd., Orp.	207	G4
Cobham Av., N.Mal.	183	G5
Cobham Cl. SW11	149	H6
Cobham Cl., Brom.	192	B7
Cobham Cl., Edg.	70	B2
Cobham Cl., Sid.	158	B6
Park Mead		
Cobham Cl., Wall.	200	E6
Cobham Ho., Bark.	117	F1
St. Margarets		
Cobham Ms. NW1	92	D7
Agar Gro.		
Cobham Pl., Bexh.	158	D5
Cobham Rd. E17	78	C1
Cobham Rd. N22	75	H3
Cobham Rd., Houns.	122	C7
Cobham Rd., Ilf.	99	H2
Cobham Rd., Kings.T.	182	A1
Cobland Rd. SE12	173	J4
Coborn Rd. E3	113	J3
Coborn St. E3	113	J3
Cobourg Rd. SE5	**37**	**F5**
Cobourg St. NW1	**9**	**G4**
Coburg Cl. SW1	**33**	**G1**
Coburg Cres. SW2	169	F1
Coburg Gdns., Ilf.	80	A2
Coburg Rd. N22	75	F3
Cochrane Ms. NW8	**7**	**F2**
Cochrane Rd. SW19	166	C7
Cochrane St. NW8	**7**	**F2**
Cochrane St. NW8	109	G2
Cock Hill E1	**21**	**E2**
Cock La. EC1	**19**	**G2**
Cock La. EC1	111	H5
Cockayne Way SE8	133	H5
Cockerell Rd. E17	77	H6
Cockfosters Rd., Barn.	41	J2
Cockpit Steps SW1	**25**	**J4**
Cockpit Yd. WC1	**18**	**D1**
Cocks Cres., N.Mal.	183	F4
Cocksett Av., Orp.	207	H6
Cockspur Ct. SW1	**25**	**J1**
Cockspur St. SW1	**25**	**J1**
Cockspur St. SW1	130	D1
Cocksure La., Sid.	177	G3
Code St. E1	**13**	**G6**
Code St. E1	112	C4
Codicote Ter. N4	93	J2
Green Las.		
Codling Cl. E1	**29**	**J2**
Codling Way, Wem.	87	G4
Codrington Hill SE23	153	H7
Codrington Ms. W11	108	B6
Blenheim Cres.		
Cody Rd. E16	114	D4
Cody Rd., Wall.	200	D7
Alcock Cl.		
Cody Rd. E16	114	D4
Cody Rd. Business	114	D4
Cen. E16		
Coe Av. SE25	188	D6
Coe's All., Barn.	40	B4
Wood St.		
Coffers Circle, Wem.	88	B3
Cogan Av. E17	77	H1
Coin St. SE1	**27**	**E1**
Coin St. SE1	131	G1
Coity Rd. NW5	92	A6
Coke St. E1	**21**	**H3**
Coke St. E1	112	D6
Cokers La. SE21	170	A1
Perifield		
Colas Ms. NW6	108	D1
Birchington Rd.		
Colbeck Ms. SW7	**30**	**B2**
Colbeck Ms. SW7	129	E4
Colbeck Rd., Har.	67	J7
Colberg Pl. N16	76	B7
Colborne Way,	197	J3
Wor.Pk.		
Colbrook Av., Hayes	121	G3
Colbrook Cl., Hayes	121	G3
Colburn Av., Pnr.	51	E6
Colburn Way, Sutt.	199	G3
Colby Ms. SE19	170	B5
Gipsy Hill		
Colby Rd. SE19	170	B5
Colchester Av. E12	98	C3
Colchester Dr., Pnr.	66	D5
Colchester Rd. E10	78	C7
Colchester Rd. E17	78	A6
Colchester Rd., Edg.	54	C7
Colchester Rd.,	66	A2
Nthwd.		
Colchester St. E1	**21**	**G3**
Cold Blow La. SE14	133	G7
Cold Blows, Mitch.	186	A3
Cold Harbour E14	134	C2
Coldbath Sq. EC1	**11**	**E5**
Coldbath St. SE13	154	B1
Coldershaw Rd. W13	124	D1
Coldfall Av. N10	73	J2
Coldharbour La. SE5	151	G4
Coldharbour La. SW9	151	G4
Coldharbour La.,	102	A7
Hayes		
Coldharbour Pl. SE5	151	J2
Denmark Hill		
Coldharbour Rd.,	201	G5
Croy.		
Coldharbour Way,	201	G5
Croy.		
Coldstream Gdns.	148	C6
SW18		
Cole Cl. SE28	138	B1
Cole Gdns., Houns.	122	A7
Cole Pk. Gdns.,	144	D6
Twick.		
Cole Pk. Rd., Twick.	144	D6
Cole Pk. Vw., Twick.	144	D6
Hill Vw. Rd.		
Cole Rd., Twick.	144	D6
Cole St. SE1	**28**	**A4**
Cole St. SE1	131	J2
Colebeck Ms. N1	93	H6
Colebert Av. E1	113	F4
Colebrook Cl. SW15	148	A7
West Hill		
Colebrook Gdns.,	49	E2
Loug.		
Colebrook Ho. E14	114	B6
Brabazon St.		
Colebrook La., Loug.	49	E2
Colebrook Path,	49	E2
Loug.		
Colebrook Ri.,	191	E2
Brom.		
Colebrooke Row N1	**11**	**G2**
Colebrooke Row N1	111	H2
Coleby Path SE5	132	A7
Harris St.		
Coledale Dr., Stan.	69	F1
Coleford Rd. SW18	149	F5
Colegrave Rd. E15	96	D5
Colegrove Rd. SE15	**37**	**G6**
Colegrove Rd. SE15	132	C7
Coleherne Ct. SW5	**30**	**B4**
Coleherne Ct. SW5	129	E5
Coleherne Ms.	**30**	**A4**
SW10		
Coleherne Rd. SW10	**30**	**A4**
Coleherne Rd. SW10	128	E5
Colehill Gdns. SW6	148	B2
Fulham Palace Rd.		
Colehill La. SW6	148	B1
Coleman Cl. SE25	188	D2
Warminster Rd.		
Coleman Flds. N1	111	J1
Coleman Rd. SE5	**36**	**D7**
Coleman Rd. SE5	132	B7
Coleman Rd., Belv.	139	G4
Coleman Rd., Dag.	101	E6
Coleman St. EC2	**20**	**B3**
Coleman St. EC2	112	A6
Colemans Heath SE9	174	E3
Colenso Dr. NW7	55	G7
Bunns La.		
Colenso Rd. E5	95	F4
Colenso Rd., Ilf.	99	H1
Colepits Wd. Rd. SE9	157	F5
Coleraine Rd. N8	75	G3
Coleraine Rd. SE3	135	F6
Coleridge Av. E12	98	B6
Coleridge Av., Sutt.	199	H4
Coleridge Cl. SW8	150	B2
Coleridge Gdns.	91	F7
NW6		
Fairhazel Gdns.		
Coleridge La. N8	74/75	E6
Coleridge Rd.		
Coleridge Rd. E17	77	J4
Coleridge Rd. N4	93	G2
Coleridge Rd. N8	74	D6
Coleridge Rd. N12	57	F5
Coleridge Rd., Croy.	189	F7
Coleridge Wk. NW11	72	D4
Coleridge Way, Hayes	102	A6
Coleridge Way,	120	C4
West Dr.		
Coles Cres., Har.	85	H2
Coles Grn., Bushey	51	J1
Coles Grn., Loug.	48	D1
Coles Grn. Ct. NW2	89	G2
Coles Grn. Rd. NW2	89	G1
Colesburg Rd., Beck.	189	J3
Coleshill Rd., Tedd.	162	B6
Colestown St. SW11	149	H2
Colet Cl. N13	59	H6
Colet Gdns. W14	128	A4
Coley St. WC1	**10**	**D6**
Coley St. WC1	111	F4
Colfe Rd. SE23	171	H1
Colham Av.,	120	B1
West Dr.		
Colham Mill Rd.,	120	A2
West Dr.		
Colin Cl. NW9	71	E4

Colin Cl., Croy. 203 J3
Colin Cl., W.Wick. 205 F3
Colin Cres. NW9 71 F4
Colin Dr. NW9 71 F5
Colin Gdns. NW9 71 F5
Colin Par. NW9 70/71 E4
Edgware Rd.
Colin Pk. Rd. NW9 70 E4
Colin Rd. NW10 89 G6
Colina Ms. N15 75 H5
Harringay Rd.
Colina Rd. N15 75 H5
Colindale Av. NW9 70 D3
Colindale Business 70 C3
  Pk. NW9
Colindeep Gdns. 71 G5
  NW4
Colindeep La. NW4 70 E3
Colindeep La. NW9 70 E3
Colinette Rd. SW15 147 J4
Colinton Rd., Ilf. 100 B2
Coliston Pas. SW18 148 D7
Coliston Rd.
Coliston Rd. SW18 148 D7
Collamore Av. SW18 167 H1
Collapit Cl., Har. 67 H5
Collard Av., Loug. 49 F2
Collard Grn., Loug. 49 F2
Collard Av.
College App. SE10 134 C6
College Av., Har. 68 B1
College Cl. E9 95 F5
Median Rd.
College Cl. N18 60 C5
College Cl., Har. 52 B7
College Cl., Twick. 162 A1
Meadway
College Cres. NW3 91 G6
College Cross N1 93 G7
College Dr., Ruis. 66 A7
College Gdns. E4 46 B7
College Gdns. N18 60 C5
College Gdns. SE21 170 B1
College Gdns. SW17 167 H2
College Gdns., Enf. 44 A1
College Gdns., Ilf. 80 B5
College Gdns., 183 F5
  N.Mal.
College Grn. SE19 170 B7
College Gro. NW1 110 D1
St. Pancras Way
College Hill EC4 20 A5
College Hill Rd., Har. 68 C1
College La. NW5 92 B4
College Ms. SW1 26 A5
College Ms. 148/149 E5
  SW18
St. Ann's Hill
College Pk. Cl. SE13 154 D4
College Pk. Rd. N17 60 C6
College Rd.
College Pl. E17 78 B4
College Pl. N1 110 C1
College Pl. SW10 30 C7
College Rd. E15 97 F6
College Rd. E17 78 C5
College Rd. N17 60 C6
College Rd. N21 59 G2
College Rd. NW10 107 J2
College Rd. SE19 170 C5
College Rd. SE21 152 B7
College Rd. SW19 167 G6
College Rd. W13 104 E6
College Rd., Brom. 173 G7
College Rd., Croy. 202 A2
College Rd., Enf. 44 A2
College Rd. (Harrow 68 B6
  on the Hill), Har.
College Rd. (Harrow 68 B1
  Weald), Har.
College Rd., Islw. 144 C1
College Rd., Wem. 87 G1
College Row E9 95 G5
College Slip, Brom. 191 G1
College St. EC4 20 B5
College Ter. E3 113 J3
College Ter. N3 72 C2
Hendon La.
College Vw. SE9 174 A1
College Wk., Kings.T. 181 H2
Grange Rd.
College Yd. NW5 92 B4
College La.
Collent St. E9 95 F6
Colless Rd. N15 76 C5
Collett Rd. SE16 29 J6
Collett Rd. SE16 132 D3
Collett Way, Sthl. 123 H1
Collier Cl. E6 116/117 E6
Trader Rd.
Collier Cl., Epsom 196 A6
Collier Dr., Edg. 70 A2
Collier Row Rd., 83 F1
  Rom.

Collier St. N1 10 C2
Collier St. N1 111 F2
Colliers Shaw, Kes. 206 A4
Colliers Water La., 187 G5
  Th.Hth.
Collindale Av., Erith 127 H1
Collindale Av., Sid. 176 A1
Collingbourne Rd. 127 H1
  W12
Collingham Gdns. 30 B2
  SW5
Collingham Gdns. 129 E4
  SW5
Collingham Pl. SW5 30 A2
Collingham Pl. SW5 128 E4
Collingham Rd. SW5 30 B1
Collingham Rd. SW5 129 E4
Collings Cl. N22 59 F6
Whittington Rd.
Collington St. SE26 171 F4
Collingtree Rd. SE26 171 F4
Collingwood Av. N10 74 A3
Collingwood Av., 196 C1
  Surb.
Collingwood Cl. 189 E1
  SE20
Collingwood Cl., 143 G6
  Twick.
Collingwood Rd. E17 78 A6
Collingwood Rd. N15 76 B4
Collingwood Rd., 185 H2
  Mitch.
Collingwood Rd., 198 D3
  Sutt.
Collingwood St. E1 113 E4
Collins Av., Stan. 69 H2
Collins Dr., Ruis. 84 C2
Collins Rd. N5 93 J4
Collins Sq. SE3 155 F2
Tranquil Vale
Collins St. SE3 155 E2
Collin's Yd. N1 111 H1
Islington Grn.
Collinson St. SE1 27 J4
Collinson Wk. SE1 27 J4
Collinwood Av., Enf. 45 F3
Collinwood Gdns., 80 C5
  Ilf.
Collis All., Twick. 162 B1
The Grn.
Colls Rd. SE15 153 F1
Collyer Av., Croy. 200 E4
Collyer Pl. SE15 152 D1
Peckham High St.
Collyer Rd., Croy. 201 E4
Colman Rd. E16 115 J5
Colmar Cl. E1 113 G4
Alderney Rd.
Colmer Pl., Har. 52 A7
Colmer Rd. SW16 187 E1
Colmore Ms. SE15 153 E1
Colmore Rd., Enf. 45 F4
Colnbrook St. SE1 27 G6
Colnbrook St. SE1 131 H3
Colne Ct., Epsom 196 C4
Colne Ho., Bark. 99 E6
Colne Rd. E5 95 H4
Colne Rd. N21 44 A7
Colne Rd., Twick. 162 B1
Colne St. E13 115 G3
Grange Rd.
Colney Hatch La. N10 74 B2
Colney Hatch La. N11 57 J6
Cologne Rd. SW11 149 G4
Colomb St. SE10 135 E5
Colombo Rd., Ilf. 99 F1
Colombo St. SE1 27 G2
Colombo St. SE1 131 H1
Colonels Wk., Enf. 43 H3
Colonial Av., Twick. 143 J5
Colonial Rd., Felt. 141 H7
Colonnade WC1 10 A6
Colonnade Wk. SW1 32 D2
Colonnades, The W2 14 B3
Colonnades, The W2 109 E6
Colson Gdns., 48/49 E4
  Loug.
Colson Rd.
Colson Grn., Loug. 48/49 E4
Colson Rd.
Colson Path, Loug. 48 D4
Colson Rd., Croy. 202 B2
Colson Rd., Loug. 48 E4
Colson Way SW16 168 C4
Colsterworth Rd. 76 C4
  N15
Colston Av., Cars. 199 H4
Colston Rd., Cars. 199 J4
West St.
Colston Rd. E7 98 A6
Colston Rd. SW14 146 C4
Colthurst Cres. N4 93 J2
Coltness Cres. SE2 138 B5
Colton Gdns. N17 75 J3

Colton Rd., Har. 68 B5
Columbia Av., Edg. 70 B1
Columbia Av., Ruis. 84 B1
Columbia Av., 183 F7
  Wor.Pk.
Columbia Ctyd. E14 134 A1
West India Av.
Columbia Rd. E2 13 F3
Columbia Rd. E2 112 C3
Columbia Rd. E13 115 F4
Columbia Sq. SW14 146 C4
Upper Richmond Rd. W.
Columbine Av. E6 116 B5
Columbine Av., 201 H7
  S.Croy.
Columbine Way SE13 154 C2
Columbus Ct. SE16 133 F1
Rotherhithe St.
Columbus Ctyd. E14 134 A1
West India Av.
Columbus Gdns., 66 A1
  Nthwd.
Colva Wk. N19 92 B2
Chester Rd.
Colvestone Cres. E8 94 C5
Colview Ct. SE9 174 A1
Mottingham La.
Colville Est. N1 112 B1
Colville Gdns. W11 108 C6
Colville Hos. W11 108 C6
Colville Ms. W11 108 C6
Lonsdale Rd.
Colville Pl. W1 17 G2
Colville Rd. E11 96 C3
Colville Rd. E17 77 H2
Colville Rd. N9 60 E1
Colville Rd. W3 126 B3
Colville Rd. W11 108 C6
Colville Sq. W11 108 C6
Colville Sq. Ms. W11 108 C6
Portobello Rd.
Colville Ter. W11 108 C6
Colvin Cl. SE26 171 F5
Colvin Gdns. E4 62 C3
Colvin Gdns. E11 79 H4
Colvin Gdns., Ilf. 81 F1
Colvin Rd. E6 98 B7
Colvin Rd., Th.Hth. 187 G5
Colwall Gdns., 63 G5
  Wdf.Grn.
Colwell Rd. SE22 152 C5
Colwick Cl. N6 74 D7
Colwith Rd. W6 127 J6
Colwood Gdns. 167 G7
  SW19
Colworth Gro. SE17 36 A2
Colworth Rd. E11 78 E6
Colworth Rd., Croy. 202 D1
Colwyn Av., Grnf. 104 C2
Colwyn Cl. SW16 168 C5
Colwyn Cres., Houns. 143 J1
Colwyn Grn. NW9 70/71 E6
Snowdon Dr.
Colwyn Rd. NW2 89 H3
Colyer Cl. N1 10 D1
Colyer Cl. N1 111 F2
Colyer Cl. SE9 175 E2
Colyers La., Erith 159 J1
Colyton Cl., Well. 158 D1
Colyton Cl., Wem. 87 F6
Bridgewater Rd.
Colyton Rd. SE22 153 E5
Colyton Way N18 60 D5
Combe Av. SE3 135 F7
Combe Lo. SE7 135 J6
Elliscombe Rd.
Combe Martin, 164 C5
  Kings.T.
Combe Ms. SE3 135 F7
Combedale Rd. SE10 135 G5
Combemartin Rd. 148 B7
  SW18
Comber Cl. NW2 89 H3
Comber Gro. SE5 151 J1
Combermere Rd. 151 F3
  SW9
Combermere Rd., 185 E6
  Mord.
Comberton Rd. E5 95 E2
Combeside SE18 137 J7
Combwell Cres. SE2 138 A3
Comely Bank Rd. E17 78 C5
Comer Cres., Sthl. 123 J2
Windmill La.
Comeragh Ms. W14 128 B5
Comeragh Rd. W14 128 B5
Comerford Rd. SE4 153 H4
Comet Cl. E12 98 A4
Comet Pl. SE8 134 A7
Comet St. SE8 134 A7
Commerce Rd. N22 75 F1
Commerce Rd., 125 F7
  Brent.

Commerce Way, 201 F2
  Croy.
Commercial Rd. E1 21 H3
Commercial Rd. E1 112 D6
Commercial Rd. E14 113 F6
Commercial Rd. N17 60 B6
Commercial Rd. N18 60 B5
Commercial St. E1 13 F6
Commercial St. E1 112 C4
Commercial Way 106 B2
  NW10
Commercial Way 132 C7
  SE15
Commerell St. SE10 135 E5
Commodity Quay E1 21 G6
Commodore Sq. 149 G1
  SW10
Commodore St. E1 113 H4
Common, The W5 105 H7
Common, The, Rich. 163 G3
Common, The, Sthl. 122 C4
Common, The, Stan. 52 B2
Common La., Esher 194 D7
Common, The, Esher 147 G3
Common Rd., Esher 194 D6
Common Rd., Stan. 52 A4
Commondale SW15 147 J3
Commonfield La. 167 H5
  SW17
Tooting Gro.
Commonside, Kes. 205 J4
Commonside E., 185 J3
  Mitch.
Commonside W., 185 J3
  Mitch.
Commonwealth Av. 107 H7
  W12
Commonwealth Rd. 60 D7
  N17
Commonwealth Way 138 B5
  SE2
Community Cl., 142 B1
  Houns.
Community La. N7 92 D5
Community Rd. E15 96 D5
Community Rd., Grnf. 103 J1
Como Rd. SE23 171 H2
Compass Hill, Rich. 145 G6
Compayne Gdns. 90 E7
  NW6
Compton Av. E6 116 A2
Compton Av. N1 93 H6
Compton Av. N6 73 H7
Compton Cl. E3 114 A5
Compton Cl. NW1 9 E4
Compton Cl. NW11 90 A3
The Vale
Compton Cl. W13 104 D6
Compton Cl., Edg. 54 C7
Pavilion Way
Compton Ct. SE19 170 B5
Victoria Cres.
Compton Cres. N17 59 J7
Compton Cres. W4 126 C6
Compton Cres., 195 H6
  Chess.
Compton Cres., Nthlt. 102 D1
Compton Pas. EC1 11 H5
Compton Pl. WC1 10 A5
Compton Pl., Wat. 50 E3
Compton Ri., Pnr. 67 E5
Compton Rd. N1 93 H6
Compton Rd. N21 59 G1
Compton Rd. NW10 108 A3
Compton Rd. SW19 166 C6
Compton Rd., Croy. 202 E1
Compton St. EC1 11 G5
Compton Ter. N1 93 H6
Comreddy Cl., Enf. 43 H1
Comus Pl. SE17 36 D2
Comus Pl. SE17 132 B4
Comyn Rd. SW11 149 H4
Comyns, The, Bushey 51 J1
Comyns Cl. E16 115 F5
Comyns Rd., Dag. 101 G7
Conant Ms. E1 21 H5
Concanon Rd. SW2 151 F4
Concert Hall App. SE1 26 D2
Concert Hall App. SE1 131 F1
Concord Cl., Nthlt. 102 D3
Britannia Cl.
Concord Rd. W3 106 B4
Concord Rd., Enf. 45 F5
Concorde Cl., 143 H2
  Houns.
Lampton Rd.
Concorde Dr. E6 116 C5
Concourse, The N9 60 D2
New Rd.
Concourse, The NW9 71 F1
Condell Rd. SW8 150 C1
Conder St. E14 113 H6
Salmon La.

Name		
Conderton Rd. SE5	151	J3
Condor Path, Nthlt.	103	G2
Brabazon Rd.		
Condover Cres. SE18	136	E7
Condray Pl. SW11	129	H7
Conduit Av. SE10	154	D1
Crooms Hill		
Conduit Ct. WC2	**18**	**A5**
Conduit La. N18	61	F5
Conduit La., Croy.	202	D5
Conduit La., Enf.	45	H6
Morson Rd.		
Conduit La., S.Croy.	202	D5
Conduit Ms. W2	**14**	**E4**
Conduit Ms. W2	109	G6
Conduit Pas. W2	**15**	**E4**
Conduit Pl. W2	**15**	**E4**
Conduit Pl. W2	109	G6
Conduit Rd. SE18	137	E5
Conduit St. W1	**17**	**E5**
Conduit St. W1	110	B7
Conduit Way NW10	88	C7
Conewood St. N5	93	H3
Coney Acre SE21	169	J1
Coney Burrows E4	62/63	E2
Wyemead Cres.		
Coney Hill Rd., W.Wick.	205	E2
Coney Way SW8	**34**	**D6**
Coney Way SW8	131	F6
Coneygrove Path, Nthlt.	84/85	E6
Arnold Rd.		
Conference Cl. E4	62	C2
Greenbank Cl.		
Conference Rd. SE2	138	C4
Congleton Gro. SE18	137	F5
Congo Rd. SE18	137	G5
Congress Rd. SE2	138	C4
Congreve Rd. SE9	156	C3
Congreve St. SE17	**36**	**D1**
Congreve St. SE17	132	B4
Congreve Wk. E16	116	A5
Conical Cor., Enf.	43	J2
Conifer Cl., Orp.	207	G4
Conifer Gdns. SW16	169	E3
Conifer Gdns., Enf.	44	B6
Conifer Gdns., Sutt.	198	E2
Conifer Way, Hayes	102	A7
Longmead Rd.		
Conifer Way, Wem.	87	F3
Conifers Cl., Tedd.	163	E7
Coniger Rd. SW6	148	D2
Coningham Ms. W12	127	G1
Percy Rd.		
Coningham Rd. W12	127	H1
Coningsby Cotts. W5	125	G2
Coningsby Rd.		
Coningsby Gdns. E4	62	B6
Coningsby Rd. N4	75	H7
Coningsby Rd. W5	125	F2
Conington Rd. SE13	154	B2
Conisbee Ct. N14	42	C5
Conisborough Cres. SE6	172	C3
Coniscliffe Cl., Chis.	192	D1
Coniscliffe Rd. N13	59	J3
Coniston Av., Bark.	99	H7
Coniston Av., Grnf.	105	E3
Coniston Av., Well.	157	H3
Coniston Cl. N20	57	F3
Coniston Cl. SW13	127	F7
Lonsdale Rd.		
Coniston Cl. SW20	184	A6
Coniston Cl. W4	146	C1
Coniston Cl., Bark.	99	H7
Coniston Av.		
Coniston Cl., Bexh.	159	J1
Coniston Gdns. N9	61	F1
Coniston Gdns. NW9	70	D5
Coniston Gdns., Ilf.	80	B4
Coniston Gdns., Pnr.	66	A4
Coniston Gdns., Sutt.	199	G6
Coniston Gdns., Wem.	87	F1
Coniston Ho. SE5	**35**	**J7**
Coniston Ho. SE5	131	J7
Coniston Rd. N10	74	B2
Coniston Rd. N17	60	D6
Coniston Rd., Bexh.	159	J1
Coniston Rd., Brom.	172	E6
Coniston Rd., Croy.	188	D7
Coniston Rd., Twick.	143	H6
Coniston Wk. E9	95	F5
Clifden Rd.		
Coniston Way, Chess.	195	H3
Conistone Way N7	93	E7
Conlan St. W10	108	B4
Conley Rd. NW10	89	E6
Conley St. SE10	134/135	E5
Pelton Rd.		
Connaught Av. E4	46	D7
Connaught Av. SW14	146	C3
Connaught Av., Barn.	57	J1
Connaught Av., Enf.	44	B2
Connaught Av., Houns.	143	E5
Connaught Av., Loug.	48	A4
Connaught Br. E16	116	A7
Connaught Cl. E10	95	H2
Connaught Cl. W2	**15**	**G4**
Connaught Cl., Enf.	44	B2
Connaught Cl., Sutt.	199	G2
Connaught Dr. NW11	72	D4
Connaught Gdns. N10	74	B5
Connaught Gdns. N13	59	H4
Connaught Gdns., Mord.	185	F4
Connaught Hill, Loug.	48	A4
Connaught La., Ilf.	99	G2
Connaught Br.		
Connaught Ms. SE18	136	D5
Connaught Ms. W2	**15**	**J4**
Connaught Ms., Ilf.	99	G2
Connaught Br.		
Connaught Pl. W2	**15**	**J5**
Connaught Pl. W2	109	J7
Connaught Rd. E4	46	E7
Connaught Rd. E11	96	D1
Connaught Rd. E16	136	A1
Connaught Rd. E17	78	A5
Connaught Rd. N4	75	G7
Connaught Rd. NW10	107	E1
Connaught Rd. SE18	136	D5
Connaught Rd. W13	104	E7
Connaught Rd., Barn.	40	A6
Connaught Rd., Har.	68	C1
Connaught Rd., Ilf.	99	G2
Connaught Rd., N.Mal.	183	E4
Connaught Rd., Rich.	145	J5
Albert Rd.		
Connaught Rd., Sutt.	199	G2
Connaught Rd., Tedd.	162	A5
Connaught Roundabout E16	116	A7
Connaught Br.		
Connaught Sq. W2	**15**	**J4**
Connaught Sq. W2	109	J6
Connaught St. W2	**15**	**G4**
Connaught St. W2	109	H6
Connaught Way N13	59	H4
Connell Cres. W5	105	J4
Connemara Cl., Borwd.	38	D6
Percheron Rd.		
Connington Cres. E4	62	D3
Connor Cl., Ilf.	80	C1
Fullwell Av.		
Connor Rd., Dag.	101	F4
Connor St. E9	113	G1
Lauriston Rd.		
Conolly Rd. W7	124	B1
Conrad Dr., Wor.Pk.	197	J1
Conrad Ho. N16	94	B5
Cons St. SE1	**27**	**F3**
Consfield Av., N.Mal.	183	G4
Consort Ms., Islw.	144	A5
Consort Rd. SE15	152	E1
Constable Av. E16	135	H1
Wesley Av.		
Constable Cl. NW11	73	E6
Constable Cres. N15	76	D5
Constable Gdns., Edg.	70	A1
Constable Gdns., Islw.	144	A5
Constable Ms., Dag.	100	B4
Stonard Rd.		
Constable Wk. SE21	170	C3
Constance Cres. Brom.	191	F7
Constance Rd., Croy.	187	H7
Constance Rd., Enf.	44	B6
Constance Rd., Sutt.	199	F4
Constance Rd., Twick.	143	H7
Constance St. E16	136	B1
Albert Rd.		
Constantine Rd. NW3	91	H4
Constitution Hill SW1	**24**	**D3**
Constitution Hill SW1	130	B2
Constitution Ri. SE18	156	D1
Consul Av., Dag.	119	J3
Content St. SE17	**36**	**A2**
Content St. SE17	132	A4
Contessa Cl., Orp.	207	H5
Control Twr. Rd., Houns.	140	D3
Convair Wk., Nthlt.	102	D3
Kittiwake Rd.		
Convent Cl., Beck.	172	C7
Convent Gdns. W5	125	F4
Convent Gdns. W11	108	C6
Kensington Pk. Rd.		
Convent Hill SE19	169	J6
Convent Way, Sthl.	122	C4
Conway Cl., Stan.	52	D6
Conway Cres., Grnf.	104	B2
Conway Cres., Rom.	82	C7
Conway Dr., Hayes	121	F3
Conway Dr., Sutt.	198	E6
Conway Gdns., Mitch.	186	D4
Conway Gdns., Wem.	69	F7
Conway Gro. W3	106	D5
Conway Ms. W1	**9**	**F6**
Conway Rd. N14	59	E3
Conway Rd. N15	75	H5
Conway Rd. NW2	89	J2
Conway Rd. SE18	137	G4
Conway Rd. SW20	183	J1
Conway Rd., Felt.	160	D5
Conway Rd., Houns.	143	F7
Conway Rd. (Heathrow Airport), Houns.	140/141	E3
Inner Ring E.		
Conway St. E13	115	G4
Conway St. W1	**9**	**F6**
Conway St. W1	110	C5
Conway Wk., Hmptn.	161	F6
Fearnley Cres.		
Conybeare NW3	91	H7
King Henry's Rd.		
Conyer St. E3	113	H2
Conyers Cl., Wdf.Grn.	62	E6
Conyers Rd. SW16	168	D5
Conyers Way, Loug.	49	E3
Cooden Cl., Brom.	173	H7
Plaistow La.		
Cooderidge Cl. N17	60	C6
Brantwood Rd.		
Cook Ct. SE16	133	F1
Rotherhithe St.		
Cook Rd., Dag.	118	E1
Cooke Cl. E14	134	A1
Cabot Sq.		
Cookes Cl. E11	97	F2
Cookes La., Sutt.	198	B6
Cookham Cl., Sthl.	123	H2
Cookham Cres. SE16	133	G2
Marlow Way		
Cookham Dene Cl., Chis.	193	G1
Cookhill Rd. SE18	138	B2
Cooks Cl., Rom.	83	J1
Cook's Rd. E15	114	B2
Cooks Rd. SE17	**35**	**G5**
Cooks Rd. SE17	131	H6
Cookson Gro., Erith	139	H7
Cool Oak La. NW9	71	E7
Coolfin Rd. E16	115	G6
Coolgardie Av. E4	62	C5
Coolgardie Av., Chig.	64	D3
Coolhurst Rd. N8	74	D6
Coomassie Rd. W9	108	C4
Bravington Rd.		
Coombe Av., Croy.	202	B4
Coombe Bank, Kings.T.	182	E1
Coombe Cl., Edg.	69	J2
Coombe Cl., Houns.	143	G4
Coombe Cor. N21	59	H1
Coombe Cres., Hmptn.	161	E7
Coombe Dr., Kings.T.	84	B1
Coombe Dr., Ruis.	84	B1
Coombe End Kings.T.	164	D7
Coombe Gdns. SW20	183	G2
Coombe Gdns., N.Mal.	183	F4
Coombe Hts., Kings.T.	165	E7
Coombe Hill Glade Kings.T.	165	E7
Coombe Hill Rd. Kings.T.	164	E7
Coombe Ho. Chase, N.Mal.	182	D1
Coombe La. SW20	183	H2
Coombe La., Croy.	202	E5
Coombe La. W., Kings.T.	183	G1
Coombe Lea, Brom.	192	B3
Coombe Neville, Kings.T.	164	D7
Coombe Pk., Kings.T.	164	D5
Coombe Ridings, Kings.T.	164	C5
Coombe Ri., Kings.T.	182	C1
Coombe Rd. N22	75	G1
Coombe Rd. NW10	88	D3
Coombe Rd. SE26	170	E4
Coombe Rd. W4	127	E5
Coombe Rd. W13	124/125	E3
Northcroft Rd.		
Coombe Rd., Croy.	202	A4
Coombe Rd., Hmptn.	161	F6
Coombe Rd., Kings.T.	182	A1
Coombe Rd., N.Mal.	182	E3
Coombe Wk., Sutt.	198	E3
Coombe Wd. Rd., Kings.T.	164	C5
Coombefield Cl., N.Mal.	183	E3
Coombehurst Cl., Barn.	41	J2
Coomber Way, Croy.	186	D7
Coombes Rd., Dag.	119	F1
Coombewood Dr., Rom.	83	F6
Coombs St. N1	**11**	**H2**
Coombs St. N1	111	H2
Coomer Ms. SW6	128	C6
Coomer Pl.		
Coomer Pl. SW6	128	C6
Coomer Pl. SW6	128	C6
Coomer Pl.		
Cooms Wk., Edg.	70	C1
East Rd.		
Cooper Av. E17	77	G1
Cooper Cl. SE1	**27**	**F4**
Cooper Cl. E15	96	B5
Clays La.		
Cooper Cres., Cars.	199	J3
Cooper Rd. NW4	72	A6
Cooper Rd. NW10	89	G5
Cooper Rd., Croy.	201	G4
Cooper St. E16	115	F5
Lawrence St.		
Cooperage Cl. N17	60	C6
Brantwood Rd.		
Coopers Cl. E1	113	F4
Coopers Cl., Dag.	101	H6
Coopers Cres., Borwd.	38	C1
Coopers La. E10	96	B1
Coopers La. NW1	**9**	**J1**
Coopers La. NW1	110	D2
Cooper's La. SE12	173	H2
Coopers Rd. SE1	**37**	**G4**
Coopers Rd. SE1	132	C5
Coopers Wk. E15	96	D5
Maryland St.		
Cooper's Row EC3	**21**	**F5**
Cooper's Yd. SE19	170	B6
Westow Hill		
Coopersale Cl., Wdf.Grn.	63	J7
Navestock Cres.		
Coopersale Rd. E9	95	G5
Coote Gdns., Dag.	101	F3
Coote Rd., Bexh.	159	F1
Coote Rd., Dag.	101	F3
Cope Pl. W8	128	D3
Cope St. SE16	133	G4
Copeland Dr. E14	134	A4
Copeland Rd. E17	78	B5
Copeland Rd. SE15	152	D2
Copeman Cl. SE26	171	F5
Copenhagen Gdns. W4	126	C2
Copenhagen Pl. E14	113	J6
Copenhagen St. N1	111	E1
Copers Cope Rd., Beck.	171	J6
Copford Cl., Wdf.Grn.	64	B6
Copford Wk. N1	111	J1
Popham St.		
Copgate Path SW16	169	F6
Copinger Wk., Edg.	70	B1
North Rd.		
Copland Av., Wem.	87	G5
Copland Cl., Wem.	87	F5
Copland Ms., Wem.	87	H6
Copland Rd.		
Copland Rd., Wem.	87	H6
Copleston Ms. SE15	152	C2
Copleston Rd.		
Copleston Pas. SE15	152	C3
Copleston Rd. SE15	152	C3
Copley Cl. SE17	**35**	**H6**
Copley Cl. W7	104	C5
Copley Dene, Brom.	192	A1
Copley Pk. SW16	169	F6
Copley Rd., Stan.	53	F5
Copley St. E1	113	G5
Stepney Grn.		
Copnor Way SE15	**37**	**E7**
Coppard Gdns., Chess.	195	F6
Copped Hall SE21	170	A2
Glazebrook Cl.		

Coppelia Rd. SE3	155	F4
Coppen Rd., Dag.	83	F7
Copper Beech Cl. NW3	91	G6
Daleham Ms.		
Copper Beech Cl., Ilf.	80	D1
Copper Beech Ct., Loug.	48	D1
Copper Beeches, Islw.	144	A1
Eversley Cres.		
Copper Cl. SE19	170	C7
Auckland Rd.		
Copper Mead Cl. NW2	89	J3
Copper Mill Dr., Islw.	144	C2
Copper Mill La. SW17	167	F4
Copper Row SE1	29	F2
Copper Row SE1	132	C1
Copperas St. SE8	134	B6
Copperbeech Cl. NW3	91	G5
Akenside Rd.		
Copperdale Rd., Hayes	122	A2
Copperfield, Chig.	65	G6
Copperfield App., Chig.	65	G6
Copperfield Ct., Pnr.	67	F4
Copperfield Way		
Copperfield Dr. N15	76	C4
Copperfield Ms. N18	60	B5
Copperfield Rd. E3	113	H4
Copperfield Rd. SE28	118	C6
Copperfield St. SE1	27	H3
Copperfield St. SE1	131	H2
Copperfield Way, Chis.	175	F6
Copperfield Way, Pnr.	67	F4
Coppergate Cl., Brom.	191	H1
Coppermill La. E17	77	F6
Coppetts Cl. N12	57	H7
Coppetts Rd. N10	74	A2
Coppice, The, Enf.	43	H4
Coppice Cl. SW20	183	J3
Coppice Cl., Stan.	52	C6
Coppice Dr. SW15	147	H6
Coppice Wk. N20	56	D3
Coppice Way E18	79	F4
Coppies Gro. N11	58	A4
Copping Cl., Croy.	202	B4
Tipton Dr.		
Coppins, The, Croy.	204	B6
Coppins, The, Har.	52	B6
Coppock Cl. SW11	149	H2
Coppsfield, W.Mol.	179	G3
Hurst Rd.		
Copse, The E4	63	F1
Copse Av., W.Wick.	204	B3
Copse Cl. SE7	135	H6
Copse Cl., West.	120	A3
Copse Glade, Surb.	195	G1
Copse Hill SW20	165	H7
Copse Hill, Sutt.	199	E7
Copsewood Cl., Sid.	157	H6
Coptefield Dr., Belv.	138	D3
Copthall Av. EC2	20	C3
Copthall Av. EC2	112	A6
Copthall Bldgs. EC2	20	B3
Copthall Cl. EC2	20	B3
Copthall Cl. EC2	112	A6
Copthall Dr. NW7	55	G7
Copthall Gdns. NW7	55	G7
Copthall Gdns., Twick.	162	C1
Copthorne Av. SW12	150	D7
Copthorne Av., Brom.	206	C2
Copthorne Cl., Ilf.	65	E6
Copthorne Ms., Hayes	121	H4
Coptic St. WC1	18	A2
Coptic St. WC1	110	E5
Copwood Cl. N12	57	G4
Coral Cl., Rom.	82	C3
Coral Row SW11	149	F3
Gartons Way		
Coral St. SE1	27	F4
Coral St. SE1	131	G2
Coraline Cl., Sthl.	103	F3
Coralline Wk. SE2	138	C2
Coram St. WC1	10	A6
Coram St. WC1	110	E4
Coran Cl. N9	45	G7
Corban Rd., Houns.	143	G3
Corbet Cl., Wall.	200	A1
Corbet Ct. EC3	20	C4
Corbet Pl. E1	21	F1
Corbett Gro. N22	58	E7
Corbett Ho., Wat.	50	C3
Corbett Rd. E11	79	J6
Corbett Rd. E17	78	C3

Corbett's La. SE16	133	F4
Rotherhithe New Rd.		
Corbetts Pas. SE16	133	F4
Rotherhithe New Rd.		
Corbicum E11	79	E7
Corbiere Ct. SW19	166	A6
Thornton Rd.		
Corbiere Ho. N1	112	B1
Corbins La., Har.	85	H3
Corbridge Cres. E2	112	E2
Corby Cres., Enf.	43	E4
Corby Rd. NW10	106	D2
Corby Way E3	114	A4
Knapp Rd.		
Corbylands Rd., Sid.	157	H7
Corbyn St. N4	93	E1
Cord Way E14	134	A3
Mellish St.		
Cordelia Cl. SE24	151	H4
Cordelia Gdns., Stai.	140	B7
Cordelia Rd., Stai.	140	B7
Cordelia St. E14	114	B6
Cording St. E14	114	B5
Chrisp St.		
Cordova Rd. E3	113	H3
Cordwainers Wk. E13	115	G2
Clegg St.		
Cordwell Rd. SE13	154	E5
Corelli Rd. SE3	156	B2
Corfe Av., Har.	85	G4
Corfe Cl., Hayes	102	C6
Corfe Twr. W3	126	B2
Corfield Rd. N21	43	F5
Corfield St. E2	113	E3
Corfton Rd. W5	105	H6
Coriander Av. E14	114	D6
Cories Cl., Dag.	100	D2
Corinium Cl., Wem.	87	J4
Corinne Rd. N19	92	C4
Corinthian Way, Stai.	140	A7
Clare Rd.		
Cork Sq. E1	132/133	E1
Smeaton St.		
Cork St. W1	17	F6
Cork St. W1	110	C7
Cork St. Ms. W1	17	F6
Cork Tree Way E4	61	H5
Corker Wk. N7	93	F2
Corkran Rd., Surb.	181	G7
Corkscrew Hill, W.Wick.	204	D2
Corlett St. NW1	15	G1
Corlett St. NW1	109	H5
Cormont Rd. SE5	151	H1
Cormorant Cl. E17	77	G7
Banbury Rd.		
Cormorant Pl., Sutt.	198	B2
Gander Grn. La.		
Cormorant Rd. E7	97	F5
Corn Mill Dr., Orp.	193	J7
Corn Way E11	96	D3
Cornbury Rd., Edg.	53	G7
Cornelia St. N7	93	F6
Cornell Cl., Sid.	177	E6
Corner Grn. SE3	155	G2
Corner Ho. St. WC2	26	A1
Corner Mead NW9	55	F7
Corney Reach Way W4	127	E7
Corney Rd. W4	127	E6
Cornflower La., Croy.	203	G1
Cornflower Ter. SE22	152	E6
Cornford Cl., Brom.	191	G5
Cornford Gro. SW12	168	B2
Cornhill EC3	20	C4
Cornhill EC3	112	A6
Cornish Ct. N9	44	E7
Cornish Gro. SE20	171	E7
Cornish Ho. SE17	35	G6
Cornish Ho., Brent.	125	J5
Green Dragon La.		
Cornmill La. SE13	154	B3
Cornmow Dr. NW10	89	F5
Cornshaw Rd., Dag.	100	D1
Cornthwaite Rd. E5	95	F3
Cornwall Av. E2	113	F3
Cornwall Av. N3	56	D7
Cornwall Av. N22	75	E1
Cornwall Av. NW10		
Cornwall Av., Sthl.	103	F5
Cornwall Av., Well.	157	H3
Cornwall Cl., Bark.	99	J6
Cornwall Cres. W11	108	B7
Cornwall Dr., Orp.	176	C7
Cornwall Gdns. NW10		
Cornwall Gdns. SW7	22	B6
Cornwall Gdns. SW7	129	F3
Cornwall Gdns. Wk. SW7	22	B6
Cornwall Gro. W4	127	E5
Cornwall Ms. S. SW7	22	C6
Cornwall Ms. S. SW7	129	F3

Cornwall Ms. W. SW7	22	B6
Cornwall Rd. N4	75	G7
Cornwall Rd. N15	76	A5
Cornwall Rd. N18	60	D5
Fairfield Rd.		
Cornwall Rd. SE1	26	E1
Cornwall Rd. SE1	131	G1
Cornwall Rd., Croy.	201	H2
Cornwall Rd., Esher	194	D7
Cornwall Rd., Har.	67	J6
Cornwall Rd., Pnr.	51	F7
Cornwall Rd., Sutt.	198	C7
Cornwall Rd., Twick.	162	D1
Cornwall St. E1	112/113	E7
Watney St.		
Cornwall Ter. NW1	8	A6
Cornwall Ter. Ms. NW1	8	A6
Cornwallis Av. N9	61	E2
Cornwallis Av. SE18	175	G2
Cornwallis Gro. N9	61	E2
Cornwallis Rd. E17	77	G4
Cornwallis Rd. N9	61	E2
Cornwallis Rd. N19	92	E2
Cornwallis Rd., Dag.	100	D4
Cornwallis Sq. N19	92	E2
Cornwallis Wk. SE9	156	C3
Cornwood Cl. N2	73	G5
Cornwood Dr. E1	113	F6
Cornworthy Rd., Dag.	100	C5
Corona Rd. SE12	155	G7
Coronation Av. N16	94	C3
Victorian Rd.		
Coronation Cl., Bex.	158	D6
Coronation Cl., Ilf.	81	F4
Coronation Rd. E13	115	J3
Coronation Rd. NW10	105	J3
Coronation Rd., Hayes	121	J4
Coronation Wk., Twick.	161	F1
Coronet St. N1	12	D4
Coronet St. N1	112	B3
Corporation Av., Houns.	142	E4
Corporation Row EC1	11	F5
Corporation Row EC1	111	G4
Corporation St. E15	115	E2
Corporation St. N7	92	E5
Corrance Rd. SW2	151	E4
Corri Av. N14	58	D4
Corrib Dr., Sutt.	199	H5
Corringham Ct. NW11	72/73	E7
Corringham Rd.		
Corringham Rd. NW11	72	D7
Corringham Rd., Wem.	88	A2
Corringway NW11	72	E7
Corringway W5	106	A4
Corsair Cl., Stai.	140	A7
Corsair Rd., Stai.	140	B7
Corscombe Cl., Kings.T.	164	C5
Corsehill St. SW16	168	C6
Corsham St. N1	12	C4
Corsham St. N1	112	A3
Corsica St. N5	93	H6
Corsley Way E9	95	J6
Osborne Rd.		
Cortayne Rd. SW6	148	C2
Cortis Rd. SW15	147	H6
Cortis Ter. SW15	147	H6
Corunna Rd. SW8	150	C1
Corunna Ter. SW8	150	C1
Corvette Sq. SE10	134	D6
Feathers Pl.		
Coryton Path W9	108	C4
Ashmore Rd.		
Cosbycote Av. SE24	151	J5
Cosdach Av., Wall.	200	D7
Cosedge Cres., Croy.	201	G5
Cosgrove Cl. N21	59	J2
Cosgrove Cl., Hayes	102/103	E4
Kingsash Dr.		
Cosmo Pl. WC1	18	B1
Cosmur Cl. W12	127	F3
Cossall Wk. SE15	153	E1
Cosser St. SE1	26	E5
Cosser St. SE1	131	G3
Costa St. SE15	152	D2
Coston Wk. SE4	153	G4
Frensbury Rd.		
Costons Av., Grnf.	104	A3
Costons La., Grnf.	104	A3
Cosway St. NW1	15	H1
Cosway St. NW1	109	H5
Cotall St. E14	114	A6
Coteford Cl., Loug.	48	E2
Coteford Cl., Pnr.	66	A5
Coteford St. SW17	167	J4

Cotelands, Croy.	202	B3
Cotesbach Rd. E5	95	F3
Cotesmore Gdns., Dag.	100	C4
Cotham St. SE17	36	A2
Cotherstone Rd. SW2	169	F1
Cotleigh Av., Bex.	176	D2
Cotleigh Rd. NW6	90	D7
Cotleigh Rd., Rom.	83	J6
Cotman Cl. NW11	73	F6
Cotman Cl. SW15	148	A6
Westleigh Av.		
Cotman Gdns., Edg.	70	A2
Cotman Ms., Dag.	100	C5
Highgrove Rd.		
Cotmandene Cres., Orp.		
Cotmans Cl., Hayes	122	A1
Coton Rd., Well.	158	A3
Cotsford Av., N.Mal.	182	C5
Cotswold Cl., Esher	194	C3
Cotswold Cl., Kings.T.	164	B6
Cotswold Ct. N11	58	A4
Cotswold Gdns. E6	116	A3
Cotswold Gdns. NW2	90	A2
Cotswold Gdns., Ilf.	81	G7
Cotswold Gate NW2	90	B1
Cotswold Gdns.		
Cotswold Grn., Enf.	43	F4
Cotswold Way		
Cotswold Ms. SW11	149	G1
Battersea High St.		
Cotswold Ri., Orp.	193	J6
Cotswold Rd., Hmptn.	161	G6
Cotswold St. SE27	169	H4
Norwood High St.		
Cotswold Way, Enf.	43	F4
Cotswold Way, Wor.Pk.	197	J2
Cottage Av., Brom.	206	B1
Cottage Fld. Cl., Sid.	176	C1
Cottage Grn. SE5	36	C7
Cottage Gro. SE5	132	A7
Cottage Gro. SW9	150	E3
Cottage Gro., Surb.	181	G6
Cottage Homes NW7	55	G4
Cottage Pl. SW3	23	G5
Cottage Pl. SW3	129	H3
Cottage Rd., Epsom	196	D7
Cottage St. E14	114	B7
Cottage Wk. N16	94	C3
Smalley Cl.		
Cottage Wk. SE15	132	C7
Sumner Est.		
Cottenham Dr. NW9	71	F3
Cottenham Dr. SW20	165	H7
Cottenham Par. SW20	183	H2
Durham Rd.		
Cottenham Pk. Rd. SW20	165	H7
Cottenham Pl. SW20	165	H7
Cottenham Rd. E17	77	J4
Cotterill Rd., Surb.	195	H2
Cottesbrook St. SE14	133	H7
Nynehead St.		
Cottesloe Ms. SE1	27	F5
Cottesmore Av., Ilf.	80	D2
Cottesmore Gdns. W8	22	B5
Cottesmore Gdns. W8	129	E3
Cottimore Cres., Walt.	178	B7
Walt.		
Cottimore Ter., Walt.	178	B7
Cottingham Chase, Ruis.	84	A3
Cottingham Rd. SE20	171	G7
Cottingham Rd. SW8	34	D6
Cottingham Rd. SW8	131	F7
Cottington Rd., Felt.	160	D4
Cottington St. SE11	35	F3
Cottle St. SE16	133	F2
St. Marychurch St.		
Cotton Av. W3	106	D6
Cotton Cl., Dag.	100	C7
Ellerton Rd.		
Cotton Hill, Brom.	172	D4
Cotton Row SW11	149	F3
Cotton St. E14	114	C7
Cottongrass Cl., Croy.	203	G1
Cornflower La.		
Cottons Gdns. E2	13	E3
Cottons La. SE1	28	C1
Cotts Cl. W7	104	C5
Westcott Cres.		
Couchman Av., Esher	194	B2
Couchmore Av., Ilf.	80	C2
Coulgate St. SE4	153	H3
Coulson Cl., Dag.	82	C7
Coulson St. SW3	31	J3
Coulson St. SW3	129	J4
Coulter Cl., Hayes	102	E4

Coulter Rd. W6 127 H3
Councillor St. SE5 131 J7
Counter Ct. SE1 132 A1
Southwark St.
Counter St. SE1 28 D2
Countess Rd. NW5 92 C5
Countisbury Av., Enf. 44 C7
Country Way, Felt. 160 B6
Country Way, Sun. 160 B6
County Gdns., Bark. 117 H2
River Rd.
County Gate SE9 175 F3
County Gate, Barn. 41 E6
County Gro. SE5 151 J1
County Rd. E6 116 E5
County Rd., Th.Hth. 187 H2
County St. SE1 28 A6
County St. SE1 132 A3
Coupland Pl. SE18 137 F5
Courcy Rd. N8 75 G3
Courier Rd., Dag. 119 J4
Courland Gro. SW8 150 D1
Courland St. SW8 150 D1
Course, The SE9 174 D3
Court, The, Ruis. 84 E4
Court Av., Belv. 139 F5
Court Cl., Har. 69 H3
Court Cl., Twick. 161 H3
Court Cl., Wall. 200 D7
Court Cl. Av., Twick. 161 H3
Court Cres., Chess. 195 G5
Court Downs Rd., Beck. 190 B2
Court Dr., Croy. 201 F4
Court Dr., Stan. 53 H4
Court Dr., Sutt. 199 H4
Court Fm. Av., Epsom 196 D5
Court Fm. Rd. SE9 174 A2
Court Fm. Rd., Nthlt. 85 G7
Court Gdns. N7 93 G6
Court Ho. Gdns. N3 56 D6
Court La. SE21 152 B6
Court La. Gdns. SE21 152 B7
Court Mead, Nthlt. 103 F3
Court Par., Wem. 86 E3
Court Rd. SE9 174 B2
Court Rd. SE25 188 C2
Court Rd., Sthl. 123 F4
Court St. E1 112/113 E5
Durward St.
Court St., Brom. 191 G2
Court Way NW9 71 E4
Court Way W3 106 C5
Court Way, Ilf. 81 F3
Court Way, Twick. 144 C7
Court Yd. SE9 156 B6
Courtauld Cl. SE28 138 A1
Pitfield Cres.
Courtauld Rd. N19 92 D1
Courtenay Av. N6 73 H7
Courtenay Av., Har. 67 J1
Courtenay Dr., Beck. 190 D2
Courtenay Gdns., Har. 67 J2
Courtenay Ms. E17 77 H5
Cranbrook Ms.
Courtenay Pl. E17 77 H5
Courtenay Rd. E11 97 F3
Courtenay Rd. E17 77 G4
Courtenay Rd. SE20 171 G7
Courtenay Rd., Wem. 87 G3
Courtenay Rd., Wor.Pk. 197 J3
Courtenay Sq. SE11 34 E4
Courtenay St. SE11 34 E3
Courtenay St. SE11 131 G5
Courtens Ms., Stan. 53 F7
Courtfield W5 105 F5
Castlebar Hill
Courtfield Av., Har. 68 C5
Courtfield Cres., Har. 68 C5
Courtfield Gdns. SW5 30 B1
Courtfield Gdns. SW5 129 E4
Courtfield Gdns. W13 104 D6
Courtfield Ms. SW5 30 C2
Courtfield Ri., W.Wick. 204 D3
Courtfield Rd. SW7 30 B2
Courtfield Rd. SW7 129 E4
Courthill Rd. SE13 154 C4
Courthope Rd. NW3 91 J4
Courthope Rd. SW19 166 B5
Courthope Rd., Grnf. 104 A2
Courthope Vil. SW19 166 B7
Courthouse Rd. N12 56 E6
Courtland Av. E4 63 F2
Courtland Av. NW7 54 D3
Courtland Av. SW16 169 F7
Courtland Av., Ilf. 98 C2
Courtland Dr., Chig. 65 E3
Courtland Gro. SE28 118 D7
Courtland Rd. E6 116 B1
Harrow Rd.
Courtlands, Rich. 146 A4
Courtlands Av. SE12 155 H5
Courtlands Av., Brom. 205 F1
Courtlands Av., Hmptn. 161 F6
Courtlands Av., Rich. 146 B2
Courtlands Dr., Epsom 197 E6
Courtlands Rd., Surb. 182 A7
Courtleet Dr., Erith 159 H1
Courtleigh Gdns. NW11 72 B4
Courtman Rd. N17 59 J7
Courtmead Cl. SE24 151 J6
Courtnell St. W2 108 D6
Courtney Cl. SE19 170 B6
Courtney Cres., Cars. 199 J7
Courtney Pl., Croy. 201 G3
Courtney Rd. N7 93 G5
Bryantwood Rd.
Courtney Rd. SW19 167 H7
Courtney Rd., Croy. 201 G3
Courtney Rd., Houns. 140 D3
Courtney Way, Houns. 140 D2
Courtrai Rd. SE23 153 H6
Courtside N8 74 D6
Courtway, Wdf.Grn. 63 J5
Courtway, The, Wat. 51 E2
Courtyard, The N1 93 F7
Cousin La. EC4 20 B6
Couthurst Rd. SE3 135 H6
Coutts Av., Chess. 195 H5
Coutts Cres. NW5 92 A3
Coval Gdns. SW14 146 B4
Coval La. SW14 146 B4
Coval Rd. SW14 146 B4
Covelees Wall E6 116 D6
Covell Ct. SE8 134 A7
Reginald Sq.
Covent Gdn. WC2 18 B5
Covent Gdn. WC2 111 E7
Coventry Cl. E6 116 C6
Harper Rd.
Coventry Cl. NW6 108 D1
Kilburn High Rd.
Coventry Cross E3 114 C4
Gillender St.
Coventry Rd. E1 113 E4
Coventry Rd. E2 113 E4
Coventry Rd. SE25 188 D4
Coventry Rd., Ilf. 98 E1
Coventry St. W1 17 H6
Coventry St. W1 110 D7
Coverack Cl. N14 42 C6
Coverack Cl., Croy. 189 H7
Coverdale Cl., Stan. 53 E5
Coverdale Gdns., Croy. 202 C3
Park Hill Ri.
Coverdale Rd. N11 58 A6
Coverdale Rd. NW2 90 A7
Coverdale Rd. W12 127 H1
Coverdales, The, Bark. 117 G2
Coverley Cl. E1 21 J1
Coverley Cl. E1 112 D5
Covert, The, Orp. 193 H6
Covert Rd., Ilf. 65 J6
Covert Way, Barn. 41 F2
Coverton Rd. SW17 167 H5
Covet Wd. Cl., Orp. 193 J6
Lockesley Dr.
Covey Cl. SW19 184 E2
Covington Gdns. SW16 169 H7
Covington Way SW16 169 F6
Cow La., Grnf. 104 A2
Cow Leaze E6 116 D6
Cowan Cl. E6 116 B5
Oliver Gdns.
Cowbridge La., Bark. 98 E7
Cowbridge Rd., Har. 69 J4
Cowcross St. EC1 19 G1
Cowcross St. EC1 111 H5
Cowden Rd., Orp. 193 J7
Cowden St. SE6 172 A4
Cowdenbeath Path N1 111 F1
Cowdrey Cl., Enf. 44 B2
Cowdrey Rd. SW19 167 E5
Cowdry Rd. E9 95 H6
Wick Rd.
Cowen Av., Har. 85 J2
Cowgate Rd., Grnf. 104 A2
Cowick Rd. SW17 167 J4
Cowings Mead, Nthlt. 85 E7
Cowland Av., Enf. 45 F4
Cowleaze Rd., Kings.T. 181 H1
Cowley La. E11 96/97 E3
Cathall Rd.
Cowley Pl. NW4 71 J5
Cowley Rd. E11 79 H5
Cowley Rd. SW9 151 G1
Cowley Rd. SW14 146 E3
Cowley Rd. W3 127 F1
Cowley Rd., Ilf. 80 C7
Cowley St. SW1 26 A5
Cowling Cl. W11 128 B1
Wilsham St.
Cowper Av. E6 98 B7
Cowper Av., Sutt. 199 G4
Cowper Cl., Brom. 192 A4
Cowper Cl., Well. 158 A5
Cowper Gdns. N14 42 C6
Cowper Gdns., Wall. 200 C6
Cowper Rd. N14 58 B1
Cowper Rd. N16 94 B5
Cowper Rd. N18 60 D5
Cowper Rd. SW19 167 F6
Cowper Rd. W3 126 D1
Cowper Rd. W7 104 C7
Cowper Rd., Belv. 139 G4
Cowper Rd., Brom. 192 A4
Cowper Rd., Kings.T. 163 J5
Cowper St. EC2 12 C5
Cowper St. EC2 112 A4
Cowper Ter. W10 108 A5
St. Marks Rd.
Cowslip Rd. E18 79 H2
Cowthorpe Rd. SW8 150 D1
Cox La., Chess. 195 J4
Cox La., Epsom 196 B5
Coxe Pl., Har. 68 D4
Coxmount Rd. SE7 136 A5
Cox's Wk. SE21 170 D1
Coxson Pl. SE1 29 F4
Coxwell Rd. SE18 137 G5
Coxwell Rd. SE19 170 B7
Coxwold Path, Chess. 195 H7
Garrison La.
Crab Hill, Beck. 172 D7
Crabbs Cft. Cl., Orp. 207 F5
Ladycroft Way
Crabtree Av., Rom. 82 D4
Crabtree Av., Wem. 105 H2
Crabtree Cl. E2 13 F2
Crabtree Cl. E2 112 C2
Crabtree Ct. E15 96 B5
Clays La.
Crabtree La. SW6 128 A7
Crabtree Manorway N., Belv. 139 J2
Crabtree Manorway S., Belv. 139 J3
Crabtree Wk. SE15 152 C1
Lisford St.
Crace St. NW1 9 H3
Craddock Rd., Enf. 44 C3
Craddock St. NW5 92 A6
Prince of Wales Rd.
Cradley Rd. SE9 175 G1
Craig Gdns. E18 79 F2
Craig Pk. Rd. N18 60 E5
Craig Rd., Rich. 163 F4
Craigen Av., Croy. 203 E1
Craigerne Rd. SE3 135 H7
Craigholm SE18 156 D2
Craigmuir Pk., Wem. 105 J1
Craignair Rd. SW2 151 G7
Craignish Av. SW16 187 F2
Craigs Ct. SW1 26 A1
Craigton Rd. SE9 156 C4
Craigweil Cl., Stan. 53 G5
Craigweil Dr., Stan. 53 G5
Craigwell Av., Felt. 160 A3
Craik Ct. NW6 108 C2
Carlton Vale
Crail Row SE17 36 C2
Cramer St. W1 16 C2
Cramond Cl. W6 128 B6
Crampton Rd. SE20 171 F6
Crampton St. SE17 35 J2
Crampton St. SE17 131 J4
Cranberry Cl., Nthlt. 102 D2
Parkfield Av.
Cranberry La. E16 114 E4
Cranborne Av., Sthl. 123 G4
Cranborne Av., Surb. 196 A3
Cranborne Rd., Bark. 117 G1
Cranborne Waye, Hayes 102 C7
Cranbourn All. WC2 17 J5
Cranbourn Pas. SE16 132/133 E2
Marigold St.
Cranbourn St. WC2 17 J5
Cranbourn St. WC2 110 D7
Cranbourne Av. E11 79 H4
Cranbourne Cl. SW16 187 E3
Cranbourne Dr., Pnr. 66 D5
Cranbourne Gdns. NW11 72 B5
Cranbourne Gdns., Ilf. 81 F3
Cranbourne Rd. E12 98 B5
High St. N.
Cranbourne Rd. E15 96 C4
Cranbourne Rd. N10 74 B2
Cranbrook Cl., Brom. 191 G6
Cranbrook Dr., Twick. 161 H1
Cranbrook Ms. E17 77 J5
Cranbrook Pk. N22 75 F1
Cranbrook Ri., Ilf. 80 C7
Cranbrook Rd. SE8 154 A1
Cranbrook Rd. SW19 166 B7
Cranbrook Rd. W4 127 E5
Cranbrook Rd., Barn. 41 G6
Cranbrook Rd., Bexh. 159 F1
Cranbrook Rd., Houns. 143 F4
Cranbrook Rd., Ilf. 98 D1
Cranbrook Rd., Th.Hth. 187 J2
Cranbrook St. E2 113 G2
Mace St.
Cranbury Rd. SW6 149 E2
Crane Av. W3 106 C7
Crane Av., Islw. 144 D5
Crane Cl., Dag. 101 G6
Crane Cl., Har. 85 J3
Crane Ct. EC4 19 F4
Crane Ct., Epsom 196 C4
Crane Gdns., Hayes 121 J4
Crane Gro. N7 93 G6
Crane Lo. Rd., Houns. 122 B6
Crane Mead SE16 133 G4
Crane Pk. Rd., Twick. 161 H2
Crane Rd., Twick. 162 B1
Crane St. SE10 134 D5
Crane St. SE15 152 C1
Crane Way, Twick. 143 J7
Cranebrook, Twick. 161 J2
Manor Rd.
Craneford Cl., Twick. 144 C7
Craneford Way, Twick. 144 B7
Cranes Dr., Surb. 181 H4
Cranes Pk., Surb. 181 H4
Cranes Pk. Av., Surb. 181 H4
Cranes Pk. Cres., Surb. 181 J4
Cranes Way, Borwd. 38 C5
Cranesbill Cl. NW9 70 D3
Colindale Av.
Craneswater, Hayes 121 J7
Craneswater Pk., Sthl. 123 F5
Cranfield Cl. SE27 169 J3
Dunelm Gro.
Cranfield Dr. NW9 54 E7
Cranfield Rd. SE4 153 J3
Cranfield Row SE1 27 F5
Cranford Av. N13 59 E5
Cranford Av., Stai. 140 B7
Cranford Cl. SW20 183 H1
Cranford Cl., Stai. 140 B7
Canopus Way
Cranford Cotts. E1 113 G7
Cranford St.
Cranford Dr., Hayes 121 J4
Cranford La., Hayes 121 G6
Cranford La. (Cranford), Houns. 141 J1
Cranford La. (Hatton Cross), Houns. 141 J3
Cranford La. (Heston), Houns. 122 D7
Cranford Pk. Rd., Hayes 121 J4
Cranford St. E1 113 G7
Cranford Way N8 75 F5
Cranhurst Rd. NW2 89 J5
Cranleigh Cl. SE20 188 E2
Cranleigh Cl., Bex. 159 H6
Cranleigh Gdns. N21 43 G5
Cranleigh Gdns. SE25 188 B3
Cranleigh Gdns., Bark. 99 G7
Cranleigh Gdns., Har. 69 H5
Cranleigh Gdns., Kings.T. 163 J6
Cranleigh Gdns., Loug. 48 C6
Cranleigh Gdns., Sthl. 103 F6
Cranleigh Gdns., Sutt. 198 E2
Cranleigh Gdns. Ind. Est., Sthl. 103 F6
Cranleigh Ms. SW11 149 H2
Cranleigh Rd. N15 75 J5
Cranleigh Rd. SW19 184 D3

Name	Page	Grid
Cranleigh St. NW1	9	G2
Cranleigh St. NW1	110	C2
Cranley Dene Ct. N10	74	B4
Cranley Dr., Ilf.	81	F7
Cranley Gdns. N10	74	C4
Cranley Gdns. N13	59	F3
Cranley Gdns. SW7	30	D3
Cranley Gdns. SW7	129	F5
Cranley Gdns. SW7	129	F5
Cranley Gdns., Wall.	200	C7
Cranley Ms. SW7	30	D3
Cranley Ms. SW7	129	F5
Cranley Par. SE9	174	B4
Beaconsfield Rd.		
Cranley Pl. SW7	31	E2
Cranley Pl. SW7	129	G4
Cranley Rd. E13	115	H5
Cranley Rd., Ilf.	81	F6
Cranmer Av. W13	125	E3
Cranmer Cl., Mord.	184	A6
Cranmer Cl., Ruis.	84	D1
Cranmer Cl., Stan.	53	F7
Cranmer Ct. SW3	31	H2
Cranmer Ct. SW4	150	D3
Cranmer Ct., Hmptn.	161	H5
Cranmer Rd.		
Cranmer Fm. Cl.,	185	J4
Mitch.		
Cranmer Gdns., Dag.	101	J4
Cranmer Rd. E7	97	H4
Cranmer Rd. SW9	35	F7
Cranmer Rd. SW9	131	G7
Cranmer Rd., Croy.	201	H3
Cranmer Rd., Edg.	54	B3
Cranmer Rd., Hmptn.	161	H5
Cranmer Rd.,	163	H5
Kings.T.		
Cranmer Rd., Mitch.	185	J4
Cranmer Ter. SW17	167	G5
Cranmore Av., Islw.	123	J7
Cranmore Rd., Brom.	173	E3
Cranmore Rd., Chis.	174	C5
Cranmore Way N10	74	C4
Cranston Est. N1	12	C2
Cranston Est. N1	112	A2
Cranston Gdns. E4	62	B5
Cranston Rd. SE23	171	H1
Cranswick Rd. SE16	133	E5
Crantock Rd. SE6	172	B2
Cranwell Cl. E3	114	B4
Cranwell Rd., Houns.	140	E2
Cranwich Av. N21	44	A7
Cranwich Rd. N16	76	A7
Cranwood St. EC1	12	B4
Cranwood St. EC1	112	A3
Cranworth Cres. E4	62	D1
Cranworth Gdns.	151	G1
SW9		
Craster Rd. SW2	151	F7
Crathie Rd. SE12	155	H6
Cravan Av., Felt.	160	A2
Craven Av. W5	105	F7
Craven Av., Sthl.	103	F5
Craven Cl., Hayes	102	A6
Craven Gdns. SW19	166	D5
Craven Gdns., Bark.	117	H2
Craven Gdns., Ilf.	81	G2
Craven Hill W2	14	D5
Craven Hill W2	109	F7
Craven Hill Gdns. W2	14	C5
Craven Hill Gdns. W2	109	F7
Craven Hill Ms. W2	14	D5
Craven Hill Ms. W2	109	F7
Craven Ms. SW11	150	A3
Taybridge Rd.		
Craven Pk. NW10	106	E1
Craven Pk. Ms.	106	E1
NW10		
Craven Pk. Rd. N15	76	C6
Craven Pk. Rd. NW10	107	E1
Craven Pas. WC2	26	A1
Craven Pas. WC2	130	E1
Craven Rd. NW10	106	D1
Craven Rd. W2	14	D5
Craven Rd. W2	109	F7
Craven Rd. W5	105	F7
Craven Rd., Croy.	202	E1
Craven Rd., Kings.T.	181	J1
Craven St. WC2	26	A1
Craven St. WC2	130	E1
Craven Ter. W2	14	D5
Craven Ter. W2	109	F7
Craven Wk. N16	76	D7
Crawford Av., Wem.	87	G5
Crawford Cl., Islw.	144	B2
Crawford Est. SE5	151	J2
Crawford Gdns. N13	59	H3
Crawford Gdns.,	103	F3
Nthlt.		
Crawford Ms. W1	15	J2
Crawford Pl. W1	15	H3
Crawford Pl. W1	109	H6
Crawford Rd. SE5	151	J1
Crawford St. W1	15	J2
Crawford St. W1	109	J5
Crawley Rd. E10	96	B1
Crawley Rd. N22	75	J2
Crawley Rd., Enf.	44	B7
Crawshay Ct. SW9	151	G1
Eythorne Rd.		
Crawthew Gro. SE22	152	C4
Cray Av., Belv.	139	G6
Cray Rd., Sid.	176	C7
Craybrooke Rd., Sid.	176	B4
Craybury End SE9	175	F2
Crayford Cl. E6	116	B5
Neatscourt Rd.		
Crayford Rd. N7	92	D4
Crayke Hill, Chess.	195	H7
Crealock Gro.,	63	F5
Wdf.Grn.		
Crealock St. SW18	149	E6
Creasy Est. SE1	28	D6
Creasy Est. SE1	132	B3
Crebor St. SE22	152	D6
Credenhall Dr., Brom.	206	C1
Credenhill St. SW16	168	C6
Crediton Hill NW6	90	E5
Crediton Rd. E16	115	G6
Pacific Rd.		
Crediton Rd. NW10	108	A1
Crediton Way, Esher	194	D6
Credon Rd. E13	115	J2
Credon Rd. SE16	133	E5
Creechurch La. EC3	21	E4
Creechurch La. EC3	112	B6
Creechurch Pl. EC3	21	E4
Creed Ct. EC4	111	H6
Ludgate Hill		
Creed La. EC4	19	H4
Creek, The, Sun.	178	A5
Creek Rd. SE8	134	A6
Creek Rd. SE10	134	A6
Creek Rd., Bark.	117	J3
Creek Rd., E.Mol.	180	B4
Creekside SE8	134	B7
Creeland Gro. SE6	171	J1
Catford Hill		
Crefeld Cl. W6	148	A6
Creffield Rd. W3	105	J7
Creffield Rd. W5	105	J7
Creighton Av. E6	116	A2
Creighton Av. N2	73	H3
Creighton Av. N10	73	H3
Creighton Cl. W12	107	H7
Bloemfontein Rd.		
Creighton Rd. N17	60	B7
Creighton Rd. NW6	108	A2
Creighton Rd. W5	125	G3
Cremer St. E2	13	F2
Cremer St. E2	112	C2
Cremorne Est. SW10	31	E7
Cremorne Rd. SW10	129	F7
Crescent EC3	21	F5
Crescent, The E17	77	H5
Crescent, The N11	57	J4
Crescent, The NW2	89	H3
Crescent, The SW13	147	F2
Crescent, The SW19	166	D3
Crescent, The W3	106	E6
Crescent, The, Barn.	40	E3
Crescent, The, Beck.	190	A1
Crescent, The, Bex.	158	C7
Crescent, The, Croy.	188	A5
Crescent, The, Har.	86	A1
Crescent, The, Hayes	121	F7
Crescent, The, Ilf.	80	D6
Crescent, The, Loug.	48	A5
Crescent, The, N.Mal.	182	C2
Crescent, The, Sid.	175	J4
Crescent, The, Sthl.	123	F2
Crescent, The, Surb.	181	H5
Crescent, The, Sutt.	199	G4
Crescent, The, Wem.	86	E2
Crescent, The,	179	G4
W.Mol.		
Crescent, The,	190	E6
W.Wick.		
Crescent Dr., Surb.	181	G5
Crescent Dr., Orp.	193	E6
Crescent Gdns.	166	D3
SW19		
Crescent Gdns., Ruis.	66	B6
Crescent Gro. SW4	150	C4
Crescent Gro., Mitch.	185	H4
Crescent La. SW4	150	D5
Crescent Ms. N22	74/75	E1
Palace Gates Rd.		
Crescent Pl. SW3	31	G1
Crescent Pl. SW3	129	H4
Crescent Ri. N22	74	D1
Crescent Ri., Barn.	41	H5
Crescent Rd. E4	47	E7
Crescent Rd. E6	116	A1
Crescent Rd. E10	96	B2
Crescent Rd. E13	115	G1
Crescent Rd. E18	79	J2
Crescent Rd. N3	72	C1
Crescent Rd. N8	74	D7
Crescent Rd. N9	60	D1
Crescent Rd. N11	57	J4
Crescent Rd. N15	75	H3
Carlingford Rd.		
Crescent Rd. N22	74	D1
Crescent Rd. SE18	136	E5
Crescent Rd. SW20	184	A1
Crescent Rd., Barn.	41	H5
Crescent Rd., Beck.	190	B2
Crescent Rd., Brom.	173	G7
Crescent Rd., Dag.	101	H4
Crescent Rd., Enf.	43	H3
Crescent Rd.,	164	A7
Kings.T.		
Crescent Rd., Sid.	175	J3
Crescent Row EC1	11	J6
Crescent Stables	148	B4
SW15		
Upper Richmond Rd.		
Crescent St. N1	93	F7
Crescent Vw., Loug.	48	A6
Crescent Way N12	57	H6
Crescent Way SE4	154	A3
Crescent Way SW16	169	F7
Crescent Way, Orp.	207	H5
Crescent Wd. Rd.	170	D3
SE26		
Cresford Rd. SW6	148	E1
Crespigny Rd. NW4	71	H6
Cressage Cl., Sthl.	103	G4
Cresset Rd. E9	95	F6
Cresset St. SW4	150	D3
Cressfield Cl. NW5	92	A5
Cressida Rd. N19	92	C1
Cressingham Gro.,	199	F4
Sutt.		
Cressingham Rd.	154	C3
SE13		
Cressingham Rd.,	54	D6
Edg.		
Cressington Cl. N16	94	B5
Wordsworth Rd.		
Cresswell Gdns. SW5	30	C3
Cresswell Gdns.	129	F5
SW5		
Cresswell Pk. SE3	155	F3
Cresswell Pl. SW10	30	C3
Cresswell Pl. SW10	129	F5
Cresswell Rd. SE25	188	D4
Cresswell Rd., Felt.	160	E4
Cresswell Rd., Twick.	145	G6
Cresswell Way N21	43	G7
Cressy Ct. E1	113	F5
Cressy Pl.		
Cressy Ct. W6	127	H3
Cressy Pl. E1	113	F5
Cressy Rd. NW3	91	J4
Crest, The N13	59	G4
Crest, The NW4	71	J5
Crest, The, Surb.	182	A5
Crest Gdns., Ruis.	84	C3
Crest Rd. NW2	89	F3
Crest Rd., Brom.	191	F7
Crest Rd., S.Croy.	202	E7
Crest Vw., Pnr.	66	D4
Crest Vw. Dr., Orp.	193	E5
Crestbrook Av. N13	59	H3
Crestbrook Pl. N13	59	H3
Crestfield St. WC1	10	B3
Crestfield St. WC1	111	E3
Creston Way, Wor.Pk.	198	A1
Crestway SW15	147	H6
Crestwood Way,	143	F5
Houns.		
Creswick Rd. W3	106	B7
Creswick Wk. NW11	72	C4
Creton St. SE18	136	D3
Crewdson Rd. SW9	131	G7
Crewe Pl. NW10	107	F3
Crews St. E14	134	A4
Crewys Rd. NW2	90	C2
Crewys Rd. SE15	153	E2
Crichton Av., Wall.	200	D5
Crichton Rd., Cars.	199	J6
Cricket Grn., Mitch.	185	J3
Cricket Grd. Rd.,	192	E1
Chis.		
Cricket La., Beck.	171	H6
Cricketers Arms Rd.,	43	J2
Enf.		
Cricketers Cl. N14	42	C7
Cricketers Cl.,	195	G4
Chess.		
Cricketers Ct. SE11	35	G2
Cricketers Ct. SE11	131	H4
Cricketers Ms.	148/149	E5
SW18		
East Hill		
Cricketers Ter., Cars.	199	H3
Wrythe La.		
Cricketfield Rd. E5	95	E4
Cricklade Av. SW2	169	E2
Cricklewood Bdy.	90	A3
NW2		
Cricklewood La. NW2	90	A4
Cricklewood Trd. Est.	90	B3
NW2		
Cridland St. E15	115	F1
Church St.		
Crieff Ct., Tedd.	163	F7
Crieff Rd. SW18	149	F6
Criffel Av. SW2	168	D2
Crimscott St. SE1	29	E6
Crimscott St. SE1	132	B3
Crimsworth Rd. SW8	150	D1
Crinan St. N1	10	B1
Crinan St. N1	111	E2
Cringle St. SW8	33	F7
Cringle St. SW8	130	C7
Cripplegate St. EC2	19	J1
Cripps Grn., Hayes	102	B4
Stratford Rd.		
Crisp Rd. W6	127	J5
Crispe Ho., Bark.	117	G2
Dovehouse Mead		
Crispen Rd., Felt.	160	E4
Crispian Cl. NW10	89	E4
Crispin Cl., Croy.	200/201	E2
Harrington Cl.		
Crispin Cres., Croy.	200	D3
Crispin Rd., Edg.	54	C6
Crispin St. E1	21	F2
Crispin St. E1	112	C5
Cristowe Rd. SW6	148	C2
Criterion Ms. N19	92	D2
Crockerton Rd. SW17	167	J2
Crockham Way SE9	174	D4
Crocus Cl., Croy.	203	G1
Cornflower La.		
Crocus Fld., Barn.	40	C6
Croft, The E4	62	E2
Croft, The NW10	107	F2
Croft, The W5	105	H5
Croft, The, Barn.	40	A4
Croft, The, Houns.	123	E6
Croft, The, Loug.	48	D2
Croft, The, Pnr.	67	F7
Rayners La.		
Croft, The, Ruis.	84	C4
Croft, The, Wem.	87	F5
Croft Av., W.Wick.	204	C1
Croft Cl. NW7	54	E3
Croft Cl., Belv.	139	F5
Croft Cl., Chis.	174	C4
Croft Cl., Hayes	121	F7
Croft End Cl., Chess.	195	J3
Ashcroft Rd.		
Croft Gdns. W7	124	D2
Croft Lo. Cl., Wdf.Grn.	63	H6
Croft Ms. N12	57	F3
Croft Rd. SW16	187	G1
Croft Rd. SW19	167	F7
Croft Rd., Brom.	173	G6
Croft Rd., Enf.	45	H1
Croft Rd., Sutt.	199	H5
Croft St. SE8	133	H4
Croft Way NW3	90	D4
Ferncroft Av.		
Croft Way, Sid.	175	H3
Croftdown Rd. NW5	92	A3
Crofters Cl., Islw.	144	A5
Ploughmans End		
Crofters Ct. SE8	133	H4
Croft St.		
Crofters Way NW1	110	D1
Crofton Av. W4	126	D7
Crofton Av., Bex.	158	D7
Crofton Av., Orp.	207	F2
Crofton Gro. E4	62	D4
Crofton La., Orp.	193	H7
Crofton Pk. Rd. SE4	153	J6
Crofton Rd. E13	115	H4
Crofton Rd. SE5	152	B1
Crofton Rd., Orp.	206	D3
Crofton Ter. E5	95	H5
Studley Cl.		
Crofton Ter., Rich.	145	J4
Crofton Way, Barn.	40/41	E6
Wycherley Cres.		
Crofton Way, Enf.	43	G2
Croftongate Way SE4	153	H5
Crofts La. N22	59	G7
Glendale Av.		
Crofts Rd., Har.	68	D6
Crofts St. E1	21	H6
Croftside SE25	188	D3
Sunny Bank		
Croftway NW3	90	D4
Croftway, Rich.	163	E3
Crogsland Rd. NW1	92	A7
Croham Cl., S.Croy.	202	B6
Croham Manor Rd.,	202	B7
S.Croy.		

Name	Page	Grid
Croham Mt., S.Croy.	202	B7
Croham Pk. Av., S.Croy.	202	C5
Croham Rd., S.Croy.	202	B5
Croham Valley Rd., S.Croy.	202	C6
Croindene Rd. SW16	187	E1
Cromartie Rd. N19	74	D7
Cromarty Rd., Edg.	54	B2
Crombie Cl., Ilf.	80	C5
Crombie Rd., Sid.	175	G1
Cromer Pl., Orp.	207	G1
Andover Rd.		
Cromer Rd. E10	78	D6
James La.		
Cromer Rd. N17	76	D2
Cromer Rd. SE25	188	E3
Cromer Rd. SW17	168	A6
Cromer Rd., Barn.	41	F4
Cromer Rd., Houns.	140	D3
Cromer Rd., Rom.	83	J6
Cromer Rd. (Chadwell Heath), Rom.	83	E6
Cromer Rd., Wdf.Grn.	63	G4
Cromer Rd. W., Houns.	140	D3
Cromer St. WC1	10	B4
Cromer St. WC1	110	E3
Cromer Ter. E8	94	D5
Ferncliff Rd.		
Cromer Vil. Rd. SW18	148	C6
Cromford Cl., Orp.	207	H3
Cromford Path E5	95	G4
Overbury St.		
Cromford Rd. SW18	148	D5
Cromford Way, N.Mal.	182	D1
Cromlix Cl., Chis.	192	E2
Crompton St. W2	6	E6
Crompton St. W2	109	G4
Cromwell Av. N6	92	B1
Cromwell Av. W6	127	H5
Cromwell Av., Brom.	191	H4
Cromwell Av., N.Mal.	183	F5
Cromwell Cl. N2	73	G4
Cromwell Cl. W3	126	C1
High St.		
Cromwell Cl., Brom.	191	H4
Cromwell Cres. SW5	128	D4
Cromwell Gdns. SW7	23	F6
Cromwell Gdns. SW7	129	G3
Cromwell Gro. W6	127	J3
Cromwell Ind. Est. E10	95	H1
Cromwell Ms. SW7	31	F1
Cromwell Ms. SW7	129	G4
Cromwell Pl. N6	92	B1
Cromwell Pl. SW7	31	F1
Cromwell Pl. SW7	129	G4
Cromwell Pl. SW14	146	C3
Cromwell Pl. W3	126	C1
Grove Pl.		
Cromwell Rd. E7	97	J7
Cromwell Rd. E17	78	C5
Cromwell Rd. N3	73	F1
Cromwell Rd. N10	58	A7
Cromwell Rd. SW5	128	E4
Cromwell Rd. SW7	30	E1
Cromwell Rd. SW7	128	E4
Cromwell Rd. SW9	151	H1
Cromwell Rd. SW19	166	D5
Cromwell Rd., Beck.	189	H2
Cromwell Rd., Croy.	188	A7
Cromwell Rd., Felt.	160	B1
Cromwell Rd., Houns.	143	G4
Cromwell Rd., Kings.T.	181	H1
Cromwell Rd., Tedd.	162	D6
Cromwell Rd., Wem.	105	H2
Cromwell Rd., Wor.Pk.	196	D3
Cromwell St., Houns.	143	G4
Crondace Rd. SW6	148	D1
Crondall St. N1	12	C2
Crondall St. N1	112	A2
Cronin St. SE15	132	C7
Crook Log, Bexh.	158	D3
Crooke Rd. SE8	133	H5
Crooked Billet SW19	165	J6
Woodhayes Rd.		
Crooked Billet Roundabout E17	62	A7
Crooked Billet Yd. E2	112	B3
Kingsland Rd.		
Crooked Usage N3	72	B3
Crookham Rd. SW6	148	C1
Crookston Rd. SE9	156	D3
Croombs Rd. E16	115	J5
Crooms Hill SE10	134	D7
Crooms Hill Gro. SE10	134	C7
Cropley Ct. N1	112	A2
Cropley St.		
Cropley St. N1	12	B1
Cropley St. N1	112	A2
Croppath Rd., Dag.	101	G4
Cropthorne Ct. W9	6	D4
Crosby Cl., Felt.	160	E4
Crosby Ct. SE1	28	B3
Crosby Rd. E7	97	G6
Crosby Rd., Dag.	119	H2
Crosby Row SE1	28	B4
Crosby Row SE1	132	A2
Crosby Sq. EC3	20	D4
Crosby Wk. E8	94	C6
Laurel St.		
Crosby Wk. SW2	151	G7
Crosland Pl. SW11	150	A3
Taybridge Rd.		
Cross Av. SE10	134	D6
Cross Cl. SE15	152/153	E1
Gordon Rd.		
Cross Deep, Twick.	162	C2
Cross Deep Gdns., Twick.	162	C2
Cross Keys Cl. N9	60	D2
Balham Rd.		
Cross Keys Cl. W1	16	C2
Cross Keys Sq. EC1	19	J2
Cross Lances Rd., Houns.	143	H4
Cross La. EC3	20	D6
Cross La. N8	75	F4
Cross La., Bex.	159	F7
Cross Rd. E4	62	E1
Cross Rd. N11	58	B5
Cross Rd. N22	59	G7
Cross Rd. SE5	152	B2
Cross Rd. SW19	166	D7
Cross Rd., Brom.	206	B2
Cross Rd., Croy.	202	A1
Cross Rd., Enf.	44	B4
Cross Rd., Felt.	160	E4
Cross Rd., Har.	68	A4
Cross Rd. (South Harrow), Har.	85	H3
Cross Rd. (Wealdstone), Har.	68	D2
Cross Rd., Kings.T.	163	J7
Cross Rd., Rom.	83	G3
Cross Rd. I (Chadwell Heath), Rom.	82	C7
Cross Rd., Sid.	176	B4
Sidcup Hill		
Cross Rd., Sutt.	199	G5
Cross Rd., Wdf.Grn.	64	C6
Cross Rds., Loug.	47	H2
Cross St. N1	111	H1
Cross St. SW13	147	E2
Cross St., Hmptn.	161	J5
Cross Way, The, Har.	68	B2
Crossbow Rd., Chig.	65	J5
Crossbrook Rd. SE3	156	B2
Crossfield Rd. N17	75	J3
Crossfield Rd. NW3	91	G7
Crossfield St. SE8	134	A7
Crossfields, Loug.	48	E5
Crossford St. SW9	151	F2
Crossgate, Edg.	54	A3
Crossgate, Grnf.	87	E6
Crossland Rd., Th.Hth.	187	H6
Crosslands Av. W5	125	J1
Crosslands Av., Sthl.	123	F5
Crosslands Rd., Epsom	196	D6
Crosslet St. SE17	36	C1
Crosslet Vale SE10	154	B1
Blackheath Rd.		
Crossley St. N7	93	G6
Crossmead SE9	174	C1
Crossmead Av., Grnf.	103	G3
Crossmount Ho. SE5	35	J7
Crossness La. SE28	118	D7
Crossness Rd., Bark.	117	J3
Crossthwaite Av. SE5	152	A4
Crosswall EC3	21	F5
Crosswall EC3	112	C7
Crossway N12	57	G6
Crossway N16	94	B5
Crossway NW9	71	F4
Crossway SE28	118	C6
Crossway SW20	183	J4
Crossway W13	104	D4
Crossway, Dag.	100	C3
Crossway, Enf.	44	B7
Crossway, Hayes	122	A1
Crossway, Orp.	193	G4
Crossway, Pnr.	66	B2
Crossway, Ruis.	84	C4
Crossway, Wdf.Grn.	63	J4
Crossway, The N22	59	H7
Crossway, The SE9	174	A2
Crossways N21	43	J6
Crossways, S.Croy.	203	H7
Crossways, The, Houns.	123	F7
Crossways, The, Wem.	88	A2
Crossways Rd., Beck.	190	A4
Crossways Rd., Mitch.	186	B3
Croston St. E8	112	D1
Crothall Cl. N13	59	F3
Crouch Av., Bark.	118	B2
Crouch Cl., Beck.	172	A6
Abbey La.		
Crouch Cft. SE9	174	D3
Crouch End Hill N8	74	D7
Crouch Hall Rd. N8	74	D6
Crouch Hill N4	74	E6
Crouch Hill N8	74	E6
Crouch Rd. NW10	88	D7
Crouchman's Cl. SE26	170	C3
Crow La., Rom.	83	F7
Crowborough Path, Wat.	50	D4
Prestwick Rd.		
Crowborough Rd. SW17	168	A6
Crowden Way SE28	118	C7
Crowder St. E1	112	E7
Crowfoot Cl. E9	95	J5
Lee Conservancy Rd.		
Crowhurst Cl. SW9	151	G2
Crowland Av., Hayes	121	H4
Crowland Gdns. N14	42	E7
Crowland Rd. N15	76	C5
Crowland Rd., Th.Hth.	188	A4
Crowland Ter. N1	94	A7
Crowland Wk., Mord.	185	E6
Crowlands Av., Rom.	83	H6
Crowley Cres., Croy.	201	G5
Crowline Wk. N1	94	A6
Clephane Rd.		
Crowmarsh Gdns. SE23	153	F7
Tyson Rd.		
Crown Arc., Kings.T.	181	G2
Union St.		
Crown Cl. E3	114	A1
Crown Cl. NW6	90	E6
Crown Cl. NW7	55	F2
Crown Cl., Hayes	121	J2
Station Rd.		
Crown Cl., Walt.	178	C7
Crown Ct. EC2	20	A4
Crown Ct. SE12	155	H6
Crown Ct. WC2	18	B4
Crown Ct., Brom.	192	A5
Victoria Rd.		
Crown Dale SE19	169	H6
Crown Hill, Croy.	201	J2
Church St.		
Crown La. N14	58	C1
Crown La. SW16	169	G5
Crown La., Brom.	192	A5
Crown La., Chis.	193	F1
Crown La., Mord.	184	E3
Crown La. Gdns. SW16	169	G5
Crown La.		
Crown La. Spur, Brom.	192	A6
Crown Ms. E13	115	J1
Waghorn Rd.		
Crown Ms. W6	127	G4
Crown Office Row EC4	19	E5
Crown Pas. SW1	25	G2
Crown Pas. SW1	130	C1
Crown Pas., Kings.T.	181	G2
Church St.		
Crown Pl. EC2	20	D1
Crown Pl. EC2	112	B5
Crown Pl. NW5	92	B6
Kentish Town Rd.		
Crown Pt. Par. SE19	169	H6
Beulah Hill		
Crown Rd. N10	58	A7
Crown Rd., Borwd.	38	A1
Crown Rd., Enf.	44	E4
Crown Rd., Ilf.	81	G4
Crown Rd., Mord.	184	E4
Crown Rd., N.Mal.	182	C2
Crown Rd., Ruis.	84	D5
Crown Rd., Sutt.	198	E4
Crown Rd., Twick.	145	E6
Crown St. SE5	36	A7
Crown St. SE5	131	J7
Crown St. W3	126	B1
Crown St., Dag.	101	J6
Crown St., Har.	86	A1
Crown Ter., Rich.	145	J4
Crown Wk., Wem.	87	J3
Crown Way, West Dr.	120	C1
Crown Wds. La. SE9	157	E2
Crown Wds. La. SE18	157	E2
Crown Wds. Way SE9	157	G5
Crown Wks. E2	112/113	E2
Temple St.		
Crown Yd., Houns.	143	J3
High St.		
Crowndale Rd. NW1	9	F1
Crowndale Rd. NW1	110	C2
Crownfield Av., Ilf.	81	H5
Crownfield Rd. E15	96	D5
Crownhill Rd. NW10	107	F1
Crownhill Rd., Wdf.Grn.	64	B7
Crownmead Way, Rom.	83	H4
Crownstone Rd. SW2	151	G5
Crowntree Cl., Islw.	124	C5
Crows Rd. E15	114	D3
Crowshott Av., Stan.	69	F1
Crowther Av., Brent.	125	H4
Crowther Rd. SE25	188	D4
Crowthorne Cl. SW18	166	C1
Crowthorne Rd. W10	108	A6
Croxden Cl., Edg.	69	J3
Croxden Wk., Mord.	185	F6
Croxford Gdns. N22	59	H7
Croxley Rd. W9	108	C3
Croxted Cl. SE21	151	J7
Croxted Rd. SE21	151	J7
Croxted Rd. SE24	151	J7
Croyde Av., Grnf.	103	J3
Croyde Av., Hayes	121	H4
Croyde Cl., Sid.	157	G7
Croydon Flyover, Croy.	201	H4
Croydon Gro., Croy.	201	H1
Croydon Rd. E13	115	F4
Croydon Rd. SE20	188	E2
Croydon Rd., Beck.	189	H4
Croydon Rd., Brom.	205	F3
Croydon Rd., Croy.	200	B4
Croydon Rd., Houns.	140	E2
Croydon Rd., Kes.	205	J3
Croydon Rd., Mitch.	186	A4
Croydon Rd., Wall.	200	B4
Croydon Rd., W.Wick.	204	E3
Croyland Rd. N9	60	D1
Croylands Dr., Surb.	181	H7
Croysdale Av., Sun.	178	A3
Crozier Ter. E9	95	G5
Crucible Cl., Rom.	82	B6
Cruden Ho. SE17	35	G6
Cruden St. N1	111	H1
Cruikshank Rd. E15	97	E4
Cruikshank St. WC1	10	E3
Cruikshank St. WC1	111	G3
Crummock Gdns. NW9	70	E5
Crumpsall St. SE2	138	C4
Crundale Av. NW9	70	A5
Crunden Rd., S.Croy.	202	A7
Crusader Gdns., Croy.	202	B3
Cotelands		
Crusoe Ms. N16	94	A2
Crusoe Rd., Mitch.	167	J7
Crutched Friars EC3	21	E5
Crutched Friars EC3	112	B7
Crutchley Rd. SE6	173	E2
Crystal Ct. SE19	170	C5
College Rd.		
Crystal Ho. SE18	137	J5
Spinel Cl.		
Crystal Palace Par. SE19	170	C6
Crystal Palace Pk. Rd. SE26	170	D5
Crystal Palace Rd. SE22	152	D4
Crystal Palace Sta. Rd. SE19	170	D6
Anerley Hill		
Crystal Ter. SE19	170	A6
Crystal Vw. Ct., Brom.	172	D4
Winlaton Rd.		
Crystal Way, Dag.	100	C1
Crystal Way, Har.	68	C5
Cuba Dr., Enf.	45	F2
Cuba St. E14	134	A2
Cubitt Sq., Sthl.	123	J2
Windmill Av.		
Cubitt Steps E14	134	A1
Cabot Sq.		
Cubitt St. WC1	10	C4
Cubitt St. WC1	111	F3
Cubitt St., Croy.	201	F5
Cubitt Ter. SW4	150	C3

Cubitts Yd. WC2	18	**B5**
Cuckoo Av. W7	104	B4
Cuckoo Dene W7	104	A5
Cuckoo Hall La. N9	45	F7
Cuckoo Hill, Pnr.	66	C3
Cuckoo Hill Dr., Pnr.	66	C3
Cuckoo Hill Rd., Pnr.	66	C4
Cuckoo La. W7	104	B7
Cudas Cl., Epsom	197	F4
Cuddington Av., Wor.Pk.	197	F3
Cudham St. SE6	154	C7
Cudworth St. E1	113	E4
Cuff Cres. SE9	156	A6
Cuff Pt. E2	13	**F3**
Cuff Pt. E2	112	C3
Culford Gdns. SW3	32	**A2**
Culford Gdns. SW3	129	J4
Culford Gro. N1	94	B6
Culford Ms. N1	94	B6
Culford Rd.		
Culford Rd. N1	94	B7
Culgaith Gdns., Enf.	42	E4
Cullen Way NW10	106	C4
Culling Rd. SE16	133	F3
Lower Rd.		
Cullington Cl., Har.	68	D4
Cullingworth Rd. NW10	89	G5
Culloden Cl. SE16	37	**J4**
Culloden Cl. SE16	132	D5
Culloden Rd., Enf.	43	H2
Culloden St. E14	114	C6
Cullum St. EC3	20	**D5**
Culmington Rd. W13	125	F2
Culmore Cross SW12	168	B1
Culmore Rd. SE15	133	E7
Culmstock Rd. SW11	150	A5
Culpeper Cl., Ilf.	65	E6
Culross Cl. N15	75	J4
Culross St. W1	16	**B6**
Culross St. W1	110	A7
Culsac Rd., Surb.	195	H2
Culver Gro., Stan.	69	F2
Culverden Rd. SW12	168	C2
Culverden Rd., Wat.	50	B3
Culverhouse Gdns. SW16	169	F3
Culverlands Cl., Stan.	52	E4
Culverley Rd. SE6	172	B1
Culvers Av., Cars.	199	J2
Culvers Retreat, Cars.	199	J1
Culvers Way, Cars.	199	J2
Culverstone Cl., Brom.	191	F6
Culvert Pl. SW11	150	A2
Culvert Rd. N15	76	B5
Culvert Rd. SW11	149	J2
Culworth St. NW8	7	**G2**
Cumberland Av. NW10	106	B3
Cumberland Av., Well.	157	H3
Cumberland Cl. E8	94	C6
Cumberland Cl. SW20	166	A7
Lansdowne Rd.		
Cumberland Cl., Ilf.	81	F1
Carrick Dr.		
Cumberland Cl., Twick.	144/145	E6
Westmorland Cl.		
Cumberland Cres. W14	128	B4
Cumberland Dr., Bexh.	138	E7
Cumberland Dr., Chess.	195	J3
Cumberland Dr., Esher	194	D2
Cumberland Gdns. NW4	72	B2
Cumberland Gdns. WC1	10	**D3**
Cumberland Gate W1	15	**J5**
Cumberland Gate W1	109	J7
Cumberland Mkt. NW1	9	**E3**
Cumberland Mkt. NW1	110	B3
Cumberland Mkt. Est. NW1	9	**E3**
Cumberland Mills Sq. E14	134	D5
Saunders Ness Rd.		
Cumberland Pk. W3	107	G3
Cumberland Pl. NW1	8	**D3**
Cumberland Pl. SE6	173	F1
Cumberland Pl., Sun.	178	A4
Cumberland Rd. E12	98	A4
Cumberland Rd. E13	115	H5
Cumberland Rd. E17	77	H2
Cumberland Rd. N9	61	F1

Cumberland Rd. N22	75	F2
Cumberland Rd. SE25	189	E6
Cumberland Rd. SW13	147	F1
Cumberland Rd. W3	106	C7
Cumberland Rd. W7	124	C2
Cumberland Rd., Brom.	191	E4
Cumberland Rd., Har.	67	H5
Cumberland Rd., Rich.	126	A7
Cumberland Rd., Stan.	69	J3
Cumberland St. SW1	32	**E3**
Cumberland St. SW1	130	B5
Cumberland Ter. NW1	8	**D3**
Cumberland Ter. Ms. NW1	8	**D2**
Cumberland Vil. W3	106	C7
Cumberland Rd.		
Cumberlow Av. SE25	188	C3
Cumberton Rd. N17	76	A1
Cumbrae Gdns., Surb.	195	F1
Cumbrian Gdns. NW2	90	A2
Cumming St. N1	10	**C2**
Cumming St. N1	111	F2
Cumnor Gdns., Epsom	197	G6
Cumnor Rd., Sutt.	199	F6
Cunard Cres. N21	44	A6
Cunard Pl. EC3	20	**E4**
Cunard Rd. NW10	106	D3
Cunard St. SE5	132	B6
Albany Rd.		
Cunard Wk. SE16	133	H4
Cundy Rd. E16	115	J6
Cundy St. SW1	32	**C2**
Cundy St. SW1	130	A4
Cundy St. Est. SW1	32	**C2**
Cunliffe Rd., Epsom	197	F4
Cunliffe St. SW16	168	C6
Cunningham Cl., Rom.	82	C5
Cunningham Cl., W.Wick.	204	B2
Cunningham Pk., Har.	67	J5
Cunningham Pl. NW8	7	**E5**
Cunningham Pl. NW8	109	G4
Cunningham Rd. N15	76	D4
Cupar Rd. SW11	150	A1
Cupola Cl., Brom.	173	H5
Cureton St. SW1	33	**J2**
Cureton St. SW1	130	D4
Curfew Ho., Bark.	117	F1
St. Ann's		
Curlew Cl. SE28	118	D7
Curlew Ct., Surb.	195	J3
Curlew St. SE1	29	**F3**
Curlew St. SE1	132	C2
Curlew Way, Hayes	102	D5
Curnick's La. SE27	169	J4
Chapel Rd.		
Curnock Est. NW1	110	C1
Plender St.		
Curran Av., Sid.	157	J5
Curran Av., Wall.	200	A3
Currey Rd., Grnf.	86	A6
Curricle St. W3	126	E1
Currie Hill Cl. SW19	166	C4
Curry Ri. NW7	56	A6
Cursitor St. EC4	18	**E3**
Cursitor St. EC4	111	G6
Curtain Pl. EC2	112	B3
Curtain Rd.		
Curtain Rd. EC2	12	**D6**
Curtain Rd. EC2	112	B4
Curthwaite Gdns., Enf.	42	D4
Curtis Dr. W3	106	D6
Curtis Fld. Rd. SW16	169	F4
Curtis La., Wem.	87	H6
Montrose Cres.		
Curtis Rd., Epsom	196	C4
Curtis Rd., Houns.	143	F7
Curtis St. SE1	37	**F1**
Curtis St. SE1	132	C4
Curtis Way SE1	37	**F1**
Curtis Way SE1	132	C4
Curtis Way SE28	118	B7
Tawney Rd.		
Curve, The W12	107	G7
Curwen Av. E7	97	H4
Woodford Rd.		
Curwen Rd. W12	127	G2
Curzon Av., Enf.	45	G5
Curzon Av., Stan.	68	D1
Curzon Cl., Orp.	207	G4
Curzon Cres. NW10	89	F7
Curzon Cres., Bark.	117	J2
Curzon Gate W1	24	**C2**
Curzon Gate W1	130	A1

Curzon Pl. W1	24	**C2**
Curzon Pl., Pnr.	66	C5
Curzon Rd. N10	74	B2
Curzon Rd. W5	105	E4
Curzon Rd., Th.Hth.	187	G6
Curzon St. W1	24	**C2**
Curzon St. W1	130	A1
Cusack Cl., Twick.	162	C4
Waldegrave Rd.		
Custom Ho. Reach SE16	133	J2
Custom Ho. Wk. EC3	20	**D6**
Custom Ho. Wk. EC3	112	B7
Cut, The SE1	27	**F3**
Cut, The SE1	131	G2
Cutcombe Rd. SE5	151	J2
Cuthberga St., Bark.	99	F7
George St.		
Cuthbert Gdns. SE25	188	B3
Cuthbert Rd. E17	78	C3
Cuthbert Rd. N18	60	D5
Fairfield Rd.		
Cuthbert Rd., Croy.	201	H2
Cuthbert St. W2	15	**E1**
Cuthbert St. W2	109	G4
Cuthill Wk. SE5	152	A1
Cutler St. E1	21	**E3**
Cutler St. E1	112	B6
Cutlers Gdns. E1	21	**E3**
Cutlers Gdns. Arc. EC2	112	B6
Cutler St.		
Cutlers Sq. E14	134	A4
Britannia Rd.		
Cutthroat All., Rich.	163	F2
Ham St.		
Cutty Sark Gdns. SE10	134	C6
King William Wk.		
Cuxton Cl., Bexh.	158	E5
Cyclamen Cl., Hmptn.	161	G6
Gresham Rd.		
Cyclamen Way, Epsom	196	B5
Cyclops Ms. E14	134	A4
Cygnet Av., Felt.	142	C7
Cygnet Cl. NW10	88	D5
Cygnet Cl., Borwd.	38	C1
Cygnet St. E1	13	**G5**
Cygnet Way, Hayes	102	D5
Cygnets, The, Felt.	160	E4
Cygnus Business Cen. NW10	89	F6
Cymbeline Ct., Har.	68	C6
Cynthia St. N1	10	**D2**
Cynthia St. N1	111	F2
Cyntra Pl. E8	94/95	E7
Mare St.		
Cypress Av., Twick.	143	J7
Cypress Gro., Ilf.	65	H6
Cypress Pl. W1	9	**G6**
Cypress Rd. SE25	188	B2
Cypress Rd., Har.	68	A2
Cypress Tree Cl. Sid.	157	J7
White Oak Gdns.		
Cyprus Av. N3	72	B2
Cyprus Cl. N4	75	H6
Atterbury Rd.		
Cyprus Gdns. N3	72	B2
Cyprus Pl. E2	113	F2
Cyprus Pl. E6	116	D7
Cyprus Rd. N3	72	C2
Cyprus Rd. N9	60	C2
Cyprus Roundabout E16	116	D7
Royal Albert Way		
Cyprus St. E2	113	F2
Cyrena Rd. SE22	152	C6
Cyril Mans. SW11	149	J1
Cyril Rd., Bexh.	159	E2
Cyrus St. EC1	11	**H5**
Cyrus St. EC1	111	H4
Czar St. SE8	134	A6

D

Da Gama Pl. E14	134	A5
Napier Av.		
Dabbs Hill La., Nthlt.	85	H5
Dabin Cres. SE10	154	C1
Dacca St. SE8	133	J6
Dace Rd. E3	96	A7
Dacre Av., Ilf.	80	D2
Dacre Cl., Chig.	65	F4
Dacre Cl., Grnf.	103	H2
Dacre Gdns. SE13	154	E4
Dacre Gdns., Borwd.	38	D5
Dacre Gdns., Chig.	65	F4
Dacre Pk. SE13	154	E3
Dacre Pl. SE13	154	E3
Dacre Rd. E11	97	F1
Dacre Rd. E13	115	H1

Dacre Rd., Croy.	187	E7
Dacre St. SW1	25	**H5**
Dacre St. SW1	130	D3
Dacres Rd. SE23	171	G3
Dade Way, Sthl.	123	F5
Daerwood Cl., Brom.	206	C1
Daffodil Cl., Croy.	203	G1
Primrose La.		
Daffodil Gdns., Ilf.	98	E5
Daffodil Pl., Hmptn.	161	G6
Gresham Rd.		
Daffodil St. W12	107	F7
Dafforne Rd. SW17	168	A3
Dagenham Av., Dag.	118	E1
Dagenham Rd. E10	95	J1
Dagenham Rd., Dag.	101	J4
Dagmar Av., Wem.	87	J4
Dagmar Gdns. NW10	108	A2
Dagmar Ms., Sthl.	122/123	E3
Dagmar Rd.		
Dagmar Pas. N1	111	H1
Cross St.		
Dagmar Rd. N4	75	G7
Dagmar Rd. N15	76	A4
Cornwall Rd.		
Dagmar Rd. N22	74	D1
Dagmar Rd. SE5	152	B1
Dagmar Rd. SE25	188	B5
Dagmar Rd., Dag.	101	J7
Dagmar Rd., Kings.T.	181	J1
Dagmar Rd., Sthl.	122	E3
Dagmar Ter. N1	111	H1
Dagnall Pk. SE25	188	B6
Dagnall Rd. SE25	188	B5
Dagnall St. SW11	149	J2
Dagnan Rd. SW12	150	B7
Dagonet Gdns., Brom.	173	G3
Shroffold Rd.		
Dagonet Rd., Brom.	173	G3
Dahlia Gdns., Ilf.	99	E6
Dahlia Gdns., Mitch.	186	D4
Dahlia Rd. SE2	138	B4
Dahomey Rd. SW16	168	C6
Daimler Way, Wall.	200	E7
Daines Cl. E12	98	C3
Colchester Av.		
Dainford Cl., Brom.	172	D5
Dainton Cl., Brom.	191	H1
Daintry Cl., Har.	68	D4
Daintry Way E9	95	J6
Eastway		
Dairsie Rd. SE9	156	D3
Dairy Cl. NW10	107	G1
Dairy Cl., Th.Hth.	187	J2
Dairy La. SE18	136	C4
Dairy Ms. SW9	151	E3
Dairy Wk. SW19	166	B4
Dairyman Cl. NW2	90	B3
Claremont Rd.		
Daisy Cl., Croy.	203	G1
Primrose La.		
Daisy La. SW6	148	D3
Daisy Rd. E16	114/115	E4
Cranberry La.		
Daisy Rd. E18	79	H2
Dakota Gdns. E6	116	B4
Dakota Gdns., Nthlt.	102/103	E3
Argus Way		
Dalberg Rd. SW2	151	G5
Dalberg Way SE2	138	D3
Lanridge Rd.		
Dalby Rd. SW18	149	F4
Dalby St. NW5	92	B6
Dalcross Rd., Houns.	142	E2
Dale, The, Kes.	206	A4
Dale Av., Edg.	69	J1
Dale Av., Houns.	143	E3
Dale Cl. SE3	155	G3
Dale Cl., Barn.	41	E6
Dale Cl., Pnr.	66	B1
Dale Grn. Rd. N11	58	B3
Dale Gro. N12	57	F5
Dale Pk. Av., Cars.	199	J2
Dale Pk. Rd. SE19	187	J1
Dale Rd. NW5	92	A5
Grafton Rd.		
Dale Rd. SE17	35	**H6**
Dale Rd. SE17	131	H6
Dale Rd., Grnf.	103	H5
Dale Rd., Sutt.	198	C4
Dale Row W11	108	B6
St. Marks Rd.		
Dale St. W4	126	E5
Dale Vw. Av. E4	62	C2
Dale Vw. Cres. E4	62	C2
Dale Vw. Gdns. E4	62	D3

Name	Page	Grid
Dale Wd. Rd., Orp.	193	H7
Dalebury Rd. SW17	167	H2
Daleham Gdns. NW3	91	G5
Daleham Ms. NW3	91	G6
Dalehead NW1	9	F2
Dalehead NW1	110	C2
Dalemain Ms. E16	135	G1
Hanover Av.		
Dales Rd., Borwd.	38	D5
Farriers Way		
Dales Rd., Borwd.	38	D5
Daleside Gdns., Chig.	65	F3
Daleside Rd. SW16	168	B5
Daleside Rd., Epsom	196	D6
Daleview Rd. N15	76	B6
Dalewood Gdns., Wor.Pk.	197	H2
Daley St. E9	95	G6
Daley Thompson Way SW8	150	B2
Dalgarno Gdns. W10	107	J5
Dalgarno Way W10	107	J4
Dalgleish St. E14	113	H6
Daling Way E3	113	H1
Dalkeith Gro., Stan.	53	G5
Dalkeith Rd. SE21	169	J1
Dalkeith Rd., Ilf.	99	F3
Dallas Rd. NW4	71	G7
Dallas Rd. SE26	170	E4
Dallas Rd. W5	105	J5
Dallas Rd., Sutt.	198	B6
Dallas Ter., Hayes	121	J3
Dallin Rd. SE18	137	E7
Dallin Rd., Bexh.	158	D4
Dalling Rd. W6	127	H3
Dallinger Rd. SE12	155	F6
Dallington St. EC1	11	H5
Dallington St. EC1	111	H4
Dalmain Rd. SE23	171	G1
Dalmally Rd., Croy.	188	C7
Dalmeny Av. N7	92	D4
Dalmeny Av. SW16	187	G2
Dalmeny Cl., Wem.	87	F6
Dalmeny Cres., Houns.	144	A4
Dalmeny Rd. N7	92	D3
Dalmeny Rd., Barn.	41	F6
Dalmeny Rd., Cars.	200	A7
Dalmeny Rd., Erith	159	H1
Dalmeny Rd., Wor.Pk.	197	H3
Dalmeyer Rd. NW10	89	F6
Dalmore Av., Esher	194	C6
Dalmore Rd. SE21	169	J2
Dalrymple Cl. N14	42	D7
Dalrymple Rd. SE4	153	H4
Dalston Cross Shop. Cen. E8	94	C6
Dalston Gdns., Stan.	69	H1
Dalston La. E8	94	C6
Dalton Av., Mitch.	185	H2
Dalton Cl., Orp.	207	H3
Dalton Rd., Har.	68	A2
Dalton St. SE27	169	H2
Dalwood St. SE5	152	B1
Daly Ct. E15	96	C5
Clays La.		
Dalyell Rd. SW9	151	F3
Damascene Wk. SE21	169	J1
Lovelace Rd.		
Damask Cres. E16	114/115	E4
Cranberry La.		
Dame St. N1	11	J1
Dame St. N1	111	J2
Damer Ter. SW10	129	F7
Tadema Rd.		
Dames Rd. E7	97	G3
Damien St. E1	113	E6
Damon Cl., Sid.	176	B3
Damsonwood Rd., Sthl.	123	G3
Dan Leno Wk. SW6	128/129	A7
Britannia Rd.		
Danbrook Rd. SW16	187	E1
Danbury Cl., Rom.	82	D3
Danbury Ms., Wall.	200	B4
Danbury Rd., Loug.	48	B7
Danbury St. N1	11	H1
Danbury St. N1	111	H2
Danbury Way, Wdf.Grn.	63	J6
Danby St. SE15	152	C3
Dancer Rd. SW6	148	C1
Dancer Rd., Rich.	146	A3
Dando Cres. SE3	155	H3
Dandridge Cl. SE10	135	F5
Dane Cl., Bex.	159	G7
Dane Cl., Orp.	207	G5
Dane Pl. E3	113	H2
Roman Rd.		
Dane Rd. N18	61	F3
Dane Rd. SW19	185	F1
Dane Rd. W13	125	F1
Dane Rd., Ilf.	99	F5
Dane Rd., Sthl.	103	E7
Dane St. WC1	18	C2
Danebury, Croy.	204	B6
Danebury Av. SW15	147	E6
Daneby Rd. SE6	172	B3
Danecourt Gdns., Croy.	202	C3
Danecroft Rd. SE24	151	J5
Danehill Wk., Sid.	176	A3
Hatherley Rd.		
Danehurst Gdns., Ilf.	80	B5
Danehurst St. SW6	148	B1
Daneland, Barn.	41	J4
Danemead Gro., Nthlt.	85	H5
Danemere St. SW15	147	J3
Danes Ct., Wem.	88	B3
Danes Gate, Har.	68	B3
Danes Rd., Rom.	83	J7
Danesbury Rd., Felt.	160	B1
Danescombe SE12	173	G1
Winn Rd.		
Danescourt Cres., Sutt.	199	F2
Danescroft NW4	72	A5
Danescroft Av. NW4	72	A5
Danescroft Gdns. NW4	72	A5
Danesdale Rd. E9	95	H6
Danesfield SE5	36	D5
Daneswood Av. SE6	172	C3
Danethorpe Rd., Wem.	87	G6
Danetree Cl., Epsom	196	C7
Danetree Rd., Epsom	196	C7
Danette Gdns., Dag.	101	F2
Daneville Rd. SE5	152	A1
Dangan Rd. E11	79	G6
Daniel Bolt Cl. E14	114	B5
Uamvar St.		
Daniel Cl. N18	61	F4
Daniel Cl. SW17	167	H6
Daniel Gdns. SE15	37	F7
Daniel Gdns. SE15	132	C7
Daniel Pl. NW4	71	H7
Daniel Rd. W5	105	J7
Daniell Way, Croy.	201	E1
Daniels Ms. SE4	153	J4
Daniels Rd. SE15	153	F3
Dansey Pl. W1	17	H5
Dansington Rd., Well.	158	A4
Danson Cres., Well.	158	B3
Danson La., Well.	158	B4
Danson Mead, Well.	158	C3
Danson Pk., Bexh.	158	C4
Danson Rd., Bex.	158	D5
Danson Rd., Bexh.	158	D5
Danson Underpass, Sid.	158	C6
Danson Rd.		
Dante Pl. SE11	35	H1
Dante Rd. SE11	35	G1
Dante Rd. SE11	131	H4
Danube St. SW3	31	H3
Danvers Rd. N8	74	D4
Danvers St. SW3	31	F6
Danvers St. SW3	129	G6
Danziger Way, Borwd.	38	C1
Daphne Gdns. E4	62	C3
Gunners Gro.		
Daphne St. SW18	149	F6
Daplyn St. E1	21	H1
D'Arblay St. W1	17	G4
D'Arblay St. W1	110	C6
Darby Cres., Sun.	178	C2
Darby Gdns., Sun.	178	C2
Darcy Av., Wall.	200	C4
D'Arcy Dr., Har.	69	G4
Darcy Gdns., Dag.	119	F1
D'Arcy Gdns., Har.	69	H4
Darcy Rd. SW16	186	E2
D'Arcy Rd., Islw.	144	D1
London Rd.		
D'Arcy Rd., Sutt.	198	A4
Dare Gdns., Dag.	100/101	E3
Grafton Rd.		
Darell Rd., Rich.	146	A3
Darenth Rd. N16	76	C7
Darenth Rd., Well.	158	A1
Darfield Rd. SE4	153	J5
Darfield Way W10	108	A6
Darfur St. SW15	148	A3
Dargate Cl. SE19	170	C7
Chipstead Cl.		
Darien Rd. SW11	149	G3
Darlan Rd. SW6	128	C7
Darlaston Rd. SW19	166	A7
Darley Cl., Croy.	189	H6
Darley Dr., N.Mal.	182	D2
Darley Gdns., Mord.	185	E6
Darley Rd. N9	60	C1
Darley Rd. SW11	149	J6
Darling Rd. SE4	154	A3
Darling Row E1	113	E4
Darlington Rd. SE27	169	H5
Darmaine Cl., S.Croy.	201	J7
Churchill Rd.		
Darndale Cl. E17	77	J2
Darnley Ho. E14	113	H6
Darnley Rd. E9	95	E6
Darnley Rd., Wdf.Grn.	79	G1
Darnley Ter. W11	128	B1
St. James's Gdns.		
Darrell Rd. SE22	152	D5
Darren Cl. N4	75	F7
Darrick Wd. Rd., Orp.	207	G2
Darris Cl., Hayes	103	E4
Darsley Dr. SW8	150	E1
Dart St. W10	108	B3
Dartford Av. N9	45	F6
Dartford Gdns., Rom.	82	B6
Heathfield Pk. Dr.		
Dartford Rd., Bex.	177	J1
Dartford St. SE17	36	A5
Dartford St. SE17	131	J6
Dartmoor Wk. E14	134	A4
Charnwood Gdns.		
Dartmouth Cl. W11	108	C6
Dartmouth Gro. SE10	154	C1
Dartmouth Hill SE10	154	C1
Dartmouth Pk. Av. NW5	92	B3
Dartmouth Pk. Hill N19	92	B1
Dartmouth Pk. Hill NW5	92	B4
Dartmouth Pk. Rd. NW5	92	B4
Dartmouth Pl. SE23	171	F2
Dartmouth Rd.		
Dartmouth Pl. W4	127	E6
Dartmouth Rd. E16	115	G6
Fords Pk. Rd.		
Dartmouth Rd. NW2	90	A6
Dartmouth Rd. NW4	71	G6
Dartmouth Rd. SE23	171	F3
Dartmouth Rd. SE26	171	F3
Dartmouth Rd., Brom.	191	G7
Dartmouth Rd., Ruis.	84	A3
Dartmouth Row SE10	154	C1
Dartmouth St. SW1	25	H4
Dartmouth St. SW1	130	D2
Dartmouth Ter. SE10	154	D1
Dartnell Rd., Croy.	188	C7
Dartrey Wk. SW10	30	D7
Darville Rd. N16	94	C3
Darwell Cl. E6	116	D2
Darwin Cl. N11	58	B3
Darwin Cl., Orp.	207	G5
Darwin Dr., Sthl.	103	H6
Darwin Gdns., Wat.	50	C5
Barnhurst Path		
Darwin Rd. N22	75	H1
Darwin Rd. W5	125	F5
Darwin Rd., Well.	157	J3
Darwin St. SE17	36	C1
Darwin St. SE17	132	A4
Daryngton Dr., Grnf.	104	A2
Dashwood Cl., Bexh.	159	G5
Dashwood Rd. N8	75	F6
Dassett Rd. SE27	169	H5
Datchelor Pl. SE5	152	A1
Datchet Rd. SE6	171	J3
Datchworth Ct. N4	93	J3
Queens Dr.		
Date St. SE17	36	B4
Date St. SE17	131	J6
Daubeney Gdns. N17	59	J7
Daubeney Rd. E5	95	H4
Daubeney Rd. N17	59	J7
Daubeney Ter. SE8	133	J4
Dault Rd. SW18	149	F6
Davema Cl., Chis.	192	D1
Brenchley Cl.		
Davenant Rd. N19	92	D2
Davenant Rd., Croy.	201	H4
Duppas Hill Rd.		
Davenant St. E1	21	J2
Davenant St. E1	112	D5
Davenport Cl., Tedd.	162	D6
Davenport Rd. SE6	154	B6
Davenport Rd., Sid.	176	D2
Daventer Dr., Stan.	52	C7
Daventry Av. E17	78	A5
Daventry St. NW1	15	G1
Daventry St. NW1	109	H5
Davern Cl. SE10	135	F4
Davey Cl. N7	93	F6
Davey Rd. E9	96	A7
Davey St. SE15	37	G6
Davey St. SE15	132	C6
David Av., Grnf.	104	B3
David Cl., Hayes	121	G7
David Ms. W1	16	A1
David Rd., Dag.	100	E2
David St. E15	96	D6
Davidge St. SE1	201	J7
Davidge St. SE1	131	H2
Davids Rd. SE23	171	F1
David's Way, Ilf.	65	H7
Davidson Gdns. SW8	130	E7
Davidson La., Har.	68	C7
Grove Rd.		
Davidson Rd., Croy.	188	C6
Davies Cl., Croy.	188	D6
Davies La. E11	97	E2
Davies Ms. W1	16	D5
Davies St. W1	16	D5
Davies St. W1	110	B7
Davington Gdns., Dag.	100	B5
Davington Rd., Dag.	100	B6
Davinia Cl., Ilf.	64	C6
Deacon Way		
Davis Rd. W3	127	F1
Davis Rd., Chess.	196	A4
Davis St. E13	115	H2
Davisville Rd. W12	127	G2
Dawes Av., Islw.	144	D5
Dawes Ho. SE17	36	C2
Dawes Rd. SW6	128	B7
Dawes St. SE17	36	C3
Dawes St. SE17	132	A5
Dawley Rd., Hayes	121	H3
Dawlish Av. N13	58	E4
Dawlish Av. SW18	166	E2
Dawlish Av., Grnf.	104	D2
Dawlish Dr., Ilf.	99	H4
Dawlish Dr., Pnr.	67	E5
Dawlish Dr., Ruis.	84	A2
Dawlish Rd. E10	96	C2
Dawlish Rd. N17	76	D3
Dawlish Rd. NW2	90	A6
Dawn Cl., Houns.	143	E3
Dawn Cres. E15	114	D1
Bridge Rd.		
Dawnay Gdns. SW18	167	G2
Dawnay Rd. SW18	167	F2
Dawpool Rd. NW2	89	F2
Daws Hill E4	46	C3
Daws La. NW7	55	F5
Dawson Av., Bark.	99	J7
Dawson Cl. SE18	137	F4
Dawson Gdns., Bark.	99	J7
Dawson Av.		
Dawson Hts. Est. SE22	152	D7
Dawson Pl. W2	108	D7
Dawson Rd. NW2	89	J5
Dawson Rd., Kings.T.	181	J3
Dawson St. E2	13	G2
Dawson St. E2	112	C2
Dax Cl., Sun.	178	C3
Thames St.		
Daybrook Rd. SW19	184	E2
Daylesford Av. SW15	147	G4
Daymer Gdns., Pnr.	66	B4
Days La., Sid.	157	H7
Daysbrook Rd. SW2	169	F1
Dayton Gro. SE15	153	F1
De Barowe Ms. N5	93	H4
Leigh Rd.		
De Beauvoir Cres. N1	112	B1
De Beauvoir Est. N1	112	A1
De Beauvoir Rd. N1	112	B1
De Beauvoir Sq. N1	94	B7
De Bohun Av. N14	42	B6
De Brome Rd., Felt.	160	C1
De Crespigny Pk. SE5	152	A2
De Frene Rd. SE26	171	G4
De Havilland Rd., Edg.	70	B2
De Havilland Rd., Houns.	122	C7
De Havilland Rd., Wall.	201	E7
De Havilland Way, Stai.	140	D2
De Laune St. SE17	35	G4
De Laune St. SE17	131	H5
De Luci Rd., Erith	139	J5
De Lucy St. SE2	138	B4
De Mandeville Gate, Enf.	44	D4
Southbury Rd.		
De Montfort Par. SW16	168/169	E3
Streatham High Rd.		
De Montfort Rd.	168	E3
De Morgan Rd. SW6	149	E3
De Quincey Ms. E16	135	G1
Wesley Av.		
De Quincey Rd. N17	76	A1
De Vere Gdns. W8	22	C4

De Vere Gdns. W8 129 F2
De Vere Gdns., Ilf. 98 C2
De Vere Ms. W8 22 C5
De Walden St. W1 16 C2
Deacon Ms. N1 94 A7
Deacon Rd. NW2 89 G5
Deacon Rd., Kings.T. 181 J1
Deacon Way SE17 35 J1
Deacon Way SE17 131 J4
Deacon Way,
  Wdf.Grn. 64 C7
Deacons Cl., Borwd. 38 A4
Deacons Cl., Pnr. 66 B2
Deacons Leas, Orp. 207 G4
Deacons Ri. N2 73 G5
Deacons Wk., Hmptn. 161 F4
  Bishops Gro.
Deal Ms. W5 125 G4
  Darwin Rd.
Deal Porters Way 133 F3
  SE16
Deal Rd. SW17 168 A6
Deal St. E1 21 H1
Deal St. E1 112 D5
Deal Wk. SW9 131 G7
  Mandela St.
Deal's Gateway SE10 154 B1
  Blackheath Rd.
Dealtry Rd. SW15 147 J4
Dean Bradley St. 26 A6
  SW1
Dean Bradley St. 130 E3
  SW1
Dean Cl. E9 95 F5
  Churchill Wk.
Dean Cl. SE16 133 G1
  Surrey Water Rd.
Dean Ct., Wem. 87 E3
Dean Dr., Stan. 69 H2
Dean Farrar St. SW1 25 H5
Dean Farrar St. SW1 130 D3
Dean Gdns. E17 78 D4
Dean Gdns. W13 124/125 E1
  Northfield Av.
Dean Rd. NW2 89 J6
Dean Rd. SE28 118 A7
Dean Rd., Croy. 202 A4
Dean Rd., Hmptn. 161 G5
Dean Rd., Houns. 143 H5
Dean Ryle St. SW1 34 A1
Dean Ryle St. SW1 130 E4
Dean Stanley St. 26 A6
  SW1
Dean Stanley St. 130 E3
  SW1
Dean St. E7 97 G5
Dean St. W1 17 H3
Dean St. W1 110 D6
Dean Trench St. SW1 26 A6
Dean Trench St. SW1 130 E3
Dean Wk., Edg. 54 C6
  Deansbrook Rd.
Dean Way, Sthl. 123 H2
Deancross St. E1 113 F6
Deane Av., Ruis. 84 C5
Deane Cft. Rd., Pnr. 66 C6
Deane Way, Ruis. 66 B6
Deanery Cl. N2 73 H4
Deanery Ms. W1 24 C1
Deanery Rd. E15 97 E6
Deanery St. W1 24 C1
Deanery St. W1 130 A1
Deanhill Rd. SW14 146 B4
Deans Bldgs. SE17 36 B2
Deans Bldgs. SE17 132 A4
Deans Cl. W4 126 B6
Deans Cl., Croy. 202 C3
Deans Cl., Edg. 54 C6
Deans Ct. EC4 19 H4
Deans Dr. N13 59 H6
Deans Dr., Edg. 54 D5
Dean's Gate Cl. SE23 171 G3
Deans La. W4 126 B6
Deans La., Edg. 54 C6
Deans Ms. W1 16 E3
Dean's Pl. SW1 33 H3
Dean's Pl. SW1 130 D5
Deans Rd. W7 124 C1
Deans Rd., Sutt. 198 E3
Deans Way, Edg. 54 C5
Dean's Yd. SW1 25 J5
Deansbrook Cl., 54 C7
  Edg.
Deansbrook Rd., 54 C6
  Edg.
Deanscroft Av. NW9 88 C2
Deansway N2 73 G4
Deansway N9 60 B3
De'Arn Gdns., Mitch. 185 H3
Dearne Cl., Stan. 52 D5
Dearsley Rd., Enf. 44 D3
Deason St. E15 114 C1
  High St.
Debden Cl., Kings.T. 163 G5

Debden Cl., 63 J7
  Wdf.Grn.
Debnams Rd. SE16 133 F4
  Rotherhithe New Rd.
Deborah Cl., Islw. 144 B1
Deburgh Rd. SW19 167 F7
Decima St. SE1 28 D5
Decima St. SE1 132 B3
Deck Cl. SE16 133 G2
  Thame Rd.
Decoy Av. NW11 72 B5
Dee Rd., Rich. 145 J4
Dee St. E14 114 C6
Deeley Rd. SW8 150 D1
Deena Cl. W3 105 J6
Deepdale SW19 166 A4
Deepdale Av., Brom. 191 F4
Deepdale Cl. N11 58 A6
  Ribblesdale Av.
Deepdene W5 105 J4
Deepdene Av., Croy. 202 C3
Deepdene Cl. E11 79 G4
Deepdene Ct. N21 43 H6
Deepdene Gdns. 151 F7
  SW2
Deepdene Path, Loug. 48 D4
Deepdene Rd. SE5 152 A4
Deepdene Rd., Loug. 48 D4
Deepdene Rd., Well. 158 A3
Deepwell Cl., Islw. 144 D1
Deepwood La., Grnf. 104 A3
  Cowgate Rd.
Deer Pk. Cl., 164 B7
  Kings.T.
Deer Pk. Gdns., 185 G3
  Mitch.
Deer Pk. Rd. SW19 185 E2
Deer Pk. Way, 205 F2
  W.Wick.
Deerbrook Rd. SE24 169 H1
Deerdale Rd. SE24 151 J4
Deerhurst Cl., Felt. 160 A4
Deerhurst Cres., 161 J5
  Hmptn.
Deerhurst Rd. NW2 90 A6
Deerhurst Rd. SW16 169 F5
Deerings Dr., Pnr. 66 A5
Deerleap Gro. E4 46 B5
Deeside Rd. SW17 167 G3
Defiance Wk. SE18 136 C3
Defiant Way, Wall. 200 E7
Defoe Av., Rich. 126 A7
Defoe Cl. SE16 133 J2
  Vaughan St.
Defoe Cl. SW17 167 H6
Defoe Rd. N16 94 B2
Degema Rd., Chis. 174 E5
Dehar Cres. NW9 71 F7
Dehavilland Cl., 102 D3
  Nthlt.
Dekker Rd. SE21 152 B6
Delacourt Rd. SE3 135 H7
  Old Dover Rd.
Delafield Rd. SE7 135 H5
Delaford Rd. SE16 133 E5
Delaford St. SW6 128 B7
Delamare Cres., 189 F6
  Croy.
Delamere Gdns. NW7 54 D6
Delamere Rd. SW20 184 A1
Delamere Rd. W5 125 H1
Delamere Rd., 38 B1
  Borwd.
Delamere Rd., Hayes 102 D7
Delamere Ter. W2 14 B1
Delancey Pas. NW1 110 B1
  Delancey St.
Delancey St. NW1 110 B1
Delaware Rd. W9 6 A5
Delaware Rd. W9 108 E4
Delawyk Cres. SE24 151 J6
Delcombe Av., 197 J1
  Wor.Pk.
Delft Way SE22 152 B5
  East Dulwich Gro.
Delhi Rd., Enf. 44 C7
Delhi St. N1 111 E1
Delia St. SW18 149 E7
Delisle Rd. SE28 137 H1
  Merbury Rd.
Delius Gro. E15 114 D2
Dell, The SE2 138 A5
Dell, The SE19 188 C1
Dell, The, Brent. 125 F6
Dell, The, Felt. 142 B7
  Harlington Rd. W.
Dell, The, Pnr. 66 D2
Dell, The, Wem. 87 E5
Dell, The, Wdf.Grn. 63 H3
Dell Cl. E15 114 D1
Dell Cl., Wall. 200 D4
Dell Cl., Wdf.Grn. 63 H3
Dell La., Epsom 197 G5

Dell Rd., Epsom 197 G6
Dell Rd., West Dr. 120 C3
Dell Wk., N.Mal. 183 E2
Dell Way W13 105 F6
Della Path E5 94/95 E3
  Napoleon Rd.
Dellbow Rd., Felt. 142 B5
  Central Way
Dellfield Cl., Beck. 172 C7
  Foxgrove Rd.
Dellors Cl., Barn. 40 A5
Dellow Cl., Ilf. 81 G7
Dellow St. E1 113 E7
Dells Cl. E4 46 B7
Dell's Ms. SW1 33 G2
Dellwood Gdns., Ilf. 80 D3
Delmare Cl. SW9 151 F4
  Brighton Ter.
Delme Cres. SE3 155 H2
Delmey Cl., Croy. 202 C3
  Radcliffe Rd.
Deloraine St. SE8 154 A1
Delorme St. W6 128 A6
Delta Cl., Wor.Pk. 197 F3
Delta Ct. NW2 89 G2
Delta Gain, Wat. 50 D2
Delta Gro., Nthlt. 102 D3
Delta Rd., Wor.Pk. 197 E3
Delta St. E2 13 H3
Delvan Cl. SE18 136 D7
  Ordnance Rd.
Delvers Mead, Dag. 101 J4
Delverton Rd. SE17 35 H4
Delverton Rd. SE17 131 H5
Delvino Rd. SW6 148 D1
Demesne Rd., Wall. 200 D5
Demeta Cl., Wem. 88 C3
Dempster Cl., Surb. 195 F1
Dempster Rd. SW18 149 F5
Den Cl., Beck. 190 D3
Den Rd., Brom. 190 D3
Denbar Par., Rom. 83 J4
  Mawney Rd.
Denberry Dr., Sid. 176 B3
Denbigh Cl. NW10 88 E7
Denbigh Cl. W11 108 C7
Denbigh Cl., Chis. 174 C6
Denbigh Cl., Sthl. 103 F6
Denbigh Cl., Sutt. 198 C5
Denbigh Dr., Hayes 121 F2
Denbigh Gdns., Rich. 145 J5
Denbigh Ms. SW1 33 F2
Denbigh Pl. SW1 33 F3
Denbigh Pl. SW1 130 C5
Denbigh Rd. E6 116 A3
Denbigh Rd. W11 108 C7
Denbigh Rd. W13 105 E7
Denbigh Rd., Houns. 143 H2
Denbigh Rd., Sthl. 103 F6
Denbigh St. SW1 33 F2
Denbigh St. SW1 130 C4
Denbigh Ter. W11 108 C7
Denbridge Rd., Brom. 192 C2
Dene, The W13 104 E5
Dene, The, Croy. 203 G4
Dene, The, Wem. 87 H4
Dene, The, W.Mol. 179 F5
Dene Av., Houns. 143 F3
Dene Av., Sid. 158 B7
Dene Cl. SE4 153 H3
Dene Cl., Brom. 205 F1
Dene Cl., Wor.Pk. 197 F2
Dene Ct., Stan. 53 F5
  Marsh La.
Dene Gdns., Stan. 53 F5
Dene Gdns., T.Ditt. 194 D2
Dene Rd. N11 57 J1
Dene Rd., Buck.H. 64 A1
Denehurst Gdns. 71 J6
  NW4
Denehurst Gdns. W3 126 B1
Denehurst Gdns., 146 A4
  Rich.
Denehurst Gdns., 144 A7
  Twick.
Denehurst Gdns., 63 H4
  Wdf.Grn.
Denewood, Barn. 41 F5
Denewood Rd. N6 73 J6
Dengie Wk. N1 111 J1
  Basire St.
Denham Cl., Well. 158 C3
  Park Vw. Rd.
Denham Cres., Mitch. 185 J4
Denham Dr., Ilf. 81 F6
Denham Rd. N20 57 J3
Denham Rd., Felt. 142 C6
Denham St. SE10 135 G5
Denham Way, Bark. 117 H1
Denham Way, Borwd. 38 D1
Denholme Rd. W9 108 C3
Denison Cl. N2 73 F3
Denison Rd. SW19 167 G6
Denison Rd. W5 105 F4

Deniston Av., Bex. 176 E1
Denleigh Gdns. N21 59 G1
Denleigh Gdns., 180 B6
  T.Ditt.
Denman Dr. NW11 72 D5
Denman Dr., Esher 194 D5
Denman Dr. N. NW11 72 D5
Denman Dr. S. NW11 72 D5
Denman Rd. SE15 152 C1
Denman St. W1 17 H6
Denmark Av. SW19 166 B7
Denmark Ct., Mord. 184 D5
Denmark Gdns., 200 A3
  Cars.
Denmark Gro. N1 11 E1
Denmark Gro. N1 111 G2
Denmark Hill SE5 152 A1
Denmark Hill Dr. 71 F4
  NW9
Denmark Hill Est. 152 A4
  SE5
Denmark Pl. WC2 17 J3
Denmark Rd. N8 75 F4
Denmark Rd. NW6 108 C2
Denmark Rd. SE5 151 J1
Denmark Rd. SE25 188 D5
Denmark Rd. SW19 166 A6
Denmark Rd. W13 105 E7
Denmark Rd., Brom. 191 H1
Denmark Rd., Cars. 199 J3
Denmark Rd., 181 H3
  Kings.T.
Denmark Rd., Twick. 162 A3
Denmark St. E11 96/97 E3
  High Rd. Leytonstone
Denmark St. E13 115 H5
Denmark St. N17 76 E1
Denmark St. WC2 17 J4
Denmark St. WC2 110 D6
Denmark Wk. SE27 169 J4
Denmead Ho. SW15 147 F6
  Highcliffe Dr.
Denmead Rd., Croy. 201 H1
Denmead Way SE15 37 F7
Dennan Rd., Surb. 195 J1
Denne Ter. E8 112 C1
Denner Rd. E4 62 A2
Dennett Rd., Croy. 187 G7
Dennetts Gro. SE14 153 G2
  Dennetts Rd.
Dennetts Rd. SE14 153 F1
Denning Av., Croy. 201 G4
Denning Cl. NW8 6 D3
Denning Cl. NW8 109 F3
Denning Cl., Hmptn. 161 F6
Denning Rd. NW3 91 G4
Dennington Cl. E5 94/95 E2
  Detmold Rd.
Dennington Pk. Rd. 90 D6
  NW6
Denningtons, The, 197 E2
  Wor.Pk.
Dennis Av., Wem. 87 J5
Dennis Gdns., Stan. 53 F5
Dennis La., Stan. 52 E3
Dennis Pk. Cres. 184 B1
  SW20
Dennis Reeve Cl., 185 J1
  Mitch.
Dennis Rd., E.Mol. 179 J4
Dennis Way SW4 150 D3
  Gauden Rd.
Dennison Pt. E15 96 C7
Denny Cl. E6 116 B5
  Linton Gdns.
Denny Cres. SE11 35 F2
Denny Gdns., Dag. 100 B7
  Canonsleigh Rd.
Denny Rd. N9 60 E1
Denny St. SE11 35 F3
Denny St. SE11 131 G5
Densham Rd. E15 115 E1
Densole Cl., Beck. 189 H1
  Kings Hall Rd.
Densworth Gro. N9 61 F2
Denton Cl., Barn. 39 J5
Denton Rd. N8 75 F5
Denton Rd. N18 60 B4
Denton Rd., Twick. 145 G6
Denton Rd., Well. 138 C7
Denton St. SW18 149 E6
Denton Way E5 95 G3
Dents Rd. SW11 149 J6
Denver Cl., Orp. 193 H6
Denver Rd. N16 76 B2
Denyer St. SW3 31 H2
Denyer St. SW3 129 H4
Denzil Rd. NW10 89 F5
Deodar Rd. SW15 148 B4
Deodora Cl. N20 57 H3
Depot Rd., Houns. 144 A3
Deptford Br. SE8 154 A1
Deptford Bdy. SE8 154 A1
Deptford Ch. St. SE8 134 A6

Deptford Ferry Rd. E14 134 A4
Deptford Grn. SE8 134 A6
Deptford High St. SE8 134 A6
Deptford Strand SE8 133 J4
Deptford Wf. SE8 133 J4
Derby Av. N12 57 F5
Derby Av., Har. 68 A1
Derby Av., Rom. 83 J6
Derby Ct. E5 95 G4
Overbury St.
Derby Est., Houns. 143 G4
Derby Gate SW1 26 A3
Derby Hill SE23 171 F2
Derby Hill Cres. SE23 171 F2
Derby Rd. E7 97 J7
Derby Rd. E9 113 G1
Derby Rd. E18 79 F1
Derby Rd. N18 61 F5
Derby Rd. SW14 146 B4
Derby Rd. SW19 166 D7
Russell Rd.
Derby Rd., Croy. 201 H2
Derby Rd., Enf. 45 E5
Derby Rd., Grnf. 103 H1
Derby Rd., Houns. 143 H4
Derby Rd., Surb. 196 A1
Derby Rd., Sutt. 198 C6
Derby St. W1 24 C2
Derbyshire St. E2 13 J4
Derbyshire St. E2 112 D3
Dereham Pl. EC2 12 E4
Dereham Rd., Bark. 99 J6
Derek Av., Epsom 196 A5
Derek Av., Wall. 200 B4
Derek Av., Wem. 88 B7
Derek Cl., Epsom 196 B5
Derek Walcott Cl. SE24 151 H5
Shakespeare Rd.
Dericote St. E8 112 D1
Deridene Cl., Stai. 140 B6
Bedfont Rd.
Derifall Cl. E6 116 C5
Dering Pl., Croy. 201 J4
Dering Rd., Croy. 201 J4
Dering St. W1 16 D4
Dering St. W1 110 B6
Derinton Rd. SW17 167 J4
Derley Rd., Sthl. 122 C3
Dermody Gdns. SE13 154 D5
Dermody Rd. SE13 154 D5
Deronda Rd. SE24 169 H1
Deroy Cl., Cars. 199 J6
Derrick Gdns. SE7 135 J4
Anchor & Hope La.
Derrick Rd., Beck. 189 J3
Derry Rd., Croy. 200 E3
Derry St. W8 22 A4
Derry St. W8 128 E2
Dersingham Av. E12 98 D5
Dersingham Rd. NW2 90 B3
Derwent Av. N18 60 A5
Derwent Av. NW7 54 D5
Derwent Av. SW15 164 E4
Derwent Av., Barn. 57 J1
Derwent Av., Pnr. 51 E6
Derwent Cl., Esher 194 B6
Derwent Cres. N20 57 F3
Derwent Cres., Bexh. 159 G2
Derwent Cres., Stan. 69 F2
Derwent Dr. NW9 70 E5
Derwent Dr., Orp. 193 G7
Derwent Gdns., Ilf. 80 B4
Derwent Gdns., Wem. 69 F7
Derwent Gro. SE22 152 C4
Derwent Ri. NW9 70 E6
Derwent Rd. N13 59 F4
Derwent Rd. SE20 188 D2
Derwent Rd. SW20 184 A6
Derwent Rd. W5 125 F3
Derwent Rd., Sthl. 103 G6
Derwent Rd., Twick. 143 H6
Derwent St. SE10 134 E5
Derwent Wk., Wall. 200 B7
Derwent Yd. W5 125 F3
Northfield Av.
Derwentwater Rd. W3 126 C1
Desborough St. W2 14 A1
Desenfans Rd. SE21 152 B6
Desford Ms. E16 114/115 E4
Desford Rd.
Desford Rd. E16 115 E4
Desmond St. SE14 133 H6
Despard Rd. N19 92 C1
Detling Rd., Brom. 173 G5
Detmold Rd. E5 95 F2
Devalls Cl. E6 116 D7
Devana End, Cars. 199 J3
Devas Rd. SW20 183 J1
Devas St. E3 114 B4
Devenay Rd. E15 97 F7
Devenish Rd. SE2 138 A2
Deventer Cres. SE22 152 B5
Deverell St. SE1 28 B6
Deverell St. SE1 132 A3
Devereux Ct. WC2 18 E4
Devereux La. SW13 127 H7
Devereux Rd. SW11 149 J6
Deverill Ct. SE20 189 F1
Devey Cl., Kings.T. 165 E7
Devizes St. N1 112 A1
Poole St.
Devon Av., Twick. 161 J1
Devon Cl. N17 76 C3
Devon Cl., Buck.H. 63 H2
Devon Cl., Grnf. 105 F1
Devon Gdns. N4 75 H6
Devon Ri. N2 73 G4
Devon Rd., Bark. 117 H1
Devon St. SE15 133 E6
Devon Way, Chess. 195 F5
Devon Way, Epsom 196 B5
Devon Waye, Houns. 123 F7
Devoncroft Gdns., Twick. 144 D7
Devonhurst Pl. W4 126 D5
Heathfield Ter.
Devonia Gdns. N18 59 J6
Devonia Rd. N1 11 H1
Devonia Rd. N1 111 H2
Devonport Gdns., Ilf. 80 C6
Devonport Ms. W12 127 H1
Devonport Rd.
Devonport Rd. W12 127 H2
Devonport St. E1 113 F6
Devons Est. E3 114 B3
Devons Rd. E3 114 A5
Devonshire Av., Sutt. 199 F7
Devonshire Cl. E15 97 E4
Devonshire Cl. N13 59 G4
Devonshire Cl. W1 16 D1
Devonshire Cl. W1 110 B5
Devonshire Cres. NW7 56 A7
Devonshire Dr. SE10 134 B7
Devonshire Dr., Surb. 195 G1
Devonshire Gdns. N17 59 J6
Devonshire Gdns. N21 43 J7
Devonshire Gdns. W4 126 C7
Devonshire Gro. SE15 133 E6
Devonshire Hill La. N17 59 J6
Devonshire Ms. W4 126/127 E5
Glebe St.
Devonshire Ms. N. W1 16 D1
Devonshire Ms. S. W1 16 D1
Devonshire Ms. S. W1 110 B5
Devonshire Ms. W. W1 8 D6
Devonshire Ms. W. W1 110 B5
Devonshire Pas. W4 126 E5
Devonshire Pl. NW2 90 D3
Devonshire Pl. W1 8 C6
Devonshire Pl. W1 110 A4
Devonshire Pl. W4 126 E5
Devonshire Pl. W8 22 A6
Devonshire Pl. Ms. W1 8 C6
Devonshire Rd. E15 96/97 E4
Janson Rd.
Devonshire Rd. E16 115 H6
Devonshire Rd. E17 78 A6
Devonshire Rd. N9 61 F1
Devonshire Rd. N13 59 F4
Devonshire Rd. N17 59 J6
Devonshire Rd. NW7 56 A7
Devonshire Rd. SE9 174 B2
Devonshire Rd. SE23 171 F1
Devonshire Rd. SW19 167 H7
Devonshire Rd. W4 126 E5
Devonshire Rd. W5 125 F3
Devonshire Rd., Bexh. 159 E4
Devonshire Rd., Cars. 200 A4
Devonshire Rd., Croy. 188 A7
Devonshire Rd., Felt. 160 E3
Devonshire Rd., Har. 68 A6
Devonshire Rd., Ilf. 81 H7
Devonshire Rd. (Eastcote), Pnr. 66 C6
Devonshire Rd. (Hatch End), Pnr. 67 F1
Devonshire Rd., Sthl. 103 G5
Devonshire Rd., Sutt. 199 F7
Devonshire Row EC2 20 E2
Devonshire Row Ms. W1 8 E6
Devonshire Sq. EC2 20 E3
Devonshire Sq., Brom. 191 H4
Devonshire St. W1 16 C1
Devonshire St. W1 110 B5
Devonshire St. W4 126 E5
Devonshire Ter. W2 14 D4
Devonshire Ter. W2 109 F6
Devonshire Way, Croy. 203 H2
Devonshire Way, Hayes 102 B6
Dewar St. SE15 152 D3
Dewberry Gdns. E6 116 B5
Dewberry St. E14 114 C5
Dewey Rd. N1 10 E1
Dewey Rd. N1 111 G2
Dewey Rd., Dag. 101 H6
Dewey St. SW17 167 J5
Dewhurst Rd. W14 128 A3
Dewlands Ct. NW4 72 A2
Holders Hill Rd.
Dewsbury Cl., Pnr. 67 F6
Dewsbury Ct. W4 126 C4
Chiswick Rd.
Dewsbury Gdns., Wor.Pk. 197 G3
Dewsbury Rd. NW10 89 G5
Dewsbury Ter. NW1 110 B1
Camden High St.
Dexter Ho., Erith 138/139 E3
Kale Rd.
Dexter Rd., Barn. 40 A6
Deyncourt Rd. N17 75 J1
Deynecourt Gdns. E11 79 J4
D'Eynsford Rd. SE5 152 A1
Diadem Ct. W1 17 H4
Dial Wk., The W8 22 B3
Dial Wk., The W8 129 E2
Diamedes Av., Stai. 140 A7
Diameter Rd., Orp. 193 E7
Diamond Cl., Dag. 100 C1
Diamond Rd., Ruis. 84 D4
Diamond St. SE15 132 B7
Diamond Ter. SE10 154 C1
Diamond Way SE8 134 A7
Deptford High St.
Diana Cl. E18 79 H1
Diana Gdns., Surb. 195 J2
Diana Ho. SW13 147 F1
Diana Pl. NW1 9 E5
Diana Pl. NW1 110 B4
Diana Rd. E17 77 J3
Dianne Way, Barn. 41 H5
Dianthus Cl. SE2 138 B5
Carnation St.
Dibden Row SE1 131 G3
Gerridge St.
Dibden St. N1 111 J1
Dibdin Cl., Sutt. 198 D3
Dibdin Rd., Sutt. 198 D3
Dicey Av. NW2 89 J5
Dick Turpin Way, Felt. 141 J4
Dickens Av. N3 73 F1
Dickens Cl., Erith 139 H7
Dickens Cl., Hayes 121 H4
Croyde Av.
Dickens Cl., Rich. 163 H2
Dickens Dr., Chis. 175 F6
Dickens Est. SE1 29 H4
Dickens Est. SE1 132 D2
Dickens Est. SE16 29 H4
Dickens Est. SE16 132 D2
Dickens La. N18 60 B5
Dickens Ri., Chig. 64 D3
Dickens Rd. E6 116 A2
Dickens Sq. SE1 28 A5
Dickens Sq. SE1 131 J3
Dickens St. SW8 150 B2
Dickenson Cl. N9 60 D1
Croyland Rd.
Dickenson Rd. N8 75 E7
Dickenson Rd., Felt. 160 C5
Dickenson St. NW5 92 B6
Dalby St.
Dickensons La. SE25 188 D5
Dickensons Pl. SE25 188 D6
Dickenswood Cl. SE19 169 H7
Dickerage La., N.Mal. 182 C3
Dickerage Rd., Kings.T. 182 C1
Dickerage Rd., N.Mal. 182 C1
Dickson Fold, Pnr. 66 D4
Dickson Rd. SE9 156 B3
Didsbury Cl. E6 116 C1
Barking Rd.
Digby Cres. N4 93 J2
Digby Gdns., Dag. 119 G1
Digby Pl., Croy. 202 C3
Digby Rd. E9 95 G5
Digby Rd., Bark. 99 J7
Digby St. E2 113 F3
Dighton Ct. SE5 35 J6
Dighton Ct. SE5 131 J6
Dighton Rd. SW18 149 F5
Digswell St. N7 93 G6
Holloway Rd.
Dilhorne Cl. SE12 173 H3
Dilke St. SW3 32 A5
Dilke St. SW3 129 J6
Dillwyn Cl. SE26 171 H4
Dilston Cl., Nthlt. 102 C3
Yeading La.
Dilston Gro. SE16 133 F4
Abbeyfield Rd.
Dilton Gdns. SW15 165 G1
Dimes Pl. W6 127 H4
King St.
Dimmock Dr., Grnf. 86 A5
Dimond Cl. E7 97 G4
Dimsdale Dr. NW9 88 C1
Dimsdale Dr., Enf. 44 D6
Dimsdale Wk. E13 115 G1
Stratford Rd.
Dimson Cres. E3 114 A4
Dingle Cl., Barn. 39 F6
Dingle Gdns. E14 114 A7
Dingley La. SW16 168 D2
Dingley Pl. EC1 12 A4
Dingley Pl. EC1 111 J3
Dingley Rd. EC1 11 J4
Dingley Rd. EC1 111 J3
Dingwall Av., Croy. 201 J2
Dingwall Gdns. NW11 72 D6
Dingwall Pl., Croy. 202 A2
Dingwall Rd.
Dingwall Rd. SW18 149 F7
Dingwall Rd., Croy. 202 A2
Dinmont St. E2 112/113 E2
Coate St.
Dinsdale Gdns. SE25 188 B5
Dinsdale Gdns., Barn. 41 E5
Dinsdale Rd. SE3 135 F6
Dinsmore Rd. SW12 150 B7
Dinton Rd. SW19 167 G6
Dinton Rd., Kings.T. 163 J7
Diploma Av. N2 73 H4
Dirleton Rd. E15 115 F1
Disbrowe Rd. W6 128 B6
Discovery Wk. E1 132 E1
Dishforth La. NW9 70 E1
Disney Ms. N4 75 H5
Chesterfield Gdns.
Disney Pl. SE1 28 A3
Disney St. SE1 28 A3
Dison Cl., Enf. 45 G1
Disraeli Cl. SE28 138 C1
Disraeli Cl. W4 126 D4
Acton La.
Disraeli Gdns. SW15 148 C4
Fawe Pk. Rd.
Disraeli Rd. E7 97 G6
Disraeli Rd. NW10 106 C2
Disraeli Rd. SW15 148 B4
Disraeli Rd. W5 125 G1
Diss St. E2 13 F3
Diss St. E2 112 C3
Distaff La. EC4 19 J5
Distaff La. EC4 111 J7
Distillery La. W6 127 J5
Fulham Palace Rd.
Distillery Rd. W6 127 J5
Distillery Wk., Brent. 125 H6
Pottery Rd.
Distin St. SE11 34 E2
Distin St. SE11 131 G4
District Rd., Wem. 86 E5
Ditch All. SE10 154 B1
Ditchburn St. E14 114 C7
Ditchfield Rd., Hayes 102 E4
Dittisham Rd. SE9 174 B4
Ditton Cl., T.Ditt. 180 D7
Ditton Gra. Cl., Surb. 195 G1
Ditton Gra. Dr., Surb. 195 G1
Ditton Hill, Surb. 195 F1
Ditton Hill Rd., Surb. 195 F1
Ditton Lawn, T.Ditt. 194 D1
Ditton Pl. SE20 189 E1
Ditton Reach, T.Ditt. 181 E6
Ditton Rd., Bexh. 158 D5
Ditton Rd., Sthl. 123 F4
Ditton Rd., Surb. 195 H1
Dittoncroft Cl., Croy. 202 B4
Divis Way SW15 147 H6
Dixon Clark Ct. N1 93 H6
Canonbury Rd.
Dixon Cl. E6 116 C6
Brandreth Rd.
Dixon Pl., W.Wick. 204 B1
Dixon Rd. SE14 153 H1
Dixon Rd. SE25 188 B3
Dixon's All. SE16 132 E2
Dobbin Cl., Har. 68 D2
Dobell Rd. SE9 156 C5

Dobree Av. NW10	89	H7
Dobson Cl. NW6	91	G7
Dock Hill Av. SE16	133	G2
Dock Rd. E16	115	F7
Dock Rd., Brent.	125	G7
Dock St. E1	21	H5
Dock St. E1	112	D7
Dockers Tanner Rd. E14	134	A3
Dockhead SE1	29	G4
Dockhead SE1	132	C2
Dockland St. E16	136	D1
Dockley Rd. SE16	29	H6
Dockley Rd. SE16	132	D3
Dockwell Cl., Felt.	142	A4
Dockyard Ind. Est. SE18	136	B3
Woolwich Ch. St.		
Doctor Johnson Av. SW17	168	B3
Doctors Cl. SE26	171	F5
Docwra's Bldgs. N1	94	B6
Dod St. E14	114	A6
Dodbrooke Rd. SE27	169	G3
Doddington Gro. SE17	35	G5
Doddington Gro. SE17	131	H6
Doddington Pl. SE17	35	G5
Doddington Pl. SE17	131	H6
Dodsley Pl. N9	61	E3
Dodson St. SE1	27	F4
Dodson St. SE1	131	G2
Doebury Wk. SE18	138	A6
Prestwood Cl.		
Doel Cl. SW19	167	F7
Dog Kennel Hill SE22	152	B3
Dog Kennel Hill Est. SE22	152	B3
Dog La. NW10	89	E4
Doggets Ct., Barn.	41	H5
Doggett Rd. SE6	154	A7
Doghurst Av., Hayes	121	E7
Doghurst Dr., West Dr.	121	E7
Doherty Rd. E13	115	G4
Dokal Incl. Est., Sthl.	122	E2
Dolben St. SE1	27	G2
Dolben St. SE1	131	H1
Dolby Ct. EC4	20	A5
Dolby Rd. SW6	148	C2
Dolland St. SE11	34	D4
Dolland St. SE11	131	F5
Dollis Av. N3	72	C1
Dollis Brook Wk., Barn.	40	B6
Dollis Cres., Ruis.	84	C1
Dollis Hill Av. NW2	89	H3
Dollis Hill Est. NW2	89	G3
Dollis Hill La. NW2	89	H3
Dollis Ms. N3	72	C1
Dollis Pk.		
Dollis Pk. N3	72	C1
Dollis Rd. N3	56	B7
Dollis Rd. NW7	56	B7
Dollis Valley Grn. Wk. N20	57	F2
Totteridge La.		
Dollis Valley Grn. Wk., Barn.	40	B6
Dollis Valley Way, Barn.	40	C6
Dolman Cl. N3	73	F2
Avondale Rd.		
Dolman Rd. W4	126	D4
Dolman St. SW4	151	F4
Dolphin Cl. SE16	133	G2
Kinburn St.		
Dolphin Cl. SE28	118	D6
Dolphin Cl., Surb.	181	G6
Dolphin Cl., NW11	72	B6
Dolphin La. E14	114	B7
Dolphin Rd., Nthlt.	103	F2
Dolphin Sq. SW1	33	G4
Dolphin Sq. SW1	130	C5
Dolphin Sq. W4	126	E6
Dolphin St., Kings.T.	181	H1
Dombey St. WC1	18	C1
Dombey St. WC1	111	F5
Dome Hill Pk. SE26	170	C4
Domett Cl. SE5	152	A4
Domfe Pl. E5	95	F4
Rushmore Rd.		
Domingo St. EC1	11	J5
Dominica Cl. E13	115	J2
Dominion Rd., Croy.	188	C7
Dominion Rd., Sthl.	123	E3
Dominion St. EC2	20	C1
Domonic Dr. SE9	174	E4
Domville Cl. N20	57	G2
Don Phelan Cl. SE5	152	A1
Donald Dr., Rom.	82	C5
Donald Rd. E13	115	H1
Donald Rd., Croy.	187	F6
Donald Wds. Gdns., Surb.	196	B2
Donaldson Rd. NW6	108	C1
Donaldson Rd. SE18	156	D1
Doncaster Dr., Nthlt.	85	F5
Doncaster Gdns. N4	75	J6
Stanhope Gdns.		
Doncaster Gdns., Nthlt.	85	F5
Doncaster Grn., Wat.	50	C5
Doncaster Rd. N9	44	E7
Doncel Ct. E4	46	D7
Donegal St. N1	10	D2
Donegal St. N1	111	F2
Doneraile St. SW6	148	A2
Dongola Rd. E13	115	H3
Dongola Rd. N17	76	B3
Dongola Rd. W. E13	115	H3
Balaam St.		
Donington Av., Ilf.	81	F5
Donkey All. SE22	152	D7
Donkey La., Enf.	44	D2
Donne Ct. SE24	151	J6
Donne Pl. SW3	31	H1
Donne Pl. SW3	129	H4
Donne Pl., Mitch.	186	B4
Donne Rd., Dag.	100	C2
Donnefield Av., Edg.	53	H7
Donnington Rd. NW10	89	H7
Donnington Rd., Har.	69	G5
Donnington Rd., Wor.Pk.	197	G2
Donnybrook Rd. SW16	168	C7
Donovan Av. N10	74	B2
Doon St. SE1	26	E2
Doone Cl., Tedd.	162	D6
Dora Rd. SW19	166	D5
Dora St. E14	113	J6
Doral Way, Cars.	199	J5
Doran Gro. SE18	137	H7
Doran Mans. N2	73	J5
Great N. Rd.		
Doran Wk. E15	96	C7
Dorchester Av. N13	59	J4
Dorchester Av., Bex.	176	D1
Dorchester Av., Har.	67	J6
Dorchester Cl., Nthlt.	85	H5
Dorchester Cl., Orp.	176	A7
Grovelands Rd.		
Dorchester Ct. N14	42	B7
Dorchester Ct. SE24	151	J5
Dorchester Dr. SE24	151	J5
Dorchester Dr., Felt.	141	H6
Dorchester Gdns. E4	62	A4
Dorchester Gdns. NW11	72	D4
Dorchester Gro. W4	127	E5
Dorchester Ms., N.Mal.	182	D4
Elm Rd.		
Dorchester Ms., Twick.	145	F7
Dorchester Rd., Mord.	185	E7
Dorchester Rd., Nthlt.	85	H5
Dorchester Rd., Wor.Pk.	197	J1
Dorchester Way, Har.	69	J6
Dorchester Waye, Hayes	102	C6
Dorcis Av., Bexh.	158	E2
Dordrecht Rd. W3	127	E1
Dore Av. E12	98	D5
Dore Gdns., Mord.	185	E7
Doreen Av. NW9	88	D1
Dorell Cl., Sthl.	103	F5
Doria Rd. SW6	148	C2
Doric Way NW1	9	H3
Doric Way NW1	110	D3
Dorien Rd. SW20	184	A2
Doris Av., Erith	159	J1
Doris Rd. E7	97	G7
Dorking Cl. SE8	133	J6
Dorking Cl., Wor.Pk.	198	A2
Dorlcote Rd. SW18	149	H7
Dorma Trcil. Plc. E10	95	C1
Dorman Pl. N9	60	D2
Balham Rd.		
Dorman Wk. NW10	88	D5
Garden Way		
Dorman Way NW8	109	G1
Dormay St. SW18	148	E5
Dormer Cl. E15	97	F6
Dormer Cl., Barn.	40	A5
Dormers Av., Sthl.	103	G6
Dormers Ri., Sthl.	103	H6
Dormers Wells La., Sthl.	103	G6
Dornberg Cl. SE3	135	G7
Dornberg Rd. SE3	135	H7
Banchory Rd.		
Dorncliffe Rd. SW6	148	B2
Dorney NW3	91	H7
Dorney Ri., Orp.	193	J4
Dorney Way, Houns.	143	E5
Dornfell St. NW6	90	C5
Dornton Rd. SW12	168	B2
Dornton Rd., S.Croy.	202	A5
Dorothy Av., Wem.	87	H7
Dorothy Evans Cl., Bexh.	159	H4
Dorothy Gdns., Dag.	100	B4
Dorothy Rd. SW11	149	J3
Dorrell Pl. SW9	151	G4
Brixton Rd.		
Dorrien Wk. SW16	168	D2
Dorrington Ct. SE25	188	B2
Dorrington Pt. E3	114	B3
Bromley High St.		
Dorrington St. EC1	19	E1
Dorrington St. EC1	111	G5
Dorrit Ms. N18	60	B4
Dorrit Way, Chis.	175	F6
Dors Cl. NW9	88	D1
Dorset Av., Sthl.	123	G4
Dorset Av., Well.	157	J4
Dorset Bldgs. EC4	19	G4
Dorset Cl. NW1	15	J1
Dorset Dr., Edg.	53	J6
Dorset Est. E2	13	G3
Dorset Est. E2	112	C3
Dorset Gdns., Mitch.	187	F4
Dorset Ms. N3	72	D1
Dorset Ms. SW1	24	D5
Dorset Pl. E15	96	D6
Dorset Ri. EC4	19	G4
Dorset Ri. EC4	111	H6
Dorset Rd. E7	97	J7
Dorset Rd. N15	76	A4
Dorset Rd. N22	75	E1
Dorset Rd. SE9	174	B2
Dorset Rd. SW8	34	B7
Dorset Rd. SW8	131	F7
Dorset Rd. SW19	184	D1
Dorset Rd. W5	125	F3
Dorset Rd., Beck.	189	G3
Dorset Rd., Har.	67	J6
Dorset Rd., Mitch.	185	H2
Dorset Sq. NW1	7	J6
Dorset Sq. NW1	109	J4
Dorset St. W1	16	A2
Dorset St. W1	110	A5
Dorset Way, Twick.	162	A1
Dorset Waye, Houns.	123	F7
Dorville Cres. W6	127	H3
Dorville Rd. SE12	155	F5
Dothill Rd. SE18	137	G7
Douai Grn., Hmptn.	179	J1
Doubleday Rd., Loug.	49	F3
Doughty Ms. WC1	10	C6
Doughty Ms. WC1	111	F4
Doughty St. WC1	10	C5
Doughty St. WC1	111	F4
Douglas Av. E17	78	A1
Douglas Av., N.Mal.	183	H4
Douglas Av., Wem.	87	H7
Douglas Cl., Stan.	52	D5
Douglas Cl., Wall.	201	E7
Douglas Cres., Hayes	102	C4
Douglas Dr., Croy.	204	A3
Douglas Est. N1	93	J6
Douglas Ms. NW2	90	B3
Douglas Rd. E4	47	E7
Douglas Rd. E16	115	G5
Douglas Rd. N1	93	J7
Douglas Rd. N22	75	G1
Douglas Rd. NW6	108	C1
Douglas Rd., Houns.	143	H3
Douglas Rd., Ilf.	82	A6
Douglas Rd., Kings.T.	182	A2
Douglas Rd., Stai.	140	A6
Douglas Rd., Surb.	195	J2
Douglas Rd., Well.	158	B1
Douglas Sq., Mord.	184	D6
Douglas St. SW1	33	H2
Douglas St. SW1	130	D4
Douglas Ter. E17	78	A1
Douglas Av.		
Douglas Way SE8	133	J7
Doulton Ms. NW6	90/91	E6
Lymington Rd.		
Dounesforth Gdns. SW18	166	E1
Douro Pl. W8	22	B5
Douro Pl. W8	129	E3
Douro St. E3	114	A2
Douthwaite Sq. E1	29	J1
Dove App. E6	116	B5
Dove Cl. NW7	55	F7
Bunns La.		
Dove Cl., Nthlt.	102	D4
Wayfarer Rd.		
Dove Ct. EC2	20	B4
Dove Ho. Gdns. E4	62	A2
Dove Ms. SW5	30	C2
Dove Ms. SW5	129	F4
Dove Pk., Pnr.	51	G7
Dove Rd. N1	94	A6
Dove Row E2	112	D1
Dove Wk. SW1	32	B3
Dovecot Cl., Pnr.	66	B5
Dovecote Av. N22	75	G3
Dovecote Gdns. SW14	146	D3
Avondale Rd.		
Dovecott Gdns. SW14	146	D3
North Worple Way		
Dovedale Av., Har.	69	F6
Dovedale Av., Ilf.	80	D2
Dovedale Cl., Well.	158	A2
Dovedale Ri., Mitch.	167	J7
Dovedale Rd. SE22	153	E5
Dovedon Cl. N14	58	E2
Dovehouse Mead, Bark.	117	G2
Dovehouse St. SW3	31	G3
Dovehouse St. SW3	129	G5
Dover Cl. NW2	90	A2
Brent Ter.		
Dover Cl., Rom.	83	J2
Dover Flats SE1	132	B4
Old Kent Rd.		
Dover Gdns., Cars.	199	J3
Dover Ho. Rd. SW15	147	G4
Dover Pk. Dr. SW15	147	H6
Dover Patrol SE3	155	H2
Kidbrooke Way		
Dover Rd. E12	97	J2
Dover Rd. N9	61	F2
Dover Rd. SE19	170	A6
Dover Rd., Rom.	82	E6
Dover St. W1	17	E6
Dover St. W1	110	B7
Dover Yd. W1	25	F1
Dovercourt Av., Th.Hth.	187	G4
Dovercourt Est. N1	94	A6
Dovercourt Gdns., Stan.	53	H5
Dovercourt La., Sutt.	199	F3
Dovercourt Rd. SE22	152	B6
Doverfield Rd. SW2	151	E6
Doveridge Gdns. N13	59	H4
Doves Cl., Brom.	206	B2
Dove's Yd. N1	111	G1
Doveton Rd., S.Croy.	202	A5
Doveton St. E1	113	F4
Malcolm Rd.		
Downhill Rd. SE6	172	D1
Dowdeswell Cl. SW15	147	E4
Dowding Pl., Stan.	52	D6
Dowgate Hill EC4	20	B5
Dowgate Hill EC4	112	A7
Dowland St. W10	108	B2
Dowlas Est. SE5	36	D7
Dowlas St. SE5	36	D7
Dowlas St. SE5	132	B7
Dowlerville Rd., Orp.	207	J6
Dowman Cl.	184/185	E1
Nelson Gro. Rd.		
Down Cl., Nthlt.	102	B2
Down Hall Rd., Kings.T.	181	G1
Down Rd. W6	127	H4
Down Rd., Tedd.	163	E6
Down St. W1	24	D2
Down St. W1	130	B1
Down St., W.Mol.	179	G5
Down St. Ms. W1	24	D2
Down Way, Nthlt.	102	B3
Downage NW4	71	J3
Downalong, Bushey	52	A1
Downbarns Rd., Ruis.	84	D3
Downbury Ms. SW18	148	D6
Merton Rd.		
Downderry Rd.,	172	D3
Brom.		
Downe Cl., Well.	138	C7
Downe Rd., Mitch.	185	J2
Downend SE18	136/137	E7
Moordown		
Downers Cotts. SW4	150	C4
The Pavement		
Downes Cl., Twick.	144/145	E6
St. Margarets Rd.		
Downes Ct. N21	59	G1
Downfield, Wor.Pk.	197	F1
Downfield Cl. W9	6	A6
Downfield Cl. W9	108	E4
Downham La., Brom.	172	D5
Downham Way		
Downham Rd. N1	94	A7
Downham Way, Brom.	172	D5
Downhills Av. N17	76	A3
Downhills Pk. Rd. N17	75	J3

Downhills Way N17 75 J3
Downhurst Av. NW7 54 D5
Downing Cl., Har. 67 J3
Downing Dr., Grnf. 104 A1
Downing Rd., Dag. 119 F1
Downing St. SW1 26 A3
Downing St. SW1 130 E2
Downings E6 116 D6
Downland Cl. N20 57 F1
Downleys Cl. SE9 174 B2
Downman Rd. SE9 156 B3
Downs, The SW20 166 A7
Downs Av., Chis. 174 C5
Downs Av., Pnr. 67 F6
Downs Br. Rd., Beck. 190 D1
Downs Hill, Beck. 190 D1
Downs La. E5 94/95 E4
Downs Rd.
Downs Pk. Rd. E5 94 D5
Downs Pk. Rd. E8 94 C5
Downs Rd. E5 94 D4
Downs Rd., Beck. 190 B2
Downs Rd., Enf. 44 B4
Downs Rd., Th.Hth. 187 J1
Downs Vw., Islw. 124 C7
Downsbury Ms. SW18 148 D5
Merton Rd.
Downsell Rd. E15 96 C4
Downsfield Rd. E17 77 H6
Downshall Av., Ilf. 81 H6
Downshire Hill NW3 91 G4
Downside, Sun. 178 A1
Downside, Twick. 162 C3
Downside Cl. SW19 167 F6
Downside Cres. NW3 91 H5
Downside Cres. W13 104 D4
Downside Rd., Sutt. 199 G6
Downside Wk., Nthlt. 103 F3
Downsview Gdns. SE19 169 H7
Downsview Rd. SE19 169 J7
Downsway, Orp. 207 H5
Downton Av. SW2 169 E2
Downtown Rd. SE16 133 H2
Downway N12 57 H7
Dowrey St. N1 111 G1
Richmond Av.
Dowsett Rd. N17 76 C2
Dowson Cl. SE5 152 A4
Doyce St. SE1 27 J3
Doyle Gdns. NW10 107 G1
Doyle Rd. SE25 188 D4
D'Oyley St. SW1 32 B1
D'Oyley St. SW1 130 A4
Doynton St. N19 92 B2
Draco St. SE17 35 J5
Draco St. SE17 131 J6
Dragmire La., Mitch. 185 G4
Dragon Rd. SE15 36 D6
Dragon Rd. SE15 132 B6
Dragonfly Cl. E13 115 H3
Hollybush St.
Dragoon Rd. SE8 133 J5
Dragor Rd. NW10 106 C4
Drake Cl. SE16 133 G2
Middleton Dr.
Drake Ct. SE19 170 C5
Drake Ct., Har. 85 F1
Drake Cres. SE28 118 C6
Drake Rd. SE4 154 A3
Drake Rd., Chess. 196 A5
Drake Rd., Croy. 187 F7
Drake Rd., Har. 85 F2
Drake Rd., Mitch. 186 A6
Drake St. WC1 18 C2
Drake St., Enf. 44 A1
Drakefell Rd. SE4 153 G2
Drakefell Rd. SE14 153 G2
Drakefield Rd. SW17 168 A3
Drakeley Ct. N5 93 H4
Highbury Hill
Drakes Ctyd. NW6 90 C7
Drakes Wk. E6 116 C1
Drakewood Rd. SW16 168 D7
Draper Cl., Belv. 139 F4
Draper Cl., Islw. 124 A7
Thornbury Rd.
Draper Pl. N1 111 H1
Essex Rd.
Drapers Gdns. EC2 112 A6
Copthall Av.
Drapers Rd. E15 96 D4
Drapers Rd. N17 76 C3
Drapers Rd., Enf. 43 H2
Drappers Way SE16 37 J1
Draven Cl., Brom. 191 F7
Drawdock Rd. SE10 134 D1
Drawell Cl. SE18 137 H5
Drax Av. SW20 165 G7
Draxmont SW19 166 B6
Dray Gdns. SW2 151 F5
Draycot Rd. E11 79 H6

Draycot Rd., Surb. 196 A1
Draycott Av. SW3 31 H1
Draycott Av. SW3 129 H4
Draycott Av., Har. 69 E6
Draycott Cl., Har. 69 E6
Draycott Ms. SW6 148 C2
New Kings Rd.
Draycott Pl. SW3 31 J2
Draycott Pl. SW3 129 J4
Draycott Ter. SW3 32 A1
Draycott Ter. SW3 129 J4
Drayford Cl. W9 108 C4
Draymans Way, Islw. 144 C3
Drayside Ms., Sthl. 123 F2
Kingston Rd.
Drayson Ms. W8 128 D2
Drayton Av. W13 104 D7
Drayton Av., Loug. 48 C6
Drayton Av., Orp. 207 E1
Drayton Br. Rd. W7 104 C7
Drayton Br. Rd. W13 104 C7
Drayton Cl., Houns. 143 F5
Bramley Way
Drayton Cl., Ilf. 99 G1
Drayton Gdns. N21 43 H7
Drayton Gdns. SW10 30 D3
Drayton Gdns. SW10 129 F5
Drayton Gdns. W13 104 D7
Drayton Gdns., 120 B2
West Dr.
Drayton Grn. W13 104 D7
Drayton Grn. Rd. W13 104 E7
Drayton Gro. W13 104 D7
Drayton Pk. N5 93 G5
Drayton Pk. Ms. N5 93 G5
Drayton Pk.
Drayton Rd. E11 96 D7
Drayton Rd. N17 76 B2
Drayton Rd. NW10 107 F1
Drayton Rd. W13 104 D7
Drayton Rd., Borwd. 38 A4
Drayton Rd., Croy. 201 H2
Drayton Waye, Har. 69 E6
Dreadnought St. SE10 135 E3
Dresden Cl. NW6 91 E6
Dresden Rd. N19 92 D1
Dressington Av. SE4 154 A6
Drew Av. NW7 56 B6
Drew Gdns., Grnf. 86 C6
Drew Rd. E16 136 B1
Drewstead Rd. SW16 168 D2
Driffield Rd. E3 113 H2
Drift, The, Brom. 206 A3
Drift Way, Rich. 163 J1
Driftway, The, Mitch. 186 A1
Drinkwater Rd., Har. 85 H2
Drive, The E4 46 D7
Drive, The E17 78 B4
Drive, The E18 79 G4
Drive, The N3 56 D7
Drive, The N6 73 J5
Fordington Rd.
Drive, The N11 58 C6
Drive, The NW10 107 F1
Longstone Av.
Drive, The NW11 72 B7
Drive, The SW6 148 B2
Fulham Rd.
Drive, The SW16 187 F3
Drive, The SW20 165 J7
Drive, The W3 106 C6
Drive, The, Bark. 99 J7
Drive, The, Barn. 40 B3
Drive, The, 41 F6
(New Barnet), Barn.
Drive, The, Beck. 190 A2
Drive, The, Bex. 158 C6
Drive, The, Buck.H. 47 J7
Drive, The, Chis. 193 J3
Drive, The, 193 H1
(Scadbury Pk.), Chis.
Drive, The, Edg. 54 A5
Drive, The, Enf. 44 A1
Drive, The, Epsom 197 F6
Drive, The, Erith 139 H7
Drive, The, Felt. 142 C7
Drive, The, Har. 67 G7
Drive, The, Houns. 144 A2
Drive, The, Ilf. 98 C1
Drive, The, Islw. 144 A2
Drive, The, Kings.T. 164 C7
Drive, The, Loug. 48 B3
Drive, The, Mord. 185 G5
Drive, The, Orp. 207 J2
Drive, The, Rom. 83 J1
Drive, The, Sid. 176 B3
Drive, The, Surb. 181 H7
Drive, The, Th.Hth. 188 A4
Drive, The, Wem. 88 C2
Drive, The, W.Wick. 190 D7
Driveway, The E17 78 B6
Hoe St.
Droitwich Cl. SE26 170 D3
Dromey Gdns., Har. 52 C7

Dromore Rd. SW15 148 B6
Dronfield Gdns., Dag. 100 C5
Droop St. W10 108 B4
Drover La. SE15 133 E7
Drovers Pl. SE15 133 E7
Drovers Rd., S.Croy. 202 A5
Droveway, Loug. 49 E2
Druce Rd. SE21 152 B6
Druid St. SE1 28 E3
Druid St. SE1 132 B2
Druids Way, Brom. 190 D4
Drum St. E1 21 G3
Drumaline Ridge, 197 E2
Wor.Pk.
Drummond Cres. 9 H3
NW1
Drummond Cres. 110 D3
NW1
Drummond Dr., Stan. 52 C7
Drummond Gate SW1 33 J3
Drummond Gate 130 D5
SW1
Drummond Pl., Rich. 145 H4
Drummond Pl., 144 E6
Twick.
Drummond Rd. E11 79 J6
Drummond Rd. SE16 132 E3
Drummond Rd., 201 J2
Croy.
Drummond St. NW1 9 F5
Drummond St. NW1 110 C4
Drummonds, The, 63 H2
Buck.H.
Drury Cres., Croy. 201 G2
Drury La. WC2 18 B4
Drury La. WC2 111 E6
Drury Rd., Har. 67 J7
Drury Way NW10 88 D5
Drury Way Ind. Est. 88 C5
NW10
Dryad St. SW15 148 A3
Dryburgh Gdns. NW9 70 A3
Dryburgh Rd. SW15 147 H3
Dryden Av. W7 104 C6
Dryden Cl., Ilf. 65 J6
Dryden Ct. SE11 35 F2
Dryden Ct. SE11 131 G4
Dryden Rd. SW19 167 F6
Dryden Rd., Enf. 44 B6
Dryden Rd., Har. 68 C1
Dryden Rd., Well. 157 H1
Dryden St. WC2 18 B4
Dryfield Cl. NW10 88 C6
Dryfield Rd., Edg. 54 C6
Dryfield Wk. SE8 134 A6
New King St.
Dryhill Rd., Belv. 139 F6
Dryland Av., Orp. 207 J4
Drylands Rd. N8 75 E6
Drysdale Av. E4 46 B7
Drysdale Pl. N1 12 E3
Drysdale St. N1 12 E3
Du Burstow Ter. W7 124 B2
Du Cane Cl. W12 107 J6
Du Cane Ct. SW17 168 A1
Du Cane Rd. W12 107 F6
Du Cros Dr., Stan. 53 F6
Du Cros Rd. W3 126/127 E1
The Vale
Dublin Av. E8 112 D1
Ducal St. E2 13 G4
Duchess Cl. N11 58 B5
Duchess Cl., Sutt. 199 F4
Duchess Gro., 63 H2
Buck.H.
Duchess Ms. W1 16 E2
Duchess of Bedford's 128 D2
Wk. W8
Duchess St. W1 16 E2
Duchess St. W1 110 B5
Duchy Cl. SE1 27 F1
Duchy St. SE1 131 G1
Ducie St. SW4 151 F4
Duck La. W1 17 H4
Duck Lees La., Enf. 45 H4
Duckett Ms. N4 75 H6
Duckett Rd. N4 75 H6
Duckett St. E1 113 G5
Ducks Wk., Twick. 145 F5
Dudden Hill La. 89 F4
NW10
Duddington Cl. SE9 174 A4
Dudley Av., Har. 69 F3
Dudley Ct. NW11 72 C4
Dudley Dr., Mord. 184 B7
Dudley Dr., Ruis. 84 B5
Dudley Gdns. W13 125 E2
Dudley Gdns., Har. 86 A1
Dudley Rd. E17 78 A2
Dudley Rd. N3 72 E2
Dudley Rd. NW6 108 B2
Dudley Rd. SW19 166 D6

Dudley Rd., Har. 85 J2
Dudley Rd., Ilf. 99 E4
Dudley Rd., Kings.T. 181 J3
Dudley Rd., Rich. 145 J2
Dudley Rd., Sthl. 122 D2
Dudley Rd., Walt. 178 A6
Dudley St. W2 14 E2
Dudley St. W2 109 G5
Dudlington Rd. E5 95 F2
Dudmaston Ms. SW3 31 F3
Dudsbury Rd., Sid. 176 B6
Dudset La., Houns. 142 A1
Duff St. E14 114 B6
Dufferin Av. EC1 12 B6
Dufferin St. EC1 12 A6
Dufferin St. EC1 111 J4
Duffield Cl., Har. 68 C5
Duffield Dr. N15 76 C7
Copperfield Dr.
Dufour's Pl. W1 17 G4
Dugard Way SE11 35 G1
Dugard Way SE11 131 H4
Duke Gdns., Ilf. 81 G4
Duke Rd.
Duke Humphrey Rd. 155 E1
SE3
Duke of Cambridge 144 A6
Cl., Twick.
Duke of Edinburgh 199 G2
Rd., Sutt.
Duke of Wellington 24 C3
Pl. SW1
Duke of Wellington 130 A2
Pl. SW1
Duke of York St. SW1 25 G1
Duke of York St. SW1 130 C1
Duke St. SW1 25 G1
Duke St. SW1 130 C1
Duke St. W1 16 C3
Duke St. W1 110 A6
Duke St., Rich. 145 G4
Duke St., Sutt. 199 G4
Duke St. Hill SE1 28 C1
Dukes Av. N3 72 E1
Dukes Av. N10 74 C3
Dukes Av. W4 126 D5
Dukes Av., Edg. 53 J6
Dukes Av., Har. 67 F6
Dukes Av. 68 B4
(Wealdstone), Har.
Dukes Av., Houns. 142 E4
Dukes Av., Kings.T. 163 F4
Dukes Av., N.Mal. 183 F3
Dukes Av., Nthlt. 85 E7
Dukes Av., Rich. 163 F4
Dukes Cl., Hmptn. 161 F5
Dukes Ct. E6 116 D1
Dukes Grn. Av., Felt. 142 A5
Dukes Head Yd. N6 92 B1
Highgate High St.
Dukes La. W8 128 D2
Duke's Meadows W4 146 C2
Great Chertsey Rd.
Dukes Ms. N10 74 B3
Dukes Av.
Duke's Ms. W1 16 C3
Dukes Orchard, Bex. 177 J1
Duke's Pas. E17 78 C4
Dukes Pl. EC3 21 E4
Dukes Pl. EC3 112 B6
Dukes Rd. E6 116 D1
Dukes Rd. W3 106 A5
Duke's Rd. WC1 9 J4
Duke's Rd. WC1 110 D3
Dukes Way, W.Wick. 205 E3
Duke's Yd. W1 16 C5
Dukesthorpe Rd. 171 G5
SE26
Dulas St. N4 93 F1
Everleigh St.
Dulford St. W11 108 B7
Dulka Rd. SW11 149 J5
Dulverton Rd. SE9 175 F2
Dulverton Rd., Ruis. 84 A1
Dulwich Common 170 B1
SE21
Dulwich Common 170 B1
SE22
Dulwich Lawn Cl. 152 C5
SE22
Colwell Rd.
Dulwich Oaks, The 170 B3
SE21
Dulwich Rd. SE24 151 G5
Dulwich Village SE21 152 B6
Dulwich Wd. Av. 170 B4
SE19
Dulwich Wd. Pk. SE19 170 B4

Entry	Page	Grid
Dumbarton Rd. SW2	151	E6
Dumbleton Cl.,	182	B1
Kings.T.		
Gloucester Rd.		
Dumbreck Rd. SE9	156	D4
Dumont Rd. N16	94	B3
Dumpton Pl. NW1	92	A7
Gloucester Av.		
Dunbar Av. SW16	187	G2
Dunbar Av., Beck.	189	H4
Dunbar Av., Dag.	101	G3
Dunbar Cl., Hayes	102	A5
Dunbar Ct., Sutt.	199	G5
Dunbar Gdns., Dag.	101	G5
Dunbar Rd. E7	97	G6
Dunbar Rd. N22	75	G1
Dunbar Rd., N.Mal.	182	C4
Dunbar St. SE27	169	J3
Dunblane Cl., Edg.	54	B2
Tayside Dr.		
Dunblane Rd. SE9	156	B3
Dunboyne Rd. NW3	91	J5
Dunbridge St. E2	**13**	**J5**
Dunbridge St. E2	112	D4
Duncan Cl., Barn.	41	F4
Duncan Gro. W3	106	E6
Duncan Rd. E8	112	E1
Duncan Rd., Rich.	145	H4
Duncan St. N1	**11**	**G1**
Duncan St. N1	111	H2
Duncan Ter. N1	**11**	**G2**
Duncan Ter. N1	111	H2
Duncannon St. WC2	**18**	**A6**
Duncannon St. WC2	110	E7
Dunch St. E1	112/113	E6
Watney St.		
Duncombe Hill SE23	153	H7
Duncombe Rd. N19	92	D1
Duncrievie Rd. SE13	154	D6
Duncroft SE18	137	H7
Dundalk Rd. SE4	153	H3
Dundas Gdns.,	179	H3
W.Mol.		
Dundas Rd. SE15	153	F2
Dundee Rd. E13	115	H2
Dundee Rd. SE25	188	E5
Dundee St. E1	132	E1
Dundee Way, Enf.	45	H3
Dundela Gdns.,	197	H4
Wor.Pk.		
Dundonald Cl. E6	116	B6
Northumberland Rd.		
Dundonald Rd. NW10	108	A1
Dundonald Rd. SW19	166	B7
Dunedin Rd. E10	96	B3
Dunedin Rd., Ilf.	99	F1
Dunedin Way, Hayes	102	C4
Dunelm Gro. SE27	169	J4
Dunelm St. E1	113	G6
Dunfield Gdns. SE6	172	B4
Dunfield Rd. SE6	172	B5
Dunford Rd. N7	93	F4
Dungarvan Av. SW15	147	G4
Dunheved Cl.,	187	G6
Th.Hth.		
Dunheved Rd. N.,	187	G6
Th.Hth.		
Dunheved Rd. S.,	187	G6
Th.Hth.		
Dunheved Rd. W.,	187	G6
Th.Hth.		
Dunholme Grn. N9	60	C3
Dunholme La. N9	60	C3
Dunholme Rd.		
Dunholme Rd. N9	60	C3
Dunkeld Rd. SE25	188	A4
Dunkeld Rd., Dag.	100	B2
Dunkery Rd. SE9	174	A4
Dunkirk St. SE27	169	J4
Waring St.		
Dunlace Rd. E5	95	F4
Dunleary Cl., Houns.	143	F7
Dunley Dr., Croy.	204	B7
Dunlin Ho. W13	104	C4
Dunloe Av. N17	76	A3
Dunloe St. E2	**13**	**F2**
Dunloe St. E2	112	C2
Dunlop Pl. SE16	**29**	**G6**
Dunmore Pt. E2	**13**	**F4**
Dunmore Rd. NW6	108	B1
Dunmore Rd. SW20	183	J1
Dunmow Cl., Felt.	160	E4
Dunmow Cl., Loug.	48	B6
Dunmow Cl., Rom.	82	C5
Dunmow Ho., Dag.	118	B1
Dunmow Rd. E15	96	D4
Dunmow Wk. N1	111	J1
Popham St.		
Dunn Mead NW9	55	F7
Field Mead		
Dunn St. E8	94	C5
Dunnage Cres. SE16	133	H4
Plough Way		
Dunnock Cl. N9	61	G1
Dunnock Cl., Borwd.	38	A4
Dunnock Rd. E6	116	B6
Dunns Pas. WC1	**18**	**B3**
Dunollie Pl. NW5	92	C5
Dunollie Rd.		
Dunollie Rd. NW5	92	C5
Dunoon Rd. SE23	153	F7
Dunraven Dr., Enf.	43	G2
Dunraven Rd. W12	127	G1
Dunraven St. W1	**16**	**A5**
Dunsany Rd. W14	128	A3
Dunsfold Way, Croy.	204	B7
Dunsford Way SW15	147	H6
Dover Pk. Dr.		
Dunsmore Cl.,	102/103	E4
Hayes		
Kingsash Dr.		
Dunsmore Rd., Walt.	178	B6
Dunsmure Rd. N16	94	B1
Dunspring La., Ilf.	80	E2
Dunstable Ms. W1	**16**	**C1**
Dunstable Rd., Rich.	145	H4
Dunstable Rd.,	179	H3
W.Mol.		
Dunstall Rd. SW20	165	H6
Dunstall Way, W.Mol.	179	H3
Dunstan Cl. N2	73	F3
Thomas More Way		
Dunstan Rd. NW11	90	C1
Dunstans Gro. SE22	152	E6
Dunstans Rd. SE22	152	D7
Dunster Av., Mord.	198	A1
Dunster Cl., Barn.	40	A4
Dunster Cl., Rom.	83	J2
Dunster Ct. EC3	**20**	**E5**
Dunster Dr. NW9	88	C1
Dunster Gdns. NW6	90	C7
Dunster Way, Har.	85	E3
Dunsterville Way SE1	**28**	**C4**
Dunston Rd. E8	112	C1
Dunston Rd. SW11	150	A2
Dunston St. E8	112	C1
Dunton Cl., Surb.	195	H1
Dunton Rd. E10	78	B7
Dunton Rd. E1	**37**	**F3**
Dunton Rd. SE1	132	C5
Dunsthill Rd. SW18	167	E1
Dunvegan Cl.,	179	H4
W.Mol.		
Dunvegan Rd. SE9	156	C4
Dunwich Rd., Bexh.	159	F1
Dunworth Ms. W11	108	C6
Portobello Rd.		
Duplex Ride SW1	**24**	**A4**
Dupont Rd. SW20	184	A2
Dupont St. E14	113	H5
Maroon St.		
Duppas Av., Croy.	201	H4
Violet La.		
Duppas Hill La., Croy.	201	H4
Duppas Hill Rd.		
Duppas Hill Rd., Croy.	201	H4
Duppas Hill Ter.,	201	H3
Croy.		
Duppas Rd., Croy.	201	G3
Dupree Rd. SE7	135	H5
Dura Den Cl., Beck.	172	B7
Durand Cl., Cars.	199	J1
Durand Gdns. SW9	151	F1
Durand Way NW10	88	C7
Durands Wk. SE16	133	J2
Durant St. E2	**13**	**H3**
Durant St. E2	112	D3
Durants Pk. Av., Enf.	45	G4
Durants Rd., Enf.	45	F4
Durban Gdns., Dag.	101	J7
Durban Rd. E15	114	E3
Durban Rd. E17	77	J1
Durban Rd. N17	60	B6
Durban Rd. SE27	169	J4
Durban Rd., Beck.	189	J2
Durban Rd., Ilf.	99	H1
Durbin Rd., Chess.	195	H4
Durdans Rd., Sthl.	103	F6
Durell Gdns., Dag.	100	D5
Durell Rd., Dag.	100	D5
Durford Cres. SW15	165	H1
Durham Av., Brom.	191	F4
Durham Av., Houns.	123	F5
Durham Av.,	64	A5
Wdf.Grn.		
Durham Cl. SW20	183	H2
Durham Rd.		
Durham Hill, Brom.	173	F4
Durham Ho. St. WC2	**18**	**B6**
Durham Pl. SW3	**31**	**J4**
Durham Pl., Ilf.	99	F4
Eton Rd.		
Durham Ri. SE18	137	F5
Durham Rd. E12	98	A4
Durham Rd. E16	115	E4
Durham Rd. N2	73	H3
Durham Rd. N7	93	F2
Durham Rd. N9	60	D2
Durham Rd. SW20	183	H1
Durham Rd. W5	125	G3
Durham Rd., Borwd.	38	C3
Durham Rd., Brom.	191	F3
Durham Rd., Dag.	101	J5
Durham Rd., Felt.	142	C7
Durham Rd., Har.	67	H5
Durham Rd., Sid.	176	B5
Durham Row E11	113	H5
Durham St. SE11	**34**	**C4**
Durham St. SE11	131	F5
Durham Ter. W2	**14**	**A3**
Durham Ter. W2	108	E6
Durham Wf., Brent.	125	F7
London Rd.		
Durham Yd. E2	112/113	E3
Teesdale St.		
Durley Av., Pnr.	67	E7
Durley Rd. N16	76	B7
Durlston Rd. E5	94	D2
Durlston Rd.,	163	H6
Kings.T.		
Durnell Way, Loug.	48	D3
Durnford St. N15	76	B5
Durnford St. SE10	134	C6
Greenwich Ch. St.		
Durning Rd. SE19	170	A5
Durnsford Av. SW19	166	D2
Durnsford Rd. N11	74	D1
Durnsford Rd. SW19	166	D2
Durrant Way, Orp.	207	G5
Durrell Rd. SW6	148	C1
Durrington Av.	183	J1
SW20		
Durrington Pk. Rd.	165	J7
SW20		
Durrington Rd. E5	95	H4
Dursley Cl. SE3	155	J2
Dursley Gdns. SE3	156	A1
Dursley Rd. SE3	155	J2
Durward St. E1	112	E5
Durweston Ms. W1	**16**	**A1**
Durweston St. W1	**16**	**A1**
Durweston St. W1	109	J5
Dury Rd., Barn.	40	C1
Dutch Barn Cl., Stai.	140	A6
Dutch Gdns.,	164	B6
Kings.T.		
Windmill Ri.		
Dutch Yd. SW18	148	D5
Wandsworth High St.		
Duthie St. E14	114	C7
Prestons Rd.		
Dutton St. SE10	154	C1
Duxberry Cl., Brom.	192	B5
Southborough La.		
Duxford Ho. SE2	138	D2
Wolvercote Rd.		
Dwight Ct. SW6	148	B2
Burlington Rd.		
Dye Ho. La. E3	114	A1
Dyer's Bldgs. EC1	**19**	**E2**
Dyers Hall Rd. E11	96	E1
Dyers La. SW15	147	H4
Dykes Way, Brom.	191	F3
Dylan Rd. SE24	151	H4
Dylan Rd., Belv.	139	G3
Dylan Thomas Ho.	75	F4
N8		
Dylways SE5	152	A4
Dymchurch Cl., Ilf.	80	D2
Dymchurch Cl., Orp.	207	H4
Dymes Path SW19	166	A2
Queensmere Rd.		
Dymock St. SW6	148	E3
Dymond Est. SW17	167	H3
Glenburnie Rd.		
Dyne Rd. NW6	90	C7
Dyneley Rd. SE12	173	J4
Dynevor Rd. N16	94	B3
Dynevor Rd., Rich.	145	H5
Dynham Rd. NW6	90	D7
Dyott St. WC1	**18**	**A3**
Dyott St. WC1	110	D6
Dysart Av., Kings.T.	163	F5
Dysart St. EC2	**12**	**D6**
Dyson Rd. E11	79	E6
Dyson Rd. E15	97	F6
Dysons Rd. N18	61	E5

E

Entry	Page	Grid
Eade Rd. N4	75	J7
Eagans Cl. N2	73	H3
Market Pl.		
Eagle Av., Rom.	82	E6
Eagle Cl. SE16	133	F5
Varcoe Rd.		
Eagle Cl., Enf.	45	F4
Eagle Cl., Wall.	201	E6
Eagle Ct. EC1	**19**	**G1**
Eagle Ct. EC1	111	H5
Eagle Dr. NW9	71	E2
Eagle Hill SE19	170	A6
Eagle La. E11	79	G4
Eagle Ms. N1	94	B6
Tottenham Rd.		
Eagle Pl. SW1	**17**	**G6**
Eagle Pl. SW7	**30**	**D3**
Eagle Rd., Wem.	87	G7
Eagle St. WC1	**18**	**C2**
Eagle St. WC1	111	F5
Eagle Ter., Wdf.Grn.	63	H7
Eagle Wf. E14	114	B5
Broomfield St.		
Eagle Wf. Rd. N1	**12**	**A1**
Eaglesfield Rd. SE18	137	E7
Ealdham Sq. SE9	155	J4
Ealing Cl., Borwd.	38	D1
Ealing Downs Ct.,	104	D3
Grnf.		
Perivale La.		
Ealing Grn. W5	125	G1
Ealing Pk. Gdns. W5	125	F4
Ealing Rd., Brent.	125	G5
Ealing Rd., Nthlt.	85	G7
Ealing Rd., Wem.	105	H1
Ealing Village W5	105	H6
Eamont St. NW8	**7**	**G1**
Eamont St. NW8	109	H2
Eardley Cres. SW5	128	D5
Eardley Pt. SE18	136/137	E4
Wilmount St.		
Eardley Rd. SW16	168	C5
Eardley Rd., Belv.	139	G5
Earl Cl. N11	58	B5
Earl Ri. SE18	137	G4
Earl Rd. SW14	146	C4
Elm Rd.		
Earl St. EC2	**20**	**D1**
Earl St. EC2	112	A5
Earldom Rd. SW15	147	J4
Earle Gdns., Kings.T.	163	H6
Earlham Gro. E7	97	F5
Earlham Gro. N22	59	F7
Earlham St. WC2	**17**	**J4**
Earlham St. WC2	110	D6
Earls Ct. Gdns. SW5	**30**	**A2**
Earls Ct. Gdns. SW5	128	E4
Earls Ct. Rd. SW5	128	D4
Earls Ct. Rd. W8	128	D3
Earls Ct. Sq. SW5	**30**	**A3**
Earls Ct. Sq. SW5	128	E5
Earls Cres., Har.	68	B4
Earl's Path, Loug.	47	J2
Earls Ter. W8	128	C3
Earls Wk. W8	128	D3
Earls Wk., Dag.	100	B4
Earls Way, Orp.	207	J2
Station Rd.		
Earlsdown Ho., Bark.	117	G2
Wheelers Cross		
Earlsferry Way N1	111	F1
Earlsfield Rd. SW18	167	F1
Earlshall Rd. SE9	156	C4
Earlsmead, Har.	85	F4
Earlsmead Rd. N15	76	C5
Earlsmead Rd. NW10	107	J2
Earlsthorpe Ms.	150	A6
SW12		
Earlsthorpe Rd. SE26	171	G4
Earlstoke St. EC1	**11**	**G3**
Earlston Gro. E9	113	E1
Earlswood Av.,	187	G5
Th.Hth.		
Earlswood Cl.	134/135	E5
SE10		
Earlswood St.		
Earlswood Gdns., Ilf.	80	D3
Earlswood St. SE10	135	E5
Early Ms. NW1	110	B1
Arlington Rd.		
East Acton La. W3	126	E1
East Arbour St. E1	113	G6
East Av. E12	98	B7
East Av. E17	78	B4
East Av., Hayes	121	J2
East Av., Sthl.	103	F7
East Av., Wall.	201	F5
East Bank N16	76	B7
East Barnet Rd., Barn.	41	H6
East Churchfield Rd.	126	D1
W3		
East Cl. W5	106	A4
East Cl., Barn.	42	A4
East Cl., Grnf.	103	J2
East Cl., Wem.	87	F2
East Cres. N11	57	J4
East Cres., Enf.	44	C5

East Cross Route E3 114 A1
East Duck Lees La., Enf. 45 H4
East Dulwich Gro. SE22 152 B6
East Dulwich Rd. SE15 152 C4
East Dulwich Rd. SE22 152 C4
East End Rd. N2 73 F3
East End Rd. N3 72 D2
East End Way, Pnr. 67 E3
East Entrance, Dag. 119 H2
East Ferry Rd. E14 134 B3
East Gdns. SW17 167 H6
East Ham Ind. Est. E6 116 B4
East Ham Manor Way E6 116 D6
East Harding St. EC4 19 F3
East Heath Rd. NW3 91 G3
East Hill SW18 149 E5
East Hill, Wem. 88 A2
East India Dock Rd. E14 114 D6
East La. SE16 29 H4
East La. SE16 132 D2
East La., Kings.T. 181 G3
High St.
East La., Wem. 87 G3
East Mascalls SE7 135 J6
Mascalls Rd.
East Mead, Ruis. 84 D3
East Mt. St. E1 113 E5
East Pk. Cl., Rom. 82 D5
East Parkside SE10 135 E2
East Pas. EC1 19 H1
East Pier E1 132/133 E1
Wapping High St.
East Pl. SE27 169 J4
Pilgrim Hill
East Poultry Av. EC1 19 G2
East Ramp, Houns. 140 E1
East Rd. E15 115 G1
East Rd. N1 12 B4
East Rd. N1 112 A3
East Rd. SW19 167 F6
East Rd., Barn. 58 A1
East Rd., Edg. 70 B1
East Rd., Felt. 141 G7
East Rd., Kings.T. 181 H1
East Rd. (Chadwell Heath), Rom. 82 E5
East Rd., Well. 158 B2
East Rd., West Dr. 120 C4
East Rochester Way SE9 157 H4
East Rochester Way, Bex. 159 J7
East Rochester Way, Sid. 157 H4
East Row E11 79 G6
East Row W10 108 B4
East Sheen Av. SW14 146 D4
East Smithfield E1 21 G6
East Smithfield E1 112 C7
East St. SE17 36 A3
East St. SE17 131 J5
East St., Bark. 99 F7
East St., Bexh. 159 G4
East St., Brent. 125 F7
East St., Brom. 191 G2
East Surrey Gro. SE15 132 C7
East Tenter St. E1 21 G4
East Tenter St. E1 112 C6
East Twrs., Pnr. 66 D5
East Vw. E4 62 C5
East Vw., Barn. 40 C3
East Wk., Barn. 42 A7
East Wk., Hayes 122 A1
East Way E11 79 H5
East Way, Brom. 191 G7
East Way, Croy. 203 H2
East Way, Hayes 122 A1
East Way, Ruis. 84 A1
East Woodside, Bex. 177 E1
Eastbank Rd., Hmptn. 161 J5
Eastbourne Av. W3 106 D6
Eastbourne Gdns. SW14 146 C3
Eastbourne Ms. W2 14 D3
Eastbourne Ms. W2 109 F6
Eastbourne Rd. E6 116 D3
Eastbourne Rd. E15 115 E1
Eastbourne Rd. N15 76 B6
Eastbourne Rd. SW17 168 A6
Eastbourne Rd. W4 126 C6
Eastbourne Rd., Brent. 125 F5
Eastbourne Rd., Felt. 160 D2
Eastbourne Ter. W2 14 D3
Eastbourne Ter. W2 109 F6
Eastbournia Av. N9 61 E3
Eastbrook Av. N9 45 F7
Eastbrook Av., Dag. 101 J4
Eastbrook Rd. SE3 135 H7
Eastbury Av., Bark. 117 H1
Eastbury Av., Enf. 44 B1
Eastbury Ct., Bark. 117 H1
Eastbury Gro. W4 127 E5
Eastbury Ho., Bark. 117 J1
Eastbury Rd. E6 116 D4
Eastbury Rd., Kings.T. 163 H7
Eastbury Rd., Orp. 193 G6
Eastbury Sq., Bark. 117 J1
Eastbury Ter. E1 113 G4
Eastcastle St. W1 17 F3
Eastcastle St. W1 110 C6
Eastcheap EC3 20 C5
Eastcheap EC3 112 A7
Eastchurch Rd., Houns. 141 H2
Eastcombe Av. SE7 135 H6
Eastcote, Orp. 207 J1
Eastcote Av., Grnf. 86 D5
Eastcote Av., Har. 85 H2
Eastcote Av., W.Mol. 179 F5
Eastcote La., Har. 85 G3
Eastcote La., Nthlt. 85 G7
Eastcote La. N., Nthlt. 85 F6
Eastcote Pl., Pnr. 66 B6
Eastcote Rd., Har. 85 J3
Eastcote Rd., Pnr. 66 D5
Eastcote Rd. (Eastcote Village), Pnr. 66 A6
Eastcote Rd., Well. 157 G2
Eastcote St. SW9 151 F2
Eastcote Vw., Pnr. 66 C4
Eastcroft Rd., Epsom 197 E7
Eastdown Pk. SE13 154 D4
Eastern Av. E11 79 J6
Eastern Av., Ilf. 80 B6
Eastern Av., Pnr. 66 D7
Eastern Av., Rom. 82 C4
Eastern Av. W., Rom. 82 E4
Eastern Ind. Est., Erith 139 G2
Eastern Perimeter Rd., Houns. 141 J3
Eastern Rd. E13 115 H2
Eastern Rd. E17 78 C5
Eastern Rd. N2 73 J3
Eastern Rd. N22 75 E1
Eastern Rd. SE4 154 A4
Eastern Way SE2 138 D1
Eastern Way SE28 138 A2
Eastern Way, Belv. 139 H2
Eastern Way, Erith 138 D1
Easternville Gdns., Ilf. 81 F6
Eastfield Cotts., Hayes 121 H5
Eastfield Gdns., Dag. 101 G4
Eastfield Rd. E17 78 A4
Eastfield Rd. N8 74 E3
Eastfield Rd., Dag. 101 G4
Eastfields, Pnr. 66 C5
Eastfields Rd. W3 106 C5
Eastfields Rd., Mitch. 186 A2
Eastgate Cl. SE28 118 D6
Eastglade, Pnr. 67 E3
Eastham Cl., Barn. 40 B5
Eastholm NW11 73 E4
Eastholme, Hayes 122 A1
Eastlake Rd. SE5 151 H2
Eastlands Cres. SE21 152 C6
Eastlea Ms. E16 114/115 E4
Desford Rd.
Eastleigh Av., Har. 85 H2
Eastleigh Cl. NW2 89 E3
Eastleigh Cl., Sutt. 199 E7
Eastleigh Rd. E17 77 J2
Eastleigh Rd., Bexh. 159 J2
Eastleigh Rd., Houns. 141 J3
Cranford La.
Eastleigh Wk. SW15 147 G7
Eastleigh Way, Felt. 160 A1
Eastman Rd. W3 126 D1
Eastmead Av., Grnf. 103 H3
Eastmead Cl., Brom. 192 B2
Eastmearn Rd. SE21 169 J2
Eastmont Rd., Esher 194 B2
Eastmoor Pl. SE7 136 A3
Eastmoor St.
Eastmoor St. SE7 136 A3
Eastney Rd., Croy. 201 H1
Eastney St. SE10 134 D5
Eastnor Rd. SE9 175 F1
Easton Gdns., Borwd. 38 D4
Easton St. WC1 10 E4
Eastry Av., Brom. 191 F6
Eastry Rd., Erith 139 G7
Eastside Rd. NW11 72 C4
Eastview Av. SE18 137 H7
Eastville Av. NW11 72 C6
Eastway E9 95 J6
Eastway E10 96 C4
Eastway E15 96 A5
Eastway, Mord. 184 A5
Eastway, Wall. 200 C4
Eastway Commercial Cen. E9 96 A5
Eastwell Cl., Beck. 189 H1
Eastwood Cl. E18 79 G2
George La.
Eastwood Cl. N17 60/61 E7
Northumberland Gro.
Eastwood Rd. E18 79 G2
Eastwood Rd. N10 74 A2
Eastwood Rd., Ilf. 82 A7
Eastwood Rd., West Dr. 120 D2
Eastwood St. SW16 168 C6
Eatington Rd. E10 78 D5
Eaton Cl. SW1 32 B2
Eaton Cl. SW1 130 A4
Eaton Cl., Stan. 53 E4
Eaton Dr. SW9 151 H4
Eaton Dr., Kings.T. 164 A7
Eaton Gdns., Dag. 100 E7
Eaton Gate SW1 32 B1
Eaton Gate SW1 130 A4
Eaton La. SW1 24 E6
Eaton La. SW1 130 B3
Eaton Ms. N. SW1 32 B1
Eaton Ms. N. SW1 130 A3
Eaton Ms. S. SW1 32 C1
Eaton Ms. S. SW1 130 B3
Eaton Ms. W. SW1 32 C1
Eaton Ms. W. SW1 130 A4
Eaton Pk. Rd. N13 59 G2
Eaton Pl. SW1 24 B6
Eaton Pl. SW1 130 A3
Eaton Ri. E11 79 J5
Eaton Ri. W5 105 G6
Eaton Rd. NW4 71 J5
Eaton Rd., Enf. 44 B3
Eaton Rd., Houns. 144 A4
Eaton Rd., Sid. 176 D2
Eaton Rd., Sutt. 199 G6
Eaton Row SW1 24 D6
Eaton Row SW1 130 B3
Eaton Sq. SW1 24 D5
Eaton Sq. SW1 130 A4
Eaton Ter. SW1 32 B1
Eaton Ter. SW1 130 A4
Eaton Ter. Ms. SW1 32 B1
Eaton Wk. SE15 132 C7
Sumner Est.
Eatons Mead E4 62 A2
Eatonville Rd. SW17 167 J2
Eatonville Vil. SW17 167 J2
Eatonville Rd.
Ebbisham Dr. SW8 34 C5
Ebbisham Dr. SW8 131 F6
Ebbisham Rd., Wor.Pk. 197 J2
Ebbsfleet Rd. NW2 90 B4
Ebdon Way SE3 155 H3
Ebenezer St. N1 12 B3
Ebenezer St. N1 112 A3
Ebenezer Wk. SW16 186 C1
Ebley Cl. SE15 37 F6
Ebley Cl. SE15 132 C6
Ebner St. SW18 149 E5
Ebor St. E1 13 F5
Ebor St. E1 112 C4
Ebrington Rd., Har. 69 G6
Ebsworth St. SE23 153 G7
Eburne Rd. N7 93 E3
Ebury Br. SW1 32 D3
Ebury Br. SW1 130 B5
Ebury Br. Est. SW1 32 D3
Ebury Br. Est. SW1 130 B5
Ebury Br. Rd. SW1 32 C4
Ebury Br. Rd. SW1 130 A5
Ebury Cl., Kes. 206 B3
Ebury Ms. SE27 169 H3
Ebury Ms. SW1 32 D1
Ebury Ms. SW1 130 B4
Ebury Ms. E. SW1 32 D1
Ebury Sq. SW1 32 C2
Ebury Sq. SW1 130 A4
Ebury St. SW1 32 D1
Ebury St. SW1 130 A4
Eccles Rd. SW11 149 J4
Ecclesbourne Cl. N13 59 G5
Ecclesbourne Gdns. N13 59 G5
Ecclesbourne Rd. N1 93 J7
Ecclesbourne Rd., Th.Hth. 187 J5
Eccleston Br. SW1 32 E1
Eccleston Br. SW1 130 B4
Eccleston Cl., Barn. 41 J4
Eccleston Cl., Orp. 207 G1
Eccleston Cres., Rom. 82 A7
Eccleston Ms. SW1 24 C6
Eccleston Ms. SW1 130 A3
Eccleston Pl. SW1 32 D1
Eccleston Pl. SW1 130 B4
Eccleston Rd. W13 104 D7
Eccleston Sq. SW1 33 E2
Eccleston Sq. SW1 130 B4
Eccleston Sq. Ms. SW1 33 F2
Eccleston St. SW1 24 D6
Eccleston St. SW1 130 A3
Ecclestone Ct., Wem. 87 H5
St. John's Rd.
Ecclestone Pl., Wem. 87 J5
Echo Hts. E4 62 B1
Mount Echo Dr.
Eckersley St. E1 112 D4
Buxton St.
Eckford St. N1 10 E1
Eckford St. N1 111 G2
Eckstein Rd. SW11 149 H4
Eclipse Rd. E13 115 H5
Ector Rd. SE6 172 E2
Edbrooke Rd. W9 108 D4
Eddiscombe Rd. SW6 148 C2
Eddy Cl., Rom. 83 H6
Eddystone Rd. SE4 153 H5
Eddystone Wk., Stai. 140 B7
Ede Cl., Houns. 143 F3
Eden Cl. NW3 90 D2
Eden Cl. W8 128 D3
Adam & Eve Ms.
Eden Cl., Wem. 105 G1
Eden Gro. E17 78 B5
Eden Gro. N7 93 F5
Eden Ms. SW17 167 F3
Huntspill St.
Eden Pk. Av., Beck. 189 H4
Eden Rd. E17 78 B5
Eden Rd. SE27 169 H5
Eden Rd., Beck. 189 H4
Eden Rd., Bex. 177 J4
Eden Rd., Croy. 202 A4
Eden St., Kings.T. 181 G2
Eden Wk., Kings.T. 181 H2
Eden St.
Eden Way, Beck. 189 J5
Edenbridge Cl. SE16 132/133 E5
Masters Dr.
Edenbridge Rd. E9 95 G7
Edenbridge Rd., Enf. 44 B6
Edencourt Rd. SW16 168 B6
Edenfield Gdns., Wor.Pk. 197 F3
Edenham Way W10 108 C5
Elkstone Rd.
Edenhurst Av. SW6 148 C3
Edensor Gdns. W4 127 E7
Edensor Rd. W4 126 E7
Edenvale Cl., Mitch. 168 A7
Edenvale Rd.
Edenvale Rd., Mitch. 168 A7
Edenvale St. SW6 149 E2
Ederline Av. SW16 187 F3
Edgar Kail Way SE22 152 B4
Edgar Rd. E3 114 B3
Edgar Rd., Houns. 143 F7
Edgar Rd., Rom. 82 D7
Edgarley Ter. SW6 148 B1
Edgbaston Rd., Wat. 50 B3
Edge Hill SE18 136 E6
Edge Hill SW19 166 A7
Edge Hill Av. N3 72 D3
Edge Hill Ct. SW19 166 A7
Edge St. W8 128 D1
Kensington Ch. St.
Edgeborough Way, Brom. 174 A7
Edgebury, Chis. 175 E4
Edgebury Wk., Chis. 175 F4
Edgecombe Ho. SW19 166 B1
Edgecoombe, S.Croy. 203 F7
Edgecoombe Cl., Kings.T. 164 D7
Edgecot Gro. N15 76 A5
Oulton Rd.
Edgecote Cl. W3 126 C1
Cheltenham Pl.
Edgefield Av., Bark. 99 J7
Edgehill Gdns., Dag. 101 G4
Edgehill Rd. W13 105 F5
Edgehill Rd., Chis. 175 F3
Edgehill Rd., Mitch. 186 B1
Edgel St. SW18 148/149 E4
Ferrier St.
Edgeley La. SW4 150 D3
Edgeley Rd.
Edgeley Rd. SW4 150 D3
Edgepoint Cl. SE27 169 H5
Knights Hill
Edgewood Dr., Orp. 207 J5
Edgewood Grn., Croy. 203 G1
Edgeworth Av. NW4 71 G5
Edgeworth Cl. NW4 71 G5
Edgeworth Cres. NW4 71 G5

Edgeworth Rd. SE9	155	J4
Edgeworth Rd., Barn.	41	H4
Edgington Rd. SW16	168	D6
Edgington Way, Sid.	176	C7
Edgware Ct., Edg.	54	A6
Cavendish Dr.		
Edgware Rd. NW2	89	H1
Edgware Rd. NW9	70	D3
Edgware Rd. W2	**15**	**H3**
Edgware Rd. W2	109	H6
Edgware Way, Edg.	53	J4
Edgwarebury Gdns.,	54	A5
Edg.		
Edgwarebury La.,	54	A4
Edg.		
Edinburgh Cl. E2	113	F2
Russia La.		
Edinburgh Cl., Pnr.	66	D7
Edinburgh Dr. SW20	184	A5
Edinburgh Dr., Rom.	83	J4
Eastern Av. W.		
Edinburgh Gate SW1	**23**	**J3**
Edinburgh Gate SW1	129	J2
Edinburgh Ho. W9	**6**	**B3**
Edinburgh Ho. W9	109	F3
Edinburgh Rd. E13	115	H2
Edinburgh Rd. E17	78	A5
Edinburgh Rd. N18	60	D5
Edinburgh Rd. W7	124	C2
Edinburgh Rd., Sutt.	199	F2
Edington Rd. SE2	138	B3
Edington Rd., Enf.	45	F2
Edis St. NW1	110	A1
Edison Cl. E17	78	A5
Exeter Rd.		
Edison Dr., Sthl.	103	H6
Edison Gro. SE18	137	J7
Edison Rd. N8	74	D6
Edison Rd., Brom.	191	G2
Edison Rd., Enf.	45	J2
Edison Rd., Well.	157	J1
Edith Cavell Cl. N19	74	D7
Hornsey Ri. Gdns.		
Edith Gdns., Surb.	182	B7
Edith Gro. SW10	**30**	**C6**
Edith Gro. SW10	129	F6
Edith Rd. E6	98	A7
Edith Rd. E15	96	D5
Chandos Rd.		
Edith Rd. N11	58	D7
Edith Rd. SE25	188	A5
Edith Rd. SW19	167	E6
Edith Rd. W14	128	B4
Edith Rd., Rom.	82	D6
Edith Row SW6	149	E1
Edith St. E2	**13**	**H1**
Edith St. E2	112	D2
Edith Ter. SW10	**30**	**C7**
Edith Ter. SW10	129	F7
Edith Turberville Ct.	74/75	E7
N19		
Hillrise Rd.		
Edith Vil. W14	128	C4
Edith Yd. SW10	**30**	**D7**
Edithna St. SW9	151	E3
Edmansons Cl. N17	76	B1
Bruce Gro.		
Edmeston Cl. E9	95	H6
Edmond Halley Way	134	E2
SE10		
Edmonds Ct., W.Mol.	179	H4
Avern Rd.		
Edmonton Grn. N9	60/61	E2
Hertford Rd.		
Edmund Gro., Felt.	161	F2
Edmund Hurst Cl. E6	116	D5
Winsor Ter.		
Edmund Rd., Mitch.	185	H3
Edmund Rd., Well.	158	A3
Edmund St. SE5	**36**	**B7**
Edmund St. SE5	132	A7
Edmunds Cl., Hayes	102	C5
Edna Rd. SW20	184	A2
Edna St. SW11	149	H1
Edric Rd. SE14	133	G7
Edrich Ho. SW4	150	E1
Edrick Rd., Edg.	54	C6
Edrick Wk., Edg.	54	C6
Edridge Rd., Croy.	201	J3
Eduff Rd., Borwd.	38	B1
Edward Av. E4	62	B6
Edward Av., Mord.	185	G5
Edward Cl. N9	44	C7
Edward Cl., Hmptn.	161	J5
Edward Rd.		
Edward Cl., Nthlt.	102	C2
Edward Cl. E16	115	G5
Alexandra St.		
Edward Gro., Barn.	41	G5
Edward Ms. NW1	**8**	**E2**
Edward Rd. SE8	133	J6
Edward Rd. E17	77	G4
Edward Rd. SE20	171	G7

Edward Rd., Barn.	41	G5
Edward Rd., Brom.	173	H7
Edward Rd., Chis.	175	E5
Edward Rd., Croy.	188	B7
Edward Rd., Felt.	141	G6
Edward Rd., Hmptn.	161	J5
Edward Rd., Har.	67	J3
Edward Rd., Nthlt.	102	C2
Edward Rd., Rom.	82	E6
Edward Sq. N1	111	F1
Caledonian Rd.		
Edward Sq. SE16	133	H1
Rotherhithe St.		
Edward St. E16	115	G4
Edward St. SE8	133	J6
Edward St. SE14	133	H7
Edward Temme Av.	97	F7
E15		
Edward Tyler Rd.	173	H2
SE12		
Edwardes Pl. W8	128	C3
Edwardes Sq.		
Edwardes Sq. W8	128	D3
Edward's Av., Ruis.	84	B6
Edwards Cl.,	198	A2
Wor.Pk.		
Edwards Cotts. N1	93	H6
Compton Av.		
Edwards Dr. N11	58	D7
Gordon Rd.		
Edwards La. N16	94	A2
Edwards Ms. N1	93	G7
Edwards Ms. W1	**16**	**B4**
Edwards Ms. W1	110	A6
Edwards Rd., Belv.	139	G4
Edwards Yd., Wem.	105	H1
Mount Pleasant		
Edwin Av. E6	116	D2
Edwin Cl., Bexh.	139	F6
Edwin Pl., Croy.	202	A1
Cross Rd.		
Edwin Rd., Edg.	54	D6
Edwin Rd., Twick.	162	C1
Edwin St. E1	113	F4
Edwin St. E16	115	G5
Edwina Gdns., Ilf.	80	B5
Edwin's Mead E9	95	H4
Lindisfarne Way		
Edwyn Cl., Barn.	39	J6
Eel Brook Studios	128	D7
SW6		
Moore Pk. Rd.		
Eel Pie Island, Twick.	162	D1
Effie Pl. SW6	128	D7
Effie Rd. SW6	128	D7
Effingham Cl., Sutt.	199	E7
Effingham Rd. N8	75	G5
Effingham Rd. SE12	155	E5
Effingham Rd., Croy.	187	F7
Effingham Rd., Surb.	181	E7
Effort St. SW17	167	H5
Effra Par. SW2	151	G5
Effra Rd. SW2	151	G4
Effra Rd. SW19	166	E6
Egbert St. NW1	110	A1
Egerton Cl., Pnr.	66	A4
Egerton Cres. SW3	**31**	**H1**
Egerton Cres. SW3	129	H4
Egerton Dr. SE10	154	B1
Egerton Gdns. NW4	71	H4
Egerton Gdns. NW10	107	J1
Egerton Gdns. SW3	**23**	**G6**
Egerton Gdns. SW3	129	H3
Egerton Gdns. W13	105	E6
Egerton Gdns., Ilf.	99	J3
Egerton Gdns. Ms.	**23**	**H6**
SW3		
Egerton Gdns. Ms.	129	H3
SW3		
Egerton Pl. SW3	**23**	**H6**
Egerton Pl. SW3	129	H3
Egerton Rd. N16	76	C7
Egerton Rd. SE25	188	B3
Egerton Rd., N.Mal.	183	F4
Egerton Rd., Twick.	144	B7
Egerton Rd., Wem.	87	J7
Egerton Ter. SW3	**23**	**H6**
Egerton Ter. SW3	129	H3
Egerton Way, Hayes	121	E7
Egham Cl. SW19	166	B2
Winterfold Cl.		
Egham Cl., Sutt.	198	B2
Egham Cres., Sutt.	198	A3
Egham Rd. E13	115	H5
Eglantine Rd. SW18	149	F5
Egleston Rd., Mord.	184	E6
Eglington Ct. SE17	**35**	**J5**
Eglington Rd. E4	46	D7
Eglinton Hill SE18	137	E6
Eglinton Rd. SE18	136	D6
Egliston Ms. SW15	147	J3
Egliston Rd. SW15	147	J3
Eglon Ms. NW1	91	J7
Berkley Rd.		

Egmont Av., Surb.	195	J1
Egmont Rd., N.Mal.	183	F4
Egmont Rd., Surb.	195	J1
Egmont Rd., Sutt.	199	F7
Egmont Rd., Walt.	178	B7
Egmont St. SE14	133	G7
Egremont Rd. SE27	169	G3
Egret Way, Hayes	102	D5
Eider Cl. E7	97	F5
Eider Cl., Hayes	102	D5
Cygnet Way		
Eighteenth Rd., Mitch.	186	E4
Eighth Av. E12	98	C4
Eighth Av., Hayes	122	A1
Eileen Rd. SE25	188	A5
Eindhoven Cl., Cars.	200	A1
Eisenhower Dr. E6	116	B5
Elaine Gro. NW5	92	A5
Elam Cl. SE5	151	H2
Elam St. SE5	151	H2
Eland Pl., Croy.	201	H3
Eland Rd.		
Eland Rd. SW11	149	J3
Eland Rd., Croy.	201	H3
Elba Pl. SE17	**36**	**A1**
Elbe St. SW6	149	F2
Elberon Av., Croy.	186	C6
Elborough Rd. SE25	188	D5
Elborough St. SW18	166	D1
Elbury Dr. E16	115	G6
Elcho St. SW11	129	H7
Elcot Av. SE15	132	E7
Elder Av. N8	74	E5
Elder Cl., Sid.	175	J1
Elder Ct., Bushey	52	B2
Elder Gdns. SE27	169	J4
Gladstone Ter.		
Elder Oak Cl. SE20	188	E1
Elder Rd. SE27	169	J5
Elder St. E1	**13**	**F6**
Elder St. E1	112	C5
Elder Wk. N1	111	H1
Essex Rd.		
Elderberry Gro. SE27	169	J5
Linton Gro.		
Elderberry Rd. W5	125	H2
Elderfield Pl. SW17	168	B4
Elderfield Rd. E5	95	F4
Elderfield Wk. E11	79	H5
Elderflower Way E15	96	E7
Elderslie Cl., Beck.	190	B5
Elderslie Rd. SE9	156	D5
Elderton Rd. SE26	171	H4
Eldertree Pl., Mitch.	186	C1
Eldertree Way		
Eldertree Way, Mitch.	186	B1
Elderwood Pl. SE27	169	J5
Elder Rd.		
Eldon Av., Borwd.	38	A2
Eldon Av., Croy.	203	F2
Eldon Av., Houns.	123	G7
Eldon Gro. NW3	91	G5
Eldon Pk. SE25	188	E4
Eldon Rd. E17	77	J4
Eldon Rd. N9	61	F2
Eldon Rd. N22	75	H1
Eldon Rd. W8	**22**	**B6**
Eldon Rd. W8	129	E3
Eldon St. EC2	**20**	**C2**
Eldon St. EC2	112	A5
Eldon Way NW10	106	B2
Eldred Rd., Bark.	117	H1
Eldridge Cl., Felt.	160	A1
Eleanor Cl. N15	76	C3
Arnold Rd.		
Eleanor Cl. SE16	133	G2
Eleanor Cres. NW7	56	A4
Eleanor Gdns., Barn.	40	A5
Eleanor Gdns., Dag.	101	F3
Eleanor Gro. SW13	147	E3
Eleanor Rd. E8	94	E7
Eleanor Rd. E15	97	F6
Eleanor Rd. N11	58	E6
Eleanor St. E3	114	A3
Eleanor Wk. SE18	136	C4
Samuel St.		
Electric Av. SW9	151	G4
Electric La. SW9	151	G4
Electric Par., Surb.	181	G6
Elephant & Castle	**27**	**H6**
SE1		
Elephant & Castle	131	H4
SE1		
Elephant La. SE16	133	F2
Elephant Rd. SE17	**35**	**J1**
Elephant Rd. SE17	131	J4
Elers Rd. W13	125	F2
Elers Rd., Hayes	121	G4
Eleven Acre Ri., Loug.	48	C3
Eley Est. N18	61	F5
Eley Rd. N18	61	G5
Elf Row E1	113	F7
Elfin Gro., Tedd.	162	C5
Broad St.		

Elfindale Rd. SE24	151	J5
Elford Cl. SE3	155	H4
Elfort Rd. N5	93	G4
Elfrida Cres. SE6	172	A4
Elgal Cl., Orp.	206/207	E5
Orchard Rd.		
Elgar Av. NW10	88	D6
Mitchellbrook Way		
Elgar Av. SW16	186	E3
Elgar Av. W5	125	H2
Elgar Av., Surb.	182	B7
Elgar Cl. E13	115	J2
Bushey Rd.		
Elgar Cl. SE8	134	A7
Comet St.		
Elgar Cl., Buck.H.	64	A2
Elgar Cl. SE16	133	H3
Elgin Av. W9	**6**	**A4**
Elgin Av. W9	108	E3
Elgin Av., Har.	68	E2
Elgin Cres. W11	108	C6
Elgin Cres., Houns.	141	H3
Eastern Perimeter Rd.		
Elgin Ms. W11	108	B6
Ladbroke Gro.		
Elgin Ms. N. W9	**6**	**B3**
Elgin Ms. S. W9	**6**	**B3**
Elgin Rd. N22	74	C2
Elgin Rd., Croy.	202	C1
Elgin Rd., Ilf.	99	H1
Elgin Rd., Sutt.	199	F3
Elgin Rd., Wall.	200	C6
Elgood Av., Nthwd.	50	A6
Elgood Cl. W11	108	B7
Avondale Pk. Rd.		
Elham Cl., Brom.	174	A7
Elia Ms. N1	**11**	**G2**
Elia Ms. N1	111	H2
Elia St. N1	**11**	**G2**
Elia St. N1	111	H2
Elias Pl. SW8	**34**	**E6**
Elias Pl. SW8	131	G6
Elibank Rd. SE9	156	D4
Elim Est. SE1	**28**	**D5**
Elim Est. SE1	132	B3
Elim Way E13	115	F3
Eliot Bank SE23	170	E2
Eliot Cotts. SE3	154/155	E2
Eliot Pl.		
Eliot Dr., Har.	85	H2
Eliot Gdns. SW15	147	G4
Eliot Hill SE13	154	C2
Eliot Ms. NW8	**6**	**D2**
Eliot Ms. NW8	109	F2
Eliot Pk. SE13	154	C3
Eliot Pl. SE3	154	E2
Eliot Rd., Dag.	100	D4
Eliot Vale SE3	154	D2
Elizabeth Av. N1	93	J7
Elizabeth Av., Enf.	43	H3
Elizabeth Av., Ilf.	99	G2
Elizabeth Blackwell	75	G1
Ho. N22		
Progress Way		
Elizabeth Br. SW1	**32**	**D2**
Elizabeth Br. SW1	130	B4
Elizabeth Cl. E14	114	B6
Grundy St.		
Elizabeth Cl. W9	**6**	**D6**
Elizabeth Cl., Barn.	40	A3
Elizabeth Cl., Rom.	83	H1
Elizabeth Cl., Sutt.	198	C4
Elizabeth Clyde Cl.	76	B4
N15		
Elizabeth Cotts., Rich.	145	J1
Elizabeth Ct. SW1	**25**	**J6**
Elizabeth Est. SE17	**36**	**B5**
Elizabeth Est. SE17	132	A6
Elizabeth Fry Rd.	94/95	E7
E8		
Lamb La.		
Elizabeth Gdns. W3	127	F1
Elizabeth Gdns., Stan.	53	F6
Stan.		
Elizabeth Gdns., Sun.	178	C3
Elizabeth Ms. NW3	91	H6
Elizabeth Pl. N15	76	A4
Elizabeth Ride N9	45	E7
Elizabeth Rd. E6	116	A1
Elizabeth Rd. N15	76	B5
Elizabeth Sq. SE16	113	H7
Rotherhithe St.		
Elizabeth St. SW1	**32**	**C1**
Elizabeth St. SW1	130	A4
Elizabeth Ter. SE9	156	C6
Elizabeth Way SE19	170	A7
Elizabeth Way, Felt.	160	C4
Elizabethan Way		
Elizabethan Way,	140	A7
Stai.		
Elkanette Ms. N20	57	F2
Ridgeview Rd.		

Elkington Rd. E13 115 H4
Elkstone Rd. W10 108 C5
Ella Rd. N8 75 E7
Ellaline Rd. W6 128 A6
Ellanby Cres. N18 60 E5
Elland Rd. SE15 153 F4
Ellement Cl., Pnr. 66 D5
Ellen Cl., Brom. 192 A3
Ellen Ct. N9 61 F2
  Densworth Gro.
Ellen St. E1 21 J4
Ellen St. E1 112 D6
Ellen Webb Dr., Har. 68 B3
Ellenborough Pl. 147 G4
  SW15
Ellenborough Rd. 75 J1
  N22
Ellenborough Rd., 176 D5
  Sid.
Elleray Rd., Tedd. 162 C6
Ellerby St. SW6 148 A1
Ellerdale Cl. NW3 91 F4
  Ellerdale Rd.
Ellerdale Rd. NW3 91 F5
Ellerdale St. SE13 154 B4
Ellerdine Rd., Houns. 143 J4
Ellerker Gdns., Rich. 145 H6
Ellerman Av., Twick. 161 F1
Ellerslie Gdns. 107 G1
  NW10
Ellerslie Rd. W12 127 H1
Ellerslie Sq. Ind. Est. 150 E5
  SW2
Ellerton Gdns., Dag. 100 C7
Ellerton Rd. SW13 147 G1
Ellerton Rd. SW18 167 G1
Ellerton Rd. SW20 165 G7
Ellerton Rd., Dag. 100 C7
Ellerton Rd., Surb. 195 J2
Ellery Rd. SE19 170 A7
Ellery St. SE15 153 E2
Ellesborough Cl., 50 C5
  Wat.
Ellesmere Av. NW7 54 D3
Ellesmere Av., Beck. 190 B2
Ellesmere Cl. E11 79 F5
Ellesmere Gdns., Ilf. 80 B5
Ellesmere Gro., Barn. 40 C5
Ellesmere Rd. E3 113 H2
Ellesmere Rd. NW10 89 G5
Ellesmere Rd. W4 126 D6
Ellesmere Rd., Grnf. 103 J4
Ellesmere Rd., Twick. 145 F6
Ellesmere St. E14 114 B6
Ellingfort Rd. E8 95 E7
Ellingham Rd. E15 96 D4
Ellingham Rd. W12 127 G2
Ellingham Rd., 195 G6
  Chess.
Ellington Rd. N10 74 B4
Ellington Rd., Houns. 143 H2
Ellington St. N7 93 G6
Elliot Cl. E15 96 E7
Elliot Rd. NW4 71 H6
Elliot Rd., Stan. 52 D6
Elliott Av., Ruis. 84 B2
Elliott Cl., Wem. 87 J3
Elliott Rd. SW9 131 H7
Elliott Rd. W4 126 E4
Elliott Rd., Brom. 192 A4
Elliott Rd., Th.Hth. 187 H4
Elliott Sq. NW3 91 H7
Elliott's Pl. N1 111 H1
  St. Peters St.
Elliotts Row SE11 35 G1
Elliotts Row SE11 131 H4
Ellis Cl. NW10 89 H6
  High Rd.
Ellis Cl. SE9 175 F2
Ellis Ct. W7 104 C5
Ellis Ms. SE7 135 J6
Ellis Rd., Mitch. 185 J6
Ellis Rd., Sthl. 123 J1
Ellis St. SW1 32 A1
Ellis St. SW1 129 J4
Elliscombe Rd. SE7 135 J5
Ellisfield Dr. SW15 147 F7
Ellison Gdns., Sthl. 123 F4
Ellison Rd. SW13 147 F2
Ellison Rd. SW16 168 D7
Ellison Rd., Sid. 175 G1
Elliston Ho. SE18 136 D4
Ellora Rd. SW16 168 D5
Ellsworth St. E2 113 E3
Ellwood Ct. W9 6 A6
Elm Av. W5 125 H1
Elm Av., Ruis. 84 A1
Elm Bank, Brom. 192 A2
Elm Bank Gdns. 147 E2
  SW13
Elm Cl. E11 79 H6
Elm Cl. N19 92 C2
  Hargrave Pk.
Elm Cl. NW4 72 A5

Elm Cl. SW20 183 J4
  Grand Dr.
Elm Cl., Buck.H. 64 A2
Elm Cl., Cars. 199 J1
Elm Cl., Har. 67 H6
Elm Cl., Hayes 102 A6
Elm Cl., Rom. 83 H2
Elm Cl., S.Croy. 202 B6
Elm Cl., Surb. 182 C7
Elm Cl., Twick. 161 H2
Elm Cl., Mitch. 185 J2
  Armfield Cres.
Elm Cres. W5 125 H1
Elm Cres., Kings.T. 181 H1
Elm Dr., Har. 67 H6
Elm Dr., Sun. 178 C2
Elm Friars Wk. NW1 92 D7
Elm Gdns. N2 73 F3
Elm Gdns., Esher 194 C6
Elm Gdns., Mitch. 186 D4
Elm Grn. W3 106 E6
Elm Gro. N8 75 E6
Elm Gro. NW2 90 A4
Elm Gro. SE15 152 C2
Elm Gro. SW19 166 B7
Elm Gro., Har. 67 G7
Elm Gro., Kings.T. 181 H1
Elm Gro., Orp. 207 J1
Elm Gro., Sutt. 199 E4
Elm Gro., Wdf.Grn. 63 F5
Elm Gro. Par., Wall. 200 A3
  Butter Hill
Elm Gro. Rd. SW13 147 G2
Elm Gro. Rd. W5 125 H2
Elm Hall Gdns. E11 79 H5
Elm La. SE6 171 J2
Elm Ms., Rich. 145 J6
  Grove Rd.
Elm Pk. SW2 151 F6
Elm Pk., Stan. 53 E5
Elm Pk. Av. N15 76 C5
Elm Pk. Ct., Pnr. 66 C3
Elm Pk. Gdns. NW4 72 A5
Elm Pk. Gdns. SW10 31 E4
Elm Pk. Gdns. SW10 129 G5
Elm Pk. La. SW3 30 E4
Elm Pk. La. SW3 129 G5
Elm Pk. Mans. SW10 30 D5
Elm Pk. Rd. E10 95 H1
Elm Pk. Rd. N3 56 C7
Elm Pk. Rd. N21 43 J7
Elm Pk. Rd. SE25 188 C3
Elm Pk. Rd. SW3 30 E5
Elm Pk. Rd. SW3 129 G6
Elm Pk. Rd., Pnr. 66 C2
Elm Pl. SW7 31 E3
Elm Pl. SW7 129 G5
Elm Quay Ct. SW8 33 H5
Elm Quay Ct. SW8 130 D6
Elm Rd. E7 97 F6
Elm Rd. E11 96 D2
Elm Rd. E17 78 C5
Elm Rd. N22 75 H1
  Granville Rd.
Elm Rd. SW14 146 C3
Elm Rd., Barn. 40 C4
Elm Rd., Beck. 189 J2
Elm Rd., Chess. 195 H4
Elm Rd., Epsom 197 F6
Elm Rd., Esher 194 C6
Elm Rd., Kings.T. 181 J1
Elm Rd., N.Mal. 182 D4
Elm Rd., Rom. 83 H2
Elm Rd., Sid. 176 A4
Elm Rd., Th.Hth. 188 A4
Elm Rd., Wall. 200 A1
Elm Rd., Wem. 87 H5
Elm Rd. W., Sutt. 184 C7
Elm Row NW3 91 F3
Elm St. WC1 10 D6
Elm St. WC1 111 F4
Elm Ter. NW2 90 D3
Elm Ter. NW3 91 H4
  Constantine Rd.
Elm Ter. SE9 156 D6
Elm Ter., Har. 52 A7
Elm Tree Av., Esher 180 A7
Elm Tree Cl. NW8 7 E3
Elm Tree Cl. NW8 109 G3
Elm Tree Cl., Nthlt. 103 F2
Elm Tree Rd. NW8 6 E3
Elm Tree Rd. NW8 109 G3
Elm Wk. NW3 90 D2
Elm Wk. SW20 183 J4
Elm Wk., Orp. 206 C3
Elm Way N11 58 A6
Elm Way NW10 88 E4
Elm Way, Epsom 196 D5
Elm Way, Wor.Pk. 197 J3
Elmar Rd. N15 76 A4
Elmbank N14 43 E7
Elmbank Av., Barn. 39 J4
Elmbank Way W7 104 A5

Elmbourne Dr., Belv. 139 H4
Elmbourne Rd. SW17 168 A3
Elmbridge Av., Surb. 182 B5
Elmbridge Cl., Ruis. 66 A6
Elmbridge Wk. E8 94 D7
  Wilman Gro.
Elmbrook Cl., Sun. 178 B1
Elmbrook Gdns. SE9 156 B4
Elmbrook Rd., Sutt. 198 C4
Elmcote Way 169 H2
Elmcourt Rd. SE27 169 H2
Elmcroft N8 75 F5
Elmcroft Av. E11 79 H5
Elmcroft Av. N9 44 E6
Elmcroft Av. NW11 72 C7
Elmcroft Av., Sid. 157 J6
Elmcroft Cl. E11 79 H4
Elmcroft Cl. W5 105 G6
Elmcroft Cl., Chess. 195 H3
Elmcroft Cl., Felt. 141 J6
Elmcroft Cres. NW11 72 B7
Elmcroft Cres., Har. 67 G3
Elmcroft Dr., Chess. 195 H3
Elmcroft Gdns. NW9 70 A5
Elmcroft St. E5 95 F4
Elmdale Rd. N13 59 F5
Elmdene, Surb. 196 C1
Elmdene Cl., Beck. 189 J5
Elmdene Rd. SE18 136 E5
Elmdon Rd., Houns. 142 D2
Elmdon Rd. 141 J3
  (Hatton Cross), Houns.
Elmer Cl., Enf. 43 F3
Elmer Gdns., Edg. 54 B7
Elmer Gdns., Islw. 144 A3
Elmer Rd. SE6 154 C7
Elmers Dr., Tedd. 162/163 E6
  Kingston Rd.
Elmers End Rd. SE20 189 F2
Elmers End Rd., Beck. 189 F2
Elmers Rd. SE25 188 D7
Elmerside Rd., Beck. 189 H4
Elmfield Av. N8 74 E5
Elmfield Av., Mitch. 186 A1
Elmfield Av., Tedd. 162 C5
Elmfield Cl., Har. 86 B2
Elmfield Pk., Brom. 191 G3
Elmfield Rd. E4 62 C2
Elmfield Rd. E17 77 G6
Elmfield Rd. N2 73 G3
Elmfield Rd. SW17 168 A2
Elmfield Rd., Brom. 191 G3
Elmfield Rd., Sthl. 123 E3
Elmfield Way W9 108 D5
Elmgate Av., Felt. 160 B3
Elmgate Gdns., Edg. 54 D5
Elmgreen Cl. E15 114/115 E1
  Church St. N.
Elmgrove Cres., Har. 68 C5
Elmgrove Gdns., Har. 68 D5
Elmgrove Rd., Croy. 188 E7
Elmgrove Rd., Har. 68 C5
Elmhurst Av. N2 73 G3
Elmhurst Av., Mitch. 168 B7
Elmhurst Dr. E18 79 G2
Elmhurst Gdns. E18 79 H1
  Elmhurst Dr.
Elmhurst Rd. E7 97 H7
Elmhurst Rd. N17 76 C2
Elmhurst Rd. SE9 174 B2
Elmhurst St. SW4 150 D3
Elmhurst Vil. SE15 153 F4
  Cheltenham Rd.
Elmhurst Way, Loug. 48 C7
Elmington Cl., Bex. 159 H6
Elmington Est. SE5 36 C7
Elmington Rd. SE5 132 A7
Elmington Rd. SE5 152 A1
Elmira St. SE13 154 B3
Elmlee Cl., Chis. 174 C6
Elmley Cl. E6 116 B5
  Northumberland Rd.
Elmley St. SE18 137 G4
Elmore Cl., Wem. 105 H2
Elmore Rd. E11 96 C3
Elmore Rd., Enf. 45 G1
Elmore St. N1 93 J7
Elms, Loug. 48 D3
Elms, The SW13 147 F3
Elms Av. N10 74 B3
Elms Av. NW4 72 A5
Elms Ct., Wem. 86 C4
Elms Cres. SW4 150 C6
Elms Gdns., Dag. 101 F4
Elms Gdns., Wem. 86 C4
Elms Ms. W2 14 E5
Elms Ms. W2 109 G7
Elms Pk. Av., Wem. 86 D4
Elms Rd. SW4 150 C5
Elms Rd., Har. 52 B7
Elmscott Gdns. N21 43 J6
Elmscott Rd., Brom. 173 F5
Elmsdale Rd. E17 77 J4

Elmshaw Rd. SW15 147 G5
Elmshurst Cres. N2 73 G4
Elmside, Croy. 204 B6
Elmside Rd., Wem. 88 A3
Elmsleigh Av., Har. 69 E4
Elmsleigh Ct., Sutt. 198 E3
Elmsleigh Rd., Twick. 162 A2
Elmslie Cl., Wdf.Grn. 64 C6
Elmslie Pt. E3 113 J5
Elmstead Av., Chis. 174 C5
Elmstead Av., Wem. 87 H1
Elmstead Cl. N20 56 D2
Elmstead Cl., Epsom 197 E5
Elmstead Cres., Well. 138 C6
Elmstead Gdns., 197 G3
  Wor.Pk.
Elmstead Glade, Chis. 174 C6
Elmstead La., Chis. 174 C5
Elmstead Rd., Ilf. 99 H2
Elmstone Rd. SW6 148 D1
Elmsworth Av., 143 H2
  Houns.
Elmton Way E5 94 D3
  Rendlesham Rd.
Elmtree Rd., Tedd. 162 B4
Elmwood Av. N13 59 E5
Elmwood Av., 38 B4
  Borwd.
Elmwood Av., Felt. 160 A2
Elmwood Av., Har. 68 D5
Elmwood Cl., Epsom 197 G7
Elmwood Cl., Wall. 200 A2
Elmwood Ct., Wem. 86 D3
Elmwood Cres. NW9 70 C4
Elmwood Dr., Bex. 158 E7
Elmwood Dr., Epsom 197 G6
Elmwood Gdns. W7 104 B6
Elmwood Rd. SE24 152 A5
Elmwood Rd. W4 126 C6
Elmwood Rd., Croy. 187 H7
Elmwood Rd., Mitch. 185 J3
Elmworth Gro. SE21 170 A2
Elnathan Ms. W9 6 B6
Elphinstone Rd. E17 77 J2
Elphinstone St. N5 93 H4
  Avenell Rd.
Elrington Rd. E8 94 D6
Elrington Rd., 63 G5
  Wdf.Grn.
Elruge Cl., West Dr. 120 A3
Elsa Rd., Well. 158 B2
Elsa St. E1 113 H5
Elsdale St. E9 95 F6
Elsden Ms. E2 113 F2
  Old Ford Rd.
Elsden Rd. N17 76 C1
Elsenham Rd. E12 98 D5
Elsenham St. SW18 166 C1
Elsham Rd. E11 96 E3
Elsham Rd. W14 128 B2
Elsham Ter. W14 128 B2
Elsie Rd. SE22 152 C4
Elsiedene Rd. N21 43 J7
Elsiemaud Rd. SE4 153 J5
Elsinore Av., Stai. 140 B7
Elsinore Gdns. NW2 90 B3
Elsinore Rd. SE23 171 H1
Elsinore Way, Rich. 146 B3
  Lower Richmond Rd.
Elsley Rd. SW11 149 J3
Elspeth Rd. SW11 149 J4
Elspeth Rd., Wem. 87 H5
Elsrick Av., Mord. 184 D5
  Chalgrove Rd.
Elstan Way, Croy. 189 H7
Elsted St. SE17 36 C2
Elsted St. SE17 132 A4
Elstow Cl. SE9 156 D5
Elstow Cl., Ruis. 66 D7
Elstow Gdns., Dag. 118 E1
Elstow Rd., Dag. 100 E7
Elstree Gdns. N9 61 E1
Elstree Gdns., Belv. 139 E4
Elstree Gdns., Ilf. 99 F5
Elstree Hill, Brom. 173 E7
Elstree Pk., Borwd. 38 D6
Elstree Way, Borwd. 38 B3
Elswick Rd. SE13 154 B2
Elswick St. SW6 149 F2
Elsworthy, T.Ditt. 180 B6
Elsworthy Ri. NW3 91 H7
Elsworthy Rd. NW3 91 H7
Elsworthy Ter. NW3 91 H7
Elsynge Rd. SW18 149 G5
Eltham Grn. SE9 155 J5
Eltham Grn. Rd. SE9 155 J4
Eltham High St. SE9 156 C6
Eltham Hill SE9 156 A5
Eltham Palace Rd. 155 J6
  SE9
Eltham Pk. Gdns. 156 D4
  SE9
Eltham Rd. SE9 155 J5
Eltham Rd. SE12 155 F5

Elthiron Rd. SW6 148 D1
Elthorne Av. W7 124 C2
Elthorne Ct., Felt. 160 C1
Elthorne Pk. Rd. W7 124 C2
Elthorne Rd. N19 92 D2
Elthorne Rd. NW9 70 D6
Elthorne Way NW9 70 D6
Elthruda Rd. SE13 154 D6
Eltisley Rd., Ilf. 98 E4
Elton Av., Barn. 40 C5
Elton Av., Grnf. 86 C6
Elton Av., Wem. 87 E5
Elton Cl., Kings.T. 163 F7
Elton Ho. E3 113 J1
Elton Pl. N16 94 B5
Elton Rd., Kings.T. 181 J1
Eltringham St. SW18 149 F4
Elvaston Ms. SW7 22 D5
Elvaston Ms. SW7 129 F3
Elvaston Pl. SW7 22 C6
Elvaston Pl. SW7 129 F3
Elveden Pl. NW10 106 A2
Elveden Rd. NW10 106 A2
Elvendon Rd. N13 58 E6
Elver Gdns. E2 13 J3
Elverson Rd. SE8 154 B2
Elverton St. SW1 33 H1
Elverton St. SW1 130 D4
Elvington Grn., Brom. 191 F5
Elvington La. NW9 70 E1
Elvino Rd. SE26 171 H5
Elvis Rd. NW2 89 J6
Elwill Way, Beck. 190 C4
Elwin St. E2 13 H3
Elwin St. E2 112 D3
Elwood St. N5 93 H3
Elwyn Gdns. SE12 155 G7
Ely Cl., N.Mal. 183 F2
Ely Ct. EC1 19 F2
Ely Gdns., Borwd. 38 D5
Ely Gdns., Dag. 101 J3
Ely Gdns., Ilf. 80 B7
  Canterbury Av.
Ely Pl. EC1 19 F2
Ely Pl., Wdf.Grn. 64 D6
Ely Rd. E10 78 C6
Ely Rd., Croy. 188 A5
Ely Rd. (Heathrow 141 J2
  Airport), Houns.
  Eastern Perimeter Rd.
Ely Rd. (Hounslow W.), 142 C3
  Houns.
Elyne Rd. N4 75 G6
Elysian Av., Orp. 193 J6
Elysium Pl. SW6 148 C2
  Fulham Pk. Gdns.
Elysium St. SW6 148 C2
  Fulham Pk. Gdns.
Elystan Business 102 C7
  Cen., Hayes
Elystan Pl. SW3 31 H3
Elystan Pl. SW3 129 H5
Elystan St. SW3 31 G2
Elystan St. SW3 129 H4
Elystan Wk. N1 111 G1
  Cloudesley Rd.
Emanuel Av. W3 106 C6
Emanuel Dr., Hmptn. 161 F5
Emba St. SE16 29 J4
Emba St. SE16 132 D2
Embankment SW15 148 A2
Embankment, The, 162 D1
  Twick.
Embankment Gdns. 32 A5
  SW3
Embankment Gdns. 129 J6
  SW3
Embankment Pl. WC2 26 B1
Embankment Pl. WC2 131 E1
Embassy Ct., Sid. 176 B3
Embassy Ct., Well. 158 B3
Embassy Gdns., 189 J1
  Beck.
  Blakeney Rd.
Ember Cl., Orp. 193 F7
Ember Fm. Av., 180 A6
  E.Mol.
Ember Fm. Way, 180 A6
  E.Mol.
Ember Gdns., T.Ditt. 180 B7
Ember La., E.Mol. 194 A1
Ember La., Esher 180 A7
Embercourt Rd., 180 B6
  T.Ditt.
Emberton SE5 36 C5
Embleton Rd. SE13 154 B3
Embleton Rd., Wat. 50 A3
Embleton Wk., 161 F6
  Hmptn.
  Fearnley Cres.
Embley Pt. E5 94/95 E4
  Tiger Way
Embry Cl., Stan. 52 D4

Embry Dr., Stan. 52 D6
Embry Way, Stan. 52 D5
Emden Cl., West Dr. 120 D2
Emden St. SW6 149 E1
Emerald Cl. E16 116 B6
Emerald Gdns., Dag. 101 G1
Emerald Sq., Sthl. 122 D3
Emerald St. WC1 18 C1
Emerald St. WC1 111 F5
Emerson Gdns., Har. 69 J6
Emerson Rd., Ilf. 80 D7
Emerson St. SE1 27 J1
Emerson St. SE1 131 J1
Emerton Cl., Bexh. 159 E4
Emery Hill St. SW1 25 G6
Emery Hill St. SW1 130 C3
Emery St. SE1 27 F5
Emes Rd., Erith 139 J7
Emilia Cl., Enf. 45 E5
Emily Pl. N7 93 G4
Emlyn Gdns. W12 127 E2
Emlyn Rd. W12 127 E3
Emma Rd. E13 115 F2
Emma St. E2 112 E2
Emmanuel Rd. SW12 168 C1
Emmaus Way, Chig. 64 D5
Emmott Av., Ilf. 81 F5
Emmott Cl. E1 113 H4
Emmott Cl. NW11 73 F6
Emms Pas., Kings.T. 181 G2
  High St.
Emperor's Gate SW7 22 B6
Emperor's Gate SW7 129 E3
Empire Av. N18 59 J5
Empire Ct., Wem. 88 B3
Empire Rd., Grnf. 105 F1
Empire Sq. N7 92/93 H3
  Holloway Rd.
Empire Way, Wem. 87 J4
Empire Wf. Rd. E14 134 D4
Empire Yd. N7 92/93 H3
  Holloway Rd.
Empress Av. E4 62 A7
Empress Av. E12 97 J2
Empress Av., Ilf. 98 C2
Empress Av., 63 F7
  Wdf.Grn.
Empress Pl. SW6 128 D5
Empress St. SE17 36 A5
Empress St. SE17 131 J6
Empson St. E3 114 B4
Emsworth Cl. N9 61 F1
Emsworth Rd., Ilf. 81 E2
Emsworth St. SW2 169 F2
Emu Rd. SW8 150 B2
Ena Rd. SW16 186 E3
Enbrook St. W10 108 B3
Endale Cl., Cars. 199 J2
Endeavour Way SW19 166 E4
Endeavour Way, Bark. 118 A2
Endeavour Way, Croy. 186 D7
Endell St. WC2 18 A3
Endell St. WC2 110 E6
Enderby St. SE10 134 E5
Enderley Cl., Har. 68 B1
  Enderley Rd.
Enderley Rd., Har. 68 B1
Endersby Rd., Barn. 39 J5
Endersleigh Gdns. 71 C3
  NW4
Endlebury Rd. E4 62 C2
Endlesham Rd. SW12 150 A7
Endsleigh Gdns. WC1 9 H5
Endsleigh Gdns. WC1 110 D4
Endsleigh Gdns., Ilf. 98 C2
Endsleigh Gdns., 181 F6
  Surb.
Endsleigh Pl. WC1 9 J5
Endsleigh Pl. WC1 110 D4
Endsleigh Rd. W13 104 D7
Endsleigh Rd., Sthl. 123 E4
Endsleigh St. WC1 9 H5
Endsleigh St. WC1 110 D4
Endway, Surb. 182 A7
Endwell Rd. SE4 153 H2
Endymion Rd. N4 75 G7
Endymion Rd. SW2 151 F6
Energen Cl. NW10 88 E6
Enfield Retail Pk., Enf. 44 E3
Enfield Rd. N1 94 B7
Enfield Rd. W3 126 B2
Enfield Rd., Brent. 125 G5
Enfield Rd., Enf. 42 D4
Enfield Rd., Houns. 141 H2
  Eastern Perimeter Rd.
Enfield Wk., Brent. 125 G5
Enford St. W1 15 J1
Enford St. W1 109 J5
Engadine Cl., Croy. 202 C3
Engadine St. SW18 166 C1
Engate St. SE13 154 C4
Engel Pk. NW7 55 J6
Engineer Cl. SE18 136 D6

Engineers Way, 88 A4
  Wem.
England Way, N.Mal. 182 C3
  California Rd.
Englands La. NW3 91 J6
Englands La., Loug. 48 D2
Englefield Cl., Croy. 187 J6
  Queen's Rd.
Englefield Cl., Enf. 43 G2
Englefield Cl., Orp. 193 J4
Englefield Cres., Orp. 193 J4
Englefield Path, Orp. 193 J4
Englefield Rd. N1 94 A6
Englehart Dr., Felt. 141 J6
Englehart Rd. SE6 154 B7
Englewood Rd. 150 B6
  SW12
English Grds. SE1 28 D2
English St. E3 113 J4
Enid St. SE16 29 G5
Enid St. SE16 132 C3
Enmore Av. SE25 188 D5
Enmore Gdns. SW14 146 D5
Enmore Rd. SE25 188 D5
Enmore Rd. SW15 147 J4
Enmore Rd., Sthl. 103 G4
Ennerdale Av., Stan. 69 F3
Ennerdale Cl. 198 C4
  (Cheam), Sutt.
Ennerdale Dr. NW9 70 E5
Ennerdale Gdns., 87 G1
  Wem.
Ennerdale Ho. E3 113 J4
Ennerdale Rd., Bexh. 159 G1
Ennerdale Rd., Rich. 145 J2
Ennersdale Rd. SE13 154 D5
Ennis Rd. N4 93 G1
Ennis Rd. SE18 137 F6
Ennismore Av. W4 127 F4
Ennismore Av., Grnf. 86 B6
Ennismore Gdns. 23 G4
  SW7
Ennismore Gdns. 129 H2
  SW7
Ennismore Gdns., 180 B6
  T.Ditt.
Ennismore Gdns. 23 G5
  Ms. SW7
Ennismore Gdns. 129 H3
  Ms. SW7
Ennismore Ms. SW7 23 G4
Ennismore Ms. SW7 129 H2
Ennismore St. SW7 23 G5
Ennismore St. SW7 129 H3
Ensign Dr. N13 59 J3
Ensign St. E1 21 H5
Ensign St. E1 112 D7
Enslin Rd. SE9 156 D6
Ensor Ms. SW7 30 E3
Enstone Rd., Enf. 45 H3
Enterprise Cl., Croy. 201 G1
Enterprise Way 107 G3
  NW10
Enterprise Way 148 D4
  SW18
Enterprise Way, 162 C5
  Tedd.
Enterprise Way SE8 133 J4
Epirus Ms. SW6 128 D7
Epirus Rd. SW6 128 C7
Epping Cl. E14 134 A4
Epping Cl., Rom. 83 H3
Epping Glade E4 46 C6
Epping New Rd., 63 H2
  Buck.H.
Epping New Rd., 47 H5
  Loug.
Epping Pl. N1 93 G6
  Liverpool Rd.
Epping Way E4 46 B6
Epple Rd. SW6 148 C1
Epsom Cl., Bexh. 159 H3
Epsom Cl., Nthlt. 85 F5
Epsom Rd. E10 78 C6
Epsom Rd., Croy. 201 G4
Epsom Rd., Ilf. 81 J6
Epsom Rd., Mord. 184 C6
Epsom Rd., Sutt. 184 C7
Epsom Sq., Houns. 141 J2
  Eastern Perimeter Rd.
Epstein Rd. SE28 138 A1
Epworth Rd., Islw. 124 E7
Epworth St. EC2 12 C6
Epworth St. EC2 112 A4
Equity Sq. E2 13 G4
  Shacklewell St.
Erasmus St. SW1 33 J2
Erasmus St. SW1 130 D4
Erconwald St. W12 107 F6
Eresby Dr., Beck. 204 A1
Eresby Pl. NW6 90 D7
Eric Clarke La., Bark. 117 E4
Eric Cl. E7 97 G4
Eric Rd. E7 97 G4

Eric Rd. NW10 89 F6
  Church Rd.
Eric Rd., Rom. 82 D7
Eric St. E3 113 J4
Erica Gdns., Croy. 204 B4
Erica St. W12 107 G7
Ericcson Cl. SW18 148 D5
Eridge Rd. W4 126 D3
Erin Cl., Brom. 172 E7
Erin Cl., Ilf. 82 A6
Erindale SE18 137 G6
Erindale Ter. SE18 137 G6
Erith Cres., Rom. 83 J1
Erith Rd., Belv. 139 G5
Erith Rd., Bexh. 159 H4
Erith Rd., Erith 159 H4
Erlanger Rd. SE14 153 G1
Erlesmere Gdns. 124 D3
  W13
Ermine Cl., Houns. 142 C2
Ermine Ho. N17 60 C7
  Moselle St.
Ermine Rd. N15 76 C6
Ermine Rd. SE13 154 B3
Ermine Side, Enf. 44 D5
Ermington Rd. SE9 175 F2
Ernald Av. E6 116 B2
Erncroft Way, Twick. 144 C6
Ernest Av. SE27 169 H4
Ernest Cl., Beck. 190 A5
Ernest Gdns. W4 126 B6
Ernest Gro., Beck. 189 J5
Ernest Rd., Kings.T. 182 B2
Ernest Sq., Kings.T. 182 B2
Ernest St. E1 113 G4
Ernle Rd. SW20 165 H7
Ernshaw Pl. SW15 148 B5
  Carlton Dr.
Erpingham Rd. SW15 147 J3
Erridge Rd. SW19 184 D2
Errington Rd. W9 108 C4
Errol Gdns., Hayes 102 B4
Errol Gdns., N.Mal. 183 G4
Errol St. EC1 12 A6
Errol St. EC1 111 J4
Erskine Cl., Sutt. 199 H3
Erskine Cres. N17 76 E4
Erskine Hill NW11 72 D5
Erskine Ms. NW3 91 J7
  Erskine Rd.
Erskine Rd. E17 77 J4
Erskine Rd. NW3 91 J7
Erskine Rd., Sutt. 199 G4
Erskine Rd., Wat. 50 C3
Erwood Rd. SE7 136 B5
Esam Way SW16 169 G5
Escot Way, Barn. 39 J5
Escott Gdns. SE9 174 B4
Escreet Gro. SE18 136 D4
Esher Av., Rom. 83 J6
Esher Av., Sutt. 198 A3
Esher Av., Walt. 178 A7
Esher Bypass, Chess. 195 F4
Esher Bypass, Cob. 195 E7
Esher Cl., Bex. 176 E1
Esher Cres., Houns. 141 H2
  Eastern Perimeter Rd.
Esher Gdns. SW19 166 A2
Esher Ms., Mitch. 185 J3
Esher Rd., E.Mol. 180 A6
Esher Rd., Ilf. 99 H3
Esk Rd. E13 115 G4
Eskdale Av., Nthlt. 103 F1
Eskdale Cl., Wem. 87 G2
Eskdale Rd., Bexh. 159 G2
Eskmont Ridge SE19 170 B7
Esmar Cres. NW9 71 G7
Esme Ho. SW15 147 F4
Esmeralda Rd. SE1 37 J2
Esmeralda Rd. SE1 132 D4
Esmond Rd. NW6 108 C1
Esmond Rd. W4 126 D4
Esmond St. SW15 148 B4
Esparto St. SW18 149 E7
Essenden Rd., Belv. 139 G5
Essenden Rd., 202 B7
  S.Croy.
Essendine Rd. W9 108 D4
Essex Av., Islw. 144 B3
Essex Cl. E17 77 H4
Essex Cl., Mord. 184 A7
Essex Cl., Rom. 83 H4
Essex Cl., Ruis. 84 D1
Essex Ct. EC4 18 E4
Essex Ct. SW13 147 F2
Essex Gdns. N4 75 H6
Essex Gro. SE19 170 A6
Essex Ho. E14 114 B6
  Giraud St.
Essex Pk. N3 56 E6
Essex Pk. Ms. W3 126 E1
Essex Pl. W4 126 C4
Essex Pl. Sq. W4 126 D4
  Essex Pl.

Name	No.	Grid
Essex Rd. E4	62	E1
Essex Rd. E10	78	C6
Essex Rd. E12	98	B5
Essex Rd. E17	77	H6
Essex Rd. E18	79	H2
Essex Rd. N1	111	H1
Essex Rd. NW10	89	E7
Essex Rd. W3	106	C7
Essex Rd. W4	126	D4
Belmont Rd.		
Essex Rd., Bark.	99	G3
Essex Rd., Borwd.	38	A3
Essex Rd., Dag.	101	J3
Essex Rd., Enf.	44	A4
Essex Rd., Rom.	83	H4
Essex Rd.	82	C7
(Chadwell Heath), Rom.		
Essex Rd. S. E11	78	D7
Essex St. E7	97	G5
Essex St. WC2	**18**	**E5**
Essex Twr. SE20	189	E1
Essex Vil. W8	128	D2
Essex Wf. E5	95	G2
Essian St. E1	113	H5
Essoldo Way, Edg.	69	J3
Estate Way E10	95	J1
Estcourt Rd. SE25	189	E6
Estcourt Rd. SW6	128	C7
Este Rd. SW11	149	H3
Estella Av., N.Mal.	183	H4
Estelle Rd. NW3	91	J4
Esterbrooke St. SW1	**33**	**H2**
Esterbrooke St. SW1	130	D4
Esther Cl. N21	43	G7
Esther Rd. E11	78	E7
Estoria Cl. SW2	151	G7
Estreham Rd. SW16	168	D6
Estridge Cl., Houns.	143	G4
Estuary Cl., Bark.	118	B3
Eswyn Rd. SW17	167	J4
Etchingham Pk. Rd. N3	57	E7
Etchingham Rd. E15	96	C4
Eternit Wk. SW6	147	J1
Etfield Gro., Sid.	176	B5
Ethel Rd. E16	115	H6
Ethel St. SE17	**35**	**J2**
Ethelbert Cl., Brom.	191	G3
Ethelbert Gdns., Ilf.	80	C5
Ethelbert Rd. SW20	184	A1
Ethelbert Rd., Brom.	191	G3
Ethelbert Rd., Erith	139	J7
Ethelbert St. SW12	168	B1
Fernlea Rd.		
Ethelburga St. SW11	149	H1
Ethelden Rd. W12	127	H1
Etheldene Av. N10	74	C4
Etheridge Grn., Loug.	49	F3
Etheridge Rd.		
Etheridge Rd. NW2	71	J7
Etheridge Rd., Loug.	49	E2
Etherley Rd. N15	75	J5
Etherow St. SE22	152	D6
Etherstone Grn. SW16	169	G4
Etherstone Rd.		
Etherstone Rd. SW16	169	G4
Ethnard Rd. SE15	132	E6
Ethronvi Rd., Bexh.	159	E3
Etloe Rd. E10	96	A2
Eton Av. N12	57	F7
Eton Av. NW3	91	G7
Eton Av., Barn.	41	H6
Eton Av., Houns.	123	F6
Eton Av., N.Mal.	182	D5
Eton Av., Wem.	87	E4
Eton Cl. SW18	149	E7
Eton College Rd. NW3	91	J6
Eton Ct. NW3	91	G7
Eton Av.		
Eton Ct., Wem.	87	F4
Eton Av.		
Eton Garages NW3	91	H6
Lambolle Pl.		
Eton Gro. NW9	70	A3
Eton Gro. SE13	154	E3
Eton Hall NW3	91	J6
Eton College Rd.		
Eton Pl. NW3	92	A7
Haverstock Hill		
Eton Ri. NW3	91	J6
Eton College Rd.		
Eton Rd. NW3	91	J7
Eton Rd., Hayes	121	J7
Eton Rd., Ilf.	99	F5
Eton St., Rich.	145	H5
Eton Vil. NW3	91	J6
Etta St. SE8	133	H6
Ettrick St. E14	114	C6
Etwell Pl., Surb.	181	J6
Eugenia Rd. SE16	133	F4
Eureka Rd., Kings.T.	182	A2
Washington Rd.		
Europa Pl. EC1	11	J4
Europe Rd. SE18	136	C3
Eustace Dr. E6	116	B3
Eustace Rd. SW6	128	D7
Eustace Rd., Rom.	82	D7
Euston Cen. NW1	110	C4
Triton Sq.		
Euston Gro. NW1	**9**	**H4**
Euston Gro. NW1	110	D3
Euston Rd. N1	**10**	**A3**
Euston Rd. N1	110	D4
Euston Rd. NW1	**9**	**E6**
Euston Rd. NW1	110	B4
Euston Rd., Croy.	201	G1
Euston Sq. NW1	**9**	**H4**
Euston Sq. NW1	110	D3
Euston Sta. Colonnade NW1	**9**	**H4**
Euston St. NW1	**9**	**G5**
Euston St. NW1	110	C3
Eva Rd., Rom.	82	C7
Evandale Rd. SW9	151	G2
Evangelist Rd. NW5	92	B4
Evans Cl. E8	94	C6
Buttermere Wk.		
Evans Gro., Felt.	161	G2
Evans Rd. SE6	173	E2
Evanston Av. E4	62	C7
Evanston Gdns., Ilf.	80	B6
Eve Rd. E11	96	E4
Eve Rd. E15	115	E2
Eve Rd. N17	76	B3
Eve Rd., Islw.	144	D4
Evelina Rd. SE15	153	F3
Evelina Rd. SE20	171	G7
Eveline Lowe Est. SE16	**29**	**H6**
Eveline Lowe Est. SE16	132	D3
Eveline Rd., Mitch.	185	J1
Evelyn Av. NW9	70	D4
Evelyn Cl., Twick.	143	H7
Evelyn Ct. N1	**12**	**B2**
Evelyn Denington Rd. E6	116	B4
Evelyn Dr., Pnr.	50	D7
Evelyn Fox Ct. W10	107	J5
Evelyn Gdns. SW7	**30**	**E4**
Evelyn Gdns. SW7	129	G5
Evelyn Gdns., Rich.	145	H4
Kew Rd.		
Evelyn Gro. W5	125	J1
Evelyn Gro., Sthl.	103	F6
Evelyn Rd. E16	135	H1
Evelyn Rd. E17	78	C4
Evelyn Rd. SW19	166	E5
Evelyn Rd. W4	126	D3
Evelyn Rd., Barn.	41	J4
Evelyn Rd., Rich.	145	H3
Evelyn Rd. (Ham.), Rich.	163	F3
Evelyn St. SE8	133	H5
Evelyn Ter., Rich.	145	H3
Evelyn Wk. N1	**12**	**B2**
Evelyn Wk. N1	112	A2
Evelyn Way, Wall.	200	D4
Evelyn Yd. W1	**17**	**H3**
Evening Hill, Beck.	172	C7
Evenwood Cl. SW15	148	B5
Everard Av., Brom.	205	G1
Everard Way, Wem.	87	H3
Everatt Cl. SW18	148	C6
Amerland Rd.		
Everdon Rd. SW13	127	G6
Everest Pl. E14	114	C5
Everest Rd. SE9	156	C5
Everest Rd., Stai.	140	A7
Everett Cl., Bushey	52	B1
Everett Wk., Belv.	139	F5
Osborne Rd.		
Everglade Strand NW9	71	F1
Evergreen Ct., Stai.	140	A7
Evergreen Way		
Evergreen Way, Stai.	140	A7
Everilda St. N1	111	F1
Evering Rd. E5	94	C3
Evering Rd. N16	94	C3
Everington Rd. N10	73	J2
Everington St. W6	128	A6
Everitt Rd. NW10	106	D3
Everleigh St. N4	93	F1
Eversfield Gdns. NW7	54	E7
Eversfield Rd., Rich.	145	J2
Evershed Wk. W4	126	D4
Eversholt St. NW1	**9**	**G1**
Eversholt St. NW1	110	C2
Evershot Rd. N4	93	F1
Eversleigh Rd. E6	116	A1
Eversleigh Rd. N3	56	C7
Eversleigh Rd. SW11	150	A2
Eversleigh Rd., Barn.	41	F5
Eversley Av., Wem.	88	A2
Eversley Cl. N21	43	F6
Eversley Cres. N21	43	F6
Eversley Cres., Islw.	144	A1
Eversley Mt. N21	43	F6
Eversley Pk. SW19	165	H5
Eversley Pk. Rd. N21	43	F6
Eversley Rd. SE7	135	H6
Eversley Rd. SE19	170	A7
Eversley Rd., Surb.	181	J4
Eversley Way, Croy.	204	A4
Everthorpe Rd. SE15	152	C3
Everton Bldgs. NW1	**9**	**F4**
Everton Dr., Stan.	69	J3
Everton Rd., Croy.	202	D1
Evesham Av. E17	78	A2
Evesham Cl., Grnf.	103	H2
Evesham Cl., Sutt.	198	D7
Evesham Grn., Mord.	184	E6
Evesham Rd. E15	115	F1
Evesham Rd. N11	58	C5
Evesham Rd., Felt.	142	C7
Sparrow Fm. Dr.		
Evesham Rd., Mord.	185	E6
Evesham St. W11	108	A7
Evesham Wk. SE5	152	A2
Love Wk.		
Evesham Wk. SW9	151	G2
Evesham Way SW11	150	A3
Evesham Way, Ilf.	80	D3
Evry Rd., Sid.	176	C6
Ewald Rd. SW6	148	C2
Ewanrigg Ter., Wdf.Grn.	63	J5
Ewart Cro. N22	75	G1
Ewart Pl. E3	113	J2
Ewart Rd. SE23	153	G7
Ewe Cl. N7	93	E6
Ewell Bypass, Epsom	197	G7
Ewell Ct. Av., Epsom	197	E5
Ewell Pk. Gdns., Epsom	197	G6
Ewell Pk. Way, Epsom	197	G6
Ewell Rd., Surb.	181	H6
Ewell Rd. (Long Ditton), Surb.	180	E7
Ewell Rd., Sutt.	198	B6
Ewellhurst Rd., Ilf.	80	B2
Ewelme Rd. SE23	171	F1
Ewen Cres. SW2	169	G1
Ewer St. SE1	**27**	**J2**
Ewer St. SE1	131	J1
Ewhurst Ho. E1	113	F5
Ewhurst Rd. SE4	153	J6
Exbury Rd. SE6	172	A2
Excel Ct. WC2	**17**	**J6**
Excelsior Cl., Kings.T.	182	A2
Washington Rd.		
Exchange Arc. EC2	20	E1
Exchange Bldgs. E1	112	B6
Cutler St.		
Exchange Ct. WC2	**18**	**B6**
Exchange Pl. EC2	**20**	**D1**
Exchange Sq. EC2	**20**	**D1**
Exchange Sq. EC2	112	B5
Exeter Cl. E6	116	C6
Harper Rd.		
Exeter Gdns., Ilf.	98	B1
Exeter Ho. SW15	147	J6
Putney Heath		
Exeter Ms. NW6	90/91	E6
West Hampstead NW6		
Exeter Rd. E16	115	G5
Exeter Rd. E17	78	A5
Exeter Rd. N9	61	F2
Exeter Rd. N14	58	B1
Exeter Rd. NW2	90	B5
Exeter Rd., Croy.	188	B7
Exeter Rd., Dag.	101	H6
Exeter Rd., Enf.	45	G3
Exeter Rd., Felt.	161	F3
Exeter Rd., Har.	85	E2
Exeter Rd., Houns.	141	H2
Exeter Rd., Well.	157	J2
Exeter St. WC2	**18**	**B5**
Exeter St. WC2	111	E7
Exeter Way SE14	133	J7
Exeter Way, Houns.	141	H3
Exford Gdns. SE12	173	H1
Exford Rd. SE12	173	H2
Exhibition Cl. W12	107	J7
Exhibition Rd. SW7	**23**	**F4**
Exhibition Rd. SW7	129	G2
Exmoor Cl., Ilf.	81	F1
Exmoor St. W10	108	A4
Exmouth Mkt. EC1	**11**	**E5**
Exmouth Mkt. EC1	111	G4
Exmouth Ms. NW1	**9**	**G4**
Exmouth Pl. E8	94	E7
Exmouth Rd. E17	77	J5
Exmouth Rd., Brom.	191	H3
Exmouth Rd., Ruis.	84	C3
Exmouth Rd., Well.	158	C1
Exmouth St. E1	113	F6
Commercial Rd.		
Exning Rd. E16	115	F4
Exon St. SE17	**36**	**D3**
Exon St. SE17	132	B5
Express Dr., Ilf.	100	B1
Exton Cres. NW10	88	C7
Exton Gdns., Dag.	100	C5
Exton St. SE1	**27**	**E2**
Exton St. SE1	131	G1
Eyebright Cl., Croy.	203	G1
Primrose La.		
Eyhurst Cl. NW2	89	G2
Eylewood Rd. SE27	169	J5
Eynella Rd. SE22	152	C7
Eynham Rd. W12	107	J6
Eynsford Cl., Orp.	193	F7
Eynsford Cres., Bex.	176	C1
Eynsford Rd., Ilf.	99	H2
Eynsham Dr. SE2	138	A4
Eynswood Dr., Sid.	176	B5
Eyot Gdns. W6	127	F5
Eyot Grn. W4	127	F6
Chiswick Mall		
Eyre Ct. NW8	**7**	**E1**
Eyre St. Hill EC1	**11**	**E6**
Eythorne Rd. SW9	151	G1
Ezra St. E2	**13**	**G3**
Ezra St. E2	112	C3

F

Name	No.	Grid
Faber Gdns. NW4	71	G5
Fabian Rd. SW6	128	C7
Fabian St. E6	116	C4
Factory La. N17	76	C2
Factory La., Croy.	201	G3
Factory Rd. E16	136	B1
Factory Sq. SW16	168	E6
Factory Yd. W7	124	B1
Uxbridge Rd.		
Faggs Rd., Felt.	142	A5
Fair Acres, Brom.	191	G5
Fair St. SE1	**29**	**E3**
Fair St. SE1	132	B2
Fair St., Houns.	143	J3
High St.		
Fairacre, N.Mal.	182	E3
Fairacres SW15	147	G4
Fairbank Av., Orp.	206	E2
Fairbanks Rd. N17	76	D3
Fairbourne Rd. N17	76	B3
Fairbridge Rd. N19	92	D2
Fairbrook Cl. N13	59	G5
Fairbrook Rd. N13	59	G6
Fairburn Cl., Borwd.	38	A1
Fairburn Ct. SW15	148	B5
Mercier Rd.		
Fairby Rd. SE12	155	H5
Faircharm Trd. Est. SE8	134	B7
Fairchild Cl. SW11	149	G2
Wye St.		
Fairchild Pl. EC2	**12**	**E6**
Fairchild St. EC2	**13**	**E6**
Fairclough St. E1	**21**	**J4**
Fairclough St. E1	112	D6
Faircross Av., Bark.	99	F6
Fairdale Gdns. SW15	147	H4
Fairdale Gdns., Hayes	122	A1
Fairey Av., Hayes	121	J4
Fairfax Gdns. SE3	156	A1
Fairfax Ms. E16	135	H1
Wesley Av.		
Fairfax Ms. SW15	147	J4
Upper Richmond Rd.		
Fairfax Pl. NW6	91	F7
Fairfax Rd. N8	75	G4
Fairfax Rd. NW6	91	F7
Fairfax Rd. W4	127	E3
Fairfax Rd., Tedd.	162	D6
Fairfax Rd. N10	58	A7
Cromwell Rd.		
Fairfield Av. NW4	71	H6
Fairfield Av., Edg.	54	B6
Fairfield Av., Twick.	161	H1
Fairfield Av., Wat.	50	C3
Fairfield Cl. N12	57	F4
Fairfield Cl., Enf.	45	H4
Scotland Grn. Rd. N.		
Fairfield Cl., Epsom	196	E5
Fairfield Cl., Mitch.	167	H7
Fairfield Cl., Sid.	157	J6
Fairfield Cl. NW10	107	G1
Fairfield Cres., Edg.	54	B6
Fairfield Dr. SW18	149	E5
Fairfield Dr., Grnf.	105	F1
Fairfield Dr., Har.	67	J3
Fairfield E., Kings.T.	181	H2
Fairfield Gdns. N8	74/75	E5
Elder Av.		
Fairfield Gro. SE7	136	A5

Name	Page	Grid
Fairfield Ind. Est., Kings.T.	181	J3
Fairfield N., Kings.T.	181	H2
Fairfield Path, Croy.	202	A3
Fairfield Pl., Kings.T.	181	H3
Fairfield Rd. E3	114	A2
Fairfield Rd. E17	77	H2
Fairfield Rd. N8	75	E5
Fairfield Rd. N18	60	D4
Fairfield Rd. W7	124	D3
Fairfield Rd., Beck.	190	A2
Fairfield Rd., Bexh.	159	F2
Fairfield Rd., Brom.	173	G7
Fairfield Rd., Croy.	202	B3
Fairfield Rd., Ilf.	99	E6
Fairfield Rd., Kings.T.	181	H2
Fairfield Rd., Orp.	193	G6
Fairfield Rd., Sthl.	103	F6
Fairfield Rd., West Dr.	120	B1
Fairfield Rd., Wdf.Grn.	63	G6
Fairfield S., Kings.T.	181	H2
Fairfield St. SW18	149	E5
Fairfield Way, Barn.	40	D5
Fairfield Way, Epsom	196	E5
Fairfield W., Kings.T.	181	H2
Fairfields Cl. NW9	70	C5
Fairfields Cres. NW9	70	C4
Fairfields Rd., Houns.	143	J3
Fairfoot Rd. E3	114	A4
Fairford Av., Croy.	189	G5
Fairford Cl., Croy.	189	H5
Fairford Gdns., Wor.Pk.	197	F2
Fairgreen, Barn.	41	J3
Fairgreen E., Barn.	41	J3
Fairgreen Rd., Th.Hth.	187	H5
Fairhaven Av., Croy.	189	G6
Fairhaven Cres., Wat.	50	A3
Fairhazel Gdns. NW6	91	E6
Fairholme, Felt.	141	G7
Fairholme Cl. N3	72	B4
Fairholme Gdns. N3	72	B3
Fairholme Rd. W14	128	B5
Fairholme Rd., Croy.	187	G7
Fairholme Rd., Har.	68	C5
Fairholme Rd., Ilf.	80	C7
Fairholme Rd., Sutt.	198	C6
Fairholt Cl. N16	94	B1
Fairholt Rd. N16	94	A1
Fairholt St. SW7	**23**	**H5**
Fairland Rd. E15	97	F6
Fairlands Av., Buck.H.	63	G2
Fairlands Av., Sutt.	198	D2
Fairlands Av., Th.Hth.	187	F4
Fairlands Ct. SE9	156	D6
North Pk.		
Fairlawn SE7	135	J6
Fairlawn Av. N2	73	H4
Fairlawn Av. W4	126	C4
Fairlawn Av., Bexh.	158	D2
Fairlawn Cl. N14	42	C6
Fairlawn Cl., Esher	194	C6
Fairlawn Cl., Felt.	161	F4
Fairlawn Cl., Kings.T.	164	C6
Fairlawn Dr., Wdf.Grn.	63	G7
Fairlawn Gdns., Sthl.	103	F7
Fairlawn Gro. W4	126	C4
Fairlawn Pk. SE26	171	H5
Fairlawn Rd. SW19	166	C7
Fairlawns, Pnr.	66	C2
Fairlawns, Sun.	178	A3
Fairlawns, Twick.	145	F6
Fairlea Pl. W5	105	G4
Fairlie Gdns. SE23	153	F7
Fairlight Av. E4	62	D2
Fairlight Av. NW10	107	E2
Fairlight Av., Wdf.Grn.	63	G6
Fairlight Cl. E4	62	D2
Fairlight Cl., Wor.Pk.	197	J4
Fairlight Rd. SW17	167	G4
Fairlop Gdns., Ilf.	65	F7
Fairlop Rd. E11	78	D7
Fairlop Rd., Ilf.	81	F2
Fairmead, Brom.	192	C4
Fairmead, Surb.	196	B1
Fairmead Cl., Brom.	192	C4
Fairmead Cl., Houns.	122	D7
Fairmead Cl., N.Mal.	182	D3
Fairmead Cres., Edg.	54	C3
Fairmead Gdns., Ilf.	80	B5
Fairmead Rd. N19	92	D3
Fairmead Rd., Croy.	201	F1
Fairmead Rd., Loug.	47	H4
Fairmead Side, Loug.	47	J5
Fairmeads, Loug.	48	E2
Fairmile Av. SW16	168	D5
Fairmont Cl., Belv.	139	F5
Lullingstone Rd.		
Fairmount Rd. SW2	151	F6
Fairoak Cl., Orp.	193	E7
Fairoak Dr. SE9	157	G5
Fairseat Cl., Bushey	52	B2
Hive Rd.		
Fairstead Wk. N1	111	J1
Popham Rd.		
Fairthorn Rd. SE7	135	G5
Fairview Av., Wem.	87	G6
Fairview Cl. E17	77	H1
Fairview Cl., Chig.	65	H4
Fairview Cres., Har.	85	G1
Fairview Dr., Chig.	65	H4
Fairview Dr., Orp.	207	G4
Fairview Gdns., Wdf.Grn.	79	H1
Fairview Pl. SW2	151	F7
Fairview Rd. N15	76	C5
Fairview Rd. SW16	187	F1
Fairview Rd., Chig.	65	H4
Fairview Rd., Enf.	43	G1
Fairview Rd., Sutt.	199	G5
Fairview Way, Edg.	54	A4
Fairwater Av., Well.	158	A4
Fairway SW20	183	J3
Fairway, Bexh.	159	E5
Fairway, Orp.	193	G5
Fairway, Wdf.Grn.	63	J5
Fairway, The N13	59	J3
Fairway, The N14	42	B6
Fairway, The NW7	54	D3
Fairway, The W3	106	E6
Fairway, The, Barn.	41	E6
Fairway, The, Brom.	192	D1
Fairway, The, N.Mal.	182	D1
Fairway, The, Nthlt.	85	J6
Fairway, The, Ruis.	84	D3
Fairway, The, Wem.	87	E3
Fairway, The, W.Mol.	179	H3
Fairway Av. NW9	70	B3
Fairway Av., Borwd.	38	B2
Fairway Cl. NW11	73	F7
Fairway Cl., Croy.	189	H5
Fairway Cl., Epsom	196	C4
Fairway Cl., Houns.	142	C5
Fairway Cl., NW7	54	D3
The Fairway		
Fairway Dr. SE28	118	D6
Fairway Dr., Grnf.	85	H7
Fairway Gdns., Beck.	190	D6
Fairway Gdns., Ilf.	99	F5
Fairways, Stan.	69	H2
Fairways, Tedd.	163	G7
Fairweather Cl. N15	76	B4
Fairweather Rd. N16	76	D6
Fairwyn Rd. SE26	171	H4
Fakenham Cl. NW7	55	G7
Fakenham Cl., Nthlt.	85	G6
Goodwood Dr.		
Fakruddin St. E1	13	J6
Fakruddin St. E1	112	D4
Falcon Av., Brom.	192	B4
Falcon Cl. SE1	**27**	**H1**
Falcon Cl. W4	126	C6
Sutton La. S.		
Falcon Ct. EC4	**19**	**E4**
Falcon Ct. EC4	111	G6
Falcon Cres., Enf.	45	G5
Falcon Dr., Stai.	140	A6
Falcon Gro. SW11	149	H3
Falcon Ho. W13	104	C4
Falcon La. SW11	149	H3
Falcon Pk. Ind. Est. NW10	89	F5
Falcon Rd. SW11	149	H2
Falcon Rd., Enf.	45	G5
Falcon Rd., Hmptn.	161	F7
Falcon St. E13	115	G4
Falcon Ter. SW11	149	H3
Falcon Way E11	79	G4
Falcon Way E14	134	B4
Falcon Way NW9	71	E2
Falcon Way, Felt.	142	B5
Falcon Way, Har.	69	H5
Falconberg Ct. W1	**17**	**J3**
Falconberg Ms. W1	**17**	**H3**
Falconer Wk. N7	93	F2
Newington Barrow Way		
Falconwood Av., Well.	157	G2
Falconwood Par., Well.	157	H4
Falconwood Rd., Croy.	204	A7
Falcourt Cl., Sutt.	198	E5
Falkirk Gdns., Wat.	50	D5
Blackford Rd.		
Falkirk Ho. W9	**6**	**B3**
Falkirk St. N1	**12**	**E2**
Falkirk St. N1	112	B2
Falkland Av. N3	54	D7
Falkland Av. N11	58	A4
Falkland Pk. Av. SE25	188	B3
Falkland Pl. NW5	92	C5
Falkland Rd.		
Falkland Rd. N8	75	G4
Falkland Rd. NW5	92	C5
Falkland Rd., Barn.	40	B2
Fallaize Av., Ilf.	98/99	E4
Riverdene Rd.		
Falloden Way NW11	72	D4
Fallow Cl., Chig.	65	J5
Fallow Ct. SE16	**37**	**J4**
Fallow Ct. Av. N12	57	F7
Fallow Flds., Loug.	47	J7
Fallowfield, Stan.	52	D3
Fallowfield Ct., Stan.	52	D3
Fallowfield Dr. N12	57	H6
Fallows Cl. N2	73	F2
Fallsbrook Rd. SW16	168	B7
Falman Cl. N9	60	D1
Croyland Rd.		
Falmer Rd. E17	78	B3
Falmer Rd. N15	75	J5
Falmer Rd., Enf.	44	B4
Falmouth Av. E4	62	D5
Falmouth Cl. N22	59	F7
Truro Rd.		
Falmouth Cl. SE12	155	F5
Falmouth Gdns., Ilf.	80	B5
Falmouth Rd. SE1	**28**	**A5**
Falmouth Rd. SE1	131	J3
Falmouth St. E15	96	D5
Falstaff Ms., Hmptn.	162	A5
Hampton Rd.		
Fambridge Cl. SE26	171	J4
Fambridge Rd., Dag.	101	G1
Fane St. W14	128	C6
North End Rd.		
Fann St. EC1	**11**	**J6**
Fann St. EC1	111	J4
Fann St. EC2	**11**	**J6**
Fann St. EC2	111	J4
Fanshaw St. N1	**12**	**D3**
Fanshaw St. N1	112	B3
Fanshawe Av., Bark.	99	F6
Fanshawe Cres., Dag.	101	E5
Fanshawe Rd., Rich.	163	F4
Fanthorpe St. SW15	147	J3
Faraday Av., Sid.	176	A2
Faraday Cl. N7	93	F6
Bride St.		
Faraday Rd. E15	97	F6
Faraday Rd. SW19	166	D6
Faraday Rd. W3	106	C7
Faraday Rd. W10	108	B5
Faraday Rd., Sthl.	103	H7
Faraday Rd., Well.	158	A3
Faraday Rd., W.Mol.	179	G4
Faraday Way SE18	136	A3
Faraday Way, Croy.	201	F1
Ampere Way		
Fareham Rd., Felt.	142	C7
Fareham St. W1	**17**	**H3**
Farewell Pl., Mitch.	185	H1
Faringdon Av., Brom.	192	E6
Faringford Rd. E15	96	E7
Farjeon Rd. SE3	156	A1
Farleigh Av., Brom.	191	F6
Farleigh Pl. N16	94	C4
Farleigh Rd.		
Farleigh Rd. N16	94	C4
Farleigh Rd., Ilf.	99	H1
Farley Dr., Ilf.	99	H1
Farley Pl. SE25	188	D4
Farley Rd. SE6	154	B7
Farley Rd., S.Croy.	202	E7
Farlington Pl. SW15	147	H7
Roehampton La.		
Farlow Rd. SW15	148	A3
Farlton Rd. SW18	149	E7
Farm Av. NW2	90	B3
Farm Av. SW16	169	E4
Farm Av., Har.	67	F5
Farm Av., Wem.	87	F6
Farm Cl., Barn.	39	J5
Farm Cl., Buck.H.	63	J3
Farm Cl., Dag.	101	J7
Farm Cl., Sthl.	103	H7
Farm Cl., Sutt.	199	G7
Farm Cl., W.Wick.	205	E3
Farm Ct. NW4	71	G3
Farm Dr., Croy.	203	J2
Farm End E4	46	E5
Farm La. N14	42	A7
Farm La. SW6	128	D6
Farm La., Croy.	203	J2
Farm Pl. W8	128	D1
Uxbridge St.		
Farm Rd. N21	59	J1
Farm Rd., Edg.	54	B6
Farm Rd., Houns.	161	E1
Farm Rd., Mord.	185	E5
Farm Rd., Sutt.	199	G7
Farm St. W1	**16**	**D6**
Farm St. W1	110	B7
Farm Vale, Bex.	159	H6
Farm Wk. NW11	72	C5
Farm Way, Buck.H.	63	J4
Farm Way, Wor.Pk.	197	J3
Farman Gro., Nthlt.	102	D3
Wayfarer Rd.		
Farmborough Cl., Har.	68	A7
Pool Rd.		
Farmcote Rd. SE12	173	G1
Farmdale Rd. SE10	135	G5
Farmdale Rd., Cars.	199	H7
Farmer Rd. E10	96	B1
Farmer St. W8	128	D1
Uxbridge St.		
Farmers Rd. SE5	**35**	**H7**
Farmers Rd. SE5	131	H7
Farmfield Rd., Brom.	172	E5
Farmhouse Rd. SW16	168	C7
Farmilo Rd. E17	77	J7
Farmington Av., Sutt.	199	G3
Farmland Wk., Chis.	174	E5
Farmlands, Enf.	43	G1
Farmlands, Pnr.	66	A4
Farmlands, The, Nthlt.	85	F6
Farmleigh N14	42	C7
Farmstead Rd. SE6	172	B6
Farmstead Rd., Har.	68	A1
Farmway, Dag.	100	C4
Farnaby Rd. SE9	155	J4
Farnaby Rd., Brom.	172	D7
Farnan Av. E17	78	A2
Farnan Rd. SW16	169	E5
Farnborough Av. E17	77	H3
Farnborough Av., S.Croy.	203	G7
Farnborough Cl., Wem.	88	B2
Chalkhill Rd.		
Farnborough Common, Orp.	206	C3
Farnborough Cres., Brom.	205	F1
Saville Row		
Farnborough Hill, Orp.	207	G5
Farnborough Way SE15	**37**	**E7**
Farnborough Way, Orp.	207	G5
Farncombe St. SE16	**29**	**J4**
Farncombe St. SE16	132	D2
Farndale Av. N13	59	H3
Farndale Cres., Grnf.	103	J3
Farnell Ms. SW5	**30**	**A3**
Farnell Rd., Islw.	144	A3
Farnham Cl. N20	41	F7
Farnham Gdns. SW20	183	H2
Farnham Pl. SE1	**27**	**H2**
Farnham Rd., Ilf.	81	J7
Farnham Rd., Well.	158	C2
Farnham Royal SE11	**34**	**D4**
Farnham Royal SE11	131	F5
Farningham Rd. N17	60	D7
Farnley Rd. E4	46	E7
Farnley Rd. SE25	188	A4
Faro Cl., Brom.	192	D2
Faroe Rd. W14	128	A3
Farorna Wk., Enf.	43	G1
Farquhar Rd. SE19	170	C5
Farquhar Rd. SW19	166	D3
Farquharson Rd., Croy.	201	J1
Farr Av., Bark.	118	A2
Farr Rd., Enf.	44	A1
Farrance Rd., Rom.	83	E6
Farrance St. E14	113	J6
Farrans Ct., Har.	69	E7
Farrant Av. N22	75	G2
Farrell Ho. E1	113	F6
Farren Rd. SE23	171	H2
Farrer Ms. N8	74	C4
Farrer Rd.		
Farrer Rd. N8	74	C4
Farrer Rd., Har.	69	H5
Farrer's Pl., Croy.	203	G4
Farrier Cl., Sun.	178	A4
Farrier Rd., Nthlt.	103	G2
Farrier St. NW1	92	B7
Farrier Wk. SW10	**30**	**C5**
Farrier Wk. SW10	129	F6
Farriers Way, Borwd.	38	C6
Farringdon La. EC1	**11**	**F6**
Farringdon La. EC1	111	G4
Farringdon Rd. EC1	**10**	**E5**
Farringdon Rd. EC1	111	G4
Farringdon St. EC4	**19**	**G3**
Farringdon St. EC4	111	H5
Farrington Pl., Chis.	175	G7

Street	Page	Grid
Farrins Rents SE16	133	H1
Farrow La. SE14	133	F7
Farrow Pl. SE16	133	H3
Ropemaker Rd.		
Farthing All. SE1	**29**	**H4**
Farthing Flds. E1	132/133	E1
Raine St.		
Farthing St., Orp.	206	C7
Farthingale Wk. E15	96	D7
Farthings, The, Kings.T.	182	A1
Brunswick Rd.		
Farthings Cl. E4	63	E3
Farthings Cl., Pnr.	66	B6
Farwell Rd., Sid.	176	B3
Farwig La., Brom.	191	F1
Fashion St. E1	**21**	**F2**
Fashion St. E1	112	C5
Fashoda Rd., Brom.	192	A4
Fassett Rd. E8	94	D6
Fassett Rd., Kings.T.	181	H4
Fassett Sq. E8	94	D6
Fauconberg Rd. W4	126	C6
Faulkner Cl., Dag.	82	D7
Faulkner St. SE14	153	F1
Faulkner's All. EC1	**19**	**G1**
Fauna Cl., Rom.	82	C7
Faunce St. SE17	**35**	**G5**
Favart Rd. SW6	148	D1
Faversham Av. E4	63	E1
Faversham Av., Enf.	44	A6
Faversham Rd. SE6	153	J7
Faversham Rd., Beck.	189	J2
Faversham Rd., Mord.	185	E6
Fawcett Cl. SW11	149	G2
Fawcett Cl. SW16	169	G4
Fawcett Est. E5	94	D1
Fawcett Rd. NW10	107	F1
Fawcett Rd., Croy.	201	H3
Fawcett St. SW10	**30**	**C5**
Fawcett St. SW10	129	F6
Fawcus Cl., Esher	194	C6
Dalmore Av.		
Fawe Pk. Rd. SW15	148	C4
Fawe St. E14	114	B5
Fawley Rd. NW6	90	E5
Fawn Rd. E13	115	J2
Fawn Rd., Chig.	65	J5
Fawnbrake Av. SE24	151	H5
Fawood Av. NW10	88	D7
Faygate Cres., Bexh.	159	G5
Faygate Rd. SW2	169	F2
Fayland Av. SW16	168	C5
Fearnley Cres., Hmptn.	161	F5
Fearon St. SE10	135	G5
Featherbed La., Croy.	203	J7
Feathers Pl. SE10	134	D6
Featherstone Av. SE23	171	E2
Featherstone Gdns., Borwd.	38	C4
Featherstone Ind. Est., Sthl.	123	E2
Featherstone Rd. NW7	55	H6
Featherstone Rd., Sthl.	122	E3
Featherstone St. EC1	**12**	**B5**
Featherstone St. EC1	112	A4
Featherstone Ter., Sthl.	123	E3
Featley Rd. SW9	151	H3
Federal Rd., Grnf.	105	F2
Federation Rd. SE2	138	B4
Fee Fm. Rd., Esher	194	C7
Felbridge Av., Stan.	68	D1
Felbridge Cl. SW16	169	G4
Felbrigge Rd., Ilf.	99	J2
Felday Rd. SE13	154	B6
Felden Cl., Pnr.	51	E7
Felden St. SW6	148	C1
Feldman Cl. N16	94	D1
Felgate Ms. W6	127	H4
Felhampton Rd. SE9	174	E2
Felhurst Cres., Dag.	101	H4
Felix Av. N8	74	E6
Felix Rd. W13	104	D7
Felix Rd., Walt.	178	A6
Felix St. E2	112/113	E2
Hackney Rd.		
Felixstowe Ct. E16	136/137	E2
Barge Ho. Rd.		
Felixstowe Rd. N9	60	D4
Felixstowe Rd. N17	76	C3
Felixstowe Rd. NW10	107	H3
Felixstowe Rd. SE2	138	B3
Fell Rd., Croy.	201	J3
Fell Wk., Edg.	70	B1
East Rd.		
Fellbrigg Rd. SE22	152	C5
Fellbrigg St. E1	112/113	E4
Headlam St.		
Fellbrook, Rich.	163	E3
Fellmongers Yd., Croy.	201	J2
Surrey St.		
Fellowes Cl., Hayes	102	D4
Paddington Cl.		
Fellowes Rd., Cars.	199	H3
Fellows Ct. E2	**13**	**F2**
Fellows Ct. E2	112	C2
Fellows Rd. NW3	91	G7
Felltram Way SE7	135	G5
Woolwich Rd.		
Felmersham Cl. SW4	150	D4
Haselrigge Rd.		
Felmingham Rd. SE20	189	F2
Felnex Trd. Est., Wall.	200	A2
Fels Cl., Dag.	101	H3
Fels Fm. Av., Dag.	101	J3
Felsberg Rd. SW2	151	E6
Felsham Rd. SW15	148	A3
Felspar Cl. SE18	137	J5
Felstead Av., Ilf.	80	D1
Felstead Gdns. E14	134	C5
Ferry St.		
Felstead Rd. E11	79	G7
Felstead Rd., Loug.	48	B7
Felstead St. E9	95	J6
Felsted Rd. E16	116	A6
Feltham Av., E.Mol.	180	B4
Feltham Business Complex, Felt.	160	B2
Feltham Hill Rd., Felt.	160	A4
Feltham Rd., Mitch.	185	J2
Felthambrook Way, Felt.	160	B3
Felton Cl., Orp.	192	E6
Felton Gdns., Bark.	117	H1
Sutton Rd.		
Felton Lea, Sid.	175	J5
Felton Rd. W13	125	F2
Camborne Av.		
Felton Rd., Bark.	117	H2
Sutton Rd.		
Felton St. N1	112	A1
Fen Ct. EC3	**20**	**D5**
Fen Gro., Sid.	157	J6
Fen St. E16	115	F7
Victoria Dock Rd.		
Fencepiece Rd., Chig.	65	F5
Fencepiece Rd., Ilf.	65	F5
Fenchurch Av. EC3	**20**	**D4**
Fenchurch Av. EC3	112	B6
Fenchurch Bldgs. EC3	**20**	**E4**
Fenchurch Pl. EC3	**20**	**E5**
Fenchurch St. EC3	**20**	**D5**
Fenchurch St. EC3	112	B7
Fendall Rd., Epsom	196	C5
Fendall St. SE1	**29**	**E6**
Fendall St. SE1	132	B3
Fendt Cl. E16	115	F7
Bowman Av.		
Fendyke Rd., Belv.	138	D3
Fenelon Pl. W14	128	C4
Fenham Rd. SE15	132	D7
Fenman Ct. N17	76/77	E1
Shelbourne Rd.		
Fenman Gdns., Ilf.	100	B1
Fenn Cl., Brom.	173	G6
Fenn St. E9	95	F5
Fennel Cl. E16	114/115	E4
Cranberry La.		
Fennel Cl., Croy.	203	G1
Primrose La.		
Fennel St. SE18	136	D6
Fenner Cl. SE16	132/133	E4
Layard Rd.		
Fenner Sq. SW11	149	G3
Thomas Baines Rd.		
Fenning St. SE1	**28**	**D3**
Fenstanton Av. N12	57	G5
Fenswood Cl., Bex.	159	G5
Fentiman Rd. SW8	**34**	**B6**
Fentiman Rd. SW8	131	E6
Fenton Cl. E8	94	C6
Laurel St.		
Fenton Cl. SW9	151	F2
Fenton Cl., Chis.	174	C5
Fenton Rd. N17	59	J7
Fentons Av. E13	115	H2
Fenwick Cl. SE18	136	D6
Ritter St.		
Fenwick Gro. SE15	152	D3
Fenwick Pl. SW9	150	E3
Fenwick Rd. SE15	152	D3
Ferdinand Pl. NW1	92	A7
Ferdinand St.		
Ferdinand St. NW1	92	A6
Fergus Rd. N5	93	H5
Calabria Rd.		
Ferguson Av., Surb.	181	J5
Ferguson Cl. E14	134	A4
Ferguson Cl., Brom.	190	C3
Ferguson Dr. W3	106	D6
Ferme Pk. Rd. N4	75	E5
Ferme Pk. Rd. N8	75	E5
Fermor Rd. SE23	171	H1
Fermoy Rd. W9	108	C4
Fermoy Rd., Grnf.	103	H4
Fern Av., Mitch.	186	D4
Fern Dene W13	104/105	E5
Templewood		
Fern Gro., Felt.	142	B7
Fern La., Houns.	123	F5
Fern St. E3	114	A4
Fern Wk. SE16	**37**	**J4**
Fernbank, Buck.H.	63	H1
Fernbank Av., Walt.	179	E7
Fernbank Av., Wem.	86	C4
Fernbank Ms. SW12	150	C6
Fernbrook Av., Sid.	157	H5
Blackfen Rd.		
Fernbrook Cres. SE13	154	E6
Fernbrook Dr., Har.	67	H7
Fernbrook Rd. SE13	154	E6
Ferncliff Rd. E8	94	D5
Ferncroft Av. N12	57	H6
Ferncroft Av. NW3	90	D3
Ferncroft Av., Ruis.	84	C2
Ferndale, Brom.	191	J2
Ferndale Av. E17	78	D5
Ferndale Av., Houns.	143	E3
Ferndale Cl., Bexh.	158	E1
Ferndale Ct. SE3	135	F7
Ferndale Rd. E7	97	H7
Ferndale Rd. E11	97	E2
Ferndale Rd. N15	76	C6
Ferndale Rd. SE25	188	E5
Ferndale Rd. SW4	150	E4
Ferndale Rd. SW9	151	F3
Ferndale Rd., Rom.	83	J2
Ferndale St. E6	116	E7
Ferndale Ter., Har.	68	C4
Ferndale Way, Orp.	207	G5
Fernden Way, Rom.	83	H6
Ferndene Rd. SE24	151	J4
Ferndown, Nthwd.	66	A2
Ferndown Av., Orp.	207	G1
Ferndown Cl., Pnr.	50	E7
Ferndown Cl., Sutt.	199	G6
Ferndown Rd. SE9	156	A7
Ferndown Rd., Wat.	50	C3
Ferney Meade Way, Islw.	144	D2
Ferney Rd., Barn.	42	A7
Fernhall Dr., Ilf.	80	A5
Fernham Rd., Th.Hth.	187	J3
Fernhead Rd. W9	108	C4
Fernhill Ct. E17	78	D2
Fernhill Gdns., Kings.T.	163	G5
Fernhill St. E16	136	C1
Fernholme Rd. SE15	153	G5
Fernhurst Gdns., Edg.	54	A6
Fernhurst Rd. SW6	148	B1
Fernhurst Rd., Croy.	188	D7
Fernlea Rd. SW12	168	B1
Fernlea Rd., Mitch.	186	A2
Fernleigh Cl., Croy.	201	G4
Stafford Rd.		
Fernleigh Ct., Har.	67	H2
Fernleigh Ct., Wem.	87	H2
Fernleigh Rd. N21	59	G2
Ferns Rd. E15	97	F6
Fernsbury St. WC1	**10**	**E4**
Fernshaw Rd. SW10	**30**	**C6**
Fernshaw Rd. SW10	129	F6
Fernside NW11	90	D2
Finchley Rd.		
Fernside, Buck.H.	63	H1
Fernside Av. NW7	54	D3
Fernside Av., Felt.	160	B4
Fernside Rd. SW12	167	J1
Fernthorpe Rd. SW16	168	C6
Ferntower Rd. N5	94	A5
Fernways, Ilf.	98/99	E4
Cecil Rd.		
Fernwood Av. SW16	168	D4
Fernwood Av., Wem.	87	F5
Bridgewater Rd.		
Fernwood Cl., Brom.	191	J2
Fernwood Cres. N20	57	J3
Ferranti Cl. SE18	136	A3
Ferraro Cl., Houns.	123	G6
Ferrers Av., Wall.	200	D4
Ferrers Av., West Dr.	120	A2
Ferrers Rd. SW16	168	D5
Ferrestone Rd. N8	75	F4
Ferriby Cl. N1	93	G7
Bewdley St.		
Ferrier Pt. E16	115	H5
Forty Acre La.		
Ferrier St. SW18	149	E4
Ferring Cl., Har.	85	J1
Ferrings SE21	170	B2
Ferris Av., Croy.	203	J3
Ferris Rd. SE22	152	D4
Ferron Rd. E5	94	E3
Ferrour Ct. N2	73	G3
Ferry La. N17	76	E4
Ferry La. SW13	127	F6
Ferry La., Brent.	125	H6
Ferry La., Rich.	125	J6
Ferry Pl. SE18	136	D3
Woolwich High St.		
Ferry Rd. SW13	127	G7
Ferry Rd., Tedd.	162	E5
Ferry Rd., T.Ditt.	180	E6
Ferry Rd., Twick.	162	E1
Ferry Rd., W.Mol.	179	G3
Ferry Sq., Brent.	125	G6
Ferry St. E14	134	C5
Ferryhills Cl., Wat.	50	C3
Ferrymead Av., Grnf.	103	G3
Ferrymead Dr., Grnf.	103	G2
Ferrymead Gdns., Grnf.	103	J2
Ferrymoor, Rich.	163	E3
Festing Rd. SW15	148	A3
Festival Cl., Bex.	176	D1
Festival Wk., Cars.	199	J5
Fetter La. EC4	**19**	**F4**
Fetter La. EC4	111	G6
Ffinch St. SE8	134	A7
Field Cl. E4	62	B6
Field Cl., Brom.	191	J2
Field Cl., Buck.H.	63	J3
Field Cl., Chess.	195	F5
Field Cl., Hayes	121	F7
Field Cl., Houns.	142	B1
Field Cl., W.Mol.	179	H5
Field Ct. WC1	**18**	**D2**
Field End, Barn.	39	H4
Field End, Nthlt.	84	D6
Field End, Ruis.	84	C6
Field End, Twick.	162	C4
Field End Rd., Pnr.	66	B6
Field End Rd., Ruis.	85	E4
Field La., Brent.	125	F7
Field La., Tedd.	162	D5
Field Mead NW7	55	E7
Field Mead NW9	55	E7
Field Pl., N.Mal.	183	F6
Field Rd. E7	97	G4
Field Rd. N17	76	A3
Field Rd. W6	128	B5
Field Rd., Felt.	142	B6
Field St. WC1	**10**	**C3**
Field St. WC1	111	F3
Field Way NW10	88	C7
Twybridge Way		
Field Way, Croy.	204	B6
Field Way, Grnf.	103	H1
Fieldcommon La., Walt.	179	F7
Fieldend Rd. SW16	186	C1
Fielders Cl., Enf.	44	B4
Woodfield Cl.		
Fielders Cl., Har.	85	J1
Fieldfare Rd. SE28	118	C7
Fieldgate La., Mitch.	185	H3
Fieldgate St. E1	**21**	**J2**
Fieldgate St. E1	112	D5
Fieldhouse Cl. E18	79	G1
Fieldhouse Rd. SW12	168	C1
Fielding Av., Twick.	161	J3
Fielding Ho. NW6	108	D3
Fielding Ms. SW13	127	H6
Castelnau		
Fielding Rd. W4	126	D3
Fielding Rd. W14	128	A3
Fielding St. SE17	**35**	**J5**
Fielding St. SE17	131	J6
Fielding Wk. W13	124	E3
Fieldings, The SE23	171	F1
Fields Est. E8	94	D7
Fields Pk. Cres., Rom.	82	D5
Fieldsend Rd., Sutt.	198	B5
Fieldside Cl., Orp.	207	F4
State Fm. Av.		
Fieldside Rd., Brom.	172	D5
Fieldview SW18	167	G1
Fieldway, Dag.	100	B4
Fieldway, Orp.	193	G6
Fieldway Cres. N5	93	G5
Fiennes Cl., Dag.	100	C1
Fiesta Dr., Dag.	119	J4
Fife Rd. E16	115	G5
Fife Rd. N22	59	H7
Fife Rd. SW14	146	C5
Fife Rd., Kings.T.	181	H2
Fife Ter. N1	**10**	**D1**
Fife Ter. N1	111	F2
Fifield Path SE23	171	G3
Bampton Rd.		
Fifth Av. E12	98	C4
Fifth Av. W10	108	B3
Fifth Av., Hayes	121	J1
Fifth Cross Rd., Twick.	162	A2

Fifth Way, Wem. 88 B4
Fig Tree Cl. NW10 106/107 E1
Craven Pk.
Figges Rd., Mitch. 168 A7
Filby Rd., Chess. 195 J6
Filey Av. N16 94 D1
Filey Cl., Sutt. 199 F7
Filey Waye, Ruis. 84 A2
Filigree Ct. SE16 133 J1
Silver Wk.
Fillebrook Av., Enf. 44 B2
Fillebrook Rd. E11 96 D1
Filmer Rd. SW6 148 B1
Filston Rd., Erith 139 H5
Riverdale Rd.
Finborough Rd. SW10 30 B5
Finborough Rd. SW10 128 E5
Finborough Rd. SW17 167 J6
Finch Av. SE27 170 A4
Finch Cl. NW10 88 D5
Finch Cl., Barn. 40 D5
Finch Dr., Felt. 142 D7
Finch La. EC3 20 C4
Finch Ms. SE15 132 C7
Finchale Rd. SE2 138 A3
Finchdean Way SE15 132 C7
Daniel Gdns.
Finchingfield Av., Wdf.Grn. 63 J7
Finchley Ct. N3 57 E6
Finchley La. NW4 71 J4
Finchley Pk. N12 57 F4
Finchley Pl. NW8 6 E1
Finchley Pl. NW8 109 G2
Finchley Rd. NW2 90 D3
Finchley Rd. NW3 91 F6
Finchley Rd. NW8 109 G1
Finchley Rd. NW11 72 C6
Finchley Way N3 56 D7
Finck St. SE1 26 D4
Finden Rd. E7 97 H5
Findhorn Av., Hayes 102 B5
Findhorn St. E14 114 C6
Findon Cl. SW18 148 D6
Wimbledon Pk. Rd.
Findon Cl., Har. 85 H3
Findon Rd. N9 60 E1
Findon Rd. W12 127 G2
Fingal St. SE10 135 F5
Finland Quay SE16 133 H3
Finland Rd. SE4 153 H3
Finland St. SE16 133 H3
Finlay St. SW6 148 A1
Finlays Cl., Chess. 196 A5
Finnis St. E2 113 E3
Finnymore Rd., Dag. 101 E7
Finsbury Av. EC2 20 C2
Finsbury Circ. EC2 20 C2
Finsbury Circ. EC2 112 A5
Finsbury Cotts. N22 58/59 E7
Clarence Rd.
Finsbury Est. EC1 11 G4
Finsbury Est. EC1 111 G3
Finsbury Ho. N22 75 E1
Finsbury Mkt. EC2 12 D6
Finsbury Mkt. EC2 112 B4
Finsbury Pk. Av. N4 75 J6
Finsbury Pk. Rd. N4 93 H3
Finsbury Pavement EC2 20 C1
Finsbury Pavement EC2 112 A5
Finsbury Rd. N22 75 F1
Finsbury Sq. EC2 20 C1
Finsbury Sq. EC2 112 A5
Finsbury St. EC2 20 B1
Finsbury St. EC2 112 A5
Finsbury Way, Bex. 159 F6
Finsen Rd. SE5 151 J3
Finstock Rd. W10 108 A6
Finucane Ri., Bushey 51 J2
Fir Cl., Walt. 178 A7
Fir Dene, Orp. 206 C3
Fir Gro., N.Mal. 183 F6
Fir Rd., Felt. 160 D5
Fir Rd., Sutt. 198 C1
Fir Tree Av., Mitch. 186 A2
Fir Tree Av., West Dr. 120 D3
Fir Tree Cl. SW16 168 C5
Fir Tree Cl. W5 105 H6
Fir Tree Cl., Epsom 197 F4
Fir Tree Cl., Orp. 207 J5
Highfield Av.
Fir Tree Gdns., Croy. 204 A4
Fir Tree Gro., Cars. 199 J7
Fir Tree Rd., Houns. 143 E4
Fir Tree Wk., Dag. 101 J3
Wheel Fm. Dr.
Fir Tree Wk., Enf. 44 A3
Fir Trees Cl. SE16 133 H1
Firbank Cl. E16 116 A5
Firbank Cl., Enf. 43 J4
Gladbeck Way
Firbank Rd. SE15 153 E2
Fircroft Gdns., Har. 86 B3
Fircroft Rd. SW17 167 J2
Fircroft Rd., Chess. 195 J4
Firdene, Surb. 196 C1
Fire Bell All., Surb. 181 H6
Fire Sta. All., Barn. 40 C2
Christchurch La.
Firecrest Dr. NW3 91 E3
Firefly Cl., Wall. 200 E7
Firefly Gdns. E6 116 B4
Jack Dash Way
Firethorn Cl., Edg. 54 C4
Larkspur Gro.
Firhill Rd. SE6 172 A4
Firs, The E17 77 H5
Leucha Rd.
Firs, The N20 57 G1
Firs, The W5 105 G5
Firs Av. N10 74 A3
Firs Av. N11 58 A6
Firs Av. SW14 146 C4
Firs Cl. N10 74 A3
Firs Av.
Firs Cl. SE23 153 G7
Firs Cl., Esher 194 B6
Firs Cl., Mitch. 186 B2
Firs Dr., Houns. 122 B7
Firs Dr., Loug. 48 D1
Firs La. N13 59 J3
Firs La. N21 59 J2
Firs Pk. Av. N21 60 A1
Firs Pk. Gdns. N21 59 J1
Firs Wk., Wdf.Grn. 63 G5
Firsby Av., Croy. 203 G1
Firsby Rd. N16 94 C1
Firscroft N13 59 J3
Firside Gro., Sid. 175 J1
First Av. E12 98 B4
First Av. E13 115 G3
First Av. E17 78 A5
First Av. N18 61 F4
First Av. NW4 71 J4
First Av. SW14 146 E3
First Av. W3 127 F1
First Av. W10 108 C4
First Av., Bexh. 138 C7
First Av., Dag. 119 H2
First Av., Enf. 44 C6
First Av., Hayes 121 J1
First Av., Rom. 82 C5
First Av., Walt. 178 B6
First Av., Wem. 87 G2
First Av., W.Mol. 179 F4
First Cl., W.Mol. 179 J3
First Cross Rd., Twick. 162 B2
First Dr. NW10 88 C7
First St. SW3 31 H1
First St. SW3 129 H4
First Way, Wem. 88 B4
Firstway SW20 183 J2
Firswood Av., Epsom 197 F5
Firth Gdns. SW6 148 B1
Fish St. Hill EC3 20 C5
Fish St. Hill EC3 112 A7
Fisher Cl., Croy. 202 C1
Grant Rd.
Fisher Cl., Grnf. 103 G3
Gosling Cl.
Fisher Rd., Har. 68 C2
Fisher St. E16 115 G5
Fisher St. WC1 18 C2
Fisher St. WC1 111 F5
Fisherman Cl., Rich. 163 F4
Locksmeade Rd.
Fishermans Dr. SE16 133 G2
Fisherman's Wk. E14 134 A1
Fishermans Wk. SE28 137 H2
Tugboat St.
Fishers Ct. SE14 153 G1
Besson St.
Fishers La. W4 126 D4
Fishers Way, Belv. 139 J1
Fishersdene, Esher 194 D7
Fisherton St. NW8 7 E6
Fisherton St. NW8 109 G4
Fishguard Way E16 136/137 E2
Barge Ho. Rd.
Fishponds Rd. SW17 167 H4
Fishponds Rd., Kes. 206 A5
Fisons Rd. E16 135 G1
Fitzalan Rd. N3 72 B3
Fitzalan Rd., Esher 194 B7
Fitzalan St. SE11 34 D1
Fitzalan St. SE11 131 F4
Fitzgeorge Av. W14 128 B4
Fitzgeorge Av., N.Mal. 182 D1
Fitzgerald Av. SW14 147 E3
Fitzgerald Cl. E11 79 G5
Fitzgerald Rd.
Fitzgerald Ho. E14 114 B6
Fitzgerald Ho., Hayes 122 B1
Fitzgerald Rd. E11 79 G5
Fitzgerald Rd. SW14 146 D3
Fitzgerald Rd., T.Ditt. 180 D6
Fitzhardinge St. W1 16 B3
Fitzhardinge St. W1 110 A6
Fitzhugh Gro. SW18 149 G6
Fitzhugh Gro. Est. SW18 149 G6
Fitzjames Av. W14 128 B4
Fitzjames Av., Croy. 202 D2
Fitzjohn Av., Barn. 40 B5
Fitzjohn's Av. NW3 91 G5
Fitzmaurice Pl. W1 24 E1
Fitzmaurice Pl. W1 110 B7
Fitzneal St. W12 107 F6
Fitzroy Cl. N6 91 J1
Fitzroy Ct. W1 9 G6
Fitzroy Cres. W4 126 D7
Fitzroy Gdns. SE19 170 B7
Fitzroy Ms. W1 9 F6
Fitzroy Pk. N6 91 J1
Fitzroy Rd. NW1 110 A1
Fitzroy Sq. W1 9 F6
Fitzroy Sq. W1 110 C4
Fitzroy St. W1 9 F6
Fitzroy St. W1 110 C4
Fitzroy Yd. NW1 110 A1
Fitzroy Rd.
Fitzstephen Rd., Dag. 100 B5
Fitzwarren Gdns. N19 92 C1
Fitzwilliam Av., Rich. 145 J2
Fitzwilliam Ms. E16 135 G1
Hanover Av.
Fitzwilliam Rd. SW4 150 C3
Fitzwygram Cl., Hmptn. 161 J5
Five Acre NW9 71 F1
Five Bell All. E14 113 J7
Three Colt St.
Five Elms Rd., Brom. 205 H3
Five Elms Rd., Dag. 101 F3
Five Flds. Cl., Wat. 51 F3
Fiveacre Cl., Th.Hth. 187 G6
Fives Ct. SE11 35 G1
Fiveways Rd. SW9 151 H2
Fladbury Rd. N15 76 A6
Fladgate Rd. E11 79 E6
Flag Cl., Croy. 203 G1
Flag Wk., Pnr. 66 A6
Eastcote Rd.
Flambard Rd., Har. 68 D6
Flamborough Rd., Ruis. 84 A3
Flamborough St. E14 113 H6
Flamingo Gdns., Nthlt. 102/103 E3
Jetstar Way
Flamstead Gdns., Dag. 100 C7
Flamstead Rd.
Flamstead Rd., Dag. 100 C7
Flamsted Av., Wem. 88 A6
Flamsteed Rd. SE7 136 B5
Flanchford Rd. W12 127 F3
Flanders Cres. SW17 167 J7
Flanders Rd. E6 116 C2
Flanders Rd. W4 127 E4
Flanders Way E9 95 G6
Flank St. E1 21 H5
Flask Cotts. NW3 91 G4
New End Sq.
Flask Wk. NW3 91 G4
Flavell Ms. SE10 135 E5
Flaxen Cl. E4 62 B3
Flaxen Rd.
Flaxen Rd. E4 62 B3
Flaxley Rd., Mord. 184 E6
Flaxman Ct. W1 17 H4
Flaxman Rd. SE5 151 H2
Flaxman Ter. WC1 9 J4
Flaxman Ter. WC1 110 D3
Flaxton Rd. SE18 157 G1
Flecker Cl., Stan. 52 C5
Fleece Dr. N9 60 D4
Fleece Rd., Surb. 195 F1
Fleece Wk. N7 92/93 E6
Manger Rd.
Fleeming Cl. E17 77 J2
Pennant Ter.
Fleeming Rd. E17 77 J2
Fleet Cl., W.Mol. 179 F5
Fleet La., W.Mol. 179 F6
Fleet Pl. EC4 111 G6
Farringdon St.
Fleet Rd. NW3 91 H5
Fleet Sq. WC1 10 C4
Fleet St. EC4 19 E4
Fleet St. EC4 111 G6
Fleet St. Hill E1 13 H6
Fleetside, W.Mol. 179 F6
Fleetway Business Pk., Grnf. 105 E2
Fleetwood Cl. E16 116 A5
Fleetwood Cl., Chess. 195 G7
Fleetwood Cl., Croy. 202 B3
Chepstow Ri.
Fleetwood Ct. E6 116 C5
Evelyn Denington Rd.
Fleetwood Gro. W3 106/107 E7
East Acton La.
Fleetwood Rd. NW10 89 G5
Fleetwood Rd., Kings.T. 182 B3
Fleetwood Sq., Kings.T. 182 B3
Fleetwood St. N16 94 B2
Stoke Newington Ch. St.
Fleetwood Way, Wat. 50 C4
Fleming Ct. W2 14 E1
Fleming Ct., Croy. 201 G5
Fleming Dr. N21 43 F5
Sydenham Av.
Fleming Mead, Mitch. 167 H7
Fleming Rd. SE17 35 H5
Fleming Rd. SE17 131 H6
Fleming Rd., Sthl. 103 H6
Fleming Way SE28 118 D7
Fleming Way, Islw. 144 C3
Flemming Av., Ruis. 84 B1
Flempton Rd. E10 95 H1
Fletcher Cl. E6 116/117 E6
Trader Rd.
Fletcher La. E10 78 C7
Fletcher Path SE8 134 A7
New Butt La.
Fletcher Rd. W4 126 C3
Fletcher Rd., Chig. 65 J5
Fletcher St. E1 21 J5
Fletcher St. E1 112 D7
Fletchers Cl., Brom. 191 H4
Fletching Rd. E5 95 F3
Fletching Rd. SE7 135 J6
Fletton Rd. N11 58 E7
Fleur de Lis St. E1 13 E6
Fleur de Lis St. E1 112 B4
Fleur Gates SW19 148 A7
Princes Way
Flexmere Gdns. N17 76 A1
Flexmere Rd.
Flexmere Rd. N17 76 A1
Flight App. NW9 71 F2
Flimwell Cl., Brom. 172 E5
Flint St. SE17 36 C2
Flint St. SE17 132 A4
Flintmill Cres. SE3 156 B2
Flinton St. SE17 36 E3
Flinton St. SE17 132 B5
Flitcroft St. WC2 17 J3
Flock Mill Pl. SW18 166 E1
Flockton St. SE16 29 H4
Flodden Rd. SE5 151 J1
Flood La., Twick. 162 D1
Church La.
Flood Pas. SE18 136 C4
Samuel St.
Flood St. SW3 31 H4
Flood St. SW3 129 H5
Flood Wk. SW3 31 H5
Flood Wk. SW3 129 H6
Flora Cl. E14 114 B6
Flora Gdns. W6 127 H4
Ravenscourt Rd.
Flora Gdns., Rom. 82 C6
Flora St., Belv. 139 F5
Victoria St.
Floral St. WC2 18 A5
Floral St. WC2 110 E7
Florence Av., Enf. 43 J3
Florence Av., Mord. 185 F5
Florence Cantwell Wk. N19 74/75 E7
Hillrise Rd.
Florence Cl., Walt. 178 B7
Florence Rd.
Florence Dr., Enf. 43 J3
Florence Elson Cl. E12 98 D4
Grantham Rd.
Florence Gdns. W4 126 C6
Florence Gdns., Rom. 82 C7
Roxy Av.
Florence Nightingale Ho. N1 94 A6
Clephane Rd.
Florence Rd. E6 115 J1
Florence Rd. E13 115 F2
Florence Rd. N4 93 G1
Florence Rd. SE2 138 C3
Florence Rd. SE14 153 J1
Florence Rd. SW19 166 E6
Florence Rd. W4 126 D3
Florence Rd. W5 105 H7

Name	Page	Grid
Florence Rd., Beck.	189	G2
Florence Rd., Brom.	191	G1
Florence Rd., Felt.	160	B1
Florence Rd., Kings.T.	163	J7
Florence Rd., Sthl.	122	D4
Florence Rd., Walt.	178	B7
Florence St. E16	115	F4
Florence St. N1	93	H7
Florence St. NW4	71	J4
Florence Ter. SE14	153	J1
Florence Way SW12	167	J1
Florfield Pas. E8	94/95	E6
Reading La.		
Florfield Rd. E8	94/95	E6
Reading La.		
Florian Av., Sutt.	199	G4
Florian Rd. SW15	148	B4
Florida Cl., Bushey	52	A2
Florida Rd., Th.Hth.	187	H1
Florida St. E2	**13**	**H4**
Florida St. E2	112	D3
Floriston Cl., Stan.	69	E1
Floriston Gdns., Stan.	69	E1
Floss St. SW15	147	J2
Flower & Dean Wk.	**21**	**G2**
E1		
Flower La. NW7	55	F5
Flower Pot Cl. N15	76	C6
St. Ann's Rd.		
Flower Wk., The SW7	**22**	**C4**
Flower Wk., The SW7	129	F2
Flowers Ms. N19	92	C2
Tollhouse Way		
Flowersmead SW17	168	A2
Floyd Rd. SE7	135	J5
Fludyer St. SE13	154	E4
Foley Ms., Esher	194	B7
Foley Rd., Esher	194	B7
Foley St. W1	**17**	**F2**
Foley St. W1	110	C5
Folgate St. E1	**21**	**E1**
Folgate St. E1	112	B5
Foliot St. W12	107	F6
Folkestone Rd. E6	116	D2
Folkestone Rd. E17	78	B4
Folkestone Rd. N18	60	D4
Folkingham La. NW9	70	D1
Folkington Cor. N12	56	C5
Follett St. E14	114	C6
Folly La. E4	61	J7
Folly La. E17	77	H1
Folly Ms. W11	108	C6
Portobello Rd.		
Folly Wall E14	134	C2
Font Hills N2	73	F2
Fontaine Rd. SW16	169	F7
Fontarabia Rd. SW11	150	A4
Fontayne Av., Chig.	65	F4
Fontenoy Rd. SW12	168	B2
Fonteyne Gdns., Wdf.Grn.	80	A2
Lechmere Av.		
Fonthill Cl. SE20	188	D2
Selby Rd.		
Fonthill Ms. N4	93	G2
Lennox Rd.		
Fonthill Rd. N4	93	F1
Fontley Way SW15	147	G7
Fontwell Cl., Har.	52	B7
Fontwell Cl., Nthlt.	85	G6
Fontwell Dr., Brom.	192	D5
Football La., Har.	86	B1
Footpath, The SW15	147	G5
Foots Cray High St., Sid.	176	C6
Foots Cray La., Sid.	176	C1
Footscray Rd. SE9	156	D6
Footway, The SE9	157	F7
Forbes Cl. NW2	89	G3
Forbes Cl. SE19	170	B5
Forbes St. E1	**21**	**J4**
Forbes Way, Ruis.	84	B2
Forburg Rd. N16	94	D1
Ford Cl. E3	113	H2
Roman Rd.		
Ford Cl., Har.	68	A7
Ford Cl., Th.Hth.	187	H6
Ford End, Wdf.Grn.	63	H6
Ford Rd. E3	113	H1
Ford Rd., Dag.	101	F7
Ford Sq. E1	113	E5
Ford St. E3	113	H1
Ford St. E16	115	F6
Forde Av., Brom.	191	J3
Fordel Rd. SE6	172	D1
Fordham Cl., Barn.	41	H3
Fordham St. E1	**21**	**J3**
Fordham St. E1	112	D6
Fordhook Av. W5	105	J7
Fordingley Rd. W9	108	C3
Fordington Rd. N6	73	J5
Fordmill Rd. SE6	172	A2
Fords Gro. N21	59	J1
Fords Pk. Rd. E16	115	G6
Fordwich Cl., Orp.	193	J7
Fordwych Rd. NW2	90	B5
Fordyce Rd. SE13	154	C6
Fordyke Rd., Dag.	101	F2
Fore St. EC2	**20**	**A2**
Fore St. EC2	111	J5
Fore St. N9	60	D5
Fore St. N18	60	C6
Fore St., Pnr.	66	A5
Fore St. Av. EC2	**20**	**B2**
Foreland Ct. NW4	72	B1
Foreland St. SE18	137	G4
Plumstead Rd.		
Foreman Ct. W6	127	J4
Hammersmith Bdy.		
Foremark Cl., Ilf.	65	J5
Foreshore SE8	133	J4
Forest, The E11	79	E4
Forest App. E4	47	F7
Forest App., Wdf.Grn.	63	F7
Forest Av. E4	47	E7
Forest Av., Chig.	64	D5
Forest Business Pk. E17	12	J1
Forest Cl. E11	79	F5
Forest Cl., Chis.	192	D1
Forest Cl., Wdf.Grn.	63	H3
Forest Ct. E4	63	F1
Forest Ct. E11	79	E4
Forest Cft. SE23	171	E2
Forest Dr. E12	98	A3
Forest Dr., Kes.	206	B4
Forest Dr., Wdf.Grn.	62	D7
Forest Dr. E. E11	78	D7
Forest Dr. W. E11	78	C7
Forest Edge, Buck.H.	63	J4
Forest Gdns. N17	76	C2
Forest Gate NW9	70	E5
Forest Glade E4	62	E4
Forest Glade E11	79	E6
Forest Gro. E8	94	C7
Forest Hts., Buck.H.	63	G2
Forest Hill Business Cen. SE23	171	F2
Forest Hill Ind. Est. SE23	171	F2
Perry Vale		
Forest Hill Rd. SE22	153	E5
Forest Hill Rd. SE23	153	E5
Forest Ind. Pk., Ilf.	81	H1
Forest La. E7	97	H5
Forest La. E15	97	E5
Forest La., Chig.	64	D5
Forest Mt. Rd., Wdf.Grn.	62	D7
Forest Ridge, Beck.	190	A3
Forest Ridge, Kes.	206	B4
Forest Ri. E17	78	D5
Forest Rd. E7	97	G4
Forest Rd. E8	94	C6
Forest Rd. E11	78	D7
Forest Rd. E17	77	F4
Forest Rd. N9	61	E1
Forest Rd. N17	77	F4
Forest Rd., Felt.	160	C2
Forest Rd., Ilf.	81	H1
Forest Rd., Loug.	48	A3
Forest Rd., Rich.	126	A7
Forest Rd., Rom.	83	H3
Forest Rd., Sutt.	198	D1
Forest Rd., Wdf.Grn.	78	B3
Forest Side E4	47	H4
Forest Side E7	97	H4
Capel Rd.		
Forest Side, Buck.H.	63	J1
Forest Side, Wor.Pk.	197	F1
Forest St. E7	97	G5
Forest Vw. E4	46	D7
Forest Vw. E11	79	F7
High St. Leytonstone		
Forest Vw. Av. E10	78	D5
Forest Vw. Rd. E12	98	B4
Forest Vw. Rd. E17	78	C1
Forest Vw. Rd., Loug.	48	A4
Forest Way N19	92	C2
Hargrave Pk.		
Forest Way, Orp.	193	J5
Forest Way, Sid.	157	G7
Forest Way, Wdf.Grn.	63	H4
Forestdale N14	58	D4
Forester Rd. SE15	153	E4
Foresters Cres., Bexh.	159	H4
Foresters Dr. E17	78	D4
Foresters Dr., Wall.	200	D7
Forestholme Cl. SE23	171	F2
Forfar Rd. N22	75	H1
Forfar Rd. SW11	150	A1
Forge Cl., Brom.	205	G1
Forge Cl., Hayes	121	G6
High St.		
Forge Cotts. W5	125	G1
Ealing Grn.		
Forge Dr., Esher	194	D7
Forge La., Felt.	160	E5
Forge La., Sun.	178	A3
Forge La., Sutt.	198	B7
Forge Ms., Sun.	178	A3
Forge La.		
Forge Pl. NW1	92	A6
Malden Cres.		
Forlong Path, Nthlt.	84/85	E6
Arnold Rd.		
Forman Pl. N16	94	C4
Farleigh Rd.		
Formby Av., Stan.	69	F3
Formosa St. W9	**6**	**C6**
Formosa St. W9	109	E4
Formunt Cl. E16	115	F5
Vincent St.		
Forres Gdns. NW11	72	D6
Forrest Gdns. SW16	187	F3
Forrester Path SE26	171	G4
Forris Av., Hayes	121	J1
Forset St. W1	**15**	**H3**
Forset St. W1	109	H6
Forstal Cl., Brom.	191	G3
Ridley Rd.		
Forster Rd. E17	77	H6
Forster Rd. N17	76	C3
Forster Rd. SW2	150	E7
Forster Rd., Beck.	189	H3
Forster Rd., Croy.	187	J7
Windmill Rd.		
Forsters Cl., Rom.	83	F6
Forster's Way SW18	166	E1
Forsters Way, Hayes	102	B6
Forston St. N1	**12**	**B1**
Forsyte Cres. SE19	188	B1
Forsyth Gdns. SE17	**35**	**H5**
Forsyth Gdns. SE17	131	H6
Forsyth Pl., Enf.	44	B5
Forsythia Cl., Ilf.	98	E5
Fort Rd. SE1	**37**	**G2**
Fort Rd. SE1	132	C4
Fort Rd., Nthlt.	85	G7
Fort St. E1	**21**	**E2**
Fort St. E16	135	H1
Forterie Gdns., Ilf.	100	A3
Fortescue Av. E8	94/95	E7
Mentmore Ter.		
Fortescue Av., Twick.	161	J3
Fortescue Rd. SW19	167	G7
Fortescue Rd., Edg.	70	D1
Fortess Gro. NW5	92	B5
Fortess Rd. NW5	92	B5
Fortess Wk. NW5	92	B5
Fortess Rd.		
Forthbridge Rd. SW11	150	A4
Fortis Cl. E16	115	J6
Fortis Grn. N2	73	H4
Fortis Grn. N10	73	H4
Fortis Grn. Av. N2	73	J3
Fortis Grn. Rd. N10	74	A3
Fortismere Av. N10	74	A3
Fortnam Rd. N19	92	D2
Fortnums Acre, Stan.	52	C6
Fortrose Gdns. SW2	168	D1
New Pk. Rd.		
Fortuna Cl. N7	93	F6
Vulcan Way		
Fortune Gate Rd. NW10	107	E1
Fortune Grn. Rd. NW6	90	D4
Fortune St. EC1	**12**	**A6**
Fortune St. EC1	111	J4
Fortune Wk. SE28	137	G3
Broadwater Rd.		
Fortune Way NW10	107	G3
Fortunes Mead, Nthlt.	85	E6
Forty Acre La. E16	115	G5
Forty Av., Wem.	87	J3
Forty Cl., Wem.	87	J2
Forty Footpath SW14	146	C3
Forty La., Wem.	88	B2
Forum, The W.Mol.	179	H4
Forum Way, Edg.	54	A6
High St.		
Forumside, Edg.	54	A6
High St.		
Forval Cl., Mitch.	185	J5
Forward Dr., Har.	68	C4
Fosbury Ms. W2	**14**	**B6**
Foscote Ms. W9	108	D5
Amberley Rd.		
Foscote Rd. NW4	71	H6
Foskett Rd. SW6	148	C2
Foss Av., Croy.	201	G5
Foss Rd. SW17	167	G4
Fossdene Rd. SE7	135	H5
Fossdyke Cl., Hayes	103	E5
Fosse Way W13	104	D5
Fossil Rd. SE13	154	A3
Fossington Rd., Belv.	138	D4
Fossway, Dag.	100	C2
Foster La. EC2	**19**	**J3**
Foster La. EC2	111	J6
Foster Rd. E13	115	G4
Foster Rd. W3	106	E7
Foster Rd. W4	126	D5
Foster St. NW4	71	J4
Foster Wk. NW4	71	J4
New Brent St.		
Fosters Cl. E18	79	H1
Fosters Cl., Chis.	174	C5
Fothergill Cl. E13	115	G2
Fothergill Dr. N21	43	F5
Fotheringham Rd., Enf.	44	C4
Foubert's Pl. W1	**17**	**F4**
Foubert's Pl. W1	110	C6
Foulden Rd. N16	94	C4
Foulden Ter. N16	94	C4
Foulden Rd.		
Foulis Ter. SW7	**31**	**F3**
Foulis Ter. SW7	129	G5
Foulser Rd. SW17	167	J3
Foulsham Rd., Th.Hth.	187	J3
Founder Cl. E6	116/117	E6
Trader Rd.		
Founders Ct. EC2	**20**	**B3**
Founders Gdns. SE19	169	J7
Foundry Cl. SE16	133	H1
Foundry Ms. NW1	**9**	**G5**
Fountain Ct. EC4	**19**	**E5**
Fountain Dr. SE19	170	C4
Fountain Dr., Cars.	199	J1
Fountain Grn. Sq. SE16	132	D2
Bermondsey Wall E.		
Fountain Ms. N5	93	J4
Kelross Rd.		
Fountain Pl. SW9	151	G1
Fountain Rd. SW17	167	G5
Fountain Rd., Th.Hth.	187	J2
Fountain Sq. SW1	**32**	**D1**
Fountain Sq. SW1	130	B4
Fountain St. E2	112	C3
Columbia Rd.		
Fountains, The, Loug.	47	J7
Fallow Flds.		
Fountains Av., Felt.	161	F3
Fountains Cl., Felt.	161	F2
Fountains Cres. N14	42	E7
Fountayne Rd. N15	76	D4
Fountayne Rd. N16	94	D2
Four Seasons Cl. E3	114	A2
Four Seasons Cres., Sutt.	198	C2
Kimpton Rd.		
Four Wents, The E4	62	D2
Kings Rd.		
Fouracres SW12	168	B2
Little Dimocks		
Fouracres, Enf.	45	H1
Fourland Wk., Edg.	54	C6
Fournier St. E1	**21**	**F1**
Fournier St. E1	112	C5
Fourth Av. E12	98	C4
Fourth Av. W10	108	B4
Fourth Av., Hayes	121	J1
Fourth Cross Rd., Twick.	162	A2
Fourth Way, Wem.	88	C4
Fowey Av., Ilf.	80	A5
Fowey Cl. E1	132/133	E1
Kennet St.		
Fowler Cl. SW11	149	G3
Fowler Rd. E7	97	G4
Fowler Rd. N1	93	H7
Halton Rd.		
Fowler Rd., Mitch.	186	A2
Fowlers Cl., Sid.	176/177	E5
Thursland Rd.		
Fownes St. SW11	149	H3
Fox & Knot St. EC1	**19**	**H1**
Fox Cl. E1	113	F4
Fox Cl. E16	115	G5
Fox Gro., Walt.	178	B7
Fox Hill SE19	170	C7
Fox Hill, Kes.	205	J5
Fox Hill Gdns. SE19	170	C7
Fox Hollow Cl. SE18	137	H5
Fox Hollow Dr., Bexh.	158	D3
Fox Ho. Rd., Belv.	139	H4
Fox La. N13	59	F3
Fox La. W5	105	H4
Fox La., Kes.	205	H5
Fox Rd. E16	115	F5
Foxberry Rd. SE4	153	H3
Foxborough Gdns. SE4	154	A5
Foxbourne Rd. SW17	168	A2

Foxbury Av., Chis. 175 G6
Foxbury Cl., Brom. 173 H6
Foxbury Rd., Brom. 173 G6
Foxcombe, Croy. 204 B6
Foxcombe Cl. E6 116 A2
Boleyn Rd.
Foxcombe Rd. SW15 165 G1
Alton Rd.
Foxcote SE5 36 E4
Foxcote SE5 132 B5
Foxcroft Rd. SE18 157 E1
Foxes Dale SE3 155 G3
Foxes Dale, Brom. 190 D3
Foxfield Rd., Orp. 207 G2
Foxglove Cl., Sthl. 103 E7
Foxglove Gdns. E11 79 J4
Foxglove La., Chess. 196 A4
Foxglove St. W12 107 F7
Foxglove Way, Wall. 200 B1
Foxgrove N14 58 E3
Foxgrove Av., Beck. 172 B7
Foxgrove Path, Wat. 50 D5
Foxgrove Rd., Beck. 172 B7
Foxham Rd. N19 92 D3
Foxhole Rd. SE9 156 B5
Foxholt Gdns. NW10 88 C7
Foxhome Cl., Chis. 174 D6
Foxlands Cres., Dag. 101 J5
Foxlands La., Dag. 101 J5
Foxlands Rd., Dag. 101 J5
Foxlees, Wem. 86 D4
Foxley Cl. E8 94 D5
Ferncliff Rd.
Foxley Cl., Loug. 49 E2
Foxley Rd. SW9 35 F7
Foxley Rd. SW9 131 G7
Foxley Rd., Th.Hth. 187 H4
Foxley Sq. SW9 131 H7
Cancell Rd.
Foxleys, Wat. 51 E3
Foxmead Cl., Enf. 43 F3
Foxmore St. SW11 149 J1
Fox's Path, Mitch. 185 H2
Foxton Gro., Mitch. 185 G2
Foxwell Ms. SE4 153 H3
Foxwell St.
Foxwell St. SE4 153 H3
Foxwood Cl. NW7 54 E4
Foxwood Cl., Felt. 160 B3
Foxwood Grn. Cl., Enf. 44 B6
Foxwood Rd. SE3 155 F4
Foyle Rd. N17 76 D1
Foyle Rd. SE3 135 F6
Framfield Cl. N12 56 D3
Framfield Ct., Enf. 44 B6
Framfield Rd. N5 93 H5
Framfield Rd. W7 104 B6
Framfield Rd., Mitch. 168 A7
Framlingham Cl. E5 95 F2
Detmold Rd.
Framlingham Cres. SE9 174 B4
Frampton Cl., Sutt. 198 D7
Frampton Pk. Rd. E9 95 F6
Frampton Rd., Houns. 142 E5
Frampton St. NW8 7 E6
Frampton St. NW8 109 G4
Francemary Rd. SE4 154 A5
Frances Rd. E4 62 A6
Frances St. SE18 136 C4
Franche Ct. Rd. SW17 167 F3
Francis Av., Bexh. 159 G2
Francis Av., Felt. 160 A3
Francis Av., Ilf. 99 G2
Francis Barber Cl. SW16 169 F4
Well Cl.
Francis Chichester Way SW11 150 A1
Francis Cl. E14 134 D4
Saunders Ness Rd.
Francis Cl., Epsom 196 D4
Francis Gro. SW19 166 C6
Francis Rd. E10 96 C1
Francis Rd. N2 73 J4
Lynmouth Rd.
Francis Rd., Croy. 187 H7
Francis Rd., Grnf. 105 F1
Francis Rd., Har. 68 D5
Francis Rd., Houns. 142 D2
Francis Rd., Ilf. 99 G2
Francis Rd., Pnr. 66 C5
Francis Rd., Wall. 200 C6
Francis St. E15 96 E5
Francis St. SW1 33 F1
Francis St. SW1 130 C4
Francis St., Ilf. 99 G2
Francis Ter. N19 92 C3
Junction Rd.
Francis Wk. N1 111 F1
Bingfield St.
Franciscan Rd. SW17 167 J5
Francklyn Gdns., Edg. 54 A3
Franconia Rd. SW4 150 C5
Frank Bailey Wk. E12 98 D5
Gainsborough Av.
Frank Burton Cl. SE7 135 H5
Victoria Way
Frank Dixon Cl. SE21 170 B1
Frank Dixon Way SE21 170 B1
Frank St. E13 115 G4
Frank Towell Ct., Felt. 160 A1
Frankfurt Rd. SE24 151 J5
Frankham St. SE8 134 A7
Frankland Cl. SE16 133 F4
Frankland Cl., Wdf.Grn. 63 J5
Frankland Rd. E4 62 A5
Frankland Rd. SW7 22 E6
Frankland Rd. SW7 129 G3
Franklin Cl. N20 41 F7
Franklin Cl. SE13 154 B1
Franklin Cl. SE27 169 H3
Franklin Cl., Kings.T. 182 A3
Franklin Cres., Mitch. 186 C4
Franklin Ho. NW9 71 F7
Franklin Pas. SE9 156 B3
Franklin Rd. SE20 171 F7
Franklin Rd., Bexh. 159 E1
Franklin Sq. W14 128 C5
Marchbank Rd.
Franklin St. E3 114 B3
St. Leonards St.
Franklin St. N15 76 B6
Franklin Way, Croy. 187 E7
Franklins Ms., Har. 85 J2
Franklin's Row SW3 32 A3
Franklin's Row SW3 129 J5
Franklyn Gdns., Ilf. 65 G6
Franklyn Rd. NW10 89 F7
Franklyn Rd., Walt. 178 A6
Franks Av., N.Mal. 182 C4
Frankswood Av., Orp. 193 E5
Franlaw Cres. N13 59 J4
Fransfield Gro. SE26 171 E3
Frant Cl. SE20 171 F7
Frant Rd., Th.Hth. 187 H5
Franthorne Way SE6 172 B2
Fraser Cl. E6 116 B6
Linton Gdns.
Fraser Cl., Bex. 177 J1
Dartford Rd.
Fraser Ho., Brent. 125 J5
Green Dragon La.
Fraser Rd. E17 78 B5
Fraser Rd. N9 60 E3
Fraser Rd., Erith 139 J5
Fraser Rd., Grnf. 105 E1
Fraser St. W4 126 E5
Frating Cres., Wdf.Grn. 63 G6
Frays Av., West Dr. 120 A2
Frays Cl., West Dr. 120 A3
Frazer Av., Ruis. 84 C5
Frazier St. SE1 26 E4
Frazier St. SE1 131 G2
Frean St. SE16 29 H5
Frean St. SE16 132 D3
Fred Wigg Twr. E11 97 F2
Freda Corbett Cl. SE15 37 H7
Frederic Ms. SW1 24 A4
Frederic St. E17 77 H5
Frederica Rd. E4 46 D7
Frederica St. N7 93 F7
Caledonian Rd.
Frederick Cl. W2 15 J5
Frederick Cl. W2 109 H7
Frederick Cl., Sutt. 198 C4
Frederick Ct. NW2 90 B3
Douglas Ms.
Frederick Cres. SW9 131 H7
Frederick Cres., Enf. 45 F2
Frederick Gdns., Sutt. 198 C5
Frederick Pl. SE18 137 E5
Frederick Rd. SE17 35 H5
Frederick Rd., Sutt. 198 C5
Frederick Sq. SE16 113 H7
Rotherhithe St.
Frederick St. WC1 10 C4
Frederick St. WC1 111 F3
Frederick Ter. E8 112 C1
Haggerston Rd.
Frederick Vil. W7 124 B1
Lower Boston Rd.
Frederick's Pl. EC2 20 B4
Fredericks Pl. N12 57 F4
Frederick's Row EC1 11 G3
Freedom Cl. E17 77 H4
Freedom Rd. N17 76 A2
Freedom St. SW11 149 J2
Freegrove Rd. N7 93 E5
Freeland Pk. NW4 72 B2
Freeland Rd. W5 105 J7
Freelands Gro., Brom. 191 H1
Freelands Rd., Brom. 191 H1
Freeling St. N1 93 F7
Caledonian Rd.
Freeman Cl., Nthlt. 85 E7
Freeman Ct. N7 92/93 E3
Tollington Way
Freeman Dr., W.Mol. 179 F3
Freeman Rd., Mord. 185 G5
Freemantle Av., Enf. 45 G5
Freemantle St. SE17 36 D3
Freemantle St. SE17 132 B5
Freemasons Rd. E16 115 H5
Freemasons Rd., Croy. 202 B1
Freesia Cl., Orp. 207 J5
Briarswood Way
Freethorpe Cl. SE19 188 A1
Freke Rd. SW11 150 A3
Fremantle Rd., Belv. 139 G4
Fremantle Rd., Ilf. 81 F2
Fremont St. E9 113 F1
French Ordinary Ct. EC3 21 E5
French Pl. E1 13 E4
French St., Sun. 178 C2
Frendsbury Rd. SE4 153 H4
Frensham Cl., Sthl. 103 F4
Frensham Ct., Mitch. 185 G3
Phipps Br. Rd.
Frensham Dr. SW15 165 G2
Frensham Dr., Croy. 204 C7
Frensham Rd. SE9 175 G2
Frensham St. SE15 37 J6
Frensham St. SE15 132 D6
Frere St. SW11 149 H2
Fresh Wf. Rd., Bark. 117 E1
Freshfield Av. E8 94 C7
Freshfield Cl. SE13 154 D4
Marischal Rd.
Freshfield Dr. N14 42 B7
Freshfields, Croy. 189 J7
Freshford St. SW18 167 F3
Freshwater Cl. SW17 168 A6
Freshwater Rd. SW17 168 A6
Freshwater Rd., Dag. 100 D1
Freshwell Av., Rom. 82 C4
Freshwood Cl., Beck. 190 B1
Freston Gdns., Barn. 42 A5
Freston Pk. N3 72 C2
Freston Rd. W10 108 A7
Freston Rd. W11 108 A7
Freta Rd., Bexh. 159 F5
Frewin Rd. SW18 167 G1
Friar Ms. SE27 169 H3
Prioress Rd.
Friar Rd., Hayes 102 D4
Friar St. EC4 19 H4
Friars, The, Chig. 65 H4
Friars Av. N20 57 H3
Friars Av. SW15 165 F3
Friars Cl. E4 62 C3
Friars Cl. N2 73 G4
Friars Cl., Nthlt. 102 D3
Broomcroft Av.
Friars Gdns. W3 106 D6
St. Dunstans Av.
Friars Gate Cl., Wdf.Grn. 63 G4
Friars La., Rich. 145 G5
Friars Mead E14 134 C3
Friars Ms. SE9 156 D5
Friars Pl. La. W3 106 D7
Friars Rd. E6 116 A1
Friars Stile Pl., Rich. 145 H6
Friars Stile Rd.
Friars Stile Rd., Rich. 145 H6
Friars Wk. N14 58 B1
Friars Wk. SE2 138 D5
Friars Way W3 106 D6
Friary Cl. N12 57 H5
Friary Ct. SW1 25 G2
Friary Est. SE15 37 J6
Friary Est. SE15 132 D6
Friary La., Wdf.Grn. 63 G4
Friary Rd. N12 57 G4
Friary Rd. SE15 37 J6
Friary Rd. SE15 132 D7
Friary Rd. W3 106 C6
Friary Way N12 57 H4
Friday Hill E4 62 E2
Friday Hill E. E4 62 E3
Friday Hill W. E4 62 E2
Friday Rd., Mitch. 167 J7
Friday St. EC4 19 J4
Friday St. EC4 111 J6
Frideswide Pl. NW5 92 C5
Islip St.
Friend St. EC1 11 G3
Friend St. EC1 111 H3
Friendly Pl. SE13 154 B1
Lewisham Rd.
Friendly St. SE8 154 A1
Friendly St. Ms. SE8 154 A2
Friendly St.
Friends Rd., Croy. 202 A3
Friendship Wk., Nthlt. 102 D3
Wayfarer Rd.
Friern Barnet La. N11 57 H4
Friern Barnet La. N20 57 H4
Friern Barnet Rd. N11 57 J5
Friern Br. Retail Pk. N11 58 B6
Friern Ct. N20 57 G3
Friern Mt. Dr. N20 41 F7
Friern Pk. N12 57 F5
Friern Rd. SE22 152 D6
Friern Watch Av. N12 57 F4
Frigate Ms. SE8 134 A6
Watergate St.
Frimley Av., Wall. 201 E5
Frimley Cl. SW19 166 B2
Frimley Cl., Croy. 204 C7
Frimley Ct., Sid. 176 B5
Frimley Cres., Croy. 204 C7
Frimley Gdns., Mitch. 185 H3
Frimley Rd., Chess. 195 H5
Frimley Rd., Ilf. 99 H3
Frimley Way E1 113 G4
Frinton Cl., Wat. 50 B2
Frinton Dr., Wdf.Grn. 62 D7
Frinton Ms., Ilf. 80 D6
Bramley Cres.
Frinton Rd. E6 116 A3
Frinton Rd. N15 76 B6
Frinton Rd. SW17 168 A6
Frinton Rd., Sid. 177 E2
Friston Path, Chig. 65 H5
Friston St. SW6 148 E2
Friswell Pl., Bexh. 159 G4
Frith Ct. NW7 56 B7
Frith La. NW7 56 B7
Frith Rd. E11 96 C4
Frith Rd., Croy. 201 J2
Frith St. W1 17 H4
Frith St. W1 110 D6
Fritham Cl., N.Mal. 182 E6
Frithville Gdns. W12 127 J1
Frizlands La., Dag. 101 H4
Frobisher Cl., Pnr. 66 D7
Frobisher Cres., Stai. 140 B7
Frobisher Gdns., Stai. 140 B7
Frobisher Pas. E14 134 A1
North Colonnade
Frobisher Rd. E6 116 C6
Frobisher Rd. N8 75 G4
Frobisher St. SE10 135 E6
Froghall La., Chig. 65 G4
Frogley Rd. SE22 152 C4
Frogmore SW18 148 D5
Frogmore Cl., Sutt. 198 A3
Frogmore Est., Ruis. 84 D5
Frogmore Gdns., Sutt. 198 B4
Frogmore Ind. Est. NW10 106 C3
Frognal NW3 91 F5
Frognal Av., Har. 68 C4
Frognal Av., Sid. 176 A6
Frognal Cl. NW3 91 F5
Frognal Ct. NW3 91 F6
Frognal Gdns. NW3 91 F4
Frognal La. NW3 91 E5
Frognal Par. NW3 91 F6
Frognal Ct.
Frognal Pl., Sid. 176 A6
Frognal Ri. NW3 91 F4
Frognal Way NW3 91 F4
Froissart Rd. SE9 156 A5
Frome Rd. N22 75 H3
Westbury Av.
Frome St. N1 11 J1
Frome St. N1 111 J2
Fromondes Rd., Sutt. 198 B5
Frostic Wk. E1 21 G2
Frostic Wk. E1 112 C5
Froude St. SW8 150 B2
Fruen Rd., Felt. 141 J7
Fry Rd. E6 98 A7
Fry Rd. NW10 107 F1
Fryatt Rd. N17 60 A7
Fryatt St. E14 114/115 E6
Orchard Pl.
Fryent Cl. NW9 70 A6
Fryent Cres. NW9 70 E6
Fryent Flds. NW9 71 E6
Fryent Gro. NW9 70 E6
Fryent Way NW9 70 A6
Frye's Bldgs. N1 11 F1
Frying Pan All. E1 21 F2
Fryston Av., Croy. 202 D2
Fuchsia St. SE2 138 B5
Fulbeck Dr. NW9 70 E1
Fulbeck Wk., Edg. 54 B2
Bushfield Cres.
Fulbeck Way, Har. 67 J2

Fulbourne Rd. E17 78 C1
Fulbourne St. E1 112/113 E5
Durward St.
Fulbrook Ms. N19 92 C4
Junction Rd.
Fulbrook Rd. N19 92 C4
Junction Rd.
Fulford Gro., Wat. 50 B2
Fulford Rd., Epsom 196 D2
Fulford St. SE16 133 E2
Fulham Bdy. SW6 128 D7
Fulham Ct. SW6 128 D7
Fulham Rd.
Fulham High St. SW6 148 B2
Fulham Palace Rd. 128 A7
SW6
Fulham Palace Rd. 127 J5
W6
Fulham Pk. Gdns. 148 C2
SW6
Fulham Pk. Rd. SW6 148 C2
Fulham Rd. SW3 30 E4
Fulham Rd. SW3 129 F6
Fulham Rd. SW6 30 B7
Fulham Rd. SW6 148 B2
Fulham Rd. SW10 30 E4
Fulham Rd. SW10 129 E7
Fullbrooks Av., 197 F1
Wor.Pk.
Fuller Cl. E2 13 H5
Fuller Cl., Orp. 207 J5
Fuller Rd., Dag. 100 B3
Fuller St. NW4 71 J4
Fuller Ter., Ilf. 99 F5
Oaktree Gro.
Fuller Way, Hayes 121 J5
Fullers Av., Surb. 195 J2
Fullers Av., Wdf.Grn. 63 F7
Fullers Rd. E18 79 F1
Fullers Way N., Surb. 195 J3
Fullers Way S., 195 H4
Chess.
Fullers Wd., Croy. 204 A5
Fullerton Rd. SW18 149 F5
Fullerton Rd., Croy. 188 C7
Fullwell Av., Ilf. 80 C1
Fullwell Cross 81 G2
Roundabout, Ilf.
Fencepiece Rd.
Fullwoods Ms. N1 12 C3
Fulmar Ct., Surb. 181 J4
Fulmead St. SW6 149 E1
Fulmer Cl., Hmptn. 161 E5
Fulmer Rd. E16 116 A5
Fulmer Way W13 124 E3
Fulready Rd. E10 78 D5
Fulstone Cl., Houns. 143 F4
Fulthorp Rd. SE3 155 F2
Fulton Ms. W2 14 C5
Fulton Rd., Wem. 88 A3
Fulwell Pk. Av., 161 H2
Twick.
Fulwell Rd., Tedd. 162 A4
Fulwood Av., Wem. 105 J1
Fulwood Gdns., 144 C6
Twick.
Fulwood Pl. WC1 18 D2
Fulwood Pl. WC1 111 F5
Fulwood Wk. SW19 166 B1
Furber St. W6 127 H3
Furham Feild, Pnr. 51 G7
Furley Rd. SE15 132 D7
Furlong Cl., Wall. 200 A1
Furlong Rd. N7 93 G6
Furmage St. SW18 149 E7
Furneaux Av. SE27 169 H5
Furness Rd. NW10 107 G2
Furness Rd. SW6 149 E2
Furness Rd., Har. 67 H7
Furness Rd., Mord. 185 E7
Furnival St. EC4 19 E3
Furnival St. EC4 111 G6
Furrow La. E9 95 F5
Fursby Av. N3 56 D6
Further Acre NW9 71 F2
Further Grn. Rd. 155 E7
SE6
Furtherfield Cl., 187 G6
Croy.
Furze Cl., Wat. 50 C5
Furze Fm. Cl., Rom. 83 E2
Furze Rd., Th.Hth. 187 J3
Furze St. E3 114 A5
Furzedown Dr. SW17 168 B5
Furzedown Rd. 168 B5
SW17
Furzefield Cl., Chis. 174 E6
Furzefield Rd. SE3 135 H6
Furzeground Way, 121 F1
Uxb.
Furzeham Rd., 120 B2
West Dr.
Furzehill Rd., Borwd. 38 A4
Furzewood, Sun. 178 A1

Fuschia Ct., 62/63 E7
Wdf.Grn.
The Bridle Path
Fyfe Way, Brom. 191 G2
Widmore Rd.
Fyfield Cl., Brom. 190 D4
Fyfield Ct. E7 97 G6
Fyfield Rd. E17 78 D3
Fyfield Rd. SW9 151 G3
Fyfield Rd., Enf. 44 B3
Fyfield Rd., Wdf.Grn. 63 J7
Fynes St. SW1 33 H1
Fynes St. SW1 130 D4

G

G.E.C. Est., Wem. 87 G3
Gable Cl., Pnr. 51 G7
Gable Ct. SE26 170/171 E5
Lawrie Pk. Av.
Gables, The, Wem. 87 J4
Gables Cl. SE5 152 B1
Gables Cl. SE12 173 G1
Gabriel Cl., Felt. 160 D4
Gabriel St. SE23 153 G7
Gabrielle Cl., Wem. 87 J3
Gabrielle Ct. NW3 91 G6
Gad Cl. E13 115 H3
Gaddesden Av., Wem. 87 J6
Gade Cl., Hayes 122 B1
Gadesden Rd., 196 C6
Epsom
Gadsbury Cl. NW9 71 F6
Gadwall Cl. E16 115 H6
Freemasons Rd.
Gadwall Way SE28 137 G2
Gage Rd. E16 114/115 E5
Malmesbury Rd.
Gage St. WC1 18 B1
Gainford St. N1 111 G1
Richmond Av.
Gainsboro Gdns., 86 B5
Grnf.
Gainsborough Av. E12 98 D5
Gainsborough Cl., 172 A7
Beck.
Gainsborough Cl., 194 B1
Esher
Lime Tree Av.
Gainsborough Ct. 57 E5
N12
Gainsborough Ct. 127 J2
W12
Lime Gro.
Gainsborough Gdns. 91 G3
NW3
Gainsborough Gdns. 72 C7
NW11
Gainsborough Gdns., 69 J2
Edg.
Gainsborough Gdns., 144 A5
Islw.
Gainsborough 170/171 E3
Ms. SE26
Panmure Rd.
Gainsborough Pl., 65 J3
Chig.
Gainsborough Rd. E11 79 E7
Gainsborough Rd. 114 E3
E15
Gainsborough Rd. 57 E5
N12
Gainsborough Rd. 127 F4
W4
Gainsborough Rd., 100 B4
Dag.
Gainsborough Rd., 182 D7
N.Mal.
Gainsborough Rd., 145 J3
Rich.
Gainsborough Rd., 64 B6
Wdf.Grn.
Gainsborough Sq., 158 D3
Bexh.
Regency Way
Gainsford Rd. E17 77 J4
Gainsford St. SE1 29 F3
Gainsford St. SE1 132 C2
Gairloch Rd. SE5 152 B2
Gaisford St. NW5 92 C6
Gaitskell Rd. SE9 175 F1
Galahad Rd., Brom. 173 G3
Galata Rd. SW13 127 G7
Galatea Sq. SE15 152/153 E3
Scylla Rd.
Galbraith St. E14 134 C3
Galdana Av., Barn. 41 F3
Gale Cl., Hmptn. 160/161 E6
Stewart Cl.
Gale Cl., Mitch. 185 G3
Gale St. E3 114 A5
Gale St., Dag. 118 D1
Galeborough Av., 62 D7
Wdf.Grn.

Galen Pl. WC1 18 B2
Galena Ho. SE18 137 J5
Grosmont Rd.
Galena Rd. W6 127 H4
Gales Gdns. E2 113 E3
Gales Way, Wdf.Grn. 64 B7
Galesbury Rd. SW18 149 F6
Galgate Cl. SW19 166 B1
Gallants Fm. Rd., 41 H7
Galleon Cl. SE16 133 G2
Kinburn St.
Galleons Dr., Bark. 117 H3
Thames Rd.
Gallery Gdns., Nthlt. 102 D2
Gallery Rd. SE21 170 A1
Galley La., Barn. 39 H3
Galleywall Rd. SE16 132 E4
Gallia Rd. N5 93 H5
Galliard Cl. N9 45 F6
Galliard Rd. N9 60 D1
Gallions Cl., Bark. 118 A3
Gallions Rd. E16 117 E7
Gallions Rd. SE7 135 H4
Gallions Roundabout 116 E7
E16
Gallions Vw. Rd. 137 G2
SE28
Goldfinch Rd.
Gallon Cl. SE7 135 J4
Gallop, The, S.Croy. 203 E7
Gallop, The, Sutt. 199 F7
Gallosson Rd. SE18 137 H4
Galloway Path, Croy. 202 A4
Galloway Rd. W12 127 G1
Gallus Cl. N21 43 F6
Gallus Sq. SE3 155 H3
Galpins Rd., Th.Hth. 187 F4
Galsworthy Av., Rom. 82 B7
Galsworthy Cl. SE28 138 B1
Galsworthy Cres. SE3 155 J1
Merriman Rd.
Galsworthy Rd. NW2 90 B4
Galsworthy Rd., 164 B7
Kings.T.
Galsworthy Ter. N16 94 B3
Hawksley Rd.
Galton St. W10 108 B4
Galva Cl., Barn. 42 A4
Galvani Way, Croy. 201 F1
Ampere Way
Galveston Rd. SW15 148 C5
Galway Cl. SE16 132/133 E5
Masters Dr.
Galway St. EC1 12 A4
Galway St. EC1 111 J3
Gambetta St. SW8 150 B2
Gambia St. SE1 27 H2
Gambole Rd. SW17 167 H4
Games Rd., Barn. 41 J3
Gamlen Rd. SW15 148 A4
Gamuel Cl. E17 78 A6
Gander Grn. Cres., 179 G1
Hmptn.
Gander Grn. La., Sutt. 198 B2
Gandhi Cl. E17 78 A6
Gandolfi St. SE15 36 E6
Gane Cl., Wall. 200/201 E7
Kingsford Av.
Ganton St. W1 17 F5
Ganton Wk., Wat. 50/51 E4
Woodhall La.
Gantshill Cres., Ilf. 80 D5
Gantshill Cross, Ilf. 80 D6
Eastern Av.
Gap Rd. SW19 166 D5
Garage Rd. W3 106 A6
Garbutt Pl. W1 16 C1
Gard St. EC1 11 H3
Garden Av., Bexh. 159 G3
Garden Av., Mitch. 168 B7
Garden City, Edg. 54 A6
Garden Cl. E4 62 A5
Garden Cl. SE12 173 H3
Garden Cl. SW15 147 H7
Garden Cl., Barn. 39 J4
Garden Cl., Hmptn. 161 F5
Garden Cl., Nthlt. 103 E1
Garden Cl., Wall. 200 E5
Garden Cl. SE4 18 E5
Garden Ct. SE15 152 C1
Sumner Est.
Garden Ct., Rich. 145 J1
Lichfield Rd.
Garden Ct., Stan. 53 F5
Marsh La.
Garden Ct., W.Mol. 179 H4
Avern Rd.
Garden La. SW2 169 F1
Christchurch Rd.
Garden La., Brom. 173 H6
Garden Ms. W2 108 D7
Linden Gdns.
Garden Rd. NW8 6 D3

Garden Rd. NW8 109 F3
Garden Rd. SE20 189 F1
Garden Rd., Brom. 173 H7
Garden Rd., Rich. 146 A3
Garden Rd., Walt. 178 B6
Garden Row SE1 27 G6
Garden Row SE1 131 H3
Garden St. E1 113 G5
Garden Ter. SW11 33 H3
Garden Wk. EC2 12 D4
Garden Wk., Beck. 189 J1
Hayne Rd.
Garden Way NW10 88 C6
Gardeners Cl. N11 58 A2
Gardeners Rd., Croy. 201 H1
Gardenia Rd., Enf. 44 B6
Gardenia Way, 63 G5
Wdf.Grn.
Gardens, The SE22 152 D4
Gardens, The, Beck. 190 C2
Gardens, The, Felt. 141 G5
Gardens, The, Har. 67 J6
Gardens, The, Pnr. 67 F6
Gardiner Av. NW2 89 J5
Gardiner Cl., Dag. 100 D4
Gardiner Cl., Enf. 45 G6
Gardner Cl. E11 79 H6
Gardner Gro., Felt. 161 F2
Gardner Rd. E13 115 H4
Gardners La. EC4 19 J5
Gardnor Rd. NW3 91 G4
Flask Wk.
Garendon Gdns., 184 E7
Mord.
Garendon Rd., Mord. 184 E7
Gareth Cl., Wor.Pk. 198 A2
Gareth Gro., Brom. 173 G4
Garfield Ms. SW11 150 A3
Garfield Rd.
Garfield Rd. E4 62 D1
Garfield Rd. E13 115 F4
Garfield Rd. SW11 150 A3
Garfield Rd. SW19 167 F5
Garfield Rd., Enf. 45 F4
Garfield Rd., Twick. 162 D1
Garford St. E14 114 A7
Garganey Wk. SE28 118 D7
Garibaldi St. SE18 137 H4
Garland Rd. SE18 137 G7
Garland Rd., Stan. 69 H1
Garlands Ct., Croy. 202 A4
Chatsworth Rd.
Garlick Hill EC4 20 A5
Garlick Hill EC4 111 J7
Garlies Rd. SE23 171 H3
Garlinge Rd. NW2 90 C6
Garman Cl. N18 60 A5
Garman Rd. N17 61 F7
Garnault Ms. EC1 11 F4
Garnault Pl. EC1 11 F4
Garner Rd. E17 78 C1
Garner St. E2 13 J2
Garnet Rd. NW10 89 E6
Garnet Rd., Th.Hth. 188 A4
Garnet St. E1 113 F7
Garnet Wk. E6 116 B5
Kingfisher St.
Garnett Cl. SE9 156 C3
Garnett Rd. NW3 91 J5
Garnett Way E17 77 H1
McEntee Av.
Garnham Cl. N16 94 C2
Garnham St.
Garnham St. N16 94 C2
Garnies Cl. SE15 37 F7
Garnies Cl. SE15 132 C7
Garrad's Rd. SW16 168 D3
Garrard Cl., Bexh. 159 G3
Garrard Cl., Chis. 175 E5
Garrard Wk. NW10 88/89 E6
Garnet Rd.
Garratt Cl., Croy. 200 E4
Garratt La. SW17 167 G4
Garratt La. SW18 148 E5
Garratt Rd., Edg. 54 A7
Garratt Ter. SW17 167 H4
Garrett Cl. W3 106 D5
Garrett St. EC1 12 A5
Garrick Av. NW11 72 B6
Garrick Cl. SW18 149 F4
Garrick Cl. W5 105 H4
Garrick Cl., Rich. 145 G5
The Grn.
Garrick Cres., Croy. 202 B2
Garrick Dr. NW4 71 J2
Garrick Dr. SE28 137 G3
Broadwater Rd.
Garrick Gdns., 179 G3
W.Mol.
Garrick Pk. NW4 72 A2
Garrick Rd. NW9 71 F6
Garrick Rd., Grnf. 103 H4

Name	Page	Grid
Garrick Rd., Rich.	146	A2
Garrick St. WC2	18	A5
Garrick St. WC2	110	E7
Garrick Way NW4	72	A4
Garrison Cl. SE18	136	D7
Red Lion La.		
Garrison Cl., Houns.	143	F5
Garrison La., Chess.	195	G7
Garsdale Cl. N11	58	A6
Garside Cl. SE28	137	G3
Goosander Way		
Garside Cl., Hmptn.	161	H6
Garsington Ms. SE4	153	J3
Garter Way SE16	133	G2
Poolmans St.		
Garth, The, Hmptn.	161	H6
Uxbridge Rd.		
Garth, The, Har.	69	J6
Garth Cl. W4	126	D5
Garth Cl., Kings.T.	163	J5
Garth Cl., Mord.	184	A7
Garth Cl., Ruis.	84	D1
Garth Cl. W4	126	D5
Garth Rd.		
Garth Ms. W5	105	H4
Greystoke Gdns.		
Garth Rd. NW2	90	C2
Garth Rd. W4	126	D6
Garth Rd., Kings.T.	163	J5
Garth Rd., Mord.	183	J6
Garth Rd. Ind. Cen., Mord.	184	A7
Garthland Dr., Barn.	39	H5
Garthorne Rd. SE23	153	G7
Garthside, Rich.	163	H5
Garthway N12	57	H6
Gartmoor Gdns. SW19	166	C1
Gartmore Rd., Ilf.	99	J1
Garton Pl. SW18	149	F6
Gartons Cl., Enf.	45	F5
Gartons Way SW11	149	F3
Garvary Rd. E16	115	H6
Garway Rd. W2	14	A4
Garway Rd. W2	108	E6
Gascoigne Gdns., Wdf.Grn.	63	E7
Gascoigne Pl. E2	13	F4
Gascoigne Pl. E2	112	C3
Gascoigne Rd., Bark.	117	F1
Gascony Av. NW6	90	D7
Gascoyne Rd. E9	95	G7
Gaselee St. E14	114	B7
Gasholder Pl. SE11	34	D4
Gaskarth Rd. SW12	150	B6
Gaskarth Rd., Edg.	70	C1
Gaskell Rd. N6	73	J6
Gaskell St. SW4	150	E2
Gaskin St. N1	111	H1
Gaspar Cl. SW5	30	B1
Gaspar Ms. SW5	30	B1
Gassiot Rd. SW17	167	J4
Gassiot Way, Sutt.	199	G3
Gastein Rd. W6	128	A6
Gaston Bell Cl., Rich.	145	J3
Gaston Rd., Mitch.	186	A3
Gataker St. SE16	133	E3
Gatcombe Rd. E16	135	G1
Gatcombe Rd. N19	92	D3
Gatcombe Way, Barn.	41	J3
Gate Cl., Borwd.	38	C1
Gate End, Nthwd.	50	A7
Gate Ms. SW7	23	H4
Gate Ms. SW7	129	H2
Gate St. WC2	18	C3
Gateforth St. NW8	7	G5
Gateforth St. NW8	109	H4
Gatehouse Cl., Kings.T.	164	C7
Gatehouse Sq. SE1	131	J1
Southwark Br. Rd.		
Gateley Rd. SW9	151	F3
Gater Dr., Enf.	44	A1
Gates Grn. Rd., Kes.	205	G4
Gates Grn. Rd., W.Wick.	205	F3
Gatesborough St. EC2	12	D5
Gateside Rd. SW17	167	J3
Gatestone Rd. SE19	170	B6
Gateway SE17	36	A5
Gateway SE17	131	J2
Gateway Arc. N1	111	H2
SET		
Gateway Ind. Est. NW10	107	A7
Gateway Ms. E8	94	C5
Shacklewell La.		
Gateway Rd. E10	96	B3
Gateways, The SW3	31	H2
Gateways, The SW3	129	J4
Gatfield Gro., Felt.	161	G2
Gathorne Rd. N22	75	G2
Gathorne St. E2	113	G2
Mace St.		
Gatley Av., Epsom	196	B5
Gatliff Rd. SW1	32	D4
Gatliff Rd. SW1	130	B5
Gatling Rd. SE2	138	A5
Gatting Cl., Edg.	54	C7
Pavilion Way		
Gatton Rd. SW17	167	H4
Gattons Way, Sid.	177	F4
Gatward Cl. N21	43	H6
Gatward Grn. N9	60	B2
Gatwick Rd. SW18	148	C7
Gauden Cl. SW4	150	D3
Gauden Rd. SW4	150	D2
Gaumont Ter. W12	127	J2
Lime Gro.		
Gaunt St. SE1	27	J5
Gauntlet Cl., Nthlt.	84	E7
Gauntlett Ct., Wem.	86	E5
Gauntlett Rd., Sutt.	199	G5
Gautrey Rd. SE15	153	F2
Gautrey Sq. E6	116	C6
Gavel St. SE17	36	C1
Gaverick St. E14	134	A4
Gavestone Cres. SE12	155	H7
Gavestone Rd. SE12	155	H7
Gaviller Pl. E5	94/95	E4
Clarence Rd.		
Gavin St. SE18	137	H4
Gavina Cl., Mord.	185	H5
Gawber St. E2	113	F3
Gawsworth Cl. E15	96/97	E5
Ash Rd.		
Gawthorne Av. NW7	56	B5
Lane Appr.		
Gawthorne Ct. E3	114	A2
Mostyn Gro.		
Gay Cl. NW2	89	H5
Gay Gdns., Dag.	101	J4
Gay Rd. E15	114	D2
Gay St. SW15	148	A3
Gaydon Ho. W2	14	B1
Gaydon Ho. W2	109	E5
Gaydon La. NW9	70	E1
Gayfere Rd., Epsom	197	G5
Gayfere Rd., Ilf.	80	C3
Gayfere St. SW1	26	A6
Gayfere St. SW1	130	E3
Gayford Rd. W12	127	F2
Gayhurst SE17	36	C5
Gayhurst Rd. E8	94	D7
Gaylor Rd., Nthlt.	85	F5
Gaynes Hill Rd., Wdf.Grn.	64	B6
Gaynesford Rd. SE23	171	G2
Gaynesford Rd., Cars.	199	J7
Gaysham Av., Ilf.	80	D5
Gaysham Hall, Ilf.	80	E3
Gayton Cl., Har.	68	C6
Gayton Cres. NW3	91	G4
Gayton Rd. NW3	91	G4
Gayton Rd. SE2	138	C3
Florence Rd.		
Gayton Rd., Har.	68	C6
Gayville Rd. SW11	149	J6
Gaywood Cl. SW2	169	F1
Gaywood Est. SE1	27	H6
Gaywood Est. SE1	131	H3
Gaywood Rd. E17	78	A3
Gaywood St. SE1	27	H6
Gaza St. SE17	35	G4
Geariesville Gdns., Ilf.	81	E4
Geary Rd. NW10	89	G5
Geary St. N7	93	F5
Geddes Pl., Bexh.	159	G4
Market Pl.		
Gedeney Rd. N17	75	J1
Gedling Pl. SE1	29	G5
Gedling Pl. SE1	132	C2
Gee St. EC1	11	J5
Gee St. EC1	111	J4
Geere Rd. E15	115	F1
Gees Ct. W1	16	C4
Geffrye Ct. N1	12	E2
Geffrye Est. N1	112	B2
Stanway St.		
Geffrye St. E2	13	F1
Geffrye St. E2	112	C2
Geldart Rd. SE15	132	E7
Geldeston Rd. E5	94	D2
Gellatly Rd. SE14	153	F2
Gemini Gro., Nthlt.	102/103	E3
Javelin Way		
General Gordon Pl. SE18	136	E4
General Wolfe Rd. SE10	154	D1
Genesta Rd. SE18	137	E6
Geneva Dr. SW9	151	G4
Geneva Gdns., Rom.	82	E5
Geneva Rd., Kings.T.	181	H4
Geneva Rd., Th.Hth.	187	J5
Genever Cl. E4	62	A5
Genista Rd. N18	61	E5
Genoa Av. SW15	147	J5
Genoa Rd. SE20	189	F1
Genotin Rd., Enf.	44	A3
Genotin Ter., Enf.	44	A3
Genotin Rd.		
Gentian Row SE13	154	C1
Sparta St.		
Gentlemans Row, Enf.	43	J3
Gentry Gdns. E13	115	G4
Whitwell Rd.		
Geoffrey Cl. SE5	151	J2
Geoffrey Gdns. E6	116	B2
Geoffrey Rd. SE4	153	J3
George Beard Rd. SE8	133	J4
George Comberton Wk. E12	98	D5
Gainsborough Av.		
George Ct. WC2	18	B6
George Cres. N10	58	A7
George Downing Est. N16	94	C2
Cazenove Rd.		
George V Av., Pnr.	67	G3
George V Cl., Pnr.	67	G3
George V Av.		
George V Way, Grnf.	105	E1
George Gange Way, Har.	68	B3
George Gro. Rd. SE20	188	D1
George Inn Yd. SE1	28	B2
George La. E18	79	G2
George La. SE13	154	C6
George La., Brom.	205	H1
George Lansbury Ho. N22	75	G1
Progress Way		
George Loveless Ho. E2	13	G3
George Lowe Ct. W2	14	A1
George Mathers Rd. SE11	35	G1
George Mathers Rd.	131	H4
George Ms. NW1	9	F4
George Ms., Enf.	44	A3
Sydney Rd.		
George Pl. N17	76	B3
Dongola Rd.		
George Rd. E4	62	A6
George Rd., Kings.T.	164	B7
George Rd., N.Mal.	183	F4
George Row SE16	29	H4
George Row SE16	132	D2
George Sq. SW19	184	C3
Mostyn Rd.		
George St. E16	115	F6
George St. W1	16	A3
George St. W1	110	A6
George St. W7	124	B1
The Bdy.		
George St., Bark.	99	F7
George St., Croy.	202	A2
George St., Houns.	143	F2
George St., Rich.	145	G5
George St., Sthl.	122	E4
George St., Sutt.	198	E5
George Wyver Cl. SW19	148	B7
Beaumont Rd.		
George Yd. EC3	20	C4
George Yd. W1	16	C5
George Yd. W1	110	A7
George's Rd. N7	93	F5
Georges Sq. SW6	128	C6
North End Rd.		
Georgetown Cl. SE19	170	A5
St. Kitts Ter.		
Georges Pl. SE10	134	C7
King George St.		
Georgeville Gdns., Ilf.	81	E4
Georgia Rd., N.Mal.	182	C4
Georgia Rd., Th.Hth.	187	H1
Georgian Cl., Brom.	191	H1
Georgian Cl., Stan.	52	D7
Georgian Ct. SW16	168/169	E4
Gleneldon Rd.		
Georgian Ct., Wem.	88	A6
Georgian Way, Har.	86	A2
Georgiana St. NW1	110	C1
Georgina Gdns. E2	13	G3
Geraint Rd., Brom.	173	G4
Gerald Ms. SW1	32	C1
Gerald Rd. E16	115	F4
Gerald Rd. SW1	32	C1
Gerald Rd. SW1	130	A4
Gerald Rd., Dag.	101	F2
Geraldine Rd. SW18	149	F5
Geraldine Rd. W4	126	A6
Geraldine St. SE11	27	G6
Geraldine St. SE11	131	H3
Gerard Av., Houns.	143	G7
Redfern Av.		
Gerard Rd. SW13	147	F1
Gerard Rd., Har.	68	D6
Gerards Cl. SE16	133	F5
Gerda Rd. SE9	175	F2
Germander Way E15	115	E3
Gernon Rd. E3	113	H2
Geron Way NW2	89	H1
Gerrard Gdns., Pnr.	66	A5
Gerrard Pl. W1	17	J5
Gerrard Rd. N1	11	H1
Gerrard Rd. N1	111	H2
Gerrard St. W1	17	H5
Gerrard St. W1	110	D7
Gerrards Cl. N14	42	C5
Gerridge St. SE1	27	F4
Gerridge St. SE1	131	G3
Gerry Raffles Sq. E15	96	D6
Salway Rd.		
Gertrude Rd., Belv.	139	G4
Gertrude St. SW10	30	D6
Gertrude St. SW10	129	F6
Gervase Cl., Wem.	88	C3
Gervase Rd., Edg.	70	C1
Gervase St. SE15	133	E7
Ghent St. SE6	172	A2
Ghent Way E8	94	C6
Tyssen St.		
Giant Arches Rd. SE24	151	J7
Giant Tree Hill, Bushey	52	A1
Gibbard Ms. SW19	166	A5
Gibbfield Cl., Rom.	82	E3
Gibbins Rd. E15	96	C7
Gibbon Rd. SE15	153	F2
Gibbon Rd. W3	106	E7
Gibbon Rd., Kings.T.	181	H1
Gibbon Wk. SW15	147	G4
Swinburne Rd.		
Gibbons Rd. NW10	88	D6
Gibbs Av. SE19	170	A5
Gibbs Cl. SE19	170	A5
Gibbs Couch, Wat.	50	D3
Gibbs Grn. W14	128	C5
Gibbs Grn., Edg.	54	C5
Gibbs Rd. N18	61	F4
Gibbs Sq. SE19	170	A5
Gibraltar Wk. E2	13	G4
Gibraltar Wk. E2	112	C3
Gibson Cl. E1	113	F4
Colebert Av.		
Gibson Cl. N21	43	G6
Gibson Cl., Chess.	195	F6
Gibson Cl., Islw.	144	A3
Gibson Gdns. N16	94	C2
Northwold Rd.		
Gibson Rd. SE11	34	D2
Gibson Rd. SE11	131	F4
Gibson Rd., Dag.	100	C1
Gibson Rd., Sutt.	198	E5
Gibson Sq. N1	111	G1
Gibson St. SE10	134	E5
Gibson's Hill SW16	169	G6
Gideon Cl., Belv.	139	H4
Gideon Ms. W5	125	G2
Gideon Rd. SW11	150	A3
Giesbach Rd. N19	92	C2
Giffard Rd. N18	60	B5
Giffin St. SE8	134	A7
Gifford Gdns. W7	104	A5
Gifford St. N1	93	E7
Gift La. E15	115	E1
Giggs Hill Gdns., T.Ditt.	194	D1
Giggs Hill Rd., T.Ditt.	180	D7
Gilbert Cl. SE18	156	C1
Gilbert Gro., Edg.	70	D1
Gilbert Ho. SE8	134	A6
McMillan St.		
Gilbert Pl. WC1	18	A2
Gilbert Rd. SE11	35	F2
Gilbert Rd. SE11	131	G4
Gilbert Rd. SW19	167	F7
Gilbert Rd., Belv.	139	G3
Gilbert Rd., Brom.	173	G6
Gilbert Rd., Pnr.	66	D4
Gilbert St. E15	96	E4
Gilbert St. W1	16	C5
Gilbert St. W1	110	A6
Gilbert St., Houns.	143	J3
High St.		
Gilbey Rd. SW17	167	H4
Gilbeys Yd. NW1	110	B1
Oval Rd.		
Gilbourne Rd. SE18	137	J6

Gilda Av., Enf. 45 H5
Gilda Cres. N16 94 D1
Gildea Cl., Pnr. 51 G7
Gildea St. W1 17 E2
Gilden Cres. NW5 92 A5
Gilders Rd., Chess. 195 J6
Gildersome St. SE18 136 D6
Nightingale Vale
Giles Coppice SE19 170 C4
Gilkes Cres. SE21 152 B6
Gilkes Pl. SE21 152 B6
Gill Av. E16 115 G6
Gill St. E14 113 J6
Gillan Grn., Bushey 51 J2
Gillards Ms. E17 78 A4
Gillards Way
Gillards Way E17 78 A4
Gillender St. E3 114 C4
Gillender St. E14 114 C4
Gillespie Rd. N5 93 G3
Gillett Av. E6 116 B2
Gillett Pl. N16 94 B5
Gillett St.
Gillett Rd., Th.Hth. 188 A4
Gillett St. N16 94 B5
Gillette Cor., Islw. 124 D7
Gillfoot NW1 9 G2
Gillfoot NW1 110 C2
Gillham Ter. N17 60 D6
Gillian Pk. Rd., Sutt. 198 C1
Gillian St. SE13 154 B5
Gillies St. NW5 92 A5
Gilling Ct. NW3 91 H6
Gillingham Ms. SW1 33 F1
Gillingham Rd. NW2 90 B3
Gillingham Row SW1 33 F1
Gillingham St. SW1 33 F1
Gillingham St. SW1 130 B4
Gillison Wk. SE16 29 J5
Gillman Dr. E15 115 F1
Gillum Cl., Barn. 57 J1
Gilmore Rd. SE13 154 D4
Gilpin Av. SW14 146 D4
Gilpin Cl., Mitch. 185 H2
Gilpin Cres. N18 60 C5
Gilpin Cres., Twick. 143 H7
Gilpin Rd. E5 95 H4
Gilpin Way, Hayes 121 G7
Gilsland Rd., Th.Hth. 188 A4
Gilstead Ho., Bark. 118 B2
Gilstead Rd. SW6 149 E2
Gilston Rd. SW10 30 D4
Gilston Rd. SW10 129 F5
Gilton Rd. SE6 173 E3
Giltspur St. EC1 19 H3
Giltspur St. EC1 111 H6
Gilwell Cl. E4 46 B4
Antlers Hill
Gilwell La. E4 46 C4
Gilwell Pk. E4 46 C3
Gippeswyck Cl., Pnr. 66 D1
Uxbridge Rd.
Gipsy Hill SE19 170 B5
Gipsy La. SW15 147 G3
Gipsy Rd. SE27 169 J4
Gipsy Rd., Well. 158 D1
Gipsy Rd. Gdns. SE27 169 J4
Giralda Cl. E16 116 A5
Fulmer Rd.
Giraud St. E14 114 B6
Girdlers Rd. W14 128 A4
Girdlestone Wk. N19 92 C2
Girdwood Rd. SW18 148 B7
Girling Way, Felt. 142 A3
Gironde Rd. SW6 128 C7
Girton Av. NW9 70 A3
Girton Cl., Nthlt. 85 J6
Girton Gdns., Croy. 204 A3
Girton Rd. SE26 171 G5
Girton Rd., Nthlt. 85 J6
Girton Vil. W10 108 A6
Gisbourne Cl., Wall. 200 D3
Gisburn Rd. N8 75 F4
Gissing Wk. N1 93 G7
Lofting Rd.
Gittens Cl., Brom. 173 F4
Given Wilson Wk. E13 115 F2
Glacier Way, Wem. 105 G2
Gladbeck Way, Enf. 43 H4
Gladding Rd. E12 98 A4
Glade, The N21 43 F6
Glade, The SE7 135 J7
Glade, The, Brom. 192 A2
Glade, The, Croy. 189 G5
Glade, The, Enf. 43 G3
Glade, The, Epsom 197 G5
Glade, The, Ilf. 80 C1
Glade, The, W.Wick. 204 B3
Glade, The, Wdf.Grn. 63 H3
Glade Cl., Surb. 195 G2
Glade Ct., Ilf. 80 C1
The Glade
Glade Gdns., Croy. 189 H7
Glade La., Sthl. 123 H2
Glades Pl., Brom. 191 G2
Widmore Rd.
Glades Shop. Cen., The, Brom. 191 G2
Gladeside N21 43 F6
Gladeside, Croy. 189 G6
Gladeside Cl., Chess. 195 G7
Leatherhead Rd.
Gladesmore Rd. N15 76 C6
Gladeswood Rd., Belv. 139 H4
Gladiator St. SE23 153 H6
Glading Ter. N16 94 C3
Gladioli Cl., Hmptn. 161 G6
Gresham Rd.
Gladsdale Dr., Pnr. 66 A4
Gladsmuir Rd. N19 92 C1
Gladsmuir Rd., Barn. 40 B2
Gladstone Av. E12 98 B7
Gladstone Av. N22 75 G2
Gladstone Av., Felt. 142 A6
Gladstone Av., Twick. 144 A7
Gladstone Gdns., Houns. 143 J1
Gresham Rd.
Gladstone Ms. NW6 90 C7
Cavendish Rd.
Gladstone Ms. SE20 171 F7
Gladstone Par. NW2 89 H1
Edgware Rd.
Gladstone Pk. Gdns. NW2 89 H3
Gladstone Pl. E3 113 J2
Roman Rd.
Gladstone Pl., Barn. 40 A4
Gladstone Rd. SW19 166 D7
Gladstone Rd. W4 126 D3
Acton La.
Gladstone Rd., Buck.H. 63 H1
Gladstone Rd., Croy. 188 A7
Gladstone Rd., Kings.T. 182 A3
Gladstone Rd., Orp. 207 F5
Gladstone Rd., Sthl. 122 E3
Gladstone Rd., Surb. 195 G2
Gladstone St. SE1 27 G5
Gladstone St. SE1 131 H3
Gladstone Ter. SE27 169 J4
Gladstone Ter. SW8 150 B1
Gladstone Way, Har. 68 B3
Gladwell Rd. N8 75 F6
Gladwell Rd., Brom. 173 G6
Gladwyn Rd. SW15 148 A3
Gladys Rd. NW6 90 D7
Glamis Cres., Hayes 121 F3
Glamis Pl. E1 113 F7
Glamis Rd. E1 113 F7
Glamis Way, Nthlt. 85 J6
Glamorgan Cl., Mitch. 187 E3
Glamorgan Rd., Kings.T. 163 F7
Glanfield Rd., Beck. 189 J4
Glanleam Rd., Stan. 53 G4
Glanville Rd. SW2 151 E5
Glanville Rd., Brom. 191 H3
Glasbrook Av., Twick. 161 F1
Glasbrook Rd. SE9 156 A7
Glaserton Rd. N16 76 B7
Glasford St. SW17 167 J6
Glasgow Ho. W9 6 B3
Glasgow Ho. W9 109 E2
Glasgow Rd. E13 115 H2
Glasgow Rd. N18 60/61 E5
Aberdeen Rd.
Glasgow Ter. SW1 33 F4
Glasgow Ter. SW1 130 C5
Glass St. E2 112/113 E4
Coventry Rd.
Glass Yd. SE18 136 D3
Woolwich High St.
Glasse Cl. W13 104 D7
Glasshill St. SE1 27 H3
Glasshill St. SE1 131 H2
Glasshouse All. EC4 19 F4
Glasshouse Flds. E1 113 G7
Glasshouse St. W1 17 G6
Glasshouse St. W1 110 C7
Glasshouse Wk. SE11 34 B3
Glasshouse Wk. SE11 131 E5
Glasshouse Yd. EC1 19 J1
Glasslyn Rd. N8 74 D5
Glassmill La., Brom. 191 F2
Glastonbury Av., Wdf.Grn. 64 A7
Glastonbury Rd. N9 60 C1
Glastonbury Rd., Mord. 184 D7
Glastonbury St. NW6 90 C5
Glaucus St. E3 114 B5
Glazbury Rd. W14 128 B4
Glazebrook Cl. SE21 170 A2
Glazebrook Rd., Tedd. 162 C7
Glebe, The SE3 154 E3
Glebe, The SW16 168 D4
Glebe, The, Chis. 193 F1
Glebe, The, West Dr. 120 C4
Glebe, The, Wor.Pk. 197 F1
Glebe Av., Enf. 43 H3
Glebe Av., Har. 69 H3
Glebe Av., Mitch. 185 H2
Glebe Av., Ruis. 84 B6
Glebe Av., Wdf.Grn. 63 G6
Glebe Cl. W4 126/127 E5
Glebe St.
Glebe Cotts., Sutt. 198/199 E4
Vale Rd.
Glebe Ct. W7 104 A7
Glebe Ct., Mitch. 185 J3
Glebe Ct., Stan. 53 F5
Glebe Rd.
Glebe Cres. NW4 71 J4
Glebe Cres., Har. 69 H3
Glebe Gdns., N.Mal. 183 E7
Glebe Ho. Dr., Brom. 205 H1
Glebe Hyrst SE19 170 C4
Giles Coppice
Glebe La., Barn. 39 G5
Glebe La., Har. 69 H4
Glebe Path, Mitch. 185 H3
Glebe Pl. SW3 31 G5
Glebe Pl. SW3 129 H6
Glebe Rd. E8 94 C7
Middleton Rd.
Glebe Rd. N3 73 F1
Glebe Rd. N8 75 F4
Glebe Rd. NW10 89 F6
Glebe Rd. SW13 147 G2
Glebe Rd., Brom. 191 G1
Glebe Rd., Cars. 199 J6
Glebe Rd., Dag. 101 H6
Glebe Rd., Hayes 121 J1
Glebe Rd., Stan. 53 F5
Glebe Side, Twick. 144 C6
Glebe St. W4 126 E5
Glebe Ter. E3 114 A3
Bow Rd.
Glebe Way, Felt. 161 G3
Glebe Way, W.Wick. 204 C2
Glebelands, W.Mol. 179 H5
Glebelands Av. E18 79 G2
Glebelands Av., Ilf. 81 G7
Glebelands Cl. SE5 152 B3
Grove Hill Rd.
Glebelands Rd., Felt. 142 A7
Glebeway, Wdf.Grn. 63 J5
Gledhow Gdns. SW5 30 C2
Gledhow Gdns. SW5 129 F4
Gledstanes Rd. W14 128 B5
Gleed Av., Bushey 52 A2
Gleeson Dr., Orp. 207 J5
Glegg Pl. SW15 148 A4
Glen, The, Brom. 190 E2
Glen, The, Croy. 203 G2
Glen, The, Enf. 43 H4
Glen, The, Orp. 206 C3
Glen, The, Pnr. 67 E7
Glen, The (Eastcote), Pnr. 66 B5
Glen, The, Sthl. 123 F5
Glen, The, Wem. 87 G4
Glen Albyn Rd. SW19 166 A2
Glen Cres., Wdf.Grn. 63 H6
Glen Gdns., Croy. 201 G3
Glen Ri., Wdf.Grn. 63 H6
Glen Rd. E13 115 J4
Glen Rd. E17 77 J5
Glen Rd., Chess. 195 H3
Glen Ter. E14 134 C2
Manchester Rd.
Glen Wk., Islw. 144 A5
Glena Mt., Sutt. 199 F4
Glenaffric Av. E14 134 D4
Glenalmond Rd., Har. 69 H4
Glenalvon Way SE18 136 B4
Glenarm Rd. E5 95 F5
Glenavon Cl., Esher 194 D7
Glenavon Rd. E15 97 E7
Glenbarr Cl. SE9 156/157 E3
Dumbreck Rd.
Glenbow Rd., Brom. 172 E6
Glenbrook N., Enf. 43 F4
Glenbrook Rd. NW6 90 D5
Glenbrook S., Enf. 43 F4
Glenbuck Ct., Surb. 181 G6
Glenbuck Rd.
Glenbuck Rd., Surb. 181 G6
Glenburnie Rd. SW17 167 J3
Glencairn Dr. W5 105 F4
Glencairn Rd. SW16 168 E7
Glencairne Cl. E16 116 A5
Glencoe Av., Ilf. 81 G7
Glencoe Dr., Dag. 101 G4
Glencoe Rd., Hayes 102 D5
Glencorse Grn., Wat. 50 D4
Caldwell Rd.
Glendale Av. N22 59 G7
Glendale Av., Edg. 53 J4
Glendale Av., Rom. 82 C7
Glendale Cl. SE9 156 D3
Dumbreck Rd.
Glendale Dr. SW19 166 C5
Glendale Gdns., Wem. 87 G1
Glendale Ms., Beck. 190 B1
Glendale Rd., Erith 139 J4
Glendale Way SE28 118 C7
Glendall St. SW9 151 F4
Glendarvon St. SW15 148 A3
Glendevon Cl., Edg. 54 B3
Tayside Dr.
Glendish Rd. N17 76 E1
Glendor Gdns. NW7 54 D4
Glendower Gdns. SW14 146 D3
Glendower Rd.
Glendower Pl. SW7 31 E1
Glendower Pl. SW7 129 G4
Glendower Rd. E4 62 D1
Glendower Rd. SW14 146 D3
Glendown Rd. SE2 138 A5
Glendun Rd. W3 107 E7
Gleneagle Ms. SW16 168 D5
Ambleside Av.
Gleneagle Rd. SW16 168 D5
Gleneagles, Stan. 52 E6
Gleneagles Cl. SE16 132/133 E5
Ryder Dr.
Gleneagles Cl., Orp. 207 G1
Gleneagles Cl., Stai. 140 A6
Gleneagles Cl., Wat. 50 D4
Gleneagles Grn., Orp. 207 G1
Tandridge Dr.
Gleneagles Twr., Sthl. 103 J6
Gleneldon Ms. SW16 168 E4
Gleneldon Rd. SW16 168 E4
Glenelg Rd. SW2 151 E5
Glenesk Rd. SE9 156 D3
Glenfarg Rd. SE6 172 D1
Glenfield Rd. SW12 168 C1
Glenfield Rd. W13 125 E2
Glenfield Ter. W13 124 E2
Glenfinlas Way SE5 35 H7
Glenfinlas Way SE5 131 H7
Glenforth St. SE10 135 F5
Glengall Causeway E14 134 A3
Glengall Gro. E14 134 C3
Glengall Rd. NW6 108 C1
Glengall Rd. SE15 37 G5
Glengall Rd. SE15 132 C6
Glengall Rd., Bexh. 159 E3
Glengall Rd., Edg. 54 B3
Glengall Rd., Wdf.Grn. 63 G6
Glengall Ter. SE15 37 G5
Glengall Ter. SE15 132 C6
Glengarnock Av. E14 134 C4
Glengarry Rd. SE22 152 B5
Glenham Dr., Ilf. 80 E5
Glenhaven Av., Borwd. 38 A3
Glenhead Cl. SE9 156/157 E3
Dumbreck Rd.
Glenhill Cl. N3 72 D2
Glenhouse Rd. SE9 156 D5
Glenhurst Av. NW5 92 A4
Glenhurst Av., Bex. 177 F1
Glenhurst Ct. SE19 170 C5
Glenhurst Ri. SE19 169 J7
Glenhurst Rd. N12 57 G5
Glenhurst Rd., Brent. 125 F6
Glenilla Rd. NW3 91 H6
Glenister Ho., Hayes 122 B1
Glenister Pk. Rd. SW16 168 D7
Glenister Rd. SE10 135 F5
Glenister St. E16 136 D1
Glenlea Rd. SE9 156 C5
Glenloch Rd. NW3 91 H6
Glenloch Rd., Enf. 45 F2
Glenluce Rd. SE3 135 G6
Glenlyon Rd. SE9 156 D5
Glenmere Av. NW7 55 G7
Glenmill, Hmptn. 161 F5
Glenmore Rd. NW3 91 H6
Glenmore Rd., Well. 157 J1
Glenmore Way, Bark. 118 A2
Glenmount Path SE18 137 F5
Raglan Rd.
Glennie Rd. SE27 169 G3
Glenny Rd., Bark. 99 F6
Glenorchy Cl., Hayes 103 E5

Name	Page	Grid
Glenparke Rd. E7	97	H6
Glenrosa St. SW6	149	F2
Glenrose Ct., Sid.	176	B5
Glenroy St. W12	107	J6
Glensdale Rd. SE4	153	J3
Glenshiel Rd. SE9	156	D5
Glenside, Chig.	65	E6
Glentanner Way SW17	167	G3
Aboyne Rd.		
Glentham Gdns. SW13	127	H6
Glentham Rd.		
Glentham Rd. SW13	127	G6
Glenthorne Av., Croy.	203	E1
Glenthorne Cl., Sutt.	198	D3
Glenthorne Gdns., Ilf.	80	D3
Glenthorne Gdns., Sutt.	198	D1
Glenthorne Ms. W6	127	H4
Glenthorne Rd.		
Glenthorne Rd. E17	77	H5
Glenthorne Rd. N11	57	J5
Glenthorne Rd. W6	127	J4
Glenthorne Rd., Kings.T.	181	J4
Glenthorpe Rd., Mord.	184	A5
Glenton Rd. SE13	154	E4
Glentrammon Av., Orp.	207	J6
Glentrammon Cl., Orp.	207	J6
Glentrammon Gdns., Orp.	207	J6
Glentrammon Rd., Orp.	207	J6
Glentworth St. NW1	**8**	**A6**
Glentworth St. NW1	109	J4
Glenure Rd. SE9	156	D5
Glenview SE2	138	D6
Glenview Rd., Brom.	192	A2
Glenville Gro. SE8	133	J7
Glenville Ms. SW18	148	E7
Glenville Rd., Kings.T.	182	A1
Glenwood Av. NW9	88	E1
Glenwood Cl., Har.	68	D5
Glenwood Gdns., Ilf.	80	D5
Glenwood Gro. NW9	88	C1
Glenwood Rd. N15	75	H5
Glenwood Rd. NW7	55	E3
Glenwood Rd. SE6	171	J1
Glenwood Rd., Epsom	197	G6
Glenwood Rd., Houns.	144	A3
Glenwood Way, Croy.	189	G6
Glenworth Av. E14	134	D4
Gliddon Rd. W14	128	B4
Glimpsing Grn., Erith	139	E3
Global App. E3	114	B2
Hancock Rd.		
Globe Pond Rd. SE16	133	H1
Globe Rd. E1	113	F3
Globe Rd. E2	113	F3
Globe Rd. E15	97	F5
Globe Rope Wk. E14	134	C4
Globe St. SE1	**28**	**A5**
Globe St. SE1	132	A3
Globe Ter. E2	113	F3
Globe Rd.		
Globe Yd. W1	**16**	**D4**
Gloster Rd., N.Mal.	182	E4
Gloucester Arc. SW7	**30**	**C1**
Gloucester Av. NW1	92	A7
Gloucester Av., Sid.	175	H2
Gloucester Av., Well.	157	J4
Gloucester Circ. SE10	134	C7
Gloucester Cl. NW10	88	D7
Gloucester Cl., T.Ditt.	194	D1
Gloucester Ct. EC3	**21**	**E6**
Gloucester Ct., Rich.	126	A7
Gloucester Cres. NW1	110	B1
Gloucester Dr. N4	93	H2
Gloucester Dr. NW11	72	D4
Gloucester Gdns. NW11	72	C7
Gloucester Gdns. W2	**14**	**B3**
Gloucester Gdns., Barn.	42	A4
Gloucester Gdns., Ilf.	80	B7
Gloucester Gdns., Sutt.	199	E2
Gloucester Gate NW1	**8**	**D1**
Gloucester Gate NW1	110	B2
Gloucester Gate Ms. NW1	**8**	**D1**
Gloucester Gro., Edg.	70	D1
Gloucester Gro. Est. SE15	**37**	**E6**
Gloucester Gro. Est. SE15	132	B6
Gloucester Ho. N7	93	E3
Gloucester Ho. NW6	108	D2
Gloucester Ms. E10	78	A7
Gloucester Rd.		
Gloucester Ms. W2	**14**	**D4**
Gloucester Ms. W2	109	F6
Gloucester Ms. W. W2	**14**	**C4**
Gloucester Par., Sid.	158	A5
Gloucester Pl. NW1	109	J4
Gloucester Pl. NW1	**7**	**J5**
Gloucester Pl. W1	**16**	**A1**
Gloucester Pl. W1	109	J5
Gloucester Pl., Enf.	43	J2
Chase Side		
Gloucester Pl. Ms. W1	**16**	**A2**
Gloucester Rd. E10	78	A7
Gloucester Rd. E11	79	H5
Gloucester Rd. E12	98	C3
Gloucester Rd. E17	77	G2
Gloucester Rd. N17	76	A2
Gloucester Rd. N18	60	C5
Gloucester Rd. SW7	**22**	**C5**
Gloucester Rd. SW7	129	F4
Gloucester Rd. W3	126	C2
Gloucester Rd. W5	125	F2
Gloucester Rd., Barn.	41	F5
Gloucester Rd., Belv.	139	F5
Gloucester Rd., Croy.	188	A6
Gloucester Rd., Felt.	160	C1
Gloucester Rd., Hmptn.	161	H7
Gloucester Rd., Har.	67	H5
Gloucester Rd., Houns.	142	E4
Gloucester Rd., Kings.T.	182	B2
Gloucester Rd., Rich.	126	A7
Gloucester Rd., Tedd.	162	B5
Gloucester Rd., Twick.	161	J1
Gloucester Sq. E2	112	D1
Whiston Rd.		
Gloucester Sq. W2	**15**	**F4**
Gloucester Sq. W2	109	G6
Gloucester St. SW1	**33**	**F4**
Gloucester St. SW1	130	C5
Gloucester Ter. W2	**14**	**C3**
Gloucester Ter. W2	109	G7
Gloucester Wk. W8	128	D2
Gloucester Way EC1	**11**	**F4**
Gloucester Way EC1	111	G3
Glover Cl. SE2	138	C4
Glover Dr. N18	61	F6
Glover Rd., Pnr.	66	D6
Gloxinia Wk., Hmptn.	161	G6
Glycena Rd. SW11	149	J3
Glyn Av., Barn.	41	G4
Glyn Cl. SE25	188	B2
Glyn Ct. SW16	169	G3
Glyn Dr., Sid.	176	B4
Glyn Rd. E5	95	G4
Glyn Rd., Enf.	45	F4
Glyn Rd., Wor.Pk.	198	A2
Glyn St. SE11	**34**	**C4**
Glynde Ms. SW3	**23**	**H6**
Glynde Rd., Bexh.	158	D3
Glynde St. SE4	153	J6
Glyndebourne Pk., Orp.	207	E2
Glyndon Rd. SE18	137	F4
Glynfield Rd. NW10	89	E7
Glyn Rd. N22	75	G2
Glynwood Ct. SE23	171	F2
Goat La., Surb.	195	F2
Goat Rd., Mitch.	186	A7
Goat St. SE1	**29**	**F3**
Goat Wf., Brent.	125	H6
Goaters All. SW6	128	C7
Godalming Av., Wall.	201	E5
Godalming Rd. E14	114	B5
Godbold Rd. E15	114	E3
Goddard Rd., Beck.	189	G4
Goddards Way, Ilf.	99	G1
Godfrey Av., Nthlt.	102	E1
Godfrey Av., Twick.	144	A7
Godfrey Hill SE18	136	B4
Godfrey Rd. SE18	136	C4
Godfrey St. E15	114	C2
Godfrey St. SW3	**31**	**H3**
Godfrey St. SW3	129	H5
Godfrey Way, Houns.	143	F7
Goding St. SE11	**34**	**B4**
Goding St. SE11	131	E5
Godley Rd. SW18	167	G1
Godliman St. EC4	**19**	**J4**
Godliman St. EC4	111	J6
Godman Rd. SE15	152	E2
Godolphin Cl. N13	59	H6
Godolphin Pl. W3	106	D7
Vyner Rd.		
Godolphin Rd. W12	127	H2
Godson Rd., Croy.	201	G3
Godson St. N1	**11**	**E1**
Godson St. N1	111	G2
Godstone Rd., Sutt.	199	F4
Godstone Rd., Twick.	144	E6
Godstow Rd. SE2	138	C2
Godwin Cl. N1	**12**	**A1**
Godwin Cl., Epsom	196	C6
Godwin Ct. NW1	**9**	**G1**
Godwin Rd. E7	97	H4
Godwin Rd., Brom.	191	J3
Goffers Rd. SE3	154	D1
Goidel Cl., Wall.	200	D4
Golborne Gdns. W10	108	C4
Golborne Rd.		
Golborne Ms. W10	108	B5
Portobello Rd.		
Golborne Rd. W10	108	B5
Gold Hill, Edg.	54	D6
Gold La., Edg.	54	D6
Golda Cl., Barn.	40	A6
Goldbeaters Gro., Edg.	54	E6
Goldcliff Cl., Mord.	184	D6
Goldcrest Cl. E16	116	A5
Sheerwater Rd.		
Goldcrest Cl. SE28	118	C7
Goldcrest Ms. W5	105	G5
Montpelier Av.		
Goldcrest Way, Bushey	51	J1
Golden Cl., Rich.	145	G5
Golden Cres., Hayes	121	J1
Golden Cross Ms. W11	108	C6
Basing St.		
Golden La. EC1	**11**	**J6**
Golden La. EC1	111	J4
Golden La. Est. EC1	**11**	**J6**
Golden Manor W7	104	B7
Golden Plover Cl. E16	115	H6
Golden Sq. W1	**17**	**G5**
Golden Sq. W1	110	C7
Golden Yd. NW3	91	F4
Heath St.		
Golders Cl., Edg.	54	B5
Golders Gdns. NW11	72	B7
Golders Grn. Cres. NW11	72	C7
Golders Grn. Rd. NW11	72	B6
Golders Manor Dr. NW11	72	A6
Golders Pk. Cl. NW11	90	E1
Golders Ri. NW4	72	A5
Golders Way NW11	72	C7
Goldfinch Rd. SE28	137	G3
Goldfinch Way, Borwd.	38	A4
Goldhawk Ms. W12	127	H2
Devonport Rd.		
Goldhawk Rd. W6	127	F4
Goldhawk Rd. W12	127	G3
Goldhawk Cl. E3, Wdf.Grn.	64	A7
Goldhurst Ter. NW6	90	E7
Golding Cl., Chess.	195	F6
Coppard Gdns.		
Golding St. E1	**21**	**J4**
Golding St. E1	112	D6
Golding Ter. SW11	150	A2
Longhedge St.		
Goldingham Av., Loug.	49	F2
Goldings Hill, Loug.	48	D1
Goldings Ri., Loug.	48	D1
Goldings Rd., Loug.	48	D1
Goldington Cres. NW1	**9**	**H1**
Goldington Cres. NW1	110	D2
Goldington St. NW1	**9**	**H1**
Goldington St. NW1	110	D2
Goldman Cl. E2	**13**	**H5**
Goldman Cl. E2	112	D4
Goldney Rd. W9	108	D4
Goldrill Dr. N11	58	A2
Goldsboro Rd. SW8	150	D1
Goldsborough Cres. E4	62	B2
Goldsdown Cl., Enf.	45	H2
Goldsdown Rd., Enf.	45	G2
Goldsmid St. SE18	137	H5
Sladedale Rd.		
Goldsmith Av. E12	98	B6
Goldsmith Av. NW9	71	F6
Goldsmith Av. W3	106	D7
Goldsmith Av., Rom.	83	G7
Goldsmith Cl. W3	126/127	E1
East Acton La.		
Goldsmith Cl., Har.	85	H1
Goldsmith La. NW9	70	B4
Goldsmith Rd. E10	96	A1
Goldsmith Rd. E17	77	G2
Goldsmith Rd. N11	57	J5
Goldsmith Rd. SE15	152	D1
Goldsmith Rd. W3	126	D1
Goldsmith St. EC2	**20**	**A3**
Goldsmith's Row E2	13	J2
Goldsmith's Row E2	112	D2
Goldsmith's Sq. E2	13	J1
Goldsmith's Sq. E2	112	D2
Goldsworthy Gdns. SE16	133	F4
Goldwell Rd., Th.Hth.	187	F4
Goldwin Cl. SE14	153	F1
Goldwing Cl. E16	115	G6
Golf Cl., Stan.	53	F7
Golf Cl., Th.Hth.	187	G1
Kensington Av.		
Golf Club Dr., Kings.T.	164	D7
Golf Rd. W5	105	J6
Boileau Rd.		
Golf Rd., Brom.	192	D3
Golf Side, Twick.	162	A3
Golfe Rd., Ilf.	99	G3
Golfside Cl. N20	57	H3
Golfside Cl., N.Mal.	183	E2
Goliath Cl., Wall.	200	E7
Gollogly Ter. SE7	135	J5
Gomer Gdns., Tedd.	162	D6
Gomer Pl., Tedd.	162	D6
Gomm Rd. SE16	133	F3
Gomshall Av., Wall.	200	E5
Gondar Gdns. NW6	90	C5
Gonson Pl. SE8	134	A6
Gonson St. SE8	134	B6
Gonston Cl. SW19	166	B2
Boddicott Cl.		
Gonville Cres., Nthlt.	85	H6
Gonville Rd., Th.Hth.	187	F5
Gonville St. SW6	148	B3
Putney Br. App.		
Goodall Rd. E11	96	C3
Gooden Ct., Har.	86	B3
Goodenough Rd. SW19	166	C7
Goodge Pl. W1	**17**	**G2**
Goodge St. W1	**17**	**G2**
Goodge St. W1	110	C5
Goodhall St. NW10	107	E3
Goodhart Pl. E14	113	H7
Goodhart Way, W.Wick.	190	E7
Goodhew Rd., Croy.	188	D6
Gooding Cl., N.Mal.	182	C4
Goodinge Cl. N7	92	E6
Goodman Cres. SW2	168	D2
Goodman Rd. E10	78	C7
Goodmans Ct., Wem.	87	G4
Goodman's Stile E1	**21**	**H4**
Goodman's Stile E1	112	D6
Goodmans Yd. E1	**21**	**F5**
Goodmans Yd. E1	112	C7
Goodmayes Av., Ilf.	100	A1
Goodmayes La., Ilf.	100	A4
Goodmayes Rd., Ilf.	100	A1
Goodrich Rd. SE22	152	C6
Goods Way NW1	**10**	**A1**
Goods Way NW1	110	E2
Goodson Rd. NW10	89	E7
Goodway Gdns. E14	114	D6
Goodwin Cl. SE16	**29**	**G6**
Goodwin Cl. SE16	132	D3
Goodwin Cl., Mitch.	185	G3
Goodwin Dr., Sid.	176	D3
Goodwin Gdns., Croy.	201	H6
Goodwin Rd. N9	61	F1
Goodwin Rd. W12	127	G2
Goodwin Rd., Croy.	201	H5
Goodwin St. N4	93	G2
Fonthill Rd.		
Goodwins Ct. WC2	**18**	**A5**
Goodwood Cl., Mord.	184	D4
Goodwood Cl., Stan.	53	F5
Goodwood Dr., Nthlt.	85	G6
Goodwood Path, Borwd.	38	A3
Stratfield Rd.		
Goodwood Rd. SE14	153	H7
Goodyers Av. NW7	55	E5
Goodyns Vale N10	74	A1
Goodyers Gdns. NW4	72	A5
Goosander Way SE28	137	G3
Goose Sq. E6	116	C6
Harper Rd.		
Gooseacre La., Har.	69	G5
Gooseley La. E6	116	D3
Goosens Cl., Sutt.	199	F5
Turnpike La.		
Gophir La. EC4	**20**	**B5**
Gopsall St. N1	112	A1
Gordon Av. E4	62	E6

Gordon Av. SW14 146 E4
Gordon Av., Stan. 52 E6
Gordon Av., Twick. 144 D5
Gordon Cl. E17 78 A6
Gordon Cl. N19 92 C1
Highgate Hill
Gordon Ct. W12 107 J6
Gordon Cres., Croy. 202 B1
Gordon Cres., Hayes 122 A3
Gordon Gdns., Edg. 70 B2
Gordon Gro. SE5 151 H2
Gordon Hill, Enf. 43 J1
Gordon Ho. Rd. NW5 92 A4
Gordon Pl. W8 128 D2
Gordon Rd. E4 47 E2
Gordon Rd. E11 79 G6
Gordon Rd. E15 96 C4
Gordon Rd. E18 79 H1
Gordon Rd. N3 56 C7
Gordon Rd. N9 61 E2
Gordon Rd. N11 58 D7
Gordon Rd. SE15 152 E2
Gordon Rd. W4 126 B6
Gordon Rd. W5 105 F7
Gordon Rd. W13 105 E7
Gordon Rd., Bark. 117 H1
Gordon Rd., Beck. 189 J3
Gordon Rd., Belv. 139 J4
Gordon Rd., Cars. 199 J6
Gordon Rd., Enf. 43 J1
Gordon Rd., Esher 194 B6
Gordon Rd., Har. 68 B3
Gordon Rd., Houns. 143 J4
Gordon Rd., Ilf. 99 G3
Gordon Rd., Kings.T. 181 J1
Gordon Rd., Rich. 145 J2
Gordon Rd., Rom. 83 F6
Gordon Rd., Sid. 157 H5
Gordon Rd., Sthl. 123 E4
Gordon Rd., Surb. 181 J7
Gordon Sq. WC1 9 J6
Gordon Sq. WC1 110 D4
Gordon St. E13 115 G3
Grange Rd.
Gordon St. WC1 9 H5
Gordon St. WC1 110 D4
Gordon Way, Barn. 40 C4
Gordon Way, Brom. 191 G1
Gordonbrock Rd. SE4 154 A5
Gordondale Rd. 166 D2
SW19
Gore Ct. NW9 70 A5
Gore Rd. E9 113 F1
Gore Rd. SW20 183 J2
Gore St. SW7 22 D5
Gore St. SW7 129 F3
Gorefield Pl. NW6 108 D2
Goresbrook Rd., Dag. 118 B1
Goresbrook Village, 118 B1
Dag.
Goresbrook Rd.
Gorham Pl. W11 108 B7
Mary Pl.
Goring Cl., Rom. 83 J1
Goring Gdns., Dag. 100 C4
Goring Rd. N11 58 E6
Goring St. EC3 21 E3
Goring St. EC3 112 B6
Goring Way, Grnf. 103 G3
Gorleston Rd. N15 76 A5
Gorleston St. W14 128 B4
Gorman Rd. SE18 136 C4
Gorringe Pk. Av., 167 J7
Mitch.
Gorse Cl. E16 115 G6
Gorse Ri. SW17 168 A5
Gorse Rd., Croy. 204 A4
Gorst Rd. NW10 106 C4
Gorst Rd. SW11 149 J6
Gorsuch Pl. E2 13 F3
Gorsuch St. E2 13 F3
Gorsuch St. E2 112 C3
Gosberton Rd. SW12 168 A1
Gosbury Hill, Chess. 195 H4
Gosfield Rd., Dag. 101 G2
Gosfield St. W1 17 F1
Gosfield St. W1 110 C5
Gosford Gdns., Ilf. 80 C5
Gosforth La., Wat. 50 C3
Gosforth Path, Wat. 50 A3
Goslett Yd. WC2 17 J4
Gosling Cl., Grnf. 103 G3
Gosling Way SW9 151 G1
Gospatrick Rd. N17 75 J1
Gospel Oak Est. NW5 91 J5
Gosport Rd. E17 77 J5
Gosport Wk. N17 76/77 E5
Yarmouth Cres.
Gosport Way SE15 132 A7
Gossage Rd. SE18 137 G5
Ancona Rd.
Gosset St. E2 13 G3
Gosset St. E2 112 C3
Gosshill Rd., Chis. 192 D2

Gossington Cl., 174/175 E4
Chis.
Beechwood Ri.
Gosterwood St. SE8 133 H6
Gostling Rd., Twick. 161 G1
Goston Gdns., Th.Hth. 187 G3
Goswell Rd. EC1 11 J6
Goswell Rd. EC1 111 H3
Gothic Ct., Hayes 121 G6
Sipson La.
Gothic Rd., Twick. 162 A2
Gottfried Ms. NW5 92 C4
Fortess Rd.
Goudhurst Rd., Brom. 173 E5
Gough Rd. E15 97 F4
Gough Rd., Enf. 44 E2
Gough Sq. EC4 19 F3
Gough Sq. EC4 111 G6
Gough St. WC1 10 D5
Gough St. WC1 111 F4
Gough Wk. E14 114 A6
Saracen St.
Gould Ct. SE19 170 C5
Gould Rd., Felt. 141 H7
Gould Rd., Twick. 162 B1
Goulds Rd. E8 94/95 E5
Kenmure Rd.
Goulding Gdns., 187 H2
Th.Hth.
Goulston St. E1 21 F3
Goulston St. E1 112 C6
Goulton Rd. E5 95 E4
Gourley Pl. N15 76 B5
Gourley St.
Gourley St. N15 76 B5
Gourock Rd. SE9 156 D5
Govan St. E2 112 D1
Whiston Rd.
Govier Cl. E15 97 E7
Gowan Av. SW6 148 B1
Gowan Rd. NW10 89 H6
Gower Cl. SW4 150 C6
Gower Ct. WC1 9 H5
Gower Ms. WC1 17 H2
Gower Ms. WC1 110 D5
Gower Pl. WC1 9 G5
Gower Pl. WC1 110 C4
Gower Rd. E7 97 G6
Gower Rd., Islw. 124 C6
Gower St. WC1 9 H6
Gower St. WC1 110 C4
Gower's Wk. E1 21 H3
Gower's Wk. E1 112 D6
Gowland Pl., Beck. 189 J2
Gowlett Rd. SE15 152 D3
Gowrie Rd. SW11 150 A3
Graburn Way, E.Mol. 180 A3
Grace Av., Bexh. 159 F2
Grace Cl. SE9 174 A3
Grace Cl., Borwd. 38 D1
Grace Cl., Edg. 54 C7
Pavilion Way
Grace Cl., Ilf. 65 J6
Grace Jones Cl. E8 94 D6
Parkholme Rd.
Grace Path SE26 171 F4
Silverdale
Grace Pl. E3 114 B3
St. Leonards St.
Grace Rd., Croy. 187 J6
Grace St. E3 114 B3
Gracechurch St. EC3 20 C5
Gracechurch St. EC3 112 A7
Gracedale Rd. SW16 168 B5
Gracefield Gdns. 169 E3
SW16
Grace's All. E1 21 H5
Grace's All. E1 112 D7
Graces Ms. SE5 152 B2
Graces Rd. SE5 152 B2
Gradient, The SE26 170 D4
Graeme Rd., Enf. 44 A2
Graemesdyke Av. 146 B4
SW14
Grafton Cl. W13 104 D6
Grafton Cl., Houns. 161 E1
Grafton Cl., Wor.Pk. 197 E3
Grafton Cres. NW1 92 B6
Grafton Gdns. N4 75 J6
Grafton Gdns., Dag. 101 E2
Grafton Ho. E3 114 A3
Grafton Ms. W1 9 F6
Grafton Pk. Rd., 196 E2
Wor.Pk.
Grafton Pl. NW1 9 H4
Grafton Pl. NW1 110 D3
Grafton Rd. NW5 92 A5
Grafton Rd. W3 106 C7
Grafton Rd., Croy. 201 G1
Grafton Rd., Dag. 101 E2
Grafton Rd., Enf. 43 E3
Grafton Rd., Har. 67 J5
Grafton Rd., N.Mal. 182 E3
Grafton Rd., Wor.Pk. 196 D3

Grafton Sq. SW4 150 C3
Grafton St. W1 17 E6
Grafton St. W1 110 B7
Grafton Ter. NW5 91 J5
Grafton Way W1 110 C4
Grafton Way W1 9 F6
Grafton Way WC1 110 C4
Grafton Way, W.Mol. 179 F4
Grafton Yd. NW5 92 B6
Prince of Wales Rd.
Graham Av. W13 124 E2
Graham Av., Mitch. 186 A1
Graham Cl., Croy. 204 A2
Graham Gdns., Surb. 195 H1
Graham Rd. E8 94 D6
Graham Rd. E13 115 G4
Graham Rd. N15 75 H3
Graham Rd. NW4 71 H6
Graham Rd. SW19 166 C7
Graham Rd. W4 126 D3
Graham Rd., Bexh. 159 G4
Graham Rd., Hmptn. 161 G4
Graham Rd., Har. 68 B3
Graham Rd., Mitch. 186 A1
Graham St. N1 11 H2
Graham St. N1 111 H2
Graham Ter. SW1 32 B2
Graham Ter. SW1 130 A4
Grahame Pk. Est. 71 F1
NW9
Grahame Pk. Way 55 F7
NW7
Grahame Pk. Way 71 F2
NW9
Grainger Cl., Nthlt. 85 J5
Lancaster Rd.
Grainger Rd. N22 75 J1
Grainger Rd., Islw. 144 C2
Gramer Cl. E11 96 D2
Norman Rd.
Grampian Cl., Hayes 121 G7
Grampian Cl., Orp. 193 J6
Cotswold Ri.
Grampian Gdns. NW2 90 B1
Granard Av. SW15 147 H5
Granard Rd. SW12 149 J7
Granary Cl. N9 45 F7
Turin Rd.
Granary Rd. E1 112 E4
Granary St. NW1 110 D1
Granby Bldgs. SE11 34 C2
Granby Rd. SE9 156 C2
Granby St. E2 13 G5
Granby St. E2 112 C4
Granby Ter. NW1 9 F2
Granby Ter. NW1 110 C2
Grand Arc. N12 57 F5
Ballards La.
Grand Av. EC1 19 H1
Grand Av. N10 74 A4
Grand Av., Surb. 182 B5
Grand Av., Wem. 88 A5
Grand Av. E., Wem. 88 B5
Grand Depot Rd. 136 D5
SE18
Grand Dr. SW20 183 J2
Grand Dr., Sthl. 123 J2
Grand Junct. Wf. N1 11 J2
Grand Junct. Wf. N1 111 J2
Grand Par. Ms. SW15 148 B5
Upper Richmond Rd.
Grand Union Canal 124 B3
Wk. W7
Grand Union Cl. W9 108 C5
Woodfield Rd.
Grand Union Cres. E8 94 D7
Grand Union Ind. Est. 106 B2
NW10
Grand Union Wk. NW1 92 B7
Grand Wk. E1 113 H4
Solebay St.
Granden Rd. SW16 187 E2
Grandison Rd. SW11 149 J5
Grandison Rd., 197 J2
Wor.Pk.
Granfield St. SW11 149 G1
Grange, The N2 73 G2
Central Av.
Grange, The SE1 29 F5
Grange, The SE1 132 C3
Grange, The SW19 166 A6
Grange, The, Croy. 203 J2
Grange, The, Wem. 88 A7
Grange, The, Wor.Pk. 196 D3
Grange Av. N12 57 F5
Grange Av. N20 40 B7
Grange Av. SE25 188 B2
Grange Av., Barn. 57 H1
Grange Av., Stan. 69 E2
Grange Av., Twick. 162 B2

Grange Av., 63 G6
Wdf.Grn.
Grange Cl., Edg. 54 C5
Grange Cl., Houns. 123 F6
Grange Cl., Sid. 176 A3
Grange Cl., W.Mol. 179 H4
Grange Cl., Wdf.Grn. 63 G7
Grange Ct. E8 94 C7
Grange Ct. WC2 18 D4
Grange Ct., Chig. 65 F2
Grange Ct., Loug. 48 A5
Grange Ct., Nthlt. 102 C2
Grange Cres. SE28 118 C6
Grange Cres., Chig. 65 G5
Grange Dr., Chis. 174 B6
Grange Frm. Cl., Har. 85 J2
Grange Gdns. N14 58 D1
Grange Gdns. NW3 91 E3
Grange Gdns. SE25 188 B2
Grange Gdns., Pnr. 67 F4
Grange Gro. N1 93 J6
Grange Hill SE25 188 B2
Grange Hill, Edg. 54 C5
Grange Ho., Bark. 117 G1
St. Margarets
Grange La. SE21 170 C2
Grange Mans., Epsom 197 F7
Grange Ms. SE10 134 D7
Crooms Hill
Grange Pk. W5 125 H1
Grange Pk. Av. N21 43 H6
Grange Pk. Pl. SW20 165 H7
Grange Pk. Rd. E10 96 B1
Grange Pk. Rd., 188 A4
Th.Hth.
Grange Pl. NW6 90 D7
Grange Rd. E10 96 A1
Grange Rd. E13 115 F3
Grange Rd. E17 77 H5
Grange Rd. N6 74 A6
Grange Rd. N17 60 D6
Grange Rd. N18 60 D6
Grange Rd. NW10 89 H6
Grange Rd. SE1 28 E6
Grange Rd. SE1 132 B3
Grange Rd. SE19 188 A4
Grange Rd. SE25 188 A4
Grange Rd. SW13 147 G1
Grange Rd. W4 126 B5
Grange Rd. W5 125 G1
Grange Rd., Chess. 195 H4
Grange Rd., Edg. 54 D6
Grange Rd., Har. 68 D6
Grange Rd. (South 86 A2
Harrow), Har.
Grange Rd., Ilf. 99 E4
Grange Rd., Kings.T. 181 H3
Grange Rd., Orp. 207 F2
Grange Rd., Sthl. 122 E2
Grange Rd., Sutt. 198 D7
Grange Rd., Th.Hth. 188 A4
Grange Rd., W.Mol. 179 H4
Grange St. N1 112 A1
Grange Vale, Sutt. 199 E7
Grange Vw. Rd. N20 57 F1
Grange Wk. SE1 28 E5
Grange Wk. SE1 132 B3
Grange Yd. SE1 29 F6
Grange Yd. SE1 132 C3
Grangecliffe Gdns. 188 B2
SE25
Grangecourt Rd. N16 94 B1
Grangehill Pl. SE9 156 C3
Westmount Rd.
Grangehill Rd. SE9 156 C3
Grangemill Rd. SE6 172 A3
Grangemill Way SE6 172 A2
Grangeway N12 57 E4
Grangeway NW6 90 D7
Messina Av.
Grangeway, Wdf.Grn. 63 J4
Grangeway, The N21 43 H6
Grangeway, The, Ilf. 80 B5
Grangeway, Bex. 177 F1
Hurst Rd.
Grangewood, Well. 66 A5
Pnr.
Grangewood La., 171 A6
Beck.
Grangewood St. E6 115 J1
Grangewood Ter. 188 A3
SE25
Grange Rd.
Granham Gdns. N9 60 C2
Granite St. SE18 137 J5
Granleigh Rd. E11 96 E2
Gransden Av. E8 95 E7
Gransden Rd. W12 127 F2
Wendell Rd.
Grant Cl. N14 42 C7
Grant Pl., Croy. 202 C1
Grant Rd. SW11 149 G4
Grant Rd., Croy. 202 C1
Grant Rd., Har. 68 C3

Grant St. E13	115	G3
Grant St. N1	**11**	**E1**
Grant Way, Islw.	124	D6
Grantbridge St. N1	**11**	**H1**
Grantbridge St. N1	111	H2
Grantchester Cl., Har.	86	C3
Grantham Cl., Edg.	53	H3
Grantham Gdns., Rom.	83	F6
Grantham Grn., Borwd.	38	C5
Grantham Pl. W1	**24**	**D2**
Grantham Rd. E12	98	D4
Grantham Rd. SW9	151	E2
Grantham Rd. W4	126	E7
Grantley Rd., Houns.	142	C2
Grantley St. E1	113	G3
Grantock Rd. E17	78	D1
Granton Rd. SW16	186	C1
Granton Rd., Ilf.	100	A1
Granton Rd., Sid.	176	C6
Grants Cl. NW7	55	J7
Grantully Rd. W9	**6**	**A4**
Grantully Rd. W9	108	E3
Granville Av. N9	61	F3
Granville Av., Felt.	160	A2
Granville Av., Houns.	143	G5
Granville Cl., Croy.	202	B2
Granville Ct. N1	112	A1
Granville Gdns. SW16	187	F1
Granville Gdns. W5	125	J1
Granville Gro. SE13	154	C3
Granville Ms., Sid.	176	A4
Granville Pk. SE13	154	C3
Granville Pl. (North Finchley) N12	57	F7
High Rd.		
Granville Pl. W1	**16**	**B4**
Granville Pl. W1	110	A6
Granville Pl., Pnr.	66	D2
Elm Pk. Rd.		
Granville Rd. E17	78	B6
Granville Rd. E18	79	H2
Granville Rd. N4	75	F6
Granville Rd. N12	57	E7
Granville Rd. N13	59	F6
Russell Rd.		
Granville Rd. N22	75	H1
Granville Rd. NW2	90	C2
Granville Rd. NW6	108	D2
Granville Rd. SW18	148	D7
Granville Rd. SW19	166	D7
Russell Rd.		
Granville Rd., Barn.	39	J4
Granville Rd., Hayes	121	J4
Granville Rd., Ilf.	98	E1
Granville Rd., Sid.	176	A4
Granville Rd., Well.	158	C3
Granville Sq. SE15	132	B7
Granville Sq. WC1	**10**	**D4**
Granville Sq. WC1	111	F3
Granville St. WC1	**10**	**D4**
Grape St. WC2	**18**	**A3**
Graphite Sq. SE11	**34**	**C3**
Grapsome Cl., Chess.	195	G6
Ashlyns Way		
Grasdene Rd. SE18	138	A7
Grasmere Av. SW15	164	D4
Grasmere Av. SW19	184	D3
Grasmere Av. W3	106	C7
Grasmere Av., Houns.	143	H6
Grasmere Av., Orp.	206	E3
Grasmere Av., Wem.	69	G7
Grasmere Cl., Loug.	48	C2
Grasmere Ct. N22	59	F6
Palmerston Rd.		
Grasmere Gdns., Har.	68	D2
Grasmere Gdns., Ilf.	80	C5
Grasmere Gdns., Orp.	206	E3
Grasmere Rd. E13	115	G2
Grasmere Rd. N10	74	B1
Grasmere Rd. N17	60	D6
Grasmere Rd. SE25	189	E6
Grasmere Rd. SW16	169	F5
Grasmere Rd., Bexh.	159	J1
Grasmere Rd., Brom.	191	F1
Grasmere Rd., Orp.	206	E3
Grass Pk. N3	72	C1
Grassington Cl. N11	58	A6
Ribblesdale Av.		
Grassington Rd., Sid.	176	A4
Grassmount SE23	171	E2
Grassway, Wall.	200	C4
Grasvenor Av., Barn.	40	D6
Grately Way SE15	**37**	**F7**
Gratton Rd. W14	128	B3
Gratton Ter. NW2	90	A3
Gravel Hill N3	72	C2
Gravel Hill, Bexh.	159	H5
Gravel Hill, Croy.	203	G6
Gravel Hill Cl., Bexh.	159	H5
Gravel La. E1	**21**	**F3**
Gravel Pit La. SE9	157	F5
Gravel Rd., Brom.	206	B2
Gravel Rd., Twick.	162	B1
Graveley Av., Borwd.	38	C4
Gravelly Ride SW19	165	H4
Gravelwood Cl., Chis.	175	F3
Graveney Gro. SE20	171	F7
Graveney Rd. SW17	167	H4
Gravesend Rd. W12	107	G7
Gray Av., Dag.	101	F1
Gray St. SE1	**27**	**F4**
Grayham Cres., N.Mal.	182	D4
Grayham Rd., N.Mal.	182	D4
Grayland Cl., Brom.	192	A1
Grayling Cl. E16	114/115	E4
Cranberry La.		
Grayling Rd. N16	94	A2
Grayling Sq. E2	**13**	**J3**
Grayling Sq. E2	112	D3
Gray's Inn WC1	**18**	**D1**
Gray's Inn WC1	111	G5
Gray's Inn Pl. WC1	**18**	**D2**
Gray's Inn Rd. WC1	**10**	**C4**
Gray's Inn Rd. WC1	111	F4
Gray's Inn Sq. WC1	**18**	**D1**
Gray's Yd. W1	**16**	**C4**
Grayscroft Rd. SW16	168	D7
Grayshott Rd. SW11	150	A2
Grayswood Gdns. SW20	183	H2
Farnham Gdns.		
Graywood Ct. N12	57	F7
Grazebrook Rd. N16	94	A2
Grazeley Cl., Bexh.	159	J5
Grazeley Ct. SE19	170	B4
Gipsy Hill		
Great Acre Ct. SW4	150	D4
St. Alphonsus Rd.		
Great Bell All. EC2	**20**	**B3**
Great Benty, West Dr.	120	B4
Great Brownings SE21	170	C4
Great Bushey Dr. N20	57	E1
Great Cambridge Rd. N9	60	C1
Great Cambridge Rd. N17	60	A5
Great Cambridge Rd. N18	60	A5
Great Cambridge Rd., Enf.	44	D4
Great Castle St. W1	**17**	**E3**
Great Castle St. W1	110	C6
Great Cen. Av., Ruis.	84	C5
Great Cen. St. NW1	**15**	**J1**
Great Cen. St. NW1	109	J5
Great Cen. Way NW10	88	E5
Great Cen. Way, Wem.	88	C4
Great Chapel St. W1	**17**	**H3**
Great Chapel St. W1	110	D6
Great Chertsey Rd. W4	146	C2
Great Chertsey Rd., Felt.	161	G3
Great Ch. La. W6	128	A5
Great College St. SW1	**26**	**A5**
Great College St. SW1	130	E3
Great Cross Av. SE10	134	E7
Great Cumberland Ms. W1	**15**	**J4**
Great Cumberland Pl. W1	**15**	**J3**
Great Cumberland Pl. W1	109	J6
Great Dover St. SE1	**28**	**A4**
Great Dover St. SE1	132	A2
Great Eastern Rd. E15	96	D7
Great Eastern St. EC2	**12**	**D4**
Great Eastern St. EC2	112	B3
Great Eastern Wk. EC2	**20**	**E2**
Great Elms Rd., Brom.	191	J4
Great Fld. NW9	71	E1
Great Fleete Way, Bark.	118	C2
Great Galley Cl., Bark.	118	B3
Great George St. SW1	**25**	**J4**
Great George St. SW1	130	D2
Great Guildford St. SE1	**27**	**J1**
Great Guildford St. SE1	131	J1
Great Harry Dr. SE9	174	D3
Great James St. WC1	**10**	**C6**
Great James St. WC1	111	F5
Great Marlborough St. W1	**17**	**F4**
Great Marlborough St. W1	110	C6
Great Maze Pond SE1	**28**	**C3**
Great Maze Pond SE1	132	A2
Great New St. EC4	**19**	**F3**
Great Newport St. WC2	110	D7
Cranbourn St.		
Great N. Rd. N2	73	H4
Great N. Rd. N6	73	H4
Great N. Rd. (New Barnet), Barn.	40	D5
Great N. Way NW4	71	J2
Great Oaks, Chig.	65	F4
Great Ormond St. WC1	**18**	**B1**
Great Ormond St. WC1	111	E5
Great Owl Rd., Chig.	64	D3
Great Percy St. WC1	**10**	**D3**
Great Percy St. WC1	111	F3
Great Peter St. SW1	**25**	**H6**
Great Peter St. SW1	130	D3
Great Portland St. W1	**17**	**E1**
Great Portland St. W1	110	B5
Great Pulteney St. W1	**17**	**G5**
Great Pulteney St. W1	110	C7
Great Queen St. WC2	**18**	**B4**
Great Queen St. WC2	111	E6
Great Russell St. WC1	**17**	**J3**
Great Russell St. WC1	110	E5
Great St. Helens EC3	**20**	**D3**
Great St. Helens EC3	112	B6
Great St. Thomas Apostle EC4	**20**	**A5**
Great Scotland Yd. SW1	**26**	**A2**
Great Scotland Yd. SW1	130	E1
Great Smith St. SW1	**25**	**J5**
Great Smith St. SW1	130	D3
Great South-West Rd., Felt.	141	F7
Great South-West Rd., Houns.	141	J4
Great Spilmans SE22	152	B5
Great Strand NW9	71	F1
Great Suffolk St. SE1	**27**	**H2**
Great Suffolk St. SE1	131	H2
Great Sutton St. EC1	**11**	**H6**
Great Sutton St. EC1	111	H4
Great Swan All. EC2	**20**	**B3**
Great Thrift, Orp.	193	F4
Great Titchfield St. W1	**17**	**F3**
Great Titchfield St. W1	110	C6
Great Twr. St. EC3	**20**	**D5**
Great Twr. St. EC3	112	B7
Great Trinity La. EC4	**20**	**A5**
Great Turnstile WC1	**18**	**D2**
Great W. Rd. W4	126	B5
Great W. Rd. W6	127	F5
Great W. Rd., Brent.	126	B5
Great W. Rd., Houns.	142	D2
Great W. Rd., Islw.	124	C7
Great Western Rd. W2	108	C5
Great Western Rd. W9	108	C5
Great Western Rd. W11	108	C5
Great Wf. Rd. E14	134	B1
Churchill Pl.		
Great Winchester St. EC2	**20**	**C3**
Great Winchester St. EC2	112	A6
Great Windmill St. W1	**17**	**H5**
Great Windmill St. W1	110	D7
Great Yd. SE1	**28**	**E3**
Greatdown Rd. W7	104	C4
Greatfield Av. E6	116	C4
Greatfield Cl. N19	92	C4
Warrender Rd.		
Greatfield Cl. SE4	154	A4
Greatfields Rd., Bark.	117	G1
Greatham Wk. SW15	165	G1
Greatorex St. E1	**21**	**H1**
Greatorex St. E1	112	D5
Greatwood, Chis.	174	D7
Greaves Cl., Bark.	99	H7
Norfolk Rd.		
Greaves Pl. SW17	167	H4
Grebe Av., Hayes	102	D6
Cygnet Way		
Grebe Cl. E7	97	F5
Cormorant Rd.		
Grebe Cl. E17	61	H7
Grebe Cl., Bark.	117	H3
Thames Rd.		
Grebe Ct., Sutt.	198	B2
Gander Grn. La.		
Grecian Cres. SE19	169	H6
Gredo Ho., Bark.	118	B3
Greek Ct. W1	**17**	**J4**
Greek St. W1	**17**	**J4**
Greek St. W1	110	D6
Greek Yd. WC2	**18**	**A5**
Green, The E4	62	C1
Green, The E11	79	H6
Green, The E15	97	E6
Green, The N9	60	D2
Green, The N14	58	D3
Green, The N21	43	G7
Green, The SW14	146	C3
Green, The SW19	166	A5
Green, The W3	107	E6
Green, The W5	125	G1
High St.		
Green, The, Bexh.	159	G1
Green, The, Brom.	191	G7
Green, The, Cars.	200	A4
Green, The, Esher	194	C6
Green, The, Felt.	160	B2
Green, The, Houns.	123	G6
Heston Rd.		
Green, The, Mord.	184	B4
Green, The, N.Mal.	182	C3
Green, The (St. Paul's Cray), Orp.	176	B7
The Av.		
Green, The, Rich.	145	G5
Green, The, Sid.	176	A4
Green, The, Sthl.	123	E3
Green, The, Sutt.	198	E3
Green, The, Twick.	162	B1
Green, The, Well.	157	H4
Green, The, Wem.	86	D2
Green, The, West Dr.	120	A3
Green, The, Wdf.Grn.	63	G5
Green Acres, Croy.	202	C3
Green Arbour Ct. EC1	**19**	**G3**
Green Av. NW7	54	D4
Green Av. W13	125	E3
Green Bank E1	132	E1
Green Bank N12	57	E4
Green Cl. NW9	70	C6
Green Cl. NW11	73	F7
Green Cl., Brom.	190	E3
Green Cl., Cars.	199	J2
Green Cl., Felt.	160	E5
Green Cft., Edg.	54	C5
Deans La.		
Green Dale SE5	152	A4
Green Dale SE22	152	B5
Green Dale Cl. SE22	152	B5
Green Dale		
Green Dragon Ct. SE1	**28**	**B1**
Green Dragon La. N21	43	H6
Green Dragon La., Brent.	125	H5
Green Dragon Yd. E1	**21**	**H2**
Green Dr., Sthl.	123	G1
Green End N21	59	H2
Green End, Chess.	195	H4
Green Gdns., Orp.	207	F5
Green Hill, Buck.H.	63	J1
Green Hundred Rd. SE15	132	D6
Green La. E4	46	E3
Green La. NW4	72	A5
Green La. SE9	174	D2
Green La. SE20	171	G7
Green La. SW16	169	F7
Green La. W7	124	B2
Green La., Chig.	65	G2
Green La., Chis.	174	E4
Green La., Dag.	100	D2
Green La., Edg.	54	A5
Green La., Felt.	160	E5
Green La., Har.	86	B3
Green La., Houns.	142	B3
Green La., Ilf.	99	F2
Green La., Mord.	184	E6
Green La., N.Mal.	182	C5
Green La., Stan.	52	E4
Green La., Th.Hth.	187	G1
Green La., Wat.	50	C1
Green La., W.Mol.	179	H5
Green La., Wor.Pk.	197	G1
Green La. Gdns., Th.Hth.	187	J2
Green Las. N4	93	J1
Green Las. N8	75	H3
Green Las. N13	59	F6
Green Las. N15	75	H3
Green Las. N16	93	J3
Green Las. N21	59	H1
Green Lawns, Ruis.	84	C1
Green Leaf Av., Wall.	200	D4
Green Man Gdns. W13	104	D7
Green Man La. W13	124	D1
Green Man La., Felt.	142	A4
Green Man Pas. W13	104	D7
Green Man Roundabout E11	79	F7

Green Moor Link N21 43 H7
Green Pk. Way, Grnf. 104 B1
Green Pt. E15 97 E6
Green Pond Cl. E17 77 J3
Green Pond Rd. E17 77 H3
Green Ride, Loug. 47 G5
Green Rd. N14 42 B6
Green Rd. N20 57 F3
Green Shield Ind. Est. E16 135 G1
Bradfield Rd.
Green St. E7 97 H6
Green St. E13 115 J1
Green St. W1 16 B5
Green St. W1 110 A7
Green St., Enf. 45 F2
Green St., Sun. 178 A1
Green Vale W5 105 J6
Green Vale, Bexh. 158 D5
Green Verges, Stan. 53 G7
Green Vw., Chess. 195 J7
Green Wk. NW4 72 A5
Green Wk. SE1 28 D6
Green Wk., Buck.H. 48 B7
Green Wk., Hmptn. 161 F6
Orpwood Cl.
Green Wk., Sthl. 123 G5
Green Wk., Wdf.Grn. 64 B6
Green Wk., The E4 62 C1
Green Way SE9 156 A5
Green Way, Brom. 192 B6
Green Way, Sun. 178 A4
Green Wrythe Cres., Cars. 199 H1
Green Wrythe La., Cars. 185 G6
Greenacre Cl., Nthlt. 85 F5
Eastcote La.
Greenacre Gdns. E17 78 C4
Greenacre Pl., Wall. 200 B2
Park Rd.
Greenacre Sq. SE16 133 G2
Fishermans Dr.
Greenacre Wk. N14 58 E3
Greenacres SE9 156 D6
Greenacres, Bushey 52 A2
Greenacres Cl., Orp. 207 F4
Greenacres Dr., Stan. 52 E7
Greenaway Gdns. NW3 90 E4
Greenbank Av., Wem. 86 D5
Greenbank Cl. E4 62 C2
Greenbank Cres. NW4 72 B4
Greenbay Rd. SE7 136 A7
Greenberry St. NW8 7 G2
Greenberry St. NW8 109 H2
Greenbrook Av., Barn. 41 F1
Greencoat Pl. SW1 33 G1
Greencoat Pl. SW1 130 C4
Greencoat Row SW1 25 G6
Greencourt Av., Croy. 203 E2
Greencourt Av., Edg. 70 B1
Greencourt Gdns., Croy. 203 E1
Greencourt Rd., Orp. 193 G5
Greencrest Pl. NW2 89 H3
Dollis Hill La.
Greencroft Av., Ruis. 84 C2
Greencroft Cl. E6 116 B5
Neatscourt Rd.
Greencroft Gdns. NW6 91 E7
Greencroft Gdns., Enf. 44 B3
Greencroft Rd., Houns. 143 F1
Greenend Rd. W4 126 E2
Greenfarm Cl., Orp. 207 J5
Greenfield Av., Surb. 182 B7
Greenfield Av., Wat. 50 D2
Greenfield Gdns. NW2 90 B2
Greenfield Gdns., Dag. 118 D1
Greenfield Gdns., Orp. 193 G7
Greenfield Rd. E1 21 J2
Greenfield Rd. E1 112 D5
Greenfield Rd. N15 76 B5
Greenfield Rd., Dag. 118 C1
Greenfield Way, Har. 67 H3
Greenfields, Loug. 48 D4
Greenfields Cl., Loug. 48 D4
Greenford Av. W7 104 B4
Greenford Av., Sthl. 103 F7
Greenford Gdns., Grnf. 103 H3
Greenford Rd., Grnf. 103 J5
Greenford Rd., Har. 104 A2
Greenford Rd., Sthl. 123 J1
Greenford Rd., Sutt. 198 E4
Greengate, Grnf. 86 E6
Greengate St. E13 115 H2
Greenhalgh Wk. N2 73 F4
Greenham Cl. SE1 27 E4
Greenham Cl. SE1 131 G2
Greenham Cres. E4 61 J6
Greenham Rd. N10 74 A2
Greenheys Dr. E18 79 F3
Greenhill NW3 91 G4
Hampstead High St.
Greenhill SE18 136 C5
Greenhill, Sutt. 199 F2
Greenhill, Wem. 88 B2
Greenhill Gdns., Nthlt. 103 F2
Greenhill Gro. E12 98 B4
Greenhill Pk. NW10 106 E1
Greenhill Pk., Barn. 40 E5
Greenhill Rd. NW10 106 E1
Greenhill Rd., Har. 68 B6
Greenhill Ter. SE18 136 C5
Greenhill Ter., Nthlt. 103 F2
Greenhill Way, Har. 68 B6
Greenhill Way, Wem. 88 B2
Greenhill's Rents EC1 19 H1
Greenhills Ter. N1 94 A6
Baxter Rd.
Greenhithe Cl., Sid. 157 H7
Greenholm Rd. SE9 156 E5
Greenhurst Rd. SE27 169 G5
Greening St. SE2 138 C4
Greenland Cres., Sthl. 122 C3
Greenland Ms. SE8 133 G5
Trundleys Rd.
Greenland Pl. NW1 110 B1
Greenland Rd.
Greenland Quay SE16 133 G4
Greenland Rd. NW1 110 C1
Greenland Rd., Barn. 39 J6
Greenland St. NW1 110 B1
Camden High St.
Greenlaw Gdns., N.Mal. 183 F7
Greenlaw St. SE18 136 D3
Greenlea Pk. SW19 185 G1
Greenleaf Cl. SW2 151 G7
Tulse Hill
Greenleaf Rd. E6 115 J1
Redclyffe Rd.
Greenleaf Rd. E17 77 J3
Greenleafe Dr., Ilf. 81 E4
Greenman St. N1 93 J7
Greenmead Cl. SE25 188 D5
Greenmoor Rd., Enf. 45 F2
Greenoak Pl., Barn. 41 J3
Cockfosters Rd.
Greenoak Way SW19 166 A4
Greenock Rd. SW16 186 D1
Greenock Rd. W3 126 B3
Greenpark Ct., Wem. 87 F7
Greens Cl., The, Loug. 48 D2
Green's Ct. W1 17 H5
Green's End SE18 136 E4
Greenshank Cl. E17 61 H7
Banbury Rd.
Greenside, Bex. 177 E1
Greenside, Dag. 100 C1
Greenside Cl. N20 57 G2
Greenside Cl. SE6 172 D2
Greenside Rd. W12 127 G3
Greenside Rd., Croy. 187 G7
Greenslade Rd., Bark. 99 G7
Greenstead Av., Wdf.Grn. 63 J7
Greenstead Cl., Wdf.Grn. 63 J6
Greenstead Gdns.
Greenstead Gdns. SW15 147 G5
Greenstead Gdns., Wdf.Grn. 63 J6
Greensted Rd., Loug. 48 B7
Greenstone Ms. E11 79 G6
Greenvale Rd. SE9 156 C4
Greenview Av., Beck. 189 H6
Greenview Av., Croy. 189 H6
Greenway N14 58 E2
Greenway N20 56 D2
Greenway SW20 183 J4
Greenway, Chis. 174 D5
Greenway, Dag. 100 C2
Greenway, Har. 69 H5
Greenway, Hayes 102 B4
Greenway, Pnr. 66 B2
Greenway, Wall. 200 C4
Greenway, Wdf.Grn. 63 J5
Greenway, The NW9 70 D2
Greenway, The, Har. 68 B1
Greenway, The, Houns. 143 F4
Greenway, The, Pnr. 67 F6
Greenway Av. E17 78 D4
Greenway Cl. N4 93 J2
Greenway Cl. N11 58 A6
Greenway Cl. N15 76 C4
Copperfield Dr.
Greenway Cl. N20 56 D2
Greenway Cl. NW9 70 D2
Greenway Gdns. NW9 70 D2
Greenway Gdns., Croy. 203 J3
Greenway Gdns., Grnf. 103 G3
Greenway Gdns., Har. 68 B1
Greenways, Beck. 190 A2
Greenways, Esher 194 B4
Greenways, The, Twick. 144 D6
South Western Rd.
Greenwell St. W1 9 E6
Greenwell St. W1 110 B4
Greenwich Ch. St. SE10 134 C6
Greenwich Cres. E6 116 B5
Swan App.
Greenwich Foot Tunnel E14 134 C5
Greenwich Foot Tunnel SE10 134 C5
Greenwich High Rd. SE10 154 B1
Greenwich Ind. Est. SE7 135 H4
Greenwich Mkt. SE10 134 C6
Greenwich Pk. SE10 134 D7
Greenwich Pk. St. SE10 134 D5
Greenwich S. St. SE10 154 B1
Greenwich Vw. Pl. E14 134 B3
Greenwood Av., Dag. 101 H4
Greenwood Av., Enf. 45 H2
Greenwood Cl., Mord. 184 B4
Greenwood Cl., Orp. 193 H6
Greenwood Cl., Sid. 176 A2
Hurst Rd.
Greenwood Cl., T.Ditt. 194 D1
Greenwood Ct. SW1 33 F3
Greenwood Ct. SW1 130 C5
Greenwood Dr. E4 62 C5
Avril Way
Greenwood Gdns. N13 59 H3
Greenwood Gdns., Ilf. 65 F7
Greenwood La., Hmptn. 161 H5
Greenwood Pk., Kings.T. 165 E7
Greenwood Pl. NW5 92 B5
Highgate Rd.
Greenwood Rd. E8 94 D6
Greenwood Rd. E13 115 F2
Maud Rd.
Greenwood Rd., Croy. 187 H7
Greenwood Rd., Islw. 144 B3
Greenwood Rd., Mitch. 186 D3
Greenwood Rd., T.Ditt. 194 D1
Greenwood Ter. NW10 106 D1
Greenwoods, The, Har. 85 J2
Sherwood Rd.
Greer Rd., Har. 67 J1
Greet St. SE1 27 F2
Greet St. SE1 131 G1
Greg Cl. E10 78 C6
Gregor Ms. SE3 135 G7
Gregory Cres. SE9 156 A7
Gregory Pl. W8 22 A3
Gregory Pl. W8 128 E2
Gregory Rd., Rom. 82 D4
Gregory Rd., Sthl. 123 G3
Gregson Cl., Borwd. 38 C1
Greig Cl. N8 74 E5
Greig Ter. SE17 35 H5
Grena Gdns., Rich. 145 J4
Grena Rd., Rich. 145 J4
Grenaby Av., Croy. 188 A7
Grenaby Rd., Croy. 188 A7
Grenada Rd. SE7 135 J7
Grenade St. E14 113 J7
Grenadier St. E16 136 D1
Grendon Gdns., Wem. 88 A2
Grendon St. NW8 7 G5
Grendon St. NW8 109 H4
Grenfell Cl., Borwd. 38 C1
Grenfell Gdns., Har. 69 H7
Grenfell Rd. W11 108 A7
Grenfell Rd., Mitch. 167 J6
Grenfell Twr. W11 108 A7
Grenfell Wk. W11 108 A7
Grennell Cl., Sutt. 199 G2
Grennell Rd., Sutt. 199 F2
Grenoble Gdns. N13 59 G6
Grenville Cl. N3 72 C1
Grenville Cl., Surb. 196 C1
Grenville Gdns., Wdf.Grn. 79 J1
Grenville Ms. SW7 30 D1
Grenville Ms. SW7 129 F4
Grenville Ms., Hmptn. 161 H5
Grenville Pl. NW7 54 D5
Grenville Pl. SW7 22 C6
Grenville Pl. SW7 129 F3
Grenville Rd. N19 92 E1
Grenville St. WC1 10 B6
Grenville St. WC1 111 E4
Gresham Av. N20 57 J4
Gresham Cl., Bex. 159 E6
Gresham Cl., Enf. 43 J3
Gresham Dr., Rom. 82 B5
Gresham Gdns. NW11 90 B1
Gresham Rd. E6 116 C2
Gresham Rd. E16 115 H6
Gresham Rd. NW10 88 D5
Gresham Rd. SE25 188 D4
Gresham Rd. SW9 151 G3
Gresham Rd., Beck. 189 H2
Gresham Rd., Edg. 53 J6
Gresham Rd., Hmptn. 161 G6
Gresham Rd., Houns. 143 J1
Gresham St. EC2 19 J3
Gresham St. EC2 111 J6
Gresham Way SW19 166 D3
Gresley Cl. E17 77 H6
Gresley Cl. N15 76 A4
Clinton Rd.
Gresley Rd. N19 92 C1
Gresse St. W1 17 H2
Gresse St. W1 110 D5
Gressenhall Rd. SW18 148 C6
Gresswell Cl., Sid. 176 A3
Greswell St. SW6 148 A1
Gretton Rd. N17 60 B7
Greville Cl., Twick. 144 E7
Greville Hall NW6 6 A1
Greville Hall NW6 109 E2
Greville Pl. NW6 6 B1
Greville Pl. NW6 109 E2
Greville Rd. E17 78 C4
Greville Rd. NW6 108 E1
Greville Rd., Rich. 145 J6
Greville St. EC1 19 F2
Greville St. EC1 111 G5
Grey Cl. NW11 73 F6
Grey Eagle St. E1 21 F1
Grey Eagle St. E1 112 C5
Greycoat Pl. SW1 25 H6
Greycoat Pl. SW1 130 D3
Greycoat St. SW1 25 H6
Greycoat St. SW1 130 D3
Greycot Rd., Beck. 172 A5
Greyfell Cl., Stan. 52/53 E5
Coverdale Cl.
Greyfriars Pas. EC1 19 H3
Greyhound Hill NW4 71 G3
Greyhound La. SW16 168 D6
Greyhound Rd. N17 76 B3
Greyhound Rd. NW10 107 H3
Greyhound Rd. W6 128 A6
Greyhound Rd. W14 128 A6
Greyhound Rd., Sutt. 199 F5
Greyhound Ter. SW16 186 C1
Greys Pk. Cl., Kes. 205 J5
Greystead Rd. SE23 153 F7
Greystoke Av., Pnr. 67 G3
Greystoke Gdns. W5 105 H4
Greystoke Gdns., Enf. 42 D4
Greystoke Pk. Ter. W5 105 G3
Greystoke Pl. EC4 19 E3
Greystone Gdns., Har. 69 F6
Greystone Gdns., Ilf. 81 F2
Greystone Path E11 79 F7
Grove Rd.
Greyswood St. SW16 168 B6
Grierson Rd. SE23 153 G7
Griffin Cen., The, Felt. 142 B5
Griffin Cl. NW10 89 H5
Griffin Manor Way SE28 137 G3
Griffin Rd. N17 76 B2
Griffin Rd. SE18 137 G5
Griffin Way, Sun. 178 A2
Griffith Cl., Dag. 100 C1
Gibson Rd.
Griffiths Cl., Wor.Pk. 197 H2
Griffiths Rd. SW19 166 D7
Griggs App., Ilf. 99 F2
Griggs Pl. SE1 28 E6
Griggs Rd. E10 78 C6

Grilse Cl. N9 61 E4
Grimsby Gro. E16 136/137 E2
Barge Ho. Rd.
Grimsby St. E2 13 G6
Grimsdyke Cres., Barn. 39 J3
Grimsdyke Rd., Pnr. 51 E7
Grimsel Path SE5 35 H7
Grimshaw Cl. N6 74 A7
Grimston Rd. SW6 148 C2
Grimwade Av., Croy. 202 D3
Grimwade Cl. SE15 153 F3
Grimwade Cres. SE15 153 F3
Evelina Rd.
Grimwood Rd., Twick. 144 C7
Grindal St. SE1 26 E4
Grindall Cl., Croy. 201 H4
Hillside Rd.
Grindleford Av. N11 58 A2
Grindley Gdns., Croy. 188 C6
Grinling Pl. SE8 134 A6
Grinstead Rd. SE8 133 H5
Grittleton Av., Wem. 88 B6
Grittleton Rd. W9 108 D4
Grizedale Ter. SE23 171 E2
Grocer's Hall Ct. EC2 20 B4
Grogan Cl., Hmptn. 161 F6
Groom Cres. SW18 149 G7
Groom Pl. SW1 24 C5
Groom Pl. SW1 130 A3
Groombridge Cl., Well. 158 A5
Groombridge Rd. E9 95 G7
Groomfield Cl. SW17 168 A4
Grooms Dr., Pnr. 66 A5
Grosmont Rd. SE18 137 J5
Grosse Way SW15 147 H6
Grosvenor Av. N5 93 J5
Grosvenor Av. SW14 146 E3
Grosvenor Av., Cars. 199 J6
Grosvenor Av., Har. 67 H6
Grosvenor Av., Rich. 145 H5
Grosvenor Rd.
Grosvenor Cl., Loug. 48 E1
Grosvenor Cotts. SW1 32 B1
Grosvenor Ct. N14 42 C7
Grosvenor Ct. NW6 108 A1
Christchurch Av.
Grosvenor Cres. NW9 70 A4
Grosvenor Cres. SW1 24 C4
Grosvenor Cres. SW1 130 A2
Grosvenor Cres. Ms. SW1 24 B4
Grosvenor Cres. Ms. SW1 130 A2
Grosvenor Dr., Loug. 49 E1
Grosvenor Est. SW1 33 J1
Grosvenor Est. SW1 130 D4
Grosvenor Gdns. E6 116 A3
Grosvenor Gdns. N10 74 C3
Grosvenor Gdns. N14 42 D5
Grosvenor Gdns. NW2 89 J5
Grosvenor Gdns. NW11 72 C6
Grosvenor Gdns. SW1 24 D5
Grosvenor Gdns. SW1 130 B3
Grosvenor Gdns. SW14 146 E3
Grosvenor Gdns., Kings.T. 163 G6
Grosvenor Gdns., Wall. 200 C7
Grosvenor Gdns., Wdf.Grn. 63 G6
Grosvenor Gdns. Ms. E. SW1 24 E5
Grosvenor Gdns. Ms. N. SW1 24 D6
Grosvenor Gdns. Ms. S. SW1 24 E6
Grosvenor Gate W1 16 A6
Grosvenor Gate W1 109 J7
Grosvenor Hill SW19 166 B6
Grosvenor Hill W1 16 D5
Grosvenor Hill W1 110 B7
Grosvenor Pk. SE5 35 J6
Grosvenor Pk. SE5 131 J6
Grosvenor Pk. Rd. E17 78 A5
Grosvenor Path, Loug. 49 E1
Grosvenor Pl. SW1 24 C4
Grosvenor Pl. SW1 130 A2
Grosvenor Ri. E. E17 78 B5
Grosvenor Rd. E6 116 A1
Grosvenor Rd. E7 97 H6
Grosvenor Rd. E10 96 C1
Grosvenor Rd. E11 79 G5
Grosvenor Rd. N3 56 C7
Grosvenor Rd. N9 60 E1
Grosvenor Rd. N10 74 B1
Grosvenor Rd. SE25 188 D4
Grosvenor Rd. SW1 33 J4
Grosvenor Rd. SW1 130 B6
Grosvenor Rd. W4 126 B5
Grosvenor Rd. W7 124 D1
Grosvenor Rd., Belv. 139 G6
Grosvenor Rd., Bexh. 158 D5
Grosvenor Rd., Borwd. 38 A3
Grosvenor Rd., Brent. 125 G6
Grosvenor Rd., Dag. 101 F1
Grosvenor Rd., Houns. 143 F3
Grosvenor Rd., Ilf. 99 F3
Grosvenor Rd., Orp. 193 H6
Grosvenor Rd., Rich. 145 H5
Grosvenor Rd., Sthl. 123 F3
Grosvenor Rd., Twick. 144 D7
Grosvenor Rd., Wall. 200 B6
Grosvenor Rd., W.Wick. 204 B1
Grosvenor Sq. W1 16 C5
Grosvenor Sq. W1 110 A7
Grosvenor St. W1 16 D5
Grosvenor St. W1 110 B7
Grosvenor Ter. SE5 35 J7
Grosvenor Ter. SE5 131 H7
Grosvenor Way E5 95 F2
Grosvenor Wf. Rd. E14 134 D4
Grote's Bldgs. SE3 155 E2
Grote's Pl. SE3 154 E2
Groton Rd. SW18 167 E2
Grotto Pas. W1 16 C1
Grotto Rd., Twick. 162 C2
Grove, The E15 96 E6
Grove, The N3 72 D1
Grove, The N4 75 F7
Grove, The N6 92 A1
Grove, The N8 74 D5
Grove, The N13 59 G4
Grove, The N14 42 C5
Grove, The NW9 70 D5
Grove, The NW11 72 B7
Grove, The W5 125 G1
Grove, The, Bexh. 158 D4
Grove, The, Edg. 54 B4
Grove, The, Enf. 43 G2
Grove, The, Grnf. 103 J6
Grove, The, Islw. 144 B1
Grove, The, Sid. 177 E4
Grove, The, Stan. 52 D2
Grove, The, Tedd. 162 D4
Grove, The, Twick. 144/145 E6
Bridge Rd.
Grove, The, Walt. 178 B7
Grove, The, W.Wick. 204 B3
Grove Av. N3 56 D7
Grove Av. N10 74 C2
Grove Av. W7 104 B6
Grove Av., Pnr. 67 E4
Grove Av., Sutt. 198 D6
Grove Av., Twick. 162 C1
Grove Bank, Wat. 50 D1
Grove Cl. N14 42 B7
Avenue Rd.
Grove Cl. SE23 171 G1
Grove Cl., Brom. 205 G2
Grove Cl., Felt. 160 E4
Grove Cl., Kings.T. 181 J4
Grove Cotts. SW3 31 H5
Grove Cotts. SW3 129 H6
Grove Ct. SE3 155 G1
Grove Ct., E.Mol. 180 A5
Walton Rd.
Grove Cres. E18 79 F2
Grove Cres. NW9 70 C4
Grove Cres. SE5 152 B2
Grove Cres., Felt. 160 E4
Grove Cres., Kings.T. 181 H3
Grove Cres., Walt. 178 B7
Grove Cres. Rd. E15 96 D6
Grove End E18 79 F2
Grove Hill
Grove End NW5 92 B4
Chetwynd Rd.
Grove End La., Esher 194 A1
Grove End Rd. NW8 6 E3
Grove End Rd. NW8 109 G3
Grove Fm. Ct., Mitch. 185 J4
Brookfields Av.
Grove Footpath, Surb. 181 H4
Grove Gdns. E15 96 E6
Grove Gdns. NW4 71 G4
Grove Gdns. NW8 7 H4
Grove Gdns., Dag. 101 J3
Grove Gdns., Enf. 45 G1
Grove Gdns., Tedd. 162 D4
Grove Grn. Rd. E11 96 C3
Grove Hall Ct. NW8 6 D3
Grove Hill E18 79 F2
Grove Hill, Har. 68 B7
Grove Hill Rd. SE5 152 B3
Grove Hill Rd., Har. 68 B7
Grove Ho. Rd. N8 74 E4
Grove La. SE5 152 A1
Grove La., Chig. 65 J3
Grove La., Kings.T. 181 H4
Grove La. Ter. SE5 152 B3
Grove La.
Grove Mkt. Pl. SE9 156 C6
Grove Ms. W6 127 J3
Grove Ms. W11 108 C6
Portobello Rd.
Grove Mill Pl., Cars. 200 A3
Grove Pk. E11 79 H6
Grove Pk. NW9 70 C4
Grove Pk. SE5 152 B2
Grove Pk. Av. E4 62 B7
Grove Pk. Br. W4 126 C7
Grove Pk. Gdns. W4 126 B6
Grove Pk. Ms. W4 126 C7
Grove Pk. Rd. N15 76 B4
Grove Pk. Rd. SE9 173 J3
Grove Pk. Rd. W4 126 B7
Grove Pk. Ter. W4 126 B6
Grove Pas. E2 113 E2
Grove Pas., Tedd. 162 D5
Grove Pl. NW3 91 G4
Christchurch Hill
Grove Pl. SW12 150 B6
Cathles Rd.
Grove Pl. W3 126 C1
Grove Pl. W5 125 G1
The Gro.
Grove Pl., Bark. 117 F1
Clockhouse Av.
Grove Rd. E3 113 G1
Grove Rd. E4 62 B4
Grove Rd. E11 79 F7
Grove Rd. E17 78 B5
Grove Rd. E18 79 F2
Grove Rd. N11 58 B5
Grove Rd. N12 57 G5
Grove Rd. N15 76 B5
Grove Rd. NW2 89 J6
Grove Rd. SW13 147 F2
Grove Rd. SW19 167 F7
Grove Rd. W3 126 C1
Grove Rd. W5 105 G7
Grove Rd., Barn. 41 H3
Grove Rd., Belv. 139 F6
Grove Rd., Bexh. 159 J4
Grove Rd., Borwd. 38 A1
Grove Rd., Brent. 125 F5
Grove Rd., E.Mol. 180 A4
Grove Rd., Edg. 54 A6
Grove Rd., Houns. 143 G4
Grove Rd., Islw. 144 B1
Grove Rd., Mitch. 186 B2
Grove Rd., Pnr. 67 F5
Grove Rd., Rich. 145 J6
Grove Rd., Rom. 82 B7
Grove Rd., Surb. 181 G5
Grove Rd., Sutt. 199 E6
Grove Rd., Th.Hth. 187 G4
Grove Rd., Twick. 162 A3
Grove St. N18 60 C6
Grove St. SE8 133 J4
Grove Ter. NW5 92 B3
Grove Ter., Tedd. 162 D4
Grove Ter. Ms. NW5 92 B3
Grove Ter.
Grove Vale SE22 152 C4
Grove Vale, Chis. 174 D6
Grove Vil. E14 114 B7
Grove Way, Esher 179 J7
Grove Way, Wem. 88 B5
Grovebury Rd. SE2 138 B2
Grovedale Rd. N19 92 D2
Groveland Av. SW16 169 F7
Groveland Ct. EC4 20 A4
Groveland Rd., Beck. 189 J3
Groveland Way, N.Mal. 182 C5
Grovelands, W.Mol. 179 G4
Grovelands Cl. SE5 152 B2
Grovelands Cl., Har. 85 H3
Grovelands Ct. N14 42 D7
Grovelands Rd. N13 59 F4
Grovelands Rd. N15 76 D6
Grovelands Rd., Orp. 176 A7
Groveside Cl. W3 106 A6
Groveside Cl., Cars. 199 H2
Groveside Rd. E4 63 E2
Grovestile Waye, Felt. 141 G7
Groveway SW9 151 F1
Groveway, Dag. 100 D4
Grovewood, Rich. 146 A1
Sandycombe Rd.
Grovewood Pl., Wdf.Grn. 64 C6
Grummant Rd. SE15 152 C1
Grundy St. E14 114 B6
Gruneisen Rd. N3 56 E7
Gubyon Av. SE24 151 H5
Guerin Sq. E3 113 J3
Malmesbury Rd.
Guernsey Cl., Houns. 143 G1
Guernsey Gro. SE24 151 J7
Guernsey Rd. E11 96 D1
Guibal Rd. SE12 155 H7
Guild Rd. SE7 136 A5
Guildersfield Rd. SW16 168 E7
Guildford Gro. SE10 154 B1
Guildford Rd. E6 116 B6
Guildford Rd. E17 78 C1
Guildford Rd. SW8 151 E1
Guildford Rd., Croy. 188 A6
Guildford Rd., Ilf. 99 H2
Guildford Way, Wall. 201 E5
Guildhall Bldgs. EC2 112 A6
Basinghall St.
Guildhall Yd. EC2 20 B3
Guildhouse St. SW1 33 F1
Guildhouse St. SW1 130 C4
Guildown Av. N12 56 E4
Guildsway E17 77 J1
Guilford Av., Surb. 181 J5
Guilford Pl. WC1 10 C6
Guilford Pl. WC1 111 F4
Guilford St. WC1 10 A6
Guilford St. WC1 111 E4
Guilford Vil., Surb. 181 J6
Alpha Rd.
Guilsborough Cl. NW10 88 E7
Guinness Bldgs. SE1 28 D6
Guinness Bldgs. SE1 132 B4
Guinness Cl. E9 95 H7
Guinness Cl., Hayes 121 G3
Guinness Sq. SE1 36 D1
Guinness Trust Bldgs. SE11 35 H3
Guinness Trust Bldgs. SE11 131 H5
Guinness Trust Bldgs. SW3 31 J2
Guinness Trust Bldgs. SW9 151 H4
Guinness Trust Est. N16 94 B1
Holmleigh Rd.
Guion Rd. SW6 148 C2
Gull Cl., Wall. 200 E7
Gulland Wk. N1 93 J6
Clephane Rd.
Gulliver Cl., Nthlt. 103 F1
Gulliver Rd., Sid. 175 H2
Gulliver St. SE16 133 J3
Gulston Wk. SW3 32 A2
Gulston Wk. W11 108 C6
Basing St.
Gumleigh Rd. W5 125 F4
Gumley Gdns., Islw. 144 D3
Gumping Rd., Orp. 207 F2
Gun St. E1 21 F2
Gun St. E1 112 C5
Gundulph Rd., Brom. 191 J3
Gunmakers La. E3 113 H1
Gunnell Cl. SE26 170 D5
Gunnell Cl., Croy. 188 D6
Gunner La. SE18 136 D5
Gunners Gro. E4 62 C3
Gunners Rd. SW18 167 G2
Gunnersbury Av. W3 126 A3
Gunnersbury Av. W4 126 A3
Gunnersbury Av. W5 125 J1
Gunnersbury Cl. W4 126 B5
Grange Rd.
Gunnersbury Ct. W3 126 B2
Bollo La.
Gunnersbury Cres. W3 126 A2
Gunnersbury Dr. W5 125 J2
Gunnersbury Gdns. W3 126 A2
Gunnersbury La. W3 126 A3
Gunnersbury Ms. W4 126 B5
Chiswick High Rd.
Gunnersbury Pk. W3 125 J4
Gunnersbury Pk. W5 125 J4
Gunning St. SE18 137 H4
Gunpowder Sq. EC4 19 F3
Gunstor Rd. N16 94 B4
Gunter Gro. SW10 30 C6
Gunter Gro. SW10 129 F6
Gunter Gro., Edg. 70 D1
Gunterstone Rd. W14 128 B4
Gunthorpe St. E1 21 G2
Gunthorpe St. E1 112 C6
Gunton Rd. E5 95 E3
Gunton Rd. SW17 168 A6
Gunwhale Cl. SE16 133 G1
Gurdon Rd. SE7 135 G5
Gurnell Gro. W13 104 C4

Name	No.	Grid
Gurney Cl. E15	96/97	E5
Gurney Rd.		
Gurney Cl. E17	77	G1
Gurney Cl., Bark.	98	E6
Gurney Cres., Croy.	201	F1
Gurney Dr. N2	73	F5
Gurney Rd. E15	96	E5
Gurney Rd., Cars.	200	A4
Gurney Rd., Nthlt.	102	B3
Guthrie St. SW3	**31**	**G3**
Gutter La. EC2	**20**	**A3**
Gutter La. EC2	111	J6
Guy Barnett Gro. SE3	155	G3
Casterbridge Rd.		
Guy Rd., Wall.	200	D3
Guy St. SE1	**28**	**C3**
Guy St. SE1	132	A2
Guyatt Gdns., Mitch.	186	A2
Ormerod Gdns.		
Guyscliff Rd. SE13	154	C5
Gwalior Rd. SW15	148	A3
Felsham Rd.		
Gwendolen Av. SW15	148	A5
Gwendolen Cl. SW15	148	A5
Gwendoline Av. E13	115	H1
Gwendwr Rd. W14	128	B5
Gwillim Cl., Sid.	158	A5
Gwydor Rd., Beck.	189	G4
Gwydyr Rd., Brom.	191	F3
Gwyn Cl. SW6	129	F7
Gwynne Av., Croy.	189	G7
Gwynne Cl. W4	127	F6
Gwynne Pk. Av.,	64	C6
Wdf.Grn.		
Gwynne Pl. WC1	**10**	**D4**
Gwynne Rd. SW11	149	G2
Gylcote Cl. SE5	152	A4
Gyles Pk., Stan.	69	F1
Gyllyngdune Gdns.,	99	J2
Ilf.		

H

Name	No.	Grid
Ha-Ha Rd. SE18	136	C6
Haarlem Rd. W14	128	A3
Haberdasher Pl. N1	**12**	**C3**
Haberdasher St. N1	**12**	**C3**
Haberdasher St. N1	112	A3
Habgood Rd., Loug.	48	B3
Haccombe Rd. SW19	167	F6
Haydons Rd.		
Hackbridge Grn.,	200	A2
Wall.		
Hackbridge Pk.	200	A2
Gdns., Cars.		
Hackbridge Rd., Wall.	200	A2
Hackford Rd. SW9	151	F1
Hackforth Cl., Barn.	39	H5
Hackington Cres.,	172	A6
Beck.		
Hackney Cl., Borwd.	38	D5
Hackney Gro. E8	94/95	E6
Reading La.		
Hackney Rd. E2	**13**	**F4**
Hackney Rd. E2	112	C3
Hadden Rd. SE28	137	H3
Hadden Way, Grnf.	86	A6
Haddington Rd.,	172	D3
Brom.		
Haddo St. SE10	134	B6
Haddon Cl., Borwd.	38	A3
Haddon Cl., Enf.	44	D6
Haddon Cl., N.Mal.	183	F5
Haddon Gro., Sid.	158	A7
Haddon Rd., Sutt.	198	E4
Haddonfield SE8	133	G4
Hadfield Cl., Sthl.	103	F3
Adrienne Av.		
Hadfield Rd., Stai.	140	A6
Hadleigh Cl. E1	113	F4
Mantus Rd.		
Hadleigh Cl. SW20	184	C2
Hadleigh Rd. N9	44	E7
Hadleigh St. E2	113	F4
Hadleigh Wk. E6	116	B6
Hadley Cl. N21	43	G6
Hadley Common,	40	D2
Barn.		
Hadley Gdns. W4	126	D5
Hadley Gdns., Sthl.	123	F5
Hadley Grn., Barn.	40	C2
Hadley Grn. Rd.,	40	C2
Barn.		
Hadley Grn. W., Barn.	40	C2
Hadley Gro., Barn.	40	B2
Hadley Highstone,	40	C1
Barn.		
Hadley Ridge, Barn.	40	C3
Hadley Rd. (New	41	E4
Barnet), Barn.		
Hadley Rd., Belv.	139	F4
Hadley Rd., Mitch.	186	D4
Hadley St. NW1	92	B6
Hadley Way N21	43	G6
Hadlow Pl. SE19	170	D7
Hadlow Rd., Sid.	176	A4
Hadlow Rd., Well.	138	C7
Hadrian Cl., Wall.	201	E7
Hadrian Est. E2	**13**	**J2**
Hadrian Est. E2	112	D2
Hadrian St. SE10	134	E5
Hadrian Way, Stai.	140	B7
Hadrians Ride, Enf.	44	C5
Hadyn Pk. Rd. W12	127	G2
Hafer Rd. SW11	149	J4
Hafton Rd. SE6	173	E1
Haggard Rd., Twick.	144	E7
Haggerston Rd. E8	94	C7
Hague St. E2	**13**	**J4**
Green La.		
Haig Pl., Mord.	184	D6
Haig Rd., Stan.	53	F5
Haig Rd. E. E13	115	J3
Haig Rd. W. E13	115	J3
Haigville Gdns., Ilf.	81	E4
Hailes Cl. SW19	167	F6
North Rd.		
Hailey Rd., Erith	139	G2
Haileybury Av., Enf.	44	C6
Hailsham Av. SW2	169	F2
Hailsham Cl., Surb.	181	G7
Hailsham Dr., Har.	68	A3
Hailsham Rd. SW17	168	A6
Hailsham Ter. N18	59	J5
Haimo Rd. SE9	156	A5
Hainault Ct. E17	78	D4
Hainault Gore, Rom.	83	E5
Hainault Gro., Chig.	65	F4
Hainault Rd. E11	96	C1
Hainault Rd., Chig.	65	E3
Hainault Rd., Rom.	83	J2
Hainault Rd.	83	F6
(Chadwell Heath), Rom.		
Hainault Rd.	82	B3
(Hainault), Rom.		
Hainault St. SE9	175	E1
Hainault St., Ilf.	99	E2
Haines Wk., Mord.	184/185	E7
Dorchester Rd.		
Hainford Cl. SE4	153	G4
Haining Cl. W4	126	A5
Wellesley Rd.		
Hainthorpe Rd. SE27	169	H3
Hainton Cl. E1	113	E6
Halberd Ms. E5	94/95	E2
Knightland Rd.		
Halbutt Gdns., Dag.	101	F3
Halbutt St., Dag.	101	F4
Halcomb St. N1	112	B1
Halcot Av., Bexh.	159	H5
Halcrow St. E1	112/113	E5
Newark St.		
Halcyon Cl., Wem.	88	B3
Coffers Circle		
Haldan Rd. E4	62	C6
Haldane Cl. N10	58	B7
Haldane Pl. SW18	166	E1
Haldane Rd. E6	116	A3
Haldane Rd. SE28	118	D7
Haldane Rd. SW6	128	C7
Haldane Rd., Sthl.	103	J6
Haldon Cl., Chig.	65	H5
Arrowsmith Rd.		
Haldon Rd. SW18	148	C5
Hale, The E4	62	D7
Hale, The N17	76	D4
Hale Cl. E4	62	C3
Hale Cl., Edg.	54	C5
Hale Cl., Orp.	207	F4
Hale Dr. NW7	54	C6
Hale End Cl., Ruis.	66	A6
Hale End Rd. E4	62	D6
Hale End Rd. E17	78	D1
Hale End Rd.,	62	D7
Wdf.Grn.		
Hale Gdns. N17	76	D3
Hale Gdns. W3	126	A1
Hale Gro. Gdns. NW7	54	D5
Hale La. NW7	54	D5
Hale La., Edg.	54	B5
Hale Path SE27	169	H4
Hale Rd. E6	116	B4
Hale Rd. N17	76	D3
Hale St. E14	114	B7
Hale Wk. W7	104	B5
Halefield Rd. N17	76	D1
Hales St. SE8	134	A7
Deptford High St.		
Halesowen Rd.,	184	E7
Mord.		
Halesworth Cl. E5	95	F2
Theydon Rd.		
Halesworth Rd. SE13	154	B3
Haley Rd. NW4	71	J6
Half Acre, Brent.	125	G6
Half Acre Rd. W7	124	B1
Half Moon Ct. EC1	**19**	**J2**
Half Moon Cres. N1	**10**	**D1**
Half Moon Cres. N1	111	F2
Half Moon La. SE24	151	J6
Half Moon Pas. E1	**21**	**G4**
Half Moon St. W1	**24**	**E1**
Half Moon St. W1	130	B1
Halford Cl., Edg.	70	B2
Halford Rd. E10	78	D5
Halford Rd. SW6	128	D6
Halford Rd., Rich.	145	H5
Halfway St., Sid.	157	G7
Haliburton Rd., Twick.	144	D5
Haliday Wk. N1	94	A6
Halidon Cl. E9	95	F5
Urswick Rd.		
Halifax Rd., Enf.	43	J2
Halifax Rd., Grnf.	103	H1
Halifax St. SE26	171	E4
Halifield Dr., Belv.	138	E3
Haling Gro., S.Croy.	201	J7
Haling Pk., S.Croy.	201	J6
Haling Pk. Gdns.,	201	H6
S.Croy.		
Haling Pk. Rd.,	201	H5
S.Croy.		
Haling Rd., S.Croy.	202	A6
Halkin Arc. SW1	**24**	**B5**
Halkin Ms. SW1	130	A3
Halkin Ms. SW1	**24**	**B5**
Halkin Pl. SW1	**24**	**B5**
Halkin Pl. SW1	130	A3
Halkin St. SW1	**24**	**C4**
Halkin St. SW1	130	A2
Hall Av. N18	60	A6
Weir Hall Av.		
Hall Cl. W5	105	H5
Hall Ct., Tedd.	162	C5
Teddington Pk.		
Hall Dr. SE26	171	F5
Hall Dr. W7	104	B6
Hall Fm. Cl., Stan.	52	E4
Hall Fm. Dr., Twick.	144	A7
Hall Gdns. E4	61	J4
Hall Gate NW8	**6**	**D3**
Hall La. E4	61	H5
Hall La. NW4	71	G1
Hall La., Hayes	121	G7
Hall Oak Wk. NW6	90	C6
Maygrove Rd.		
Hall Pl. W2	**7**	**E6**
Hall Pl. W2	109	G4
Hall Pl. Cres., Bex.	159	J5
Hall Rd. E6	116	C1
Hall Rd. E15	96	D4
Hall Rd. NW8	**6**	**D4**
Hall Rd. NW8	109	F3
Hall Rd., Islw.	144	A5
Hall Rd., Rom.	82	C6
Hall St. EC1	**11**	**H3**
Hall St. EC1	111	H3
Hall St. N12	57	F5
Hall Vw. SE9	174	A2
Hallam Cl., Chis.	174	C5
Hallam Gdns., Pnr.	51	E7
Hallam Ms. W1	**16**	**E1**
Hallam Rd. N15	75	H4
Hallam Rd. SW13	147	H3
Hallam St. W1	**8**	**E6**
Halley Gdns. SE13	154	D4
Halley Rd. E7	97	J6
Halley Rd. E12	98	A6
Halley St. E14	113	H5
Hallfield Est. W2	**14**	**C4**
Hallfield Est. W2	109	F6
Halliards, The, Walt.	178	A3
Felix Rd.		
Halliday Sq., Sthl.	124	A1
Halliford St. N1	93	J7
Hallingbury Ct. E17	78	B3
Halliwell Rd. SW2	151	F6
Halliwick Rd. N10	74	A1
Hallmark Trd. Est.	88	C4
NW10		
Great Cen. Way		
Hallowell Av., Croy.	200	E4
Hallowell Cl., Mitch.	186	A3
Hallowes Cres., Wat.	50	A3
Hayling Rd.		
Hallowfield Way,	185	H3
Mitch.		
Hallsville Rd. E16	115	F6
Hallswelle Rd. NW11	72	C5
Hallywell Cres. E6	116	C5
Halons Rd. SE9	156	D7
Halpin Pl. SE17	**36**	**C2**
Halsbrook Rd. SE3	156	A3
Halsbury Cl., Stan.	52	E4
Halsbury Rd. W12	127	H1
Halsbury Rd. E., Nthlt.	85	J4
Halsbury Rd. W.,	85	H5
Nthlt.		
Halsend, Hayes	122	B1
Halsey Ms. SW3	**31**	**J1**
Halsey St. SW3	**31**	**J1**
Halsey St. SW3	129	J4
Halsham Cres., Bark.	99	J6
Halsmere Rd. SE5	151	H1
Halstead Cl., Croy.	201	J3
Charles St.		
Halstead Ct. N1	**12**	**C2**
Halstead Gdns. N21	60	A1
Halstead Rd. E11	79	G5
Halstead Rd. N21	59	J1
Halstead Rd., Enf.	44	B4
Halstow Rd. NW10	108	A3
Halstow Rd. SE10	135	G5
Halsway, Hayes	122	A1
Halt Robin La., Belv.	139	H4
Halt Robin Rd.		
Halt Robin Rd., Belv.	139	G4
Halter Cl., Borwd.	38	D5
Clydesdale Rd.		
Halton Cross St. N1	111	H1
Halton Pl. N1	111	J1
Dibden St.		
Halton Rd. N1	93	H7
Ham, The, Brent.	125	F7
Ham Cl., Rich.	163	F3
Ham Common, Rich.	163	J4
Ham Fm. Rd., Rich.	163	G4
Ham Gate Av., Rich.	163	G3
Ham Pk. Rd. E7	97	F7
Ham Pk. Rd. E15	97	F7
Ham Ridings, Rich.	163	J5
Ham St., Rich.	163	F2
Ham Vw., Croy.	189	H6
Ham Yd. W1	**17**	**H5**
Hambalt Rd. SW4	150	C5
Hamble Ct., Kings.T.	163	G7
Hamble St. SW6	149	E3
Hamble Wk., Nthlt.	103	G2
Brabazon Rd.		
Hambledon Gdns.	188	C3
SE25		
Hambledon Pl. SE21	170	B1
Hambledon Rd. SW18	148	C7
Hambledown Rd.,	157	G7
Sid.		
Hambleton Cl.,	197	J2
Wor.Pk.		
Cotswold Way		
Hambridge Way SW2	151	G7
Hambro Av., Brom.	205	G1
Hambro Rd. SW16	168	D6
Hambrook Rd. SE25	188	E3
Hambrough Rd., Sthl.	122	E1
Hamden Cres., Dag.	101	H3
Hamel Cl., Har.	69	G3
Hamelin St. E14	114	C6
Halley St.		
Hameway E6	116	D4
Hamfrith Rd. E15	97	F6
Hamilton Av. N9	44	D7
Hamilton Av., Ilf.	81	E4
Hamilton Av., Surb.	196	B1
Hamilton Av., Sutt.	198	B2
Hamilton Cl. N17	76	C3
Hamilton Cl. NW8	**6**	**E4**
Hamilton Cl. NW8	109	G3
Hamilton Cl. SE16	133	H2
Somerford Way		
Hamilton Cl., Barn.	41	H4
Hamilton Cl., Stan.	52	C2
Hamilton Ct. W5	105	J7
Hamilton Ct. W9	**6**	**C3**
Hamilton Cres. N13	59	G4
Hamilton Cres., Har.	85	F3
Hamilton Cres.,	143	H5
Houns.		
Hamilton Gdns. NW8	**6**	**D3**
Hamilton Gdns. NW8	109	F3
Hamilton La. N5	93	H4
Hamilton Pk.		
Hamilton Ms. W1	**24**	**D3**
Hamilton Pk. N5	93	H4
Hamilton Pk. W. N5	93	H4
Hamilton Pl. N19	92	D3
Wedmore St.		
Hamilton Pl. W1	**24**	**C2**
Hamilton Pl. W1	130	A1
Hamilton Pl., Sun.	160	B7
Hamilton Rd. E15	115	E3
Hamilton Rd. E17	77	H2
Hamilton Rd. N2	73	F3
Hamilton Rd. N9	60	C7
Hamilton Rd. NW10	89	G5
Hamilton Rd. NW11	72	A7
Hamilton Rd. SE27	170	A4
Hamilton Rd. SW19	167	E7
Hamilton Rd. W4	126	E2
Hamilton Rd. W5	105	H7
Hamilton Rd., Barn.	41	H4
Hamilton Rd., Bexh.	159	E2
Hamilton Rd., Brent.	125	G6

Entry	Page	Grid
Hamilton Rd., Har.	68	B5
Hamilton Rd., Hayes	102	B7
Hamilton Rd., Ilf.	98	E4
Hamilton Rd., Sid.	176	A4
Hamilton Rd., Sthl.	123	F1
Hamilton Rd., Th.Hth.	188	A3
Hamilton Rd., Twick.	162	B1
Hamilton Rd., Wat.	50	B3
Hamilton Sq. SE1	**28**	**C3**
Hamilton St. SE8	134	A6
Deptford High St.		
Hamilton Ter. NW8	**6**	**D3**
Hamilton Ter. NW8	109	E2
Hamilton Way N3	56	D6
Hamilton Way N13	59	H4
Hamlea Cl. SE12	155	F5
Hamlet, The SE5	152	A3
Hamlet Cl. SE13	154/155	E4
Old Rd.		
Hamlet Gdns. W6	127	G4
Hamlet Rd. SE19	170	C7
Hamlet Sq. NW2	90	B3
The Vale		
Hamlet Way SE1	**28**	**C3**
Hamlets Way E3	113	J4
Hamlin Cres., Pnr.	66	C5
Hamlyn Cl., Edg.	53	H3
Hamlyn Gdns. SE19	170	B7
Hammelton Grn. SW9	151	H1
Cromwell Rd.		
Hammelton Rd., Brom.	191	F1
Hammers La. NW7	55	G5
Hammersmith Br. SW13	127	H5
Hammersmith Br. W6	127	H5
Hammersmith Br. Rd. W6	127	J5
Hammersmith Bdy. W6	127	J4
Hammersmith Flyover W6	127	J5
Hammersmith Gro. W6	127	J3
Hammersmith Rd. W6	128	A4
Hammersmith Rd. W14	128	A4
Hammersmith Ter. W6	127	G5
Hammet Cl., Hayes	102	D5
Willow Tree La.		
Hammett St. EC3	**21**	**F5**
Hammond Av., Mitch.	186	B2
Hammond Cl., Barn.	40	B5
Hammond Cl., Grnf.	86	A5
Lilian Board Way		
Hammond Cl., Hmptn.	179	G1
Hammond Rd., Enf.	45	E2
Hammond Rd., Sthl.	123	E3
Hammond St. NW5	92	C6
Hammond Way SE28	118	B7
Oriole Way		
Hammonds Cl., Dag.	100	C3
Hamonde Cl., Edg.	54	B2
Hampden Av., Beck.	189	H2
Hampden Cl. NW1	**9**	**J2**
Hampden Gurney St. W1	**15**	**J4**
Hampden La. N17	76	C1
Hampden Rd. N8	75	G4
Hampden Rd. N10	58	A7
Hampden Rd. N17	76	D1
Hampden Rd. N19	92	D2
Holloway Rd.		
Hampden Rd., Beck.	189	H2
Hampden Rd., Har.	67	J3
Hampden Rd., Kings.T.	182	A3
Hampden Sq. N14	58	B1
Osidge La.		
Hampden Way N14	58	B2
Hampshire Cl. N18	60/61	E5
Berkshire Gdns.		
Hampshire Hog La. W6	127	H4
King St.		
Hampshire Rd. N22	59	F7
Hampshire St. NW5	92	D6
Torriano Av.		
Hampson Way SW8	151	F1
Hampstead Cl. SE28	138	B1
Hampstead Gdns. NW11	72	D6
Hampstead Gdns., Rom.	82	B5
Hampstead Grn. NW3	91	H5
Hampstead Gro. NW3	91	F3
Hampstead Hts. N2	73	F4
Hampstead High St. NW3	91	F4
Hampstead Hill Gdns. NW3	91	G4
Hampstead La. N6	73	G7
Hampstead La. NW3	73	G7
Hampstead Rd. NW1	**9**	**F2**
Hampstead Rd. NW1	110	C2
Hampstead Sq. NW3	91	F3
Hampstead Wk. E3	113	J1
Parnell Rd.		
Hampstead Way NW11	91	F1
Hampton Cl. N11	58	B5
Balmoral Av.		
Hampton Cl. NW6	108	D3
Hampton Cl. SW20	165	J7
Hampton Cl. N1	93	H6
Upper St.		
Hampton Ct. Av., E.Mol.	180	A5
Hampton Ct. Cres., E.Mol.	180	A3
Hampton Ct. Palace, E.Mol.	180	C3
Hampton Ct. Par., E.Mol.	180	B4
Creek Rd.		
Hampton Ct. Rd., E.Mol.	180	C3
Hampton Ct. Rd., Hmptn.	179	J2
Hampton Ct. Rd., Kings.T.	180	C3
Hampton Ct. Way, E.Mol.	180	B6
Hampton Ct. Way, T.Ditt.	194	B2
Hampton Fm. Ind. Est., Felt.	161	F3
Hampton La., Felt.	161	E4
Hampton Mead, Loug.	48	E3
Hampton Ms. NW10	106	D3
Minerva Rd.		
Hampton Ri., Har.	69	H6
Hampton Rd. E4	61	J5
Hampton Rd. E7	97	H5
Hampton Rd. E11	96	D1
Hampton Rd., Croy.	187	J6
Hampton Rd., Hmptn.	162	A5
Hampton Rd., Ilf.	99	E4
Hampton Rd., Tedd.	162	A5
Hampton Rd., Twick.	162	A3
Hampton Rd., Wor.Pk.	197	G2
Hampton Rd. E., Felt.	161	F3
Hampton Rd. W., Felt.	160	E2
Hampton St. SE1	**35**	**H2**
Hampton St. SE1	131	H4
Hampton St. SE17	**35**	**H2**
Hampton St. SE17	131	H4
Hamshades Cl., Sid.	175	J3
Hanah Ct. SW19	166	A7
Hanameel St. E16	135	H1
Hanbury Cl. NW4	71	J3
Parson St.		
Hanbury Dr. N21	43	F5
Hanbury Ms. N1	111	J1
Mary St.		
Hanbury Rd. N17	76	E2
Hanbury Rd. W3	126	B2
Hanbury St. E1	**21**	**F1**
Hanbury St. E1	112	C5
Hancock Ct., Borwd.	38	C1
Hancock Rd. E3	114	C3
Hancock Rd. SE19	170	A6
Hand Ct. WC1	**18**	**D2**
Hand Ct. WC1	111	F5
Handa Wk. N1	94	A6
Clephane Rd.		
Handcroft Rd., Croy.	187	H7
Handel Cl., Edg.	53	J6
Handel Pl. NW10	88	D6
Mitchellbrook Way		
Handel St. WC1	**10**	**A5**
Handel St. WC1	110	E4
Handel Way, Edg.	54	A7
Handen Rd. SE12	155	E5
Handforth Rd. SW9	**34**	**E7**
Handforth Rd. SW9	131	G7
Handforth Rd., Ilf.	98/99	E3
Winston Way		
Handley Rd. E9	95	F7
Handowe Cl. NW4	71	G4
Hands Wk. E16	115	G6
Handside Cl., Wor.Pk.	198	A1
Carters Cl.		
Handsworth Av. E4	62	D6
Handsworth Rd. N17	76	A3
Handsworth Way, Wat.	50	A3
Hayling Rd.		
Handtrough Way, Bark.	116/117	E2
Fresh Wf. Rd.		
Hanford Cl. SW18	166	D1
Hanford Row SW19	165	J6
Hangar Ruding, Wat.	51	F3
Hanger Grn. W5	105	J3
Hanger La. W5	105	J4
Hanger Vale La. W5	105	J6
Hanger Vw. Way W3	106	A6
Hankey Pl. SE1	**28**	**C4**
Hankey Pl. SE1	132	A2
Hankins La. NW7	54	E3
Hanley Pl., Beck.	172	A7
Hanley Rd. N4	93	E1
Hanmer Wk. N7	93	F3
Newington Barrow Way		
Hannah Cl. NW10	88	C4
Hannah Cl., Beck.	190	C3
Hannah Mary Way SE1	**37**	**J2**
Hannah Ms., Wall.	200	C7
Hannay La. N8	74	D7
Hannay Wk. SW16	168	D2
Hannell Rd. SW6	128	B7
Hannen Rd. SE27	169	H3
Norwood High St.		
Hannibal Rd. E1	113	F5
Hannibal Rd., Stai.	140	A7
Hannibal Way, Croy.	201	F5
Hannington Rd. SW4	150	B3
Hanover Av. E16	135	G1
Hanover Av., Felt.	160	A1
Hanover Cl., Rich.	126	A7
Hanover Cl., Sutt.	198	C4
Hanover Ct. W12	127	G1
Uxbridge Rd.		
Hanover Dr., Chis.	175	F4
Hanover Gdns. SE11	**34**	**E6**
Hanover Gdns. SE11	131	G6
Hanover Gdns., Ilf.	65	F7
Hanover Gate NW1	**7**	**H4**
Hanover Gate Mans. NW1	109	H3
Hanover Pk. SE15	152	D1
Hanover Pl. E3	113	J3
Brokesley St.		
Hanover Pl. WC2	**18**	**B4**
Hanover Rd. N15	76	C4
Hanover Rd. NW10	89	J7
Hanover Rd. SW19	167	F7
Hanover Sq. W1	**17**	**E4**
Hanover St. W1	**17**	**E4**
Hanover St. W1	110	B6
Hanover St., Croy.	201	H3
Abbey Rd.		
Hanover Ter. NW1	**7**	**J4**
Hanover Ter. NW1	109	H3
Hanover Ter. Ms. NW1	**7**	**H4**
Hanover Ter., Islw.	144	D1
Hanover W. Ind. Est. NW10	106	D2
Hanover Yd. N1	**11**	**H1**
Hans Cres. SW1	**23**	**J5**
Hans Cres. SW1	129	J3
Hans Pl. SW1	**24**	**A5**
Hans Pl. SW1	129	J3
Hans Rd. SW3	**23**	**J5**
Hans Rd. SW3	129	J3
Hans St. SW1	**24**	**A6**
Hansard Ms. W14	128	A2
Holland Rd.		
Hansart Way, Enf.	43	G1
The Ridgeway		
Hanselin Cl., Stan.	52	C5
Chenduit Way		
Hansen Dr. N21	43	F5
Hansha Dr., Edg.	70	D1
Hansler Gro., E.Mol.	180	A4
Hansler Rd. SE22	152	C5
Hansol Rd., Bexh.	158	E5
Hanson Cl. SW12	150	B7
Hanson Cl. SW14	146	C3
Hanson Cl., Beck.	172	B6
Hanson Cl., Loug.	49	F2
Hanson Dr.		
Hanson Cl., West Dr.	120	C3
Hanson Dr., Loug.	49	F2
Hanson Gdns., Sthl.	123	E2
Hanson Grn., Loug.	49	F2
Hanson Dr.		
Hanson St. W1	**17**	**F1**
Hanson St. W1	110	C5
Hanway Pl. W1	**17**	**H3**
Hanway Rd. W7	104	A6
Hanway St. W1	**17**	**H3**
Hanway St. W1	110	D6
Hanworth Rd., Felt.	160	B1
Hanworth Rd., Hmptn.	161	H6
Hanworth Rd., Houns.	143	H3
Hanworth Rd., Sun.	160	A7
Hanworth Ter., Houns.	143	H4
Hanworth Trd. Est., Felt.	161	E3
Hapgood Cl., Grnf.	86	A5
Harads Pl. E1	**21**	**H6**
Harben Rd. NW6	91	F7
Harberson Rd. E15	115	F1
Harberson Rd. SW12	168	B1
Harberton Rd. N19	92	C1
Harbet Rd. E4	61	G5
Harbet Rd. N18	61	G5
Harbet Rd. W2	**15**	**F2**
Harbex Cl., Bex.	159	H1
Harbinger Rd. E14	134	B4
Harbledown Rd. SW6	148	D1
Harborough Av., Sid.	157	H7
Harborough Rd. SW16	169	F4
Harbour Av. SW10	149	F1
Harbour Ex. Sq. E14	134	B2
Harbour Rd. SE5	151	J3
Harbridge Av. SW15	147	F7
Harbut Rd. SW11	149	G4
Harcombe Rd. N16	94	B3
Harcourt Av. E12	98	C4
Harcourt Av., Edg.	54	C3
Harcourt Av., Sid.	158	C6
Harcourt Av., Wall.	200	B4
Harcourt Cl., Islw.	144	D3
Harcourt Fld., Wall.	200	B4
Harcourt Rd. E15	115	F2
Harcourt Rd. N22	74	D1
Harcourt Rd. SE4	153	H4
Harcourt Rd. SW19	166	D7
Russell Rd.		
Harcourt Rd., Bexh.	159	E4
Harcourt Rd., Th.Hth.	187	F6
Harcourt Rd., Wall.	200	B4
Harcourt St. W1	**15**	**H2**
Harcourt St. W1	109	H5
Harcourt Ter. SW10	**30**	**B4**
Harcourt Ter. SW10	129	E5
Hardcastle Cl., Croy.	188	D6
Hardcourts Cl., W.Wick.	204	B3
Hardel Ri. SW2	169	H2
Hardel Wk. SW2	151	G7
Papworth Way		
Hardens Manorway SE7	136	A3
Harders Rd. SE15	152	E2
Hardess St. SE24	151	J3
Herne Hill Rd.		
Hardie Cl. NW10	88	D5
Hardie Rd., Dag.	101	J3
Harding Cl. SE17	**35**	**J5**
Harding Cl., Croy.	202	C3
Harding Ho., Hayes	102	B6
Harding Rd., Bexh.	159	F2
Hardinge La. E1	113	F6
Hardinge St.		
Hardinge Rd. N18	60	B5
Hardinge Rd. NW10	107	H1
Hardinge St. E1	113	F6
Harding's Cl., Kings.T.	181	J1
Hardings La. SE20	171	G6
Hardman Rd. SE7	135	H5
Hardman Rd., Kings.T.	181	H2
Hardwick Cl., Stan.	53	F5
Hardwick Grn. W13	105	E5
Hardwick St. EC1	**11**	**F4**
Hardwick St. EC1	111	G3
Hardwicke Av., Houns.	143	G1
Hardwicke Rd. N13	58	E6
Hardwicke Rd. W4	126	D4
Hardwicke Rd., Rich.	163	F4
Hardwicke St., Bark.	117	F1
Hardwicks Way SW18	148	D5
Buckhold Rd.		
Hardwidge St. SE1	**28**	**D3**
Hardy Av. E16	135	G1
Wesley Av.		
Hardy Av., Ruis.	84	B5
Hardy Cl., Barn.	40	B6
Hardy Cl., Pnr.	66	D7
Hardy Rd. E4	61	J6
Hardy Rd. SE3	135	F7
Hardy Rd. SW19	167	E7
Hardy Way, Enf.	43	G1
Hare & Billet Rd. SE3	154	D1
Hare Ct. EC4	**19**	**E4**
Hare La., Esher	194	B6
Hare Marsh E2	**13**	**H5**
Hare Pl. EC4	**19**	**F4**
Hare Row E2	113	E2
Hare St. SE18	136	D3
Hare Wk. N1	**13**	**E2**
Hare Wk. N1	112	B2
Harebell Dr. E6	116	D5

Harecastle Cl., Hayes 102/103 E4
Braunston Dr.
Harecourt Rd. N1 93 J6
Haredale Rd. SE24 151 J4
Haredon Cl. SE23 153 F7
Harefield, Esher 194 B4
Harefield Cl., Enf. 43 G1
Harefield Ms. SE4 153 J3
Harefield Rd. N8 74 D5
Harefield Rd. SE4 153 J3
Harefield Rd. SW16 169 F7
Harefield Rd., Sid. 176 D2
Haresfield Rd., Dag. 101 G6
Harewood Av. NW1 7 H6
Harewood Av. NW1 109 H4
Harewood Av., Nthlt. 85 E7
Harewood Cl., Nthlt. 85 F7
Harewood Dr., Ilf. 80 C2
Harewood Pl. W1 16 E4
Harewood Rd. SW19 167 H6
Harewood Rd., Islw. 124 C7
Harewood Rd., S.Croy. 202 B6
Harewood Rd., Wat. 50 B3
Harewood Row NW1 15 H1
Harewood Ter., Sthl. 123 F4
Harfield Gdns. SE5 152 B3
Harfield Rd., Sun. 178 D2
Harford Cl. E4 46 B7
Harford Rd. E4 46 B7
Harford St. E1 113 H4
Harford Wk. N2 73 G5
Hargood Cl., Har. 69 H6
Hargood Rd. SE3 155 J1
Hargrave Pk. N19 92 C2
Hargrave Pl. N7 92 D5
Brecknock Rd.
Hargrave Rd. N19 92 C2
Hargwyne St. SW9 151 F3
Haringey Pk. N8 75 E6
Haringey Pas. N4 75 H6
Haringey Pas. N8 75 G4
Haringey Rd. N8 74 E4
Harington Ter. N9 60 A3
Harington Ter. N18 60 A3
Harkett Cl., Har. 68 C2
Byron Rd.
Harkett Ct., Har. 68 C2
Harland Av., Croy. 202 C3
Harland Av., Sid. 175 G3
Harland Cl. SW19 184 E3
Harland Rd. SE12 173 G1
Harlands Gro., Orp. 206/207 E4
Pinecrest Gdns.
Harlech Gdns., Houns. 122 C6
Harlech Gdns., Pnr. 66 D7
Harlech Rd. N14 59 E3
Harlech Twr. W3 126 B2
Harlequin Av., Brent. 124 D6
Harlequin Cl., Hayes 102 D5
Cygnet Way
Harlequin Cl., Islw. 144 B5
Harlequin Ho., Erith 138/139 E3
Kale Rd.
Harlequin Rd., Tedd. 162 E7
Harlescott Rd. SE15 153 G4
Harlesden Gdns. NW10 107 F1
Harlesden La. NW10 107 G1
Harlesden Rd. NW10 107 G1
Harleston Cl. E5 95 F2
Theydon Rd.
Harley Cl., Wem. 87 G6
Harley Ct. E11 79 G7
Blake Hall Rd.
Harley Cres., Har. 68 A4
Harley Gdns. SW10 30 D4
Harley Gdns. SW10 129 F5
Harley Gdns., Orp. 207 H4
Harley Gro. E3 113 J3
Harley Pl. W1 16 D2
Harley Pl. W1 110 B5
Harley Rd. NW3 91 G7
Harley Rd. NW10 106 E2
Harley Rd., Har. 68 A4
Harley St. W1 16 D2
Harley St. W1 110 B4
Harleyford, Brom. 191 H1
Harleyford Rd. SE11 34 C5
Harleyford Rd. SE11 131 F6
Harleyford St. SE11 34 E6
Harleyford St. SE11 131 G6
Harlinger St. SE18 136 B3
Harlington Cl., Hayes 121 F7
New Rd.
Harlington Rd., Bexh. 159 E3
Harlington Rd., Houns. 141 J4
Harlington Rd. E., Felt. 142 B7
Harlington Rd. W., Felt. 142 B6
Harlow Rd. N13 60 A3
Harlyn Dr., Pnr. 66 B3
Harman Av., Wdf.Grn. 63 F7
Harman Cl. E4 62 D4
Harman Cl. NW2 90 B3
Harman Dr. NW2 90 B3
Harman Dr., Sid. 157 J6
Harman Rd., Enf. 44 C5
Harmondsworth La., West Dr. 120 B6
Harmondsworth Rd., West Dr. 120 B5
Harmony Cl. NW11 72 B5
Harmony Way NW4 71 J4
Victoria Rd.
Harmood Gro. NW1 92 B7
Clarence Way
Harmood Pl. NW1 92 B7
Harmood St.
Harmood St. NW1 92 B7
Harmsworth Ms. SE11 27 G6
Harmsworth St. SE17 35 G4
Harmsworth St. SE17 131 H5
Harmsworth Way N20 56 C1
Harness Rd. SE28 138 A2
Harold Av., Belv. 139 F5
Harold Av., Hayes 121 J3
Harold Est. SE1 28 E6
Harold Est. SE1 132 B3
Harold Gibbons Ct. SE7 135 J6
Victoria Way
Harold Pl. SE11 34 E4
Harold Pl. SE11 131 G5
Harold Rd. E4 62 C4
Harold Rd. E11 96 E1
Harold Rd. E13 115 H1
Harold Rd. N8 75 F5
Harold Rd. N15 76 C5
Harold Rd. NW10 106 D3
Harold Rd. SE19 170 A7
Harold Rd., Sutt. 199 G4
Harold Rd., Wdf.Grn. 79 G1
Haroldstone Rd. E17 77 G5
Harp All. EC4 19 G3
Harp Island Cl. NW10 88 D2
Harp La. EC3 20 D6
Harp Rd. W7 104 C4
Harpenden Rd. E12 97 J2
Harpenden Rd. SE27 169 H3
Harper Cl. N14 42 C5
Alexandra Ct.
Harper Rd. E6 116 C6
Harper Rd. SE1 27 J5
Harper Rd. SE1 131 J3
Harpers Yd. N17 76 C1
Ruskin Rd.
Harpley Sq. E1 113 F3
Harpour Rd., Bark. 99 F6
Harpsden St. SW11 150 A1
Harpur Ms. WC1 18 C1
Harpur St. WC1 18 C1
Harpur St. WC1 111 F5
Harraden Rd. SE3 155 J1
Harrap St. E14 114 C7
Harrier Av. E11 79 H6
Eastern Av.
Harrier Ms. SE28 137 G3
Harrier Rd. NW9 71 E2
Harrier Way E6 116 C5
Harriers Cl. W5 105 H7
Harries Rd., Hayes 102 C4
Harriet Cl. E8 112 D1
Harriet Gdns., Croy. 202 D2
Harriet St. SW1 24 A4
Harriet Tubman Cl. SW2 151 G7
Harriet Wk. SW1 24 A4
Harriet Wk. SW1 129 J2
Harringay Gdns. N8 75 H4
Harringay Rd. N15 75 H5
Harrington Cl. NW10 88 D3
Harrington Cl., Croy. 200 E2
Harrington Ct. W10 108 C3
Dart St.
Harrington Gdns. SW7 30 B2
Harrington Gdns. SW7 129 E4
Harrington Hill E5 95 E1
Harrington Rd. E11 97 E1
Harrington Rd. SE25 188 E4
Harrington Rd. SW7 30 E1
Harrington Rd. SW7 129 G4
Harrington Sq. NW1 9 F2
Harrington Sq. NW1 110 C2
Harrington St. NW1 9 F3
Harrington St. NW1 110 C3
Harrington Way SE18 136 A3
Harriott Cl. SE10 135 F4
Harris Cl., Enf. 43 H1
Harris Cl., Houns. 143 G1
Harris Rd., Bexh. 159 E1
Harris Rd., Dag. 101 F5
Harris St. E17 77 J7
Harris St. SE5 132 A7
Harrison Cl. N20 57 H1
Harrison Rd., Dag. 101 H6
Harrison St. WC1 10 B4
Harrison St. WC1 111 E3
Harrisons Ri., Croy. 201 H3
Harrogate Rd., Wat. 50 C3
Harrold Rd., Dag. 100 B5
Harrow Av., Enf. 44 C6
Harrow Cl., Chess. 195 G7
Harrow Dr. N9 60 C1
Harrow Flds. Gdns., Har. 86 B3
Harrow Grn. E11 96/97 E3
Harrow Rd.
Harrow La. E14 114 C7
Harrow Manorway SE2 138 C1
Harrow Pk., Har. 86 B2
Harrow Pas., Kings.T. 181 G2
Market Pl.
Harrow Pl. E1 21 E3
Harrow Pl. E1 112 B6
Harrow Rd. E6 116 B1
Harrow Rd. E11 97 E3
Harrow Rd. NW10 107 H3
Harrow Rd. W2 14 A2
Harrow Rd. W2 108 C4
Harrow Rd. W9 108 C4
Harrow Rd. W10 108 A4
Harrow Rd., Bark. 117 H1
Harrow Rd., Cars. 199 H5
Harrow Rd., Ilf. 99 F4
Harrow Rd., Wem. 87 F5
Harrow Rd. (Tokyngton), Wem. 88 B6
Harrow Vw., Har. 68 A4
Harrow Vw., Hayes 102 A6
Harrow Vw. Rd. W5 105 E4
Harrow Way, Wat. 50 E3
Harrow Weald Pk., Har. 52 A6
Harroway Rd. SW11 149 G2
Harrowby St. W1 15 H3
Harrowby St. W1 109 H6
Harrowdene Cl., Wem. 87 G4
Harrowdene Gdns., Tedd. 162 D6
Harrowdene Rd., Wem. 87 G3
Harrowes Meade, Edg. 54 A3
Harrowgate Rd. E9 95 H6
Hart Cres., Chig. 65 J5
Hart Gro. W5 126 A1
Hart Gro., Sthl. 103 G5
Hart St. EC3 20 E5
Harte Rd., Houns. 143 F2
Hartfield Av., Borwd. 38 A5
Hartfield Av., Nthlt. 102 B2
Hartfield Cl., Borwd. 38 A5
Hartfield Cres. SW19 166 C7
Hartfield Cres., W.Wick. 205 G3
Hartfield Gro. SE20 189 E1
Hartfield Rd. SW19 166 C7
Hartfield Rd., Chess. 195 G5
Hartfield Rd., W.Wick. 205 G4
Hartfield Ter. E3 114 A2
Hartford Av., Har. 68 D3
Hartford Rd., Bex. 159 G6
Hartford Rd., Epsom 196 A6
Hartforde Rd., Borwd. 38 A2
Hartham Cl. N7 93 E5
Hartham Cl., Islw. 144 D1
Hartham Rd. N7 92 E5
Hartham Rd. N17 76 C2
Hartham Rd., Islw. 144 C1
Harting Rd. SE9 174 B4
Hartington Cl., Har. 86 B4
Hartington Ct. W4 126 B7
Hartington Rd. E16 115 H6
Hartington Rd. E17 77 H6
Hartington Rd. SW8 150 E1
Hartington Rd. W4 126 B7
Hartington Rd. W13 105 E7
Hartington Rd., Sthl. 122 E2
Hartington Rd., Twick. 144 E7
Hartismere Rd. SW6 128 C7
Hartlake Rd. E9 95 G6
Hartland Cl. N21 43 J6
Elmscott Gdns.
Hartland Cl., Edg. 54 A2
Hartland Dr., Edg. 54 A2
Hartland Dr., Ruis. 84 B3
Hartland Rd. E15 97 F7
Hartland Rd. N11 57 J5
Hartland Rd. NW1 92 B7
Hartland Rd. NW6 108 C2
Hartland Rd., Hmptn. 161 H4
Hartland Rd., Islw. 144 D3
Hartland Rd., Mord. 184 D7
Hartland Way, Croy. 203 H2
Hartland Way, Mord. 184 C7
Hartlands Cl., Bex. 159 F6
Hartlepool Ct. E16 136/137 E2
Barge Ho. Rd.
Hartley Av. E6 116 B1
Hartley Av. NW7 55 F5
Hartley Cl. NW7 55 F5
Hartley Cl., Brom. 192 C2
Hartley Rd. E11 97 F1
Hartley Rd., Croy. 187 H7
Hartley Rd., Well. 138 C7
Hartley St. E2 113 F3
Hartmann Rd. E16 136 A1
Hartnoll St. N7 93 F5
Eden Gro.
Harton Cl., Brom. 192 A1
Harton Rd. N9 61 E2
Harton St. SE8 154 A1
Harts Gro., Wdf.Grn. 63 G5
Harts La. SE14 133 H7
Harts La., Bark. 98 E6
Hartsbourne Av., Bushey 51 J2
Hartsbourne Cl., Bushey 52 A2
Hartsbourne Rd., Bushey 52 A2
Hartshorn All. EC3 21 E4
Hartshorn Gdns. E6 116 D4
Hartslock Dr. SE2 138 D2
Hartsmead Rd. SE9 174 C2
Hartsway, Enf. 45 F4
Hartswood Gdns. W12 127 F3
Hartswood Grn., Bushey 52 A2
Hartswood Rd. W12 127 F2
Hartsworth Cl. E13 115 F2
Hartville Rd. SE18 137 H4
Hartwell Dr. E4 62 C6
Hartwell St. E8 94 C6
Dalston La.
Harvard Hill W4 126 B6
Harvard La. W4 126 B5
Harvard Rd. SE13 154 C5
Harvard Rd. W4 126 B5
Harvard Rd., Islw. 144 B1
Harvel Cres. SE2 138 D5
Harvest Bank Rd., W.Wick. 205 F3
Harvest La., Loug. 47 J7
Fallow Flds.
Harvest La., T.Ditt. 180 D6
Harvest Rd., Felt. 160 A4
Harvesters Cl., Islw. 144 A5
Harvey Dr., Hmptn. 179 H1
Harvey Gdns. E11 97 F1
Harvey Rd.
Harvey Gdns. SE7 136 A4
Harvey Gdns., Loug. 49 E3
Harvey Ho., Brent. 125 H5
Green Dragon La.
Harvey Pt. E16 115 H5
Fife Rd.
Harvey Rd. E11 97 F1
Harvey Rd. N8 75 F5
Harvey Rd. SE5 152 A1
Harvey Rd., Houns. 143 F7
Harvey Rd., Ilf. 99 E5
Harvey Rd., Nthlt. 84 C7
Harvey Rd., Walt. 178 A7
Harvey St. N1 112 A1
Harvill Rd., Sid. 176 D5
Harvington Wk. E8 94 D7
Wilman Gro.
Harvist Est. N7 93 G4
Harvist Rd. NW6 108 A2
Harwater Dr., Loug. 48 C2
Harwell Pas. N2 73 J4
Harwich La. EC2 20 E1
Harwich La. EC2 112 B5
Harwood Av., Brom. 191 H2
Harwood Av., Mitch. 185 H3
Harwood Cl. N12 57 H6
Summerfields Av.
Harwood Cl., Wem. 87 G4
Harrowdene Rd.
Harwood Rd. SW6 128 D7
Harwood Ter. SW6 148 E1
Harwoods Yd. N21 43 G7
Wades Hill
Hascombe Ter. SE5 152 A2
Haselbury Rd. N9 60 B4
Haselbury Rd. N18 60 B4
Haseley End SE23 153 F7
Tyson Rd.
Haselrigge Rd. SW4 150 D4
Haseltine Rd. SE26 171 J4
Haselwood Dr., Enf. 43 H4
Haskard Rd., Dag. 100 D4
Haskell Ho. NW10 106 D1
Hasker St. SW3 31 H1
Hasker St. SW3 129 H4

Name	Page	Ref
Haslam Av., Sutt.	198	B1
Haslam Cl. N1	93	G7
Haslam St. SE15	132	C7
Haslemere Av. NW4	72	A6
Haslemere Av. SW18	166	E2
Haslemere Av. W7	124	D3
Haslemere Av. W13	124	D3
Haslemere Av., Barn.	57	J1
Haslemere Av., Houns.	142	C2
Haslemere Av., Mitch.	185	G2
Haslemere Cl., Hmptn.	161	F5
Haslemere Cl., Wall.	200/201	E5
Stafford Rd.		
Haslemere Gdns. N3	72	C3
Haslemere Heathrow Est., Houns.	142	B2
Haslemere Rd. N8	74	D7
Haslemere Rd. N21	59	H2
Haslemere Rd., Bexh.	159	F2
Haslemere Rd., Ilf.	99	J2
Haslemere Rd., Th.Hth.	187	H5
Hasler Cl. SE28	118	B7
Hasluck Gdns., Barn.	41	F6
Hassard St. E2	**13**	**G2**
Hassendean Rd. SE3	135	H6
Hassett Rd. E9	95	G6
Hassock Wd., Kes.	206	A4
Hassocks Cl. SE26	171	E3
Hassocks Rd. SW16	186	D1
Hassop Rd. NW2	90	A4
Hassop Wk. SE9	174	B4
Hasted Rd. SE7	136	A5
Hastings Av., Ilf.	81	F4
Hastings Cl. SE15	132	D7
Hastings Cl., Barn.	41	F4
Leicester Rd.		
Hastings Dr., Surb.	181	F6
Hastings Ho. SE18	136	C4
Hastings Rd. N11	58	C5
Hastings Rd. N17	76	A3
Hastings Rd. W13	105	E7
Hastings Rd., Brom.	206	B1
Hastings Rd., Croy.	202	C1
Hastings St. WC1	**10**	**A4**
Hastings St. WC1	110	E3
Hastingwood Trd. Est. N18	61	G6
Hastoe Cl., Hayes	102/103	E4
Kingsash Dr.		
Hat and Mitre Ct. EC1	**11**	**H6**
Hatch, The, Enf.	45	G1
Hatch Gro., Rom.	83	E4
Hatch La. E4	62	D4
Hatch La., Houns.	120	A7
Hatch Pl., Kings.T.	163	J5
Hatch Rd. SW16	187	E2
Hatch Side, Chig.	64	D5
Hatcham Pk. Ms. SE14	153	G1
Hatcham Pk. Rd.		
Hatcham Pk. Rd. SE14	153	G1
Hatcham Rd. SE15	133	F6
Hatchard Rd. N19	92	D2
Hatchcroft NW4	71	H3
Hatchwood Cl., Wdf.Grn.	63	F4
Sunset Av.		
Hatcliffe Cl. SE3	155	F3
Hatcliffe St. SE10	135	F5
Woolwich Rd.		
Hatfield Cl. SE14	133	G7
Reaston St.		
Hatfield Cl., Ilf.	81	E3
Hatfield Cl., Mitch.	185	G4
Hatfield Mead, Mord.	184	D5
Central Rd.		
Hatfield Rd. E15	97	E5
Hatfield Rd. W4	126	D2
Hatfield Rd. W13	124	D1
Hatfield Rd., Dag.	101	E7
Hatfields SE1	**27**	**F1**
Hatfields SE1	131	H1
Hatfields, Loug.	48	E3
Hathaway Cl., Brom.	206	C1
Hathaway Cl., Stan.	52	D5
Hathaway Cres. E12	98	C6
Hathaway Gdns. W13	104	C5
Hathaway Gdns., Rom.	82	D5
Hathaway Rd., Croy.	187	H7
Hatherleigh Cl., Chess.	195	G5
Hatherleigh Cl., Mord.	184	D4
Hatherleigh Rd., Ruis.	84	A2
Hatherley Cres., Sid.	176	A2
Hatherley Gdns. E6	116	A3
Hatherley Gdns. N8	74	E6
Hatherley Gro. W2	**14**	**A3**
Hatherley Gro. W2	108	E6
Hatherley Ms. E17	78	A4
Hatherley Rd. E17	77	J4
Hatherley Rd., Rich.	145	J2
Hatherley Rd., Sid.	176	A4
Hatherley St. SW1	**33**	**G1**
Hathern Gdns. SE9	174	D4
Hatherop Rd., Hmptn.	161	F7
Hathorne Cl. SE15	153	E2
Hathway St. SE15	153	F2
Gibbon Rd.		
Hathway Ter. SE14	153	F2
Gibbon Rd.		
Hatley Av., Ilf.	81	F4
Hatley Cl. N11	57	J5
Hatley Rd. N4	93	F2
Hatteraick St. SE16	133	F2
Brunel Rd.		
Hattersfield Cl., Belv.	139	F4
Hatton Cl. SE18	137	G7
Hatton Ct. E5	95	H4
Gilpin Rd.		
Hatton Gdn. EC1	**19**	**F1**
Hatton Gdn. EC1	111	G5
Hatton Gdns., Mitch.	185	J5
Hatton Grn., Felt.	142	A4
Hatton Gro., West Dr.	120	A2
Hatton Ho. E1	**21**	**J5**
Hatton Pl. EC1	**11**	**F6**
Hatton Pl. EC1	111	G4
Hatton Rd., Croy.	201	G1
Hatton Rd., Felt.	141	H5
Hatton Row NW8	**7**	**F6**
Hatton St. NW8	**7**	**F6**
Hatton Wall EC1	**19**	**E1**
Hatton Wall EC1	111	G5
Haunch of Venison Yd. W1	**16**	**D4**
Havana Rd. SW19	166	D2
Havannah St. E14	134	A2
Havant Rd. E17	78	C3
Havant Way SE15	**37**	**F7**
Havelock Pl., Har.	68	B6
Havelock Rd. N17	76	D2
Havelock Rd. SW19	167	F5
Havelock Rd., Belv.	139	F4
Havelock Rd., Brom.	191	J4
Havelock Rd., Croy.	202	C1
Havelock Rd., Har.	68	B3
Havelock Rd., Sthl.	123	F3
Havelock St. N1	111	E1
Havelock St., Ilf.	98	E2
Havelock Ter. SW8	130	B7
Havelock Wk. SE23	171	F1
Haven, The SE26	170/171	E5
Springfield Rd.		
Haven, The, Rich.	146	A3
Haven Cl. SE9	174	C3
Haven Cl. SW19	166	A3
Haven Cl., Sid.	176	B6
Haven Grn. W5	105	G6
Haven Grn. Ct. W5	105	G6
Haven Grn.		
Haven La. W5	105	H6
Haven Pl. W5	105	G7
The Bdy.		
Haven St. NW1	92	B7
Castlehaven Rd.		
Haven Ter. W5	105	G7
The Bdy.		
Havenhurst Ri., Enf.	43	G2
Havenwood, Wem.	88	B3
Haverfield Gdns., Rich.	126	A7
Haverfield Rd. E3	113	H3
Haverhill Rd. E4	62	C1
Haverhill Rd. SW12	168	C1
Havering Gdns., Rom.	82	C5
Havering St. E1	113	G6
Devonport St.		
Havering Way, Bark.	118	B3
Haversfield Est., Brent.	125	H5
Haversham Cl., Twick.	145	G6
Haversham Pl. N6	91	J2
Haverstock Hill NW3	91	H5
Haverstock Rd. NW5	92	A5
Haverstock St. N1	**11**	**H2**
Haverstock St. N1	111	H2
Haverthwaite Rd. Orp.	207	G2
Havil St. SE5	132	B7
Havisham Pl. SE19	169	H6
Hawarden Gro. SE24	151	J7
Hawarden Hill NW2	89	G3
Hawarden Rd. E17	77	G4
Hawbridge Rd. E11	96	D1
Hawes La., W.Wick.	204	D1
Hawes Rd. N18	60	E6
Hawes Rd., Brom.	191	H1
Hawes St. N1	93	H7
Haweswater Ho., Islw.	144	C5
Summerwood Rd.		
Hawgood St. E3	114	A5
Hawk Ter., Ilf.	80	D3
Tiptree Cres.		
Hawkdene E4	46	B6
Hawke Pk. Rd. N22	75	H3
Hawke Pl. SE16	133	G2
Middleton Dr.		
Hawke Rd. SE19	170	B6
Hawker Cl., Wall.	201	E7
Hawkes Rd., Mitch.	185	H1
Hawkesbury Rd. SW15	147	H5
Hawkesfield Rd. SE23	171	H2
Hawkesley Cl., Twick.	162	D4
Hawkewood Rd., Sun.	178	A3
Hawkhurst Gdns., Chess.	195	H4
Hawkhurst Rd. SW16	186	D1
Hawkhurst Way, N.Mal.	182	D5
Hawkhurst Way, W.Wick.	204	B2
Hale La.		
Hawkins Cl. NW7	54	D5
Hawkins Cl., Borwd.	38	C2
Banks Rd.		
Hawkins Cl., Har.	68	A7
Hawkins Rd., Tedd.	163	E6
Hawkins Way SE6	172	A4
Hawkley Gdns. SE27	169	H2
Hawkridge Cl., Rom.	82	C7
Hawks Ms. SE10	134	C7
Luton Pl.		
Hawks Rd., Kings.T.	181	J2
Hawksbrook La., Beck.	190	B6
Hawkshaw Cl. SW2	150/151	E7
Tierney Rd.		
Hawkshead Cl., Brom.	173	E7
Hawkshead Rd. NW10	89	F7
Hawkshead Rd. W4	126	E2
Hawkslade Rd. SE15	153	G5
Hawksley Rd. N16	94	B3
Hawksmoor Cl. E6	116	B6
Allhallows Rd.		
Hawksmoor Cl. SE18	137	H5
Hawksmoor Ms. E1	112/113	E7
Cable St.		
Hawksmoor St. W6	128	A6
Hawksmouth E4	46	B7
Hawkstone Rd. SE16	133	F4
Hawkwell Ct. E4	62	C3
Colvin Gdns.		
Hawkwell Ho., Dag.	101	G1
Hawkwell Wk. N1	111	J1
Basire St.		
Hawkwood Cres. E4	46	B6
Hawkwood La., Chis.	193	F1
Hawkwood Mt. E5	95	E1
Hawlands Dr., Pnr.	66	E7
Hawley Cl., Hmptn.	161	F6
Hawley Cres. NW1	92	B7
Hawley Ms. NW1	92	B7
Hawley Rd.		
Hawley Rd. N18	61	G5
Hawley Rd. NW1	92	B7
Hawley St. NW1	92	B7
Hawstead Rd. SE6	154	B6
Hawsted, Buck.H.	47	H1
Hawthorn Av. N13	59	E5
Hawthorn Av., Cars.	200	A7
Hawthorn Av., Rich.	145	H2
Kew Rd.		
Hawthorn Av., Th.Hth.	187	H1
Hawthorn Cen., Har.	68	C4
Hawthorn Cl., Hmptn.	161	G5
Hawthorn Cl., Houns.	122	B7
Hawthorn Cl., Orp.	193	G6
Hawthorn Cotts., Well.	158	A3
Hook La.		
Hawthorn Ct., Rich.	146	B1
West Hall Rd.		
Hawthorn Cres. SW17	168	A5
Hawthorn Dr., Har.	67	F6
Hawthorn Dr., W.Wick.	205	E4
Hawthorn Gdns. W5	125	G3
Hawthorn Gro. SE20	171	E7
Hawthorn Gro., Barn.	39	F6
Hawthorn Hatch, Brent.	125	E7
Hawthorn Ms. NW7	72	B1
Holders Hill Rd.		
Hawthorn Pl., Erith	139	J5
Hawthorn Rd. N8	74	D3
Hawthorn Rd. N18	60	C5
Hawthorn Rd. NW10	89	G7
Hawthorn Rd., Bexh.	159	F4
Hawthorn Rd., Brent.	125	E7
Hawthorn Rd., Buck.H.	64	C3
Hawthorn Rd., Sutt.	199	H6
Hawthorn Rd., Wall.	200	B7
Hawthorn Wk. W10	108	B4
Droop St.		
Hawthornden Cl. N12	57	H6
Fallowfields Dr.		
Hawthorndene Cl., Brom.	205	G2
Hawthorndene Rd., Brom.	205	F2
Hawthorne Av., Har.	68	D6
Hawthorne Av., Mitch.	185	G2
Hawthorne Av., Ruis.	66	B6
Hawthorne Cl. N1	94	B6
Hawthorne Cl., Brom.	192	C3
Hawthorne Cl., Sutt.	198/199	E2
Aultone Way		
Hawthorne Ct., Nthwd.	66	A2
Ryefield Cres.		
Hawthorne Cres., West Dr.	120	C2
Hawthorne Fm. Av., Nthlt.	103	E1
Hawthorne Gro. NW9	70	C7
Hawthorne Ms., Grnf.	103	J6
Greenford Rd.		
Hawthorne Rd. E17	78	A3
Hawthorne Rd., Brom.	192	C3
Hawthorne Way N9	60	B2
Hawthorne Way, Stai.	140	A7
Hawthorns, Wdf.Grn.	63	G3
Hawthorns, The, Epsom	197	F6
Ewell Bypass		
Hawthorns, The, Loug.	48	D4
Hawtrey Av., Nthlt.	102	D2
Hawtrey Dr., Ruis.	66	A7
Hawtrey Rd. NW3	91	H7
Haxted Rd., Brom.	191	H1
North Rd.		
Hay Cl. E15	97	E7
Hay Cl., Borwd.	38	C2
Hay Currie St. E14	114	B6
Hay Hill W1	**17**	**E6**
Hay Hill W1	110	B7
Hay La. NW9	70	D4
Hay St. E2	112	D1
Haycroft Gdns. NW10	107	G1
Haycroft Rd. SW2	151	E5
Haycroft Rd., Surb.	195	H3
Hayday Rd. E16	115	G5
Hayden Way, Rom.	83	J2
Haydens Pl. W11	108	C6
Portobello Rd.		
Haydns Ms. W3	106	C6
Emanuel Av.		
Haydock Av., Nthlt.	85	G6
Haydock Grn., Nthlt.	85	G6
Haydock Av.		
Haydon Cl. NW9	70	C4
Haydon Cl., Enf.	44	B6
Mortimer Dr.		
Haydon Dr., Pnr.	66	A4
Haydon Pk. Rd. SW19	166	E5
Haydon Rd., Dag.	100	C2
Haydon St. EC3	**21**	**F5**
Haydon Wk. E1	**21**	**G5**
Haydon Way SW11	149	G4
St. John's Hill		
Haydons Rd. SW19	167	E5
Hayes Bypass, Hayes	102	D4
Hayes Chase, W.Wick.	190	E5
Hayes Cl., Brom.	205	G2
Hayes Ct. SW2	168	E1
Hayes Cres. NW11	72	C5
Hayes Cres., Sutt.	198	A4
Hayes Gdn., Brom.	205	G2
Hayes Hill, Brom.	205	E1
Hayes Hill Rd., Brom.	205	F1
Hayes La., Beck.	190	C3
Hayes La., Brom.	191	G5
Hayes Mead Rd., Brom.	205	E1
Hayes Metro Cen., Hayes	102	C7
Hayes Pl. NW1	**7**	**H6**
Hayes Rd., Brom.	191	G4
Hayes Rd., Sthl.	122	B4
Hayes St., Brom.	205	H1
Hayes Way, Beck.	190	C4
Hayes Wd. Av., Brom.	205	H1
Hayesford Pk. Dr., Brom.	191	F5

Hayfield Pas. E1 113 F4
  Stepney Grn.
Hayfield Yd. E1 113 F4
  Mile End Rd.
Haygarth Pl. SW19 166 A5
Haygreen Cl., 164 B6
  Kings.T.
Hayland Cl. NW9 70 D4
Hayles St. SE11 35 G1
Hayles St. SE11 131 H4
Haylett Gdns., 181 G4
  Kings.T.
  Anglesea Rd.
Hayling Av., Felt. 160 A3
Hayling Cl. N16 94 B5
  Pellerin Rd.
Hayling Rd., Wat. 50 B2
Hayman St. N1 93 H7
  Cross St.
Haymarket SW1 17 H6
Haymarket SW1 110 D7
Haymarket Arc. SW1 17 H6
Haymer Gdns., 197 G3
  Wor.Pk.
Haymerle Rd. SE15 37 H6
Haymerle Rd. SE15 132 D6
Haymill Cl., Grnf. 104 C3
Hayne Rd., Beck. 189 J2
Haynes St. EC1 19 H1
Haynes Cl. N11 58 A3
Haynes Cl. N17 60 E7
Haynes Cl. SE3 155 E3
Haynes La. SE19 170 B6
Haynes Rd., Wem. 87 H7
Haynt Wk. SW20 184 B3
Hay's La. SE1 28 D2
Hay's Ms. W1 16 D6
Hay's Ms. W1 110 B7
Haysleigh Gdns. 188 D2
  SE20
Hayter Rd. SW2 151 E5
Hayton Cl. E8 94 C6
  Buttermere Wk.
Hayward Cl. SW19 185 E1
Hayward Gdns. SW15 147 J6
Hayward Rd. N20 57 F2
Hayward Rd., T.Ditt. 194 D1
Haywards Cl., Rom. 82 B5
Hayward's Pl. EC1 11 G5
Haywood Cl., Pnr. 66 D2
Haywood Ri., Orp. 207 H4
Haywood Rd., Brom. 192 A4
Hayworth Cl., Enf. 45 H2
  Green Cl.
Hazel Av., West Dr. 120 D3
Hazel Cl. N13 60 A3
Hazel Cl. N19 92 C2
  Hargrave Pk.
Hazel Cl. SE15 152 D2
Hazel Cl., Brent. 125 E7
Hazel Cl., Croy. 189 G7
Hazel Cl., Mitch. 186 D4
Hazel Cl., Twick. 143 J7
Hazel Gdns., Edg. 54 B4
Hazel Gro. SE26 171 G4
Hazel Gro., Enf. 44 D6
  Dimsdale Dr.
Hazel Gro., Orp. 206 E2
Hazel Gro., Rom. 82 E3
Hazel Gro., Wem. 105 H1
  Carlyon Rd.
Hazel Gro. Est. SE26 171 G4
Hazel La., Rich. 163 H2
Hazel Mead, Barn. 39 H5
Hazel Rd. E15 96/97 E5
  Wingfield Rd.
Hazel Rd. NW10 107 J3
Hazel Wk., Brom. 192 D6
Hazel Way E4 61 J6
Hazel Way SE1 37 F1
Hazelbank, Surb. 196 C1
Hazelbank Rd. SE6 172 D2
Hazelbourne Rd. 150 B6
  SW12
Hazelbrouck Gdns., 65 G7
  Ilf.
Hazelbury Cl. SW19 184 D2
Hazelbury Grn. N9 60 B3
Hazelbury La. N9 60 B3
Hazelcroft, Pnr. 51 G6
Hazeldean Rd. NW10 88 D7
Hazeldene Dr., Pnr. 66 C3
Hazeldene Rd., Ilf. 100 B2
Hazeldene Rd., Well. 158 C2
Hazeldon Rd. SE4 153 H5
Hazeleigh Gdns. 64 B5
  Wdf.Grn.
Hazelgreen Cl. N21 59 H1
Hazelhurst, Beck. 190 C1
Hazelhurst Rd. SW17 167 F4
Hazell Cres., Rom. 83 H1
Hazellville Rd. N19 74 D7
Hazelmere Cl., Felt. 141 G6
Hazelmere Cl., Nthlt. 103 F2

Hazelmere Dr., Nthlt. 103 F2
Hazelmere Rd. NW6 108 D1
Hazelmere Rd., Nthlt. 103 F2
Hazelmere Rd., Orp. 193 F4
Hazelmere Wk., Nthlt. 103 F2
Hazelmere Way, 191 G6
  Brom.
Hazeltree La., Nthlt. 103 E3
Hazelwood, Loug. 48 A5
Hazelwood Av., 185 E4
  Mord.
Hazelwood Cl. W5 125 H2
Hazelwood Cl., Har. 67 H4
Hazelwood Ct. 88/89 E3
  NW10
  Neasden La. N.
Hazelwood Cres. N13 59 G4
Hazelwood Cft., 181 H6
  Surb.
Hazelwood Dr., Pnr. 66 B2
Hazelwood La. N13 59 G4
Hazelwood Pk. Cl., 65 H5
  Chig.
Hazelwood Rd. E17 77 H5
Hazelwood Rd., Enf. 44 C6
Hazlebury Rd. SW6 149 E2
Hazledean Rd., Croy. 202 A2
Hazledene Rd. W4 126 C6
Hazlemere Gdns., 197 H1
  Wor.Pk.
Hazlewell Rd. SW15 147 J5
Hazlewood Cl. E5 95 H3
  Mandeville St.
Hazlitt Ms. W14 128 B3
  Hazlitt Rd.
Hazlitt Rd. W14 128 B3
Head St. E1 113 G6
Headcorn Pl., Th.Hth. 187 F4
  Headcorn Rd.
Headcorn Rd. N17 60 C7
Headcorn Rd., Brom. 173 F5
Headcorn Rd., Th.Hth. 187 F4
Headfort Pl. SW1 24 C4
Headfort Pl. SW1 130 A2
Headingley Cl., Ilf. 65 J6
Headington Rd. SW18 167 F2
Headlam Rd. SW4 150 D6
Headlam St. E1 113 E4
Headley App., Ilf. 80 D5
Headley Av., Wall. 201 F5
Headley Cl., Epsom 196 A6
Headley Ct. SE26 171 E5
Headley Dr., Croy. 204 B7
Headley Dr., Ilf. 80 E6
Head's Ms. W11 108 D6
  Artesian Rd.
Headstone Dr., Har. 68 B3
Headstone Gdns., 67 J4
  Har.
Headstone La., Har. 67 H4
Headstone Rd., Har. 68 B5
Headway Cl., Rich. 163 F4
  Locksmeade Rd.
Heald St. SE14 153 J1
Healey Dr., Orp. 207 J4
Healey St. NW1 92 B6
Heanor Ct. E5 95 G3
  Pedro St.
Hearn Ri., Nthlt. 102 D1
Hearn St. EC2 12 E6
Hearn St. EC2 112 B4
Hearne Rd. W4 126 A6
Hearn's Bldgs. SE17 36 C2
Hearnville Rd. SW12 168 A1
Heath, The W7 124 B1
  Lower Boston Rd.
Heath Av., Bexh. 138 D6
Heath Brow NW3 91 F3
  North End Way
Heath Cl. NW11 72 E7
Heath Cl. W5 105 J4
Heath Cl., Hayes 121 G7
Heath Cl., Houns. 143 F4
Heath Dr. NW3 90 E4
Heath Dr. SW20 183 J4
Heath Gdns., Twick. 162 C1
Heath Gro. SE20 171 F7
  Maple Rd.
Heath Hurst Rd. NW3 91 H4
Heath La. SE3 154 D7
Heath Mead SW19 166 A3
Heath Pk. Dr., Brom. 192 B3
Heath Pas. NW3 91 E2
Heath Ri. SW15 148 A6
Heath Ri., Brom. 191 F6
Heath Rd. SW8 150 B2
Heath Rd., Bex. 177 J1
Heath Rd., Har. 67 J7
Heath Rd., Houns. 143 H4
Heath Rd., Rom. 82 D7
Heath Rd., Th.Hth. 187 J3
Heath Rd., Twick. 162 C1
Heath Side NW3 91 G4

Heath Side, Orp. 207 F1
Heath St. NW3 91 F4
Heath Vw. N2 73 F4
Heath Vw. Cl. N2 73 F4
Heath Vil. SE18 137 J5
Heath Vil. SW18 167 F1
  Cargill Rd.
Heath Way, Erith 159 J1
Heatham Pk., Twick. 144 C7
Heathbourne Rd., 52 B2
  Bushey
Heathbourne Rd., 52 B2
  Stan.
Heathcock Ct. WC2 110/111 E7
  Strand
Heathcote Av., Ilf. 80 C3
Heathcote Gro. E4 62 C3
Heathcote Rd., Twick. 145 E6
Heathcote St. WC1 10 C5
Heathcote St. WC1 111 F4
Heathcote Way, 120 A1
  West Dr.
  Tavistock Rd.
Heathcroft NW11 91 E1
Heathcroft W5 105 J4
Heathcroft Gdns. E17 78 D1
  Hale End Rd.
Heathdale Av., 143 E3
  Houns.
Heathdene Dr., Belv. 139 H4
Heathdene Rd. SW16 169 F7
Heathdene Rd., Wall. 200 B7
Heathedge SE26 170 E2
Heather Cl. E6 116 E6
Heather Cl. SE13 154 D7
Heather Cl. SW8 150 B3
Heather Cl., Hmptn. 179 F1
Heather Cl., Islw. 144 A5
  Harvesters Cl.
Heather Dr., Enf. 43 H2
  Chasewood Av.
Heather Gdns. NW11 72 B6
Heather Gdns., Sutt. 198 D6
Heather Pk. Dr., Wem. 88 A7
Heather Rd. E4 61 J6
Heather Rd. NW2 89 F2
Heather Rd. SE12 173 G2
Heather Wk. W10 108 B4
  Droop St.
Heather Wk., Edg. 54 B5
Heather Wk., Twick. 143 G7
  Stephenson Rd.
Heather Way, Stan. 52 C6
Heatherbank SE9 156 C2
Heatherbank, Chis. 192 D2
Heatherdale Cl., 164 A6
  Kings.T.
Heatherdene Cl. N12 73 F1
  Bow La.
Heatherdene Cl., 185 H4
  Mitch.
Heatherlands, Sun. 160 A6
Heatherley Dr., Ilf. 80 B3
Heathers, The, Stai. 140 C7
Heatherset Gdns. 169 F7
  SW16
Heatherside Rd., 196 D7
  Epsom
Heatherside Rd., Sid. 176 D3
  Wren Rd.
Heatherwood Cl. E12 97 J2
Heathfield E4 62 C3
Heathfield, Chis. 175 F6
Heathfield Av. SW18 149 G7
  Heathfield Rd.
Heathfield Cl. E16 116 A5
Heathfield Cl., Kes. 205 J5
Heathfield Dr., Mitch. 185 H1
Heathfield Gdns. 72 A6
  NW11
Heathfield Gdns. 149 G6
  SW18
  Heathfield Rd.
Heathfield Gdns. W4 126 C5
Heathfield Gdns., 202 A4
  Croy.
  Coombe Rd.
Heathfield La., Chis. 175 E6
Heathfield N., Twick. 144 C7
Heathfield Pk. NW2 89 J6
Heathfield Pk. Dr., 82 B5
  Rom.
Heathfield Rd. SW18 149 F6
Heathfield Rd. W3 126 B2
Heathfield Rd., Bexh. 159 F4
Heathfield Rd., Brom. 173 F7
Heathfield Rd., Croy. 202 A4
Heathfield Rd., Kes. 205 J5
Heathfield S., Twick. 144 C7
Heathfield Sq. SW18 149 G7
Heathfield St. W11 108 B7
  Portland Rd.
Heathfield Ter. SE18 137 J6
Heathfield Ter. W4 126 C5

Heathfields Ct., 142/143 E5
  Houns.
  Frampton Rd.
Heathgate NW11 72 E6
Heathgate Pl. NW3 91 J5
  Agincourt Rd.
Heathland Rd. N16 94 B1
Heathlands Cl., Sun. 178 A2
Heathlands Cl., 162 C2
  Twick.
Heathlands Way, 142/143 E5
  Houns.
  Frampton Rd.
Heathlee Rd. SE3 155 F4
Heathley End, Chis. 175 F6
Heathmans Rd. SW6 148 C1
Heathrow 122 C1
  Interchange, Hayes
Heathrow Int. Trd. 142 B3
  Est., Houns.
Heathrow Tunnel 140 E3
  App., Houns.
Heathrow Vehicle 140 E1
  Tunnel, Houns.
Heathside NW11 91 E1
Heathside, Esher 194 B3
Heathside, Houns. 143 F7
Heathside Av., Bexh. 159 E1
Heathside Cl., Esher 194 B3
Heathside Cl., Ilf. 80 D3
Heathstan Rd. W12 107 G6
Heathview Ct. SW19 166 A2
Heathview Dr. SE2 138 D6
Heathview Gdns. 147 J7
  SW15
Heathview Rd., 187 G4
  Th.Hth.
Heathville Rd. N19 74 E7
Heathwall St. SW11 149 J3
Heathway SE3 135 F7
Heathway, Croy. 203 J3
Heathway, Dag. 101 G7
Heathway, Wdf.Grn. 63 J4
Heathway Ind. Est., 101 H4
  Dag.
  Manchester Way
Heathwood Gdns. SE7 136 B4
Heaton Cl. E4 62 C3
  Friars Cl.
Heaton Rd. SE15 152 D3
Heaton Rd., Mitch. 168 A7
Heaver Rd. SW11 149 G3
  Wye St.
Heavitree Cl. SE18 137 G5
Heavitree Rd. SE18 137 G5
Hebden Cl. E2 112 C1
  Laburnum St.
Hebden Ter. N17 60 B6
  Commercial Rd.
Hebdon Rd. SW17 167 H3
Heber Rd. NW2 90 A5
Heber Rd. SE22 152 C6
Hebron Rd. W6 127 H3
Hecham Cl. E17 77 H2
Heckfield Pl. SW6 128 D7
  Fulham Rd.
Heckford St. E1 113 G7
  The Highway
Hector St. SE18 137 H4
Heddington Gro. N7 93 F5
Heddon Cl., Islw. 144 D4
Heddon Ct. Av., 41 J5
  Barn.
Heddon St. W1 17 F5
Heddon St. W1 110 C7
Hedge Hill, Enf. 43 H1
Hedge La. N13 59 H3
Hedge Wk. SE6 172 B4
Hedgeley, Ilf. 80 C4
Hedgemans Rd., Dag. 100 D7
Hedgemans Way, 100 E6
  Dag.
Hedger St. SE11 35 G1
Hedgerley Gdns., 103 J3
  Grnf.
Hedgers Cl., Loug. 48 D4
  Newmans La.
Hedgers Gro. E9 95 H6
Hedgewood Gdns., 80 D5
  Ilf.
Hedgley St. SE12 155 F5
Hedingham Cl. N1 93 J7
  Popham Rd.
Hedingham Rd., Dag. 100 D7
Hedley Rd., Twick. 143 G7
Hedley Row N5 94 A5
  Poets Rd.
Heenan Cl., Bark. 99 F6
  Glenny Rd.
Heene Rd., Enf. 44 A1
Heidegger Cres. SW13 127 H6
  Trinity Ch. Rd.
Heigham Rd. E6 98 A7
Heighton Gdns., Croy. 201 H5

Heights, The SE7 135 J5
Heights, The, Beck. 172 C7
Heights, The, Loug. 48 C2
Heights, The, Nthlt. 85 F5
Heights Cl. SW20 165 H7
Heiron St. SE17 35 H6
Heiron St. SE17 131 H6
Helby Rd. SW4 150 D6
Helder Gro. SE12 155 F7
Helder St., S.Croy. 202 A6
Heldmann Cl., Houns. 144 A4
Helen Av., Felt. 142 B7
Helen Cl. N2 73 F3
Thomas More Way
Helen Cl., W.Mol. 179 H4
Helen St. SE18 136/137 E4
Wilmount St.
Helena Cl., Wall. 201 E7
Helena Pl. E9 113 F1
Fremont St.
Helena Rd. E13 115 F2
Helena Rd. E17 78 A5
Helena Rd. NW10 89 H5
Helena Rd. W5 105 G5
Helena Sq. SE16 113 H7
Rotherhithe St.
Helen's Pl. E2 113 F3
Roman Rd.
Helenslea Av. NW11 90 C1
Helix Gdns. SW2 151 F6
Helix Rd.
Helix Rd. SW2 151 F6
Hellings St. E1 29 J2
Helme Cl. SW19 166 C5
Helmet Row EC1 12 A5
Helmet Row EC1 111 J4
Helmsdale Cl., Hayes 102/103 E4
Berrydale Rd.
Helmsdale Rd. SW16 186 C1
Helmsley Pl. E8 94 E7
Helsinki Sq. SE16 133 H3
Finland St.
Helston Cl., Pnr. 51 F7
Helvetia St. SE6 171 J2
Hemans St. SW8 33 J7
Hemans St. SW8 130 D7
Hemberton Rd. SW9 150 E3
Hemery Rd., Grnf. 86 A5
Heming Rd., Edg. 54 B7
Hemingford Cl. N12 57 G5
Hemingford Rd. N1 111 F1
Hemingford Rd., Sutt. 197 J4
Hemington Av. N11 57 J5
Hemlock Rd. W12 107 F7
Hemming Cl., Hmptn. 179 G1
Chandler Cl.
Hemming St. E1 13 J6
Hemming St. E1 112 D4
Hemmings Cl., Sid. 176 B2
Hemp Wk. SE17 36 C1
Hemp Wk. SE17 132 A4
Hempstead Cl., Buck.H. 63 G2
Hempstead Rd. E17 78 D2
Hemsby Rd., Chess. 195 J6
Hemstal Rd. NW6 90 D7
Hemswell Dr. NW9 70 E1
Hemsworth St. N1 12 D1
Hemsworth St. N1 112 B2
Hemus Pl. SW3 31 H4
Hen & Chicken Ct. EC4 111 G6
Fleet St.
Henbury Way, Wat. 50 D3
Henchman St. W12 107 F6
Hendale Av. NW4 71 G3
Henderson Cl. NW10 88 C6
Henderson Dr. NW8 7 E5
Henderson Rd. E7 97 J6
Henderson Rd. N9 60 E1
Henderson Rd. SW18 149 H7
Henderson Rd., Croy. 188 A6
Henderson Rd., Hayes 102 A3
Hendham Rd. SW17 167 H2
Hendon Av. N3 72 B1
Hendon Hall Ct. NW4 72 A3
Hendon La. N3 72 B3
Hendon Pk. Row NW11 72 C6
Hendon Rd. N9 60 D2
Hendon Way NW2 90 C3
Hendon Way NW4 71 H6
Hendon Way, Stai. 140 A6
Hendon Wd. La. NW7 39 F6
Hendre Rd. SE1 36 E2
Hendren Cl., Grnf. 86 A5
Dimmock Dr.
Hendrick Av. SW12 149 J7
Heneage La. EC3 21 E4
Heneage St. E1 21 G1
Heneage St. E1 112 C5
Henfield Cl. N19 92 C1
Henfield Cl., Bex. 159 G6
Henfield Rd. SW19 184 C1
Hengelo Gdns., Mitch. 185 G4
Hengist Rd. SE12 155 H7
Hengist Rd., Erith 139 H7
Hengist Way, Brom. 190 E4
Hengrave Rd. SE23 153 G7
Hengrove Ct., Bex. 176/177 E1
Hurst Rd.
Henley Av., Sutt. 198 B3
Henley Cl., Grnf. 103 J2
Henley Cl., Islw. 144 C1
Henley Ct. N14 42 C7
Henley Cross SE3 155 H3
Henley Dr. SE1 37 G1
Henley Dr. SE1 132 C4
Henley Dr., Kings.T. 165 F7
Henley Gdns., Pnr. 66 B3
Henley Gdns., Rom. 82 E5
Henley Rd. E16 136 C2
Henley Rd. N18 60 B4
Henley Rd. NW10 107 J1
Henley Rd., Ilf. 99 F4
Henley St. SW11 150 A2
Henley Way, Felt. 160 D5
Henlow Pl., Rich. 163 G2
Sandpits Rd.
Hennel Cl. SE23 171 F3
Henniker Gdns. E6 116 A3
Henniker Ms. SW3 30 E5
Henniker Pt. E15 96 E5
Henniker Rd. E15 96 D5
Henning St. SW11 149 H1
Henningham Rd. N17 76 A1
Henrietta Cl. SE8 134 A6
Henrietta Ms. WC1 10 B5
Henrietta Pl. W1 16 D4
Henrietta Pl. W1 110 B6
Henrietta St. E15 96 C5
Henrietta St. WC2 18 B5
Henrietta St. WC2 111 E7
Henriques St. E1 21 J3
Henriques St. E1 112 D6
Henry Addlington Cl. E6 116 D5
Winsor Ter.
Henry Cooper Way SE9 174 A3
Henry Darlot Dr. NW7 56 A5
Henry Dickens Ct. W11 128 A1
Henry Doulton Dr. SW17 168 B4
Henry Jackson Rd. SW15 148 A3
Henry Macaulay Av., Kings.T. 181 G1
Henry Rd. E6 116 B2
Henry Rd. N4 93 J1
Henry Rd., Barn. 41 G5
Henry St., Brom. 191 H1
Henry's Av., Wdf.Grn. 63 F5
Henry's Wk., Ilf. 65 G7
Henryson Rd. SE4 154 A5
Hensford Gdns. SE26 170/171 E4
Wells Pk. Rd.
Henshall St. N1 94 A6
Henshaw St. SE17 36 B1
Henshaw St. SE17 132 A4
Henshawe Rd., Dag. 100 D3
Henshill Pt. E3 114 B3
Bromley High St.
Henslowe Rd. SE22 152 D5
Henson Av. NW2 89 J5
Henson Cl., Orp. 207 E2
Henson Path, Har. 69 G3
Henson Pl., Nthlt. 102 C1
Henstridge Pl. NW8 7 G1
Henstridge Pl. NW8 109 H2
Henty Cl. SW11 129 H7
Henty Wk. SW15 147 H5
Henville Rd., Brom. 191 H1
Henwick Rd. SE9 156 A3
Henwood Side, Wdf.Grn. 64 C6
Love La.
Hepburn Gdns., Brom. 205 E1
Hepburn Ms. SW11 149 J5
Webbs Rd.
Hepple Cl., Islw. 144 E2
Hepplestone Cl. SW15 147 H6
Dover Pk. Dr.
Hepscott Rd. E9 96 A7
Hepworth Ct., Bark. 100 A5
Hepworth Gdns., Bark. 100 A5
Hepworth Rd. SW16 169 E7
Hepworth Wk. NW3 91 H5
Haverstock Hill
Heracles Cl., Wall. 200 E7
Herald Gdns., Wall. 200 B3
Herald St. E2 112/113 E4
Three Colts La.
Herald's Ct. SE11 35 G2
Herald's Pl. SE11 35 F1
Herbal Hill EC1 11 F6
Herbal Hill EC1 111 G4
Herbert Cres. SW1 24 A5
Herbert Gdns. NW10 107 H2
Herbert Gdns. W4 126 B6
Magnolia Rd.
Herbert Gdns., Rom. 82 D7
Herbert Pl. SE18 136/137 E6
Plumstead Common Rd.
Herbert Rd. E12 98 B4
Herbert Rd. E17 77 J7
Herbert Rd. N11 58 E7
Herbert Rd. N15 76 C5
Herbert Rd. NW9 71 G6
Herbert Rd. SE18 136 D7
Herbert Rd. SW19 166 C7
Herbert Rd., Bexh. 159 E2
Herbert Rd., Brom. 192 A5
Herbert Rd., Ilf. 99 H2
Herbert Rd., Kings.T. 181 J3
Herbert Rd., Sthl. 123 F1
Herbert St. E13 115 G2
Herbert St. NW5 92 A6
Herbert Ter. SE18 136/137 E6
Herbert Rd.
Herbrand St. WC1 10 A5
Herbrand St. WC1 110 E4
Hercules Pl. N7 92/93 E3
Hercules St.
Hercules Rd. SE1 26 D6
Hercules Rd. SE1 131 F3
Hercules St. N7 93 E3
Hercules Twr. SE14 133 H6
Milton Ct. Rd.
Hereford Av., Barn. 57 J1
Hereford Gdns. SE13 154/155 E5
Longhurst Rd.
Hereford Gdns., Ilf. 80 B7
Hereford Gdns., Pnr. 66 E5
Hereford Gdns., Twick. 161 J1
Hereford Ho. NW6 108 D2
Hereford Ms. W2 108 D6
Hereford Rd.
Hereford Pl. SE14 133 J7
Hereford Retreat SE15 37 H6
Hereford Rd. E11 79 H5
Hereford Rd. W2 108 D6
Hereford Rd. W3 106 B7
Hereford Rd. W5 125 F3
Hereford Rd., Felt. 160 C1
Hereford Sq. SW7 30 D2
Hereford Sq. SW7 129 F4
Hereford St. E2 13 H5
Hereford St. E2 112 D4
Hereford Way, Chess. 195 F5
Herent Dr., Ilf. 80 C3
Hereward Gdns. N13 59 G5
Hereward Grn., Loug. 49 F1
Hereward Rd. SW17 167 J4
Herga Ct., Har. 86 B3
Herga Rd., Har. 68 C4
Heriot Av. E4 62 A2
Heriot Rd. NW4 71 J5
Heriots Cl., Stan. 52 D4
Heritage Cl. SW9 151 H3
Heritage Hill, Kes. 205 J5
Heritage Vw., Har. 86 C3
Herlwyn Gdns. SW17 167 J4
Hermes Pt. W9 108 D4
Hermes St. N1 10 E2
Hermes Wk., Nthlt. 103 G2
Hotspur Rd.
Hermes Way, Wall. 200 D7
Hermiston Av. N8 75 E5
Hermit Pl. NW6 108/109 E1
Belsize Rd.
Hermit Rd. E16 115 F5
Hermit St. EC1 11 G3
Hermit St. EC1 111 H3
Hermitage, The SE23 171 F1
Hermitage, The SW13 147 F1
Hermitage, The, Rich. 145 G5
Hermitage Cl. E18 79 F4
Hermitage Cl., Enf. 43 H2
Hermitage Cl., Esher 194 D6
Hermitage Ct. E18 79 G4
Hermitage Ct. NW2 90 D3
Hermitage La.
Hermitage Gdns. NW2 90 D3
Hermitage Gdns. SE19 169 J6
Hermitage La. N18 60 A5
Hermitage La. NW2 90 D3
Hermitage La. SE25 188 D6
Hermitage La. SW16 169 F7
Hermitage La., Croy. 188 D6
Hermitage Path SW16 187 E1
Hermitage Rd. N4 75 H7
Hermitage Rd. N15 75 H7
Hermitage Rd. SE19 169 J7
Hermitage Row E8 94 D5
Hermitage St. W2 15 E2
Hermitage St. W2 109 G5
Hermitage Wk. E18 79 F4
Hermitage Wall E1 29 J2
Hermitage Wall E1 132 D1
Hermitage Way, Stan. 68 D1
Hermon Gro., Hayes 122 A1
Hermon Hill E11 79 G5
Hermon Hill E18 79 G5
Herndon Rd. SW18 149 F5
Herne Cl. NW10 88 D5
North Circular Rd.
Herne Hill SE24 151 J6
Herne Hill Rd. SE24 151 J3
Herne Ms. N18 60 D4
Lyndhurst Rd.
Herne Pl. SE24 151 H5
Herne Rd., Surb. 195 G2
Heron Cl. E17 77 J2
Heron Cl. NW10 89 E6
Heron Cl., Buck.H. 63 G1
Heron Cl., Sutt. 198 B2
Gander Grn. La.
Heron Ct., Brom. 191 J4
Heron Cres., Sid. 175 H3
Heron Dr. N4 93 J2
Heron Hill, Belv. 139 F4
Heron Ms., Ilf. 98/99 E2
Balfour Rd.
Heron Pl. SE16 133 H1
Heron Quay E14 134 A1
Heron Rd. SE24 151 J4
Heron Rd., Croy. 202 B2
Tunstall Rd.
Heron Rd., Twick. 144 D4
Heron Sq., Rich. 145 G5
Bridge St.
Herondale Av. SW18 167 G1
Herongate Rd. E12 97 J2
Herons, The E11 79 F6
Heron's Pl., Islw. 144 E3
Herons Ri., Barn. 41 H4
Heronsforde W13 105 F6
Heronsgate, Edg. 54 A5
Heronslea Dr., Stan. 53 H5
Heronway, Wdf.Grn. 63 J4
Herrick Rd. N5 93 J3
Herrick St. SW1 33 J1
Herrick St. SW1 130 D4
Herries St. W10 108 B2
Herringham Rd. SE7 135 J3
Herrongate Cl., Enf. 44 C2
Hersant Cl. NW10 107 G1
Herschell Rd. SE23 153 H7
Hersham Cl. SW15 147 G7
Hertford Av. SW14 146 E5
Hertford Cl., Barn. 41 G3
Hertford Pl. W1 9 F6
Hertford Rd. N1 112 B1
Hertford Rd. N2 73 H3
Hertford Rd. N9 60 E2
Hertford Rd., Bark. 98 E7
Hertford Rd., Barn. 41 F3
Hertford Rd., Enf. 45 F3
Hertford Rd., Ilf. 81 H6
Hertford Sq., Mitch. 186/187 E4
Hertford Way
Hertford St. W1 24 D1
Hertford St. W1 130 B1
Hertford Wk., Belv. 139 G5
Hoddesdon Rd.
Hertford Way, Mitch. 186 E4
Hertslet Rd. N7 93 F3
Hertsmere Rd. E14 114 A7
Hervey Cl. N3 72 D1
Hervey Pk. Rd. E17 77 H4
Hervey Rd. SE3 155 H1
Hesa Rd., Hayes 102 A6
Hesewall Cl. SW4 150 C2
Brayburne Av.
Hesketh Pl. W11 108 B7
Hesketh Rd. E7 97 G3
Heslop Rd. SW12 167 J1
Hesper Ms. SW5 30 A3
Hesper Ms. SW5 128 E5
Hesperus Cres. E14 134 B4
Hessel Rd. W13 124 D2
Hessel St. E1 112 E6
Hester Rd. N18 60 D5
Hester Rd. SW11 129 H7
Hester Ter., Rich. 146 A3
Chilton Rd.
Hestercombe Av. SW6 148 B2
Hesterman Way, Croy. 201 F1
Heston Av., Houns. 123 E7
Heston Gra. La., Houns. 123 F6
Heston Ind. Mall, Houns. 123 F7

Heston Rd., Houns.	123	G7
Heston St. SE14	153	J1
Heswell Grn., Wat.	50	A3
Fairhaven Cres.		
Hetherington Rd. SW4	150	E4
Hetley Gdns. SE19	170	C7
Fox Hill		
Hetley Rd. W12	127	H1
Heton Gdns. NW4	71	G4
Hevelius Cl. SE10	135	F5
Hever Cft. SE9	174	D4
Hever Gdns., Brom.	192	D3
Heverham Rd. SE18	137	H4
Heversham Rd., Bexh.	159	G2
Hewer St. W10	108	A5
Hewett Cl., Stan.	53	E4
Hewett Rd., Dag.	100	D4
Hewett St. EC2	**12**	**E6**
Hewish Rd. N18	60	B4
Hewison St. E3	113	J2
Hewitt Av. N22	75	H2
Hewitt Cl., Croy.	204	A3
Hewitt Rd. N8	75	G5
Hewlett Rd. E3	113	H3
Hexagon, The N6	91	J1
Hexal Rd. SE6	172	E3
Hexham Gdns., Islw.	124	D7
Hexham Rd. SE27	169	J2
Hexham Rd., Barn.	41	E4
Hexham Rd., Mord.	198	E1
Heybourne Rd. N17	61	E7
Heybridge Av. SW16	169	E7
Heybridge Dr., Ilf.	81	G3
Heybridge Way E10	77	H7
Heyford Av. SW8	**34**	**B7**
Heyford Av. SW8	131	E7
Heyford Rd. SW20	184	C3
Heyford Rd., Mitch.	185	H2
Heyford Ter. SW8	130/131	E7
Heyford Av.		
Heygate St. SE17	**35**	**J2**
Heygate St. SE17	131	J4
Heylyn Sq. E3	113	J3
Malmesbury Rd.		
Heynes Rd., Dag.	100	C4
Heysham Dr., Wat.	50	C5
Heysham La. NW3	91	E3
Heysham Rd. N15	76	A6
Heythorp St. SW18	166	C1
Heywood Av. NW9	70	E1
Heyworth Rd. E5	94	E4
Heyworth Rd. E15	97	F5
Hibbert Rd. E17	77	J7
Hibbert Rd., Har.	68	C2
Hibbert St. SW11	149	G3
Hibernia Gdns.,	143	G4
Houns.		
Hibernia Pt. SE2	138	D2
Wolvercote Rd.		
Hibernia Rd., Houns.	143	G4
Hibiscus Cl., Edg.	54	C4
Campion Way		
Hichisson Rd. SE15	153	F5
Hickin Cl. SE7	136	A4
Hickin St. E14	134	C3
Plevna St.		
Hickling Rd., Ilf.	99	E5
Hickman Av. E4	62	C6
Hickman Cl. E16	116	A5
Hickman Rd., Rom.	82	C7
Hickmore Wk. SW4	150	C3
Hickory Cl. N9	44	D7
Hicks Av., Grnf.	104	A3
Hicks Cl. SW11	149	H3
Hicks St. SE8	133	H5
Hidcote Gdns. SW20	183	H3
Hide E6	116	D6
Downings		
Hide Pl. SW1	**33**	**H2**
Hide Pl. SW1	130	D4
Hide Rd., Har.	68	A4
Hides St. N7	93	F6
Sheringham Rd.		
Higgins Wk., Hmptn.	160/161	E6
Abbott Cl.		
High Beech, S.Croy.	202	B7
High Beech Rd.,	48	A4
Loug.		
High Beeches, Sid.	176	E3
High Br. SE10	134	D5
High Br. Wf. SE10	134	D5
High Broom Cres.,	190	B7
W.Wick.		
High Cedar Dr. SW20	165	H7
High Coombe Pl.,	164	D6
Kings.T.		
High Cross Cen. N15	76	D4
High Cross Rd. N17	76	D3
High Dr., N.Mal.	182	C1
High Elms, Chig.	65	H4
High Elms, Wdf.Grn.	63	G5
High Foleys, Esher	194	E7
High Gables, Loug.	48	A5
High Gro. SE18	137	G7
High Gro., Brom.	191	J1
High Hill Est. E5	94/95	E1
Mount Pleasant La.		
High Hill Ferry E5	95	E1
High Holborn WC1	**18**	**B3**
High Holborn WC1	111	E6
High La. W7	104	A6
High Lawns, Har.	86	B3
High Level Dr. SE26	170	D4
High Mead, Chig.	65	F2
High Mead, Har.	68	B5
High Mead, W.Wick.	204	D2
High Meadow Cl.,	66	B4
Pnr.		
High Meadow Cres.	70	D5
NW9		
High Meadows, Chig.	65	G5
High Meads Rd. E16	116	A6
Fulmer Rd.		
High Mt. NW4	71	G6
High Pk. Av., Rich.	146	A1
High Pk. Rd., Rich.	146	A1
High Path SW19	185	E1
High Pt. N6	74	A7
High Rd. SE9	175	E3
High Rd. N2	73	G2
High Rd. N11	58	B5
High Rd. N12	57	F6
High Rd. N15	76	C6
High Rd. N17	76	C1
High Rd. N20	41	F7
High Rd. N22	75	G3
High Rd. (Willesden)	89	F6
NW10		
High Rd., Buck.H.	63	H2
High Rd., Bushey	52	A1
High Rd., Chig.	64	C5
High Rd. (Harrow	52	B7
Weald), Har.		
High Rd., Ilf.	98	E3
High Rd. (Seven	99	J1
Kings), Ilf.		
High Rd., Loug.	47	J7
High Rd., Pnr.	66	B4
High Rd. (Chadwell	100	B1
Heath), Rom.		
High Rd., Wem.	87	G5
High Rd., Leyton E10	96	B1
High Rd. Leyton E15	96	C3
High Rd. Leytonstone	96	E4
E11		
High Rd. Leytonstone	96	E4
E15		
High Rd. Woodford	79	G2
Grn. E18		
High Rd. Woodford	63	F7
Grn., Wdf.Grn.		
High Silver, Loug.	48	A4
High St. E11	79	G5
High St. E13	115	G2
High St. E15	114	C2
High St. E17	77	J5
High St. N8	74	E4
High St. N14	58	D1
High St. NW7	55	H4
High St. (Harlesden)	107	F2
NW10		
High St. SE20	171	E6
High St. (South	188	C4
Norwood) SE25		
High St. W3	126	B1
High St. W5	105	G7
High St., Barn.	40	B3
High St., Beck.	190	A1
High St., Brent.	125	G6
High St., Brom.	191	G2
High St., Cars.	200	A4
High St., Chis.	175	E6
High St., Croy.	201	J2
High St., Edg.	54	A6
High St. (Ponders	45	F4
End), Enf.		
High St. (Claygate),	194	C6
Esher		
High St., Felt.	160	A3
High St., Hmptn.	161	J6
High St., Har.	86	B1
High St.	68	B3
(Wealdstone), Har.		
High St., Hayes	121	H5
High St., Houns.	143	J3
High St. (Cranford)	142	A1
Houns.		
High St., Ilf.	81	F2
High St., Kings.T.	181	G2
High St. (Hampton	181	F1
Wick), Kings.T.		
High St., N.Mal.	183	E3
High St.	207	E5
(Farnborough), Orp.		
High St. (Green St.	207	J7
Grn.), Orp.		
High St., Pnr.	66	E3
High St., Sthl.	123	F1
High St. (Stanwell),	140	A6
Stai.		
High St., Sutt.	198	E4
High St. (Cheam),	198	B6
Sutt.		
High St., Tedd.	162	D5
High St., T.Ditt.	180	C7
High St., Th.Hth.	187	J4
High St. (Whitton),	143	J7
Twick.		
High St., Wem.	87	J4
High St., West Dr.	120	A6
High St. (Yiewsley),	120	A1
West Dr.		
High St., W.Mol.	179	G4
High St., W.Wick.	204	B1
High St. Colliers Wd.	167	G7
SW19		
High St. Ms. SW19	166	B5
High St. N. E6	116	B1
High St. N. E12	98	B5
High St. S. E6	116	C2
High St. Wimbledon	166	B5
SW19		
High Timber St. EC4	**19**	**J5**
High Timber St. EC4	111	J7
High Tor Cl., Brom.	173	H7
Babbacombe Rd.		
High Tree Cl. W7	104	B7
High Trees SW2	169	G1
High Trees, Barn.	41	H5
High Trees, Croy.	203	H1
High Vw., Pnr.	66	C4
High Vw. Cl. SE19	188	C2
High Vw. Cl., Loug.	47	J5
High Vw. Rd. E18	79	F3
High Worple, Har.	67	F7
Higham Hill Rd. E17	77	H2
Higham Pl. E17	77	H3
Higham Rd. N17	76	A3
Higham Rd., Wdf.Grn.	63	G6
Higham Sta. Av. E4	62	B6
Higham St. E17	77	H3
Highams Lo.	77	H3
Business Cen. E17		
Highams Pk. Ind. Est.	62	C6
E4		
Highbank Way N8	75	G6
Highbanks Cl., Well.	138	B7
Highbanks Rd., Pnr.	51	H5
Highbarrow Rd.,	188	D7
Croy.		
Highbridge Rd., Bark.	116	E1
Highbrook Rd. SE3	156	A3
Highbury Av.,	187	G2
Th.Hth.		
Highbury Cl., N.Mal.	182	C4
Highbury Cl.,	204	B2
W.Wick.		
Highbury Cor. N5	93	G6
Highbury Cres. N5	93	G5
Highbury Est. N5	93	J5
Highbury Gdns., Ilf.	99	H2
Highbury Gra. N5	93	H4
Highbury Gro. N5	93	H6
Highbury Hill N5	93	G3
Highbury Ms. N7	93	G6
Holloway Rd.		
Highbury New Pk. N5	93	J5
Highbury Pk. N5	93	H3
Highbury Pk. Ms. N5	93	J4
Highbury Gra.		
Highbury Pl. N5	93	H6
Highbury Quad. N5	93	J3
Highbury Rd. SW19	166	B5
Highbury Sta. Rd. N1	93	G6
Highbury Ter. N5	93	H5
Highbury Ter. Ms. N5	93	H5
Highclere Rd., N.Mal.	182	D3
Highclere St. SE26	171	H4
Highcliffe Dr. SW15	147	F6
Highcliffe Gdns., Ilf.	80	B6
Highcombe SE7	135	H6
Highcombe Cl. SE9	174	A1
Highcroft NW9	70	D5
Highcroft Av., Wem.	106	A1
Highcroft Gdns.	72	C6
NW11		
Highcroft Rd. N19	74	E7
Highcross Way SW15	165	G1
Highdaun Dr. SW16	187	F4
Highdown, Wor.Pk.	197	F2
Highdown Rd. SW15	147	H6
Highfield, Felt.	160	A1
Highfield, Wat.	51	F3
Highfield Av. NW9	70	C5
Highfield Av. NW11	72	A7
Highfield Av., Erith	139	H6
Highfield Av., Grnf.	86	B5
Highfield Av., Orp.	207	J5
Highfield Av., Pnr.	67	F5
Highfield Av., Wem.	87	J3
Highfield Cl. N22	75	G1
Highfield Cl. NW9	70	C5
Highfield Cl. SE13	154	D7
Highfield Cl., Surb.	195	F1
Highfield Ct. N14	42	C6
Highfield Dr., Brom.	191	E4
Highfield Dr., Epsom	197	F7
Highfield Dr., W.Wick.	204	B2
Highfield Gdns. NW11	72	B6
Highfield Hill SE19	170	A7
Highfield Rd. N21	59	H2
Highfield Rd. NW11	72	B6
Highfield Rd. W3	106	B5
Highfield Rd., Bexh.	159	F5
Highfield Rd., Brom.	192	C4
Highfield Rd., Chis.	193	J3
Highfield Rd., Felt.	160	A2
Highfield Rd., Islw.	144	C1
Highfield Rd., Surb.	182	C7
Highfield Rd., Sutt.	199	H5
Highfield Rd.,	64	B7
Wdf.Grn.		
Highfields Gro. N6	91	J1
Highgate Av. N6	74	B6
Highgate Cl. N6	74	A7
Highgate High St. N6	92	A1
Highgate Hill N6	92	B1
Highgate Hill N19	92	B1
Highgate Rd. NW5	92	B4
Highgate Wk. SE23	171	F2
Highgate W. Hill N6	92	A2
Highgrove Cl. N11	58	A5
Balmoral Av.		
Highgrove Cl., Chis.	192	B1
Highgrove Ct., Beck.	172	A7
Park Rd.		
Highgrove Ms., Cars.	199	J3
Highgrove Rd., Dag.	100	C5
Highgrove Way, Ruis.	66	A6
Highland Av. W7	104	B6
Highland Av., Dag.	101	J3
Highland Av., Loug.	48	B6
Highland Cotts., Wall.	200	B4
Highland Ct. E18	79	H1
Highland Cft., Beck.	172	B5
Highland Dr. SE19	170	B6
Highland Rd., Bexh.	159	G5
Highland Rd., Brom.	191	F1
Highlands, Wat.	50	C1
Highlands, The, Edg.	70	B2
Highlands, The, Pot.B.	40	E5
Highlands Av. N21	43	F5
Highlands Av. W3	106	C7
Highlands Cl. N4	74/75	E7
Mount Vw. Rd.		
Highlands Cl., Houns.	143	H1
Highlands Gdns., Ilf.	98	C1
Highlands Heath	147	J7
SW15		
Highlands Rd., Barn.	40	D5
Highlea Cl. NW9	71	E1
Highlever Rd. W10	107	J5
Highmead SE18	137	J7
Highmead Cres.,	87	J7
Wem.		
Highmore Rd. SE3	135	E6
Highshore Rd. SE15	152	C2
Highstone Av. E11	79	G6
Highview, Nthlt.	103	E3
Highview Av., Edg.	54	C4
Highview Av., Wall.	201	F5
Highview Gdns. N3	72	B3
Highview Gdns. N11	58	C5
Highview Gdns., Edg.	54	C4
Highview Ho., Rom.	83	E4
Highview Rd. SE19	170	A6
Highview Rd. W13	104	D5
Highview Rd., Sid.	176	B4
Highway, The E1	**21**	**J6**
Highway, The E1	112	E7
Highway, The E14	112	E7
Highway, The, Stan.	68	C1
Highwood, Brom.	190	D3
Highwood Av. N12	57	F4
Highwood Av., Orp.	207	F2
Highwood Dr., Orp.	207	F2
Highwood Gdns., Ilf.	80	C5
Highwood Gro. NW7	54	D5
Highwood Hill NW7	55	F3
Highwood La., Loug.	48	D5
Highwood Rd. N19	92	E3
Highworth Rd. N11	58	D6
Hilary Av., Mitch.	186	A3
Hilary Cl. SW6	**30**	**A7**
Hilary Cl. SW6	128	E7
Hilary Cl., Erith	159	J1
Hilary Rd. W12	107	F6
Hilbert Rd., Sutt.	198	A3
Hilborough Way, Orp.	207	G5
Hilda Rd. E6	98	A7
Hilda Rd. E16	115	E4
Hilda Ter. SW9	151	G2
Hilda Vale Cl., Orp.	206	E4
Hilda Vale Rd., Orp.	206	D4

Hildenborough Gdns., Brom. 173 E6
Hildenlea Pl., Brom. 190 E2
Hildreth St. SW12 168 B1
Hildyard Rd. SW6 128 D6
Hiley Rd. NW10 107 J3
Hilgrove Rd. NW6 91 F7
Hiliary Gdns., Stan. 69 F2
Hill Brow, Brom. 192 A1
Hill Cl. NW2 89 H3
Hill Cl. NW11 72 D6
Hill Cl., Barn. 39 J5
Hill Cl., Chis. 174 E5
Hill Cl., Har. 86 B3
Hill Cl., Stan. 52 E4
Hill Ct., Nthlt. 85 G5
Hill Cres. N20 56 E2
Hill Cres., Bex. 177 J1
Hill Cres., Har. 68 D5
Hill Cres., Surb. 181 J5
Hill Cres., Wor.Pk. 197 J2
Hill Crest, Sid. 158 A7
Hill Dr. NW9 88 C1
Hill Dr. SW16 187 F3
Hill End, Orp. 207 J2
The App.
Hill Fm. Rd. W10 107 J5
Hill Gro., Felt. 161 F2
Watermill Way
Hill Ho. Av., Stan. 52 C7
Hill Ho. Cl. N21 43 G7
Hill Ho. Dr., Hmptn. 179 G1
Hill Ho. Rd. SW16 169 F5
Hill Path SW16 169 F5
Valley Rd.
Hill Ri. N9 45 E6
Hill Ri. NW11 73 E4
Hill Ri. SE23 170/171 E1
London Rd.
Hill Ri., Esher 194 E2
Hill Ri., Grnf. 85 J7
Hill Ri., Rich. 145 G5
Hill Rd. N10 73 J1
Hill Rd. NW8 6 D2
Hill Rd. NW8 109 F2
Hill Rd., Cars. 199 H6
Hill Rd., Har. 68 D5
Hill Rd., Mitch. 186 B1
Hill Rd., Pnr. 66 E5
Hill Rd., Sutt. 199 E5
Hill Rd., Wem. 86 E3
Hill St. W1 24 C1
Hill St. W1 130 B1
Hill St., Rich. 145 G5
Hill Top NW11 73 E4
Hill Top, Loug. 48 D2
Hill Top, Mord. 184 D6
Hill Top, Sutt. 184 C7
Hill Top Cl., Loug. 48 D3
Hill Top Pl., Loug. 48 D3
Hill Top Vw., Wdf.Grn. 64 C6
Hill Vw. Cres., Orp. 207 J1
Hill Vw. Dr., Well. 157 H2
Hill Vw. Gdns. NW9 70 D5
Hill Vw. Rd., Esher 194 D7
Hill Vw. Rd., Orp. 207 J1
Hill Vw. Rd., Twick. 144 D6
Hillary Ri., Barn. 40 D4
Hillary Rd., Sthl. 123 G3
Hillbeck Cl. SE15 133 F7
Hillbeck Way, Grnf. 104 A1
Hillborne Cl., Hayes 122 A5
Hillborough Cl. SW19 167 F7
Hillbrook Rd. SW17 167 J3
Hillbrow, N.Mal. 183 F3
Hillbrow Rd., Brom. 172 E7
Hillbury Av., Har. 69 E5
Hillbury Rd. SW17 168 B3
Hillcote Av. SW16 169 G7
Hillcourt Av. N12 56 E6
Hillcourt Est. N16 94 A1
Hillcourt Rd. SE22 152 E6
Hillcrest N6 74 A7
Hillcrest N21 43 H7
Hillcrest Av. NW11 72 B5
Hillcrest Av., Edg. 54 B4
Hillcrest Av., Pnr. 66 D4
Hillcrest Cl. SE26 170 D4
Hillcrest Cl., Beck. 189 J5
Hillcrest Gdns. N3 72 B4
Hillcrest Gdns. NW2 89 G3
Hillcrest Gdns., Esher 194 C3
Hillcrest Rd. E17 78 D2
Hillcrest Rd. E18 79 F2
Hillcrest Rd. W3 126 A1
Hillcrest Rd. W5 105 H5
Hillcrest Rd., Brom. 173 G5
Hillcrest Rd., Loug. 48 A6
Hillcrest Vw., Beck. 189 J6
Hillcroft, Loug. 48 D2
Hillcroft Av., Pnr. 67 F6
Hillcroft Cres. W5 105 H6
Hillcroft Cres., Ruis. 84 D3
Hillcroft Cres., Wat. 50 B1
Hillcroft Cres., Wem. 87 J4
Hillcroft Rd. E6 116 E5
Hillcroome Rd., Sutt. 199 G6
Hillcross Av., Mord. 184 C5
Hilldale Rd., Sutt. 198 C4
Hilldown Rd. SW16 169 E7
Hilldown Rd., Brom. 205 E1
Hilldrop Cres. N7 92 D5
Hilldrop Est. N7 92 D5
Hilldrop La. N7 92 D5
Hilldrop Rd. N7 92 D5
Hilldrop Rd., Brom. 173 G6
Hillend SE18 156 D1
Hillersdon Av. SW13 147 G2
Hillersdon Av., Edg. 53 J5
Hillery Cl. SE17 36 C2
Hillfield Av. N8 75 E5
Hillfield Av. NW9 71 E5
Hillfield Av., Wem. 87 H7
Hillfield Cl., Har. 67 J4
Hillfield Ct. NW3 91 H5
Hillfield Par., Mord. 185 H6
Hillfield Pk. N10 74 B4
Hillfield Pk. N21 59 G2
Hillfield Pk. Ms. N10 74 B4
Hillfield Rd. NW6 90 C5
Hillfield Rd., Hmptn. 161 F7
Hillfoot Av., Rom. 83 J1
Hillfoot Rd., Rom. 83 J1
Hillgate Pl. SW12 150 B7
Hillgate Pl. W8 128 D1
Hillgate St. W8 128 D1
Hilliards Ct. E1 132/133 E1
Wapping High St.
Hillier Cl., Barn. 40 E6
Hillier Gdns., Croy. 201 G5
Crowley Cres.
Hillier Pl., Chess. 195 F6
Hillier Rd. SW11 149 J6
Hilliers La., Croy. 200 E3
Hillingdon Rd., Bexh. 159 J2
Hillingdon St. SE5 35 H6
Hillingdon St. SE5 131 H6
Hillingdon St. SE17 35 H6
Hillingdon St. SE17 131 H6
Hillington Gdns., Wdf.Grn. 80 A2
Hillman Dr. W10 107 J4
Hillman St. E8 95 E6
Hillmarton Rd. N7 93 E5
Hillmead Dr. SW9 151 H4
Hillmont Rd., Esher 194 B3
Hillmore Gro. SE26 171 G5
Hillreach SE18 136 C5
Hillrise Rd. N19 74 E7
Hills Ms. W5 105 H7
Hills Pl. W1 17 F4
Hills Rd., Buck.H. 63 H1
Hillsborough Grn., Wat. 50 A3
Ashburnham Dr.
Hillsborough Rd. SE22 152 B5
Hillsgrove, Well. 138 C7
Hillside NW9 70 D4
Hillside NW10 106 C1
Hillside SW19 166 A6
Hillside, Barn. 41 F5
Hillside Av. N11 57 J6
Hillside Av., Borwd. 38 B4
Hillside Av., Wem. 87 J4
Hillside Av., Wdf.Grn. 63 J5
Hillside Cl. NW8 6 B1
Hillside Cl. NW8 109 E2
Hillside Cl., Mord. 184 B4
Hillside Cl., Wdf.Grn. 63 J5
Hillside Cres., Har. 85 J1
Hillside Cres., Nthwd. 66 A1
Hillside Dr., Edg. 54 A6
Hillside Est. N15 76 C6
Hillside Gdns. E17 78 D3
Hillside Gdns. N6 74 A6
Hillside Gdns. SW2 169 G2
Hillside Gdns., Barn. 40 B4
Hillside Gdns., Edg. 53 J4
Hillside Gdns., Har. 69 H7
Hillside Gdns., Nthwd. 50 A7
Hillside Gdns., Wall. 200 C7
Hillside Gro. N14 42 D7
Hillside Gro. NW7 55 G7
Hillside La., Brom. 205 G2
Hillside Pas. SW2 169 F2
Hillside Ri., Nthwd. 50 A7
Hillside Rd. N15 76 B7
Hillside Rd. SW2 169 G2
Hillside Rd. W5 105 H5
Hillside Rd., Brom. 191 F3
Hillside Rd., Croy. 201 H5
Hillside Rd., Nthwd. 50 A7
Hillside Rd., Pnr. 50 B7
Hillside Rd., Sthl. 103 G4
Hillside Rd., Surb. 181 J5
Hillside Rd., Sutt. 198 C7
Hillsleigh Rd. W8 128 C1
Hillstowe St. E5 95 F2
Hilltop Gdns. NW4 71 H1
Great N. Way
Hilltop Gdns., Orp. 207 H2
Hilltop Rd. NW6 90 D7
Hilltop Way, Stan. 52 D3
Hillview SW20 165 H7
Hillview, Mitch. 186 E4
Hillview Av., Har. 69 H5
Hillview Cl., Pnr. 51 F6
Hillview Cres., Ilf. 80 C6
Hillview Gdns. NW4 72 A4
Hillview Gdns., Har. 67 G3
Hillview Rd. NW7 56 A4
Hillview Rd., Chis. 174 D5
Hillview Rd., Pnr. 51 F7
Hillview Rd., Sutt. 199 F3
Hillway N6 92 A2
Hillway NW9 88 E1
Hillworth Rd. SW2 151 G7
Hilly Flds. Cres. SE4 154 A3
Hillyard Rd. W7 104 B5
Hillyard St. SW9 151 G1
Hillyfield E17 77 H3
Hillyfields, Loug. 48 D2
Hilsea St. E5 95 F4
Hilton Av. N12 57 G5
Hilversum Cres. SE22 152 B5
East Dulwich Gro.
Himley Rd. SW17 167 H5
Hinchcliffe Cl., Wall. 201 F7
Hinchley Cl., Esher 194 C3
Hinchley Dr., Esher 194 C3
Hinchley Way, Esher 194 D3
Hinckley Rd. SE15 152 D4
Hind Cl., Chig. 65 J5
Hind Ct. EC4 19 F4
Hind Gro. E14 114 A6
Hinde Ms. W1 110 A6
Marylebone La.
Hinde St. W1 16 C3
Hinde St. W1 110 A6
Hindes Rd., Har. 68 A5
Hindhead Cl. N16 94 B1
Hindhead Gdns., Nthlt. 102 E1
Hindhead Grn., Wat. 50 C5
Hindhead Way, Wall. 200 E5
Hindmans Rd. SE22 152 D5
Hindmans Way, Dag. 119 F4
Hindmarsh Cl. E1 21 J5
Hindrey Rd. E5 95 E5
Hindsley's Pl. SE23 171 F2
Hinkler Cl., Wall. 201 E7
Hinkler Rd., Har. 69 G3
Hinksey Path SE2 138 D3
Hinstock Rd. SE18 137 F6
Hinton Av., Houns. 142 D4
Hinton Cl. SE9 174 B1
Hinton Rd. N18 60 B4
Hinton Rd. SE24 151 H3
Hinton Rd., Wall. 200 C6
Hippodrome Ms. W11 108 B7
Portland Rd.
Hippodrome Pl. W11 108 B7
Hiscocks Ho. NW10 88 C7
Hitcham Rd. E17 77 J7
Hitchin Sq. E3 113 H2
Hither Fm. Rd. SE3 155 J3
Hither Grn. La. SE13 154 C5
Hitherbroom Rd., Hayes 122 A1
Hitherfield Rd. SW16 169 F2
Hitherfield Rd., Dag. 101 E2
Hitherlands SW12 168 B2
Hitherwell Dr., Har. 68 A1
Hitherwood Dr. SE19 170 C4
Hive Cl., Bushey 52 A2
Hive Rd., Bushey 52 A2
Hoadly Rd. SW16 168 D3
Hobart Cl. N20 57 H2
Oakleigh Rd. N.
Hobart Cl., Hayes 102 D4
Hobart Dr., Hayes 102 D4
Hobart Gdns., Th.Hth. 188 A3
Hobart La., Hayes 102 D4
Hobart Pl. SW1 24 D5
Hobart Pl. SW1 130 B3
Hobart Pl., Rich. 145 J6
Chisholm Rd.
Hobart Rd., Dag. 100 D4
Hobart Rd., Hayes 102 D4
Hobart Rd., Ilf. 81 F2
Hobart Rd., Wor.Pk. 197 H3
Hobbayne Rd. W7 104 A6
Hobbes Wk. SW15 147 H5
Hobbs Grn. N2 73 F3
Hobbs Ms., Ilf. 99 J2
Ripley Rd.
Hobbs Pl. Est. N1 112 B1
Pitfield St.
Hobbs Rd. SE27 169 J4
Hobday St. E14 114 B5
Hobill Wk., Surb. 181 J6
Hoblands End, Chis. 175 H6
Hobsons Pl. E1 21 H1
Hobury St. SW10 30 D6
Hobury St. SW10 129 F6
Hocker St. E2 13 F4
Hockett Cl. SE8 133 H4
Hockley Av. E6 116 B2
Hockley Ms., Bark. 117 H2
Hocroft Av. NW2 90 C3
Hocroft Rd. NW2 90 C4
Hocroft Wk. NW2 90 C3
Hodder Dr., Grnf. 104 C2
Hoddesdon Rd., Belv. 139 G5
Hodford Rd. NW11 90 C2
Hodgkin Cl. SE28 118 D7
Fleming Way
Hodister Cl. SE5 131 J7
Badsworth Rd.
Hodnet Gro. SE16 133 G4
Hodson Cl., Har. 85 F3
Hoe, The, Wat. 50 D2
Hoe St. E17 78 A4
Hofland Rd. W14 128 A3
Hogan Ms. W2 14 E1
Hogan Way E5 94 D2
Geldeston Rd.
Hogarth Cl. E16 116 A5
Hogarth Cl. W5 105 H5
Hogarth Ct. EC3 20 E5
Hogarth Ct. SE19 170 C4
Fountain Dr.
Hogarth Cres. SW19 185 G1
Hogarth Cres., Croy. 187 J7
Hogarth Gdns., Houns. 123 G7
Hogarth Hill NW11 72 C4
Hogarth La. W4 126 E6
Hogarth Pl. SW5 30 A2
Hogarth Reach, Loug. 48 C5
Hogarth Rd. SW5 30 A2
Hogarth Rd. SW5 128 E4
Hogarth Rd., Dag. 100 B5
Hogarth Rd., Edg. 70 A2
Hogarth Roundabout W4 127 E6
Hogarth Roundabout Flyover W4 126/127 E6
Burlington La.
Hogarth Way, Hmptn. 179 J1
Hogshead Pas. E1 112/113 E7
Pennington St.
Hogsmill Way, Epsom 196 C5
Holbeach Gdns., Sid. 157 H6
Holbeach Ms. SW12 168 B1
Harberson Rd.
Holbeach Rd. SE6 154 A7
Holbeck Row SE15 132 D7
Holbein Ms. SW1 32 B3
Holbein Ms. SW1 130 A5
Holbein Pl. SW1 32 B2
Holbein Pl. SW1 130 A4
Holbein Ter., Dag. 100 B4
Marlborough Rd.
Holberton Gdns. NW10 107 H3
Holborn EC1 18 E2
Holborn EC1 111 G5
Holborn Circ. EC1 19 F2
Holborn Pl. WC1 18 C2
Holborn Rd. E13 115 H4
Holborn Viaduct EC1 19 F2
Holborn Viaduct EC1 111 G5
Holborn Way, Mitch. 185 J2
Holbrook Cl. N19 92 B1
Dartmouth Pk. Hill
Holbrook Cl., Enf. 44 C1
Holbrook La., Chis. 175 G7
Holbrook Rd. E15 115 F2
Holbrook Way, Brom. 192 C6
Holbrooke Ct. N7 93 E4
Holbrooke Pl., Rich. 145 G5
Hill Ri.
Holburne Cl. SE3 155 J1
Holburne Gdns. SE3 156 A1
Holburne Rd. SE3 155 J1
Holcombe Hill NW7 55 G3
Highwood Hill
Holcombe Rd. N17 76 C3
Holcombe Rd., Ilf. 80 D7
Holcombe St. W6 127 H4
Holcote Cl., Belv. 138/139 E3
Blakemore Way
Holcroft Rd. E9 95 F7
Holden Av. N12 57 E5
Holden Av. NW9 88 C1
Holden Cl., Dag. 100 B3
Holden Pt. E15 96 D6
Waddington Rd.
Holden Rd. N12 56 E5
Holden St. SW11 150 A2
Holdenby Rd. SE4 153 H5
Holdenhurst Av. N12 57 E7
Holder Cl. N3 57 E7
Holderness Way SE27 169 H5

Holdernesse Cl., Islw. 144 D1
Holdernesse Rd. SW17 167 J3
Holders Hill Av. NW4 72 A2
Holders Hill Circ. NW7 56 B7
Dollis Rd.
Holders Hill Cres. NW4 72 A2
Holders Hill Dr. NW4 72 A3
Holders Hill Gdns. NW4 72 B2
Holders Hill Rd. NW4 72 A2
Holders Hill Rd. NW7 72 B1
Holdgate St. SE7 136 A3
Westmoor St.
Holford Pl. WC1 10 D3
Holford Rd. NW3 91 F3
Holford St. WC1 10 E3
Holford St. WC1 111 G3
Holgate Av. SW11 149 G3
Holgate Gdns., Dag. 101 G5
Holgate Rd., Dag. 101 G5
Holland Av. SW20 183 F1
Holland Cl., Barn. 41 G7
Holland Cl., Brom. 205 F2
Holland Cl., Rom. 83 J5
Holland Cl., Stan. 52 E5
Holland Dr. SE23 171 H3
Holland Gdns. W14 128 B3
Holland Gro. SW9 131 G7
Holland Pk. W8 128 C2
Holland Pk. W11 128 C2
Holland Pk. Av. W11 128 B2
Holland Pk. Av., Ilf. 81 H6
Holland Pk. Gdns. W14 128 B1
Holland Pk. Ms. W11 128 B1
Holland Pk. Rd. W14 128 C3
Holland Pas. N1 111 J1
Basire St.
Holland Pl. W8 22 A3
Holland Rd. E6 116 C1
Holland Rd. E15 115 E3
Holland Rd. NW10 107 G1
Holland Rd. SE25 188 D5
Holland Rd. W14 128 A2
Holland Rd., Wem. 87 G6
Holland St. SE1 27 H1
Holland St. SE1 131 H1
Holland St. W8 128 D2
Holland Vil. Rd. W14 128 B2
Holland Wk. N19 92 D1
Duncombe Rd.
Holland Wk. W8 128 C2
Holland Wk., Stan. 52 D5
Holland Way, Brom. 205 F2
Hollands, The, Felt. 160 D4
Hollands, The, Wor.Pk. 197 F1
Hollar Rd. N16 94 C3
Stoke Newington High St.
Hollen St. W1 17 H3
Hollen St. W1 110 C6
Holles Cl., Hmptn. 161 G6
Holles St. W1 16 E3
Holles St. W1 110 B6
Holley Rd. W3 127 E2
Hollickwood Av. N12 57 J6
Holliday Sq. SW11 149 G3
Fowler Cl.
Hollidge Way, Dag. 101 H6
Hollies, The E11 79 G5
Hollies, The N20 57 G1
Oakleigh Pk. N.
Hollies, The, Har. 68 D4
Hollies Av., Sid. 175 J2
Hollies Cl. SW16 169 G6
Hollies Cl., Twick. 162 C2
Hollies End NW7 55 H5
Hollies Rd. W5 125 F4
Hollies Way SW12 150 A7
Bracken Av.
Holligrave Rd., Brom. 191 G1
Hollingbourne Av., Bexh. 139 F7
Hollingbourne Gdns. W13 104 E5
Hollingbourne Rd. SE24 151 J5
Hollingsworth Rd., Croy. 203 E6
Hollington Cres., N.Mal. 183 F6
Hollington Rd. E6 116 C3
Hollington Rd. N17 76 D2
Hollingworth Cl., W.Mol. 179 F4
Hollingworth Rd., Orp. 192 E6
Hollman Gdns. SW16 169 H6
Hollow, The, Wdf.Grn. 63 F4
Hollow Wk., Rich. 125 H7
Kew Rd.
Holloway Cl., West Dr. 120 B5
Holloway La., West Dr. 120 B6
Holloway Rd. E6 116 C3
Holloway Rd. E11 96 E3
Holloway Rd. N7 93 G6
Holloway Rd. N19 92 D2
Holloway St., Houns. 143 H3
Hollowfield Wk., Nthlt. 84 E6
Hollows, The, Brent. 125 J6
Kew Br. Rd.
Holly Av., Stan. 69 H2
Holly Bush Hill NW3 91 F4
Holly Bush La., Hmptn. 161 F7
Holly Bush Steps NW3 91 F4
Heath St.
Holly Bush Vale NW3 91 F4
Heath St.
Holly Cl. NW10 88 E7
Holly Cl., Buck.H. 64 A3
Holly Cl., Felt. 160 E5
Holly Cl., Wall. 200 B7
Holly Cres., Beck. 189 J5
Holly Cres., Wdf.Grn. 62 D7
Holly Dr. E4 46 B7
Holly Dr., Brent. 124 D6
Holly Fm. Rd., Sthl. 122 E5
Holly Gdns., West Dr. 120 C2
Holly Gro. NW9 70 C7
Holly Gro. SE15 152 C2
Holly Gro., Pnr. 67 E1
Holly Hedge Ter. SE13 154 D5
Holly Hill N21 43 F6
Holly Hill NW3 91 F4
Holly Hill Rd., Belv. 139 H5
Holly Hill Rd., Erith 139 H5
Holly Lo. Gdns. N6 92 A2
Holly Ms. SW10 30 D4
Holly Mt. NW3 91 F4
Holly Bush Hill
Holly Pk. N3 72 C3
Holly Pk. N4 75 F7
Holly Pk. Est. N4 75 F7
Blythwood Rd.
Holly Pk. Gdns. N3 72 D3
Holly Pk. Rd. N11 58 A5
Holly Pk. Rd. W7 124 C1
Holly Pl. NW3 91 F4
Holly Wk.
Holly Rd. E11 79 F7
Holly Rd. W4 126 D4
Dolman Rd.
Holly Rd., Hmptn. 161 J6
Holly Rd., Houns. 143 H4
Holly Rd., Twick. 162 D1
Holly St. E8 94 C6
Holly St. Est. E8 94 C7
Holly Ter. N6 92 A1
Highgate W. Hill
Holly Ter. N20 57 F2
Swan La.
Holly Vw. Cl. NW4 71 G6
Holly Village N6 92 B2
Swains La.
Holly Wk. NW3 91 F4
Holly Wk., Enf. 44 A3
Holly Wk., Rich. 145 H2
Holly Way, Mitch. 186 D4
Hollybank Cl., Hmptn. 161 G5
Hollyberry La. NW3 91 F4
Holly Wk.
Hollybrake Cl., Chis. 175 G7
Hollybush Cl. E11 79 G5
Hollybush Cl., Har. 68 B1
Hollybush Gdns. E2 113 E3
Hollybush Hill E11 79 F6
Hollybush Pl. E2 112/113 E3
Bethnal Grn. Rd.
Hollybush Rd., Kings.T. 163 H5
Hollybush St. E13 115 H3
Hollybush Wk. SW9 151 H4
Hollycroft Av. NW3 90 D3
Hollycroft Av., Wem. 87 J2
Hollycroft Cl., S.Croy. 202 B5
Hollycroft Cl., West Dr. 120 D6
Hollycroft Gdns., West Dr. 120 D6
Hollydale Cl., Nthlt. 85 H4
Dorchester Rd.
Hollydale Dr., Brom. 206 C3
Hollydale Rd. SE15 153 F1
Hollydene SE15 152 E1
Hollydown Way E11 96 D3
Hollyfield Av. N11 57 J5
Hollyfield Rd., Surb. 181 J7
Hollymead, Cars. 199 J3
Hollymount Cl. SE10 154 C1
Hollytree Cl. SW19 166 A1
Hollywood Gdns., Hayes 102 B6
Hollywood Ms. SW10 30 C5
Hollywood Rd. E4 61 H5
Hollywood Rd. SW10 30 C5
Hollywood Rd. SW10 129 F6
Hollywood Way, Wdf.Grn. 62 D7
Holm Oak Cl. SW15 148 C6
West Hill
Holm Oak Ms. SW4 150/151 E5
King's Av.
Holm Wk. SE3 155 G2
Blackheath Pk.
Holman Rd. SW11 149 G2
Holman Rd., Epsom 196 C5
Holmbridge Gdns., Enf. 45 G4
Holmbrook Dr. NW4 72 A5
Holmbury Ct. SW17 167 J3
Holmbury Ct. SW19 167 H7
Cavendish Rd.
Holmbury Gdns., Hayes 121 J1
Church Rd.
Holmbury Gro., Croy. 203 J7
Holmbury Pk., Brom. 174 B7
Holmbury Vw. E5 95 E1
Holmbush Rd. SW15 148 B6
Holmcote Gdns. N5 93 J5
Holmcroft Way, Brom. 192 C5
Holmdale Gdns. NW4 72 A5
Holmdale Rd. NW6 90 D5
Holmdale Rd., Chis. 175 F5
Holmdale Ter. N15 76 B7
Holmdene Av. NW7 55 G6
Holmdene Av. SE24 151 J5
Holmdene Av., Har. 67 H3
Holmdene Cl., Beck. 190 C2
Holme Lacey Rd. SE12 155 F6
Holme Rd. E6 116 B1
Holme Way, Stan. 52 C6
Holmead Rd. SW6 129 E7
Holmebury Cl., Bushey 52 B2
Holmefield Ct. NW3 91 H6
Holmes Av. E17 77 J3
Holmes Av. NW7 56 B5
Holmes Pl. SW10 30 D5
Holmes Rd. NW5 92 B5
Holmes Rd. SW19 167 F7
Holmes Rd., Twick. 162 C2
Holmes Ter. SE1 27 E3
Holmes Ter. SE1 131 G2
Holmesdale Av. SW14 146 B3
Holmesdale Cl. SE25 188 C3
Holmesdale Rd. N6 74 B7
Holmesdale Rd. SE25 188 A5
Holmesdale Rd., Bexh. 158 D2
Holmesdale Rd., Croy. 188 A5
Holmesdale Rd., Rich. 145 J1
Holmesdale Rd., Tedd. 163 F6
Holmesley Rd. SE23 153 H6
Holmewood Gdns. SW2 151 F7
Holmewood Rd. SE25 188 B3
Holmewood Rd. SW2 151 E7
Holmfield Av. NW4 72 A5
Holmhurst Rd., Belv. 139 H5
Holmleigh Rd. N16 94 B1
Holmleigh Rd. Est. N16 94 C1
Holmleigh Rd.
Holms St. E2 13 H1
Holms St. E2 112 D2
Holmshaw Cl. SE26 171 H4
Holmside Ri., Wat. 50 B3
Holmside Rd. SW12 150 A6
Holmsley Cl., N.Mal. 183 F6
Holmstall Av., Edg. 70 C3
Holmwood Cl., Har. 67 J3
Holmwood Cl., Nthlt. 85 H6
Holmwood Gdns. N3 72 D2
Holmwood Gdns., Wall. 200 B6
Holmwood Gro. NW7 54 D5
Holmwood Rd., Chess. 195 G5
Holmwood Rd., Ilf. 99 H2
Holmwood Vil. SE7 135 G5
Woolwich Rd.
Holne Chase N2 73 F6
Holne Chase, Mord. 184 C6
Holness Rd. E15 97 F6
Holroyd Rd. SW15 147 J4
Holstein Way, Erith 138 E3
Holstock Rd., Ilf. 99 F3
Holsworth Cl., Har. 67 J5
Holsworthy Sq. WC1 10 D6
Holsworthy Way, Chess. 195 F5
Holt, The, Ilf. 65 F6
Holt, The, Wall. 200 C4
Holt Cl. N10 74 A4
Holt Cl. SE28 118 B7
Holt Cl., Chig. 65 J5
Holt Ct. E15 96 C5
Clays La.
Holt Rd. E16 136 B1
Holt Rd., Wem. 87 E3
Holt Way, Chig. 65 J5
Holton St. E1 113 G4
Holtwhite Av., Enf. 43 J2
Holtwhites Hill, Enf. 43 H1
Holwell Pl., Pnr. 66 E4
Holwood Pk. Av., Orp. 206 C4
Holwood Pl. SW4 150 D4
Holybourne Av. SW15 147 G7
Holyhead Cl. E3 114 A3
Holyhead Cl. E6 116 C5
Valiant Way
Holyoak Rd. SE11 35 G1
Holyoake Ct. SE16 133 J2
Bryan Rd.
Holyoake Wk. N2 73 F3
Holyoake Wk. W5 105 F4
Holyport Rd. SW6 127 J7
Holyrood Av., Har. 85 E4
Holyrood Gdns., Edg. 70 B3
Holyrood Ms. E16 135 G1
Wesley Av.
Holyrood Rd., Barn. 41 F6
Holyrood St. SE1 28 D2
Holywell Cl. SE3 135 G6
Holywell Cl. SE16 132/133 E5
Masters Dr.
Holywell La. EC2 12 E5
Holywell La. EC2 112 B4
Holywell Row EC2 12 D6
Holywell Row EC2 112 B4
Home Cl., Cars. 199 J2
Home Cl., Nthlt. 103 F3
Home Ct., Felt. 160 A1
Home Fm. Cl., T.Ditt. 180 C7
Home Gdns., Dag. 101 J3
Home Lea, Orp. 207 J5
Home Mead, Stan. 69 F1
Home Pk. Rd. SW19 166 D3
Home Pk. Wk., Kings.T. 181 G4
Home Rd. SW11 149 H2
Homecroft Gdns., Loug. 48 E4
Homecroft Rd. N22 75 J1
Homecroft Rd. SE26 171 F5
Homefarm Rd. W7 104 B6
Homefield Av., Ilf. 81 H5
Homefield Cl. NW10 88 C6
Homefield Cl., Hayes 102 C4
Homefield Gdns. N2 73 G3
Homefield Gdns., Mitch. 185 F2
Homefield Ms., Beck. 190 A1
Homefield Pk., Sutt. 198 E6
Homefield Rd. SW19 166 A6
Homefield Rd. W4 127 F4
Homefield Rd., Brom. 191 J1
Homefield Rd., Edg. 54 D6
Homefield Rd., Walt. 179 E7
Homefield Rd., Wem. 86 D4
Homefield St. N1 12 D2
Homefield St. N1 112 B2
Homelands Dr. SE19 170 B7
Homeleigh Rd. SE15 153 G5
Homemead SW12 168 C2
Homemead Rd., Brom. 192 C5
Homemead Rd., Croy. 186 C6
Homer Cl., Bexh. 159 J1
Homer Dr. E14 134 A4
Homer Rd. E9 95 H6
Homer Rd., Croy. 189 G6
Homer Row W1 15 H2
Homer Row W1 109 H5
Homer St. W1 15 H2
Homer St. W1 109 H5
Homersham Rd., Kings.T. 182 A2
Homerton Gro. E9 95 G5
Homerton High St. E9 95 F5
Homerton Rd. E9 95 H5
Homerton Row E9 95 F5
Homerton Ter. E9 95 F6
Morning La.
Homesdale Cl. E11 79 G5
Homesdale Rd., Brom. 191 J4
Homesdale Rd., Orp. 193 H7
Homesfield NW11 72 D5
Homestall Rd. SE22 153 F5
Homestead, The N11 58 B4
Homestead Gdns., Esher 194 B5

Homestead Paddock N14	42	B5
Homestead Pk. NW2	89	F3
Homestead Rd. SW6	128	C7
Homestead Rd., Dag.	101	F2
Homewillow Cl. N21	43	H6
Homewood Cl., Hmptn.	161	F6
Fearnley Cres.		
Homewood Cres., Chis.	175	H6
Honduras St. EC1	11	J5
Honey Cl., Dag.	101	H6
Honey La. EC2	20	A4
Honeybourne Rd. NW6	90	E5
Honeybourne Way, Orp.	207	G1
Honeybrook Rd. SW12	150	C7
Honeycroft, Loug.	48	D4
Honeyden Rd., Sid.	177	E6
Honeyman Cl. NW6	90	A7
Honeypot Cl. NW9	69	J4
Honeypot La. NW9	69	J3
Honeypot La., Stan.	69	J3
Honeysett Rd. N17	76	C2
Reform Row		
Honeysuckle Cl., Sthl.	102	E7
Honeysuckle Gdns., Croy.	203	G1
Primrose La.		
Honeywell Rd. SW11	149	J6
Honeywood Rd. NW10	107	F2
Honeywood Rd., Islw.	144	D4
Honeywood Wk., Cars.	199	J4
Honister Cl., Stan.	69	J6
Honister Gdns., Stan.	53	E7
Honister Pl., Stan.	69	E1
Honiton Rd. NW6	108	C7
Honiton Rd., Well.	157	J2
Honley Rd. SE6	154	B7
Honnor Gdns., Islw.	143	J3
London Rd.		
Honor Oak Pk. SE23	153	F6
Honor Oak Ri. SE23	153	F6
Honor Rd. SE23	171	F1
Hood Av. N14	42	B6
Hood Av. SW14	146	C5
Hood Cl., Croy.	201	H1
Parson's Mead		
Hood Ct. EC4	19	F4
Hood Rd. SW20	165	F7
Hood Wk., Rom.	83	H1
Hoodcote Gdns. N21	43	H7
Hook, The, Barn.	41	G6
Hook Fm. Rd., Brom.	192	A5
Hook La., Well.	157	J5
Hook Ri. N., Surb.	196	A3
Hook Ri. S., Surb.	196	A3
Hook Ri. S. Ind. Pk., Surb.	196	A3
Hook Rd., Chess.	195	G5
Hook Rd., Surb.	195	H3
Hook Wk., Edg.	54	C6
Hookers Rd. E17	77	G3
Hooking Grn., Har.	67	H5
Hooks Cl. SE15	152/153	E1
Woods Rd.		
Hooks Hall Dr., Dag.	101	J3
Hooks Way SE22	170	D1
Dulwich Common		
Hookstone Way, Wdf.Grn.	64	A7
Hoop La. NW11	72	C7
Hooper Rd. E16	115	G6
Hooper St. E1	21	H5
Hooper St. E1	112	D6
Hooper's Ct. SW3	23	J4
Hop Gdns. WC2	18	A6
Hope Cl. N1	93	J6
Wallace Rd.		
Hope Cl. SE12	173	H3
Hope Cl., Sutt.	199	F5
Hope Cl., Wdf.Grn.	63	J6
West Gro.		
Hope Pk., Brom.	173	F7
Hope St. SW11	149	G3
Hope Wf. SE16	133	F2
St. Marychurch St.		
Hopedale Rd. SE7	135	H6
Hopefield Av. NW6	108	B2
Hopes Cl., Houns.	123	G6
Old Cote Dr.		
Hopetown St. E1	21	G2
Hopewell St. SE5	132	A7
Hopewell Yd. SE5	132	A7
Hopewell St.		
Hopgood St. W12	127	J1
Macfarlane Rd.		
Hopkins Cl. N10	58	A7
Cromwell Rd.		
Hopkins Ms. E15	115	F1
West Rd.		
Hopkins St. W1	17	G4
Hopkinsons Pl. NW1	110	A1
Fitzroy Rd.		
Hoppers Rd. N13	59	G3
Hoppers Rd. N21	59	G2
Hoppett Rd. E4	62	E3
Hopping La. N1	93	H6
St. Mary's Gro.		
Hoppingwood Av., N.Mal.	183	E3
Hopton Gdns. SE1	27	H1
Hopton Gdns., N.Mal.	183	G6
Hopton Rd. SW16	168	E5
Hopton St. SE1	27	H1
Hopton St. SE1	131	H1
Hopwood Cl. SW17	167	F3
Hopwood Rd. SE17	36	C5
Hopwood Rd. SE17	132	A6
Hopwood Wk. E8	94	D7
Wilman Gro.		
Horace Av., Rom.	101	J1
Horace Rd. E7	97	H4
Horace Rd., Ilf.	81	F3
Horace Rd., Kings.T.	181	J3
Horatio Ct. SE16	133	F1
Rotherhithe St.		
Horatio Pl. E14	134	C2
Cold Harbour		
Horatio Pl. SW19	166	D7
Kingston Rd.		
Horatio St. E2	13	H2
Horatio St. E2	112	C2
Horatius Way, Croy.	201	F5
Horbury Cres. W11	108	D7
Horbury Ms. W11	108	C7
Ladbroke Rd.		
Horder Rd. SW6	148	B1
Hordle Prom. E. SE15	37	G7
Hordle Prom. N. SE15	37	E7
Hordle Prom. S. SE15	37	E7
Hordle Prom. W. SE15	37	E7
Horizon Way SE7	135	H4
Horle Wk. SE5	151	H2
Lilford Rd.		
Horley Cl., Bexh.	159	G5
Horley Rd. SE9	174	B4
Hormead Rd. W9	108	C4
Horn La. SE10	135	G4
Horn La. W3	106	C7
Horn La., Wdf.Grn.	63	G6
Horn Link Way SE10	135	G4
Horn Pk. Cl. SE12	155	H5
Horn Pk. La. SE12	155	H5
Hornbeam Cl. NW7	55	F3
Marsh La.		
Hornbeam Cl. SE11	34	E1
Hornbeam Cl., Borwd.	38	A1
Hornbeam Cl., Buck.H.	64	A3
Hornbeam Rd.		
Hornbeam Cl., Ilf.	99	G5
Hornbeam Cl., Nthlt.	85	F5
Hornbeam Cres., Brent.	125	E7
Hornbeam Gro. E4	63	E3
Hornbeam La. E4	47	E5
Hornbeam La., Bexh.	159	J2
Hornbeam Rd., Buck.H.	64	A3
Hornbeam Rd., Hayes	102	C5
Hornbeam Ter., Cars.	199	H1
Hornbeam Twr. E11	96	D3
Hollydown Way		
Hornbeam Wk., Rich.	163	J3
Hornbeam Way, Brom.	192	D6
Hornbeams Ri. N11	58	A6
Hornblower Cl. SE16	133	H4
Greenland Quay		
Hornbuckle Cl., Har.	86	A2
Hornby Cl. NW3	91	G7
Horncastle Cl. SE12	155	G7
Horncastle Rd. SE12	155	G7
Hornchurch Cl., Kings.T.	163	G4
Horndean Cl. SW15	165	G1
Bessborough Rd.		
Horndon Cl., Rom.	83	J1
Horndon Grn., Rom.	83	J1
Horndon Rd., Rom.	83	J2
Horne Way SW15	147	J2
Horner La., Mitch.	185	G2
Hornfair Rd. SE7	135	J6
Horniman Dr. SE23	171	E1
Horning Cl. SE9	174	B4
Horns End Pl., Pnr.	66	C4
Horns Rd., Ilf.	81	F6
Hornsey La. N6	92	B1
Hornsey La. N19	74	C7
Hornsey La. Est. N19	74	D7
Hornsey La.		
Hornsey La. Gdns. N6	74	C7
Hornsey Pk. Rd. N8	75	F3
Hornsey Ri. N19	74	D7
Hornsey Ri. Gdns. N19	74	D7
Hornsey Rd. N7	93	E2
Hornsey Rd. N19	93	E2
Hornsey St. N7	93	F5
Hornshay St. SE15	133	F6
Hornton Pl. W8	22	A4
Hornton St. W8	128	D2
Hornton St. W8	128	D2
Horsa Cl., Wall.	201	E7
Horsa Rd. SE12	155	J7
Horsa Rd., Erith	139	J7
Horse & Dolphin Yd. W1	17	J5
Horse Fair, Kings.T.	181	G2
Horse Guards Av. SW1	26	A2
Horse Guards Av. SW1	130	E1
Horse Guards Rd. SW1	25	J2
Horse Guards Rd. SW1	130	D1
Horse Leaze E6	116	D6
Horse Ride SW1	25	H2
Horse Ride SW1	130	C1
Horse Rd. E7	97	H3
Centre Rd.		
Horse Shoe Cres., Nthlt.	103	G2
Horse Shoe Grn., Sutt.	198/199	E2
Aultone Way		
Horse Yd. N1	111	H1
Essex Rd.		
Horsebridge Cl., Dag.	119	E1
Horsecroft Rd., Edg.	54	D7
Horseferry Pl. SE10	134	C6
Horseferry Rd. E14	113	H7
Horseferry Rd. SW1	25	H6
Horseferry Rd. SW1	130	D4
Horsell Rd. N5	93	G5
Horselydown La. SE1	29	F3
Horselydown La. SE1	132	C2
Horsenden Av., Grnf.	86	B5
Horsenden Cres., Grnf.	86	C5
Horsenden La. N., Grnf.	86	C6
Horsenden La. S., Grnf.	104	D2
Horseshoe Cl. E14	134	C5
Ferry St.		
Horseshoe Cl. NW2	89	H2
Horseshoe La. N20	56	A1
Horseshoe La., Enf.	43	J3
Chase Side		
Horsfeld Gdns. SE9	156	B5
Horsfeld Rd. SE9	156	A5
Horsford Rd. SW2	151	F5
Horsham Av. N12	57	H5
Horsham Rd., Bexh.	159	G5
Horsham Rd., Felt.	141	F6
Horsley Dr., Croy.	204	C7
Horsley Dr., Kings.T.	163	G5
Horsley Rd. E4	62	C2
Horsley Rd., Brom.	191	H1
Palace Rd.		
Horsley St. SE17	36	B5
Horsley St. SE17	132	A6
Horsmonden Cl., Orp.	193	H7
Horsmonden Rd. SE4	153	J5
Hortensia Rd. SW10	30	C7
Hortensia Rd. SW10	129	F6
Horticultural Pl. W4	126	D5
Heathfield Ter.		
Horton Av. NW2	90	B4
Horton Br. Rd., West Dr.	120	C1
Horton Cl., West Dr.	120	C1
Horton Ind. Pk., West Dr.	120	C1
Horton Rd. E8	94	E6
Horton Rd., West Dr.	120	D1
Horton St. SE13	154	B3
Horton Way, Croy.	189	G5
Hortus Rd. E4	62	C2
Hortus Rd., Sthl.	123	F2
Horwood Sq. SW17	167	J2
Hosack Rd. SW17	167	J2
Hoser Av. SE12	173	G2
Hosier La. EC1	19	G2
Hosier La. EC1	111	H5
Hoskins Cl. E16	115	J6
Hoskins Cl., Hayes	121	J5
Cranford Dr.		
Hoskins St. SE10	134	D5
Hospital Br. Rd., Twick.	143	H7
Hospital Rd. E9	95	G5
Homerton Row		
Hospital Rd., Houns.	143	G3
Hotham Cl., W.Mol.	179	G3
Garrick Gdns.		
Hotham Rd. SW15	147	J3
Hotham Rd. SW19	167	F7
Hotham Rd. Ms. SW19	167	F7
Haydons Rd.		
Hotham St. E15	114	E1
Hothfield Pl. SE16	133	F3
Lower Rd.		
Hotspur Rd., Nthlt.	103	G2
Hotspur St. SE11	34	E3
Hotspur St. SE11	131	G5
Houblon Rd., Rich.	145	H5
Houghton Cl. E8	94	C6
Buttermere Wk.		
Houghton Cl., Hmptn.	161	E6
Houghton Rd. N15	76	C5
West Grn. Rd.		
Houghton St. WC2	18	D4
Houlder Cres., Croy.	201	H6
Hounsden Rd. N21	43	F6
Houndsditch EC3	20	E3
Houndsditch EC3	112	B6
Houndsfield Rd. N9	44	E7
Hounslow Av., Houns.	143	H5
Hounslow Gdns., Houns.	143	H5
Hounslow Rd. (Feltham), Felt.	160	B1
Hounslow Rd. (Hanworth), Felt.	160	D4
Hounslow Rd., Twick.	143	J6
Houseman Way SE5	132	A7
Hopewell St.		
Houston Pl., Esher	194	B1
Lime Tree Av.		
Houston Rd. SE23	171	H2
Houston Rd., Surb.	181	E6
Hove Av. E17	77	J5
Hove Gdns., Sutt.	199	E1
Hoveden Rd. NW2	90	B5
Hoveton Rd. SE28	118	C6
Howard Av., Bex.	176	C1
Howard Cl. N11	58	A2
Howard Cl. NW2	90	B4
Howard Cl. W3	106	B6
Howard Cl., Hmptn.	161	J6
Howard Cl., Loug.	48	B6
Howard Cl., Borwd.	38	D4
Howard Ms. N5	93	H4
Hamilton Pk.		
Howard Pl. SW1	25	F6
Howard Rd. E6	116	C2
Howard Rd. E11	97	E3
Howard Rd. E17	78	A3
Howard Rd. N15	76	B6
Howard Rd. N16	94	A4
Howard Rd. NW2	90	A4
Howard Rd. SE20	189	F1
Howard Rd. SE25	188	D5
Howard Rd., Bark.	117	G1
Howard Rd., Brom.	173	G7
Howard Rd., Ilf.	99	E4
Howard Rd., Islw.	144	C3
Howard Rd., N.Mal.	183	E3
Howard Rd., Sthl.	103	H6
Howard Rd., Surb.	181	J6
Howard St., T.Ditt.	181	E7
Howard Wk. N2	73	F4
Howard Way, Barn.	40	A5
Howards Cl., Pnr.	66	B2
Howards Crest Cl., Beck.	190	C2
Howards La. SW15	147	H4
Howards Rd. E13	115	G3
Howarth Ct. E15	96	C5
Clays La.		
Howarth Rd. SE2	138	A5
Howberry Cl., Edg.	53	G6
Howberry Rd., Edg.	53	G6
Howberry Rd., Stan.	53	G6
Howberry Rd., Th.Hth.	188	A1
Howbury Rd. SE15	153	F3
Howcroft Cres. N3	56	D7
Howcroft La., Grnf.	104	A3
Cowgate Rd.		
Howden Cl. SE28	118	D7
Howden Rd. SE25	188	C2
Howden St. SE15	152	D3
Howe Cl., Rom.	83	G1
Howell Cl., Rom.	82	D5
Howell Wk. SE1	35	H2
Howes Cl. N3	72	D3
Howfield Pl. N17	76	C3
Howgate Rd. SW14	146	D3

Howick Pl. SW1 25 G6
Howick Pl. SW1 130 C3
Howie St. SW11 129 H7
Howitt Cl. NW3 91 H6
Howitt Rd.
Howitt Rd. NW3 91 H6
Howland Est. SE16 133 F3
Howland Ms. E. W1 17 G1
Howland St. W1 17 F1
Howland St. W1 110 C5
Howland Way SE16 133 H2
Howletts Rd. SE24 151 J6
Howley Pl. W2 14 D1
Howley Pl. W2 109 F5
Howley Rd., Croy. 201 H3
Hows St. E2 13 F1
Hows St. E2 112 C2
Howsman Rd. SW13 127 G6
Howson Rd. SE4 153 H4
Howson Ter., Rich. 145 H6
Howton Pl., Bushey 52 A1
Hoxton Mkt. N1 12 D4
Hoxton Sq. N1 12 D4
Hoxton St. N1 112 B3
Hoxton St. N1 12 E4
Hoxton St. N1 112 B1
Hoy St. E16 115 F6
Hoylake Gdns., Mitch. 186 C3
Hoylake Gdns., Ruis. 84 B1
Hoylake Gdns., Wat. 50 D4
Hoylake Rd. W3 107 E6
Hoyland Cl. SE15 132/133 E7
Commercial Way
Hoyle Rd. SW17 167 H5
Hubbard Dr., Chess. 195 F6
Hubbard Rd. SE27 169 J4
Hubbard St. E15 114 E1
Hubbinet Ind. Est., 83 J3
Rom.
Hubert Gro. SW9 151 E3
Hubert Rd. E6 116 A3
Huddart St. E3 114 A5
Huddleston Cl. E2 113 F2
Huddleston Rd. N7 92 D4
Huddlestone Rd. E7 97 F4
Huddlestone Rd. NW2 89 H6
Hudson Ct. E14 134 A5
Napier Av.
Hudson Ct. SW19 167 E7
Superior Dr.
Hudson Pl. SE18 137 F5
Hudson Rd., Bexh. 159 F2
Hudson Rd., Hayes 121 G6
Hudson's Pl. SW1 33 E1
Huggin Ct. EC4 20 A5
Huggin Hill EC4 20 A5
Huggins Pl. SW2 169 F1
Roupell Rd.
Hugh Dalton Av. 128 C6
SW6
Hugh Gaitskell Cl. 128 C6
SW6
Hugh Ms. SW1 33 E2
Hugh Pl. SW1 33 H1
Hugh St. SW1 32 E2
Hugh St. SW1 130 B4
Hughan Rd. E15 96 D5
Hughenden Av., Har. 69 E5
Hughenden Gdns., 102 C3
Nthlt.
Hughenden Rd., 183 G7
Wor.Pk.
Hughenden Ter. E15 96 C4
Westdown Rd.
Hughes Rd., Hayes 102 B7
Hughes Wk., Croy. 187 J7
St. Saviours Rd.
Hugo Rd. N19 92 C4
Hugon Rd. SW6 148 E3
Huguenot Pl. E1 21 G1
Huguenot Pl. E1 112 C5
Huguenot Pl. SW18 149 F5
Huguenot Sq. 152/153 E3
SE15
Scylla Rd.
Hull Cl. SE16 133 G2
Hull Pl. E16 136/137 E2
Barge Ho. Rd.
Hull St. EC1 11 J4
Hullbridge Ms. N1 112 A1
Sherborne St.
Hulse Av., Bark. 99 G6
Hulse Av., Rom. 83 H1
Hulse Cl., Ilf. 99 F5
Buttsbury Rd.
Humber Cl., West 120 A1
Dr.
Humber Dr. W10 108 A4
Humber Rd. NW2 89 H2
Humber Rd. SE3 135 F6
Humberstone Rd. E13 115 J3
Humberton Cl. E9 95 H5
Marsh Hill

Humbolt Rd. W6 128 B6
Hume Ter. E16 115 J6
Prince Regent La.
Hume Way, Ruis. 66 A6
Humes Av. W7 124 B3
Humphrey Cl., Ilf. 80 C1
Humphrey St. SE1 37 F3
Humphrey St. SE1 132 C5
Humphries Cl., Dag. 101 F4
Hundred Acre NW9 71 F2
Hungerford Br. SE1 26 B1
Hungerford Br. SE1 131 E1
Hungerford Br. WC2 26 B1
Hungerford Br. WC2 131 E1
Hungerford La. WC2 26 A1
Hungerford Rd. N7 92 E5
Hungerford St. E1 112/113 E6
Commercial Rd.
Hunsdon Cl., Dag. 101 E6
Hunsdon Rd. SE14 133 G6
Hunslett St. E2 113 F2
Royston St.
Hunston Rd., Mord. 198 E1
Hunt Rd., Sthl. 123 G3
Hunt St. W11 128 A1
Hunt Way SE22 170 D1
Dulwich Common
Hunter Cl. SE1 28 C6
Hunter Cl. SW12 168 A1
Balham Pk. Rd.
Hunter Cl., Borwd. 38 C5
Hunter Ho., Felt. 160 A1
Hunter Rd. SW20 183 J1
Hunter Rd., Ilf. 99 E5
Hunter Rd., Th.Hth. 188 A3
Hunter St. WC1 10 B5
Hunter St. WC1 111 E4
Hunter Wk. E13 115 G2
Hunter Wk., Borwd. 38 C5
Ashley Dr.
Huntercombe Gdns., 50 C4
Wat.
Hunters, The, Beck. 190 C1
Hunters Ct., Rich. 145 G5
Friars La.
Hunters Gro., Har. 69 F4
Hunters Gro., Hayes 122 A1
Hunters Gro., Orp. 207 E4
Hunters Hall Rd., 101 G4
Dag.
Hunters Hill, Ruis. 84 C3
Hunters Meadow 170 B4
SE19
Dulwich Wd. Av.
Hunters Rd., Chess. 195 H3
Hunters Sq., Dag. 101 G4
Hunters Way, Croy. 202 B4
Brownlow Rd.
Hunters Way, Enf. 43 G1
Hunting Gate Cl., 43 G3
Enf.
Hunting Gate Dr., 195 H7
Chess.
Hunting Gate Ms., 199 E3
Sutt.
Hunting Gate Ms., 162 B1
Twick.
Colne Rd.
Huntingdon Cl., 187 E3
Mitch.
Huntingdon Gdns., 126 C7
W4
Huntingdon Gdns., 197 J3
Wor.Pk.
Huntingdon Rd. N2 73 H3
Huntingdon Rd. N9 61 F1
Huntingdon St. E16 115 F6
Huntingdon St. N1 93 F7
Huntingfield, Croy. 203 J7
Huntingfield Rd. 147 G5
SW15
Huntings Rd., Dag. 101 G6
Huntley Dr. N3 56 D6
Huntley St. WC1 9 G6
Huntley St. WC1 110 C4
Huntley Way SW20 183 G2
Hunton St. E1 13 H6
Hunton St. E1 112 D4
Hunt's Cl. SE3 155 G2
Hunt's Ct. WC2 17 J6
Hunts La. E15 114 C2
Hunts Mead, Enf. 45 G3
Hunts Mead Cl., 174 C7
Chis.
Hunts Slip Rd. SE21 170 B3
Huntsman St. SE17 36 C2
Huntsman St. SE17 132 A4
Huntsmans Cl., Felt. 160 B4
Huntsmoor Rd., 196 D5
Epsom
Huntspill St. SW17 167 F3
Huntsworth Ms. NW1 7 J6

Hurley Cres. SE16 133 G2
Marlow Way
Hurley Rd. SE11 35 F2
Hurley Rd. SE11 131 G4
Hurley Rd., Grnf. 103 H6
Hurlingham Ct. SW6 148 C3
Hurlingham Gdns. 148 C3
SW6
Hurlingham Rd. SW6 148 C2
Hurlingham Rd., 139 F7
Bexh.
Hurlingham Sq. 148/149 E3
SW6
Peterborough Rd.
Hurlock St. N5 93 H3
Hurlstone Rd. SE25 188 A5
Hurn Ct. Rd., Houns. 142 D2
Renfrew Rd.
Huron Cl., Orp. 207 J6
Huron Rd. SW17 168 A2
Hurren Cl. SE3 154 E3
Hurry Cl. E15 97 E7
Hursley Rd., Chig. 65 J5
Tufter Rd.
Hurst Av. E4 62 A4
Hurst Av. N6 74 C6
Hurst Cl. E4 62 A3
Hurst Cl. NW11 72 E6
Hurst Cl., Brom. 205 F1
Hurst Cl., Chess. 196 A5
Hurst Cl., Nthlt. 85 F5
Hurst Est. SE2 138 D5
Hurst La. SE2 138 D5
Hurst La., E.Mol. 179 J4
Hurst Ri., Barn. 40 D3
Hurst Rd. E17 78 B3
Hurst Rd. N21 59 G1
Hurst Rd., Bex. 176 D1
Hurst Rd., Buck.H. 64 A1
Hurst Rd., Croy. 202 A5
Hurst Rd., E.Mol. 179 H3
Hurst Rd., Erith 139 J7
Hurst Rd., Sid. 176 A2
Hurst Rd., Walt. 178 C5
Hurst Rd., W.Mol. 179 E3
Hurst Springs, Bex. 177 E1
Hurst St. SE24 151 H6
Hurst Vw. Rd., 202 B7
S.Croy.
Hurst Way, S.Croy. 202 B6
Hurstbourne, Esher 194 C6
Hurstbourne Gdns., 99 H6
Bark.
Hurstbourne Ho. 147 H1
SE23
Compton Av.
Hurstcourt Rd., Sutt. 198 E2
Hurstdene Av., 205 F1
Brom.
Hurstdene Gdns. N15 76 B7
Hurstfield, Brom. 191 G5
Hurstfield Rd., W.Mol. 179 G3
Hurstleigh Gdns., Ilf. 80 C1
Hurstmead Ct., Edg. 54 B4
Hurstway Wk. W11 108 A7
Hurstwood Av. E18 79 H4
Hurstwood Av., Bex. 176 E1
Hurstwood Dr., Brom. 192 C3
Hurstwood Rd. NW11 72 B4
Hurstwood Rd., Walt. 179 F7
Huson Cl. NW3 91 H7
Hussars Cl., Houns. 142 E3
Husseywell Cres., 205 G1
Brom.
Hutchings St. E14 134 A2
Hutchings Wk. NW11 73 E4
Hutchins Cl. E15 96 C7
Gibbins Rd.
Hutchins Rd. SE28 118 A7
Hutchinson Ter., Wem. 87 G3
Hutton Cl., Grnf. 86 A5
Mary Peters Dr.
Hutton Cl., Wdf.Grn. 63 H6
Hutton Gdns., Har. 51 J7
Hutton Gro. N12 57 E5
Hutton La., Har. 51 J7
Hutton Row, Edg. 54 C7
Pavilion Way
Hutton St. EC4 19 F4
Hutton Wk., Har. 51 J7
Huxbear St. SE4 153 J5
Huxley Cl., Nthlt. 103 E1
Huxley Dr., Rom. 82 B7
Huxley Gdns. NW10 105 J3
Huxley Par. N18 60 A5
Huxley Pl. N13 59 H4
Huxley Rd. E10 96 C2
Huxley Rd. N18 60 A4
Huxley Rd., Well. 157 J3
Huxley Sayze N18 60 A5
Huxley St. W10 108 B3
Hyacinth Cl., Hmptn. 161 G6
Gresham Rd.
Hyacinth Cl., Ilf. 98 E6

Hyacinth Ct., Pnr. 66 C3
Tulip Ct.
Hyacinth Rd. SW15 165 G1
Hycliffe Gdns., Chig. 65 F4
Hyde, The NW9 71 E5
Hyde Cl. E13 115 G2
Hyde Cl., Barn. 40 C3
Hyde Ct. N20 57 G3
Hyde Cres. NW9 71 E5
Hyde Est. Rd. NW9 71 F5
Hyde Ho. NW9 71 E5
Hyde La. SW11 149 H1
Battersea Br. Rd.
Hyde Pk. SW7 23 G1
Hyde Pk. SW7 129 J1
Hyde Pk. W1 23 G1
Hyde Pk. W1 129 J1
Hyde Pk. W2 23 G1
Hyde Pk. W2 129 J1
Hyde Pk. Av. N21 59 J2
Hyde Pk. Cor. W1 24 C3
Hyde Pk. Cor. W1 130 A2
Hyde Pk. Cres. W2 15 G4
Hyde Pk. Cres. W2 109 H6
Hyde Pk. Gdns. N21 59 J1
Hyde Pk. Gdns. W2 15 F5
Hyde Pk. Gdns. W2 109 G7
Hyde Pk. Gdns. Ms. 15 F5
W2
Hyde Pk. Gate SW7 22 D4
Hyde Pk. Gate SW7 129 F2
Hyde Pk. Gate Ms. 22 D4
SW7
Hyde Pk. Pl. W2 15 H5
Hyde Pk. Pl. W2 109 H7
Hyde Pk. Sq. W2 15 G4
Hyde Pk. Sq. W2 109 H6
Hyde Pk. Sq. Ms. W2 15 G4
Hyde Pk. St. W2 15 G4
Hyde Pk. St. W2 109 H6
Hyde Rd. N1 112 A1
Hyde Rd., Bexh. 159 F2
Hyde Rd., Rich. 145 J5
Albert Rd.
Hyde St. SE8 134 A6
Deptford High St.
Hyde Vale SE10 134 C7
Hyde Wk., Mord. 184 D7
Hyde Way N9 60 C2
Hyde Way, Hayes 121 J4
Hydefield Cl. N21 60 A1
Hydefield Ct. N9 60 A1
Hyderabad Way E15 96 E7
Hydes Pl. N1 93 H7
Compton Av.
Hydeside Gdns. N9 60 C2
Hydethorpe Av. N9 60 C2
Hydethorpe Rd. SW12 168 C1
Hylands Rd. E17 78 D2
Hylton St. SE18 137 J4
Hyndewood SE23 171 G3
Hyndman St. SE15 132 E6
Hynton Rd., Dag. 100 C2
Hyrstdene, S.Croy. 201 H4
Hyson Rd. SE16 132/133 E4
Galleywall Rd.
Hythe Av., Bexh. 139 F7
Hythe Cl. N18 60 D4
Hythe Path, Th.Hth. 188 A3
Hythe Rd. NW10 107 G4
Hythe Rd., Th.Hth. 188 A2
Hyver Hill NW7 38 D6

I

Ian Sq., Enf. 45 G1
Lansbury Rd.
Ibbetson Path, Loug. 49 E3
Ibbotson Av. E16 115 F6
Ibbott St. E1 113 F4
Mantus Rd.
Iberian Av., Wall. 200 D4
Ibis La. W4 146 C1
Ibis Way, Hayes 102 D6
Cygnet Way
Ibscott Cl., Dag. 101 J6
Ibsley Gdns. SW15 165 G1
Ibsley Way, Barn. 41 H5
Ice Wf. Marina N1 10 B1
Iceland Rd. E3 114 A1
Iceni Ct. E3 113 J1
Roman Rd.
Ickburgh Est. E5 94/95 E3
Ickburgh Rd. E5 94 E3
Ickleton Rd. SE9 174 B4
Icknield Dr., Ilf. 81 E5
Ickworth Pk. Rd. E17 77 H4
Ida Rd. N15 76 A5
Ida St. E14 114 C6
Iden Cl., Brom. 191 E3
Idlecombe Rd. SW17 168 A6
Idmiston Rd. E15 97 F5
Idmiston Rd. SE27 169 J3

Idmiston Rd., Wor.Pk.	183	F7
Idmiston Sq., Wor.Pk.	183	F7
Idol La. EC3	**20**	**D6**
Idonia St. SE8	133	J7
Iffley Rd. W6	127	H3
Ifield Rd. SW10	**30**	**B5**
Ifield Rd. SW10	129	E6
Ifor Evans Pl. E1	113	G4
Mile End Rd.		
Ightham Rd., Erith	139	G7
Ikea Twr. NW10	88	D5
Ilbert St. W10	108	A3
Ilchester Gdns. W2	**14**	**A5**
Ilchester Gdns. W2	108	E7
Ilchester Pl. W14	128	C3
Ilchester Rd., Dag.	100	B5
Ildersly Gro. SE21	170	A2
Ilderton Rd. SE15	133	F7
Ilderton Rd. SE16	133	E5
Ilex Cl., Sun.	178	C2
Oakington Dr.		
Ilex Ho. N4	75	F7
Ilex Rd. NW10	89	F6
Ilex Way SW16	169	G5
Ilford Hill, Ilf.	98	D3
Ilford La., Ilf.	98	E3
Ilfracombe Gdns.,	82	B7
Rom.		
Ilfracombe Rd., Brom.	173	F3
Iliffe St. SE17	**35**	**H3**
Iliffe St. SE17	131	H5
Iliffe Yd. SE17	**35**	**H3**
Ilkeston Ct. E5	95	G4
Overbury St.		
Ilkley Cl. SE19	170	A6
Ilkley Rd. E16	115	J5
Ilkley Rd., Wat.	50	D5
Illingworth Cl.,	185	G3
Mitch.		
Illingworth Way, Enf.	44	B4
Ilmington Rd., Har.	69	G6
Ilminster Gdns. SW11	149	H4
Imber Cl. N14	42	C7
Imber Cl., Esher	194	A1
Ember La.		
Imber Ct. Trd. Est.,	180	A6
E.Mol.		
Imber Gro., Esher	180	A7
Imber Pk. Rd., Esher	194	A1
Imber St. N1	112	A1
Imer Pl., T.Ditt.	180	C7
Imperial Av. N16	94	C3
Victorian Rd.		
Imperial Cl., Har.	67	G6
Imperial College Rd.	**22**	**E6**
SW7		
Imperial College Rd.	129	G3
SW7		
Imperial Dr., Har.	67	G7
Imperial Gdns.,	186	B3
Mitch.		
Imperial Ms. E6	115	J2
Central Pk. Rd.		
Imperial Rd. N22	74	E1
Imperial Rd. SW6	149	F1
Imperial Rd., Felt.	141	H7
Imperial Sq. SW6	149	E1
Imperial St. E3	114	C3
Imperial Way, Chis.	175	F3
Imperial Way, Croy.	201	F6
Imperial Way, Har.	69	H6
Imre Cl. W12	127	H1
Ellerslie Rd.		
Inca Dr. SE9	156	E7
Inchmery Rd. SE6	172	B2
Inchwood, Croy.	204	B4
Independent Pl. E8	94	C5
Downs Pk. Rd.		
Independents Rd.	155	F3
SE3		
Blackheath Village		
Inderwick Rd. N8	75	F5
Indescon Ct. E14	134	B2
India Pl. WC2	**18**	**C5**
India St. EC3	**21**	**F4**
India Way W12	107	H7
Indigo Ms. E14	114	C7
Ashton St.		
Indigo Ms. N16	94	A3
Indus Rd. SE7	135	J7
Industry Ter. SW9	151	G3
Canterbury Cres.		
Ingal Rd. E13	115	G4
Ingate Pl. SW8	150	B1
Ingatestone Rd. E12	97	J1
Ingatestone Rd. SE25	188	E4
Ingatestone Rd.,	63	G7
Wdf.Grn.		
Ingelow Rd. SW8	150	B2
Ingersoll Rd. W12	127	H1
Ingestre Pl. W1	**17**	**G4**
Ingestre Rd. E7	97	G4
Ingestre Rd. NW5	92	B4
Ingham Rd. NW6	90	D4

Ingle Cl., Pnr.	67	E3
Inglebert St. EC1	**11**	**E3**
Ingleborough St. SW9	151	G2
Ingleby Dr., Har.	86	A3
Ingleby Rd., Dag.	101	H6
Ingleby Rd., Ilf.	98	E1
Ingleby Way, Chis.	174	D5
Ingledew Rd. SE18	137	G5
Inglehurst Gdns., Ilf.	80	C5
Inglemere Rd. SE23	171	G3
Inglemere Rd., Mitch.	167	J7
Inglesham Wk. E9	95	J6
Ingleside Cl., Beck.	172	A1
Ingleside Gro. SE3	135	F6
Inglethorpe St. SW6	148	A1
Ingleton Av., Well.	158	A5
Ingleton Rd. N18	60	D6
Ingleton St. SW9	151	G2
Ingleway N12	57	G6
Inglewood Cl. E14	134	A4
Inglewood Cl., Ilf.	65	J6
Inglewood Copse,	192	B2
Brom.		
Inglewood Rd. NW6	90	D5
Inglis Barracks NW7	56	B6
Inglis Rd. W5	105	J7
Inglis Rd., Croy.	202	C1
Inglis St. SE5	151	H1
Ingram Av. NW11	73	F7
Ingram Cl. SE11	**34**	**D1**
Ingram Cl., Stan.	53	F5
Ingram Rd. N2	73	H4
Ingram Rd., Th.Hth.	187	J1
Ingram Way, Grnf.	104	A1
Ingrave Ho., Dag.	118	B1
Ingrave St. SW11	149	G3
Ingress St. W4	126/127	E5
Devonshire Rd.		
Inigo Jones Rd. SE7	136	B7
Inigo Pl. WC2	**18**	**A5**
Inkerman Rd. NW5	92	B6
Inkerman Ter. W8	128	D3
Allen St.		
Inks Grn. E4	62	C5
Inman Rd. NW10	106	E1
Inman Rd. SW18	149	F7
Inmans Row, Wdf.Grn.	63	G4
Inner Circle NW1	**8**	**B3**
Inner Circle NW1	110	A3
Inner Pk. Rd. SW19	166	A1
Inner Ring E., Houns.	140	E3
Inner Ring W., Houns.	140	D3
Inner Temple La. EC4	**19**	**E4**
Innes Cl. SW20	184	B2
Innes Gdns. SW15	147	H6
Innes Yd., Croy.	201	J3
Whitgift St.		
Inniskilling Rd. E13	115	J2
Innovation Cl., Wem.	105	H1
Inskip Cl. E10	96	B2
Inskip Rd., Dag.	100	D1
Institute Pl. E8	94/95	E5
Amhurst Rd.		
Instone Cl., Wall.	201	E7
Integer Gdns. E11	78	D7
Forest Rd.		
Interchange E. Ind.	95	F1
Est. E5		
Theydon Rd.		
International Av.,	122	C5
Houns.		
International Trd.	122	B3
Est., Sthl.		
Inver Cl. E5	95	F2
Theydon Rd.		
Inver Ct. W2	**14**	**B4**
Inverary Pl. SE18	137	G6
Old Mill Rd.		
Inverclyde Gdns.,	82	D4
Rom.		
Inveresk Gdns.,	197	F3
Wor.Pk.		
Inverforth Cl. NW3	91	F2
North End Way		
Inverforth Rd. N11	58	B5
Invermore Pl. SE18	137	F4
Inverness Av., Enf.	44	B1
Inverness Dr., Ilf.	65	H6
Inverness Gdns. W8	**22**	**A2**
Inverness Ms.	136/137	E2
E16		
Barge Ho. Rd.		
Inverness Ms. W2	**14**	**B5**
Inverness Pl. W2	**14**	**B5**
Inverness Pl. W2	109	E7
Inverness Rd. N18	60/61	E5
Aberdeen Rd.		
Inverness Rd., Houns.	143	F4
Inverness Rd., Sthl.	123	E4
Inverness Rd.,	198	A1
Wor.Pk.		
Inverness St. NW1	110	B1
Inverness Ter. W2	**14**	**B5**

Inverness Ter. W2	109	E7
Inverton Rd. SE15	153	G4
Invicta Cl., Chis.	174	D5
Invicta Gro., Nthlt.	103	F3
Invicta Plaza SE1	**27**	**G1**
Invicta Rd. SE3	135	G7
Inville Rd. SE17	**36**	**C4**
Inville Rd. SE17	132	A5
Inwen Ct. SE8	133	H5
Inwood Av., Houns.	143	J3
Inwood Cl., Croy.	203	H2
Inwood Rd., Houns.	143	H4
Inworth St. SW11	149	H2
Inworth Wk. N1	111	J1
Popham St.		
Ion Sq. E2	**13**	**H2**
Iona Cl. SE6	154	A7
Iona Cl., Mord.	184	E7
Ipswich Rd. SW17	168	A6
Ireland Cl. E6	116	C5
Bradley Stone Rd.		
Ireland Pl. N22	58/59	E7
Whittington Rd.		
Ireland Yd. EC4	**19**	**H4**
Ireland Yd. EC4	111	H6
Irene Rd. SW6	148	D1
Irene Rd., Orp.	193	J7
Ireton Cl. N10	58	A7
Cromwell Rd.		
Ireton St. E3	114	A4
Tidworth Rd.		
Iris Av., Bex.	159	E5
Iris Cl. E6	116	B4
Iris Cl., Croy.	203	G1
Iris Cl., Surb.	181	J7
Iris Ct., Pnr.	66	C3
Iris Cres., Bexh.	139	F6
Iris Rd., Epsom	196	B5
Iris Wk., Edg.	54	C4
Ash Cl.		
Iris Way E4	61	J6
Irkdale Av., Enf.	44	C1
Iron Br. Cl. NW10	88	E5
Iron Br. Cl., Sthl.	123	J1
Iron Br. Rd., Uxb.	120	D2
Iron Br. Rd., West Dr.	120	D2
Iron Mill Pl.	148/149	E6
SW18		
Garratt La.		
Iron Mill Rd. SW18	149	E6
Ironmonger La. EC2	**20**	**B4**
Ironmonger Pas. EC1	**12**	**A5**
Ironmonger Row EC1	**12**	**A5**
Ironmonger Row EC1	111	J3
Ironmongers Pl. E14	134	A4
Spindrift Av.		
Ironside Cl. SE16	133	G2
Kinburn St.		
Irvine Av., Har.	68	D3
Irvine Cl. N20	57	H2
Irvine Way, Orp.	193	J7
Irving Av., Nthlt.	102	D1
Irving Gro. SW9	151	F2
Irving Rd. W14	128	A3
Irving St. WC2	**17**	**J5**
Irving St. WC2	110	D7
Irving Way NW9	71	F5
Irwin Av. SE18	137	H7
Irwin Gdns. NW10	107	H1
Isabel Hill Cl., Hmptn.	179	H1
Upper Sunbury Rd.		
Isabel St. SW9	151	F1
Isabella Cl. N14	42	C7
Isabella Dr., Orp.	207	F4
Isabella Rd. E9	95	F5
Isabella St. SE1	**27**	**G2**
Isabella St. SE1	131	H1
Isambard Ms. E14	134	C3
Isambard Pl. SE16	133	F1
Rotherhithe St.		
Isel Way SE22	152	B5
East Dulwich Gro.		
Isham Rd. SW16	186	E2
Isis Cl. SW15	147	J4
Isis St. SW18	167	F2
Isla Rd. SE18	137	F6
Island Fm. Av.,	179	F5
W.Mol.		
Island Fm. Rd.,	179	F5
W.Mol.		
Island Rd., Mitch.	167	J7
Island Row E14	113	J6
Commercial Rd.		
Islay Gdns., Houns.	142	D5
Islay Wk. N1	93	J7
Douglas Rd.		
Isledon Rd. N7	93	G3
Islehurst Cl., Chis.	192	D1
Isleworth Business	144	C2
Complex, Islw.		
St. John's Rd.		
Isleworth Prom.,	144	E4
Twick.		
Islington Grn. N1	111	H1

Islington High St. N1	**11**	**F2**
Islington High St. N1	111	H2
Islington Pk. Ms. N1	93	G7
Islington Pk. St.		
Islington Pk. St. N1	93	G7
Islip Gdns., Edg.	54	D7
Islip Gdns., Nthlt.	85	E7
Islip Manor Rd., Nthlt.	85	E7
Islip St. NW5	92	C5
Ismailia Rd. E7	97	H7
Isom Cl. E13	115	J4
Belgrave Rd.		
Ivanhoe Dr., Har.	68	D3
Ivanhoe Rd. SE5	152	C3
Ivanhoe Rd., Houns.	142	D3
Ivatt Pl. W14	128	C5
Ivatt Way N17	75	H3
Ive Fm. Cl. E10	96	A2
Ive Fm. La. E10	96	A2
Iveagh Av. NW10	106	A2
Iveagh Cl. E9	113	G1
Iveagh Cl. NW10	106	A2
Iveagh Ter. NW10	106	A2
Iveagh Av.		
Ivedon Rd., Well.	158	C2
Iveley Rd. SW4	150	C2
Ivere Dr., Barn.	40	E6
Iverhurst Cl., Bexh.	158	D5
Iverna Ct. W8	128	D3
Iverna Gdns. W8	128	D3
Iverna Gdns., Felt.	141	G5
Ivers Way, Croy.	204	B7
Iverson Rd. NW6	90	C6
Ives Rd. E16	114	E5
Ives St. SW3	**31**	**H1**
Ives St. SW3	129	H4
Ivestor Ter. SE23	153	F7
Ivimey St. E2	**13**	**J3**
Ivimey St. E2	112	D3
Ivinghoe Cl., Enf.	44	B2
Ivinghoe Rd., Dag.	100	B5
Ivor Gro. SE9	175	E1
Ivor Pl. NW1	**7**	**J6**
Ivor Pl. NW1	109	J4
Ivor St. NW1	92	C7
Ivory Sq. SW11	149	F3
Gartons Way		
Ivorydown, Brom.	173	G4
Ivy Cl., Har.	85	F4
Ivy Cl., Pnr.	66	C7
Ivy Cl., Sun.	178	C2
Ivy Cotts. E14	114	B7
Grove Vil.		
Ivy Ct. SE16	**37**	**J4**
Ivy Cres. W4	126	C4
Ivy Gdns. N8	74	E6
Ivy Gdns., Mitch.	186	D3
Ivy La., Houns.	143	F4
Ivy Pl., Surb.	181	J6
Alpha Rd.		
Ivy Rd. E16	115	G6
Pacific Rd.		
Ivy Rd. E17	78	A6
Ivy Rd. N14	42	C7
Ivy Rd. NW2	89	J4
Ivy Rd. SE4	153	J4
Ivy Rd. SW17	167	H5
Tooting High St.		
Ivy Rd., Houns.	143	H4
Ivy Rd., Surb.	196	A1
Ivy St. N1	**12**	**D1**
Ivy St. N1	112	B2
Ivy Wk., Dag.	100	E6
Ivybridge Cl. WC2	**18**	**B6**
Ivybridge Est., Islw.	144	C5
Ivychurch Cl. SE20	171	F7
Ivychurch La. SE17	**37**	**F3**
Ivydale Rd. SE15	153	G3
Ivydale Rd., Cars.	199	J2
Ivyday Gro. SW16	169	F3
Ivydene, W.Mol.	179	F5
Ivydene Cl., Sutt.	199	F4
Ivyhouse Rd., Dag.	100	D6
Ivymount Rd. SE27	169	G3
Ixworth Pl. SW3	**31**	**G3**
Ixworth Pl. SW3	129	H5
Izane Rd., Bexh.	159	F4

J

Jacaranda Cl.,	182	E3
N.Mal.		
Jacaranda Gro. E8	94	C7
Queensbridge Rd.		
Jack Barnett Way N22	75	F2
Jack Clow Rd. E15	115	E2
Jack Cornwell St. E12	98	D4
Jack Dash Way E6	116	B4
Jack Walker Ct. N5	93	H4
Jackass La., Kes.	205	H6
Jacklin Grn., Wdf.Grn.	63	G4
Jackman Ms. NW10	88	E3
Jackman St. E8	112	E1

Name	Page	Grid
Jackson Cl. E9	95	F7
Jackson Rd. N7	93	F4
Jackson Rd., Bark.	117	G1
Jackson Rd., Barn.	41	H6
Jackson Rd., Brom.	206	B2
Jackson St. SE18	136	D6
Jackson Way, Sthl.	123	H2
Jacksons La. N6	74	A7
Jacksons Pl., Croy.	202	A1
Cross Rd.		
Jacksons Way, Croy.	204	A3
Jacob Ho., Erith	138	D2
Kale Rd.		
Jacob St. SE1	**29**	**G3**
Jacob St. SE1	132	D2
Jacobs Cl., Dag.	101	H4
Jacobs Ho. E13	115	J3
Jacob's Well Ms. W1	**16**	**C3**
Jacqueline Cl., Nthlt.	103	F1
Canford Av.		
Jade Cl. E16	116	A6
Jade Cl. NW2	72	A7
Marble Dr.		
Jade Cl., Dag.	100	C1
Jaffe Rd., Ilf.	99	F1
Jaffray Pl. SE27	169	H4
Chapel Rd.		
Jaffray Rd., Brom.	192	A4
Jaggard Way SW12	149	J7
Jago Cl. SE18	137	F6
Jago Wk. SE5	132	A7
Jamaica Rd. SE1	**29**	**G4**
Jamaica Rd. SE1	132	D2
Jamaica Rd. SE16	132	E2
Jamaica Rd., Th.Hth.	187	H6
Jamaica St. E1	113	F6
James Av. NW2	89	J5
James Av., Dag.	101	F1
James Bedford Cl.,	66	C2
Pnr.		
James Boswell Cl.	169	G4
SW16		
Curtis Fld. Rd.		
James Cl. E13	115	G2
Richmond St.		
James Cl. NW11	72	B6
Woodlands		
James Collins Cl. W9	108	C4
Fermoy Rd.		
James Ct. N1	93	J7
Morton Rd.		
James Dudson Ct.	88	C7
NW10		
James Gdns. N22	59	H7
James Hammett Ho.	**13**	**G2**
E2		
James Joyce Wk.	151	H4
SE24		
Shakespeare Rd.		
James La. E10	78	D7
James La. E11	78	D6
James Newman Ct.	174	D3
SE9		
Great Harry Dr.		
James Pl. N17	76	C1
James Sinclair Pt. E13	115	J1
James St. W1	**16**	**C3**
James St. W1	110	A6
James St. WC2	**18**	**B5**
James St., Bark.	99	F7
James St., Enf.	44	C5
James St., Houns.	144	A3
James Ter. SW14	146	D3
Addington Ct.		
James Yd. E4	62	D6
Larkshall Rd.		
Jameson Cl. W3	126	C2
Acton La.		
Jameson St. W8	128	D1
James's Cotts., Rich.	126	A7
Kew Rd.		
Jamestown Rd. NW1	110	B1
Jamestown Way E14	114	D7
Jamieson Ho., Houns.	143	F7
Jane St. E1	112/113	E6
Commercial Rd.		
Janet St. E14	134	A3
Janeway Pl. SE16	132/133	E2
Janeway St.		
Janeway St. SE16	**29**	**J4**
Janeway St. SE16	132	D2
Janice Ms., Ilf.	98/99	E3
Oakfield Rd.		
Jansen Wk. SW11	149	G4
Hope St.		
Janson Cl. E15	96/97	E5
Janson Rd.		
Janson Cl. NW10	88	D3
Janson Rd. E15	96	E5
Jansons Rd. N15	76	B3
Japan Cres. N4	75	F7
Japan Rd., Rom.	82	D6
Jardine Rd. E1	113	G7
Jarrett Cl. SW2	169	H1
Jarrow Cl., Mord.	184	E5
Jarrow Rd. N17	76	E4
Jarrow Rd. SE16	133	F4
Jarrow Rd., Rom.	82	C6
Jarrow Way E9	95	H4
Jarvis Cl., Bark.	117	G1
Westbury Rd.		
Jarvis Cl., Barn.	40	A5
Jarvis Rd. SE22	152	B4
Melbourne Gro.		
Jarvis Rd., S.Croy.	202	A6
Jasmin Rd., Epsom	196	B5
Jasmine Cl., Ilf.	99	E5
Jasmine Cl., Orp.	206	E2
Jasmine Cl., Sthl.	103	E7
Jasmine Gdns., Croy.	204	B3
Jasmine Gdns., Har.	85	G2
Jasmine Gro. SE20	189	E1
Jasmine Ter.,	120	D2
West Dr.		
Jasmine Way, E.Mol.	180	B4
Hampton Ct. Way		
Jason Cl. W1	110	A6
Marylebone La.		
Jason Wk. SE9	174	D4
Jasper Pas. SE19	170	C6
Jasper Rd. E16	116	A6
Jasper Rd. SE19	170	C5
Jasper Wk. N1	**12**	**B3**
Javelin Way, Nthlt.	102	D3
Jay Gdns., Chis.	174	C4
Jay Ms. SW7	**22**	**D4**
Jay Ms. SW7	129	F2
Jaycroft, Enf.	43	G1
The Ridgeway		
Jebb Av. SW2	151	E6
Jebb St. E3	114	A2
Jedburgh Rd. E13	115	J3
Jedburgh St. SW11	150	A4
Jeddo Rd. W12	127	F2
Jefferson Cl. W13	125	E3
Jefferson Cl., Ilf.	81	E5
Jefferson Wk. SE18	136	D6
Kempt St.		
Jeffreys Pl. NW1	92	C7
Jeffreys St.		
Jeffreys Rd. SW4	150	E2
Jeffreys Rd., Enf.	45	J3
Jeffreys St. NW1	92	B7
Jeffreys Wk. SW4	150	E2
Jeffries Ho. NW10	106	D1
Jeffs Cl., Hmptn.	161	H6
Uxbridge Rd.		
Jeffs Rd., Sutt.	198	C4
Jeger Av. E2	112	C1
Jeken Rd. SE9	155	J4
Jelf Rd. SW2	151	G5
Jellicoe Gdns., Stan.	52	C6
Jellicoe Rd. E13	115	G4
Jutland Rd.		
Jellicoe Rd. N17	60	A7
Jemmett Cl.,	182	B1
Kings.T.		
Jengar Cl., Sutt.	199	E4
Jenkins La. E6	116	D2
Jenkins La., Bark.	117	E2
Jenkins Rd. E13	115	H4
Jenner Av. W3	106	D5
Jenner Ho. SE3	135	E6
Jenner Pl. SW13	127	H6
Jenner Rd. N16	94	C2
Jennett Rd., Croy.	201	G3
Jennifer Rd., Brom.	173	F3
Jennings Cl., Surb.	181	F7
Jennings Rd. SE22	152	C6
Jennings Way, Barn.	39	J3
Jenningtree Way,	139	J2
Belv.		
Jenny Hammond Cl.	97	F3
E11		
Newcomen Rd.		
Jenson Way SE19	170	C7
Jenton Av., Bexh.	158	E1
Jephson Rd. E7	97	J7
Jephson St. SE5	152	A1
Grove La.		
Jephtha Rd. SW18	148	D6
Jeppos La., Mitch.	185	J4
Jerdan Pl. SW6	128	D7
Jeremiah St. E14	114	B6
Jeremys Grn. N18	61	E4
Jermyn St. SW1	**25**	**F1**
Jermyn St. SW1	110	D7
Jerningham Av., Ilf.	80	E2
Jerningham Rd. SE14	153	H2
Jerome Cres. NW8	**7**	**G5**
Jerome Cres. NW8	109	H4
Jerome St. E1	**21**	**F1**
Jerrard St. N1	**12**	**E2**
Jerrard St. SE13	154	B3
Jersey Av., Stan.	69	E2
Jersey Dr., Orp.	193	G6
Jersey Par., Houns.	143	H1
Jersey Rd. E11	96	D1
Jersey Rd. E16	115	J6
Prince Regent La.		
Jersey Rd. SW17	168	B6
Jersey Rd. W7	124	D2
Jersey Rd., Houns.	143	H1
Jersey Rd., Ilf.	99	E4
Jersey Rd., Islw.	124	B6
Jersey St. E2	112/113	E3
Bethnal Grn. Rd.		
Jerusalem Pas. EC1	**11**	**G6**
Jervis Ct. W1	**17**	**E4**
Jerviston Gdns.	169	G6
SW16		
Jesmond Av., Wem.	87	J6
Jesmond Cl., Mitch.	186	B3
Jesmond Rd., Croy.	188	C7
Jesmond Way, Stan.	53	H5
Jessam Av. E5	94	E1
Jessamine Rd. W7	124	B1
Jesse Rd. E10	96	C1
Jessel Dr., Loug.	49	F1
Jessica Rd. SW18	149	F6
Jessie Blythe La. N19	74	E7
Jessop Av., Sthl.	123	F4
Jessop Rd. SE24	151	H4
Milkwood Rd.		
Jessop Sq. E14	134	A1
Heron Quay		
Jessops Way, Croy.	186	C6
Jessup Cl. SE18	137	F4
Jetstar Way, Nthlt.	102	E3
Jevington Way SE12	173	H1
Jewel Rd. E17	78	A3
Jewry St. EC3	**21**	**F4**
Jewry St. EC3	112	C6
Jew's Row SW18	149	F4
Jews Wk. SE26	171	E4
Jeymer Av. NW2	89	H5
Jeymer Dr., Grnf.	103	J1
Jeypore Pas. SW18	149	F6
Jeypore Rd.		
Jeypore Rd. SW18	149	F7
Jillian Cl., Hmptn.	161	G7
Jim Bradley Cl. SE18	136	D4
John Wilson St.		
Joan Cres. SE9	156	A7
Joan Gdns., Dag.	100	E2
Joan Rd., Dag.	100	E2
Joan St. SE1	**27**	**F2**
Joan St. SE1	131	H1
Jocelyn Rd., Rich.	145	H3
Jocelyn St. SE15	152	D1
Jockey's Flds. WC1	**18**	**D1**
Jockey's Flds. WC1	111	F5
Jodane St. SE8	133	J4
Jodrell Cl., Islw.	144	D1
Jodrell Rd. E3	113	J1
Joel St., Nthwd.	66	A3
Joel St., Pnr.	66	A3
Johanna St. SE1	**27**	**E4**
John Adam St. WC2	**18**	**B6**
John Adam St. WC2	111	E7
John Aird Ct. W2	**14**	**D1**
John Aird Ct. W2	109	F5
John Archer Way	149	G6
SW18		
John Ashby Cl. SW2	151	E6
John Austin Cl.,	181	J1
Kings.T.		
Queen Elizabeth Rd.		
John Barnes Wk. E15	97	F6
John Bradshaw Rd.	58	D1
N14		
High St.		
John Burns Dr., Bark.	99	H7
John Campbell Rd.	94	B5
N16		
John Carpenter St.	**19**	**G5**
EC4		
John Carpenter St.	111	H7
EC4		
John Cornwell VC Ho.	98	D5
E12		
John Felton Rd. SE16	**29**	**H4**
John Felton Rd. SE16	132	D2
John Fisher St. E1	**21**	**H5**
John Fisher St. E1	112	D7
John Gooch Dr., Enf.	43	H1
John Harrison Way	135	F3
SE10		
John Horner Ms. N1	111	J2
Frome St.		
John Islip St. SW1	**34**	**A2**
John Islip St. SW1	130	E4
John Keats Ho. N22	59	F7
John Maurice Cl.	**36**	**B1**
SE17		
John Maurice Cl.	132	A4
SE17		
John McKenna Wk.	**29**	**J5**
SE16		
John Newton Ct.,	158	B3
Well.		
Danson La.		
John Parker Cl., Dag.	101	H7
John Parker Sq. SW11	149	G3
Thomas Baines Rd.		
John Penn St. SE13	154	B1
John Perrin Pl., Har.	69	H7
John Princes St. W1	**17**	**E3**
John Princes St. W1	110	B6
John Rennie Wk.	132/133	E1
Wine Cl.		
John Roll Way SE16	**29**	**J5**
John Roll Way SE16	132	D3
John Ruskin St. SE5	**35**	**G7**
John Ruskin St. SE5	131	H7
John Silkin La. SE8	133	G4
John Smith Av. SW6	128	C7
John Spencer Sq. N1	93	H6
John St. E15	115	F1
John St. SE25	188	D4
John St. WC1	**10**	**D6**
John St. WC1	111	F4
John St., Enf.	44	D5
John St., Houns.	143	E2
John Walsh Twr. E11	97	F2
John Williams Cl.	133	G6
SE14		
John Williams Cl.,	181	G1
Kings.T.		
Henry Macaulay Av.		
John Wilson St. SE18	136	D3
John Woolley Cl.	154	E4
SE13		
Johns Av. NW4	71	J4
Johns La., Mord.	185	F5
John's Ms. WC1	**10**	**D6**
John's Ms. WC1	111	F4
John's Pl. E1	112/113	E6
Damien St.		
John's Ter., Croy.	202	A1
Johnson Cl. E8	112	D1
Johnson Rd., Brom.	192	A5
Johnson Rd., Croy.	188	A7
Johnson Rd., Houns.	122	C7
Johnson St. E1	113	F7
Cable St.		
Johnson St., Sthl.	122	C3
Johnsons Cl., Cars.	199	J3
Johnson's Ct. EC4	111	G6
Fleet St.		
Johnsons Dr., Hmptn.	179	J1
Johnson's Pl. SW1	**33**	**G4**
Johnson's Pl. SW1	130	C5
Johnsons Way NW10	106	B4
Johnston Cl. SW9	151	F1
Hackford Rd.		
Johnston Rd.,	63	G5
Wdf.Grn.		
Johnston Ter. NW2	90	A3
Campion Ter.		
Johnstone Rd. E6	116	C3
Joiner St. SE1	**28**	**C2**
Joiner's Arms Yd. SE5	152	A1
Denmark Hill		
Jollys La., Har.	86	A1
Jollys La., Hayes	102	E6
Jonathan Ct. W4	126/127	E4
Windmill Rd.		
Jonathan St. SE11	**34**	**C3**
Jonathan St. SE11	131	F5
Jones Rd. E13	115	H4
Holborn Rd.		
Jones St. W1	**16**	**D6**
Jones Wk., Rich.	145	J6
Pyrland Rd.		
Jonquil Gdns.,	161	F6
Hmptn.		
Partridge Rd.		
Jonson Cl., Hayes	102	A5
Jonson Cl., Mitch.	186	B4
Jordan Cl., Dag.	101	H4
Muggeridge Rd.		
Jordan Cl., Har.	85	F3
Hamilton Cres.		
Jordan Rd., Grnf.	105	E1
Jordans Cl., Islw.	144	B1
Joseph Av. W3	106	D6
Joseph Powell Cl.	150	B6
SW12		
Hazelbourne Rd.		
Joseph Ray Rd. E11	97	E2
Joseph St. E3	113	J4
Josephine Av. SW2	151	F5
Joshua St. E14	114	C6
St. Leonards Rd.		
Joubert St. SW11	149	J2
Jowett St. SE15	132	C7
Joyce Av. N18	60	C5
Joyce Dawson Way	118	A7
SE28		
Thamesmere Dr.		
Joyce Page Cl. SE7	136	A6
Lansdowne La.		
Joyce Wk. SW2	151	G6
Joydon Dr., Rom.	82	B6

Joyners Cl., Dag.	101	F4
Jubb Powell Ho. N15	76	B6
Jubilee Av. E4	62	C6
Jubilee Av., Rom.	83	H5
Jubilee Av., Twick.	161	J1
Jubilee Cl. NW9	70	D6
Jubilee Cl., Pnr.	66	C2
Jubilee Cl., Rom.	83	H5
Jubilee Cres. E14	134	C3
Jubilee Cres. N9	60	D1
Jubilee Dr., Ruis.	84	D4
Jubilee Gdns., Sthl.	103	G6
Jubilee Pl. SW3	**31**	**H3**
Jubilee Pl. SW3	129	H5
Jubilee Rd., Grnf.	104	E1
Jubilee Rd., Sutt.	198	A7
Jubilee St. E1	113	F6
Jubilee Wk., Wat.	50	B4
Jubilee Way SW19	185	E1
Jubilee Way, Chess.	196	A4
Jubilee Way, Sid.	176	A2
Judd St. WC1	**10**	**A4**
Judd St. WC1	110	E3
Jude St. E16	115	F6
Judge Wk., Esher	194	B6
Juer St. SW11	129	H7
Julia Gdns., Bark.	118	D2
Julia Garfield Ms.	135	H1
E16		
Wesley Av.		
Julia St. NW5	92	A4
Oak Village		
Julian Av. W3	106	B7
Julian Cl., Barn.	40	E3
Julian Hill, Har.	86	B2
Julian Pl. E14	134	B5
Juliana Cl. N2	72/73	E3
East End Rd.		
Julien Rd. W5	125	F3
Juliette Rd. E13	115	F2
Junction App. SE13	154	C3
Junction App. SW11	149	H3
Junction Av. W10	107	J3
Harrow Rd.		
Junction Ms. W2	**15**	**G3**
Junction Pl. W2	**15**	**G3**
Junction Rd. E13	115	H2
Junction Rd. N9	60	D1
Junction Rd. N17	76	D3
Junction Rd. N19	92	C4
Junction Rd. W5	125	G4
Junction Rd., Brent.	125	G4
Junction Rd., Har.	68	B6
Junction Rd., S.Croy.	202	A5
Junction Rd. E.,	82/83	E7
Rom.		
Kenneth Rd.		
Junction Rd. W.,	82	E7
Rom.		
Juniper Cl., Barn.	40	A5
Juniper Cl., Chess.	195	J6
Juniper Cl., Wem.	87	J5
Juniper Cres. NW1	92	A7
Juniper Gdns. SW16	186	C1
Leonard Rd.		
Juniper La. E6	116	B5
Juniper Rd., Ilf.	98	D4
Juniper St. E1	113	F7
Juno Way SE14	133	G6
Jupiter Way N7	93	F6
Jupp Rd. E15	96	D7
Jupp Rd. W. E15	114	C1
Justice Wk. SW3	**31**	**G6**
Justin Cl., Brent.	125	G7
Justin Rd. E4	61	J6
Jute La., Enf.	45	H2
Jutland Cl. N19	92/93	E1
Sussex Way		
Jutland Rd. E13	115	G4
Jutland Rd. SE6	154	C7
Jutsums Av., Rom.	83	H4
Jutsums La., Rom.	83	H5
Juxon Cl., Har.	67	H1
Augustine Rd.		
Juxon St. SE11	**34**	**D1**
Juxon St. SE11	131	F4

K		
Kaduna Cl., Pnr.	66	A5
Kale Rd., Erith	138	E2
Kambala Rd. SW11	149	G3
Kangley Br. Rd. SE26	171	J5
Kaplan Dr. N21	43	F5
Kara Way NW2	90	A4
Karen Ct. SE4	153	J2
Wickham Rd.		
Karen Ct., Brom.	191	F1
Blyth Rd.		
Karen Ter. E11	97	F2
Montague Rd.		
Karenza Ct., Wem.	69	F7
Lulworth Av.		
Karina Cl., Chig.	65	H5

Karoline Gdns., Grnf.	104	A2
Oldfield La. N.		
Kashgar Rd. SE18	137	J4
Kashmir Rd. SE7	136	A7
Kassala Rd. SW11	149	J1
Katella Trd. Est.,	117	H3
Bark.		
Kates Cl., Barn.	39	G5
Katharine St., Croy.	201	J3
Katherine Cl. SE16	133	G1
Rotherhithe St.		
Katherine Gdns. SE9	156	A4
Katherine Gdns., Ilf.	65	F7
Katherine Rd. E6	98	A7
Katherine Rd. E7	97	J5
Katherine Rd., Twick.	162	D1
London Rd.		
Katherine Sq. W11	128	B1
Wilsham St.		
Kathleen Av. W3	106	C5
Kathleen Av., Wem.	87	H7
Kathleen Rd. SW11	149	J3
Kay St. E2	**13**	**J1**
Kay St. E2	112	D2
Kay St. E15	96	D7
Kay St., Well.	158	B1
Kaymoor Rd., Sutt.	199	H7
Kean St. WC2	**18**	**C4**
Kean St. WC2	111	F6
Keatley Grn. E4	61	J6
Keats Av. E16	135	H1
Wesley Av.		
Keats Cl. E11	79	H5
Nightingale La.		
Keats Cl. NW3	91	H4
Keats Gro.		
Keats Cl. SE1	**37**	**F2**
Keats Cl. SW19	167	G6
North Rd.		
Keats Cl., Chig.	65	F6
Keats Cl., Enf.	45	G5
Keats Cl., Hayes	102	A5
Keats Gro. NW3	91	G4
Keats Ho., Beck.	172	A6
Keats Pl. EC2	**20**	**B2**
Keats Rd., Belv.	139	J3
Keats Rd., Well.	157	H1
Keats Way, Croy.	189	F6
Keats Way, Grnf.	103	H5
Keats Way, West Dr.	120	C4
Keble Cl., Nthlt.	85	J5
Keble Cl., Wor.Pk.	197	F1
Keble Pl. SW13	127	H6
Somerville Av.		
Keble St. SW17	167	F4
Kechill Gdns., Brom.	191	G7
Kedelston Dr., Orp.	95	G4
Redwald Rd.		
Kedleston Dr., Orp.	193	J6
Kedleston Wk. E2	112/113	E3
Middleton St.		
Keedonwood Rd.,	172	E5
Brom.		
Keel Cl. SE16	133	G1
Keel Cl., Bark.	118/119	E3
Choats Rd.		
Keeley Rd., Croy.	201	J2
Keeley St. WC2	**18**	**C4**
Keeley St. WC2	111	F6
Keeling Rd. SE9	156	A5
Keely Cl., Barn.	41	H5
Keemor Cl. SE18	136	D7
Llanover Rd.		
Keens Cl. SW16	168	D5
Keens Rd., Croy.	201	J4
Keens Yd. N1	93	H6
St. Paul's Rd.		
Keep, The SE3	155	G2
Keep, The, Kings.T.	163	J6
Keep La. N11	58	A2
Gardeners Cl.		
Keepers Ms., Tedd.	163	F6
Keesey St. SE17	**36**	**B5**
Keesey St. SE17	132	A6
Keetons Rd. SE16	132	E3
Keevil Dr. SW19	148	A7
Keighley Cl. N7	92/93	E5
Penn Rd.		
Keightley Dr. SE9	175	F1
Keildon Rd. SW11	149	J4
Keir, The SW19	165	J5
West Side Common		
Keir Hardie Est. E5	94/95	E4
Springfield		
Keir Hardie Ho. W6	127	J6
Lochaline St.		
Keir Hardie Way,	100	A7
Bark.		
Keir Hardie Way,	102	A3
Hayes		
Keith Connor Cl. SW8	150	B3
Daley Thompson Way		
Keith Gro. W12	127	G2

Keith Rd. E17	77	J1
Keith Rd., Bark.	117	G2
Keith Rd., Hayes	121	H3
Kelbrook Rd. SE3	156	B3
Kelby Path SE9	175	E3
Kelceda Cl. NW2	89	G2
Kelfield Gdns. W10	107	J6
Kelfield Ms. W10	108	A6
Kelfield Gdns.		
Kell St. SE1	**27**	**H5**
Kelland Cl. N8	74	D5
Palace Rd.		
Kelland Rd. E13	115	G4
Kellaway Rd. SE3	155	J2
Keller Cres. E12	98	A4
Kellerton Rd. SE13	154	E5
Kellett Rd. SW2	151	G4
Kelling Gdns., Croy.	187	H7
Kellino St. SW17	167	J4
Kellner Rd. SE28	137	J3
Kelly Av. SE15	132	C7
Kelly Cl. NW10	88	D3
Kelly Ct., Borwd.	38	C2
Kelly Ms. W9	108	C5
Woodfield Rd.		
Kelly Rd. NW7	56	B6
Kelly St. NW1	92	B6
Kelly Way, Rom.	82	E5
Kelman Cl. SW4	150	D2
Kelmore Gro. SE22	152	D4
Kelmscott Cl. E17	77	J2
Kelmscott Gdns. W12	127	G3
Kelmscott Rd. SW11	149	J5
Kelross Pas. N5	93	J4
Kelross Rd.		
Kelross Rd. N5	93	J4
Kelsall Cl. SE3	155	H2
Kelsey La., Beck.	190	A2
Kelsey Pk. Av., Beck.	190	B2
Kelsey Pk. Rd., Beck.	190	A2
Kelsey Sq., Beck.	190	A2
Kelsey St. E2	**13**	**J5**
Kelsey St. E2	112	E4
Kelsey Way, Beck.	190	A3
Kelshall Ct. N4	93	J2
Brownswood Rd.		
Kelsie Way, Ilf.	65	H7
Kelso Pl. W8	**22**	**B6**
Kelso Pl. W8	128	E3
Kelso Rd., Cars.	185	F7
Kelson Ho. E14	134	C3
Kelston Rd., Ilf.	81	E2
Kelvedon Cl., Kings.T.	163	J6
Kelvedon Rd. SW6	128	C7
Kelvedon Way,	64	C6
Wdf.Grn.		
Kelvin Av. N13	59	F6
Kelvin Av., Tedd.	162	B6
Kelvin Cl., Epsom	196	A6
Kelvin Cres., Har.	52	B7
Kelvin Dr., Twick.	145	E6
Kelvin Gdns., Croy.	187	E7
Kelvin Gdns., Sthl.	103	G6
Kelvin Gro. SE26	170	E3
Kelvin Gro., Chess.	195	H3
Kelvin Ind. Est., Grnf.	85	H7
Kelvin Par., Orp.	207	H1
Kelvin Rd. N5	93	J4
Kelvin Rd., Well.	158	A3
Kelvinbrook, W.Mol.	179	H3
Kelvington Cl., Croy.	189	H7
Kelvington Rd. SE15	153	G5
Kember St. N1	93	F7
Carnoustie Dr.		
Kemble Dr., Brom.	206	B3
Kemble Rd. N17	76	D1
Kemble Rd. SE23	171	G1
Kemble Rd., Croy.	201	G3
Kemble St. WC2	**18**	**C4**
Kemble St. WC2	111	F6
Kemerton Rd. SE5	151	J3
Kemerton Rd., Beck.	190	B2
Kemerton Rd., Croy.	188	C7
Kemeys St. E9	95	H5
Kemnal Rd., Chis.	175	G4
Kemp Gdns., Croy.	187	J6
St. Saviours Rd.		
Kemp Rd., Dag.	100	D1
Kempe Rd. NW6	108	A2
Kempis Way SE22	152	B5
East Dulwich Gro.		
Kemplay Rd. NW3	91	G4
Kemp's Ct. W1	**17**	**G4**
Kemps Dr. E14	114	A7
Morant St.		
Kemps Gdns. SE13	154	C5
Thornford Rd.		
Kempsford Gdns.	128	D5
SW5		
Kempsford Rd. SE11	**35**	**G1**
Kempsford Rd. SE11	131	G4
Kempshott Rd. SW16	168	D7
Kempson Rd. SW6	148	D1
Kempt St. SE18	136	D6

Kempthorne Rd. SE8	133	H4
Kempton Av., Nthlt.	85	G6
Kempton Av., Sun.	178	B1
Kempton Cl., Erith	139	J6
Kempton Ct., Sun.	178	B1
Kempton Rd. E6	116	C1
Kempton Rd., Hmptn.	179	F2
Kempton Wk., Croy.	189	H6
Kemsing Cl., Bex.	159	E7
Kemsing Cl., Brom.	205	F2
Kemsing Cl., Th.Hth.	187	J4
Kemsing Rd. SE10	135	G5
Ken Way, Wem.	88	C2
Kenbury Gdns. SE5	151	J2
Kenbury St.		
Kenbury St. SE5	151	J2
Kenchester Cl. SW8	131	E7
Kencot Cl., Erith	139	F2
Kendal Av. N18	60	A4
Kendal Av. W3	106	A5
Kendal Av., Bark.	99	H7
Kendal Cl., Felt.	160	A1
Kendal Cl. SW9	**35**	**G7**
Kendal Cl. SW9	131	H7
Kendal Cl., Wdf.Grn.	63	F2
Kendal Gdns. N18	60	A4
Kendal Gdns., Sutt.	199	F2
Kendal Par. N18	60	A4
Great Cambridge Rd.		
Kendal Pl. SW15	148	C5
Upper Richmond Rd.		
Kendal Rd. NW10	89	G4
Kendal St. W2	**15**	**H4**
Kendal St. W2	109	H6
Kendale Rd., Brom.	172	E5
Kendall Av., Beck.	189	H2
Kendall Cl. SW19	167	G6
Byegrove Rd.		
Kendall Pl. W1	**16**	**B2**
Kendall Pl. W1	110	A5
Kendall Rd., Beck.	189	H2
Kendall Rd., Islw.	144	D2
Kendalmere Cl. N10	74	B1
Kender St. SE14	133	F7
Kendoa Rd. SW4	150	D4
Kendon Cl. E11	79	H5
The Av.		
Kendra Hall Rd.,	201	H7
S.Croy.		
Kendrey Gdns.,	144	B6
Twick.		
Kendrick Ms. SW7	**31**	**E1**
Kendrick Pl. SW7	**31**	**E2**
Kendrick Pl. SW7	129	G4
Kenelm Cl., Har.	86	D3
Kenerne Dr., Barn.	40	B5
Kenilford Rd. SW12	150	B7
Kenilworth Av. E17	78	A2
Kenilworth Av. SW19	166	D5
Kenilworth Av., Har.	85	F4
Kenilworth Cl.,	38	C3
Borwd.		
Kenilworth Ct. SW15	148	A3
Lower Richmond Rd.		
Kenilworth Cres., Enf.	44	B1
Kenilworth Dr.,	38	C3
Borwd.		
Kenilworth Gdns.	156	E2
SE18		
Kenilworth Gdns., Ilf.	99	J2
Kenilworth Gdns.,	48	C6
Loug.		
Kenilworth Gdns.,	103	F3
Sthl.		
Kenilworth Gdns.,	50	C5
Wat.		
Kenilworth Rd. E3	113	H2
Kenilworth Rd. NW6	108	C1
Kenilworth Rd. SE20	189	G1
Kenilworth Rd. W5	125	H1
Kenilworth Rd., Edg.	54	C3
Kenilworth Rd.,	197	G6
Epsom		
Kenilworth Rd., Orp.	193	F6
Kenley Av. NW9	70	E1
Kenley Cl., Barn.	41	H4
Kenley Cl., Bex.	159	G7
Kenley Cl., Chis.	193	H3
Kenley Gdns., Th.Hth.	187	H4
Kenley Rd. SW19	184	C2
Kenley Rd., Kings.T.	182	B2
Kenley Rd., Twick.	144	D6
Kenley Wk. W11	108	B7
Kenley Wk., Sutt.	198	A4
Kenlor Rd. SW17	167	G5
Kenmare Dr., Mitch.	167	J7
Kenmare Gdns. N13	59	H4
Kenmare Rd., Th.Hth.	187	G6
Kenmere Gdns.,	106	A1
Wem.		
Kenmere Rd., Well.	158	C2
Kenmont Gdns. NW10	107	H3
Kenmore Av., Har.	68	D4
Kenmore Cl., Rich.	126	A7
Kent Rd.		
Kenmore Gdns., Edg.	70	B2

Name	No.	Grid
Kenmore Rd., Har.	69	G3
Kenmure Rd. E8	95	E5
Kenmure Yd. E8	94/95	E5
Kenmure Rd.		
Kennacraig Cl. E16	135	G1
Hanameel St.		
Kennard Rd. E15	96	D7
Kennard Rd. N11	57	J5
Kennard St. E16	136	C1
Kennard St. SW11	150	A2
Kennedy Av., Enf.	45	F6
Kennedy Cl. E13	115	G2
Kennedy Cl., Mitch.	186	A2
Kennedy Cl., Pnr.	51	F6
Kennedy Path W7	104	C4
Harp Rd.		
Kennedy Rd. W7	104	B5
Kennedy Rd., Bark.	117	H1
Kennedy Wk. SE17	132	A4
Flint St.		
Kennet Cl. SW11	149	G4
Maysoule Rd.		
Kennet Rd. W9	108	C4
Kennet Rd., Islw.	144	C3
Kennet Sq., Mitch.	185	H1
Kennet St. E1	**29**	**J1**
Kennet St. E1	132	D1
Kennet Wf. La. EC4	**20**	**A5**
Kenneth Av., Ilf.	98	E4
Kenneth Cres. NW2	89	H5
Kenneth Gdns., Stan.	52	D6
Kenneth More Rd., Ilf.	98/99	E3
Oakfield Rd.		
Kenneth Rd., Rom.	82	D7
Kenneth Robbins Ho. N17	60	E7
Kennett Dr., Hayes	102	E5
Kenning St. SE16	133	F2
Railway Av.		
Kenning Ter. N1	112	B1
Kenninghall Rd. E5	94	D3
Kenninghall Rd. N18	61	F5
Kennings Way SE11	**35**	**G3**
Kennings Way SE11	131	G5
Kennington Grn. SE11	**35**	**E4**
Kennington Gro. SE11	**34**	**D5**
Kennington La. SE11	**35**	**F3**
Kennington La. SE11	131	F5
Kennington Oval SE11	**34**	**D5**
Kennington Oval SE11	131	F6
Kennington Pk. Est. SE11	**35**	**E6**
Kennington Pk. Gdns. SE11	**35**	**E4**
Kennington Pk. Gdns. SE11	131	H6
Kennington Pk. Pl. SE11	**35**	**F4**
Kennington Pk. Pl. SE11	131	G6
Kennington Pk. Rd. SE11	**35**	**F5**
Kennington Pk. Rd. SE11	131	G6
Kennington Rd. SE1	**27**	**E5**
Kennington Rd. SE1	131	G3
Kennington Rd. SE11	**27**	**E6**
Kennington Rd. SE11	131	G4
Kenny Dr., Cars.	199	J7
Fountain Rd.		
Kenny Rd. NW7	56	B7
Kenrick Pl. W1	**16**	**B1**
Kensal Rd. W10	108	B4
Kensington Av. E12	98	B6
Kensington Av., Th.Hth.	187	G1
Kensington Ch. Ct. W8	**22**	**A4**
Kensington Ch. Ct. W8	128	E2
Kensington Ch. St. W8	128	D1
Kensington Ch. Wk. W8	**22**	**A4**
Kensington Ch. Wk. W8	128	E2
Kensington Ct. N11	58	A6
Kensington Ct. W8	**22**	**B4**
Kensington Ct. W8	129	E2
Kensington Ct. Gdns. W8	128/129	E3
Kensington Ct. Pl.		
Kensington Ct. Ms. W8	**22**	**B4**
Kensington Ct. Pl. W8	**22**	**B5**
Kensington Ct. Pl. W8	129	E3
Kensington Dr., Wdf.Grn.	80	A1
Kensington Gdns. W2	**22**	**D2**
Kensington Gdns. W2	129	F1
Kensington Gdns., Ilf.	98	C1
Kensington Gdns., Kings.T.	181	G3
Portsmouth Rd.		
Kensington Gdns. Sq. W2	**14**	**A4**
Kensington Gdns. Sq. W2	108	E6
Kensington Gate W8	**22**	**C5**
Kensington Gate W8	129	F3
Kensington Gore SW7	**22**	**E4**
Kensington Gore SW7	129	G2
Kensington Hall Gdns. W14	128	C5
Beaumont Av.		
Kensington High St. W8	128	D3
Kensington High St. W8	128	B4
Kensington Mall W8	128	D1
Kensington Palace Gdns. W8	**22**	**A1**
Kensington Palace Gdns. W8	128	E1
Kensington Pk. Gdns. W11	108	C7
Kensington Pk. Ms. W11	108	C6
Kensington Pk. Rd.		
Kensington Pk. Rd. W11	108	C7
Kensington Pl. W8	128	D1
Kensington Rd. SW7	**23**	**F4**
Kensington Rd. SW7	129	G2
Kensington Rd. W8	**22**	**B4**
Kensington Rd. W8	129	E2
Kensington Rd., Nthlt.	103	G3
Kensington Rd., Rom.	83	J6
Kensington Sq. W8	**22**	**A4**
Kensington Sq. W8	128	E2
Kensington Ter., S.Croy.	202	A7
Sanderstead Rd.		
Kent Av. W13	104	E5
Kent Av., Dag.	119	G4
Kent Av., Well.	157	J5
Kent Cl., Mitch.	187	E4
Kent Cl., Orp.	207	H6
Kent Dr., Barn.	42	A4
Kent Dr., Tedd.	162	B5
Kent Gdns. W13	105	E5
Kent Gdns., Ruis.	66	B6
Kent Gate Way, Croy.	204	A5
Kent Ho. La., Beck.	171	H5
Kent Ho. Rd. SE26	189	G1
Kent Ho. Rd., Beck.	171	H5
Kent Pas. NW1	**7**	**J5**
Kent Pas. NW1	109	J3
Kent Rd. N21	60	A4
Kent Rd. W4	126	C3
Kent Rd., Dag.	101	H5
Kent Rd., E.Mol.	179	J4
Kent Rd., Kings.T.	181	G3
The Bittoms		
Kent Rd., Rich.	126	A7
Kent Rd., W.Wick.	204	B1
Kent St. E2	**13**	**G1**
Kent St. E2	112	C2
Kent St. E13	115	J3
Kent Ter. NW1	**7**	**H4**
Kent Ter. NW1	109	H3
Kent Twr. SE20	171	E7
Kent Vw. Gdns., Ilf.	99	H2
Kent Wk. SW9	151	H4
Moorland Rd.		
Kent Way SE15	152	C1
Sumner Est.		
Kent Way, Surb.	195	H3
Kent Yd. SW7	**23**	**H4**
Kentford Way, Nthlt.	102	E1
Kentish Bldgs. SE1	**28**	**B2**
Kentish Rd., Belv.	139	G4
Kentish Town Rd. NW1	92	B7
Kentish Town Rd. NW5	92	B7
Kentish Way, Brom.	191	G2
Kentmere Rd. SE18	137	H4
Kenton Av., Har.	68	C7
Kenton Av., Sthl.	103	G7
Kenton Av., Sun.	178	E2
Kenton Ct. W14	128	C3
Kensington High St.		
Kenton Gdns., Har.	69	F5
Kenton La., Har.	69	F3
Kenton Pk. Av., Har.	69	G4
Kenton Pk. Cl., Har.	69	F4
Kenton Pk. Cres., Har.	69	G4
Kenton Pk. Rd., Har.	69	F4
Kenton Rd. E9	95	G6
Kenton Rd., Har.	69	G5
Kenton St. WC1	**10**	**A5**
Kenton St. WC1	110	E4
Kents Pas., Hmptn.	179	F1
Kentwode Grn. SW13	127	G7
Kenver Av. N12	57	G6
Kenward Rd. SE9	155	J5
Kenway, Rom.	83	J2
Kenway Rd. SW5	**30**	**A2**
Kenway Rd. SW5	128	E4
Kenwood Av. N14	42	D5
Kenwood Av. SE14	153	G1
Besson St.		
Kenwood Cl. NW3	91	G1
Kenwood Cl., West Dr.	120	D6
Kenwood Dr., Beck.	190	C3
Kenwood Gdns. E18	79	H3
Kenwood Gdns., Ilf.	80	D4
Kenwood Rd. N6	73	J6
Kenwood Rd. N9	60	D1
Kenworthy Rd. E9	95	H5
Kenwyn Dr. NW2	89	E3
Kenwyn Rd. SW4	150	D4
Kenwyn Rd. SW20	183	J1
Kenya Rd. SE7	136	A7
Kenyngton Dr., Sun.	160	A5
Kenyngton Pl., Har.	69	F5
Kenyon St. SW6	148	A1
Keogh Rd. E15	97	E6
Kepler Rd. SW4	150	E4
Keppel Rd. E6	98	C7
Keppel Rd., Dag.	100	E4
Keppel Row SE1	**27**	**J2**
Keppel St. WC1	**17**	**J1**
Keppel St. WC1	110	D5
Kerbela St. E2	**13**	**H5**
Kerbey St. E14	114	B6
Kerfield Cres. SE5	152	A1
Kerfield Pl. SE5	152	A1
Kerri Cl., Barn.	39	J4
Kerridge Ct. N1	94	B6
Kerrison Pl. W5	125	G1
Kerrison Rd. E15	114	D1
Kerrison Rd. SW11	149	H3
Kerrison Rd. W5	125	G1
Kerrison Vil. W5	125	G1
Kerrison Pl.		
Kerry Av., Stan.	53	G4
Kerry Cl. E16	115	H6
Kerry Cl. N13	59	F2
Kerry Ct., Stan.	53	G4
Kerry Path SE14	133	J6
Kerry Rd.		
Kerry Rd. SE14	133	J6
Kersey Gdns. SE9	174	B4
Kersfield Rd. SW15	148	A6
Kershaw Cl. SW18	149	G6
Westover Rd.		
Kershaw Rd., Dag.	101	G3
Kersley Ms. SW11	149	J2
Kersley Rd. N16	94	B3
Kersley St. SW11	149	J2
Kerswell Cl. N15	76	B5
Kerwick Cl. N7	93	F7
Sutterton St.		
Keslake Rd. NW6	108	A2
Kessock Cl. N17	76	E5
Kesteven Cl., Ilf.	65	J6
Kestlake Rd., Bex.	158	C6
East Rochester Way		
Keston Av., Kes.	205	J5
Keston Cl. N18	60	A3
Keston Cl., Well.	138	C7
Keston Gdns., Kes.	205	J4
Keston Pk. Cl., Kes.	206	C3
Keston Rd. N17	76	A3
Keston Rd. SE15	152	D3
Keston Rd., Th.Hth.	187	G6
Kestrel Av. E6	116	B5
Swan App.		
Kestrel Av. SE24	151	H5
Kestrel Cl. NW9	71	E2
Kestrel Cl. NW10	88	D5
Kestrel Cl., Kings.T.	163	G4
Kestrel Ho. EC1	**11**	**J3**
Kestrel Ho. EC1	111	H3
Kestrel Ho. W13	104	C4
Kestrel Pl. SE14	133	H6
Milton Ct. Rd.		
Keswick Av. SW15	164	E5
Keswick Av. SW19	184	D2
Keswick Bdy. SW15	148	B5
Upper Richmond Rd.		
Keswick Cl., Sutt.	199	F4
Keswick Gdns., Ilf.	80	B5
Keswick Gdns., Wem.	87	H4
Keswick Ms. W5	125	H1
Keswick Rd. SW15	148	B5
Keswick Rd., Bexh.	159	G2
Keswick Rd., Orp.	207	J1
Keswick Rd., Twick.	143	J6
Keswick Rd., W.Wick.	204	E2
Kett Gdns. SW2	151	F5
Kettering St. SW16	168	C6
Kettlebaston Rd. E10	95	J1
Kettlewell Cl. N11	58	A6
Kevan Ho. SE5	131	J7
Kevelioc Rd. N17	75	J1
Kevin Cl., Houns.	142	D2
Kevington Cl., Orp.	193	J4
Kevington Dr., Chis.	193	J4
Kevington Dr., Orp.	193	J4
Kew Br., Brent.	125	J6
Kew Br., Rich.	125	J6
Kew Br. Arches, Rich.	125	J6
Kew Br.		
Kew Br. Ct. W4	126	A5
Kew Br. Rd., Brent.	125	J6
Kew Cres., Sutt.	198	B3
Kew Foot Rd., Rich.	145	H4
Kew Gdns. Rd., Rich.	125	J7
Kew Grn., Rich.	126	A6
Kew Meadow Path, Rich.	146	A1
Kew Palace, Rich.	125	H7
Kew Rd., Rich.	145	H3
Key Cl. E1	113	E4
Keybridge Ho. SW8	**34**	**B6**
Keybridge Ho. SW8	131	E6
Keyes Rd. NW2	90	A5
Keymer Rd. SW2	169	F2
Keynes Cl. N2	73	J3
Keynsham Av., Wdf.Grn.	63	E4
Keynsham Gdns. SE9	156	B5
Keynsham Rd. SE9	156	A5
Keynsham Rd., Mord.	198	E1
Keyse Rd. SE1	**29**	**F6**
Keysham Av., Houns.	142	A1
The Av.		
Keystone Cres. N1	**10**	**B2**
Keywood Dr., Sun.	160	A6
Keyworth Cl. E5	95	H4
Keyworth St. SE1	**27**	**H5**
Keyworth St. SE1	131	H3
Kezia St. SE8	133	H5
Trundleys Rd.		
Khama Rd. SW17	167	H4
Khartoum Rd. E13	115	H3
Khartoum Rd. SW17	167	G4
Khartoum Rd., Ilf.	99	E5
Khyber Rd. SW11	149	H2
Kibworth St. SW8	131	F7
Kidbrooke Gdns. SE3	155	G2
Kidbrooke Gro. SE3	155	G1
Kidbrooke La. SE9	156	B4
Kidbrooke Pk. Cl. SE3	155	H1
Kidbrooke Pk. Rd. SE3	155	H1
Kidbrooke Way SE3	155	H2
Kidd Pl. SE7	136	B5
Kidderminster Pl., Croy.	201	H1
Kidderminster Rd.		
Kidderminster Rd., Croy.	201	H1
Kidderpore Av. NW3	90	D4
Kidderpore Gdns. NW3	90	D4
Kidlington Way NW9	70	E2
Kielder Cl., Ilf.	65	J6
Kiffen St. EC2	**12**	**C5**
Kilberry Cl., Islw.	144	A1
Kilburn Br. NW6	90	C7
Kilburn High Rd.		
Kilburn Bldgs. NW6	108/109	E1
Kilburn Gate NW6	**6**	**A1**
Kilburn High Rd. NW6	90	C7
Kilburn La. W9	108	A3
Kilburn La. W10	108	A3
Kilburn Pk. Rd. NW6	108	D3
Kilburn Pl. NW6	108	D1
Kilburn Priory NW6	108	E1
Kilburn Sq. NW6	108	D1
Kilburn High Rd.		
Kilburn Vale NW6	108/109	E1
Belsize Rd.		
Kildare Cl., Ruis.	84	C1
Kildare Gdns. W2	108	D6
Kildare Rd. E16	115	G5
Kildare Ter. W2	108	D6
Farrance St.		
Kildare Wk. E14	114	A6
Kildonan Rd. SW2	150	E5
Kildown Rd., Ilf.	100	A1
Kilgour Rd. SE23	153	H6
Kilkie St. SW6	149	F2
Killarney Rd. SW18	149	F6
Killburns Mill Cl., Wall.	200	B4
London Rd.		
Killearn Rd. SE6	172	D1
Killester Gdns., Wor.Pk.	197	H4
Killick St. N1	**10**	**C1**
Killick St. N1	111	F2
Killieser Av. SW2	168	E2
Killip Cl. E16	115	F6
Killowen Av., Nthlt.	85	J5
Killowen Rd. E9	95	G6
Killyon Rd. SW8	150	C2

Killyon Ter. SW8	150	C2
Kilmaine Rd. SW6	128	B7
Kilmarnock Gdns.,	100	C3
Dag.		
Lindsey Rd.		
Kilmarnock Rd., Wat.	50	D4
Kilmarsh Rd. W6	127	J4
Kilmartin Av. SW16	187	F3
Kilmartin Rd., Ilf.	100	A2
Kilmeston Way SE15	**37**	**F7**
Kilmington Rd.	127	G6
SW13		
Kilmorey Gdns.,	144	E5
Twick.		
Kilmorey Rd., Twick.	144	E4
Kilmorie Rd. SE23	171	H1
Kiln Cl., Hayes	121	G6
Brickfield La.		
Kiln Ms. SW17	167	G5
Kiln Pl. NW5	92	A5
Kilner St. E14	114	A5
Kilnside, Esher	194	D7
Kilpatrick Way, Hayes	103	E5
Kilravock St. W10	108	B3
Kilsby Wk., Dag.	100	B6
Rugby Rd.		
Kilsha Rd., Walt.	178	B6
Kimbell Gdns. SW6	148	B1
Kimbell Pl. SE3	155	J4
Tudway Rd.		
Kimber Rd. SW18	148	D7
Kimberley Av. E6	116	B2
Kimberley Av. SE15	153	E2
Kimberley Av., Ilf.	81	G7
Kimberley Av., Rom.	83	J6
Kimberley Dr., Sid.	176	D2
Kimberley Gdns. N4	75	H5
Kimberley Gdns.,	44	C3
Enf.		
Kimberley Gate,	173	F7
Brom.		
Oaklands Rd.		
Kimberley Rd. E4	62	E1
Kimberley Rd. E11	96	D2
Kimberley Rd. E16	115	F4
Kimberley Rd. E17	77	J1
Kimberley Rd. N17	76	D2
Kimberley Rd. N18	61	E6
Kimberley Rd. NW6	108	B1
Kimberley Rd. SW9	151	E2
Kimberley Rd., Beck.	189	G2
Kimberley Rd., Croy.	187	H6
Kimberley Way E4	63	E1
Kimble Rd. SW19	167	G6
Kimbolton Cl. SE12	155	F6
Kimbolton Grn.,	38	C4
Borwd.		
Kimbolton Row SW3	**31**	**G2**
Kimmeridge Gdns.,	174	B4
SE9		
Kimmeridge Rd. SE9	174	B4
Kimpton Rd. SE5	152	A1
Kimpton Rd., Sutt.	198	C2
Kimpton Trade	198	C2
Business Cen., Sutt.		
Kinburn St. SE16	133	G2
Kincaid Rd. SE15	132	E7
Kincardine Gdns. W9	108	C4
Harrow Rd.		
Kinch Gro., Wem.	69	J7
Kinder Cl. SE28	118	D7
Kinder St. E1	112/113	E6
Cannon St. Rd.		
Kinfauns Rd. SW2	169	G2
Kinfauns Rd., Ilf.	100	A1
King Alfred Av. SE6	172	A3
King & Queen Cl. SE9	174	B4
St. Keverne Rd.		
King & Queen St.	**36**	**A2**
SE17		
King & Queen St.	131	J5
SE17		
King Arthur Cl. SE15	133	F7
King Charles Cres.,	181	J7
Surb.		
King Charles Rd.,	181	J6
Surb.		
King Charles St. SW1	**25**	**J3**
King Charles St.	130	D2
SW1		
King Charles Ter.	112/113	E7
E1		
Sovereign Cl.		
King Charles Wk.	166	B1
SW19		
Princes Way		
King David La. E1	113	F7
King Edward Dr.,	195	H3
Chess.		
Kelvin Gro.		
King Edward Ms.	147	G1
SW13		
King Edward Rd. E10	96	C1
King Edward Rd. E17	77	H3
King Edward Rd.,	40	D4
Barn.		
King Edward St. EC1	**19**	**J3**
King Edward St. EC1	111	J6
King Edward III	132/133	E2
Ms. SE16		
Paradise St.		
King Edward Wk. SE1	**27**	**F5**
King Edward Wk. SE1	131	G3
King Edward's Gdns.	126	A1
W3		
King Edwards Gro.,	163	E6
Tedd.		
King Edward's Pl. W3	126	A1
King Edward's Gdns.		
King Edwards Rd. E9	113	E1
King Edwards Rd. N9	44	E7
King Edwards Rd.,	117	G1
Bark.		
King Edward's Rd.,	45	G4
Enf.		
King Frederik IX Twr.	133	J3
SE16		
Finland St.		
King Gdns., Croy.	201	H5
King George Av. E16	116	A6
King George Av., Ilf.	81	G5
King George Cl., Rom.	83	J3
King George VI Av.,	185	J4
Mitch.		
King George Sq.,	145	J6
Rich.		
King George St. SE10	134	C7
King Georges Dr.,	103	F5
Sthl.		
King George's Trd.	196	A4
Est., Chess.		
King Harolds Way,	138	D7
Bexh.		
King Henry Ms., Orp.	207	J5
Osgood Av.		
King Henry St. N16	94	B5
King Henry Ter. E1	112/113	E7
Sovereign Cl.		
King Henry's Rd. NW3	91	H7
King Henry's Rd.,	182	B3
Kings.T.		
King Henry's Wk. N1	94	B6
King James St. SE1	**27**	**H4**
King James St. SE1	131	H2
King John Ct. EC2	**12**	**E5**
King John St. E1	113	G5
King Johns Wk. SE9	174	A1
King Sq. EC1	**11**	**J4**
King Stairs Cl. SE16	132/133	E2
Elephant La.		
King St. E13	115	G4
King St. EC2	**20**	**A4**
King St. EC2	111	J6
King St. N2	73	G3
King St. N17	76	C1
King St. SW1	**25**	**G2**
King St. SW1	130	C1
King St. W3	126	B1
King St. W6	127	G4
King St. WC2	**18**	**A5**
King St. WC2	110	E7
King St., Rich.	145	G5
King St., Sthl.	123	E3
King St., Twick.	162	D1
King William IV Gdns.	171	F6
SE20		
St. John's Rd.		
King William La.	134/135	E5
SE10		
Orlop St.		
King William St. EC4	**20**	**C6**
King William St. EC4	112	A7
King William Wk.	134	C6
SE10		
Kingcup Cl., Croy.	203	G1
Primrose Fld.		
Kingdon Rd. NW6	90	D6
Kingfield Rd. W5	105	G4
Kingfield St. E14	134	C4
Kingfisher Av. E11	79	H6
Eastern Av.		
Kingfisher Cl. SE28	118	C7
Kingfisher Cl., Har.	52	C7
Kingfisher Cl. SW19	166	B2
Queensmere Rd.		
Kingfisher Cl., Sutt.	198	B2
Gander Grn. La.		
Kingfisher Dr., Rich.	163	E4
Kingfisher Sq. SE8	133	J6
Kingfisher St. E6	116	B5
Kingfisher Wk. NW9	70/71	E2
Eagle Dr.		
Kingfisher Way NW10	88	D6
Kingfisher Way, Beck.	189	G5
Kingham Cl. SW18	149	F7
Kingham Cl. W11	128	B2
Kinghorn St. EC1	**19**	**J2**
Kinglake Est. SE17	**37**	**E3**
Kinglake St. SE17	**36**	**D4**
Kinglake St. SE17	132	B5
Kingly Ct. W1	**17**	**F5**
Kingly St. W1	**17**	**F4**
Kingly St. W1	110	C6
Kings Arbour, Sthl.	122	E5
Kings Arms Ct. E1	**21**	**H2**
Kings Arms Yd. EC2	**20**	**B3**
Kings Av. N10	74	A3
Kings Av. N21	59	H1
King's Av. SW4	150	D7
King's Av. SW12	168	D1
Kings Av. W5	105	G6
Kings Av., Brom.	173	F6
Kings Av., Buck.H.	64	A2
Kings Av., Cars.	199	H7
Kings Av., Grnf.	103	H6
Kings Av., Houns.	143	H1
Kings Av., N.Mal.	183	E4
Kings Av., Rom.	83	F6
Kings Av., Wdf.Grn.	63	H5
Kings Bench St. SE1	**27**	**H3**
Kings Bench Wk. EC4	**19**	**F4**
Kings Chace Vw., Enf.	43	G2
Crofton Way		
Kings Chase, E.Mol.	179	J3
Kings Cl. E10	78	B7
Kings Cl. NW4	72	A4
Kings Cl., T.Ditt.	180	D6
Kings College Rd.	91	H7
NW3		
Kings Ct. E13	115	H1
Kings Ct. W6	127	G4
King St.		
Kings Ct., Wem.	88	B2
Kings Cres. N4	93	J3
Kings Cres. Est. N4	93	J2
King's Cross Br. N1	**10**	**B3**
King's Cross Rd. WC1	**10**	**D3**
King's Cross Rd. WC1	111	F3
Kings Dr., Edg.	53	J4
Kings Dr., Surb.	182	A7
Kings Dr., Tedd.	162	A5
Kings Dr., T.Ditt.	180	E6
Kings Dr., Wem.	88	B2
Kings Fm. Av., Rich.	146	A4
Kings Gdns. NW6	90	D7
West End La.		
Kings Gdns., Ilf.	99	G1
King's Garth Ms.	171	F2
SE23		
London Rd.		
Kings Grn., Loug.	48	B3
Kings Gro. SE15	133	E7
Kings Hall Rd., Beck.	171	H7
Kings Head Hill E4	46	B7
Kings Head Yd. SE1	**28**	**B2**
Kings Highway SE18	137	H6
Kings Hill, Loug.	48	B2
Kings Keep, Kings.T.	181	H4
Beaufort Rd.		
Kings La., Sutt.	199	G6
Kings Mead Pk.,	194	B7
Esher		
Kings Ms. SW4	150/151	E5
King's Av.		
King's Ms. WC1	**10**	**D6**
King's Ms. WC1	111	F5
Kings Ms., Chig.	65	F2
Kings Oak, Rom.	83	G3
King's Orchard SE9	156	B6
Kings Paddock,	179	J1
Hmptn.		
Kings Par., Cars.	199	H3
Wrythe La.		
Kings Pas. E11	78	E7
Kings Pas., Kings.T.	181	G2
Kings Pl. SE1	**27**	**J4**
Kings Pl. W4	126	C5
Kings Pl., Buck.H.	63	J2
Kings Pl., Loug.	47	J7
Fallow Flds.		
King's Reach Twr. SE1	**27**	**F1**
King's Reach Twr. SE1	131	G1
Kings Ride Gate, Rich.	146	A4
Kings Rd. E4	62	D1
Kings Rd. E6	115	J1
Kings Rd. E11	78	E7
Kings Rd. N17	76	C1
Kings Rd. N18	60	D5
Kings Rd. N22	75	F1
Kings Rd. NW10	89	H7
Kings Rd. SE25	188	D3
King's Rd. SW1	**31**	**H3**
King's Rd. SW1	129	J5
King's Rd. SW3	**31**	**H3**
King's Rd. SW3	129	J5
King's Rd. SW6	149	E1
King's Rd. SW10	149	E1
King's Rd. SW14	146	D3
Kings Rd. SW19	166	D6
Kings Rd. W5	105	G5
Kings Rd., Bark.	99	F7
North St.		
Kings Rd., Barn.	39	J3
Kings Rd., Felt.	160	C1
Kings Rd., Har.	85	F2
Kings Rd., Kings.T.	163	H7
Kings Rd., Mitch.	186	A3
Kings Rd., Orp.	207	J4
Kings Rd., Rich.	145	J5
Kings Rd., Surb.	195	F1
Kings Rd., Tedd.	162	A5
Kings Rd., Twick.	145	E6
Kings Rd., West Dr.	120	C2
Kings Rd.	85	F3
Bungalows, Har.		
Kings Rd.		
King's Scholars' Pas.	**33**	**F1**
SW1		
King's Ter. NW1	110	C1
Plender St.		
Kings Ter., Islw.	144	D3
Worple Rd.		
King's Wk., Kings.T.	181	G1
Kings Way, Har.	68	B4
Kingsand Rd. SE12	173	G2
Kingsash Dr., Hayes	102	E4
Kingsbridge Av. W3	125	J2
Kingsbridge Cres.,	103	F5
Sthl.		
Kingsbridge Rd. W10	107	J6
Kingsbridge Rd.,	117	G2
Bark.		
Kingsbridge Rd.,	184	A7
Mord.		
Kingsbridge Rd., Sthl.	123	F4
Kingsbridge Rd.,	178	B7
Walt.		
Kingsbury Circle NW9	70	A5
Kingsbury Rd. N1	94	B6
Kingsbury Rd. NW9	70	B5
Kingsbury Ter. N1	94	B6
Kingsbury Trd. Est.	70	D6
NW9		
Kingsclere Cl. SW15	**147**	**G7**
Kingsclere Pl., Enf.	43	J2
Chase Side		
Kingscliffe Gdns.	166	C1
SW19		
Kingscote Rd. W4	126	D3
Kingscote Rd., Croy.	188	D7
Kingscote Rd., N.Mal.	182	D3
Kingscote St. EC4	**19**	**G5**
Kingscourt Rd. SW16	168	D3
Kingscroft Rd. NW2	90	C6
Kingsdale Gdns. W11	128	A1
Kingsdale Rd. SE18	137	J7
Kingsdale Rd. SE20	171	G7
Kingsdown Av. W3	107	E7
Kingsdown Av. W13	125	E2
Kingsdown Cl.	132/133	E5
SE16		
Masters Dr.		
Kingsdown Cl. W10	108	A6
Kingsdown Rd. E11	97	E3
Kingsdown Rd. N19	92	E2
Kingsdown Rd., Sutt.	198	B5
Kingsdown Way,	191	G7
Brom.		
Kingsdowne Rd.,	181	H7
Surb.		
Kingsfield Av., Har.	67	H4
Kingsfield Ho. SE9	174	A3
Kingsfield Rd., Har.	68	A7
Kingsford Av., Wall.	201	E7
Kingsford St. NW5	91	J5
Kingsford Way E6	116	C5
Kingsgate, Wem.	88	C3
Kingsgate Av. N3	72	D3
Kingsgate Cl., Bexh.	158	E1
Kingsgate Pl. NW6	90	D7
Kingsgate Rd. NW6	90	D7
Kingsgate Rd.,	181	H1
Kings.T.		
Kingsground SE9	156	B7
Kingshall Ms. SE13	154	C3
Lewisham Rd.		
Kingshill Av., Har.	69	E4
Kingshill Av., Nthlt.	102	A3
Kingshill Av.,	183	G7
Wor.Pk.		
Kingshill Dr., Har.	68	E3
Kingshold Rd. E9	95	F7
Kingsholm Gdns. SE9	156	A4
Kingshurst Rd. SE12	155	G7
Kingsland NW8	109	H1
Broxwood Way		
Kingsland Grn. E8	94	B6
Kingsland High St. E8	94	C5
Kingsland Pas. E8	94	B6
Kingsland Rd. E2	**13**	**E3**
Kingsland Rd. E2	112	B2
Kingsland Rd. E8	112	B2
Kingsland Rd. E13	115	J3
Kingslawn Cl. SW15	147	H5
Howards La.		

Kingsleigh Pl., Mitch. 185 J3
Chatsworth Pl.
Kingsleigh Wk., Brom. 191 F4
Stamford Dr.
Kingsley Av. W13 104 D6
Kingsley Av., Houns. 143 J2
Kingsley Av., Sthl. 103 G7
Kingsley Av., Sutt. 199 G4
Kingsley Cl. N2 73 F5
Kingsley Cl., Dag. 101 H4
Kingsley Ct., Edg. 54 B2
Kingsley Dr., Wor.Pk. 197 F2
Badgers Copse
Kingsley Flats SE1 132 B4
Old Kent Rd.
Kingsley Gdns. E4 62 A5
Kingsley Ms. E1 112/113 E7
Wapping La.
Kingsley Ms. W8 22 B6
Kingsley Ms., Chis. 175 E6
Kingsley Pl. N6 74 A7
Kingsley Rd. E7 97 G7
Kingsley Rd. E17 78 C2
Kingsley Rd. N13 59 G4
Kingsley Rd. NW6 108 C1
Kingsley Rd. SW19 167 E5
Kingsley Rd., Croy. 201 G1
Kingsley Rd., Har. 85 J4
Kingsley Rd., Houns. 143 J2
Kingsley Rd., Ilf. 81 F1
Kingsley Rd., Loug. 49 G3
Kingsley Rd., Orp. 207 J7
Kingsley Rd., Pnr. 67 F4
Kingsley St. SW11 149 J3
Kingsley Way N2 73 F6
Kingsley Wd. Dr. SE9 174 C3
Kingslyn Cres. SE19 188 B1
Kingsman Par. SE18 136 C3
Woolwich Ch. St.
Kingsman St. SE18 136 C3
Kingsmead, Barn. 40 D4
Kingsmead, Rich. 145 J6
Kingsmead Av. N9 60 E1
Kingsmead Av. NW9 70 D7
Kingsmead Av., Mitch. 186 C3
Kingsmead Av., Sun. 178 C3
Kingsmead Av., Surb. 196 A2
Kingsmead Av., Wor.Pk. 197 H3
Kingsmead Cl., Epsom 196 D7
Kingsmead Cl., Sid. 176 A2
Kingsmead Cl., Tedd. 162 D6
Kingsmead Dr., Nthlt. 85 F7
Kingsmead Est. E9 95 H4
Kingsmead Way
Kingsmead Rd. SW2 169 G2
Kingsmead Way E9 95 H4
Kingsmere Cl. SW15 148 B3
Felsham Rd.
Kingsmere Pk. NW9 88 B1
Kingsmere Rd. SW19 166 A2
Kingsmill Gdns., Dag. 101 F5
Kingsmill Rd., Dag. 101 F5
Kingsmill Ter. NW8 7 F1
Kingsmill Ter. NW8 109 G2
Kingsnympton Pk., Kings.T. 164 B6
Kingspark Ct. E18 79 G3
Kingsridge SW19 166 B2
Kingsthorpe Rd. SE26 171 G4
Kingston Av., Felt. 141 H6
Kingston Av., Sutt. 198 B3
Kingston Br., Kings.T. 181 G2
Kingston Bypass SW15 165 E4
Kingston Bypass SW20 165 E4
Kingston Bypass, Esher 194 D3
Kingston Bypass, N.Mal. 183 F1
Kingston Bypass, Surb. 195 H3
Kingston Cl., Nthlt. 103 F1
Kingston Cl., Rom. 82 E3
Kingston Cl., Tedd. 162 E6
Kingston Ct. N4 75 J6
Wiltshire Gdns.
Kingston Cres., Beck. 189 J1
Kingston Gdns., Croy. 200/201 E3
Wandle Rd.
Kingston Hall Rd., Kings.T. 181 G3
Kingston Hill, Kings.T. 164 C6
Kingston Hill Av., Rom. 83 E3
Kingston Hill Pl., Kings.T. 164 C4
Kingston La., Tedd. 162 D5
Kingston La., West Dr. 120 C2
Kingston Pk. Est., Kings.T. 164 B6
Kingston Pl., Har. 52 C7
Richmond Gdns.
Kingston Rd. N9 60 D2
Kingston Rd. SW15 165 G1
Kingston Rd. SW19 184 C1
Kingston Rd. SW20 184 A2
Kingston Rd., Barn. 41 G5
Kingston Rd., Epsom 197 E5
Kingston Rd., Ilf. 99 E4
Kingston Rd., Kings.T. 182 B3
Kingston Rd., N.Mal. 182 D4
Kingston Rd., Sthl. 123 F2
Kingston Rd., Surb. 196 B2
Kingston Rd., Tedd. 162 E5
Kingston Rd., Wor.Pk. 196 B2
Kingston Sq. SE19 170 A5
Kingston Vale SW15 164 D4
Kingstown St. NW1 110 A1
Kingswater Pl. SW11 129 H7
Battersea Ch. Rd.
Kingsway N12 57 F6
Kingsway SW14 146 B3
Kingsway WC2 18 C3
Kingsway WC2 111 F6
Kingsway, Croy. 201 F5
Kingsway, Enf. 45 E5
Kingsway, N.Mal. 183 J4
Kingsway, Orp. 193 H5
Kingsway, Wem. 87 H4
Kingsway, W.Wick. 205 E3
Kingsway, Wdf.Grn. 63 J5
Kingsway Business Pk., Hmptn. 179 F1
Kingsway Cres., Har. 67 J4
Kingsway Rd., Sutt. 198 B7
Kingswear Rd. NW5 92 B3
Kingswear Rd., Ruis. 84 A2
Kingswood Av. NW6 108 B1
Kingswood Av., Belv. 139 F4
Kingswood Av., Brom. 190 E3
Kingswood Av., Hmptn. 161 H6
Kingswood Av., Houns. 143 F1
Kingswood Av., Th.Hth. 187 G5
Kingswood Cl. N20 41 F6
Kingswood Cl. SW8 131 E7
Kingswood Cl., Enf. 44 B5
Kingswood Cl., N.Mal. 183 F6
Motspur Pk.
Kingswood Cl., Orp. 193 G7
Kingswood Cl., Surb. 181 H7
Kingswood Dr. SE19 170 B4
Kingswood Dr., Cars. 199 J1
Kingswood Est. SE21 170 B4
Bowen Dr.
Kingswood Pk. N3 72 C2
Kingswood Pl. SE13 155 E4
Kingswood Rd. E11 96 D2
Grove Grn. Rd.
Kingswood Rd. SE20 171 F6
Kingswood Rd. SW2 150 E6
Kingswood Rd. SW19 166 C7
Kingswood Rd. W4 126 C3
Kingswood Rd., Brom. 190 D4
Kingswood Rd., Ilf. 100 A1
Kingswood Rd., Wem. 88 A3
Kingswood Ter. W4 126 C3
Kingswood Rd.
Kingswood Way, Wall. 201 E5
Kingsworth Cl., Beck. 189 H5
Kingsworthy Cl., Kings.T. 181 J3
Kingthorpe Rd. NW10 88 D7
Kingthorpe Ter. NW10 88 D6
Kingwood Rd. SW6 148 B1
Kinlet Rd. SE18 157 F1
Kinloch Dr. NW9 70 E7
Kinloch St. N7 93 F3
Hornsey Rd.
Kinloss Ct. N3 72 C4
Haslemere Gdns.
Kinloss Gdns. N3 72 C4
Kinloss Rd., Cars. 185 F7
Kinnaird Av. W4 126 C7
Kinnaird Av., Brom. 173 F6
Kinnaird Cl., Brom. 173 F6
Kinnaird Way, Wdf.Grn. 64 C6
Kinnear Rd. W12 127 F2
Kinnerton Pl. N. SW1 24 A4
Kinnerton Pl. S. SW1 24 A4
Kinnerton St. SW1 24 B4
Kinnerton St. SW1 130 A2
Kinnerton Yd. SW1 24 A4
Kinnoul Rd. W6 128 B6
Kinross Av., Wor.Pk. 197 G2
Kinross Cl., Edg. 54 B2
Tayside Dr.
Kinross Cl., Har. 69 J5
Kinsale Rd. SE15 152 D3
Kintore Way SE1 37 F1
Kintyre Cl. SW16 187 F3
Kinveachy Gdns. SE7 136 B5
Kinver Rd. SE26 171 F4
Kipling Dr. SW19 167 G6
Kipling Est. SE1 28 C4
Kipling Est. SE1 132 A2
Kipling Pl., Stan. 52 C6
Uxbridge Rd.
Kipling Rd., Bexh. 159 E1
Kipling St. SE1 28 C4
Kipling St. SE1 132 A2
Kipling Ter. N9 60 A3
Kippington Dr. SE9 174 A1
Kirby Cl., Epsom 197 F5
Kirby Cl., Ilf. 65 H6
Kirby Cl., Loug. 48 B7
Kirby Est. SE16 132 E3
Kirby Gro. SE1 28 D3
Kirby Gro. SE1 132 B2
Kirby St. EC1 19 F1
Kirby Way, Walt. 178 C6
Kirchen Rd. W13 104 E7
Kirk La. SE18 137 F6
Kirk Ri., Sutt. 199 E3
Kirk Rd. E17 77 J6
Kirkby Cl. N11 58 A6
Coverdale Rd.
Kirkcaldy Grn., Wat. 50 C3
Trevose Way
Kirkdale SE26 170 E2
Kirkdale Rd. E11 97 E1
Kirkfield Cl. W13 124/125 E1
Broomfield Rd.
Kirkham Rd. E6 116 B6
Kirkham St. SE18 137 H6
Kirkland Av., Ilf. 80 D2
Kirkland Cl., Sid. 157 H6
Kirkland Wk. E8 94 C6
Kirkleas Rd., Surb. 195 H1
Kirklees Rd., Dag. 100 C5
Kirklees Rd., Th.Hth. 187 G5
Kirkley Rd. SW19 184 D1
Kirkman Pl. W1 17 H2
Kirkmichael Rd. E14 114 C6
Dee St.
Kirks Pl. E14 113 J5
Rhodeswell Rd.
Kirkside Rd. SE3 135 G6
Kirkstall Av. N17 76 A4
Kirkstall Gdns. SW2 168 E1
Kirkstall Rd. SW2 168 D1
Kirkstead Ct. E5 95 H3
Mandeville St.
Kirksted Rd., Mord. 198 E1
Kirkstone Way, Brom. 173 E7
Kirkton Rd. N15 76 B4
Kirkwall Pl. E2 113 F3
Kirkwood Rd. SE15 153 E2
Kirn Rd. W13 104/105 E7
Kirchen Rd.
Kirrane Cl., N.Mal. 183 F5
Kirtley Rd. SE26 171 H4
Kirtling St. SW8 33 F7
Kirtling St. SW8 130 C7
Kirton Cl. W4 126 D4
Dolman Rd.
Kirton Gdns. E2 13 G4
Kirton Rd. E13 115 J2
Kirton Wk., Edg. 54 C7
Kirwyn Way SE5 35 H7
Kirwyn Way SE5 131 H7
Kitcat Ter. E3 114 A3
Kitchener Rd. E7 97 H6
Kitchener Rd. E17 78 B1
Kitchener Rd. N2 73 H3
Kitchener Rd. N17 76 A3
Kitchener Rd., Dag. 101 H6
Kitchener Rd., Th.Hth. 188 A3
Kite Pl. E2 13 J3
Kite Yd. SW11 149 J1
Cambridge Rd.
Kitley Gdns. SE19 188 C1
Kitson Rd. SE5 36 A7
Kitson Rd. SE5 132 A7
Kitson Rd. SW13 147 G1
Kittiwake Pl., Sutt. 198 B2
Gander Grn. La.
Kittiwake Rd., Nthlt. 102 D3
Kittiwake Way, Hayes 102 D5
Kitto Rd. SE14 153 G2
Kiver Rd. N19 92 D2
Kiwi Cl., Twick. 144/145 E6
Crown Rd.
Klea Av. SW4 150 C6
Knapdale Cl. SE23 171 E2
Knapmill Rd. SE6 172 A2
Knapmill Way SE6 172 B2
Knapp Cl. NW10 89 E6
Knapp Rd. E3 114 A4
Knapton Ms. SW17 168 A6
Seely Rd.
Knaresborough Dr. SW18 166 E1
Knaresborough Pl. SW5 30 A1
Knaresborough Pl. SW5 128 E4
Knatchbull Rd. NW10 106 D1
Knatchbull Rd. SE5 151 J1
Knebworth Av. E17 78 A1
Knebworth Path, Borwd. 38 D4
Knebworth Rd. N16 94 B4
Nevill Rd.
Knee Hill SE2 138 C4
Knee Hill Cres. SE2 138 C4
Kneller Gdns., Islw. 144 A5
Kneller Rd. SE4 153 H4
Kneller Rd., N.Mal. 182 E7
Kneller Rd., Twick. 143 J6
Knighten St. E1 29 J2
Knighten St. E1 132 D1
Knightland Rd. E5 94 E2
Knighton Cl., S.Croy. 201 H7
Knighton Cl., Wdf.Grn. 63 H4
Knighton Dr., Wdf.Grn. 63 G4
Knighton La., Buck.H. 63 H2
Knighton Pk. Rd. SE26 171 G5
Knighton Rd. E7 97 G3
Knighton Rd., Rom. 83 J6
Knightrider Ct. EC4 19 J5
Knightrider St. EC4 111 J7
Godliman St.
Knights Arc. SW1 23 J4
Knights Av. W5 125 H2
Knights Cl. E9 95 F5
Churchill Wk.
Knights Ct., Kings.T. 181 H3
Knights Ct., Rom. 83 E6
Knights Hill SE27 169 H5
Knights Hill Sq. SE27 169 H4
Knights Hill
Knights La. N9 60 D3
Knights Pk., Kings.T. 181 H3
Knights Rd. E16 135 G2
Knights Rd., Stan. 53 F4
Knights Wk. SE11 35 G2
Knights Way, Ilf. 65 F6
Knightsbridge SW1 24 A4
Knightsbridge SW1 129 J2
Knightsbridge SW7 23 H4
Knightsbridge SW7 129 H2
Knightsbridge Grn. SW1 23 J4
Knightsbridge Grn. SW1 129 J2
Knightswood Cl., Edg. 54 C2
Knightwood Cres., N.Mal. 182 E6
Knivet Rd. SW6 128 D6
Knobs Hill Rd. E15 114 B1
Knockholt Rd. SE9 156 A5
Knole, The SE9 174 D4
Knole Cl., Croy. 189 F6
Stockbury Rd.
Knole Gate, Sid. 175 H3
Woodside Cres.
Knoll, The W13 105 F5
Knoll, The, Beck. 190 B1
Knoll, The, Brom. 205 G2
Knoll Ct. SE19 170 C5
Knoll Dr. N14 42 A7
Knoll Ri., Orp. 207 J1
Knoll Rd. SW18 149 F5
Knoll Rd., Bex. 159 G7
Knoll Rd., Sid. 176 B5
Knollmead, Surb. 196 C1
Knolls Cl., Wor.Pk. 197 H3
Knollys Cl. SW16 169 G3
Knollys Rd. SW16 169 G3
Knottisford St. E2 113 F3
Knotts Grn. Ms. E10 78 B6
Knotts Grn. Rd. E10 78 B6
Knowle Av., Bexh. 139 E7
Knowle Cl. SW9 151 G3
Knowle Rd., Brom. 206 B2
Knowle Rd., Twick. 162 B1
Knowles Cl., West Dr. 120 B1
Knowles Hill Cres. SE13 154 D5
Knowles Wk. SW4 150 C3
Knowlton Grn., Brom. 191 F5
Knowsley Av., Sthl. 123 G1
Knowsley Rd. SW11 149 J2
Knox Rd. E7 97 F6
Knox St. W1 15 J1
Knox St. W1 109 J5
Knoyle St. SE14 133 H6
Chubworthy St.

Kohat Rd. SW19	167	E5
Kossuth St. SE10	134	E5
Kotree Way SE1	37	J2
Kramer Ms. SW5	128	D5
Kempsford Gdns.		
Kreedman Wk. E8	94	D5
Kreisel Wk., Rich.	125	J6
Kuala Gdns. SW16	187	F1
Kuhn Way E7	97	G5
Forest La.		
Kydbrook Cl., Orp.	193	G7
Kylemore Cl. E6	116	A2
Parr Rd.		
Kylemore Rd. NW6	90	D7
Kymberley Rd., Har.	68	B6
Kynance Gdns., Stan.	69	F1
Kynance Ms. SW7	**22**	**C6**
Kynance Ms. SW7	129	E3
Kynance Pl. SW7	**22**	**C6**
Kynance Pl. SW7	129	F3
Kynaston Av. N16	94	C3
Dynevor Rd.		
Kynaston Av.,	187	J5
Th.Hth.		
Kynaston Cl., Har.	52	A7
Kynaston Cres.,	187	J5
Th.Hth.		
Kynaston Rd. N16	94	B3
Kynaston Rd., Brom.	173	G5
Kynaston Rd., Enf.	44	A1
Kynaston Rd., Th.Hth.	187	J5
Kynaston Wd., Har.	52	A7
Kynersley Cl., Cars.	199	J3
William St.		
Kynock Rd. N18	61	F4
Kyrle Rd. SW11	150	A5
Kyverdale Rd. N16	94	C2
L		
La Tourne Gdns.,	207	F3
Orp.		
Laburnum Av. N9	60	B2
Laburnum Av. N17	60	A7
Laburnum Av., Sutt.	199	H3
Laburnum Cl. E4	61	J6
Laburnum Cl. N11	58	A6
Laburnum Cl. SE15	133	F7
Clifton Way		
Laburnum Ct. E2	112	C1
Laburnum St.		
Laburnum Ct., Stan.	53	F4
Laburnum Cres., Sun.	178	B1
Batavia Rd.		
Laburnum Gdns. N21	59	J2
Laburnum Gdns.,	189	G7
Croy.		
Laburnum Gro. N21	59	J2
Laburnum Gro. NW9	70	C7
Laburnum Gro.,	143	F4
Houns.		
Laburnum Gro.,	182	D2
N.Mal.		
Laburnum Gro., Sthl.	103	F4
Laburnum Ho., Dag.	101	G2
Bradwell Av.		
Laburnum Rd. SW19	167	F7
Laburnum Rd.,	121	J4
Hayes		
Laburnum Rd., Mitch.	186	A2
Laburnum St. E2	112	C1
Laburnum Way,	192	D7
Brom.		
Lacebark Cl., Sid.	157	J7
Lacey Cl. N9	60	D2
Lacey Dr., Dag.	100	B4
Lacey Dr., Edg.	53	H4
Lacey Dr., Hmptn.	179	F1
Lacey Wk. E3	114	A2
Lackington St. EC2	**20**	**C1**
Lackington St. EC2	112	A5
Lacock Cl. SW19	167	F6
Lacon Rd. SE22	152	D4
Lacy Rd. SW15	148	A4
Ladas Rd. SE27	169	J4
Ladbroke Cres. W11	108	B6
Ladbroke Gro.		
Ladbroke Gdns. W11	108	C7
Ladbroke Gro. W10	108	A4
Ladbroke Gro. W11	108	B6
Ladbroke Ms. W11	128	B1
Ladbroke Rd.		
Ladbroke Rd. W11	108	C7
Ladbroke Rd., Enf.	44	C6
Ladbroke Sq. W11	108	C7
Ladbroke Ter. W11	108	C7
Ladbroke Wk. W11	128	C1
Ladbrook Cl., Pnr.	67	F5
Ladbrook Rd. SE25	188	A3
Ladbrooke Cres., Sid.	176	D3
Ladderstile Ride,	164	B5
Kings.T.		
Ladderswood Way	58	C5
N11		
Lady Booth Rd.,	181	H2
Kings.T.		
Lady Dock Path SE16	133	H2
Salter Rd.		
Lady Hay, Wor.Pk.	197	F2
Lady Margaret Rd.	92	C4
N19		
Lady Margaret Rd.	92	C5
NW5		
Lady Margaret Rd.,	103	F5
Sthl.		
Lady Somerset Rd.	92	B4
NW5		
Ladybower Ct. E5	95	H4
Gilpin Rd.		
Ladycroft Gdns., Orp.	207	F5
Ladycroft Rd. SE13	154	B3
Ladycroft Wk., Stan.	69	G1
Ladycroft Way, Orp.	207	F5
Ladyfield Cl., Loug.	49	E4
Ladyfields, Loug.	49	E4
Ladysmith Av. E6	116	B2
Ladysmith Av., Ilf.	81	G7
Ladysmith Rd. E16	115	F3
Ladysmith Rd. N17	76	D2
Ladysmith Rd. N18	61	E5
Ladysmith Rd. SE9	156	D6
Ladysmith Rd., Enf.	44	B3
Ladysmith Rd., Har.	68	B2
Ladywell Cl. SE4	153	J4
Adelaide Av.		
Ladywell Hts. SE4	153	J6
Ladywell Rd. SE13	154	A5
Ladywell St. E15	115	F1
Plaistow Gro.		
Ladywood Av., Orp.	193	H5
Ladywood Rd., Surb.	196	A2
Lafone Av., Felt.	160	C1
Alfred Rd.		
Lafone St. SE1	**29**	**F3**
Lafone St. SE1	132	C2
Lagado Ms. SE16	133	G1
Lagonda Av., Ilf.	65	J6
Laidlaw Dr. N21	43	F5
Chadwick Av.		
Laing Cl., Ilf.	65	G6
Laing Dean, Nthlt.	102	C1
Laings Av., Mitch.	185	J2
Lainlock Pl., Houns.	143	H1
Spring Gro. Rd.		
Lainson St. SW18	148	D7
Laird Ho. SE5	131	J7
Lairdale Cl. SE21	169	J1
Lairs Cl. N7	92/93	E6
Manger Rd.		
Laitwood Rd. SW12	168	B1
Lake, The, Bushey	51	J1
Lake Av., Brom.	173	G6
Lake Cl. SW19	166	C5
Lake Rd.		
Lake Dr., Bushey	51	J2
Lake Gdns., Dag.	101	G5
Lake Gdns., Rich.	163	E2
Lake Gdns., Wall.	200	B3
Lake Ho. Rd. E11	97	G3
Lake Rd. SW19	166	C5
Lake Rd., Croy.	203	J2
Lake Rd., Rom.	82	D4
Lake Vw., Edg.	53	J5
Lakedale Rd. SE18	137	H6
Lakefield Rd. N22	75	H2
Lakehall Gdns.,	187	H5
Th.Hth.		
Lakehall Rd., Th.Hth.	187	H5
Lakehurst Rd., Epsom	196	E5
Lakeland Cl., Har.	52	A6
Lakenheath N14	42	D6
Laker Pl. SW15	148	C6
Lakes Rd., Kes.	205	J5
Lakeside N3	73	E2
Lakeside W13	105	F6
Edgehill Rd.		
Lakeside, Beck.	190	B3
Lakeside, Enf.	42	D4
Lakeside, Wall.	200	B3
Derek Av.		
Lakeside Av. SE28	138	A1
Lakeside Av., Ilf.	80	A4
Lakeside Cl. SE25	188	D2
Lakeside Cl., Chig.	65	J4
Lakeside Cl., Sid.	158	C5
Lakeside Ct. N4	93	H2
Lakeside Ct., Borwd.	38	A5
Cavendish Cres.		
Lakeside Cres., Barn.	41	J5
Lakeside Dr., Brom.	206	B3
Lakeside Rd. N13	59	F4
Lakeside Rd. W14	128	A3
Lakeside Way, Wem.	88	A4
Lakeswood Rd., Orp.	193	E6
Lakeview Ct. SW19	166	B2
Victoria Dr.		
Lakeview Rd. SE27	169	G5
Lakeview Rd., Well.	158	B4
Lakis Cl. NW3	91	F4
Flask Wk.		
Laleham Av. NW7	54	D3
Laleham Rd. SE6	154	C6
Lalor St. SW6	148	B2
Lamb La. E8	94	E7
Lamb St. E1	**21**	**F1**
Lamb St. E1	112	C5
Lamb Wk. SE1	**28**	**D4**
Lambarde Av. SE9	174	D4
Lamberhurst Rd.	169	G4
SE27		
Lamberhurst Rd.,	101	F1
Dag.		
Lambert Av., Rich.	146	B3
Lambert Rd. E16	115	H6
Lambert Rd. N12	57	G5
Lambert Rd. SW2	151	E5
Lambert St. N1	93	G7
Lambert Wk., Wem.	87	G3
Lambert Way N12	57	F5
Woodhouse Rd.		
Lamberts Pl., Croy.	202	A1
Lamberts Rd., Surb.	181	H5
Lambeth Br. SE1	**34**	**B1**
Lambeth Br. SE1	131	E4
Lambeth Br. SW1	**34**	**B1**
Lambeth Br. SW1	131	E4
Lambeth High St.	**34**	**C2**
SE1		
Lambeth High St.	131	F4
SE1		
Lambeth Hill EC4	**19**	**J5**
Lambeth Hill EC4	111	J7
Lambeth Palace Rd.	**26**	**C6**
SE1		
Lambeth Palace Rd.	131	F3
SE1		
Lambeth Rd. SE1	**26**	**D6**
Lambeth Rd. SE1	131	F4
Lambeth Rd. SE11	**26**	**D6**
Lambeth Rd. SE11	131	F4
Lambeth Rd., Croy.	187	G7
Lambeth Wk. SE11	**34**	**D1**
Lambeth Wk. SE11	131	F4
Lamble St. NW5	92	A5
Lambley Rd., Dag.	100	B6
Lambolle Pl. NW3	91	H6
Lambolle Rd. NW3	91	H6
Lambourn Cl. W7	124	C2
Lambourn Rd. SW4	150	B3
Lambourne Av.	166	C4
SW19		
Lambourne Gdns. E4	62	A2
Lambourne Gdns.,	99	J7
Bark.		
Lambourne Rd.		
Lambourne Gdns.,	44	C2
Enf.		
Lambourne Gro.,	182	B2
Kings.T.		
Kenley Rd.		
Lambourne Pl. SE3	155	H1
Shooter's Hill Rd.		
Lambourne Rd. E11	78	C7
Lambourne Rd., Bark.	99	H7
Lambourne Rd., Chig.	65	H4
Lambourne Rd., Ilf.	99	H2
Lambrook Ter. SW6	148	B1
Lamb's Bldgs. EC1	**12**	**B6**
Lambs Conduit Pas.	**18**	**C1**
WC1		
Lamb's Conduit St.	**10**	**C6**
WC1		
Lamb's Conduit St.	111	F4
WC1		
Lambs Meadow,	80	A2
Wdf.Grn.		
Lambs Ms. N1	111	H1
Colebrooke Row		
Lamb's Pas. EC1	**12**	**B6**
Lamb's Pas. EC1	112	A5
Lambs Ter. N9	60	A2
Lambs Wk., Enf.	43	J2
Lambscroft Av. SE9	173	J3
Lambton Pl. W11	108	C6
Westbourne Gro.		
Lambton Rd. N19	92	E1
Lambton Rd. SW20	183	J1
Lamerock Rd., Brom.	173	F4
Lamerton Rd., Ilf.	81	E2
Lamerton St. SE8	134	A6
Lamford Cl. N17	60	A7
Lamington St. W6	127	H4
Lamlash St. SE11	**35**	**G1**
Lammas Av., Mitch.	186	A2
Lammas Grn. SE26	170	E3
Lammas Pk. W5	125	F2
Lammas Pk. Gdns.	125	F2
W5		
Lammas Rd. E9	95	G7
Lammas Rd. E10	95	H2
Lammas Rd., Rich.	163	F4
Lammermoor Rd.	150	B7
SW12		
Lamont Rd. SW10	30	D6
Lamont Rd. SW10	129	F6
Lamorbey Cl., Sid.	175	J1
Lamorna Cl. E17	78	C1
Lamorna Gro., Stan.	69	G1
Lamp Office Ct. WC1	**10**	**C6**
Lampard Gro. N16	94	C1
Lampern Sq. E2	**13**	**J3**
Humbolt Rd.		
Lampeter Sq. W6	128	B6
Lamplighter Cl. E1	113	F4
Cleveland Way		
Lampmead Rd.	155	E5
SE12		
Lamport Cl. SE18	136	C4
Lampton Av., Houns.	143	H1
Lampton Ho. Cl.	166	A4
SW19		
Lampton Pk. Rd.,	143	H2
Houns.		
Lampton Rd., Houns.	143	H2
Lanacre Av. NW9	71	F1
Lanark Cl. W5	105	F5
Lanark Pl. W9	**6**	**D5**
Lanark Pl. W9	109	F4
Lanark Rd. W9	**6**	**C4**
Lanark Rd. W9	109	E2
Lanark Sq. E14	134	B3
Lanata Wk., Hayes	102	D4
Ramulis Dr.		
Lancashire Ct. W1	**16**	**E5**
Lancaster Av. E18	79	H4
Lancaster Av. SE27	169	H2
Lancaster Av. SW19	166	A5
Lancaster Av., Bark.	99	H7
Lancaster Av., Mitch.	186	E5
Lancaster Cl. N1	94	B7
Hertford Rd.		
Lancaster Cl. N17	60	D7
Park La.		
Lancaster Cl. NW9	55	F7
Lancaster Cl., Brom.	191	F4
Lancaster Cl.,	163	G5
Kings.T.		
Lancaster Cl., Stai.	140	B6
Lancaster Cotts.,	145	H6
Rich.		
Lancaster Pk.		
Lancaster Ct. SE27	169	H2
Lancaster Ct. SW6	128	C7
Lancaster Ct. W2	**14**	**D6**
Lancaster Ct., Walt.	178	A7
Lancaster Dr. E14	134	C1
Prestons Rd.		
Lancaster Dr. NW3	91	H6
Lancaster Dr., Loug.	48	B6
Lancaster Gdns.	166	B5
SW19		
Lancaster Gdns. W13	125	E2
Lancaster Gdns.,	163	G5
Kings.T.		
Lancaster Gate W2	**14**	**D6**
Lancaster Gate W2	109	F7
Lancaster Gro. NW3	91	G6
Lancaster Ms.	148/149	E5
SW18		
East Hill		
Lancaster Ms. W2	**14**	**D5**
Lancaster Ms. W2	109	F7
Lancaster Ms., Rich.	145	H6
Richmond Hill		
Lancaster Pk., Rich.	145	H5
Lancaster Pl. SW19	166	A5
Lancaster Rd.		
Lancaster Pl. WC2	**18**	**C5**
Lancaster Pl. WC2	111	F7
Lancaster Pl., Houns.	142	C2
Lancaster Pl., Ilf.	99	F5
Staines Rd.		
Lancaster Pl., Twick.	144	D6
Lancaster Rd. E7	97	G7
Lancaster Rd. E11	97	E2
Lancaster Rd. E17	77	G2
Lancaster Rd. N4	75	G7
Lancaster Rd. N11	58	D6
Lancaster Rd. N18	60	C5
Lancaster Rd. NW10	89	G5
Lancaster Rd. SE25	188	C2
Lancaster Rd. SW19	166	A5
Lancaster Rd. W11	108	B6
Lancaster Rd., Barn.	41	G5
Lancaster Rd., Enf.	44	A1
Lancaster Rd., Har.	67	G5
Lancaster Rd., Nthlt.	85	J6
Lancaster Rd., Sthl.	103	E7
Lancaster St. SE1	**27**	**H4**
Lancaster St. SE1	131	H2
Lancaster Ter. W2	**15**	**E5**
Lancaster Ter. W2	109	G7
Lancaster Wk. W2	**22**	**E3**
Lancaster Wk. W2	129	F1

Lancaster W. W11 108 A7
Grenfell Rd.
Lance Rd., Har. 67 J7
Lancefield St. W10 108 C3
Lancell St. N16 94 B2
Stoke Newington Ch. St.
Lancelot Av., Wem. 87 G4
Lancelot Cres., Wem. 87 G4
Lancelot Gdns., Barn. 42 A7
Lancelot Pl. SW7 23 J4
Lancelot Pl. SW7 129 J2
Lancelot Rd., Ilf. 65 H6
Lancelot Rd., Well. 158 A4
Lancelot Rd., Wem. 87 G5
Lancer Sq. W8 22 A3
Lancey Cl. SE7 136 A4
Cleveley Cl.
Lanchester Rd. N6 73 J5
Lancing Gdns. N9 60 C1
Lancing Rd. W13 104/105 E7
Drayton Grn. Rd.
Lancing Rd., Croy. 187 F6
Lancing Rd., Ilf. 81 G6
Lancing St. NW1 9 H4
Lancresse Ct. N1 112 B1
Landcroft Rd. SE22 152 C6
Landells Rd. SE22 152 C6
Landford Rd. SW15 147 J3
Landgrove Rd. SW19 166 D5
Landmann Way SE14 133 G5
Landon Pl. SW1 23 J5
Landon Pl. SW1 129 J3
Landon Wk. E14 114 B7
Cottage St.
Landons Cl. E14 134 C1
Landor Rd. SW9 150 E3
Landor Wk. W12 127 G2
Landport Way SE15 37 G7
Landra Gdns. N21 43 H6
Landridge Rd. SW6 148 C2
Landrock Rd. N8 75 E6
Landscape Rd., 63 H7
Wdf.Grn.
Landseer Av. E12 98 D5
Landseer Cl. SW19 185 F1
Brangwyn Cres.
Landseer Cl., Edg. 70 A2
Landseer Rd. N19 92 E3
Landseer Rd., Enf. 44 D5
Landseer Rd., N.Mal. 182 D7
Landseer Rd., Sutt. 198 D6
Landstead Rd. SE18 137 G7
Lane, The NW8 6 C1
Lane, The SE3 155 G3
Lane App. NW7 56 B5
Lane Cl. NW2 89 H3
Lane End, Bexh. 159 H3
Lane Ms. E12 98 C3
Colchester Rd.
Lanercost Cl. SW2 169 G2
Lanercost Gdns. N14 42 E7
Lanercost Rd. SW2 169 G2
Lanesborough Pl. 24 B3
SW1
Laneside, Chis. 175 E5
Laneside, Edg. 54 C5
Laneside Av., Dag. 83 F7
Laneway SW15 147 H5
Lanfranc Rd. E3 113 H2
Lanfrey Pl. W14 128 C5
North End Rd.
Lang St. E1 113 F4
Langbourne Av. N6 92 A2
Langbourne Pl. E14 134 A2
Westferry Rd.
Langbourne Way, 194 D6
Esher
Langbrook Rd. SE3 156 A3
Langcroft Cl., Cars. 199 J3
Langdale Av., Mitch. 185 J3
Langdale Cl. SE17 35 J5
Langdale Cl. SE17 131 J6
Langdale Cl. SW14 146 B4
Clifford Av.
Langdale Cl., Dag. 100 C1
Langdale Cl., Orp. 206/207 E3
Grasmere Rd.
Langdale Cres., Bexh. 139 G7
Langdale Gdns., Grnf. 105 E3
Langdale Rd. SE10 134 C7
Langdale Rd., Th.Hth. 187 G4
Langdale St. E1 112/113 E6
Burslem St.
Langdon Ct. NW10 106 E1
Langdon Cres. E6 116 D2
Langdon Dr. NW9 88 C1
Langdon Pk. Rd. N6 74 C7
Langdon Pl. SW14 146 C3
Rosemary La.
Langdon Rd. E6 116 D1
Langdon Rd., Brom. 191 H3
Langdon Rd., Mord. 185 F5
Langdon Shaw, Sid. 175 J5
Langdon Wk., Mord. 185 F5

Langdon Way SE1 37 J2
Langdons Ct., Sthl. 123 G3
Langford Cl. E8 94 D5
Langford Cl. N15 76 B6
Langford Cl. NW8 6 D1
Langford Cl. NW8 6 C2
Langford Cl. NW8 109 F2
Langford Cres., Barn. 41 J4
Langford Grn. SE5 152 B3
Langford Pl. NW8 6 D1
Langford Pl. NW8 109 F2
Langford Pl., Sid. 176 A3
Langford Rd. SW6 149 E2
Langford Rd., Barn. 41 H4
Langford Rd., 63 J6
Wdf.Grn.
Langfords, Buck.H. 64 A2
Langham Cl. N15 75 H3
Langham Rd.
Langham Dr., Rom. 82 B6
Langham Gdns. N21 43 G5
Langham Gdns. W13 105 E7
Langham Gdns., Edg. 54 C7
Langham Gdns., Rich. 163 F4
Langham Gdns., 87 F2
Wem.
Langham Ho. Cl., 163 G4
Rich.
Langham Pl. N15 75 H3
Langham Pl. W1 16 E2
Langham Pl. W1 110 B5
Langham Pl. W4 126/127 E6
Hogarth Roundabout
Langham Rd. N15 75 H3
Langham Rd. SW20 183 J1
Langham Rd., Edg. 54 C6
Langham Rd., Tedd. 162 E5
Langham St. W1 17 E2
Langham St. W1 110 B5
Langhedge Cl. N18 60 C6
Langhedge La. 60 C5
Langhedge La. N18 60 C5
Langhedge La. Ind. 60 C6
Est. N18
Langholm Cl. SW12 150 D7
King's Av.
Langholme, Bushey 51 J1
Langhorne Rd., Dag. 101 G7
Langland Cres., Stan. 69 H3
Langland Dr., Pnr. 50 E7
Langland Gdns. NW3 91 E5
Langland Gdns., 203 J2
Croy.
Langler Rd. NW10 107 J2
Langley Av., Ruis. 84 B1
Langley Av., Surb. 195 G1
Langley Av., Wor.Pk. 198 A2
Langley Ct. SE9 156 D6
Langley Ct. WC2 18 A5
Langley Ct., Beck. 190 B5
Langley Cres. E11 79 J7
Langley Cres., Dag. 100 C7
Langley Cres., Edg. 54 C3
Langley Cres., Hayes 121 J7
Langley Dr. E11 79 H7
Langley Dr. W3 126 B2
Langley Gdns., Brom. 191 J4
Langley Gdns., Dag. 100 D7
Langley Gdns., Orp. 193 E6
Langley Gro., N.Mal. 182 E2
Langley La. SW8 34 B5
Langley La. SW8 131 F6
Langley Meadow, 49 G2
Loug.
Langley Pk. NW7 54 E6
Langley Pk. Rd., Sutt. 199 F5
Langley Rd. SW19 184 C1
Langley Rd., Beck. 189 H4
Langley Rd., Islw. 144 C2
Langley Rd., Surb. 181 H7
Langley Rd., Well. 138 C6
Langley Row, Barn. 40 C1
Langley St. WC2 18 A4
Langley St. WC2 110 E6
Langley Way, W.Wick. 204 D1
Langmead Dr., 52 A1
Bushey
Langmead St. SE27 169 H4
Beadman St.
Langmore Ct., Bexh. 158 D3
Regency Way
Langridge Ms., 161 F6
Hmptn.
Oak Av.
Langroyd Rd. SW17 167 J2
Langside Av. SW15 147 G4
Langside Cres. N14 58 D3
Langston Hughes Cl. 151 H4
SE24
Shakespeare Rd.
Langston Rd., Loug. 49 F5
Langthorn Ct. EC2 20 B3
Langthorne Rd. E11 96 C3
Langthorne St. SW6 128 A7

Langton Av. E6 116 D3
Langton Av. N20 41 F7
Langton Cl. WC1 10 D4
Langton Pl. SW18 166 D1
Merton Rd.
Langton Ri. SE23 152 E7
Langton Rd. NW2 89 J3
Langton Rd. SW9 131 H7
Langton Rd., Har. 51 J7
Langton Rd., W.Mol. 179 J4
Langton St. SW10 30 D6
Langton St. SW10 129 F6
Langton Way SE3 155 F1
Langton Way, Croy. 202 B4
Langtry Rd. NW8 108 E1
Langtry Rd., Nthlt. 102 D2
Langtry Wk. NW8 91 F7
Alexandra Pl.
Langwood Chase, 163 F6
Tedd.
Langworthy Dr., Hayes 102 A6
Lanhill Rd. W9 108 D4
Lanier Rd. SE13 154 C6
Lanigan Dr., Houns. 143 H5
Lankaster Gdns. N2 73 G1
Lankers Dr., Har. 67 F6
Lankton Cl., Beck. 190 C1
Lannock Rd., Hayes 121 H1
Lannoy Rd. SE9 175 F1
Lanrick Rd. E14 114 D6
Lanridge Rd. SE2 138 D3
Lansbury Av. N18 60 A5
Lansbury Av., Bark. 100 A7
Lansbury Av., Felt. 142 B6
Lansbury Av., Rom. 83 E5
Lansbury Cl. NW10 88 C5
Lansbury Est. E14 114 B6
Lansbury Gdns. E14 114 D6
Lansbury Way N18 60 B5
Lanscombe Wk. SW8 150 E1
Lansdell Rd., Mitch. 186 A2
Lansdowne Av., Bexh. 138 D7
Lansdowne Av., Orp. 207 E1
Lansdowne Cl. SW20 166 A7
Lansdowne Cl., Surb. 196 B2
Kingston Rd.
Lansdowne Cl., 162 C1
Twick.
Lion Rd.
Lansdowne Ct., 197 G2
Wor.Pk.
The Av.
Lansdowne Cres. W11 108 B7
Lansdowne Dr. E8 94 D6
Lansdowne Gdns. 150 E1
SW8
Lansdowne Grn. 150/151 E1
SW8
Hartington Rd.
Lansdowne Gro. 89 E4
NW10
Lansdowne Hill SE27 169 H3
Lansdowne La. SE7 136 A6
Lansdowne Ms. SE7 136 A5
Lansdowne Ms. W11 128 C1
Lansdowne Rd.
Lansdowne Pl. SE1 28 C6
Lansdowne Pl. SE19 170 C7
Lansdowne Ri. W11 108 B7
Lansdowne Rd. E4 62 A2
Lansdowne Rd. E11 97 F2
Lansdowne Rd. E17 78 A5
Lansdowne Rd. E18 79 G3
Lansdowne Rd. N3 56 C7
Lansdowne Rd. N10 74 C2
Lansdowne Rd. N17 76 C1
Lansdowne Rd. SW20 165 J7
Lansdowne Rd. W11 108 B7
Lansdowne Rd., 173 G7
Brom.
Lansdowne Rd., Croy. 202 A2
Lansdowne Rd., 196 C7
Epsom
Lansdowne Rd., Har. 68 D7
Lansdowne Rd., 143 H3
Houns.
Lansdowne Rd., Ilf. 99 J1
Lansdowne Rd., Stan. 53 F6
Lansdowne Row W1 24 E1
Lansdowne Ter. WC1 10 B6
Lansdowne Ter. WC1 111 E4
Lansdowne Wk. W11 128 B1
Lansdowne Way 150 E1
SW8
Lansdowne Wd. Cl. 169 H3
SE27

Lantern Cl., Wem. 87 G5
Lantern Way, West Dr. 120 B2
Warwick Rd.
Lanterns Ct. E14 134 A2
Lanvanor Rd. SE15 153 F2
Lapford Cl. W9 108 C4
Lappmore Wk., 102 D5
Hayes
Lochan Cl.
Lapse Wd. Wk. SE23 170 E1
Lapstone Gdns., Har. 69 F6
Lapwing Ct., Surb. 196 A3
Chaffinch Cl.
Lapwing Way, Hayes 102 D6
Lara Cl. SE13 154 C6
Lara Cl., Chess. 195 H7
Larbert Rd. SW16 186 C1
Larch Av. W3 126 E1
Larch Cl. E13 115 H4
Larch Cl. N11 58 A7
Larch Cl. N19 92 C2
Bredgar Rd.
Larch Cl. SE8 133 J6
Clyde St.
Larch Cl. SW12 168 B2
Larch Cres., Epsom 196 B6
Larch Cres., Hayes 102 C4
Larch Dr. W4 126 A5
Gunnersbury Av.
Larch Grn. NW9 70/71 E2
Clayton Fld.
Larch Gro., Sid. 175 J1
Larch Ms. N19 92 C2
Bredgar Rd.
Larch Rd. E10 96 A2
Walnut Rd.
Larch Rd. NW2 89 J4
Larch Tree Way, Croy. 204 A3
Larch Way, Brom. 192 D7
Larchdene, Orp. 206 D2
Larches, The N13 59 J3
Larches Av. SW14 146 D4
Larchwood Rd. SE9 175 E2
Larcom St. SE17 36 A2
Larcom St. SE17 131 J4
Larcombe Cl., Croy. 202 C4
Larden Rd. W3 127 E1
Largewood Av., 196 A2
Surb.
Larissa St. SE17 36 C3
Lark Row E2 113 F1
Lark Way, Cars. 185 H7
Larkbere Rd. SE26 171 H4
Larken Dr., Bushey 51 J1
Larkfield Av., Har. 69 E3
Larkfield Cl., Brom. 205 F2
Larkfield Rd., Rich. 145 H4
Larkfield Rd., Sid. 175 J3
Larkhall La. SW4 150 D2
Larkhall Ri. SW4 150 C3
Larkhill Ter. SE18 136 D7
Larks Gro., Bark. 99 H7
Larksfield Gro., Enf. 45 E1
Larkshall Ct., Rom. 83 J2
Larkshall Cres. E4 62 C4
Larkshall Rd. E4 62 C5
Larkspur Cl. E6 116 B5
Larkspur Cl. N17 60 A7
Fryatt Rd.
Larkspur Cl. NW9 70 B5
Larkspur Gro., Edg. 54 C4
Larkspur Way, Epsom 196 C5
Larkswood Cl. E4 62 D5
Larkswood Ri., Pnr. 66 C4
Larkswood Rd. E4 62 A4
Larkway Cl. NW9 70 D4
Larnach Rd. W6 128 A6
Larpent Av. SW15 147 J5
Larwood Cl., Grnf. 86 A5
Lascelles Av., Har. 68 A7
Lascelles Cl. E11 96 D2
Lascotts Rd. N22 59 F6
Lassa Rd. SE9 156 B5
Lassell St. SE10 134 D5
Lasseter Pl. SE3 135 F6
Vanbrugh Hill
Latchett Rd. E18 79 H1
Latchingdon Cl. E17 77 G4
Latchingdon Gdns., 64 B6
Wdf.Grn.
Latchmere Cl., Rich. 163 H5
Latchmere La. 163 J6
Kings.T.
Latchmere Pas. SW11 149 H2
Cabul Rd.
Latchmere Rd. SW11 149 J2
Latchmere Rd., 163 H7
Kings.T.
Latchmere St. SW11 149 J2
Lateward Rd., Brent. 125 G6
Latham Cl. E6 116 B6
Oliver Gdns.
Latham Cl., Twick. 144 D7
Latham Ho. E1 113 G6

Latham Rd., Bexh. 159 G5
Latham Rd., Twick. 144 C7
Lathams Way, Croy. 201 F1
Lathkill Cl., Enf. 44 D7
Lathom Rd. E6 98 C7
Latimer SE17 36 D4
Latimer Av. E6 116 C1
Latimer Cl., Pnr. 66 C1
Latimer Cl., Wor.Pk. 197 H4
Latimer Gdns., Pnr. 66 C1
Latimer Pl. W10 107 J6
Latimer Rd. E7 97 H4
Latimer Rd. N15 76 B6
Latimer Rd. SW19 166 E6
Latimer Rd. W10 107 J6
Latimer Rd., Barn. 40 E3
Latimer Rd., Croy. 201 H3
Abbey Rd.
Latimer Rd., Tedd. 162 C5
Latona Rd. SE15 37 H6
Latona Rd. SE15 132 D6
Lattimer Pl. W4 127 E6
Latton Cl., Walt. 179 E7
Latymer Ct. W6 128 A4
Latymer Rd. N9 60 C1
Latymer Way N9 60 A2
Laud St. SE11 34 C3
Laud St., Croy. 201 J3
Lauder Cl., Nthlt. 102 D2
Lauderdale Dr., Rich. 163 G3
Lauderdale Pl. EC2 111 J5
Beech St.
Lauderdale Rd. W9 6 A4
Lauderdale Rd. W9 108 E3
Laughton Ct., Borwd. 38 D2
Banks Rd.
Laughton Rd., Nthlt. 102 D1
Launcelot Rd., Brom. 173 G4
Launcelot St. SE1 26 E4
Launceston Gdns., Grnf. 105 F1
Launceston Pl. W8 22 C5
Launceston Pl. W8 129 F3
Launceston Rd., Grnf. 105 F1
Launch St. E14 134 C3
Laundress La. N16 94 D3
Laundry La. N1 111 J1
Greenman St.
Laundry Rd. W6 128 B6
Laura Cl. E11 79 J5
Laura Cl., Enf. 44 B5
Laura Pl. E5 95 F4
Lauradale Rd. N2 73 J4
Laurel Av., Twick. 162 C1
Laurel Bank Gdns. SW6 148 C2
New Kings Rd.
Laurel Bank Rd., Enf. 43 J1
Laurel Bank Vil. W7 124 B1
Lower Boston Rd.
Laurel Cl. N19 92 C2
Hargrave Pk.
Laurel Cl. SW17 167 H5
Laurel Cl., Ilf. 65 F6
Laurel Cl., Sid. 176 A3
Laurel Cres., Croy. 204 A3
Laurel Dr. N21 43 G7
Laurel Gdns. E4 46 B7
Laurel Gdns. NW7 54 D3
Laurel Gdns. W7 124 B1
Laurel Gdns., Houns. 142 E4
Laurel Gro. SE20 171 E7
Laurel Gro. SE26 171 G4
Laurel La., West Dr. 120 B4
Laurel Pk., Har. 52 C7
Laurel Rd. SW13 147 G2
Laurel Rd. SW20 183 H1
Laurel Rd., Hmptn. 162 A5
Laurel St. E8 94 C6
Laurel Vw. N12 56 E3
Laurel Way E18 79 F4
Laurel Way N20 56 D3
Laurence Ms. W12 127 G2
Askew Rd.
Laurence Pountney Hill EC4 20 B5
Laurence Pountney La. EC4 20 B5
Laurie Gro. SE14 153 H1
Laurie Rd. W7 104 B5
Laurier Rd. NW5 92 B3
Laurier Rd., Croy. 188 C7
Laurimel Cl., Stan. 52/53 E6
September Way
Laurino Pl., Bushey 51 J2
Lauriston Rd. E9 113 G1
Lauriston Rd. SW19 166 A6
Lausanne Rd. N8 75 G4
Lausanne Rd. SE15 153 F1
Lavell St. N16 94 A4
Lavender Av. NW9 88 C1
Lavender Av., Mitch. 185 H1
Lavender Av., Wor.Pk. 197 J3
Lavender Cl. SW3 31 F6
Lavender Cl., Brom. 192 B6
Lavender Cl., Cars. 200 A4
Lavender Ct., W.Mol. 179 H3
Molesham Way
Lavender Gdns. SW11 149 J4
Lavender Gdns., Enf. 43 H1
Lavender Gdns., Har. 52 B6
Uxbridge Rd.
Lavender Gro. E8 94 C7
Lavender Gro., Mitch. 185 H1
Lavender Hill SW11 149 H4
Lavender Hill, Enf. 43 G1
Lavender Ms., Wall. 200 E6
Lavender Pl., Ilf. 98 E5
Lavender Ri., West Dr. 120 D2
Lavender Rd. SE16 133 H1
Lavender Rd. SW11 149 G3
Lavender Rd., Cars. 200 A4
Lavender Rd., Croy. 187 F6
Lavender Rd., Enf. 44 A1
Lavender Rd., Epsom 196 B5
Lavender Rd., Sutt. 199 G4
Lavender Sq. E11 96 D3
Anglian Rd.
Lavender St. E15 96/97 E6
Manbey Gro.
Lavender Sweep SW11 149 J4
Lavender Ter. SW11 149 H3
Falcon Rd.
Lavender Vale, Wall. 200 D6
Lavender Wk. SW11 149 J4
Lavender Wk., Mitch. 186 A3
Lavender Way, Croy. 189 G6
Lavengro Rd. SE27 169 J2
Lavenham Rd. SW18 166 C2
Lavernock Rd., Bexh. 159 G2
Lavers Rd. N16 94 B3
Laverstoke Gdns. SW15 147 G7
Laverton Ms. SW5 30 B2
Laverton Pl. SW5 30 B2
Laverton Pl. SW5 129 E4
Lavidge Rd. SE9 174 B2
Lavina Gro. N1 10 C1
Lavington Rd. W13 125 E1
Lavington Rd., Croy. 201 F3
Lavington St. SE1 27 H2
Lavington St. SE1 131 H1
Law Ho., Bark. 118 A2
Law St. SE1 28 C5
Law St. SE1 132 A3
Lawdons Gdns., Croy. 201 H4
Lawford Rd. N1 94 B7
Lawford Rd. NW5 92 C6
Lawford Rd. W4 126 C7
Lawless St. E14 114 B7
Lawley Rd. N14 42 B7
Lawley St. E5 95 F4
Lawn, The, Sthl. 123 G5
Lawn Cl. N9 44 C7
Lawn Cl., Brom. 173 H6
Lawn Cl., N.Mal. 182 E2
Lawn Cres., Rich. 146 A2
Lawn Fm. Gro., Rom. 82 E4
Lawn Gdns. W7 124 B1
Lawn Ho. Cl. E14 134 C2
Lawn La. SW8 34 B6
Lawn La. SW8 131 E6
Lawn Pl. SE15 152 C1
Sumner Est.
Lawn Rd. NW3 91 J5
Lawn Rd., Beck. 171 J7
Lawn Ter. SE3 155 E3
Lawn Vale, Pnr. 66 D2
Lawnfield NW2 90 A7
Coverdale Rd.
Lawns, The E4 62 A5
Lawns, The SE3 154/155 E3
Lee Ter.
Lawns, The SE19 188 A1
Lawns, The, Pnr. 51 H7
Lawns, The, Sid. 176 B4
Lawns, The, Sutt. 198 B7
Lawns Ct., Wem. 87 J2
The Av.
Lawnside SE3 155 F4
Lawrence Av. E12 98 D4
Lawrence Av. E17 77 G1
Lawrence Av. N13 59 H4
Lawrence Av. NW7 55 E4
Lawrence Av., N.Mal. 182 D6
Lawrence Bldgs. N16 94 C3
Lawrence Campe Cl. N20 57 G3
Friern Barnet La.
Lawrence Cl. E3 114 A2
Lawrence Cl. N15 76 B3
Lawrence Rd.
Lawrence Ct. NW7 55 E5
Lawrence Cres., Dag. 101 H3
Lawrence Cres., Edg. 70 A2
Lawrence Gdns. NW7 55 F3
Lawrence Hill E4 62 A2
Lawrence La. EC2 20 A4
Lawrence Pl. N1 110/111 E1
Outram Pl.
Lawrence Rd. E6 116 A1
Lawrence Rd. E13 115 H1
Lawrence Rd. N15 76 B4
Lawrence Rd. N18 60 E4
Lawrence Rd. SE25 188 C4
Lawrence Rd. W5 125 G4
Lawrence Rd., Erith 139 H7
Lawrence Rd., Hmptn. 161 F7
Lawrence Rd., Houns. 142 C4
Lawrence Rd., Pnr. 66 D5
Lawrence Rd., Rich. 163 F4
Lawrence Rd., W.Wick. 205 G4
Lawrence St. E16 115 F5
Lawrence St. NW7 55 F4
Lawrence St. SW3 31 G6
Lawrence St. SW3 129 H6
Lawrence Way NW10 88 C4
Lawrence Weaver Cl., Mord. 184/185 E6
Green La.
Lawrie Pk. Av. SE26 171 E5
Lawrie Pk. Cres. SE26 171 E5
Lawrie Pk. Gdns. SE26 171 E4
Lawrie Pk. Rd. SE26 171 E6
Lawson Cl. E16 115 J5
Lawson Cl. SW19 166 A3
Lawson Est. SE1 28 B6
Lawson Est. SE1 132 A3
Lawson Gdns., Pnr. 66 B3
Lawson Rd., Enf. 45 F1
Lawson Rd., Sthl. 103 F4
Lawson Wk., Cars. 199 J7
Fountain Dr.
Lawton Rd. E3 113 H3
Lawton Rd. E10 96 C1
Lawton Rd., Barn. 41 G3
Lawton Rd., Loug. 48 E3
Laxcon Cl. NW10 88 C5
Laxey Rd., Orp. 207 J6
Laxley Cl. SE5 35 H7
Laxley Cl. SE5 131 H7
Laxton Pl. NW1 9 E5
Layard Rd. SE16 133 E4
Layard Rd., Enf. 44 C1
Layard Rd., Th.Hth. 188 A2
Layard Sq. SE16 133 E4
Laycock St. N1 93 G6
Layer Gdns. W3 106 A7
Layfield Cl. NW4 71 H7
Layfield Cres. NW4 71 H7
Layfield Rd. NW4 71 H7
Layhams Rd., Kes. 205 F5
Layhams Rd., W.Wick. 204 D3
Laymarsh Cl., Belv. 139 F3
Laymead Cl., Nthlt. 84 E6
Laystall St. EC1 10 E6
Laystall St. EC1 111 G4
Layton Cres., Croy. 201 G5
Layton Rd. N1 11 F1
Layton Rd., Brent. 125 G5
Layton Rd., Houns. 143 H4
Laytons Bldgs. SE1 28 A3
Layzell Wk. SE9 174 A1
Mottingham La.
Lazar Wk. N7 93 F2
Briset Way
Le May Av. SE12 173 H3
Lea Br. Rd. E5 95 F3
Lea Br. Rd. E10 95 H1
Lea Br. Rd. E17 78 D4
Lea Gdns., Wem. 87 H4
Lea Hall Rd. E10 96 A1
Lea Rd., Beck. 190 A2
Fairfield Rd.
Lea Rd., Enf. 44 A1
Lea Rd., Sthl. 122 E4
Lea Valley Rd. E4 45 G5
Lea Valley Rd., Enf. 45 G5
Lea Valley Trd. Est. N18 61 G5
Lea Valley Viaduct E4 61 G5
Lea Valley Viaduct N18 61 G5
Lea Vw. Hos. E5 94/95 E1
Springfield
Leabank Cl., Har. 86 B3
Leabank Sq. E9 96 A6
Leabank Vw. N15 76 D6
Leabourne Rd. N16 76 D6
Leacroft Av. SW12 149 J7
Leadale Av. E4 62 A2
Leadale Rd. N15 76 D6
Leadale Rd. N16 76 D6
Leadbeaters Cl. N11 57 J5
Goldsmith Rd.
Leadenhall Mkt. EC3 20 D4
Leadenhall Pl. EC3 20 D4
Leadenhall St. EC3 20 D4
Leadenhall St. EC3 112 B6
Leader Av. E12 98 D5
Leadings, The, Wem. 88 C3
Leaf Cl., T.Ditt. 180 B5
Leaf Gro. SE27 169 G5
Leafield Cl. SW16 169 H6
Leafield La., Sid. 177 F4
Leafield Rd. SW20 184 C3
Leafield Rd., Sutt. 198 D2
Leafy Gro., Kes. 205 J5
Leafy Oak Rd. SE12 173 J3
Leafy Way, Croy. 202 C2
Leagrave St. E5 95 F3
Leahurst Rd. SE13 154 D5
Leake Ct. SE1 26 D4
Leake St. SE1 26 D3
Leake St. SE1 131 F2
Lealand Rd. N15 76 C6
Leamington Av. E17 78 A5
Leamington Av., Brom. 173 J5
Leamington Av., Mord. 184 C4
Leamington Av., Orp. 207 H4
Leamington Cl. E12 98 B5
Leamington Cl., Brom. 173 J5
Leamington Cl., Houns. 143 J5
Leamington Cres., Har. 85 E3
Leamington Gdns., Ilf. 99 J2
Leamington Pk. W3 106 D5
Leamington Rd., Sthl. 122 D4
Leamington Rd. Vil. W11 108 C5
Leamore St. W6 127 H4
Leamouth Rd. E6 116 B6
Remington Rd.
Leamouth Rd. E14 114 D6
Leander Ct. SE8 154 A1
Leander Rd. SW2 151 F6
Leander Rd., Nthlt. 103 G2
Leander Rd., Th.Hth. 187 F4
Learner Dr., Har. 85 G2
Learoyd Gdns. E6 116 D7
Leas Cl., Chess. 195 J7
Leas Dale SE9 174 D3
Leas Grn., Chis. 175 J6
Leaside Av. N10 74 A3
Leaside Rd. E5 95 F1
Leasowes Rd. E10 96 A1
Leather Bottle La., Belv. 139 E4
Leather Cl., Mitch. 186 A2
Leather Gdns. E15 114/115 E1
Abbey Rd.
Leather La. EC1 19 F2
Leather La. EC1 111 G5
Leatherbottle Grn., Erith 139 F3
Leatherdale St. E1 113 F4
Portelet Rd.
Leatherhead Cl. N16 94 C1
Leathermarket Ct. SE1 28 D4
Leathermarket Ct. SE1 132 B2
Leathermarket St. SE1 28 D4
Leathermarket St. SE1 132 B2
Leathersellers Cl., Barn. 40 B4
The Av.
Leathsail Rd., Har. 85 H3
Leathwaite Rd. SW11 149 J4
Leathwell Rd. SE8 154 B2
Leaveland Cl., Beck. 190 A4
Leaver Gdns., Grnf. 104 A2
Leavesden Rd., Stan. 52 D6
Leaway E10 95 G1
Lebanon Av., Felt. 160 D5
Lebanon Ct., Twick. 144 E7
Lebanon Gdns. SW18 148 D6
Lebanon Pk., Twick. 144 E7
Lebanon Rd. SW18 148 D5
Lebanon Rd., Croy. 202 B1
Lebrun Sq. SE3 155 H3
Lechmere App., Wdf.Grn. 79 J2
Lechmere Av., Chig. 65 F4
Lechmere Av., Wdf.Grn. 80 A2
Lechmere Rd. NW2 89 H6
Leckford Rd. SW18 167 F2
Leckwith Av., Bexh. 138 E6
Lecky St. SW7 31 E3
Lecky St. SW7 129 G5
Leconfield Av. SW13 147 F3
Leconfield Rd. N5 94 A4

Name	Page	Grid
Leda Av., Enf.	45	G1
Leda Rd. SE18	136	C3
Ledbury Est. SE15	132	E7
Ledbury Ms. N. W11	108	D7
Ledbury Rd.		
Ledbury Ms. W. W11	108	D7
Ledbury Rd.		
Ledbury Pl., Croy.	201	J4
Ledbury Rd.		
Ledbury Rd. W11	108	C6
Ledbury Rd., Croy.	201	J4
Ledbury St. SE15	132	D7
Ledrington Rd. SE19	170	D6
Anerley Hill		
Ledway Dr., Wem.	69	J7
Lee Av., Rom.	82	E6
Lee Br. SE13	154	C3
Lee Ch. St. SE13	155	E4
Lee Cl. E17	77	G1
Lee Cl., Barn.	41	F4
Lee Conservancy Rd. E9	95	J5
Lee Grn. SE12	155	F5
Lee High Rd.		
Lee Gro., Chig.	64	D2
Lee High Rd. SE12	154	D3
Lee High Rd. SE13	154	D3
Lee Pk. SE3	155	F4
Lee Pk. Way N9	61	G4
Lee Pk. Way N18	61	G4
Lee Rd. NW7	56	A7
Lee Rd. SE3	155	F3
Lee Rd. SW19	185	E1
Lee Rd., Enf.	44	D6
Lee Rd., Grnf.	105	F1
Lee St. E8	112	C1
Lee Ter. SE3	154	E3
Lee Ter. SE13	154	E3
Lee Valley Technopark N17	76	D3
Lee Vw., Enf.	43	H1
Leechcroft Av., Sid.	157	J3
Leechcroft Rd., Wall.	200	A3
Leecroft Rd., Barn.	40	B5
Leeds Pl. N4	93	F2
Tollington Pk.		
Leeds Rd., Ilf.	99	G1
Leeds St. N18	60	D5
Leefern Rd. W12	127	G2
Leegate SE12	155	F5
Leeke St. WC1	10	C3
Leeke St. WC1	111	F3
Leeland Rd. W13	124	D1
Leeland Ter. W13	124	D1
Leeland Way NW10	89	F4
Leerdam Dr. E14	134	C3
Lees, The, Croy.	203	J2
Lees Pl. W1	**16**	**B5**
Lees Pl. W1	110	A7
Leeside, Barn.	40	B5
Leeside Cres. NW11	72	C6
Leeside Rd. N17	61	E6
Leeson Rd. SE24	151	G4
Leesons Hill, Chis.	193	J3
Leesons Way, Orp.	193	J2
Leeward Gdns. SW19	166	C6
Leeway SE8	133	J5
Leeway Cl., Pnr.	51	F7
Leewood Cl. SE12	155	F6
Upwood Rd.		
Lefevre Wk. E3	114	A1
Lefroy Rd. W12	127	F2
Legard Rd. N5	93	H3
Legatt Rd. SE9	156	A5
Leggatt Rd. E15	114	C2
Legge St. SE13	154	C5
Leghorn Rd. NW10	107	F2
Leghorn Rd. SE18	137	G5
Legion Cl. N1	93	G6
Legion Ct., Mord.	184	D6
Legion Rd., Grnf.	103	J1
Legion Way N12	57	H7
Legon Av., Rom.	101	J1
Legrace Av., Houns.	142	D2
Leicester Av., Mitch.	187	E4
Leicester Cl., Wor.Pk.	197	J4
Leicester Ct. WC2	**17**	**J5**
Leicester Gdns., Ilf.	81	H7
Leicester Pl. WC2	**17**	**J5**
Leicester Rd. E11	79	H5
Leicester Rd. N2	73	H3
Leicester Rd. NW10	88	D7
Leicester Rd., Barn.	40	E5
Leicester Rd., Croy.	188	B7
Leicester Sq. WC2	**17**	**J6**
Leicester Sq. WC2	110	D7
Leicester St. WC2	**17**	**J5**
Leigh Av., Ilf.	80	A4
Leigh Cl., N.Mal.	182	D4
Leigh Ct., Borwd.	38	D2
Banks Rd.		
Leigh Ct., Har.	86	B1
Leigh Cres., Croy.	204	B7
Leigh Gdns. NW10	107	J2
Leigh Hunt Dr. N14	58	D1
Leigh Hunt St. SE1	**27**	**J3**
Leigh Orchard Cl. SW16	169	F3
Leigh Pl. EC1	**19**	**E1**
Leigh Pl., Well.	158	A2
Leigh Rd. E6	98	D6
Leigh Rd. E10	78	C7
Leigh Rd. N5	93	H4
Leigh Rd., Houns.	144	A4
Leigh Rodd, Wat.	51	F3
Leigh St. WC1	**10**	**A5**
Leigh St. WC1	110	E4
Leigham Av. SW16	169	E3
Leigham Ct., Wall.	200	C6
Stafford Rd.		
Leigham Ct. Rd. SW16	169	E2
Leigham Dr., Islw.	124	B7
Leigham Vale SW2	169	F3
Leigham Vale SW16	169	F3
Leighton Av. E12	98	D5
Leighton Av., Pnr.	66	E3
Leighton Cl., Edg.	70	A2
Leighton Cres. NW5	92	C5
Leighton Gro.		
Leighton Gdns. NW10	107	H2
Leighton Gro. NW5	92	C5
Leighton Pl. NW5	92	C5
Leighton Rd. NW5	92	D5
Leighton Rd. W13	124	D2
Leighton Rd., Enf.	44	C5
Leighton Rd., Har.	68	A2
Leighton St., Croy.	201	H1
Leila Parnell Pl. SE7	135	J6
Leinster Av. SW14	146	C3
Leinster Gdns. W2	**14**	**C4**
Leinster Gdns. W2	109	F6
Leinster Ms. W2	**14**	**C5**
Leinster Ms. W2	109	F7
Leinster Pl. W2	**14**	**C4**
Leinster Pl. W2	109	F6
Leinster Rd. N10	74	B4
Leinster Rd. NW6	108	D3
Stafford Rd.		
Leinster Sq. W2	108	D6
Leinster Ter. W2	**14**	**C5**
Leinster Ter. W2	109	F7
Leisure Way N12	57	G7
Leith Cl. NW9	88	D1
Leith Rd. N22	75	H1
Leith Yd. NW6	108	D1
Quex Rd.		
Leithcote Gdns. SW16	169	F4
Leithcote Path SW16	169	F3
Lela Av., Houns.	142	C2
Lelitia Cl. E8	112	D1
Pownall Rd.		
Leman St. E1	**21**	**G4**
Leman St. E1	112	C6
Lemark Cl., Stan.	53	F5
Lemmon Rd. SE10	134	E6
Lemna Rd. E11	79	E7
Lemonwell Ct. SE9	157	F5
Lemonwell Dr.		
Lemonwell Dr. SE9	157	F5
Lemsford Cl. N15	76	D5
Lemsford Ct. N4	93	J2
Brownswood Rd.		
Lemsford Ct., Borwd.	38	C4
Lemuel St. SW18	149	E6
Len Freeman Pl. SW6	128	C7
John Smith Av.		
Lena Gdns. W6	127	J3
Lena Kennedy Cl. E4	62	B6
Lenanton Steps E14	134	A2
Manilla St.		
Lendal Ter. SW4	150	D3
Lenelby Rd., Surb.	196	A1
Lenham Rd. SE12	155	F4
Lenham Rd., Bexh.	139	F6
Lenham Rd., Sutt.	199	E4
Lenham Rd., Th.Hth.	188	A2
Lennard Av., W.Wick.	205	E2
Lennard Cl., W.Wick.	205	E2
Lennard Rd. SE20	171	F6
Lennard Rd., Beck.	171	G6
Lennard Rd., Brom.	206	C1
Lennard Rd., Croy.	201	J1
Lennon Rd. NW2	89	J5
Lennox Gdns. NW10	89	F4
Lennox Gdns. SW1	**23**	**J6**
Lennox Gdns. SW1	129	J3
Lennox Gdns., Croy.	201	H4
Lennox Gdns., Ilf.	98	C1
Lennox Gdns. Ms. SW1	**23**	**J6**
Lennox Gdns. Ms. SW1	129	J3
Lennox Rd. E17	77	J6
Lennox Rd. N4	93	F2
Lenor Cl., Bexh.	159	E4
Lens Rd. E7	97	J7
Lensbury Way SE2	138	C3
Lenthall Rd. E8	94	D7
Lenthall Rd., Loug.	49	G4
Lenthorp Rd. SE10	135	F4
Lentmead Rd., Brom.	173	F3
Lenton Path SE18	137	G6
Lenton Ri., Rich.	145	H3
Evelyn Ter.		
Lenton St. SE18	137	G4
Leo St. SE15	133	E7
Leo Yd. EC1	**11**	**H6**
Leof Cres. SE6	172	B5
Leominster Rd., Mord.	185	F6
Leominster Wk., Mord.	185	F6
Leonard Av., Mord.	185	F5
Leonard Rd. E4	62	A6
Leonard Rd. E7	97	G4
Leonard Rd. N9	60	C3
Leonard Rd. SW16	186	C1
Leonard Rd., Sthl.	122	D3
Leonard Robbins Path SE28	118	B7
Tawney Rd.		
Leonard St. E16	136	B1
Leonard St. EC2	**12**	**C5**
Leonard St. EC2	112	A4
Leontine Cl. SE15	132	D7
Leopold Av. SW19	166	C5
Leopold Ms. E9	113	F1
Fremont St.		
Leopold Rd. E17	78	A5
Leopold Rd. N2	73	G3
Leopold Rd. N18	61	E5
Leopold Rd. NW10	89	E7
Leopold Rd. SW19	166	C4
Leopold St. E3	113	J5
Leopold Ter. SW19	166	D5
Dora Rd.		
Leppoc Rd. SW4	150	D5
Leroy St. SE1	**36**	**D1**
Leroy St. SE1	132	B4
Lescombe Cl. SE23	171	H3
Lescombe Rd. SE23	171	H3
Lesley Cl., Bex.	159	H7
Leslie Gdns., Sutt.	198	D7
Leslie Gro., Croy.	202	A1
Leslie Gro. Pl., Croy.	202	A1
Leslie Gro.		
Leslie Pk. Rd., Croy.	202	B1
Leslie Rd. E11	96	C4
Leslie Rd. E16	115	H6
Leslie Rd. N2	73	G3
Leslie Smith Sq. SE18	136	D6
Nightingale Vale		
Lessar Av. SW4	150	C5
Lessing St. SE23	153	H7
Lessingham Av. SW17	167	J4
Lessingham Av., Ilf.	80	D3
Lessington Av., Rom.	83	J6
Lessness Av., Bexh.	138	D7
Lessness Pk., Belv.	139	F5
Lessness Rd., Belv.	139	G5
Stapley Rd.		
Lessness Rd., Mord.	185	F6
Lester Av. E15	115	E3
Leswin Pl. N16	94	C3
Leswin Rd.		
Leswin Rd. N16	94	C3
Letchford Gdns. NW10	107	G3
Letchford Ms. NW10	107	G3
Letchford Gdns.		
Letchford Ter., Har.	67	H1
Letchworth Av., Felt.	141	J7
Letchworth Cl., Brom.	191	G5
Letchworth Cl., Wat.	50	D5
Letchworth Dr., Brom.	191	G5
Letchworth St. SW17	167	J4
Lethbridge Cl. SE13	154	C1
Lett Rd. E15	96	D7
Letterstone Rd. SW6	128	C7
Varna Rd.		
Lettice St. SW6	148	C1
Lettsom St. SE5	152	B2
Lettsom Wk. E13	115	G2
Leucha Rd. E17	77	H5
Levana Cl. SW19	166	B1
Levehurst Way SW4	151	E2
Leven Cl., Wat.	50	D5
Leven Rd. E14	114	C5
Levendale Rd. SE23	171	H2
Lever St. EC1	**11**	**H4**
Lever St. EC1	111	H3
Leverett St. SW3	**31**	**H1**
Leverholme Gdns. SE9	174	D3
Leverson St. SW16	168	C6
Leverton Pl. NW5	92	C5
Leverton St.		
Leverton St. NW5	92	C5
Levett Gdns., Ilf.	99	J4
Levett Rd., Bark.	99	H6
Levine Gdns., Bark.	118	D2
Levison Way N19	92	D2
Grovedale Rd.		
Lewes Cl., Nthlt.	85	G6
Lewes Rd. N12	57	H5
Lewes Rd., Brom.	192	A2
Lewesdon Cl. SW19	166	A1
Leweston Pl. N16	76	C7
Lewey Ho. E3	113	J4
Lewgars Av. NW9	70	C6
Lewin Rd. SW14	146	D3
Lewin Rd. SW16	168	D6
Lewin Rd., Bexh.	159	E4
Lewis Av. E17	78	A1
Lewis Cl. N14	42	C7
Orchid Rd.		
Lewis Cres. NW10	88	C5
Lewis Gdns. N2	73	G2
Lewis Gro. SE13	154	C3
Lewis Rd., Mitch.	185	G2
Lewis Rd., Rich.	145	G5
Red Lion St.		
Lewis Rd., Sid.	176	C3
Lewis Rd., Sthl.	123	E2
Lewis Rd., Sutt.	199	E4
Lewis Rd., Well.	158	C3
Lewis St. NW1	92	B7
Lewis Way, Dag.	101	H6
Lewisham High St. SE13	154	C3
Lewisham Hill SE13	154	C2
Lewisham Pk. SE13	154	B6
Lewisham Rd. SE13	154	B1
Lewisham St. SW1	**25**	**J4**
Lewisham Way SE4	153	J1
Lewisham Way SE14	153	J1
Lexden Dr., Rom.	82	B6
Lexden Rd. W3	106	B7
Lexden Rd., Mitch.	186	D4
Lexham Ct., Grnf.	104	A1
Lexham Gdns. W8	**30**	**B1**
Lexham Gdns. W8	128	E3
Lexham Gdns. Ms. W8	**22**	**B6**
Lexham Gdns. Ms. W8	129	E3
Lexham Ms., Bark.	117	G1
St. Margarets		
Lexham Ms. W8	128	D4
Lexham Wk. W8	**22**	**B6**
Lexington St. W1	**17**	**G4**
Lexington St. W1	110	C6
Lexington Way, Barn.	40	A4
Lexton Gdns. SW12	168	D1
Ley St., Ilf.	99	E2
Leyborne Av. W13	125	E2
Leyborne Pk., Rich.	146	A1
Leybourne Cl., Brom.	191	G6
Leybourne Rd. E11	97	F1
Leybourne Rd. NW1	92	B7
Leybourne Rd. NW9	70	A5
Leybourne Rd. NW1	92	B7
Hawley St.		
Leybridge Ct. SE12	155	G5
Leyburn Cl. E17	78	B4
Church La.		
Leyburn Gdns., Croy.	202	B2
Leyburn Gro. N18	60	D6
Leyburn Rd. N18	60	D6
Leycroft Cl., Loug.	48	D5
Leyden St. E1	**21**	**F2**
Leydon Cl. SE16	133	G1
Lagado Ms.		
Leyfield, Wor.Pk.	197	E1
Leyland Av., Enf.	45	H2
Leyland Gdns., Wdf.Grn.	63	J5
Leyland Rd. SE12	155	G5
Leylang Rd. SE14	133	G7
Leys, The N2	73	F4
Leys, The, Har.	69	J6
Leys Av., Dag.	101	J7
Leys Cl., Dag.	101	J7
Leys Cl., Har.	68	A5
Leys Gdns., Barn.	42	A5
Leys Rd. E., Enf.	45	H1
Leys Rd. W., Enf.	45	H1
Leysdown Av., Bexh.	159	J4
Leysdown Rd. SE9	174	B2
Leysfield Rd. W12	127	G2
Leyspring Rd. E11	97	F1
Leyswood Dr., Ilf.	81	H5
Leythe Rd. W3	126	C2

Leyton Business Cen. E10 96 A2
Leyton Gra. E10 96 B1
Goldsmith Rd.
Leyton Gra. Est. E10 96 B1
Leyton Grn. Rd. E10 78 C6
Leyton Ind. Village E10 77 G7
Leyton Pk. Rd. E10 96 C3
Leyton Rd. E15 96 D5
Leyton Rd. SW19 167 F7
Leyton Way E11 79 E7
Leytonstone Rd. E15 96 E5
Leywick St. E15 114 E2
Lezayre Rd., Orp. 207 J6
Liardet St. SE14 133 H6
Liberia Rd. N5 93 H6
Liberty Av. SW19 185 G1
Liberty Ms. SW12 150 B6
Liberty St. SW9 151 F1
Libra Rd. E3 113 J1
Libra Rd. E13 115 G2
Library Pl. E1 112/113 E7
Cable St.
Library St. SE1 27 G4
Library St. SE1 131 H2
Library Way, Twick. 143 J7
Nelson Rd.
Lichfield Cl., Barn. 41 J3
Lichfield Gdns., Rich. 145 H4
Lichfield Gro. N3 72 E2
Lichfield Rd. E3 113 H3
Lichfield Rd. E6 116 A3
Lichfield Rd. N9 60 D2
Winchester Rd.
Lichfield Rd. NW2 90 B4
Lichfield Rd., Dag. 100 B4
Lichfield Rd., Houns. 142 C3
Lichfield Rd., Nthwd. 66 A3
Lichfield Rd., Rich. 145 J1
Lichfield Rd., Wdf.Grn. 63 E4
Lichfield Sq., Rich. 145 H4
Lichfield Gdns.
Lichlade Cl., Orp. 207 J4
Lidbury Rd. NW7 56 B6
Lidcote Gdns. SW9 151 G2
Liddall Way, West Dr. 120 C1
Liddell Cl., Har. 69 G3
Liddell Gdns. NW10 107 J2
Liddell Rd. NW6 90 D6
Lidding Rd., Har. 69 G5
Liddington Rd. E15 115 F1
Liddon Rd. E13 115 H3
Liddon Rd., Brom. 191 J3
Liden Cl. E17 95 J1
Hitcham Rd.
Lidfield Rd. N16 94 A4
Lidgate Rd. SE15 132 C7
Chandler Way
Lidiard Rd. SW18 167 F2
Lidlington Pl. NW1 9 G2
Lidlington Pl. NW1 110 C2
Lido Sq. N17 76 A2
Lidyard Rd. N19 92 C1
Liffler Rd. SE18 137 H5
Lifford St. SW15 148 A4
Liffords Pl. SW13 147 F2
Lightcliffe Rd. N13 59 G4
Lighter Cl. SE16 133 H4
Lighterman Ms. E1 113 G6
Lightermans Rd. E14 134 A2
Lightermans Wk. SW18 148 D4
Lightfoot Rd. N8 74 E5
Lightley Cl., Wem. 87 J7
Stanley Av.
Ligonier St. E2 13 F5
Lilac Cl. E4 61 J6
Lilac Gdns. W5 125 G3
Lilac Gdns., Croy. 204 A3
Lilac Pl. SE11 34 C2
Lilac Pl. SE11 131 F4
Lilac St. W12 107 G7
Lilburne Gdns. SE9 156 B5
Lilburne Rd. SE9 156 B5
Lilburne Wk. NW10 88 C6
Lile Cres. W7 104 B5
Lilestone Est. NW8 7 E6
Lilestone St. NW8 7 G5
Lilestone St. NW8 109 H4
Lilford Rd. SE5 151 H2
Lilian Barker Cl. SE12 155 G5
Lilian Board Way, Grnf. 86 A5
Lilian Cl. N16 94 B3
Barbauld Rd.
Lilian Gdns., Wdf.Grn. 79 H1
Lilian Rd. SW16 186 C1
Lillechurch Rd., Dag. 100 B6
Lilleshall Rd., Mord. 185 G6
Lilley Cl. E1 29 J2
Lilley La. NW7 54 D5
Lillian Av. W3 126 A2
Lillian Rd. SW13 127 G6
Lillie Rd. SW6 128 B7
Lillie Yd. SW6 128 D6
Lillieshall Rd. SW4 150 B3
Lillington Gdns. Est. SW1 33 G2
Lilliput Av., Nthlt. 103 F1
Lily Cl. W14 128 B4
Lily Dr., West Dr. 120 A3
Wise La.
Lily Gdns., Wem. 105 F2
Lily Pl. EC1 19 F1
Lily Pl. EC1 111 G5
Lily Rd. E17 78 A6
Lilyville Rd. SW6 148 C1
Limbourne Av., Dag. 83 F7
Limburg Rd. SW11 149 J4
Lime Cl. E1 29 J1
Lime Cl. E1 132 D1
Lime Cl., Brom. 192 B4
Lime Cl., Buck.H. 64 A3
Lime Cl., Cars. 199 J2
Lime Cl., Har. 68 D2
Lime Cl., Rom. 83 J4
Lime Ct., Mitch. 185 G2
Lewis Rd.
Lime Cres., Sun. 178 C2
Lime Gro. E4 61 J6
Burnside Av.
Lime Gro. N20 56 C1
Lime Gro. W12 127 J2
Lime Gro., Ilf. 65 J6
Lime Gro., N.Mal. 182 D3
Lime Gro., Orp. 207 E2
Lime Gro., Ruis. 66 B7
Lime Gro., Sid. 157 J6
Lime Gro., Twick. 144 C6
Lime Rd., Rich. 145 J4
St. Mary's Gro.
Lime Row, Erith 139 F3
Northwood Pl.
Lime St. E17 77 H4
Lime St. EC3 20 D5
Lime St. EC3 112 B7
Lime St. Pas. EC3 20 D4
Lime Ter. W7 104 B7
Manor Ct. Rd.
Lime Tree Av., Esher 194 A1
Lime Tree Av., T.Ditt. 194 A1
Lime Tree Gro., Croy. 203 J3
Lime Tree Pl., Mitch. 186 B1
Lime Tree Rd., Houns. 143 H1
Lime Tree Ter. SE6 171 J1
Winterstoke Rd.
Lime Tree Wk., Bushey 52 B1
Lime Tree Wk., W.Wick. 205 F4
Lime Wk. E15 114/115 E1
Church St. N.
Limeburner La. EC4 19 G4
Limeburner La. EC4 111 H6
Limecroft Cl., Epsom 196 D7
Limedene Cl., Pnr. 66 D1
Limeharbour E14 134 B3
Limehouse Causeway E14 113 J7
Limehouse Flds. Est. E14 113 H5
Limehouse Link E14 113 H7
Limekiln Dr. SE7 135 H6
Limekiln Pl. SE19 170 C7
Limerick Cl. SW12 150 C7
Limerston St. SW10 30 D5
Limerston St. SW10 129 F6
Limes, The W2 108 D7
Linden Gdns.
Limes, The, Brom. 206 B2
Limes, The, Har. 68 C2
Limes Av. E11 79 H4
Limes Av. N12 57 F4
Limes Av. NW7 54 E6
Limes Av. NW11 72 B7
Limes Av. SE20 171 E7
Limes Av. SW13 147 F2
Limes Av., Cars. 199 J1
Limes Av., Chig. 65 G6
Limes Av., Croy. 201 G3
Limes Av., The N11 58 B5
Limes Fld. Rd. SW14 146/147 E3
White Hart La.
Limes Gdns. SW18 148 D6
Limes Gro. SE13 154 C4
Limes Pl., Croy. 188 A7
Limes Rd., Beck. 190 B2
Limes Rd., Croy. 188 A6
Limes Row, Orp. 206/207 E5
Orchard Rd.
Limes Wk. SE15 153 E4
Limes Wk. W5 125 G2
Chestnut Gro.
Limesdale Gdns., Edg. 70 C2
Limesford Rd. SE15 153 G4
Limestone Wk., Erith 138 D3
Limetree Cl. SW2 169 F1
Limetree Ter., Well. 158 A3
Hook La.
Limetree Wk. SW17 168 A5
Church La.
Limewood Cl. E17 77 J4
Limewood Cl. W13 104/105 E6
St. Stephens Rd.
Limewood Ct., Ilf. 80 C5
Limewood Rd., Erith 139 J7
Limpsfield Av. SW19 166 A2
Limpsfield Av., Th.Hth. 187 F5
Linacre Ct. W6 128 A5
Linacre Rd. NW2 89 H6
Linberry Wk. SE8 133 J4
Linchmere Rd. SE12 155 F7
Lincoln Av. N14 58 C3
Lincoln Av. SW19 166 A3
Lincoln Av., Twick. 161 J2
Lincoln Cl. SE25 188 D6
Woodside Grn.
Lincoln Cl., Grnf. 103 J1
Lincoln Cl., Har. 67 F5
Lincoln Ct. N16 76 A7
Lincoln Ct., Borwd. 38 D5
Lincoln Cres., Enf. 44 B5
Lincoln Dr., Wat. 50 C3
Lincoln Gdns., Ilf. 80 B7
Lincoln Grn. Rd., Orp. 193 J5
Lincoln Ms. NW6 108 C1
Willesden La.
Lincoln Ms. SE21 170 A1
Lincoln Rd. E7 98 A6
Lincoln Rd. E13 115 H4
Lincoln Rd. E18 79 G1
Grove Rd.
Lincoln Rd. N2 73 H3
Lincoln Rd. SE25 188 E3
Lincoln Rd., Enf. 44 D5
Lincoln Rd., Felt. 161 F3
Lincoln Rd., Har. 67 F5
Lincoln Rd., Mitch. 186 E5
Lincoln Rd., N.Mal. 182 C3
Lincoln Rd., Sid. 176 B5
Lincoln Rd., Wem. 87 G6
Lincoln Rd., Wor.Pk. 197 H1
Lincoln St. E11 96 E2
Lincoln St. SW3 31 J2
Lincoln St. SW3 129 J4
Lincoln Way, Enf. 44 E5
Lincolns, The NW7 55 F3
Lincoln's Inn WC2 18 D3
Lincoln's Inn WC2 111 G6
Lincoln's Inn Flds. WC2 18 C3
Lincoln's Inn Flds. WC2 111 F6
Lincombe Rd., Brom. 173 F3
Lind Rd., Sutt. 199 F5
Lind St. SE8 154 B2
Lindal Cres., Enf. 43 E4
Lindal Rd. SE4 153 J5
Lindales, The N17 60 C6
Brantwood Rd.
Linden Av. NW10 108 A2
Linden Av., Enf. 44 D1
Linden Av., Houns. 143 H5
Linden Av., Ruis. 84 A1
Linden Av., Th.Hth. 187 H4
Linden Av., Wem. 87 J5
Linden Cl. N14 42 C6
Linden Cl., Ruis. 84 A1
Linden Cl., Stan. 52 E5
Linden Cl., T.Ditt. 180 C7
Linden Ct. W12 127 J1
Linden Cres., Grnf. 86 C6
Linden Cres., Kings.T. 181 J2
Linden Cres., Wdf.Grn. 63 H6
Linden Gdns. W2 108 D7
Linden Gdns. W4 126 D5
Linden Gdns., Enf. 44 D1
Linden Gro. SE15 153 F3
Linden Gro. SE26 171 F6
Linden Gro., N.Mal. 182 E3
Linden Gro., Tedd. 162 C5
Waldegrave Rd.
Linden Lawns, Wem. 87 J4
Linden Lea N2 73 F5
Linden Leas, W.Wick. 204 D2
Linden Ms. N1 94 A5
Mildmay Gro. N.
Linden Ms. W2 108 D7
Linden Gdns.
Linden Pas. W4 126 D5
Linden Gdns.
Linden Pl., Mitch. 185 H4
Linden Rd. E17 77 J5
High St.
Linden Rd. N10 74 B4
Linden Rd. N11 57 J2
Linden Rd. N15 75 J4
Linden Rd., Hmptn. 161 G7
Linden Wk. N19 92 C2
Hargrave Pk.
Linden Way N14 42 C6
Lindenfield, Chis. 192 E2
Lindens, The N12 57 G5
Lindens, The W4 146 C1
Hartington Rd.
Lindens, The, Croy. 204 C6
Lindens, The, Loug. 48 C5
Lindeth Cl., Stan. 53 F6
Old Ch. La.
Lindfield Gdns. NW3 91 E5
Lindfield Rd. W5 105 F4
Lindfield Rd., Croy. 188 C6
Lindfield St. E14 114 A6
Lindhill Cl., Enf. 45 G1
Lindisfarne Rd. SW20 165 G7
Lindisfarne Rd., Dag. 100 C3
Lindisfarne Way E9 95 H4
Lindley Est. SE15 37 H7
Lindley Rd. E10 96 B2
Lindley St. E1 113 F5
Lindo St. SE15 153 F2
Selden Rd.
Lindore Rd. SW11 149 J4
Lindores Rd., Cars. 185 F7
Lindrop St. SW6 149 F2
Lindsay Cl., Chess. 195 H7
Lindsay Cl., Stai. 140 A5
Lindsay Dr., Har. 69 H6
Lindsay Rd., Hmptn. 161 H4
Lindsay Rd., Wor.Pk. 197 H2
Lindsay Sq. SW1 33 J3
Lindsay Sq. SW1 130 D5
Lindsell St. SE10 154 C1
Lindsey Cl., Brom. 192 A3
Lindsey Cl., Mitch. 187 E4
Lindsey Gdns., Felt. 141 G7
Lindsey Ms. N1 93 J7
Lindsey Rd., Dag. 100 C4
Lindsey St. EC1 19 H1
Lindsey St. EC1 111 H5
Lindum Rd., Tedd. 163 F7
Lindway SE27 169 H5
Lindwood Cl. E6 116 B5
Northumberland Rd.
Linfield Cl. NW4 71 J3
Linford Rd. E17 78 C3
Linford St. SW8 150 C1
Ling Rd. E16 115 G5
Ling Rd., Erith 139 J6
Lingards Rd. SE13 154 C4
Lingey Cl., Sid. 175 J2
Lingfield Av., Kings.T. 181 H4
Lingfield Cl., Enf. 44 B6
Lingfield Cres. SE9 157 G4
Lingfield Gdns. N9 45 E7
Lingfield Rd. SW19 166 A5
Lingfield Rd., Wor.Pk. 197 J3
Lingham St. SW9 151 E2
Lingholm Way, Barn. 40 A5
Lingmere Cl., Chig. 65 F2
Lingrove Gdns., Buck.H. 63 H2
Beech La.
Lings Coppice SE21 170 A2
Lingwell Rd. SW17 167 H3
Lingwood Gdns., Islw. 124 B7
Lingwood Rd. E5 76 D7
Linhope St. NW1 7 J5
Linhope St. NW1 109 J4
Link, The SE9 174 D3
Link, The W3 106 B6
Link, The, Enf. 45 H1
Link, The, Nthlt. 85 F5
Eastcote La.
Link, The, Pnr. 66 C7
Link, The, Wem. 87 F1
Nathans Rd.
Link La., Wall. 200 D6
Link Rd. N11 58 A4
Link Rd., Dag. 119 H2
Link Rd., Felt. 141 J7
Link Rd., Wall. 200 A1
Link St. E9 95 F6
Link Way, Brom. 192 B7
Link Way, Pnr. 66 D1
Linkfield, Brom. 191 G6
Linkfield, W.Mol. 179 G3
Linkfield Rd., Islw. 144 C2
Linklea Cl. NW9 55 E7
Links, The E17 77 H4

Links Av., Mord. 184 D4
Links Dr. N20 56 D1
Links Gdns. SW16 169 G7
Links Rd. NW2 89 F2
Links Rd. SW17 168 A6
Links Rd. W3 106 A6
Links Rd., W.Wick. 204 C1
Links Rd., Wdf.Grn. 63 G5
Links Side, Enf. 43 G3
Links Vw. N3 56 C7
Links Vw. Cl., Stan. 52 D6
Links Vw. Rd., Croy. 204 A3
Links Vw. Rd., Hmptn. 161 J5
Links Way, Beck. 190 A6
Links Yd. E1 21 H1
Linkside N12 56 C6
Linkside, Chig. 65 F5
Linkside, N.Mal. 183 E2
Linkside Cl., Enf. 43 F3
Linkside Gdns., Enf. 43 F3
Linksway NW4 72 A2
Linkway N4 75 J7
Linkway SW20 183 H3
Linkway, Dag. 100 C4
Linkway, Rich. 163 E2
Linkway, The, Barn. 40 E6
Linkwood Wk. NW1 92 D7
Maiden La.
Linley Cres., Rom. 83 H3
Linley Rd. N17 76 B2
Linnell Cl. NW11 72 E6
Linnell Dr. NW11 72 E6
Linnell Rd. N18 60 D5
Fairfield Rd.
Linnell Rd. SE5 152 B2
Linnet Cl. N9 61 G1
Linnet Cl. SE28 118 C7
Linnet Ms. SW12 150 A7
Linnet Ter., Ilf. 80 D3
Tiptree Cres.
Linnett Cl. E4 62 C4
Linom Rd. SW4 150 E4
Linscott Rd. E5 95 F4
Linsdell Rd., Bark. 117 F1
Linsey St. SE16 37 H1
Linsey St. SE16 132 D4
Linslade Cl., Houns. 142/143 E5
Frampton Rd.
Linslade Cl., Pnr. 66 B3
Linstead Ct. SE9 157 H6
Linstead St. NW6 90 D7
Linstead Way SW18 148 B7
Linster Gro., Borwd. 38 C5
Lintaine Cl. W6 128 B6
Moylan Rd.
Linthorpe Av., Wem. 87 F6
Linthorpe Rd. N16 76 B7
Linthorpe Rd., Barn. 41 H3
Linton Cl., Mitch. 185 J7
Linton Cl., Well. 158 B1
Anthony Rd.
Linton Gdns. E6 116 B6
Linton Gro. SE27 169 H5
Linton Rd., Bark. 99 F7
Linton St. N1 111 J1
Lintons, The, Bark. 99 F7
Lintott Ct., Stai. 140 A6
Linver Rd. SW6 148 D2
Linwood Cl. SE5 152 C2
Linwood Cres., Enf. 44 D1
Linwood Way SE15 37 F7
Linzee Rd. N8 74 E4
Lion Av., Twick. 162 C1
Lion Rd.
Lion Cl. SE4 154 A6
Lion Ct., Borwd. 38 C1
Lion Gate Gdns., Rich. 145 J3
Lion Pk. Av., Chess. 196 A4
Lion Rd. E6 116 C5
Lion Rd. N9 60 D2
Lion Rd., Bexh. 159 F4
Lion Rd., Croy. 187 J5
Lion Rd., Twick. 162 C1
Lion Way, Brent. 125 G7
Lion Wf. Rd., Islw. 144 E3
Lion Yd. SW4 150 D4
Tremadoc Rd.
Lionel Gdns. SE9 156 A5
Lionel Ms. W10 108 B5
Telford Rd.
Lionel Rd. SE9 156 A5
Lionel Rd., Brent. 125 J5
Lions Cl. SE9 173 J3
Liphook Cres. SE23 153 F7
Liphook Rd., Wat. 50 D4
Lippitts Hill, Loug. 47 E1
Lipton Cl. SE28 118 C7
Aisher Rd.
Lipton Rd. E1 113 G6
Bower St.
Lisbon Av., Twick. 161 J2
Lisburne Rd. NW3 91 J4
Lisford St. SE15 152 C1
Lisgar Ter. W14 128 C4
Liskeard Cl., Chis. 175 F6
Liskeard Gdns. SE3 155 G1
Lisle Cl. SW17 168 B4
Lisle St. WC2 17 J5
Lisle St. WC2 110 D7
Lismore Circ. NW5 92 A5
Lismore Cl., Islw. 144 D2
Lismore Rd. N17 76 A3
Lismore Rd., S.Croy. 202 B6
Lismore Wk. N1 93 J6
Clephane Rd.
Liss Way SE15 37 G7
Lissenden Gdns. NW5 92 A4
Lisson Grn. Est. NW8 7 G4
Lisson Grn. Est. NW8 109 H3
Lisson Gro. NW1 7 G6
Lisson Gro. NW1 109 H4
Lisson Gro. NW8 7 F4
Lisson Gro. NW8 109 G3
Lisson St. NW1 15 G1
Lisson St. NW1 109 H5
Lister Cl. W3 106 D5
Lister Cl., Mitch. 185 H1
Lister Gdns. N18 59 J5
Lister Ho. SE3 135 E6
Lister Rd. E11 97 E1
Lister St. E13 115 G3
Sewell St.
Lister Wk. SE28 118 D7
Haldane Rd.
Liston Rd. N17 76 D1
Liston Rd. SW4 150 C3
Liston Way, Wdf.Grn. 63 J7
Listowel Cl. SW9 35 F7
Listowel Rd., Dag. 101 G3
Listria Pk. N16 94 B2
Litchfield Av. E15 96 E6
Litchfield Av., Mord. 184 C7
Litchfield Gdns. NW10 89 G6
Litchfield Rd., Sutt. 199 F4
Litchfield St. WC2 17 J5
Litchfield St. WC2 110 D7
Litchfield Way NW11 73 E5
Lithos Rd. NW3 91 E6
Little Acre, Beck. 190 A3
Little Albany St. NW1 8 E5
Little Argyll St. W1 17 F4
Little Benty, West Dr. 120 A5
Little Birches, Sid. 175 H2
Little Boltons, The SW5 30 B3
Little Boltons, The SW5 129 E5
Little Boltons, The SW10 30 B3
Little Boltons, The SW10 129 E5
Little Bornes SE21 170 B4
Little Britain EC1 19 H2
Little Britain EC1 111 H5
Little Brownings SE23 170 E2
Little Bury St. N9 60 A1
Little Cedars N12 57 F4
Woodside Av.
Little Chester St. SW1 24 C5
Little Chester St. SW1 130 B3
Little College La. EC4 112 A7
Garlick Hill
Little College St. SW1 26 A5
Little Common, Stan. 52 D3
Little Ct., W.Wick. 204 E2
Little Dean's Yd. SW1 26 A5
Little Dimocks SW12 168 B2
Little Dorrit Ct. SE1 28 A3
Little Dorrit Ct. SE1 131 J2
Little Dragons, Loug. 48 A4
Little Ealing La. W5 125 F4
Little Edward St. NW1 8 E3
Little Elms, Hayes 121 G7
Little Essex St. WC2 18 E5
Little Ferry Rd., Twick. 162/163 E1
Ferry Rd.
Little Friday Rd. E4 62 E2
Little Gearies, Ilf. 80 E4
Little George St. SW1 26 A4
Little Gra., Grnf. 104 D3
Perivale La.
Little Grn., Rich. 145 G4
Little Grn. St. NW5 92 B4
College La.
Little Halliards, Walt. 178 A6
Felix Rd.
Little Heath SE7 136 B6
Little Heath, Rom. 82 B4
Little Heath Rd., Bexh. 159 F1
Little Ilford La. E12 98 C4
Little Marlborough St. W1 17 F4
Little Moss La., Pnr. 67 E2
Little New St. EC4 19 F3
Little Newport St. WC2 17 J5
Little Newport St. WC2 110 D7
Little Orchard Cl., Pnr. 66/67 E2
Barrow Pt. La.
Little Oxhey La., Wat. 50 D5
Little Pk. Dr., Felt. 160 D2
Little Pk. Gdns., Enf. 43 J3
Little Pluckets Way, Buck.H. 63 J1
Little Portland St. W1 17 F3
Little Portland St. W1 110 B6
Little Queens Rd., Tedd. 162 C6
Little Redlands, Brom. 192 B2
Little Rd., Croy. 202 B1
Lower Addiscombe Rd.
Little Rd., Hayes 121 J2
Little Russell St. WC1 18 A2
Little Russell St. WC1 110 E5
Little St. James's St. SW1 25 F2
Little St. James's St. SW1 130 C1
Little St. Leonards SW14 146 C3
Little Sanctuary SW1 25 J4
Little Smith St. SW1 25 J5
Little Somerset St. E1 21 F4
Little Strand NW9 71 F2
Little Thrift, Orp. 193 F4
Little Titchfield St. W1 17 F2
Little Trinity La. EC4 20 A5
Little Turnstile WC1 18 C2
Littlebrook Cl., Croy. 189 G6
Littlebury Rd. SW4 150 D3
Littlecombe SE7 135 H6
Littlecombe Cl. SW15 148 A6
Littlecote Cl. SW19 148 A7
Littlecote Pl., Pnr. 67 E1
Littlecroft SE9 156 D3
Littledale SE2 138 A6
Littlefield Cl. N19 92 C4
Tufnell Pk. Rd.
Littlefield Cl., Kings.T. 181 H2
Fairfield W.
Littlefield Rd., Edg. 54 C7
Littlegrove, Barn. 41 H6
Littleheath Rd., S.Croy. 202 E7
Littlejohn Rd. W7 104 C6
Littlemead, Esher 194 A4
Littlemede SE9 174 C3
Littlemoor Rd., Ilf. 99 G3
Littlemore Rd. SE2 138 A2
Littlers Cl. SW19 185 G1
Runnymede
Littlestone Cl., Beck. 172 A6
Abbey La.
Littleton Av. E4 63 F1
Littleton Cres., Har. 86 C2
Littleton Rd., Har. 86 C2
Littleton St. SW18 167 F2
Littlewood SE13 154 C5
Littlewood Cl. W13 125 E3
Littleworth Av., Esher 194 A5
Littleworth Common Rd., Esher 194 A3
Littleworth La., Esher 194 A4
Littleworth Pl., Esher 194 A4
Littleworth Rd., Esher 194 B4
Livermere Rd. E8 112 C1
Liverpool Gro. SE17 36 A4
Liverpool Gro. SE17 132 A5
Liverpool Rd. E10 78 C6
Liverpool Rd. E16 115 E5
Liverpool Rd. N1 111 G2
Liverpool Rd. N7 93 G5
Liverpool Rd. W5 125 G2
Liverpool Rd., Kings.T. 164 A7
Liverpool Rd., Th.Hth. 187 J3
Liverpool St. EC2 20 D2
Liverpool St. EC2 112 B5
Livesey Cl., Kings.T. 181 J3
Livesey Pl. SE15 37 J5
Livingston College Twrs. E10 78 C6
Essex Rd.
Livingstone Pl. E14 134 C5
Ferry St.
Livingstone Rd. E15 114 C1
Livingstone Rd. E17 78 B6
Livingstone Rd. N13 59 E6
Livingstone Rd. SW11 149 G3
Winstanley Rd.
Livingstone Rd., Houns. 143 J4
Livingstone Rd., Sthl. 102 D7
Livingstone Rd., Th.Hth. 187 J2
Livingstone Wk. SW11 149 G3
Livonia St. W1 17 G4
Lizard St. EC1 12 A4
Lizard St. EC1 111 J3
Lizban St. SE3 135 H7
Llanelly Rd. NW2 90 C2
Llanover Rd. SE18 136 D6
Llanover Rd., Wem. 87 G3
Llanthony Rd., Mord. 185 G6
Llanvanor Rd. NW2 90 C2
Llewellyn St. SE16 29 J4
Lloyd Av. SW16 187 E1
Lloyd Baker St. WC1 10 D4
Lloyd Baker St. WC1 111 F3
Lloyd Ct., Pnr. 66 D5
Lloyd Pk. Av., Croy. 202 C4
Lloyd Rd. E6 116 C1
Lloyd Rd. E17 77 G4
Lloyd Rd., Dag. 101 F6
Lloyd Rd., Wor.Pk. 197 J3
Lloyd Sq. WC1 10 E3
Lloyd Sq. WC1 111 G3
Lloyd St. WC1 10 E3
Lloyd St. WC1 111 G3
Lloyd's Av. EC3 21 E4
Lloyd's Av. EC3 112 B6
Lloyds Pl. SE3 155 E2
Lloyd's Row EC1 11 F4
Lloyds Way, Beck. 189 H5
Loampit Hill SE13 154 A2
Loampit Vale SE13 154 B3
Loanda Cl. E8 112 C1
Clarissa St.
Loats Rd. SW2 150 E6
Lobelia Cl. E6 116 B5
Sorrel Gdns.
Locarno Rd. W3 126 C1
High St.
Locarno Rd., Grnf. 103 J4
Lochaber Rd. SE13 154 E4
Lochaline St. W6 127 J6
Lochan Cl., Hayes 102 E4
Lochinvar St. SW12 150 B7
Lochmere Cl., Erith 139 H6
Lochnagar St. E14 114 C5
Lock Chase SE3 155 F3
Lock Cl., Sthl. 123 J2
Navigator Dr.
Lock Rd., Rich. 163 F4
Lockesfield Pl. E14 134 B5
Lockesley Dr., Orp. 193 J6
Lockesley Sq., Surb. 181 G6
Locket Rd., Har. 68 B3
Lockfield Av., Enf. 45 H2
Lockgate Cl. E9 95 J5
Lee Conservancy Rd.
Lockhart Cl. N7 93 F6
Lockhart Cl., Enf. 44/45 E5
Derby Rd.
Lockhart St. E3 113 J4
Lockhurst St. E5 95 G4
Lockie Pl. SE25 188 D3
Lockier Wk., Wem. 87 G3
Lockington Rd. SW8 150 B1
Lockmead Rd. N15 76 D6
Lockmead Rd. SE13 154 C3
Locks La., Mitch. 185 J1
Locksley Est. E14 113 J6
Locksley St. E14 113 J5
Locksmeade Rd., Rich. 163 F4
Lockswood Cl., Barn. 41 J4
Lockwood Cl. SE26 171 G4
Lockwood Ind. Pk. N17 76 E3
Lockwood Sq. SE16 132 E3
Lockwood Way E17 77 G2
Lockwood Way, Chess. 196 A5
Lockyer Est. SE1 28 C3
Lockyer St. SE1 28 C4
Loddiges Rd. E9 95 F7
Loder St. SE15 153 F1
Lodge Av. SW14 146 E3
Lodge Av., Croy. 201 G3
Lodge Av., Dag. 118 A1

Lodge Av., Har. 69 H4
Lodge Cl. N18 59 J5
Lodge Cl., Edg. 53 J6
Lodge Cl., Islw. 144 E1
Lodge Cl., Wall. 200 A1
Lodge Ct., Wem. 87 H5
Lodge Dr. N13 59 G4
Lodge Gdns., Beck. 189 J5
Lodge Hill SE2 138 B7
Lodge Hill, Ilf. 80 B4
Lodge Hill, Well. 138 B7
Lodge La. N12 57 F5
Lodge La., Bex. 158 D6
Lodge La., Croy. 204 A6
Lodge Pl., Sutt. 199 E5
Lodge Rd. NW4 71 J4
Lodge Rd. NW8 7 F4
Lodge Rd. NW8 109 G3
Lodge Rd., Brom. 173 H7
Lodge Rd., Croy. 187 H6
Lodge Rd., Sutt. 198/199 E5
Throwley Way
Lodge Rd., Wall. 200 B5
Lodge Vil., Wdf.Grn. 63 F7
Lodgehill Pk. Cl., Har. 85 H2
Lodore Gdns. NW9 70 E5
Lodore St. E14 114 C6
Lofthouse Pl., Chess. 195 F6
Loftie St. SE16 29 J4
Loftie St. SE16 132 D2
Lofting Rd. N1 93 F7
Loftus Rd. W12 127 H1
Logan Cl., Enf. 45 G1
Logan Cl., Houns. 143 F3
Logan Ms. W8 128 D4
Logan Pl. W8 128 D4
Logan Rd. N9 61 E2
Logan Rd., Wem. 87 H2
Loggetts, The SE21 170 B2
Logs Hill, Brom. 174 B7
Logs Hill, Chis. 174 B7
Logs Hill Cl., Chis. 192 B1
Lolesworth Cl. E1 21 G2
Lollard St. SE11 34 D1
Lollard St. SE11 131 F4
Loman St. SE1 27 H3
Loman St. SE1 131 H2
Lomas Cl., Croy. 204 C7
Lomas Ct. E8 94 C7
Lomas St. E1 21 J1
Lomas St. E1 112 D5
Lombard Av., Enf. 45 F1
Lombard Av., Ilf. 99 H1
Lombard Business Pk. SW19 185 F2
Lombard Ct. EC3 20 C5
Lombard Ct. W3 126 B1
Crown St.
Lombard La. EC4 19 F4
Lombard Rd. N11 58 B5
Lombard Rd. SW11 149 G2
Lombard Rd. SW19 185 E2
Lombard St. EC3 20 C4
Lombard St. EC3 112 A6
Lombard Wall SE7 135 H3
Lombardy Pl. W2 14 A6
Lomond Cl. N15 76 B4
Lomond Cl., Wem. 87 J7
Lomond Gdns., S.Croy. 203 H7
Lomond Gro. SE5 36 B7
Lomond Gro. SE5 132 A7
Loncroft Rd. SE5 37 E5
Loncroft Rd. SE5 132 B6
Londesborough Rd. N16 94 B4
London Br. EC4 28 C1
London Br. EC4 132 A1
London Br. SE1 28 C1
London Br. SE1 132 A1
London Br. St. SE1 28 B2
London Br. St. SE1 132 A1
London Br. Wk. SE1 28 C1
London Br. Wk. SE1 132 B1
London City Airport E16 136 C1
London Flds. E8 94 E7
London Flds. E. Side E8 94 E7
London Flds. W. Side E8 94 D7
London La. E8 95 E7
London La., Brom. 173 F7
London Ms. W2 15 F4
London Rd. E13 115 G2
London Rd. SE1 27 G5
London Rd. SE1 131 H3
London Rd. SE23 170 D1
London Rd. SW16 187 F1
London Rd. SW17 185 J2
London Rd., Bark. 98 E7
London Rd., Brent. 125 F7
London Rd., Brom. 173 F7
London Rd., Croy. 187 H7
London Rd., Enf. 44 A3
London Rd., Har. 86 B2
London Rd., Houns. 144 A3
London Rd., Islw. 144 C2
London Rd., Kings.T. 181 J2
London Rd., Mitch. 185 J2
London Rd. (Beddington Cor.), Mitch. 186 A7
London Rd., Mord. 184 D5
London Rd., Rom. 83 G6
London Rd. (Abridge), Rom. 49 J4
London Rd., Stan. 53 F5
London Rd., Sutt. 198 A3
London Rd., Th.Hth. 187 G5
London Rd., Twick. 144 D5
London Rd., Wall. 200 B4
London Rd., Wem. 87 H6
London Stile W4 126 A5
Wellesley Rd.
London St. EC3 20 E5
London St. W2 15 F4
London St. W2 109 G6
London Wall EC2 20 A2
London Wall EC2 111 J5
London Wall Bldgs. EC2 20 C2
Lonesome Way SW16 186 B1
Long Acre WC2 18 A5
Long Acre WC2 110 E7
Long Deacon Rd. E4 62 E1
Long Dr. W3 106 E6
Long Dr., Grnf. 103 H1
Long Dr., Ruis. 84 D4
Long Elmes, Har. 67 H1
Long Fld. NW9 55 E7
Long Grn., Chig. 65 H4
Long Hedges, Houns. 143 G1
Long La. EC1 19 H1
Long La. EC1 111 H5
Long La. N2 73 F2
Long La. N3 73 F2
Long La. SE1 28 B4
Long La. SE1 132 A2
Long La., Bexh. 138 D7
Long La., Croy. 189 F5
Long Leys E4 62 B6
Long Mark Rd. E16 116 A5
Fulmer Rd.
Long Mead NW9 71 F1
Long Meadow NW5 92 D5
Torriano Av.
Long Meadow Cl., W.Wick. 190 C7
Long Pond Rd. SE3 154 E1
Long Reach Ct., Bark. 117 G2
Long Rd. SW4 150 C4
Long St. E2 13 F3
Long St. E2 112 C3
Long Wk. SE1 29 E5
Long Wk. SE18 136 E6
Long Wk. SW13 147 E2
Long Wk., N.Mal. 182 C3
Long Yd. WC1 10 C6
Long Yd. WC1 111 F4
Longacre Pl., Cars. 200 A6
Beddington Gdns.
Longacre Rd. E17 78 D1
Longbeach Rd. SW11 149 J3
Longberrys NW2 90 C3
Longboat Row, Sthl. 103 F6
Longbridge Rd., Bark. 99 F7
Longbridge Rd., Dag. 100 A4
Longbridge Way SE13 154 C5
Longcliffe Path, Wat. 50 A3
Gosforth La.
Longcroft SE9 174 C3
Longcroft Ri., Loug. 48 D5
Longcrofte Rd., Edg. 53 G7
Longdon Wd., Kes. 206 B4
Longdown Rd. SE6 172 A4
Longfellow Rd. E17 77 J6
Longfellow Rd., Wor.Pk. 197 G2
Longfellow Way SE1 37 G2
Longfield, Brom. 191 F1
Longfield, Loug. 47 J5
Longfield Av. E17 77 H4
Longfield Av. NW7 55 G7
Longfield Av. W5 105 F7
Longfield Av., Wall. 200 A1
Longfield Av., Wem. 87 H1
Longfield Cres. SE26 171 F3
Longfield Dr. SW14 146 B5
Longfield Dr., Mitch. 167 H7
Longfield Est. SE1 37 G2
Longfield Est. SE1 132 C4
Longfield Rd. W5 105 F7
Longfield St. SW18 148 D7
Longfield Wk. W5 105 F6
Longford Av., Felt. 141 H6
Longford Av., Sthl. 103 G7
Longford Cl., Hmptn. 161 G4
Longford Cl., Hayes 102 D7
Longford Gdns.
Longford Ct. E5 95 G4
Pedro St.
Longford Ct. NW4 72 A4
Longford Ct., Epsom 196 C4
Longford Gdns., Hayes 102 D7
Longford Gdns., Sutt. 199 F3
Longford Rd., Twick. 161 G1
Longford St. NW1 8 E5
Longford St. NW1 110 B4
Longford Wk. SW2 151 G7
Longhayes Av., Rom. 82 D4
Longhayes Ct., Rom. 82 D4
Longhayes Av.
Longheath Gdns., Croy. 189 F5
Longhedge Ho. SE26 170 C4
Longhedge St. SW11 150 A2
Longhill Rd. SE6 172 D2
Longhook Gdns., Nthlt. 102 A2
Longhope Cl. SE15 37 E6
Longhope Cl. SE15 132 B6
Longhurst Rd. SE13 154 D5
Longhurst Rd., Croy. 189 E6
Longland Ct. SE1 37 H3
Longland Dr. N20 56 E3
Longlands Ct. W11 108 C7
Portobello Rd.
Longlands Ct., Mitch. 186 A1
Summerhill Way
Longlands Pk. Cres., Sid. 175 H3
Longlands Rd., Sid. 175 H3
Longleat Rd., Enf. 44 B5
Longleat Way, Felt. 141 G7
Longleigh La. SE2 138 C6
Longleigh La., Bexh. 138 C6
Longlents Ho. NW10 106 D1
Longley Av., Wem. 105 J1
Longley Rd. SW17 167 H6
Longley Rd., Croy. 187 H7
Longley Rd., Har. 67 J5
Longley St. SE1 37 H2
Longley St. SE1 132 D4
Longley Way NW2 89 J3
Longmead, Chis. 192 D2
Longmead Dr., Sid. 176 D2
Longmead Rd. SW17 167 J5
Longmead Rd., T.Ditt. 180 B7
Longmeadow Rd., Sid. 175 H1
Longmoor Pt. SW15 165 H1
Norley Vale
Longmoore St. SW1 33 F2
Longmoore St. SW1 130 C4
Longmore Av., Barn. 41 F6
Longnor Rd. E1 113 G3
Longreach Rd., Bark. 117 J4
Longridge La., Sthl. 103 H7
Longridge Rd. SW5 128 D4
Long's Ct. WC2 17 H5
Long's Ct. WC2 110 D7
Longs Ct., Rich. 145 J4
Crown Ter.
Longshaw Rd. E4 62 D3
Longshore SE8 133 J4
Longstaff Cres. SW18 148 D6
Longstaff Rd. SW18 148 D6
Longstone Av. NW10 89 F7
Longstone Rd. SW17 168 B5
Longthornton Rd. SW16 186 C2
Longton Av. SE26 170 D4
Longton Gro. SE26 170 E4
Longville Rd. SE11 35 G1
Longwalk Rd., Uxb. 121 E1
Longwood Dr. SW15 147 G6
Longwood Gdns., Ilf. 80 C4
Longworth Cl. SE28 118 D6
Loning, The NW9 71 E4
Lonsdale Av. E6 116 A4
Lonsdale Av., Rom. 83 J6
Lonsdale Av., Wem. 87 H5
Lonsdale Cl. E6 116 B4
Lonsdale Av.
Lonsdale Cl. SE9 174 A3
Lonsdale Cl., Edg. 53 J5
Orchard Dr.
Lonsdale Cl., Pnr. 51 E7
Lonsdale Cres., Ilf. 80 E6
Lonsdale Dr., Enf. 43 E5
Lonsdale Gdns., Th.Hth. 187 F4
Lonsdale Ms., Rich. 146 A1
Elizabeth Cotts.
Lonsdale Pl. N1 93 G7
Barnsbury St.
Lonsdale Rd. E11 79 F7
Lonsdale Rd. NW6 108 C2
Lonsdale Rd. SE25 188 E4
Lonsdale Rd. SW13 127 G6
Lonsdale Rd. W4 127 F4
Lonsdale Rd. W11 108 C6
Lonsdale Rd., Bexh. 159 F2
Lonsdale Rd., Sthl. 122 D3
Lonsdale Sq. N1 93 G7
Loobert Rd. N15 76 B3
Looe Gdns., Ilf. 81 E3
Loom Ct. E1 13 E6
Loop Rd., Chis. 175 F6
Lopen Rd. N18 60 B4
Loraine Cl., Enf. 45 F5
Loraine Rd. N7 93 F4
Loraine Rd. W4 126 B6
Lord Amory Way E14 134 C2
Lord Av., Ilf. 80 C4
Lord Chancellor Wk., Kings.T. 182 C1
Lord Gdns., Ilf. 80 B4
Lord Hills Br. W2 14 B2
Lord Hills Rd. W2 14 B1
Lord Hills Rd. W2 109 E5
Lord Holland La. SW9 151 G1
Myatt's Flds. S.
Lord Knyvett Cl., Stai. 140 A6
Lord Napier Pl. W6 127 G5
Upper Mall
Lord N. St. SW1 26 A6
Lord N. St. SW1 130 E3
Lord Roberts Ms. SW6 128/129 E7
Moore Pk. Rd.
Lord Roberts Ter. SE18 136 D5
Lord St. E16 136 B1
Lord Warwick St. SE18 136 C3
Lordell Pl. SW19 165 J6
Lorden Wk. E2 13 H4
Lorden Wk. E2 112 D3
Lord's Cl. SE21 169 J2
Lords Cl., Felt. 161 E2
Lord's Vw. NW8 7 F4
Lordship Gro. N16 94 A2
Lordship La. N17 75 J1
Lordship La. N22 75 G2
Lordship La. SE22 152 C6
Lordship La. Est. SE22 170 D1
Lordship Pk. N16 93 J2
Lordship Pk. Ms. N16 93 J2
Allerton Rd.
Lordship Pl. SW3 31 G6
Lordship Rd. N16 94 A2
Lordship Rd., Nthlt. 84 E7
Lordship Ter. N16 94 A2
Lordsmead Rd. N17 76 B1
Lorenzo St. WC1 10 C3
Lorenzo St. WC1 111 F3
Loretto Gdns., Har. 69 H4
Lorian Cl. N12 56 E4
Loring Rd. N20 57 H2
Loring Rd., Islw. 144 C2
Loris Rd. W6 127 J3
Lorn Ct. SW9 151 G2
Lorn Rd. SW9 151 F2
Lorne Av., Croy. 189 G7
Lorne Cl. NW8 7 H4
Lorne Gdns. E11 79 J4
Lorne Gdns. W11 128 A2
Lorne Gdns., Croy. 189 H7
Lorne Rd. E7 97 H4
Lorne Rd. E17 78 A5
Lorne Rd. N4 93 F1
Lorne Rd., Har. 68 C2
Lorne Rd., Rich. 145 J5
Albert Rd.
Lorraine Pk., Har. 52 B7
Lorrimore Rd. SE17 35 H5
Lorrimore Rd. SE17 131 H6
Lorrimore Sq. SE17 35 H5
Lorrimore Sq. SE17 131 H6
Loseberry Rd., Esher 194 A5
Lothair Rd. W5 125 G2
Lothair Rd. N. N4 75 H6
Lothair Rd. S. N4 75 G7
Lothbury EC2 20 B3
Lothbury EC2 112 A6
Lothian Av., Hayes 102 B5
Lothian Cl., Wem. 86 D4
Lothian Rd. SW9 151 H1
Lothrop St. W10 108 B3
Lots Rd. SW10 129 F7
Lotus Cl. SE21 169 J3
Loubet St. SW17 167 J6
Loudoun Av., Ilf. 81 E5

Name	Page	Grid
Loudoun Rd. NW8	6	D1
Loudoun Rd. NW8	91	F7
Loudoun Rd. Ms. NW8	109	F1
Loudoun Rd.		
Loudwater Cl., Sun.	178	A4
Loudwater Rd., Sun.	178	A4
Lough Rd. N7	93	F6
Loughborough Est. SW9	151	H2
Loughborough Rd.		
Loughborough Pk. SW9	151	H4
Loughborough Rd. SW9	151	G2
Loughborough St. SE11	**34**	**D3**
Loughborough St. SE11	131	F5
Loughton Way, Buck.H.	64	A1
Louis Ms. N10	74	B1
Louisa Gdns. E1	113	G4
Louisa St.		
Louisa Ho. SW15	147	E4
Louisa St. E1	113	G4
Louise Aumonier Wk. N19	74/75	E7
Hillrise Rd.		
Louise Bennett Cl. SE24	151	H4
Shakespeare Rd.		
Louise Rd. E15	97	E6
Louisville Rd. SW17	168	A3
Louvaine Rd. SW11	149	G4
Lovage App. E6	116	B5
Lovat Cl. EC3	**20**	**D6**
Lovat Wk., Houns.	122/123	E7
Cranford La.		
Lovatt Cl., Edg.	54	B6
Lovatt Dr., Ruis.	66	A5
Love La. EC2	**20**	**A3**
Love La. EC2	111	J6
Love La. N17	60	C7
Love La. SE18	136	E4
Love La. SE25	189	E3
Love La., Bex.	159	F6
Love La., Mitch.	185	H3
Love La., Mord.	184	D7
Love La., Pnr.	66	E3
Love La., Surb.	195	G2
Love La., Sutt.	198	B5
Love La., Wdf.Grn.	64	C6
Love Wk. SE5	152	A2
Loveday Rd. W13	125	E1
Lovegrove St. SE1	**37**	**J4**
Lovegrove St. SE1	132	D5
Lovegrove Wk. E14	134	C1
Lovekyn Cl., Kings.T.	181	J2
Queen Elizabeth Rd.		
Lovel Av., Well.	158	A2
Lovelace Av., Brom.	192	D6
Lovelace Gdns., Bark.	100	A4
Lovelace Gdns., Surb.	181	G7
Lovelace Grn. SE9	156	C3
Lovelace Rd. SE21	169	J2
Lovelace Rd., Barn.	41	H7
Lovelace Rd., Surb.	181	F7
Lovelinch Cl. SE15	133	F6
Lovell Ho. E8	112	D1
Lovell Pl. SE16	133	H3
Ropemaker Rd.		
Lovell Rd., Rich.	163	F3
Lovell Rd., Sthl.	103	H6
Loveridge Ms. NW6	90	C6
Loveridge Rd.		
Loveridge Rd. NW6	90	C6
Lovers Wk. N3	56	D7
Lovers Wk. NW7	56	C6
Lovers Wk. SE10	134	E6
Lover's Wk. W1	**24**	**B1**
Lover's Wk. W1	130	A1
Lovett Dr., Cars.	185	F7
Lovett Way NW10	88	C5
Lovett's Pl. SW18	148/149	E4
Old York Rd.		
Lovibonds Av., Orp.	207	E3
Low Cross Wd. La. SE21	170	C3
Low Hall Cl. E4	46	A7
Low Hall La. E17	77	H6
Lowbrook Rd., Ilf.	99	E5
Lowden Rd. N9	61	E1
Lowden Rd. SE24	151	H4
Lowden Rd., Sthl.	102	E7
Lowe Av. E16	115	G5
Lowell St. E14	113	H6
Lower Aberdeen Wf. E14	133	J1
Lower Addiscombe Rd., Croy.	202	B1
Lower Addison Gdns. W14	128	B2
Lower Alderton Hall La., Loug.	48	D5
Lower Belgrave St. SW1	**24**	**D6**
Lower Belgrave St. SW1	130	B3
Lower Boston Rd. W7	124	B1
Lower Broad St., Dag.	119	G1
Lower Camden, Chis.	174	C7
Lower Ch. St., Croy.	201	H2
Waddon New Rd.		
Lower Clapton Rd. E5	95	E5
Lower Clarendon Wk. W11	108	B6
Lancaster Rd.		
Lower Common S. SW15	147	H3
Lower Coombe St., Croy.	201	J4
Lower Downs Rd. SW20	184	A1
Lower Drayton Pl., Croy.	201	H2
Drayton Rd.		
Lower George St., Rich.	145	G5
George St.		
Lower Gravel Rd., Brom.	206	B1
Lower Grn. W., Mitch.	185	H3
Lower Grosvenor Pl. SW1	**24**	**D5**
Lower Grosvenor Pl. SW1	130	B3
Lower Gro. Rd., Rich.	145	J6
Lower Hall La. E4	61	H5
Lower Ham Rd., Kings.T.	163	G6
Lower Hampton Rd. Sun.	178	C3
Lower James St. W1	**17**	**G5**
Lower John St. W1	**17**	**G5**
Lower Kenwood Av., Enf.	42	D5
Lower Lea Crossing E14	114	E7
Lower Lea Crossing E16	114	E7
Lower Maidstone Rd. N11	58	C6
Telford Rd.		
Lower Mall W6	127	H5
Lower Mardyke Av., Rain.	119	J2
Lower Marsh SE1	**26**	**E4**
Lower Marsh SE1	131	G2
Lower Marsh La., Kings.T.	181	J4
Lower Merton Ri. NW3	91	H7
Lower Morden La., Mord.	183	J6
Lower Mortlake Rd., Rich.	145	H4
Lower Pk. Rd. N11	58	C5
Lower Pk. Rd., Belv.	139	G3
Lower Pk. Rd., Loug.	48	A5
Lower Queens Rd., Buck.H.	64	A2
Lower Richmond Rd. SW14	146	B3
Lower Richmond Rd. SW15	147	J3
Lower Richmond Rd., Rich.	146	A3
Lower Rd. SE8	133	F3
Lower Rd. SE16	133	F3
Lower Rd., Belv.	139	H3
Lower Rd., Har.	86	A1
Lower Rd., Loug.	48	D2
Lower Rd., Sutt.	199	F4
Lower Robert St. WC2	110/111	E7
John Adam St.		
Lower Sand Hills, T.Ditt.	181	G7
Lower Sloane St. SW1	**32**	**B2**
Lower Sloane St. SW1	130	A4
Lower Sq., Islw.	144	E3
Lower Strand NW9	71	F2
Lower Sunbury Rd. Hmptn.	179	F2
Lower Sydenham Ind. Est. SE26	171	J5
Lower Tail, Wat.	51	E3
Lower Talbot Wk. W11	108	B6
Lancaster Rd.		
Lower Teddington Rd., Kings.T.	181	G1
Lower Ter. NW3	91	F3
Lower Thames St. EC3	**20**	**C6**
Lower Thames St. EC3	112	A7
Lower Wd. Rd., Esher	194	D6
Lowestoft Cl. E5	95	F2
Theydon Rd.		
Lowestoft Ms. E16	136/137	E2
Barge Ho. Rd.		
Loweswater Cl., Wem.	87	G2
Lowfield Rd. NW6	90	D7
Lowfield Rd. W3	106	C6
Lowick Rd., Har.	68	B4
Lowlands Dr., Stai.	140	A5
Lowlands Gdns., Rom.	83	H6
Lowlands Rd., Har.	68	B7
Lowlands Rd., Pnr.	66	C7
Lowman Rd. N7	93	F4
Lowndes Cl. SW1	**24**	**C6**
Lowndes Cl. SW1	130	A3
Lowndes Ct. W1	**17**	**F4**
Lowndes Pl. SW1	**24**	**B6**
Lowndes Pl. SW1	130	A3
Lowndes Sq. SW1	**24**	**A4**
Lowndes Sq. SW1	129	J2
Lowndes St. SW1	**24**	**A5**
Lowndes St. SW1	130	A3
Lowood Ct. SE19	170	C5
Lowood St. E1	112/113	E7
Dellow St.		
Lowry Cres., Mitch.	185	H2
Lowry Rd., Dag.	100	B4
Lowshoe La., Rom.	83	H1
Lowth Rd. SE5	151	J2
Lowther Dr., Enf.	42	E4
Lowther Gdns. SW7	**23**	**F4**
Lowther Gdns. SW7	129	G2
Lowther Hill SE23	153	H7
Lowther Rd. E17	77	H2
Lowther Rd. N7	93	G5
Mackenzie Rd.		
Lowther Rd. SW13	147	F1
Lowther Rd., Kings.T.	181	J1
Lowther Rd., Stan.	69	J3
Loxford Av. E6	116	A2
Loxford La., Ilf.	99	F5
Loxford Rd., Bark.	99	E6
Loxford Ter., Bark.	99	F6
Fanshawe Av.		
Loxham Rd. E4	62	A7
Loxham St. WC1	**10**	**B4**
Loxley Cl. SE26	171	G5
Loxley Rd. SW18	167	G1
Loxley Rd., Hmptn.	161	F4
Loxton Rd. SE23	171	G1
Loxwood Rd. N17	76	B3
Lubbock Rd., Chis.	174	C7
Lubbock St. SE14	133	F7
Lucan Pl. SW3	**31**	**G2**
Lucan Pl. SW3	129	H4
Lucan Rd., Barn.	40	B3
Lucas Av. E13	115	H1
Lucas Av., Har.	85	G2
Lucas Cl. NW10	89	G7
Pound La.		
Lucas Ct., Har.	85	G1
Lucas Gdns. N2	73	F2
Lucas Rd. SE20	171	F6
Lucas Sq. NW11	72	D6
Hampstead Way		
Lucas St. SE8	154	A1
Lucerne Cl. N13	58	E4
Lucerne Ct., Erith	138/139	E3
Middle Way		
Lucerne Gro. E17	78	D4
Lucerne Ms. W8	128	D1
Kensington Mall		
Lucerne Rd. N5	93	H4
Lucerne Rd., Orp.	207	J1
Lucerne Rd., Th.Hth.	187	H5
Lucey Rd. SE16	**29**	**H6**
Lucey Rd. SE16	132	D3
Lucey Way SE16	**29**	**J6**
Lucien Rd. SW17	168	A4
Lucien Rd. SW19	166	E2
Lucknow St. SE18	137	H7
Lucorn Cl. SE12	155	F6
Lucton Ms., Loug.	48	E4
Luctons Av., Buck.H.	63	J1
Lucy Cres. W3	106	C5
Lucy Gdns., Dag.	100/101	E3
Grafton Rd.		
Luddesdon Rd., Erith	139	G7
Ludford Cl. NW9	70	E2
Ludford Cl., Croy.	201	H4
Warrington Rd.		
Ludgate Bdy. EC4	**19**	**G4**
Ludgate Circ. EC4	**19**	**G4**
Ludgate Hill EC4	**19**	**G4**
Ludgate Hill EC4	111	H6
Ludgate Sq. EC4	**19**	**H4**
Ludham Cl. SE28	118	C6
Rollesby Way		
Ludlow Cl., Brom.	191	G3
Aylesbury Rd.		
Ludlow Cl., Har.	85	F4
Ludlow Mead, Wat.	50	B3
Ludlow Rd. W5	105	F4
Ludlow Rd., Felt.	160	A4
Ludlow St. EC1	**11**	**J5**
Ludlow Way N2	73	F4
Ludovick Wk. SW15	147	E4
Ludwick Ms. SE14	133	H7
Luffield Rd. SE2	138	B3
Luffman Rd. SE12	173	H3
Lugard Rd. SE15	153	E2
Lugg App. E12	98	D3
Luke Ho. E1	113	E6
Luke St. EC2	**12**	**D5**
Luke St. EC2	112	B4
Lukin Cres. E4	62	D3
Lukin St. E1	113	F6
Lukintone Cl., Loug.	48	B6
Lullingstone Cl., Orp.	176	B7
Lullingstone Cres.		
Lullingstone Cres., Orp.	176	A7
Lullingstone La. SE13	154	D7
Lullingstone Rd., Belv.	139	F6
Lullington Garth N12	56	C5
Lullington Garth, Borwd.	38	B5
Lullington Garth, Brom.	173	E7
Lullington Rd. SE20	170	D7
Lullington Rd., Dag.	100	E7
Lulot Gdns. N19	92	B2
Lulworth SE17	**36**	**B3**
Lulworth Av., Houns.	123	H7
Lulworth Av., Wem.	69	F7
Lulworth Cl., Har.	85	F3
Lulworth Cres., Mitch.	185	H2
Lulworth Dr., Pnr.	66	D6
Lulworth Gdns., Har.	85	E2
Lulworth Rd. SE9	174	B2
Lulworth Rd. SE15	153	E2
Lulworth Rd., Well.	157	J2
Lulworth Waye, Hayes	102	C6
Lumen Rd., Wem.	87	G2
Lumley Cl., Belv.	139	G6
Lumley Ct. WC2	**18**	**B6**
Lumley Gdns., Sutt.	198	B5
Lumley Rd., Sutt.	198	B6
Lumley St. W1	**16**	**C4**
Luna Rd., Th.Hth.	187	J3
Lunar Ho., Croy.	201	J1
Woodhall La.		
Lundy Dr., Hayes	121	H4
Lundy Wk. N1	93	J6
Clephane Rd.		
Lunham Rd. SE19	170	B6
Lupin Cl. SW2	169	H2
Palace Rd.		
Lupin Cl., Croy.	203	G1
Primrose La.		
Lupin Cl., West Dr.	120	A5
Magnolia St.		
Lupin Cres., Ilf.	98/99	E5
Bluebell Way		
Lupton Cl. SE12	173	H3
Lupton St. NW5	92	C4
Lupus St. SW1	**33**	**G3**
Lupus St. SW1	130	B6
Luralda Gdns. E14	134	C5
Saunders Ness Rd.		
Lurgan Av. W6	128	A6
Lurline Gdns. SW11	150	A1
Luscombe Ct., Brom.	190	E2
Luscombe Way SW8	**34**	**A7**
Luscombe Way SW8	130	J7
Lushes Ct., Loug.	48/49	E5
Lushes Rd.		
Lushes Rd., Loug.	49	E5
Lushington Rd. NW10	107	H2
Lushington Rd. SE6	172	B5
Lushington Ter. E8	94	D5
Wayland Av.		
Luther Cl., Edg.	54	C2
Luther King Cl. E17	77	H6
Luther Rd., Tedd.	162	C5
Luton Pl. SE10	134	C7
Luton Rd. E17	77	J3
Luton Rd., Sid.	176	C3
Luton St. NW8	**7**	**F6**

Luton St. NW8 109 G4
Lutton Ter. NW3 91 G4
  Flask Wk.
Luttrell Av. SW15 147 H5
Lutwyche Rd. SE6 171 J2
Luxborough La., 64 B3
  Chig.
Luxborough St. W1 16 B1
Luxborough St. W1 110 A4
Luxemburg Gdns. 128 A4
  W6
Luxfield Rd. SE9 174 B1
Luxford St. SE16 133 G4
Luxmore St. SE4 153 J1
Luxor St. SE5 151 J3
Lyal Rd. E3 113 H2
Lyall Av. SE21 170 B3
Lyall Ms. SW1 24 B6
Lyall Ms. SW1 130 A3
Lyall Ms. W. SW1 24 B6
Lyall St. SW1 24 B6
Lyall St. SW1 130 A3
Lycett Pl. W12 127 G2
  Becklow Rd.
Lyconby Gdns., Croy. 189 H7
Lydd Cl., Sid. 175 H3
Lydd Rd., Bexh. 139 F7
Lydden Ct. SE9 157 H6
Lydden Gro. SW18 148 E7
Lydden Rd. SW18 148 E7
Lydeard Rd. E6 98 C7
Lydford Cl. N16 94 B5
  Pellerin Rd.
Lydford Rd. N15 76 A5
Lydford Rd. NW2 90 A6
Lydford Rd. W9 108 C4
Lydhurst Av. SW2 169 F2
Lydney Cl. SE15 36 E7
Lydney Cl. SE15 132 B7
Lydney Cl. SW19 166 B2
  Princes Way
Lydon Rd. SW4 150 C3
Lydstep Rd., Chis. 174 D4
Lyford Rd. SW18 149 G7
Lygon Pl. SW1 24 D6
Lyham Cl. SW2 151 E6
Lyham Rd. SW2 150 E5
Lyle Cl., Mitch. 186 A7
Lyme Fm. Rd. SE12 155 G4
Lyme Gro. E9 95 F7
  St. Thomas's Sq.
Lyme Rd., Well. 158 B1
Lyme St. NW1 92 C7
Lyme Ter. NW1 92 C7
  Royal College St.
Lymer Av. SE19 170 C5
Lymescote Gdns., 198 D2
  Sutt.
Lyminge Cl., Sid. 175 J4
Lyminge Gdns. 167 H1
  SW18
Lymington Av. N22 75 G2
Lymington Cl. E6 116 C5
  Valiant Way
Lymington Cl. SW16 186 D2
Lymington Gdns., 197 F5
  Epsom
Lymington Rd. NW6 90 E6
Lymington Rd., Dag. 100 D1
Lympstone Gdns. 37 J7
  SE15
Lympstone Gdns. 132 D7
  SE15
Lyn Ms. E3 113 J3
  Tredegar Sq.
Lynbridge Gdns. N13 59 H4
Lynbrook Cl. SE15 36 E7
Lynch Wk. SE8 133 J6
  Prince St.
Lynchen Cl., Houns. 142 A1
  The Av.
Lyncott Cres. SW4 150 B4
Lyncroft Gdns., Pnr. 66 E5
Lyncroft Gdns. NW6 90 D5
Lyncroft Gdns. W13 125 F2
Lyncroft Gdns., 143 J4
  Houns.
Lyndale NW2 90 C4
Lyndale Av. NW2 90 C3
Lyndale Cl. SE3 135 F6
Lyndhurst Av. N12 57 J6
Lyndhurst Av. NW7 54 E6
Lyndhurst Av. SW16 186 D2
Lyndhurst Av., Pnr. 66 B1
Lyndhurst Av., Sthl. 123 H1
Lyndhurst Av., Sun. 178 A3
Lyndhurst Av., Surb. 196 B1
Lyndhurst Av., 161 F1
  Twick.
Lyndhurst Cl. NW10 88 D3
Lyndhurst Cl., Bexh. 159 H3
Lyndhurst Cl., Croy. 202 C3
Lyndhurst Cl., Orp. 207 E4
Lyndhurst Dr. E10 78 C7

Lyndhurst Dr., N.Mal. 183 E6
Lyndhurst Gdns. N3 72 B1
Lyndhurst Gdns. 91 G5
  NW3
Lyndhurst Gdns., 99 H6
  Bark.
Lyndhurst Gdns., Enf. 44 A4
Lyndhurst Gdns., Ilf. 81 G6
Lyndhurst Gdns., 66 B1
  Pnr.
Lyndhurst Gro. SE15 152 B2
Lyndhurst Ri., Chig. 64 D4
Lyndhurst Rd. E4 62 C7
Lyndhurst Rd. N18 60 D4
Lyndhurst Rd. N22 59 F6
Lyndhurst Rd. NW3 91 G5
Lyndhurst Rd., Bexh. 159 H3
Lyndhurst Rd., Grnf. 103 H4
Lyndhurst Rd., 187 G4
  Th.Hth.
Lyndhurst Sq. SE15 152 C1
Lyndhurst Ter. NW3 91 G5
Lyndhurst Way SE15 152 C1
Lyndhurst Way, Sutt. 198 D7
Lyndon Av., Pnr. 51 E6
Lyndon Av., Sid. 157 J5
Lyndon Av., Wall. 200 A3
Lyndon Rd., Belv. 139 G4
Lyne Cres. E17 77 J1
Lyneham Wk. E5 95 H5
Lynett Rd., Dag. 100 D2
Lynette Av. SW4 150 B6
Lynford Cl., Barn. 39 F5
  Rowley La.
Lynford Cl., Edg. 54 C7
Lynford Gdns., Edg. 54 B3
Lynford Gdns., Ilf. 99 J2
Lynmere Rd., Well. 158 B2
Lynmouth Av., Enf. 44 C6
Lynmouth Av., Mord. 184 A7
Lynmouth Dr., Ruis. 84 B2
Lynmouth Gdns., 105 E1
  Grnf.
Lynmouth Gdns., 142 D1
  Houns.
Lynmouth Rd. E17 77 H6
Lynmouth Rd. N2 73 J3
Lynmouth Rd. N16 94 C1
Lynmouth Rd., Grnf. 105 E1
Lynn Cl., Har. 68 A2
Lynn Ms. E11 96/97 E2
  Lynn Rd.
Lynn Rd. E11 96 E2
Lynn Rd. SW12 150 B7
Lynn Rd., Ilf. 81 G7
Lynn St., Enf. 44 A1
Lynne Cl., Orp. 207 J6
Lynne Way NW10 88 E6
Lynne Way, Nthlt. 102 D2
Lynsted Cl., Bexh. 159 H5
Lynsted Cl., Brom. 191 J2
Lynsted Ct., Beck. 189 H2
  Churchfields Rd.
Lynsted Gdns. SE9 156 A3
Lynton Av. N12 57 G4
Lynton Av. NW9 71 F4
Lynton Av. W13 104 D6
Lynton Cl. NW10 88 E5
Lynton Cl., Chess. 195 H4
Lynton Cl., Islw. 144 C4
Lynton Cres., Ilf. 80 E6
Lynton Est. SE1 37 H2
Lynton Gdns. N11 58 D6
Lynton Gdns., Enf. 44 B7
Lynton Mead N20 56 D3
Lynton Rd. E4 62 B5
Lynton Rd. N8 74 D5
Lynton Rd. NW6 108 C1
Lynton Rd. SE1 37 G2
Lynton Rd. SE1 132 C4
Lynton Rd. W3 106 A7
Lynton Rd., Croy. 187 G6
Lynton Rd., Har. 85 E2
Lynton Rd., N.Mal. 182 D5
Lynton Rd. W3 106 C6
  Lynton Rd.
Lynwood Cl. E18 79 J1
Lynwood Cl., Har. 85 E3
Lynwood Dr., Wor.Pk. 197 G2
Lynwood Gdns., 201 F4
  Croy.
Lynwood Gdns., Sthl. 103 F6
Lynwood Gro. N21 59 G1
Lynwood Gro., Orp. 193 H7
Lynwood Rd. SW17 167 J3
Lynwood Rd. W5 105 H4
Lynwood Rd., T.Ditt. 194 C2
Lyon Business Pk., 117 H2
  Bark.
Lyon Meade, Stan. 69 F1
Lyon Pk. Av., Wem. 87 H6
Lyon Rd. SW19 185 F1
Lyon Rd., Har. 68 C6

Lyon St. N1 93 F7
  Caledonian Rd.
Lyon Way, Grnf. 104 B1
Lyons Pl. NW8 7 E5
Lyons Pl. NW8 109 G4
Lyons Wk. W14 128 B4
Lyonsdown Av., 41 F6
  Barn.
Lyonsdown Rd., 41 F6
  Barn.
Lyoth Rd., Orp. 207 F2
Lyric Dr., Grnf. 103 H4
Lyric Rd. SW13 147 F1
Lysander Gdns., 181 J6
  Surb.
  Ewell Rd.
Lysander Gro. N19 92 D1
Lysander Rd., Croy. 201 F6
Lysander Way, Orp. 207 F3
Lysia St. SW6 128 A7
Lysias Rd. SW12 150 B6
Lysons Wk. SW15 147 G5
  Swinburne Rd.
Lytchet Rd., Brom. 173 H7
Lytchet Way, Enf. 45 F1
Lytchgate Cl., S.Croy. 202 B7
Lytcott Dr., W.Mol. 179 F3
  Freeman Dr.
Lytcott Gro. SE22 152 C5
Lyte St. E2 113 F2
  Bishops Way
Lytham Av., Wat. 50 D5
Lytham Gro. W5 105 H3
Lytham St. SE17 36 B4
Lytham St. SE17 132 A5
Lytton Cl. NW3 91 H7
Lytton Cl., Nthlt. 85 F7
Lytton Gdns., Wall. 200 D4
Lytton Gro. SW15 148 A5
Lytton Rd. E11 78 E7
Lytton Rd., Barn. 41 F4
Lytton Rd., Pnr. 50 E7
Lytton Strachey Path 118 B7
  SE28
  Titmuss Av.
Lyveden Rd. SE3 135 H7
Lyveden Rd. SW17 167 H6

M

Maberley Cres. SE19 170 D7
Maberley Rd. SE19 188 C1
Maberley Rd., Beck. 189 G3
Mabledon Pl. WC1 9 J4
Mabledon Pl. WC1 110 D3
Mablethorpe Rd. 128 B7
  SW6
Mabley St. E9 95 H6
Macaret Cl. N20 41 E7
MacArthur Cl. E7 97 G6
MacArthur Ter. SE7 136 B6
Macaulay Av., Esher 194 C2
Macaulay Ct. SW4 150 B3
Macaulay Rd. E6 116 A2
Macaulay Rd. SW4 150 B3
Macaulay Sq. SW4 150 B4
Macaulay Way SE28 118 B7
  Booth Cl.
Macauley Ms. SE13 154 C2
Macbean St. SE18 136 D3
Macbeth St. W6 127 H5
Macclesfield Br. NW1 7 H1
Macclesfield Rd. EC1 11 J3
Macclesfield Rd. EC1 111 J3
Macclesfield Rd. 189 F7
  SE25
Macclesfield St. W1 17 J5
Macclesfield St. W1 110 D7
Macdonald Av., Dag. 101 H3
Macdonald Rd. E7 97 G4
Macdonald Rd. E17 78 C2
Macdonald Rd. N11 57 J5
Macdonald Rd. N19 92 C2
Mace Cl. E1 132/133 E1
  Kennet St.
Mace St. E2 113 G2
MacFarlane La., Islw. 124 C6
Macfarlane Rd. W12 127 J1
Macfarren Pl. NW1 8 C6
Macgregor Rd. E16 115 J5
Machell Rd. SE15 153 F3
Mackay Rd. SW4 150 B3
Mackennal St. NW8 7 H2
Mackennal St. NW8 109 H2
Mackenzie Rd. N7 93 F6
Mackenzie Rd., Beck. 189 F2

Mackenzie Wk. E14 134 A1
Mackeson Rd. NW3 91 J4
Mackie Rd. SW2 151 G7
Mackintosh La. E9 95 G5
  Homerton High St.
Macklin St. WC2 18 B3
Macklin St. WC2 111 E6
Mackrow Wk. E14 114 C7
  Robin Hood La.
Macks Rd. SE16 37 J1
Macks Rd. SE16 132 D4
Mackworth St. NW1 9 F3
Mackworth St. NW1 110 C3
Maclaren Ms. SW15 147 J4
  Clarendon Dr.
Maclean Rd. SE23 153 H6
Macleod Rd. N21 43 E5
Macleod St. SE17 36 A4
Macleod St. SE17 131 J5
Maclise Rd. W14 128 B3
Macoma Rd. SE18 137 G6
Macoma Ter. SE18 137 G6
Maconochies Rd. E14 134 B5
Macquarie Way E14 134 B4
Macready Pl. N7 92/93 E4
  Warlters Rd.
Macroom Rd. W9 108 C3
Mada Rd., Orp. 206 E3
Maddams St. E3 114 B4
Maddison Cl., Tedd. 162 C6
Maddock Way SE17 35 H6
Maddock Way SE17 131 H6
Maddocks Cl., Sid. 176 E5
Maddox St. W1 17 E5
Maddox St. W1 110 B7
Madeira Av., Brom. 173 E7
Madeira Gro., 63 J6
  Wdf.Grn.
Madeira Rd. E11 96 D1
Madeira Rd. N13 59 H4
Madeira Rd. SW16 169 E5
Madeira Rd., Mitch. 185 J4
Madeley Rd. W5 105 H6
Madeline Gro., Ilf. 99 G5
Madeline Rd. SE20 188 D1
Madge Gill Way E6 116 B1
  Ron Leighton Way
Madinah Rd. E8 94 D6
Madison Cres., Bexh. 138 C7
Madison Gdns., 138 C7
  Bexh.
Madison Gdns. 191 F3
  Brom.
Madras Pl. N7 93 G6
Madras Rd., Ilf. 99 E4
Madrid Rd. SW13 147 G1
Madrigal La. SE5 131 H7
Madron St. SE17 37 E3
Madron St. SE17 132 B5
Mafeking Av. E6 116 A2
Mafeking Av., Brent. 125 H6
Mafeking Av., Ilf. 81 G7
Mafeking Rd. E16 115 F4
Mafeking Rd. N17 76 D2
Mafeking Rd., Enf. 44 C3
Magdala Av. N19 92 B2
Magdala Rd., Islw. 144 D3
Magdala Rd., S.Croy. 202 A7
  Napier Rd.
Magdalen Pas. E1 21 G5
Magdalen Rd. SW18 167 F1
Magdalen St. SE1 28 D2
Magdalen St. SE1 132 B1
Magdalene Cl. 152/153 E2
  SE15
  Heaton Rd.
Magdalene Gdns. E6 116 D4
Magee St. SE11 35 E5
Magee St. SE11 131 G6
Magellan Pl. E14 134 A5
  Napier Av.
Maggie Blake's 29 F2
  Cause SE1
Magnet Rd., Wem. 87 G2
Magnin Cl. E8 112 D1
  Wilde Cl.
Magnolia Cl. E10 96 A2
Magnolia Cl., 164 C6
  Kings.T.
Magnolia Ct., Har. 69 J3
Magnolia Ct., Rich. 146 B1
  West Hall Rd.
Magnolia Gdns., Edg. 54 C4
  Ash Cl.
Magnolia Pl. SW4 150 E5
Magnolia Pl. W5 105 H5
  Montpelier Rd.
Magnolia Rd. W4 126 B6
Magnolia St., 120 A4
  West Dr.
Magnolia Way, 196 C5
  Epsom
Magpie All. EC4 19 F4
Magpie Cl. E7 97 F5

Magpie Cl. NW9 70/71 E2
Eagle Dr.
Magpie Cl., Enf. 44 D1
Magpie Hall Cl., 192 B6
Brom.
Magpie Hall La., 192 C5
Brom.
Magpie Hall Rd., 52 B2
Bushey
Magpie Pl. SE14 133 H6
Milton Ct. Rd.
Magri Wk. E1 113 F5
Ashfield St.
Maguire Dr., Rich. 163 F4
Maguire St. SE1 29 G3
Maguire St. SE1 132 C2
Mahatma Gandhi Ho., 88 A5
Wem.
Mahlon Av., Ruis. 84 B5
Mahogany Cl. SE16 133 H1
Mahon Cl., Enf. 44 C1
Maida Av. E4 46 B7
Maida Av. W2 14 D1
Maida Av. W2 109 F5
Maida Rd., Belv. 139 G3
Maida Vale W9 6 C4
Maida Vale W9 109 E2
Maida Way E4 46 B7
Maiden Erlegh Av., 176 E1
Bex.
Maiden La. NW1 92 D7
Maiden La. SE1 28 A1
Maiden La. WC2 18 B6
Maiden La. WC2 111 E7
Maiden Rd. E15 97 E7
Maidenstone Hill 154 C1
SE10
Maids of Honour 145 G5
Row, Rich.
The Grn.
Maidstone Av., Rom. 83 J2
Maidstone Bldgs. SE1 28 A2
Maidstone Ho. E14 114 B6
Carmen St.
Maidstone Rd. N11 58 D6
Maidstone Rd., Sid. 176 D6
Maidstone St. E2 13 J1
Main Av., Enf. 44 C5
Main Dr., Wem. 87 G3
Main Rd., Sid. 175 H3
Main St., Felt. 160 D5
Mainridge Rd., Chis. 174 D4
Maisemore St. SE15 37 J7
Maitland Cl. SE10 134 B7
Maitland Cl., Houns. 143 F3
Maitland Pk. Est. 91 J6
NW3
Maitland Pk. Rd. 91 J6
NW3
Maitland Pk. Vil. 91 J6
NW3
Maitland Pl. E5 94/95 E4
Clarence Rd.
Maitland Rd. E15 97 F6
Maitland Rd. SE26 171 G6
Maize Row E14 113 J7
Commercial Rd.
Majendie Rd. SE18 137 G5
Majestic Way, Mitch. 185 J2
Major Rd. E15 96 D5
Major Rd. SE16 29 J5
Makepeace Av. N6 92 A2
Makepeace Rd. E11 79 G4
Makepeace Rd., 102 E2
Nthlt.
Makins St. SW3 31 H2
Makins St. SW3 129 H4
Malabar St. E14 134 A2
Malam Gdns. E14 114 B7
Wades Pl.
Malbrook Rd. SW15 147 H4
Malcolm Ct., Stan. 53 F5
Malcolm Cres. NW4 71 G6
Malcolm Dr., Surb. 195 H1
Malcolm Pl. E2 113 F4
Malcolm Rd. E1 113 F4
Malcolm Rd. SE20 171 F7
Malcolm Rd. SE25 188 D6
Malcolm Rd. SW19 166 B6
Malcolm Way E11 79 G5
Malcolms Way N14 42 C5
Malden Av. SE25 188 E4
Malden Av., Grnf. 86 B5
Malden Cres. NW1 92 A6
Malden Grn. Av., 197 F1
Wor.Pk.
Malden Hill, N.Mal. 183 F3
Malden Hill Gdns., 183 F3
N.Mal.
Malden Pk., N.Mal. 183 F6
Malden Pl. NW5 92 A5
Grafton Ter.
Malden Rd. NW5 92 A5
Malden Rd., Borwd. 38 A3

Malden Rd., N.Mal. 183 E5
Malden Rd., Sutt. 198 A4
Malden Rd., Wor.Pk. 183 F7
Malden Way, N.Mal. 183 F5
Maldon Cl. E15 96 D5
David St.
Maldon Cl. N1 111 J1
Maldon Cl. SE5 152 B3
Maldon Ct., Wall. 200 C5
Maldon Rd.
Maldon Rd. N9 60 C3
Maldon Rd. W3 106 C7
Maldon Rd., Rom. 83 J7
Maldon Rd., Wall. 200 B5
Maldon Wk., 63 J6
Wdf.Grn.
Malet Pl. WC1 9 H6
Malet Pl. WC1 110 D4
Malet St. WC1 9 H6
Malet St. WC1 110 D4
Maley Av. SE27 169 H2
Malford Ct. E18 79 G2
Malford Gro. E18 79 F4
Malfort Rd. SE5 152 B3
Malham Cl. N11 58 A6
Catterick Cl.
Malham Rd. SE23 171 G1
Malins Cl., Barn. 39 H5
Mall, The E15 96 D7
Mall, The N14 58 E3
Mall, The SW1 25 G3
Mall, The SW1 130 C2
Mall, The SW14 146 C5
Mall, The W5 105 H7
Mall, The, Brom. 191 G3
High St.
Mall, The, Croy. 201 J2
Mall, The, Har. 69 J6
Mall, The, Surb. 181 G5
Mall Rd. W6 127 H4
Mallams Ms. SW9 151 H3
St. James's Cres.
Mallard Cl. E9 95 J6
Mallard Cl. NW6 108 D2
Mallard Cl. W7 124 B2
Mallard Cl., Barn. 41 G6
The Hook
Mallard Cl., Twick. 143 G7
Stephenson Rd.
Mallard Path SE28 137 G3
Mallard Pl., Twick. 162 D3
Mallard Wk., Beck. 189 G5
Mallard Wk., Sid. 176 C5
Mallard Way NW9 70 C7
Mallards Rd., Bark. 117 H3
Thames Rd.
Mallards Rd., 63 H7
Wdf.Grn.
Mallet Dr., Nthlt. 85 F5
Mallet Rd. SE13 154 D6
Malling Cl., Croy. 189 F6
Malling Gdns., Mord. 185 F6
Malling Way, Brom. 191 F7
Mallinson Rd. SW11 149 H5
Mallinson Rd., Croy. 200 D3
Mallord St. SW3 31 F5
Mallord St. SW3 129 G6
Mallory Cl. SE4 153 H4
Mallory Gdns., Barn. 42 A7
Mallory St. NW8 7 G5
Mallory St. NW8 109 H4
Mallow Cl., Croy. 203 G1
Marigold Way
Mallow Mead NW7 56 B7
Mallow St. EC1 12 B5
Malmains Cl., Beck. 190 D5
Malmains Way, Beck. 190 C4
Malmesbury Rd. E3 113 J3
Malmesbury Rd. 115 E5
E16
Malmesbury Rd. E18 79 F1
Malmesbury Rd., 185 F7
Mord.
Malmesbury Ter. 115 F5
E16
Malpas Dr., Pnr. 66 D5
Malpas Rd. E8 94 E6
Malpas Rd. SE4 153 J2
Malpas Rd., Dag. 100 D6
Malt St. SE1 37 H5
Malt St. SE1 132 D6
Malta Rd. E10 96 A1
Malta St. EC1 11 H5
Maltby Rd., Chess. 196 A6
Maltby St. SE1 29 F4
Maltby St. SE1 132 C2
Malthouse Dr. W4 127 E6
Malthouse Dr., Felt. 160 D5
Malthouse Pas. 146/147 E2
SW13
The Ter.
Malthus Path SE28 138 C1
Owen Cl.
Malting Ho. E14 113 J7

Malting Way, Islw. 144 C3
Maltings, The, Orp. 207 J1
Maltings Cl. 146/147 E2
SW13
Cleveland Gdns.
Maltings Ms., Sid. 176 A3
Station Rd.
Maltings Pl. SW6 149 F1
Malton Ms. SE18 137 H6
Malton St.
Malton Ms. W10 108 B6
Cambridge Gdns.
Malton Rd. W10 108 B6
St. Marks Rd.
Malton St. SE18 137 H6
Maltravers St. WC2 18 D5
Malva Cl. SW18 148/149 E5
St. Ann's Hill
Malvern Av. E4 62 D7
Malvern Av., Bexh. 138 E7
Malvern Av., Har. 85 E3
Renforth St.
Malvern Cl. SE20 188 D2
Derwent Rd.
Malvern Cl. W10 108 C5
Malvern Cl., Mitch. 186 C3
Malvern Cl., Surb. 195 H1
Malvern Cl., Surb. 133 F7
Avonley Rd.
Malvern Ct. SW7 31 F2
Malvern Ct. SW7 129 G4
Malvern Dr., Felt. 160 D5
Malvern Dr., Ilf. 99 J4
Malvern Dr., Wdf.Grn. 63 J5
Malvern Gdns. NW2 90 B2
Malvern Gdns. NW6 108 C2
Carlton Vale
Malvern Gdns., Har. 69 H3
Malvern Gdns., Loug. 48 C6
Malvern Ms. NW6 108 D3
Malvern Rd.
Malvern Pl. NW6 108 C3
Malvern Rd. E6 116 B1
Malvern Rd. E8 94 D7
Malvern Rd. E11 97 E2
Malvern Rd. N8 75 F3
Malvern Rd. N17 76 D3
Malvern Rd. NW6 108 D3
Malvern Rd., Hmptn. 161 G7
Malvern Rd., Hayes 121 H7
Malvern Rd., Surb. 195 H2
Malvern Rd., Th.Hth. 187 G4
Malvern Ter. N1 111 G1
Malvern Ter. N9 60 C1
Latymer Rd.
Malvern Way 104/105 E5
W13
Templewood
Malwood Rd. SW12 150 B6
Malyons Rd. SE13 154 B5
Malyons Ter. SE13 154 B5
Managers St. E14 134 C1
Prestons Rd.
Manatee Pl., Wall. 200 D3
Croydon Rd.
Manaton Cl. SE15 152 E3
Manaton Cres., Sthl. 103 G6
Manbey Gro. E15 96 E6
Manbey Pk. Rd. E15 96 E6
Manbey Rd. E15 96 E6
Manbey St. E15 96 E6
Manbre Rd. W6 127 J6
Manbrough Av. E6 116 C3
Manchester Dr. W10 108 B4
Manchester Gro. E14 134 C5
Manchester Ms. W1 16 B2
Manchester Rd. E14 134 C5
Manchester Rd. N15 76 A6
Manchester Rd., 187 J3
Th.Hth.
Manchester Sq. W1 16 B3
Manchester Sq. W1 110 A6
Manchester St. W1 16 B2
Manchester St. W1 110 A5
Manchester Way, 101 H4
Dag.
Manchuria Rd. SW11 150 A6
Manciple St. SE1 28 B4
Manciple St. SE1 132 A3
Mandalay Rd. SW4 150 C5
Mandarin St. E14 114 A7
Salter St.
Mandarin Way, 102 D5
Hayes
Mandela Cl. NW10 88 C7
Mandela Rd. E16 115 G6
Mandela St. NW1 110 C1
Mandela St. SW9 131 G7
Mandela Way SE1 37 F2
Mandela Way SE1 132 B4
Mandeville Cl. SE3 135 F7
Vanbrugh Pk.
Mandeville Cl. SW20 184 B1
Mandeville Ct. E4 61 H4
Mandeville Dr., Surb. 195 G1

Mandeville Pl. W1 16 C3
Mandeville Pl. W1 110 A6
Mandeville Rd. N14 58 B2
Mandeville Rd., Islw. 144 D2
Mandeville Rd., 85 G7
Nthlt.
Mandeville St. E5 95 H3
Mandrake Rd. SW17 167 J3
Mandrake Way E15 96 E7
Mandrell Rd. SW2 150 E5
Manette St. W1 17 J4
Manette St. W1 110 D6
Manford Way, Chig. 65 H5
Manfred Rd. SW15 148 C5
Manger Rd. N7 93 E6
Mangold Way, Erith 138 E3
Manhattan Wf. E16 135 G2
Manilla St. E14 134 A2
Manister Rd. SE2 138 A3
Manitoba Cl. SE16 133 F2
Manitoba Gdns., Orp. 207 J6
Superior Dr.
Manley Ct. N16 94 C3
Stoke Newington High St.
Manley St. NW1 110 A1
Mann Cl., Croy. 201 J3
Salem Rd.
Mannin Rd., Rom. 82 B7
Manning Gdns., Har. 69 G7
Manning Pl., Rich. 145 J6
Grove Rd.
Manning Rd. E17 77 H5
Southcote Rd.
Manning Rd., Dag. 101 G6
Manningford Cl. EC1 11 G3
Manningtree Cl. 166 B1
SW19
Manningtree Rd., 84 B4
Ruis.
Manningtree St. E1 21 H3
Mannock Dr., Loug. 49 F2
Mannock Rd. N22 75 H3
Manns Cl., Islw. 144 C5
Manns Rd., Edg. 54 A6
Manoel St. E14 ... 161 J2
Manor Av. SE4 153 J2
Manor Av., Houns. 142 D3
Manor Av., Nthlt. 85 F7
Manor Cl. E17 77 H2
Manor Rd.
Manor Cl. NW7 54 D5
Manor Dr.
Manor Cl. NW9 70 B5
Manor Cl. SE28 118 C7
Manor Cl., Barn. 40 B4
Manor Cl., Wor.Pk. 197 E1
Manor Cotts. App. N2 73 F2
Manor Ct. E10 96 B1
Manor Ct. N2 73 J5
Manor Ct. SW6 148/149 E1
Bagley's La.
Manor Ct., Twick. 161 J2
Manor Ct., Wem. 87 H5
Manor Ct. Rd. W7 104 B7
Manor Cres., Surb. 182 A6
Manor Dr. N14 42 B7
Manor Dr. N20 57 H3
Manor Dr. NW7 54 D5
Manor Dr., Epsom 196 E6
Manor Dr., Esher 194 C2
Manor Dr., Felt. 160 D5
Lebanon Av.
Manor Dr., Sun. 178 A2
Manor Dr., Surb. 181 J6
Manor Dr., Wem. 87 J4
Manor Dr., The, 197 E1
Wor.Pk.
Manor Dr. N., N.Mal. 182 D7
Manor Dr. N., Wor.Pk. 196 E1
Manor Est. SE16 132 E4
Manor Fm. Cl., 196 E1
Wor.Pk.
Manor Fm. Dr. E4 63 E3
Manor Fm. Rd., 187 G2
Th.Hth.
Manor Fm. Rd., Wem. 105 G2
Manor Flds. SW15 148 A6
Manor Gdns. N7 93 E3
Manor Gdns. SW20 184 C2
Manor Gdns. W3 126 A4
Manor Gdns. W4 126/127 E5
Devonshire Rd.
Manor Gdns., Hmptn. 161 H7
Manor Gdns., Rich. 145 J4
Manor Gdns., Ruis. 84 C5
Manor Gdns., S.Croy. 202 C6
Manor Gate, Nthlt. 84 E7
Manor Gro. SE15 133 F6
Manor Gro., Beck. 190 B2
Manor Gro., Rich. 146 A4
Manor Hall Av. NW4 71 J2

Manor Hall Dr. NW4 72 A2
Manor Ho. Dr. NW6 90 A7
Manor Ho. Est., Stan. 52/53 E6
Old Ch. La.
Manor Ho. Way, Islw. 144 E3
Manor La. SE12 155 E6
Manor La. SE13 154 E4
Manor La., Felt. 160 A2
Manor La., Hayes 121 G6
Manor La., Sun. 178 A2
Manor La., Sutt. 199 F5
Manor La. Ter. SE13 154 E4
Manor Ms. NW6 108 D2
Cambridge Av.
Manor Ms. SE4 154 A2
Manor Mt. SE23 171 F1
Manor Par. NW10 107 F2
Station Rd.
Manor Pk. SE13 154 D4
Manor Pk., Chis. 193 G2
Manor Pk., Rich. 145 J4
Manor Pk. Cl., W.Wick. 204 B1
Manor Pk. Cres., Edg. 54 A6
Manor Pk. Dr., Har. 67 H3
Manor Pk. Gdns., Edg. 54 A5
Manor Pk. Par. SE13 154 D4
Lee High Rd.
Manor Pk. Rd. E12 98 A4
Manor Pk. Rd. N2 73 G3
Manor Pk. Rd. NW10 107 F1
Manor Pk. Rd., Chis. 193 F1
Manor Pk. Rd., Sutt. 199 F5
Manor Pk. Rd., W.Wick. 204 B1
Manor Pl. SE17 35 H4
Manor Pl. SE17 131 H5
Manor Pl., Chis. 193 G1
Manor Pl., Felt. 160 A1
Manor Pl., Mitch. 186 C3
Manor Pl., Sutt. 199 E4
Manor Rd. E10 78 A7
Manor Rd. E15 114 E2
Manor Rd. E16 114 E3
Manor Rd. E17 77 H2
Manor Rd. N16 94 A1
Manor Rd. N17 76 D1
Manor Rd. N22 59 E6
Manor Rd. SE25 188 D4
Manor Rd. SW20 184 C2
Manor Rd. W13 104 D7
Manor Rd., Bark. 99 J6
Manor Rd., Barn. 40 B5
Manor Rd., Beck. 190 B2
Manor Rd., Bex. 177 H1
Manor Rd., Chig. 64 E5
Manor Rd., Dag. 101 J6
Manor Rd., E.Mol. 180 A4
Manor Rd., Enf. 44 A2
Manor Rd., Har. 68 D6
Manor Rd., Hayes 102 A6
Manor Rd., Loug. 47 H6
Manor Rd., Mitch. 186 C4
Manor Rd., Rich. 145 J3
Manor Rd. (Chadwell Heath), Rom. 82 D6
Manor Rd., Sid. 175 J3
Manor Rd., Sutt. 198 C7
Manor Rd., Tedd. 162 E5
Manor Rd., Twick. 161 J2
Manor Rd., Wall. 200 B4
Manor Rd., W.Wick. 204 B2
Manor Rd., Wdf.Grn. 64 C6
Manor Rd. N., Esher 194 C3
Manor Rd. N., T.Ditt. 194 D2
Manor Rd. N., Wall. 200 B4
Manor Rd. S., Esher 194 B4
Manor Sq., Dag. 100 D2
Manor Vale, Brent. 125 F5
Manor Vw. N3 72 E2
Manor Way E4 62 D4
Manor Way NW9 70 E3
Manor Way SE3 155 F4
Manor Way SE28 138 C1
Manor Way, Beck. 190 A2
Manor Way, Bex. 177 G1
Manor Way, Borwd. 38 C4
Manor Way, Brom. 192 B6
Manor Way, Har. 67 H4
Manor Way, Mitch. 186 C3
Manor Way, Orp. 193 F4
Manor Way, S.Croy. 202 B6
Manor Way, Sthl. 122 D4
Manor Way, Wor.Pk. 197 E1
Manor Way, The, Wall. 200 B4
Manorbrook SE3 155 G4
Manordene Cl., T.Ditt. 194 D1
Manordene Rd. SE28 118 C6
Manorfield Cl. N19 92 C4
Tufnell Pk. Rd.
Manorfields Cl., Chis. 193 J3
Manorgate Rd., Kings.T. 182 A1
Manorhall Gdns. E10 96 A1
Manorside, Barn. 40 B4
Manorside Cl. SE2 138 C4
Manorway, Enf. 44 B7
Manorway, Wdf.Grn. 63 J5
Manpreet Ct. E12 98 C5
Morris Av.
Manresa Rd. SW3 31 G4
Manresa Rd. SW3 129 H5
Mansard Beeches SW17 168 A5
Mansard Cl., Pnr. 66 D3
Manse Cl., Hayes 121 G6
Manse Rd. N16 94 C3
Mansel Gro. E17 78 A1
Mansel Rd. SW19 166 B6
Mansell Rd. W3 126 D2
Mansell Rd., Grnf. 103 H5
Mansell St. E1 21 G6
Mansell St. E1 112 C6
Mansergh Cl. SE18 136 B7
Mansfield Av. N15 76 A4
Mansfield Av., Barn. 41 J6
Mansfield Av., Ruis. 84 B1
Mansfield Cl. N9 44 D6
Mansfield Hill E4 62 B1
Mansfield Ms. W1 16 D2
Mansfield Pl. NW3 91 F4
New End
Mansfield Rd. E11 79 H6
Mansfield Rd. E17 77 J4
Mansfield Rd. NW3 91 J5
Mansfield Rd. W3 106 B4
Mansfield Rd., Chess. 195 F5
Mansfield Rd., Ilf. 98 D2
Mansfield Rd., S.Croy. 202 A6
Mansfield St. W1 16 D2
Mansfield St. W1 110 B5
Mansford St. E2 13 J2
Mansford St. E2 112 D2
Manship Rd., Mitch. 168 A7
Mansion Cl. SW9 151 G1
Cowley Rd.
Mansion Gdns. NW3 91 E3
Mansion Ho. EC4 20 B4
Mansion Ho. EC4 112 A6
Mansion Ho. Pl. EC4 20 B4
Mansion Ho. St. EC4 20 B4
Manson Ms. SW7 30 D2
Manson Ms. SW7 129 F4
Manson Pl. SW7 30 E2
Manson Pl. SW7 129 G4
Mansted Gdns., Rom. 82 C7
Manston Av., Sthl. 123 G4
Manston Cl. SE20 189 F1
Garden Rd.
Manston Gro., Kings.T. 163 G5
Manstone Rd. NW2 90 B5
Manthorp Rd. SE18 137 F5
Mantilla Rd. SW17 168 A4
Mantle Rd. SE4 153 H3
Mantle Way E15 96/97 E7
Romford Rd.
Mantlet Cl. SW16 168 C7
Manton Av. W7 124 C2
Manton Rd. SE2 138 A4
Mantua St. SW11 149 G3
Mantus Cl. E1 113 F4
Mantus Rd.
Mantus Rd. E1 113 F4
Manus Way N20 57 F2
Blakeney Cl.
Manville Gdns. SW17 168 B2
Manville Rd. SW17 168 A2
Manwood Rd. SE4 153 J5
Manwood St. E16 136 C1
Manygates SW12 168 B2
Mape St. E2 112 E4
Mapesbury Rd. NW2 90 B6
Mapeshill Pl. NW2 89 J6
Maple Av. E4 61 J5
Maple Av. W3 127 E1
Maple Av., Har. 85 H2
Maple Cl. N3 56 D6
Maple Cl. N16 76 D6
Maple Cl. SW4 150 D6
Maple Cl., Buck.H. 64 A3
Maple Cl., Hmptn. 161 F6
Maple Cl., Hayes 102 D3
Maple Cl., Ilf. 65 H5
Maple Cl., Mitch. 186 B1
Maple Cl., Orp. 193 G5
Maple Cl., Ruis. 66 B6
Maple Ct., N.Mal. 182 E3
Maple Cres., Sid. 158 A6
Maple Gdns., Edg. 54 E7
Maple Gate, Loug. 48 D2
Maple Gro. NW9 70 C7
Maple Gro. W5 125 G3
Maple Gro., Brent. 124 E7
Maple Gro., Sthl. 103 F5
Maple Ind. Est., Felt. 160 A3
Maple Way
Maple Leaf Dr., Sid. 175 J1
Maple Leaf Sq. SE16 133 G2
St. Elmos Rd.
Maple Ms. NW6 6 A1
Maple Ms. SW16 169 F5
Maple Pl. W1 9 G6
Maple Rd. E11 79 E6
Maple Rd. SE20 189 E1
Maple Rd., Hayes 102 C3
Maple Rd., Surb. 181 H5
Maple St. W1 17 F1
Maple St. W1 110 C5
Maple St., Rom. 83 J4
Maple Wk. W10 108 A4
Droop St.
Maple Way, Felt. 160 B3
Maplecroft Cl. E6 116 B6
Allhallows Rd.
Mapledale Av., Croy. 202 D2
Mapledene, Chis. 175 F5
Kemnal Rd.
Mapledene Rd. E8 94 C7
Maplehurst Cl., Kings.T. 181 H4
Mapleleafe Gdns., Ilf. 80 E3
Maples Pl. E1 112/113 E5
Raven Row
Maplestead Rd. SW2 151 F7
Maplestead Rd., Dag. 118 B1
Maplethorpe Rd., Th.Hth. 187 H4
Mapleton Cl., Brom. 191 G6
Mapleton Cres. SW18 148 E6
Mapleton Rd. E4 62 C3
Mapleton Rd. SW18 148 E6
Mapleton Rd., Enf. 45 E2
Maplin Cl. N21 43 F6
Maplin Ho. SE2 138 D2
Wolvercote Rd.
Maplin Rd. E16 115 G6
Maplin St. E3 113 J3
Mapperley Dr., Wdf.Grn. 62/63 E7
Forest Dr.
Maran Way, Erith 138 D2
Marban Rd. W9 108 C3
Marble Arch W1 16 A5
Marble Arch W1 109 J7
Marble Cl. W3 126 B1
Marble Dr. NW2 72 A7
Marble Hill Cl., Twick. 145 E7
Marble Hill Gdns., Twick. 144 E7
Marble Ho. SE18 137 J5
Felspar Cl.
Marble Quay E1 29 H1
Marble Quay E1 132 D1
Marbrook Ct. SE12 173 J3
Marcellina Way, Orp. 207 H3
March Rd., Twick. 144 D7
Marchant Rd. E11 96 D2
Marchant St. SE14 133 H6
Sanford St.
Marchbank Rd. W14 128 C6
Marchmont Gdns., Rich. 145 J5
Marchmont Rd.
Marchmont Rd., Rich. 145 J5
Marchmont Rd., Wall. 200 C7
Marchmont St. WC1 10 A5
Marchmont St. WC1 110 E4
Marchside Cl., Houns. 142 D1
Springwell Rd.
Marchwood Cl. SE5 132 B7
Marchwood Cres. W5 105 F6
Marcia Rd. SE1 37 E2
Marcia Rd. SE1 132 B4
Marcilly Rd. SW18 149 G5
Marco Rd. W6 127 J3
Marcon Pl. E8 94 E6
Marconi Rd. E10 96 A1
Marconi Way, Sthl. 103 H6
Marcourt Lawns W5 105 H4
Marcus Ct. E15 115 E1
Marcus Garvey Ms. SE22 152/153 E5
St. Aidan's Rd.
Marcus Garvey Way SE24 151 G4
Marcus St. E15 115 F1
Marcus St. SW18 149 E6
Marcus Ter. SW18 149 E6
Mardale Dr. NW9 70 D5
Mardell Rd., Croy. 189 G5
Marden Av., Brom. 191 G6
Marden Cres., Bex. 159 J5
Marden Cres., Croy. 187 F6
Marden Rd. N17 76 B3
Marden Rd., Croy. 187 F6
Marden Sq. SE16 132 E3
Marder Rd. W13 124 D2
Mare St. E8 113 E1
Marechal Niel Av., Sid. 175 G3
Maresfield, Croy. 202 B3
Maresfield Gdns. NW3 91 F5
Marfleet Cl., Cars. 199 H2
Margaret Av. E4 46 B6
Margaret Bondfield Av., Bark. 100 A7
Margaret Bldgs. N16 94 C1
Margaret Rd.
Margaret Ct. W1 17 F3
Margaret Gardner Dr. SE9 174 C2
Margaret Ingram Cl. SW6 128 C6
John Smith Av.
Margaret Lockwood Cl., Kings.T. 181 J4
Margaret Rd. N16 94 C1
Margaret Rd., Barn. 41 G4
Margaret Rd., Bex. 158 D6
Margaret St. W1 17 E3
Margaret St. W1 110 B6
Margaret Way, Ilf. 80 B6
Margaretta Ter. SW3 31 G5
Margaretta Ter. SW3 129 H6
Margaretting Rd. E12 97 J1
Margate Rd. SW2 150 E5
Margeholes, Wat. 50 E2
Margery Pk. Rd. E7 97 G6
Margery Rd., Dag. 100 D3
Margery St. WC1 10 E4
Margery St. WC1 111 G3
Margin Dr. SW19 166 A5
Margravine Gdns. W6 128 A5
Margravine Rd. W6 128 A6
Marham Gdns. SW18 167 H1
Marham Gdns., Mord. 185 F6
Maria Ter. E1 113 G4
Maria Theresa Cl., N.Mal. 182 D5
Marian Cl., Hayes 102 D4
Marian Ct., Sutt. 198 E5
Marian Pl. E2 112 E2
Marian Rd. SW16 186 C1
Marian Sq. E2 13 J1
Marian St. E2 112/113 E2
Hackney Rd.
Marian Way NW10 89 F7
Maricas Av., Har. 68 A1
Marie Lloyd Gdns. N19 74/75 E7
Hornsey Ri. Gdns.
Marie Lloyd Wk. E8 94 D6
Forest Rd.
Marigold All. SE1 19 G6
Marigold Cl., Sthl. 102/103 E7
Lancaster Rd.
Marigold Rd. N17 61 F7
Marigold St. SE16 132 E2
Marigold Way E4 61 J6
Silver Birch Av.
Marigold Way, Croy. 203 G1
Marina App., Hayes 103 E5
Marina Av., N.Mal. 183 H5
Marina Cl., Brom. 191 G3
Marina Dr., Well. 157 H2
Marina Gdns., Rom. 83 J6
Marina Way, Tedd. 163 G7
Fairways
Marine Dr. SE18 136 C4
Marine Dr., Bark. 117 H3
Thames Rd.
Marine St. SE16 29 H5
Marinefield Rd. SW6 149 E2
Mariner Gdns., Rich. 163 F3
Mariner Rd. E12 98 C4
Dersingham Av.
Mariners Ms. E14 134 D4
Marion Cl., Ilf. 65 G7
Marion Gro., Wdf.Grn. 63 E5
Marion Rd. NW7 55 G5
Marion Rd., Th.Hth. 187 J5
Marischal Rd. SE13 154 D3
Maritime Quay E14 134 A5
Maritime St. E3 113 J4

Name	Page	Grid
Marius Pas. SW17	168	A2
Marius Rd.		
Marius Rd. SW17	168	A2
Marjorams Av., Loug.	48	C2
Marjorie Gro. SW11	149	J4
Marjorie Ms. E1	113	G6
Arbour Sq.		
Mark Av. E4	46	B6
Mark Cl., Bexh.	158	E1
Mark Cl., Sthl.	123	H1
Longford Av.		
Mark La. EC3	**20**	**E5**
Mark La. EC3	112	B7
Mark Rd. N22	75	H2
Mark Sq. EC2	**12**	**D5**
Mark St. E15	96	E7
Mark St. EC2	**12**	**D5**
Marke Cl., Kes.	206	B4
Markeston Grn., Wat.	50	D4
Market Ct. W1	**17**	**F3**
Market Est. N7	92	E6
Market Hill SE18	136	D3
Market La., Edg.	70	C1
Market Ms. W1	**24**	**D2**
Market Ms. W1	130	B1
Market Par. SE15	152	D2
Rye La.		
Market Pl. N2	73	H3
Market Pl. NW11	73	F4
Market Pl. SE16	**37**	**J1**
Market Pl. W1	**17**	**F3**
Market Pl. W1	110	C6
Market Pl. W3	126	C1
Market Pl., Bexh.	159	G4
Market Pl., Brent.	125	F7
Market Pl., Enf.	44	A3
The Town		
Market Pl., Kings.T.	181	G2
Market Rd. N7	92	E6
Market Rd., Rich.	146	A3
Market Row SW9	151	G4
Atlantic Rd.		
Market Sq. E2	**13**	**F3**
Market Sq. E14	114	B6
Chrisp St.		
Market Sq. N9	60	D2
New Rd.		
Market Sq., Brom.	191	G2
Market St. E6	116	C2
Market St. SE18	136	D4
Market Way E14	114	B6
Kerbey St.		
Market Way, Wem.	87	H5
Turton Rd.		
Markfield Gdns. E4	46	B7
Markfield Rd. N15	76	D4
Markham Pl. SW3	**31**	**J3**
Markham Sq. SW3	**31**	**J3**
Markham Sq. SW3	129	J5
Markham St. SW3	**31**	**H3**
Markham St. SW3	129	H5
Markhole Cl., Hmptn.	161	F7
Priory Rd.		
Markhouse Av. E17	77	H6
Markhouse Rd. E17	77	J5
Markmanor Av. E17	77	H7
Marks Rd., Rom.	83	J5
Marksbury Av., Rich.	146	A3
Markway, Sun.	178	C2
Markwell Cl. SE26	170/171	E4
Longton Gro.		
Markyate Rd., Dag.	100	B5
Marl Rd. SW18	149	E4
Marl St. SW18	149	F4
Marl Rd.		
Marlands Rd., Ilf.	80	B3
Marlborough Av. E8	112	D1
Marlborough Av. N14	58	C3
Marlborough Av., Edg.	54	B3
Marlborough Bldgs. SW3	**31**	**H1**
Marlborough Bldgs. SW3	129	H4
Marlborough Cl. N20	57	J3
Marlborough Gdns.		
Marlborough Cl. SE17	**35**	**H2**
Marlborough Cl. SW19	167	H6
Marlborough Cl., Orp.	193	J7
Aylesham Rd.		
Marlborough Ct. W1	**17**	**F4**
Marlborough Ct. W8	128	D4
Marlborough Ct., Wall.	200	C7
Cranley Gdns.		
Marlborough Cres. W4	126	D3
Marlborough Dr., Ilf.	80	B3
Marlborough Gdns. N20	57	J3
Marlborough Gate Ho. W2	**14**	**E5**
Marlborough Gro. SE1	**37**	**H4**
Marlborough Gro. SE1	132	D5
Marlborough Hill NW8	109	F1
Marlborough Hill, Har.	68	C4
Marlborough La. SE7	135	J6
Marlborough Pk. Av., Sid.	158	A7
Marlborough Pl. NW8	**6**	**C2**
Marlborough Pl. NW8	109	F2
Marlborough Rd. E4	62	A6
Marlborough Rd. E7	97	J7
Marlborough Rd. E15	96/97	E4
Borthwick Rd.		
Marlborough Rd. E18	79	G3
Marlborough Rd. N9	60	C1
Marlborough Rd. N19	92	D2
Marlborough Rd. N22	59	E7
Marlborough Rd. SW1	**25**	**G2**
Marlborough Rd. SW1	130	C1
Marlborough Rd. SW19	167	G6
Marlborough Rd. W4	126	C5
Marlborough Rd. W5	125	G2
Marlborough Rd., Bexh.	158	D3
Marlborough Rd., Brom.	191	J4
Marlborough Rd., Dag.	100	B4
Marlborough Rd., Felt.	160	D2
Marlborough Rd., Hmptn.	161	G6
Marlborough Rd., Islw.	144	E1
Marlborough Rd., Rich.	145	H6
Marlborough Rd., Rom.	83	G4
Marlborough Rd., S.Croy.	201	J7
Marlborough Rd., Sthl.	122	C3
Marlborough Rd., Sutt.	198	D3
Marlborough St. SW3	**31**	**G2**
Marlborough St. SW3	129	H4
Marlborough Yd. N19	92	D2
Marlborough Rd.		
Marler Rd. SE23	171	H1
Marlescroft Way, Loug.	48	E5
Marley Av., Bexh.	138	D6
Marley Cl. N15	75	H4
Stanmore Rd.		
Marley Cl., Grnf.	103	G3
Marley Wk. NW2	89	J5
Lennon Rd.		
Marlingdene Cl., Hmptn.	161	G6
Marlings Cl., Chis.	193	H4
Marlings Pk. Av., Chis.	193	H4
Marlins Cl., Sutt.	199	F5
Turnpike La.		
Marloes Cl., Wem.	87	G4
Marloes Rd. W8	**22**	**A6**
Marloes Rd. W8	128	E3
Marlow Cl. SE20	189	E3
Marlow Ct. NW6	90	A7
Marlow Ct. NW9	71	F3
Marlow Cres., Twick.	144	C6
Marlow Dr., Sutt.	198	A2
Marlow Gdns., Hayes	121	G3
Marlow Rd. E6	116	C3
Marlow Rd. SE20	189	E3
Marlow Rd., Sthl.	123	F3
Marlow Way SE16	133	G2
Marlowe Cl., Chis.	175	G6
Marlowe Cl., Ilf.	81	F1
Marlowe Gdns. SE9	156	D6
Marlowe Rd. E17	78	C4
Marlowe Sq., Mitch.	186	C4
Marlowe Way, Croy.	201	E2
Marlowes, The NW8	109	G1
Marlton St. SE10	135	F5
Woolwich Rd.		
Marlwood Cl., Sid.	175	H2
Marmadon Rd. SE18	137	J4
Marmion App. E4	62	A4
Marmion Av. E4	61	J4
Marmion Cl. E4	61	J4
Marmion Ms. SW11	150	A3
Taybridge Rd.		
Marmion Rd. SW11	150	A4
Marmont Rd. SE15	152	D1
Marmora Rd. SE22	153	F6
Marmot Rd., Houns.	142	D3
Marne Av. N11	58	B4
Marne Av., Well.	158	A3
Marne St. W10	108	B3
Marnell Way, Houns.	142	D3
Marney Rd. SW11	150	A4
Marnfield Cres. SW2	151	F7
Marnham Av. NW2	90	B4
Marnham Cres., Grnf.	103	H3
Marnock Rd. SE4	153	H5
Maroon St. E14	113	H5
Maroons Way SE6	172	A5
Marquess Rd. N1	94	A6
Marquis Cl., Wem.	87	J7
Marquis Rd. N4	93	F1
Marquis Rd. N22	59	F6
Marquis Rd. NW1	92	D6
Marrabon Cl., Sid.	176	A1
Marrick Cl. SW15	147	G4
Marriots Cl. NW9	71	F6
Marriott Cl., Felt.	141	G6
Marriott Rd. E15	114	E1
Marriott Rd. N4	93	F1
Marriott Rd. N10	73	J1
Marriott Rd., Barn.	40	A3
Marryat Pl. SW19	166	B4
Marryat Rd. SW19	166	A5
Marryat Sq. SW6	148	B1
Marsala Rd. SE13	154	B4
Marsden Rd. N9	60	E2
Marsden Rd. SE15	152	C3
Marsden St. NW5	92	A6
Marsden Way, Orp.	207	J4
Marsh Av., Mitch.	186	A2
Marsh Cl. NW7	55	F3
Marsh Ct. SW19	185	F1
Marsh Dr. NW9	71	F6
Marsh Fm. Rd., Twick.	162	C1
Marsh Grn. Rd., Dag.	119	G1
Marsh Hill E9	95	H5
Marsh La. E10	96	A2
Marsh La. N17	61	E7
Marsh La. NW7	54	E4
Marsh La., Stan.	53	F5
Marsh Rd., Pnr.	66	E4
Marsh Rd., Wem.	105	G2
Marsh St. E14	134	B4
Harbinger Rd.		
Marsh Wall E14	134	A1
Marshall Cl. SW18	149	F6
Allfarthing La.		
Marshall Cl., Har.	68	A7
Bowen Rd.		
Marshall Cl., Houns.	143	F5
Marshall Path SE28	118	B7
Attlee Rd.		
Marshall Rd. E10	96	B3
Marshall Rd. N17	76	A1
Marshall St. W1	**17**	**G4**
Marshall St. W1	110	C6
Marshalls Cl. N11	58	B4
Marshall's Gro. SE18	136	B4
Marshalls Pl. SE16	**29**	**G6**
Marshall's Rd., Sutt.	198	E4
Marshalsea Rd. SE1	**28**	**A3**
Marshalsea Rd. SE1	131	J2
Marsham Cl., Chis.	174	E5
Marsham St. SW1	**25**	**J6**
Marsham St. SW1	130	D3
Marshbrook Cl. SE3	156	A3
Marshfield St. E14	134	C3
Marshgate La. E15	114	B1
Marshgate Path SE28	137	F7
Tom Cribb Rd.		
Marshgate Sidings E15	96	B7
Marshgate La.		
Marshside Cl. N9	61	F1
Marsland Cl. SE17	**35**	**H4**
Marsland Cl. SE17	131	H5
Marston Av., Chess.	195	H6
Marston Av., Dag.	101	G2
Marston Cl. NW6	91	F7
Marston Cl., Dag.	101	G3
Marston Rd., Ilf.	80	B1
Marston Rd., Tedd.	162	E5
Marston Way SE19	169	H7
Marsworth Av., Pnr.	66	D1
Marsworth Cl., Hayes	103	E5
Mart St. WC2	**18**	**B4**
Martaban Rd. N16	94	B2
Martel Pl. E8	94	C6
Dalston La.		
Martell Rd. SE21	170	A3
Martello St. E8	94	E7
Martello Ter. E8	94	E7
Marten Rd. E17	78	A2
Martens Av., Bexh.	159	J4
Martens Cl., Bexh.	159	J4
Martha Ct. E2	112/113	E2
Cambridge Heath Rd.		
Martha Rd. E4	61	J6
Martha Rd. E15	97	E6
Martha St. E1	113	E6
Marthorne Cres., Har.	68	A2
Martin Bowes Rd. SE9	156	C3
Martin Cl. N9	61	G1
Martin Cres., Croy.	201	G1
Martin Dene, Bexh.	159	F5
Martin Dr., Nthlt.	85	F5
Martin Gdns., Dag.	100	C4
Martin Gro., Mord.	184	D3
Martin La. EC4	**20**	**C5**
Martin Ri., Bexh.	159	F5
Martin Rd., Dag.	100	C4
Martin St. SE28	137	H1
Merbury Rd.		
Martin Way SW20	184	B3
Martin Way, Mord.	184	B3
Martinbridge Ind. Est., Enf.	44	D5
Martindale SW14	146	C5
Martindale Av. E16	115	G7
Martindale Rd. SW12	150	B7
Martindale Rd., Houns.	142	E3
Martineau Cl., Esher	194	A4
Martineau Ms. N5	93	H4
Martineau Rd.		
Martineau Rd. N5	93	H4
Martineau St. E1	113	F7
Martineau Cl., Sun.	178	A4
Martingales Cl., Rich.	163	G3
Martins Cl., W.Wick.	204	D1
Martins Mt., Barn.	40	D4
Martins Rd., Brom.	191	E2
Martins Wk. N10	74	A1
Martins Wk., Borwd.	38	A4
Siskin Cl.		
Martinsfield Cl., Chig.	65	H4
Martlet Gro., Nthlt.	102	D3
Javelin Way		
Martlett Ct. WC2	**18**	**B4**
Martley Dr., Ilf.	80	E5
Martock Cl., Har.	68	D4
Marton Cl. SE6	172	A3
Marton Rd. N16	94	B2
Martys Yd. NW3	91	G4
Hampstead High St.		
Marvell Av., Hayes	102	A5
Marvels Cl. SE12	173	H2
Marvels La. SE12	173	H2
Marville Rd. SW6	128	C7
Marvin St. E8	94/95	E6
Sylvester Rd.		
Marwell Cl., W.Wick.	205	F2
Deer Pk. Way		
Marwood Cl., Well.	158	B3
Mary Adelaide Cl. SW15	164	E4
Mary Ann Gdns. SE8	134	A6
Mary Cl., Stan.	69	J4
Mary Datchelor Cl. SE5	152	A1
Mary Grn. NW8	109	E1
Mary Kingsley Ct. N19	74/75	E7
Hillrise Rd.		
Mary Lawrenson Pl. SE3	135	F7
Mary Macarthur Ho. W6	128	B6
Field Rd.		
Mary Peters Dr., Grnf.	86	A5
Mary Pl. W11	108	B7
Mary Rose Cl., Hmptn.	179	G3
Ashley Rd.		
Mary Rose Mall E6	116	D5
Frobisher Rd.		
Mary Seacole Cl. E8	112	C1
Clarissa St.		
Mary St. E16	115	F5
Barking Rd.		
Mary St. N1	111	J1
Mary Ter. NW1	110	B1
Maryatt Av., Har.	85	H2

Marybank SE18　136　C4
Maryland Ind. Est.　96　D5
　E15
　Maryland Rd.
Maryland Pk. E15　96　E5
Maryland Pt. E15　96/97　E6
　Leytonstone Rd.
Maryland Rd. E15　96　D5
Maryland Rd. N22　59　F6
Maryland Rd.,　187　H1
　Th.Hth.
Maryland Sq. E15　97　E5
Maryland St. E15　96　D5
Maryland Wk. N1　111　J1
　Popham St.
Maryland Way, Sun.　178　A2
Marylands Rd. W9　108　D4
Marylebone Flyover　15　F2
　NW1
Marylebone Flyover　15　F2
　W2
Marylebone High St.　16　C1
　W1
Marylebone High St.　110　A5
　W1
Marylebone La. W1　16　D4
Marylebone La. W1　110　A6
Marylebone Ms. W1　16　D2
Marylebone Ms. W1　110　B5
Marylebone Pas. W1　17　G3
Marylebone Rd. NW1　15　H1
Marylebone Rd. NW1　109　H5
Marylebone St. W1　16　C2
Marylebone St. W1　110　A5
Marylee Way SE11　34　D3
Marylee Way SE11　131　F4
Maryon Gro. SE7　136　B4
Maryon Ms. NW3　91　H4
　South End Rd.
Maryon Rd. SE7　136　B4
Maryon Rd. SE18　136　B4
Maryrose Way N20　57　G1
Mary's Cl. N17　76　C1
　Kemble Rd.
Mary's Ter., Twick.　144　D7
Masbro Rd. W14　128　A3
Mascalls Ct. SE7　135　J6
　Victoria Way
Mascalls Rd. SE7　135　J6
Mascotte Rd. SW15　148　A4
Mascotts Cl. NW2　89　H3
Masefield Av., Sthl.　103　G7
Masefield Av., Stan.　52　C5
Masefield Cres. N14　42　C6
Masefield Gdns. E6　116　D4
Masefield La., Hayes　102　B4
Masefield Rd.,　161　F4
　Hmptn.
　Wordsworth Rd.
Masefield Vw., Orp.　207　F3
Masham Ho., Erith　138　D2
　Kale Rd.
Mashie Rd. W3　106　E6
Maskall Cl. SW2　169　G1
Maskani Wk. SW16　168　C7
　Bates Cres.
Maskell Rd. SW17　167　F3
Maskelyne Cl. SW11　149　H1
Mason Bradbear Ct.　94　A6
　N1
　St. Paul's Rd.
Mason Cl. E16　115　G7
Mason Cl. SE16　37　J3
Mason Cl. SW20　184　A1
Mason Cl., Bexh.　159　H3
Mason Cl., Borwd.　38　C2
Mason Cl., Hmptn.　179　F1
Mason Rd., Sutt.　198/199　E5
　Manor Pl.
Mason St. SE17　36　C1
Mason St. SE17　132　A4
Masons Arms Ms.　17　E4
　W1
Masons Av. EC2　20　B3
Masons Av., Croy.　201　J3
Masons Av., Har.　68　C4
Masons Ct., Wem.　88　B1
　Mayfields
Masons Grn. La. W3　106　A5
Masons Hill SE18　137　E4
Masons Hill, Brom.　191　G3
Mason's Pl. EC1　11　H3
Mason's Pl. EC1　111　H3
Masons, Mitch.　185　J1
Mason's Yd. SW1　25　G1
Mason's Yd. SW19　166　A5
　High St. Wimbledon
Massey Cl. N11　58　B5
　Grove Rd.
Massie Rd. E8　94　D6
　Graham Rd.

Massingberd Way　168　B4
　SW17
Massinger St. SE17　36　D2
Massingham St. E1　113　G4
Masson Av., Ruis.　84　C6
Mast Ho. Ter. E14　134　A4
Mast Leisure Pk.　133　G3
　SE16
Master Gunner Pl.　136　B7
　SE18
Masterman Ho. SE5　36　B7
Masterman Ho. SE5　132　A7
Masterman Rd. E6　116　B3
Masters Dr. SE16　132　E5
Masters St. E1　113　G5
Mastmaker Rd. E14　134　A2
Maswell Pk. Cres.,　143　J5
　Houns.
Maswell Pk. Rd.,　143　H5
　Houns.
Matcham Rd. E11　97　E3
Matchless Dr. SE18　136　D7
Matfield Cl., Brom.　191　G5
Matfield Rd., Belv.　139　G6
Matham Gro. SE22　152　C4
Matham Rd., E.Mol.　180　A5
Matheson Rd. W14　128　C4
Mathews Av. E6　116　D2
Mathews Pk. Av. E15　97　F6
Matilda Cl. SE19　170　A7
　Elizabeth Way
Matilda St. N1　111　F1
Matlock Cl. SE24　151　J4
Matlock Cl., Barn.　40　A6
Matlock Cl. SE5　152　A4
　Denmark Hill Est.
Matlock Cres., Sutt.　198　B4
Matlock Cres., Wat.　50　C3
Matlock Gdns., Sutt.　198　B4
Matlock Pl., Sutt.　198　B4
Matlock Rd. E10　78　C6
Matlock St. E14　113　H6
Matlock Way, N.Mal.　182　D1
Matrimony Pl. SW8　150　C2
Matson Ct.,　62/63　E7
　Wdf.Grn.
　The Bridle Path
Matthew Cl. W10　108　A4
Matthew Cl., Mitch.　186　D5
Matthew Parker St.　25　J4
　SW1
Matthew Parker St.　130　D2
　SW1
Matthews Rd., Grnf.　86　A5
Matthews St. SW11　149　J2
Matthews Yd. WC2　18　A4
Matthias Rd. N16　94　A5
Mattingley Way SE15　132　C7
　Daniel Gdns.
Mattison Rd. N4　75　G6
Mattock La. W5　125　E1
Mattock La. W13　125　E1
Maud Cashmore Way　136　C3
　SE18
Maud Gdns. E13　115　F1
Maud Gdns., Bark.　117　J2
Maud Rd. E10　96　C3
Maud Rd. E13　115　F2
Maud St. E16　115　F5
Maude Rd. E17　77　H5
Maude Rd. SE5　152　B1
Maude Ter. E17　77　H4
Maudesville Cotts.　124　B1
　W7
　The Bdy.
Maudlin's Grn. E1　29　H1
Maudslay Rd. SE9　156　C3
Maudsley Ho., Brent.　125　H5
　Green Dragon La.
Mauleverer Rd. SW2　150　E5
Maundeby Wk.　88/89　E6
　NW10
　Neasden La.
Maunder Rd. W7　124　C1
Maunsel St. SW1　33　H1
Maunsel St. SW1　130　D4
Maurice Av. N22　75　H2
Maurice Brown Cl.　56　A5
　NW7
Maurice St. W12　107　H6
Maurice Wk. NW11　73　F4
Maurier Cl., Nthlt.　102　C1
Mauritius Rd. SE10　135　E4
Maury Rd. N16　94　D2
Mavelstone Cl.,　192　B1
　Brom.
Mavelstone Rd.,　192　B1
　Brom.
Maverton Rd. E3　114　A1
Mavis Av., Epsom　197　E5
Mavis Cl., Epsom　197　E5
Mavis Wk. E6　116　B5
Mawbey Est. SE1　37　H4
Mawbey Est. SE1　132　D5

Mawbey Pl. SE1　37　G4
Mawbey Pl. SE1　132　C5
Mawbey Rd. SE1　37　G4
Mawbey St. SW8　130　E7
Mawney Cl., Rom.　83　H2
Mawney Rd., Rom.　83　J4
Mawson Cl. SW20　184　B2
Mawson La. W4　127　F6
Maxey Gdns., Dag.　101　E4
Maxey Rd. SE18　137　F4
Maxey Rd., Dag.　100　E4
Maxfield Cl. N20　41　F7
Maxilla Gdns. W10　108　A6
　Cambridge Gdns.
Maxilla Wk. W10　108　A6
　Kingsdown Cl.
Maxim Rd. N21　43　G6
Maxted Pk., Har.　68　B7
Maxted Rd. SE15　152　C3
Maxwell Cl., Croy.　201　E1
Maxwell Gdns., Orp.　207　J3
Maxwell Rd. SW6　128　E7
Maxwell Rd., Borwd.　38　B3
Maxwell Rd., Well.　158　A3
Maxwell Rd.,　120　C4
　West Dr.
Maxwelton Av. NW7　54　D5
Maxwelton Cl. NW7　54　D5
May Bate Av.,　181　G1
　Kings.T.
May Cl., Chess.　195　J6
May Ct. SW19　185　F1
May Gdns., Wem.　105　F2
May Rd. E4　62　A6
May Rd. E13　115　G2
May Rd., Twick.　162　B1
May St. W14　128　C5
　North End Rd.
May Tree La., Stan.　52　C7
May Wk. E13　115　H2
Maya Rd. N2　73　F4
Mayall Rd. SE24　151　H5
Maybank Av. E18　79　H2
Maybank Av., Wem.　86　C5
Maybank Gdns., Pnr.　66　A5
Maybank Rd. E18　79　H1
Maybells Commercial　118　D2
　Est., Bark.
Maybourne Pl., Surb.　181　J7
Maybourne Cl. SE26　171　E5
Maybrook Meadow　100　A7
　Est., Bark.
Maybury Cl., Loug.　48　E4
Maybury Cl., Orp.　193　E5
Maybury Gdns.　89　H6
　NW10
Maybury Ms. N6　74　C7
Maybury Rd. E13　115　J4
Maybury Rd., Bark.　117　J2
Maybury St. SW17　167　H5
Maychurch Cl., Stan.　53　G7
Maycroft, Pnr.　66　B2
Maycross Av., Mord.　184　C3
Mayday Gdns. SE3　156　B2
Mayday Rd., Th.Hth.　187　H6
Mayerne Rd. SE9　156　A5
Mayes Rd. N22　75　G2
Mayesbrook Rd.,　117　J1
　Bark.
Mayesbrook Rd.,　100　A3
　Dag.
Mayesbrook Rd., Ilf.　100　A3
Mayesford Rd., Rom.　82　C7
Mayeswood Rd.　173　J3
　SE12
Mayfair Av., Bexh.　158　D1
Mayfair Av., Ilf.　98　C2
Mayfair Av., Rom.　82　D6
Mayfair Av., Twick.　143　J7
Mayfair Av., Wor.Pk.　197　G1
Mayfair Cl., Beck.　190　B1
Mayfair Cl., Surb.　195　H1
Mayfair Gdns. N17　60　A6
Mayfair Gdns.,　63　G7
　Wdf.Grn.
Mayfair Ms. NW1　91　J7
　Regents Pk. Rd.
Mayfair Pl. W1　25　E1
Mayfair Pl. W1　130　B1
Mayfair Ter. N14　42　D7
Mayfield Av. N12　57　F4
Mayfield Av. N14　58　D2
Mayfield Av. W4　127　E4
Mayfield Av. W13　124　E3
Mayfield Av., Har.　68　E5
Mayfield Av., Orp.　207　J1
Mayfield Av.,　63　G7
　Wdf.Grn.
Mayfield Cl. E8　94　C6
　Forest Rd.
Mayfield Cl. SW4　150　D5
Mayfield Cl., T.Ditt.　194　E1

Mayfield Cres. N9　44　E6
Mayfield Cres.,　187　F4
　Th.Hth.
Mayfield Dr., Pnr.　67　F4
Mayfield Gdns. NW4　72　A6
Mayfield Gdns. W7　104　A6
Mayfield Mans.　148　A7
　SW18
　West Hill
Mayfield Rd. E4　62　C2
Mayfield Rd. E8　94　C7
Mayfield Rd. E13　115　F4
Mayfield Rd. E17　77　H2
Mayfield Rd. N8　75　F6
Mayfield Rd. SW19　184　C1
Mayfield Rd. W3　106　B7
Mayfield Rd. W12　127　E2
Mayfield Rd., Belv.　139　J4
Mayfield Rd., Brom.　192　B5
Mayfield Rd., Dag.　100　C1
Mayfield Rd., Enf.　45　G2
Mayfield Rd., Sutt.　199　G6
Mayfield Rd., Th.Hth.　187　F4
Mayfields, Wem.　88　A2
Mayfields Cl., Wem.　88　A2
Mayflower Cl. SE16　133　G4
　Greenland Quay
Mayflower Ct. SE16　133　F2
　St. Marychurch St.
Mayflower Rd. SW9　150　E3
Mayflower St. SE16　133　F2
Mayfly Cl., Pnr.　66　C7
Mayfly Gdns., Nthlt.　102　D3
　Ruislip Rd.
Mayford Cl. SW12　149　J7
Mayford Cl., Beck.　189　G3
Mayford Rd. SW12　149　J7
Maygood St. N1　10　D1
Maygood St. N1　111　F2
Maygrove Rd. NW6　90　C6
Mayhew Cl. E4　62　A3
Mayhill Rd. SE7　135　H6
Mayhill Rd., Barn.　40　B6
Maylands Dr., Sid.　176　D3
Maylands Rd., Wat.　50　C4
Maynard Cl. N15　76　B4
　Brunswick Rd.
Maynard Cl.,　128/129　E7
　SW6
　Cambria St.
Maynard Path E17　78　C5
　Maynard Rd.
Maynard Rd. E17　78　C5
Maynards Quay E1　113　F7
　Garnet St.
Maynooth Gdns.,　185　J7
　Cars.
　Middleton Rd.
Mayo Rd. NW10　88　E6
Mayo Rd., Croy.　188　A5
Mayola Rd. E5　95　F4
Mayow Rd. SE23　171　G3
Mayow Rd. SE26　171　G4
Mayplace Cl., Bexh.　159　H3
Mayplace La. SE18　137　E7
Mayplace Rd. E.,　159　H3
　Bexh.
Mayplace Rd. E.,　159　J3
　Dart.
Mayplace Rd. W.,　159　G4
　Bexh.
Maypole Cres., Ilf.　65　G7
Mayroyd Av., Surb.　196　A2
Mays Ct. WC2　18　A6
Mays Hill Rd., Brom.　191　E2
Mays La. E4　62　D2
Mays La., Barn.　39　H7
Mays Rd., Tedd.　162　A5
Maysoule Rd. SW11　149　G4
Mayston Ms. SE10　135　G5
　Westcombe Hill
Mayswood Gdns.,　101　J6
　Dag.
Mayton St. N7　93　F3
Maytree Cl., Edg.　54　C3
Maytree Gdns. W5　125　G2
　South Ealing Rd.
Maytree Wk. SW2　169　G2
Mayville Est. N16　94　B5
　King Henry St.
Mayville Rd. E11　96　E3
Mayville Rd., Ilf.　98　E5
Maywood Cl., Beck.　172　B7
Maze Hill SE3　134　E6
Maze Hill SE10　134　E6
Maze Rd., Rich.　126　A7
McAdam Dr., Enf.　43　H2
　Rowantree Rd.
McAuley Cl. SE1　26　E5
McAuley Cl. SE1　131　G3
McAuley Cl. SE9　156　E5
McCall Cl. SW4　150/151　E2
　Jeffreys Rd.

Name	Page	Grid
McCall Cres. SE7	136	B5
McCarthy Rd., Felt.	160	D5
McCoid Way SE1	**27**	**J4**
McCrone Ms. NW3	91	G6
Belsize La.		
McCullum Rd. E3	113	J1
McDermott Cl. SW11	149	H3
McDermott Rd. SE15	152	D3
McDonough Cl.,	195	H4
Chess.		
McDowall Cl. E16	115	F5
McDowall Rd. SE5	151	J1
McEntee Av. E17	77	H1
McEwen Way E15	114	D1
McGrath Rd. E15	97	F6
McGregor Rd. W11	108	C6
McIntosh Cl., Wall.	200	E7
McKay Rd. SW20	165	H7
McKellar Cl., Bushey	51	J2
McKerrell Rd. SE15	152	D1
McLeod Rd. SE2	138	B4
McLeod's Ms. SW7	**30**	**B1**
McLeod's Ms. SW7	129	E4
McMillan St. SE8	134	A6
McNair Rd., Sthl.	123	H2
McNeil Rd. SE5	152	B2
McNicol Dr. NW10	106	C2
McRae La., Mitch.	185	J7
Mead, The W13	104	E5
Mead, The, Beck.	190	C1
Mead, The, Wall.	200	D6
Mead, The, Wat.	50	E3
Mead, The, W.Wick.	204	D1
Mead Cl., Har.	68	A1
Mead Cl., Loug.	48	E2
Mead Cl. NW9	70	C5
Mead Cres. E4	62	C4
Mead Cres., Sutt.	199	H4
Mead Fld., Har.	85	F3
Kings Rd.		
Mead Gro., Rom.	82	E3
Mead Path SW17	167	F5
Mead Pl. E9	95	F6
Mead Pl., Croy.	201	H1
Mead Plat NW10	88	C6
Mead Rd., Chis.	175	F6
Mead Rd., Edg.	54	A6
Mead Rd., Rich.	163	F3
Mead Row SE1	**27**	**E5**
Mead Ter., Wem.	87	G4
Meadow Way		
Mead Way, Brom.	191	F6
Mead Way, Croy.	203	H2
Meadcroft St. SE11	**35**	**G6**
Meadcroft Rd. SE11	131	H6
Meade Cl. W4	126	A6
Meadfield, Edg.	54	B2
Meadfield Grn., Edg.	54	B2
Meadfoot Rd. SW16	168	C7
Meadgate Av.,	64	B5
Wdf.Grn.		
Meadlands Dr., Rich.	163	G2
Meadow, The, Chis.	175	F6
Meadow Av., Croy.	189	G6
Meadow Bank N21	43	F6
Meadow Cl. E4	62	C1
Mount Echo Av.		
Meadow Cl. E9	95	J5
Meadow Cl. SE6	172	A5
Meadow Cl. SW20	183	J4
Meadow Cl., Barn.	40	C6
Meadow Cl., Bexh.	159	F5
Meadow Cl., Chis.	174	E5
Meadow Cl., Esher	194	C3
Meadow Cl., Houns.	143	G6
Meadow Cl., Nthlt.	103	G2
Meadow Cl., Rich.	163	J1
Meadow Cl.,	198/199	E2
Sutt.		
Aultone Way		
Meadow Dr. N10	74	B3
Meadow Dr. NW4	71	J2
Meadow Gdns., Edg.	54	B6
Meadow Garth	88	C6
NW10		
Meadow Hill, N.Mal.	182	E6
Meadow Ms. SW8	**34**	**C6**
Meadow Ms. SW8	131	F6
Meadow Pl. SW8	**34**	**B7**
Meadow Pl. SW8	131	E7
Meadow Pl. W4	126/127	E7
Edensor Rd.		
Meadow Rd. SW8	**34**	**C7**
Meadow Rd. SW8	131	F6
Meadow Rd. SW19	167	F7
Meadow Rd., Bark.	99	J7
Meadow Rd., Borwd.	38	B2
Meadow Rd., Brom.	191	E1
Meadow Rd., Dag.	101	F6
Meadow Rd., Esher	194	B6
Meadow Rd., Felt.	160	E2
Meadow Rd., Loug.	48	B5
Meadow Rd., Pnr.	66	D4
Meadow Rd., Rom.	101	J1
Meadow Rd., Sthl.	103	F7
Meadow Rd., Sutt.	199	H5
Meadow Row SE1	**27**	**J6**
Meadow Row SE1	131	J3
Meadow Stile, Croy.	201	J3
High St.		
Meadow Vw., Har.	86	B1
Meadow Vw., Sid.	158	B7
Meadow Vw. Rd.,	187	H5
Th.Hth.		
Meadow Wk. E18	79	G4
Meadow Wk., Dag.	101	F6
Meadow Wk., Epsom	197	E6
Meadow Wk., Wall.	200	B3
Meadow Way NW9	70	D5
Meadow Way, Chess.	195	H5
Meadow Way, Chig.	65	F3
Meadow Way, Orp.	206	D3
Meadow Way, Ruis.	66	B6
Meadow Way, Wem.	87	G4
Meadow Way, The,	68	B1
Har.		
Meadow Waye,	123	E6
Houns.		
Meadowbank NW3	91	J7
Meadowbank SE3	155	F3
Meadowbank, Surb.	181	J6
Meadowbank Cl.,	127	J7
SW6		
Meadowbank Cl.,	39	F5
Barn.		
Meadowbank Gdns.,	142	A2
Houns.		
Meadowbank Rd.	70	D7
NW9		
Meadowbanks, Barn.	39	G5
Barnet Rd.		
Meadowcourt Rd.	155	F4
SE3		
Meadowcroft, Brom.	192	C3
Meadowcroft Rd.	59	G2
N13		
Meadowlea Cl.,	120	A6
West Dr.		
Meadows Cl. E10	96	A2
Meadows End, Sun.	178	A1
Meadowside SE9	155	J4
Meadowsweet Cl.	116	A5
E16		
Monarch Dr.		
Meadowview Rd.	171	J5
SE6		
Meadowview Rd.,	159	E6
Bex.		
Meads, The, Edg.	54	D6
Meads, The, Sutt.	198	B3
Meads La., Ilf.	81	H7
Meads Rd. N22	75	H2
Meads Rd., Enf.	45	H1
Meadvale Rd. W5	105	E4
Meadvale Rd., Croy.	188	C7
Meadway N14	58	D2
Meadway NW11	73	E6
Meadway SW20	183	J4
Meadway, Barn.	40	D4
Meadway, Beck.	190	C1
Meadway, Ilf.	99	H4
Meadway, Surb.	196	C1
Meadway, Twick.	162	A1
Meadway, Wdf.Grn.	63	J5
Meadway, The SE3	154	D2
Heath La.		
Meadway, The,	64	A1
Buck.H.		
Meadway, The, Loug.	48	C6
Meadway Cl. NW11	73	E6
Meadway Cl., Barn.	40	D4
Meadway Cl., Pnr.	51	H6
Highbanks Rd.		
Meadway Ct. NW11	73	E6
Meadway Gate	72	D6
NW11		
Meaford Way SE20	171	E7
Meakin Est. SE1	**28**	**D5**
Meakin Est. SE1	132	B3
Meanley Rd. E12	98	B4
Meard St. W1	**17**	**H4**
Meard St. W1	110	D6
Meath Rd. E15	115	F2
Meath Rd., Ilf.	99	F3
Meath St. SW11	150	B1
Mechanics Path SE8	134	A7
Deptford High St.		
Mecklenburgh Pl.	**10**	**C5**
WC1		
Mecklenburgh Pl.	111	F4
WC1		
Mecklenburgh Sq.	**10**	**C5**
WC1		
Mecklenburgh Sq.	111	F4
WC1		
Mecklenburgh St.	**10**	**C5**
WC1		
Medburn St. NW1	**9**	**H1**
Medburn St. NW1	110	D2
Medcroft Gdns.	146	C4
SW14		
Medebourne Cl. SE3	155	G3
Medesenge Way	59	H6
N13		
Medfield St. SW15	147	H7
Medhurst Cl. E3	113	H2
Arbery Rd.		
Medhurst Rd. E3	113	H2
Arbery Rd.		
Median Rd. E5	95	F5
Medina Av., Esher	194	B3
Medina Gro. N7	93	G3
Medina Rd.		
Medina Rd. N7	93	G3
Medland Cl., Wall.	200	A1
Medland Cl., Nthlt.	102/103	E2
Parkfield Av.		
Medlar St. SE5	151	J1
Medley Rd. NW6	90	D6
Medora Rd. SW2	151	F7
Medusa Rd. SE6	154	B6
Medway Bldgs. E3	113	H2
Medway Rd.		
Medway Cl., Croy.	189	F6
Medway Cl., Ilf.	99	F5
Medway Dr., Grnf.	104	C2
Medway Gdns., Wem.	86	D4
Medway Ms. E3	113	H2
Medway Rd.		
Medway Par., Grnf.	104	C2
Medway Rd. E3	113	H2
Medway St. SW1	**25**	**J6**
Medway St. SW1	130	D3
Medwin St. SW4	151	F4
Meerbrook Rd. SE3	155	J3
Meeson Rd. E15	115	F1
Meeson St. E5	95	H4
Meeting Flds. Path E9	95	F6
Morning La.		
Meeting Ho. La.	152	E1
SE15		
Meetinghouse	132/133	E7
All. E1		
Wapping La.		
Mehetabel Rd. E9	95	F6
Meister Cl., Ilf.	99	G1
Melancholy Wk.,	163	F2
Rich.		
Melanda Cl., Chis.	174	C5
Melanie Cl., Bexh.	158	E1
Melba Way SE13	154	B1
Melbourne Av. N13	59	F6
Melbourne Av. W13	124	D1
Melbourne Av., Pnr.	67	H3
Melbourne Cl., Orp.	193	H7
Melbourne Cl., Wall.	200	C5
Melbourne Rd.		
Melbourne Ct. E5	95	H4
Daubeney Rd.		
Melbourne Ct. N10	58	B7
Sydney Rd.		
Melbourne Ct. SE20	170	D7
Melbourne Gdns.,	82	E5
Rom.		
Melbourne Gro.	152	B4
SE22		
Melbourne Ho.,	102	C4
Hayes		
Melbourne Ms. SE6	154	C7
Melbourne Ms.	151	G1
SW9		
Melbourne Pl. WC2	**18**	**D5**
Melbourne Pl. WC2	111	F6
Melbourne Rd. E6	116	C1
Melbourne Rd. E10	78	B7
Melbourne Rd. E17	77	H4
Melbourne Rd.	184	D1
SW19		
Melbourne Rd., Ilf.	99	E1
Melbourne Rd., Tedd.	163	F6
Melbourne Rd., Wall.	200	B5
Melbourne Sq. SW9	151	G1
Melbourne Ms.		
Melbourne Ter.	128/129	E7
SW6		
Waterford Rd.		
Melbourne Way, Enf.	44	C6
Melbury Av., Sthl.	123	H3
Melbury Cl., Chis.	174	C6
Melbury Cl., Esher	194	E6
Melbury Ct. W8	128	C3
Melbury Dr. SE5	132	B7
Sedgmoor Pl.		
Melbury Gdns. SW20	183	H1
Melbury Rd. W14	128	C3
Melbury Rd., Har.	69	J5
Melbury Ter. NW1	**7**	**H6**
Melbury Ter. NW1	109	H4
Melcombe Gdns.,	69	J6
Har.		
Melcombe Pl. NW1	**15**	**J1**
Melcombe Pl. NW1	109	J5
Melcombe St. NW1	**8**	**A6**
Melcombe St. NW1	109	J4
Meldex Cl. NW7	55	J6
Meldon Cl. SW6	148/149	E1
Bagley's La.		
Meldone Cl., Surb.	182	B6
Meldrum Rd., Ilf.	100	A2
Melfield Gdns. SE6	172	B4
Melford Av., Bark.	99	H6
Melford Cl., Chess.	195	J5
Melford Rd. E6	116	C4
Melford Rd. E11	96	E2
Melford Rd. E17	77	H4
Melford Rd. SE22	152	D7
Melford Rd., Ilf.	99	G2
Melfort Av., Th.Hth.	187	H3
Melfort Rd., Th.Hth.	187	H3
Melgund Rd. N5	93	G5
Melina Pl. NW8	**6**	**E4**
Melina Pl. NW8	109	G3
Melina Rd. W12	127	H2
Melior Pl. SE1	**28**	**D3**
Melior St. SE1	**28**	**C3**
Melior St. SE1	132	A2
Meliot Rd. SE6	172	D2
Mell St. SE10	134/135	E5
Trafalgar Rd.		
Meller Cl., Croy.	200	E3
Melling Dr., Enf.	44	D1
Melling St. SE18	137	H6
Mellish Cl., Bark.	117	J1
Mellish Gdns.,	63	G5
Wdf.Grn.		
Mellish Ind. Est.	136	B3
SE18		
Harrington Way		
Mellish St. E14	134	A3
Mellison Rd. SW17	167	H5
Mellitus St. W12	107	F6
Mellor Cl., Walt.	179	F7
Mellows Rd., Ilf.	80	C3
Mellows Rd., Wall.	200	D5
Mells Cres. SE9	174	C4
Melody La. N5	93	H5
Melody Rd. SW18	149	F5
Melon Pl. W8	**22**	**A3**
Melon Rd. E11	96	E3
Melon Rd. SE15	152	D1
Melrose Av. N22	75	H1
Melrose Av. NW2	89	J5
Melrose Av. SW16	187	F3
Melrose Av. SW19	166	D2
Melrose Av., Borwd.	38	B5
Melrose Av., Grnf.	103	H2
Melrose Av., Mitch.	168	B7
Melrose Av., Twick.	143	H7
Melrose Cl. SE12	173	G1
Melrose Cl., Grnf.	103	H2
Melrose Cl., Hayes	102	A5
Melrose Cres., Orp.	207	G4
Melrose Dr., Sthl.	123	G1
Melrose Gdns. W6	127	J3
Melrose Gdns., Edg.	70	B2
Melrose Gdns.,	182	D3
N.Mal.		
Melrose Rd. SW13	147	F2
Melrose Rd. SW18	148	C6
Melrose Rd. SW19	184	D2
Melrose Rd. W3	126	C3
Stanley Rd.		
Melrose Rd., Pnr.	67	F4
Melrose Ter. W6	127	J2
Melsa Rd., Mord.	185	F6
Melthorne Dr., Ruis.	84	C3
Melthorpe Gdns.	156	B1
SE3		
Melton Cl., Ruis.	84	C1
Melton Ct. SW7	31	F2
Melton Ct. SW7	129	G4
Melton St. NW1	**9**	**G4**
Melton St. NW1	110	D3
Melville Av. SW20	165	G7
Melville Av., Grnf.	86	C5
Melville Av., S.Croy.	202	C5
Melville Gdns. N13	59	H5
Melville Pl. N1	111	H1
Essex Rd.		
Melville Rd. E17	77	J3
Melville Rd. NW10	88	D7
Melville Rd. SW13	147	G1
Melville Rd., Sid.	176	C2
Melville Vil. Rd. W3	126	D1
High St.		
Melvin Rd. SE20	189	F1
Melyn Cl. N7	92	C4
Anson Rd.		
Memel Ct. EC1	**11**	**J6**
Memel St. EC1	**11**	**J6**
Memess Path SE18	136	D6
Memorial Av. E15	114	E3
Memorial Cl.,	123	F6
Houns.		
Mendip Cl. SE26	171	F4

Mendip Cl. SW19	166	B2
Queensmere Rd.		
Mendip Cl., Hayes	121	G7
Mendip Cl., Wor.Pk.	197	J1
Mendip Dr. NW2	90	A2
Mendip Rd. SW11	149	F3
Mendip Rd., Ilf.	81	H5
Mendora Rd. SW6	128	B7
Menelik Rd. NW2	90	B4
Menlo Gdns. SE19	170	A7
Menotti St. E2	**13**	**J5**
Mentmore Cl., Har.	69	F6
Mentmore Ter. E8	95	E7
Meon Ct., Islw.	144	B2
Meon Rd. W3	126	C2
Meopham Rd., Mitch.	186	C1
Mepham Cres., Har.	51	J7
Mepham Gdns., Har.	51	J7
Mepham St. SE1	**26**	**D2**
Mepham St. SE1	131	F1
Mera Dr., Bexh.	159	G4
Merantun Way SW19	185	F1
Merbury Cl. SE13	154	C5
Merbury Rd. SE28	137	H2
Mercator Pl. E14	134	A5
Napier Av.		
Mercator Rd. SE13	154	D4
Mercer Cl., T.Ditt.	180	C7
Mercer Pl., Pnr.	66	C2
Crossway		
Mercer St. WC2	**18**	**A4**
Mercer St. WC2	110	E6
Merceron St. E1	112	E4
Mercers Cl. SE10	135	F4
Mercers Pl. W6	127	J4
Mercers Rd. N19	92	D3
Merchant St. E3	113	J3
Merchiston Rd. SE6	172	D2
Merchland Rd. SE9	175	F1
Mercia Gro. SE13	154	C4
Mercier Rd. SW15	148	B5
Mercury Cen., Felt.	142	B5
Mercury Way SE14	133	G6
Mercy Ter. SE13	154	B4
Mere Cl. SW15	148	A7
Mere Cl., Orp.	206	E2
Mere End, Croy.	189	G7
Mere Side, Orp.	206	D2
Merebank La., Croy.	201	F5
Meredith Av. NW2	89	J5
Meredith Cl., Pnr.	50	D7
Meredith St. E13	115	G3
Meredith St. EC1	**11**	**G4**
Meredyth Rd. SW13	147	G2
Meretone Cl. SE4	153	H4
Merevale Cres.,	185	F6
Mord.		
Mereway Rd., Twick.	162	A1
Merewood Cl.,	192	D2
Brom.		
Merewood Rd.,	159	J2
Bexh.		
Mereworth Cl.,	191	F5
Brom.		
Mereworth Dr. SE18	137	F7
Merganser Gdns.	137	G3
SE28		
Avocet Ms.		
Meriden Cl., Brom.	174	A7
Meriden Cl., Ilf.	81	F1
Meridian Gate E14	134	C2
Meridian Pl. E14	134	B2
Meridian Rd. SE7	136	A7
Meridian Trd. Est.	135	H4
SE7		
Meridian Wk. N17	60	B6
Commercial Rd.		
Meridian Way N9	61	F5
Meridian Way N18	61	F6
Meridian Way, Enf.	45	G6
Merifield Rd. SE9	155	J4
Merino Cl. E11	79	J4
Merino Pl., Sid.	158	A6
Blackfen Rd.		
Merivale Rd. SW15	148	B4
Merivale Rd., Har.	67	J3
Merlewood Dr., Chis.	192	C1
Merley Ct. NW9	88	C1
Merlin Cl., Croy.	202	B4
Minster Dr.		
Merlin Cl., Mitch.	185	H3
Merlin Cl., Nthlt.	102	C3
Merlin Cres., Edg.	69	J1
Merlin Gdns., Brom.	173	G3
Merlin Gro., Beck.	189	J4
Merlin Gro., Ilf.	65	E7
Merlin Rd. E12	98	A2
Merlin Rd., Well.	158	A4
Merlin Rd. N., Well.	158	A4
Merlin St. WC1	**11**	**E4**
Merling Cl., Chess.	195	G5
Coppard Gdns.		
Merlins Av., Har.	85	F3
Mermaid Ct. SE1	**28**	**B3**
Mermaid Ct. SE1	132	A2
Mermaid Ct. SE16	133	J1
Merredene St. SW2	151	F6
Merriam Cl. E4	62	C5
Merrick Rd., Sthl.	123	F2
Merrick Sq. SE1	**28**	**A5**
Merrick Sq. SE1	131	J3
Merridene N21	43	H6
Merrielands Cres.,	119	F1
Dag.		
Merrilands Rd.,	197	J1
Wor.Pk.		
Merrilees Rd., Sid.	157	H7
Merrilyn Cl., Esher	194	D6
Merriman Rd. SE3	155	J1
Merrington Rd. SW6	128	D6
Merrion Av., Stan.	53	G5
Merrion Wk. SE17	132	A5
Dawes St.		
Merritt Gdns., Chess.	195	F6
Merritt Rd. SE4	153	J5
Merrivale N14	42	D6
Merrivale Av., Ilf.	80	A4
Merrow St. SE17	**36**	**C4**
Merrow St. SE17	131	J6
Merrow Wk. SE17	**36**	**C3**
Merrow Way, Croy.	204	C6
Merry Hill Mt.,	51	H1
Bushey		
Merry Hill Rd.,	51	H1
Bushey		
Merrydown Way,	192	B1
Chis.		
Merryfield SE3	155	F2
Merryfield Gdns.,	53	F5
Stan.		
Merryfields Way	154	B7
SE6		
Merryhill Cl. E4	46	B7
Merryhills Ct. N14	42	C5
Merryhills Dr., Enf.	42	D4
Mersea Ho., Bark.	98	E6
Mersey Rd. E17	77	J3
Mersey Wk., Nthlt.	103	G2
Brabazon Rd.		
Mersham Dr. NW9	70	A5
Mersham Pl. SE20	189	E1
Mersham Rd.,	188	A3
Th.Hth.		
Merten Rd., Rom.	83	E7
Merthyr Ter. SW13	127	H6
Merton Av. W4	127	F4
Merton Av., Nthlt.	85	J5
Merton Gdns., Orp.	193	E5
Merton Hall Gdns.	184	B1
SW20		
Merton Hall Rd.	184	B1
SW19		
Merton High St.	167	E7
SW19		
Merton Ind. Pk.	185	F1
SW19		
Merton La. N6	91	J2
Merton Mans. SW20	184	A2
Merton Pk. Par.	184	C1
SW19		
Kingston Rd.		
Merton Ri. NW3	91	H7
Merton Rd. E17	78	C5
Merton Rd. SE25	188	D5
Merton Rd. SW18	148	D6
Merton Rd. SW19	166	E7
Merton Rd., Bark.	99	J7
Merton Rd., Har.	85	J1
Merton Rd., Ilf.	81	J7
Merton Way, W.Mol.	179	H4
Merttins Rd. SE15	153	G5
Meru Cl. NW5	92	A4
Mervan Rd. SW2	151	G4
Mervyn Av. SE9	175	F3
Mervyn Rd. W13	124	D3
Messaline Av. W3	106	C6
Messent Rd. SE9	155	J5
Messeter Pl. SE9	156	D6
Messina Av. NW6	90	D7
Metcalf Wk.,	160/161	E4
Felt.		
Gabriel Cl.		
Meteor St. SW11	150	A4
Meteor Way, Wall.	200	E7
Metheringham Way	70	E1
NW9		
Methley St. SE11	**35**	**F4**
Methley St. SE11	131	G5
Methuen Cl., Edg.	54	A7
Methuen Pk. N10	74	B2
Methuen Rd., Belv.	139	H4
Methuen Rd., Bexh.	159	F4
Methuen Rd., Edg.	54	A7
Methwold Rd. W10	108	A5
Metro Cen., The,	144	B2
Islw.		
Metropolitan Cen.,	103	H1
The, Grnf.		
Metropolitan Cl. E14	114	A5
Broomfield St.		
Mews, The N1	111	J1
St. Paul St.		
Mews, The, Ilf.	80	A5
Mews, The,	144/145	E6
Twick.		
Bridge Rd.		
Mews Deck E1	113	E7
Mews Pl., Wdf.Grn.	63	G4
Mews St. E1	**29**	**H1**
Mews St. E1	132	D1
Mexfield Rd. SW15	148	C5
Meyer Rd., Erith	139	J6
Meymott St. SE1	**27**	**G2**
Meymott St. SE1	131	H1
Meynell Cres. E9	95	G7
Meynell Gdns. E9	95	G7
Meynell Rd. E9	95	G7
Meyrick Rd. NW10	89	G6
Meyrick Rd. SW11	149	G3
Miah Ter. E1	132	D1
Wapping High St.		
Miall Wk. SE26	171	H4
Micawber St. N1	**12**	**A3**
Micawber St. N1	111	J3
Michael Faraday Ho.	**36**	**C4**
SE17		
Michael Gaynor Cl.	124	C1
W7		
Michael Rd. E11	97	E1
Michael Rd. SE25	188	B3
Michael Rd. SW6	149	E1
Michaelmas Cl.	183	J3
SW20		
Michaels Cl. SE13	154	E4
Micheldever Rd.	155	E6
SE12		
Michelham Gdns.,	162	C3
Twick.		
Michels Row, Rich.	145	H4
Kew Foot Rd.		
Michigan Av. E12	98	B4
Michleham Down	56	C4
N12		
Mickleham Cl., Orp.	193	J2
Mickleham Gdns.,	198	B6
Sutt.		
Mickleham Rd., Orp.	193	J1
Micklethwaite Rd.	128	D6
SW6		
Midas Metropolitan	198	A1
Ind. Est., The, Mord.		
Garth Rd.		
Middle Dene NW7	54	D3
Middle Fld. NW8	109	G1
Middle Grn. Cl.,	181	J6
Surb.		
Alpha Rd.		
Middle La. N8	74	E5
Middle La., Tedd.	162	C6
Middle La. Ms. N8	74/75	E5
Middle La.		
Middle Pk. Av. SE9	156	A6
Middle Path, Har.	86	A1
Middle Rd.		
Middle Rd. E13	115	G2
London Rd.		
Middle Rd. SW16	186	D2
Middle Rd., Barn.	41	H6
Middle Rd., Har.	86	A2
Middle Row W10	108	B4
Middle St. EC1	**19**	**J1**
Middle St., Croy.	201	J3
Surrey St.		
Middle Temple EC4	**19**	**E5**
Middle Temple La.	**19**	**E4**
EC4		
Middle Temple La.	111	G6
EC4		
Middle Way SW16	186	D2
Middle Way, Erith	138	E3
Middle Way, Hayes	102	C4
Middle Way, The,	68	C2
Har.		
Middle Yd. SE1	**28**	**C1**
Middlefield Gdns.,	81	E6
Ilf.		
Middlefielde W13	104	E5
Middleham Gdns.	60	D6
N18		
Middleham Rd. N18	60	D6
Middlesborough Rd.	60	D6
N18		
Middlesex Business	123	G2
Cen., Sthl.		
Middlesex Ct. W4	127	F4
British Gro.		
Middlesex Pas. EC1	**19**	**H2**
Middlesex Rd., Mitch.	186	E5
Middlesex St. E1	**21**	**E2**
Middlesex St. E1	112	B5
Middlesex Wf. E5	95	F2
Middleton Av. E4	61	J4
Middleton Av., Grnf.	104	A2
Middleton Av., Sid.	176	C6
Middleton Bldgs. W1	**17**	**F2**
Middleton Cl. E4	61	J3
Middleton Dr. SE16	133	G2
Middleton Dr., Pnr.	66	A3
Middleton Gdns., Ilf.	81	E6
Middleton Gro. N7	92	E5
Middleton Ms. N7	92/93	E5
Middleton Gro.		
Middleton Rd. E8	94	C7
Middleton Rd. NW11	72	D7
Middleton Rd., Cars.	185	H7
Middleton Rd.,	185	F6
Mord.		
Middleton St. E2	112	E3
Middleton Way	154	D4
SE13		
Middleway NW11	73	E5
Midfield Av., Bexh.	159	J3
Midfield Par., Bexh.	159	J3
Midford Pl. W1	**9**	**G6**
Midholm NW11	72	E4
Midholm, Wem.	88	A1
Midholm Cl. NW11	72	E4
Midholm Rd., Croy.	203	H2
Midhope St. WC1	**10**	**B4**
Midhurst Av. N10	74	A3
Midhurst Av., Croy.	187	G7
Midhurst Hill, Bexh.	159	G6
Midhurst Rd. W13	124	D2
Midland Cres. NW3	91	F6
Finchley Rd.		
Midland Pl. E14	134	C5
Midland Rd. E10	78	C7
Midland Rd. NW1	**9**	**J2**
Midland Rd. NW1	110	D2
Midland Rd. NW2	90	A3
Kara Way		
Midland Ter. NW10	107	E4
Midland Ter. NW2	182	C3
Midlothian Rd. E3	113	J5
Midmoor Rd. SW12	168	C1
Midmoor Rd. SW19	184	A1
Midship Cl. SE16	133	G1
Surrey Water Rd.		
Midship Pt. E14	134	A2
Midstrath Rd. NW10	89	E4
Midsummer Av.,	143	F4
Houns.		
Midway, Sutt.	184	C7
Midwinter Cl., Well.	158	A3
Hook La.		
Midwood Cl. NW2	89	H3
Miers Cl. E6	116	D1
Mighell Av., Ilf.	80	A5
Milan Rd., Sthl.	123	F2
Milborne Gro. SW10	**30**	**D4**
Milborne Gro. SW10	129	F5
Milborne St. E9	95	F6
Milborough Cres.	155	E6
SE12		
Milcote St. SE1	**27**	**G4**
Milcote St. SE1	131	H2
Mildenhall Rd. E5	95	F4
Mildmay Av. N1	94	A6
Mildmay Gro. N. N1	94	A5
Mildmay Gro. S. N1	94	A5
Mildmay Pk. N1	94	A5
Mildmay Pl. N16	94	B5
Boleyn Rd.		
Mildmay Rd. N1	94	B5
Mildmay Rd., Ilf.	98/99	E3
Winston Way		
Mildmay Rd., Rom.	83	J5
Mildmay St. N1	94	A6
Mildred Av., Borwd.	38	A4
Mildred Av., Hayes	121	G4
Mildred Av., Nthlt.	85	H5
Mile End, The, E17	77	G1
Mile End Pl. E1	113	G4
Mile End Rd. E1	113	F5
Mile End Rd. E3	113	F5
Mile Rd., Wall.	200	C1
Miles Dr. SE28	137	H1
Merbury Rd.		
Miles Pl. NW1	**15**	**F1**
Miles Pl., Surb.	181	J4
Villiers Av.		
Miles Rd. N8	75	E3
Miles Rd., Mitch.	185	H3
Miles St. SW8	**34**	**B6**
Miles St. SW8	131	E6
Miles Way N20	57	H2
Milespit Hill NW7	55	H5
Milestone Cl. N9	60	D2
Chichester Rd.		
Milestone Cl.,	199	G6
Sutt.		
Milestone Rd. SE19	170	C6
Milfoil St. W12	107	G7
Milford Cl. SE2	139	E6

Milford Gdns., Croy. 189 G5
Tannery Cl.
Milford Gdns., Edg. 54 A7
Milford Gdns. 87 G5
Wem.
Milford Gro., Sutt. 199 F4
Milford La. WC2 18 D5
Milford La. WC2 111 F7
Milford Ms. SW16 169 F3
Milford Rd. W13 124 E1
Milford Rd., Sthl. 103 G7
Milford Way SE15 152 C1
Sumner Est.
Milk St. E16 136 E1
Milk St. EC2 20 A4
Milk St., Brom. 173 H6
Milk Yd. E1 113 F7
Milkwell Gdns., 63 H7
Wdf.Grn.
Milkwell Yd. SE5 151 J1
Milkwood Rd. SE24 151 H5
Mill Cl., Cars. 200 A2
Mill Cl., West Dr. 120 A3
Mill Cor., Barn. 40 C1
Mill Ct. E10 96 C3
Mill Fm. Cl., Pnr. 66 C2
Mill Fm. Cres., 161 E1
Houns.
Mill Gdns. SE26 171 E4
Mill Grn., Mitch. 186 A7
Mill Grn. Rd., Mitch. 185 J7
Mill Hill SW13 147 H5
Mill Hill Rd.
Mill Hill Circ. NW7 55 F5
Watford Way
Mill Hill Gro. W3 126 B1
Mill Hill Rd.
Mill Hill Rd. SW13 147 G2
Mill Hill Rd. W3 126 B2
Mill La. E4 46 B3
Mill La. NW6 90 C5
Mill La. SE18 136 D5
Mill La., Cars. 199 J4
Mill La., Croy. 201 F3
Mill La. 82 E6
(Chadwell Heath), Rom.
Mill La., Wdf.Grn. 63 F5
Mill La. Trd. Est., 201 F3
Croy.
Mill Mead Rd. N17 76 E3
Mill Pl. E14 113 J6
East India Dock Rd.
Mill Pl., Chis. 192 E1
Mill Pl., Kings.T. 181 J3
Mill Plat, Islw. 144 D2
Mill Plat Av., Islw. 144 D2
Mill Ridge, Edg. 53 J5
Mill Rd. E16 135 H1
Mill Rd. SE13 154 C3
Loampit Vale
Mill Rd. SW19 167 F7
Mill Rd., Erith 139 J7
Mill Rd., Ilf. 98 D3
Mill Rd., Twick. 161 J2
Mill Row N1 112 B1
Mill Shot Cl. SW6 127 J7
Mill St. SE1 29 G4
Mill St. SE1 132 C2
Mill St. W1 17 F5
Mill St. W1 110 C7
Mill St., Kings.T. 181 H3
Mill Vale, Brom. 191 F2
Mill Vw. Cl., Epsom 197 F7
Mill Vw. Gdns., 203 G3
Croy.
Mill Way, Felt. 142 B5
Mill Yd. E1 21 H5
Millais Av. E12 98 D5
Millais Gdns., Edg. 70 A2
Millais Rd. E11 96 C4
Millais Rd., Enf. 44 C5
Millais Rd., N.Mal. 182 E6
Millais Way, Epsom 196 C4
Milland Ct., Borwd. 38 D1
Millard Cl. N16 94 B5
Boleyn Rd.
Millard Ter., Dag. 101 G6
Church Elm La.
Millbank SW1 26 A6
Millbank SW1 130 E3
Millbank Twr. SW1 34 A2
Millbank Twr. SW1 130 E4
Millbank Way SE12 155 G5
Millbourne Rd., Felt. 161 E4
Millbrook Av., Well. 157 G4
Millbrook Gdns. 83 F6
(Chadwell Heath), Rom.
Millbrook Rd. N9 60 E1
Millbrook Rd. SW9 151 H3
Millender Wk. SE16 133 F4
Millennium Cl. E16 115 G6
Russell Rd.
Millennium Dr. E14 134 D4

Millennium Mile 26 C2
SE1
Millennium Mile 111 H7
SE1
Millennium Pl. E2 113 E2
Millennium Pt. E14 134 A2
Millennium Sq. SE1 29 G3
Millennium Way 134 E2
SE10
Miller Cl., Mitch. 185 J7
Miller Cl., Pnr. 66 C2
Miller Rd. SW19 167 G6
Miller Rd., Croy. 201 F1
Miller St. NW1 9 F1
Miller St. NW1 110 C2
Miller Wk. SE1 27 F2
Miller Wk. SE1 131 G1
Miller's Av. E8 94 C5
Millers Cl. NW7 55 G4
Millers Ct. W4 127 F5
Chiswick Mall
Millers Grn. Cl., Enf. 43 H3
Millers Meadow Cl. 155 F5
SE3
Meadowcourt Rd.
Miller's Ter. E8 94 C5
Millers Way W6 127 J2
Millet Rd., Grnf. 103 H3
Millfield Av. E17 77 H1
Millfield La. N6 91 J2
Millfield Pl. N6 92 A2
Millfield Rd., Edg. 70 C2
Millfield Rd., Houns. 161 E1
Millfields Est. E5 95 G3
Denton Way
Millfields Rd. E5 95 F4
Millgrove St. SW11 150 A2
Millharbour E14 134 B3
Millhaven Cl., Rom. 82 B6
Millhouse Pl. SE27 169 H4
Millicent Rd. E10 95 J1
Milligan St. E14 113 J7
Milliners Ct., Loug. 48 D2
The Cft.
Milling Rd., Edg. 54 D7
Millington Rd., 121 H3
Hayes
Millman Ms. WC1 10 C6
Millman Ms. WC1 111 F4
Millman Pl. WC1 111 F4
Millman St.
Millman St. WC1 10 C6
Millman St. WC1 111 F4
Millmark Gro. SE14 153 H2
Millmarsh La., Enf. 45 J2
Millpond Est. 132/133 E2
SE16
West La.
Mills Cl. EC2 12 E4
Mills Gro. E14 114 C5
Dewberry St.
Mills Gro. NW4 72 A3
Mills Row W4 126 D4
Millside, Cars. 199 J2
Millside Pl., Islw. 144 E2
Millsmead Way, 48 C2
Loug.
Millson Cl. N20 57 G2
Millstream Cl. N13 59 G5
Millstream Rd. SE1 29 F4
Millwall Dock Rd. 134 A3
E14
Millway NW7 54 E5
Millway Gdns., Nthlt. 85 F6
Millwell Cres., Chig. 65 G5
Millwood Rd., 143 H5
Houns.
Millwood St. W10 108 B5
St. Charles Sq.
Milman Cl., Pnr. 66 D3
Milman Rd. NW6 108 B2
Milman's St. SW10 31 E6
Milman's St. SW10 129 G6
Milmead Ind. Cen. 76 C2
N17
Milne Feild, Pnr. 51 G7
Milne Gdns. SE9 156 B5
Milner Dr., Twick. 144 A7
Milner Pl. N1 111 G1
Milner Pl., Cars. 200 A4
High St.
Milner Rd. E15 114 E3
Milner Rd. SW19 184 E1
Milner Rd., Dag. 100 C2
Milner Rd., Kings.T. 181 G3
Milner Rd., Mord. 185 G5
Milner Rd., Th.Hth. 188 A3
Milner Sq. N1 93 H7
Milner St. SW3 31 J1
Milner St. SW3 129 J4
Milner Wk. SE9 175 G1
Milnthorpe Rd. W4 126 D6
Milo Rd. SE22 152 C6

Milroy Wk. SE1 27 G1
Milson Rd. W14 128 B3
Milton Av. E6 98 A7
Milton Av. N6 74 C7
Milton Av. NW9 70 C3
Milton Av. NW10 106 C1
Milton Av., Barn. 40 C5
Milton Av., Croy. 188 A7
Milton Av., Sutt. 199 G3
Milton Cl. N2 73 F5
Milton Cl. SE1 37 F2
Milton Cl. SE1 132 C4
Milton Cl., Hayes 102 A6
Milton Cl., Sutt. 199 G3
Milton Ct. EC2 20 B1
Milton Ct. Rd. SE14 133 H6
Milton Cres., Ilf. 81 F7
Milton Dr., Borwd. 38 B5
Milton Gdn. Est. N16 94 B4
Milton Gro.
Milton Gro. N11 58 C5
Milton Gro. N16 94 A4
Milton Pk. N6 74 C7
Milton Pl. N7 93 G5
George's Rd.
Milton Rd. E17 78 A4
Milton Rd. N6 74 C7
Milton Rd. N15 75 H4
Milton Rd. NW7 55 G5
Milton Rd. NW9 71 G7
West Hendon Bdy.
Milton Rd. SE24 151 H6
Milton Rd. SW14 146 D3
Milton Rd. SW19 167 F6
Milton Rd. W3 126 D1
Milton Rd. W7 104 C7
Milton Rd., Belv. 139 G4
Milton Rd., Croy. 202 A1
Milton Rd., Hmptn. 161 G7
Milton Rd., Har. 68 B4
Milton Rd., Mitch. 168 A7
Milton Rd., Sutt. 198 D3
Milton Rd., Wall. 200 C6
Milton Rd., Well. 157 J1
Milton St. EC2 20 B1
Milton St. EC2 112 A5
Milton Way 120 C4
West Dr.
Milverton Gdns., Ilf. 99 J2
Milverton Rd. NW6 89 J7
Milverton St. SE11 35 F4
Milverton St. SE11 131 G5
Milverton Way SE9 174 D4
Milward St. E1 112/113 E5
Stepney Way
Milward Wk. SE18 136 D6
Spearman St.
Mimosa Rd., Hayes 102 C5
Mimosa St. SW6 148 C1
Mina Rd. SE17 37 E4
Mina Rd. SE17 132 B5
Mina Rd. SW19 184 D1
Minard Rd. SE6 154 E7
Minchenden Cres. 58 C3
N14
Mincing La. EC3 20 D5
Mincing La. EC3 112 B7
Minden Rd. SE20 188 E1
Minden Rd., Sutt. 198 C2
Minehead Rd. SW16 169 F5
Minehead Rd., Har. 85 G3
Minera Ms. SW1 32 C1
Minera Ms. SW1 130 A4
Mineral St. SE18 137 H4
Minerva Cl. SW9 131 G7
Minerva Cl., Sid. 175 H3
Minerva Rd. E4 62 B7
Minerva Rd. NW10 106 C3
Minerva Rd., 181 J2
Kings.T.
Minerva St. E2 112 E2
Minet Av. NW10 106 E2
Minet Dr., Hayes 122 A1
Minet Gdns. NW10 106 E2
Minet Gdns., Hayes 122 A1
Minet Rd. SW9 151 H2
Minford Gdns. W14 128 A2
Ming St. E14 114 A7
Mingard Wk. N7 93 F2
Hornsey Rd.
Ministry Way SE9 174 C2
Miniver Pl. EC4 111 J7
Garlick Hill
Mink Ct., Houns. 142 C3
Minniedale, Surb. 181 J5
Minnow St. SE17 132 B4
East St.
Minnow Wk. SE17 36 E2
Minories EC3 21 F5
Minories EC3 112 C6
Minshull Pl., Beck. 172 A7
Minshull St. SW8 150 D1
Wandsworth Rd.
Minson Rd. E9 113 G1

Minstead Gdns. 147 F7
SW15
Minstead Way, 182 E6
N.Mal.
Minster Av., Sutt. 198 D2
Leafield Rd.
Minster Ct. EC3 112 A7
Mincing La.
Minster Dr., Croy. 202 B4
Minster Gdns., 179 F5
W.Mol.
Molesey Av.
Minster Pavement 112 A7
EC3
Mincing La.
Minster Rd. NW2 90 B5
Minster Rd., Brom. 173 H7
Minster Wk. N8 74/75 E4
Lightfoot Rd.
Minstrel Gdns., Surb. 181 J4
Mint Business Pk. 115 G3
E16
Mint Rd., Wall. 200 B4
Mint St. SE1 27 J3
Mint Wk., Croy. 201 J3
High St.
Mintern Cl. N13 59 H3
Mintern St. N1 12 C1
Mintern St. N1 112 A2
Minterne Av., Sthl. 123 G4
Minterne Rd., Har. 69 J5
Minterne Waye, 102 C6
Hayes
Minton Ms. NW6 90/91 E6
Lymington Rd.
Mirabel Rd. SW6 128 C7
Miranda Cl. E1 113 F5
Sidney St.
Miranda Ct. W3 105 J6
Queens Dr.
Miranda Rd. N19 92 C1
Mirfield St. SE7 136 A4
Miriam Rd. SE18 137 H5
Mirravale Trd. Est., 83 F7
Dag.
Mirren Cl., Har. 85 F4
Mirror Path SE9 173 J3
Lambscroft Av.
Missenden Gdns., 185 F6
Mord.
Mission Gro. E17 77 H5
Mission Pl. SE15 152 D1
Mission Sq., Brent. 125 H6
Mistletoe Cl., Croy. 203 G1
Marigold Way
Mitali Pas. E1 21 H4
Mitcham Gdn. 186 A5
Village, Mitch.
Mitcham Ind. Est., 186 A1
Mitch.
Mitcham La. SW16 168 C6
Mitcham Pk., Mitch. 185 J4
Mitcham Rd. E6 116 B3
Mitcham Rd. SW17 167 J5
Mitcham Rd., Croy. 186 E6
Mitcham Rd., Ilf. 81 J7
Mitchell Cl. SE2 138 C4
Mitchell Cl., Belv. 139 J3
Mitchell Rd. N13 59 H5
Mitchell Rd., Orp. 207 J4
Mitchell St. EC1 11 J5
Mitchell St. EC1 111 J4
Mitchell Wk. E6 116 B5
Mitchell Way NW10 88 C6
Mitchell Way, Brom. 191 G1
Mitchellbrook Way 88 D6
NW10
Mitchison Rd. N1 94 A6
Mitchley Rd. N17 76 D3
Mitford Cl., Chess. 195 F6
Merritt Gdns.
Mitford Rd. N19 93 E2
Mitre, The E14 113 J7
Three Colt St.
Mitre Av. E17 77 J3
Greenleaf Rd.
Mitre Cl., Brom. 191 F2
Beckenham La.
Mitre Cl., Sutt. 199 F7
Mitre Ct. EC2 20 A3
Mitre Ct. EC4 19 F4
Mitre Rd. E15 115 E2
Mitre Rd. SE1 27 F3
Mitre Sq. EC3 21 E4
Mitre St. EC3 21 E4
Mitre St. EC3 112 B6
Mitre Way W10 107 H4
Moat Cl., Orp. 207 J6
Moat Cres. N3 72 E3

Name	Page	Grid
Moat Cft., Well.	158	C3
Moat Dr. E13	115	J2
Boundary Rd.		
Moat Dr., Har.	67	J4
Moat Fm. Rd., Nthlt.	85	F6
Moat Pl. SW9	151	F3
Moat Pl. W3	106	B6
Moatside, Enf.	45	G4
Moatside, Felt.	160	C4
Moberley Rd. SW4	150	D7
Modbury Gdns. NW5	92	A6
Queens Cres.		
Modder Pl. SW15	148	A4
Model Cotts. SW14	146	C4
Upper Richmond Rd. W.		
Model Fm. Cl. SE9	174	B3
Modling Ho. E2	113	G2
Moelwyn Hughes Ct. N7	92	D5
Hilldrop Cres.		
Moelyn Ms., Har.	68	D5
Moffat Rd. N13	59	E6
Moffat Rd. SW17	167	H4
Moffat Rd., Th.Hth.	187	J2
Mogden La., Islw.	144	B5
Mohmmad Khan Rd. E11	97	F1
Harvey Rd.		
Moira Cl. N17	76	B2
Moira Rd. SE9	156	C4
Moland Mead SE16	133	G5
Crane Mead		
Molasses Row SW11	149	F3
Cinnamon Row		
Mole Abbey Gdns. W.Mol.	179	G3
New Rd.		
Mole Ct., Epsom	196	C4
Molember Ct., E.Mol.	180	B5
Molember Rd., E.Mol.	180	B5
Molescroft SE9	175	F3
Molesey Av., W.Mol.	179	F4
Molesey Dr., Sutt.	198	B2
Molesey Pk. Av., W.Mol.	179	H5
Molesey Pk. Cl., E.Mol.	179	J5
Molesey Pk. Rd., E.Mol.	180	A5
Molesey Pk. Rd., W.Mol.	179	H5
Molesey Rd., W.Mol.	179	E5
Molesford Rd. SW6	148	D1
Molesham Cl., W.Mol.	179	H3
Molesham Way, W.Mol.	179	H3
Molesworth St. SE13	154	C3
Molineaux Pl., Tedd.	162	D5
Mollison Av., Enf.	45	H2
Mollison Dr., Wall.	201	E6
Mollison Way, Edg.	70	A2
Molly Huggins Cl. SW12	150	C7
Molyneux Dr. SW17	168	B4
Molyneux St. W1	15	H2
Molyneux St. W1	109	H5
Mona Rd. SE15	153	F2
Mona St. E16	115	F5
Monarch Cl., Felt.	141	H7
Monarch Cl., W.Wick.	205	F4
Monarch Dr. E16	116	A5
Monarch Ms. E17	78	B5
Monarch Ms. SW16	169	G5
Monarch Pl., Buck.H.	63	J2
Monarch Rd., Belv.	139	G3
Monastery Gdns., Enf.	44	A2
Monaveen Gdns., W.Mol.	179	G3
Monck St. SW1	25	J6
Monck St. SW1	130	D3
Monclar Rd. SE5	152	A4
Moncorvo Cl. SW7	23	G4
Moncrieff Cl. E6	116	B6
Linton Gdns.		
Moncrieff Pl. SE15	152	D2
Rye La.		
Moncrieff St. SE15	152	D2
Mondial Way, Hayes	121	F7
Monega Rd. E7	97	J6
Monega Rd. E12	98	A6
Money La., West Dr.	120	A3
Monier Rd. E3	96	A7
Monivea Rd., Beck.	171	J7
Monk Dr. E16	115	G6
Monk Pas. E16	115	G7
Monk Dr.		
Monk St. SE18	136	D4
Monkchester Cl., Loug.	48	D1
Monkfrith Av. N14	42	B6
Monkfrith Cl. N14	42	B7
Monkfrith Way N14	42	A7
Monkhams Av., Wdf.Grn.	63	G5
Monkhams Dr., Wdf.Grn.	63	H4
Monkhams La., Buck.H.	63	H3
Monkhams La., Wdf.Grn.	63	G5
Monkleigh Rd., Mord.	184	B3
Monks Av., Barn.	41	F6
Monks Av., W.Mol.	179	F5
Monks Cl. SE2	138	D4
Monks Cl., Enf.	43	J2
Monks Cl., Har.	85	H2
Monks Cl., Ruis.	84	D4
Monks Dr. W3	106	A5
Monks Orchard Rd., Beck.	204	A1
Monks Pk., Wem.	88	C6
Monks Pk. Gdns. Wem.	88	B6
Monks Rd., Enf.	43	J2
Monks Way NW11	72	C4
Hurstwood Rd.		
Monks Way, Beck.	190	A5
Monks Way, Orp.	207	F1
Monks Way, West Dr.	120	B6
Harmondsworth La.		
Monksdene Gdns., Sutt.	199	E3
Monksgrove, Loug.	48	D5
Monksmead, Borwd.	38	C4
Monkswell Ct. N10	74	A1
Pembroke Rd.		
Monkswood Gdns., Borwd.	38	D4
Monkswood Gdns., Ilf.	80	D3
Monkton Rd., Well.	157	J2
Monkton St. SE11	35	F1
Monkton St. SE11	131	G4
Monkville Av. NW11	72	C4
Monkwell Sq. EC2	20	A2
Monmouth Av. E18	79	H3
Monmouth Av., Kings.T.	163	F7
Monmouth Cl. W4	126	D3
Beaumont Rd.		
Monmouth Cl., Mitch.	186/187	E4
Recreation Way		
Monmouth Cl., Well.	158	A4
Monmouth Gro., Brent.	125	H4
Sterling Pl.		
Monmouth Pl. W2	108	D6
Monmouth Rd.		
Monmouth Rd. E6	116	C3
Monmouth Rd. N9	60	E2
Monmouth Rd. W2	108	E6
Monmouth Rd., Dag.	101	F5
Monmouth Rd., Hayes	121	H4
Monmouth St. WC2	18	A4
Monmouth St. WC2	110	E7
Monnery Rd. N19	92	C3
Monnow Rd. SE1	37	H2
Monnow Rd. SE1	132	D4
Mono La., Felt.	160	B2
Monoux Gro. E17	78	A1
Monro Gdns., Har.	52	B7
Monroe Cres., Enf.	44	E1
Monroe Dr. SW14	146	B5
Mons Way, Brom.	192	B6
Monsal Ct. E5	95	G4
Redwald Rd.		
Monsell Rd. N4	93	H3
Monson Rd. NW10	107	G2
Monson Rd. SE14	133	G7
Montacute Rd. SE6	153	J7
Montacute Rd., Mord.	185	G6
Montagu Cres. N18	61	E4
Montagu Gdns. N18	61	E4
Montagu Gdns., Wall.	200	C4
Montagu Mans. W1	16	A1
Montagu Ms. N. W1	16	A2
Montagu Ms. S. W1	16	A3
Montagu Ms. W. W1	16	A3
Montagu Pl. W1	15	J2
Montagu Pl. W1	109	J5
Montagu Rd. N9	61	F3
Montagu Rd. N18	61	E5
Montagu Rd. NW4	71	G6
Montagu Rd. Ind. Est. N18	61	F4
Montagu Row W1	16	A2
Montagu Sq. W1	16	A2
Montagu Sq. W1	109	J5
Montagu St. W1	16	A3
Montagu St. W1	109	J6
Montague Av. SE4	153	J4
Montague Av. W7	124	C1
Montague Cl. SE1	28	B1
Montague Cl. SE1	132	A1
Montague Cl., Walt.	178	A7
Montague Gdns. W3	106	A7
Montague Pl. WC1	17	J1
Montague Pl. WC1	110	D5
Montague Rd. E8	94	D5
Montague Rd. E11	97	F2
Montague Rd. N8	75	F5
Montague Rd. N15	76	D4
Montague Rd. SW19	166	E7
Montague Rd. W7	124	C1
Montague Rd. W13	105	E6
Montague Rd., Croy.	201	H1
Montague Rd., Houns.	143	H3
Montague Rd., Rich.	145	H6
Montague Rd., Sthl.	122	E4
Montague Sq. SE15	133	F7
Clifton Way		
Montague St. EC1	19	J2
Montague St. EC1	111	J5
Montague St. WC1	18	A1
Montague St. WC1	110	E5
Montague Waye, Sthl.	122	E3
Montalt Rd., Wdf.Grn.	63	F5
Montana Gdns. SE26	171	J4
Worsley Br. Rd.		
Montana Gdns., Sutt.	199	F5
Lind Rd.		
Montana Rd. SW17	168	A4
Montana Rd. SW20	183	J1
Montbelle Rd. SE9	174	E3
Montcalm Cl., Brom.	191	G6
Montcalm Cl., Hayes	102	B3
Ayles Rd.		
Montcalm Rd. SE7	136	A7
Montclare St. E2	13	F4
Monteagle Av., Bark.	99	F6
Monteagle Way E5	94	D3
Rendlesham Rd.		
Monteagle Way SE15	153	E3
Montefiore St. SW8	150	B2
Montego Cl. SE24	151	G4
Railton Rd.		
Monteith Rd. E3	113	J1
Montem Rd. SE23	153	J7
Montem Rd., N.Mal.	182	E4
Montem St. N4	93	F1
Thorpedale Rd.		
Montenotte Rd. N8	74	C5
Monterey Cl., Bex.	177	J2
Montesole Ct., Pnr.	66	C2
Montford Pl. SE11	34	E4
Montford Pl. SE11	131	G5
Montford Rd., Sun.	178	A4
Montfort Gdns., Ilf.	65	F6
Montfort Pl. SW19	166	A1
Montgolfier Wk., Nthlt.	102/103	E3
Jetstar Way		
Montgomery Av., Esher	194	B3
Montgomery Cl., Mitch.	187	E4
Montgomery Cl., Sid.	157	J6
Montgomery Rd. W4	126	C4
Montgomery Rd., Edg.	53	J6
Montholme Rd. SW11	149	J6
Monthope Rd. E1	21	H2
Montolieu Gdns. SW15	147	H5
Montpelier Av. W5	105	F5
Montpelier Av., Bex.	158	D7
Montpelier Gdns. E6	116	A3
Montpelier Gdns., Rom.	82	C7
Montpelier Gro. NW5	92	C5
Montpelier Ms. SW7	23	H5
Montpelier Pl. E1	113	F6
Montpelier Pl. SW7	23	H5
Montpelier Ri. NW11	72	B7
Montpelier Ri., Wem.	87	G1
Montpelier Rd. N3	73	F1
Montpelier Rd. SE15	153	E1
Montpelier Rd. W5	105	G5
Montpelier Rd., Sutt.	199	F4
Montpelier Row SE3	155	F2
Montpelier Row, Twick.	145	F7
Montpelier Sq. SW7	23	H4
Montpelier Sq. SW7	129	H2
Montpelier St. SW7	23	H4
Montpelier St. SW7	129	H2
Montpelier Ter. SW7	23	H4
Montpelier Vale SE3	155	F2
Montpelier Wk. SW7	23	H5
Montpelier Wk. SW7	129	H3
Montpelier Way NW11	72	B7
Montrave Rd. SE20	171	F6
Montreal Pl. WC2	18	C5
Montreal Rd., Ilf.	81	F7
Montrell Rd. SW2	169	E1
Montrose Av. NW6	108	B2
Montrose Av., Edg.	70	C2
Montrose Av., Sid.	158	A7
Montrose Av., Twick.	143	H7
Montrose Av., Well.	157	H3
Montrose Cl., Well.	157	J3
Montrose Cl., Wdf.Grn.	63	G4
Montrose Ct. SW7	23	H4
Montrose Ct. SW7	129	G2
Montrose Cres. N12	57	F6
Montrose Cres., Wem.	87	H6
Montrose Gdns., Mitch.	185	J3
Montrose Gdns., Sutt.	199	E2
Montrose Pl. SW1	24	C4
Montrose Pl. SW1	130	A2
Montrose Rd., Felt.	141	G6
Montrose Rd., Har.	68	B2
Montrose Way SE23	171	G1
Montserrat Av. Wdf.Grn.	62	D7
Montserrat Cl. SE19	170	A5
Montserrat Rd. SW15	148	B4
Monument Gdns. SE13	154	C5
Monument St. EC3	20	C5
Monument St. EC3	112	A7
Monument Way N17	76	C3
Monza St. E1	113	F7
Moodkee St. SE16	133	F3
Moody Rd. SE15	152	C1
Moody St. E1	113	G3
Moon La., Barn.	40	C3
Moon St. N1	111	H1
Moor La. EC2	20	B2
Moor La. EC2	112	A5
Moor La., Chess.	195	H4
Moor Mead Rd., Twick.	144	D6
Moor Pk. Gdns., Kings.T.	165	E7
Moor Pl. EC2	20	B2
Moor St. W1	17	J4
Moorcroft Gdns., Brom.	192	B5
Southborough Rd.		
Moorcroft Rd. SW16	168	E3
Moorcroft Way, Pnr.	66	E5
Moordown SE18	156	D1
Moore Cl. SW14	146	C3
Little St. Leonards		
Moore Cl., Mitch.	186	B2
Moore Cres., Dag.	118	B1
Moore Pk. Rd. SW6	128	E7
Moore Rd. SE19	169	J6
Moore St. SW3	31	J1
Moore St. SW3	129	J4
Moore Wk. E7	97	G4
Stracey Rd.		
Moore Way SE22	170	D1
Lordship La.		
Moorefield Rd. N17	76	C2
Moorehead Way SE3	155	H3
Moreland Rd., Brom.	173	F7
Moorey Cl. E15	115	F1
Stephen's Rd.		
Moorfield Av. W5	105	G4
Moorfield Rd., Chess.	195	H5
Moorfield Rd., Enf.	45	F1
Moorfields EC2	20	B2
Moorfields EC2	112	A5
Moorfields Highwalk EC2	112	A5
Fore St.		
Moorgate EC2	20	B3
Moorgate EC2	112	A6
Moorgate Pl. EC2	20	B3
Moorhouse Rd. W2	108	D6
Moorhouse Rd., Har.	69	G3
Moorings SE28	118	B7
Moorland Cl., Twick.	143	G7
Telford Rd.		
Moorland Rd. SW9	151	H4
Moorlands Av. NW7	55	H6
Moorlands Est. SW9	151	G4
Moormead Dr., Epsom	197	E5
Moorside Rd., Brom.	173	E3

Moortown Rd., Wat.	50	C4
Moot Ct. NW9	70	A5
Mora Rd. NW2	89	J4
Mora St. EC1	**12**	**A4**
Mora St. EC1	111	J3
Morant Pl. N22	75	F1
Commerce Rd.		
Morant St. E14	114	A7
Morat St. SW9	151	F1
Moravian Pl. SW10	**31**	**F6**
Moravian St. E2	113	F3
Moray Av., Hayes	121	J1
Moray Cl., Edg.	54	B2
Pentland Av.		
Moray Ms. N7	93	F2
Durham Rd.		
Moray Rd. N4	93	F2
Mordaunt Gdns.,	100	E7
Dag.		
Mordaunt Ho. NW10	106	D1
Mordaunt Rd. NW10	106	D1
Mordaunt St. SW9	151	F3
Morden Cl. SE13	154	C2
Morden Ct., Mord.	184	E4
Morden Gdns., Grnf.	86	C5
Morden Gdns.,	185	G4
Mitch.		
Morden Hall Rd.,	185	E3
Mord.		
Morden Hill SE13	154	C2
Morden La. SE13	154	C1
Morden Rd. SE3	155	G2
Morden Rd. SW19	185	E1
Morden Rd., Mitch.	185	F4
Morden Rd., Rom.	83	E7
Morden Rd. Ms. SE3	155	G2
Morden St. SE13	154	B1
Morden Way, Sutt.	184	D7
Morden Wf. Rd.	134	E3
SE10		
Mordon Rd., Ilf.	81	J7
Mordred Rd. SE6	172	E2
More Cl. E16	115	F6
More Cl. W14	128	B4
Morecambe Cl. E1	113	G5
Morecambe Gdns.,	53	G4
Stan.		
Morecambe St. SE17	**36**	**A2**
Morecambe St. SE17	131	J4
Morecambe Ter. N18	60	A4
Morecoombe Cl.,	164	B7
Kings.T.		
Moree Way N18	60	D4
Moreland St. EC1	**11**	**H3**
Moreland St. EC1	111	H3
Moreland Way E4	62	B3
Morell Cl., Barn.	41	F3
Galdana Av.		
Morella Rd. SW12	149	J7
Moremead Rd. SE6	171	J4
Morena St. SE6	154	B7
Moresby Av., Surb.	182	B7
Moresby Rd. E5	94	E1
Moresby Wk. SW8	150	C2
Moreton Av., Islw.	144	B1
Moreton Cl. E5	95	F2
Moreton Cl. N15	76	A6
Moreton Cl. NW7	55	J6
Moreton Gdns.,	64	B5
Wdf.Grn.		
Moreton Pl. SW1	**33**	**G3**
Moreton Pl. SW1	130	C5
Moreton Rd. N15	76	A6
Moreton Rd., S.Croy.	202	A5
Moreton Rd., Wor.Pk.	197	G2
Moreton St. SW1	**33**	**G3**
Moreton St. SW1	130	D5
Moreton Ter. SW1	**33**	**G3**
Moreton Ter. SW1	130	C5
Moreton Ter. Ms. N.	**33**	**G3**
SW1		
Moreton Ter. Ms. S.	**33**	**G3**
SW1		
Moreton Twr. W3	126	B1
Morford Cl., Ruis.	66	B7
Morford Way, Ruis.	66	B7
Morgan Av. E17	78	D4
Morgan Cl., Dag.	101	G7
Morgan Rd. N7	93	G5
Morgan Rd. W10	108	C5
Morgan Rd., Brom.	173	G7
Morgan St. E3	113	H3
Morgan St. E16	115	F5
Morgan Way,	64	B6
Wdf.Grn.		
Morgans La. SE1	**28**	**D2**
Morgans La. SE1	132	B1
Moriatry Cl. N7	92	E4
Morie St. SW18	149	E5
Morieux Rd. E10	95	J1
Moring Rd. SW17	168	A4
Morkyns Wk. SE21	170	B3
Morland Av., Croy.	202	B1
Morland Cl. NW11	91	E1
Morland Cl., Hmptn.	161	F5
Morland Cl., Mitch.	185	H3
Morland Gdns.	88	D7
NW10		
Morland Gdns., Sthl.	123	H1
Morland Ms. N1	93	G7
Lofting Rd.		
Morland Rd. E17	77	G5
Morland Rd. SE20	171	G6
Morland Rd., Croy.	202	B1
Morland Rd., Dag.	101	G7
Morland Rd., Har.	69	H5
Morland Rd., Ilf.	98	E2
Morland Rd., Sutt.	199	F5
Morley Av. E4	62	D7
Morley Av. N18	60	D4
Morley Av. N22	75	G2
Morley Cl., Orp.	207	E2
Morley Cres., Edg.	54	C2
Morley Cres., Ruis.	84	C2
Morley Cres. E., Stan.	69	F2
Morley Cres. W.,	69	F2
Stan.		
Morley Rd. E10	96	C1
Morley Rd. E15	115	F2
Morley Rd. SE13	154	C4
Morley Rd., Bark.	117	G1
Morley Rd., Chis.	193	F1
Morley Rd., Rom.	82	E5
Morley Rd., Sutt.	198	C1
Morley Rd., Twick.	145	G6
Morley St. SE1	**27**	**F5**
Morley St. SE1	131	G2
Morna Rd. SE5	151	J2
Morning La. E9	95	F6
Morningside Rd.,	197	H2
Wor.Pk.		
Mornington Av. W14	128	C4
Mornington Av.,	191	J3
Brom.		
Mornington Av., Ilf.	80	D7
Mornington Cl.,	63	G4
Wdf.Grn.		
Mornington Ct., Bex.	177	J1
Mornington Cres.	**9**	**F1**
NW1		
Mornington Cres.	110	C2
NW1		
Mornington Cres.,	142	B1
Houns.		
Mornington Gro. E3	114	A3
Mornington Ms. SE5	151	J1
Mornington Pl. NW1	**9**	**E1**
Mornington Pl. NW1	8	E4
Mornington Rd. E11	97	F1
Mornington Rd. SE8	133	J7
Mornington Rd.,	103	H5
Grnf.		
Mornington Rd.,	49	F3
Loug.		
Mornington Rd.,	63	F4
Wdf.Grn.		
Mornington St. NW1	**8**	**E1**
Mornington St. NW1	110	B2
Mornington Ter. NW1	110	B1
Mornington Wk.,	163	G4
Rich.		
Morocco St. SE1	**28**	**D4**
Morocco St. SE1	132	B2
Morpeth Gro. E9	113	G1
Morpeth Rd. E9	113	F1
Morpeth St. E2	113	G3
Morpeth Ter. SW1	**25**	**F6**
Morpeth Ter. SW1	130	C3
Morpeth Wk. N17	60/61	E7
West Rd.		
Morrab Gdns., Ilf.	99	J3
Morris Av. E12	98	C5
Morris Cl., Croy.	189	H6
Morris Cl., Orp.	207	H3
Morris Ct. E4	62	B3
Flaxen Rd.		
Morris Gdns. SW18	148	D7
Morris Pl. N4	93	G2
Morris Rd. E14	114	B5
Morris Rd. E15	96	E4
Morris Rd., Dag.	101	F2
Morris Rd., Islw.	144	C3
Morris St. E1	113	E6
Morrish Rd. SW2	151	E7
Morrison Av. N17	76	B3
Morrison Rd., Bark.	118	E2
Morrison Rd., Hayes	102	B3
Morrison St. SW11	150	A3
Morriston Cl., Wat.	50	C5
Morse Cl. E13	115	G3
Morshead Rd. W9	108	D3
Morson Rd., Enf.	45	H6
Morston Gdns. SE9	174	C4
Morten Cl. SW4	150	D6
Morteyne Rd. N17	76	A1
Mortgramit Sq. SE18	136	D3
Powis St.		
Mortham St. E15	114	E1
Mortimer Cl. NW2	90	C3
Mortimer Cl. SW16	168	D2
Mortimer Cres. NW6	108	E1
Mortimer Cres.,	196	D3
Wor.Pk.		
Mortimer Dr., Enf.	44	B5
Mortimer Est. NW6	108	E1
Mortimer Mkt. WC1	**9**	**G6**
Mortimer Pl. NW6	108	E1
Mortimer Rd. E6	116	C3
Mortimer Rd. N1	94	B7
Mortimer Rd. NW10	107	J3
Mortimer Rd. W13	105	F6
Mortimer Rd., Mitch.	185	J1
Mortimer Sq. W11	108	A7
St. Anns Rd.		
Mortimer St. W1	**17**	**F2**
Mortimer St. W1	110	C6
Mortimer Ter. NW5	92	B4
Gordon Ho. Rd.		
Mortlake Cl.,	200/201	E3
Croy.		
Richmond Rd.		
Mortlake Dr., Mitch.	185	H1
Mortlake High St.	146	D3
SW14		
Mortlake Rd. E16	115	H6
Mortlake Rd., Ilf.	99	F4
Mortlake Rd., Rich.	126	A7
Mortlake Ter., Rich.	126	A7
Kew Rd.		
Mortlock Cl.	152/153	E1
SE15		
Cossall Wk.		
Morton Cres. N14	58	D4
Morton Gdns., Wall.	200	C5
Morton Ms. SW5	**30**	**A2**
Morton Pl. SE1	**26**	**E6**
Morton Rd. E15	97	F3
Morton Rd. N1	93	J7
Morton Rd., Mord.	185	G5
Morton Way N14	58	C3
Morval Rd. SW2	151	G5
Morvale Cl., Belv.	139	F4
Morven Rd. SW17	167	J3
Morville St. E3	114	A2
Morwell St. WC1	**17**	**J2**
Moscow Pl. W2	**14**	**A5**
Moscow Pl. W2	108	D7
Moscow Rd. W2	14	A5
Moselle Av. N22	75	G2
Moselle Cl. N8	75	F3
Miles Rd.		
Moselle Ho. N17	60	C7
William St.		
Moselle Pl. N17	60	C7
High Rd.		
Moselle St. N17	60	C7
Moss Cl. E1	**21**	**J1**
Moss Cl., Pnr.	67	F2
Moss Gdns., Felt.	160	A2
Moss Gdns., S.Croy.	203	G7
Warren Av.		
Moss Hall Cres. N12	57	E6
Moss Hall Gro. N12	56	E6
Moss La., Pnr.	67	F3
Moss Rd., Dag.	101	G7
Mossborough Cl.	57	E6
N12		
Mossbury Rd. SW11	149	H3
Mossdown Cl., Belv.	139	G4
Mossford Ct., Ilf.	81	E3
Mossford Grn., Ilf.	81	E3
Mossford La., Ilf.	81	E2
Mossford St. E3	113	J4
Mossington Gdns.	133	F4
SE16		
Abbeyfield Rd.		
Mosslea Rd. SE20	171	F6
Mosslea Rd., Brom.	192	A5
Mosslea Rd., Orp.	207	F3
Mossop St. SW3	**31**	**H1**
Mossop St. SW3	129	H4
Mossville Gdns.,	184	C3
Mord.		
Moston Cl., Hayes	121	J5
Fuller Way		
Mostyn Av., Wem.	87	J5
Mostyn Gdns.	108	A2
NW10		
Mostyn Gro. E3	113	J2
Mostyn Rd. SW9	151	G1
Mostyn Rd. SW19	184	C1
Mostyn Rd., Edg.	54	D7
Mosul Way, Brom.	192	B6
Motcomb St. SW1	**24**	**A5**
Motcomb St. SW1	130	A3
Mothers' Sq. E5	95	E4
Motley Av. EC2	112	B4
Scrutton St.		
Motley St. SW8	150	C2
St. Rule St.		
Motspur Pk., N.Mal.	183	F6
Mott St., Loug.	47	F1
Mottingham Gdns.	174	A1
SE9		
Mottingham La. SE9	173	J1
Mottingham La.	173	J1
SE12		
Mottingham Rd. N9	45	G6
Mottingham Rd.	174	B2
SE9		
Mottisfont Rd. SE2	138	A3
Moulins Rd. E9	113	F1
Moulton Av., Houns.	143	E2
Mound, The SE9	174	D3
Moundfield Rd. N16	76	D6
Mount, The N20	57	F2
Mount, The NW3	91	F4
Heath St.		
Mount, The W3	126	C1
High St.		
Mount, The N.Mal.	183	F3
Mount, The, Wem.	88	B2
Mount, The, Wor.Pk.	197	H4
Mount Adon Pk.	152	D7
SE22		
Mount Angelus Rd.	147	F7
SW15		
Mount Ararat Rd.,	145	H5
Rich.		
Mount Ash Rd. SE26	170	E3
Mount Av. E4	62	A3
Mount Av. W5	105	G5
Mount Av., Sthl.	103	G6
Mount Cl. W5	105	F5
Mount Cl., Barn.	42	A4
Mount Cl., Brom.	192	B1
Mount Cor., Felt.	160	D2
Mount Cl. SW15	148	B3
Weimar St.		
Mount Ct., W.Wick.	204	E2
Mount Culver Av.,	176	D6
Sid.		
Mount Dr., Bexh.	158	E5
Mount Dr., Har.	67	F5
Mount Dr., Wem.	88	C2
Mount Echo Av. E4	62	B2
Mount Echo Dr. E4	62	B1
Mount Ephraim La.	168	D3
SW16		
Mount Ephraim Rd.	168	D3
SW16		
Mount Est., The E5	94/95	E2
Mount Pleasant La.		
Mount Gdns. SE26	170	E3
Mount Gro., Edg.	54	C3
Mount Ms., Hmptn.	179	H1
Mount Mills EC1	**11**	**H4**
Mount Nod Rd.	169	F3
SW16		
Mount Pk. Av., Har.	86	A2
Mount Pk. Cres. W5	105	G6
Mount Pk. Rd. W5	105	G5
Mount Pk. Rd., Har.	86	A3
Mount Pk. Rd., Pnr.	66	A5
Mount Pl. W3	126	B1
High St.		
Mount Pleasant SE27	169	J4
Mount Pleasant WC1	**10**	**D6**
Mount Pleasant WC1	111	G4
Mount Pleasant,	41	H4
Barn.		
Mount Pleasant, Ruis.	84	C2
Mount Pleasant,	105	H1
Wem.		
Mount Pleasant Cres.	75	F7
N4		
Mount Pleasant Hill	95	F2
E5		
Mount Pleasant La.	94	E2
E5		
Mount Pleasant Pl.	137	G4
SE18		
Orchard Rd.		
Mount Pleasant Rd.	77	H2
E17		
Mount Pleasant Rd.	76	B2
N17		
Mount Pleasant Rd.	89	J7
NW10		
Mount Pleasant Rd.	154	B6
SE13		
Mount Pleasant Rd.	105	F4
W5		
Mount Pleasant Rd.,	65	G4
Chig.		
Mount Pleasant Rd.,	182	C3
N.Mal.		
Mount Pleasant Vil.	75	F7
N4		
Mount Pleasant Wk.,	159	J5
Bex.		
Mount Rd. NW2	89	H3
Mount Rd. NW4	71	G6
Mount Rd. SE19	170	A6
Mount Rd. SW19	166	D2
Mount Rd., Barn.	41	H5

Name	Page	Grid
Mount Rd., Bexh.	158	D5
Mount Rd., Chess.	195	J5
Mount Rd., Dag.	101	F1
Mount Rd., Felt.	160	E3
Mount Rd., Hayes	122	A2
Mount Rd., Ilf.	98	E5
Mount Rd., Mitch.	185	H2
Mount Rd., N.Mal.	182	D3
Mount Row W1	**16**	**D6**
Mount Row W1	110	B7
Mount Sq., The NW3	91	F3
Heath St.		
Mount Stewart Av.,	69	G6
Har.		
Mount St. W1	**16**	**C6**
Ryder St.		
Mount St. W1	110	A7
Mount Ter. E1	112/113	E5
New Rd.		
Mount Vernon NW3	91	F4
Mount Vw. NW7	54	D3
Mount Vw. W5	105	G4
Mount Vw. Rd. E4	46	C7
Mount Vw. Rd. N4	75	E7
Mount Vw. Rd. NW9	70	D4
Mount Vil. SE27	169	H3
Mountacre Cl. SE26	170	C4
Mountague Pl. E14	114	C7
Mountbatten Cl. SE18	137	H6
Mountbatten Cl.	170	B5
SE19		
Mountbatten Cl.	133	F1
SE16		
Rotherhithe St.		
Mountbatten Ct.,	64	A2
Buck.H.		
Mountbatten Gdns.,	189	H4
Beck.		
Balmoral Av.		
Mountbatten Ms.	167	F1
SW18		
Inman Rd.		
Mountbel Rd., Stan.	68	D1
Mountcombe Cl.,	181	H7
Surb.		
Mountearl Gdns.	169	F3
SW16		
Mountfield Cl. SE6	154	D7
Mountfield Rd. E6	116	D2
Mountfield Rd. N3	72	D3
Mountfield Rd. W5	105	G6
Mountford St. E1	**21**	**H3**
Mountfort Cres. N1	93	G7
Barnsbury Sq.		
Mountfort Ter. N1	93	G7
Barnsbury Sq.		
Mountgrove Rd. N5	93	H3
Mounthurst Rd.,	191	F7
Brom.		
Mountington Pk. Cl.,	69	G6
Har.		
Mountjoy Cl. SE2	138	B2
Mounts Pond Rd.	154	D2
SE3		
Mountsfield Ct. SE13	154	D6
Mountside, Felt.	160/161	E3
Hampton Rd. W.		
Mountside, Stan.	68	C1
Mountview Ct. N8	75	H4
Green Las.		
Mountview Rd.,	194	E7
Esher		
Mountwood, W.Mol.	179	G3
Movers La., Bark.	117	H2
Mowatt Cl. N19	92	D1
Mowbray Rd. NW6	90	B7
Mowbray Rd. SE19	188	C1
Mowbray Rd., Barn.	41	F4
Mowbray Rd., Edg.	54	A4
Mowbray Rd., Rich.	163	F3
Mowbrays Cl., Rom.	83	J1
Mowbrays Rd., Rom.	83	J2
Mowbray Gdns.,	49	F2
Loug.		
Mowlem St. E2	113	E2
Mowlem Trd. Est.	61	F7
N17		
Mowll St. SW9	131	G2
Moxon Cl. E13	115	F2
Whitelegg Rd.		
Moxon St. W1	**16**	**B2**
Moxon St. W1	110	A5
Moxon St., Barn.	40	C3
Moye Cl. E2	**13**	**J1**
Moyers Rd. E10	78	C7
Moylan Rd. W6	128	B6
Moyne Pl. NW10	106	A2
Moynihan Dr. N21	43	E5
Moys Cl., Croy.	186	E6
Moyser Rd. SW16	168	B5
Mozart St. W10	108	B5
Mozart Ter. SW1	**32**	**C2**
Mozart Ter. SW1	130	A4
Muchelney Rd.,	185	F6
Mord.		
Mud La. W5	105	G5
Mudlarks Way SE7	135	G3
Mudlarks Way SE10	135	G3
Muggeridge Cl.,	202	A5
S.Croy.		
Muggeridge Rd.,	101	H4
Dag.		
Muir Dr. SW18	149	G6
Muir Rd. E5	94	D4
Muir St. E16	136	C1
Newland St.		
Muirdown Av. SW14	146	D4
Muirfield W3	107	E6
Muirfield Cl.	132/133	E5
SE16		
Muirfield Cl., Wat.	50	C4
Muirfield Cres. E14	134	B3
Millharbour		
Muirfield Grn., Wat.	50	C4
Muirfield Rd., Wat.	50	D4
Muirkirk Rd. SE6	172	C1
Mulberry Cl. E4	62	A2
Mulberry Cl. N8	74	E5
Mulberry Cl. NW3	91	G4
Hampstead High St.		
Mulberry Cl. NW4	71	J3
Mulberry Cl. SE7	136	A6
Mulberry Cl. SE22	152	D5
Mulberry Cl. SW3	129	G6
Beaufort St.		
Mulberry Cl. SW16	168	C4
Mulberry Cl., Barn.	41	G4
Mulberry Cl.,	102/103	E2
Nthlt.		
Parkfield Av.		
Mulberry Cl., Bark.	99	J7
Westrow Dr.		
Mulberry Cres.,	125	E7
Brent.		
Mulberry Cres.	120	D2
West Dr.		
Mulberry La., Croy.	202	C1
Mulberry Ms., Wall.	200	C6
Ross Rd.		
Mulberry Par.	120	D3
West Dr.		
Mulberry Pl. W6	127	G5
Chiswick Mall		
Mulberry Rd. E8	94	C7
Mulberry St. E1	**21**	**H3**
Mulberry Wk. SW3	**31**	**F5**
Mulberry Wk. SW3	129	G6
Mulberry Way E18	79	H2
Mulberry Way, Belv.	139	J2
Mulberry Way, Ilf.	81	F4
Mulgrave Rd. NW10	89	F4
Mulgrave Rd. SW6	128	C6
Mulgrave Rd. W5	105	G3
Mulgrave Rd., Croy.	202	A3
Mulgrave Rd., Har.	86	D2
Mulgrave Rd., Sutt.	198	D6
Mulholland Cl.,	186	B2
Mitch.		
Mulkern Rd. N19	92	D1
Mull Wk. N1	93	J6
Clephane Rd.		
Mullards Cl., Mitch.	199	J1
Muller Rd. SW4	150	D6
Mullet Gdns. E2	**13**	**J2**
Mullins Path SW14	146	D3
Mullion Cl., Har.	67	H1
Mullion Wk., Wat.	50	D4
Ormskirk Rd.		
Mulready St. NW8	**7**	**G6**
Multi Way W3	126/127	E2
Valetta Rd.		
Multon Rd. SW18	149	G7
Mulvaney Way SE1	**28**	**C4**
Mulvaney Way SE1	132	A2
Mumford Ct. EC2	**20**	**A3**
Mumford Rd. SE24	151	H5
Railton Rd.		
Muncaster Rd. SW11	149	J5
Muncies Ms. SE6	172	C2
Mund St. W14	128	C5
Mundania Rd. SE22	153	E6
Munday Rd. E16	115	G6
Munden St. W14	128	B4
Mundesley Cl., Wat.	50	C4
Mundford Rd. E5	95	F2
Mundon Gdns., Ilf.	99	G1
Mundy St. N1	**12**	**D3**
Mundy St. N1	112	B3
Mungo Pk. Cl.,	51	J2
Bushey		
Munnery Way, Orp.	206	D3
Munnings Gdns.,	144	A5
Islw.		
Munro Dr. N11	58	C6
Munro Ms. W10	108	B5
Munro Ter. SW10	**31**	**E7**
Munro Ter. SW10	129	G7
Munslow Gdns., Sutt.	199	G4
Munster Av., Houns.	143	F4
Munster Ct., Tedd.	163	F6
Munster Gdns. N13	59	H4
Munster Ms. SW6	128	B7
Munster Rd.		
Munster Rd. SW6	148	C1
Munster Rd., Tedd.	163	F6
Munster Sq. NW1	**9**	**E5**
Munster Sq. NW1	110	B3
Munton Rd. SE17	**36**	**A1**
Munton Rd. SE17	131	J4
Murchison Av., Bex.	176	D1
Murchison Rd. E10	96	C2
Murdock Cl. E16	115	F6
Rogers Rd.		
Murdock St. SE15	132	E6
Murfett Cl. SW19	166	B2
Muriel St. N1	**10**	**D1**
Muriel St. N1	111	F2
Murillo Rd. SE13	154	D4
Murphy St. SE1	**27**	**E4**
Murphy St. SE1	131	G2
Murray Av., Brom.	191	H2
Murray Av., Houns.	143	H5
Murray Cres., Pnr.	66	D1
Murray Gro. N1	**12**	**B2**
Murray Gro. N1	111	J2
Murray Ms. NW1	92	D7
Murray Rd. SW19	166	A6
Murray Rd. W5	125	F4
Murray Rd., Rich.	163	E2
Murray Sq. E16	115	G6
Murray St. NW1	92	D7
Murray Ter. NW3	91	G4
Flask Wk.		
Murray Ter. W5	125	G4
Murray Rd.		
Mursell Est. SW8	151	F1
Murtwell Dr., Chig.	65	F6
Musard Rd. W6	128	B6
Musard Rd. W14	128	B6
Musbury St. E1	113	F6
Muscal W6	128	B6
Muscatel Pl. SE5	152	B1
Dalwood St.		
Muschamp Rd. SE15	152	C3
Muschamp Rd.,	199	H2
Cars.		
Muscovy Ho.,	138/139	E2
Erith		
Kale Rd.		
Muscovy St. EC3	**21**	**E6**
Museum La. SW7	**23**	**E6**
Museum Pas. E2	112/113	E3
Victoria Pk. Sq.		
Museum St. WC1	**18**	**A2**
Museum St. WC1	110	E5
Musgrave Cl., Barn.	41	F1
Musgrave Cres. SW6	148	D1
Musgrave Rd., Islw.	144	C1
Musgrove Rd. SE14	153	G1
Musjid Rd. SW11	149	G2
Kambala Rd.		
Musket Cl., Barn.	41	G5
East Barnet Rd.		
Musquash Way,	142	C2
Houns.		
Muston Rd. E5	94	E2
Mustow Pl. SW6	148	C2
Munster Rd.		
Muswell Av. N10	74	B2
Muswell Hill N10	74	B3
Muswell Hill Bdy. N10	74	B3
Muswell Hill Pl. N10	74	B4
Muswell Hill Rd. N6	74	A6
Muswell Hill Rd. N10	74	A4
Muswell Ms. N10	74	B3
Muswell Rd.		
Muswell Rd. N10	74	B3
Mutrix Rd. NW6	108	D1
Mutton Pl. NW1	92	B6
Harmood St.		
Muybridge Rd.,	182	C2
N.Mal.		
Myatt Rd. SW9	151	H1
Myatt's Flds. N. SW9	151	G1
Eythorne Rd.		
Myatt's Flds. S. SW9	151	G2
Mycenae Rd. SE3	135	G7
Myddelton Cl., Enf.	44	C1
Myddelton Gdns.	43	H7
N21		
Myddelton Pk. N20	57	G3
Myddelton Pas. EC1	**11**	**F3**
Myddelton Rd. N8	75	E4
Myddelton Sq. EC1	**11**	**F3**
Myddelton Sq. EC1	111	G3
Myddelton St. EC1	**11**	**F4**
Myddelton St. EC1	111	G3
Myddleton Av. N4	93	J2
Myddleton Ms. N22	59	E7
Myddleton Rd. N22	59	E7
Myers La. SE14	133	G6
Mylis Cl. SE26	171	E4
Mylius Cl. SE14	153	F1
Kender St.		
Mylne St. EC1	**11**	**E2**
Mylne St. EC1	111	G3
Myra St. SE2	138	A4
Myrdle St. E1	**21**	**J2**
Myrdle St. E1	112	D5
Myrna Cl. SW19	167	H7
Myron Pl. SE13	154	C3
Myrtle Av., Felt.	141	H4
Myrtle Av., Ruis.	66	A7
Myrtle Cl., Barn.	57	J1
Myrtle Cl., West Dr.	120	C3
Myrtle Gdns. W7	124	B1
Myrtle Gro., N.Mal.	182	C2
Myrtle Rd. E6	116	B1
Myrtle Rd. E17	77	H6
Myrtle Rd. N13	59	J3
Myrtle Rd. W3	126	C1
Myrtle Rd., Croy.	204	A3
Myrtle Rd., Hmptn.	161	J6
Myrtle Rd., Houns.	143	J2
Myrtle Rd., Ilf.	99	E2
Myrtle Rd., Sutt.	199	F5
Myrtle Wk. N1	**12**	**D2**
Myrtle Wk. N1	112	B2
Myrtleberry Cl. E8	94	C6
Beechwood Rd.		
Myrtledene Rd. SE2	138	A5
Mysore Rd. SW11	149	J3
Myton Rd. SE21	170	A3

N

Name	Page	Grid
Nadine St. SE7	135	J5
Nafferton Ri., Loug.	48	A5
Nagle Cl. E17	78	D2
Nag's Head Ct. EC1	**11**	**J6**
Nag's Head La., Well.	158	B3
Nags Head Rd., Enf.	45	F4
Nairn Grn., Wat.	50	A3
Nairn Rd., Ruis.	84	C6
Nairn St. E14	114	C5
Nairne Gro. SE24	152	A5
Naish Ct. N1	111	E1
Nallhead Rd., Felt.	160	C5
Namba Roy Cl. SW16	169	F4
Valley Rd.		
Namton Dr., Th.Hth.	187	F4
Nan Clark's La. NW7	55	F2
Nankin St. E14	114	A6
Nansen Rd. SW11	150	A4
Nant Rd. NW2	90	C2
Nant St. E2	112/113	E3
Cambridge Heath Rd.		
Nantes Cl. SW18	149	F4
Nantes Pas. E1	**21**	**F1**
Naoroji St. WC1	**11**	**E4**
Napier Av. E14	134	A5
Napier Av. SW6	148	C3
Napier Cl. SE8	133	J7
Amersham Vale		
Napier Cl. W14	128	C3
Napier Rd.		
Napier Cl., West Dr.	120	C3
Napier Cl. SW6	148	C3
Ranelagh Gdns.		
Napier Gro. N1	**12**	**A2**
Napier Gro. N1	111	J2
Napier Pl. W14	128	C3
Napier Rd. E6	116	D1
Napier Rd. E11	96	E4
Napier Rd. E15	115	E2
Napier Rd. N17	76	B3
Napier Rd. NW10	107	H3
Napier Rd. SE25	188	E4
Napier Rd. W14	128	C3
Napier Rd., Belv.	139	F4
Napier Rd., Brom.	191	H4
Napier Rd., Enf.	45	G5
Napier Rd., Houns.	140	A1
Napier Rd., Islw.	144	D4
Napier Rd., S.Croy.	202	A7
Napier Rd., Wem.	87	G5
Napier Ter. N1	93	H7
Napoleon Rd. E5	94	E3
Napoleon Rd., Twick.	145	E7
Napton Cl.,	102/103	E4
Hayes		
Kingsash Dr.		
Narbonne Av. SW4	150	C5
Narborough St. SW6	148	E2
Narcissus Rd. NW6	90	D5
Naresby Fold, Stan.	53	F6
Bernays Cl.		
Narford Rd. E5	94	D3
Narrow St. E14	113	H7
Narrow Way, Brom.	192	B6
Nascot St. W12	107	J6
Naseby Cl. NW6	91	F7
Fairfax Rd.		
Naseby Cl., Islw.	144	B1
Naseby Rd. SE19	170	A6
Naseby Rd., Dag.	101	G3

Naseby Rd., Ilf. 80 C1
Nash Cl., Sutt. 199 G3
Nash Grn., Brom. 173 G6
Nash La., Kes. 205 G5
Nash Pl. E14 134 B1
South Colonnade
Nash Rd. N9 61 F2
Nash Rd. SE4 153 H4
Nash Rd., Rom. 82 D4
Nash St. NW1 8 E4
Nash Way, Har. 69 E6
Nasmyth St. W6 127 H3
Nassau Path SE28 138 C1
Disraeli Cl.
Nassau Rd. SW13 147 F1
Nassau St. W1 17 F2
Nassau St. W1 110 C5
Nassington Rd. NW3 91 H4
Natal Rd. N11 58 E6
Natal Rd. SW16 168 D6
Natal Rd., Ilf. 98 E4
Natal Rd., Th.Hth. 188 A3
Natalie Cl., Felt. 141 G7
Natalie Ms., Twick. 162 A3
Sixth Cross Rd.
Nathan Way SE28 137 H4
Nathaniel Cl. E1 21 G2
Nathans Rd., Wem. 87 F1
Nation Way E4 62 C1
Naval Row E14 114 C7
Naval Wk., Brom. 191 G3
High St.
Navarino Gro. E8 94 D6
Navarino Rd. E8 94 D6
Navarre Rd. E6 116 B2
Navarre St. E2 13 F5
Navarre St. E2 112 C4
Navenby Wk. E3 114 A4
Rounton Rd.
Navestock Cl. E4 62 C3
Mapleton Rd.
Navestock Cres., 79 J1
Wdf.Grn.
Navestock Ho., Bark. 118 B2
Navigator Dr., Sthl. 123 J2
Navy St. SW4 150 D3
Naylor Gro., Enf. 45 G5
South St.
Naylor Rd. N20 57 F2
Naylor Rd. SE15 132 E7
Nazareth Gdns. SE15 152 E2
Nazrul St. E2 13 F3
Nazrul St. E2 112 C3
Neagle Cl., Borwd. 38 C1
Balcon Way
Neal Av., Sthl. 103 F4
Neal Cl., Nthwd. 66 A1
Neal St. WC2 18 A4
Neal St. WC2 110 E6
Nealden St. SW9 151 F3
Neale Cl. N2 73 F3
Neal's Yd. WC2 18 A4
Near Acre NW9 71 F1
Neasden Cl. NW10 89 E5
Neasden La. NW10 89 E4
Neasden La. N. 88 D3
NW10
Neasham Rd., Dag. 100 B5
Neate St. SE5 37 F5
Neate St. SE5 132 C6
Neath Gdns., Mord. 185 F6
Neathouse Pl. SW1 33 F1
Neatscourt Rd. E6 116 A5
Nebraska St. SE1 28 B4
Nebraska St. SE1 132 A2
Neckinger SE16 29 G5
Neckinger St. SE16 132 C3
Neckinger Est. SE16 29 G5
Neckinger Est. SE16 132 C3
Neckinger St. SE1 29 G4
Neckinger St. SE1 132 C2
Nectarine Way SE13 154 B2
Needham Rd. W11 108 D6
Westbourne Gro.
Needham Ter. NW2 90 A3
Needleman St. SE16 133 G2
Neeld Cres. NW4 71 H5
Neeld Cres., Wem. 88 A5
Neeld Par., Wem. 88 A5
Harrow Rd.
Neil Wates Cres. 169 G1
SW2
Nelgarde Rd. SE6 154 A7
Nella Rd. W6 128 A6
Nelldale Rd. SE16 133 F4
Nello James Gdns. 170 A4
SE27
Nelson Cl., Croy. 201 H1
Nelson Cl., Rom. 83 H1
Nelson Ct. SE16 133 F1
Brunel Rd.
Nelson Gdns. E2 13 J3
Nelson Gdns. E2 112 D3
Nelson Gdns., Houns. 143 G6

Nelson Gro. Rd. 185 E1
SW19
Nelson Mandela Cl. 74 A2
N10
Nelson Mandela Rd. 155 J3
SE3
Nelson Pas. EC1 12 A4
Nelson Pl. N1 11 H2
Nelson Pl. N1 111 H2
Nelson Pl., Sid. 176 A4
Nelson Rd. E4 62 B6
Nelson Rd. E11 79 G4
Nelson Rd. N8 75 F5
Nelson Rd. N9 61 E2
Nelson Rd. N15 76 B4
Nelson Rd. SE10 134 C6
Nelson Rd. SW19 167 E7
Nelson Rd., Belv. 139 F5
Nelson Rd., Brom. 191 J4
Nelson Rd., Enf. 45 G6
Nelson Rd., Har. 86 A1
Nelson Rd., Houns. 143 J7
Nelson Rd. 140 C1
(Heathrow Airport), Houns.
Nelson Rd., N.Mal. 182 D5
Nelson Rd., Sid. 176 A4
Nelson Rd., Stan. 53 F6
Nelson Rd., Twick. 143 J6
Nelson Sq. SE1 27 G3
Nelson Sq. SE1 131 H2
Nelson St. E1 112 E6
Nelson St. E6 116 C2
Nelson St. E16 115 F7
Huntingdon St.
Nelson Ter. N1 11 H2
Nelson Ter. N1 111 H2
Nelson Trd. Est. 184 E1
SW19
Nelson Wk. SE16 133 H1
Rotherhithe St.
Nelson's Row SW4 150 D4
Nelsons Yd. NW1 9 F1
Nemoure Rd. W3 106 C7
Nene Gdns., Felt. 161 F2
Nene Rd., Houns. 141 E1
Nepaul Rd. SW11 149 H2
Nepean St. SW15 147 G6
Neptune Rd., Har. 68 A6
Neptune Rd. 141 G1
(Heathrow Airport), Houns.
Neptune St. SE16 133 F3
Nesbit Rd. SE9 156 A4
Nesbitt Cl. SE3 154/155 E3
Hurren Cl.
Nesbitt Sq. SE19 170 B7
Coxwell Rd.
Nesbitts All., Barn. 40 C3
Bath Pl.
Nesham St. E1 29 H1
Nesham St. E1 132 D1
Ness St. SE16 29 H5
Nesta Rd., Wdf.Grn. 63 E6
Nestles Av., Hayes 121 J3
Nestor Av. N21 43 H6
Nether Cl. N3 56 D7
Nether St. N3 72 D1
Nether St. N12 56 D7
Netheravon Rd. W4 127 F4
Netheravon Rd. W7 124 C1
Netheravon Rd. S. 127 F5
W4
Netherbury Rd. W5 125 G3
Netherby Gdns., Enf. 42 E4
Netherby Rd. SE23 153 F7
Nethercourt Av. N3 56 D6
Netherfield Gdns., 99 G6
Bark.
Netherfield Rd. N12 57 E5
Netherfield Rd. SW17 168 A3
Netherford Rd. SW4 150 C2
Netherhall Gdns. 91 F6
NW3
Netherhall Way NW3 91 F5
Netherhall Gdns.
Netherlands Rd., 41 G6
Barn.
Netherleigh Cl. N6 92 B1
Netherton Gro. 30 D6
SW10
Netherton Gro. 129 F6
SW10
Netherton Rd. N15 76 A6
Netherton Rd., Twick. 144 E5
Netherwood N2 73 G2
Netherwood Pl. W14 128 A3
Netherwood Rd.
Netherwood Rd. 128 A3
W14
Netherwood St. NW6 90 C7
Netley Cl., Croy. 204 C7
Netley Cl., Sutt. 198 A5
Netley Dr., Walt. 179 F7
Netley Gdns., Mord. 185 F7
Netley Rd. E17 77 J5

Netley Rd., Brent. 125 H6
Netley Rd. 141 G1
(Heathrow Airport), Houns.
Netley Rd., Ilf. 81 G5
Netley Rd., Mord. 185 F7
Netley St. NW1 9 F4
Nettleden Av., Wem. 88 A6
Nettlefold Pl. SE27 169 H3
Nettlestead Cl., 171 J7
Beck.
Copers Cope Rd.
Nettleton Rd. SE14 153 G1
Nettleton Rd., Houns. 141 E1
Nettlewood Rd. 168 D7
SW16
Neuchatel Rd. SE6 171 J2
Nevada Cl., N.Mal. 182 C4
Georgia Rd.
Nevada St. SE10 134 C6
Nevern Pl. SW5 128 D4
Nevern Rd. SW5 128 C4
Nevern Sq. SW5 128 D5
Nevill Rd. N16 94 B4
Nevill Way, Loug. 48 B7
Valley Hill
Neville Av., N.Mal. 182 D1
Neville Cl. E11 97 F3
Neville Cl. NW1 9 J2
Neville Cl. NW6 108 C2
Neville Cl. SE15 132 D7
Neville Cl. W3 126 C2
Acton La.
Neville Cl., Houns. 143 H2
Neville Cl., Sid. 175 J4
Neville Dr. N2 73 F6
Neville Gdns., Dag. 100 D3
Neville Gill Cl. SW18 148 D6
Neville Pl. N22 75 F1
Neville Rd. E7 97 G7
Neville Rd. NW6 108 C2
Neville Rd. W5 105 G4
Neville Rd., Croy. 188 A7
Neville Rd., Dag. 100 D2
Neville Rd., Ilf. 81 F1
Neville Rd., Kings.T. 182 A2
Neville Rd., Rich. 163 F3
Neville St. SW7 31 E3
Neville St. SW7 129 G5
Neville Ter. SW7 31 E3
Neville Ter. SW7 129 G5
Neville Wk., Cars. 185 H7
Green Wrythe La.
Nevilles Ct. NW2 89 G3
Nevin Dr. E4 62 B1
Nevinson Cl. SW18 149 G6
Nevis Rd. SW17 168 A2
Nevis Ash Cl. N2 73 G3
Oakridge Dr.
New Barn St. E13 115 G4
New Barns Av., 186 D4
Mitch.
New Barns Way, Chig. 64 E3
New Bond St. W1 17 E5
New Bond St. W1 110 B7
New Brent St. NW4 71 J5
New Br. St. EC4 19 G4
New Br. St. EC4 111 H6
New Broad St. EC2 20 D2
New Broad St. EC2 112 B5
New Bdy. W5 105 G4
New Bdy., Hmptn. 162 A5
Hampton Rd.
New Burlington Ms. 17 F5
W1
New Burlington Pl. 17 F5
W1
New Burlington St. 17 F5
W1
New Burlington St. 110 C7
W1
New Butt La. SE8 134 A7
New Butt La. N. SE8 134 A7
Reginald Rd.
New Cavendish St. 17 E1
W1
New Cavendish St. 110 A5
W1
New Change EC4 19 J4
New Change EC4 111 J6
New Chapel Sq., Felt. 160 B1
New Charles St. EC1 11 H3
New Ch. Rd. SE5 36 A7
New Ch. Rd. SE5 131 J7
New City Rd. E13 115 J3
New Cl. SW19 185 F3
New Cl., Felt. 160 E5
New College Ct. NW3 91 F7
College Cres.
New College Ms. N1 93 G7
Islington Pk. St.
New College Par. NW3 91 G6
College Cres.
New Compton St. 17 J4
WC2

New Compton St. 110 D6
WC2
New Ct. EC4 18 E5
New Covent Gdn. 130 D7
Mkt. SW8
New Coventry St. W1 17 J6
New Crane Pl. E1 133 F1
Garnet St.
New Cross Rd. SE14 133 F7
New End NW3 91 F4
New End Sq. NW3 91 G4
New Era Est. N1 112 B1
Phillipp St.
New Fm. Av., Brom. 191 G4
New Ferry App. 136 D3
SE18
New Fetter La. EC4 19 F3
New Fetter La. EC4 111 G6
New Forest La., Chig. 64 D6
New Gdn. Dr., 120 B2
West Dr.
Drayton Gdns.
New Globe Wk. SE1 27 J1
New Globe Wk. SE1 131 J1
New Goulston St. E1 21 F3
New Grn. Pl. SE19 170 B6
Hawke Rd.
New Heston Rd., 123 F7
Houns.
New Horizons Ct., 124 D6
Brent.
Shield Dr.
New Inn Bdy. EC2 12 E5
New Inn Pas. WC2 18 D4
New Inn St. EC2 12 E5
New Inn Yd. EC2 12 E5
New Inn Yd. EC2 112 B4
New James Ct. 152/153 E3
SE15
Nunhead La.
New Kent Rd. SE1 27 J6
New Kent Rd. SE1 131 J3
New King St. SE8 134 A6
New Kings Rd. SW6 148 C2
New London St. EC3 21 E5
New Lydenburg St. 135 J3
SE7
New Mt. St. E15 96 D7
Bridge Rd.
New N. Pl. EC2 12 D6
New N. Rd. N1 12 C2
New N. Rd. N1 112 A2
New N. Rd., Ilf. 65 G7
New N. St. WC1 18 C1
New N. St. WC1 111 F5
New Oak Rd. N2 73 F2
New Orleans Wk. N19 74 D7
New Oxford St. WC1 17 J3
New Oxford St. WC1 110 D6
New Pk. Av. N13 59 J3
New Pk. Cl., Nthlt. 84 E6
New Pk. Ct. SW2 151 E7
New Pk. Par. 150/151 E7
SW2
Doverfield Rd.
New Pk. Rd. SW2 168 D1
New Pl. Sq. SE16 132 E3
New Plaistow Rd. 115 E1
E15
New Printing Ho. Sq. 111 F4
WC1
Gray's Inn Rd.
New Priory Cl. NW6 90 D7
Mazenod Av.
New Quebec St. W1 16 A4
New Quebec St. W1 109 J6
New Ride SW7 23 J3
New Ride SW7 129 H2
New River Cres. N13 59 H4
New River Wk. N1 93 J6
New River Way N4 76 A7
New Rd. E1 112 E5
New Rd. E4 62 B4
New Rd. N8 74 E5
New Rd. N9 60 D3
New Rd. N17 76 C1
New Rd. N22 75 J1
New Rd. NW7 56 B7
New Rd. 39 F7
(Barnet Gate) NW7
New Rd. SE2 138 D4
New Rd., Brent. 125 G6
New Rd., Dag. 119 G1
New Rd., Felt. 141 G6
New Rd. 160 B1
(East Bedfont), Felt.
New Rd. (Hanworth), 160 E5
Felt.
New Rd., Har. 86 C4
New Rd., Hayes 121 F7
New Rd., Houns. 143 H4
Station Rd.
New Rd., Ilf. 99 H2
New Rd., Kings.T. 164 A7

New Rd., Mitch. 199 J1
New Rd., Rich. 163 F4
New Rd., Well. 158 B2
New Rd., W.Mol. 179 G3
New Row WC2 18 A5
New Row WC2 110 E7
New Spring Gdns. Wk. SE11 34 B4
New Sq. WC2 18 D3
New Sq. WC2 111 F6
New Sq. Pas. WC2 111 F6 *New Sq.*
New St. EC2 20 E2
New St. EC2 112 B5
New St. Hill, Brom. 173 H5
New St. Sq. EC4 19 F3
New Trinity Rd. N2 73 G3
New Turnstile WC1 18 C2
New Union Cl. E14 134 C3
New Union St. EC2 20 B2
New Union St. EC2 112 A5
New Wanstead E11 79 F6
New Way Rd. NW9 71 E4
New Wf. Rd. N1 10 B1
New Wf. Rd. N1 111 E2
New Zealand Way W12 107 H7
Newall Rd., Houns. 141 F1
Newark Cres. NW10 106 D3
Newark Grn., Borwd. 38 D3
Newark Knok E6 116 D6
Newark Par. NW4 71 G3 *Greyhound Hill*
Newark Rd., S.Croy. 202 A6
Newark St. E1 112 E5
Newark Way NW4 71 G4
Newbiggin Path, Wat. 50 C4
Newbolt Av., Sutt. 197 J5
Newbolt Rd., Stan. 52 C6
Newborough Grn., N.Mal. 182 D4
Newburgh Rd. W3 126 C1
Newburgh St. W1 17 F4
Newburgh St. W1 110 C6
Newburn St. SE11 34 D3
Newburn St. SE11 131 F5
Newbury Cl., Nthlt. 85 F6
Newbury Gdns., Epsom 197 F4
Newbury Ho. N22 75 E1
Newbury Ms. NW5 92 A6 *Malden Rd.*
Newbury Rd. E4 62 C6
Newbury Rd., Brom. 191 G3
Newbury Rd., Houns. 140 C1
Newbury Rd., Ilf. 81 H6
Newbury St. EC1 19 J2
Newbury Way, Nthlt. 85 E6
Newby Cl., Enf. 44 B2
Newby Pl. E14 114 C7
Newby St. SW8 150 B3
Newcastle Cl. EC4 19 G3
Newcastle Pl. W2 15 F2
Newcastle Pl. W2 109 G5
Newcastle Row EC1 11 F5
Newcombe Gdns. SW16 169 E4
Newcombe Pk. NW7 55 E5
Newcombe Pk., Wem. 105 J1
Newcombe St. W8 128 D1 *Kensington Pl.*
Newcomen Rd. E11 97 F3
Newcomen Rd. SW11 149 G3
Newcomen St. SE1 28 B3
Newcomen St. SE1 132 A2
Newcourt St. NW8 7 G2
Newcourt St. NW8 109 H2
Newdales Cl. N9 60 D2 *Balham Rd.*
Newdene Av., Nthlt. 102 D2
Newell St. E14 113 J6
Newent Cl. SE15 36 D7
Newent Cl. SE15 132 B7
Newent Cl., Cars. 199 J1
Newfield Cl., Hmptn. 179 G1 *Percy Rd.*
Newfield Ri. NW2 89 H3
Newgale Gdns., Edg. 69 J1
Newgate, Croy. 201 J1
Newgate Cl., Felt. 161 E2
Newgate St. E4 63 F3
Newgate St. EC1 19 H3
Newgate St. EC1 111 H6
Newham Way E6 115 J5
Newham Way E16 115 F5
Newhams Row SE1 28 E4
Newhaven Cl., Hayes 121 J4
Newhaven Gdns. SE9 156 A4
Newhaven La. E16 115 F4
Newhaven Rd. SE25 188 A5
Newhouse Av., Rom. 82 D3
Newhouse Cl., N.Mal. 183 E7
Newhouse Wk., Mord. 185 F7
Newick Cl., Bex. 159 H6
Newick Rd. E5 95 E3
Newing Grn., Brom. 174 A7
Newington Barrow Way N7 93 F3
Newington Butts SE1 35 H2
Newington Butts SE1 131 H4
Newington Butts SE11 35 H2
Newington Butts SE11 131 H4
Newington Causeway SE1 27 H6
Newington Causeway SE1 131 H3
Newington Grn. N1 94 A5
Newington Grn. N16 94 A5
Newington Grn. Rd. N1 94 A6
Newington Way N7 93 F2 *Hornsey Rd.*
Newland Cl., Pnr. 51 E6
Newland Ct., Wem. 88 A2 *Forty Av.*
Newland Dr., Enf. 44 E1
Newland Gdns. W13 124 D2
Newland Rd. N8 74 E3
Newland St. E16 136 B1
Newlands, The, Wall. 200 C7
Newlands Av., T.Ditt. 194 B1
Newlands Cl., Edg. 53 H3
Newlands Cl., Sthl. 122 E5
Newlands Cl., Wem. 87 F6
Newlands Ct. SE9 156 D6
Newlands Pk. SE26 171 G5
Newlands Pl., Barn. 40 A5
Newlands Quay E1 113 F7
Newlands Rd. SW16 187 E2
Newlands Rd., Wdf.Grn. 63 F2
Newlands Way, Chess. 195 F5
Newling Cl. E6 116 C6 *Porter Rd.*
Newlyn Gdns., Har. 67 F7
Newlyn Rd. N17 76 C1
Newlyn Rd. NW2 89 J1 *Tilling Rd.*
Newlyn Rd., Barn. 40 C4
Newlyn Rd., Well. 157 J2
Newman Pas. W1 17 G2
Newman Rd. E13 115 H3
Newman Rd. E17 77 G5 *Southcote Rd.*
Newman Rd., Brom. 191 G1
Newman Rd., Croy. 201 F1
Newman Rd., Hayes 102 B7
Newman St. W1 17 G2
Newman St. W1 110 C5
Newman Yd. W1 17 H3
Newmans Cl., Loug. 48 E3
Newman's Ct. EC3 20 C4
Newmans La., Loug. 48 D3
Newmans La., Surb. 181 G6
Newman's Row WC2 18 D2
Newmans Way, Barn. 41 F1
Newmarket Av., Nthlt. 85 G5
Newmarket Grn. SE9 156 A7 *Middle Pk. Av.*
Newminster Rd., Mord. 185 F6
Newnes Path SW15 147 H4 *Putney Pk. La.*
Newnham Av., Ruis. 84 C1
Newnham Cl., Loug. 48 A6
Newnham Cl., Nthlt. 85 J5
Newnham Cl., Th.Hth. 187 J2
Newnham Gdns., Nthlt. 85 J5
Newnham Ms. N22 75 F1 *Newnham Rd.*
Newnham Rd. N22 75 F1
Newnham Ter. SE1 26 E5
Newnham Way, Har. 69 H5
Newnhams Cl., Brom. 192 C3
Newnton Cl. N4 76 A7
Newpiece, Loug. 48 E3
Newport Av. E13 115 H4
Newport Av. E14 114 D7
Newport Ct. WC2 17 J5
Newport Mead, Wat. 50 D4 *Kilmarnock Rd.*
Newport Pl. WC2 17 J5
Newport Pl. WC2 110 D7
Newport Rd. E10 96 C2
Newport Rd. E17 77 H4
Newport Rd. SW13 147 G1
Newport Rd., Houns. 140 D1
Newport St. SE11 34 C2
Newport St. SE11 131 F4
Newquay Cres., Har. 85 E2
Newquay Gdns., Wat. 50 B2 *Fulford Gro.*
Newquay Rd. SE6 172 B2
Newry Rd., Twick. 144 D4
Newsam Av. N15 76 A5
Newsholme Dr. N21 43 F5
Newstead Av., Orp. 207 G3
Newstead Rd. SE12 155 E7
Newstead Wk., Cars. 185 F7
Newstead Way SW19 166 A4
Newton Av. N10 74 A1
Newton Av. W3 126 C2
Newton Cl. E17 77 H6
Newton Cl., Har. 85 G2
Newton Cres., Borwd. 38 C4
Newton Gro. W4 126 E4
Newton Rd. E15 96 D5
Newton Rd. N15 76 C5
Newton Rd. NW2 89 J3
Newton Rd. SW19 166 B7
Newton Rd. W2 14 A4
Newton Rd. W2 108 D6
Newton Rd., Har. 68 B2
Newton Rd., Islw. 144 C2
Newton Rd., Well. 158 A3
Newton Rd., Wem. 87 J7
Newton St. WC2 18 B3
Newton St. WC2 111 E6
Newton Wk., Edg. 70 B1 *North Rd.*
Newton Way N18 59 J5
Newtons Yd. SW18 148/149 E5 *Wandsworth High St.*
Newtown St. SW11 150 B1 *Strasburg Rd.*
Niagara Av. W5 125 F4
Nibthwaite Rd., Har. 68 B5
Nichol Cl. N14 58 D1
Nichol La., Brom. 173 G7
Nicholas Cl., Grnf. 103 H2
Nicholas Ct. E13 115 H3 *Tunmarsh La.*
Nicholas Gdns. W5 125 G2
Nicholas La. EC4 20 C5
Nicholas Pas. EC4 20 C5
Nicholas Rd. E1 113 F4
Nicholas Rd., Croy. 201 E4
Nicholas Rd., Dag. 101 F2
Nicholay Rd. N19 92 D1
Nicholes Rd., Houns. 143 G4
Nicholl St. E2 112 D1
Nichollsfield Wk. N7 93 F5 *Hillmarton Rd.*
Nichols Cl. N4 93 G1 *Osborne Rd.*
Nichols Cl., Chess. 195 F6 *Merritt Gdns.*
Nichols Grn. W5 105 H5 *Montpelier Rd.*
Nicholson Rd., Croy. 202 C1
Nicholson St. SE1 27 G2
Nicholson St. SE1 131 H1
Nickelby Cl. SE28 118 C6
Nicol Cl., Twick. 144/145 E6 *Cassilis Rd.*
Nicola Cl., Har. 68 A2
Nicola Cl., S.Croy. 201 J6
Nicola Ms., Ilf. 65 E7
Nicoll Pl. NW4 71 H6
Nicoll Rd. NW10 107 E1
Nicoll Way, Borwd. 38 D5
Nicolson Dr., Bushey 51 J1
Nicosia Rd. SW18 149 H7
Niederwald Rd. SE26 171 H4
Nield Rd., Hayes 121 J2
Nigel Cl., Nthlt. 102/103 E1 *Church Rd.*
Nigel Fisher Way, Chess. 195 G6 *Ashlyns Way*
Nigel Ms., Ilf. 98 E4
Nigel Playfair Av. W6 127 H4 *King St.*
Nigel Rd. E7 97 J5
Nigel Rd. SE15 152 D3
Nigeria Rd. SE7 135 J7
Nightingale Av. E4 62 E5
Nightingale Cl. E4 62 E4
Nightingale Cl. W4 126 C6 *Grove Pk. Ter.*
Nightingale Cl., Cars. 200 A2
Nightingale Cl., Pnr. 66 C5
Nightingale Dr., Epsom 196 B6
Nightingale Est. E5 94 D3
Nightingale Gro. SE13 154 D5
Nightingale La. E11 79 H5
Nightingale La. N6 91 H1
Nightingale La. N8 74 E4
Nightingale La. SW4 149 J7
Nightingale La. SW12 149 J7
Nightingale La., Brom. 191 J2
Nightingale La., Rich. 145 H7
Nightingale Ms. E3 113 H2 *Chisenhale Rd.*
Nightingale Ms., Kings.T. 181 G3 *South La.*
Nightingale Pl. SE18 136 D6
Nightingale Pl. SW10 30 D5
Nightingale Rd. E5 94 E3
Nightingale Rd. N9 45 F6
Nightingale Rd. N22 75 E1
Nightingale Rd. NW10 107 F2
Nightingale Rd. W7 124 C1
Nightingale Rd., Cars. 199 J3
Nightingale Rd., Hmptn. 161 G5
Nightingale Rd., Orp. 193 F6
Nightingale Rd., Walt. 178 B7
Nightingale Rd., W.Mol. 179 H5
Nightingale Sq. SW12 150 A7
Nightingale Vale SE18 136 D6
Nightingale Wk. SW4 150 B6
Nightingale Way E6 116 B5
Nightingales, The, Stai. 140 C7
Nile Path SE18 136 D6 *Jackson St.*
Nile Rd. E13 115 J2
Nile St. N1 12 A3
Nile St. N1 112 A3
Nile Ter. SE15 37 F4
Nile Ter. SE15 132 C5
Nimegen Way SE22 152 B5
Nimrod Cl., Nthlt. 102 D3 *Britannia Cl.*
Nimrod Pas. N1 94 B6 *Tottenham Rd.*
Nimrod Rd. SW16 168 B6
Nina Mackay Cl. E15 114/115 E1 *Arthingworth St.*
Nine Acres Cl. E12 98 B5
Nine Elms La. SW8 33 G7
Nine Elms La. SW8 130 C6
Nineteenth Rd., Mitch. 186 E4
Ninhams Wd., Orp. 206 D4
Ninth Av., Hayes 102 A7
Nisbet Ho. E9 95 G5 *Homerton High St.*
Nithdale Rd. SE18 137 E7
Niton Cl., Barn. 40 A6
Niton Rd., Rich. 146 A3
Niton St. SW6 128 A7
Niven Cl., Borwd. 38 C1
Nobel Dr., Hayes 121 G7
Nobel Rd. N18 61 F5
Noble St. EC2 19 J3
Noble St. EC2 111 J6
Noel Pk. Rd. N22 75 G2
Noel Rd. E6 116 B4
Noel Rd. N1 11 G1
Noel Rd. N1 111 H2
Noel Rd. W3 106 B6
Noel Sq., Dag. 100 C4
Noel St. W1 17 G4
Noel St. W1 110 C6
Noel Ter. SE23 171 F2 *Dartmouth Rd.*
Nolan Way E5 94 D4
Nolton Pl., Edg. 69 J1
Nonsuch Cl., Ilf. 65 E6
Nora Gdns. NW4 72 A4
Norbiton Av., Kings.T. 182 A2
Norbiton Common Rd., Kings.T. 182 B3
Norbiton Rd. E14 113 J6
Norbreck Gdns. NW10 105 J3 *Lytham Gro.*
Norbreck Par. NW10 105 J3 *Lytham Gro.*
Norbroke St. W12 107 F7
Norburn St. W10 108 B5 *Chesterton Rd.*
Norbury Av. SW16 187 F1
Norbury Av., Houns. 144 A5
Norbury Av., Th.Hth. 187 G2
Norbury Cl. SW16 187 G1

Norbury Ct. Rd. 186 E2
SW16
Norbury Cres. SW16 187 F1
Norbury Cross SW16 186 E3
Norbury Gdns., Rom. 82 D5
Norbury Gro. NW7 54 E3
Norbury Hill SW16 169 G7
Norbury Ri. SW16 186 E3
Norbury Rd. E4 62 A5
Norbury Rd., Th.Hth. 187 J2
Norcombe Gdns., 69 F6
Har.
Norcott Cl., Hayes 102 C4
Willow Tree La.
Norcott Rd. N16 94 D2
Norcroft Gdns. SE22 152 D7
Norcutt Rd., Twick. 162 B1
Norfield Rd., Dart. 177 J4
Norfolk Av. N13 59 H6
Norfolk Av. N15 76 C6
Norfolk Cl. N2 73 H3
Park Rd.
Norfolk Cl. N13 59 H6
Norfolk Cl., Barn. 42 A4
Norfolk Cl., Twick. 144/145 E6
Cassilis Rd.
Norfolk Cres. W2 15 H3
Norfolk Cres. W2 109 H6
Norfolk Cres., Sid. 157 H7
Norfolk Gdns., Bexh. 159 F1
Norfolk Gdns., 38 D4
Borwd.
Norfolk Ho. SE3 135 E6
Norfolk Ho. Rd. 168 D3
SW16
Norfolk Ms. W10 108 C5
Blagrove Rd.
Norfolk Pl. W2 15 F3
Norfolk Pl. W2 109 G6
Norfolk Pl., Well. 158 A2
Norfolk Rd. E6 116 C1
Norfolk Rd. E17 77 G2
Norfolk Rd. NW8 109 G1
Norfolk Rd. NW10 88 E7
Norfolk Rd. SW19 167 H7
Norfolk Rd., Bark. 99 H7
Norfolk Rd., Barn. 40 D3
Norfolk Rd., Dag. 101 H5
Norfolk Rd., Enf. 45 E6
Norfolk Rd., Esher 194 B5
Norfolk Rd., Felt. 160 C1
Norfolk Rd., Har. 67 H5
Norfolk Rd., Ilf. 99 H1
Norfolk Rd., Rom. 83 J6
Norfolk Rd., Th.Hth. 187 J3
Norfolk Row SE1 34 C1
Norfolk Sq. W2 15 F4
Norfolk Sq. W2 109 G6
Norfolk Sq. Ms. W2 15 F4
Norfolk St. E7 97 G4
Norfolk Ter. W6 128 B5
Field Rd.
Norgrove St. SW12 150 A7
Norhyrst Av. SE25 188 C3
Norland Pl. W11 128 B1
Norland Rd. W11 128 A1
Norland Sq. W11 128 B1
Norlands Cres., Chis. 192 E1
Norlands Gate, Chis. 193 E1
Norley Vale SW15 165 G1
Norlington Rd. E10 96 C1
Norlington Rd. E11 96 C1
Norman Av. N22 75 H1
Norman Av., Felt. 161 E2
Norman Av., Sthl. 103 E7
Norman Av., Twick. 145 E7
Norman Cl., Orp. 207 F3
Norman Cl., Rom. 83 H2
Norman Cl., Ilf. 81 G7
Norman Cres., 142 D1
Houns.
Norman Cres., Pnr. 66 C1
Norman Gro. E3 113 H2
Norman Rd. E6 116 C4
Norman Rd. E11 96 D2
Norman Rd. N15 76 C5
Norman Rd. SE10 134 B7
Norman Rd. SW19 167 F7
Norman Rd., Belv. 139 H3
Norman Rd., Ilf. 99 E5
Norman Rd., Sutt. 198 D5
Norman Rd., Th.Hth. 187 H5
Norman St. EC1 11 J4
Norman Way N14 58 E2
Norman Way W3 106 B5
Normanby Cl. SW15 148 C5
Manfred Rd.
Normanby Rd. NW10 89 F4
Normand Gdns. W14 128 B6
Greyhound Rd.
Normand Ms. W14 128 B6
Normand Rd.
Normand Rd. W14 128 C6
Normandy Av., Barn. 40 C5

Normandy Rd. SW9 151 G1
Normandy Ter. E16 115 H6
Normanhurst Av., 158 D1
Bexh.
Normanhurst Dr., 144/145 E5
Twick.
St. Margarets Rd.
Normanhurst Rd. 169 F2
SW2
Norman's Bldgs. 111 J3
EC1
Ironmonger Row
Normans Cl. NW10 88 D6
Normans Mead 88 D6
NW10
Normansfield Av., 163 F7
Tedd.
Normanshire Av. E4 62 C4
Normanshire Dr. E4 62 A4
Normanton Av. SW19 166 D2
Normanton Pk. E4 62 E3
Normanton Rd., 202 B6
S.Croy.
Normanton St. SE23 171 G2
Norrice Lea N2 73 G5
Norris St. SW1 17 H6
Norroy Rd. SW15 148 A4
Norrys Cl., Barn. 41 J5
Norrys Rd., Barn. 41 J4
Norseman Cl., Ilf. 100 B1
Norseman Way, Grnf. 103 H1
Olympic Way
Norstead Pl. SW15 165 G2
North Access Rd. E17 77 G6
North Acre NW9 71 E1
North Acton Rd. 106 D2
NW10
North Audley St. W1 16 B4
North Audley St. W1 110 A6
North Av. N18 60 D4
North Av. W13 104 E6
North Av., Cars. 199 J7
North Av., Har. 67 H6
North Av., Hayes 102 A7
North Av., Rich. 146 A1
Sandycombe Rd.
North Av., Sthl. 103 F7
North Bank NW8 7 G4
North Bank NW8 109 H3
North Birkbeck Rd. 96 D3
E11
North Branch Av. 107 J3
W10
Harrow Rd.
North Carriage Dr. 15 G5
W2
North Carriage Dr. 109 G7
W2
North Circular Rd. E4 61 J7
North Circular Rd. 79 J2
E18
North Circular Rd. N3 72 E3
North Circular Rd. 73 G1
N12
North Circular Rd. 59 G5
N13
North Circular Rd. 88 E3
NW2
North Circular Rd. 88 C7
NW10
North Circular Rd. 72 B4
NW11
North Cl., Barn. 39 J5
North Cl., Bexh. 158 D4
North Cl., Dag. 119 G1
North Cl., Felt. 141 G6
North Rd.
North Cl., Mord. 184 B4
North Colonnade E14 134 A1
North Common Rd. 105 H7
W5
North Countess Rd. 77 J1
E17
North Ct. W1 17 G1
North Cray Rd., Bex. 177 F3
North Cray Rd., Sid. 176 E6
North Cres. E16 114 D4
North Cres. N3 72 C2
North Cres. WC1 17 H1
North Cres. WC1 110 D5
North Cross Rd. 152 C5
SE22
North Cross Rd., Ilf. 81 F4
North Dene NW7 54 D3
North Dene, Houns. 143 H1
North Dr. SW16 168 C4
North Dr., Houns. 143 J2
North Dr., Orp. 207 H4
North End NW3 91 F2
North End, Buck.H. 47 J7
North End, Croy. 201 J2
North End Av. NW3 91 F2

North End Cres. 128 C4
W14
North End Ho. W14 128 B4
North End Par. W14 128 B4
North End Rd.
North End Rd. NW11 90 D1
North End Rd. SW6 128 C6
North End Rd. W14 128 B4
North End Rd., Wem. 88 A3
North End Way NW3 91 F2
North Eyot Gdns. 127 F5
W6
St. Peter's Sq.
North Flockton St. 29 H3
SE16
North Gdn. E14 133 J1
Westferry Circ.
North Gdns. SW19 167 G7
North Glade, The, 159 F7
Bex.
North Gower St. NW1 9 G4
North Gower St. 110 C3
NW1
North Grn. NW9 54/55 E7
Clayton Fld.
North Gro. N6 74 A7
North Gro. N15 76 A5
North Hatton Rd. 141 G1
(Heathrow Airport), Houns.
North Hill N6 73 J6
North Hill Av. N6 74 A6
North Hyde Gdns. 122 A4
Hayes
North Hyde La. 123 E5
Houns.
North Hyde La., Sthl. 123 E5
North Hyde Rd., 121 J3
Hayes
North La., Tedd. 162 C6
North Lo. Cl. SW15 148 A5
Westleigh Av.
North Mall N9 60/61 E2
St. Martins Rd.
North Ms. WC1 10 D6
North Ms. WC1 111 F4
North Par., Chess. 195 H5
North Pk. SE9 156 C6
North Pas. SW18 148 D4
North Peckham Est. 37 E7
SE15
North Peckham Est. 132 C7
SE15
North Pl., Mitch. 167 J7
North Pl., Tedd. 162 C6
North Pole La., Kes. 205 F6
North Pole Rd. W10 107 J5
North Ride W2 15 G6
North Ride W2 109 H7
North Rd. N6 74 A7
North Rd. N7 92 E6
North Rd. N9 60 E1
North Rd. SE18 137 H4
North Rd. SW19 167 F6
North Rd. W5 125 G3
North Rd., Belv. 139 H3
North Rd., Brent. 125 H6
North Rd., Brom. 191 H1
North Rd., Edg. 70 B1
North Rd., Felt. 141 G6
North Rd., Ilf. 99 H2
North Rd., Rich. 146 A3
North Rd., Rom. 82 E5
North Rd., Sthl. 103 G7
North Rd., Surb. 181 G6
North Rd., West Dr. 120 C3
North Rd., W.Wick. 204 B1
North Row W1 16 A5
North Row W1 109 J7
North Several SE3 154 D2
Orchard Dr.
North Side 149 G5
Wandsworth Common
SW18
North Sq. N9 60/61 E2
St. Martins Rd.
North Sq. NW11 72 D5
North St. E13 115 H2
North St. NW4 71 J5
North St. SW4 150 C3
North St., Bark. 99 E6
North St., Bexh. 159 G4
North St., Brom. 191 G1
North St., Cars. 199 J3
North St., Islw. 144 D3
North Tenter St. E1 21 G4
North Tenter St. E1 112 C6
North Ter. SW3 23 G6
North Ter. SW3 129 H3
North Verbena Gdns. 127 G5
W6
St. Peter's Sq.
North Vw. SW19 165 H5
North Vw. W5 105 F4

North Vw., Pnr. 66 C7
North Vw. Dr., 80 A2
Wdf.Grn.
North Vw. Rd. N8 74 D3
North Vil. NW1 92 D6
North Wk. W2 14 C6
North Wk., Croy. 204 B5
North Way N9 61 F2
North Way N11 58 C6
North Way NW9 70 B3
North Way, Pnr. 66 C3
North Wf. Rd. W2 14 E2
North Wf. Rd. W2 109 G5
North Woolwich Rd. 135 G1
E16
North Woolwich 136 A1
Roundabout E16
North Woolwich Rd.
North Worple Way 146 D3
SW14
Northall Rd., Bexh. 159 J2
Northampton Gro. 94 A5
N1
Northampton Pk. N1 93 J6
Northampton Rd. 11 F5
EC1
Northampton Rd. EC1 111 G4
Northampton Rd., 202 D2
Croy.
Northampton Rd., 45 H4
Enf.
Northampton Sq. 11 G4
EC1
Northampton Sq. 111 H3
EC1
Northampton St. N1 93 J7
Northanger Rd. SW16 168 E6
Northbank Rd. E17 78 C2
Northborough Rd. 186 D3
SW16
Northbourne, Brom. 191 G7
Northbourne Rd. 150 D4
SW4
Northbrook Rd. N22 59 E7
Northbrook Rd. SE13 154 D5
Northbrook Rd., Barn. 40 B6
Northbrook Rd., Croy. 188 A5
Northbrook Rd., Ilf. 98 D2
Northburgh St. EC1 11 H5
Northburgh St. EC1 111 H4
Northchurch SE17 36 C3
Northchurch Rd. N1 94 A7
Northchurch Rd., 87 J7
Wem.
Northchurch Ter. N1 94 B7
Northcliffe Cl., 197 E3
Wor.Pk.
Northcliffe Dr. N20 56 C1
Northcote, Pnr. 66 C2
Northcote Av. W5 105 H7
Northcote Av., Islw. 144 D5
Northcote Av., Sthl. 103 E7
Northcote Av., Surb. 182 A7
Northcote Rd. E17 77 H4
Northcote Rd. NW10 89 E7
Northcote Rd. SW11 149 H4
Northcote Rd., Croy. 188 A6
Northcote Rd., N.Mal. 182 C3
Northcote Rd., Sid. 175 H4
Northcote Rd., Twick. 144 D5
Northcott Av. N22 75 E1
Northcroft Rd. W13 124 E2
Northcroft Rd., 196 D7
Epsom
Northcroft Ter. 124/125 E2
W13
Northcroft Rd.
Northdene, Chig. 65 G5
Northdene Gdns. N15 76 C6
Northdown Gdns., Ilf. 81 H5
Northdown Rd., Well. 158 B2
Northdown St. N1 10 B1
Northdown St. N1 111 F2
Northern Av. N9 60 C2
Northern Perimeter 141 F1
Rd., Houns.
Northern Perimeter 140 A1
Rd. W., Houns.
Northern Relief Rd., 99 E7
Bark.
Northern Rd. E13 115 H1
Northern Service Rd., 40 B3
Barn.
Northernhay Wk., 184 B4
Mord.
Northey St. E14 113 H7
Northfield, Loug. 48 A4
Northfield Av. W5 125 E2
Northfield Av. W13 125 E2
Northfield Av., Pnr. 66 D4
Northfield Cl., Brom. 192 B1
Northfield Cl., Hayes 121 J3
Northfield Cres., 198 B4
Sutt.

Northfield Gdns., Dag. 101 F4
Northfield Rd.
Northfield Pk., Hayes 121 J3
Northfield Path, Dag. 101 F3
Northfield Rd. E6 98 C7
Northfield Rd. N16 76 B7
Northfield Rd. W13 124 E2
Northfield Rd., Barn. 41 H3
Northfield Rd., 38 B1
Borwd.
Northfield Rd., Dag. 101 F4
Northfield Rd., Enf. 45 E5
Northfield Rd., 122 D6
Houns.
Northfields SW18 148 D4
Northfields Ind. Est., 106 A1
Wem.
Northfields Rd. W3 106 B5
Northgate Dr. NW9 70 E6
Northiam N12 56 D3
Northiam St. E9 113 E1
Northington St. WC1 10 D6
Northington St. WC1 111 F4
Northlands Av., Orp. 207 H4
Northlands St. SE5 151 J2
Northolm, Edg. 54 D4
Northolme Gdns., 70 A1
Edg.
Northolme Ri., Orp. 207 H2
Northolme Rd. N5 93 J4
Northolt Av., Ruis. 84 B5
Northolt Gdns., Grnf. 86 C5
Northolt Rd., Har. 85 H4
Northolt Rd., Houns. 140 A1
Northover, Brom. 173 F3
Northport St. N1 112 A1
Northrop Rd., Houns. 141 H1
Northside Rd., Brom. 191 G1
Mitchell Way
Northspur Rd., Sutt. 198 D3
Northstead Rd. SW2 169 G2
**Northumberland All. 21 E4
EC3**
Northumberland All. 112 B6
EC3
**Northumberland Av. 97 J1
E12**
**Northumberland Av. 26 A1
WC2**
Northumberland Av. 130 E1
WC2
Northumberland Av., 45 E1
Enf.
Northumberland Av., 144 C1
Islw.
Northumberland Av., 157 H4
Well.
Northumberland Cl., 139 J7
Erith
Northumberland Cl., 140 B6
Stai.
Northumberland 141 H6
Cres., Felt.
Northumberland 60 C3
Gdns. N9
Northumberland 192 D4
Gdns., Brom.
Northumberland 124 D7
Gdns., Islw.
Northumberland 186 D5
Gdns., Mitch.
Northumberland Gro. 60 E7
N17
Northumberland Pk. 60 C7
N17
Northumberland Pk., 139 J7
Erith
Northumberland Pl. 108 D6
W2
Northumberland Pl., 145 G5
Rich.
Northumberland Rd. 116 B6
E6
Northumberland Rd. 78 A7
E17
Northumberland Rd., 41 F6
Barn.
Northumberland Rd., 67 F5
Har.
Northumberland 162 B1
Row, Twick.
Colne Rd.
**Northumberland St. 26 A1
WC2**
Northumberland St. 130 E1
WC2
Northumberland 159 J1
Way, Erith
Northumbria St. E14 114 A6
Northview Cres. 89 F4
NW10
Northway NW11 72 E5
Northway, Mord. 184 B3
Northway, Wall. 200 C4

Northway Circ. NW7 54 D4
Northway Cres. NW7 54 D4
Northway Rd. SE5 151 J3
Northway Rd., Croy. 188 C6
Northways Par. NW3 91 G7
College Cres.
Northwold La., 163 G5
Kings.T.
Northwest Av., Har. 68 D6
Northwick Circle, Har. 69 F6
Northwick Cl. NW8 7 E5
Northwick Cl. NW8, 68 C6
Har.
Northwick Rd., Wat. 50 C4
Northwick Rd., Wem. 105 G1
Northwick Ter. NW8 6 E5
Northwick Ter. NW8 109 G4
Northwick Wk., Har. 68 C7
Northwold Dr., Pnr. 66 C3
Cuckoo Hill
Northwold Est. E5 94 D2
Northwold Rd. E5 94 C2
Northwold Rd. N16 94 C2
Northwood Gdns. N12 57 G5
Northwood Gdns., 86 C5
Grnf.
Northwood Gdns., Ilf. 80 D4
Northwood Hall N6 74 C7
Northwood Ho. SE27 170 A4
Northwood Pl., Erith 139 F3
Northwood Rd. N6 74 B7
Northwood Rd. SE23 171 J1
Northwood Rd., Cars. 200 A6
Northwood Rd., 140 A1
Houns.
Northwood Rd., 187 H2
Th.Hth.
Northwood Way 170 A6
SE19
Northwood Way, 50 A7
Nthwd.
Norton Av., Surb. 182 B7
Norton Cl. E4 62 A5
Norton Cl., Borwd. 38 A1
Norton Cl., Enf. 44/45 E2
Brick La.
Norton Folgate E1 21 E1
Norton Folgate E1 112 B5
Norton Gdns. SW16 186 E2
Norton Rd. E10 95 J1
Norton Rd., Wem. 87 G6
Norval Rd., Wem. 86 E2
Norway Gate SE16 133 H3
Norway Pl. E14 113 J6
Norway St. SE10 134 B6
Norwich Ho. E14 114 B6
Cordelia St.
Norwich Ms., Ilf. 100 A1
Ashgrove Rd.
Norwich Pl., Bexh. 159 G4
Norwich Rd. E7 97 G5
Norwich Rd., Dag. 119 G2
Norwich Rd., Grnf. 103 H1
Norwich Rd., Th.Hth. 187 J3
Norwich St. EC4 19 E3
Norwich St. EC4 111 G6
Norwich Wk., Edg. 54 C7
Norwood Av., Wem. 105 J1
Norwood Cl., Sthl. 123 G4
Norwood Cl., Twick. 162 A2
Fourth Cross Rd.
Norwood Cres., 141 F1
Houns.
Norwood Dr., Har. 67 F6
Norwood Gdns., 102 C4
Hayes
Norwood Gdns., Sthl. 123 F4
Norwood Grn. Rd., 123 G4
Sthl.
Norwood High St. 169 H3
SE27
Norwood Pk. Rd. SE27 169 J5
Norwood Rd. SE24 169 H1
Norwood Rd. SE27 169 H2
Norwood Rd., Sthl. 123 F4
Norwood Ter., Sthl. 123 H4
Tentelow La.
Nota Ms. N3 72 D1
Station Rd.
Notley St. SE5 36 B7
Notley St. SE5 132 A7
Notre Dame Est. 150 C4
SW4
Notson Rd. SE25 188 E4
Notting Barn Rd. 108 A4
W10
Notting Hill Gate 128 D1
W11
Nottingdale Sq. W11 128 B1
Wilsham St.
Nottingham Av. E16 115 J5

Nottingham Ct. WC2 18 A4
Nottingham Pl. W1 8 B6
Nottingham Pl. W1 110 A4
Nottingham Rd. E10 78 C6
Nottingham Rd. 167 J1
SW17
Nottingham Rd., Islw. 144 C2
Nottingham Rd., 201 J4
S.Croy.
Nottingham St. W1 16 B1
Nottingham St. W1 110 A5
Nottingham Ter. NW1 8 B6
Nova Ms., Sutt. 198 B1
Nova Rd., Croy. 187 H7
Novar Cl., Orp. 193 J7
Novar Rd. SE9 175 F1
Novello St. SW6 148 D1
Novello Way, Borwd. 38 D1
Nowell Rd. SW13 127 G6
Nower Hill, Pnr. 67 F4
Noyna Rd. SW17 167 J3
Nuding Cl. SE13 154 A3
Nugent Rd. N19 93 E1
Nugent Rd. SE25 188 C3
Nugent Ter. NW8 6 D2
Nugent Ter. NW8 109 F2
Nugents Ct., Pnr. 66/67 E1
St. Thomas' Dr.
Nugents Pk., Pnr. 67 E1
Nun Ct. EC2 20 B3
Nuneaton Rd., Dag. 100 D7
Nunhead Cres. SE15 152 E3
Nunhead Est. SE15 152 E3
Nunhead Grn. SE15 153 E3
Nunhead Gro. SE15 153 E3
Nunhead La. SE15 152 E3
Nunhead Pas. SE15 152 D3
Peckham Rye
Nunnington Cl. SE9 174 B3
Nunns Rd., Enf. 43 J2
Nupton Dr., Barn. 39 J6
Nursery Av. N3 73 F2
Nursery Av., Bexh. 159 F3
Nursery Av., Croy. 203 G2
Nursery Cl. SE4 153 J2
Nursery Cl. SW15 148 A4
Nursery Cl., Croy. 203 G2
Nursery Cl., Enf. 45 G1
Nursery Cl., Felt. 142 B7
Nursery Cl., Rom. 82 D6
Nursery Cl., Wdf.Grn. 63 H5
Nursery Cl. N17 60 C7
Nursery St.
Nursery Gdns., Chis. 174 E6
Nursery Gdns., Enf. 45 G1
Nursery Gdns., 143 F5
Houns.
Nursery La. E2 112 C1
Nursery La. E7 97 G6
Nursery La. W10 107 J5
Nursery Rd. E9 95 F6
Morning La.
Nursery Rd. N2 73 G1
Nursery Rd. N14 42 C7
Nursery Rd. SW9 151 F4
Nursery Rd., Loug. 47 J5
Nursery Rd. 47 H1
(High Beach), Loug.
Nursery Rd., Pnr. 66 C3
Nursery Rd., Sutt. 199 F4
Nursery Rd., Th.Hth. 188 A4
Nursery Rd. Merton 185 E2
SW19
Nursery Rd., Mitch. 185 H3
Nursery Rd. 166 B7
Wimbledon SW19
Worple Rd.
Nursery Row SE17 36 B2
Nursery Row SE17 132 A4
Nursery Row, Barn. 40 B3
St. Albans Rd.
Nursery St. N17 60 C7
Nursery Wk. NW4 71 H3
Nurserymans Rd. 58 A2
N11
Nurstead Rd., Erith 139 G7
Nutbourne St. W10 108 B3
Nutbrook St. SE15 152 D3
Nutbrowne Rd., Dag. 119 F1
Nutcroft Rd. SE15 132 E7
Nutfield Cl. N18 60 D6
Nutfield Cl., Cars. 199 H3
Nutfield Gdns., Ilf. 99 J2
Nutfield Gdns., Nthlt. 102 C2
Nutfield Rd. E15 96 C4
Nutfield Rd. NW2 89 G2
Nutfield Rd. SE22 152 C5
Nutfield Rd., Th.Hth. 187 H4
Nutfield Way, Orp. 206 D2
Nutford Pl. W1 15 H3
Nutford Pl. W1 109 H6
Nuthatch Gdns. SE28 137 G2
Nuthurst Av. SW2 169 F2
Nutley Ter. NW3 91 F6

Nutmead Cl., Bex. 177 J1
Nutmeg Cl. E16 114/115 E4
Cranberry La.
Nutmeg La. E14 114 D6
Nutt Gro., Edg. 53 G2
Nutt St. SE15 37 G7
Nutt St. SE15 132 C7
Nuttall St. N1 12 E1
Nuttall St. N1 112 B2
Nutter La. E11 79 J6
Nutwell St. SW17 167 H5
Nuxley Rd., Belv. 139 F6
Nyanza St. SE18 137 G6
Nye Bevan Est. E5 95 G3
Nylands Av., Rich. 146 A1
Nymans Gdns. SW20 183 H3
Hidcote Gdns.
Nynehead St. SE14 133 H7
Nyon Gro. SE6 171 J2
Nyssa Cl., Wdf.Grn. 64 C6
Gwynne Pk. Av.
Nyton Cl. N19 92/93 E2
Courtauld Rd.

O

Oak Apple Ct. SE12 173 G2
Oak Av. N8 74 E4
Oak Av. N10 58 B7
Oak Av. N17 60 A7
Oak Av., Croy. 204 A2
Oak Av., Hmptn. 161 E5
Oak Av., Houns. 122 D7
Oak Av., West Dr. 120 D3
Oak Bank, Croy. 204 C6
Oak Cl. N14 42 B7
Oak Cl., Sutt. 199 F2
Oak Cottage Cl. SE6 173 F1
Oak Cres. E16 115 E5
Oak Dene W13 104/105 E5
The Dene
Oak Fm., Borwd. 38 C5
Oak Gdns., Croy. 204 A2
Oak Gdns., Edg. 70 C2
Oak Gro. NW2 90 B4
Oak Gro., Ruis. 84 B1
Oak Gro., Sun. 160 B7
Oak Gro., W.Wick. 204 C2
Oak Gro. Rd. SE20 189 F1
Oak Hall Rd. E11 79 H6
Oak Hill, Surb. 181 H7
Oak Hill, Wdf.Grn. 62 D7
Oak Hill Cl., Wdf.Grn. 62 D7
Oak Hill Cres., Surb. 181 H7
Oak Hill Cres., 62 D7
Wdf.Grn.
Oak Hill Gdns., 79 E1
Wdf.Grn.
Oak Hill Gro., Surb. 181 H6
Oak Hill Pk. NW3 91 E4
Oak Hill Pk. Ms. 91 F4
NW3
Oak Hill Rd., Surb. 181 H6
Oak Hill Way NW3 91 F4
Oak La. E14 113 J7
Oak La. N2 73 G2
Oak La. N11 58 D6
Oak La., Islw. 144 B4
Oak La., Twick. 144 D7
Oak La., Wdf.Grn. 63 F4
Oak Lo. Av., Chig. 65 G5
Oak Lo. Cl., Stan. 53 F5
Dennis La.
Oak Lo. Dr., W.Wick. 190 B7
Oak Manor Dr., Wem. 87 J5
Oakington Manor Dr.
Oak Pk. Gdns. SW19 148 A7
Oak Pk. SW18 148/149 E5
East Hill
Oak Ri., Buck.H. 64 A3
Oak Rd. W5 105 G7
The Bdy.
Oak Rd. 139 J7
(Northumberland
Heath), Erith
Oak Rd., N.Mal. 182 D2
Oak Row SW16 186 C2
Oak St., Rom. 83 J5
Oak Tree Cl. W5 105 F6
Pinewood Gro.
Oak Tree Cl., Loug. 49 F1
Oak Tree Cl., Stan. 53 F7
Oak Tree Dell NW9 70 C5
Oak Tree Dr. N20 57 E1
Oak Tree Gdns., 173 H5
Brom.
Oak Tree Rd. NW8 7 F4
Oak Tree Rd. NW8 109 H3
Oak Village NW5 92 A4
Oak Way N14 42 B7
Oak Way W3 126 E1
Oak Way, Croy. 189 G6
Oakbank Av., Walt. 179 F7
Oakbank Gro. SE24 151 J4

Oakbrook Cl., Brom. 173 H4
Oakbury Rd. SW6 149 E2
Oakcombe Cl., 182/183 E1
  N.Mal.
  Traps La.
Oakcroft Cl., Pnr. 66 B2
Oakcroft Rd. SE13 154 D2
Oakcroft Rd., Chess. 195 J4
Oakcroft Vil., Chess. 195 J4
Oakdale N14 58 B1
Oakdale Av., Har. 69 H5
Oakdale Av., Nthwd. 66 A2
Oakdale Cl., Wat. 50 C4
Oakdale Gdns. E4 62 C5
Oakdale Rd. E7 97 H7
Oakdale Rd. E11 96 D2
Oakdale Rd. E18 79 H2
Oakdale Rd. N4 75 J6
Oakdale Rd. SE15 153 F3
Oakdale Rd. SW16 169 E5
Oakdale Rd., Wat. 50 C3
Oakdale Way, Mitch. 186 A7
  Wolseley Rd.
Oakden St. SE11 35 F1
Oakden St. SE11 131 G4
Oakdene SE15 152/153 E1
  Carlton Gro.
Oakdene Av., Chis. 174 D5
Oakdene Av., Erith 139 J6
Oakdene Av., T.Ditt. 194 D1
Oakdene Cl., Pnr. 51 F7
Oakdene Dr., Surb. 182 C7
Oakdene Ms., Sutt. 198 C1
Oakdene Pk. N3 56 C7
Oakdene Rd., Orp. 193 J5
Oake Ct. SW15 148 B5
Oaken Dr., Esher 194 C6
Oaken La., Esher 194 B5
Oakenholt Ho. SE2 138 D2
  Hartslock Dr.
Oakenshaw Cl., 181 H7
  Surb.
Oakes Cl. E6 116 C6
  Savage Gdns.
Oakeshott Av. N6 92 A2
Oakey La. SE1 27 E5
Oakey La. SE1 131 G3
Oakfield E4 62 B5
Oakfield Av., Har. 69 E3
Oakfield Cl., N.Mal. 183 F5
  Blakes La.
Oakfield Ct. N8 74 E7
Oakfield Ct. NW2 72 A7
  Hendon Way
Oakfield Ct., Borwd. 38 B3
Oakfield Gdns. N18 60 B4
Oakfield Gdns. SE19 170 B5
Oakfield Gdns., 190 A5
  Beck.
Oakfield Gdns., Cars. 199 H1
Oakfield Gdns., 104 A4
  Grnf.
Oakfield La., Kes. 205 J4
Oakfield Rd. E6 116 B1
Oakfield Rd. E17 77 H2
Oakfield Rd. N3 72 E1
Oakfield Rd. N4 75 G6
Oakfield Rd. N14 58 E3
Oakfield Rd. SE20 171 E7
Oakfield Rd. SW19 166 A3
Oakfield Rd., Croy. 201 J1
Oakfield Rd., Ilf. 99 E2
Oakfield St. SW10 30 C5
Oakfield St. SW10 129 F6
Oakfields Rd. NW11 72 B6
Oakford Rd. NW5 92 C4
Oakhall Ct. E11 79 H6
Oakham Cl. SE6 171 J2
  Rutland Wk.
Oakham Cl., Barn. 41 J3
Oakham Dr., Brom. 191 F4
Oakhampton Rd. 56 A7
  NW7
Oakhill, Esher 194 D6
Oakhill Av. NW3 90 E4
Oakhill Av., Pnr. 66 E2
Oakhill Ct. SW19 166 A7
Oakhill Dr., Surb. 181 H7
Oakhill Path, Surb. 181 H6
Oakhill Pl. SW15 148 D5
  Oakhill Rd.
Oakhill Rd. SW15 148 C5
Oakhill Rd. SW16 187 E1
Oakhill Rd., Beck. 190 C2
Oakhill Rd., Orp. 207 J1
Oakhill Rd., Sutt. 199 E3
Oakhouse Rd., Bexh. 159 G5
Oakhurst Av., Barn. 41 H7
Oakhurst Av., Bexh. 138 E7
Oakhurst Cl. E17 78 E4
Oakhurst Cl., Ilf. 81 F1
Oakhurst Cl., Tedd. 162 B5
Oakhurst Gdns. E4 63 F1
Oakhurst Gdns. E17 78 E4

Oakhurst Gdns., 139 E7
  Bexh.
Oakhurst Gro. SE22 152 D4
Oakhurst Rd., Epsom 196 C6
Oakington Av., Har. 67 G7
Oakington Av., Hayes 121 G4
Oakington Av., Wem. 87 J3
Oakington Dr., Sun. 178 C2
Oakington Manor Dr., 88 A5
  Wem.
Oakington Rd. W9 108 D4
Oakington Way N8 75 E6
Oakland Pl., Buck.H. 63 G2
Oakland Rd. E15 96 D4
Oakland Way, Epsom 196 D6
Oaklands N21 59 F2
Oaklands, Twick. 143 J7
Oaklands Av. N9 44 E6
Oaklands Av., Esher 194 A1
Oaklands Av., Islw. 124 C6
Oaklands Av., Sid. 157 J7
Oaklands Av., Th.Hth. 187 G4
Oaklands Av., Wat. 50 B1
Oaklands Av., 204 B3
  W.Wick.
Oaklands Cl., Bexh. 159 F5
Oaklands Cl., Chess. 195 F4
Oaklands Cl., Orp. 193 H6
Oaklands Cl., Wem. 87 G5
Oaklands Est. SW4 150 C6
Oaklands Gro. W12 127 G1
Oaklands La., Barn. 39 H4
Oaklands Pk. Av., Ilf. 99 G2
  High Rd.
Oaklands Pl. SW4 150 C4
  St. Alphonsus Rd.
Oaklands Rd. N20 40 C7
Oaklands Rd. NW2 90 A4
Oaklands Rd. SW14 146 D3
Oaklands Rd. W7 124 C2
Oaklands Rd., Bexh. 159 F4
Oaklands Rd., Brom. 173 E7
Oaklands Way, Wall. 200 D7
Oaklea Pas., Kings.T. 181 G3
Oakleafe Gdns., Ilf. 80 E3
Oakleigh Av. N20 57 G2
Oakleigh Av., Edg. 70 B2
Oakleigh Av., Surb. 196 A1
Oakleigh Cl. N20 57 J3
Oakleigh Cl., Barn. 41 H6
  Church Hill Rd.
Oakleigh Ct., Edg. 70 C2
Oakleigh Cres. N20 57 H3
Oakleigh Gdns. N20 57 F1
Oakleigh Gdns., Edg. 53 J5
Oakleigh Gdns., Orp. 207 H4
Oakleigh Ms. N20 57 F2
  Oakleigh Rd. N.
Oakleigh Pk. Av., Chis. 192 D1
Oakleigh Pk. N. N20 57 G1
Oakleigh Pk. S. N20 57 H2
Oakleigh Rd., Pnr. 51 F6
Oakleigh Rd. N. N20 57 G2
Oakleigh Rd. S. N11 58 A3
Oakleigh Way, Mitch. 186 B1
Oakleigh Way, Surb. 196 A1
Oakley Av. W5 106 A7
Oakley Av., Bark. 99 J7
Oakley Av., Croy. 201 E4
Oakley Cl. E4 62 C3
  Mapleton Rd.
Oakley Cl. E6 116 B6
  Northumberland Rd.
Oakley Cl. W7 104 B7
Oakley Cl., Islw. 144 A1
Oakley Ct., Loug. 48 D2
  Hillyfields
Oakley Ct., Mitch. 200 A1
  London Rd.
Oakley Cres. EC1 11 H2
Oakley Dr. SE9 175 G1
Oakley Dr. SE13 154 C5
  Hither Grn. La.
Oakley Dr., Brom. 206 B3
Oakley Gdns. N8 75 F5
Oakley Gdns. SW3 31 H5
Oakley Gdns. SW3 129 H6
Oakley Pk., Bex. 158 C7
Oakley Pl. SE1 37 F4
Oakley Pl. SE1 132 C5
Oakley Rd. N1 94 A7
Oakley Rd. SE25 188 E5
Oakley Rd., Brom. 206 B3
Oakley Rd., Har. 68 B6
Oakley Sq. NW1 9 G1
Oakley Sq. NW1 110 C2
Oakley St. SW3 31 G6
Oakley St. SW3 129 H6
Oakley Wk. W6 128 A6
Oakley Yd. E2 13 G5

Oakmead Pl., Mitch. 185 H1
Oakmead Rd. SW12 168 A1
Oakmead Rd., Croy. 186 D6
Oakmeade, Pnr. 51 G6
Oakmere Rd. SE2 138 A6
Oakmoor Way, Chig. 65 H5
Oakmount Pl., Orp. 207 G2
Oakridge Dr. N2 73 G3
Oakridge La., Brom. 172 D5
  Downham Way
Oakridge Rd., Brom. 172 D4
Oaks, The N12 57 E4
Oaks, The SE18 137 F5
Oaks, The, Wat. 50 C1
Oaks, The, Wdf.Grn. 63 E6
Oaks Av. SE19 170 B5
Oaks Av., Felt. 160 E2
Oaks Av., Rom. 83 J2
Oaks Av., Wor.Pk. 197 H3
Oaks Gro. E4 62 E2
Oaks La., Croy. 203 F3
Oaks La., Ilf. 81 H5
Oaks Rd., Croy. 202 E5
Oaks Rd., Stai. 140 A6
Oaks Way, Cars. 199 J7
Oaks Way, Surb. 195 G2
Oaksford Av. SE26 170 E3
Oakshade Rd., Brom. 172 D4
Oakshaw Rd. SW18 149 E7
Oakthorpe Rd. N13 59 G5
Oaktree Av. N13 59 H3
Oaktree Gro., Ilf. 99 G5
Oakview Gdns. N2 73 G4
Oakview Gro., Croy. 203 H1
Oakview Rd. SE6 172 B5
Oakway SW20 183 J4
Oakway, Brom. 190 D2
Oakway, Cl., Bex. 159 E6
Oakways SE9 156 E6
Oakwood Av. N14 42 D7
Oakwood Av., Beck. 190 C2
Oakwood Av., Borwd. 38 B4
Oakwood Av., Brom. 191 H3
Oakwood Av., Mitch. 185 G2
Oakwood Av., Sthl. 103 G7
Oakwood Cl. N14 42 C6
Oakwood Cl., Chis. 174 C6
Oakwood Cl., 64 B6
  Wdf.Grn.
  Green Wk.
Oakwood Ct. W14 128 C3
Oakwood Cres. N21 43 E6
Oakwood Cres., Grnf. 86 D6
Oakwood Dr. SE19 170 A6
Oakwood Dr., Edg. 54 C6
Oakwood Gdns., Ilf. 99 J2
Oakwood Gdns., Orp. 207 F2
Oakwood Gdns., Sutt. 198 D2
Oakwood Hill, Loug. 48 C6
Oakwood Hill Ind. 49 F5
  Est., Loug.
Oakwood La. W14 128 C3
Oakwood Pk. Rd. 42 D7
  N14
Oakwood Rd., Croy. 187 G6
Oakwood Rd. NW11 72 E5
Oakwood Rd. SW20 183 G1
Oakwood Rd., Croy. 187 G6
Oakwood Rd., Orp. 207 F2
Oakwood Rd., Pnr. 66 B3
Oakwood Vw. N14 42 D6
Oakworth Rd. W10 107 J5
Oarsman Pl., E.Mol. 180 B4
Oat La. EC2 19 J3
Oat La. EC2 111 J6
Oates Cl., Brom. 190 D3
Oatfield Rd., Orp. 207 J1
Oatland Ri. E17 77 H2
Oatlands Rd., Enf. 45 F1
Oban Cl. E13 115 J4
Oban Ho., Bark. 117 G2
  Wheelers Cross
Oban Rd. E13 115 J3
Oban Rd. SE25 188 A4
Oban St. E14 114 D6
Oberon Cl., Borwd. 38 C1
Oberstein Rd. SW11 149 G4
Oborne Cl. SE24 151 H5
Observatory Gdns. 128 D2
  W8
Observatory Ms. E14 134 D4
  Storers Quay
Observatory Rd. 146 C3
  SW14
Occupation La. SE18 156 E1
Occupation La. W5 125 G4
Occupation Rd. SE17 35 J3
Occupation Rd. SE17 131 J5
Occupation Rd. W13 125 E2
Ocean Est. E1 113 G4
Ocean St. E1 113 G5
Ocean Wf. E14 134 A2
Ockendon Rd. N1 94 A6
Ockham Dr., Orp. 176 A7

Ockley Rd. SW16 168 E3
Ockley Rd., Croy. 187 F7
Octagon Arc. EC2 20 D2
Octavia Cl., Mitch. 185 H5
Octavia Rd., Islw. 144 C2
Octavia St. SW11 149 H1
Octavia Way SE28 118 B7
  Booth Cl.
Octavius St. SE8 134 A7
Odard Rd., W.Mol. 179 G4
  Down St.
Oddesey Rd., Borwd. 38 B1
Odessa Rd. E7 97 F4
Odessa Rd. NW10 107 G2
Odessa St. SE16 133 J2
Odger St. SW11 149 J2
Odhams Wk. WC2 18 A4
Odyssey Business Pk., 84 B5
  Ruis.
Offa's Mead E9 95 H4
  Lindisfarne Way
Offenbach Ho. E2 113 G2
Offenham Rd. SE9 174 C4
Offerton Rd. SW4 150 C3
Offham Slope N12 56 C5
Offley Pl., Islw. 124 A7
  Thornbury Rd.
Offley Rd. SW9 35 E7
Offley Rd. SW9 131 G7
Offord Cl. N17 60 D7
Offord Rd. N1 93 F7
Offord St. N1 93 F7
Ogilby St. SE18 136 C4
Oglander Rd. SE15 152 C4
Ogle St. W1 17 F1
Ogle St. W1 110 C5
Oglethorpe Rd., Dag. 101 F3
Ohio Rd. E13 115 F4
Oil Mill La. W6 127 G5
Okeburn Rd. SW17 168 A5
Okehampton Cl. N12 57 G5
Okehampton Cres., 158 B1
  Well.
Okehampton Rd. 107 J1
  NW10
Olaf St. W11 108 A7
Old Bailey EC4 19 H4
Old Bailey EC4 111 H6
Old Barge Ho. All. 27 E1
  SE1
Old Barn Cl., Sutt. 198 B7
Old Barrack Yd. SW1 24 B4
Old Barrowfield 114/115 E1
  E15
  New Plaistow Rd.
Old Bellgate Wf. E14 134 A4
Old Bethnal Grn. Rd. 13 J3
  E2
Old Bethnal Grn. Rd. 112 D3
  E2
Old Bond St. W1 17 F6
Old Bond St. W1 110 C7
Old Brewers Yd. 18 A4
  WC2
Old Brewery Ms. 91 G4
  NW3
  Hampstead High St.
Old Br. Cl., Nthlt. 103 G2
Old Br. St., Kings.T. 181 G2
Old Broad St. EC2 20 C4
Old Broad St. EC2 112 A6
Old Bromley Rd., 172 D5
  Brom.
Old Brompton Rd. 128 D5
  SW5
Old Brompton Rd. 30 C3
  SW7
Old Brompton Rd. 128 D5
  SW7
Old Bldgs. WC2 18 E3
Old Burlington St. 17 F5
  W1
Old Burlington St. W1 110 C7
Old Castle St. E1 21 F3
Old Castle St. E1 112 C6
Old Cavendish St. 16 D3
  W1
Old Cavendish St. 110 B6
  W1
Old Change Ct. EC4 111 J6
  Carter La.
Old Chelsea Ms. SW3 31 F6
Old Ch. La. NW9 88 C2
Old Ch. La., Grnf. 104 D3
  Perivale La.
Old Ch. La., Stan. 53 F7
Old Ch. Rd. E1 113 G6
Old Ch. Rd. E4 62 A4
Old Ch. St. SW3 31 F4
Old Ch. St. SW3 129 G5
Old Claygate La., 194 D6
  Esher
Old Clem Sq. SE18 136 D6
  Kempt St.

Name	Page	Grid
Old Compton St. W1	17	H5
Old Compton St. W1	110	D7
Old Cote Dr., Houns.	123	G6
Old Ct. Pl. W8	**22**	**A3**
Old Ct. Pl. W8	128	E2
Old Deer Pk. Gdns., Rich.	145	H3
Old Devonshire Rd. SW12	150	B7
Old Dock Cl., Rich.	126	A6
Watcombe Cotts.		
Old Dover Rd. SE3	135	H7
Old Fm. Av. N14	42	C7
Old Fm. Av., Sid.	175	G1
Old Fm. Cl., Houns.	143	F4
Old Fm. Pas., Hmptn.	179	J1
Old Fm. Rd. N2	73	G1
Old Fm. Rd., Hmptn.	161	F6
Old Fm. Rd., West Dr.	120	A2
Old Fm. Rd. E., Sid.	176	A2
Old Fm. Rd. W., Sid.	175	J2
Old Fish St. Hill EC4	**19**	**J5**
Old Fleet La. EC4	**19**	**G3**
Old Fold Cl., Barn.	40	C1
Old Fold La.		
Old Fold La., Barn.	40	C1
Old Fold Vw., Barn.	39	J3
Old Ford Rd. E2	113	F2
Old Ford Rd. E3	113	H2
Old Forge Cl., Stan.	52	D4
Old Forge Ms. W12	127	H2
Goodwin Rd.		
Old Forge Way, Sid.	176	B4
Old Fox Footpath, S.Croy.	202	B7
Essenden Rd.		
Old Gloucester St. WC1	**18**	**B1**
Old Gloucester St. WC1	111	E5
Old Hall Cl., Pnr.	67	E1
Old Hall Dr., Pnr.	66	E1
Old Hill, Chis.	192	D1
Old Hill, Orp.	207	G6
Old Homesdale Rd., Brom.	191	J4
Old Hospital Cl. SW12	167	J1
Old Ho. Cl. SW19	166	B5
Old Ho. Gdns., Twick.	145	F5
Old Jamaica Rd. SE16	**29**	**H5**
Old Jamaica Rd. SE16	132	D3
Old James St. SE15	152	E3
Old Jewry EC2	**20**	**B4**
Old Jewry EC2	112	A6
Old Kent Rd. SE1	**36**	**D1**
Old Kent Rd. SE1	132	B4
Old Kent Rd. SE15	132	B4
Old Kenton La. NW9	70	B5
Old Kingston Rd., Wor.Pk.	196	C3
Old Lo. Pl., Twick.	144/145	E6
St. Margarets Rd.		
Old Lo. Way, Stan.	52	D5
Old Maidstone Rd., Sid.	177	F7
Old Malden La., Wor.Pk.	196	D2
Old Manor Dr., Islw.	143	J6
Old Manor Way, Chis.	174	C5
Old Marylebone Rd. NW1	**15**	**H2**
Old Marylebone Rd. NW1	109	H5
Old Ms., Har.	68	B5
Hindes Rd.		
Old Mill Ct. E18	79	J3
Old Mill Rd. SE18	137	G6
Old Mitre Ct. EC4	19	G1
Fleet St.		
Old Montague St. E1	**21**	**H2**
Old Montague St. E1	112	D5
Old Nichol St. E2	**13**	**F5**
Old Nichol St. E2	112	C4
Old N. St. WC1	**18**	**C1**
Old Oak Cl., Chess.	195	J4
Old Oak Common La. NW10	107	E4
Old Oak Common La. W3	107	E5
Old Oak La. NW10	107	E3
Old Oak Rd. W3	107	F7
Old Orchard, Sun.	178	C2
Old Orchard, The NW3	91	J4
Nassington Rd.		
Old Palace La., Rich.	145	F5
Old Palace Rd., Croy.	201	H3
Old Palace Ter., Rich.	145	G5
King St.		
Old Palace Yd. SW1	**26**	**A5**
Old Palace Yd. SW1	130	E3
Old Palace Yd., Rich.	145	F5
Old Paradise St. SE11	**34**	**C1**
Old Paradise St. SE11	131	F4
Old Pk. Av. SW12	150	A6
Old Pk. Av., Enf.	43	J4
Old Pk. Gro., Enf.	43	J4
Old Pk. La. W1	**24**	**C2**
Old Pk. La. W1	130	A1
Old Pk. Ms., Houns.	123	F7
Old Pk. Ridings N21	43	H6
Old Pk. Rd. N13	59	F4
Old Pk. Rd. SE2	138	A5
Old Pk. Rd., Enf.	43	H3
Old Pk. Rd. S., Enf.	43	H4
Old Pk. Vw., Enf.	43	G3
Old Perry St., Chis.	175	H7
Old Pound Cl., Islw.	144	D1
Old Pye St. SW1	**25**	**H5**
Old Pye St. SW1	130	D3
Old Quebec St. W1	**16**	**A4**
Old Quebec St. W1	109	J6
Old Queen St. SW1	**25**	**J4**
Old Queen St. SW1	130	D2
Old Rectory Gdns., Edg.	54	A6
Old Redding, Har.	51	J4
Old Rd. SE13	155	E4
Old Rd., Enf.	45	F1
Old Rope Wk., Sun.	178	B3
The Av.		
Old Royal Free Pl. N1	111	G1
Liverpool Rd.		
Old Royal Free Sq. N1	111	G1
Old Ruislip Rd., Nthlt.	102	D2
Old Savill's Cotts., Chig.	65	F4
The Chase		
Old Sch. Cl. SW19	184	D2
Old Sch. Cl., Beck.	189	G2
Old Sch. Cres. E7	97	F6
Old Sch. Sq., T.Ditt.	180	C6
Old Seacoal La. EC4	**19**	**G3**
Old S. Cl., Pnr.	66	D1
Old S. Lambeth Rd. SW8	**34**	**B7**
Old S. Lambeth Rd. SW8	131	E7
Old Spitalfields Mkt. E1	**21**	**F1**
Old Spitalfields Mkt. E1	112	C5
Old Sq. WC2	**18**	**D3**
Old Sq. WC2	111	F6
Old Sta. Rd., Hayes	121	J3
Old Sta. Rd., Loug.	48	B5
Old Stockley Rd., West Dr.	120	E2
Old St. E13	115	H2
Old St. EC1	**11**	**J5**
Old St. EC1	111	J4
Old Swan Yd., Cars.	199	J4
Old Town SW4	150	C3
Old Town, Croy.	201	H3
Old Tram Yd. SE18	137	H4
Lakedale Rd.		
Old Woolwich Rd. SE10	134	D6
Old York Rd. SW18	149	E5
Oldacre Ms. SW12	150	B7
Balham Gro.		
Oldberry Rd., Edg.	54	D6
Oldborough Rd., Wem.	87	F2
Oldbury Pl. W1	**16**	**C1**
Oldbury Pl. W1	110	A4
Oldbury Rd., Enf.	44	D2
Oldfield Cl., Brom.	192	C4
Oldfield Cl., Grnf.	86	B5
Oldfield Cl., Stan.	52	D5
Oldfield Fm. Gdns., Grnf.	104	A1
Oldfield Gro. SE16	133	G4
Oldfield La. N., Grnf.	86	B6
Oldfield La. S., Grnf.	103	J4
Oldfield Ms. N6	74	C7
Oldfield Rd. N16	94	B3
Oldfield Rd. NW10	89	F7
Oldfield Rd. SW19	166	B6
Oldfield Rd. W3	127	F2
Valetta Rd.		
Oldfield Rd., Bexh.	159	E2
Oldfield Rd., Brom.	192	C4
Oldfield Rd., Hmptn.	179	F1
Oldfields Circ., Nthlt.	85	J6
Oldfields Rd., Sutt.	198	C3
Oldfields Trd. Est., Sutt.	198	D3
Oldfields Rd.		
Oldham Ter. W3	126	C1
Oldhill St. N16	94	D1
Oldridge Rd. SW12	150	A7
Oldstead Rd., Brom.	172	D4
Oleander Cl., Orp.	207	G5
O'Leary Sq. E1	113	F5
Olinda Rd. N16	76	C6
Oliphant St. W10	108	A3
Olive Rd. E13	115	J3
Olive Rd. NW2	89	J4
Olive Rd. SW19	167	F7
Norman Rd.		
Olive Rd. W5	125	G3
Oliver Av. SE25	188	C3
Oliver Cl. E10	96	B2
Oliver Rd.		
Oliver Cl. W4	126	B6
Oliver Gdns. E6	116	B6
Oliver Gro. SE25	188	C4
Oliver Rd. E10	96	B2
Oliver Rd. E17	78	C5
Oliver Rd., N.Mal.	182	C2
Oliver Rd., Sutt.	199	G4
Oliver-Goldsmith Est. SE15	152	D1
Olivers Yd. EC1	12	C5
Olivette St. SW15	148	A4
Ollards Gro., Loug.	48	A4
Ollerton Grn. E3	113	J1
Ollerton Rd. N11	58	D5
Olley Cl., Wall.	200	E7
Ollgar Cl. W12	127	F1
Olliffe St. E14	134	C3
Olmar St. SE1	**37**	**H5**
Olmar St. SE1	132	D6
Olney Rd. SE17	**35**	**J5**
Olney Rd. SE17	131	H6
Olron Cres., Bexh.	158	D5
Olven Rd. SE18	137	F7
Olveston Wk., Cars.	185	G6
Olwen Ms., Pnr.	66	D2
Olyffe Av., Well.	158	A2
Olyffe Dr., Beck.	190	C1
Olympia Ms. W2	**14**	**B6**
Olympia Way W14	128	B3
Olympic Retail Pk., Wem.	88	B4
Olympic Way, Grnf.	103	H1
Olympic Way, Wem.	88	A4
Olympus Sq. E5	94	D4
Nolan Way		
Oman Av. NW2	89	J4
O'Meara St. SE1	**28**	**A2**
O'Meara St. SE1	131	J1
Omega Cl. E14	134	B3
Tiller Rd.		
Omega Pl. N1	**10**	**B2**
Omega St. SE14	154	A1
Ommaney Rd. SE14	153	G1
Omnibus Way E17	78	A2
On The Hill, Wat.	50	E2
Ondine Rd. SE15	152	C4
One Tree Cl. SE23	153	F6
Onega Gate SE16	133	H3
O'Neill Path SE18	136	D6
Kempt St.		
Ongar Cl., Rom.	82	C5
Ongar Rd. SW6	128	D6
Onra Rd. E17	78	A7
Onslow Av., Rich.	145	H5
Onslow Cl. E4	62	C2
Onslow Cl., T.Ditt.	194	B1
Onslow Cres., Chis.	192	E1
Onslow Gdns. E18	79	H3
Onslow Gdns. N10	74	B5
Onslow Gdns. N21	43	G5
Onslow Gdns. SW7	**31**	**E3**
Onslow Gdns. SW7	129	G5
Onslow Gdns., T.Ditt.	194	B1
Onslow Gdns., Wall.	200	C6
Onslow Ms. E. SW7	**31**	**E2**
Onslow Ms. W. SW7	**30**	**E2**
Onslow Rd., Croy.	187	F7
Onslow Rd., N.Mal.	183	G4
Onslow Rd., Rich.	145	H5
Onslow Sq. SW7	**31**	**F1**
Onslow Sq. SW7	129	G4
Onslow St. EC1	**11**	**F6**
Ontario St. SE1	**27**	**H6**
Ontario St. SE1	131	H3
Ontario Way E14	114	A7
Opal Cl. E16	116	A6
Opal Ms. NW6	108	C1
Priory Pk. Rd.		
Opal Ms., Ilf.	98/99	E2
Ley St.		
Opal St. SE11	**35**	**G2**
Opal St. SE11	131	H4
Openshaw Rd. SE2	138	B4
Openview SW18	167	F1
Ophelia Gdns. NW2	90	B3
The Vale		
Ophir Ter. SE15	152	D1
Opossum Way, Houns.	142	C2
Oppenheim Rd. SE13	154	C2
Oppidans Ms. NW3	91	J7
Meadowbank		
Oppidans Rd. NW3	91	J7
Orange Ct. E1	**29**	**J2**
Orange Ct. La., Orp.	207	J6
Orange Gro. E11	96	E3
Orange Gro., Chig.	65	F6
Orange Hill Rd., Edg.	54	C7
Orange Pl. SE16	133	F3
Lower Rd.		
Orange St. WC2	**17**	**H6**
Orange St. WC2	110	D7
Orange Yd. W1	**17**	**J4**
Orangery, The, Rich.	163	F2
Orangery La. SE9	156	C5
Oratory La. SW3	**31**	**F3**
Orb St. SE17	**36**	**B2**
Orb St. SE17	132	A4
Orbain Rd. SW6	128	B7
Orbel St. SW11	149	H1
Orchard, The N14	42	B5
Orchard, The N21	44	A6
Orchard, The NW11	72	D5
Orchard, The SE3	154	D2
Orchard, The W4	126	D4
Orchard, The W5	105	G5
Orchard, The, Epsom	197	F7
Orchard, The, Houns.	143	J2
Orchard Av. N3	72	D3
Orchard Av. N14	42	C6
Orchard Av. N20	57	G2
Orchard Av., Belv.	139	E6
Orchard Av., Croy.	189	H7
Orchard Av., Felt.	141	G5
Orchard Av., Houns.	123	E7
Orchard Av., Mitch.	200	A1
Orchard Av., N.Mal.	183	E2
Orchard Av., Sthl.	123	E1
Orchard Av., T.Ditt.	194	D1
Orchard Cl. E4	62	A4
Chingford Mt. Rd.		
Orchard Cl. E11	79	H4
Orchard Cl. N1	93	J7
Morton Rd.		
Orchard Cl. NW2	89	G3
Orchard Cl. SE23	153	F6
Brenchley Gdns.		
Orchard Cl. SW20	183	J4
Grand Dr.		
Orchard Cl. W10	108	B5
Orchard Cl., Bexh.	52	A1
Orchard Cl., Bushey	52	A1
Orchard Cl., Edg.	53	H6
Orchard Cl., Epsom	196	B6
Orchard Cl., Nthlt.	85	J5
Orchard Cl., Surb.	181	E7
Orchard Cl., Walt.	178	B7
Garden Rd.		
Orchard Cl., Wem.	105	H1
Orchard Cl., Islw.	144	A1
Thornbury Av.		
Orchard Ct., Twick.	162	A2
Orchard Ct., Wor.Pk.	197	G1
The Av.		
Orchard Cres., Edg.	54	C5
Orchard Cres., Enf.	44	C1
Orchard Dr. SE3	154	E2
Orchard Dr., Edg.	53	J5
Orchard Gdns., Chess.	195	H4
Orchard Gdns., Sutt.	198	D5
Orchard Gate NW9	70	E4
Orchard Gate, Esher	194	A1
Orchard Gate, Grnf.	86	E6
Orchard Grn., Orp.	207	H2
Orchard Gro. SE20	170	D7
Orchard Gro., Croy.	189	H7
Orchard Gro., Edg.	70	A1
Orchard Gro., Har.	69	J5
Orchard Gro., Orp.	207	J2
Orchard Hill SE13	154	B2
Coldbath St.		
Orchard Hill, Cars.	199	J5
Orchard La. SW20	183	H1
Orchard La., E.Mol.	180	A6
Orchard La., Wdf.Grn.	63	J4
Orchard Ms. N1	94	A7
Southgate Gro.		
Orchard Pl. E14	115	G7
Orchard Pl. N17	60	C7
Orchard Ri., Croy.	203	H1
Orchard Ri., Kings.T.	182	C1
Orchard Ri., Rich.	146	B4
Orchard Ri. E., Sid.	157	J5
Orchard Ri. W., Sid.	157	H5
Orchard Rd. N6	74	B7
Orchard Rd. SE3	154/155	E3
Eliot Pl.		
Orchard Rd. SE18	137	G4
Orchard Rd., Barn.	40	C4
Orchard Rd., Belv.	139	G4
Orchard Rd., Brent.	125	F6
Orchard Rd., Brom.	191	J1
Orchard Rd., Chess.	195	H4
Orchard Rd., Dag.	119	G1

Name	Page	Grid
Orchard Rd., Enf.	45	F5
Orchard Rd., Hmptn.	161	F7
Orchard Rd., Hayes	102	A7
Orchard Rd., Houns.	143	F5
Orchard Rd., Kings.T.	181	H2
Orchard Rd., Mitch.	200	A1
Orchard Rd.	207	E5
(Farnborough), Orp.		
Orchard Rd., Rich.	146	A3
Orchard Rd., Rom.	83	H1
Orchard Rd., Sid.	175	H4
Orchard Rd., Sun.	160	B7
Hanworth Rd.		
Orchard Rd., Sutt.	198	D5
Orchard Rd., Twick.	144	D5
Orchard Rd., Well.	158	B3
Orchard Sq. W14	128	C5
Sun Rd.		
Orchard St. E17	77	H4
Orchard St. W1	16	B4
Orchard St. W1	110	A6
Orchard Ter., Enf.	44	D6
Great Cambridge Rd.		
Orchard Way, Beck.	189	H5
Orchard Way, Croy.	189	H7
Orchard Way, Enf.	44	B3
Orchard Way, Sutt.	199	G4
Orchardleigh Av., Enf.	45	F2
Orchardmede N21	44	A6
Orchardson St. NW8	7	E6
Orchardson St. NW8	109	G4
Orchid Cl. E6	116	B5
Orchid Cl., Sthl.	103	E6
Orchid Rd. N14	42	C7
Orchid St. W12	107	G7
Orde Hall St. WC1	10	C6
Orde Hall St. WC1	111	F4
Ordell Rd. E3	113	J2
Ordnance Cl., Felt.	160	A3
Ordnance Cres. SE10	134	D2
Ordnance Hill NW8	109	G1
Ordnance Ms. NW8	7	F1
Ordnance Rd. E16	115	F5
Ordnance Rd. SE18	136	C6
Oregano Dr. E14	114	D6
Oregon Av. E12	98	C4
Oregon Cl., N.Mal.	182	C4
Georgia Rd.		
Oregon Sq., Orp.	207	G1
Orestes Ms. NW6	90	D5
Aldred Rd.		
Orford Ct. SE27	169	H2
Orford Gdns., Twick.	162	C2
Orford Rd. E17	78	A5
Orford Rd. E18	79	H3
Orford Rd. SE6	172	B3
Organ La. E4	62	C2
Oriel Cl., Mitch.	186	D4
Oriel Ct. NW3	91	F4
Heath St.		
Oriel Dr. SW13	127	H6
Oriel Gdns., Ilf.	80	C3
Oriel Pl. NW3	91	F4
Heath St.		
Oriel Rd. E9	95	G6
Oriel Way, Nthlt.	85	H7
Orient Ind. Pk. E10	96	A2
Orient St. SE11	35	G1
Orient Way E5	95	G3
Orient Way E10	95	H2
Oriental Rd. E16	136	A1
Oriental St. E14	114	A7
Morant St.		
Oriole Way SE28	118	B7
Orion Rd. N11	58	B6
Orissa Rd. SE18	137	H5
Orkney St. SW11	150	A2
Orlando Rd. SW4	150	C3
Orleans Cl., Esher	194	A2
Orleans Rd. SE19	170	A6
Orleans Rd., Twick.	145	E7
Orleston Ms. N7	93	G6
Orleston Rd. N7	93	G6
Orley Frm. Rd., Har.	86	B3
Orlop St. SE10	134	E5
Ormanton Rd. SE26	170	D4
Orme Ct. W2	14	A6
Orme Ct. W2	108	E7
Orme Ct. Ms. W2	14	B6
Orme La. W2	14	A6
Orme La. W2	108	E7
Orme Rd., Kings.T.	182	B2
Orme Sq. W2	14	A6
Ormeley Rd. SW12	168	B1
Ormerod Gdns.,	186	A2
Mitch.		
Ormesby Cl. SE28	118	D7
Wroxham Rd.		
Ormesby Way, Har.	69	J6
Ormiston Gro. W12	127	H1
Ormiston Rd. SE10	135	G5
Ormond Av., Hmptn.	179	H1
Ormond Av., Rich.	145	G5
Ormond Rd.		
Ormond Cl. WC1	18	B1
Ormond Cres.,	179	H1
Hmptn.		
Ormond Dr., Hmptn.	161	H7
Ormond Ms. WC1	10	B6
Ormond Rd. N19	93	E1
Ormond Rd., Rich.	145	G5
Ormond Yd. SW1	25	G1
Ormonde Av., Orp.	207	F2
Ormonde Gate SW3	32	A4
Ormonde Gate SW3	129	J5
Ormonde Pl. SW1	32	B2
Ormonde Ri.,	63	J1
Buck.H.		
Ormonde Rd. SW14	146	B3
Ormonde Ter. NW8	109	J1
Ormsby Gdns.,	103	J2
Grnf.		
Ormsby Pl. N16	94	C3
Victorian Gro.		
Ormsby St. SE18	136/137	E4
Troy Ct.		
Ormsby St. E2	13	F1
Ormsby St. E2	112	C2
Ormside St. SE15	133	F6
Ornskirk Rd., Wat.	50	D4
Ornan Rd. NW3	91	H5
Oronsay Wk. N1	93	J6
Clephane Rd.		
Orpen Wk. N16	94	B3
Orpheus St. SE5	152	A1
Orpington Gdns.	60	B3
N18		
Orpington Rd. N21	59	H1
Orpington Rd., Chis.	193	H3
Orpwood Cl.,	161	F5
Hmptn.		
Orsett St. SE11	34	D3
Orsett St. SE11	131	F5
Orsett Ter. W2	14	B3
Orsett Ter. W2	109	F6
Orsett Ter., Wdf.Grn.	79	J1
Orsman Rd. N1	112	B1
Orton St. E1	29	H2
Orville Rd. SW11	149	G2
Orwell Cl. N5	93	J4
Orwell Rd. E13	115	J2
Osbaldeston Rd. N16	94	D2
Osbert St. SW1	33	H2
Osberton Rd. SE12	155	G5
Osborn Cl. E8	112	D1
Osborn Gdns. NW7	56	A7
Osborn La. SE23	153	H7
Osborn St. E1	21	G2
Osborn St. E1	112	C5
Osborn Ter. SE3	155	F4
Lee Rd.		
Osborne Cl., Barn.	41	J3
Osborne Cl., Beck.	189	H4
Osborne Cl., Felt.	160	D5
Osborne Cl.,	187	J2
Th.Hth.		
Osborne Gro. E17	77	J4
Osborne Gro. N4	93	G1
Osborne Ms. E17	77	J4
Osborne Gro.		
Osborne Pl., Sutt.	199	G5
Osborne Rd. E7	97	H5
Osborne Rd. E9	95	J6
Osborne Rd. E10	96	B3
Osborne Rd. N4	93	G1
Osborne Rd. N13	59	G3
Osborne Rd. NW2	89	H6
Osborne Rd. W3	126	B3
Osborne Rd., Belv.	139	F5
Osborne Rd.,	63	H1
Buck.H.		
Osborne Rd., Dag.	101	F5
Osborne Rd., Enf.	45	H2
Osborne Rd., Houns.	143	F3
Osborne Rd.,	163	H7
Kings.T.		
Osborne Rd., Sthl.	103	J6
Osborne Rd., Th.Hth.	187	J2
Osborne Sq., Dag.	101	F5
Osborne Ter. SW17	168	A5
Church La.		
Oscar St. SE8	154	A1
Oseney Cres. NW5	92	C6
Osgood Av., Orp.	207	J5
Osgood Gdns., Orp.	207	J5
O'Shea Gro. E3	113	J1
Osidge La. N14	58	A1
Osier Ms. W4	127	F6
Osier St. E1	113	F4
Osier Way E10	96	B3
Osier Way, Mitch.	185	H5
Osiers Rd. SW18	148	D4
Oslac Rd. SE6	172	B5
Oslo Ct. NW8	7	G2
Oslo Sq. SE16	133	H3
Norway Gate		
Osman Cl. N15	76	A6
Tewkesbury Rd.		
Osman Rd. N9	60	D3
Osman Rd. W6	127	J3
Batoum Gdns.		
Osmond Cl., Har.	85	J2
Osmond Gdns.,	200	C5
Wall.		
Osmund St. W12	107	F6
Braybrook St.		
Osnaburgh St. NW1	9	E6
Osnaburgh St. NW1	110	B4
Osnaburgh Ter. NW1	8	E5
Osney Ho. SE2	138	D2
Hartslock Dr.		
Osney Wk., Cars.	185	G6
Osprey Cl. E6	116	B5
Dove App.		
Osprey Cl. E11	79	G4
Osprey Cl. E17	61	H7
Osprey Cl., Sutt.	198	B2
Gander Grn. La.		
Osprey Cl., West Dr.	120	B2
Osprey Cl. SE9	157	G6
Alderwood Rd.		
Osprey Ms., Enf.	45	E5
Ospringe Cl. SE20	171	F7
Ospringe Rd. NW5	92	C4
Osram Rd., Wem.	87	G3
Osric Path N1	12	D2
Osric Path N1	112	B2
Ossian Ms. N4	75	F7
Ossian Rd. N4	75	F7
Ossington Bldgs. W1	16	B1
Ossington St. W2	14	A6
Ossington St. W2	108	E7
Ossory Rd. SE1	37	H4
Ossory Rd. SE1	132	D5
Ossulston St. NW1	9	H2
Ossulston St. NW1	110	D3
Ossulton Pl. N2	73	F3
East End Rd.		
Ossulton Way N2	73	F4
Ostade Rd. SW2	151	F7
Osten Ms. SW7	22	B6
Oster Ter. E17	77	F5
Southcote Rd.		
Osterley Av., Islw.	124	A7
Osterley Cl., Islw.	144	A1
Osterley Cres., Islw.	144	B1
Osterley Gdns.,	187	J2
Th.Hth.		
Osterley Ho. E14	114	B6
Giraud St.		
Osterley La., Islw.	124	B5
Osterley La., Sthl.	123	G5
Osterley La., Islw.	124	A5
Osterley Pk. Rd., Sthl.	123	F3
Osterley Pk. Vw. Rd.	124	B2
W7		
Osterley Rd. N16	94	B4
Osterley Rd., Islw.	124	B7
Osterley Views, Sthl.	123	J1
West Pk. Rd.		
Ostliffe Rd. N13	59	H5
Oswald Rd., Sthl.	123	E1
Oswald St. E5	95	G3
Oswald Ter. NW2	89	J3
Temple Rd.		
Oswald's Mead E9	95	H4
Lindisfarne Way		
Osward Pl. N9	60	E2
Osward Rd. SW17	167	J2
Oswell Ho. E1	133	E1
Oswin St. SE11	35	H1
Oswin St. SE11	131	H4
Oswyth Rd. SE5	152	B2
Otford Cl. SE20	189	F1
Otford Cl., Bex.	159	H6
Southwold Rd.		
Otford Cl., Brom.	192	D3
Otford Cres. SE4	153	J6
Othello Cl. SE11	35	G3
Otis St. E3	114	C3
Otley App., Ilf.	81	E6
Otley Dr., Ilf.	80	E5
Otley Rd. E16	115	J6
Otley Ter. E5	95	G2
Otley Way, Wat.	50	C3
Ottaway St. E5	94	D3
Stellman Cl.		
Ottenden Cl., Orp.	207	H4
Southfleet Rd.		
Otter Rd., Grnf.	103	J4
Otterbourne Rd. E4	62	D3
Otterbourne Rd.,	201	J2
Croy.		
Otterburn Gdns.,	124	D7
Islw.		
Otterburn Ho. SE5	35	J7
Otterburn Ho. SE5	131	J7
Otterburn St. SW17	167	J6
Otterden St. SE6	172	A4
Otto Cl. SE26	170	E3
Otto St. SE17	35	G6
Otto St. SE17	131	H6
Oulton Cl. E5	95	F2
Mundford Rd.		
Oulton Cl. SE28	118	C6
Rollesby Way		
Oulton Cres., Bark.	99	J8
Oulton Rd. N15	76	A5
Oulton Way, Wat.	51	E4
Ouseley Rd. SW12	167	J1
Outer Circle NW1	8	B6
Outer Circle NW1	110	B2
Outgate Rd. NW10	89	F7
Outram Pl. N1	111	E1
Outram Rd. E6	116	B1
Outram Rd. N22	74	D1
Outram Rd., Croy.	202	C1
Outwich St. EC3	20	E3
Oval, The E2	112	E2
Oval, The, Sid.	158	A7
Oval Pl. SW8	34	C7
Oval Pl. SW8	131	F7
Oval Rd. NW1	110	B1
Oval Rd., Croy.	202	B1
Oval Rd. N., Dag.	119	H1
Oval Rd. S., Dag.	119	H2
Oval Way SE11	34	D4
Oval Way SE11	131	F5
Overbrae, Beck.	172	A6
Overbrook Wk., Edg.	54	A7
Overbury Av., Beck.	190	B3
Overbury Rd. N15	76	A6
Overbury St. E5	95	G4
Overcliff Rd. SE13	154	A3
Overcourt Cl., Sid.	158	B6
Overdale Av., N.Mal.	182	C2
Overdale Rd. W5	125	F3
Overdown Rd. SE6	172	A4
Overhill Rd. SE22	152	D7
Overhill Way, Beck.	190	D5
Overlea Rd. E5	76	D7
Overmead, Sid.	157	G7
Oversley Ho. W2	108	D5
Overstand Cl., Beck.	190	A5
Overstone Gdns.,	189	J7
Croy.		
Overstone Rd. W6	127	J3
Overton Cl. NW10	88	C6
Overton Cl., Islw.	144	C1
Avenue Rd.		
Overton Ct. E11	79	G7
Overton Dr. E11	79	H7
Overton Dr., Rom.	82	C7
Overton Rd. E10	95	H1
Overton Rd. N14	42	E5
Overton Rd. SE2	138	C3
Overton Rd. SW9	151	G2
Overton Rd., Sutt.	198	D6
Overton Rd. E. SE2	138	D3
Overtons Yd., Croy.	201	J3
Ovesdon Av., Har.	85	F1
Ovett Cl. SE19	170	B6
Ovex Cl. E14	134	C2
Ovington Gdns. SW3	23	H6
Ovington Gdns. SW3	129	H3
Ovington Ms. SW3	23	H6
Ovington Ms. SW3	129	H3
Ovington Sq. SW3	23	H6
Ovington Sq. SW3	129	H3
Ovington St. SW3	23	H6
Ovington St. SW3	129	H3
Owen Cl. SE28	138	C1
Owen Cl., Croy.	188	A6
Owen Cl., Hayes	102	B3
Owen Gdns.,	64	B6
Wdf.Grn.		
Owen Rd. N13	59	J5
Owen Rd., Hayes	102	B3
Owen St. EC1	11	G2
Owen Wk. SE20	170	D7
Sycamore Gro.		
Owen Waters Ho., Ilf.	80	C1
Owen Way NW10	88	C6
Owenite St. SE2	138	B4
Owen's Ct. EC1	11	G3
Owen's Row EC1	11	G3
Owens Way SE23	153	H7
Owgan Cl. SE5	132	A7
Benhill Rd.		
Oxberry Av. SW6	148	B2
Oxendon St. SW1	17	H6
Oxendon St. SW1	110	D7
Oxenford St. SE15	152	C3
Oxenholme NW1	9	G2
Oxenholme NW1	110	C2
Oxenpark Av., Wem.	69	H7
Oxestalls Rd. SE8	133	H5
Oxford Av. SW20	184	B2
Oxford Av., Hayes	121	J7
Oxford Av., Houns.	123	G5
Oxford Circ. Av. W1	17	F4
Oxford Cl. N9	60	E2
Oxford Cl., Mitch.	186	C3
Oxford Ct. EC4	20	B5
Oxford Ct. W3	106	A6

Oxford Ct., Felt. 160 D4
Oxford Way
Oxford Cres., N.Mal. 182 D6
Oxford Dr., Ruis. 84 C2
Oxford Gdns. N20 57 G1
Oxford Gdns. N21 43 J7
Oxford Gdns. W4 126 A5
Oxford Gdns. W10 108 B6
Oxford Gate W6 128 A4
Oxford Ms., Bex. 159 G7
Bexley High St.
Oxford Pl. NW10 88 D3
Neasden La. N.
Oxford Rd. E15 96 D6
Oxford Rd. N4 93 G1
Oxford Rd. N9 61 E2
Oxford Rd. NW6 108 D2
Oxford Rd. SE19 170 A6
Oxford Rd. SW15 148 B4
Oxford Rd. W5 105 G7
Oxford Rd., Cars. 199 H6
Oxford Rd., Enf. 45 E5
Oxford Rd., Har. 67 J6
Oxford Rd. 68 C3
(Wealdstone), Har.
Oxford Rd., Ilf. 99 F4
Oxford Rd., Sid. 176 B5
Oxford Rd., Tedd. 162 A5
Oxford Rd., Wall. 200 C5
Oxford Rd., Wdf.Grn. 63 J5
Oxford Rd. N. W4 126 B5
Oxford Rd. S. W4 126 A5
Oxford Sq. W2 15 H4
Oxford Sq. W2 109 H6
Oxford St. W1 16 B4
Oxford St. W1 110 B6
Oxford Wk., Sthl. 123 F1
Oxford Way, Felt. 160 D4
Oxgate Gdns. NW2 89 H3
Oxgate La. NW2 89 H2
Oxhawth Cres., 192 D5
Brom.
Oxhey Dr., Nthwd. 50 B5
Oxhey Dr., Wat. 50 C3
Oxhey La., Har. 51 H5
Oxhey La., Pnr. 51 H5
Oxhey La., Wat. 51 F3
Oxhey Ridge Cl., 50 A5
Nthwd.
Oxleas E6 116 E6
Oxleas Cl., Well. 157 G2
Oxleay Ct., Har. 85 G1
Oxleay Rd., Har. 85 G1
Oxleigh Cl., N.Mal. 183 E5
Oxley Cl. SE1 37 G3
Oxley Cl. SE1 132 C5
Oxleys Rd. NW2 89 H3
Oxlip Cl., Croy. 203 G1
Marigold Way
Oxlow La., Dag. 101 G4
Oxonian St. SE22 152 C4
Oxted Cl., Mitch. 185 G3
Oxtoby Way SW16 186 D2
Oyster Catchers Cl. 115 H6
E16
Freemasons Rd.
Oyster Row E1 113 F6
Lukin St.
Ozolins Way E16 115 G6

P

Pablo Neruda Cl. 151 H4
SE24
Shakespeare Rd.
Pace Pl. E1 112/113 E6
Bigland St.
Pacific Rd. E16 115 G6
Packington Rd. W3 126 C3
Packington Sq. N1 111 J1
Packington St. N1 111 H1
Packmores Rd. SE9 157 G5
Padbury SE17 36 D4
Padbury SE17 132 B5
Padbury Ct. E2 13 G4
Padbury Ct. E2 112 C3
Padcroft Rd., West Dr. 120 A1
Paddenswick Rd. W6 127 G3
Paddington Cl., 102 D4
Hayes
Paddington Grn. W2 15 F1
Paddington Grn. W2 109 G5
Paddington St. W1 16 B1
Paddington St. W1 110 A5
Paddock Cl. SE3 155 G2
Paddock Cl. SE26 171 G4
Paddock Cl., Nthlt. 103 G2
Paddock Cl., Orp. 206/207 E4
State Fm. Av.
Paddock Cl., Wor.Pk. 196 E1
Paddock Gdns. SE19 170 B6
Westow St.
Paddock Rd. NW2 89 G3
Paddock Rd., Bexh. 159 E4

Paddock Rd., Ruis. 84 D3
Paddock Way, Chis. 175 G2
Paddocks, The, Barn. 41 J3
Paddocks, The, Wem. 88 B2
Paddocks Cl., Har. 85 H4
Padfield Rd. SE5 151 J3
Padnall Ct., Rom. 82 D3
Padnall Rd.
Padnall Rd., Rom. 82 D4
Padstow Rd., Enf. 43 H2
Padua Rd. SE20 189 F1
Pagden St. SW8 150 B1
Page Cl., Dag. 101 E5
Page Cl., Hmptn. 161 E6
Page Cl., Har. 69 J6
Page Cres., Croy. 201 G5
Page Grn. Rd. N15 76 D5
Page Grn. Ter. N15 76 C5
Page Heath La., 192 A3
Brom.
Page Heath Vil., 192 A3
Brom.
Page Meadow NW7 55 G7
Page Rd., Felt. 141 G6
Page St. NW7 71 G1
Page St. SW1 33 J1
Page St. SW1 130 E4
Pageant Av. NW9 70 D1
Pageant Cres. SE16 133 H1
Rotherhithe St.
Pageant Wk., Croy. 202 B3
Pageantmaster Ct. 19 G4
EC4
Pagehurst Rd., Croy. 188 E7
Pages Hill N10 74 A2
Pages La. N10 74 A2
Pages Wk. SE1 36 D1
Pages Yd. W4 126/127 E6
Church St.
Paget Av., Sutt. 199 G3
Paget Cl., Hmptn. 162 A4
Paget Gdns., Chis. 193 E1
Paget La., Islw. 144 A3
Paget Pl., Kings.T. 164 C6
Paget Pl., T.Ditt. 194 D1
Brooklands Rd.
Paget Rd. N16 94 A1
Paget Rd., Ilf. 98 E4
Paget St. EC1 11 G3
Paget Ter. SE18 136 D6
Pagitts Gro., Barn. 40 E1
Pagnell St. SE14 133 J7
Pagoda Av., Rich. 145 J3
Pagoda Gdns. SE3 154 D2
Pagoda Vista, Rich. 145 J2
Paignton Rd. N15 76 B6
Paignton Rd., Ruis. 84 A3
Paines Cl., Pnr. 67 E3
Paines La., Pnr. 66 E1
Pains Cl., Mitch. 186 B2
Painsthorpe Rd. N16 94 B3
Oldfield Rd.
Painters Rd., Ilf. 81 J3
Paisley Rd. N22 75 H1
Paisley Rd., Cars. 199 G1
Pakeman St. N7 93 F3
Pakenham Cl. SW12 168 A1
Balham Pk. Rd.
Pakenham St. WC1 10 D5
Pakenham St. WC1 111 F3
Palace Av. W8 22 B2
Palace Av. W8 129 E1
Palace Ct. NW3 91 E5
Palace Ct. W2 14 A5
Palace Ct. W2 108 E7
Palace Ct., Brom. 191 H1
Palace Gro.
Palace Ct., Har. 69 H6
Palace Ct. Gdns. N10 74 C3
Palace Gdns., Buck.H. 64 A1
Palace Gdns., Enf. 44 A3
Palace Gdns. Ms. W8 128 D1
Palace Gdns. Ter. W8 128 D1
Palace Gate W8 22 C4
Palace Gate W8 129 F2
Palace Gates Rd. N22 74 D1
Palace Grn. W8 22 B3
Palace Grn. W8 129 E2
Palace Grn., Croy. 203 J7
Palace Gro. SE19 170 C7
Palace Gro., Brom. 191 H1
Palace Ms. E17 77 J4
Palace Ms. SW1 32 C2
Palace Ms. SW6 128 C7
Hartismere Rd.
Palace of Industry, 88 A4
Wem.
Palace Pl. SW1 25 F5
Palace Rd. N8 74 D5
Palace Rd. N11 58 E7
Palace Rd. SE19 170 C7
Palace Rd. SW2 169 F1

Palace Rd., Brom. 191 H1
Palace Rd., E.Mol. 180 A3
Palace Rd., Kings.T. 181 G4
Palace Rd., Ruis. 84 E4
Palace Rd. Est. SW2 169 F1
Palace Sq. SE19 170 C7
Palace St. SW1 25 F5
Palace St. SW1 130 C3
Palace Vw. SE12 173 G2
Palace Vw., Brom. 191 G3
Palace Vw., Croy. 203 J4
Palace Vw. Rd. E4 62 B5
Palamos Rd. E10 96 A1
Palatine Av. N16 94 C4
Stoke Newington Rd.
Palatine Rd. N16 94 B4
Palermo Rd. NW10 107 G2
Palestine Gro. SW19 185 G1
Palewell Common 146 D5
Dr. SW14
Palewell Pk. SW14 146 D5
Paley Gdns., Loug. 49 F3
Palfrey Pl. SW8 34 D7
Palfrey Pl. SW8 131 F7
Palgrave Av., Sthl. 103 G7
Palgrave Rd. W12 127 F3
Palissy St. E2 13 F4
Pall Mall SW1 25 G2
Pall Mall SW1 130 C1
Pall Mall E. SW1 25 J1
Pall Mall E. SW1 130 D1
Pall Mall Pl. SW1 25 G2
Pall Mall Pl. SW1 130 C1
Pallant Way, Orp. 206 D3
Pallet Way SE18 156 B1
Palliser Rd. W14 128 B5
Palm Av., Sid. 176 D6
Palm Cl. E10 96 B3
Palm Gro. W5 125 H3
Palm Rd., Rom. 83 J5
Palmar Cres., Bexh. 159 G3
Palmar Rd., Bexh. 159 G2
Palmeira Rd., Bexh. 158 D3
Palmer Av., Sutt. 197 J4
Palmer Cl., Houns. 143 G1
Palmer Cl., W.Wick. 204 D3
Palmer Cres., Kings.T. 181 H3
Palmer Gdns., Barn. 40 A5
Palmer Pl. N7 93 G5
Palmer Rd. E13 115 H4
Palmer Rd., Dag. 100 D1
Palmer St. SW1 25 H4
Palmer St. SW1 130 D3
Palmers Gro., W.Mol. 179 G4
Palmers La., Enf. 45 E1
Palmers Pas. SW14 146 C3
Palmers Rd.
Palmers Rd. E2 113 G2
Palmers Rd. N11 58 C5
Palmers Rd. SW14 146 C3
Palmers Rd. SW16 187 F2
Palmers Rd., Borwd. 38 B1
Palmerston Cres. N13 59 G5
Palmerston Cres. 137 F6
SE18
Palmerston Gro. 166 D7
SW19
Palmerston Rd. E7 97 H5
Palmerston Rd. E17 77 J4
Palmerston Rd. N22 59 F7
Palmerston Rd. NW6 90 D7
Palmerston Rd. 146 C4
SW14
Palmerston Rd. 166 D7
SW19
Palmerston Rd. W3 126 C3
Palmerston Rd., 63 H2
Buck.H.
Palmerston Rd., Cars. 199 J4
Palmerston Rd., Croy. 188 A5
Palmerston Rd., Har. 68 C3
Palmerston Rd., 143 J1
Houns.
Gresham Rd.
Palmerston Rd., Orp. 207 F4
Palmerston Rd., Sutt. 199 F5
Vernon Rd.
Palmerston Rd., 144 C6
Twick.
Palmerston Way SW8 130 B7
Bradmead
Pamela Gdns., Pnr. 66 B5
Pamela Wk. E8 112 D1
Marlborough Av.
Pampisford Rd., 201 H7
S.Croy.
Pams Way, Epsom 196 D5
Pancras La. EC4 20 A4
Pancras Rd. NW1 9 H1
Pancras Rd. NW1 110 D2
Pandora Rd. NW6 90 D6
Panfield Ms., Ilf. 80 D6
Cranbrook Rd.
Panfield Rd. SE2 138 A3

Pangbourne Av. W10 107 J5
Pangbourne Dr., Stan. 53 G5
Panhard Pl., Sthl. 103 H7
Pank Av., Barn. 41 F5
Pankhurst Cl. SE14 133 G7
Briant St.
Pankhurst Cl., Islw. 144 C3
Pankhurst Rd., Walt. 178 C7
Panmuir Rd. SW20 183 H1
Panmure Cl. N5 93 H4
Panmure Rd. SE26 170 E3
Pansy Gdns. W12 107 G7
Panther Dr. NW10 88 D5
Pantiles, The NW11 72 C5
Willifield Way
Pantiles, The, Bexh. 139 F7
Pantiles, The, Brom. 192 B3
Pantiles Cl. N13 59 H5
Panton St. SW1 17 H6
Panyer All. EC4 19 J3
Papermill Cl., Cars. 200 A4
Papillons Wk. SE3 155 G2
Papworth Gdns. N7 93 F5
Liverpool Rd.
Papworth Way SW2 151 G7
Parade, The SW11 32 A7
Parade, The SW11 129 J7
Parade, The, Esher 194 B6
Parade, The, Hmptn. 162 A5
Hampton Rd.
Parade, The 50 E3
(Carpenders Pk.), Wat.
Parade Ms. SE27 169 H2
Norwood Rd.
Paradise Pas. N7 93 G5
Paradise Pl. SE18 136 B4
Woodhill
Paradise Rd. SW4 150 E2
Paradise Rd., Rich. 145 G5
Paradise Row E2 112/113 E3
Bethnal Grn. Rd.
Paradise St. SE16 132 E2
Paradise Wk. SW3 31 J5
Paradise Wk. SW3 129 J6
Paragon, The SE3 155 F2
Paragon Cl. E16 115 G6
Paragon Gro., Surb. 181 J6
Paragon Ms. SE1 36 C1
Paragon Pl. SE3 155 F2
Paragon Pl., Surb. 181 J6
Berrylands Rd.
Paragon Rd. E9 95 E6
Parbury Ri., Chess. 195 H6
Parbury Rd. SE23 153 H6
Parchmore Rd., 187 H2
Th.Hth.
Parchmore Way, 187 H2
Th.Hth.
Pardon St. EC1 11 H5
Pardoner St. SE1 28 C5
Pardoner St. SE1 132 A3
Parfett St. E1 21 J2
Parfett St. E1 112 D5
Parfitt Cl. NW3 91 F2
North End
Parfrey St. W6 127 J6
Pargan Dr., Ilf. 80 E6
Parham Way N10 74 C2
Paris Gdn. SE1 27 G1
Paris Gdn. SE1 131 H1
Parish Gate Dr., Sid. 157 H6
Parish La. SE20 171 G6
Parish Ms. SE20 171 G7
Parish Wf. Pl. SE18 136 B4
Woodhill
Park, The N6 74 A6
Park, The NW11 90 E1
Park, The SE19 170 B7
Park, The SE23 170/171 E1
Park Hill
Park, The W5 125 G1
Park, The, Cars. 199 J5
Park, The, Sid. 175 J5
Park App., Well. 158 B4
Park Av. E6 116 D1
Park Av. E15 96 E6
Park Av. N3 73 E1
Park Av. N13 59 G3
Park Av. N18 60 D4
Park Av. N22 75 E2
Park Av. NW2 89 H6
Park Av. NW10 105 J3
Park Av. NW11 90 E1
Park Av. SW14 146 D4
Park Av., Bark. 99 F6
Park Av., Brom. 173 F6
Park Av., Cars. 200 A6
Park Av., Enf. 44 B6
Park Av., Houns. 143 H6
Park Av., Ilf. 98 D1
Park Av., Mitch. 168 B7
Park Av. 206 C3
(Farnborough), Orp.
Park Av., Sthl. 123 G1

Par–Par 325

Park Av., W.Wick. 204 C2
Park Av., Wdf.Grn. 63 H5
Park Av. E., Epsom 197 G6
Park Av. Ms., Mitch. 168 B7
Park Av.
Park Av. N. N8 74 D3
Park Av. N. NW10 89 H5
Park Av. Rd. N17 61 E7
Park Av. S. N8 74 D4
Park Av. W., Epsom 197 G6
Park Chase, Wem. 87 J4
Park Cl. E9 113 F1
Park Cl. NW2 89 H3
Park Cl. NW10 105 J3
Park Cl. SW1 23 J4
Park Cl. SW1 129 J2
Park Cl. W4 126 D5
Park Cl. W14 128 C3
Park Cl., Cars. 199 J6
Park Cl., Hmptn. 179 J1
Park Cl., Har. 68 B1
Park Cl., Houns. 143 J5
Park Cl., Kings.T. 182 A1
Park Ct. SE26 171 E6
Park Ct., Kings.T. 181 F1
Park Ct., N.Mal. 182 D4
Park Ct., Wem. 87 H5
Park Cres. N3 57 E7
Park Cres. W1 8 D6
Park Cres. W1 110 B4
Park Cres., Enf. 44 A4
Park Cres., Har. 68 B1
Park Cres., Twick. 162 A1
Park Cres. Ms. E. W1 8 E6
Park Cres. Ms. W. W1 16 D1
Park Cft., Edg. 70 C1
Park Dale N11 58 D6
Park Dr. N21 43 J6
Park Dr. NW11 90 E1
Park Dr. SE7 136 B6
Park Dr. SW14 146 D4
Park Dr. W3 126 A3
Park Dr., Dag. 101 J3
Park Dr., Har. 67 G7
Park Dr. 52 B6
(Harrow Weald), Har.
Park Dr. Cl. SE7 136 B5
Park End NW3 91 H4
South Hill Pk.
Park End, Brom. 191 F1
Park Fm. Cl. N2 73 F3
Park Fm. Cl., Pnr. 66 B5
Field End Rd.
Park Fm. Rd., Brom. 192 A1
Park Fm. Rd., 163 H7
Kings.T.
Park Gdns. NW9 70 B3
Park Gdns., Kings.T. 163 J5
Park Gate N2 73 G3
Park Gate N21 43 F7
Park Gate W5 105 G5
Mount Av.
Park Gates, Har. 85 G4
Park Gro. E15 115 G1
Park Gro. N11 58 D7
Park Gro., Bexh. 159 J4
Park Gro., Brom. 191 H1
Park Gro., Edg. 53 J5
Park Gro. Rd. E11 96 E2
Park Hall Rd. N2 73 H4
Park Hall Rd. SE21 169 J3
Park Hill SE23 171 E2
Park Hill SW4 150 D5
Park Hill W5 105 G5
Park Hill, Brom. 192 B4
Park Hill, Cars. 199 H6
Park Hill, Loug. 48 A5
Park Hill, Rich. 145 J6
Park Hill Cl., Cars. 199 H5
Park Hill Ct. SW17 167 J3
Beeches Rd.
Park Hill Ri., Croy. 202 B2
Park Hill Rd., Brom. 190 E2
Park Hill Rd., Croy. 202 B4
Park Hill Rd., Wall. 200 B7
Park Ho. N21 43 F7
Park Ho. Gdns., 145 F6
Twick.
Park La. E15 114 D1
High St.
Park La. N9 60 C3
Park La. N17 60 D7
Park La. N18 60 B4
Sheldon Rd.
Park La. W1 24 C2
Park La. W1 110 A7
Park La., Cars. 200 A4
Park La., Croy. 202 A3
Park La., Har. 85 H3
Park La., Houns. 122 A7
Park La., Rich. 145 G4
Park La. 82 D6
(Chadwell Heath), Rom.
Park La., Stan. 52 D3
Park La., Sutt. 198 B6
Park La., Tedd. 162 C6
Park La., Wall. 200 A4
Park La., Wem. 87 H5
Park La. Cl. N17 60 D7
Park Lawns, Wem. 87 J4
Park Mead, Har. 85 H3
Park Mead, Sid. 158 B5
Park Ms. SE24 151 J6
Croxted Rd.
Park Ms., Chis. 175 E6
Park Ms., E.Mol. 179 J4
Park Ms., Hmptn. 161 J5
Park Rd.
Park Par. NW10 107 F2
Park Pl. E14 134 A1
Park Pl. SW1 25 F2
Park Pl. SW1 130 C1
Park Pl. W3 126 A4
Park Pl. W5 125 G1
Park Pl., Hmptn. 161 J6
Park Pl., Wem. 87 J4
Park Pl. Vil. W2 14 D1
Park Pl. Vil. W2 109 F5
Park Ridings N8 75 G3
Park Ri. SE23 171 H1
Park Ri., Har. 68 B1
Park Ri. Rd. SE23 171 H1
Park Rd. E6 115 J1
Park Rd. E10 96 A1
Park Rd. E12 97 H1
Park Rd. E15 115 G1
Park Rd. E17 77 J5
Park Rd. N2 73 G3
Park Rd. N8 74 C4
Park Rd. N11 58 D7
Park Rd. N14 42 D7
Park Rd. N15 75 H4
Park Rd. N18 60 C4
Park Rd. NW1 7 G3
Park Rd. NW1 109 H3
Park Rd. NW4 71 G7
Park Rd. NW8 7 G3
Park Rd. NW8 109 H3
Park Rd. NW9 70 D7
Park Rd. NW10 106 E1
Park Rd. SE25 188 B4
Park Rd. SW19 167 G6
Park Rd. W4 126 C7
Park Rd. W7 104 C7
Park Rd., Barn. 40 C4
Park Rd. 41 H4
(New Barnet), Barn.
Park Rd., Beck. 171 J7
Park Rd., Brom. 191 H1
Park Rd., Chis. 175 E6
Park Rd., E.Mol. 179 J4
Park Rd., Felt. 160 D4
Park Rd., Hmptn. 161 H4
Park Rd., Houns. 143 J4
Park Rd., Ilf. 99 G3
Park Rd., Islw. 144 E1
Park Rd., Kings.T. 163 J5
Park Rd. 162 C6
(Hampton Wick), Kings.T.
Park Rd., N.Mal. 182 D4
Park Rd., Rich. 145 J6
Park Rd., Sun. 160 B7
Park Rd., Surb. 181 J5
Park Rd., Sutt. 198 B6
Park Rd., Tedd. 181 F1
Park Rd., Twick. 145 F6
Park Rd., Wall. 200 B5
Park Rd. (Hackbridge), 200 B2
Wall.
Park Rd., Wem. 87 H6
Park Rd. E. W3 126 B2
Park Rd. N. W3 126 B2
Park Rd. N. W4 126 D5
Park Row SE10 134 D6
Park Royal Rd. NW10 106 C3
Park Royal Rd. W3 106 C3
Park Sq. E. NW1 8 D5
Park Sq. E. NW1 110 B4
Park Sq. Ms. NW1 8 D5
Park Sq. Ms. NW1 110 B4
Park Sq. W. NW1 8 D5
Park Sq. W. NW1 110 B4
Park St. SE1 27 J1
Park St. SE1 131 J1
Park St. W1 16 B5
Park St. W1 110 A7
Park St., Croy. 201 J2
Park St., Tedd. 162 B6
Park Ter., Wor.Pk. 197 G1
Park Vw. N21 43 F7
Park Vw. W3 106 C5
Park Vw., N.Mal. 183 F3
Park Vw., Pnr. 67 F1
Park Vw., Wem. 88 B5
Park Vw. Ct., Ilf. 81 H6
Brancaster Rd.
Park Vw. Cres. N11 58 B4
Park Vw. Est. E2 113 G2
Park Vw. Gdns. NW4 71 J5
Park Vw. Gdns., Bark. 117 H2
River Rd.
Park Vw. Gdns., Ilf. 80 C4
Park Vw. Rd. N3 73 E1
Park Vw. Rd. N17 76 D3
Park Vw. Rd. NW10 89 F4
Park Vw. Rd. W5 105 H5
Park Vw. Rd., Pnr. 50 B7
Park Vw. Rd., Sthl. 123 G1
Park Vw. Rd., Well. 158 C3
Park Village E. NW1 110 B2
Park Village W. NW1 8 D1
Park Village W. NW1 110 B2
Park Vil., Rom. 82 D6
Park Vista SE10 134 D6
Park Wk. N6 74 A7
North Rd.
Park Wk. SE10 134 D7
Crooms Hill
Park Wk. SW10 30 D5
Park Wk. SW10 129 F6
Park Way N20 57 J4
Park Way NW11 72 B5
Park Way, Edg. 70 B1
Park Way, Enf. 43 G2
Park Way, Felt. 142 B7
Park Way, Ruis. 84 A1
Park Way, W.Mol. 179 H3
Park W. W2 15 H4
Park W. Pl. W2 15 H3
Parkcroft Rd. SE12 155 F7
Parkdale Cres., 196 D3
Wor.Pk.
Parkdale Rd. SE18 137 H5
Parke Rd. SW13 147 G1
Parke Rd., Sun. 178 A4
Parker Cl. E16 136 B1
Parker Ms. WC2 18 B3
Parker Rd., Croy. 201 J4
Parker St. E16 136 B1
Parker St. WC2 18 B3
Parker St. WC2 111 E6
Parkers Row SE1 29 G4
Parkes Rd., Chig. 65 H5
Parkfield Av. SW14 146 E4
Parkfield Av., Felt. 160 A3
Parkfield Av., Har. 67 J2
Parkfield Av., Nthlt. 102 D2
Parkfield Cl., Edg. 54 B6
Parkfield Cl., Nthlt. 102 E2
Parkfield Cres., Felt. 160 A3
Parkfield Cres., Har. 67 J2
Parkfield Cres., Ruis. 84 E3
Parkfield Dr., Nthlt. 102 D2
Parkfield Gdns., Har. 67 H3
Parkfield Rd. NW10 89 G7
Parkfield Rd. SE14 153 J1
Parkfield Rd., Felt. 160 A3
Parkfield Rd., Har. 85 J3
Parkfield Rd., Nthlt. 102 E2
Parkfield St. N1 11 F1
Parkfield St. N1 111 G2
Parkfield Way, Brom. 192 C6
Parkfields SW15 147 J4
Parkfields, Croy. 203 J1
Parkfields Av. NW9 88 D1
Parkfields Av. SW20 183 H1
Parkfields Cl., Cars. 200 A4
Devonshire Rd.
Parkfields Rd., 163 J5
Kings.T.
Parkgate SE3 155 F3
Parkgate Av., Barn. 41 F1
Parkgate Cl., Kings.T. 164 B6
Warboys App.
Parkgate Cres., Barn. 41 F2
Parkgate Gdns. SW14 146 D5
Parkgate Ms. N6 74 C7
Stanhope Rd.
Parkgate Rd. SW11 129 H7
Parkgate Rd., Wall. 200 A5
Parkham Ct., Brom. 191 E2
Parkham St. SW11 149 H1
Parkhill Rd. E4 62 C1
Parkhill Rd. NW3 91 J5
Parkhill Rd., Bex. 159 F7
Parkhill Rd., Sid. 175 G3
Parkhill Wk. NW3 91 J5
Parkholme Rd. E8 94 C6
Parkhouse St. SE5 36 C7
Parkhouse St. SE5 132 A7
Parkhurst Av. E16 135 H1
Wesley Av.
Parkhurst Gdns., Bex. 159 G7
Parkhurst Rd. E12 98 D4
Parkhurst Rd. E17 77 H4
Parkhurst Rd. N7 92 E4
Parkhurst Rd. N11 58 A4
Parkhurst Rd. N17 76 D2
Parkhurst Rd. N22 59 F7
Parkhurst Rd., Bex. 159 G7
Parkhurst Rd., Sutt. 199 G4
Parkland Cl., Chig. 65 F3
Parkland Gdns. SW19 166 A1
Parkland Rd. N22 75 F2
Parkland Rd., Wdf.Grn. 63 G7
Parkland Wk. N4 75 F7
Parkland Wk. N6 74 D7
Parkland Wk. N10 74 B4
Parklands N6 74 B7
Parklands, Chig. 65 F3
Parklands, Surb. 181 J5
Parklands Cl. SW14 146 C5
Parklands Ct., Houns. 142 D2
Parklands Dr. N3 72 B3
Parklands Rd. SW16 168 B5
Parklands Way, 197 E3
Wor.Pk.
Parklea Cl. NW9 71 E1
Parkleigh Rd. SW19 184 E2
Parkleys, Rich. 163 G4
Parkmead SW15 147 H6
Parkmead, Loug. 48 D5
Parkmead Gdns. NW7 55 F6
Parkmore Cl., 63 G4
Wdf.Grn.
Parkshot, Rich. 145 H4
Parkside N3 72 E1
Parkside NW2 89 H3
Parkside NW7 55 G6
Parkside SE3 135 F7
Parkside SW19 166 A4
Parkside, Buck.H. 63 H2
Parkside, Hmptn. 162 A5
Parkside, Sid. 176 B2
Parkside, Sutt. 198 B6
Parkside Av. SW19 166 A5
Parkside Av., Brom. 192 B4
Parkside Cl. SE20 171 F7
Parkside Cres. N7 93 G3
Parkside Cres., Surb. 182 C6
Parkside Dr., Edg. 54 A3
Parkside Est. E9 113 F1
Rutland Rd.
Parkside Gdns. SW19 166 A4
Parkside Gdns., Barn. 57 J1
Parkside Ho., Dag. 101 J3
Parkside Rd. SW11 150 A1
Parkside Rd., Belv. 139 J4
Parkside Rd., Houns. 143 H5
Parkside Ter. N18 60 A4
Great Cambridge Rd.
Parkside Wk. SE10 134 E5
Parkside Way, Har. 67 H4
Parkstead Rd. SW15 147 G5
Parkstone Av. N18 60 C5
Parkstone Rd. E17 78 C3
Parkstone Rd. SE15 152 D2
Rye La.
Parkthorne Cl., Har. 67 H6
Parkthorne Dr., Har. 67 G6
Parkthorne Rd. SW12 150 D7
Parkview Ct. SW18 148 D6
Broomhill Rd.
Parkview Dr., Mitch. 185 G2
Parkview Rd. SE9 174 E2
Parkview Rd., Croy. 202 D1
Parkville Rd. SW6 128 C7
Parkway N14 58 E2
Parkway NW1 110 B1
Parkway SW20 184 A4
Parkway, Erith 139 E3
Parkway, Ilf. 99 J3
Parkway, Wdf.Grn. 63 J5
Parkway, The, Hayes 102 C6
Parkway, The 142 B2
(Cranford), Houns.
Parkway, The, Nthlt. 102 D3
Parkway, The, Sthl. 122 A5
Parkway Ms., Mitch. 168 B7
Park Av.
Parkway Trd. Est., 122 C6
Houns.
Parkwood N20 57 J3
Parkwood, Beck. 190 A1
Parkwood Gro., Sun. 178 A3
Parkwood Ms. N6 74 B6
Parkwood Rd. SW19 166 C5
Parkwood Rd., Bex. 159 F7
Parkwood Rd., Islw. 144 C1
Parliament Ct. E1 112 B5
Sandy's Row
Parliament Hill NW3 91 H4
Parliament Ms. SW14 146 C2
Thames Bank
Parliament Sq. SW1 26 A4
Parliament Sq. SW1 130 E2
Parliament St. SW1 26 A4
Parliament St. SW1 130 E2
Parma Cres. SW11 149 J4
Parmiter St. E2 113 E2
Parnell Cl., Edg. 54 B4
Parnell Rd. E3 113 J1
Parnham St. E14 113 H6
Blount St.
Parolles Rd. N19 92 C1
Paroma Rd., Belv. 139 G3

Parr Cl. N9 60 E4
Parr Cl. N18 60 E4
Parr Ct., Felt. 160 C4
Parr Rd. E6 116 A1
Parr Rd., Stan. 69 G1
Parr St. N1 12 B1
Parr St. N1 112 A2
Parrs Pl., Hmptn. 161 G7
Parry Av. E6 116 C6
Parry Cl., Epsom 197 G7
Parry Pl. SE18 137 E4
Parry Rd. SE25 188 B3
Parry Rd. W10 108 B3
Parry St. SW8 34 A5
Parry St. SW8 130 E6
Parsifal Rd. NW6 90 D5
Parsley Gdns., Croy. 203 G1
  Primrose La.
Parsloes Av., Dag. 100 D4
Parson St. NW4 71 J4
Parsonage Gdns., Enf. 43 J2
Parsonage La., Enf. 44 A2
Parsonage La., Sid. 177 E4
Parsonage 139 G6
  Manorway, Belv.
Parsonage St. E14 134 C4
Parsons Cres., Edg. 54 A3
Parsons Grn. SW6 148 D1
Parsons Grn. La. SW6 148 D1
Parsons Gro., Edg. 54 A3
Parsons Hill SE18 136 D3
  Powis St.
Parson's Ho. W2 7 E6
Parson's Ho. W2 109 G4
Parson's Mead, Croy. 201 H1
Parson's Mead, E.Mol. 179 J3
Parsons Rd. E13 115 J2
  Old St.
Parthenia Rd. SW6 148 D1
Partingdale La. NW7 56 A5
Partington Cl. N19 92 D1
Partridge Cl. E16 116 A5
  Fulmer Rd.
Partridge Cl., Barn. 39 J6
Partridge Cl., Bushey 51 H1
Partridge Cl., Stan. 53 H4
Partridge Ct. EC1 111 H4
  Percival St.
Partridge Dr., Orp. 207 F3
Partridge Grn. SE9 174 D3
Partridge Rd., Hmptn. 161 F6
Partridge Rd., Sid. 175 H3
Partridge Sq. E6 116 B5
  Nightingale Way
Partridge Way N22 75 E1
Parvin St. SW8 150 D1
Pasadena Cl., Hayes 122 B2
Pasadena Cl. Trd. 122 B2
  Est., Hayes
  Pasadena Cl.
Pascal St. SW8 33 J7
Pascal St. SW8 130 D7
Pascoe Rd. SE13 154 D5
Pasley Cl. SE17 35 J4
Pasquier Rd. E17 77 H3
Passey Pl. SE9 156 C6
Passfield Dr. E14 114 B5
  Uamvar St.
Passfield Path SE28 118 B7
  Booth St.
Passing All. EC1 11 H6
Passmore Gdns. N11 58 D6
Passmore St. SW1 32 B2
Passmore St. SW1 130 A4
Pasteur Cl. NW9 71 E2
Pasteur Gdns. N18 59 H5
Paston Cl. E5 95 G3
  Caldecott Way
Paston Cl., Wall. 200 C3
Paston Cres. SE12 155 H7
Pastor St. SE11 35 H1
Pastor St. SE11 131 H4
Pasture Cl., Wem. 86 E3
Pasture Rd. SE6 173 F1
Pasture Rd., Dag. 101 F4
Pasture Rd., Wem. 86 E3
Pastures, The N20 56 C1
Patcham Ter. SW8 150 B1
Pater St. W8 128 D3
Paternoster Row 19 J4
EC4
Paternoster Sq. EC4 19 H3
Pates Manor Dr., Felt. 141 G7
Path, The SW19 184 E1
Pathfield Rd. SW16 168 D6
Pathway, The, Wat. 50 D1
  Anthony Cl.
Patience Rd. SW11 149 H2
Patio Cl. SW4 150 D6
Patmore Est. SW8 150 C1
Patmore St. SW8 150 C1
Patmos Rd. SW9 131 H7
Paton Cl. E3 114 A3
Paton St. EC1 11 J4

Patricia Ct., Chis. 193 G1
  Manor Pk. Rd.
Patricia Ct., Well. 138 B7
Patrick Connolly 114 B3
  Gdns. E3
  Talwin St.
Patrick Pas. SW11 149 H2
Patrick Rd. E13 115 J3
Patriot Sq. E2 113 E2
Patrol Pl. SE6 154 B6
Patshull Pl. NW5 92 C6
  Patshull Rd.
Patshull Rd. NW5 92 C6
Patten All., Rich. 145 G5
  The Hermitage
Patten Rd. SW18 149 H7
Pattenden Rd. SE6 171 J1
Patterdale Cl., Brom. 173 F6
Patterdale Rd. SE15 133 F7
Patterson Ct. SE19 170 C7
Patterson Rd. SE19 170 C6
Pattina Wk. SE16 133 J1
Pattison Pl. E16 115 G5
  Fife Rd.
Pattison Rd. NW2 90 D3
Pattison Wk. SE18 137 F5
Paul Cl. E15 96/97 E7
  Paul St.
Paul Gdns., Croy. 202 C2
Paul Julius Cl. E14 114 D7
Paul Robeson Cl. E6 116 D3
  Eastbourne Rd.
Paul St. E15 114 D1
Paul St. EC2 12 C6
Paul St. EC2 112 A4
Paulet Rd. SE5 151 H2
Paulhan Rd., Har. 69 G4
Paulin Dr. N21 43 G7
Pauline Cres., Twick. 161 J1
Paul's Wk. E3 19 H5
Paul's Wk. EC4 111 J7
Paultons Sq. SW3 31 F5
Paultons Sq. SW3 129 G6
Paultons St. SW3 31 F6
Paultons St. SW3 129 G6
Pauntley St. N19 92 C1
Paved Ct., Rich. 145 G5
Paveley Dr. SW11 129 H7
Paveley St. NW8 7 H5
Paveley St. NW8 109 H4
Pavement, The SW4 150 C4
Pavement, The W5 125 H3
  Popes La.
Pavement Ms., Rom. 82 D7
  Clarissa Rd.
Pavement Sq., Croy. 202 D1
Pavet Cl., Dag. 101 H6
Pavilion Ms. N3 72 D2
  Windermere Av.
Pavilion Rd. SW1 24 A6
Pavilion Rd. SW1 129 J2
Pavilion Rd., Ilf. 80 C7
Pavilion St. SW1 24 A6
Pavilion Ter., E.Mol. 180 C4
Pavilion Ter., Ilf. 81 H5
  Southdown Cres.
Pavilion Way, Edg. 54 B7
Pavilion Way, Ruis. 84 C2
Pawleyne Cl. SE20 171 F7
Pawsey Cl. E13 115 G1
  Plashet Rd.
Pawson's Rd., Croy. 187 J6
Paxford Rd., Wem. 86 E2
Paxton Cl., Rich. 145 J2
Paxton Cl., Walt. 178 C7
  Shaw Dr.
Paxton Pl. SE27 170 B4
Paxton Rd. N17 60 C7
Paxton Rd. SE23 171 H3
Paxton Rd. W4 126 E6
Paxton Rd., Brom. 173 G7
Paxton Ter. SW1 33 E5
Paxton Ter. SW1 130 B6
Payne Rd. E3 114 B2
Payne St. SE8 133 J6
Paynell Ct. SE3 154/155 E3
  Lawn Ter.
Paynes Wk. W6 128 B6
Paynesfield Av. 146 D3
  SW14
Peabody Av. SW1 32 D3
Peabody Cl. SE10 154 B1
  Devonshire Dr.
Peabody Cl., Croy. 203 F1
  Shirley Rd.
Peabody Dws. WC1 10 A5
Peabody Est. EC1 12 A6
Peabody Est. EC1 111 J4
Peabody Est. N17 76 B1
Peabody Est. SE1 27 F2
Peabody Est. SE24 151 J7
Peabody Est. SW3 31 H5
Peabody Est. W6 127 J5
  The Sq.
Peabody Est. W10 107 J5

Peabody Hill SE21 169 H1
Peabody Hill Est. 151 H7
  SE21
Peabody Sq. N1 111 H1
  Essex Rd.
Peabody Sq. SE1 27 G4
Peabody Sq. SE1 131 H2
Peabody Trust SE1 27 J2
Peabody Trust SE1 131 J1
Peabody Yd. N1 111 J1
  Greenman St.
Peace Cl. N14 42 B5
Peace Cl. SE25 188 B4
Peace Gro., Wem. 88 B3
Peace St. SE18 136/137 E6
  Nightingale Vale
Peach Rd. W10 108 A3
Peaches Cl., Sutt. 198 B7
Peacock St. SE17 35 H2
Peacock Wk. E16 115 H6
Peacock Yd. SE17 35 H2
Peak, The SE26 171 F3
Peak Hill SE26 171 F4
Peak Hill Av. SE26 171 F4
Peak Hill Gdns. SE26 171 F4
Peaketon Av., Ilf. 80 A4
Peal Gdns. W13 104 D4
  Ruislip Rd. E.
Peall Rd., Croy. 187 F6
Pear Cl. NW9 70 D4
Pear Cl. SE14 133 H7
  Southerngate Way
Pear Pl. SE1 27 E3
Pear Rd. E11 96 D3
Pear Tree Cl. E2 112 C1
Pear Tree Cl., Chess. 196 A5
Pear Tree Cl., Mitch. 185 H2
Pear Tree Ct. EC1 11 F5
Pear Tree Ct. EC1 111 G4
Pear Tree Ct. EC1 11 H5
Pear Tree Ct. EC1 111 H4
Pearce Cl., Mitch. 186 A2
Pearce Rd., W.Mol. 179 H3
Pearcefield Av. SE23 171 F1
Pearcroft Rd. E11 96 D2
Peardon St. SW8 150 B2
Pearswood Gdns., 69 G1
  Stan.
Pearfield Rd. SE23 171 H3
Pearl Cl. E6 116 D6
Pearl Cl. NW2 72 A7
  Marble Dr.
Pearl Rd. E17 78 A3
Pearl St. E1 132/133 E1
  Penang St.
Pearman St. SE1 27 F5
Pearman St. SE1 131 G2
Pears Rd., Houns. 143 J3
Pearscroft Ct. SW6 149 E1
Pearscroft Rd. SW6 149 E1
Pearse St. SE15 36 E6
Pearson Ms. SW4 150 D3
  Edgeley Rd.
Pearson St. E2 13 E1
Pearson St. E2 112 C2
Pearson's Av. SE14 154 A1
  Tanners Hill
Peartree Av. SW17 167 F3
Peartree Gdns., Dag. 100 B4
Peartree Gdns., Rom. 83 H2
Peartree La. E1 113 F7
  Glamis Rd.
Peartree Rd., Enf. 44 B3
Peartree Way SE10 135 G4
Peary Pl. E2 113 F3
  Kirkwall Pl.
Peatfield Cl., Sid. 175 H3
  Woodside Rd.
Pebble Way W3 126 B1
Pebworth Rd., Har. 86 D2
Peckarmans Wd. 170 D3
  SE26
Peckett Sq. N5 93 J4
  Highbury Gra.
Peckford Pl. SW9 151 G2
Peckham Gro. SE15 36 E7
Peckham Gro. SE15 132 B7
Peckham High St. 152 D1
  SE15
Peckham Hill St. 37 H7
SE15
Peckham Hill St. 132 D7
  SE15
Peckham Pk. Rd. 37 J7
SE15
Peckham Pk. Rd. 132 D7
  SE15
Peckham Rd. SE5 152 B1
Peckham Rd. SE15 152 B1
Peckham Rye SE15 152 D3
Peckham Rye SE22 152 D4
Pecks Yd. E1 21 F1
Peckwater St. NW5 92 C5

Pedlars Wk. N7 93 E6
Pedley Rd., Dag. 100 C1
Pedley St. E1 13 G6
Pedley St. E1 112 C4
Pedro St. E5 95 G3
Pedworth Gdns. 133 F4
  SE16
Peek Cres. SW19 166 A5
Peel Cl. E4 62 B2
Peel Cl. N9 60 D3
  Plevna Rd.
Peel Dr., NW9 71 F3
Peel Dr., Ilf. 80 B3
Peel Gro. E2 113 F2
Peel Pas. W8 128 D1
  Peel St.
Peel Pl., Ilf. 80 B2
Peel Prec. NW6 108 D2
Peel Rd. E18 79 F1
Peel Rd. NW6 108 C3
Peel Rd., Har. 68 C3
Peel Rd., Orp. 207 F5
Peel Rd., Wem. 87 G3
Peel St. W8 128 D1
Peerless St. EC1 12 B4
Peerless St. EC1 112 A3
Pegamoid Rd. N18 61 F3
Pegasus Cl. N16 94 A4
  Green Las.
Pegasus Pl. SE11 35 E5
Pegasus Way N11 58 B6
Pegg Rd., Houns. 122 D7
Pegley Gdns. SE12 173 G2
Pegwell St. SE18 137 H7
Pekin Cl. E14 114 A6
  Pekin St.
Pekin St. E14 114 A6
Peldon Ct., Rich. 145 J4
Peldon Pas., Rich. 145 J4
  Worple Way
Peldon Wk. N1 111 H1
  Britannia Row
Pelham Av., Bark. 117 J1
Pelham Cl. SE5 152 B2
Pelham Cres. SW7 31 G2
Pelham Cres. SW7 129 H4
Pelham Pl. SW7 31 G2
Pelham Pl. SW7 129 H4
Pelham Rd. E18 79 H3
Pelham Rd. N15 76 C4
Pelham Rd. N22 75 G2
Pelham Rd. SW19 166 D7
Pelham Rd., Beck. 189 F2
Pelham Rd., Bexh. 159 G3
Pelham Rd., Ilf. 99 G2
Pelham St. SW7 31 F1
Pelham St. SW7 129 H4
Pelican Est. SE15 152 C1
Pelican Pas. E1 113 F4
  Cambridge Heath Rd.
Pelican Wk. SW9 151 H4
  Loughborough Pk.
Pelier St. SE17 36 A5
Pelinore Rd. SE6 172 E2
Pellant Rd. SW6 128 B7
Pellatt Gro. N22 75 G1
Pellatt Rd. SE22 152 C5
Pellatt Rd., Wem. 87 G2
Pellerin Rd. N16 94 B5
Pelling St. E14 114 A6
Pellipar Cl. N13 59 G3
Pellipar Gdns. SE18 136 C5
Pelly Rd. E13 115 G2
Pelter St. E2 13 F3
Pelter St. E2 112 C3
Pelton Rd. SE10 134 E5
Pember Av. E17 77 H3
Pember Rd. NW10 108 A3
Pemberley Chase 196 B5
  (West Ewell), Epsom
Pemberley Cl. 196 B5
  (West Ewell), Epsom
  Ruxley Cl.
Pemberton Gdns. N19 92 C3
Pemberton Gdns., 82 E5
  Rom.
Pemberton Ho. SE26 170 D4
  High Level Dr.
Pemberton Pl. E8 94/95 E7
  Mare St.
Pemberton Rd. N4 75 G5
Pemberton Rd., 179 J4
  E.Mol.
Pemberton Row EC4 19 F3
Pemberton Ter. N19 92 C3
Pembridge Av., 161 F1
  Twick.
Pembridge Cres. W11 108 D7
Pembridge Gdns. W2 108 D7
Pembridge Ms. W11 108 D7
Pembridge Pl. SW15 148 D5
  Oakhill Rd.
Pembridge Pl. W2 108 D7

Pembridge Rd. W11	108	D7
Pembridge Sq. W2	108	D7
Pembridge Vil. W2	108	D7
Pembridge Vil. W11	108	D7
Pembroke Av., Har.	68	D3
Pembroke Av., Pnr.	84	D1
Pembroke Av., Surb.	182	B5
Pembroke Cl. SW1	**24**	**C4**
Pembroke Cl. SW1	130	A2
Pembroke Cotts. W8	128	D3
Pembroke Sq.		
Pembroke Gdns. W8	128	C4
Pembroke Gdns., Dag.	101	H3
Pembroke Gdns. Cl. W8	128	D3
Pembroke Ms. E3	113	H3
Morgan St.		
Pembroke Ms. N10	74	A1
Pembroke Rd.		
Pembroke Ms. W8	128	D3
Earls Wk.		
Pembroke Pl. W8	128	D3
Pembroke Pl., Edg.	54	A7
Pembroke Pl., Islw.	144	B2
Thornbury Rd.		
Pembroke Rd. E6	116	C5
Pembroke Rd. E17	78	B5
Pembroke Rd. N8	74	E4
Pembroke Rd. N10	74	A1
Pembroke Rd. N13	59	J3
Pembroke Rd. N15	76	C5
Pembroke Rd. SE25	188	B4
Pembroke Rd. W8	128	D4
Pembroke Rd., Brom.	191	J2
Pembroke Rd., Erith	139	J5
Pembroke Rd., Grnf.	103	H4
Pembroke Rd., Ilf.	99	J1
Pembroke Rd., Mitch.	186	A2
Pembroke Rd., Wem.	87	G3
Pembroke Sq. W8	128	D3
Pembroke St. N1	93	E7
Pembroke Studios W8	128	C3
Pembroke Vil. W8	128	D4
Pembroke Vil., Rich.	145	G4
Pembroke Wk. W8	128	D4
Pembroke Way, Hayes	121	F3
Pembury Av., Wor.Pk.	183	G7
Pembury Cl., Brom.	191	F7
Pembury Ct., Hayes	121	G6
Pembury Cres., Sid.	176	E2
Pembury Pl. E5	94	E5
Pembury Rd. E5	94	E5
Pembury Rd. N17	76	C2
Pembury Rd. SE25	188	D4
Pembury Rd., Bexh.	139	E7
Pemdevon Rd., Croy.	187	G7
Pemell Cl. E1	113	F4
Colebert Av.		
Pemerich Cl., Hayes	121	J5
Pempath Pl., Wem.	87	G2
Penally Pl. N1	112	A1
Shepperton Rd.		
Penang St. E1	133	E1
Penard Rd., Sthl.	123	G3
Penarth St. SE15	133	F6
Penates, Esher	194	A4
Penberth Rd. SE6	172	C1
Penbury Rd., Sthl.	123	F4
Pencombe Ms. W11	108	C7
Denbigh Rd.		
Pencraig Way SE15	132	E6
Penda Rd., Erith	139	H7
Pendall Cl., Barn.	41	H4
Pendarves Rd. SW20	183	J1
Penda's Mead E9	95	H4
Lindisfarne Way		
Pendell Av., Hayes	121	J7
Pendennis Rd. N17	76	A3
Pendennis Rd. SW16	168	E4
Penderel Rd., Houns.	143	G5
Penderry Ri. SE6	172	D2
Penderyn Way N7	92	D4
Pendle Rd. SW16	168	B6
Pendlestone Rd. E17	78	B5
Pendragon Rd., Brom.	173	F3
Pendragon Wk. NW9	70	E6
Pendrell Rd. SE4	153	H2
Pendrell St. SE18	137	G7
Pendula Dr., Hayes	102	D4
Pendulum Ms. E8	94	C5
Birkbeck Rd.		
Penerley Rd. SE6	172	B1
Penfold Cl., Croy.	201	G3
Epsom Rd.		
Penfold La., Bex.	176	D2
Penfold Pl. NW1	**15**	**G1**
Penfold Pl. NW1	109	H5
Penfold Rd. N9	61	G1
Penfold St. NW1	**7**	**F6**
Penfold St. NW1	109	G4
Penfold St. NW8	**7**	**F6**
Penfold St. NW8	109	G4
Penford Gdns. SE9	156	A3
Penford St. SE5	151	H2
Pengarth Rd., Bex.	158	D5
Penge Ho. SW11	149	G3
Wye St.		
Penge La. SE20	171	F7
Penge Rd. E13	97	J7
Penge Rd. SE20	188	D3
Penge Rd. SE25	188	D3
Penhall Rd. SE7	136	A4
Penhill Rd., Bex.	158	C7
Penhurst Rd., Ilf.	65	E7
Penifather La., Grnf.	104	A3
Peninsular Cl., Felt.	141	G6
Peninsular Pk. Rd. SE7	135	G4
Penistone Rd. SW16	168	E7
Penketh Dr., Har.	86	A3
Penmon Rd. SE2	138	A3
Penn Cl., Grnf.	103	H2
Penn Cl., Har.	69	F4
Penn Gdns., Chis.	192	E2
Penn La., Bex.	158	D5
Penn Rd. N7	93	E5
Penn St. N1	112	A1
Pennack Rd. SE15	**37**	**G6**
Pennack Rd. SE15	132	C6
Pennant Ms. W8	**30**	**A1**
Pennant Ms. W8	128	E4
Pennant Ter. E17	77	J2
Pennard Rd. W12	127	J2
Pennards, The, Sun.	178	C2
Penner Cl. SW19	166	B2
Victoria Dr.		
Penners Gdns., Surb.	181	H7
Pennethorne Cl. E9	113	F1
Victoria Pk. Rd.		
Pennethorne Rd. SE15	132	E7
Pennine Dr. NW2	90	B2
Pennine La. NW2	90	B2
Pennine Dr.		
Pennine Way, Hayes	121	G7
Pennington Cl. SE27	170	A4
Hamilton Rd.		
Pennington Dr. N21	43	E5
Pennington St. E1	**21**	**J6**
Pennington St. E1	112	D7
Pennington Way SE12	173	H2
Penniston Cl. N17	75	J2
Penny Ms. SW12	150	B7
Caistor Rd.		
Penny Rd. NW10	106	B3
Pennyfather La., Enf.	43	J3
Pennyfields E14	114	A7
Pennymoor Wk. W9	108	C3
Ashmore Rd.		
Pennyroyal Av. E6	116	D6
Penpoll Rd. E8	94	E6
Penpool La., Well.	158	B3
Penrhyn Av. E17	77	J1
Penrhyn Cres. E17	78	A1
Penrhyn Cres. SW14	146	C4
Penrhyn Gro. E17	78	A1
Penrhyn Rd., Kings.T.	181	H3
Penrith Cl. SW15	148	B5
Penrith Cl., Beck.	190	B1
Albemarle Rd.		
Penrith Pl. SE27	169	H2
Harpenden Rd.		
Penrith Rd. N15	76	A5
Penrith Rd., Ilf.	65	J6
Penrith Rd., N.Mal.	182	D4
Penrith Rd., Th.Hth.	187	J2
Penrith St. SW16	168	C6
Penrose Av., Wat.	50	D2
Penrose Gro. SE17	**35**	**J4**
Penrose Gro. SE17	131	J5
Penrose Ho. SE17	**35**	**J4**
Penrose Ho. SE17	131	J5
Penrose St. SE17	**35**	**J4**
Penrose St. SE17	131	J5
Penry St. SE1	**37**	**E2**
Penryn St. NW1	**9**	**H1**
Penryn St. NW1	110	D2
Pensbury Pl. SW8	150	C2
Pensbury St. SW8	150	C2
Penscroft Gdns., Borwd.	38	D4
Pensford Av., Rich.	146	A2
Penshurst Av., Sid.	158	A6
Penshurst Gdns., Edg.	54	B5
Penshurst Grn., Brom.	191	F5
Penshurst Rd. E9	95	G7
Penshurst Rd. N17	60	C7
Penshurst Rd., Bexh.	159	F1
Penshurst Rd., Th.Hth.	187	H5
Penshurst Wk., Brom.	191	F5
Hayesford Pk. Dr.		
Penshurst Way, Sutt.	198	D7
Pensilver Cl., Barn.	41	H4
Penstemon Cl. N3	56	D7
Penstock Footpath N22	75	E3
Pentavia Retail Pk. NW7	55	F7
Bunns La.		
Pentelow Gdns., Felt.	142	A6
Pentire Rd. E17	78	D1
Pentland Av., Edg.	54	B2
Pentland Cl. NW11	90	B2
Pentland Gdns. SW18	149	F6
St. Ann's Hill		
Pentland Pl., Nthlt.	102	E1
Pentland St. SW18	149	F6
Pentlands Cl., Mitch.	186	B3
Pentlow St. SW15	147	J3
Pentlow Way, Buck.H.	48	B7
Pentney Rd. E4	62	D1
Pentney Rd. SW12	168	C1
Pentney Rd. SW19	184	B1
Midmoor Rd.		
Penton Gro. N1	**11**	**E2**
Penton Ho. SE2	138	D2
Hartslock Dr.		
Penton Pl. SE17	**35**	**H3**
Penton Pl. SE17	131	H5
Penton Ri. WC1	**10**	**D3**
Penton Ri. WC1	111	F3
Penton St. N1	**10**	**E1**
Penton St. N1	111	G2
Pentonville Rd. N1	**10**	**C2**
Pentonville Rd. N1	111	F2
Pentridge St. SE15	132	C7
Pentyre Av. N18	60	A5
Penwerris Av., Islw.	123	J7
Penwith Rd. SW18	166	E2
Penwortham Rd. SW16	168	B6
Penylan Pl., Edg.	54	A7
Penywern Rd. SW5	128	D5
Penzance Pl. W11	128	B1
Penzance St. W11	128	B1
Peony Ct., Wdf.Grn.	62/63	E7
The Bridle Path		
Peony Gdns. W12	107	G7
Peploe Rd. NW6	108	A2
Peplow Cl., West Dr.	120	A1
Tavistock Rd.		
Pepper All., Loug.	47	G1
Pepper Cl. E6	116	C5
Pepper St. E14	134	B3
Pepper St. SE1	**27**	**J3**
Peppermead Sq. SE13	154	A5
Peppermint Cl., Croy.	186	E7
Peppermint Pl. E11	96/97	E3
Birch Gro.		
Peppie Cl. N16	94	B2
Bouverie Rd.		
Pepys Cres. E16	135	G1
Britannia Gate		
Pepys Cres., Barn.	39	J5
Pepys Ri., Orp.	207	J1
Pepys Rd. SE14	153	G1
Pepys Rd. SW20	183	J1
Pepys St. EC3	**21**	**E5**
Pepys St. EC3	112	B7
Perceval Av. NW3	91	H5
Perch St. E8	94	C4
Percheron Cl., Islw.	144	D3
Percheron Rd., Borwd.	38	D6
Percival Ct. N17	60	C7
High Rd.		
Percival Ct., Nthlt.	85	G5
Percival Gdns., Rom.	82	C6
Percival Rd. SW14	146	C4
Percival Rd., Enf.	44	C4
Percival Rd., Orp.	207	E2
Percival St. EC1	**11**	**G5**
Percival St. EC1	111	H4
Percival Way, Epsom	196	C4
Percy Bush Rd., West Dr.	120	C3
Percy Circ. WC1	**10**	**D3**
Percy Circ. WC1	111	F3
Percy Gdns., Enf.	45	G5
Percy Gdns., Islw.	144	D2
Percy Gdns., Wor.Pk.	196	E1
Percy Ms. W1	**17**	**H2**
Percy Pas. W1	**17**	**G2**
Percy Rd. E11	78	E7
Percy Rd. E16	115	E5
Percy Rd. N12	57	F5
Percy Rd. N21	43	J7
Percy Rd. NW6	108	D3
Stafford Rd.		
Percy Rd. SE20	189	G1
Percy Rd. SE25	188	D5
Percy Rd. W12	127	G2
Percy Rd., Bexh.	159	E2
Percy Rd., Hmptn.	161	G7
Percy Rd., Ilf.	82	A7
Percy Rd., Islw.	144	D4
Percy Rd., Mitch.	186	A7
Percy Rd., Rom.	83	H3
Percy Rd., Twick.	161	H1
Percy St. W1	**17**	**H2**
Percy St. W1	110	D5
Percy Way, Twick.	161	J1
Percy Yd. WC1	**10**	**D3**
Peregrine Cl. NW10	88	D5
Peregrine Ct. SW16	169	F4
Leithcote Gdns.		
Peregrine Ct., Well.	157	J1
Peregrine Gdns., Croy.	203	H2
Peregrine Ho. EC1	**11**	**H3**
Peregrine Ho. EC1	111	H3
Peregrine Way SW19	165	J7
Perham Rd. W14	128	B5
Peridot St. E6	116	B5
Perifield SE21	169	J1
Perimeade Rd., Grnf.	105	F2
Periton Rd. SE9	156	A4
Perivale Gdns. W13	104/105	E4
Bellevue Rd.		
Perivale Gra., Grnf.	104	D3
Perivale Ind. Pk., Grnf.	104	E2
Perivale La., Grnf.	104	D3
Perivale New Business Cen., Grnf.	105	E2
Perkin Cl., Wem.	86	E5
Perkin's Rents SW1	**25**	**H5**
Perkin's Rents SW1	130	D3
Perkins Rd., Ilf.	81	G5
Perkins Sq. SE1	**28**	**A1**
Perks Cl. SE3	154/155	E3
Hurren Cl.		
Perpins Rd. SE9	157	H6
Perran Rd. SW2	169	H2
Christchurch Rd.		
Perran Wk., Brent.	125	H5
Perren St. NW5	92	B6
Ryland Rd.		
Perrers Rd. W6	127	H4
Perrin Rd., Wem.	86	D4
Perrins Ct. NW3	91	F4
Hampstead High St.		
Perrins La. NW3	91	F4
Perrin's Wk. NW3	91	F4
Perrott St. SE18	137	F4
Perry Av. W3	106	D6
Perry Ct. E14	134	A5
Napier Av.		
Perry Ct. N15	76	B6
Albert Rd.		
Perry Gdns. N9	60	B3
Deansway		
Perry Garth, Nthlt.	102	C1
Perry Hall Rd., Orp.	193	J6
Perry Hill SE6	171	J3
Perry How, Wor.Pk.	197	F1
Perry Mead, Enf.	43	H2
Perry Ri. SE23	171	H3
Perry Rd., Dag.	119	F4
Perry St., Chis.	175	G6
Perry St. Gdns., Chis.	175	H6
Old Perry St.		
Perry Vale SE23	171	F2
Perryfield Way NW9	71	F6
Perryfield Way, Rich.	163	E2
Perryman Ho., Bark.	117	F1
The Shaftesburys		
Perrymans Fm. Rd., Ilf.	81	G6
Perrymead St. SW6	148	D1
Perryn Rd. SE16	132/133	E3
Drummond Rd.		
Perryn Rd. W3	106	D7
Perrys Pl. W1	**17**	**H3**
Persant Rd. SE6	172	E2
Perseverance Pl. SW9	131	G7
Perseverance Pl., Rich.	145	H3
Shaftesbury Rd.		
Pershore Cl., Ilf.	81	E5
Pershore Gro., Cars.	185	G6
Pert Cl. N10	58	B7
Perth Av. NW9	70	D7
Perth Av., Hayes	102	C4
Perth Cl. SW20	183	G2
Huntley Way		
Perth Rd. E10	95	H1
Perth Rd. E13	115	H2
Perth Rd. N4	93	G1
Perth Rd. N22	75	H1
Perth Rd., Bark.	117	G2
Perth Rd., Beck.	190	C2
Perth Rd., Ilf.	80	D6
Perth Ter., Ilf.	81	F7
Perwell Av., Har.	85	F1

Perwell Ct., Har.	85	F1
Peter Av. NW10	89	H7
Peter James	122	A2
Business Cen., Hayes		
Peter St. W1	**17**	**G5**
Peter St. W1	110	D7
Peterboat Cl.	134/135	E4
SE10		
Tunnel Av.		
Peterborough Gdns.,	80	B7
Ilf.		
Peterborough Ms.	148	D2
SW6		
Peterborough Rd. E10	78	C5
Peterborough Rd.,	148	D2
SW6		
Peterborough Rd.,	185	H6
Cars.		
Peterborough Rd.,	86	B1
Har.		
Peterborough Vil.	148	E1
SW6		
Peterchurch Ho.	132/133	E6
SE15		
Commercial Way		
Petergate SW11	149	F4
Peters Cl., Dag.	100	D1
Peters Cl., Stan.	53	G6
Peters Cl., Well.	157	H2
Peters Hill EC4	**19**	**J5**
Peter's La. EC1	**19**	**H1**
Peters Path SE26	170	E4
Petersfield Cl. N18	59	J5
Petersfield Ri. SW15	165	H1
Petersfield Rd. W3	126	C2
Petersham Cl., Rich.	163	G2
Petersham Cl., Sutt.	198	D5
Petersham Dr., Orp.	193	J2
Petersham Gdns.,	193	J2
Orp.		
Petersham La. SW7	**22**	**C5**
Petersham La. SW7	129	F3
Petersham Ms. SW7	**22**	**C6**
Petersham Ms. SW7	129	F3
Petersham Pl. SW7	**22**	**C5**
Petersham Pl. SW7	129	F3
Petersham Rd., Rich.	145	H6
Petersham Ter.,	200/201	E3
Croy.		
Richmond Grn.		
Peterstone Rd. SE2	138	B3
Peterstow Cl. SW19	166	B2
Peterwood Way,	201	F2
Croy.		
Petherton Rd. N5	93	J5
Petley Rd. W6	127	A6
Peto Pl. NW1	**8**	**E5**
Peto Pl. NW1	110	B4
Peto St. N. E16	115	F7
Victoria Dock Rd.		
Petrie Cl. NW2	90	B6
Pett St. SE18	136	B4
Petticoat La. E1	**21**	**E2**
Petticoat La. E1	112	B5
Petticoat Sq. E1	**21**	**F3**
Petticoat Sq. E1	112	C6
Pettits Pl., Dag.	101	G5
Pettits Rd., Dag.	101	G5
Pettiward Cl. SW15	147	J4
Pettman Cres. SE28	137	G3
Petts Hill, Nthlt.	85	H5
Petts Wd. Rd., Orp.	193	H5
Pettsgrove Av., Wem.	87	F5
Petty France SW1	**25**	**G5**
Petty France SW1	130	C3
Petworth Cl., Nthlt.	85	F7
Petworth Gdns.	183	H3
SW20		
Hidcote Gdns.		
Petworth Rd. N12	57	H5
Petworth Rd., Bexh.	159	G5
Petworth St. SW11	149	H1
Petyt Pl. SW3	**31**	**G6**
Petyward SW3	**31**	**H2**
Petyward SW3	129	H4
Pevel Ho., Dag.	101	G2
Pevensey Av. N11	58	D5
Pevensey Av., Enf.	44	A2
Pevensey Cl., Islw.	123	J2
Pevensey Rd. E7	97	F4
Pevensey Rd. SW17	167	G4
Pevensey Rd., Felt.	160	E1
Peverel E6	116	D6
Downings		
Peveret Cl. N11	58	B5
Woodland Rd.		
Peveril Dr., Tedd.	162	A5
Pewsey Cl. E4	62	A5
Peyton Pl. SE10	134	C7
Pharaoh Cl., Mitch.	185	J7
Pheasant Cl. E16	115	G6
Maplin Rd.		
Phelp St. SE17	**36**	**B5**
Phelp St. SE17	132	A6
Phelps Way, Hayes	121	J4
Phene St. SW3	**31**	**H5**
Phene St. SW3	129	H6
Phil Brown Pl. SW8	150	B2
Heath Rd.		
Philbeach Gdns. SW5	128	D5
Philchurch Pl. E1	**21**	**J4**
Philimore Cl. SE18	137	H5
Philip Gdns., Croy.	203	J2
Philip La. N15	76	A4
Philip Rd. SE15	152	D3
Peckham Rye		
Philip St. E13	115	G4
Philip Wk. SE15	152	D3
Philipot Path SE9	156	C6
Philippa Gdns. SE9	156	A5
Philips Cl., Cars.	200	A1
Phillimore Gdns.	107	J1
NW10		
Phillimore Gdns. W8	128	D2
Phillimore Gdns. Cl.	128	D3
W8		
Phillimore Gdns.		
Phillimore Pl. W8	128	D2
Phillimore Wk. W8	128	D3
Phillipp St. N1	112	B1
Philpot La. EC3	**20**	**D5**
Philpot Path, Ilf.	99	F3
Sunnyside Rd.		
Philpot Sq. SW6	148/149	E3
Peterborough Rd.		
Philpot St. E1	113	E6
Phineas Pett Rd. SE9	156	B3
Phipp St. EC2	**12**	**D5**
Phipp St. EC2	112	B4
Phipps Br. Rd. SW19	185	F2
Phipps Br. Rd.,	185	F2
Mitch.		
Phipp's Ms. SW1	**24**	**D6**
Phoebeth Rd. SE4	154	A5
Phoenix Cl. E8	112	C1
Stean St.		
Phoenix Cl., W.Wick.	204	E2
Phoenix Dr., Kes.	206	A3
Phoenix Pk., Brent.	125	G5
Phoenix Pl. WC1	**10**	**D5**
Phoenix Pl. WC1	111	F4
Phoenix Rd. NW1	**9**	**H3**
Phoenix Rd. NW1	110	D3
Phoenix Rd. SE20	171	F6
Phoenix St. WC2	**17**	**J4**
Phoenix Way, Houns.	122	C6
Phoenix Wf. SE10	135	F2
Phoenix Wf. Rd.	**29**	**G4**
SE1		
Phyllis Av., N.Mal.	183	H5
Physic Pl. SW3	**31**	**J5**
Piazza, The WC2	110/111	E7
Covent Gdn.		
Picardy Manorway,	139	H3
Belv.		
Picardy Rd., Belv.	139	G4
Picardy St., Belv.	139	G3
Piccadilly W1	**24**	**E2**
Piccadilly W1	130	B1
Piccadilly Arc. SW1	**25**	**F1**
Piccadilly Circ. W1	**17**	**H6**
Piccadilly Circ. W1	110	D7
Piccadilly Pl. W1	**17**	**G6**
Pickard St. EC1	**11**	**H3**
Pickering Av. E6	116	D2
Pickering Cl. E9	95	G7
Cassland Rd.		
Pickering Gdns.	188	C6
Croy.		
Pickering Ms. W2	**14**	**B3**
Pickering Pl. SW1	**25**	**G2**
Pickering St. N1	111	H1
Essex Rd.		
Pickets Cl., Bushey	52	A1
Pickets St. SW12	150	B7
Pickett Cft., Stan.	69	G1
Picketts Lock La. N9	61	F2
Pickford Cl., Bexh.	158	E2
Pickford La., Bexh.	159	E2
Pickford Rd., Bexh.	158	E3
Pickfords Wf. N1	**11**	**J2**
Pickfords Wf. N1	111	J2
Pickhurst Grn., Brom.	191	F7
Pickhurst La., Brom.	205	F1
Pickhurst La.,	191	E6
W.Wick.		
Pickhurst Mead,	191	F7
Brom.		
Pickhurst Pk., Brom.	191	E5
Pickhurst Ri., W.Wick.	190	C7
Pickle Herring St.	132	B1
SE1		
Tooley St.		
Pickwick Cl.,	142/143	E5
Houns.		
Dorney Way		
Pickwick Ct. SE9	174	B1
West Pk.		
Pickwick Ms. N18	60	B5
Pickwick Pl., Har.	68	B7
Pickwick Rd. SE21	152	A7
Pickwick St. SE1	**27**	**J4**
Pickwick Way, Chis.	175	F6
Pickworth Cl.	130/131	E7
SW8		
Kenchester Cl.		
Picton Pl. W1	**16**	**C4**
Picton Pl., Surb.	196	A1
Picton St. SE5	132	A7
Piedmont Rd. SE18	137	G5
Pier Head E1	132/133	E1
Wapping High St.		
Pier Par. E16	136	D2
Pier Rd.		
Pier Rd. E16	136	C2
Pier Rd., Felt.	142	B5
Pier Rd. E14	134	C4
Pier Ter. SW18	149	F4
Jew's Row		
Pier Way SE28	137	G3
Piermont Grn. SE22	152	E5
Piermont Pl., Brom.	192	B2
Piermont Rd. SE22	152	E5
Pierrepoint Arc. N1	111	H2
Islington High St.		
Pierrepoint Rd. W3	106	B7
Pierrepoint Row N1	**11**	**G1**
Pigeon La., Hmptn.	161	G4
Pigott St. E14	114	A6
Pike Cl., Brom.	173	H5
Pike Rd. NW7	54	D4
Ellesmere Av.		
Pikes End, Pnr.	66	B4
Pikestone Cl.,	102/103	E4
Hayes		
Berrydale Rd.		
Pilgrim Cl., Mord.	185	E7
Pilgrim Hill SE27	169	J4
Pilgrim St. EC4	**19**	**G4**
Pilgrimage St. SE1	**28**	**B4**
Pilgrimage St. SE1	132	A2
Pilgrims Cl. N13	59	F4
Pilgrims Cl., Nthlt.	85	J5
Pilgrims Cl. SE3	155	G1
Pilgrim's La. NW3	91	G4
Pilgrims Ms. E14	114	C7
Blackwall Way		
Pilgrims Pl. NW3	91	G4
Hampstead High St.		
Pilgrims Ri., Barn.	41	H5
Pilgrims Way E6	116	B1
High St. N.		
Pilgrims Way N19	92	D1
Pilgrim's Way, Wem.	88	B1
Pilkington Rd. SE15	152	E2
Pilkington Rd., Orp.	207	F2
Pilsdon Cl. SW19	166	A1
Inner Pk. Rd.		
Piltdown Rd., Wat.	50	D4
Pilton Est., The, Croy.	201	H2
Pitlake		
Pimento Ct. W5	125	G3
Olive Rd.		
Pimlico Rd. SW1	**32**	**B3**
Pimlico Rd. SW1	130	A5
Pimlico Wk. N1	**12**	**D3**
Pinchbeck Rd., Orp.	207	J6
Pinchin St. E1	**21**	**J5**
Pinchin St. E1	112	D7
Pincott Pl. SE4	153	G3
Billingford Cl.		
Pincott Rd. SW19	185	F1
Pincott Rd., Bexh.	159	G5
Pindar St. EC2	**20**	**D1**
Pindar St. EC2	112	B5
Pindock Ms. W9	**6**	**B6**
Pine Av. E15	96	D5
Pine Av., W.Wick.	204	B1
Pine Cl. E10	96	B2
Walnut Rd.		
Pine Cl. N14	42	C7
Pine Cl. N19	92	C2
Hargrave Rd.		
Pine Cl. SE20	189	F1
Pine Cl., Stan.	52	E4
Pine Coombe, Croy.	203	G4
Pine Gdns., Ruis.	84	B1
Pine Gdns., Surb.	182	A6
Pine Glade, Orp.	206	C4
Pine Gro. N4	93	E2
Pine Gro. N20	56	C1
Pine Gro. SW19	166	C5
Pine Ms. NW10	108	A2
Clifford Gdns.		
Pine Rd. N11	58	A2
Pine Rd. NW2	89	J4
Pine St. EC1	**11**	**E5**
Pine St. EC1	111	G4
Pine Tree Cl., Houns.	142	B1
Pine Wk., Brom.	191	J1
Pine Wk., Surb.	182	A6
Pine Wd., Sun.	178	A1
Pineapple Ct. SW1	**25**	**F5**
Pinecrest Gdns., Orp.	207	E4
Pinecroft Cres., Barn.	40	B4
Hillside Gdns.		
Pinedene SE15	152/153	E1
Meeting Ho. La.		
Pinefield Cl. E14	114	A7
Pinehurst Wk., Orp.	207	H1
Pinelands Cl. SE3	135	F7
St. John's Pk.		
Pinemartin Cl. NW2	89	J3
Pines, The N14	42	C5
Pines, The, Sun.	178	A3
Pines, The, Wdf.Grn.	63	G3
Pines Rd., Brom.	192	B2
Pinewood Av., Pnr.	51	H6
Pinewood Av., Sid.	175	H1
Pinewood Cl., Borwd.	38	D1
Pinewood Cl., Croy.	203	H3
Pinewood Cl., Nthwd.	50	B5
Pinewood Cl., Orp.	207	G1
Pinewood Cl., Pnr.	51	H6
Pinewood Dr., Orp.	207	H5
Pinewood Gro. W5	105	F6
Pinewood Rd. SE2	138	D6
Pinewood Rd., Brom.	191	G4
Pinewood Rd., Felt.	160	B3
Pinfold Rd. SW16	168	E4
Pinglestone Cl.,	120	B7
West Dr.		
Pinkcoat Cl., Felt.	160	B3
Tanglewood Way		
Pinkerton Pl. SW16	168	D4
Riggindale Rd.		
Pinkham Way N11	58	A7
Pinkwell Av., Hayes	121	G4
Pinkwell La., Hayes	121	F4
Pinley Gdns., Dag.	118	B7
Stamford Rd.		
Pinnacle Hill, Bexh.	159	H4
Pinnacle Hill N., Bexh.	159	H4
Pinnell Rd. SE9	156	A4
Pinnell Rd. SE9	156	A4
Pinner Ct., Pnr.	67	G4
Pinner Grn., Pnr.	66	C2
Pinner Gro., Pnr.	67	E4
Pinner Hill, Pnr.	66	C1
Pinner Hill Rd., Pnr.	66	C2
Pinner Pk., Pnr.	67	G1
Pinner Pk. Av., Har.	67	H3
Pinner Pk. Gdns., Har.	67	J2
Pinner Rd., Har.	67	H5
Pinner Rd., Pnr.	67	F4
Pinner Vw., Har.	67	J6
Pintail Cl. E6	116	B5
Swan App.		
Pintail Rd., Wdf.Grn.	63	H7
Pintail Way, Hayes	102	D5
Pinto Cl., Borwd.	38	D6
Percheron Rd.		
Pinto Way SE3	155	H4
Pioneer St. SE15	152	D1
Pioneer Way W12	107	H6
Du Cane Rd.		
Pioneers Ind. Pk.,	200	E1
Croy.		
Piper Cl. N7	93	F5
Piper Rd., Kings.T.	182	A3
Piper's Gdns., Croy.	189	H7
Pipers Grn. NW9	70	C5
Pipers Grn. La., Edg.	53	H3
Pipewell Rd., Cars.	185	H6
Pippin Cl. NW2	89	H3
Pippin Cl., Croy.	203	J1
Pippins Cl., West Dr.	120	A3
Piquet Rd. SE20	189	F2
Pirbright Cres., Croy.	204	C6
Pirbright Rd. SW18	166	C1
Pirie Cl. SE5	152	A3
Denmark Hill		
Pirie St. E16	135	H1
Pitcairn Cl., Rom.	83	G4
Pitcairn Rd., Mitch.	167	J7
Pitcairn's Path, Har.	85	J3
Eastcote Rd.		
Pitchford St. E15	96	D7
Pitfield Cres. SE28	138	A1
Pitfield Est. N1	**12**	**C3**
Pitfield Est. N1	112	A3
Pitfield St. N1	**12**	**D3**
Pitfield St. N1	112	B3
Pitfield Way NW10	88	C6
Pitfield Way, Enf.	45	F1
Pitfold Cl. SE12	155	G6
Pitfold Rd. SE12	155	G6
Pitlake, Croy.	201	H2
Pitman St. SE5	**35**	**J7**
Pitman St. SE5	131	J7
Pitsea Pl. E1	**113**	**G6**
Pitsea St.		
Pitsea St. E1	113	G6
Pitshanger La. W5	105	E4
Pitshanger Pk. W13	105	F3

Name	Page	Grid
Pitt Cres. SW19	166	E4
Pitt Rd., Croy.	187	J5
Pitt Rd., Orp.	207	F4
Pitt Rd., Th.Hth.	187	J5
Pitt St. W8	128	D2
Pittman Gdns., Ilf.	99	F5
Pitt's Head Ms. W1	24	C2
Pitt's Head Ms. W1	130	A1
Pittsmead Av., Brom.	191	G7
Pittville Gdns. SE25	188	D3
Pixfield Ct., Brom.	191	F2
Beckenham La.		
Pixley St. E14	113	J6
Place Fm. Av., Orp.	207	G1
Plaistow Gro. E15	115	F1
Plaistow Gro., Brom.	173	H7
Plaistow La., Brom.	173	H7
Plaistow Pk. Rd. E13	115	H2
Plaistow Rd. E13	115	F1
Plaistow Rd. E15	115	F1
Plane St. SE26	170	E3
Plane Tree Cres., Felt.	160	B3
Plane Tree Wk. SE19	170	B6
Central Hill		
Plantagenet La., Wor.Pk.	196	D4
Plantagenet Gdns., Rom.	82	D7
Broomfield Rd.		
Plantagenet Pl., Rom.	82	D7
Broomfield Rd.		
Plantagenet Rd., Barn.	41	F4
Plantain Gdns. E11	96	D3
Hollydown Way		
Plantain Pl. SE1	28	B3
Plantation, The SE3	155	G2
Plantation Wf. SW11	149	F3
Plasel Ct. E13	115	G1
Plashet Rd.		
Plashet Gro. E6	115	J1
Plashet Rd. E13	115	G1
Plassy Rd SE6	154	B7
Platina St. EC2	12	C5
Plato Rd. SW2	151	E4
Platt, The SW15	148	A3
Platt St. NW1	9	H1
Platt St. NW1	110	D2
Platt's Eyot, Hmptn.	179	G2
Platt's La. NW3	90	D4
Platts Rd., Enf.	45	F1
Plawsfield Rd., Beck.	189	G1
Plaxtol Cl., Brom.	191	J1
Plaxtol Rd., Erith	139	G7
Playfair St. W6	127	J5
Winslow Rd.		
Playfield Av., Rom.	83	J1
Playfield Cres. SE22	152	C5
Playfield Rd., Edg.	70	C2
Playford Rd. N4	93	F2
Playgreen Way SE6	172	A4
Playground Cl., Beck.	189	G2
Churchfields Rd.		
Playhouse Yd. EC4	19	G4
Plaza W., Houns.	143	H1
Pleasance, The SW15	147	H4
Pleasance Rd. SW15	147	H5
Pleasant Gro., Croy.	203	J3
Pleasant Pl. N1	93	H7
Pleasant Row NW1	110	B1
Pleasant Vw. Pl., Orp.	206/207	E5
High St.		
Pleasant Way, Wem.	105	F2
Plender St. NW1	110	C1
Plender St. Est. NW1	110	C1
Plender St.		
Pleshey Rd. N7	92	D4
Plevna Cres. N15	76	B6
Plevna Rd. N9	60	D3
Plevna Rd., Hmptn.	179	H1
Plevna St. E14	134	C3
Pleydell Av. SE19	170	C7
Pleydell Av. W6	127	F4
Pleydell Ct. EC4	19	F4
Pleydell Est. EC1	111	J3
Radnor St.		
Pleydell St. EC4	19	F4
Plimsoll Cl. E14	114	B6
Grundy St.		
Plimsoll Rd. N4	93	G3
Plough Cl. EC3	20	C5
Plough La. SE22	152	C6
Plough La. SW17	167	E5
Plough La. SW19	167	E5
Plough La., Tedd.	162	D5
Plough La., Wall.	200	E5
Plough La. Cl., Wall.	200	E5
Plough Ms. SW11	149	G4
Plough Ter.		
Plough Pl. EC4	19	F3
Plough Rd. SW11	149	G3
Plough St. E1	21	H3
Plough Ter. SW11	149	G4
Plough Way SE16	133	G4
Plough Yd. EC2	12	E6
Plough Yd. EC2	112	B4
Ploughmans Cl. NW1	110	D1
Crofters Way		
Ploughmans End, Islw.	144	A5
Plover Way SE16	133	H3
Plover Way, Hayes	102	D6
Plowden Bldgs. EC4	111	G6
Middle Temple La.		
Plowman Cl. N18	60	A5
Plowman Way, Dag.	100	C1
Plum Cl., Felt.	160	A1
Highfield Rd.		
Plum Garth, Brent.	125	G4
Plum La. SE18	137	F7
Plumbers Row E1	21	H2
Plumbers Row E1	112	D5
Plumbridge St. SE10	154	C1
Blackheath Hill		
Plummer La., Mitch.	185	J2
Plummer Rd. SW4	150	D7
Plumpton Cl., Nthlt.	85	G6
Plumpton Way, Cars.	199	H3
Plumstead Common Rd. SE18	136	E6
Plumstead High St. SE18	137	H4
Plumstead Rd. SE18	137	E4
Plumtree Cl., Dag.	101	H6
Plumtree Cl., Wall.	200	D7
Plumtree Ct. EC4	19	F3
Plumtree Mead, Loug.	48	D3
Plymouth Rd. E16	115	G5
Plymouth Rd., Brom.	191	H1
Plymouth Wf. E14	134	D4
Plympton Av. NW6	90	C7
Plympton Cl., Belv.	138/139	E3
Halifield Dr.		
Plympton Pl. NW8	7	G6
Plympton Rd. NW6	90	C7
Plympton St. NW8	7	G6
Plympton St. NW8	109	H4
Plymstock Rd., Well.	138	C7
Pocklington Cl. NW9	70	E2
Pocock Av., West Dr.	120	C3
Pocock St. SE1	27	G3
Pocock St. SE1	131	H2
Podmore Rd. SW18	149	F4
Poets Rd. N5	94	A5
Poets Way, Har.	68	B4
Blawith Rd.		
Point Cl. SE10	154	C1
Point Hill		
Point Hill SE10	134	C7
Point of Thomas Path E1	113	F7
Glamis Rd.		
Point Pl., Wem.	88	B7
Point Pleasant SW18	148	D4
Pointalls Cl. N3	73	F2
Pointer Cl. SE28	118	D6
Pointers Cl. E14	134	B5
Poland St. W1	17	G4
Poland St. W1	110	C6
Pole Cat All., Brom.	205	F2
Pole Hill Rd. E4	46	C7
Polebrook Rd. SE3	155	J3
Polecroft La. SE6	171	J2
Polehamptons, The, Hmptn.	161	J7
High St.		
Polesden Gdns. SW20	183	H2
Polesworth Ho. W2	108	D5
Polesworth Rd., Dag.	100	D7
Pollard Cl. E16	115	G6
Pollard Cl. N7	93	F4
Pollard Rd. N20	57	H2
Pollard Rd., Mord.	185	G5
Pollard Row E2	13	J3
Pollard Row E2	112	D3
Pollard St. E2	13	J3
Pollard St. E2	112	D3
Pollard Wk., Sid.	176	C6
Pollards Cl., Loug.	47	J5
Pollards Cres. SW16	187	E3
Pollards Hill E. SW16	187	F3
Pollards Hill N. SW16	187	F3
Pollards Hill S. SW16	187	E3
Pollards Hill W. SW16	187	E3
Pollards Wd. Rd. SW16	187	E2
Pollen St. W1	17	E4
Pollitt Dr. NW8	7	E5
Polperro Cl., Orp.	193	J6
Cotswold Ri.		
Polsted Rd. SE6	153	J7
Polthorne Est. SE18	137	G4
Polthorne Gro. SE18	137	F4
Polworth Rd. SW16	168	E5
Polygon, The SW4	150	C4
Old Town		
Polygon Rd. NW1	9	H2
Polygon Rd. NW1	110	D2
Polytechnic St. SE18	136	D4
Pomell Way E1	21	G3
Pomeroy St. SE14	153	F1
Pomfret Rd. SE5	151	H3
Flaxman Rd.		
Pomoja La. N19	92	D2
Pond Cl. N12	57	H6
Summerfields Av.		
Pond Cl. SE3	155	F2
Pond Cottage La., W.Wick.	204	A1
Pond Cotts. SE21	170	B1
Pond Fld. End, Loug.	47	J7
Pond Hill Gdns., Sutt.	198	B6
Pond Mead SE21	152	A6
Pond Path, Chis.	174/175	E6
Heathfield La.		
Pond Pl. SW3	31	G2
Pond Pl. SW3	129	H4
Pond Rd. E15	114	E2
Pond Rd. SE3	155	F2
Pond Sq. N6	92	A1
South Gro.		
Pond St. NW3	91	H5
Pond Way, Tedd.	163	F6
Holmesdale Rd.		
Ponder St. N7	93	F7
Ponders End Ind. Est., Enf.	45	J4
Pondfield Rd., Brom.	205	E1
Pondfield Rd., Dag.	101	H5
Pondfield Rd., Orp.	207	E3
Pondside Cl., Hayes	121	G7
Providence La.		
Pondwood Ri., Orp.	193	H7
Ponler St. E1	112	E6
Ponsard Rd. NW10	107	H3
Ponsford St. E9	95	F6
Ponsonby Pl. SW1	33	J3
Ponsonby Pl. SW1	130	D5
Ponsonby Rd. SW15	147	H7
Ponsonby Ter. SW1	33	J3
Ponsonby Ter. SW1	130	D5
Pont St. SW1	23	J6
Pont St. SW1	129	J3
Pont St. Ms. SW1	23	J6
Pont St. Ms. SW1	129	J3
Pontefract Rd., Brom.	173	F5
Ponton Rd. SW8	33	J6
Ponton Rd. SW8	130	D6
Pontypool Pl. SE1	27	G3
Pool Cl., Beck.	172	A5
Pool Cl., W.Mol.	179	F5
Pool Ct. SE6	172	A2
Pool Rd., Har.	68	A7
Pool Rd., W.Mol.	179	F5
Poole Ct. Rd., Houns.	142/143	E2
Vicarage Fm. Rd.		
Poole Rd. E9	95	G6
Poole Rd., Epsom	196	D6
Poole St. N1	112	A1
Pooles Bldgs. EC1	10	E6
Pooles La. SW10	129	F7
Lots Rd.		
Pooles La., N17	119	E2
Pooles Pk. N4	93	G2
Seven Sisters Rd.		
Poolmans St. SE16	133	G2
Poolsford Rd. NW9	71	E4
Poonah St. E1	113	F6
Hardinge St.		
Pope Cl. SW19	167	G6
Shelley Way		
Pope Rd., Brom.	192	A5
Pope St. SE1	29	E4
Pope St. SE1	132	B2
Popes Av., Twick.	162	B2
Popes Dr. N3	72	D1
Popes Gro., Croy.	203	J3
Popes Gro., Twick.	162	C2
Pope's Head All. EC3	112	A6
Cornhill		
Popes La. W5	125	G3
Popes Rd. SW9	151	G3
Popham Cl., Felt.	161	F3
Popham Gdns., Rich.	146	A3
Lower Richmond Rd.		
Popham Rd. N1	111	J1
Popham St. N1	111	H1
Poplar Av., Mitch.	185	J1
Poplar Av., Orp.	207	E2
Poplar Av., Sthl.	123	H3
Poplar Bath St. E14	114	B7
Lawless St.		
Poplar Business Pk. E14	114	C7
Poplar Cl. E9	95	J5
Lee Conservancy Rd.		
Poplar Cl., Pnr.	66	D1
Poplar Ct. SW19	166	D5
Poplar Cres., Epsom	196	C6
Poplar Fm. Cl., Epsom	196	C6
Poplar Gdns., N.Mal.	182	D2
Poplar Gro. N11	58	A6
Poplar Gro. W6	127	J2
Poplar Gro., N.Mal.	182	D3
Poplar Gro., Wem.	88	C3
Poplar High St. E14	114	A7
Poplar Mt., Belv.	139	H4
Poplar Pl. SE28	118	C1
Poplar Pl. W2	14	A5
Poplar Pl. W2	109	E7
Poplar Pl., Hayes	102	A7
Central Av.		
Poplar Rd. SE24	151	J4
Poplar Rd. SW19	184	D2
Poplar Rd., Sutt.	198	C1
Poplar Rd. S. SW19	184	D3
Poplar St., Rom.	83	J4
Poplar Vw., Wem.	87	G2
Magnet Rd.		
Poplar Wk. SE24	151	J4
Poplar Wk., Croy.	201	J2
Poplar Way, Felt.	160	A3
Poplar Way, Ilf.	81	F4
Poplars Av. NW10	42	B5
Poplars Rd. E17	78	B6
Poppins Ct. EC4	19	G4
Poppleton Rd. E11	79	E6
Poppy Cl., Wall.	200	A1
Porch Way N20	57	J3
Porchester Cl. SE5	151	J4
Porchester Gdns. W2	14	B5
Porchester Gdns. Ms. W2	14	B4
Porchester Mead, Beck.	172	B5
Porchester Ms. W2	14	B3
Porchester Ms. W2	109	E6
Porchester Pl. W2	15	H4
Porchester Pl. W2	109	H6
Porchester Rd. W2	14	A3
Porchester Rd. W2	109	E6
Porchester Rd., Kings.T.	182	B2
Porchester Sq. W2	14	B3
Porchester Sq. W2	109	E6
Porchester Ter. W2	14	C4
Porchester Ter. W2	109	F7
Porchester Ter. N. W2	14	B3
Porchester Ter. N. W2	109	E6
Porcupine Cl. SE9	174	B2
Porden Rd. SW2	151	F4
Porlock Rd. W10	108	A4
Ladbroke Gro.		
Porlock Rd., Enf.	44	C7
Porlock St. SE1	28	B3
Porlock St. SE1	132	A2
Porrington Cl., Chis.	192	C1
Port Cres. E13	115	H4
Jenkins Rd.		
Portal Cl. SE27	169	G3
Portal Cl., Ruis.	84	A4
Portbury Cl. SE15	152	D1
Clayton Rd.		
Portcullis Lo. Rd., Enf.	44	A3
Portelet Rd. E1	113	G3
Porten Rd. W14	128	B3
Porter Rd. E6	116	C6
Porter Sq. N19	92/93	E1
Hornsey Rd.		
Porter St. SE1	28	A1
Porter St. W1	16	A1
Porters Av., Dag.	100	B6
Porters Wk. E1	112/113	E7
Pennington St.		
Porters Way, West Dr.	120	C3
Portersfield Rd., Enf.	44	B4
Porteus Rd. W2	14	D1
Porteus Rd. W2	109	F5
Portgate Cl. W9	108	C4
Porthcawe Rd. SE26	171	H4
Porthkerry Av., Well.	158	A4
Portia Way E3	113	J4
Portinscale Rd. SW15	148	B5
Portland Av. N16	76	C7
Portland Av., N.Mal.	183	F7
Portland Av., Sid.	158	A6
Portland Cl., Rom.	82	E5
Portland Cres. SE9	174	B2
Portland Cres., Grnf.	103	H4
Portland Cres., Stan.	69	G2
Portland Gdns. N4	75	H4
Portland Gdns., Rom.	82	D5
Portland Gro. SW8	151	F1

Name	Map	Grid
Portland Ms. W1	17	G4
Portland Pl. W1	16	E2
Portland Pl. W1	110	B5
Portland Ri. N4	93	H1
Portland Ri. Est. N4	93	J1
Portland Rd. N15	76	C4
Portland Rd. SE9	174	B2
Portland Rd. SE25	188	D2
Portland Rd. W11	128	B1
Portland Rd., Brom.	173	J4
Portland Rd., Kings.T.	181	H3
Portland Rd., Mitch.	185	H2
Portland Rd., Sthl.	123	F3
Portland Sq. E1	132/133	E1
Watts St.		
Portland St. SE17	36	B3
Portland St. SE17	132	A5
Portland Ter., Rich.	145	G4
Portland Wk. SE17	36	C5
Portman Av. SW14	146	D3
Portman Cl. W1	16	A3
Portman Cl. W1	109	J6
Portman Cl., Bexh.	158	D3
Queen Anne's Gate		
Portman Dr., Wdf.Grn.	80	A2
Portman Gdns. NW9	70	D2
Portman Gate NW1	7	H6
Portman Ms. S. W1	16	B4
Portman Ms. S. W1	110	A6
Portman Pl. E2	113	F3
Portman Rd., Kings.T.	181	J2
Portman Sq. W1	16	B3
Portman Sq. W1	109	J6
Portman St. W1	16	B4
Portman St. W1	110	A6
Portmeadow Wk. SE2	138	D2
Portmeers Cl. E17	77	J4
Lennox Rd.		
Portnall Rd. W9	108	C3
Portobello Ct. W11	108	C7
Westbourne Gro.		
Portobello Ms. W11	108	D7
Portobello Rd.		
Portobello Rd. W10	108	C6
Portobello Rd. W11	108	C6
Porton Ct., Surb.	181	F6
Portpool La. EC1	18	E1
Portpool La. EC1	111	G5
Portree Cl. N22	59	F7
Nightingale Rd.		
Portree St. E14	114	D6
Portsdown, Edg.	54	A5
Rectory La.		
Portsdown Av. NW11	72	C6
Portsdown Ms. NW11	72	C6
Portsea Ms. W2	15	H4
Portsea Pl. W2	15	H4
Portside Rd. SW8	150	C2
Portsmouth Av., T.Ditt.	180	D7
Portsmouth Ms. E16	135	H1
Wesley Av.		
Portsmouth Rd. SW15	147	H7
Portsmouth Rd., Kings.T.	181	F5
Portsmouth Rd., Surb.	181	F5
Portsmouth Rd., T.Ditt.	194	B2
Portsmouth St. WC2	18	C4
Portsoken St. E1	21	F5
Portsoken St. E1	112	C7
Portugal Gdns., Twick.	161	J2
Fulwell Pk. Av.		
Portugal St. WC2	18	C4
Portugal St. WC2	111	F6
Portway E15	115	F1
Portway Gdns. SE18	136	A7
Shooter's Hill Rd.		
Post La., Twick.	162	A1
Post Office Ct. EC3	20	C4
Post Office Way SW8	33	H7
Post Office Way SW8	130	D7
Post Rd., Sthl.	123	H3
Postern Grn., Enf.	43	G2
Postmill Cl., Croy.	203	G3
Postway Ms., Ilf.	98/99	E3
Clements Rd.		
Potier St. SE1	28	C6
Potier St. SE1	132	A3
Pott St. E2	113	E3
Potter Cl., Mitch.	186	B2
Potter St., Nthwd.	66	A1
Potter St., Pnr.	66	A1
Potter St. Hill, Pnr.	50	B6
Potterne Cl. SW19	148	A7
Potters Cl., Croy.	203	H1
Potters Cl., Loug.	48	B2
Potters Flds. SE1	132	B3
Tooley St.		
Potters Gro., N.Mal.	182	C4
Potters Hts. Cl., Pnr.	50	B7
Potters La. SW16	168	D6
Potters La., Barn.	40	D4
Potters La., Borwd.	38	C1
Potters Rd. SW6	149	F2
Potters Rd., Barn.	40	E4
Pottery La. W11	108	B7
Portland Rd.		
Pottery Rd., Bex.	177	J2
Pottery Rd., Brent.	125	H6
Pottery St. SE16	132	E2
Poulett Gdns., Twick.	162	D1
Poulett Rd. E6	116	C2
Poulner Way SE15	132	C7
Daniel Gdns.		
Poulters Wd., Kes.	206	A5
Poulton Av., Sutt.	199	G3
Poulton Cl. E8	94/95	E5
Spurstowe Ter.		
Poultry EC2	20	B4
Poultry EC2	112	A6
Pound Cl., Orp.	207	G2
Pound Cl., Surb.	195	F1
Pound Ct. Dr., Orp.	207	G2
Pound La. NW10	89	G6
Pound Pk. Rd. SE7	136	A4
Pound Pl. SE9	156	D6
Pound St., Cars.	199	J5
Pound Way, Chis.	175	F7
Royal Par.		
Poundfield Rd., Loug.	48	D5
Pountney Rd. SW11	150	A3
Poverest Rd., Orp.	193	J5
Powder Mill La., Twick.	161	F1
Powell Cl., Chess.	195	G5
Coppard Gdns.		
Powell Cl., Edg.	53	J6
Powell Cl., Wall.	200	D7
Powell Gdns., Dag.	101	G4
Powell Rd. E5	95	E3
Powell Rd., Buck.H.	47	J7
Powell's Wk. W4	127	E6
Power Rd. W4	126	A4
Powers Ct., Twick.	145	G7
Powerscroft Rd. E5	95	F4
Powerscroft Rd., Sid.	176	C6
Powis Gdns. NW11	72	C7
Powis Gdns. W11	108	C6
Powis Ms. W11	108	C6
Westbourne Pk. Rd.		
Powis Pl. WC1	10	B6
Powis Pl. WC1	111	E4
Powis Rd. E3	114	B3
Powis Sq. W11	108	C6
Powis St. SE18	136	D3
Powis Ter. W11	108	C6
Powle Ter., Ilf.	99	F5
Oaktree Gro.		
Powlett Pl. NW1	92	B6
Harmood St.		
Pownall Gdns., Houns.	143	H4
Pownall Rd. E8	112	C1
Pownall Rd., Houns.	143	H4
Pownsett Ter., Ilf.	99	F5
Buttsbury Rd.		
Powster Rd., Brom.	173	H5
Powys Cl., Bexh.	138	D6
Powys La. N13	58	E5
Powys La. N14	58	E4
Poynders Ct. SW4	150	C6
Poynders Rd.		
Poynders Gdns. SW4	150	C7
Poynders Rd. SW4	150	C6
Poynings Rd. N19	92	C3
Poynings Way N12	56	D5
Poyntell Cres., Chis.	193	G1
Poynter Rd., Enf.	44	D5
Poynton Rd. N17	76	D2
Poyntz Rd. SW11	149	J2
Poyser St. E2	113	E2
Praed Ms. W2	15	F3
Praed St. W2	15	G2
Praed St. W2	109	G6
Pragel St. E13	115	H2
Pragnell Rd. SE12	173	H2
Prague Pl. SW2	150	E5
Prah Rd. N4	93	G2
Prairie St. SW8	150	A2
Pratt Ms. NW1	110	C1
Pratt St.		
Pratt St. NW1	110	C1
Pratt Wk. SE11	34	D1
Pratt Wk. SE11	131	F4
Pratts Pas., Kings.T.	181	H2
Eden St.		
Prayle Gro. NW2	90	A1
Prebend Gdns. W4	127	F3
Prebend Gdns. W6	127	F3
Prebend St. N1	111	J1
Precinct, The, W.Mol.	179	H3
Victoria Av.		
Precinct Rd., Hayes	102	A7
Precincts, The, Mord.	184/185	E6
Green La.		
Premier Cor. W9	108	C2
Kilburn La.		
Premier Pk. NW10	106	B1
Premier Pl. SW15	148	B4
Putney High St.		
Premiere Pl. E14	114	A7
Garford St.		
Prendergast Rd. SE3	155	E3
Prentis Rd. SW16	168	D4
Prentiss Ct. SE7	136	A4
Presburg Rd., N.Mal.	183	E5
Presburg St. E5	95	G3
Glyn Rd.		
Prescelly Pl., Edg.	69	J1
Prescot St. E1	21	G5
Prescot St. E1	112	C7
Prescott Av., Orp.	192	E6
Prescott Cl. SW16	168	E7
Prescott Grn., Loug.	49	F3
Prescott Ho. SE17	35	H6
Prescott Pl. SW4	150	D3
Presentation Ms. SW2	169	F1
President Dr. E1	132/133	E1
Waterman Way		
President St. EC1	11	J3
Press Rd. NW10	88	D3
Prestage Way E14	114	C7
Prestbury Rd. E7	97	J7
Prestbury Sq. SE9	174	C4
Prested Rd. SW11	149	H4
St. John's Hill		
Prestige Way NW4	71	J5
Heriot Rd.		
Preston Av. E4	62	D6
Preston Cl. SE1	36	D1
Preston Cl., Twick.	162	B3
Preston Dr. E11	79	J5
Preston Dr., Bexh.	158	D1
Preston Dr., Epsom	197	E6
Preston Gdns. NW10	88/89	E6
Church Rd.		
Preston Gdns., Ilf.	80	B6
Preston Hill, Har.	69	J6
Preston Pl. NW2	89	G6
Preston Pl., Rich.	145	H5
Preston Rd. E11	79	E6
Preston Rd. SE19	169	H6
Preston Rd. SW20	165	F7
Preston Rd., Har.	69	H7
Preston Rd., Wem.	87	H2
Preston Waye, Har.	87	H1
Prestons Rd. E14	134	C2
Prestons Rd., Brom.	205	G3
Prestwick Cl., Sthl.	122/123	E5
Ringway		
Prestwick Rd., Wat.	50	D5
Prestwood Av., Har.	69	E4
Prestwood Cl. SE18	138	A7
Prestwood Cl., Har.	69	F4
Prestwood Gdns., Croy.	187	J7
Prestwood St. N1	12	A2
Pretoria Av. E17	77	H4
Pretoria Cl. N17	60	C7
Pretoria Rd.		
Pretoria Cres. E4	62	C1
Pretoria Rd. E4	62	C1
Pretoria Rd. E11	96	D1
Pretoria Rd. E16	115	F3
Pretoria Rd. N17	60	C7
Pretoria Rd. SW16	168	B6
Pretoria Rd., Ilf.	98	E5
Pretoria Rd., Rom.	83	J4
Pretoria Rd. N. N18	60	C6
Prevost Rd. N11	58	A2
Price Cl. NW7	56	B6
Price Cl. SW17	167	J3
Price Rd., Croy.	201	H5
Price Way, Hmptn.	160/161	E6
Victors Dr.		
Price's Yd. N1	111	F1
Pricklers Hill, Barn.	41	E6
Prickley Rd., Brom.	205	F1
Priddy's Yd., Croy.	201	J2
Church St.		
Prideaux Pl. W3	106	D7
Friars Pl. La.		
Prideaux Pl. WC1	10	D3
Prideaux Pl. WC1	111	F3
Prideaux Rd. SW9	151	E3
Pridham Rd., Th.Hth.	188	A4
Priest Ct. EC2	19	J3
Priest Pk. Av., Har.	85	G2
Priestfield Rd. SE23	171	H3
Priestlands Pk. Rd., Sid.	175	J3
Priestley Cl. N16	76	C7
Ravensdale Rd.		
Priestley Gdns., Rom.	82	B6
Priestley Rd., Mitch.	186	A2
Priestley Way E17	77	G3
Priestley Way NW2	89	G1
Priests Br. SW14	147	E3
Priests Br. SW15	147	E3
Prima Rd. SW9	35	E7
Prima Rd. SW9	131	G7
Primrose Av., Enf.	44	A1
Primrose Av., Rom.	82	B7
Primrose Cl. SE6	172	C5
Primrose Cl., Har.	85	F4
Primrose Cl., Wall.	200	B1
Primrose Dr., West Dr.	120	A3
Wise La.		
Primrose Gdns. NW3	91	H6
Primrose Gdns., Ruis.	84	C5
Primrose Hill EC4	19	F4
Primrose Hill Ct. NW3	91	J7
Primrose Hill Rd. NW3	91	H7
Primrose Hill Studios NW1	110	A1
Fitzroy Rd.		
Primrose La., Croy.	203	G1
Primrose Ms. NW1	91	J7
Sharpleshall St.		
Primrose Ms. SE3	135	H7
Primrose Ms. W5	125	G2
St. Mary's Rd.		
Primrose Rd. E10	96	B1
Primrose Rd. E18	79	H2
Primrose Sq. E9	95	F7
Primrose St. EC2	20	D1
Primrose St. EC2	112	B5
Primrose Wk., Epsom	197	F7
Primrose Way, Wem.	105	G2
Primula St. W12	107	G6
Prince Albert Rd. NW1	7	H2
Prince Albert Rd. NW1	109	H2
Prince Albert Rd. NW8	7	H2
Prince Albert Rd. NW8	109	H2
Prince Arthur Ms. NW3	91	F4
Perrins La.		
Prince Arthur Rd. NW3	91	F5
Prince Charles Dr. NW4	71	J7
Prince Charles Rd. SE3	155	F1
Prince Charles Way, Wall.	200	B3
Prince Consort Dr., Chis.	193	G1
Prince Consort Rd. SW7	22	E5
Prince Consort Rd. SW7	129	F3
Prince Edward Rd. E9	95	J6
Prince George Av. N14	42	C5
Prince George Duke of Kent Ct., Chis.	175	G7
Holbrook La.		
Prince George Rd. N16	94	B4
Prince George's Av. SW20	183	J2
Prince George's Rd. SW19	185	G1
Prince Henry Rd. SE7	136	A7
Prince Imperial Rd. SE18	156	C1
Prince Imperial Rd., Chis.	175	E7
Prince John Rd. SE9	156	B5
Prince of Orange La. SE10	134	C7
Greenwich High Rd.		
Prince of Wales Cl. NW4	71	H4
Church Ter.		
Prince of Wales Dr. SW8	130	B7
Prince of Wales Dr. SW11	149	J1
Prince of Wales Gate SW7	23	G3
Prince of Wales Gate SW7	129	H2
Prince of Wales Pas. NW1	9	F4
Prince of Wales Rd. NW5	92	A6
Prince of Wales Rd. SE3	155	F1

Prince of Wales Rd., 199 G2
Sutt.
Prince of Wales Ter. 126 E5
W4
Prince of Wales Ter. 22 B4
W8
Prince Regent Ct. 133 H1
SE16
Rotherhithe St.
Prince Regent La. 115 H3
E13
Prince Regent La. 115 J5
E16
Prince Regent Rd., 143 J3
Houns.
Prince Rd. SE25 188 B5
Prince Rupert Rd. 156 C4
SE9
Prince St. SE8 133 J6
Princedale Rd. W11 128 B1
Princelet St. E1 21 G1
Princelet St. E1 112 C5
Prince's Arc. SW1 25 G1
Princes Av. N3 72 D1
Princes Av. N10 74 A3
Princes Av. N13 59 G5
Princes Av. N22 74 D1
Princes Av. NW9 70 B4
Princes Av. W3 126 A3
Princes Av., Cars. 199 J7
Princes Av., Grnf. 103 H6
Princes Av., Orp. 193 H5
Princes Av., Surb. 196 A1
Princes Av., 63 H4
Wdf.Grn.
Princes Cl. N4 93 H1
Princes Cl. NW9 70 A4
Princes Cl. SW4 150 C3
Old Town
Princes Cl., Edg. 54 A5
Princes Cl., Sid. 176 D3
Princes Cl., Tedd. 162 A4
Princes Cl. E1 113 E7
Princes Cl. SE16 133 J3
Princes Cl., Wem. 87 H5
Princes Dr., Har. 68 B3
Princes Gdns. SW7 23 F5
Princes Gdns. SW7 129 G3
Princes Gdns. W3 106 A5
Princes Gdns. W5 105 F4
Princes Gate SW7 23 G4
Princes Gate SW7 129 H2
Princes Gate Ct. SW7 23 F4
Princes Gate Ms. 23 F5
SW7
Princes Gate Ms. 129 G3
SW7
Princes La. N10 74 B3
Princes Ms. W2 14 A5
Princes Pk. Av. 72 B6
NW11
Princes Pl. SW1 25 G1
Princes Pl. W11 128 B1
Princes Ri. SE13 154 C3
Princes Riverside Rd. 133 G1
SE16
Princes Rd. N18 61 F4
Princes Rd. SE20 171 G6
Princes Rd. SW14 146 D3
Princes Rd. SW19 166 D6
Princes Rd. W13 124/125 E1
Broomfield Rd.
Princes Rd., Buck.H. 63 J2
Princes Rd., Ilf. 81 G4
Princes Rd., Kings.T. 164 A7
Princes Rd., Rich. 145 J5
Princes Rd. (Kew), 145 J1
Rich.
Princes Rd., Tedd. 162 A4
Princes Sq. W2 14 A5
Princes Sq. W2 108 E7
Princes St. EC2 20 B4
Princes St. EC2 112 A6
Princes St. N17 60 B6
Queen St.
Princes St. W1 17 E4
Princes St. W1 110 B6
Princes St., Bexh. 159 F4
Princes St., Rich. 145 H5
Sheen Rd.
Princes St., Sutt. 199 G4
Princes Ter. E13 115 H1
Princes Way SW19 148 A7
Princes Way, Buck.H. 63 J2
Princes Way, Croy. 201 F5
Princes Way, Ruis. 84 E4
Princes Way, W.Wick. 205 F4
Princes Yd. W11 128 B1
Princedale Rd.
Princess Alice Way 137 G2
SE28
Princess Av., Wem. 87 H2
Princess Cres. N4 93 H2

Princess May Rd. N16 94 B4
Princess Ms. NW3 91 G6
Belsize Cres.
Princess Par., Orp. 206 D3
Crofton Rd.
Princess Pk. Manor 58 A5
N11
Princess Rd. NW1 110 A1
Princess Rd. NW6 108 D2
Princess Rd., Croy. 187 J6
Princess St. SE1 27 H6
Princess St. SE1 131 H3
Princesses Wk., Rich. 125 H7
Kew Rd.
Princethorpe Ho. W2 14 A1
Princethorpe Rd. W2 108 E5
Princethorpe Rd. 171 G4
SE26
Princeton Ct. SW15 148 A3
Felsham Rd.
Princeton St. WC1 18 C1
Princeton St. WC1 111 F5
Pringle Gdns. SW16 168 C4
Print Village SE15 152 C2
Chadwick Rd.
Printer St. EC4 19 F3
Printers Inn Ct. EC4 19 E3
Printing Ho. La., 121 H2
Hayes
Printing Ho. Yd. E2 13 E3
Priolo Rd. SE7 135 J5
Prior Av., Sutt. 199 H7
Prior Bolton St. N1 93 H6
Prior Rd., Ilf. 98 D3
Prior St. SE10 134 C7
Prioress Rd. SE27 169 H3
Prioress St. SE1 28 C6
Prioress St. SE1 132 A3
Priors Cft. E17 77 H2
Priors Fld., Nthlt. 84/85 E6
Arnold Rd.
Priors Gdns., Ruis. 84 C5
Priors Mead, Enf. 44 B1
Priory, The SE3 155 F4
Priory Av. E4 61 J3
Priory Av. E17 78 A5
Priory Av. N8 74 D4
Priory Av. W4 127 E4
Priory Av., Orp. 193 G6
Priory Av., Sutt. 198 A4
Priory Av., Wem. 86 C4
Priory Cl. E4 61 J3
Priory Cl. E18 79 G1
Priory Cl. N3 72 C1
Church Cres.
Priory Cl. N14 42 B5
Priory Cl. N20 40 C7
Priory Cl. SW19 184/185 E1
High Path
Priory Cl., Beck. 189 H3
Priory Cl., Chis. 192 C1
Priory Cl., Hmptn. 179 F1
Priory Gdns.
Priory Cl., Hayes 102 B7
Priory Cl., Stan. 52 C3
Priory Cl., Sun. 160 A7
Staines Rd. E.
Priory Cl. 86 C4
(Sudbury), Wem.
Priory Ct. E17 77 J3
Priory Ct. EC4 111 H6
Ludgate Hill
Priory Ct. SW8 150 D1
Priory Ct. Est. E17 77 J2
Priory Cres. SE19 169 J7
Priory Cres., Sutt. 198 A4
Priory Cres., Wem. 86 D3
Priory Dr. SE2 138 D5
Priory Dr., Stan. 52 B3
Priory Fld. Dr., Edg. 54 B4
Priory Gdns. N6 74 B6
Priory Gdns. SW13 148 C3
Priory Gdns. W4 127 E4
Priory Gdns. W5 105 H3
Hanger La.
Priory Gdns., Hmptn. 161 F7
Priory Gdns., Wem. 86 D4
Priory Grn. Est. N1 10 D1
Priory Grn. Est. N1 111 F2
Priory Gro. SW8 150 E1
Priory Hill, Wem. 86 D4
Priory La. SW15 147 E6
Priory La., Rich. 126 A7
Forest Rd.
Priory La., W.Mol. 179 H4
Priory Ms. SW8 150 D1
Priory Pk. SE3 155 F3
Priory Pk. Rd. NW6 108 C1
Priory Pk. Rd., Wem. 86 D4
Priory Rd. E6 116 A1
Priory Rd. N8 74 D4
Priory Rd. NW6 108 E1
Priory Rd. SW19 167 G7

Priory Rd. W4 126 D3
Priory Rd., Bark. 99 G7
Priory Rd., Chess. 195 H3
Priory Rd., Croy. 187 G7
Priory Rd., Hmptn. 161 F7
Priory Rd., Houns. 143 J5
Priory Rd., Loug. 48 B4
Priory Rd., Rich. 126 A6
Priory Rd., Sutt. 198 A4
Priory St. E3 114 B3
St. Leonards St.
Priory Ter. NW6 108 E1
Priory Ter., Sun. 160 A7
Staines Rd. E.
Priory Wk. SW10 30 D4
Priory Wk. SW10 129 F5
Priory Way, Har. 67 H4
Priory Way, Sthl. 122 D3
Priory Way, West Dr. 120 B6
Pritchard's Rd. E2 112 D1
Priter Rd. SE16 29 J6
Priter Rd. SE16 132 D3
Priter Way SE16 132 D3
Dockley Rd.
Private Rd., Enf. 44 B5
Probert Rd. SW2 151 G5
Probyn Rd. SW2 169 H2
Procter St. WC1 18 C2
Procter St. WC1 111 F5
Proctor Cl., Mitch. 186 A1
Proctors Cl., Felt. 160 A1
Progress Business 201 F2
Pk., Croy.
Progress Way N22 75 G1
Progress Way, Croy. 201 F2
Progress Way, Enf. 44 D5
Promenade, The W4 147 E1
Promenade App. Rd. 126 E7
W4
Promenade Mans., 54 B5
Edg.
Hale La.
Prospect Business 49 F4
Pk., Loug.
Prospect Cl. SE26 170 E4
Prospect Cl., Belv. 139 G4
Prospect Cl., Houns. 143 F1
Prospect Cl., Ruis. 66 D7
Prospect Cotts. SW18 148 D4
Point Pleasant
Prospect Cres., 143 J6
Twick.
Prospect Hill E17 78 B4
Prospect Pl. E1 133 F1
Prospect Pl. N2 73 G4
Prospect Pl. N17 76 B1
Prospect Pl. NW2 90 C3
Ridge Rd.
Prospect Pl. NW3 91 F4
Holly Wk.
Prospect Pl., Brom. 191 H3
Prospect Pl., Rom. 83 J2
Prospect Quay SW18 148 D4
Point Pleasant
Prospect Ring N2 73 G3
Prospect Rd. NW2 90 C3
Prospect Rd., Barn. 40 D5
Prospect Rd., Surb. 181 F6
Prospect Rd., Wdf.Grn. 63 J5
Prospect St. SE16 132/133 E2
Jamaica Rd.
Prospect Vale SE18 136 B4
Prospero Rd. N19 92 C1
Protea Cl. E16 115 F4
Hermit Rd.
Prothero Gdns. NW4 71 H5
Prothero Rd. NW10 88 D7
Prothero Rd. SW6 128 B7
Prout Gro. NW10 89 E4
Prout Rd. E5 95 E3
Provence St. N1 111 J2
St. Peters St.
Providence Ct. W1 16 C5
Providence Ct. W1 110 A7
Providence La., 121 G7
Hayes
Providence Pl. N1 111 H1
Upper St.
Providence Pl., Rom. 83 F2
Providence Rd., 120 B1
West Dr.
Providence Row N1 10 C2
Providence Row Cl. E2 112/113 E3
Ainsley St.
Providence Sq. SE1 132 C2
Mill St.
Providence St. N1 111 J2
St. Peters St.
Providence Yd. E2 13 H3
Provident Ind. Est., 122 A2
Hayes
Provost Est. N1 12 B3
Provost Est. N1 112 A2

Provost Rd. NW3 91 J7
Provost St. N1 12 B4
Provost St. N1 112 A3
Prowse Av., Bushey 51 J2
Prowse Pl. NW1 92 B7
Bonny St.
Pruden Cl. N14 58 C2
Prudent Pas. EC2 20 A3
Prusom St. E1 133 E1
Pryors, The NW3 91 G3
Pudding La. EC3 20 C6
Pudding La. EC3 112 A7
Pudding La., Chig. 65 J1
Pudding Mill La. E15 114 B1
Puddle Dock EC4 19 H5
Puffin Cl., Bark. 117 H3
Thames Rd.
Puffin Cl., Beck. 189 G5
Pulborough Rd. 148 C7
SW18
Pulborough Way, 142 C4
Houns.
Pulford Rd. N15 76 A6
Pulham Av. N2 73 F4
Puller Rd., Barn. 40 B2
Pulleyns Av. E6 116 B3
Pullman Ct. SW2 169 E1
Pullman Gdns. SW15 147 J6
Pullman Pl. SE9 156 B5
Pulross Rd. SW9 151 F3
Pulteney Cl. E3 113 J1
Pulteney Gdns. E18 79 H3
Pulteney Rd.
Pulteney Rd. E18 79 H3
Pulteney Ter. N1 111 F1
Pulton Pl. SW6 128 D7
Puma Ct. E1 21 F1
Pump All., Brent. 125 G7
Pump Cl., Nthlt. 103 G2
Union Rd.
Pump Ct. EC4 19 E4
Pump Hill, Loug. 48 C2
Pump Ho. Cl., Brom. 191 F2
Pump La. SE14 133 F7
Farrow La.
Pump La., Hayes 122 A2
Pump Pail N., Croy. 201 J3
Old Town
Pump Pail S., Croy. 201 J3
Southbridge Rd.
Pumping Sta. Rd. W4 127 E7
Pundersons Gdns. E2 113 E3
Punjab La., Sthl. 123 F1
Herbert Rd.
Purbeck Av., N.Mal. 183 F6
Purbeck Dr. NW2 90 B2
Purbrook Est. SE1 29 E4
Purbrook St. SE1 29 E5
Purbrook St. SE1 132 B3
Purcell Cres. SW6 128 B7
Purcell Ms. NW10 88/89 E7
Suffolk Rd.
Purcell Rd., Grnf. 103 H5
Purcell St. N1 12 D1
Purcell St. N1 112 B2
Purcells Av., Edg. 54 A5
Purchese St. NW1 9 J1
Purchese St. NW1 110 D2
Purdy St. E3 114 B4
Purelake Ms. SE13 154 D3
Purland Cl., Dag. 101 F1
Purland Rd. SE28 137 J2
Purleigh Av., 64 B6
Wdf.Grn.
Purley Av. NW2 90 B3
Purley Cl., Ilf. 80 D2
Purley Pl. N1 93 H7
Islington Pk. St.
Purley Rd. N9 60 A3
Purley Rd., S.Croy. 202 A7
Purley Way, Croy. 187 F7
Purley Way, Pur. 201 G7
Purley Way Cres., 187 F7
Croy.
Purley Way
Purneys Rd. SE9 156 A4
Purrett Rd. SE18 137 J5
Purser's Cross Rd. 148 C1
SW6
Pursewardens Cl. 125 J1
W13
Pursley Rd. NW7 55 H7
Purves Rd. NW10 107 J2
Puteaux Ho. E2 113 G2
Putney Br. SW6 148 B3
Putney Br. SW15 148 B3
Putney Br. App. SW6 148 B3
Putney Br. Rd. SW15 148 B4
Putney Br. Rd. SW18 148 B5
Putney Common 147 J3
SW15
Putney Gdns., Rom. 82 B6
Heathfield Pk. Dr.
Putney Heath SW15 147 J6

Putney Heath La. 148 A6
SW15
Putney High St. 148 A4
SW15
Putney Hill SW15 148 A6
Putney Pk. Av. SW15 147 G4
Putney Pk. La. SW15 147 H4
Puttenham Cl., Wat. 50 C3
Pycroft Way N9 60 C4
Pyecombe Cor. N12 56 C4
Pylbrook Rd., Sutt. 198 D3
Pylon Way, Croy. 201 E1
Pym Cl., Barn. 41 G5
Pymers Mead SE21 169 J1
Pymmes Cl. N13 59 F5
Pymmes Cl. N17 76 E1
Pymmes Gdns. N. N9 60 C3
Pymmes Gdns. S. N9 60 C3
Pymmes Grn. Rd. N11 58 B4
Pymmes Rd. N13 59 E6
Pymms Brook Dr., 41 H4
Barn.
Pyne Rd. SW19 196 A1
Pyne Ter. SW19 166 A1
Windlesham Gro.
Pynfolds SE16 132/133 E2
Paradise St.
Pynham Cl. SE2 138 A3
Pynnacles Cl., Stan. 53 E5
Pyrland Rd. N5 94 A5
Pyrland Rd., Rich. 145 J6
Pyrles Grn., Loug. 48 E1
Pyrles La., Loug. 48 E2
Pyrmont Gro. SE27 169 H3
Pyrmont Rd. W4 126 A6
Pyrmont Rd., Ilf. 99 F2
High Rd.
Pytchley Cres. SE19 169 J6
Pytchley Rd. SE22 152 B3

Q

Quad Rd., Wem. 87 G3
Courtenay Rd.
Quadrangle, The W2 15 G3
Quadrangle Ms., 53 F7
Stan.
Quadrant, The SE24 151 J6
Herne Hill
Quadrant, The SW20 184 B1
Quadrant, The, Bexh. 138 D7
Quadrant, The, Rich. 145 H4
Quadrant, The, Sutt. 199 F6
Quadrant Arc. W1 17 G6
Quadrant Gro. NW5 91 J5
Quadrant Rd., Rich. 145 G4
Quadrant Rd., Th.Hth. 187 H4
Quaggy Wk. SE3 155 G4
Quainton St. NW10 88 D3
Quaker Ct. E1 13 F6
Quaker La., Sthl. 123 G3
Quaker St. E1 13 F6
Quaker St. E1 112 C4
Quakers Course 71 F1
NW9
Quakers La., Islw. 144 D1
Quaker's Pl. E7 98 A5
Quakers Wk. N21 44 A6
Quality Ct. WC2 18 E3
Quality Ct. WC2 111 G6
Quantock Cl., Hayes 121 G7
Quantock Dr., Wor.Pk. 197 J2
Quantock Gdns. 90 A2
NW2
Quarley Way SE15 37 F7
Quarr Rd., Cars. 185 G6
Quarrendon St. SW6 148 D2
Quarry Pk. Rd., Sutt. 198 C6
Quarry Ri., Sutt. 198 C6
Quarry Rd. SW18 149 F6
Quarter Mile La. E10 96 B4
Quarterdeck, The E14 134 A2
Quay W., Tedd. 162 E5
Quebec Ms. W1 16 A4
Quebec Rd., Hayes 102 C7
Quebec Rd., Ilf. 81 E7
Quebec Way SE16 133 G2
Queen Adelaide Rd. 171 F6
SE20
Queen Alexandra's 166 C5
Ct. SW19
Suffield Rd.
Queen Anne Av. N15 76 C5
Queen Anne Av., 191 F3
Brom.
Queen Anne Dr., 194 B7
Esher
Queen Anne Ms. W1 16 E2
Queen Anne Rd. E9 95 G6
Queen Anne St. W1 16 D3
Queen Anne St. W1 110 B6
Queen Anne Ter. 112/113 E7
E1
Sovereign Cl.

Queen Anne's Cl., 162 A3
Twick.
Queen Anne's Gdns. 127 E3
W4
Queen Annes Gdns. 125 H2
W5
Queen Anne's Gdns., 44 B6
Enf.
Queen Anne's Gdns., 185 J3
Mitch.
Queen Anne's Gate 25 H4
SW1
Queen Anne's Gate 130 D2
SW1
Queen Anne's Gate, 158 D3
Bexh.
Queen Annes Gro. 126 E3
W4
Queen Annes Gro. 125 H2
W5
Queen Annes Gro., 44 A7
Enf.
Queen Annes Pl., Enf. 44 B6
Queen Caroline Est. 127 J5
W6
Queen Caroline St. 127 J4
W6
Queen Elizabeth 184 D4
Gdns., Mord.
Queen Elizabeth Rd. 77 H3
E17
Queen Elizabeth Rd., 181 J1
Kings.T.
Queen Elizabeth St. 29 E3
SE1
Queen Elizabeth St. 132 C2
SE1
Queen Elizabeth Wk. 147 H1
SW13
Queen Elizabeths Cl. 94 A2
N16
Queen Elizabeths Dr. 58 E1
N14
Queen Elizabeths Wk. 94 A2
N16
Queen Elizabeth's Wk. 200 D4
Wall.
Queen Margaret's Gro. 94 B5
N1
Queen Mary Av., 184 A5
Mord.
Queen Mary Cl., Surb. 196 A3
Queen Mary Rd. SE19 169 H6
Queen Mary's Av., 199 J7
Cars.
Queen of Denmark 133 J3
Ct. SE16
Queen Sq. WC1 10 B6
Queen Sq. WC1 111 E4
Queen Sq. Pl. WC1 10 B6
Queen St. EC4 20 A5
Queen St. EC4 111 J7
Queen St. N17 60 B6
Queen St. W1 24 D1
Queen St. W1 130 B1
Queen St., Bexh. 159 F3
Queen St., Croy. 201 J3
Church La.
Queen St. Pl. EC4 20 A6
Wem.
Queen Victoria Av., 87 G7
Wem.
Queen Victoria St. EC4 19 H5
Queen Victoria St. 111 H7
EC4
Queen Victoria Ter. 112/113 E7
E1
Sovereign Cl.
Queenborough Gdns. 175 G6
Chis.
Queenborough Gdns., 80 D4
Ilf.
Queenhithe EC4 20 A5
Queenhithe EC4 111 J7
Queens Acre, Sutt. 198 A7
Queens Av. N3 57 F7
Queens Av. N10 74 A3
Queens Av. N20 57 G2
Queen's Av. N21 59 H1
Queens Av., Felt. 160 C4
Queens Av., Grnf. 103 H6
Queens Av., Stan. 69 F3
Queens Av., Wdf.Grn. 63 H5
Queen's Circ. SW8 130 B7
Queenstown Rd.
Queen's Circ. SW11 130 B7
Queenstown Rd.
Queens Cl., Edg. 54 A5
Queens Cl., Wall. 200 B5
Queens Pl.
Queens Club Gdns. 128 B6
W14
Queens Ct. SE23 171 F1
Queens Ct., Rich. 145 J6
Queens Cres. NW5 92 A6

Queens Cres., Rich. 145 J5
Queens Dr. E10 78 A7
Queens Dr. N4 93 H2
Queens Dr. W3 105 J6
Queens Dr. W5 105 J6
Queens Dr., Surb. 182 D7
Queens Dr., T.Ditt. 180 D7
Queen's Elm Sq. SW3 31 F4
Queens Gdns. NW4 71 J5
Queens Gdns. NW4 14 C5
Queens Gdns. W2 109 F7
Queens Gdns. W5 105 F4
Queen's Gdns., 143 E1
Houns.
Queen's Gate SW7 30 E1
Queen's Gate SW7 129 F3
Queen's Gate Gdns. 22 D6
SW7
Queen's Gate Gdns. 129 F3
SW7
Queens Gate Gdns. 147 H4
SW15
Upper Richmond Rd.
Queen's Gate Ms. SW7 22 D4
SW7
Queen's Gate Ms. SW7 129 F2
SW7
Queen's Gate Pl. SW7 22 D6
SW7
Queen's Gate Pl. SW7 129 F3
SW7
Queen's Gate Pl. Ms. 22 D6
SW7
Queen's Gate Pl. Ms. 129 F3
SW7
Queen's Gate Ter. 22 C5
SW7
Queen's Gate Ter. 129 F3
SW7
Queen's Gro. NW8 109 G1
Queen's Gro. Ms. 109 G1
NW8
Queens Gro. Rd. E4 62 D1
Queen's Head St. N1 111 H1
Queen's Head Yd. SE1 28 B2
Queens Ho., Tedd. 162 C6
Queens La. N10 74 B3
Queens Mkt. E13 115 J1
Green St.
Queens Ms. W2 14 B5
Queens Ms. W2 109 E7
Queens Par. N11 57 J5
Colney Hatch La.
Queens Par. W5 105 J6
Queens Par. Cl. N11 57 J5
Colney Hatch La.
Queens Pk. Ct. W10 108 A3
Queens Pas., 174/175 E6
Chis.
High St.
Queens Pl., Mord. 184 D4
Queen's Prom., 181 G3
Kings.T.
Portsmouth Rd.
Queens Reach, E.Mol. 180 B4
Queens Ride SW13 147 G3
Queens Ride SW15 147 G3
Queen's Ride, Rich. 164 B1
Queens Ri., Rich. 145 J6
Queens Rd. E11 78 D7
Queens Rd. E13 115 H1
Queen's Rd. E17 77 J6
Queens Rd. N3 73 F1
Queen's Rd. N9 60 E3
Queens Rd. N11 58 E7
Queens Rd. NW4 71 J5
Queens Rd. SE14 152 E1
Queens Rd. SE15 152 E1
Queens Rd. SW14 146 D3
Queens Rd. SW19 166 C6
Queens Rd. W5 105 H6
Queens Rd., Bark. 99 F6
Queens Rd., Barn. 40 A3
Queens Rd., Beck. 189 H2
Queens Rd., Brom. 191 G2
Queen's Rd., Buck.H. 63 H2
Queens Rd., Chis. 175 E6
Queen's Rd., Croy. 187 H6
Queens Rd., Enf. 44 B4
Queens Rd., Felt. 160 B1
Queen's Rd., Hmptn. 161 H4
Queen's Rd., Houns. 143 H3
Queen's Rd., Kings.T. 164 A7
Queens Rd., Loug. 48 B3
Queen's Rd., Mitch. 185 G3
Queens Rd., Mord. 184 D4
Queen's Rd., N.Mal. 183 F4
Queens Rd., Rich. 145 H7
Queens Rd., Sthl. 122 D2
Queen's Rd., Tedd. 162 C6
Queen's Rd., T.Ditt. 180 C5
Queens Rd., Twick. 162 C1
Queens Rd., Wall. 200 B5
Queens Rd., Well. 158 B2
Queen's Rd., West Dr. 120 C2
Queen's Rd. W. E13 115 G2
Queen's Row SE17 36 B5

Queen's Row SE17 132 A6
Queens Ter. E13 115 H1
Queen's Ter. NW8 7 E1
Queen's Ter. NW8 109 G2
Queen's Ter., Islw. 144 D4
Queens Ter. Cotts. W7 124 B2
Boston Rd.
Queens Wk. E4 62 D1
The Grn. Wk.
Queens Wk. NW9 88 C2
Queen's Wk. SW1 25 F2
Queen's Wk. SW1 130 C1
Queens Wk. W5 105 F4
Queens Wk., Har. 68 B4
Queens Wk., Ruis. 84 D3
Queen's Wk., The 28 E1
SE1
Queen's Wk., The SE1 132 B1
Queens Way NW4 71 J5
Queens Way, Croy. 201 F6
Queens Way, Felt. 160 C4
Queens Well Av. N20 57 H3
Queen's Wd. Rd. N10 74 B6
Queens Yd. WC1 9 G6
Queensberry Ms. W. 30 E1
SW7
Queensberry Pl. SW7 30 E1
Queensberry Pl. SW7 129 G4
Queensberry Way 31 E1
SW7
Queensborough Ms. 14 C5
W2
Queensborough Pas. 14 C5
W2
Queensborough S. 109 F7
Bldgs. W2
Porchester Ter.
Queensborough 14 C5
Studios W2
Queensborough Ter. 14 B5
W2
Queensborough Ter. 109 E7
W2
Queensbridge Pk., 144 B5
Islw.
Queensbridge Rd. E2 112 C1
Queensbridge Rd. E8 94 C7
Queensbury Circle 69 H3
Par., Har.
Streatfield Rd.
Queensbury Circle 69 H3
Par., Stan.
Streatfield Rd.
Queensbury Pl., Rich. 145 G5
Friars La.
Queensbury Rd. NW9 70 D7
Queensbury Rd., 105 J2
Wem.
Queensbury Sta. 69 J3
Par., Edg.
Queensbury St. N1 93 J7
Queenscourt, Wem. 87 H4
Queenscroft Rd. SE9 156 A5
Queensdale Cres. 128 A1
W11
Queensdale Pl. W11 128 B1
Queensdale Rd. W11 128 B1
Queensdale Wk. W11 128 B1
Queensdown Rd. E5 94 E4
Queensferry Wk. 76/77 E4
N17
Jarrow Rd.
Queensgate Gdns., 193 G1
Chis.
Queensgate Pl. NW6 90 D7
Queensland Av. N18 59 J6
Queensland Av. 184 E1
SW19
Queensland Pl. N7 93 G4
Queensland Rd.
Queensland Rd. N7 93 G4
Queensmead NW8 109 G1
Queensmead Rd., 191 F2
Brom.
Queensmere Cl. 166 A2
SW19
Queensmere Rd. 166 A2
SW19
Queensmill Rd. SW6 128 A7
Queensthorpe Rd. 171 G4
SE26
Queenstown Ms. SW8 150 B2
Queenstown Rd.
Queenstown Rd. 32 D6
SW8
Queenstown Rd. 130 B6
SW8
Queensville Rd. 150 D7
SW12
Queensway W2 14 B4
Queensway W2 109 E6
Queensway, Enf. 45 E4
Queensway, Orp. 193 F5
Queensway, Sun. 178 B2

Name	Page	Grid
Queensway, W.Wick.	205	E3
Queenswood Av. E17	78	C1
Queenswood Av., Hmptn.	161	H6
Queenswood Av., Houns.	143	F2
Queenswood Av., Th.Hth.	187	G5
Queenswood Av., Wall.	200	D4
Queenswood Gdns. E11	97	H1
Queenswood Pk. N3	72	B2
Queenswood Rd. SE23	171	G3
Queenswood Rd., Sid.	157	J5
Quemerford Rd. N7	93	F5
Quentin Pl. SE13	155	E3
Quentin Rd. SE13	155	E3
Quernmore Cl., Brom.	173	G6
Quernmore Rd. N4	75	G6
Quernmore Rd., Brom.	173	G6
Querrin St. SW6	149	F2
Quex Ms. NW6	108	D1
Quex Rd.		
Quex Rd. NW6	108	D1
Quick Pl. N1	111	H1
Quick Rd. W4	126	E5
Quick St. N1	11	H2
Quick St. N1	111	H2
Quick St. Ms. N1	11	G2
Quicks Rd. SW19	167	E7
Quickswood NW3	91	H7
King Henry's Rd.		
Quiet Nook, Brom.	206	A3
Croydon Rd.		
Quill La. SW15	148	A4
Quill St. N4	93	G3
Quill St. W5	105	H3
Quilp St. SE1	27	J3
Quilter St. E2	13	H3
Quilter St. E2	112	D3
Quilter St. SE18	137	J5
Quinta Dr., Barn.	39	H5
Quintin Av. SW20	184	C1
Quintin Cl., Pnr.	66	B5
High Rd.		
Quinton Cl., Beck.	190	C3
Quinton Cl., Houns.	122	B7
Quinton Cl., Wall.	200	B4
Quinton Rd., T.Ditt.	194	D1
Quinton St. SW18	167	F2
Quixley St. E14	114	D7
Quorn Rd. SE22	152	B4
R		
Rabbit Row W8	128	D1
Kensington Mall		
Rabbits Rd. E12	98	B4
Rabournmead Dr., Nthlt.	84	E5
Raby Rd., N.Mal.	182	D4
Raby St. E14	113	H6
Salmon La.		
Raccoon Way, Houns.	142	C2
Rachel Cl., Ilf.	81	G3
Rachel Pt. E5	94	D4
Muir Rd.		
Rackham Cl., Well.	158	B2
Rackham Ms. SW16	168	C6
Westcote Rd.		
Racton Rd. SW6	128	D6
Radbourne Av. W5	125	F4
Radbourne Cl. E5	95	G2
Overbury Rd.		
Radbourne Cres. E17	78	D2
Radbourne Rd. SW12	150	C7
Radcliffe Av. NW10	107	G2
Radcliffe Av., Enf.	43	J1
Radcliffe Gdns., Cars.	199	H7
Radcliffe Ms., Hmptn.	161	J5
Taylor Cl.		
Radcliffe Path SW8	150	C2
St. Rule St.		
Radcliffe Rd. N21	59	H1
Radcliffe Rd. SE1	29	E5
Radcliffe Rd., Croy.	202	C2
Radcliffe Rd., Har.	68	D2
Radcliffe Sq. SW15	148	A6
Radcliffe St., Nthlt.	102	D3
Radcot Pt. SE23	171	G3
Radcot St. SE11	35	F4
Radcot St. SE11	131	G5
Raddington Rd. W10	108	B5
Radfield Way, Sid.	157	G7
Radford Rd. SE13	154	C6
Radford Way, Bark.	117	J3
Radipole Rd. SW6	148	C1
Radius Pk., Felt.	141	J4
Radland Rd. E16	115	F6
Radlet Av. SE26	171	E3
Radlett Cl. E7	97	F6
Radlett Pl. NW8	109	H1
Radley Av., Ilf.	99	J4
Radley Ct. SE16	133	G2
Thame Rd.		
Radley Gdns., Har.	69	H4
Radley Ho. SE2	138	D2
Wolvercote Rd.		
Radley Ms. W8	128	D3
Radley Rd. N17	76	B2
Radley's La. E18	79	G2
Radleys Mead, Dag.	101	H6
Radlix Rd. E10	96	A1
Radnor Av., Har.	68	B5
Radnor Av., Well.	158	B5
Radnor Cl., Chis.	175	H6
Homewood Cres.		
Radnor Cl., Mitch.	187	E4
Radnor Cres. SE18	138	A7
Radnor Cres., Ilf.	80	C5
Radnor Gdns., Enf.	44	B1
Radnor Gdns., Twick.	162	C2
Radnor Ms. W2	15	F4
Radnor Pl. W2	15	G4
Radnor Rd. NW6	109	H6
Radnor Rd. NW6	108	B1
Radnor Rd. SE15	37	H7
Radnor Rd. SE15	132	D7
Radnor Rd., Har.	68	A5
Radnor Rd., Twick.	162	C2
Radnor St. EC1	12	A4
Radnor St. EC1	111	J3
Radnor Ter. W14	128	C4
Radnor Wk. E14	134	A4
Copeland Dr.		
Radnor Wk. SW3	31	H4
Radnor Wk. SW3	129	H5
Radnor Wk., Croy.	189	J6
Radnor Way NW10	106	B4
Radstock Av., Har.	68	D3
Radstock St. SW11	129	H7
Raebarn Gdns., Barn.	39	H5
Raeburn Av., Surb.	182	B6
Raeburn Cl. NW11	73	F6
Raeburn Cl., Kings.T.	163	G7
Raeburn Rd., Edg.	70	A1
Raeburn Rd., Sid.	157	H6
Raeburn St. SW2	151	E4
Rafford Way, Brom.	191	H2
Raft Rd. SW18	148	D4
North Pas.		
Ragglesswood, Chis.	192	D1
Raglan Cl., Houns.	142/143	E5
Vickers Way		
Raglan Ct. SE12	155	G5
Raglan Ct., S.Croy.	201	H5
Raglan Ct., Wem.	87	J4
Raglan Gdns., Wat.	50	B1
Raglan Rd. E17	78	C5
Raglan Rd. SE18	137	F5
Raglan Rd., Belv.	139	F4
Raglan Rd., Brom.	191	J4
Raglan Rd., Enf.	44	B7
Raglan St. NW5	92	B6
Raglan Ter., Har.	85	H4
Raglan Way, Nthlt.	85	J6
Ragley Cl. W3	126	C2
Church Rd.		
Raider Cl., Rom.	83	G1
Railey Ms. NW5	92	C5
Railshead Rd., Islw.	144	E4
Railton Rd. SE24	151	G5
Railway App. N4	75	G6
Wightman Rd.		
Railway App. SE1	28	C1
Railway App., Har.	68	C4
Railway App., Twick.	162	D1
Railway App., Wall.	200	B6
Railway Av. SE16	133	F2
Railway Ms. E3	114	A3
Wellington Way		
Railway Ms. W10	108	B6
Ladbroke Gro.		
Railway Pas., Tedd.	162	D6
Victoria Rd.		
Railway Pl. SW19	166	C6
Hartfield Rd.		
Railway Pl., Belv.	139	G3
Railway Ri. SE22	152	B4
Grove Vale		
Railway Rd., Tedd.	162	C4
Railway Side SW13	147	E3
Railway St. N1	10	B2
Railway St. N1	111	E2
Railway St., Rom.	100	C1
Railway Ter. SE13	154	B5
Ladywell Rd.		
Railway Ter., Felt.	160	A1
Rainbow Av. E14	134	B5
Rainbow Quay SE16	133	H3
Rope St.		
Rainbow St. SE5	132	B7
Raine St. E1	133	E1
Rainham Cl. SE9	157	G6
Rainham Cl. SW11	149	H6
Rainham Rd. NW10	107	J3
Rainham Rd. N., Dag.	101	H2
Rainham Rd. S., Dag.	101	H4
Rainhill Way E3	114	A3
Rainsborough Av. SE8	133	H4
Rainsford Cl., Stan.	53	F5
Coverdale Cl.		
Rainsford Rd. NW10	106	B3
Rainsford St. W2	15	G3
Rainton Rd. SE7	135	G5
Rainville Rd. W6	127	J6
Raisins Hill, Pnr.	66	C3
Raith Av. N14	58	D3
Raleana Rd. E14	134	C1
Raleigh Av., Hayes	102	B5
Raleigh Av., Wall.	200	D4
Raleigh Cl. NW4	71	J5
Raleigh Cl., Pnr.	66	D7
Raleigh Cl. SE16	133	G1
Rotherhithe St.		
Raleigh Ct., Wall.	200	B6
Raleigh Dr. N20	57	H3
Raleigh Dr., Esher	194	A5
Raleigh Dr., Surb.	196	C1
Raleigh Gdns. SW2	151	F6
Brixton Hill		
Raleigh Gdns., Mitch.	185	J2
Raleigh Ms. N1	111	H1
Queen's Head St.		
Raleigh Ms., Orp.	207	J5
Osgood Av.		
Raleigh Rd. N8	75	G4
Raleigh Rd. SE20	171	G7
Raleigh Rd., Enf.	44	A4
Raleigh Rd., Rich.	145	J3
Raleigh Rd., Sthl.	122	E5
Raleigh St. N1	111	H1
Raleigh Way N14	58	D1
Raleigh Way, Felt.	160	C5
Ralph Ct. W2	14	B3
Ralph Perring Ct., Beck.	190	A4
Ralston St. SW3	31	J4
Ralston Way, Wat.	50	D2
Ram Pas., Kings.T.	181	G2
High St.		
Ram Pl. E9	95	F6
Chatham Pl.		
Ram St. SW18	148	E5
Rama Cl. SW16	168	D7
Rama Ct., Har.	86	B2
Ramac Way SE7	135	H4
Rambler Cl. SW16	168	C4
Rame Cl. SW17	168	A5
Ramilles Cl. SW2	151	E6
Ramillies Pl. W1	17	F4
Ramillies Pl. W1	110	C6
Ramillies Rd. NW7	54	E2
Ramillies Rd. W4	126	D4
Ramillies Rd., Sid.	158	B6
Ramillies St. W1	17	F4
Rampart St. E1	112/113	E6
Commercial Rd.		
Rampayne St. SW1	33	H2
Rampayne St. SW1	130	D5
Rampton Cl. E4	62	A3
Rams Gro., Rom.	83	E4
Ramsay Ms. SW3	31	G5
Ramsay Pl., Har.	86	B1
Ramsay Rd. E7	97	F4
Ramsay Rd. W3	126	C3
Ramscroft Cl. N9	44	B7
Ramsdale Rd. SW17	168	A5
Ramsden Rd. N11	57	J5
Ramsden Rd. SW12	150	A6
Ramsey Cl. NW9	71	F6
West Hendon Bdy.		
Ramsey Cl., Grnf.	85	J5
Ramsey Ho., Wem.	87	H6
Ramsey Ms. N4	93	H3
Monsell Rd.		
Ramsey Rd., Th.Hth.	187	F6
Ramsey St. E2	13	J5
Ramsey St. E2	112	D4
Ramsey Wk. N1	94	A6
Clephane Rd.		
Ramsey Way N14	42	C7
Ramsgate Cl. E16	135	H1
Hanameel St.		
Ramsgate St. E8	94	C6
Dalston La.		
Ramsgill App., Ilf.	81	J4
Ramsgill Dr., Ilf.	81	J5
Ramulis Dr., Hayes	102	D4
Ramus Wd. Av., Orp.	207	H5
Rancliffe Gdns. SE9	156	B4
Rancliffe Rd. E6	116	B2
Randall Av. NW2	89	F3
Randall Cl. SW11	149	H1
Randall Cl., Erith	139	J6
Randall Pl. SE10	134	C7
Randall Rd. SE11	34	C3
Randall Rd. SE11	131	F4
Randall's Rd. N1	111	E1
Randle Rd., Rich.	163	F4
Randlesdown Rd., SE6	172	A4
Randolph App. E16	116	A6
Randolph Av. W9	6	D6
Randolph Av. W9	109	F4
Randolph Cl., Bexh.	159	J3
Randolph Cl., Kings.T.	164	C5
Randolph Cres. W9	6	C6
Randolph Cres. W9	109	F4
Randolph Gdns. NW6	6	A2
Randolph Gdns. NW6	108	E2
Randolph Gro., Rom.	82	C5
Donald Dr.		
Randolph Ho., Croy.	201	J1
Randolph Ms. W9	6	D6
Randolph Ms. W9	109	F4
Randolph Rd. E17	78	B5
Randolph Rd. W9	6	C6
Randolph Rd. W9	109	F4
Randolph Rd., Sthl.	123	F2
Randolph St. NW1	92	C7
Randon Cl., Har.	67	H2
Ranelagh Av. SW6	148	C3
Ranelagh Av. SW13	147	G2
Ranelagh Br. W2	108/109	E5
Gloucester Ter.		
Ranelagh Cl., Edg.	54	A4
Ranelagh Dr., Edg.	54	A4
Ranelagh Dr., Twick.	145	E5
Ranelagh Gdns. E11	79	J5
Ranelagh Gdns. SW6	148	C3
Ranelagh Gdns. W4	126	C7
Grove Pk. Gdns.		
Ranelagh Gdns. W6	127	F3
Ranelagh Gdns., Ilf.	98	D1
Ranelagh Gro. SW1	32	C3
Ranelagh Gro. SW1	130	A5
Ranelagh Ms. W5	125	G2
Ranelagh Rd.		
Ranelagh Pl., N.Mal.	182/183	E5
Rodney Rd.		
Ranelagh Rd. E6	116	D1
Ranelagh Rd. E11	96	E4
Ranelagh Rd. E15	115	E1
Ranelagh Rd. N17	76	B3
Ranelagh Rd. N22	75	F1
Ranelagh Rd. NW10	107	F2
Ranelagh Rd. SW1	33	G4
Ranelagh Rd. W5	125	G2
Ranelagh Rd., Sthl.	122	D1
Ranelagh Rd., Wem.	87	G5
Ranfurly Rd., Sutt.	198	D2
Rangefield Rd., Brom.	172	E5
Rangemoor Rd. N15	76	C5
Rangers Rd. E4	47	E7
Rangers Rd., Loug.	47	E7
Rangers Sq. SE10	154	D1
Rangeworth Pl., Sid.	175	J3
Priestlands Pk. Rd.		
Rangoon St. EC3	112	C6
Northumberland All.		
Rankin Cl. NW9	71	E3
Ranleigh Gdns., Bexh.	139	F7
Ranmere St. SW12	168	B1
Ormeley Rd.		
Ranmoor Cl., Har.	68	A4
Ranmoor Gdns., Har.	68	A4
Ranmore Av., Croy.	202	C3
Rannoch Cl., Edg.	54	B2
Rannoch Rd. W6	127	J6
Rannock Av. NW9	70	E7
Ranskill Rd., Borwd.	38	A1
Ransom Rd. SE7	135	J5
Harvey Gdns.		
Ransom Wk. SE7	135	J5
Woolwich Rd.		
Ranston St. NW1	15	G1
Ranulf Rd. NW2	90	C4
Ranwell Cl. E3	113	J1
Beale Rd.		
Ranwell St. E3	113	J1
Ranworth Rd. N9	61	F2
Ranyard Cl., Chess.	195	J3
Raphael Dr., T.Ditt.	180	C7
Raphael St. SW7	23	J4
Raphael St. SW7	129	J2
Rashleigh St. SW8	150	B2
Peardon St.		
Rasper Rd. N20	57	F2
Rastell Av. SW2	168	D2
Ratcliff Rd. E7	97	J5
Ratcliffe Cl. SE12	155	G7
Ratcliffe Cross St. E1	113	G6
Ratcliffe La. E14	113	H6
Ratcliffe Orchard E1	113	G7

Rathbone Mkt. E16 115 F5
Barking Rd.
Rathbone Pl. W1 17 H3
Rathbone Pl. W1 110 D6
Rathbone Pt. E5 94 D4
Nolan Way
Rathbone St. E16 115 F5
Rathbone St. W1 17 G2
Rathbone St. W1 110 C5
Rathcoole Av. N8 75 F4
Rathcoole Gdns. N8 75 F5
Rathfern Rd. SE6 171 J1
Rathgar Av. W13 125 E1
Rathgar Cl. N3 72 C2
Rathgar Rd. SW9 151 H3
Coldharbour La.
Rathlin Wk. N1 93 J6
Clephane Rd.
Rathmell Dr. SW4 150 D6
Rathmore Rd. SE7 135 H5
Rattray Rd. SW2 151 G4
Raul Rd. SE15 152 D1
Raveley St. NW5 92 C4
Raven Cl. NW9 70/71 E2
Eagle Dr.
Raven Ct. E5 94 D3
Stellman Cl.
Raven Rd. E18 79 J2
Raven Row E1 113 E6
Ravenet St. SW11 150 B1
Strasburg Rd.
Ravenfield Rd. SW17 167 J3
Ravenhill Rd. E13 115 J2
Ravenna Rd. SW15 148 A5
Ravenoak Way, Chig. 65 H5
Ravenor Pk. Rd., Grnf. 103 H3
Ravens Cl., Brom. 191 F2
Ravens Cl., Enf. 44 B2
Ravens Ms. SE12 155 G5
Ravens Way
Ravens Way SE12 155 G5
Ravensbourne Av., 172 D7
Beck.
Ravensbourne Av., 172 D7
Brom.
Ravensbourne Gdns. 104 E5
W13
Ravensbourne Gdns., 80 D1
Ilf.
Ravensbourne Pk. 154 A7
SE6
Ravensbourne Pk. 153 J7
Cres. SE6
Ravensbourne Pl. 154 B2
SE13
Ravensbourne Rd. 153 J7
SE6
Ravensbourne Rd. 191 G3
Brom.
Ravensbourne Rd. 145 F6
Twick.
Ravensbury Av. 185 F5
Mord.
Ravensbury Ct., Mitch. 185 G4
Ravensbury Gro.
Ravensbury Gro. 185 G4
Mitch.
Ravensbury La. 185 G4
Mitch.
Ravensbury Path 185 G4
Mitch.
Ravensbury Rd. 166 D2
SW18
Ravensbury Rd., Orp. 193 J4
Ravensbury Ter. 167 E1
SW18
Ravenscar Rd., Brom. 172 E4
Ravenscar Rd., Surb. 195 J2
Ravenscourt Av. W6 127 G4
Ravenscourt Gdns. 127 G4
W6
Ravenscourt Pk. W6 127 G3
Ravenscourt Pl. W6 127 H4
Ravenscourt Rd. W6 127 H4
Ravenscourt Sq. W6 127 G3
Ravenscraig Rd. N11 58 B4
Ravenscroft Av. NW11 72 C7
Ravenscroft Av., Wem. 87 J1
Ravenscroft Cl. E16 115 G5
Ravenscroft Cres. 174 C3
SE9
Ravenscroft Pk., Barn. 40 A4
Ravenscroft Rd. E16 115 G5
Ravenscroft Rd. W4 126 C4
Ravenscroft Rd., 189 F2
Beck.
Ravenscroft St. E2 13 G2
Ravenscroft St. E2 112 C2
Ravensdale Av. N12 57 F4
Ravensdale Gdns. 170 A7
SE19
Ravensdale Gdns., 142 E3
Houns.
Ravensdale Rd. N16 76 C7

Ravensdale Rd., 142 E3
Houns.
Ravensdon St. SE11 35 F4
Ravensfield Cl., Dag. 100 D4
Ravensfield Gdns., 197 E5
Epsom
Ravenshaw St. NW6 90 C5
Ravenshill, Chis. 192 E1
Ravenshurst Av. NW4 71 J4
Ravenside Cl. N18 61 G6
Ravenside Retail Pk. 61 G5
N18
Ravenslea Rd. SW12 149 J7
Ravensmead Rd., 172 D7
Brom.
Ravensmede Way W4 127 F4
Ravenstone SE17 36 E4
Ravenstone SE17 132 B5
Ravenstone Rd. N8 75 G3
Ravenstone Rd. NW9 71 F6
Ravenstone St. SW12 168 A1
Ravenswood, Bex. 177 E1
Ravenswood Av., 195 J2
Surb.
Ravenswood Av., 204 C1
W.Wick.
Ravenswood Ct., 164 B6
Kings.T.
Ravenswood Cres. 85 F2
Har.
Ravenswood Cres. 204 C1
W.Wick.
Ravenswood Gdns., 144 B1
Islw.
Ravenswood Pk., 50 A6
Nthwd.
Ravenswood Rd. E17 78 B4
Ravenswood Rd. 150 B7
SW12
Ravenswood Rd., 201 H3
Croy.
Ravensworth Rd. 107 H3
NW10
Ravensworth Rd. SE9 174 C4
Ravent Rd. SE11 34 D2
Ravent Rd. SE11 131 F4
Ravey St. EC2 12 D5
Ravine Gro. SE18 137 H6
Rawlings St. SW3 31 J1
Rawlings St. SW3 129 J4
Rawlins Cl. N3 72 B3
Rawlins Cl., S.Croy. 203 H7
Rawnsley Av., Mitch. 185 G5
Rawreth Wk. N1 111 J1
Basire St.
Rawson St. SW11 150 A1
Strasburg Rd.
Rawsthorne Cl. E16 136 C1
Kennard St.
Rawstone Wk. E13 115 G2
Rawstorne Pl. EC1 11 G3
Rawstorne St. EC1 11 G3
Rawstorne St. EC1 111 H3
Ray Cl., Chess. 195 F6
Merritt Gdns.
Ray Gdns., Bark. 118 A2
Ray Gdns., Stan. 53 E5
Ray Lo. Rd., Wdf.Grn. 63 J6
Ray Massey Way E6 116 B1
Ron Leighton Way
Ray Rd., W.Mol. 179 H5
Ray St. EC1 11 F6
Ray St. EC1 111 G4
Ray St. Br. EC1 11 F6
Ray Wk. N7 93 F2
Andover Rd.
Raydean Rd., Barn. 40 E5
Raydon St. N19 92 B2
Raydons Gdns., Dag. 101 E5
Raydons Rd., Dag. 100 E5
Rayfield Cl., Brom. 192 B6
Rayford Av. SE12 155 F7
Rayleas Cl. SE18 156 E1
Rayleigh Av., Tedd. 162 B6
Rayleigh Cl. N13 60 A3
Rayleigh Rd.
Rayleigh Ct., Kings.T. 181 J2
Rayleigh Ri., S.Croy. 202 B6
Rayleigh Rd. E16 135 H1
Wesley Av.
Rayleigh Rd. N13 59 J3
Rayleigh Rd. SW19 184 C1
Rayleigh Rd., 63 J6
Wdf.Grn.
Raymead NW4 71 J4
Tenterden Gro.
Raymead Av., Th.Hth. 187 G5
Raymere Gdns. SE18 137 G7
Raymond Av. E18 79 F3
Raymond Av. W13 124 D3
Raymond Bldgs. WC1 18 D1
Raymond Cl. SE26 171 F5

Raymond Ct. N10 58 A7
Pembroke Rd.
Raymond Rd. E13 97 J7
Raymond Rd. SW19 166 B6
Raymond Rd., Beck. 189 H4
Raymond Rd., Ilf. 81 G7
Raymond Way, Esher 194 D6
Raymouth Rd. SE16 133 E4
Rayne Ct. E18 79 F4
Rayner Twr. E10 78 A7
Rayners Av. Wem. 87 G5
Rayners Ct., Har. 85 G1
Rayners Cres., Nthlt. 102 B3
Rayners Gdns., Nthlt. 102 B2
Rayners La., Har. 85 H2
Rayners La., Pnr. 67 F6
Rayners La. SE18 148 B5
Raynes Av. E11 79 J7
Raynham Av. N18 60 D6
Raynham Rd. N18 60 D5
Raynham Rd. W6 127 H4
Raynham Ter. N18 60 D5
Raynor Cl., Sthl. 123 F1
Raynor Pl. N1 111 J1
Elizabeth Av.
Raynton Cl., Har. 85 E1
Rays Av. N18 61 F4
Rays Rd. N18 61 F4
Rays Rd., W.Wick. 190 C7
Raywood Cl., Hayes 121 F7
Raywood St. SW8 150 B1
Gladstone Ter.
Reachview Cl. NW1 92 C7
Baynes St.
Read Cl., T.Ditt. 180 D7
Reade Wk. NW10 88/89 E7
Denbigh Cl.
Reading La. E8 94 E6
Reading Rd., Nthlt. 85 H5
Reading Rd., Sutt. 199 F5
Reading Way NW7 56 A5
Reads Cl., Ilf. 98/99 E3
Chapel Rd.
Reapers Cl. NW1 110 D1
Crofters Way
Reapers Way, Islw. 144 A5
Hall Rd.
Reardon Ct. N21 59 J2
Cosgrove Cl.
Reardon Path E1 133 E1
Reardon St. E1 132 E1
Reaston St. SE14 133 G7
Reckitt Rd. W4 126 E5
Record St. SE15 133 F6
Recovery St. SW17 167 H5
Recreation Av., Rom. 83 J5
Recreation Rd. SE26 171 G4
Recreation Rd., Brom. 191 F2
Recreation Rd., Sid. 175 H3
Recreation Rd., Sthl. 122 E4
Recreation Way, 186 D3
Mitch.
Rector St. N1 111 J1
Rectory Cl. E4 62 A3
Rectory Cl. N3 72 C1
Rectory Cl. SW20 183 J3
Rectory Cl., Sid. 176 B4
Rectory Cl., Stan. 53 E6
Rectory Cl., Surb. 195 F1
Rectory Cres. E11 79 J6
Rectory Fld. Cres. 135 J7
SE7
Rectory Gdns. N8 74 E4
Rectory Gdns. SW4 150 C3
Rectory Gdns., Nthlt. 103 F1
Rectory Grn., Beck. 189 J1
Rectory Gro. SW4 150 C3
Rectory Gro., Croy. 201 H2
Rectory Gro., Hmptn. 161 F4
Rectory La. SW17 168 A6
Rectory La., Edg. 54 A6
Rectory La., Loug. 48 D2
Rectory La., Sid. 176 B4
Rectory La., Stan. 52 E5
Rectory La., Surb. 195 F1
Rectory La., Wall. 200 C4
Rectory Orchard 166 B4
SW19
Rectory Pk. Av., 103 F3
Nthlt.
Rectory Pl. SE18 136 D4
Rectory Rd. E12 98 C5
Rectory Rd. E17 78 B3
Rectory Rd. N16 94 C3
Rectory Rd. SW13 147 G2
Rectory Rd. W3 126 B1
Rectory Rd., Beck. 190 A1
Rectory Rd., Dag. 101 G7
Rectory Rd., Hayes 102 A6
Rectory Rd., Houns. 142 A1
Rectory Rd., Kes. 206 A7
Rectory Rd., Sthl. 123 F3
Rectory Rd., Sutt. 198 D3

Rectory Sq. E1 113 G5
Reculver Ms. N18 60 D4
Reculver Rd. SE16 133 G5
Red Anchor Cl. SW3 31 G6
Red Barracks Rd. 136 C4
SE18
Red Cedars Rd., Orp. 193 H7
Red Hill, Chis. 174 D5
Red Hill Cl., La., Bexh. 158 D4
Red Ho. Sq. N1 93 J6
Clephane Rd.
Red La., Esher 194 D6
Red Lion Cl. SE17 36 A5
Red Lion Ct. EC4 19 F3
Red Lion Hill N2 73 G2
Red Lion La. SE18 156 D7
Red Lion Pl. SE18 156 D1
Shooter's Hill Rd.
Red Lion Rd., Surb. 195 J2
Red Lion Row SE17 36 A5
Red Lion Row SE17 131 J6
Red Lion Sq. SW18 148 D5
Wandsworth High St.
Red Lion Sq. WC1 18 C2
Red Lion Sq. WC1 111 F5
Red Lion St. WC1 18 C1
Red Lion St. WC1 111 F5
Red Lion Yd. W1 24 C1
Red Lo. Rd., W.Wick. 190 D6
Red Oak Cl., Orp. 207 E3
Red Path E9 95 J6
Red Pl. W1 16 B5
Red Post Hill SE21 152 A5
Red Post Hill SE24 152 A4
Redan Pl. W2 14 A4
Redan Pl. W2 108 E6
Redan St. W14 128 A3
Redan Ter. SE5 151 J2
Flaxman Rd.
Redberry Gro. SE26 171 F3
Redbourne Av. N3 72 D1
Redbridge Enterprise 99 F2
Cen., Ilf.
Redbridge Gdns. SE5 132 B7
Redbridge La. E., Ilf. 80 A6
Redbridge La. W. E11 79 H6
Redburn St. SW3 31 J5
Redburn St. SW3 129 J6
Redcar Cl., Nthlt. 85 H5
Redcar St. SE5 131 J7
Redcastle Cl. E1 113 F7
Redchurch St. E2 13 F5
Redchurch St. E2 112 C4
Redcliffe Cl. SW5 128/129 E5
Warwick Rd.
Redcliffe Gdns. SW5 30 B4
Redcliffe Gdns. SW5 129 E5
Redcliffe Gdns. SW10 30 B4
Redcliffe Gdns. SW10 129 E5
Redcliffe Gdns., Ilf. 98 D1
Redcliffe Ms. SW10 30 B4
Redcliffe Ms. SW10 129 E5
Redcliffe Pl. SW10 30 C6
Redcliffe Pl. SW10 129 F6
Redcliffe Rd. SW10 30 C4
Redcliffe Rd. SW10 129 F5
Redcliffe Sq. SW10 30 B5
Redcliffe Sq. SW10 129 E5
Redcliffe St. SW10 30 B5
Redcliffe St. SW10 129 E6
Reddcliffe Av., Mord. 184 D5
Chalgrove Av.
Redclyffe Rd. E6 115 J1
Redcroft Rd., Sthl. 103 J7
Redcross Way SE1 28 A3
Redcross Way SE1 131 J2
Reddings, The NW7 55 F3
Reddings Cl. NW7 55 F4
Reddins Rd. SE15 37 H6
Reddins Rd. SE15 132 D6
Reddons Rd., Beck. 171 H7
Rede Pl. W2 108 D6
Chepstow Pl.
Redesdale Gdns., 124 D7
Islw.
Redesdale St. SW3 31 H5
Redesdale St. SW3 129 H6
Redfern Av., Houns. 143 G7
Redfern Rd. NW10 89 E7
Redfern Rd. SE6 154 C7
Redfield La. SW5 128 D4
Redfield Ms. SW5 128 D4
Redfield La.
Redford Av., Th.Hth. 187 F4
Redford Av., Wall. 200 E6
Redford Wk. N1 111 H1
Britannia Row
Redgate Dr., Brom. 205 H2
Redgate Ter. SW15 148 A6
Lytton Gro.
Redgrave Cl., Croy. 188 C6
Redgrave Rd. SW15 148 A3

Red–Ric 335

Redhill Dr., Edg. 70 C2
Redhill St. NW1 8 E3
Redhill St. NW1 110 B2
Redhouse Rd., Croy. 186 D6
Redington Gdns. NW3 91 E4
Redington Rd. NW3 90 E4
Redland Gdns., W.Mol. 179 F4
Dunstable Rd.
Redlands Ct., Brom. 173 F7
Redlands Rd., Enf. 45 H1
Redlands Way SW2 151 F7
Redleaf Cl., Belv. 139 G6
Redlees Cl., Islw. 144 D4
Redman Cl., Nthlt. 102 C2
Redman's Rd. E1 113 F5
Redmead La. E1 29 H2
Redmead Rd., Hayes 121 H4
Redmore Rd. W6 127 H4
Redpoll Way, Erith 138 D3
Redriff Est. SE16 133 J3
Redriff Rd. SE16 133 G4
Redriff Rd., Rom. 83 H2
Redriffe Rd. E13 115 F1
Redroofs Cl., Beck. 190 B1
Redruth Cl. N22 59 F7
Palmerston Rd.
Redruth Rd. E9 113 G1
Redstart Cl. E6 116 B5
Columbine Av.
Redstart Cl. SE14 133 H7
Southerngate Way
Redston Rd. N8 74 D4
Redvers Rd. N22 75 G2
Redvers St. N1 13 E2
Redwald Rd. E5 95 G4
Redway Dr., Twick. 143 J7
Redwing Path SE28 137 G2
Redwood Cl. N14 42 D7
The Vale
Redwood Cl. SE16 133 H1
Redwood Cl., Sid. 158 A7
Redwood Cl., Wat. 50 C4
Redwood Est., Houns. 122 B6
Redwood Gdns. E4 46 B6
Redwood Ms. SW4 150 B3
Hannington Rd.
Redwood Twr. E11 96 D3
Hollydown Way
Redwood Wk., Surb. 195 G1
Redwood Way, Barn. 40 A5
Redwoods SW15 165 G1
Redwoods Cl., Buck.H. 63 H2
Beech La.
Ree La. Cotts., Loug. 48 D2
Englands La.
Reece Ms. SW7 30 E1
Reece Ms. SW7 129 G4
Reed Av., Orp. 207 H3
Reed Cl. E16 115 G5
Reed Cl. SE12 155 G5
Reed Rd. N17 76 C2
Reede Gdns., Dag. 101 H5
Reede Rd., Dag. 101 G6
Reede Way, Dag. 101 H6
Reedham Cl. N17 76 E4
Reedham St. SE15 152 D2
Reedholm Vil. N16 94 A4
Winston Rd.
Reeds Pl. NW1 92 C7
Royal College St.
Reedworth St. SE11 35 F2
Reedworth St. SE11 131 G4
Reenglass Rd., Stan. 53 G4
Rees Dr., Stan. 53 H4
Rees Gdns., Croy. 188 C6
Rees St. N1 111 J1
Reesland Cl. E12 98 D5
Reets Fm. Cl. NW9 71 E6
Reeves Av. NW9 70 D7
Reeves Cor., Croy. 201 H2
Roman Way
Reeves Ms. W1 16 B6
Reeves Ms. W1 110 A7
Reeves Rd. E3 114 B4
Reeves Rd. SE18 136 E6
Reform Row N17 76 C2
Reform St. SW11 149 J2
Regal Cl. E1 21 J1
Regal Cl. W5 105 G5
Regal Ct. N18 60 C5
College Cl.
Regal Cres., Wall. 200 B3
Regal Dr. N11 58 B5
Regal La. NW1 110 A1
Regents Pk. Rd.
Regal Pl. E3 113 J3
Coborn St.
Regal Pl. SW6 128/129 E7
Maxwell Rd.
Regal Row SE15 153 F1
Queens Rd.
Regal Way, Har. 69 H6
Regan Way N1 12 D2
Regan Way N1 112 B2
Regency Cl. W5 105 H6
Regency Cl., Chig. 65 F5
Regency Cl., Hmptn. 161 F5
Regency Cres. NW4 72 A2
Regency Lo., Buck.H. 64 A2
Regency Ms. NW10 89 G6
High Rd.
Regency Ms., Beck. 190 C1
Regency Ms., Islw. 144 B5
Queensbridge Pk.
Regency Pl. SW1 33 J1
Regency St. SW1 33 J1
Regency St. SW1 130 D4
Regency Ter. SW7 129 G5
Fulham Rd.
Regency Wk., Croy. 189 H6
Regency Wk., Rich. 145 H6
Friars Stile Rd.
Regency Way, Bexh. 158 D3
Regent Cl. N12 57 F5
Nether St.
Regent Cl., Har. 69 H6
Regent Cl., Houns. 142 B1
Regent Gdns., Ilf. 82 A6
Regent Pl. SW19 166/167 E5
Haydons Rd.
Regent Pl. W1 17 G5
Regent Pl., Croy. 202 C1
Grant Rd.
Regent Rd. SE24 151 H6
Regent Rd., Surb. 181 J5
Regent Sq. E3 114 B3
Regent Sq. WC1 10 B4
Regent Sq. WC1 111 E3
Regent Sq., Belv. 139 H4
Regent St. NW10 108 A3
Wellington Rd.
Regent St. SW1 17 H6
Regent St. SW1 110 D7
Regent St. W1 17 E3
Regent St. W1 110 B6
Regent St. W4 126 A5
Regents Av. N13 59 F5
Regents Br. Gdns. SW8 34 B7
Regents Br. Gdns. SW8 131 E7
Regents Cl., S.Croy. 202 B6
Regents Dr., Kes. 206 A5
Regents Ms. NW8 6 D1
Regent's Pk. NW1 7 J2
Regent's Pk. NW1 110 A2
Regent's Pk. Est. NW1 9 F4
Regents Pk. Rd. N3 72 C3
Regents Pk. Rd. NW1 109 J1
Regents Pk. Ter. NW1 110 B1
Oval Rd.
Regent's Pl. NW1 9 F5
Regent's Pl. NW1 110 C4
Regent's Pl. SE3 155 G2
Regents Pl., Loug. 47 J7
Fallow Flds.
Regents Row E8 112 D1
Regina Cl., Barn. 40 A3
Regina Rd. N4 93 F1
Regina Rd. SE25 188 D3
Regina Rd. W13 124 D1
Regina Rd., Sthl. 122 E4
Regina Ter. W13 124 E1
Reginald Rd. E7 97 G7
Reginald Rd. SE8 134 A7
Reginald Sq. SE8 134 A7
Regis Pl. SW2 151 F4
Regis Rd. NW5 92 B5
Regnart Bldgs. NW1 9 G5
Reid Cl., Pnr. 66 A4
Reidhaven Rd. SE18 137 H4
Reigate Av., Sutt. 198 D1
Reigate Rd., Brom. 173 F3
Reigate Rd., Ilf. 99 J2
Reigate Way, Wall. 201 E5
Reighton Rd. E5 94 D3
Relay Rd. W12 107 J7
Relf Rd. SE15 152 D3
Relko Gdns., Sutt. 199 G5
Relton Ms. SW7 23 H5
Rembrandt Cl. E14 134 D3
Rembrandt Cl. SW1 32 B2
Rembrandt Ct., Epsom 197 F6
Rembrandt Rd. SE13 154 E4
Rembrandt Rd., Edg. 70 A2
Remington Rd. E6 116 B6
Remington Rd. N15 76 A6
Remington St. N1 11 H2
Remington St. N1 111 H2
Remnant St. WC2 18 C3
Rempstone Ms. N1 12 C1
Remus Rd. E3 96 A7
Monier Rd.
Rendle Cl., Croy. 188 C5
Rendlesham Rd. E5 94 D4
Rendlesham Rd., Enf. 43 H1
Renforth St. SE16 133 F2
Renfrew Cl. E6 116 D7
Renfrew Rd. SE11 35 G1
Renfrew Rd. SE11 131 H4
Renfrew Rd., Houns. 142 D2
Renfrew Rd., Kings.T. 164 B7
Renmuir St. SW17 167 J6
Rennell St. SE13 154 C3
Rennels Way, Islw. 144 B2
St. John's Rd.
Renness Rd. E17 77 H3
Rennets Cl. SE9 157 H5
Rennets Wd. Rd. SE9 157 G5
Rennie Est. SE16 133 E4
Rennie St. SE1 27 G1
Rennie St. SE1 131 H1
Renown Cl., Croy. 201 H1
Renown Cl., Rom. 83 G1
Rensburg Rd. E17 77 G5
Renshaw Cl., Belv. 139 F6
Grove Rd.
Renters Av. NW4 71 J6
Renwick Ind. Est., Bark. 118 B1
Renwick Rd., Bark. 118 B4
Repens Way, Hayes 102 D4
Stipularis Dr.
Rephidim St. SE1 28 D6
Replingham Rd. SW18 166 C1
Reporton Rd. SW6 148 B1
Repository Rd. SE18 136 C6
Repton Av., Hayes 121 G4
Repton Av., Wem. 87 F4
Repton Cl., Cars. 199 H5
Repton Ct., Beck. 190 B1
Repton Gro., Ilf. 80 C1
Repton Rd., Har. 69 J4
Repton St. E14 113 H6
Repulse Cl., Rom. 83 H1
Reservoir Cl., Th.Hth. 188 A4
Reservoir Rd. N14 42 C5
Reservoir Rd. SE4 153 H2
Resolution Wk. SE18 136 C3
Restell Cl. SE3 135 E6
Restmor Way, Wall. 200 A2
Reston Pl. SW7 22 C4
Restons Cres. SE9 157 G6
Restormel Cl., Houns. 143 G5
Retcar Cl. N19 92 B2
Dartmouth Pk. Hill
Retcar Pl. N19 92 B2
Retford St. N1 13 E2
Retingham Way E4 62 B2
Retreat, The NW9 70 D5
Retreat, The SW14 146/147 E3
South Worple Way
Retreat, The, Har. 67 G7
Retreat, The, Surb. 181 J6
Retreat, The, Th.Hth. 188 A4
Retreat, The, Wor.Pk. 197 H2
Retreat Cl., Har. 69 F5
Retreat Pl. E9 95 F6
Retreat Rd., Rich. 145 G5
Reunion Row E1 112/113 E7
Pennington St.
Reveley Sq. SE16 133 H2
Howland Way
Revell Ri. SE18 137 J6
Revell Rd., Kings.T. 182 B1
Revell Rd., Sutt. 198 C6
Revelon Rd. SE4 153 H4
Revelstoke Rd. SW18 166 C2
Reventlow Rd. SE9 175 F1
Reverdy Rd. SE1 37 H2
Reverdy Rd. SE1 132 D4
Reverend Cl., Har. 85 H3
Revesby Rd., Cars. 185 G6
Review Rd. NW2 89 F2
Review Rd., Dag. 119 H1
Rewell St. SW6 129 F7
Rewley Rd., Cars. 185 G6
Rex Pl. W1 16 C6
Reydon Av. E11 79 J6
Reynard Cl. SE4 153 H3
Foxwell St.
Reynard Cl., Brom. 192 C3
Reynard Dr. SE19 170 C7
Reynard Pl. SE14 133 H6
Milton Ct. Rd.
Reynardson Rd. N17 59 J7
Reynolds Av. E12 98 D5
Reynolds Av., Chess. 195 H7
Reynolds Av., Rom. 82 C7
Reynolds Cl. NW11 72 E7
Reynolds Cl. SW19 185 G1
Reynolds Cl., Cars. 199 J1
Reynolds Ct. E11 97 F3
Cobbold Rd.
Reynolds Ct., Rom. 82 D3
Reynolds Dr., Edg. 69 J3
Reynolds Pl. SE3 135 H7
Reynolds Pl., Rich. 145 J6
Cambrian Rd.
Reynolds Rd. SE15 153 F5
Reynolds Rd. W4 126 C3
Reynolds Rd., Hayes 102 C4
Reynolds Rd., N.Mal. 182 D7
Reynolds Way, Croy. 202 B4
Rheidol Ms. N1 11 J1
Rheidol Ter. N1 11 H1
Rheidol Ter. N1 111 H2
Rheola Cl. N17 76 C1
Rhoda St. E2 13 G5
Rhodes Av. N22 74 C1
Rhodes Moorhouse Ct., Mord. 184 D6
Rhodes St. N7 93 F5
Mackenzie Rd.
Rhodesia Rd. E11 96 D2
Rhodesia Rd. SW9 151 E2
Rhodeswell Rd. E14 113 J6
Rhodrons Av., Chess. 195 H5
Rhondda Gro. E3 113 H3
Rhyl Rd., Grnf. 104 C2
Rhyl St. NW5 92 A6
Rhys Av. N11 58 D7
Rialto Rd., Mitch. 186 A2
Ribble Cl., Wdf.Grn. 63 J6
Prospect Rd.
Ribblesdale Av. N11 58 A6
Ribblesdale Av., Nthlt. 85 H6
Ribblesdale Rd. N8 75 F4
Ribblesdale Rd. SW16 168 B6
Ribbon Dance Ms. SE5 152 A1
Camberwell Gro.
Ribchester Av., Grnf. 104 C3
Ribston Cl., Brom. 206 C1
Ricardo Path SE28 138 C1
Byron Cl.
Ricardo St. E14 114 B6
Ricards Rd. SW19 166 C5
Rich La. SW5 30 A4
Rich St. E14 113 J7
Richard Cl. SE18 136 B4
Richard Foster Cl. E17 77 J7
Richard Ho. Dr. E16 116 A6
Richard St. E1 112/113 E6
Commercial Rd.
Richards Av., Rom. 83 J5
Richards Cl., Har. 68 D5
Richards Cl., Hayes 121 G6
Richards Pl. E17 78 A3
Richards Pl. SW3 31 H1
Richardson Cl. E8 112 C1
Clarissa St.
Richardson Rd. E15 114 E2
Richardson's Ms. W1 9 F6
Richbell Pl. WC1 18 C1
Richborne Ter. SW8 34 D7
Richborne Ter. SW8 131 F7
Richborough Rd. NW2 90 A4
Richens Cl., Houns. 144 A2
Riches Rd., Ilf. 99 F2
Richford Rd. E15 115 F1
Richford St. W6 127 J2
Richlands Av., Epsom 197 G4
Richmond Av. E4 62 D5
Richmond Av. N1 111 F1
Richmond Av. NW10 89 J6
Richmond Av. SW20 184 B1
Richmond Av., Felt. 141 H6
Richmond Br., Rich. 145 G6
Richmond Br., Twick. 145 G6
Richmond Bldgs. W1 17 H4
Richmond Cl. E17 77 J6
Richmond Cl., Borwd. 38 D5
Richmond Cres. E4 62 D5
Richmond Cres. N1 111 F1
Richmond Cres. N9 60 D1
Richmond Gdns. NW4 71 G5
Richmond Gdns., Har. 52 C6
Richmond Grn., Croy. 201 E3
Richmond Gro. N1 93 H7
Richmond Gro., Surb. 181 J6
Richmond Hill, Rich. 145 H6
Richmond Hill Ct., Rich. 145 H6
Richmond Ms. W1 17 H4
Richmond Ms., Tedd. 162 C6
Broad St.
Richmond Pk., Kings.T. 146 C7
Richmond Pk., Loug. 47 J7
Fallow Flds.
Richmond Pk., Rich. 146 C7
Richmond Pk. Rd. SW14 146 C5

Name	Page	Grid
Richmond Pk. Rd., Kings.T.	163	H7
Richmond Pl. SE18	137	F4
Richmond Rd. E4	62	D1
Richmond Rd. E7	97	H5
Richmond Rd. E8	94	C7
Richmond Rd. E11	96	D2
Richmond Rd. N2	73	F2
Richmond Rd. N11	58	E6
Richmond Rd. N15	76	B6
Richmond Rd. SW20	183	H1
Richmond Rd. W5	125	H2
Richmond Rd., Barn.	41	E5
Richmond Rd., Croy.	200	E3
Richmond Rd., Ilf.	99	F3
Richmond Rd., Islw.	144	D3
Richmond Rd., Kings.T.	163	G5
Richmond Rd., Th.Hth.	187	H3
Richmond Rd., Twick.	145	F6
Richmond St. E13	115	G2
Richmond Ter. SW1	26	A3
Richmond Ter. SW1	130	E2
Richmond Ter. Ms. SW1	130/131	E2
Parliament St.		
Richmond Way E11	97	G2
Richmond Way W12	128	A2
Richmond Way W14	128	A3
Richmount Gdns. SE3	155	G3
Rick Roberts Way E15	114	C1
Rickard Cl. NW4	71	H4
Rickard Cl. SW2	169	F1
Rickard Cl., West Dr.	120	A3
Rickards Cl., Surb.	195	H1
Rickett St. SW6	128	E2
Rickman St. E1	113	F3
Mantus Rd.		
Rickmansworth Rd., Pnr.	66	B2
Rickthorne Rd. N19	92/93	E2
Landseer Rd.		
Rickyard Path SE9	156	B4
Ridding La., Grnf.	86	C5
Riddons Rd. SE12	173	J3
Ride, The, Brent.	125	E5
Ride, The, Enf.	45	F3
Rideout St. SE18	136	C4
Rider Cl., Sid.	157	H6
Ridgdale St. E3	114	B2
Ridge, The, Bex.	159	F7
Ridge, The, Orp.	207	G2
Ridge, The, Surb.	182	A5
Ridge, The, Twick.	144	A7
Ridge Av. N21	43	J7
Ridge Cl. NW4	72	A2
Ridge Cl. NW9	70	D4
Ridge Cl. SE28	137	G2
Ridge Crest, Enf.	43	F1
Ridge Hill NW11	90	B1
Ridge Rd. N8	75	H4
Ridge Rd. N21	59	J1
Ridge Rd. NW2	90	C3
Ridge Rd., Mitch.	168	B7
Ridge Rd., Sutt.	198	B1
Ridge Way SE19	170	B6
Central Hill		
Ridge Way, Felt.	160	E3
Ridgebrook Rd. SE3	155	J3
Ridgecroft Cl., Bex.	177	J1
Ridgemont Gdns., Edg.	54	C4
Ridgemount Av., Croy.	203	G1
Ridgemount Cl. SE20	170/171	E7
Anerley Pk.		
Ridgemount Gdns. Enf.	43	H2
Ridgeview Cl., Barn.	40	A6
Ridgeview Rd. N20	57	E3
Ridgeway, Brom.	205	G2
Ridgeway, Wdf.Grn.	63	J4
Ridgeway, The E4	62	B2
Ridgeway, The N3	56	E7
Ridgeway, The N11	57	J4
Ridgeway, The N14	59	E2
Ridgeway, The NW7	55	H4
Ridgeway, The NW9	70	E4
Ridgeway, The NW11	90	C1
Ridgeway, The SE28	137	G4
Pettman Cres.		
Ridgeway, The W3	126	A3
Ridgeway, The, Croy.	201	F3
Ridgeway, The, Enf.	43	G1
Ridgeway, The, Har.	67	F5
Ridgeway, The (Kenton), Har.	69	F6
Ridgeway, The, Ruis.	67	G6
Ridgeway, The, Stan.	53	F6
Ridgeway Av., Barn.	41	J6
Ridgeway Cres., Orp.	207	H3
Ridgeway Cres. Gdns., Orp.	207	H2
Ridgeway Dr., Brom.	173	H4
Ridgeway E., Sid.	157	J5
Ridgeway Gdns. N6	74	C7
Ridgeway Gdns., Ilf.	80	B5
Ridgeway Rd. SW9	151	H3
Ridgeway Rd., Islw.	124	B7
Ridgeway Rd. N., Islw.	124	B6
Ridgeway Wk., Nthlt.	84/85	E6
Fortunes Mead		
Ridgeway W., Sid.	157	H5
Ridgewell Cl. N1	111	J1
Basire St.		
Ridgewell Cl. SE26	171	J4
Ridgewell Cl., Dag.	119	H1
Ridgmount Gdns. WC1	9	H6
Ridgmount Pl. WC1	17	H1
Ridgmount Rd. SW18	149	E5
Ridgmount St. WC1	17	H1
Ridgway SW19	166	A6
Ridgway, The, Sutt.	199	G7
Ridgway Gdns. SW19	166	A7
Ridgway Pl. SW19	166	B6
Ridgwell Rd. E16	115	J5
Riding, The NW11	72	C7
Golders Grn. Rd.		
Riding Ho. St. W1	17	F2
Riding Ho. St. W1	110	B5
Ridings, The W5	105	J4
Ridings, The, Sun.	178	A1
Ridings, The, Surb.	182	A5
Ridings Av. N21	43	H4
Ridings Cl. N6	74	C7
Hornsey La. Gdns.		
Ridley Av. W13	124	E3
Ridley Rd. E7	97	J4
Ridley Rd. E8	94	C5
Ridley Rd. NW10	107	G2
Ridley Rd. SW19	166	E7
Ridley Rd., Brom.	191	F3
Ridley Rd., Well.	158	B1
Ridley Several SE3	155	H2
Blackheath Pk.		
Ridsdale Rd. SE20	188	E1
Riefield Rd. SE9	157	F4
Riesco Dr., Croy.	203	F6
Riffel Rd. NW2	89	J5
Rifle Pl. SE11	35	F5
Rifle Pl. SE11	131	G6
Rifle Pl. W11	128	A1
Rifle St. E14	114	B5
Rigault Rd. SW6	148	B2
Rigby Cl., Croy.	201	G3
Rigby La., Hayes	121	G2
Rigby Ms., Ilf.	98/99	E2
Cranbrook Rd.		
Rigden St. E14	114	B6
Rigeley Rd. NW10	107	G3
Rigg App. E10	95	G1
Rigge Pl. SW4	150	D4
Riggindale Rd. SW16	168	D5
Riley Rd. SE1	29	E5
Riley Rd. SE1	132	C3
Riley St. SW10	31	E7
Riley St. SW10	129	G6
Rinaldo Rd. SW12	150	B7
Ring, The W2	15	G5
Ring, The W2	109	G7
Ring Cl., Brom.	173	H7
Garden Rd.		
Ring Rd. W12	107	J7
Ringcroft St. N7	93	G5
Ringers Rd., Brom.	191	G3
Ringford Rd. SW18	148	C5
Ringlet Cl. E16	115	H6
Ringlewell Cl., Enf.	44/45	E2
Central Av.		
Ringmer Av. SW6	148	B1
Ringmer Gdns. N19	92/93	E2
Sussex Way		
Ringmer Pl. N21	44	A5
Ringmer Way, Brom.	192	C5
Ringmore Ri. SE23	153	E7
Ringslade Rd. N22	75	F2
Ringstead Rd. SE6	154	B7
Ringstead Rd., Sutt.	199	G4
Ringway N11	58	C6
Ringway, Sthl.	123	E5
Ringwold Cl., Beck.	171	H7
Ringwood Av. N2	73	J2
Ringwood Av., Croy.	187	E7
Ringwood Cl., Pnr.	66	C3
Ringwood Gdns. E14	134	A4
Inglewood Cl.		
Ringwood Gdns. SW15	165	G2
Ringwood Rd. E17	77	J6
Ringwood Way N21	59	H1
Ringwood Way, Hmptn.	161	G4
Ripley Cl., Brom.	192	C5
Ringmer Way		
Ripley Cl., Croy.	204	C6
Ripley Gdns. SW14	146	D3
Ripley Gdns., Sutt.	199	F4
Ripley Ms. E11	78/79	E7
Wadley Rd.		
Ripley Rd. E16	115	J6
Ripley Rd., Belv.	139	G4
Ripley Rd., Enf.	43	J1
Ripley Rd., Hmptn.	161	G7
Ripley Rd., Ilf.	99	J2
Ripley Vil. W5	105	F6
Castlebar Rd.		
Riplington Ct. SW15	147	G7
Longwood Dr.		
Ripon Cl., Nthlt.	85	G5
Ripon Gdns., Chess.	195	F5
Ripon Gdns., Ilf.	80	B6
Ripon Rd. N9	44	E7
Ripon Rd. N17	76	A3
Ripon Rd. SE18	136	E6
Ripon Way, Borwd.	38	C5
Rippersley Rd., Well.	158	A1
Ripple Rd., Bark.	99	F7
Ripple Rd., Dag.	118	B1
Rippleside	118	C2
Commercial Est., Bark.		
Ripplevale Gro. N1	93	F7
Rippolson Rd. SE18	137	J5
Risborough Dr., Wor.Pk.	183	G7
Risborough St. SE1	27	H3
Risdon St. SE16	133	F2
Renforth St.		
Rise, The E11	79	G5
Rise, The N13	59	G4
Rise, The NW7	55	F6
Rise, The NW10	88	D4
Rise, The, Bex.	158	C7
Rise, The, Buck.H.	48	A7
Rise, The, Edg.	54	B5
Rise, The, Grnf.	86	D5
Risedale Rd., Bexh.	159	H3
Riseldine Rd. SE23	153	H6
Rising Sun Ct. EC1	19	H2
Risinghill St. N1	10	E1
Risinghill St. N1	111	F2
Risingholme Cl., Har.	68	B3
Risingholme Rd., Har.	68	B2
Risings, The E17	78	D4
Risley Av. N17	75	J1
Rita Rd. SW8	34	B6
Rita Rd. SW8	131	E7
Ritches Rd. N15	75	J5
Ritchie Rd., Croy.	189	E6
Ritchie St. N1	11	F1
Ritchie St. N1	111	G2
Ritchings Av. E17	77	H4
Ritherdon Rd. SW17	168	A2
Ritson Rd. E8	94	D6
Ritter St. SE18	136	D6
Ritz Par. W5	105	J4
Connell Cres.		
Rivaz Pl. E9	95	F6
Rivenhall Gdns. E18	79	F4
River Av. N13	59	H3
River Av., T.Ditt.	180	D7
River Bank N21	43	J7
River Bank, E.Mol.	180	A3
River Bank, T.Ditt.	180	C5
River Bank, W.Mol.	179	F3
River Barge Cl. E14	134	C2
Stewart St.		
River Brent Business Pk. W7	124	B3
River Cl. E11	79	J6
River Cl., Sthl.	123	J2
River Cl., Surb.	181	G5
Catherine Rd.		
River Crane Wk., Felt.	160	D1
River Crane Wk., Houns.	160	D1
River Crane Way, Felt.	161	F2
Watermill Way		
River Front, Enf.	44	A3
River Gdns., Cars.	200	A2
River Gdns., Felt.	142	B4
River Gro. Pk., Beck.	189	J1
River La., Rich.	163	G1
River Pk. Gdns., Brom.	172	D7
River Pk. Rd. N22	75	F2
River Pl. N1	93	J7
River Reach, Tedd.	163	F5
River Rd., Bark.	117	H2
River Rd., Buck.H.	64	B1
River Rd. Business Pk., Bark.	117	J3
River St. EC1	11	E3
River St. EC1	111	G3
River Ter. W6	127	J5
Crisp Rd.		
River Vw., Enf.	43	J3
Chase Side		
River Wk., Walt.	178	A6
River Way, Epsom	196	D5
River Way, Loug.	48	D6
River Way, Twick.	161	H2
Riverbank Way, Brent.	125	F6
Rivercourt Rd. W6	127	H4
Riverdale SE13	154	C3
Lewisham High St.		
Riverdale Cl., Bark.	117	H3
Thames Rd.		
Riverdale Dr. SW18	166/167	E1
Strathville Rd.		
Riverdale Gdns., Twick.	145	F6
Riverdale Rd. SE18	137	J5
Riverdale Rd., Bex.	159	F7
Riverdale Rd., Erith	139	H5
Riverdale Rd., Felt.	161	E4
Riverdale Rd., Twick.	145	F6
Riverdene, Edg.	54	C3
Riverdene Rd., Ilf.	98	D3
Riverhead Cl. E17	77	G2
Rivermead, E.Mol.	179	J3
Rivermead Cl., Tedd.	163	E5
Rivermead Ct. SW6	148	C3
Rivermeads Av., Twick.	161	G3
Rivernook Cl., Walt.	178	C5
Riversdale Rd. N5	93	H3
Riversdale Rd., T.Ditt.	180	D5
Riversfield Rd., Enf.	44	B3
Riverside NW4	71	H7
Riverside SE7	135	H3
Riverside, Twick.	162	E1
Riverside, The, E.Mol.	180	A3
Riverside Av., E.Mol.	180	A5
Riverside Business Cen. SW18	167	E1
Riverside Cl. E5	95	F1
Riverside Cl. W7	104	B4
Riverside Cl., Kings.T.	181	G4
Riverside Cl., Wall.	200	B3
Riverside Ct. E4	46	B6
Chelwood Cl.		
Riverside Ct. SW8	33	J5
Riverside Ct. SW8	130	D6
Riverside Dr. NW11	72	B6
Riverside Dr. W4	126	D7
Riverside Dr., Mitch.	185	H5
Riverside Dr., Rich.	163	E2
Riverside Gdns. N3	72	B3
Riverside Gdns. W6	127	H5
Riverside Gdns., Enf.	43	J2
Riverside Gdns., Wem.	105	H2
Riverside Ind. Est., Bark.	118	A3
Riverside Ind. Est., Enf.	45	H6
Riverside Ms., Croy.	200/201	E3
Wandle Rd.		
Riverside Pl., Stai.	140	A6
Riverside Rd. E15	114	C2
Riverside Rd. N15	76	D6
Riverside Rd. SW17	167	E4
Riverside Rd., Sid.	177	E3
Riverside Rd. (Stanwell), Stai.	140	A5
Riverside Wk. SE1	26	C2
Riverside Wk. SE1	131	F1
Riverside Wk., Bex.	158	C7
Riverside Wk., Islw.	144	B3
Riverside Wk., Kings.T.	181	G2
High St.		
Riverside W., Loug.	48	E6
Riverside W. SW18	148/149	E4
Smugglers Way		
Riverton Cl. W9	108	C3
Riverview Gdns. SW13	127	H6
Riverview Gdns., Twick.	162	C2
Riverview Gro. W4	126	B6
Riverview Pk. SE6	172	A2
Riverview Rd. W4	126	B6
Riverview Rd., Epsom	196	C4
Riverway N13	59	G5
Riverwood La., Chis.	193	G1
Rivington Av., Wdf.Grn.	80	A2
Rivington Cres. NW10	107	G1
Rivington Cres. NW7	55	F7
Rivington Pl. EC2	12	E4
Rivington St. EC2	12	D4
Rivington St. EC2	112	B3
Rivington Wk. E8	112	D1
Wilde Cl.		
Rivulet Rd. N17	59	J7
Rixon Ho. SE18	136/137	E6
Barnfield Rd.		

Rixon St. N7	93	G3
Rixsen Rd. E12	98	B5
Roach Rd. E3	96	A7
Roads Pl. N19	92/93	E2
Hornsey Rd.		
Roan St. SE10	134	C6
Robarts Cl., Pnr.	66	B5
Field End Rd.		
Robb Rd., Stan.	52	D6
Robert Adam St. W1	**16**	**B3**
Robert Adam St. W1	110	A6
Robert Cl. W9	**6**	**D6**
Robert Cl., Chig.	65	J5
Robert Dashwood Way SE17	**35**	**J2**
Robert Dashwood Way SE17	131	J4
Robert Gentry Ho. W14	128	B5
Comeragh Rd.		
Robert Keen Cl. SE15	152	D1
Cicely Rd.		
Robert Lowe Cl. SE14	133	G7
Robert Owen Ho. SW6	148	A1
Robert St. E16	136	E1
Robert St. NW1	**8**	**E4**
Robert St. NW1	110	B3
Robert St. SE18	137	G4
Robert St. WC2	**18**	**B6**
Robert St., Croy.	201	J3
High St.		
Roberta St. E2	**13**	**H3**
Roberta St. E2	112	D3
Roberton Dr., Brom.	191	J1
Roberts Cl. SE9	175	G1
Roberts Cl., Pnr.	66	B5
Field End Rd.		
Roberts Cl., Sutt.	198	A7
Roberts Cl., West Dr.	120	B1
Roberts Ms. SW1	**24**	**B6**
Robert's Pl. EC1	**11**	**F5**
Roberts Rd. E17	78	B1
Roberts Rd. NW7	56	B6
Roberts Rd., Belv.	139	G5
Robertsbridge Rd., Cars.	199	F1
Robertson Rd. E15	114	C1
Robertson St. SW8	150	B2
Robeson St. E3	113	J5
Ackroyd Dr.		
Robeson Way, Borwd.	38	C1
Robin Cl. NW7	54	E3
Robin Cl., Hmptn.	161	E5
Robin Ct. SE16	**37**	**H1**
Robin Ct. SE16	132	D4
Robin Cres. E6	116	A5
Robin Gro. N6	92	A2
Robin Gro., Brent.	125	F6
Robin Gro., Har.	69	J6
Robin Hill Dr., Chis.	174	B6
Robin Hood Dr., Har.	52	C7
Robin Hood La. E14	114	C7
Robin Hood La. SW15	164	E4
Robin Hood La., Bexh.	159	E5
Robin Hood La., Sutt.	198	D5
Robin Hood Rd. SW19	165	H5
Robin Hood Way SW15	165	E4
Robin Hood Way SW20	165	E4
Robin Hood Way, Grnf.	86	C6
Robina Cl., Bexh.	158	D4
Robinhood Cl., Mitch.	186	C3
Robinhood La., Mitch.	186	C3
Robinia Cl., Ilf.	65	H6
Robinia Cres. E10	96	B2
Robins Ct. SE12	173	J3
Robins Gro., W.Wick.	205	G3
Robinscroft Ms. SE10	154	B1
Sparta St.		
Robinson Cres., Bushey	51	J1
Robinson Rd. E2	113	F2
Robinson Rd. SW17	167	H6
Robinson Rd., Dag.	101	G4
Robinson St. SW3	**31**	**J5**
Robinsons Cl. W13	104	D5
Robinwood Pl. SW15	164	D4
Robsart St. SW9	151	F2
Robson Av. NW10	107	G1
Robson Cl. E6	116	B6
Linton Gdns.		
Robson Cl., Enf.	43	H2
Robson Rd. SE27	169	H3
Roch Av., Edg.	69	J2
Rochdale Rd. E17	78	A7
Rochdale Rd. SE2	138	B5
Rochdale Way SE8	134	A7
Octavius St.		
Roche Rd. SW16	187	F1
Roche Wk., Cars.	185	G6
Rochelle Cl. SW11	149	G4
Rochelle St. E2	**13**	**F4**
Rochemont Wk. E8	112	C1
Pownall Rd.		
Rochester Av. E13	115	J1
Rochester Av., Brom.	191	H2
Rochester Cl. SW16	169	E7
Rochester Cl., Enf.	44	B1
Rochester Cl., Sid.	158	B6
Rochester Dr., Bex.	159	F6
Rochester Dr., Pnr.	66	D5
Rochester Gdns., Croy.	202	B3
Rochester Gdns., Ilf.	80	C7
Rochester Ms. NW1	92	C7
Rochester Pl. NW1	92	C6
Rochester Rd. NW1	92	C6
Rochester Rd., Cars.	199	J4
Rochester Row SW1	**33**	**G1**
Rochester Row SW1	130	C4
Rochester Sq. NW1	92	C7
Rochester St. SW1	**25**	**H6**
Rochester St. SW1	130	D3
Rochester Ter. NW1	92	C6
Rochester Wk. SE1	**28**	**B1**
Rochester Way SE3	155	H1
Rochester Way SE9	156	C3
Rochester Way Relief Rd. SE3	155	H1
Rochester Way Relief Rd. SE9	156	B4
Rochford Av., Loug.	49	F3
Rochford Av., Rom.	82	C5
Rochford Cl. E6	116	A2
Boleyn Rd.		
Rochford Grn., Loug.	49	F3
Rochford St. NW5	91	J5
Rochford Wk. E8	94	D7
Wilman Gro.		
Rochford Way, Croy.	186	E6
Rock Av. SW14	146	D3
South Worple Way		
Rock Gdns., Dag.	101	H5
Rock Gro. Way SE16	**37**	**J1**
Rock Hill SE26	170	C4
Rock St. N4	93	G2
Rockbourne Rd. SE23	171	G1
Rockells Pl. SE22	153	E6
Rockford Av., Grnf.	104	D2
Rockhall Rd. NW2	90	A4
Rockhampton Cl. SE27	169	G4
Rockhampton Rd.		
Rockhampton Rd. SE27	169	G4
Rockhampton Rd., S.Croy.	202	B6
Rockingham Cl. SW15	147	F4
Rockingham Est. SE1	**27**	**J6**
Rockingham Est. SE1	131	J3
Rockingham St. SE1	**27**	**J6**
Rockingham St. SE1	131	J3
Rockland Rd. SW15	148	B4
Rocklands Dr., Stan.	69	E2
Rockley Rd. W14	128	A2
Rockmount Rd. SE18	137	J5
Rockmount Rd. SE19	170	A6
Rocks La. SW13	147	G1
Rockware Av., Grnf.	104	A1
Rockways, Barn.	39	F6
Rockwell Gdns. SE19	170	B5
Rockwell Rd., Dag.	101	H5
Rockwood Pl. W12	127	J2
Rocliffe St. N1	**11**	**H2**
Rocombe Cres. SE23	153	F7
Rocque La. SE3	155	F3
Rodborough Rd. NW11	90	D1
Roden Ct. N6	74	D7
Hornsey La.		
Roden Gdns., Croy.	188	B6
Roden St. N7	93	F3
Roden St., Ilf.	98	D3
Rodenhurst Rd. SW4	150	C6
Roderick Rd. NW3	91	J4
Roding Av., Wdf.Grn.	64	B6
Roding Gdns., Loug.	48	B6
Roding La., Buck.H.	64	B1
Roding La., Chig.	64	D1
Roding La. N., Wdf.Grn.	80	A2
Roding La. S., Ilf.	80	A4
Roding La. S., Wdf.Grn.	80	A4
Roding Ms. E1	**29**	**J1**
Roding Rd. E5	95	G4
Roding Rd. E6	116	E5
Roding Rd., Loug.	48	B5
Roding Trd. Est., Bark.	98	E7
Roding Vw., Buck.H.	64	A1
Rodings, The, Wdf.Grn.	63	J6
Rodings Row, Barn.	40	B5
Leecroft Rd.		
Rodmarton St. W1	**16**	**A2**
Rodmarton St. W1	109	J5
Rodmell Cl., Hayes	102	E4
Rodmell Slope N12	56	C5
Rodmere St. SE10	134/135	E5
Trafalgar Rd.		
Rodmill La. SW2	151	E7
Rodney Cl., Croy.	201	H1
Rodney Cl., N.Mal.	182	E5
Rodney Cl., Pnr.	66	E7
Rodney Ct. W9	**6**	**D5**
Rodney Gdns., Pnr.	66	B5
Rodney Gdns., W.Wick.	205	G4
Rodney Pl. E17	77	H2
Rodney Pl. SE17	**36**	**A1**
Rodney Pl. SE17	131	J4
Rodney Pl. SW19	185	F1
Rodney Rd. E11	79	H4
Rodney Rd. SE17	**36**	**A1**
Rodney Rd. SE17	132	A4
Rodney Rd., Mitch.	185	H2
Rodney Rd., N.Mal.	182	E5
Rodney Rd., Twick.	143	G6
Rodney St. N1	**10**	**D1**
Rodney St. N1	111	F2
Rodney Way, Rom.	83	G1
Rodway Rd. SW15	147	G7
Rodway Rd., Brom.	191	H1
Rodwell Cl., Ruis.	66	C7
Rodwell Pl., Edg.	54	A6
Whitchurch La.		
Rodwell Rd. SE22	152	C6
Roe End NW9	70	C4
Roe Grn. NW9	70	C5
Roe La. NW9	70	B4
Roe Way, Wall.	201	E7
Roebourne Way E16	136	D2
Roebuck Cl., Felt.	160	B4
Roebuck La. N17	60	C6
High Rd.		
Roebuck La., Buck.H.	47	J7
Roebuck Rd., Chess.	196	A5
Roedean Av., Enf.	45	F1
Roedean Cl., Enf.	45	F1
Roedean Cres. SW15	146	E6
Roehampton Cl. SW15	147	G4
Roehampton Dr., Chis.	175	F6
Roehampton Gate SW15	146	E6
Roehampton High St. SW15	147	H7
Roehampton La. SW15	147	G4
Roehampton Vale SW15	165	E3
Roffey St. E14	134	C2
Rogate Ho. E5	94	D3
Muir Rd.		
Roger St. WC1	**10**	**D6**
Roger St. WC1	111	F4
Rogers Gdns., Dag.	101	G5
Rogers Rd. E16	115	F6
Rogers Rd. SW17	167	G4
Rogers Rd., Dag.	101	G5
Rogers Wk. N12	56/57	E3
Brook Meadow		
Rojack Rd. SE23	171	G1
Rokeby Gdns., Wdf.Grn.	79	G1
Rokeby Pl. SW20	165	H7
Rokeby Rd. SE4	153	J2
Rokeby St. E15	114	E1
Rokesby Cl., Well.	157	G2
Rokesby Pl., Wem.	87	G5
Rokesly Av. N8	74	E5
Roland Gdns. SW7	**30**	**D3**
Roland Gdns. SW7	129	F5
Roland Gdns., Felt.	161	F3
Hampton Rd. W.		
Roland Ms. E1	113	G5
Stepney Grn.		
Roland Rd. E17	78	D4
Roland Way SE17	**36**	**C4**
Roland Way SE17	132	A5
Roland Way SW7	**30**	**D3**
Roland Way, Wor.Pk.	197	F2
Roles Gro., Rom.	82	D4
Rolfe Cl., Barn.	41	H4
Rolinsden Way, Kes.	206	A4
Roll Gdns., Ilf.	80	D5
Rollesby Rd., Chess.	196	A6
Rollesby Way SE28	118	C7
Rolleston Av., Orp.	193	E6
Rolleston Cl., Orp.	193	E7
Rolleston Rd., S.Croy.	202	A7
Rollins St. SE15	133	F6
Rollit Cres., Houns.	143	G5
Rollit St. N7	93	F5
Hornsey Rd.		
Rolls Bldgs. EC4	**19**	**E3**
Rolls Pk. Av. E4	62	A6
Rolls Pk. Rd. E4	62	B5
Rolls Pas. EC4	**18**	**E3**
Rolls Rd. SE1	**37**	**G3**
Rolls Rd. SE1	132	C5
Rollscourt Av. SE24	151	J5
Rolt St. SE8	133	H6
Rolvenden Gdns., Brom.	174	A7
Rolvenden Pl. N17	76	D1
Manor Rd.		
Roma Read Cl. SW15	147	H7
Bessborough Rd.		
Roma Rd. E17	77	H3
Roman Cl. W3	126	B2
Avenue Gdns.		
Roman Cl., Felt.	142	C5
Roman Ind. Est., Croy.	188	B7
Roman Ri. SE19	170	A6
Roman Rd. E2	113	F3
Roman Rd. E3	113	H2
Roman Rd. E6	116	B4
Roman Rd. N10	58	B7
Roman Rd. NW2	89	J3
Roman Rd. W4	127	F4
Roman Rd., Ilf.	99	E6
Roman Sq. SE28	138	A1
Roman Way N7	93	F6
Roman Way SE15	133	F7
Clifton Way		
Roman Way, Cars.	199	J7
Fountain Dr.		
Roman Way, Croy.	201	H2
Roman Way, Enf.	44	C5
Roman Way Ind. Est. N1	93	F7
Offord St.		
Romanfield Rd. SW2	151	F7
Romanhurst Av., Brom.	191	E4
Romanhurst Gdns., Brom.	190	E4
Romany Gdns. E17	77	H1
McEntee Av.		
Romany Gdns., Sutt.	184	D7
Romany Ri., Orp.	207	F1
Romberg Rd. SW17	168	A3
Romborough Gdns. SE13	154	C5
Romborough Way SE13	154	C5
Romero Cl. SW9	151	F3
Stockwell Rd.		
Romero Sq. SE3	155	J4
Romeyn Rd. SW16	169	F3
Romford Rd. E7	97	H5
Romford Rd. E12	98	B4
Romford Rd. E15	96	E7
Romford St. E1	**21**	**J2**
Romford St. E1	112	D5
Romilly Dr., Wat.	51	E3
Romilly Rd. N4	93	H2
Romilly St. W1	**17**	**H5**
Romilly St. W1	110	D7
Rommany Rd. SE27	170	A4
Romney Cl. N17	76	E1
Romney Cl. NW11	91	F1
Romney Cl. SE14	133	F7
Kender St.		
Romney Cl., Chess.	195	H4
Romney Cl., Har.	67	G7
Romney Dr., Brom.	174	A7
Romney Dr., Har.	67	G7
Romney Gdns., Bexh.	159	F1
Romney Ms. W1	**16**	**B1**
Romney Rd. SE10	134	C6
Romney Rd., N.Mal.	182	D6
Romney Row NW2	90	A2
Brent Ter.		
Romney St. SW1	**25**	**J6**
Romney St. SW1	130	E3
Romola Rd. SE24	169	H1
Romsey Cl., Orp.	207	E4
Romsey Gdns., Dag.	118	D1
Romsey Rd. W13	104	D7
Romsey Rd., Dag.	118	D1
Ron Leighton Way E6	116	B1
Rona Rd. NW3	92	A4
Rona Wk. N1	94	A6
Clephane Rd.		
Ronald Av. E15	115	E3
Ronald Cl., Beck.	189	J4
Ronald St. E1	113	F6
Devonport St.		
Ronalds Rd. N5	93	G5
Ronalds Rd., Brom.	191	G1
Ronaldstone Rd., Sid.	157	H6

Ronart St., Har. 68 C3
Stuart Rd.
Rondu Rd. NW2 90 B5
Ronelean Rd., Surb. 195 J3
Ronver Rd. SE12 155 F7
Rood La. EC3 20 D5
Rood La. EC3 112 B7
Rook Wk. E6 116 B6
Allhallows Rd.
Rookby Ct. N21 59 H2
Carpenter Gdns.
Rooke Way SE10 135 F5
Rookeries Cl., Felt. 160 B3
Rookery Cl. NW9 71 F5
Rookery Cres., Dag. 101 H7
Rookery Dr., Chis. 192 D1
Rookery La., Brom. 192 A5
Rookery Rd. SW4 150 C4
Rookery Way NW9 71 F5
Rookfield Av. N10 74 C4
Rookfield Cl. N10 74 C4
Cranmore Way
Rookstone Rd. SW17 167 J5
Rookwood Av., Loug. 49 F3
Rookwood Av., 183 G4
  N.Mal.
Rookwood Av., Wall. 200 D4
Rookwood Gdns. E4 63 F1
Whitehall Rd.
Rookwood Gdns., 49 F3
  Loug.
Rookwood Ho., Bark. 117 G2
St. Marys
Rookwood Rd. N16 76 C7
Rootes Dr. W10 108 A4
Rope St. SE16 133 H4
Rope Wk., Sun. 178 C3
Rope Wk. Gdns. E1 21 J4
Ropemaker Rd. SE16 133 H3
Ropemaker St. EC2 20 B1
Ropemaker St. EC2 112 A5
Ropemakers Flds. E14 113 J7
Narrow St.
Roper La. SE1 29 E4
Roper St. SE9 156 C6
Roper Way, Mitch. 186 A2
Ropers Av. E4 62 C5
Ropers Wk. SW2 151 G7
Brockwell Pk. Gdns.
Ropery St. E3 113 J4
Ropley St. E2 13 H2
Ropley St. E2 112 D2
Rosa Alba Ms. N5 93 J4
Kelross Rd.
Rosaline Rd. SW6 128 B7
Rosamond St. SE26 170 E3
Rosamun St., Sthl. 123 E4
Rosamund Cl., 202 A4
  S.Croy.
Rosary Cl., Houns. 142 E2
Rosary Gdns. SW7 30 C2
Rosary Gdns. SW7 129 F4
Rosaville Rd. SW6 128 C7
Roscoe St. EC1 12 A6
Roscoff Cl., Edg. 70 C1
Rose All. SE1 28 A1
Rose All. SE1 131 J1
Rose & Crown Ct. 19 J3
  EC2
Rose & Crown Yd. 25 G1
  SW1
Rose Av. E18 79 H2
Rose Av., Mitch. 185 J1
Rose Av., Mord. 185 F5
Rose Bates Dr. NW9 70 A4
Rose Ct. E1 112 B5
Sandy's Row
Rose Ct. SE26 170 E2
Rose Ct., Pnr. 66 C3
Nursery Rd.
Rose Dale, Orp. 207 E2
Rose End, Wor.Pk. 198 A1
Rose Gdn. Cl., Edg. 53 H4
Rose Gdns. W5 125 G3
Rose Gdns., Felt. 160 A2
Rose Gdns., Sthl. 103 G4
Rose Gdns., Stai. 140 A7
Diamedes Av.
Rose Glen NW9 70 D4
Rose Hill, Sutt. 199 E2
Rose La., Rom. 82 D3
Rose Lawn, Bushey 51 J1
Rose Sq. SW3 31 F3
Rose Sq. SW3 129 G5
Rose St. WC2 18 A5
Rose Wk., Surb. 182 B5
Rose Wk., W.Wick. 204 D2
Rose Way SE12 155 G5
Rose Way, Edg. 54 C4
Stoneyfields La.
Roseacre Cl. W13 104/105 E5
Middlefielde
Roseacre Rd., Well. 158 B3

Rosary Cl., West Dr. 120 A4
Rosebank SE20 170 E7
Rosebank Av., Wem. 86 C4
Rosebank Cl. N12 57 H5
Rosebank Cl., Tedd. 162 D6
Rosebank Gdns. E3 113 J2
Rosebank Gro. E17 77 J3
Rosebank Rd. E17 78 B6
Rosebank Rd. W7 124 B2
Rosebank Vil. E17 78 A4
Rosebank Wk. NW1 92 D7
Maiden La.
Rosebank Wk. SE18 136 B4
Woodhill
Roseberry Gdns. N4 75 H6
Roseberry Gdns., 207 H3
  Orp.
Roseberry Pl. E8 94 C6
Roseberry St. SE16 132 E4
Rosebery Av. E12 98 B6
Rosebery Av. EC1 10 E6
Rosebery Av. EC1 111 G4
Rosebery Av. N17 76 D2
Rosebery Av., Har. 85 F4
Rosebery Av., N.Mal. 183 F2
Rosebery Av., Sid. 157 H7
Rosebery Av., 187 J2
  Th.Hth.
Rosebery Cl., Mord. 184 A6
Rosebery Ct. EC1 111 G4
Rosebery Av.
Rosebery Gdns. N8 74 E5
Rosebery Gdns. W13 104 D6
Rosebery Gdns., Sutt. 199 E4
Rosebery Ms. N10 74 C2
Rosebery Ms. 150/151 E6
  SW2
Rosebery Rd.
Rosebery Rd. N9 60 D3
Rosebery Rd. N10 74 C2
Rosebery Rd. SW2 150 E6
Rosebery Rd., Houns. 143 J5
Rosebery Rd., 182 B2
  Kings.T.
Rosebery Rd., Sutt. 198 C6
Rosebery Sq. EC1 10 E6
Rosebery Sq., 182 A2
  Kings.T.
Rosebine Av., 144 A7
  Twick.
Rosebury Rd. SW6 149 E2
Rosecourt Rd., Croy. 187 F6
Rosecroft Av. NW3 90 D3
Rosecroft Gdns. NW2 89 G3
Rosecroft Gdns., 162 A1
  Twick.
Rosecroft Rd., Sthl. 103 G4
Rosecroft Wk., Pnr. 66 D5
Rosecroft Wk., Wem. 87 G5
Rosedale Cl. SE2 138 B3
Finchale Rd.
Rosedale Cl. W7 124 C2
Boston Rd.
Rosedale Cl., Stan. 53 E6
Rosedale Ct. N5 93 H4
Rosedale Gdns., Dag. 100 B7
Rosedale Rd. E7 97 J5
Rosedale Rd., Dag. 100 B7
Rosedale Rd., Epsom 197 G5
Rosedale Rd., Rich. 145 H4
Rosedale Rd., Rom. 83 J2
Rosedale Ter. W6 127 H3
Dalling Rd.
Rosedene NW6 108 A1
Christchurch Av.
Rosedene Av. SW16 169 F3
Rosedene Av., Croy. 187 F7
Rosedene Av., Grnf. 103 G3
Rosedene Av., Mord. 184 D5
Rosedene Gdns., Ilf. 80 D4
Rosedene Ter. E10 96 B2
Rosedew Rd. W6 128 A6
Rosefield Cl., Cars. 199 H5
Alma Rd.
Rosefield Gdns. E14 114 A7
Roseford Ct. W12 128 A2
Rosehart Ms. W11 108 D6
Westbourne Gro.
Rosehatch Av., Rom. 82 D3
Roseheath Rd., 143 F5
  Houns.
Rosehill, Esher 194 D6
Rosehill, Hmptn. 179 G1
Rosehill Av., Sutt. 199 F1
Rosehill Gdns., Grnf. 86 C5
Rosehill Gdns., Sutt. 199 E2
Rosehill Pk. W., Sutt. 199 F1
Rosehill Rd. SW18 149 F6
Roseland Cl. N17 60 A7
Cavell Rd.
Roseleigh Av. N5 93 H4
Roseleigh Cl., Twick. 145 G6
Rosemary Av. N3 73 E2

Rosemary Av. N9 60 E1
Rosemary Av., Enf. 44 A1
Rosemary Av., Houns. 142 D2
Rosemary Av., W.Mol. 179 G3
Rosemary Cl., Croy. 186 E6
Rosemary Dr. E14 114 D6
Rosemary Dr., Ilf. 80 A5
Rosemary Gdns. 146 C3
  SW14
Rosemary La.
Rosemary Gdns., 195 H4
  Chess.
Rosemary Gdns., Dag. 101 F1
Rosemary La. SW14 146 C3
Rosemary Rd. SE15 37 G7
Rosemary Rd. SE15 132 C7
Rosemary Rd. SW17 167 F3
Rosemary Rd., Well. 157 J1
Rosemary St. N1 112 A1
Shepperton Rd.
Rosemead NW9 71 F7
Rosemead Av., Mitch. 186 C2
Rosemead Av., Wem. 87 H5
Rosemont Av. N12 57 F6
Rosemont Rd. NW3 91 F6
Rosemont Rd. W3 106 B7
Rosemont Rd., N.Mal. 182 C3
Rosemont Rd., Rich. 145 H6
Rosemont Rd., Wem. 105 H1
Rosemoor St. SW3 31 J2
Rosemoor St. SW3 129 J4
Rosemount Cl., 64 C6
  Wdf.Grn.
Chapelmount Rd.
Rosemount Dr., 192 C4
  Brom.
Rosemount Rd. W13 104 D6
Rosenau Cres. SW11 149 H1
Rosenau Rd. SW11 149 H1
Rosendale Rd. SE21 151 J7
Rosendale Rd. SE24 151 J7
Roseneath Av. N21 59 H1
Roseneath Rd. SW11 150 A6
Roseneath Wk., Enf. 44 B4
Rosens Wk., Edg. 54 B3
Rosenthal Rd. SE6 154 B6
Rosenthorpe Rd. 153 G5
  SE15
Roserton St. E14 134 C2
Rosery, The, Croy. 189 G6
Roses, The, Wdf.Grn. 63 F7
Rosethorn Cl. SW12 150 C7
Rosetta Cl. SW8 131 E7
Rosetti Ter., Dag. 100 B4
Marlborough Rd.
Roseveare Rd. SE12 173 J4
Roseville Av., Houns. 143 G5
Roseville Rd., Hayes 122 A5
Rosevine Rd. SW20 183 J1
Roseway SE21 152 A6
Rosewell Cl. SE20 170 E7
Rosewood, Esher 194 D2
Rosewood Av., Grnf. 86 D5
Rosewood Cl., Sid. 176 C3
Rosewood Ct., Brom. 191 J1
Rosewood Ct., Rom. 82 C5
Rosewood Gdns. 154 C2
  SE13
Lewisham Rd.
Rosewood Gro., Sutt. 199 F2
Rosewood Sq. W12 107 G6
Primula St.
Rosewood Ter. SE20 171 F7
Laurel Gro.
Rosher Cl. E15 96 D7
Rosina St. E9 95 G5
Roskell Rd. SW15 148 A3
Roslin Rd. W3 126 B3
Roslin Way, Brom. 173 G5
Roslyn Cl., Mitch. 185 G2
Roslyn Rd. N15 76 A5
Rosman Pl. EC1 11 F5
Rosman Rd. EC1 11 F4
Rosoman St. EC1 111 G3
Ross Av. NW7 56 B5
Ross Av., Dag. 101 F2
Ross Cl., Har. 51 J7
Ross Cl., Hayes 121 G4
Ross Ct. SW15 148 A7
Ross Par., Wall. 200 B6
Ross Rd. SE25 188 A3
Ross Rd., Twick. 161 H1
Ross Rd., Wall. 200 C5
Ross Way SE9 156 B3
Rossall Cres. NW10 105 J3
Rossdale, Sutt. 199 H5
Rossdale Dr. N9 45 F6
Rossdale Dr. NW9 88 C1
Rossdale Rd. SW15 147 J4
Rosse Ms. SE3 155 H1
Rossendale St. E5 94 E2
Rossendale Way NW1 92 C7

Rossetti Rd. SE16 132 E5
Rossignol Gdns., 200 A2
  Cars.
Rossindel Rd., Houns. 143 G5
Rossington St. E5 94 D2
Rossiter Flds., Barn. 40 B6
Rossiter Rd. SW12 168 B1
Rossland Cl., Bexh. 159 H5
Rosslyn Av. E4 63 F2
Rosslyn Av. SW13 147 E3
Rosslyn Av., Barn. 41 H6
Rosslyn Av., Dag. 83 F7
Rosslyn Av., Felt. 142 A6
Rosslyn Av., W.Wick. 205 F3
Rosslyn Cl., W.Wick. 205 F3
Rosslyn Cres., Har. 68 C5
Rosslyn Cres., Wem. 87 H4
Rosslyn Gdns., Wem. 87 H3
Rosslyn Cres.
Rosslyn Hill NW3 91 G4
Rosslyn Ms. NW3 91 G4
Rosslyn Rd.
Rosslyn Pk. Ms. NW3 91 G5
Lyndhurst Rd.
Rosslyn Rd. E17 78 C4
Rosslyn Rd., Bark. 99 G7
Rosslyn Rd., Twick. 145 F6
Rossmore Rd. NW1 7 H6
Rossmore Rd. NW1 109 H4
Rosswood Gdns., 200 C6
  Wall.
Rostella Rd. SW17 167 G4
Rostrevor Av. N15 76 C6
Rostrevor Gdns., 121 H1
  Hayes
Rostrevor Gdns., 123 E5
  Sthl.
Rostrevor Ms. SW6 148 C1
Rostrevor Rd. SW6 148 C1
Rostrevor Rd. SW19 166 D5
Rotary St. SE1 27 G5
Roth Wk. N7 93 F3
Durham Rd.
Rothbury Gdns., Islw. 124 D7
Rothbury Rd. E9 95 J2
Rothbury Wk. N17 60 D7
Rotherfield Rd., Cars. 200 A4
Rotherfield St. N1 93 J7
Rotherham Wk. SE1 27 G2
Rotherhill Av. SW16 168 D6
Rotherhithe New Rd. 37 J4
  SE16
Rotherhithe New Rd. 132 D5
  SE16
Rotherhithe Old Rd. 133 G4
  SE16
Rotherhithe St. SE16 133 F2
Rotherhithe Tunnel E1 133 F1
Rotherhithe Tunnel 133 F2
  App. E14
Rotherhithe Tunnel 133 F2
  App. SE16
Rothermere Rd., 201 F5
  Croy.
Rotherwick Hill W5 105 J4
Rotherwick Rd. NW11 72 D7
Rotherwood Cl. 184 B1
  SW20
Rotherwood Rd. 148 A3
  SW15
Rothery St. N1 111 H1
Gaskin St.
Rothery Ter. SW9 131 H7
Rothesay Av. SW20 184 B2
Rothesay Av., Grnf. 86 A6
Rothesay Av., Rich. 146 B4
Rothesay Rd. SE25 188 B4
Rothsay Rd. E7 97 J6
Rothsay St. SE1 28 D5
Rothsay St. SE1 132 B3
Rothsay Wk. E14 134 A4
Charnwood Gdns.
Rothschild Rd. W4 126 C4
Rothschild St. SE27 169 H4
Rothwell Gdns., Dag. 100 C7
Rothwell Rd., Dag. 118 C1
Rothwell St. NW1 109 J1
Rotten Row SW1 24 B3
Rotten Row SW1 129 H2
Rotten Row SW7 23 G3
Rotten Row SW7 129 H2
Rotterdam Dr. E14 134 C3
Rouel Rd. SE16 29 H6
Rouel Rd. SE16 132 D3
Rougemont Av., 184 D6
  Mord.
Round Gro., Croy. 189 G7
Round Hill SE26 171 F2
Roundacre SW19 166 A2
Inner Pk. Rd.
Roundaway Rd., Ilf. 80 C2
Roundel Cl. SE4 153 J4
Adelaide Av.
Roundhay Cl. SE23 171 G2
Roundhill Dr., Enf. 43 F4

Roundmead Av., Loug.	48	D3	
Roundmead Cl., Loug.	48	D3	
Roundshaw	200/201	E7	
Meter Way			
Roundtable Rd., Brom.	173	F3	
Roundtree Rd., Wem.	86	E5	
Roundway, The N17	75	J1	
Roundway, The, Esher	194	C5	
Roundwood, Chis.	192	E2	
Roundwood Av., Uxb.	121	F1	
Roundwood Rd. NW10	89	F6	
Rounton Rd. E3	114	A4	
Roupell Rd. SW2	169	F1	
Roupell St. SE1	**27**	**F2**	
Roupell St. SE1	131	G1	
Rous Rd., Buck.H.	64	B1	
Rousden St. NW1	92	C7	
Rouse Gdns. SE21	170	B4	
Routemaster Cl. E13	115	H3	
Routh Rd. SW18	149	H7	
Routh St. E6	116	C5	
Routledge Cl. N19	92	D1	
Rover Av., Ilf.	65	J6	
Rowallan Rd. SW6	128	B7	
Rowan Av. E4	61	J6	
Rowan Cl. SW16	186	C1	
Rowan Cl. W5	125	H2	
Rowan Cl., Ilf.	99	G5	
Rowan Cl., N.Mal.	182	E2	
Rowan Cl., Stan.	52	C6	
Woodlands Dr.			
Rowan Cl., Wem.	86	D3	
Rowan Cres. SW16	186	C1	
Rowan Dr. NW9	71	G4	
Rowan Gdns., Croy.	202	C3	
Radcliffe Rd.			
Rowan Rd. SW16	186	C2	
Rowan Rd. W6	128	A4	
Rowan Rd., Bexh.	159	E3	
Rowan Rd., Brent.	125	E7	
Rowan Rd., West Dr.	120	A4	
Rowan Ter. W6	128	A4	
Bute Gdns.			
Rowan Wk. N2	73	F6	
Rowan Wk. N19	92	C2	
Bredgar Rd.			
Rowan Wk. W10	108	B4	
Droop St.			
Rowan Wk., Barn.	40/41	E5	
Station Rd.			
Rowan Wk., Brom.	206	C3	
Rowan Way, Rom.	82	C3	
Rowans, The N13	59	H3	
Rowans Way, Loug.	48	C4	
Rowantree Cl. N21	60	A1	
Rowantree Rd. N21	60	A1	
Rowantree Rd., Enf.	43	H2	
Rowanwood Av., Sid.	176	A1	
Rowben Cl. N20	56	E1	
Rowberry Cl. SW6	127	J7	
Rowcross St. SE1	**37**	**F3**	
Rowcross St. SE1	132	C5	
Rowdell Rd., Nthlt.	103	G1	
Rowden Pk. Gdns. E4	62	A6	
Rowden Rd.			
Rowden Rd. E4	62	A6	
Rowden Rd., Beck.	189	H1	
Rowden Rd., Epsom	196	B4	
Rowditch La. SW11	150	A2	
Rowdon Av. NW10	89	H7	
Rowdowns Rd., Dag.	119	F1	
Rowe Gdns., Bark.	117	J2	
Rowe La. E9	95	F5	
Rowe Wk., Har.	85	G3	
Rowena Cres. SW11	149	H2	
Rowfant Rd. SW17	168	A1	
Rowhill Rd. E5	95	E4	
Rowington Cl. W2	**14**	**A1**	
Rowington Cl. W2	108	E5	
Rowland Av., Har.	69	F3	
Rowland Ct. E16	115	F4	
Rowland Cres., Chig.	65	H4	
Rowland Gro. SE26	170/171	E3	
Dallas Rd.			
Rowland Hill Av. N17	59	J7	
Rowland Hill St. NW3	91	H5	
Rowland Way SW19	184/185	E1	
Hayward Cl.			
Rowlands Av., Pnr.	51	G6	
Rowlands Cl. N6	74	A6	
North Hill			
Rowlands Cl. NW7	55	G7	
Rowlands Rd., Dag.	101	F2	
Rowley Av., Sid.	158	B7	
Rowley Cl., Wem.	87	J7	
Rowley Gdns. N4	75	J7	
Rowley Grn. Rd., Barn.	39	F5	
Rowley Ind. Pk. W3	126	B3	
Rowley La., Barn.	39	F5	
Rowley La., Borwd.	38	D1	
Rowley Rd. N15	75	J5	
Rowley Way NW8	109	E1	
Rowlheys Pl., West Dr.	120	B3	
Rowlls Rd., Kings.T.	181	J3	
Rowney Gdns., Dag.	100	B6	
Rowney Rd., Dag.	100	B6	
Rowntree Clifford Cl. E13	115	H3	
Liddon Rd.			
Rowntree Path SE28	118	B7	
Booth Cl.			
Rowntree Rd., Twick.	162	B1	
Rowse Cl. E15	96	C7	
Rowsley Av. NW4	71	J3	
Rowstock Gdns. N7	92	D5	
Rowton Rd. SE18	137	F7	
Roxborough Av., Har.	68	A7	
Roxborough Av., Islw.	124	C7	
Roxborough Pk., Har.	68	B7	
Roxborough Rd., Har.	68	A6	
Roxbourne Cl., Nthlt.	84	D6	
Roxburgh Rd. SE27	169	H5	
Roxby Pl. SW6	128	D6	
Roxeth Grn. Av., Har.	85	H3	
Roxeth Gro., Har.	85	H4	
Roxeth Hill, Har.	86	A2	
Roxley Rd. SE13	154	B6	
Roxton Gdns., Croy.	204	A5	
Roxwell Rd. W12	127	G2	
Roxwell Rd., Bark.	118	A2	
Roxwell Trd. Pk. E10	77	H7	
Roxwell Way, Wdf.Grn.	63	J7	
Roxy Av., Rom.	82	C7	
Roy Gdns., Ilf.	81	H4	
Roy Gro., Hmptn.	161	H6	
Roy Sq. E14	113	H7	
Narrow St.			
Royal Albert Dock E16	116	C7	
Royal Albert Roundabout E16	116	B7	
Royal Albert Way			
Royal Albert Way E16	116	A7	
Royal Arc. W1	**17**	**F6**	
Royal Artillery Barracks SE18	136	D5	
Repository Rd.			
Royal Av. SW3	**31**	**J3**	
Royal Av. SW3	129	J5	
Royal Av., Wor.Pk.	197	E2	
Royal Circ. SE27	169	G3	
Royal Cl. N16	94	B1	
Manor Rd.			
Royal Cl., Ilf.	82	A7	
Royal Cl., Wor.Pk.	196	E2	
Royal College St. NW1	92	C7	
Royal Ct. EC3	112	A6	
Cornhill			
Royal Ct. SE16	133	J3	
Royal Cres. W11	128	A1	
Royal Cres., Ruis.	84	C4	
Royal Cres. Ms. W11	128	A1	
Queensdale Rd.			
Royal Docks Rd. E6	117	E6	
Royal Dr. N11	58	A5	
Royal Ex. EC3	20	C4	
Royal Ex. EC3	112	A6	
Royal Ex. Av. EC3	20	C4	
Royal Ex. Bldgs. EC3	**20**	**C4**	
Royal Ex. Steps EC3	112	A6	
Cornhill			
Royal Gdns. W7	124	D3	
Royal Hill SE10	134	C7	
Royal Hospital Rd. SW3	**31**	**J5**	
Royal Hospital Rd. SW3	129	J6	
Royal London Est., The N17	60	E6	
Royal Ms., The SW1	**25**	**E5**	
Royal Ms., The SW1	130	B3	
Royal Mint Ct. EC3	**21**	**G6**	
Royal Mint Ct. EC3	112	C7	
Royal Mint Pl. E1	**21**	**G5**	
Royal Mint St. E1	**21**	**G5**	
Royal Mint St. E1	112	C7	
Royal Mt. Ct., Twick.	162	B3	
Royal Naval Pl. SE14	133	J7	
Royal Oak Ct. N1	112	B3	
Pitfield St.			
Royal Oak Pl. SE22	153	E6	
Royal Oak Rd. E8	94	E6	
Royal Oak Rd., Bexh.	159	F5	
Royal Opera Arc. SW1	**25**	**H1**	
Royal Opera Arc. SW1	130	D1	
Royal Orchard Cl. SW18	148	B7	
Royal Par. SE3	155	E2	
Royal Par. SW6	128	B7	
Dawes Rd.			
Royal Par. W5	105	H3	
Western Av.			
Royal Par., Chis.	175	F7	
Royal Par., Rich.	146	A1	
Station App.			
Royal Par. Ms. SE3	155	F2	
Royal Par.			
Royal Par. Ms., Chis.	175	F7	
Royal Pl. SE10	134	C7	
Royal Rd. E16	116	A6	
Royal Rd. SE17	**35**	**G5**	
Royal Rd. SE17	131	H6	
Royal Rd., Sid.	176	D3	
Royal Rd., Tedd.	162	A5	
Royal Route, Wem.	87	J4	
Monsell Rd.			
Royal St. SE1	**26**	**D5**	
Royal St. SE1	131	F3	
Royal Victor Pl. E3	113	G2	
Royal Victoria Dock E16	115	H7	
Royal Victoria Pl. E16	135	H1	
Wesley Av.			
Royal Wk., Wall.	200	B3	
Prince Charles Way			
Royal Windsor Ct. Surb.	196	A1	
Royalty Ms. W1	**17**	**H4**	
Roycraft Av., Bark.	117	J2	
Roycraft Cl., Bark.	117	J2	
Roycroft Cl. E18	79	H1	
Roycroft Cl. SW2	169	G1	
Roydene Rd. SE18	137	H6	
Roydon Cl. SW11	150	B1	
Reform St.			
Roydon Cl., Loug.	48	B7	
Roydon St. SW11	150	B1	
Southolm St.			
Royle Cres. W13	104	D4	
Royston Av. E4	62	A5	
Royston Av., Sutt.	199	G3	
Royston Av., Wall.	200	D4	
Royston Cl., Houns.	142	B1	
Royston Ct. SE24	151	J6	
Burbage Rd.			
Royston Ct., Rich.	145	J1	
Lichfield Rd.			
Royston Ct., Surb.	196	A3	
Hook Ri. N.			
Royston Gdns., Ilf.	80	A6	
Royston Gro., Pnr.	51	F6	
Royston Par., Ilf.	80	A6	
Royston Pk. Rd., Pnr.	51	F6	
Royston Rd. SE20	189	G1	
Royston Rd., Rich.	145	H5	
Royston St. E2	113	F2	
Roystons, The, Surb.	182	B5	
Rozel Ct. N1	112	B1	
Rozel Rd. SW4	150	C2	
Rubastic Rd., Sthl.	122	B3	
Rubens Rd., Nthlt.	102	C2	
Rubens St. SE6	171	J2	
Ruberoid Rd., Enf.	45	J3	
Ruby Ms. E17	78	A3	
Ruby Rd.			
Ruby Rd. E17	78	A3	
Ruby St. SE15	132	E6	
Ruby Triangle SE15	132/133	E6	
Sandgate St.			
Ruckholt Cl. E10	96	B3	
Ruckholt Rd. E10	96	A4	
Rucklidge Av. NW10	107	F2	
Rudall Cres. NW3	91	G4	
Willoughby Rd.			
Ruddington Cl. E5	95	H4	
Ruddock Cl., Edg.	54	C7	
Orange Hill Rd.			
Ruddstreet Cl. SE18	137	E4	
Ruddy Way NW7	55	G6	
Flower La.			
Rudland Rd., Bexh.	159	H3	
Rudloe Rd. SW12	150	C7	
Rudolf Pl. SW8	**34**	**B6**	
Rudolph Ct. SE22	152	D7	
Rudolph Rd. E13	115	F2	
Rudolph Rd. NW6	108	D2	
Rudyard Gro. NW7	54	C6	
Ruffetts, The, S.Croy.	203	E7	
Ruffetts Cl., S.Croy.	202	E7	
Rufford Cl., Har.	68	D6	
Rufford St. N1	111	E1	
Rufford Twr. W3	126	B1	
Rufus Cl., Ruis.	84	E3	
Rufus St. N1	**12**	**D4**	
Rugby Av. N9	60	C1	
Rugby Av., Grnf.	86	A6	
Rugby Av., Wem.	87	E5	
Rugby Cl., Har.	68	B5	
Rugby Gdns., Dag.	100	C6	
Rugby Rd. NW9	70	B4	
Rugby Rd. W4	126	E2	
Rugby Rd., Dag.	100	B7	
Rugby Rd., Twick.	144	B6	
Rugby St. WC1	**10**	**C6**	
Rugby St. WC1	111	F4	
Rugg St. E14	114	A7	
Ruislip Cl., Grnf.	103	H4	
Ruislip Rd., Grnf.	103	G3	
Ruislip Rd., Nthlt.	102	D3	
Ruislip Rd. E. W7	104	B4	
Ruislip Rd. E. W13	104	A4	
Ruislip Rd. E., Grnf.	103	G3	
Ruislip St. SW17	167	J4	
Rum Cl. E1	113	F7	
Rumbold Rd. SW6	129	E7	
Rumsey Cl., Hmptn.	161	F6	
Rumsey Ms. N4	93	H3	
Monsell Rd.			
Rumsey Rd. SW9	151	F3	
Runbury Circle NW9	88	D2	
Runcorn Cl. N17	76	E4	
Runcorn Pl. W11	108	B7	
Rundell Cres. NW4	71	H5	
Runes Cl., Mitch.	185	G4	
Runnel Fld., Har.	86	B3	
Running Horse Yd., Brent.	125	H6	
Pottery Rd.			
Runnymede SW19	185	G1	
Runnymede Cl., Twick.	143	H6	
Runnymede Ct., Croy.	202	C2	
Runnymede Cres. SW16	186	D1	
Runnymede Gdns., Grnf.	104	A2	
Runnymede Gdns., Twick.	143	H6	
Runnymede Rd., Twick.	143	H6	
Runway, The, Ruis.	84	B5	
Rupack St. SE16	133	F2	
St. Marychurch St.			
Rupert Av., Wem.	87	H5	
Rupert Ct. W1	**17**	**H5**	
Rupert Ct., W.Mol.	179	G4	
St. Peter's Rd.			
Rupert Gdns. SW9	151	H2	
Rupert Rd. N19	92	D3	
Holloway Rd.			
Rupert Rd. NW6	108	C2	
Rupert Rd. W4	127	E3	
Rupert St. W1	**17**	**H5**	
Rupert St. W1	110	D7	
Rural Way SW16	168	B7	
Ruscoe Rd. E16	115	F6	
Ruscombe Way, Felt.	141	J7	
Rush, The SW19	184	C1	
Kingston Rd.			
Rush Grn. Gdns., Rom.	101	J1	
Rush Grn. Rd., Rom.	101	J1	
Rush Gro. St. SE18	136	C4	
Rush Hill Ms. SW11	150	A3	
Rush Hill Rd.			
Rush Hill Rd. SW11	150	A3	
Rusham Rd. SW12	149	J6	
Rushbrook Cres. E17	77	J1	
Rushbrook Rd. SE9	175	F2	
Rushcroft Rd. E4	62	A7	
Rushcroft Rd. SW2	151	G4	
Rushden Cl. SE19	170	A7	
Rushden Gdns. NW7	55	J6	
Rushden Gdns., Ilf.	80	D3	
Rushdene SE2	138	D3	
Rushdene Av., Barn.	41	H7	
Rushdene Cl., Nthlt.	102	C3	
Rushdene Cres., Nthlt.	102	C2	
Rushdene Rd., Pnr.	66	D6	
Rushden Wk., Cars.	199	G1	
Paisley Rd.			
Rushett Cl., T.Ditt.	194	E1	
Rushett Rd., T.Ditt.	180	E7	
Rushey Cl., N.Mal.	182	D4	
Rushey Grn. SE6	154	B7	
Rushey Hill, Enf.	43	F4	
Rushey Mead SE4	154	A5	
Rushford Rd. SE4	153	J6	
Rushley Cl., Kes.	206	A4	
Rushmead E2	112/113	E3	
Florida St.			
Rushmead, Rich.	163	E3	
Rushmead Cl., Croy.	202	C4	

Rushmere Ct., Wor.Pk. 197 G2
The Av.
Rushmere Pl. SW19 166 A5
Rushmoor Cl., Pnr. 66 B4
Rushmore Cl., Brom. 192 B3
Rushmore Cres. E5 95 G4
Rushmore Rd.
Rushmore Rd. E5 95 F4
Rusholme Av., Dag. 101 G3
Rusholme Gro. SE19 170 B5
Rusholme Rd. SW15 148 B6
Rushout Av., Har. 68 E6
Rushton St. N1 12 C1
Rushton St. N1 112 A2
Rushworth Av. NW4 71 G3
Rushworth Gdns.
Rushworth Gdns. NW4 71 G4
Rushworth St. SE1 27 H3
Rushworth St. SE1 131 H2
Rushy Meadow La., Cars. 199 H2
Ruskin Av. E12 98 B6
Ruskin Av., Felt. 141 J6
Ruskin Av., Rich. 126 A7
Ruskin Av., Well. 158 A2
Ruskin Cl. NW11 72 E6
Ruskin Dr., Orp. 207 H3
Ruskin Dr., Well. 158 A3
Ruskin Dr., Wor.Pk. 197 H2
Ruskin Gdns. W5 105 G4
Ruskin Gdns., Har. 69 J4
Ruskin Gro., Well. 158 A2
Ruskin Pk. Ho. SE5 152 A3
Ruskin Rd. N17 76 C1
Ruskin Rd., Belv. 139 G4
Ruskin Rd., Cars. 199 J5
Ruskin Rd., Croy. 201 H2
Ruskin Rd., Islw. 144 C3
Ruskin Rd., Sthl. 102 E7
Ruskin Wk. N9 60 D2
Durham Rd.
Ruskin Wk. SE24 151 J5
Ruskin Wk., Brom. 192 C6
Ruskin Way SW19 185 G1
Rusland Av., Orp. 207 G3
Rusland Hts., Har. 68 B4
Rusland Pk. Rd.
Rusland Pk. Rd., Har. 68 B4
Rusper Cl. NW2 89 J3
Rusper Cl., Stan. 53 F4
Rusper Rd. N22 75 J2
Rusper Rd., Dag. 100 C6
Russell Av. N22 75 H2
Russell Cl. NW10 88 C7
Russell Cl. SE7 135 J7
Russell Cl. W4 127 F6
Russell Cl., Beck. 190 B3
Russell Cl., Bexh. 159 G4
Russell Cl., Ruis. 84 C2
Russell Ct. SW1 25 G2
Russell Dr., Stai. 140 A6
Russell Gdns. N20 57 H2
Russell Gdns. NW11 72 B6
Russell Gdns. W14 128 B3
Russell Gdns., Rich. 163 F2
Russell Gdns., West Dr. 120 D5
Russell Gdns. Ms. W14 128 B2
Russell Gro. NW7 54 E5
Russell Gro. SW9 131 G7
Russell Kerr Cl. W4 126 C7
Burlington La.
Russell La. N20 57 H2
Russell Mead, Har. 68 C1
Russell Pl. NW3 91 H5
Aspern Gro.
Russell Pl. SE16 133 H3
Onega Gate
Russell Rd. E4 61 J4
Russell Rd. E10 78 B6
Russell Rd. E16 115 G6
Russell Rd. E17 77 J3
Russell Rd. N8 74 D6
Russell Rd. N13 59 F6
Russell Rd. N15 76 B5
Russell Rd. N20 57 H2
Russell Rd. NW9 71 F6
Russell Rd. SW19 166 D7
Russell Rd. W14 128 B3
Russell Rd., Buck.H. 63 H1
Russell Rd., Mitch. 185 H3
Russell Rd., Nthlt. 85 J5
Russell Rd., Twick. 144 C6
Russell Rd., Walt. 178 A6
Russell Sq. WC1 10 A6
Russell Sq. WC1 110 D5
Russell St. WC2 18 B5
Russell St. WC2 111 F6
Russell Wk., Rich. 145 J6
Park Hill
Russell Way, Sutt. 198 D5
Russell's Footpath SW16 169 E5
Russet Cres. N7 93 F5
Stock Orchard Cres.
Russet Dr., Croy. 203 H1
Russets Cl. E4 62 D4
Larkshall Rd.
Russett Way SE13 154 B2
Conington Rd.
Russia Ct. EC2 20 A3
Russia Dock Rd. SE16 133 H1
Russia La. E2 113 F2
Russia Row EC2 20 A4
Russia Wk. SE16 133 H2
Rust Sq. SE5 36 B7
Rust Sq. SE5 132 A7
Rusthall Av. W4 126 D4
Rusthall Cl., Croy. 189 F6
Rustic Av. SW16 168 B7
Rustic Pl., Wem. 87 G4
Rustic Wk. E16 115 H6
Lambert Rd.
Rustington Wk., Mord. 184 C7
Ruston Av., Surb. 182 B7
Ruston Gdns. N14 42 A6
Farm La.
Ruston Ms. W11 108 B6
St. Marks Rd.
Ruston Rd. SE18 136 B3
Ruston St. E3 113 J1
Rutford Rd. SW16 168 E5
Ruth Cl., Stan. 69 J4
Rutherford Cl., Borwd. 38 C2
Rutherford Cl., Sutt. 199 G6
Rutherford St. SW1 33 H1
Rutherford St. SW1 130 D4
Rutherford Twr., Sthl. 103 H6
Rutherford Way, Bushey 52 A1
Rutherford Way, Wem. 88 A4
Rutherglen Rd. SE2 138 A6
Rutherwyke Cl., Epsom 197 G6
Ruthin Cl. NW9 70 E6
Ruthin Rd. SE3 135 G6
Ruthven St. E9 113 G1
Lauriston Rd.
Rutland Av., Sid. 158 A7
Rutland Cl. SW14 146 C3
Rutland Cl. SW19 167 H7
Rutland Rd.
Rutland Cl., Bex. 176 D1
Rutland Cl., Chess. 195 J6
Rutland Ct., Enf. 45 F5
Rutland Dr., Mord. 184 C6
Rutland Dr., Rich. 163 G1
Rutland Gdns. N4 75 H6
Rutland Gdns. SW7 23 H4
Rutland Gdns. SW7 129 H2
Rutland Gdns. W13 104 D5
Rutland Gdns., Croy. 202 B4
Rutland Gdns., Dag. 100 C5
Rutland Gdns. Ms. SW7 23 H4
Rutland Gate SW7 23 H4
Rutland Gate SW7 129 H2
Rutland Gate, Belv. 139 H5
Rutland Gate, Brom. 191 F4
Rutland Gate Ms. SW7 23 G4
Rutland Gro. W6 127 H5
Rutland Ms. NW8 108/109 E1
Boundary Rd.
Rutland Ms. E. SW7 23 G5
Rutland Ms. S. SW7 23 G5
Rutland Pk. NW2 89 J6
Rutland Pk. SE6 171 J2
Rutland Pk. Gdns. NW2 89 J6
Rutland Pk.
Rutland Pk. Mans. NW2 89 J6
Walm La.
Rutland Pl. EC1 11 J6
Rutland Pl., Bushey 52 A1
The Rutts
Rutland Rd. E7 98 A7
Rutland Rd. E9 113 F1
Rutland Rd. E11 79 H5
Rutland Rd. E17 78 A6
Rutland Rd. SW19 167 H7
Rutland Rd., Har. 67 J6
Rutland Rd., Hayes 121 G4
Rutland Rd., Ilf. 99 E4
Rutland Rd., Sthl. 103 G5
Rutland Rd., Twick. 162 A2
Rutland St. SW7 23 H5
Rutland St. SW7 129 H3
Rutland Wk. SE6 171 J2
Rutley Cl. SE17 35 G5
Rutlish Rd. SW19 184 D1
Rutter Gdns., Mitch. 185 F4
Rutters Cl., West Dr. 120 D2
Rutts, The, Bushey 52 A1
Rutts Ter. SE14 153 G1
Ruvigny Gdns. SW15 148 A3
Ruxley Cl., Epsom 196 B5
Ruxley Cl., Sid. 176 D6
Ruxley Cor. Ind. Est., Sid. 176 D6
Ruxley Cres., Esher 194 E6
Ruxley La., Epsom 196 D5
Ruxley Ms., Epsom 196 B5
Ruxley Ridge, Esher 194 D7
Ryalls Ct. N20 57 J3
Ryan Cl. SE3 155 J4
Ryan Cl., Ruis. 84 B1
Ryan Dr., Brent. 124 D6
Ryarsh Cres., Orp. 207 H4
Rycott Path SE22 152 D7
Lordship La.
Rycroft Way N17 76 C3
Ryculff Sq. SE3 155 F2
Rydal Cl. NW4 72 B1
Rydal Cres., Grnf. 105 E3
Rydal Dr., Bexh. 159 G1
Rydal Dr., W.Wick. 205 E2
Rydal Gdns. NW9 71 E5
Rydal Gdns. SW15 164 E5
Rydal Gdns., Houns. 143 H6
Rydal Gdns., Wem. 87 F1
Rydal Rd. SW16 168 D4
Rydal Way, Enf. 45 F6
Rydal Way, Ruis. 84 C4
Ryde Pl., Twick. 145 F6
Ryde Vale Rd. SW12 168 B2
Ryder Cl., Brom. 173 H5
Ryder Ct. SW1 25 G1
Ryder Dr. SE16 132 E5
Ryder Ms. E9 95 F5
Homerton High St.
Ryder St. SW1 25 G1
Ryder St. SW1 130 C1
Ryder Yd. SW1 25 G1
Ryders Ter. NW8 6 C1
Rydon St. N1 111 J1
St. Paul St.
Rydons Cl. SE9 156 B3
Rydston Cl. N7 93 F7
Sutterton St.
Rye, The N14 42 C7
Rye Cl., Bex. 159 H6
Rye Hill Pk. SE15 153 F4
Rye La. SE15 152 D1
Rye Pas. SE15 152 D3
Rye Rd. SE15 153 G4
Rye Wk. SW15 148 A5
Chartfield Av.
Rye Way, Edg. 53 J6
Canons Dr.
Ryecotes Mead SE21 170 B1
Ryecroft Av., Ilf. 80 E2
Ryecroft Av., Twick. 143 H7
Ryecroft Cres., Barn. 39 H5
Ryecroft Rd. SE13 154 C5
Ryecroft Rd. SW16 169 G6
Ryecroft Rd., Orp. 193 G6
Ryecroft St. SW6 148 E1
Ryedale SE22 152 E6
Ryefield Ct., Nthwd. 66 A2
Ryefield Cres.
Ryefield Cres., Nthwd. 66 A2
Ryefield Par., Nthwd. 66 A2
Ryefield Cres.
Ryefield Path SW15 165 G1
Ryefield Rd. SE19 169 J6
Ryelands Cres. SE12 155 J6
Ryfold Rd. SW19 166 D3
Ryhope Rd. N11 58 B4
Ryland Ho., Croy. 201 J3
Ryland Rd. NW5 92 B6
Rylandes Rd. NW2 89 G3
Rylett Cres. W12 127 F3
Rylett Rd. W12 127 F2
Rylston Rd. N13 60 A3
Rylston Rd. SW6 128 C6
Rymer Rd., Croy. 188 B7
Rymer St. SE24 151 H6
Rymill St. E16 136 D1
Rysbrack St. SW3 23 J5
Rysbrack St. SW3 129 J3
Rythe Cl., Chess. 195 G6
Ashlyns Way
Rythe Ct., T.Ditt. 180 D7
Rythe Rd., Esher 194 A5

S

Sabbarton St. E16 115 F6
Victoria Dock Rd.
Sabella Ct. E3 113 J2
Sabine Rd. SW11 149 J3
Sable Cl., Houns. 142 C3
Sable St. N1 93 H7
Canonbury Rd.
Sach Rd. E5 95 E2
Sackville Av., Brom. 205 G1
Sackville Cl., Har. 86 A3
Sackville Est. SW16 169 E3
Sackville Gdns., Ilf. 98 C1
Sackville Rd., Sutt. 198 D7
Sackville St. W1 17 G6
Sackville St. W1 110 C7
Sackville Way SE22 170 D1
Dulwich Common
Saddle Yd. W1 24 D1
Saddlers Cl., Barn. 39 H5
Barnet Rd.
Saddlers Cl., Borwd. 38 D6
Farriers Way
Saddlers Cl., Pnr. 51 G6
Saddlers Ms. SW8 151 F1
Portland Gro.
Saddlers Ms., Wem. 86 C4
The Boltons
Saddlers Path, Borwd. 38 D5
Saddlescombe Way N12 56 D5
Sadler Cl., Mitch. 185 J2
Sadlers Ride, W.Mol. 179 J2
Saffron Av. E14 114 D7
Saffron Cl. NW11 72 C5
Saffron Cl., Croy. 186 E6
Saffron Ct., Felt. 141 F7
Staines Rd.
Saffron Hill EC1 11 F6
Saffron Hill EC1 111 G4
Saffron Rd., Rom. 83 J2
Saffron St. EC1 19 F1
Saffron Way, Surb. 195 G1
Sage Cl. E6 116 C5
Bradley Stone Rd.
Sage St. E1 113 F7
Cable St.
Sage Way WC1 10 C4
Saigasso Cl. E16 116 A6
Royal Rd.
Sail St. SE11 34 D1
Sail St. SE11 131 F4
Sainfoin Rd. SW17 168 A2
Sainsbury Rd. SE19 170 B5
St. Agatha's Dr., Kings.T. 163 J6
St. Agathas Gro., Cars. 199 J1
St. Agnes Cl. E9 113 F1
Gore Rd.
St. Agnes Pl. SE11 35 G6
St. Agnes Pl. SE11 131 G6
St. Agnes Well EC1 112 A4
Old St.
St. Aidans Ct. W13 124/125 E2
St. Aidans Rd.
St. Aidans Ct., Bark. 118 B3
Choats Rd.
St. Aidan's Rd. SE22 152 E6
St. Aidans Rd. W13 125 E2
St. Albans Av. E6 116 C3
St. Alban's Av. W4 126 D4
St. Albans Av., Felt. 160 D5
St. Albans Cl. NW11 90 D1
St. Albans Cres. N22 75 G1
St. Alban's Cres., Wdf.Grn. 63 G7
St. Alban's Gdns., Tedd. 162 D5
St. Albans Gro. W8 22 B5
St. Albans Gro. W8 129 E3
St. Alban's Gro., Cars. 185 H7
St. Albans La. NW11 90 D1
West Heath Dr.
St. Albans Ms. W2 15 F1
St. Albans Ms. W2 109 G5
St. Alban's Pl. N1 111 H1
St. Albans Rd. NW5 92 A3
St. Albans Rd. NW10 106 E1
St. Albans Rd., Barn. 40 B1
St. Albans Rd., Ilf. 99 J1
St. Alban's Rd., Kings.T. 163 H6
St. Alban's Rd., Sutt. 198 C4
St. Alban's Rd., Wdf.Grn. 63 G7
St. Albans St. SW1 17 H6
St. Albans Ter. W6 128 B6
Margravine Rd.
St. Albans Twr. E4 61 J6
St. Alban's Vil. NW5 92 A3
Highgate Rd.
St. Alfege Pas. SE10 134 C6
St. Alfege Rd. SE7 136 A6
St. Alphage Gdns. EC2 20 A2

St. Alphage	112	A5
Highwalk EC2		
London Wall		
St. Alphage Wk., Edg.	70	C2
St. Alphege Rd. N9	45	F7
St. Alphonsus Rd.	150	C4
SW4		
St. Amunds Cl. SE6	172	A4
St. Andrew St. EC4	**19**	**F2**
St. Andrew St. EC4	111	G5
St. Andrews Av.,	86	D4
Wem.		
St. Andrew's Cl. N12	57	F4
Woodside Av.		
St. Andrews Cl. NW2	89	H3
St. Andrews Cl.	132/133	E5
SE16		
Ryder Dr.		
St. Andrew's Cl., Islw.	144	A1
St. Andrews Cl., Ruis.	84	D2
St. Andrews Cl., Stan.	69	F2
St. Andrew's Ct.	167	F2
SW18		
Waynflete St.		
St. Andrews Dr.,	69	F1
Stan.		
St. Andrew's Gro.	94	A1
N16		
St. Andrew's Hill EC4	**19**	**H5**
St. Andrew's Hill EC4	111	H7
St. Andrew's Ms. N16	94	B1
St. Andrews Ms. SE3	135	G7
Mycenae Rd.		
St. Andrews Pl. NW1	**8**	**E5**
St. Andrews Pl. NW1	110	B4
St. Andrews Rd. E11	78	E6
St. Andrews Rd. E13	115	H3
St. Andrews Rd. E17	77	G2
St. Andrews Rd. N9	45	F7
St. Andrews Rd. NW9	88	D1
St. Andrews Rd.	89	H6
NW10		
St. Andrews Rd.	72	C6
NW11		
St. Andrews Rd. W3	107	E7
St. Andrews Rd. W7	124	B2
Church Rd.		
St. Andrews Rd.	128	B6
W14		
St. Andrews Rd.,	199	H3
Cars.		
St. Andrews Rd.,	201	J4
Croy.		
Lower Coombe St.		
St. Andrews Rd., Enf.	44	A3
St. Andrew's Rd., Ilf.	80	C7
St. Andrew's Rd., Sid.	176	D3
St. Andrew's Rd.,	181	G6
Surb.		
St. Andrews Rd., Wat.	50	D3
St. Andrews Sq. W11	108	B6
St. Marks Rd.		
St. Andrew's Sq.,	181	G6
Surb.		
St. Andrews Twr.,	103	J7
Sthl.		
St. Andrews Way E3	114	B4
St. Anna Rd., Barn.	40	A5
Sampson Av.		
St. Anne St. E14	113	J6
Commercial Rd.		
St. Annes Av., Stai.	140	A7
St. Anne's Cl. N6	92	A3
Highgate W. Hill		
St. Anne's, Wat.	50	C4
St. Anne's Ct. W1	**17**	**H4**
St. Annes Gdns.	105	J3
NW10		
St. Annes Pas. E14	113	J6
Newell St.		
St. Annes Rd. E11	96	D2
St. Anne's Rd., Wem.	87	G5
St. Anne's Row E14	113	J6
Commercial Rd.		
St. Ann's, Bark.	117	F1
St. Ann's Cres. SW18	149	F6
St. Ann's Gdns. NW5	92	A6
Queens Cres.		
St. Ann's Hill SW18	149	E5
St. Ann's La. SW1	**25**	**J5**
St. Ann's Pk. Rd.	149	F6
SW18		
St. Ann's Pas. SW13	147	E3
St. Anns Rd. N9	60	C2
St. Ann's Rd. N15	75	H5
St. Ann's Rd. SW13	147	F2
St. Ann's Rd. W11	108	A7
St. Ann's Rd., Bark.	117	F1
Axe St.		
St. Ann's Rd., Har.	68	B6
St. Ann's St. SW1	**25**	**J5**
St. Ann's St. SW1	130	D3
St. Ann's Ter. NW8	**7**	**F1**
St. Ann's Ter. NW8	109	G2

St. Anns Vil. W11	128	A1
St. Anns Way,	201	H6
S.Croy.		
St. Anselm's Pl. W1	**16**	**D4**
St. Anselms Rd.,	121	J2
Hayes		
St. Anthonys Av.,	63	J6
Wdf.Grn.		
St. Anthonys Cl. E1	**29**	**H1**
St. Anthonys Cl. E1	132	D1
St. Anthonys Cl.	167	H2
SW17		
College Gdns.		
St. Anthony's Way,	141	J4
Felt.		
St. Antony's Rd. E7	97	H7
St. Arvans Cl., Croy.	202	B3
St. Asaph Rd. SE4	153	G3
St. Aubyn's Av.	166	C5
SW19		
St. Aubyns Av.,	143	G5
Houns.		
St. Aubyns Cl., Orp.	207	J3
St. Aubyns Gdns.,	207	J2
Orp.		
St. Aubyn's Rd.	170	C6
SE19		
St. Audrey Av., Bexh.	159	G2
St. Augustine's Av.	105	H2
W5		
St. Augustines Av.,	192	B5
Brom.		
St. Augustine's Av.,	201	J6
S.Croy.		
St. Augustine's Path	93	H5
N5		
St. Augustines Rd.	92	D7
NW1		
St. Augustine's Rd.,	139	F4
Belv.		
St. Austell Cl., Edg.	69	J2
St. Austell Rd. SE13	154	C2
St. Awdry's Rd., Bark.	99	G7
St. Awdry's Wk., Bark.	99	F7
Station Par.		
St. Barnabas Cl.	152	B5
SE22		
East Dulwich Gro.		
St. Barnabas Cl.,	190	C2
Beck.		
St. Barnabas Ct., Har.	67	J1
St. Barnabas Gdns.,	179	G5
W.Mol.		
St. Barnabas Rd. E17	78	A6
St. Barnabas Rd.,	168	A7
Mitch.		
St. Barnabas Rd.,	199	G5
Sutt.		
St. Barnabas Rd.,	79	H1
Wdf.Grn.		
St. Barnabas St. SW1	**32**	**C3**
St. Barnabas St. SW1	130	A5
St. Barnabas Ter. E9	95	G5
St. Barnabas Vil. SW8	151	E1
St. Bartholomews Cl.	171	F4
SE26		
St. Bartholomew's Rd.	116	B1
E6		
St. Benedict's Cl.	168	A5
SW17		
Church La.		
St. Benet's Cl. SW17	167	H2
College Gdns.		
St. Benet's Gro.,	185	F7
Cars.		
St. Bernards, Croy.	202	B3
St. Bernard's Cl.	170	A4
SE27		
St. Gothard Rd.		
St. Bernard's Rd. E6	116	A1
St. Blaise Av., Brom.	191	H2
St. Botolph Row EC3	**21**	**F4**
St. Botolph St. EC3	**21**	**F4**
St. Botolph St. EC3	112	C6
St. Bride St. EC4	**19**	**G3**
St. Bride St. EC4	111	H6
St. Bride's Av. EC4	111	H6
New Br. St.		
St. Brides Av., Edg.	69	J1
St. Brides Cl., Erith	138	D2
St. Katherines Rd.		
St. Bride's Pas. EC4	**19**	**G4**
St. Catherines Cl.	167	H2
SW17		
College Gdns.		
St. Catherines Dr.	153	G2
SE14		
Kitto Rd.		
St. Catherine's Ms.	**31**	**J1**
SW3		
St. Catherines Rd. E4	62	A2

St. Chads Cl., Surb.	181	F7
St. Chad's Gdns.,	82	E7
Rom.		
St. Chad's Pl. WC1	**10**	**B3**
St. Chad's Pl. WC1	111	E3
St. Chad's Rd., Rom.	82	E6
St. Chad's St. WC1	**10**	**B3**
St. Chad's St. WC1	111	E3
St. Charles Pl. W10	108	B5
Chesterton Rd.		
St. Charles Sq. W10	108	A5
St. Christopher's Cl.	144	B1
Islw.		
St. Christopher's Dr.,	102	B7
Hayes		
St. Christophers	187	G3
Gdns., Th.Hth.		
St. Christophers Ms.,	200	C5
Wall.		
St. Christopher's Pl.	**16**	**C3**
W1		
St. Clair Dr., Wor.Pk.	197	H3
St. Clair Rd. E13	115	H2
St. Clair's Rd., Croy.	202	B2
St. Clare Business	161	J6
Pk., Hmptn.		
St. Clare Cl., Ilf.	80	C2
St. Clare St. EC3	**21**	**F4**
St. Clements Cl. EC4	112	A7
Clements La.		
St. Clements Cl. N7	93	G6
Arundel Sq.		
St. Clements Hts.	170	D3
SE26		
St. Clement's La. WC2	**18**	**D4**
St. Clements St. N7	93	G6
St. Cloud Rd. SE27	169	J4
St. Crispins Cl. NW3	91	H4
St. Crispins Cl., Sthl.	103	F6
St. Cross St. EC1	**19**	**F1**
St. Cross St. EC1	111	G5
St. Cuthberts Gdns.,	51	F7
Pnr.		
Westfield Pk.		
St. Cuthberts Rd. N13	59	G6
St. Cuthberts Rd.	90	C6
NW2		
St. Cyprian's St.	167	J4
SW17		
St. Davids Cl.	132/133	E5
SE16		
Masters Dr.		
St. Davids Cl., Wem.	88	C3
St. David's Cl.,	190	B7
W.Wick.		
St. David's Ct. E17	78	C3
St. Davids Dr., Edg.	69	J1
St. Davids Pl. NW4	71	H7
St. Davids Sq. E14	134	B5
St. Denis Rd. SE27	170	A4
St. Dionis Rd. SW6	148	C2
St. Donatts Rd. SE14	153	J1
St. Dunstan's All. EC3	**20**	**D5**
St. Dunstans Av. W3	106	D7
St. Dunstans Cl.,	121	J4
Hayes		
St. Dunstan's Ct. EC4	111	G6
Fleet St.		
St. Dunstans Gdns.	106	D7
W3		
St. Dunstans Av.		
St. Dunstan's Hill EC3	**20**	**D6**
St. Dunstan's Hill EC3	112	B7
St. Dunstan's Hill,	198	B5
Sutt.		
St. Dunstan's La. EC3	**20**	**D6**
St. Dunstan's La.,	190	C6
Beck.		
St. Dunstan's Rd. E7	97	J6
St. Dunstans Rd.	188	C4
SE25		
St. Dunstans Rd. W6	128	A5
St. Dunstans Rd. W7	124	B2
St. Dunstans Rd.,	142	C2
Houns.		
St. Edmunds Cl. NW8	109	J1
St. Edmunds Ter.		
St. Edmunds Cl.	167	H2
SW17		
College Gdns.		
St. Edmunds Cl.,	138	D2
Erith		
St. Katherines Rd.		
St. Edmunds Dr., Stan.	68	D1
St. Edmund's La.,	143	H7
Twick.		
St. Edmunds Rd. N9	44	D7
St. Edmunds Rd., Ilf.	80	C6
St. Edmunds Sq.	127	J6
SW13		
St. Edmunds Ter.	**7**	**H1**
NW8		
St. Edmunds Ter.	109	H1
NW8		

St. Edwards Cl.	72	D6
NW11		
St. Egberts Way E4	62	C1
St. Elmo Rd. W12	127	F1
St. Elmos Rd. SE16	133	H2
St. Erkenwald Ms.,	117	G1
Bark.		
St. Erkenwald Rd.		
St. Erkenwald Rd.	117	G1
Bark.		
St. Ermin's Hill SW1	**25**	**H5**
St. Ervans Rd. W10	108	B5
St. Fabian Twr. E4	61	J6
Iris Way		
St. Faiths Cl., Enf.	43	J1
St. Faith's Rd. SE21	169	H1
St. Fillans Rd. SE6	172	C1
St. Francis Cl., Orp.	193	H6
St. Francis Cl., Wat.	50	B1
St. Francis Rd. SE22	152	B4
St. Francis Twr. E4	61	J6
Iris Way		
St. Francis Way, Ilf.	99	H4
St. Frideswides Ms.	114	C6
E14		
Lodore St.		
St. Gabriel's Cl. E11	97	H1
St. Gabriels Rd. NW2	90	A5
St. George St. W1	**17**	**E4**
St. George St. W1	110	B6
St. Georges Av. E7	97	H7
St. Georges Av. N7	92	D4
St. Georges Av. NW9	70	C4
St. George's Av. W5	125	G2
St. Georges Av.,	103	F7
Sthl.		
St. Georges Circ. SE1	**27**	**G5**
St. Georges Circ. SE1	131	H3
St. Georges Cl.	72	C6
NW11		
St. George's Cl. SW8	150	C1
Patmore Est.		
St. Georges Cl.,	86	D3
Wem.		
St. Georges Ct. E6	116	C4
St. Georges Ct. EC4	**19**	**G3**
St. Georges Ct. SW7	**22**	**C5**
St. George's Dr. SW1	**33**	**F3**
St. George's Dr. SW1	130	B4
St. Georges Dr., Wat.	50	E3
St. Georges Flds. W2	**15**	**H4**
St. Georges Flds. W2	109	H6
St. George's Gdns.,	196	B2
Surb.		
Hamilton Av.		
St. Georges Gro.	167	G3
SW17		
St. Georges Gro. Est.	167	G3
SW17		
St. Georges Ind. Est.,	163	G5
Kings.T.		
St. Georges La. EC3	**20**	**D5**
St. Georges Ms. NW1	91	J7
Regents Pk. Rd.		
St. Georges Pl.,	162	D1
Twick.		
Church St.		
St. Georges Rd. E7	97	H6
St. Georges Rd. E10	96	C3
St. Georges Rd. N9	60	D3
St. Georges Rd. N13	59	F3
St. Georges Rd.	72	C6
NW11		
St. Georges Rd. SE1	**27**	**F5**
St. Georges Rd. SE1	131	G3
St. Georges Rd.	166	C6
SW19		
St. Georges Rd. W4	126	B2
St. Georges Rd. W7	124	C1
St. George's Rd.,	190	B1
Beck.		
St. Georges Rd.,	192	C2
Brom.		
St. George's Rd., Dag.	100	E5
St. Georges Rd., Felt.	160	D4
St. George's Rd., Ilf.	80	C7
St. George's Rd.,	164	A7
Kings.T.		
St. George's Rd.,	186	B3
Mitch.		
St. George's Rd., Orp.	193	G6
St. Georges Rd., Rich.	145	J3
St. George's Rd., Sid.	176	D6
St. Georges Rd.,	145	E5
Twick.		
St. George's Rd., Wall.	200	B5
St. Georges Rd. W.,	192	B1
Brom.		
St. Georges Sq. E7	97	H7
St. Georges Sq. E14	113	H7
Narrow St.		
St. Georges Sq. SE8	133	J4
St. George's Sq. SW1	**33**	**H3**
St. George's Sq. SW1	130	D5

Name	Page	Grid
St. George's Sq., N.Mal.	182/183	E3
High St.		
St. George's Sq. Ms. SW1	**33**	**H4**
St. George's Sq. Ms. SW1	130	D5
St. Georges Ter. NW1	91	J7
Regents Pk. Rd.		
St. Georges Wk., Croy.	201	J3
St. Georges Way SE15	**36**	**D6**
St. Georges Way SE15	132	B6
St. Gerards Cl. SW4	150	C5
St. German's Pl. SE3	155	G1
St. Germans Rd. SE23	171	H1
St. Giles Av., Dag.	101	H7
St. Giles Cl., Dag.	101	H7
St. Giles Av.		
St. Giles Cl., Orp.	207	G5
St. Giles High St. WC2	**17**	**J3**
St. Giles High St. WC2	110	D6
St. Giles Pas. WC2	**17**	**J4**
St. Gilles Rd. SE5	132	B7
St. Gilles Ho. E2	113	G2
St. Gothard Rd. SE27	170	A4
St. Gregory Cl., Ruis.	84	C4
St. Helena Rd. SE16	133	G4
St. Helena St. WC1	**10**	**E4**
St. Helens Cres. SW16	187	F1
St. Helens Rd.		
St. Helens Gdns. W10	108	A6
St. Helens Pl. EC3	**20**	**D3**
St. Helens Rd. SW16	187	F1
St. Helen's Rd. W13	124/125	E1
Dane Rd.		
St. Helens Rd., Erith	138	D2
St. Helens Rd., Ilf.	80	C6
St. Helier Av., Mord.	185	F7
St. Heliers Av., Houns.	143	G5
St. Heliers Rd. E10	78	C6
St. Hildas Cl. NW6	90	A7
St. Hildas Cl. SW17	167	H2
St. Hilda's Wk. SW13	127	H6
St. Hughe's Cl. SW17	167	H2
College Gdns.		
St. Hughs Rd. SE20	188/189	E1
Ridsdale Rd.		
St. James Av. N20	57	H3
St. James Av. W13	124	D1
St. James Av., Sutt.	198	D5
St. James Cl. N20	57	H3
St. James Cl. SE18	137	F5
Congleton Gro.		
St. James Cl., Barn.	41	G4
St. James Cl., N.Mal.	183	F5
St. James Cl., Ruis.	84	C2
St. James Gdns., Wem.	87	G7
St. James Gate NW1	92	D7
St. Paul's Cres.		
St. James Gro. SW11	149	J2
Reform St.		
St. James Ms. E14	134	C3
St. James Ms. E17	77	H5
St. James's St.		
St. James Rd. E15	97	F5
St. James Rd. N9	60/61	E2
Queens Rd.		
St. James Rd., Cars.	199	H3
St. James Rd., Kings.T.	181	H2
St. James Rd., Mitch.	168	A7
St. James Rd., Surb.	181	G6
St. James Rd., Sutt.	198	D5
St. James St. W6	127	J5
St. James Wk. SE15	132	C7
Commercial Way		
St. James Way, Sid.	177	E5
St. James's SE14	153	H1
St. James's Av. E2	113	F2
St. James's Av., Beck.	189	H3
St. James's Av., Hmptn.	161	J5
St. James's Cl. SW17	167	J2
St. James's Dr.		
St. James's Cotts., Rich.	145	G5
Paradise Rd.		
St. James's Ct. SW1	**25**	**G5**
St. James's Ct. SW1	130	C3
St. James's Cres. SW9	151	G3
St. James's Dr. SW12	167	J1
St. James's Dr. SW17	167	J1
St. James's Gdns. W11	128	B1
St. James's La. N10	74	B4
St. James's Mkt. SW1	**17**	**H6**
St. James's Palace SW1	**25**	**G3**
St. James's Palace SW1	130	C1
St. James's Pk. SW1	**25**	**H3**
St. James's Pk. SW1	130	D2
St. James's Pk., Croy.	187	J7
St. James's Pas. EC3	**21**	**E4**
St. James's Pl. SW1	**25**	**F2**
St. James's Pl. SW1	130	C1
St. James's Rd. SE1	**37**	**J3**
St. James's Rd. SE1	132	D5
St. James's Rd. SE16	**29**	**J5**
St. James's Rd. SE16	132	D3
St. James's Rd., Croy.	187	H7
St. James's Row EC1	**11**	**F5**
St. James's Sq. SW1	25	G1
St. James's Sq. SW1	130	C1
St. James's St. E17	77	H5
St. James's St. SW1	**25**	**F1**
St. James's St. SW1	130	C1
St. James's Ter. NW8	**7**	**J1**
St. James's Ter. Ms. NW8	109	J1
St. James's Wk. EC1	**11**	**G5**
St. James's Wk. EC1	111	H4
St. Joans Rd. N9	60	C1
St. John Fisher Rd., Erith	138	D3
St. John St. EC1	11	H6
St. John St. EC1	111	H4
St. Johns Av. N11	57	J5
St. John's Av. NW10	107	F1
St. John's Av. SW15	148	A5
St. John's Ch. Rd. E9	95	F5
St. Johns Cl. N14	42	C6
Chase Rd.		
St. John's Cl. SW6	128	D7
Dawes Rd.		
St. John's Cl., Wem.	87	H5
St. John's Cotts. SE20	171	F7
Maple Rd.		
St. Johns Cotts., Rich.	145	H4
Kew Foot Rd.		
St. Johns Ct., Buck.H.	63	H1
St. John's Ct., Islw.	144	C2
St. Johns Cres. SW9	151	G3
St. Johns Dr. SW18	166	E1
St. John's Est. N1	**12**	**C2**
St. John's Est. N1	112	A2
St. John's Est. SE1	**29**	**F3**
St. John's Gdns. W11	108	C7
St. Johns Gro. N19	92	C2
St. Johns Gro. SW13	147	F2
Terrace Gdns.		
St. Johns Gro., Rich.	145	H4
Kew Foot Rd.		
St. John's Hill SW11	149	G4
St. John's Hill Gro. SW11	149	G4
St. John's La. EC1	**11**	**G6**
St. John's La. EC1	111	H4
St. John's Ms. W11	108	D6
Ledbury Rd.		
St. Johns Par., Sid.	176	A4
Church Rd.		
St. John's Pk. SE3	135	F7
St. Johns Pas. SE23	171	F1
Davids Rd.		
St. John's Pas. SW19	166	B6
Ridgway Pl.		
St. John's Path EC1	**11**	**G6**
St. Johns Pathway SE23	171	F1
Devonshire Rd.		
St. John's Pl. EC1	**11**	**G6**
St. John's Rd. E4	62	B3
St. John's Rd. E6	116	B1
Ron Leighton Way		
St. Johns Rd. E16	115	G6
St. John's Rd. E17	78	B2
St. John's Rd. N15	76	B6
St. Johns Rd. NW11	72	C6
St. John's Rd. SE20	171	F7
St. John's Rd. SW11	149	H4
St. John's Rd. SW19	166	B7
St. John's Rd., Bark.	117	H1
St. John's Rd., Cars.	199	H3
St. Johns Rd., Croy.	201	H3
Sylverdale Rd.		
St. John's Rd., E.Mol.	180	A4
St. John's Rd., Felt.	161	E4
St. John's Rd., Har.	68	C6
St. Johns Rd., Ilf.	81	G7
St. John's Rd., Islw.	144	C2
St. John's Rd., Kings.T.	181	F2
St. Johns Rd., Loug.	48	C2
St. John's Rd., N.Mal.	182	C3
St. John's Rd., Orp.	193	G6
St. John's Rd., Rich.	145	H4
St. John's Rd., Sid.	176	B4
St. Johns Rd., Sthl.	122	E3
St. Johns Rd., Sutt.	198	D2
St. John's Rd., Well.	158	B3
St. John's Rd., Wem.	87	G4
St. John's Sq. EC1	**11**	**G6**
St. Johns Ter. E7	97	H6
St. Johns Ter. SE18	137	F6
St. Johns Ter. SW15	164	D4
Kingston Vale		
St. Johns Ter. W10	108	A4
Harrow Rd.		
St. Johns Vale SE8	154	A2
St. Johns Vil. N19	92	D2
St. John's Vil. W8	**22**	**B6**
St. Johns Way N19	92	D1
St. John's Wd. Ct. NW8	**7**	**F4**
St. John's Wd. High St. NW8	**7**	**F2**
St. John's Wd. High St. NW8	109	G2
St. John's Wd. Pk. NW8		
St. John's Wd. Pk. NW8	109	G1
St. John's Wd. Rd. NW8	**6**	**E5**
St. John's Wd. Rd. NW8	109	G4
St. John's Wd. Ter. NW8	**7**	**G1**
St. John's Wd. Ter. NW8	109	G2
St. Josephs Cl. W10	108	B5
Bevington Rd.		
St. Joseph's Cl., Orp.	207	J4
St. Josephs Ct. SE7	135	H6
St. Josephs Dr., Sthl.	123	E1
St. Josephs Gro. NW4	71	H4
St. Josephs Rd. N9	45	E7
St. Joseph's Vale SE3	154	D2
St. Jude St. N16	94	B5
St. Jude's Rd. E2	113	E2
St. Julian's Cl. SW16	169	G4
St. Julian's Fm. Rd. SE27	169	G4
St. Julian's Rd. NW6	90	C7
St. Katharines Prec. NW1	**8**	**D1**
St. Katharine's Way E1	**29**	**G1**
St. Katharine's Way E1	132	C1
St. Katherines Rd., Erith	138	D2
St. Katherine's Row EC3	**21**	**E4**
St. Katherine's Wk. W11	108	A7
Hunt St.		
St. Keverne Rd. SE9	174	B4
St. Kilda Rd. W13	124	D1
St. Kilda Rd., Orp.	207	J1
St. Kilda's Rd. N16	94	A1
St. Kilda's Rd., Har.	68	B6
St. Kitts Ter. SE19	170	B5
St. Laurence Cl. NW6	108	A1
St. Lawrence Cl., Edg.	53	J7
St. Lawrence Dr., Pnr.	66	B6
St. Lawrence St. E14	134	C1
St. Lawrence Ter. W10	108	B5
St. Lawrence Way SW9	151	G2
St. Leonards Av. E4	62	E6
St. Leonards Av., Har.	69	G4
St. Leonard's Cl., Well.	158	A3
Hook La.		
St. Leonards Ct. N1	**12**	**A3**
St. Leonards Ct. N1	112	A3
St. Leonard's Gdns., Houns.	122	E7
St. Leonards Gdns., Ilf.	99	F5
St. Leonards Ri., Orp.	207	H4
St. Leonards Rd. E14	114	B5
St. Leonards Rd. NW10	106	D4
St. Leonard's Rd. SW14	146	B3
St. Leonards Rd. W13	105	F7
St. Leonards Rd., Croy.	201	H3
St. Leonards Rd., Esher	194	C6
St. Leonard's Rd., Surb.	181	G5
St. Leonards Rd., T.Ditt.	180	D6
St. Leonards Sq. NW5	92	A6
St. Leonard's Sq., Surb.	181	G5
St. Leonard's Rd.		
St. Leonards St. E3	114	B3
St. Leonard's Ter. SW3	**31**	**J4**
St. Leonard's Ter. SW3	129	J5
St. Leonards Wk. SW16	169	F7
St. Loo Av. SW3	31	H5
St. Loo Av. SW3	129	H6
St. Louis Rd. SE27	169	J4
St. Loy's Rd. N17	76	B2
St. Lucia Dr. E15	115	F1
St. Luke's Av. SW4	150	D4
St. Luke's Av., Ilf.	99	E5
St. Lukes Cl. EC1	111	J4
Old St.		
St. Luke's Cl. SE25	189	E6
St. Luke's Est. EC1	**12**	**B4**
St. Lukes Est. EC1	112	A3
St. Lukes Ms. W11	108	C6
Basing St.		
St. Lukes Pas., Kings.T.	181	J1
St. Lukes Rd. W11	108	C5
St. Lukes Sq. E16	115	F6
St. Luke's St. SW3	**31**	**G3**
St. Luke's St. SW3	129	H5
St. Luke's Yd. W9	108	C2
St. Malo Av. N9	61	F3
St. Margarets, Bark.	117	G1
St. Margarets Av. N15	75	H4
St. Margarets Av. N20	57	F2
St. Margarets Av., Har.	85	J3
St. Margaret's Av., Sid.	175	G3
St. Margaret's Av., Sutt.	198	B3
St. Margaret's Ct. SE1	**28**	**A2**
St. Margarets Cres. SW15	147	H5
St. Margaret's Dr., Twick.	144	E5
St. Margaret's Gro. E11	97	F3
St. Margarets Gro. SE18	137	F6
St. Margarets Gro., Twick.	144	D6
St. Margarets La. W8	**22**	**A6**
St. Margarets La. W8	128	E3
St. Margarets Pas. SE13	154/155	E3
Church Ter.		
St. Margarets Rd. E12	97	J2
St. Margaret's Rd. N17	76	B3
St. Margaret's Rd. NW10	107	J3
St. Margarets Rd. SE4	153	J4
St. Margarets Rd. W7	124	B2
St. Margarets Rd., Edg.	54	B5
St. Margarets Rd., Islw.	144	E4
St. Margarets Rd., Twick.	144	E4
St. Margarets Sq. SE4	153	J4
Adelaide Av.		
St. Margaret's St. SW1	**26**	**A4**
St. Margaret's St. SW1	130	D4
St. Margaret's Ter. SE18	137	F5
St. Mark St. E1	**21**	**G4**
St. Mark St. E1	112	C6
St. Marks Cl. SE10	134	C7
Ashburnham Pl.		
St. Mark's Cl. W11	108	B6
Lancaster Rd.		
St. Mark's Cl., Barn.	40	E3
St. Marks Cres. NW1	110	A1
St. Marks Gate E9	95	J7
Cadogan Ter.		
St. Mark's Gro. SW10	**30**	**B7**
St. Mark's Gro. SW10	129	E6
St. Mark's Hill, Surb.	181	H6
St. Mark's Pl. SW19	166	C6
Wimbledon Hill Rd.		

Name	Page	Grid
St. Marks Pl. W11	108	B6
St. Marks Ri. E8	94	C5
St. Marks Rd. SE25	188	D4
Coventry Rd.		
St. Mark's Rd. W5	125	H1
The Common		
St. Marks Rd. W7	124	B2
St. Marks Rd. W10	108	A6
St. Marks Rd. W11	108	B6
St. Marks Rd., Brom.	191	H3
St. Marks Rd., Enf.	44	C6
St. Marks Rd., Mitch.	185	J2
St. Mark's Rd., Tedd.	163	E7
St. Marks Sq. NW1	110	A1
St. Martins Av. E6	116	A2
St. Martins Cl. NW1	110	C1
St. Martins Cl., Enf.	44	E1
St. Martins Cl., Erith	138	D2
St. Helens Rd.		
St. Martin's Cl., Wat.	50	C4
Muirfield Rd.		
St. Martin's Cl., West Dr.	120	A3
St. Martin's Rd.		
St. Martins Ct. WC2	110	D7
St. Martin's La.		
St. Martins Est. SW2	169	G1
St. Martin's La. WC2	**18**	**A5**
St. Martin's La. WC2	110	E7
St. Martin's Ms. WC2	**18**	**A6**
St. Martin's Pl. WC2	**18**	**A6**
St. Martins Pl. WC2	110	E7
St. Martins Rd. N9	60	E2
St. Martin's Rd. SW9	151	F2
St. Martin's Rd., West Dr.	120	A3
St. Martin's St. WC2	**17**	**J6**
St. Martins Way SW17	167	F3
St. Martin's-le-Grand EC1	**19**	**J3**
St. Martin's-le-Grand EC1	111	J6
St. Mary Abbots Pl. W8	128	C3
St. Mary Abbots Ter. W14	128	C3
St. Mary at Hill EC3	**20**	**D6**
St. Mary at Hill EC3	112	B7
St. Mary Av., Wall.	200	A3
St. Mary Axe EC3	**20**	**D4**
St. Mary Axe EC3	112	B6
St. Mary Rd. E17	78	A4
St. Mary St. SE18	136	C4
St. Marychurch St. SE16	133	F2
St. Marys, Bark.	117	G1
St. Marys App. E12	98	C5
St. Marys Av. E11	79	H6
St. Mary's Av. N3	72	B2
St. Mary's Av., Brom.	191	E3
St. Mary's Av., Stai.	140	A7
St. Mary's Av., Tedd.	162	C6
St. Mary's Av. Cen., Sthl.	123	H4
St. Mary's Av. N., Sthl.	123	H4
St. Mary's Av. S., Sthl.	123	H4
St. Marys Cl. N17	76	D1
Kemble Rd.		
St. Marys Cl., Epsom	197	G7
St. Mary's Cl., Stai.	140	A7
St. Mary's Cl., Sun.	178	A4
Green Way		
St. Marys Ct. E6	116	C4
St. Mary's Ct. SE7	136	A7
St. Mary's Ct. W5	125	G2
St. Mary's Rd.		
St. Mary's Cres. NW4	71	H3
St. Marys Cres., Islw.	124	A7
St. Mary's Cres., Stai.	140	A7
St. Marys Dr., Felt.	141	F7
St. Mary's Gdns. SE11	**35**	**F1**
St. Mary's Gdns. SE11	131	G4
St. Mary's Gate W8	**22**	**A6**
St. Mary's Gate W8	128	E3
St. Marys Grn. W2	73	F3
Thomas More Way		
St. Mary's Gro. N1	93	H6
St. Mary's Gro. SW13	147	H3
St. Mary's Gro. W4	126	B6
St. Mary's Gro., Rich.	145	J4
St. Marys Mans. W2	**14**	**E1**
St. Marys Mans. W2	109	E5
St. Mary's Ms. NW6	90/91	E7
Priory Rd.		
St. Mary's Ms., Rich.	163	F3
Back La.		
St. Marys Path N1	111	H1
St. Mary's Pl. SE9	156	D6
Eltham High St.		
St. Mary's Pl. W5	125	G2
St. Mary's Rd.		
St. Mary's Pl. W8	**22**	**B6**
St. Mary's Pl. W8	128	E3
St. Marys Rd. E10	96	C3
St. Mary's Rd. E13	115	H2
St. Marys Rd. N8	74/75	E4
High St.		
St. Marys Rd. N9	61	F1
St. Mary's Rd. NW10	107	E1
St. Mary's Rd. NW11	72	B7
St. Mary's Rd. SE15	153	F1
St. Mary's Rd. SE25	188	B3
St. Mary's Rd. (Wimbledon) SW19	166	B5
St. Mary's Rd. W5	125	G2
St. Mary's Rd., Barn.	41	J7
St. Mary's Rd., Bex.	177	J1
St. Mary's Rd., E.Mol.	180	A5
St. Mary's Rd., Ilf.	99	F2
St. Marys Rd., Surb.	181	G6
St. Marys Rd. (Long Ditton), Surb.	181	F7
St. Mary's Rd., Wor.Pk.	197	E2
St. Marys Sq. W2	**14**	**E1**
St. Marys Sq. W2	109	G5
St. Mary's Sq. W5	125	G2
St. Mary's Rd.		
St. Marys Ter. W2	**14**	**E1**
St. Marys Ter. W2	109	G5
St. Marys Vw., Har.	69	F5
St. Mary's Wk. SE11	**35**	**F1**
St. Mary's Wk. SE11	131	G4
St. Mary's Way, Chig.	64	D5
St. Matthew St. SW1	**25**	**H6**
St. Matthew's Av., Surb.	195	H1
St. Matthew's Dr., Brom.	192	C3
St. Matthew's Rd. SW2	151	F4
St. Matthews Rd. W5	125	H1
The Common		
St. Matthew's Row E2	**13**	**H4**
St. Matthew's Row E2	112	D1
St. Matthias Cl. NW9	71	F5
St. Maur Rd. SW6	148	C1
St. Merryn Cl. SE18	137	G7
St. Michael's All. EC3	**20**	**C4**
St. Michaels Av. N9	45	F7
St. Michael's Av., Wem.	88	A6
St. Michaels Cl. E16	116	A5
Fulmer Rd.		
St. Michael's Cl. N3	72	C2
St. Michael's Cl. N12	57	H5
St. Michaels Cl., Brom.	192	B3
St. Michaels Cl., Erith	138	D2
St. Helens Rd.		
St. Michaels Cl., Wor.Pk.	197	F2
St. Michaels Cres., Pnr.	67	E6
St. Michaels Gdns. W10	108	B5
St. Lawrence Ter.		
St. Michaels Rd. NW2	89	J4
St. Michael's Rd. SW9	151	F2
St. Michaels Rd., Croy.	201	J1
St. Michaels Rd., Wall.	200	C6
St. Michaels Rd., Well.	158	B3
St. Michaels St. W2	**15**	**F3**
St. Michael's St. W2	109	H5
St. Michaels Ter. N22	75	E2
St. Mildred's Ct. EC2	112	A6
Poultry		
St. Mildreds Rd. SE12	155	E7
St. Nicholas Glebe SW17	168	A5
St. Nicholas Rd. SE18	137	J5
St. Nicholas Rd., Sutt.	198	E5
St. Nicholas Rd., T.Ditt.	180	C6
St. Nicholas St. SE8	154	A1
Lucas St.		
St. Nicholas Way, Sutt.	198	E4
St. Nicolas La., Chis.	192	B1
St. Ninian's Ct. N20	57	J3
St. Norbert Grn. SE4	153	H4
St. Norbert Rd. SE4	153	H5
St. Olaf's Rd. SW6	128	B7
St. Olaves Ct. EC2	**20**	**B4**
St. Olave's Est. SE1	**29**	**E3**
St. Olaves Gdns. SE11	**34**	**E1**
St. Olaves Rd. E6	116	D1
St. Olave's Wk. SW16	186	C2
St. Olav's Sq. SE16	133	F3
St. Oswald's Pl. SE11	**34**	**C4**
St. Oswald's Pl. SE11	131	F5
St. Oswald's Rd. SW16	187	H1
St. Oswulf St. SW1	**33**	**J2**
St. Pancras Way NW1	92	C7
St. Patrick's Ct., Wdf.Grn.	63	E7
St. Paul St. N1	111	J1
St. Paul's All. EC4	111	H6
St. Paul's Chyd.		
St. Paul's Av. NW2	89	H6
St. Paul's Av. SE16	133	G1
St. Pauls Av., Har.	69	J5
St. Paul's Chyd. EC4	**19**	**H4**
St. Paul's Chyd. EC4	111	H6
St. Paul's Cl. SE7	136	A5
St. Paul's Cl. W5	125	J1
St. Paul's Cl., Cars.	199	H1
St. Pauls Cl., Chess.	195	G4
St. Paul's Cl., Hayes	121	G5
St. Paul's Cl., Houns.	143	E2
St. Paul's Ct. W14	128	A4
Colet Gdns.		
St. Pauls Ctyd. SE8	134	A7
Deptford High St.		
St. Pauls Cray Rd., Chis.	193	G1
St. Paul's Cres. NW1	92	D7
St. Pauls Dr. E15	96	D5
St. Paul's Ms. NW1	92	D7
St. Paul's Cres.		
St. Paul's Pl. N1	94	A6
St. Paul's Ri. N13	59	H6
St. Paul's Rd. N1	93	H6
St. Paul's Rd. N17	60	D7
St. Paul's Rd., Bark.	117	F1
St. Paul's Rd., Brent.	125	G6
St. Paul's Rd., Erith	139	J7
St. Paul's Rd., Rich.	145	J3
St. Paul's Rd., Th.Hth.	187	J3
St. Paul's Shrubbery N1	94	A6
St. Pauls Sq., Brom.	191	G2
St. Paul's Ter. SE17	**35**	**H5**
St. Pauls Twr. E10	78	B7
St. Pauls Wk., Kings.T.	164	A7
Alexandra Rd.		
St. Paul's Way E3	113	J5
St. Paul's Way E14	113	J5
St. Paul's Way N3	56	E7
St. Pauls Wd. Hill, Orp.	193	H2
St. Peter's All. EC3	**20**	**C4**
St. Peter's Av. E2	**13**	**J2**
St. Peter's Av. E17	78	E4
St. Peters Av. N18	60	D4
St. Peter's Cl. E2	**13**	**J2**
St. Peter's Cl. E2	112	D2
St. Peter's Cl. SW17	167	H2
College Gdns.		
St. Peter's Cl., Barn.	39	H5
St. Peters Cl., Bushey	52	A1
St. Peter's Cl., Chis.	175	G7
St. Peter's Cl., Ilf.	81	H4
St. Peter's Cl., Ruis.	84	D2
St. Peters Cl. NW4	71	J5
St. Peters Cl. SE3	155	F4
Eltham Rd.		
St. Peters Cl. SE4	153	J2
Wickham Rd.		
St. Peters Ct., W.Mol.	179	G4
St. Peter's Gdns. SE27	169	G3
St. Peter's Gro. W6	127	G4
St. Peter's Pl. W9	**6**	**A6**
St. Peters Rd. W6	127	G4
St. Peter's Rd. N9	61	F1
St. Peter's Rd., Croy.	202	A4
St. Peters Rd., Kings.T.	182	A2
St. Peters Rd., Sthl.	103	G5
St. Peters Rd., Twick.	145	E5
St. Peter's Rd., W.Mol.	179	G4
St. Peter's Sq. E2	**13**	**J2**
St. Peter's Sq. W6	127	G5
St. Peters St. N1	111	H1
St. Peters St., S.Croy.	202	A5
St. Peter's Ter. SW6	128	B7
St. Peter's Vil. W6	127	G4
St. Peters Way N1	94	B7
St. Peters Way W5	105	G5
St. Peters Way, Hayes	121	G5
St. Petersburgh Ms. W2	**14**	**A5**
St. Petersburgh Ms. W2	108	E7
St. Petersburgh Pl. W2	**14**	**A5**
St. Petersburgh Pl. W2	108	E7
St. Philip Sq. SW8	150	B2
St. Philip St. SW8	150	B2
St. Philip's Av., Wor.Pk.	197	H2
St. Philip's Rd. E8	94	D6
St. Philips Rd., Surb.	181	G6
St. Philip's Way N1	111	J1
Linton St.		
St. Quentin Rd., Well.	157	J3
St. Quintin Av. W10	107	J5
St. Quintin Gdns. W10	107	J5
St. Quintin Rd. E13	115	H2
St. Raphael's Way NW10	88	C3
St. Regis Cl. N10	74	B2
St. Ronans Cres., Wdf.Grn.	63	G7
St. Rule St. SW8	150	C2
St. Saviour's Est. SE1	**29**	**F5**
St. Saviour's Est. SE1	132	C3
St. Saviour's Rd. SW2	151	F5
St. Saviours Rd., Croy.	187	J6
St. Silas Pl. NW5	92	A6
St. Silas St. Est. NW5	92	A6
St. Simon's Av. SW15	147	J5
St. Stephens Av. E17	78	C5
St. Stephens Av. W12	127	H2
St. Stephens Av. W13	104	E6
St. Stephens Cl. E17	78	B5
St. Stephens Cl. NW8	109	H1
St. Stephens Cl., Sthl.	103	G5
St. Stephens Cres. W2	108	D6
St. Stephens Cres., Th.Hth.	187	G3
St. Stephens Gdn. Est. W2	108	D6
Shrewsbury Rd.		
St. Stephens Gdns. SW15	148	C5
Manfred Rd.		
St. Stephens Gdns. W2	108	D6
St. Stephens Gdns., Twick.	145	F6
St. Stephens Gro. SE13	154	C3
St. Stephens Ms. W2	108	D5
Chepstow Rd.		
St. Stephen's Par. E7	97	J7
Green St.		
St. Stephen's Pas., Twick.	145	F6
Richmond Rd.		
St. Stephen's Rd. E3	113	J2
St. Stephen's Rd. E6	97	J7
St. Stephen's Rd. E17	78	B5
Grove Rd.		
St. Stephens Rd. W13	105	E6
St. Stephen's Rd., Barn.	40	A5
St. Stephens Rd., Houns.	143	G6
St. Stephen's Rd., West Dr.	120	A1
St. Stephens Row EC4	**20**	**B4**
St. Stephens Ter. SW8	131	F7
St. Stephen's Wk. SW7	**30**	**C1**
St. Stephen's Wk. SW7	129	F4
St. Swithin's La. EC4	**20**	**B5**
St. Swithin's La. EC4	112	A7
St. Swithun's Rd. SE13	154	D5
St. Theresa's Rd., Felt.	141	J4
St. Thomas' Cl., Surb.	195	J1
St. Thomas Cl., Bex.	159	G7
St. Thomas Dr., Orp.	207	F1
St. Thomas' Dr., Pnr.	67	E1
St. Thomas Gdns., Ilf.	99	F6
St. Thomas Pl. NW1	92	D7
St. Thomas Rd. E16	115	G6
St. Thomas' Rd. N14	42	D7
St. Thomas' Rd. W4	126	C6
St. Thomas Rd., Belv.	139	J2

Name	Pg	Grid
St. Thomas St. SE1	28	B2
St. Thomas St. SE1	132	A1
St. Thomas's Gdns. NW5	92	A6
Queens Cres.		
St. Thomas's Pl. E9	95	F7
St. Thomas's Rd. N4	93	G2
St. Thomas's Rd. NW10	107	E1
St. Thomas's Sq. E9	95	E7
St. Thomas's Way SW6	128	C7
St. Timothy's Ms., Brom.	191	H1
Wharton Rd.		
St. Ursula Gro., Pnr.	66	D5
St. Ursula Rd., Sthl.	103	G6
St. Vincent Cl. SE27	169	H5
St. Vincent Rd., Twick.	143	J6
St. Vincent St. W1	16	C2
St. Wilfrids Cl., Barn.	41	H5
St. Wilfrids Rd., Barn.	41	G5
St. Winefride's Av. E12	98	C5
St. Winifreds Cl., Chig.	65	F5
St. Winifred's Rd., Tedd.	163	E6
Saints Cl. SE27	169	H4
Wolfington Rd.		
Saints Dr. E7	98	A5
Salamanca Pl. SE1	34	C2
Salamanca St. SE1	34	B2
Salamanca St. SE1	131	F4
Salamander Cl., Kings.T.	163	F5
Salcombe Dr., Mord.	198	A1
Salcombe Dr., Rom.	83	F6
Salcombe Gdns. NW7	55	J6
Salcombe Pk., Loug.	48	A5
High Rd.		
Salcombe Rd. E17	77	J7
Salcombe Rd. N16	94	B5
Salcombe Way, Ruis.	84	A2
Salcott Rd. SW11	149	H5
Salcott Rd., Croy.	201	E3
Sale Pl. W2	15	G2
Sale Pl. W2	109	H5
Sale St. E2	13	H5
Salehurst Cl., Har.	69	H5
Salehurst Rd. SE4	153	J6
Salem Pl., Croy.	201	J3
Salem Rd. W2	14	B5
Salem Rd. W2	109	E7
Salford Rd. SW2	168	D1
Salhouse Cl. SE28	118	C6
Rollesby Way		
Salisbury Av. N3	72	C3
Salisbury Av., Bark.	99	H7
Salisbury Av., Sutt.	198	C6
Salisbury Cl. SE17	36	B1
Salisbury Cl., Wor.Pk.	197	F3
Salisbury Ct. EC4	19	G4
Salisbury Ct. EC4	111	H6
Salisbury Gdns. SW19	166	B7
Salisbury Gdns., Buck.H.	64	A2
Salisbury Hall Gdns. E4	62	A6
Salisbury Ho. E14	114	B6
Hobday St.		
Salisbury Ms. SW6	128	C7
Dawes Rd.		
Salisbury Ms., Brom.	192	B5
Salisbury Rd.		
Salisbury Pl. SW9	131	H7
Salisbury Pl. W1	15	J1
Salisbury Pl. W1	109	J5
Salisbury Rd. E4	62	A3
Salisbury Rd. E7	97	G6
Salisbury Rd. E10	96	C2
Salisbury Rd. E12	98	A5
Salisbury Rd. E17	78	C5
Salisbury Rd. N4	75	H5
Salisbury Rd. N9	60	D3
Salisbury Rd. N22	75	H1
Salisbury Rd. SE25	188	D6
Salisbury Rd. SW19	166	B7
Salisbury Rd. W13	124	D2
Salisbury Rd., Barn.	40	B3
Salisbury Rd., Bex.	177	G1
Salisbury Rd., Brom.	192	B5
Salisbury Rd., Cars.	199	J6
Salisbury Rd., Dag.	101	H6
Salisbury Rd., Felt.	160	C1
Salisbury Rd., Har.	68	A5
Salisbury Rd., Houns.	142	C3
Salisbury Rd. (Heathrow Airport), Houns.	141	F5
Salisbury Rd., Ilf.	99	H2
Salisbury Rd., N.Mal.	182	D3
Salisbury Rd., Pnr.	66	A4
Salisbury Rd., Rich.	145	H4
Salisbury Rd., Sthl.	123	E4
Salisbury Rd., Wor.Pk.	197	F3
Salisbury Sq. EC4	19	F4
Salisbury St. NW8	7	G6
Salisbury St. NW8	109	H4
Salisbury St. W3	126	C2
Salisbury Ter. SE15	153	F3
Salix Cl., Sun.	160	B7
Oak Way		
Salliesfield, Twick.	144	A6
Sally Murray Cl. E12	98	D4
Salmen Rd. E13	115	F2
Salmon La. E14	113	H6
Salmon Rd., Belv.	139	G5
Salmon St. E14	113	J6
Salmon La.		
Salmon St. NW9	88	B1
Salmon Cl., Stan.	52	D6
Robb Rd.		
Salmons Rd. N9	60	D1
Salmons Rd., Chess.	195	G6
Salomons Rd. E13	115	J5
Chalk Rd.		
Salop Rd. E17	77	G6
Saltash Cl., Sutt.	198	C4
Saltash Rd., Ilf.	65	G7
Saltash Rd., Well.	158	C1
Saltcoats Rd. W4	126	E2
Saltcroft Cl., Wem.	88	B1
Salter Cl., Har.	85	F3
Salter Rd. SE16	133	G1
Salter St. E14	114	A7
Salter St. NW10	107	G3
Salterford Rd. SW17	168	A6
Salters Hall Ct. EC4	20	B5
Salters Hill SE19	170	A5
Salters Rd. E17	78	D4
Salters Rd. W10	108	A4
Salterton Rd. N7	93	E3
Saltley Cl. E6	116	B6
Dunnock Rd.		
Saltoun Rd. SW2	151	G4
Saltram Cl. N15	76	C4
Saltram Cres. W9	108	C3
Saltwell St. E14	114	A7
Saltwood Gro. SE17	36	B4
Salusbury Rd. NW6	108	B1
Salutation Rd. SE10	135	E4
Salvia Gdns., Grnf.	104	D2
Selborne Gdns.		
Salvin Rd. SW15	148	A3
Salway Cl., Wdf.Grn.	63	F7
Salway Pl. E15	96/97	E6
Broadway		
Salway Rd. E15	96	D6
Sam Bartram Cl. SE7	135	J5
Samantha Cl. E17	77	J7
Sambruck Ms. SE6	172	B1
Samels Ct. W6	127	G5
South Black Lion La.		
Samford St. NW8	7	F6
Samford St. NW8	109	G4
Samos Rd. SE20	189	E2
Sampson Av., Barn.	40	A5
Sampson Cl., Belv.	138	D3
Carrill Way		
Sampson St. E1	29	J2
Sampson St. E1	132	D1
Samson St. E13	115	J2
Samuel Cl. E8	112	C1
Samuel Cl. SE14	133	G6
Samuel Cl. SE18	136	B4
Samuel Gray Gdns., Kings.T.	181	G1
Samuel Johnson Cl. SW16	169	G4
Curtis Fld. Rd.		
Samuel Lewis Trust Dws. E8	94	D4
Amhurst Rd.		
Samuel Lewis Trust Dws. N1	93	G7
Liverpool Rd.		
Samuel Lewis Trust Dws. SW3	31	G2
Samuel Lewis Trust Dws. SW6	128	D7
Samuel St. SE15	37	F7
Samuel St. SE15	132	C7
Samuel St. SE18	136	C4
Samuels Cl. W6	127	G5
South Black Lion La.		
Sancroft Cl. NW2	89	H3
Sancroft Rd., Har.	68	C2
Sancroft St. SE11	34	D3
Sancroft St. SE11	131	F5
Sanctuary, The SW1	25	J4
Sanctuary, The, Bex.	158	D6
Sanctuary, The, Mord.	184	D6
Sanctuary Rd., Houns.	140	D6
Sanctuary St. SE1	28	A4
Sandal Rd. N18	60	D5
Sandal Rd., N.Mal.	182	D5
Sandal St. E15	114	E1
Sandale Cl. N16	94	A3
Stoke Newington Ch. St.		
Sandall Cl. W5	105	H4
Sandall Rd. NW5	92	C6
Sandall Rd. W5	105	H4
Sandalwood Cl. E1	113	H4
Sandalwood Rd., Felt.	160	B3
Sandbach Pl. SE18	137	F4
Sandbourne Av. SW19	184	E3
Sandbourne Rd. SE4	153	H2
Sandbrook Cl. NW7	54	D6
Sandbrook Rd. N16	94	B3
Sandby Grn. SE9	156	B3
Sandcroft Cl. N13	59	H6
Sandell St. SE1	27	E3
Sanders Cl., Hmptn.	161	J5
Sanders La. NW7	56	A7
Sanders Way N19	92	D1
Sussex Way		
Sanderson Cl. NW5	92	B4
Sanderstead Av. NW2	90	B2
Sanderstead Cl. SW12	150	C7
Atkins Rd.		
Sanderstead Rd. E10	95	H1
Sanderstead Rd., S.Croy.	202	A7
Sandfield Gdns., Th.Hth.	187	H3
Sandfield Pas., Th.Hth.	187	J3
Sandfield Rd., Th.Hth.	187	H3
Sandford Av. N22	59	J7
Sandford Av., Loug.	49	F3
Sandford Cl. E6	116	C4
Sandford Ct. N16	94	B1
Sandford La. N16	94	C2
Lawrence Bldgs.		
Sandford Rd. E6	116	B4
Sandford Rd., Bexh.	159	E4
Sandford Rd., Brom.	191	G4
Sandford St. SW6	128/129	E7
King's Rd.		
Sandgate La. SW18	167	H1
Sandgate Rd., Well.	138	C7
Sandgate St. SE15	132	E6
Sandham Pt. SE18	136/137	E4
Troy Ct.		
Sandhills, Wall.	200	D4
Sandhurst Av., Har.	67	H6
Sandhurst Av., Surb.	182	B7
Sandhurst Cl. NW9	70	A3
Sandhurst Dr., Ilf.	99	J4
Sandhurst Rd. N9	45	F6
Sandhurst Rd. NW9	70	A3
Sandhurst Rd. SE6	172	D1
Sandhurst Rd., Bex.	158	D5
Sandhurst Rd., Sid.	175	J3
Sandhurst Way, S.Croy.	202	B7
Sandiford Rd., Sutt.	198	C2
Sandiland Cres., Brom.	205	F2
Sandilands, Croy.	202	D2
Sandilands Rd. SW6	148	E1
Sandison St. SE15	152	C3
Sandland St. WC1	18	D2
Sandland St. WC1	111	F5
Sandling Ri. SE9	174	D3
Sandlings, The N22	75	G2
Sandlings Cl. SE15	152/153	E2
Pilkington Rd.		
Sandmere Rd. SW4	150	E4
Sandon Cl., Esher	180	A7
Sandow Cres., Hayes	121	J3
Sandown Av., Dag.	101	J6
Sandown Cl., Houns.	142	A1
Sandown Rd. SE25	188	E5
Sandown Way, Nthlt.	85	E6
Sandpiper Cl. E17	77	G1
Sandpiper Cl. SE16	133	J2
Sandpiper Rd., Sutt.	198	B2
Garder Grn. La.		
Sandpit Pl. SE7	136	B5
Sandpit Rd., Brom.	172	E5
Sandpits Rd., Croy.	203	G4
Sandpits Rd., Rich.	163	G2
Sandra Cl. N22	75	J1
New Rd.		
Sandra Cl., Houns.	143	H5
Sandridge Cl., Har.	68	B4
Sandridge Ct. N4	93	J3
Queens Dr.		
Sandridge St. N19	92	C2
Sandringham Av. SW20	184	B2
Sandringham Cl. SW19	166	A1
Sandringham Cl., Enf.	44	B2
Sandringham Cl., Ilf.	81	F3
Sandringham Ct. W9	6	D4
Sandringham Cres. Har.	85	G2
Sandringham Dr., Well.	157	H2
Sandringham Gdns. N8	75	E6
Sandringham Gdns. N12	57	G6
Sandringham Gdns. Houns.	142	A1
Sandringham Gdns., Ilf.	81	F3
Sandringham Ms. W5	105	G2
High St.		
Sandringham Rd. E7	97	J5
Sandringham Rd. E8	94	C5
Sandringham Rd. E10	78	D6
Sandringham Rd. N22	75	J3
Sandringham Rd. NW2	89	H6
Sandringham Rd. NW11	72	B7
Sandringham Rd. Bark.	99	J6
Sandringham Rd. Brom.	173	G5
Sandringham Rd. Houns.	140	B5
Sandringham Rd. Nthlt.	85	G7
Sandringham Rd. Th.Hth.	187	J5
Sandringham Rd. Wor.Pk.	197	G3
Sandrock Pl., Croy.	203	G4
Sandrock Rd. SE13	154	A3
Sand's End La. SW6	149	E1
Sands Way, Wdf.Grn.	64	B6
Sandstone Pl. N19	92	B2
Sandstone Rd. SE12	173	H2
Sandtoft Rd. SE7	135	H6
Sandwell Cres. NW6	90	D6
Sandwich St. WC1	10	A4
Sandwich St. WC1	110	E3
Sandwich Cl. NW7	55	G7
Sebergham Gro.		
Sandy Bury, Orp.	207	G3
Sandy Hill Av. SE18	136	E5
Sandy Hill Rd. SE18	136	E5
Sandy La., Har.	69	J6
Sandy La., Kings.T.	162	D7
Sandy La., Mitch.	186	A1
Sandy La., Nthwd.	50	A5
Sandy La., Rich.	163	F2
Sandy La., Sid.	176	D7
Sandy La., Sutt.	198	B7
Sandy La., Tedd.	162	D7
Sandy La., Walt.	178	B6
Sandy La. Est., Rich.	163	G2
Sandy La. N., Wall.	200	D6
Sandy La. S., Wall.	200	D6
Sandy Ridge, Chis.	174	D6
Sandy Rd. NW3	90	E3
Sandy Way, Croy.	203	J3
Sandycombe Rd., Felt.	160	A1
Sandycombe Rd. Rich.	146	A3
Sandycoombe Rd., Twick.	145	F6
Sandycroft SE2	138	A6
Sandyhill Rd., Ilf.	98	E4
Sandymount Av., Stan.	53	F5
Sandy's Row E1	21	E2
Sandy's Row E1	112	B5
Sanford La. N16	94	C2
Stoke Newington High St.		
Sanford St. SE14	133	H6
Sanford Ter. N16	94	C3
Sanford Wk. N16	94	C2
Sanford St.		
Sanford Wk. SE14	133	H6
Cold Blow La.		
Sanger Av., Chess.	195	H5
Sangley Rd. SE6	154	B7
Sangley Rd. SE25	188	B4
Sangora Rd. SW11	149	G4
Sans Wk. EC1	11	F5
Sans Wk. EC1	111	G4
Sansom Rd. E11	97	E2

Name	Page	Grid
Sansom St. SE5	132	A7
Santley St. SW4	151	F4
Santos Rd. SW18	148	D5
Santway, The, Stan.	52	B5
Sapcote Trd. Cen. NW10	89	F5
Saperton Wk. SE11	**34**	**D1**
Saperton Wk. SE11	131	F4
Saphora Cl., Orp.	207	G5
Oleander Cl.		
Sapphire Cl. E6	116	D6
Sapphire Cl., Dag.	100	C1
Sapphire Rd. SE8	133	H4
Sara Ct., Beck.	190	B1
Albemarle Rd.		
Saracen Cl., Croy.	188	A6
Saracen St. E14	114	A6
Saracen's Head Yd. EC3	**21**	**F4**
Sarah Ho. SW15	147	F4
Sarah St. N1	**12**	**E3**
Saratoga Rd. E5	95	F4
Sardinia St. WC2	**18**	**C4**
Sarita Cl., Har.	68	A2
Sarjant Path SW19	166	A2
Queensmere Rd.		
Sark Cl., Houns.	123	G7
Sark Wk. E16	115	H6
Sarnesfield Ho. SE15	132/133	E3
Pencraig Way		
Sarnesfield Rd., Enf.	44	A3
Church St.		
Sarre Rd. NW2	90	C5
Sarsen Av., Houns.	143	F2
Sarsfeld Rd. SW12	167	J1
Sarsfield Rd., Grnf.	105	E2
Sartor Rd. SE15	153	G4
Sarum Ter. E3	113	J4
Satanita Cl. E16	116	A6
Fulmer Rd.		
Satchell Mead NW9	71	F1
Satchwell Rd. E2	**13**	**H4**
Satchwell Rd. E2	112	D3
Sauls Grn. E11	96/97	E3
Napier Rd.		
Saunders Cl. E14	113	J7
Limehouse Causeway		
Saunders Ness Rd. E14	134	C5
Saunders Rd. SE18	137	J5
Saunders St. SE11	**34**	**E1**
Saunders St. SE11	131	G4
Saunders Way SE28	118	B7
Oriole Way		
Saunderton Rd., Wem.	86	E5
Saunton Av., Hayes	121	J7
Savage Gdns. E6	116	C6
Savage Gdns. EC3	**21**	**E5**
Savernake Rd. N9	44	D6
Savernake Rd. NW3	91	J4
Savery Dr., Surb.	181	F7
Savile Cl., N.Mal.	183	E5
Savile Cl., T.Ditt.	194	C1
Savile Gdns., Croy.	202	C2
Savile Row W1	**17**	**F5**
Savile Row W1	110	C7
Savill Gdns. SW20	183	G3
Bodnant Gdns.		
Savill Row, Wdf.Grn.	63	F6
Saville Rd. E16	136	B1
Saville Rd. W4	126	D3
Saville Rd., Rom.	83	F6
Saville Rd., Twick.	162	C1
Saville Row, Brom.	205	F1
Saville Row, Enf.	45	G2
Savona Cl. SW19	166	B7
Savona Est. SW8	130	C7
Savona St. SW8	130	C7
Savoy Av., Hayes	121	H5
Savoy Bldgs. WC2	**18**	**C6**
Savoy Cl. E15	114/115	E1
Arthingworth St.		
Savoy Cl., Edg.	54	A5
Savoy Ct. WC2	**18**	**B6**
Savoy Hill WC2	**18**	**C6**
Savoy Pl. WC2	**18**	**B6**
Savoy Pl. WC2	111	E7
Savoy Row WC2	**18**	**C5**
Savoy Steps WC2	111	F7
Savoy St.		
Savoy St. WC2	**18**	**C5**
Savoy St. WC2	111	F7
Savoy Way WC2	**18**	**C6**
Sawbill Cl., Hayes	102	D5
Sawkins Cl. SW19	166	B2
Sawley Rd. W12	127	G1
Sawtry Cl., Cars.	185	H7
Sawyer Cl. N9	60	D2
Lion Rd.		
Sawyer St. SE1	**27**	**J3**
Sawyer St. SE1	131	J2
Sawyers Cl., Dag.	101	J6
Sawyer's Hill, Rich.	146	B7
Sawyers Lawn W13	104	C6
Saxby Rd. SW2	150	E7
Saxham Rd., Bark.	117	J1
Saxlingham Rd. E4	62	D3
Saxon Av., Felt.	161	F2
Saxon Cl. E17	78	A7
Saxon Cl., Surb.	181	G6
Saxon Dr. W3	106	B6
Saxon Gdns., Sthl.	102/103	E7
Saxon Rd.		
Saxon Rd. E3	113	J2
Saxon Rd. E6	116	C4
Saxon Rd. N22	75	H1
Saxon Rd. SE25	188	A5
Saxon Rd., Brom.	173	F7
Saxon Rd., Ilf.	99	E6
Saxon Rd., Sthl.	123	E1
Saxon Rd., Wem.	88	C3
Saxon Wk., Sid.	176	C6
Saxon Way N14	42	D6
Saxonbury Av., Sun.	178	B3
Saxonbury Cl., Mitch.	185	G3
Saxonbury Gdns., Surb.	195	F1
Saxonfield Cl. SW2	151	F7
Saxton Cl. SE13	154	D3
Sayers Wk., Rich.	145	J7
Stafford Pl.		
Sayes Ct. SE8	133	J5
Sayes Ct. St.		
Sayes Ct. St. SE8	133	J6
Sayesbury La. N18	60	D5
Scadbury Pk., Chis.	175	J6
Scads Hill Cl., Orp.	193	J6
Scala St. W1	**17**	**G1**
Scala St. W1	110	C5
Scales Rd. N17	76	C3
Scampston Ms. W10	108	A6
Scampton Rd., Houns.	140	C6
Southampton Rd.		
Scandrett St. E1	132	E1
Scarba Wk. N1	94	A6
Marquess Rd.		
Scarborough Rd. E11	96	D1
Scarborough Rd. N4	75	G7
Scarborough Rd. N9	45	F7
Scarborough Rd., Houns.	141	F6
Southern Perimeter Rd.		
Scarborough St. E1	**21**	**G4**
Scarbrook Rd., Croy.	201	J3
Scarle Rd., Wem.	87	G6
Scarlet Rd. SE6	172	E3
Scarlette Manor Way SW2	151	G7
Papworth Way		
Scarsbrook Rd. SE3	156	A3
Scarsdale Pl. W8	**22**	**A5**
Scarsdale Rd., Har.	85	J3
Scarsdale Vil. W8	128	D3
Scarth Rd. SW13	147	F3
Scawen Cl., Cars.	200	A4
Scawen St. SE8	133	H5
Scawfell St. E2	**13**	**G2**
Scawfell St. E2	112	C2
Scaynes Link N12	56	D5
Sceaux Est. SE5	152	B1
Sceaux Gdns. SE5	152	C1
Sceptre Rd. E2	113	F3
Schofield Wk. SE3	135	H7
Dornberg Cl.		
Scholars Rd. E4	62	C1
Scholars Rd. SW12	168	C1
Scholefield Rd. N19	92	D1
Schonfeld Sq. N16	94	A2
School Ho. La., Tedd.	163	E7
School La. SE23	170	E2
School La., Kings.T.	181	F1
School Rd.		
School La., Pnr.	66	E4
School La., Surb.	196	A1
School La., Well.	158	B3
School Pas., Kings.T.	181	J2
School Pas., Sthl.	123	F1
School Rd. E12	98	C4
School Rd. NW10	106	D4
School Rd., Chis.	193	F1
School Rd., Dag.	119	G1
School Rd., E.Mol.	180	A4
School Rd., Hmptn.	161	J6
School Rd., Houns.	143	J3
School Rd., Kings.T.	181	F1
School Rd., West Dr.	120	A6
School Rd. Av., Hmptn.	161	J6
School Way N12	57	F4
High Rd.		
School Way, Dag.	100	C3
Schoolbell Ms. E3	113	H2
Arbery Rd.		
Schoolhouse Gdns., Loug.	48	E4
Schoolhouse La. E1	113	G7
Schoolway N12	57	G6
Schooner Cl. E14	134	D3
Schooner Cl. SE16	133	G2
Kinburn St.		
Schooner Cl., Bark.	117	H3
Thames Rd.		
Schubert Rd. SW15	148	C5
Sclater St. E1	**13**	**F5**
Sclater St. E1	112	C4
Scoble Pl. N16	94	C4
Scoles Cres. SW2	169	G1
Scoresby St. SE1	**27**	**G2**
Scoresby St. SE1	131	H1
Scorton Av., Grnf.	104	D2
Scot Gro., Pnr.	50	D7
Scotch Common W13	104	D5
Scoter Cl., Wdf.Grn.	63	H7
Mallards Rd.		
Scotia Rd. SW2	151	G7
Scotland Grn. N17	76	D2
Scotland Grn. Rd., Enf.	45	G5
Scotland Grn. Rd. N., Enf.	45	G4
Scotland Pl. SW1	**26**	**A1**
Scotland Rd., Buck.H.	63	J1
Scotsdale Cl., Orp.	193	H4
Scotsdale Cl., Sutt.	198	B7
Scotsdale Rd. SE12	155	H5
Scotswood St. EC1	**11**	**F5**
Scotswood Wk. N17	60	D7
Scott Cl. SW16	187	F1
Scott Cl., Epsom	196	C5
Scott Cl., West Dr.	120	C4
Scott Ct. W3	126	C2
Petersfield Rd.		
Scott Cres., Har.	85	H1
Scott Ellis Gdns. NW8	**6**	**E4**
Scott Ellis Gdns. NW8	109	G3
Scott Fm. Cl., T.Ditt.	194	E1
Scott Gdns., Houns.	122	D7
Scott Ho. N18	60	D5
Scott Lidgett Cres. SE16	**29**	**H4**
Scott Lidgett Cres. SE16	132	D2
Scott Russell Pl. E14	134	B5
Westferry Rd.		
Scott St. E1	112	E4
Scott Trimmer Way, Houns.	143	E2
Scottes La., Dag.	100	D1
Valence Av.		
Scotts Av., Brom.	190	D2
Scotts Dr., Hmptn.	161	H7
Scotts Fm. Rd., Epsom	196	C6
Scotts La., Brom.	190	D3
Scotts Rd. E10	96	C1
Scotts Rd. W12	127	H2
Scotts Rd., Brom.	173	G7
Scotts Rd., Sthl.	122	C3
Scott's Yd. EC4	20	B5
Scottwell Dr. NW9	71	F5
Crossway		
Scoulding Rd. E16	115	F6
Scouler St. E14	114	D7
Quixley St.		
Scout App. NW10	88	E4
Scout La. SW4	150	C3
Old Town		
Scout Way NW7	54	D4
Scovell Cres. SE1	**27**	**J4**
Scovell Rd. SE1	**27**	**J4**
Scrattons Ter., Bark.	118	D2
Scriven St. E8	112	C1
Scrooby St. SE6	154	B6
Scrubs La. NW10	107	G3
Scrubs La. W10	107	G3
Scrutton Cl. SW12	150	D7
Scrutton St. EC2	**12**	**D6**
Scrutton St. EC2	112	B4
Scudamore La. NW9	70	C3
Scutari Rd. SE22	153	F5
Scylla Cres., Houns.	141	E7
Scylla Pl. SE15	152	E3
Scylla Rd., Houns.	141	E6
Seabright St. E2	112/113	E3
Bethnal Grn. Rd.		
Seabrook Dr., W.Wick.	204	E2
Seabrook Gdns., Rom.	83	G7
Seabrook Rd., Dag.	100	D3
Seacole Cl. W3	106	D5
Seacourt Rd. SE2	138	D2
Seacroft Gdns., Wat.	50	D3
Seafield Rd. N11	58	D4
Seaford Rd. E17	78	B3
Seaford Rd. N15	76	A5
Seaford Rd. W13	124	E1
Seaford Rd., Enf.	44	B4
Seaford Rd., Houns.	140	A5
Seaford St. WC1	**10**	**B4**
Seaford St. WC1	111	E3
Seaforth Av., N.Mal.	183	H5
Seaforth Cres. N5	93	J5
Seaforth Gdns. N21	43	F7
Seaforth Gdns., Epsom	197	F4
Seaforth Gdns., Wdf.Grn.	63	J5
Seaforth Pl. SW1	130	C3
Buckingham Gate		
Seagrave Rd. SW6	128	D6
Seagry Rd. E11	79	G6
Seagull Cl., Bark.	117	H3
Thames Rd.		
Seal St. E8	94	C4
Sealand Rd., Houns.	140	D6
Sealand Wk., Nthlt.	102/103	E3
Wayfarer Rd.		
Searle Pl. N4	93	F1
Evershot Rd.		
Searles Cl. SW11	129	H7
Searles Dr. E6	116	D5
Winsor Ter.		
Searles Rd. SE1	**36**	**C1**
Searles Rd. SE1	132	A4
Sears St. SE5	**36**	**B7**
Sears St. SE5	132	A7
Seasprite Cl., Nthlt.	102	D3
Seaton Av., Ilf.	99	H5
Seaton Cl. E13	115	H4
New Barn St.		
Seaton Cl. SE11	**35**	**F3**
Seaton Cl. SE11	131	G5
Seaton Cl. SW15	165	H1
Seaton Cl., Twick.	144	A6
Seaton Gdns., Ruis.	84	A3
Seaton Pt. E5	94	D4
Nolan Way		
Seaton Rd., Hayes	121	G4
Seaton Rd., Mitch.	185	H2
Seaton Rd., Twick.	143	J6
Seaton Rd., Well.	138	C7
Seaton Rd., Wem.	105	H2
Seaton St. N18	60	D5
Sebastian St. EC1	**11**	**H4**
Sebastian St. EC1	111	H3
Sebastopol Rd. N9	60	D4
Sebbon St. N1	93	H7
Sebergham Gro. NW7	55	G7
Sebert Rd. E7	97	H5
Sebright Pas. E2	**13**	**J2**
Sebright Rd., Barn.	40	A2
Secker Cres., Har.	67	J1
Secker St. SE1	**27**	**E2**
Second Av. E12	98	B4
Second Av. E13	115	G3
Second Av. E17	78	A5
Second Av. N18	61	F4
Second Av. NW4	72	A4
Second Av. SW14	146	E3
Second Av. W3	127	F1
Second Av. W10	108	B4
Second Av., Dag.	119	H1
Second Av., Enf.	44	C5
Second Av., Hayes	121	J1
Second Av., Rom.	82	C5
Second Av., Walt.	178	B6
Second Av., Wem.	87	G2
Second Cl., W.Mol.	179	J4
Second Cross Rd., Twick.	162	B2
Second Way, Wem.	88	B4
Sedan Way SE17	**36**	**D3**
Sedcombe Cl., Sid.	176	B4
Knoll Rd.		
Sedcote Rd., Enf.	45	F5
Sedding St. SW1	**32**	**B1**
Sedding St. SW1	130	A4
Seddon Rd., Mord.	185	G5
Seddon St. WC1	**10**	**D4**
Sedge Rd. N17	61	F7
Sedgebrook Rd. SE3	156	A2
Sedgecombe Av., Har.	69	F5
Sedgeford Rd. W12	127	F1
Sedgehill Rd. SE6	172	A4
Sedgemere Av. N2	73	F3
Sedgemere Rd. SE2	138	C3
Sedgemoor Dr., Dag.	101	G4
Sedgeway SE6	173	F1
Sedgewood Cl., Brom.	191	F7
Sedgmoor Pl. SE5	132	B7
Sedgwick Rd. E10	96	C2
Sedgwick St. E9	95	G5
Sedleigh Rd. SW18	148	C6

Sedlescombe Rd. 128 C6
SW6
Sedley Pl. W1 **16 D4**
Sedley Ri., Loug. 48 C2
Sedum Cl. NW9 70 B5
Seeley Dr. SE21 170 B4
Seelig Av. NW9 71 G7
Seely Rd. SW17 168 A6
Seething La. EC3 **21 E6**
Seething La. EC3 112 B7
Seething Wells La., 181 F6
Surb.
Sefton Av. NW7 54 D5
Sefton Av., Har. 68 A1
Sefton Cl., Orp. 193 J4
Sefton Rd., Croy. 202 D1
Sefton Rd., Orp. 193 J4
Sefton St. SW15 147 J2
Segal Cl. SE23 153 H7
Sekforde St. EC1 **11 G6**
Sekforde St. EC1 111 H4
Sekhon Ter., Felt. 161 G3
Selan Gdns., Hayes 102 B5
Selbie Av. NW10 89 F5
Selborne Av. E12 98 D4
Walton Rd.
Selborne Av., Bex. 176 E1
Selborne Gdns. NW4 71 G4
Selborne Gdns., Grnf. 104 D1
Selborne Rd. E17 77 J5
Selborne Rd. N14 58 E3
Selborne Rd. N22 75 F1
Selborne Rd. SE5 152 A2
Denmark Hill
Selborne Rd., Croy. 202 B3
Selborne Rd., Ilf. 98 D2
Selborne Rd., N.Mal. 182 E2
Selborne Rd., Sid. 176 B4
Selborne Wk. E17 77 J4
Selbourne Av., 195 J2
Surb.
Selby Chase, Ruis. 84 B2
Selby Cl. E6 116 B5
Linton Gdns.
Selby Cl., Chess. 195 H7
Selby Cl., Chis. 174 D6
Selby Gdns., Sthl. 103 G4
Selby Grn., Cars. 185 H7
Selby Rd. E11 96 E3
Selby Rd. E13 115 H5
Selby Rd. N17 60 B6
Selby Rd. SE20 188 D2
Selby Rd. W5 105 E4
Selby Rd., Cars. 185 H7
Selby St. E1 **13 J6**
Selby St. E1 112 D4
Selden Rd. SE15 153 F2
Selden Wk. N7 93 F2
Durham Rd.
Selhurst Cl. SW19 166 A1
Selhurst New Rd. 188 B6
SE25
Selhurst Pl. SE25 188 B6
Selhurst Rd. N9 60 A3
Selhurst Rd. SE25 188 B5
Selinas La., Dag. 83 E7
Selkirk Rd. SW17 167 H4
Selkirk Rd., Twick. 161 J2
Sellers Cl., Borwd. 38 C1
Sellers Hall Cl. N3 56 D7
Sellincourt Rd. SW17 167 H5
Sellindge Cl., Beck. 171 J7
Sellon Ms. SE11 **34 D2**
Sellons Av. NW10 107 F1
Sellwood Dr., Barn. 40 A5
Selsdon Av., S.Croy. 202 A6
Selsdon Rd.
Selsdon Cl., Rom. 83 J1
Selsdon Cl., Surb. 181 H5
Selsdon Rd. E11 79 G7
Selsdon Rd. E13 115 J1
Selsdon Rd. NW2 89 F2
Selsdon Rd. SE27 169 H3
Selsdon Rd., S.Croy. 202 A5
Selsdon Rd. Ind. Est., 202 A6
S.Croy.
Selsdon Rd.
Selsdon Way E14 134 B3
Selsea Pl. N16 94 B5
Crossway
Selsey Cres., Well. 158 D1
Selsey St. E14 114 A5
Selvage La. NW7 54 D5
Selway Cl., Pnr. 66 B4
Selwood Pl. SW7 **30 E3**
Selwood Pl. SW7 129 G5
Selwood Rd., Chess. 195 G4
Selwood Rd., Croy. 202 E2
Selwood Rd., Sutt. 198 C1
Selwood Ter. SW7 **31 E3**
Selworthy Cl. E11 79 G5
Selworthy Rd. SE6 171 J3
Selwyn Av. E4 62 C6
Selwyn Av., Ilf. 81 H6

Selwyn Av., Rich. 145 H3
Selwyn Cl., Houns. 143 E4
Selwyn Cl. SE3 155 E3
Selwyn Ct., Edg. 54 B7
Camrose Av.
Selwyn Cres., Well. 158 B4
Selwyn Rd. E3 113 J2
Selwyn Rd. E13 115 H1
Selwyn Rd. NW10 88 D7
Selwyn Rd., N.Mal. 182 D5
Semley Gate E9 95 J6
Eastway
Semley Pl. SW1 **32 C2**
Semley Pl. SW1 130 A4
Semley Rd. SW16 187 E2
Senate St. SE15 153 F2
Senator Wk. SE28 137 G3
Broadwater Rd.
Seneca Rd., Th.Hth. 187 J4
Senga Rd., Wall. 200 A1
Senhouse Rd., Sutt. 198 A3
Senior St. W2 **14 A1**
Senior St. W2 108 E5
Senlac Rd. SE12 173 H1
Sennen Rd., Enf. 44 C7
Sennen Wk. SE9 174 B3
Senrab St. E1 113 G6
Sentinel Cl., Nthlt. 103 E4
Sentinel Sq. NW4 71 J4
September Way, 53 E6
Stan.
Sequoia Cl., Bushey 52 A1
Giant Tree Hill
Sequoia Gdns., Orp. 193 J7
Sequoia Pk., Pnr. 51 H6
Serbin Cl. E10 78 C7
Serjeants Inn EC4 **19 F4**
Serle St. WC2 **18 D3**
Serle St. WC2 111 F6
Sermon La. EC4 19 J4
Serpentine Rd. W2 **23 J2**
Serpentine Rd. W2 129 J1
Servian Dr., Brom. 192 A1
Setchell Rd. SE1 **37 F1**
Setchell Way SE1 **37 F1**
Seth St. SE16 133 F2
Swan Rd.
Seton Gdns., Dag. 100 C7
Settle Pt. E13 115 G2
London Rd.
Settle Rd. E13 115 G2
London Rd.
Settles St. E1 **21 J2**
Settles St. E1 112 D5
Settrington Rd. SW6 148 E2
Seven Acres, Cars. 199 H2
Seven Acres, Nthwd. 50 A6
Seven Kings Rd., Ilf. 99 J2
Seven Sisters Rd. N4 93 F3
Seven Sisters Rd. N7 93 F3
Seven Sisters Rd. N15 76 A6
Seven Stars Cor. 127 G3
W12
Goldhawk Rd.
Sevenoaks Cl., Bexh. 159 J4
Sevenoaks Ho. SE25 188 D3
Sevenoaks Rd. SE4 153 H6
Sevenoaks Rd., Orp. 207 J4
Sevenoaks Rd. 207 J7
(Green St. Grn.), Orp.
Sevenoaks Way, Orp. 176 C7
Sevenoaks Way, Sid. 176 C7
Seventh Av. E12 98 C4
Seventh Av., Hayes 122 A1
Severn Dr., Esher 194 D2
Severn Way NW10 89 F5
Severnake Cl. E14 134 A4
Severus Rd. SW11 149 H4
Seville Ms. N1 94 B7
Seville St. SW1 **24 A4**
Seville St. SW1 129 J2
Sevington Rd. NW4 71 H6
Sevington St. W9 **6 A6**
Sevington St. W9 108 E4
Seward Rd. W7 124 D2
Seward Rd., Beck. 189 G2
Seward St. EC1 **11 H5**
Seward St. EC1 111 J3
Sewardstone Gdns. 46 B5
E4
Sewardstone Rd. E2 113 F2
Sewardstone Rd. E4 46 B7
Sewdley St. E5 95 G3
Sewell Rd. SE2 138 A3
Sewell St. E13 115 G3
Sextant Av. E14 134 D4
Seymour Av. N17 76 D2
Seymour Av., Mord. 184 A7
Seymour Cl., E.Mol. 179 J5
Seymour Cl., Loug. 48 B6
Seymour Cl., Pnr. 67 F1
Seymour Ct. E4 63 F2
Seymour Dr., Brom. 206 C1
Seymour Gdns. SE4 153 H3

Seymour Gdns., Felt. 160 C4
Seymour Gdns., Ilf. 98 C1
Seymour Gdns., Ruis. 84 D1
Seymour Gdns., 181 J5
Surb.
Seymour Gdns., 144 E7
Twick.
Seymour Ms. W1 **16 B3**
Seymour Ms. W1 110 A6
Seymour Pl. SE25 188 E4
Seymour Pl. W1 **15 J2**
Seymour Pl. W1 109 H5
Seymour Rd. E4 62 B1
Seymour Rd. E6 116 A2
Seymour Rd. E10 95 J1
Seymour Rd. N3 57 E7
Seymour Rd. N8 75 G5
Seymour Rd. N9 61 E2
Seymour Rd. SW18 148 C7
Seymour Rd. SW19 166 A2
Seymour Rd. W4 126 C4
Seymour Rd., Cars. 200 A5
Seymour Rd., E.Mol. 179 J5
Seymour Rd., Hmptn. 161 J5
Seymour Rd., 181 G1
Kings.T.
Seymour Rd., Mitch. 186 A7
Seymour St. W1 **15 J4**
Seymour St. W1 109 J6
Seymour St. W2 **15 J4**
Seymour St. W2 109 J6
Seymour Ter. SE20 188 E1
Seymour Vil. SE20 188 E1
Seymour Wk. SW10 **30 C5**
Seymour Wk. SW10 129 F6
Seymours, The, 48 D1
Loug.
Seyssel St. E14 134 C4
Shaa Rd. W3 106 D7
Shacklegate La., 162 B4
Tedd.
Shackleton Cl. 170/171 E2
SE23
Featherstone Av.
Shackleton Ct. E14 134 A5
Napier Av.
Shackleton Rd., Sthl. 103 F7
Shacklewell Grn. E8 94 C4
Shacklewell La. E8 94 C5
Shacklewell Rd. N16 94 C4
Shacklewell Row E8 94 C4
Shacklewell St. E2 **13 G5**
Shacklewell St. E2 112 C4
Shad Thames SE1 **29 F2**
Shad Thames SE1 132 C1
Shadbolt Av. E4 61 H5
Shadbolt Cl., 197 F2
Wor.Pk.
Shadwell Ct., Nthlt. 103 F2
Shadwell Dr.
Shadwell Dr., Nthlt. 103 F3
Shadwell Gdns. E1 113 F6
Martha St.
Shadwell Pierhead E1 113 F7
Glamis Rd.
Shadwell Pl. E1 113 F7
Sutton St.
Shaef Way, Tedd. 162 D7
Shafter Rd., Dag. 101 J6
Shaftesbury, Loug. 48 A3
Shaftesbury Av. W1 **17 H5**
Shaftesbury Av. W1 110 D7
Shaftesbury Av. WC2 **17 H5**
Shaftesbury Av. WC2 110 D7
Shaftesbury Av., 45 G2
Barn.
Shaftesbury Av., 142 A6
Felt.
Shaftesbury Av., Har. 85 H1
Shaftesbury Av. 69 G6
(Kenton), Har.
Shaftesbury Av., Sthl. 123 G4
Shaftesbury Circle, 85 J1
Har.
Shaftesbury Av.
Shaftesbury Ct. N1 112 A2
Shaftesbury St.
Shaftesbury Gdns. 107 E4
NW10
Shaftesbury Ms. SW4 150 C5
Clapham Common S. Side
Shaftesbury Ms. W8 128 D3
Stratford Rd.
Shaftesbury Pl. W14 128 C4
Warwick Rd.
Shaftesbury Pt. E13 115 H2
High St.
Shaftesbury Rd. E4 62 D1
Shaftesbury Rd. E7 97 J7
Shaftesbury Rd. E10 96 A1
Shaftesbury Rd. E17 78 B6
Shaftesbury Rd. N18 60 B6
Shaftesbury Rd. N19 92 E1

Shaftesbury Rd., 189 J2
Beck.
Shaftesbury Rd., 185 G7
Cars.
Shaftesbury Rd., 145 H3
Rich.
Shaftesbury St. N1 **12 A2**
Shaftesbury St. N1 111 J2
Shaftesbury Way, 162 A3
Twick.
Shaftesbury Waye, 102 B5
Hayes
Shaftesburys, The, 98 D7
Bark.
Shafto Ms. SW1 **23 J6**
Shafton Rd. E9 113 G1
Shakespeare Av. N11 58 C5
Shakespeare Av. 106 D1
NW10
Shakespeare Av., 142 A6
Felt.
Shakespeare Av., 102 B4
Hayes
Shakespeare Cres. 98 C6
E12
Shakespeare Cres. 106 D1
NW10
Shakespeare Dr., Har. 70 A6
Shakespeare Gdns. 73 J4
N2
Shakespeare Ho. N14 58 D2
High St.
Shakespeare Rd. E17 77 G2
Shakespeare Rd. N3 72 D1
Popes Dr.
Shakespeare Rd. NW7 55 F4
Shakespeare Rd. 151 H5
SE24
Shakespeare Rd. W3 126 C1
Shakespeare Rd. W7 104 C7
Shakespeare Rd., 158 E1
Bexh.
Shakespeare Sq., Ilf. 65 F6
Shakespeare Way, 160 C4
Felt.
Shakspeare Ms. N16 94 B4
Shakspeare Wk.
Shakspeare Wk. N16 94 B4
Shalcomb St. SW10 **30 D6**
Shalcomb St. SW10 129 F6
Shaldon Dr., Mord. 184 B5
Shaldon Dr., Ruis. 84 C3
Shaldon Rd., Edg. 69 J1
Shalfleet Dr. W10 108 A7
Shalford Cl., Orp. 207 F4
Shalimar Gdns. W3 106 C7
Shalimar Rd. W3 106 C7
Hereford Rd.
Shallons Rd. SE9 174 E4
Shalston Vil., Surb. 181 J6
Shalstone Rd. SW14 146 B3
Shamrock Rd., Croy. 187 F6
Shamrock St. SW4 150 D3
Shamrock Way N14 58 B1
Shand St. SE1 **28 E3**
Shand St. SE1 132 B2
Shandon Rd. SW4 150 C6
Shandy St. E1 113 G5
Shanklin Gdns., Wat. 50 C4
Shanklin Rd. N8 74 D5
Shanklin Rd. N15 76 D4
Shanklin Way SE15 132 C7
Pentridge St.
Shannon Cl. NW2 90 A3
Shannon Cl., Sthl. 122 D5
Shannon Gro. SW9 151 F4
Shannon Pl. NW8 **7 H1**
Shannon Way, Beck. 172 B6
Shap Cres., Cars. 199 J1
Shapland Way N13 59 F5
Shardcroft Av. SE24 151 H5
Shardeloes Rd. SE14 153 J2
Sharland Cl., Th.Hth. 187 G6
Dunheved Rd. N.
Sharman Ct., Sid. 176 A4
Sharnbrooke Cl., 158 C3
Well.
Sharon Cl., Surb. 195 G1
Sharon Gdns. E9 113 F1
Sharon Rd. W4 126 D5
Sharon Rd., Enf. 45 H2
Sharpe Cl. W7 104 C5
Templeman Rd.
Sharpleshall St. NW1 91 J7
Sharpness Cl., 102 E5
Hayes
Sharratt St. SE15 133 F6
Sharsted St. SE17 **35 G4**
Sharsted St. SE17 131 H5
Sharvel La., Nthlt. 102 A1
Shavers Pl. SW1 **17 H6**
Shaw Av., Bark. 118 E2
Shaw Cl. SE28 138 B1
Shaw Cl., Bushey 52 B2

Shaw Dr., Walt.	178	C7
Shaw Gdns., Bark.	118	E2
Shaw Rd. SE22	152	B4
Shaw Rd., Brom.	173	F3
Shaw Rd., Enf.	45	G1
Shaw Sq. E17	77	H1
Shaw Way, Wall.	200	E7
Shawbrooke Rd. SE9	155	J5
Shawbury Rd. SE22	152	C5
Shawfield Ct.,	120	B3
West Dr.		
Shawfield Pk., Brom.	192	A2
Shawfield St. SW3	**31**	**H4**
Shawfield St. SW3	129	H5
Shawford Cl. SW15	147	G7
Shawford Rd., Epsom	196	D6
Shaws Cotts. SE23	171	H3
Shearing Dr., Cars.	185	F7
Stavordale Rd.		
Shearling Way N7	93	E6
Shearman Rd. SE3	155	F4
Shearsmith Ho. E1	**21**	**J5**
Shearwater Cl., Bark.	117	H3
Thames Rd.		
Shearwater Rd., Sutt.	198	B2
Gander Grn. La.		
Shearwater Way,	102	D6
Hayes		
Sheaveshill Av. NW9	71	E4
Sheen Common Dr.,	146	A4
Rich.		
Sheen Ct., Rich.	146	A4
Sheen Ct. Rd., Rich.	146	A4
Sheen Gate Gdns.	146	C4
SW14		
Sheen Gro. N1	111	G1
Richmond Av.		
Sheen La. SW14	146	C3
Sheen Pk., Rich.	145	J4
Sheen Rd., Orp.	193	J4
Sheen Rd., Rich.	145	H5
Sheen Way, Wall.	201	F5
Sheen Wd. SW14	146	C5
Sheendale Rd., Rich.	145	J4
Sheenewood SE26	171	E5
Sheep La. E8	112	E1
Sheep Wk. Ms.	166	A6
SW19		
Sheepcote Cl.,	122	A7
Houns.		
Sheepcote La. SW11	149	J2
Sheepcote Rd., Har.	68	C6
Sheepcotes Rd., Rom.	82	D4
Sheephouse Way,	182	E7
N.Mal.		
Sheerness Ms.	136/137	E2
E16		
Barge Ho. Rd.		
Sheerwater Rd. E16	116	A5
Sheffield Rd., Houns.	141	G5
Southern Perimeter Rd.		
Sheffield Sq. E3	113	J3
Malmesbury Rd.		
Sheffield St. WC2	**18**	**C4**
Sheffield Ter. W8	128	D1
Shefton Ri., Nthwd.	50	A7
Shelbourne Cl., Pnr.	67	F3
Shelbourne Rd. N17	76	E2
Shelburne Rd. N7	93	F4
Shelbury Cl., Sid.	176	A3
Shelbury Rd. SE22	153	E5
Sheldon Av. N6	73	H7
Sheldon Av., Ilf.	80	E2
Sheldon Cl. SE12	155	H5
Sheldon Cl. SE20	189	E1
Sheldon Rd. N18	60	B4
Sheldon Rd. NW2	90	A4
Sheldon Rd., Bexh.	159	F1
Sheldon Rd., Dag.	100	E7
Sheldon St., Croy.	201	J3
Wandle Rd.		
Sheldrake Cl. E16	136	C1
Newland St.		
Sheldrake Pl. W8	128	C2
Sheldrick Cl. SW19	185	G2
Shelduck Cl. E15	97	F5
Sheldwich Ter.,	192	B6
Brom.		
Shelford Pl. N16	94	A3
Stoke Newington Ch. St.		
Shelford Ri. SE19	170	C7
Shelford Rd., Barn.	39	J6
Shelgate Rd. SW11	149	J5
Shell Cl., Brom.	192	C6
Shell Rd. SE13	154	B3
Shellduck Cl. NW9	70/71	E2
Swan Dr.		
Shelley Av. E12	98	B6
Shelley Av., Grnf.	104	A3
Shelley Cl. SE15	153	E2
Shelley Cl., Edg.	54	A4
Shelley Cl., Grnf.	104	A3
Shelley Cl., Hayes	102	A5
Shelley Cl., Orp.	207	H3
Shelley Cres., Houns.	142	D2
Shelley Cres., Sthl.	103	F6
Shelley Dr., Well.	157	H1
Shelley Gdns., Wem.	87	F2
Shelley Way SW19	167	G6
Shellness Rd. E5	94	E5
Shellwood Rd. SW11	149	J2
Shelmerdine Cl. E3	114	A6
Shelton Rd. SW19	184	D1
Shelton St. WC2	**18**	**A4**
Shelton St. WC2	110	E6
Shenfield Ho. SE18	136	A7
Shooter's Hill Rd.		
Shenfield Rd.,	63	H7
Wdf.Grn.		
Shenfield St. N1	**12**	**E2**
Shenley Rd. N13	112	B2
Shenley Rd. SE5	152	B1
Shenley Rd., Borwd.	38	A4
Shenley Rd., Houns.	142	E1
Shepcot Ho. N14	42	C6
Shepherd Mkt. W1	**24**	**D1**
Shepherd St. W1	**24**	**D2**
Shepherdess Pl. N1	**12**	**A3**
Shepherdess Wk. N1	**12**	**A1**
Shepherdess Wk. N1	111	J2
Shepherds Bush Grn.	127	J2
W12		
Shepherds Bush	127	J2
Mkt. W12		
Shepherds Bush Pl.	128	A2
W12		
Shepherds Bush Rd.	127	J4
W6		
Shepherds Cl. N6	74	B6
Shepherds Cl., Orp.	207	J3
Stapleton Rd.		
Shepherds Cl., Rom.	82	D5
Shepherds Ct. W12	128	A2
Shepherds Grn., Chis.	175	G7
Shepherds Hill N6	74	B6
Shepherds La. E9	95	G5
Shepherds Path,	84/85	E6
Nthlt.		
Fortunes Mead		
Shepherds Pl. W1	**16**	**B5**
Shepherds Pl. W1	110	A7
Shepherds Wk. NW2	89	G2
Shepherds Wk. NW3	91	G5
Shepherds Wk.,	52	A2
Bushey		
Shepherds Way,	203	G7
S.Croy.		
Shepiston La., Hayes	121	G4
Shepiston La.,	121	F4
West Dr.		
Shepley Cl., Cars.	200	A3
Sheppard Cl., Enf.	45	E1
Sheppard Cl.,	181	H4
Kings.T.		
Beaufort Rd.		
Sheppard Dr. SE16	132	E5
Sheppard St. E16	115	F4
Shepperton Cl.,	38	D1
Borwd.		
Shepperton Rd. N1	111	J1
Shepperton Rd., Orp.	193	F6
Sheppey Gdns., Dag.	100	C7
Sheppey Rd.		
Sheppey Rd., Dag.	100	B7
Sheppey Wk. N1	93	J7
Clephane Rd.		
Sherard Ct. N7	92/93	E3
Manor Gdns.		
Sherard Rd. SE9	156	B5
Sheraton Business	105	E2
Cen., Grnf.		
Sheraton St. W1	**17**	**H4**
Sherborne Av., Enf.	45	F2
Sherborne Av., Sthl.	123	G4
Sherborne Cl., Hayes	102	C6
Sherborne Cres.,	185	H7
Cars.		
Sherborne Gdns.	70	A3
NW9		
Sherborne Gdns.	105	E6
W13		
Sherborne La. EC4	**20**	**B5**
Sherborne Rd.,	195	H5
Chess.		
Sherborne Rd., Felt.	141	G7
Sherborne Rd., Orp.	193	J4
Sherborne Rd., Sutt.	198	D2
Sherboro Rd. N15	76	C6
Ermine Rd.		
Sherbrook Gdns. N21	43	H7
Sherbrooke Cl.,	159	G4
Bexh.		
Sherbrooke Rd. SW6	128	C7
Shere Cl., Chess.	195	G5
Shere Rd., Ilf.	80	D5
Sheredan Rd. E4	62	D5
Sherfield Cl., N.Mal.	182	C3
California Rd.		
Sherfield Gdns.	147	F6
SW15		
Sheridan Ct., Houns.	143	F5
Vickers Way		
Sheridan Cres., Chis.	192	E2
Sheridan Gdns., Har.	69	G6
Sheridan Ms. E11	79	G6
Woodbine Pl.		
Sheridan Pl. SW13	147	F2
Brookwood Av.		
Sheridan Pl., Hmptn.	179	H1
Sheridan Rd. E7	97	F3
Sheridan Rd. E12	98	B5
Sheridan Rd. SW19	184	C1
Sheridan Rd., Belv.	139	G4
Sheridan Rd., Bexh.	158	E3
Sheridan Rd., Rich.	163	F3
Sheridan St. E1	112/113	E6
Watney St.		
Sheridan Ter., Nthlt.	85	H5
Whitton Av. W.		
Sheridan Wk. NW11	72	D6
Sheridan Wk., Cars.	199	J5
Carshalton Pk. Rd.		
Sheridan Way, Beck.	171	J7
Turners Meadow Way		
Sheringham Av. E12	98	C4
Sheringham Av. N14	42	D5
Sheringham Av.,	160	A3
Felt.		
Sheringham Av., Rom.	83	J6
Sheringham Av.,	161	F1
Twick.		
Sheringham Dr.,	99	J5
Bark.		
Sheringham Rd. N7	93	F6
Sheringham Rd.	189	E3
SE20		
Sheringham Twr.,	103	H7
Sthl.		
Sherington Av., Pnr.	51	G7
Sherington Rd. SE7	135	H6
Sherland Rd., Twick.	162	C1
Sherlies Av., Orp.	207	H2
Sherlock Ms. W1	**16**	**B1**
Sherman Rd., Brom.	191	G1
Shernhall St. E17	78	C5
Sherrard Rd. E7	97	J6
Sherrard Rd. E12	98	A5
Sherrards Way, Barn.	40	D5
Sherrick Grn. Rd.	89	H5
NW10		
Sherriff Rd. NW6	90	D6
Sherrin Rd. E10	96	A4
Sherringham Av.	76	D2
N17		
Sherrock Gdns. NW4	71	G4
Sherry Ms., Bark.	99	G7
Cecil Av.		
Sherwin Rd. SE14	153	G1
Sherwood Av. E18	79	H3
Sherwood Av. SW16	168	D7
Sherwood Av., Grnf.	86	B6
Sherwood Av.,	102	B4
Hayes		
Sherwood Cl. SW13	147	H3
Lower Common S.		
Sherwood Cl. W13	124	E1
Sherwood Cl., Bex.	158	C6
Sherwood Gdns. E14	134	A4
Sherwood Gdns.	**37**	**J4**
SE16		
Sherwood Gdns.	132	D5
SE16		
Sherwood Gdns.,	99	G7
Bark.		
Sherwood Pk. Av.	158	A7
Sid.		
Sherwood Pk. Rd.	186	C4
Mitch.		
Sherwood Pk. Rd.,	198	D5
Sutt.		
Sherwood Rd. NW4	71	J3
Sherwood Rd. SW19	166	C7
Sherwood Rd., Croy.	188	E7
Sherwood Rd.,	179	G1
Hmptn.		
Sherwood Rd., Har.	85	J2
Sherwood Rd., Ilf.	81	G4
Sherwood Rd., Well.	157	H2
Sherwood St. N20	57	G3
Sherwood St. W1	**17**	**G5**
Sherwood Ter. N20	57	G3
Green Rd.		
Sherwood Way,	204	B2
W.Wick.		
Shetland Cl., Borwd.	38	D6
Percheron Rd.		
Shetland Rd. E3	113	J2
Shield Dr., Brent.	124	D6
Shieldhall St. SE2	138	C4
Shifford Path SE23	171	G3
Shillibeer Pl. W1	**15**	**H1**
Shillibeer Wk., Chig.	65	J3
Shillingford St. N1	93	H7
Cross St.		
Shinfield St. W12	107	J6
Shinglewell Rd., Erith	139	G7
Shinners Cl. SE25	188	D5
Ship All. W4	126	A6
Thames Rd.		
Ship & Mermaid	**28**	**C3**
Row SE1		
Ship La. SW14	146	C2
Ship St. SE8	154	A1
Ship Tavern Pas. EC3	**20**	**D5**
Ship Yd. E14	134	B5
Napier Av.		
Shipka Rd. SW12	168	B1
Shipman Rd. E16	115	H6
Shipman Rd. SE23	171	G2
Shipton Cl., Dag.	100	D3
Shipton St. E2	**13**	**G3**
Shipton St. E2	112	C3
Shipwright Rd. SE16	133	H2
Shirburn Cl. SE23	153	F7
Tyson Rd.		
Shirbutt St. E14	114	B7
Shire Cl., Epsom	197	F7
Shire Cl., Erith	138	D3
St. John Fisher Rd.		
Shire Horse Way,	144	C3
Islw.		
Shire La., Kes.	206	C7
Shire La., Orp.	206	C7
Shire Pl. SW18	149	F7
Whitehead Cl.		
Shirebrook Rd. SE3	156	A3
Shirehall Cl. NW4	72	A6
Shirehall Gdns. NW4	72	A6
Shirehall La. NW4	72	A6
Shirehall Pk. NW4	72	A6
Shires, The, Rich.	163	H4
Shirland Ms. W9	108	C3
Shirland Rd. W9	108	D4
Shirley Av., Bex.	158	D7
Shirley Av., Croy.	203	F1
Shirley Av., Sutt.	199	H4
Shirley Ch. Rd., Croy.	203	G3
Shirley Cl. E17	78	B5
Addison Rd.		
Shirley Cl., Houns.	143	J5
Shirley Cl., Croy.	203	G3
Shirley Cres., Beck.	189	H4
Shirley Dr., Houns.	143	J5
Shirley Gdns. W7	124	D1
Shirley Gdns., Bark.	99	H6
Shirley Gro. N9	45	F7
Shirley Gro. SW11	150	A3
Shirley Hills Rd.,	203	G5
Croy.		
Shirley Ho. Dr. SE7	135	J7
Shirley Oaks Rd.,	203	G1
Croy.		
Shirley Pk. Rd., Croy.	203	E1
Shirley Rd. E15	97	E7
Shirley Rd. W4	126	D2
Shirley Rd., Croy.	189	E7
Shirley Rd., Enf.	43	J3
Shirley Rd., Sid.	175	H3
Shirley St. E16	115	F6
Shirley Way, Croy.	203	H3
Shirlock Rd. NW3	91	J4
Shobden Rd. N17	76	A1
Shobroke Cl. NW2	89	J3
Shoe La. EC4	**19**	**F3**
Shoe La. EC4	111	G6
Shoebury Rd. E6	98	C7
Sholto Rd., Houns.	140	C5
Shoot Up Hill NW2	90	B5
Shooters Av., Har.	69	F4
Shooter's Hill SE18	156	D1
Shooter's Hill, Well.	156	D1
Shooter's Hill Rd.	135	H7
SE3		
Shooter's Hill Rd.	154	D1
SE10		
Shooter's Hill Rd.	135	H7
SE18		
Shooters Rd., Enf.	43	H1
Shore Cl., Felt.	142	A7
Shore Cl., Hmptn.	160/161	E5
Stewart Cl.		
Shore Gro., Felt.	161	G2
Shore Pl. E9	95	F7
Shore Rd. E9	95	F7
Shoreditch High St.	**13**	**G3**
E1		
Shoreditch High St.	112	B4
E1		
Shoreham Cl.	148/149	D1
SW18		
Ram St.		
Shoreham Cl., Bex.	176	D1
Stansted Cres.		

Shoreham Cl., Croy. 189 F6
Shoreham Rd. E., 140 B5
  Houns.
Shoreham Rd. W., 140 B5
  Houns.
Shoreham Way, 191 G6
  Brom.
Shorncliffe Rd. SE1 37 F3
Shorncliffe Rd. SE1 132 C5
Shorndean St. SE6 172 C1
Shorne Cl., Sid. 158 B6
Shornefield Cl., 192 D3
  Brom.
Shornells Way SE2 138 C5
  Willrose Cres.
Shorrolds Rd. SW6 128 C7
Short Hedges, Houns. 143 H1
Short Hill, Har. 86 B1
  High St.
Short Path SE18 136/137 E6
  Westdale Rd.
Short Rd. E11 96 E2
Short Rd. E15 114 D1
Short Rd. W4 126 E6
Short Rd., Houns. 140 B6
Short St. NW4 71 J4
  New Brent St.
Short St. SE1 27 F3
Short Wall E15 114 C3
Short Way SE9 156 B3
Short Way, Twick. 143 J7
Shortcroft Rd., 197 F7
  Epsom
Shortcrofts Rd., Dag. 101 F6
Shorter St. E1 21 F5
Shorter St. E1 112 C7
Shortgate N12 56 C4
Shortlands W6 128 A4
Shortlands, Hayes 121 G6
Shortlands Cl. N18 60 A3
Shortlands Cl., Belv. 139 F3
Shortlands Gdns., 191 E2
  Brom.
Shortlands Gro., 190 D3
  Brom.
Shortlands Rd. E10 78 B7
Shortlands Rd., 190 D3
  Brom.
Shortlands Rd., 163 J7
  Kings.T.
Shorts Cft. NW9 70 B4
Shorts Gdns. WC2 18 A4
Shorts Gdns. WC2 110 E6
Shorts Rd., Cars. 199 H4
Shortway N12 57 H6
Shotfield, Wall. 200 B6
Shott Cl., Sutt. 199 F5
  Turnpike La.
Shottendane Rd. 148 D1
  SW6
Shottery Cl. SE9 174 B3
Shottfield Av. SW14 146 E4
Shoulder of Mutton 113 H7
  All. E14
  Narrow St.
Shouldham St. W1 15 H2
Shouldham St. W1 109 H5
Showers Way, Hayes 122 A1
Shrapnel Cl. SE18 136 B7
Shrapnel Rd. SE9 156 C3
Shrewsbury Av. 146 C4
  SW14
Shrewsbury Av., Har. 69 H4
Shrewsbury Cl., 195 H2
  Surb.
Shrewsbury Ct. EC1 111 J4
  Whitecross St.
Shrewsbury Cres. 106 D1
  NW10
Shrewsbury La. SE18 156 E1
Shrewsbury Ms. W2 108 D5
  Chepstow Rd.
Shrewsbury Rd. E7 98 A5
Shrewsbury Rd. N11 58 C6
Shrewsbury Rd. W2 108 D6
Shrewsbury Rd., 189 H3
  Beck.
Shrewsbury Rd., 185 H6
  Cars.
Shrewsbury Rd., Felt. 141 G5
  Great South-West Rd.
Shrewsbury Rd., 141 G5
  Houns.
  Great South-West Rd.
Shrewsbury St. W10 107 J4
Shrewsbury Wk., 144 D3
  Islw.
  South St.
Shrewton Rd. SW17 167 J7
Shroffold Rd., Brom. 173 E4
Shropshire Cl., 187 E4
  Mitch.
Shropshire Pl. WC1 9 G6
Shropshire Rd. N22 59 F7

Shroton St. NW1 15 G1
Shroton St. NW1 109 H5
Shrubberies, The E18 79 G2
Shrubberies, The, 65 F5
  Chig.
Shrubbery Cl. N1 111 J1
  St. Paul St.
Shrubbery Gdns. 43 H7
  N21
Shrubbery Rd. N9 60 D3
Shrubbery Rd. SW16 168 E4
Shrubbery Rd., Sthl. 123 F1
Shrubland Gro. 197 J3
  Wor.Pk.
Shrubland Rd. E8 112 D1
Shrubland Rd. E10 78 A7
Shrubland Rd. E17 78 A5
Shrublands Av., 204 A4
  Croy.
Shrublands Cl. N20 57 G1
Shrublands Cl. SE26 171 F3
Shrublands Cl., Chig. 65 F6
Shrubsall Cl. SE9 174 B1
Shuna Wk. N1 94 A6
  St. Paul's Rd.
Shurland Av., Barn. 41 G6
Shurland Gdns. 37 G7
  SE15
Shurlock Dr., Orp. 207 F4
Shuters Sq. W14 128 C5
  Sun Rd.
Shuttle Cl., Sid. 157 J7
Shuttle St. E1 13 H6
Shuttlemead, Bex. 159 F7
Shuttleworth Rd. 149 H2
  SW11
Sibella Rd. SW4 150 D2
Sibley Cl., Bexh. 159 E5
Sibley Gro. E12 98 B7
Sibthorpe Rd. SE12 155 H6
Sibton Rd., Cars. 185 H7
Sicilian Av. WC1 18 B2
Sidbury St. SW6 148 B1
Sidcup Bypass, Chis. 174 E2
Sidcup Bypass, Orp. 176 D7
Sidcup Bypass, Sid. 175 H4
Sidcup High St., Sid. 176 A4
Sidcup Hill, Sid. 176 B4
Sidcup Hill Gdns., 176 C5
  Sid.
  Sidcup Hill
Sidcup Pl., Sid. 176 A5
Sidcup Rd. SE9 156 A7
Sidcup Rd. SE12 155 H5
Sidcup Technology 176 D5
  Cen., Sid.
Siddeley Dr., Houns. 142 E3
Siddons La. NW1 8 A6
Siddons Rd. N17 76 D1
Siddons Rd. SE23 171 H2
Siddons Rd., Croy. 201 G3
Side Rd. E17 77 J5
Sidewood Rd. SE9 175 G1
Sidford Pl. SE1 26 D6
Sidings, The E11 96 C1
Sidings, The, Loug. 48 B6
Sidings Ms. N7 93 G3
Sidmouth Av., Islw. 144 B2
Sidmouth Cl., Wat. 50 B2
Sidmouth Dr., Ruis. 84 A3
Sidmouth Par. NW2 89 J7
  Sidmouth Rd.
Sidmouth Rd. E10 96 C3
Sidmouth Rd. NW2 89 J7
Sidmouth Rd. SE15 152 C1
Sidmouth Rd., Well. 138 C7
Sidmouth St. WC1 10 B4
Sidmouth St. WC1 111 E3
Sidney Av. N13 59 F5
Sidney Elson Way E6 116 D2
  Edwin Av.
Sidney Gdns., Brent. 125 F6
Sidney Gro. EC1 11 G2
Sidney Rd. E7 97 G3
Sidney Rd. N22 59 F7
Sidney Rd. SE25 188 D5
Sidney Rd. SW9 151 F2
Sidney Rd., Beck. 189 H2
Sidney Rd., Har. 67 J3
Sidney Rd., Twick. 144 D6
Sidney Rd., Walt. 178 A7
Sidney Sq. E1 113 F6
Sidney St. E1 113 E5
Sidworth St. E8 95 E7
Siebert Rd. SE3 135 G6
Siemens Rd. SE18 136 A3
Sigdon Rd. E8 94 D5
Sigers, The, Pnr. 66 B6
Signmakers Yd. NW1 110 B1
  Delancey St.
Sigrist Sq., Kings.T. 181 H1
Silbury Av., Mitch. 185 H1
Silbury St. N1 12 B3
Silchester Rd. W10 108 A6

Silecroft Rd., Bexh. 159 G1
Silesia Bldgs. E8 94/95 E7
  London La.
Silex St. SE1 27 H4
Silex St. SE1 131 H2
Silk Cl. SE12 155 G5
Silk Mills Path SE13 154 C2
  Lewisham Rd.
Silk St. EC2 20 A1
Silk St. EC2 111 J5
Silkfield Rd. NW9 71 E5
Silkin Ho., Wat. 50 C3
Silkmills Sq. E9 95 J6
Silkstream Rd., Edg. 70 C1
Silsoe Rd. N22 75 F2
Silver Birch Av. E4 61 J6
Silver Birch Cl. N11 58 A6
Silver Birch Cl. SE28 138 A1
Silver Birch Gdns. E6 116 C4
Silver Birch Ms., Ilf. 65 F6
  Fencepiece Rd.
Silver Cl. SE14 133 H7
  Southerngate Way
Silver Cl., Har. 52 A7
Silver Cres. W4 126 B4
Silver Jubilee Way, 142 B2
  Houns.
Silver La., W.Wick. 204 D2
Silver Pl. W1 17 G5
Silver Rd. SE13 154 B3
  Elmira St.
Silver Rd. W12 108 A7
Silver Spring Cl., 139 H6
  Erith
Silver St. N18 60 B4
Silver St., Enf. 44 A3
Silver Wk. SE16 133 J1
Silver Way, Rom. 83 H3
Silverbirch Wk. NW3 92 A6
  Queens Cres.
Silvercliffe Gdns., 41 H4
  Barn.
Silverdale SE26 171 F4
Silverdale, Enf. 43 E4
Silverdale Av., Ilf. 81 H5
Silverdale Cl. W7 124 B1
Silverdale Cl., Nthlt. 85 F5
Silverdale Cl., Sutt. 198 C4
Silverdale Dr. SE9 174 B2
Silverdale Dr., Sun. 178 B2
Silverdale Gdns., 122 A2
  Hayes
Silverdale Rd. E4 62 D6
Silverdale Rd., Bexh. 159 H2
Silverdale Rd., Hayes 122 A2
Silverdale Rd. 193 F4
  (Petts Wd.), Orp.
Silverhall St., Islw. 144 D3
Silverholme Cl., Har. 69 G7
Silverland St. E16 136 C1
Silverleigh Rd., 187 F4
  Th.Hth.
Silvermere Rd. SE6 154 B6
Silverston Way, Stan. 53 F6
Silverthorn Gdns. E4 62 A2
Silverthorne Rd. SW8 150 B2
Silverton Rd. W6 128 A6
Silvertown Way E16 115 F6
Silvertree La., Grnf. 104 A3
  Cowgate Rd.
Silverwood Cl., 172 A7
  Beck.
Silvester Rd. SE22 152 C5
Silvocea Way E14 114 D6
Silwood Est. SE16 133 F4
Silwood St. SE16 133 F4
Simla Cl. SE14 133 H6
Simla Ho. SE1 28 C4
Simmil Rd., Esher 194 B5
Simmons Cl. N20 57 H1
Simmons Cl., 195 F7
  Chess.
Simmons La. E4 62 D1
Simmons Rd. SE18 136 E5
Simmons Way N20 57 H2
Simms Cl., Cars. 199 H2
Simms Gdns. N2 73 F2
  Tarling Rd.
Simms Rd. SE1 37 H2
Simms Rd. SE1 132 D4
Simnel Rd. SE12 155 H7
Simon Cl. W11 108 C7
  Portobello Rd.
Simonds Rd. E10 96 A2
Simone Cl., Brom. 192 A1
Simons Wk. E15 96 D5
  Waddington St.
Simpson Cl. N21 42/43 E5
  Macleod Rd.
Simpson Dr. W3 106 D6
Simpson Rd., Houns. 143 F6
Simpson Rd., Rich. 163 F4
Simpson St. SW11 149 G2

Simpsons Rd. E14 114 B7
Simpsons Rd., Brom. 191 G3
Simrose Ct. SW18 148 D5
  Wandsworth High St.
Sims Wk. SE3 155 F4
Sinclair Cl., Beck. 172 A7
Sinclair Gdns. W14 128 A2
Sinclair Gro. NW11 72 A6
Sinclair Rd. E4 61 J5
Sinclair Rd. W14 128 A2
Sinclare Cl., Enf. 44 C1
Singapore Rd. W13 124 D1
Singer St. EC2 12 C4
Singleton Cl. SW17 167 J7
Singleton Cl., Croy. 187 J7
  St. Saviours Rd.
Singleton Rd., Dag. 101 F5
Singleton Scarp N12 56 D5
Sinnott Rd. E17 77 G1
Sion Rd., Twick. 162 E1
Sipson Cl., West Dr. 120 D6
Sipson La., Hayes 120 D6
Sipson La., West Dr. 120 D6
Sipson Rd., West Dr. 120 D5
Sipson Way, West Dr. 120 D7
Sir Alexander Cl. W3 127 F1
Sir Alexander Rd. W3 127 F1
Sir Cyril Black Way 166 D7
  SW19
Sir Thomas More 31 F6
  Est. SW3
Sirdar Rd. N22 75 H3
Sirdar Rd. W11 108 A7
Sirdar Rd., Mitch. 168 A6
  Grenfell Rd.
Sirinham Pt. SW8 34 D6
Sirinham Pt. SW8 131 F6
Sirius Rd., Nthwd. 50 A5
Sise La. EC4 20 B4
Siskin Cl., Borwd. 38 A4
Sisley Rd., Bark. 117 H1
Sispara Gdns. SW18 148 C6
Sissinghurst Rd., 188 D7
  Croy.
Sissulo Ct. E6 115 J1
  Redclyffe Rd.
Sister Mabel's Way 37 H7
  SE15
Sisters Av. SW11 149 J4
Sistova Rd. SW12 168 B1
Sisulu Pl. SW9 151 G3
Sittingbourne Av., 44 A6
  Enf.
Sitwell Gro., Stan. 52 C5
Siverst Cl., Nthlt. 85 H6
Sivill Ho. E2 13 G3
Sivill Ho. E2 112 C3
Siviter Way, Dag. 101 H7
Siward Rd. N17 76 A1
Siward Rd. SW17 167 F3
Siward Rd., Brom. 191 H3
Six Acres Est. N4 93 G2
Six Bridges Trd. Est. 37 J4
  SE1
Six Bridges Trd. Est. 132 D5
  SE1
Sixth Av. E12 98 C4
Sixth Av. W10 108 B3
Sixth Av., Hayes 121 J1
Sixth Cross Rd., 161 J3
  Twick.
Skardu Rd. NW2 90 B5
Skeena Hill SW18 148 B7
Skeffington Rd. E6 116 C1
Skelbrook St. SW18 167 E2
Skelgill Rd. SW15 148 C4
Skelley Rd. E15 97 F7
Skelton Cl. E8 94 C6
  Buttermere Wk.
Skelton Rd. E7 97 G6
Skeltons La. E10 78 B7
Skelwith Rd. W6 127 J6
Skenfrith Ho. 132/133 E6
  SE15
  Commercial Way
Skerne Rd., Kings.T. 181 G1
Sketchley Gdns. 133 G5
  SE16
Sketty Rd., Enf. 44 B3
Skiers St. E15 114 E1
Skiffington Cl. SW2 169 G1
Skinner Ct. E2 112/113 E2
  Parmiter St.
Skinner Pl. SW1 32 B2
Skinner St. EC1 11 F4
Skinner St. EC1 111 G3
Skinners La. EC4 20 A5
Skinners La., Houns. 143 H1
Skinner's Row SE10 154 B1
  Blackheath Rd.
Skipsey Av. E6 116 C3
Skipton Cl. N11 58 A6
  Ribblesdale Av.
Skipton Dr., Hayes 121 F3

Name			Name			Name			Name		
Skipworth Rd. E9	113	F1	Smokehouse Yd. EC1	111	H5	Somerset Cl. N17	76	A2	South Carriage Dr. SW7	23	F4
Skomer Wk. N1	93	J6	Smugglers Way SW18	149	E4	Somerset Cl., N.Mal.	183	E6	South Carriage Dr. SW7	129	H2
Clephane Rd.			Smyrks Rd. SE17	36	E4	Somerset Cl., SW7	79	G1	South Cl. N6	74	B6
Sky Peals Rd., Wdf.Grn.	78	D1	Smyrks Rd. SE17	132	B5	Somerset Est. SW11	149	G1	South Cl., Barn.	40	C3
Skyport Dr., West Dr.	120	A7	Smyrna Rd. NW6	90	D7	Somerset Gdns. N6	74	A7	South Cl., Bexh.	158	D4
Slade, The SE18	137	H6	Smythe St. E14	114	B7	Somerset Gdns. N17	60	B7	South Cl., Dag.	119	G1
Slade Ho., Houns.	143	F6	Snakes La., Barn.	42	B3	Somerset Gdns. SE13	154	B2	South Cl., Mord.	184/185	E6
Slade Twr. E10	96	B2	Snakes La. E. Wdf.Grn.	63	J6	Somerset Gdns. SW16	187	F3	*Green La.*		
Slade Wk. SE17	35	H6	Snakes La. W., Wdf.Grn.	63	G6	Somerset Gdns., Tedd.	162	B5	South Cl., Pnr.	67	F7
Sladebrook Rd. SE3	156	A2	Snaresbrook Dr., Stan.	53	G4	Somerset Rd. E17	78	A5	South Cl., Twick.	161	G3
Sladedale Rd. SE18	137	H5	Snaresbrook Rd. E11	78	E4	Somerset Rd. N17	76	C3	South Cl., West Dr.	120	C3
Slades Cl., Enf.	43	G3	Snarsgate St. W10	107	J5	Somerset Rd. N18	60	C5	South Colonnade E14	134	A1
Slades Dr., Chis.	175	F3	Sneath Av. NW11	72	C7	Somerset Rd. NW4	71	J4	South Countess Rd. E17	77	J3
Slades Gdns., Enf.	43	G2	Snells Pk. N18	60	C6	Somerset Rd. SW19	166	B4	South Cres. E16	114	D4
Slades Hill, Enf.	43	G3	Sneyd Rd. NW2	89	J4	Somerset Rd. W4	126	D3	South Cres. WC1	17	H2
Slades Ri., Enf.	43	G3	Snow Hill EC1	19	G2	Somerset Rd. W13	125	E1	South Cres. WC1	110	D5
Slagrove Pl. SE13	154	B5	Snow Hill EC1	111	H5	Somerset Rd., Barn.	41	E5	South Cross Rd., Ilf.	81	F5
Slaidburn St. SW10	30	D6	Snow Hill Ct. EC1	19	H3	Somerset Rd., Brent.	125	F6	South Croxted Rd. SE21	170	A3
Slaidburn St. SW10	129	F6	Snowberry Cl. E15	96	D4	Somerset Rd., Har.	67	J5	South Dene NW7	54	D3
Slaithwaite Rd. SE13	154	C4	Snowbury Rd. SW6	149	E2	Somerset Rd., Kings.T.	181	J2	South Dr., Orp.	207	H5
Slaney Pl. N7	93	G5	Snowden St. EC2	12	D6	Somerset Rd., Sthl.	103	F5	South Ealing Rd. W5	125	G2
Hornsey Rd.			Snowden St. EC2	112	B4	Somerset Rd., Tedd.	162	B5	South Eastern Av. N9	60	C3
Slater Cl. SE18	136	D5	Snowdon Cres., Hayes	121	F3	Somerset Sq. W14	128	B2	South Eaton Pl. SW1	32	C1
Woolwich New Rd.			Snowdon Dr. NW9	70	E6	Somerset Waye, Houns.	122	E6	South Eaton Pl. SW1	130	A4
Slattery Rd., Felt.	160	C1	Snowdon Rd., Houns.	141	F5	Somersham Rd., Bexh.	159	E2	South Eden Pk. Rd., Beck.	190	B6
Sleaford Grn., Wat.	50	D3	*Southern Perimeter Rd.*			Somerton Av., Rich.	146	B3	South Edwardes Sq. W8	128	C3
Sleaford St. SW8	33	F7	Snowdown Cl. SE20	189	G1	Somerton Rd. NW2	90	B3	South End W8	22	B5
Sleaford St. SW8	130	C7	Snowdrop Cl., Hmptn.	161	G6	Somerton Rd. SE15	153	E4	South End, Croy.	201	J4
Slievemore Cl. SW4	150	D3	*Gresham Rd.*			Somertrees Av. SE12	173	H2	South End Cl. NW3	91	H4
Voltaire Rd.			Snowman Ho. NW6	109	E1	Somervell Rd., Har.	85	F5	South End Grn. NW3	91	H4
Slingsby Pl. WC2	18	A5	Snowsfields SE1	28	C3	Somerville Av. SW13	127	H6	South End Rd. NW3	91	H4
Slippers Pl. SE16	133	E3	Snowsfields SE1	132	A2	Somerville Rd. SE20	171	G7	South End Row W8	22	B5
Sloane Av. SW3	31	G2	Snowshill Rd. E12	98	B5	Somerville Rd., Rom.	82	C6	South End Row W8	129	E3
Sloane Av. SW3	129	H4	Snowy Fielder Waye, Islw.	144	E2	Sonderburg Rd. N7	93	F2	South Esk Rd. E7	97	J6
Sloane Ct. E. SW3	32	B3	Soames St. SE15	152	C3	Sondes St. SE17	36	B5	South Gipsy Rd., Well.	158	D3
Sloane Ct. W. SW3	32	B3	Soames Wk., N.Mal.	182	E1	Sondes St. SE17	132	A6	South Glade, The, Bex.	177	F1
Sloane Ct. W. SW3	130	A5	Socket La., Brom.	191	H7	Sonia Ct., Har.	68	C6	South Grn. NW9	70/71	E1
Sloane Gdns. SW1	32	B2	Soho Sq. W1	17	H3	Sonia Gdns. N12	57	F4	*Clayton Fld.*		
Sloane Gdns. SW1	130	A4	Soho Sq. W1	110	D6	Sonia Gdns. NW10	89	F4	South Gro. E17	77	J5
Sloane Gdns., Orp.	207	F3	Soho St. W1	17	H3	Sonia Gdns., Houns.	123	G7	South Gro. N6	92	A1
Sloane Sq. SW1	32	B2	Sojourner Truth Cl. E8	94/95	E6	Sonning Gdns., Hmptn.	161	E6	South Gro. N15	76	A5
Sloane Sq. SW1	129	J4	*Richmond Rd.*			Sonning Rd. SE25	188	D6	South Gro. Ho. N6	92	A1
Sloane St. SW1	24	A5	Solander Gdns. E1	112/113	E7	Soper Cl. E4	61	J5	*Highgate W. Hill*		
Sloane St. SW1	129	J2	*Dellow St.*			Sophia Cl. N7	93	F6	South Hill, Chis.	174	C6
Sloane Ter. SW1	32	A1	Solebay St. E1	113	H4	*Mackenzie Rd.*			South Hill Av., Har.	85	J3
Sloane Ter. SW1	129	J4	Solent Ri. E13	115	G3	Sophia Rd. E10	96	B1	South Hill Gro., Har.	86	B4
Sloane Wk., Croy.	189	J6	Solent Rd. NW6	90	D5	Sophia Rd. E16	115	H6	South Hill Pk. NW3	91	H4
Slocum Cl. SE28	118	C7	Solent Rd., Houns.	140	C6	Sophia Sq. SE16	113	H7	South Hill Pk. Gdns. NW3	91	H4
Slough La. NW9	70	C6	Soley Ms. WC1	10	E3	*Rotherhithe St.*			South Hill Rd., Brom.	190	E3
Sly St. E1	112/113	E6	Solna Av. SW15	147	J5	Sopwith Av., Chess.	195	H5	South Huxley N18	60	A5
Cannon St. Rd.			Solna Rd. N21	60	A1	Sopwith Cl., Kings.T.	163	J5	South Island Pl. SW9	131	F7
Smaldon Cl., West Dr.	120	D3	Solomon Av. N9	60	D4	Sopwith Rd., Houns.	122	C7	South Kensington Sta. Arc. SW7	129	G4
Walnut Av.			Solomon's Pas. SE15	152	E4	Sopwith Way SW8	32	D7	*Pelham St.*		
Smallberry Av., Islw.	144	C2	Solon New Rd. SW4	150	E4	Sopwith Way SW8	130	B7	South Lambeth Pl. SW8	34	B5
Smallbrook Ms. W2	14	E4	Solon New Rd. Est. SW4	150/151	E4	Sopwith Way, Kings.T.	181	H1	South Lambeth Pl. SW8	131	E6
Smalley Cl. N16	94	C3	*Solon New Rd.*			Sorrel Cl. SE28	138	A1	South Lambeth Rd. SW8	131	E7
Smalley Rd. Est. N16	94	C3	Solon Rd. SW2	151	E4	Sorrel Gdns. E6	116	B5	South La., Kings.T.	181	G3
Smalley Cl.			Solway Cl. E8	94	C6	Sorrel La. E14	114	D6	South La., N.Mal.	182	D4
Smallwood Rd. SW17	167	G4	*Buttermere Wk.*			Sorrell Cl. SE14	133	H7	South La. W., N.Mal.	182	D4
Smardale Rd. SW18	149	F5	Solway Cl., Houns.	143	E3	*Southerngate Way*			South Lo. Av., Mitch.	186	E4
Alma Rd.			Solway Rd. N22	75	H1	Sorrento Rd., Sutt.	198	E3	South Lo. Cres., Enf.	42	D4
Smarden Cl., Belv.	139	G5	Solway Rd. SE22	152	D4	Sotheby Rd. N5	93	H3	South Lo. Dr. N14	42	E5
Essenden Rd.			Somaford Gro., Barn.	41	G6	Sotheran Cl. E8	112	D1	South Mall N9	60	D3
Smarden Gro. SE9	174	C4	Somali Rd. NW2	90	C4	Sotheron Rd. SW6	129	E7	*Plevna Rd.*		
Smart St. E2	113	G3	Somerby Rd., Bark.	99	G7	Soudan Rd. SW11	149	J1	South Mead NW9	71	F1
Smarts La., Loug.	48	A4	Somercoates Cl., Barn.	41	H3	Souldern Rd. W14	128	A3	South Mead, Epsom	197	E7
Smarts Pl. N18	60	D5	Somerfield Rd. N4	93	H2	South Access Rd. E17	77	H7	South Meadows, Wem.	87	J5
Fore St.			Somerford Cl., Pnr.	66	A4	South Acre NW9	71	E2	South Molton La. W1	16	D4
Smart's Pl. WC2	18	B3	Somerford Gro. N16	94	C4	South Africa Rd. W12	127	H1	South Molton La. W1	110	B6
Smeaton Cl., Chess.	195	G6	Somerford Gro. N17	60	D7	South Audley St. W1	16	C6	South Molton Rd. E16	115	G6
Merritt Gdns.			Somerford Gro. Est. N16	94	C4	South Audley St. W1	110	A7	South Molton St. W1	16	D4
Smeaton Rd. SW18	148	D7	*Somerford Gro.*			South Av. E4	46	B7	South Molton St. W1	110	B6
Smeaton Rd., Wdf.Grn.	64	C5	Somerford St. E1	112	E4	South Av., Cars.	199	J7	South Norwood Hill SE25	188	B2
Smeaton St. E1	132	E1	Somerford Way SE16	133	H2	South Av., Rich.	146	A2	South Oak Rd. SW16	169	F4
Smedley St. SW4	150	D2	Somerhill Av., Sid.	158	B7	*Sandycombe Rd.*			South Par. SW3	31	F3
Smedley St. SW8	150	D2	Somerhill Rd., Well.	158	B2	South Av. Gdns., Sthl.	103	F7	South Par. SW3	129	G5
Smeed Rd. E3	96	A7	Somerleyton Pas. SW9	151	H4	South Bank, Chis.	175	F4	South Par. W4	126	D4
Smiles Pl. SE13	154	C2	Somerleyton Rd. SW9	151	H4	South Bank, Surb.	181	H6	South Pk. SW6	148	D2
Smith Cl. SE16	133	G1	Somers Cl. NW1	9	H1	South Bank Ter., Surb.	181	H6	South Pk. Cres. SE6	173	F1
Smith Sq. SW1	26	A6	Somers Cres. W2	15	G4	South Birkbeck Rd. E11	96	D3	South Pk. Cres., Ilf.	99	G3
Smith Sq. SW1	130	E3	Somers Ms. W2	15	G4	South Black Lion La. W6	127	G5	South Pk. Dr., Bark.	99	H4
Smith St. SW3	31	J3	Somers Pl. SW2	151	F7	South Bolton Gdns. SW5	30	B3	South Pk. Dr., Ilf.	99	H4
Smith St. SW3	129	J5	Somers Rd. E17	77	J4	South Bolton Gdns. SW5	129	E5	South Pk. Gro., N.Mal.	182	C4
Smith St., Surb.	181	J6	Somers Rd. SW2	151	F6	South Carriage Dr. SW1	23	J3	South Pk. Hill Rd., S.Croy.	202	A5
Smith Ter. SW3	31	J4	Somersby Gdns., Ilf.	80	C5	South Carriage Dr. SW1	129	H2			
Smith Ter. SW3	129	J5	Somerset Av. SW20	183	H3						
Smithfield St. EC1	19	G2	Somerset Av., Well.	157	J5						
Smithies Ct. E15	96	C5									
Smithies Rd. SE2	138	B4									
Smith's Ct. W1	17	G5									
Smiths Fm. Est., Nthlt.	103	G2									
Smiths Yd. SW18	167	F2									
Summerley St.											
Smith's Yd., Croy.	201	J3									
St. Georges Wk.											
Smithson Rd. N17	76	A1									
Smithwood Cl. SW19	166	B1									
Smithy St. E1	113	F5									
Smock Wk., Croy.	187	J6									
Smokehouse Yd. EC1	19	H1									

Name	Page	Grid
South Pk. Ms. SW6	148	E3
South Pk. Rd. SW19	166	D6
South Pk. Rd., Ilf.	99	G3
South Pk. Ter., Ilf.	99	H3
South Pk. Way, Ruis.	84	C6
South Penge Pk. Est. SE20	188	E2
South Pl. EC2	**20**	**C1**
South Pl. EC2	112	A5
South Pl., Enf.	45	F5
South Pl., Surb.	181	J7
South Pl. Ms. EC2	**20**	**C1**
South Ri. Way SE18	137	G5
South Rd. N9	60	D1
South Rd. SE23	171	G2
South Rd. SW19	167	F6
South Rd. W5	125	G4
South Rd., Edg.	70	B1
South Rd., Felt.	160	D5
South Rd., Hmptn.	161	G6
South Rd. (Chadwell Heath), Rom.	82	C5
South Rd. (Little Heath), Rom.	82	E6
South Rd., Sthl.	123	F2
South Rd., Twick.	162	A3
South Rd., West Dr.	120	D3
South Row SE3	155	F2
South Sea St. SE16	133	J3
South Side W6	127	F3
South Sq. NW11	72	E6
South Sq. WC1	**18**	**E2**
South St. W1	**24**	**C1**
South St. W1	130	A1
South St., Brom.	191	G2
South St., Enf.	45	G5
South St., Islw.	144	D3
South St., Rain.	119	J2
South Tenter St. E1	**21**	**G5**
South Tenter St. E1	112	C7
South Ter. SW7	**31**	**G1**
South Ter. SW7	129	H4
South Ter., Surb.	181	H6
South Vale SE19	170	B6
South Vale, Har.	86	B4
South Vw., Brom.	191	H2
South Vw. Dr. E18	79	H3
South Vw. Rd. N8	74	D3
South Vw. Rd., Loug.	48	C1
South Vw. Rd., Pnr.	50	B6
South Vil. NW1	92	D6
South Wk., W.Wick.	204	E3
South Way N9	61	F2
South Way N11 *Ringway*	58	C6
South Way, Brom.	191	G7
South Way, Croy.	203	H3
South Way, Har.	67	G4
South Way, Wem.	88	A5
South W. India Dock Entrance E14 *Prestons Rd.*	134	C2
South Western Rd., Twick.	144	D6
South Wf. Rd. W2	**15**	**E3**
South Wf. Rd. W2	109	G6
South Woodford to Barking Relief Rd. E11	79	J4
South Woodford to Barking Relief Rd. E12	98	D3
South Woodford to Barking Relief Rd. E18	79	J4
South Woodford to Barking Relief Rd., Bark.	98	D3
South Woodford to Barking Relief Rd., Ilf.	98	D3
South Worple Av. SW14	146	E3
South Worple Way SW14	146	D3
Southacre Way, Pnr.	66	C1
Southall La., Houns.	122	B6
Southall La., Sthl.	122	C4
Southall Pl. SE1	**28**	**B4**
Southall Pl. SE1	132	A2
Southam St. W10	108	B4
Southampton Bldgs. WC2	**18**	**E3**
Southampton Gdns. Mitch.	186	E5
Southampton Ms. E16 *Wesley Av.*	135	H1
Southampton Pl. WC1	**18**	**B2**
Southampton Pl. WC1	111	E5
Southampton Rd. NW5	91	J5
Southampton Rd., Houns.	140	D6
Southampton Row WC1	**18**	**B1**
Southampton Row WC1	111	E5
Southampton St. WC2	**18**	**B5**
Southampton St. WC2	111	E7
Southampton Way SE5	**36**	**C7**
Southampton Way SE5	132	A7
Southbank, T.Ditt.	180	E7
Southborough Cl., Surb.	195	G1
Southborough La., Brom.	192	B5
Southborough Rd. E9	113	F1
Southborough Rd., Brom.	192	B3
Southborough Rd., Surb.	195	H1
Southbourne, Brom.	191	G7
Southbourne Av. NW9	70	C2
Southbourne Cl., Pnr.	67	E7
Southbourne Cres. NW4	72	B4
Southbourne Gdns. SE12	155	H5
Southbourne Gdns. Ilf.	99	F5
Southbourne Gdns., Ruis.	84	B1
Southbridge Pl., Croy.	201	J4
Southbridge Rd., Croy.	201	J4
Southbridge Way, Sthl.	123	E2
Southbrook Ms. SE12	155	F6
Southbrook Rd. SE12	155	F6
Southbrook Rd. SW16	187	E1
Southbury Av., Enf.	44	D5
Southbury Rd., Enf.	44	A3
Southchurch Rd. E6	116	C2
Southcombe St. W14	128	B4
Southcote Av., Surb.	182	B7
Southcote Rd. E17	77	G5
Southcote Rd. N19	92	C4
Southcote Rd. SE25	189	E6
Southcroft Av., Well.	157	H3
Southcroft Av., W.Wick.	204	C2
Southcroft Rd. SW16	168	A6
Southcroft Rd. SW17	168	A6
Southcroft Rd., Orp.	207	H3
Southdale, Chig.	65	G6
Southdean Gdns. SW19	166	C2
Southdown Av. W7	124	D3
Southdown Cres., Har.	85	H1
Southdown Cres., Ilf.	81	H5
Southdown Dr. SW20 *Crescent Rd.*	166	A7
Southdown Rd. SW20	184	A1
Southend Cl. SE9	156	E6
Southend Cres. SE9	156	D6
Southend La. SE6	171	J4
Southend La. SE26	171	J4
Southend Rd. E4	61	H5
Southend Rd. E6	98	C7
Southend Rd. E17	78	B1
Southend Rd. E18	79	G1
Southend Rd., Beck.	172	A7
Southend Rd., Wdf.Grn.	79	J2
Southern Av. SE25	188	C3
Southern Av., Felt.	160	A1
Southern Dr., Loug.	48	C6
Southern Gro. E3	113	J3
Southern Perimeter Rd., Houns.	141	G5
Southern Rd. E13	115	H2
Southern Rd. N2	73	J4
Southern Row W10	108	B4
Southern St. N1	**10**	**C1**
Southern St. N1	111	F2
Southern Way, Rom.	83	G6
Southernhay, Loug.	48	A5
Southerngate Way SE14	133	H7
Southerton Rd. W6	127	J3
Southey Ms. E16 *Wesley Av.*	135	G1
Southey Rd. N15	76	B5
Southey Rd. SW9	151	G1
Southey Rd. SW19	166	D7
Southey St. SE20	171	G7
Southfield, Barn.	40	A6
Southfield Cotts. W7 *Oaklands Rd.*	124	C2
Southfield Gdns. Twick.	162	C4
Southfield Pk., Har.	67	H4
Southfield Rd. N17 *The Av.*	76	B2
Southfield Rd. W4	126	E3
Southfield Rd., Chis.	193	J3
Southfield Rd., Enf.	45	E6
Southfields NW4	71	G2
Southfields, E.Mol.	180	B6
Southfields Ct. SW19	166	B1
Southfields Pas. SW18	148	D6
Southfields Rd. SW18	148	D6
Southfleet Rd., Orp.	207	H3
Southgate Circ. N14 *The Bourne*	58	D1
Southgate Gro. N1	94	A7
Southgate Rd. N1	94	A7
Southholme Cl. SE19	188	B1
Southill La., Pnr.	66	A4
Southill Rd., Chis.	174	B7
Southill St. E14 *Chrisp St.*	114	B6
Southland Rd. SE18	137	J7
Southland Way, Houns.	144	A5
Southlands Av., Orp.	207	G4
Southlands Dr. SW19	166	A2
Southlands Gro. Brom.	192	B3
Southlands Rd., Brom.	191	J4
Southly Cl., Sutt.	198	D3
Southmead Rd. SW19	166	B1
Southmont Rd., Esher	194	B2
Southmoor Way E9	95	J6
Southold Ri. SE9	174	C3
Southolm St. SW11	150	B1
Southover N12	56	D4
Southover, Brom.	173	G5
Southport Rd. SE18	137	G4
Southridge Pl. SW20	166	A7
Sonsea Rd., Kings.T.	181	H4
Southside Common SW19	165	J6
Southspring, Sid.	157	G7
Southvale Rd. SE3	155	E2
Southview Av. NW10	89	F5
Southview Cl. SW17	168	A5
Southview Cl., Bex.	159	F6
Southview Cres., Ilf.	80	E6
Southview Gdns., Wall.	200	C7
Southview Rd., Brom.	172	D4
Southville SW8	150	D1
Southville, T.Ditt.	180	E7
Southwark Br. EC4	**28**	**A1**
Southwark Br. EC4	131	J1
Southwark Br. SE1	**28**	**A1**
Southwark Br. SE1	131	J1
Southwark Br. Rd. SE1	**27**	**H5**
Southwark Br. Rd. SE1	131	H3
Southwark Gro. SE1	**27**	**J2**
Southwark Pk. Est. SE16	133	E4
Southwark Pk. Rd. SE16	**37**	**G1**
Southwark Pk. Rd. SE16	132	C4
Southwark Pl., Brom. *St. Georges Rd.*	192	C3
Southwark St. SE1	**27**	**H1**
Southwark St. SE1	131	H1
Southwater Cl. E14	113	J6
Southwater Cl., Beck.	172	B7
Southway N20	56	D2
Southway NW11	73	E6
Southway SW20	183	J4
Southway, Wall.	200	C4
Southwell Av., Nthlt.	85	G6
Southwell Gdns. SW7	**30**	**C1**
Southwell Gdns. SW7	129	F4
Southwell Gro. Rd. E11	96	E2
Southwell Rd. SE5	151	J3
Southwell Rd., Croy.	187	G6
Southwell Rd., Har.	69	G6
Southwest Rd. E11	96	D1
Southwick Ms. W2	**15**	**F3**
Southwick Pl. W2	**15**	**G4**
Southwick St. W2	**15**	**G3**
Southwick St. W2	109	H6
Southwold Dr., Bark.	100	A5
Southwold Rd. E5	95	E2
Southwold Rd., Bex.	159	H6
Southwood Av. N6	74	B7
Southwood Av., Kings.T.	182	C1
Southwood Cl., Brom.	192	C4
Southwood Cl., Wor.Pk.	198	A1
Southwood Dr., Surb.	182	C7
Southwood Gdns., Esher	194	D3
Southwood Gdns., Ilf.	80	E4
Southwood La. N6	74	A7
Southwood Lawn Rd. N6	74	A7
Southwood Rd. SE9	174	E2
Southwood Rd. SE28	138	B1
Southwood Smith St. N1 *Barford St.*	111	G1
Sovereign Cl. E1	113	E7
Sovereign Cl. W5	105	F5
Sovereign Ct., Brom.	192	C5
Sovereign Ct., W.Mol.	179	F4
Sovereign Cres. SE16 *Rotherhithe St.*	133	H1
Sovereign Gro., Wem.	87	G3
Sovereign Ms. E2	**13**	**F1**
Sovereign Pk. NW10	106	B4
Sovereign Rd., Bark.	118	C3
Sowerby Cl. SE9	156	B5
Spa Cl. SE19	170	A3
Spa Grn. Est. EC1	**11**	**F3**
Spa Grn. Est. EC1	111	G3
Spa Hill SE19	188	A1
Spa Rd. SE16	**29**	**F6**
Spa Rd. SE16	132	C3
Space Waye, Felt.	142	A5
Spafield St. EC1 *Blundell St.*	**11**	**E5**
Spalding Cl., Edg. *Blundell St.*	54/55	E7
Spalding Rd. NW4	71	J6
Spalding Rd. SW17	168	B5
Spanby Rd. E3	114	A4
Spaniards Cl. NW11	91	G1
Spaniards End NW3	91	F1
Spaniards Rd. NW3	91	F2
Spanish Pl. W1	**16**	**C2**
Spanish Pl. W1	110	A6
Spanish Rd. SW18	149	F5
Spareleaze Hill, Loug.	48	B4
Sparkbridge Rd., Har.	68	B4
Sparks Cl. W3 *Joseph Av.*	106	D6
Sparks Cl., Dag.	100	D2
Sparks Cl., Hmptn. *Victors Dr.*	160/161	E6
Sparrow Cl., Hmptn.	160	E6
Sparrow Dr., Orp.	207	F1
Sparrow Fm. Dr., Felt.	142	D7
Sparrow Fm. Rd., Epsom	197	G4
Sparrow Grn., Dag.	101	H3
Sparrows La. SE9	157	F7
Sparsholt Rd. N19	93	F1
Sparsholt Rd., Bark.	117	H1
Sparta St. SE10	154	B1
Spear Ms. SW5	128	D4
Spearman St. SE18	136	D6
Spearpoint Gdns., Ilf.	81	J4
Spears Rd. N19	92	E1
Speart La., Houns.	122	E7
Spedan Cl. NW3	91	E3
Speedwell St. SE8 *Comet St.*	134	A7
Speedy Pl. WC1	**10**	**A4**
Speer Rd., T.Ditt.	180	C5
Speirs Cl., N.Mal.	183	F6
Speke Ho. SE5	131	J7
Speke Rd., Th.Hth.	188	A2
Spekehill SE9	174	C3
Speldhurst Cl., Brom.	191	F5
Speldhurst Rd. E9	95	G7
Speldhurst Rd. W4	126	D3
Spellbrook Wk. N1 *Basire St.*	111	J1
Spelman St. E1	**21**	**H1**
Spelman St. E1	112	D5
Spence Cl. SE16 *Vaughan St.*	133	J2
Spencer Av. N13	59	F6
Spencer Av., Hayes	102	B5
Spencer Cl. N3	72	D2
Spencer Cl. NW10	105	J3
Spencer Cl., Orp.	207	H2
Spencer Cl., Wdf.Grn.	63	J5
Spencer Dr. N2	73	F6
Spencer Gdns. SE9	156	C5
Spencer Gdns. SW14	146	C5
Spencer Hill SW19	166	B6
Spencer Hill Rd. SW19	166	B7
Spencer Ms. SW8 *Lansdowne Way*	151	F1
Spencer Ms. W6 *Greyhound Rd.*	128	B6
Spencer Pk. SW18	149	G5
Spencer Pas. E2 *Pritchard's Rd.*	112/113	E2

Spencer Pl. N1 93 H7
Canonbury La.
Spencer Pl., Croy. 188 A7
Gloucester Rd.
Spencer Ri. NW5 92 B4
Spencer Rd. E6 116 A1
Spencer Rd. E17 78 C1
Spencer Rd. N8 75 F5
Spencer Rd. N11 58 B4
Spencer Rd. N17 76 D1
Spencer Rd. SW18 149 G4
Spencer Rd. SW20 183 H1
Spencer Rd. W3 126 C1
Spencer Rd. W4 126 C7
Spencer Rd., Brom. 173 E7
Spencer Rd., E.Mol. 179 J5
Spencer Rd., Har. 68 B2
Spencer Rd., Ilf. 99 J1
Spencer Rd., Islw. 144 A1
Spencer Rd., Mitch. 186 A3
Spencer Rd. (Beddington Cor.), Mitch. 186 A7
Spencer Rd., S.Croy. 202 B5
Spencer Rd., Twick. 162 B3
Spencer Rd., Wem. 87 F2
Spencer St. EC1 11 G4
Spencer St. EC1 111 H3
Spencer St., Sthl. 122 D2
Spencer Wk. NW3 91 F4
Hampstead High St.
Spencer Wk. SW15 148 A4
Spenser Gro. N16 94 B4
Spenser Ms. SE21 170 A1
Croxted Rd.
Spenser Rd. SE24 151 G5
Spenser St. SW1 25 G5
Spenser St. SW1 130 C3
Spensley Wk. N16 94 A3
Clissold Rd.
Speranza St. SE18 137 J5
Sperling Rd. N17 76 B2
Spert St. E14 113 H7
Spey St. E14 114 C5
Speyside N14 42 C6
Spezia Rd. NW10 107 G2
Spicer Cl. SW9 151 H2
Spicer Cl., Walt. 178 C6
Spice's Yd., Croy. 201 J4
Spigurnell Rd. N17 76 A1
Spikes Br. Rd., Sthl. 103 E6
Spilsby Cl. NW9 70/71 E2
Kenley Av.
Spindle Cl. SE18 136 B3
Spindlewood Gdns., Croy. 202 B4
Spindrift Av. E14 134 B4
Spinel Cl. SE18 137 J5
Spinnaker Cl., Bark. 117 H3
Thames Rd.
Spinnells Rd., Har. 85 F1
Spinney, The N21 43 G7
Spinney, The SW16 168 D3
Spinney, The, Barn. 41 E2
Spinney, The, Sid. 176 E5
Spinney, The, Stan. 53 H4
Spinney, The, Sun. 178 A1
Spinney, The, Sutt. 197 J4
Spinney, The, Wem. 86 D3
Spinney Cl., N.Mal. 182 E5
Spinney Cl., Wor.Pk. 197 F2
Spinney Dr., Felt. 141 F7
Spinney Gdns. SE19 170 C5
Spinney Gdns., Dag. 101 E5
Spinney Oak, Brom. 192 B2
Spinneys, The, Brom. 192 C2
Spirit Quay E1 29 J1
Spital Sq. E1 21 E1
Spital Sq. E1 112 B5
Spital St. E1 21 H1
Spital St. E1 112 D4
Spital Yd. E1 21 E1
Spitfire Est., Houns. 122 C5
Spitfire Way, Houns. 122 C5
Splendour Wk. SE16 133 F5
Verney Rd.
Spode Wk. NW6 90/91 E6
Lymington Rd.
Spondon Rd. N15 76 D4
Spoonbill Way, Hayes 102 D5
Spooner Wk., Wall. 200 D5
Spooners Ms. W3 126 D1
Churchfield Rd.
Sportsbank St. SE6 154 C7
Spottons Gro. N17 75 J1
Gospatrick Rd.
Spout Hill, Croy. 204 A5
Spratt Hall Rd. E11 79 G6
Spray La., Twick. 144 B6
Spray St. SE18 137 E4
Spreighton Rd., W.Mol. 179 H4
Sprimont Pl. SW3 31 J3
Sprimont Pl. SW3 129 J5
Spring Br. Ms. W5 105 G7
Spring Br. Rd.
Spring Br. Rd. W5 105 G7
Spring Cl., Barn. 40 A5
Spring Cl., Borwd. 38 A1
Spring Cl., Dag. 100 D1
Spring Cl. La., Sutt. 198 B6
Spring Cotts., Surb. 181 G5
St. Leonard's Rd.
Spring Ct., Sid. 176 A3
Station Rd.
Spring Dr., Pnr. 66 A6
Eastcote Rd.
Spring Gdns. N5 93 J5
Grosvenor Av.
Spring Gdns. SW1 25 J1
Spring Gdns., Rom. 83 J5
Spring Gdns., Wall. 200 C5
Spring Gdns., W.Mol. 179 J5
Spring Gdns., Wdf.Grn. 63 J7
Spring Gdns. Ind. Est., Rom. 83 J5
Spring Gro. SE19 170 C7
Alma Pl.
Spring Gro. W4 126 A5
Spring Gro., Hmptn. 179 H1
Plevna Rd.
Spring Gro., Loug. 48 A6
Spring Gro., Mitch. 186 A1
Spring Gro. Cres., Houns. 143 J1
Spring Gro. Rd., Houns. 143 J1
Spring Gro. Rd., Islw. 143 J1
Spring Gro. Rd., Rich. 145 J5
Spring Hill E5 76 D7
Spring Hill SE26 171 F4
Spring Lake, Stan. 52 E4
Spring La. E5 95 E1
Spring La. N10 74 A3
Spring La. SE25 188 E6
Spring Ms. W1 16 A1
Spring Pk. Av., Croy. 203 G2
Spring Pk. Dr. N4 93 J1
Spring Pk. Rd., Croy. 203 G2
Spring Pas. SW15 148 A3
Embankment
Spring Path NW3 91 G5
Spring Pl. NW5 92 B5
Spring St. W2 15 E4
Spring St. W2 109 G6
Spring Ter., Rich. 145 H5
Spring Vale, Bexh. 159 H4
Spring Vil. Rd., Edg. 54 A7
Spring Wk. E1 21 H1
Springall St. SE15 133 E7
Springbank N21 43 F6
Springbank Rd. SE13 154 D6
Springbank Wk. NW1 92 D7
St. Paul's Cres.
Springbourne Ct., Beck. 190 C1
Springcroft Av. N2 73 J4
Springdale Ms. N16 94 A4
Springdale Rd.
Springdale Rd. N16 94 A4
Springfield E5 94 E1
Springfield, Bushey 52 A1
Springfield Av. N10 74 C3
Springfield Av. SW20 184 C3
Springfield Av., Hmptn. 161 H6
Springfield Cl. N12 56 E5
Springfield Cl., Stan. 52 D3
Springfield Dr., Ilf. 81 F6
Springfield Gdns. E5 95 E1
Springfield Gdns. NW9 70 D5
Springfield Gdns., Brom. 192 C4
Springfield Gdns., Ruis. 84 B1
Springfield Gdns., W.Wick. 204 B2
Springfield Gdns., Wdf.Grn. 63 J7
Springfield Gro. SE7 135 J6
Springfield La. NW6 108 E1
Springfield Mt. NW9 70 E5
Springfield Pl., N.Mal. 182 C4
Springfield Ri. SE26 170 E3
Springfield Rd. E4 62 E1
Springfield Rd. E6 98 C7
Springfield Rd. E15 115 E3
Springfield Rd. E17 77 J6
Springfield Rd. N11 58 B5
Springfield Rd. N15 76 D4
Springfield Rd. NW8 109 F1
Springfield Rd. SE26 171 E5
Springfield Rd. SW19 166 C5
Springfield Rd. W7 124 B1
Springfield Rd., Bexh. 159 H3
Springfield Rd., Brom. 192 C4
Springfield Rd., Har. 68 B6
Springfield Rd., Hayes 122 C1
Springfield Rd., Kings.T. 181 H3
Springfield Rd., Tedd. 162 D5
Springfield Rd., Th.Hth. 187 J1
Springfield Rd., Twick. 161 G1
Springfield Rd., Wall. 200 B5
Springfield Rd., Well. 158 B3
Springfield Wk. NW6 108 E1
Springfield Wk., Orp. 207 G1
Place Fm. Av.
Springhill Cl. SE5 152 A3
Springhurst Cl., Croy. 203 J4
Springpark Dr., Beck. 190 C3
Springpond Rd., Dag. 101 E5
Springrice Rd. SE13 154 D6
Springvale Av., Brent. 125 G5
Springvale Est. W14 128 B3
Blythe Rd.
Springvale Ter. W14 128 A3
Springwater Cl. SE18 156 D1
Springway, Har. 68 A7
Springwell Av. NW10 107 F1
Springwell Cl. SW16 169 G4
Etherstone Rd.
Springwell Ct., Houns. 142 D2
Springwell Rd. SW16 169 G4
Springwell Rd., Houns. 142 D1
Springwood Cres., Edg. 54 B2
Sprowston Ms. E7 97 G6
Sprowston Rd. E7 97 G5
Spruce Ct. W5 125 H3
Elderberry Rd.
Spruce Hills Rd. E17 78 C2
Spruce Pk., Brom. 191 F4
Cumberland Rd.
Sprucedale Gdns., Croy. 203 G4
Sprules Rd. SE4 153 H2
Spur Rd. N15 76 A4
Philip La.
Spur Rd. SE1 27 E3
Spur Rd. SE1 131 G2
Spur Rd. SW1 25 F4
Spur Rd. SW1 130 C2
Spur Rd., Bark. 117 F3
Spur Rd., Edg. 53 H4
Spur Rd., Felt. 142 B5
Spur Rd., Islw. 124 E7
Spur Rd. Est., Edg. 53 J4
Spurfield, W.Mol. 179 H3
Spurgeon Av. SE19 188 A1
Spurgeon Rd. SE19 188 A1
Spurgeon St. SE1 28 B6
Spurgeon St. SE1 132 A3
Spurling Rd. SE22 152 C4
Spurling Rd., Dag. 101 F6
Spurstowe Rd. E8 94/95 E6
Marcon Pl.
Spurstowe Ter. E8 94 E5
Square, The W6 127 J5
Square, The, Cars. 200 A5
Square, The, Hayes 121 G1
Square, The, Ilf. 80 D7
Square, The, Rich. 145 G5
Square, The, Wdf.Grn. 63 G5
Square Rigger Row SW11 149 F3
York Pl.
Squarey St. SW17 167 F3
Squires Ct. SW19 166 D4
Squires La. N3 73 E2
Squires Mt. NW3 91 G3
East Heath Rd.
Squires Wd. Dr., Chis. 174 B7
Squirrel Cl., Houns. 142 C2
Squirrel Ms. W13 104 D7
Squirrels, The SE13 154 D3
Belmont Hill
Squirrels, The, Pnr. 67 F3
Squirrels Cl. N12 57 F4
Woodside Av.
Squirrels Grn., Wor.Pk. 197 F1
Squirrels La., Buck.H. 64 A3
Squirrels Trd. Est., The, Hayes 122 A3
Squirries St. E2 13 J3
Squirries St. E2 112 D3
Stable Cl., Nthlt. 103 G2
Stable Wk. N2 73 G1
Old Fm. Rd.
Stable Way W10 107 J6
Latimer Rd.
Stable Yd. SW1 25 F3
Stable Yd. SW9 151 F2
Broomgrove Rd.
Stable Yd. SW15 147 J3
Danemere St.
Stable Yd. Rd. SW1 25 F2
Stable Yd. Rd. SW1 130 C1
Stables, The, Buck.H. 47 J7
Stables End, Orp. 207 F3
Stables Ms. SE27 169 J5
Stables Way SE11 35 E3
Stables Way SE11 131 G5
Stacey Av. N18 61 F4
Stacey Cl. E10 78 D5
Halford Rd.
Stacey St. N7 93 G3
Stacey St. WC2 17 J4
Stacey St. WC2 110 D6
Stackhouse St. SW3 23 J5
Stacy Path SE5 132 B7
Harris St.
Stadium Rd. NW2 71 J7
Stadium Rd. SE18 136 C7
Stadium St. SW10 129 F7
Stadium Way, Wem. 87 J4
Staff St. EC1 12 C4
Staffa Rd. E10 95 H1
Stafford Cl. E17 77 J6
Stafford Cl. N14 42 C5
Stafford Cl. NW6 108 D3
Stafford Cl., Sutt. 198 B6
Stafford Ct. W8 128 D3
Stafford Cross, Croy. 201 F5
Stafford Gdns., Croy. 201 F5
Stafford Pl. SW1 25 F5
Stafford Pl. SW1 130 C3
Stafford Pl., Rich. 145 J7
Stafford Rd. E3 113 J2
Stafford Rd. E7 97 J7
Stafford Rd. NW6 108 D3
Stafford Rd., Croy. 201 G4
Stafford Rd., Har. 51 J7
Stafford Rd., N.Mal. 182 C3
Stafford Rd., Sid. 175 H4
Stafford Rd., Wall. 200 C6
Stafford St. W1 25 F1
Stafford St. W1 130 C1
Stafford Ter. W8 128 D3
Staffordshire St. SE15 152 D1
Stag Cl., Edg. 70 C2
Stag La. NW9 70 B2
Stag La. SW15 165 F2
Stag La., Buck.H. 63 H2
Stag La., Edg. 70 B2
Stag Pl. SW1 25 F5
Stag Pl. SW1 130 C3
Stag Ride SW19 165 F3
Staggart Grn., Chig. 65 J6
Stags Way, Islw. 124 C6
Stainbank Rd., Mitch. 186 B3
Stainby Cl., West Dr. 120 B3
Stainby Rd. N15 76 C4
Stainer St. SE1 28 C2
Stainer St. SE1 132 A1
Staines Av., Sutt. 198 A2
Staines Rd., Felt. 141 G7
Staines Rd., Houns. 143 H3
Staines Rd., Ilf. 99 G4
Staines Rd., Twick. 161 G3
Staines Rd. E., Sun. 160 A7
Staines Wk., Sid. 176 C6
Evry Rd.
Stainforth Rd. E17 78 A4
Stainforth Rd., Ilf. 81 G7
Staining La. EC2 20 A3
Staining La. EC2 111 J6
Stainmore Cl., Chis. 193 G1
Stainsbury St. E2 113 F2
Royston St.
Stainsby Pl. E14 114 A6
Stainsby Rd.
Stainsby Rd. E14 114 A6
Stainton Rd. SE6 154 D6
Stainton Rd., Enf. 45 F1
Stalbridge St. NW1 15 H1
Stalham St. SE16 133 E3
Stambourne Way SE19 170 B7
Stambourne Way, W.Wick. 204 C3
Stamford Brook Av. W6 127 F3
Stamford Brook Rd. W6 127 F3
Stamford Cl. N15 76 D4
Stamford Cl. NW3 91 F4
Heath St.
Stamford Cl., Har. 52 B7
Stamford Cl., Sthl. 103 G7

Stamford Cotts. SW10	128/129	E7
Billing St.		
Stamford Ct. W6	127	F4
Goldhawk Rd.		
Stamford Dr., Brom.	191	F4
Stamford Gdns., Dag.	100	C7
Stamford Gro. E. N16	94	D1
Oldhill St.		
Stamford Gro. W. N16	94	D1
Oldhill St.		
Stamford Hill N16	94	C2
Stamford Hill Est. N16	94	C1
Stamford Rd. E6	116	B1
Stamford Rd. N1	94	B7
Stamford Rd. N15	76	D5
Stamford Rd., Dag.	118	B1
Stamford St. SE1	**27**	**E2**
Stamford St. SE1	131	G1
Stamp Pl. E2	**13**	**F3**
Stamp Pl. E2	112	C3
Stanard Cl. N16	76	B7
Stanborough Cl., Hmptn.	161	F6
Stanborough Pas. E8	94	C6
Abbot St.		
Stanborough Rd., Houns.	144	A3
Stanbridge Pl. N21	59	H2
Stanbridge Rd. SW15	147	J3
Stanbrook Rd. SE2	138	B2
Stanbury Rd. SE15	153	E1
Stancroft NW9	70	E4
Standard Ind. Est. E16	136	C2
Standard Pl. EC2	**12**	**E4**
Standard Rd. NW10	106	C4
Standard Rd., Belv.	139	G5
Standard Rd., Bexh.	159	E4
Standard Rd., Houns.	143	E3
Standen Rd. SW18	148	C7
Standfield Gdns., Dag.	101	G6
Standfield Rd.		
Standfield Rd., Dag.	101	G5
Standish Rd. W6	127	G4
Standlake Pt. SE23	171	G3
Stane Cl. SW19	184/185	E1
Hayward Cl.		
Stane Way SE18	136	A7
Stanfield Rd. E3	113	H2
Stanford Cl., Hmptn.	161	F6
Stanford Cl., Rom.	83	H6
Stanford Cl., Wdf.Grn.	64	B5
Stanford Ho., Bark.	118	B2
Stanford Pl. SE17	**36**	**D2**
Stanford Rd. N11	57	J5
Stanford Rd. SW16	186	D2
Stanford Rd. W8	**22**	**B5**
Stanford Rd. W8	129	E3
Stanford St. SW1	**33**	**H2**
Stanford Way SW16	186	D2
Stangate Cres., Borwd.	38	E5
Stangate Gdns., Stan.	53	E4
Stanger Rd. SE25	188	D4
Stanhope Av. N3	72	C3
Stanhope Av., Brom.	205	F1
Stanhope Av., Har.	68	A1
Stanhope Cl. SE16	133	G2
Middleton Dr.		
Stanhope Gdns. N4	75	H6
Stanhope Gdns. N6	74	B6
Stanhope Gdns. NW7	55	F5
Stanhope Gdns. SW7	**30**	**D1**
Stanhope Gdns. SW7	129	F4
Stanhope Gdns., Dag.	101	F3
Stanhope Gdns., Ilf.	98	C1
Stanhope Gate W1	**24**	**C1**
Stanhope Gate W1	130	A1
Stanhope Gro., Beck.	189	J5
Stanhope Ms. E. SW7	**30**	**D1**
Stanhope Ms. E. SW7	129	F4
Stanhope Ms. S. SW7	**30**	**D2**
Stanhope Ms. W. SW7	**30**	**D1**
Stanhope Ms. W. SW7	129	F4
Stanhope Par. NW1	**9**	**F3**
Stanhope Pk. Rd., Grnf.	103	J4
Stanhope Pl. W2	**15**	**J4**
Stanhope Pl. W2	109	J6
Stanhope Rd. E17	78	B5
Stanhope Rd. N6	74	C6
Stanhope Rd. N12	57	F5
Stanhope Rd., Barn.	39	J6
Stanhope Rd., Bexh.	159	E2
Stanhope Rd., Cars.	200	A7
Stanhope Rd., Croy.	202	B3
Stanhope Rd., Dag.	101	F2
Stanhope Rd., Grnf.	103	J5
Stanhope Rd., Sid.	176	A4
Stanhope Row W1	**24**	**D2**
Stanhope St. NW1	**9**	**F4**
Stanhope St. NW1	110	C3
Stanhope Ter. W2	**15**	**F5**
Stanhope Ter. W2	109	G7
Stanier Cl. W14	128	C5
Aisgill Av.		
Stanlake Ms. W12	127	J1
Stanlake Rd. W12	127	H1
Stanlake Vil. W12	127	H1
Stanley Av., Bark.	117	J2
Stanley Av., Beck.	190	C2
Stanley Av., Dag.	101	F1
Stanley Av., Grnf.	103	J1
Stanley Av., N.Mal.	183	G5
Stanley Av., Wem.	87	H7
Stanley Cl. SW8	**34**	**C6**
Stanley Cl. SW8	131	F6
Stanley Cl., Wem.	87	H7
Stanley Cres. W11	108	C7
Stanley Gdns. NW2	89	J5
Stanley Gdns. W3	126	E1
Stanley Gdns. W11	108	C7
Stanley Gdns., Mitch.	168	A6
Ashbourne Rd.		
Stanley Gdns., Wall.	200	C6
Stanley Gdns. Ms. W11	108	C7
Stanley Cres.		
Stanley Gdns. Rd., Tedd.	162	B5
Stanley Gro. SW8	150	A2
Stanley Gro., Croy.	187	G6
Stanley Pk. Dr., Wem.	87	J7
Stanley Pk. Rd., Cars.	199	J7
Stanley Pk. Rd., Wall.	200	B6
Stanley Pas. NW1	**10**	**A2**
Stanley Rd. E4	62	D1
Stanley Rd. E10	78	B6
Stanley Rd. E12	98	B5
Stanley Rd. E15	114	D1
Stanley Rd. E18	79	F1
Stanley Rd. N2	73	G3
Stanley Rd. N9	60	C1
Stanley Rd. N10	58	B7
Stanley Rd. N11	58	D6
Stanley Rd. N15	75	H4
Stanley Rd. NW9	71	G7
West Hendon Bdy.		
Stanley Rd. SW14	146	B4
Stanley Rd. SW19	166	D7
Stanley Rd. W3	126	C3
Stanley Rd., Brom.	191	H4
Stanley Rd., Cars.	200	A7
Stanley Rd., Croy.	187	G7
Stanley Rd., Enf.	44	B3
Stanley Rd., Har.	85	J2
Stanley Rd., Houns.	143	J4
Stanley Rd., Ilf.	99	G2
Stanley Rd., Mitch.	168	A7
Stanley Rd., Mord.	184	D4
Stanley Rd., Nthwd.	66	A1
Stanley Rd., Sid.	176	A3
Stanley Rd., Sthl.	102	E7
Stanley Rd., Sutt.	198	E6
Stanley Rd., Tedd.	162	B4
Stanley Rd., Twick.	162	A3
Stanley Rd., Wem.	87	J6
Stanley St. SE8	133	J7
Stanley Ter. N19	92	E2
Stanleycroft Cl., Islw.	144	B1
Stanmer St. SW11	149	H1
Stanmore Gdns., Rich.	145	J3
Stanmore Gdns., Sutt.	199	F3
Stanmore Hall, Stan.	52	E3
Stanmore Hill, Stan.	52	D3
Stanmore Pk., Stan.	52	E5
Stanmore Pl. NW1	110	B1
Arlington Rd.		
Stanmore Rd. E11	97	F1
Stanmore Rd. N15	75	H4
Stanmore Rd., Belv.	139	J4
Stanmore Rd., Rich.	145	J3
Stanmore St. N1	111	F1
Caledonian Rd.		
Stanmore Ter., Beck.	190	A2
Stanmore Way, Loug.	48	D1
Stannard Ms. E8	94	D6
Stannard Rd. E8	94	D6
Stannary Pl. SE11	**35**	**F4**
Stannary Pl. SE11	131	G5
Stannary St. SE11	**35**	**F5**
Stannary St. SE11	131	G6
Stannet Way, Wall.	200	C4
Stannington Path, Borwd.	38	A1
Stansfeld Rd. E6	116	A5
Stansfield Rd. SW9	151	F3
Stansfield Rd., Houns.	142	B2
Stansgate Rd., Dag.	101	G2
Stanstead Cl., Brom.	191	F5
Stanstead Gro. SE6	171	J1
Catford Hill		
Stanstead Manor, Sutt.	198	D6
Stanstead Rd. E11	79	H5
Stanstead Rd. SE6	171	G1
Stanstead Rd. SE23	171	G1
Stanstead Rd., Houns.	140	C6
Stansted Cres., Bex.	176	D1
Stanswood Gdns. SE5	132	B7
Sedgmoor Pl.		
Stanthorpe Cl. SW16	168/169	E5
Stanthorpe Rd.		
Stanthorpe Rd. SW16	168	E5
Stanton Av., Tedd.	162	B5
Stanton Cl., Epsom	196	B5
Stanton Cl., Wor.Pk.	198	A1
Stanton Rd. SE26	171	J4
Stanton Way		
Stanton Rd. SW13	147	F2
Stanton Rd. SW20	184	A2
Stanton Rd., Croy.	187	J7
Stanton Sq. SE26	171	J4
Stanton Way		
Stanton Way SE26	171	J4
Stanway Cl., Chig.	65	H5
Stanway Ct. N1	112	B2
Hoxton St.		
Stanway Gdns. W3	126	A1
Stanway Gdns., Edg.	54	C5
Stanway St. N1	**12**	**E1**
Stanway St. N1	112	B2
Stanwell Cl., Stai.	140	A6
Stanwell Gdns., Stai.	140	A6
Stanwell Rd., Felt.	141	F7
Stanwick Rd. W14	128	C4
Stanworth St. SE1	**29**	**F4**
Stanworth St. SE1	132	C2
Stanwyck Dr., Chig.	65	F5
Stapenhill Rd., Wem.	86	E3
Staple Inn WC1	**19**	**E2**
Staple Inn Bldgs. WC1	**18**	**E2**
Staple Inn Bldgs. WC1	111	G5
Staple St. SE1	**28**	**C4**
Staple St. SE1	132	A2
Staplefield Cl. SW2	169	E1
Staplefield Cl., Pnr.	50	E7
Stapleford Av., Ilf.	81	H5
Stapleford Cl. E4	62	C3
Stapleford Cl. SW19	148	B7
Stapleford Cl., Kings.T.	182	A3
Stapleford Rd., Wem.	87	G7
Stapleford Way, Bark.	118	B3
Staplehurst Rd. SE13	154	E5
Staplehurst Rd., Cars.	199	H7
Staples Cl. SE16	133	H1
Staples Cor. NW2	89	H1
Staples Cor. Business Pk. NW2	89	H1
Staples Rd., Loug.	48	B3
Stapleton Gdns., Croy.	201	G5
Stapleton Hall Rd. N4	75	F7
Stapleton Rd. SW17	168	A3
Stapleton Rd., Bexh.	139	F7
Stapleton Rd., Orp.	207	J3
Stapley Rd., Belv.	139	G5
Stapylton Rd., Barn.	40	B3
Star & Garter Hill, Rich.	163	H1
Star La. E16	115	E4
Star Path, Nthlt.	103	G2
Brabazon Rd.		
Star Pl. E1	**21**	**G6**
Star Rd. W14	128	C6
Star Rd., Islw.	144	A2
Star St. E16	115	F5
Star St. W2	**15**	**F3**
Star St. W2	109	H5
Star Yd. WC2	**18**	**E3**
Starboard Way E14	134	A3
Starch Ho. La., Ilf.	81	G2
Starcross St. NW1	**9**	**G4**
Starcross St. NW1	110	C3
Starfield Rd. W12	127	G2
Starling Cl., Buck.H.	63	G1
Starling Cl., Pnr.	66	C3
Starling Ms. SE28	137	G2
Whinchat Rd.		
Starling Wk., Hmptn.	160/161	E6
Oak Av.		
Starmans Cl., Dag.	119	E1
Starts Cl., Orp.	206	D3
Starts Hill Av., Orp.	207	E4
Starts Hill Rd., Orp.	206	D3
Starveall Cl., West Dr.	120	C3
State Fm. Av., Orp.	207	E4
Staten Gdns., Twick.	162	C1
Lion Rd.		
Statham Gro. N16	93	J4
Green Las.		
Statham Gro. N18	60	B5
Station App. E7	97	H4
Woodford Rd.		
Station App. (Snaresbrook) E11	79	G5
High St.		
Station App. N11	58	B5
Friern Barnet Rd.		
Station App. N12	56/57	E5
Holden Rd.		
Station App. (Woodside Pk.) N12	56	E4
Station App. (Stoke Newington) N16	94	C2
Stamford Hill		
Station App. NW10	107	F3
Station Rd.		
Station App. SE1	**26**	**D4**
Station App. SE1	131	G2
Station App. SE3	155	H3
Kidbrooke Pk. Rd.		
Station App. (Mottingham) SE9	174	C1
Station App. (Lower Sydenham) SE26	171	J5
Worsley Br. Rd.		
Station App. (Sydenham) SE26	171	F4
Sydenham Rd.		
Station App. SW6	148	B3
Station App. SW16	168	D5
Station App. W7	124	B1
Station App., Barn.	41	F4
Station App., Bex.	159	G7
Bexley High St.		
Station App., Bexh.	158/159	E2
Avenue Rd.		
Station App. (Barnehurst), Bexh.	159	J2
Station App., Brom.	205	G1
Station App., Buck.H.	64	A4
Cherry Tree Ri.		
Station App., Chis.	192	D1
Station App. (Elmstead Wds.), Chis.	174	B6
Station App. (Stoneleigh), Epsom	197	G5
Station App. (Hinchley Wd.), Esher	194	C3
Station App., Grnf.	86	A7
Station App., Hmptn.	179	G1
Milton Rd.		
Station App., Har.	68	B7
Station App., Hayes	121	J2
Station App., Kings.T.	182	A1
Station App., Loug.	48	B5
Station App. (Debden), Loug.	49	F4
Station App., Orp.	207	J2
Station App., Pnr.	66	E3
Station App. (Hatch End), Pnr.	51	G7
Uxbridge Rd.		
Station App., Rich.	146	A1
Station App., Ruis.	84	B5
Station App., Sun.	178	A1
Station App. (Cheam), Sutt.	198	B7
Station App. (Carpenders Pk.), Wat.	50	D3
Prestwick Rd.		
Station App., Well.	157	J2
Station App., Wem.	87	E6
Station App., West Dr.	120	B1
Station App. N., Sid.	176	A2
Station App. Rd. W4	126	C7
Station Av. SW9	151	H3
Coldharbour La.		
Station Av., N.Mal.	183	E3
Station Av., Rich.	146	A1
Station Par.		
Station Cl. N3	72	D1
Station Cl. (Woodside Pk.) N12	56	E4
Station Cl., Hmptn.	179	H1
Station Cres. N15	76	A4
Station Cres. SE3	135	G5
Station Cres., Wem.	87	E6
Station Est., Beck.	189	G4
Elmers End Rd.		
Station Est. Rd., Felt.	160	B1
Station Garage Ms. SW16	168	D6
Estreham Rd.		
Station Gdns. W4	126	C7
Station Gro., Wem.	87	H6
Station Hill, Brom.	205	G2

Station Ho. Ms. N9 60 D4
Fore St.
Station Par. E11 79 G5
Station Par. N14 58 D1
High St.
Station Par. NW2 89 J6
Station Par. SW12 168 A1
Balham High Rd.
Station Par. W3 106 A6
Station Par., Bark. 99 F7
Station Par., Felt. 142 B7
Station Par., Rich. 146 A1
Station Pas. E18 79 H2
Maybank Rd.
Station Pas. SE15 152/153 E1
Asylum Rd.
Station Path E8 94/95 E6
Amhurst Rd.
Station Pl. N4 93 G2
Seven Sisters Rd.
Station Ri. SE27 169 H2
Norwood Rd.
Station Rd. (Chingford) E4 62 D1
Station Rd. E7 97 G4
Station Rd. E12 98 A4
Station Rd. E17 77 H6
Station Rd. N3 72 D1
Station Rd. N11 58 B5
Station Rd. N17 76 D3
Hale Rd.
Station Rd. N19 92 C3
Station Rd. N21 59 H1
Station Rd. N22 75 F2
Station Rd. NW4 71 G6
Station Rd. NW7 55 E5
Station Rd. NW10 107 F2
Station Rd. SE13 154 C3
Station Rd. SE20 171 F6
Station Rd. (Norwood Junct.) SE25 188 C4
Station Rd. SW13 147 G3
Station Rd. SW19 185 F1
Station Rd. W5 105 J6
Station Rd. (Hanwell) W7 124 B1
Station Rd., Barn. 40 E5
Station Rd., Belv. 139 G3
Station Rd., Bexh. 159 E3
Station Rd., Borwd. 38 A4
Station Rd., Brent. 125 F6
Station Rd., Brom. 191 G1
Station Rd. (Shortlands), Brom. 191 E2
Station Rd., Cars. 199 J4
Station Rd., Chess. 195 H5
Station Rd., Chig. 64 E3
Station Rd. (East Croydon), Croy. 202 A2
Station Rd. (West Croydon), Croy. 201 J1
Station Rd., Edg. 54 A6
Station Rd., Esher 194 A2
Station Rd. (Claygate), Esher 194 A5
Station Rd., Hmptn. 179 G1
Station Rd., Har. 68 C7
Station Rd. (North Harrow), Har. 67 H5
Station Rd., Hayes 121 J3
Station Rd., Houns. 143 H4
Station Rd., Ilf. 98 E3
Station Rd. (Barkingside), Ilf. 81 G3
Station Rd., Kings.T. 182 A1
Station Rd. (Hampton Wick), Kings.T. 181 F1
Station Rd., Loug. 48 B4
Station Rd. (Motspur Pk.), N.Mal. 183 H5
Station Rd., Orp. 207 J2
Station Rd. (Chadwell Heath), Rom. 82 D7
Station Rd., Sid. 176 A4
Station Rd., Sun. 160 A7
Station Rd., Tedd. 162 C5
Station Rd., T.Ditt. 180 C7
Station Rd., Twick. 162 C1
Station Rd., West Dr. 120 B1
Station Rd., W.Wick. 204 C1
Station Rd. N., Belv. 139 H3
Station Sq. (Petts Wd.), Orp. 193 F5
Station St. E15 96 D7
Station St. E16 136 E1
Station Ter. NW10 108 A2
Station Ter. SE5 151 J1
Station Vw., Grnf. 104 A1
Station Way SE15 152 D2
Rye La.
Station Way (Roding Valley), Buck.H. 63 J4
Station Way (Claygate), Esher 194 B6
Station Way (Cheam), Sutt. 198 B6
Station Yd., Twick. 144 D7
Stationers Hall Ct. EC4 111 H6
Ludgate Hill
Staunton Rd., Kings.T. 163 H6
Staunton St. SE8 133 J6
Stave Yd. Rd. SE16 133 H1
Staveley Cl. E9 95 F5
Churchill Wk.
Staveley Cl. N7 92/93 E4
Penn Rd.
Staveley Cl. SE15 152/153 E1
Asylum Rd.
Staveley Gdns. W4 146 D1
Staveley Rd. W4 126 D7
Staverton Rd. NW2 89 J7
Stavordale Rd. N5 93 H4
Stavordale Rd., Cars. 185 F7
Stayner's Rd. E1 113 G4
Stayton Rd., Sutt. 198 D3
Stead St. SE17 36 B2
Stead St. SE17 132 A4
Steadfast Rd., Kings.T. 181 G1
Steam Fm. La., Felt. 141 J4
Stean St. E8 112 C1
Stebbing Way, Bark. 118 A2
Stebondale St. E14 134 C5
Stedham Pl. WC1 18 A3
Steedman St. SE17 35 J2
Steeds Rd. N10 73 J1
Steeds Way, Loug. 48 B3
Steele Rd. E11 96 E4
Steele Rd. N17 76 B3
Steele Rd. NW10 106 C2
Steele Rd. W4 126 C3
Steele Rd., Islw. 144 D4
Steele Wk., Erith 139 H6
Steeles Ms. N. NW3 91 J6
Steeles Rd.
Steeles Ms. S. NW3 91 J6
Steeles Rd.
Steeles Rd. NW3 91 J6
Steel's La. E1 113 F6
Devonport St.
Steelyard Pas. EC4 112 A7
Upper Thames St.
Steen Way SE22 152 B5
East Dulwich Gro.
Steep Cl., Orp. 207 J6
Steep Hill SW16 168 D3
Steep Hill, Croy. 202 B4
Steeple Cl. SW6 148 B2
Steeple Cl. SW19 166 B5
Steeple Ct. E1 112/113 E4
Coventry Rd.
Steeple Wk. N1 111 J1
Basire St.
Steeplestone Cl. N18 59 J5
Steerforth St. SW18 167 E2
Steers Mead, Mitch. 185 J1
Steers Way SE16 133 H2
Stella Rd. SW17 167 J6
Stellar Ho. N17 60 C6
Stellman Cl. E5 94 D3
Stembridge Rd. SE20 188 E2
Stephan Cl. E8 112 D1
Stephen Cl., Orp. 207 J3
Stephen Ms. W1 17 H2
Stephen Rd., Bexh. 159 J3
Stephen St. W1 17 H2
Stephen St. W1 110 D5
Stephendale Rd. SW6 149 E2
Stephen's Rd. E15 115 E1
Stephenson Rd. E17 77 H5
Stephenson Rd. W7 104 C6
Stephenson Rd., Twick. 143 G7
Stephenson St. E16 114 E4
Stephenson St. NW10 107 E3
Stephenson Way NW1 9 G5
Stephenson Way NW1 110 C4
Stepney Causeway E1 113 G6
Stepney Grn. E1 113 F5
Stepney High St. E1 113 G5
Stepney Way E1 112 E5
Sterling Av., Edg. 53 J4
Sterling Av., Pnr. 66 E7
Sterling Cl., Pnr. 84 D1
Sterling Gdns. SE14 133 H6
Sterling Ind. Est., Dag. 101 H4
Sterling Pl. W5 125 H4
Sterling St. SW7 23 H5
Sterling Way N18 60 A5
Stern Cl., Bark. 118/119 E3
Choats Rd.
Sterndale Rd. W14 128 A3
Sterne St. W12 128 A2
Sternhall La. SE15 152 D3
Sternhold Av. SW2 168 D2
Sterry Cres., Dag. 101 G5
Alibon Rd.
Sterry Dr., Epsom 196 E4
Sterry Dr., T.Ditt. 180 B6
Sterry Gdns., Dag. 101 G6
Sterry Rd., Bark. 117 J1
Sterry Rd., Dag. 101 G4
Sterry St. SE1 28 B4
Sterry St. SE1 132 A2
Steucers La. SE23 153 H7
Steve Biko La. SE6 172 A4
Steve Biko Rd. N7 93 G3
Steve Biko Way, Houns. 143 G3
Stevedale Rd., Well. 158 C2
Stevedore St. E1 132/133 E1
Waterman Way
Stevenage Rd. E6 98 D6
Stevenage Rd. SW6 128 A7
Stevens Av. E9 95 F6
Stevens Cl., Beck. 172 A6
Stevens Cl., Hmptn. 161 F6
Stevens Cl., Pnr. 66 C5
Bridle Rd.
Stevens Grn., Bushey 51 J1
Stevens La., Esher 194 D7
Stevens Rd., Dag. 100 B3
Stevens St. SE1 29 E5
Stevens Way, Chig. 65 H4
Stevenson Cl., Barn. 41 G6
Stevenson Cres. SE16 37 J3
Stevenson Cres. SE16 132 E5
Steventon Rd. W12 107 F7
Stew La. EC4 19 J5
Steward St. E1 21 E2
Steward St. E1 112 B5
Stewards Holte Wk. N11 58 B4
Coppies Gro.
Stewart Cl. NW9 70 C6
Stewart Cl., Chis. 175 E5
Stewart Cl., Hmptn. 161 E5
Stewart Rainbird Ho. E12 98 D5
Stewart Rd. E15 96 D4
Stewart St. E14 134 C2
Stewart's Gro. SW3 31 F3
Stewart's Gro. SW3 129 G4
Stewart's Rd. SW8 130 C7
Stewartsby Cl. N18 59 J5
Steyne Rd. W3 126 C1
Steyning Gro. SE9 174 C4
Steyning Way, Houns. 142 C4
Steynings Way N12 56 D5
Steynton Av., Bex. 176 D2
Stickland Rd., Belv. 139 G4
Picardy Rd.
Stickleton Cl., Grnf. 103 H3
Stile Hall Gdns. W4 126 A5
Stile Hall Par. W4 126 A5
Chiswick High Rd.
Stile Path, Sun. 178 A3
Stilecroft Gdns., Wem. 86 E3
Stiles Cl., Brom. 192 C6
Stiles Cl., Erith 139 H5
Riverdale Rd.
Stillingfleet Rd. SW13 127 G6
Stillington St. SW1 33 G1
Stillington St. SW1 130 C4
Stillness Rd. SE23 153 H6
Stilton Cres. NW10 88 C7
Stipularis Dr., Hayes 102 D4
Stirling Cl. SW16 186 C1
Stirling Cor., Barn. 38 D6
Stirling Cor., Borwd. 38 D6
Stirling Gro., Houns. 143 J2
Stirling Rd. E13 115 H2
Stirling Rd. E17 77 H3
Stirling Rd. N17 76 D1
Stirling Rd. N22 75 H1
Stirling Rd. SW9 150 E2
Stirling Rd. W3 126 B3
Stirling Rd., Har. 68 C3
Stirling Rd., Hayes 102 B7
Stirling Rd., Houns. 140 C6
Stirling Rd., Twick. 143 G7
Stirling Rd. Path E17 77 H3
Stirling Wk., N.Mal. 182 C5
Stirling Wk., Surb. 182 B6
Stirling Way, Borwd. 38 D6
Stirling Way, Croy. 186 E7
Stiven Cres., Har. 85 F3
Stock Orchard Cres. N7 93 F5
Stock Orchard St. N7 93 F5
Stock St. E13 115 G2
Stockbury Rd., Croy. 189 F6
Stockdale Rd., Dag. 101 F2
Stockdove Way, Grnf. 104 C3
Stocker Gdns., Dag. 100 C7
Ellerton Rd.
Stockfield Rd. SW16 169 F3
Stockfield Rd., Esher 194 B5
Stockholm Rd. SE16 133 F5
Stockholm Way E1 29 H1
Stockholm Way E1 132 D1
Stockhurst Cl. SW15 147 J2
Stockingswater La., Enf. 45 H3
Stockley Cl., West Dr. 120 E2
Stockley Fm. Rd., West Dr. 120/121 E3
Stockley Rd.
Stockley Pk., Uxb. 121 E1
Stockley Pk. Roundabout, Uxb. 120 E1
Stockley Rd., West Dr. 120 E4
Stockport Rd. SW16 186 D1
Stocks Pl. E14 113 J7
Grenade St.
Stocksfield Rd. E17 78 C3
Stockton Gdns. N17 59 J7
Stockton Rd.
Stockton Gdns. NW7 54 E3
Stockton Rd. N17 59 J7
Stockton Rd. N18 60 D6
Stockwell Av. SW9 151 F3
Stockwell Cl., Brom. 191 H2
Stockwell Gdns. SW9 151 F2
Stockwell Gdns. Est. SW9 151 E2
Stockwell Grn. SW9 151 F2
Stockwell La. SW9 151 F2
Stockwell Ms. SW9 151 F2
Stockwell Rd.
Stockwell Pk. Cres. SW9 151 F2
Stockwell Pk. Est. SW9 151 G2
Stockwell Pk. Rd. SW9 151 F1
Stockwell Pk. Wk. SW9 151 F3
Stockwell Rd. SW9 151 F2
Stockwell St. SE10 134 C6
Stockwell Ter. SW9 151 F1
Stodart Rd. SE20 189 F1
Stofield Gdns. SE9 174 A3
Aldersgrove Av.
Stoford Cl. SW19 148 B7
Stoke Newington Ch. St. N16 94 A3
Stoke Newington Common N16 94 C3
Stoke Newington High St. N16 94 C3
Stoke Newington Rd. N16 94 C5
Stoke Pl. NW10 107 F3
Stoke Rd., Kings.T. 164 C7
Stokenchurch St. SW6 148 E1
Stokes Rd. E6 116 B4
Stokes Rd., Croy. 189 G6
Stokesby Rd., Chess. 195 J6
Stokesley St. W12 107 F6
Stoll Cl. NW2 89 J3
Stoms Path SE6 172 A5
Stonard Rd. N13 59 G3
Stonard Rd., Dag. 100 B5
Stonards Hill, Loug. 48 C6
Stondon Pk. SE23 153 H7
Stondon Wk. E6 116 A2
Stone Bldgs. WC2 18 D2
Stone Bldgs. WC2 111 F5
Stone Cl. SW4 150 C2
Larkhall Ri.
Stone Cl., Dag. 101 F2
Stone Cl., West Dr. 120 C1
Stone Cres., Felt. 141 J7
Stone Hall Gdns. W8 22 A6
Stone Hall Pl. W8 22 A6
Stone Hall Rd. N21 43 F7
Stone Ho. Ct. EC3 20 D3
Stone Pk. Av., Beck. 190 A4
Stone Pl., Wor.Pk. 197 G2
Stone Rd., Brom. 191 F5
Stone St., Croy. 201 G5
Stonebanks, Walt. 178 A7
Stonebridge Common E8 94 C7
Mayfield Rd.
Stonebridge Pk. NW10 88 D7
Stonebridge Rd. N15 76 B5
Stonebridge Way, Wem. 88 B6
Stonechat Sq. E6 116 B5
Peridot St.
Stonecot Cl., Sutt. 198 B1
Stonecot Hill, Sutt. 198 B1
Stonecroft Cl., Barn. 39 H4
Stonecroft Rd., Erith 139 J7

Name	Page	Grid
Stonecroft Way, Croy.	187	E7
Stonecrop Cl. NW9	70	D3
Colindale Av.		
Stonecutter Ct. EC4	111	H6
Stonecutter St.		
Stonecutter St. EC4	**19**	**G3**
Stonecutter St. EC4	111	H6
Stonefield Cl., Bexh.	159	G3
Stonefield Cl., Ruis.	84	E5
Stonefield St. N1	111	H1
Stonefield Way SE7	136	A7
Greenbay Rd.		
Stonefield Way, Ruis.	84	A4
Stonegrove, Edg.	53	H4
Stonegrove Est., Edg.	53	J5
Stonegrove Gdns.,	53	J5
Edg.		
Stonehall Av., Ilf.	80	B6
Stoneham Rd. N11	58	C6
Stonehill Cl. SW14	146	D5
Stonehill Grn., Dart.	167	J7
Stonehill Rd. SW14	146	C5
Stonehill Rd. W4	126	A5
Wellesley Rd.		
Stonehill Wds.	177	H6
Caravan Pk., Sid.		
Stonehills Ct. SE21	170	B3
Stonehorse Rd., Enf.	45	H5
Stoneleigh Av., Enf.	45	E1
Stoneleigh Av.,	197	G4
Wor.Pk.		
Stoneleigh Bdy.,	197	G5
Epsom		
Stoneleigh Cres.,	197	F5
Epsom		
Stoneleigh Pk. Av.,	189	G6
Croy.		
Stoneleigh Pk. Rd.,	197	F6
Epsom		
Stoneleigh Pl. W11	108	A7
Stoneleigh Rd. N17	76	C3
Stoneleigh Rd., Cars.	185	H7
Stoneleigh Rd., Ilf.	80	B3
Stoneleigh St. W11	108	A7
Stoneleigh Ter. N19	92	B2
Stonells Rd. SW11	149	J5
Chatham Rd.		
Stonemasons Cl. N15	76	A4
Stonenest St. N4	93	F1
Stones End St. SE1	**27**	**J4**
Stones End St. SE1	131	J2
Stonewall E6	116	D5
Stoney All. SE18	156	D2
Stoney La. E1	**21**	**E3**
Stoney La. SE19	170	C6
Church Rd.		
Stoney St. SE1	**28**	**B1**
Stoney St. SE1	132	A1
Stoneyard La. E14	114	B7
Poplar High St.		
Stoneycroft Cl. SE12	155	F7
Stoneycroft Rd.,	64	B6
Wdf.Grn.		
Stoneydeep, Tedd.	162	D4
Twickenham Rd.		
Stoneydown E17	77	H4
Stoneydown Av. E17	77	H4
Stoneyfields Gdns.,	54	C4
Edg.		
Stoneyfields La., Edg.	54	C5
Stonhouse St. SW4	150	D3
Stonor Rd. W14	128	C4
Stony Path, Loug.	48	C2
Stonycroft Cl., Enf.	45	H2
Brimsdown Av.		
Stopes St. SE15	132	C7
Stopford Rd. E13	115	G1
Stopford Rd. SE17	**35**	**H4**
Stopford Rd. SE17	131	H5
Store Rd. E16	136	D2
Store St. E15	96	D5
Store St. WC1	**17**	**H2**
Store St. WC1	110	D5
Storers Quay E14	134	D4
Storey Rd. E17	77	J4
Storey Rd. N6	73	J6
Storey St. E16	136	D1
Storey's Gate SW1	**25**	**J4**
Storey's Gate SW1	130	D2
Stories Ms. SE5	152	B2
Stories Rd. SE5	152	B3
Stork Rd. E7	97	F6
Storks Rd. SE16	**29**	**J6**
Storks Rd. SE16	132	D3
Storksmead Rd., Edg.	54	E7
Stormont Rd. N6	73	J7
Stormont Rd. SW11	150	A3
Stormont Way,	195	F5
Chess.		
Stormount Dr.,	121	F2
Hayes		
Storrington Rd., Croy.	202	C1
Story St. N1	93	F7
Carnoustie Dr.		
Stothard Pl. EC2	112	B5
Bishopsgate		
Stothard St. E1	113	F4
Colebert Av.		
Stott Cl. SW18	149	G6
Stoughton Av., Sutt.	198	A5
Stoughton Cl. SE11	**34**	**D2**
Stoughton Cl. SW15	165	G1
Bessborough Rd.		
Stour Av., Sthl.	123	G3
Stour Cl., Kes.	205	J4
Stour Rd. E3	96	A7
Stour Rd., Dag.	101	G2
Stourcliffe St. W1	**15**	**J4**
Stourcliffe St. W1	109	J6
Stourhead Cl. SW19	148	A7
Castlecombe Dr.		
Stourhead Gdns.	183	G3
SW20		
Stourton Av., Felt.	161	F4
Stow Cres. E17	61	H7
Stowage SE8	134	A6
Stowe Gdns. N9	60	C1
Latymer Rd.		
Stowe Pl. N15	76	B3
Stowe Rd. W12	127	H2
Stowting Rd., Orp.	207	H4
Stox Mead, Har.	68	A1
Stracey Rd. E7	97	G4
Stracey Rd. NW10	106	D1
Strachan Pl. SW19	165	J6
Woodhayes Rd.		
Stradbroke Dr., Chig.	64	D6
Stradbroke Gro.,	64	A1
Buck.H.		
Stradbroke Gro., Ilf.	80	B3
Stradbroke Pk., Chig.	64	E6
Stradbroke Rd. N5	93	J4
Stradbrook Cl., Har.	85	F3
Stiven Cres.		
Stradella Rd. SE24	151	J6
Strafford Av., Ilf.	80	D2
Strafford Rd. W3	126	C2
Strafford Rd., Barn.	40	B3
Strafford Rd., Houns.	143	F3
Strafford Rd., Twick.	144	D7
Strafford St. E14	134	A2
Strahan Rd. E3	113	H3
Straight, The, Sthl.	122	D2
Straightsmouth SE10	134	C7
Strait Rd. E6	116	B7
Straker's Rd. SE15	152	E4
Strand WC2	**18**	**A6**
Strand WC2	111	E7
Strand La. WC2	**18**	**D5**
Strand on the Grn.	126	A6
W4		
Strand Pl. N18	60	A4
Strand Sch. App. W4	126	A6
Thames Rd.		
Strandfield Cl. SE18	137	H5
Strangways Ter. W14	128	C3
Melbury Rd.		
Stranraer Rd., Houns.	140	B6
Stranraer Way N1	93	E7
Strasburg Rd. SW11	150	B1
Stratfield Pk. Cl. N21	43	H7
Stratfield Rd., Borwd.	38	A3
Stratford Av. W8	128	D3
Stratford Rd.		
Stratford Cen., The	96	D7
E15		
Stratford Cl., Bark.	100	A7
Stratford Cl., Dag.	101	J7
Stratford Cl., N.Mal.	182	D4
Kingston Rd.		
Stratford Gro. SW15	148	A4
Stratford Ho. Av.,	192	B3
Brom.		
Stratford Pl. W1	**16**	**D4**
Stratford Pl. W1	110	B6
Stratford Rd. E13	115	F1
Stratford Rd. NW4	72	A4
Stratford Rd. W8	128	D3
Stratford Rd., Hayes	102	B4
Stratford Rd., Houns.	141	E6
Stratford Rd., Sthl.	122	E4
Stratford Rd., Th.Hth.	187	G4
Stratford Vil. NW1	92	C7
Strath Ter. SW11	149	H4
Stratham Cl. SW18	148	B6
Strathaven Rd. SE12	155	H6
Strathblaine Rd.	149	G4
SW11		
Strathbrook Rd.	169	F7
SW16		
Strathcona Rd., Wem.	87	G2
Strathdale SW16	169	F5
Strathdon Dr. SW17	167	G3
Strathearn Av.,	121	J7
Hayes		
Strathearn Av.	161	H1
Twick.		
Strathearn Pl. W2	**15**	**F5**
Strathearn Pl. W2	109	H7
Strathearn Rd. SW19	166	D5
Strathearn Rd., Sutt.	198	D5
Stratheden Par. SE3	135	G7
Stratheden Rd.		
Stratheden Rd. SE3	155	G1
Strathfield Gdns.,	99	G6
Bark.		
Strathleven Rd. SW2	151	E5
Strathmore Gdns. N3	72	E1
Strathmore Gdns. W8	128	D1
Palace Gdns. Ter.		
Strathmore Gdns.,	70	B2
Edg.		
Strathmore Rd. SW19	166	D3
Strathmore Rd., Croy.	187	J7
Strathmore Rd.,	162	B4
Tedd.		
Strathnairn St. SE1	**37**	**J2**
Strathnairn St. SE1	132	D4
Strathray Gdns. NW3	91	H6
Strathville Rd. SW18	166	E2
Strathyre Av. SW16	187	G3
Stratton Cl. SW19	184	D2
Stratton Cl., Bexh.	159	E3
Stratton Cl., Edg.	53	J6
Stratton Cl., Houns.	143	F1
Stratton Cl., Walt.	178	C7
Stratton Dr., Bark.	99	J5
Stratton Gdns., Sthl.	103	F6
Stratton Rd. SW19	184	D2
Stratton Rd., Bexh.	159	E3
Stratton St. W1	**25**	**E1**
Stratton St. W1	130	B1
Strattondale St. E14	134	C3
Strauss Rd. W4	126	D2
Strawberry Hill,	162	C3
Twick.		
Strawberry Hill Cl.,	162	C3
Twick.		
Strawberry Hill Rd.,	162	C3
Twick.		
Strawberry Vale N2	73	G1
Strawberry Vale,	162	D1
Twick.		
Streakes Fld. Rd. NW2	89	G2
Stream La., Edg.	54	B5
Streamdale SE2	138	A6
Streamside Cl. N9	60	C1
Streamside Cl.,	191	G4
Brom.		
Streamway, Belv.	139	G6
Streatfield Av. E6	116	C1
Streatfield Rd., Har.	69	G3
Streatham Cl. SW16	169	E2
Streatham Common	169	E5
N. SW16		
Streatham Common	169	E6
S. SW16		
Streatham Ct. SW16	168	E3
Streatham High Rd.	168	E5
SW16		
Streatham Hill SW2	169	E2
Streatham Pl. SW2	150	E7
Streatham Rd. SW16	186	A1
Streatham Rd., Mitch.	186	A1
Streatham St. WC1	**17**	**J3**
Streatham St. WC1	110	D6
Streatham Vale SE6	168	C7
Streathbourne Rd.	168	A2
SW17		
Streatley Pl. NW3	91	F4
New End Sq.		
Streatley Rd. NW6	90	C7
Streeters La., Wall.	200	D3
Streetfield Ms. SE3	155	G3
Streimer Rd. E15	114	C2
Strelley Way W3	106	E7
Stretton Pl., Rich.	163	F2
Stretton Rd., Croy.	188	B7
Stretton Rd., Rich.	163	F2
Strickland Row	149	G7
SW18		
Strickland St. SE8	154	A2
Strickland Way, Orp.	207	J4
Stride E13	115	F2
Strode Cl. N10	58	A7
Pembroke Rd.		
Strode Rd. E7	97	G4
Strode Rd. N17	76	B2
Strode Rd. NW10	89	G6
Strode Rd. SW6	128	A7
Strone Rd. E7	97	J6
Strone Rd. E12	98	A6
Strone Way, Hayes	102	E4
Strongbow Cres. SE9	156	C5
Strongbow Rd. SE9	156	C5
Strongbridge Cl.,	85	G1
Har.		
Stronsa Rd. W12	127	F2
Stroud Cres. SW15	165	G3
Stroud Fld., Nthlt.	84	E6
Stroud Grn. Gdns.,	189	F7
Croy.		
Stroud Grn. Rd. N4	93	F1
Stroud Grn. Way,	189	E7
Croy.		
Stroud Rd. SE25	188	D6
Stroud Rd. SW19	166	D3
Stroudes Cl., Wor.Pk.	183	E7
Stroudley Wk. E3	114	B3
Strouds Cl.	82	B5
(Chadwell Heath), Rom.		
Strouts Pl. E2	**13**	**F3**
Strutton Grd. SW1	**25**	**H5**
Strutton Grd. SW1	130	D3
Strype St. E1	**21**	**F2**
Stuart Av. NW9	71	G7
Stuart Av. W5	125	J1
Stuart Av., Brom.	205	G1
Stuart Av., Har.	85	F3
Stuart Cres. N22	75	F1
Stuart Cres., Croy.	203	J3
Stuart Evans Cl.,	158	C3
Well.		
Stuart Gro., Tedd.	162	B5
Stuart Pl., Mitch.	185	J1
Stuart Rd. NW6	108	D3
Stuart Rd. SE15	153	F4
Stuart Rd. SW19	166	D3
Stuart Rd. W3	126	C1
Stuart Rd., Bark.	99	J7
Stuart Rd., Barn.	41	H7
Stuart Rd., Grav.	68	C2
Stuart Rd., Rich.	163	E2
Stuart Rd., Th.Hth.	187	J4
Stuart Rd., Well.	158	B1
Stuart Twr. W9	**6**	**C4**
Stuart Twr. W9	109	F3
Stubbs Dr. SE16	132	E5
Stubbs Ms., Dag.	100	B4
Marlborough Rd.		
Stubbs Pt. E13	115	H4
Stubbs Way SW19	185	G1
Brangwyn Cres.		
Stucley Pl. NW1	92	B7
Hawley Cres.		
Stucley Rd., Houns.	123	J7
Studd St. N1	111	H1
Studdridge St. SW6	148	D2
Studholme Ct. NW3	90	D4
Studholme St. SE15	132	E7
Studio Ct., Borwd.	38	C2
Studio Pl. SW1	**24**	**A4**
Studio Way, Borwd.	38	C2
Studland SE17	**36**	**B3**
Studland Cl., Sid.	175	J3
Studland Rd. SE26	171	G5
Studland Rd. W7	104	A6
Studland Rd.,	163	H6
Kings.T.		
Studland St. W6	127	H4
Studley Av. E4	62	D7
Studley Cl. E5	95	H5
Studley Ct., Sid.	176	B5
Studley Dr., Ilf.	80	A6
Studley Est. SW4	151	E1
Studley Gra. Rd. W7	124	B2
Studley Rd. E7	97	H6
Studley Rd. SW4	150	E1
Studley Rd., Dag.	100	D7
Stukeley Rd. E7	97	H7
Stukeley St. WC2	**18**	**B3**
Stukeley St. WC2	111	E6
Stumps Hill La., Beck.	172	A6
Sturdy Rd. SE15	153	E2
Sturge Av. E17	78	B2
Sturge St. SE1	**27**	**J3**
Sturgeon Rd. SE17	35	J4
Sturgeon Rd. SE17	131	J5
Sturges Fld., Chis.	175	G6
Sturgess Av. NW4	71	H7
Sturmer Way N7	93	F5
Stock Orchard Cres.		
Sturminster Cl.,	102	C6
Hayes		
Sturrock Cl. N15	76	A4
Sturry St. E14	114	B6
Sturt St. N1	**12**	**A2**
Sturt St. N1	111	J2
Stutfield St. E1	**21**	**J4**
Stutfield St. E1	112	D6
Styles Gdns. SW9	151	H3
Styles Way, Beck.	190	C4
Sudbourne Rd. SW2	151	E5
Sudbrook Gdns.,	163	G3
Rich.		
Sudbrook La., Rich.	163	H1
Sudbrooke Rd. SW12	149	J6
Sudbury E6	116	D6
Newark Knok		
Sudbury Av., Wem.	87	G3
Sudbury Ct. E5	95	H4
Sudbury Ct. Dr., Har.	86	C3
Sudbury Ct. Rd., Har.	86	C3
Sudbury Cres., Brom.	173	G6
Sudbury Cres., Wem.	87	E5
Sudbury Cft., Wem.	86	C4

Sudbury Gdns., Croy. 202 B4 *Langton Way*
Sudbury Hts. Av., Grnf. 86 C5
Sudbury Hill, Har. 86 B2
Sudbury Hill Cl., Wem. 86 C4
Sudbury Rd., Bark. 99 J5
Sudeley St. N1 11 H2
Sudeley St. N1 111 H2
Sudlow Rd. SW18 148 D4
Sudrey St. SE1 27 J4
Suez Av., Grnf. 104 C2
Suez Rd., Enf. 45 H4
Suffield Rd. E4 62 B3
Suffield Rd. N15 76 C5
Suffield Rd. SE20 189 F2
Suffolk Cl., Borwd. 38 D5 *Clydesdale Cl.*
Suffolk Ct. E10 78 A7
Suffolk Ct., Ilf. 81 H6
Suffolk Ct., Surb. 181 G6 *St. James Rd.*
Suffolk La. EC4 20 B5
Suffolk Pk. Rd. E17 77 H4
Suffolk Pl. SW1 25 J1
Suffolk Rd. E13 115 F3
Suffolk Rd. N15 76 A6
Suffolk Rd. NW10 89 E7
Suffolk Rd. SE25 188 C4
Suffolk Rd. SW13 127 F7
Suffolk Rd., Bark. 99 G7
Suffolk Rd., Dag. 101 J5
Suffolk Rd., Enf. 45 E5
Suffolk Rd., Har. 67 F6
Suffolk Rd., Ilf. 81 H6
Suffolk Rd., Sid. 176 C6
Suffolk Rd., Wor.Pk. 197 F2
Suffolk St. E7 97 G5
Suffolk St. SW1 25 J1
Sugar Bakers Ct. EC3 112 B6 *Creechurch La.*
Sugar Ho. La. E15 114 C2
Sugar Loaf Wk. E2 113 F3 *Victoria Pk. Sq.*
Sugar Quay Wk. EC3 20 E6
Sugar Quay Wk. EC3 112 B7
Sugden Rd. SW11 150 A3
Sugden Rd., T.Ditt. 194 E1
Sugden Way, Bark. 117 J2
Sulgrave Gdns. W6 127 J2 *Sulgrave Rd.*
Sulgrave Rd. W6 127 J2
Sulina Rd. SW2 151 E7
Sulivan Ct. SW6 148 D3
Sulivan Rd. SW6 148 D3
Sullivan Av. E16 116 A5
Sullivan Cl. SW11 149 H3
Sullivan Cl., W.Mol. 179 G3 *Victoria Av.*
Sullivan Rd. SE11 35 F1
Sullivan Rd. SE11 131 H4
Sultan Rd. E11 79 H4
Sultan St. SE5 35 J7
Sultan St. SE5 131 J7
Sultan St., Beck. 189 G2
Sumatra Rd. NW6 90 D5
Sumburgh Rd. SW12 150 A6
Summer Av., E.Mol. 180 B5
Summer Gdns., E.Mol. 180 B5
Summer Hill, Borwd. 38 A5
Summer Hill, Chis. 192 D2
Summer Hill Vil., Chis. 192 D1
Summer Rd., E.Mol. 180 B5
Summer Rd., T.Ditt. 180 C5
Summer St. EC1 11 E6
Summer Trees, Sun. 178 B1 *The Av.*
Summercourt Rd. E1 113 F6
Summerene Cl. SW16 168 C7 *Bates Cres.*
Summerfield Av. NW6 108 B2
Summerfield La., Surb. 195 G2
Summerfield Rd. W5 105 E4
Summerfield Rd., Loug. 48 A6
Summerfield St. SE12 155 F7
Summerfields Av. N12 57 H6
Summerhill Cl., Orp. 207 H3
Summerhill Gro., Enf. 44 B6
Summerhill Rd. N15 76 A4
Summerhill Way, Mitch. 186 A1
Summerhouse Av., Houns. 142 E1
Summerhouse La., West Dr. 120 A6
Summerhouse Rd. N16 94 B2
Summerland Gdns. N10 74 B3
Summerlands Av. W3 106 C7
Summerlee Av. N2 73 J4
Summerlee Gdns. N2 73 J4
Summerley St. SW18 167 E2
Summers Cl., Sutt. 198 D7 *Overton Rd.*
Summers Cl., Wem. 88 B1
Summers La. N12 57 G7
Summers Row N12 57 H6
Summersby Rd. N6 74 B6
Summerstown SW17 167 F3
Summerton Way SE28 118 D6
Summerville Gdns., Sutt. 198 C6
Summerwood Rd., Islw. 144 C5
Summit, The, Loug. 48 C1
Summit Av. NW9 70 D5
Summit Cl. N14 58 C2
Summit Cl. NW9 70 D4
Summit Cl., Edg. 54 A7
Summit Ct. NW2 90 B5
Summit Dr., Wdf.Grn. 80 A2
Summit Est. N16 76 D7
Summit Rd. E17 78 B4
Summit Rd., Nthlt. 85 G7
Summit Way N14 58 B2
Summit Way SE19 170 B7
Sumner Av. SE15 152 C1 *Sumner Rd.*
Sumner Cl., Orp. 207 F4
Sumner Est. SE15 132 C7
Sumner Gdns., Croy. 201 G1
Sumner Pl. SW7 31 F2
Sumner Pl. SW7 129 G4
Sumner Pl. Ms. SW7 31 F2
Sumner Rd. SE15 37 G6
Sumner Rd. SE15 132 C7
Sumner Rd., Croy. 201 G1
Sumner Rd., Har. 67 J7
Sumner Rd. S., Croy. 201 G1
Sumner St. SE1 27 H1
Sumner St. SE1 131 J1
Sumpter Cl. NW3 91 F6
Sun All., Rich. 145 H4 *Kew Rd.*
Sun Ct. EC3 20 C4
Sun La. SE3 135 H7
Sun Pas. SE16 29 H5
Sun Rd. W14 128 C5
Sun St. EC2 20 D2
Sun St. EC2 112 A5
Sun St. Pas. EC2 20 D2
Sun Wk. E1 21 H6
Sunbeam Cres. W10 107 J4
Sunbeam Rd. NW10 106 C4
Sunbury Av. NW7 54 D5
Sunbury Av. SW14 146 D4
Sunbury Ct., Sun. 178 D2
Sunbury Ct. Island, Sun. 178 D3
Sunbury Ct. Ms., Sun. 178 D2 *Lower Hampton Rd.*
Sunbury Ct. Rd., Sun. 178 C2
Sunbury Gdns. NW7 54 D5
Sunbury La. SW11 149 G1
Sunbury La., Walt. 178 A6
Sunbury Lock Ait, Walt. 178 B4
Sunbury Rd., Sutt. 198 A3
Sunbury St. SE18 136 C3
Sunbury Way, Felt. 160 C5
Suncroft Pl. SE26 171 F3
Sunderland Ct. SE22 152 D7
Sunderland Mt. SE23 171 G2 *Sunderland Rd.*
Sunderland Rd. SE23 171 G1
Sunderland Rd. W5 125 G3
Sunderland Ter. W2 14 A3
Sunderland Ter. W2 108 E6
Sunderland Way E12 98 A2
Sundew Av. W12 107 G7
Sundial Av. SE25 188 C3
Sundorne Rd. SE7 135 J5
Sundra Wk. E1 113 G4 *Beaumont Gro.*
Sundridge Av., Brom. 174 A7
Sundridge Av., Chis. 174 A7
Sundridge Av., Well. 157 G2
Sundridge Ho., Brom. 173 H5 *Burnt Ash La.*
Sundridge Pl., Croy. 202 D1 *Inglis Rd.*
Sundridge Rd., Croy. 188 C7
Sunfields Pl. SE3 135 H7
Sunland Av., Bexh. 159 E4
Sunleigh Rd., Wem. 105 H1
Sunley Gdns., Grnf. 104 D1
Sunlight Cl. SW19 167 F6
Sunlight Sq. E2 113 E3
Sunmead Rd., Sun. 178 A3
Sunna Gdns., Sun. 178 B2
Sunningdale N14 58 D5 *Wilmer Way*
Sunningdale Av. W3 107 E7
Sunningdale Av., Bark. 117 G1
Sunningdale Av., Felt. 160 E2
Sunningdale Av., Ruis. 84 C1
Sunningdale Cl. E6 116 C3 *Ascot Rd.*
Sunningdale Cl. SE16 132/133 E5 *Ryder Dr.*
Sunningdale Cl. SE28 118 E6
Sunningdale Cl., Stan. 52 D7
Sunningdale Cl., Surb. 195 H2 *Culsac Rd.*
Sunningdale Gdns. NW9 70 C5
Sunningdale Gdns. W8 128 D3 *Lexham Ms.*
Sunningdale Rd., Brom. 192 B4
Sunningdale Rd., Sutt. 198 C4
Sunningfields Cres. NW4 71 H2
Sunningfields Rd. NW4 71 H2
Sunninghill Rd. SE13 154 B2
Sunny Bank SE25 188 D3
Sunny Cres. NW10 88 C7
Sunny Gdns. Par. NW4 71 J2 *Great N. Way*
Sunny Gdns. Rd. NW4 71 H2
Sunny Hill NW4 71 H3
Sunny Nook Gdns., S.Croy. 202 A6 *Selsdon Rd.*
Sunny Rd., The, Enf. 45 G1
Sunny Vw. NW9 70 D5
Sunny Way N12 57 H7
Sunnycroft Rd. SE25 188 D3
Sunnycroft Rd., Houns. 143 H2
Sunnycroft Rd., Sthl. 103 G5
Sunnydale, Orp. 206 D2
Sunnydale Gdns. NW7 54 D6
Sunnydale Rd. SE12 155 H5
Sunnydene Av. E4 62 D5
Sunnydene Av., Ruis. 84 A2
Sunnydene Gdns., Wem. 87 F6
Sunnydene St. SE26 171 H4
Sunnyfield NW7 55 F4
Sunnyhill Cl. E5 95 H4
Sunnyhill Rd. SW16 168 E4
Sunnyhurst Cl., Sutt. 198 D3
Sunnymead Av., Mitch. 186 C3
Sunnymead Rd. NW9 70 D7
Sunnymead Rd. SW15 147 H5
Sunnymede Dr., Ilf. 80 E4
Sunnyside NW2 90 C3
Sunnyside SW19 166 B6
Sunnyside, Walt. 178 C5
Sunnyside Dr. E4 46 C7
Sunnyside Pas. SW19 166 B6
Sunnyside Pl. SW19 166 B6 *Sunnyside*
Sunnyside Rd. E10 96 A1
Sunnyside Rd. N19 74 D7
Sunnyside Rd. W5 125 G1
Sunnyside Rd., Ilf. 99 F3
Sunnyside Rd., Tedd. 162 A4
Sunnyside Rd. E. N9 60 D3
Sunnyside Rd. N. N9 60 C3
Sunnyside Rd. S. N9 60 C3
Sunnyside Ter. NW9 70 D3 *Edgware Rd.*
Sunray Av. SE24 152 A4
Sunray Av., Brom. 192 B6
Sunray Av., Surb. 196 B2
Sunray Av., West Dr. 120 A2
Sunrise Cl., Felt. 161 F3 *Exeter Rd.*
Sunset Av. E4 62 B1
Sunset Av., Wdf.Grn. 63 F4
Sunset Gdns. SE25 188 C2
Sunset Rd. SE5 151 J4
Sunset Rd. SE28 138 A2
Sunset Vw., Barn. 40 B2
Sunshine Way, Mitch. 185 J2
Sunwell Cl. SE15 152/153 E1 *Cossall Wk.*
Superior Dr., Orp. 207 J6
Surbiton Ct., Surb. 181 F6
Surbiton Cres., Kings.T. 181 H4
Surbiton Hall Cl., Kings.T. 181 H4
Surbiton Hill Pk., Surb. 182 A5
Surbiton Hill Rd., Surb. 181 H4
Surbiton Par., Surb. 181 H6 *St. Mark's Hill*
Surbiton Rd., Kings.T. 181 H4
Surlingham Cl. SE28 118 D7
Surma Cl. E1 13 J6
Surma Cl. E1 112 E4
Surr St. N7 93 E5
Surrendale Pl. W9 108 D4
Surrey Canal Rd. SE14 133 F6
Surrey Canal Rd. SE15 133 F6
Surrey Cres. W4 126 A5
Surrey Gdns. N4 75 J6 *Finsbury Pk. Av.*
Surrey Gro. SE17 36 D4
Surrey Gro., Sutt. 199 G3
Surrey La. SW11 149 H1
Surrey La. Est. SW11 149 H1
Surrey Lo. SE1 26 E6
Surrey Ms. SE27 170 B4 *Hamilton Rd.*
Surrey Mt. SE23 171 E1
Surrey Quays Rd. SE16 133 G2
Surrey Rd. SE15 153 G5
Surrey Rd., Bark. 117 H1
Surrey Rd., Dag. 101 H5
Surrey Rd., Har. 67 J5
Surrey Rd., W.Wick. 204 B1
Surrey Row SE1 27 G3
Surrey Row SE1 131 H2
Surrey Sq. SE17 36 D3
Surrey Sq. SE17 132 B5
Surrey St. E13 115 H3
Surrey St. WC2 18 D5
Surrey St. WC2 111 F7
Surrey St., Croy. 201 J3
Surrey Ter. SE17 36 E3
Surrey Ter. SE17 132 B5
Surrey Twr. SE20 171 F7
Surrey Water Rd. SE16 133 G1
Surridge Gdns. SE19 170 A6 *Hancock Rd.*
Susan Cl., Rom. 83 J3
Susan Rd. SE3 155 H2
Susan Wd., Chis. 192 D1
Susannah St. E14 114 B6
Sussex Av., Islw. 144 B3
Sussex Cl. N19 92/93 E2 *Cornwallis Rd.*
Sussex Cl., Ilf. 80 C5
Sussex Cl., N.Mal. 183 E4
Sussex Cl., Twick. 144/145 E6 *Westmorland Cl.*
Sussex Cres., Nthlt. 85 G6
Sussex Gdns. N4 75 J5
Sussex Gdns. N6 73 J5 *Great N. Rd.*
Sussex Gdns. W2 15 E4
Sussex Gdns. W2 109 G6
Sussex Gdns., Chess. 195 G6
Sussex Ms. E. W2 15 F4
Sussex Ms. W. W2 15 F5
Sussex Pl. NW1 7 J5
Sussex Pl. NW1 109 J4
Sussex Pl. W2 15 F4
Sussex Pl. W2 109 G6
Sussex Pl. W6 127 J5
Sussex Pl., Erith 139 H7
Sussex Pl., N.Mal. 183 E4
Sussex Ring N12 56 D5
Sussex Rd. E6 116 D1
Sussex Rd., Cars. 199 J6
Sussex Rd., Erith 139 H7
Sussex Rd., Har. 67 J5
Sussex Rd., Mitch. 186/187 E5 *Lincoln Rd.*
Sussex Rd., N.Mal. 183 E4
Sussex Rd., Sid. 176 B5
Sussex Rd., S.Croy. 202 A6
Sussex Rd., Sthl. 122 D3
Sussex Rd., W.Wick. 204 B1
Sussex Sq. W2 15 F5
Sussex Sq. W2 109 G7
Sussex St. E13 115 H3
Sussex St. SW1 32 E4
Sussex St. SW1 130 B5
Sussex Wk. SW9 151 H4
Sussex Way N7 93 E2
Sussex Way N19 92 E1
Sussex Way, Barn. 42 A5
Sutcliffe Cl. NW11 73 E5
Sutcliffe Ho., Hayes 102 A6
Sutcliffe Rd. SE18 137 H6

Sutcliffe Rd., Well.	158	C2
Sutherland Av. W9	**6**	**C4**
Sutherland Av. W9	109	F3
Sutherland Av. W13	104	E6
Sutherland Av.,	122	A4
Hayes		
Sutherland Av., Orp.	193	J6
Sutherland Av., Well.	157	H4
Sutherland Cl., Barn.	40	B4
Sutherland Ct. NW9	70	B5
Sutherland Dr. SW19	185	G1
Willow Vw.		
Sutherland Gdns.	147	E3
SW14		
Sutherland Gdns.,	197	H1
Wor.Pk.		
Sutherland Gro.	148	B6
SW18		
Sutherland Gro.,	162	B5
Tedd.		
Sutherland Pl. W2	108	D6
Sutherland Pt. E5	94/95	E4
Tiger Way		
Sutherland Rd. E17	77	G2
Sutherland Rd. N9	60	D1
Sutherland Rd. N17	60	D7
Sutherland Rd. W4	126	E6
Sutherland Rd. W13	104	D6
Sutherland Rd., Belv.	139	G3
Sutherland Rd., Croy.	187	G7
Sutherland Rd., Enf.	45	G5
Sutherland Rd., Sthl.	103	F6
Sutherland Rd. Path	77	G3
E17		
Sutherland Row SW1	**32**	**E3**
Sutherland Row SW1	130	B5
Sutherland Sq. SE17	**35**	**J4**
Sutherland Sq. SE17	131	J5
Sutherland St. SW1	**32**	**D3**
Sutherland St. SW1	130	B5
Sutherland Wk. SE17	**36**	**A4**
Sutherland Wk. SE17	131	J5
Highbury Sta. Rd.		
Sutlej Rd. SE7	135	J7
Sutterton St. N7	93	F6
Sutton Cl., Beck.	190	B1
Albemarle Rd.		
Sutton Cl., Loug.	48	B7
Sutton Cl., Pnr.	66	A5
Sutton Common Rd.,	184	C1
Sutt.		
Sutton Ct. W4	126	C6
Sutton Ct. Rd. E13	115	J3
Sutton Ct. Rd. W4	126	C7
Sutton Ct. Rd., Sutt.	199	F6
Sutton Cres., Barn.	40	A5
Sutton Dene, Houns.	143	H1
Sutton Est. SW3	**31**	**H3**
Sutton Est. SW3	129	H5
Sutton Est. W10	107	J5
Sutton Est., The N1	93	H7
Sutton Gdns., Bark.	117	H1
Sutton Rd.		
Sutton Gdns., Croy.	188	C5
Sutton Grn., Bark.	117	H1
Sutton Rd.		
Sutton Gro., Sutt.	199	G4
Sutton Hall Rd.,	123	G7
Houns.		
Sutton La., Houns.	143	F3
Sutton La. N. W4	126	C5
Sutton La. S. W4	126	C6
Sutton Par. NW4	71	J4
Church Rd.		
Sutton Pk. Rd., Sutt.	198	E6
Sutton Path, Borwd.	38	A2
Stratfield Rd.		
Sutton Pl. E9	95	F5
Sutton Rd. E13	115	F4
Sutton Rd. E17	77	G1
Sutton Rd. N10	74	A2
Sutton Rd., Bark.	117	H2
Sutton Rd., Houns.	143	G1
Sutton Row W1	**17**	**J3**
Sutton Row W1	110	D6
Sutton Sq. E9	95	F5
Urswick Rd.		
Sutton Sq., Houns.	143	F1
Sutton St. E1	113	F6
Sutton Way W10	107	J5
Sutton Way, Houns.	143	F1
Sutton's Way EC1	**12**	**A6**
Swaby Rd. SW18	167	F1
Swaffham Way N22	59	H7
White Hart La.		
Swaffield Rd. SW18	149	E7
Swain Cl. SW16	168	B6
Swain Rd., Th.Hth.	187	J5
Swains Cl., West Dr.	120	B2
Swains La. N6	92	A3
Swains Rd. SW17	167	J7
Swainson Rd. W3	127	F2
Swaledale Cl. N11	58	A6
Ribblesdale Av.		
Swallands Rd. SE6	172	A3

Swallow Cl. SE14	153	F1
Swallow Cl., Bushey	51	J1
Swallow Dr. NW10	88	D6
Kingfisher Way		
Swallow Dr., Nthlt.	103	G2
Swallow Gdns. SW16	168	D5
Swallow Pas. W1	**17**	**E4**
Swallow Pl. W1	**17**	**E4**
Swallow Pl. W1	116	B5
Swallow St. W1	**17**	**G6**
Swallowfield Rd. SE7	135	H5
Swallowfield Way,	121	G2
Hayes		
Swan App. E6	116	B5
Swan Cl. E17	77	H1
Swan Cl., Croy.	188	B7
Swan Cl., Felt.	161	E4
Swan Ct. SW3	**31**	**H4**
Swan Dr. NW9	70	E2
Swan La. EC4	**20**	**B6**
Swan La. N20	57	F3
Swan La., Loug.	47	J7
Swan Mead SE1	**28**	**D6**
Swan Mead SE1	132	B3
Swan Pas. E1	112	C7
Cartwright St.		
Swan Path E10	96	C1
Jesse Rd.		
Swan Pl. SW13	147	F2
Swan Rd. SE16	133	F2
Swan Rd. SE18	136	A3
Swan Rd., Felt.	160	E5
Swan Rd., Sthl.	103	H6
Swan Rd., West Dr.	120	A2
Swan St. SE1	28	A5
Swan St. SE1	131	J3
Swan St., Islw.	144	E3
Swan Wk. SW3	**31**	**J5**
Swan Wk. SW3	129	J6
Swan Way, Enf.	45	G2
Swan Yd. N1	93	H6
Highbury Sta. Rd.		
Swanage Rd. E4	62	C7
Swanage Rd. SW18	149	F6
Swanage Waye,	102	C6
Hayes		
Swanbridge Rd.,	159	G1
Bexh.		
Swanfield St. E2	**13**	**F4**
Swanfield St. E2	112	C3
Swanley Rd., Well.	158	C1
Swanscombe Rd.	127	E5
W4		
Swanscombe Rd.	128	A1
W11		
Swansea Ct. E16	136/137	E2
Barge Ho. Rd.		
Swansea Rd., Enf.	45	F4
Swansea Rd., Felt.	141	F6
Southern Perimeter Rd.		
Swansea Rd., Houns.	141	F6
Southern Perimeter Rd.		
Swanshope, Loug.	49	E2
McEntee Av.		
Swansland Gdns. E17	77	H1
Swanston Path, Wat.	50	C3
Swanton Gdns.	166	A1
SW19		
Swanton Rd., Erith	139	H7
Swanwick Cl. SW15	147	F7
Swaton Rd. E3	114	A4
Swaylands Rd., Belv.	139	G6
Swaythling Cl. N18	61	E4
Sweden Gate SE16	133	H3
Swedenborg Gdns.	**21**	**J5**
E1		
Swedenborg Gdns.	112	D7
E1		
Sweeney Cres. SE1	**29**	**G4**
Sweeney Cres. SE1	132	C2
Sweet Briar Grn. N9	60	C3
Sweet Briar Gro. N9	60	C3
Sweet Briar Wk. N18	60	C4
Sweetmans Av., Pnr.	66	D3
Sweets Way N20	57	G2
Swete St. E13	115	G2
Swetenham Wk. SE18	137	F5
Sandbach Pl.		
Sweyn Pl. SE3	155	G2
Swift Cl. E17	61	H7
Swift Cl., Har.	85	H2
Swift Rd., Felt.	161	E3
Swift Rd., Sthl.	123	F3
Swift St. SW6	148	C1
Swiftsden Way,	173	E6
Brom.		
Swinbrook Rd. W10	108	B5
Swinburne Ct. SE5	152	A4
Basingdon Way		
Swinburne Cres.,	189	F6
Croy.		
Swinburne Rd. SW15	147	G4
Swinderby Rd., Wem.	87	H6

Swindon Cl., Ilf.	99	H2
Salisbury Rd.		
Swindon Rd., Houns.	141	F5
Swindon St. W12	127	H1
Swinfield Cl., Felt.	160	E4
Swinford Gdns. SW9	151	H3
Swingate La. SE18	137	H6
Swinnerton St. E9	95	H5
Swinton Cl., Wem.	88	B1
Swinton Pl. WC1	**10**	**C3**
Swinton Pl. WC1	111	F3
Swinton St. WC1	**10**	**C3**
Swinton St. WC1	111	F3
Swires Shaw, Kes.	206	A4
Swiss Ter. NW6	91	G7
Swithland Gdns. SE9	174	D4
Swyncombe Av. W5	125	E4
Swynford Gdns. NW4	71	G4
Handowe Cl.		
Sybil Ms. N4	75	H6
Lothair Rd. N.		
Sybil Phoenix Cl. SE8	133	G5
Sybil Thorndike Ho.	93	J6
N1		
Clephane Rd.		
Sybourn St. E17	77	J7
Sycamore Av. W5	125	G3
Sycamore Av., Sid.	157	J6
Sycamore Cl. E16	114/115	E4
Clarence Rd.		
Sycamore Cl. N9	60	D4
Pycroft Way		
Sycamore Cl. SE9	174	B2
Sycamore Cl. SW3	126/127	E1
Bromyard Av.		
Sycamore Cl., Barn.	41	G6
Sycamore Cl., Cars.	199	J4
Sycamore Cl., Edg.	54	C4
Ash Cl.		
Sycamore Cl., Felt.	160	A3
Sycamore Cl., Loug.	48/49	E2
Cedar Dr.		
Sycamore Cl., Nthlt.	103	E1
Sycamore Cl., Surb.	181	H7
Penners Gdns.		
Sycamore Gdns. W6	127	H2
Sycamore Gdns.,	185	G2
Mitch.		
Sycamore Gro. NW9	70	C7
Sycamore Gro. SE6	154	C6
Sycamore Gro. SE20	170	D7
Sycamore Gro.,	182	D3
N.Mal.		
Sycamore Hill N11	58	A6
Sycamore Ms. SW4	150	C3
Sycamore Rd. SW19	165	J6
Sycamore St. EC1	**11**	**J6**
Sycamore Wk. W10	108	B4
Fifth Av.		
Sycamore Wk., Ilf.	81	F4
Civic Way		
Sycamore Way, Tedd.	163	F6
Sycamore Way,	187	G5
Th.Hth.		
Sydenham Av. N21	43	F5
Sydenham Av. SE26	171	E5
Sydenham Cotts.	173	J2
SE12		
Sydenham Hill SE23	170	E1
Sydenham Hill SE26	170	D3
Sydenham Hill Est.	170	D3
SE26		
Sydenham Pk. SE26	171	F3
Sydenham Pk. Rd.	171	F3
SE26		
Sydenham Ri. SE23	170	E2
Sydenham Rd. SE26	171	F5
Sydenham Rd., Croy.	188	A7
Sydmons Ct. SE23	153	F7
Sydner Ms. N16	94	C4
Sydner Rd.		
Sydner Rd. N16	94	C4
Sydney Cl. SW3	31	F2
Sydney Cl. SW3	129	G4
Sydney Ms. SW3	**31**	**F2**
Sydney Ms. SW3	129	G4
Sydney Pl. SW7	**31**	**F2**
Sydney Pl. SW7	129	G4
Sydney Rd. E11	79	H6
Mansfield Rd.		
Sydney Rd. N8	75	G4
Sydney Rd. N10	74	A1
Sydney Rd. SE2	138	C3
Sydney Rd. SW20	184	A2
Sydney Rd. W13	124	D1
Sydney Rd., Bexh.	158	D4
Sydney Rd., Enf.	44	A4
Sydney Rd., Felt.	160	A1
Sydney Rd., Ilf.	81	F2
Sydney Rd., Rich.	145	H4
Sydney Rd., Sid.	175	H4
Sydney Rd., Sutt.	198	D4
Sydney Rd., Tedd.	162	C5

Sydney Rd., Wdf.Grn.	63	G4
Sydney St. SW3	**31**	**G3**
Sydney St. SW3	129	H4
Sylvan Av. N3	72	D2
Sylvan Av. N22	59	F7
Sylvan Av. NW7	55	F6
Sylvan Av., Rom.	83	F6
Sylvan Est. SE19	188	C1
Sylvan Gdns., Surb.	181	G7
Sylvan Gro. NW2	90	A4
Sylvan Gro. SE15	133	E6
Sylvan Hill SE19	188	B1
Sylvan Rd. E7	97	G6
Sylvan Rd. E11	79	G5
Sylvan Rd. E17	78	A5
Sylvan Rd. SE19	188	C1
Sylvan Rd., Ilf.	99	F2
Hainault La.		
Sylvan Wk., Brom.	192	C3
Sylvan Way, Dag.	100	B3
Sylvan Way, W.Wick.	204	E4
Sylverdale Rd., Croy.	201	H3
Sylvester Av., Chis.	174	C6
Sylvester Path E8	94/95	E6
Sylvester Rd.		
Sylvester Rd. E8	95	E6
Sylvester Rd. E17	77	J7
Sylvester Rd. N2	73	F2
Sylvester Rd., Wem.	87	F4
Sylvestrus Cl., Kings.T.	182	A1
Sylvia Av., Pnr.	51	F6
Sylvia Ct., Wem.	88	B7
Harrow Rd.		
Sylvia Gdns., Wem.	88	B7
Symes Ms. NW1	**9**	**F1**
Symons St. SW3	**32**	**A2**
Symons St. SW3	129	J4
Syon Gate Way,	124	D7
Brent.		
Syon La., Islw.	124	E7
Syon Pk. Gdns., Islw.	124	C7
Syon Vista, Rich.	145	G1
T		
Tabard Gdn. Est. SE1	**28**	**C4**
Tabard Gdn. Est. SE1	132	A2
Tabard St. SE1	**28**	**B4**
Tabard St. SE1	132	A2
Tabernacle Av. E13	115	G4
Barking Rd.		
Tabernacle St. EC2	**12**	**C4**
Tabernacle St. EC2	112	A4
Tableer Av. SW4	150	D5
Tabley Rd. N7	92	E4
Tabor Gdns., Sutt.	198	C6
Tabor Gro. SW19	166	B7
Tabor Rd. W6	127	H3
Tachbrook Est. SW1	**33**	**J4**
Tachbrook Est. SW1	130	D5
Tachbrook Ms. SW1	**33**	**F1**
Tachbrook Rd., Felt.	141	J7
Tachbrook Rd., Sthl.	122	D4
Tachbrook St. SW1	**33**	**G2**
Tachbrook St. SW1	130	C4
Tack Ms. SE4	154	A3
Tadema Rd. SW10	**30**	**D7**
Tadema Rd. SW10	129	F7
Tadmor St. W12	128	A1
Tadworth Av., N.Mal.	183	F5
Tadworth Rd. NW2	89	G2
Taeping St. E14	134	B4
Taffy's How, Mitch.	185	H3
Taft Way E3	114	B3
St. Leonards St.		
Tagg's Island, Hmptn.	180	A2
Tailworth St. E1	**21**	**H2**
Tait Rd., Croy.	188	B7
Takhar Ms. SW11	149	H2
Cabul Rd.		
Talacre Rd. NW5	92	A6
Talbot Av. N2	73	G3
Talbot Cl. N15	76	C4
Talbot Ct. EC3	**20**	**C5**
Talbot Cres. NW4	71	G5
Talbot Gdns., Ilf.	100	A2
Talbot Ho. E14	114	B6
Giraud St.		
Talbot Pl. SE3	154	E2
Talbot Rd. E6	116	D2
Talbot Rd. E7	97	G4
Talbot Rd. N6	74	A6
Talbot Rd. N15	76	C4
Talbot Rd. N22	74	C2
Talbot Rd. SE22	152	B4
Talbot Rd. W2	108	C6
Talbot Rd. W11	108	C6
Talbot Rd. W13	104	D7
Talbot Rd., Brom.	191	H4
Masons Hill		
Talbot Rd., Cars.	200	A5
Talbot Rd., Dag.	101	F6
Talbot Rd., Har.	68	C2
Talbot Rd., Islw.	144	D4

Talbot Rd., Sthl. 123 E4
Talbot Rd., Th.Hth. 188 A4
Talbot Rd., Twick. 162 B1
Talbot Rd., Wem. 87 G5
Talbot Sq. W2 15 F4
Talbot Sq. W2 109 G6
Talbot Wk. NW10 88/89 E6
Garnet Rd.
Talbot Wk. W11 108 B6
Talbot Yd. SE1 28 B2
Marquess Rd.
Talfourd Pl. SE15 152 C1
Talfourd Rd. SE15 152 C1
Talgarth Rd. W6 128 B5
Talgarth Rd. W14 128 B5
Talgarth Wk. NW9 70 E5
Talisman Cl., Ilf. 100 B1
Talisman Sq. SE26 170 D4
Talisman Way, Wem. 87 J3
Tall Elms Cl., Brom. 191 F5
Tall Trees SW16 187 F3
Tallack Cl., Har. 52 B7
College Hill Rd.
Tallack Rd. E10 95 J1
Tallis Cl. E16 115 H6
Tallis Gro. SE7 135 H6
Tallis St. EC4 19 F5
Tallis St. EC4 111 G7
Tallis Vw. NW10 88 D6
Tally Ho Cor. N12 57 F5
Talma Gdns., Twick. 144 B6
Talma Rd. SW2 151 G4
Talmage Cl. SE23 153 F7
Tyson Rd.
Talman Gro., Stan. 53 G6
Talwin St. E3 114 B3
Tamar Cl. E3 113 J1
Lefevre Wk.
Tamar Sq., Wdf.Grn. 63 H6
Tamar St. SE7 136 B3
Woolwich Rd.
Tamar Way N17 76 D3
Tamarind Yd. E1 29 J1
Tamarisk Sq. W12 107 F7
Tamesis Gdns., 196 E1
Wor.Pk.
Tamian Way, Houns. 142 C4
Tamworth Av., 63 E6
Wdf.Grn.
Tamworth La., Mitch. 186 B2
Tamworth Pk., Mitch. 186 B4
Tamworth Pl., Croy. 201 J2
Tamworth Rd., Croy. 201 H2
Tamworth St. SW6 128 D6
Tancred Rd. N4 75 H6
Tandridge Dr., Orp. 207 G1
Tandridge Pl., Orp. 193 G7
Tandridge Dr.
Tanfield Av. NW2 89 F4
Tanfield Rd., Croy. 201 J4
Tangier Rd., Rich. 146 B3
Tangle Tree Cl. N3 73 E2
Tanglebury Cl., Brom. 192 C4
Tanglewood Cl., Croy. 203 F3
Tanglewood Cl., Stan. 52 B2
Tanglewood Way, 160 B3
Felt.
Tangley Gro. SW15 147 F6
Tangley Pk. Rd., 161 F6
Hmptn.
Tangmere Gdns., 102 C2
Nthlt.
Tangmere Gro., 163 G5
Kings.T.
Tangmere Way NW9 71 E2
Tanhurst Wk. SE2 138 D3
Alsike Rd.
Tankerton Rd., Surb. 195 J2
Tankerton St. WC1 10 B4
Tankerville Rd. SW16 168 D6
Tankridge Rd. NW2 89 H2
Tanner St. SE1 28 E4
Tanner St. SE1 132 B2
Tanner St., Bark. 99 F6
Tanners Cl., Walt. 178 B6
Tanners End La. N18 60 B4
Tanners Hill SE8 153 J1
Tanners La., Ilf. 81 F3
Tannery Cl., Beck. 189 G5
Tannery Cl., Dag. 101 H3
Tannington Ter. N5 93 G3
Tannsfeld Rd. SE26 171 G5
Tansley Cl. N7 92 D5
Hilldrop Rd.
Tanswell Est. SE1 27 F4
Tanswell St. SE1 27 F4
Tansy Cl. E6 116 D6
Tant Av. E16 115 F6
Tantallon Rd. SW12 168 A1
Tantony Gro., Rom. 82 D3
Tanworth Gdns., Pnr. 66 B2
Tanyard La., Bex. 159 G7
Bexley High St.
Tanza Rd. NW3 91 J4
Tapestry Cl., Sutt. 198 E7

Taplow NW3 91 G7
Taplow SE17 36 D4
Taplow Rd. N13 59 J4
Taplow St. N1 12 A2
Taplow St. N1 111 J2
Tapp St. E1 113 E4
Tappesfield Rd. SE15 153 F3
Tapster St., Barn. 40 C4
Taransay Wk. N1 94 A6
Marquess Rd.
Tarbert Rd. SE22 152 B5
Tarbert Wk. E1 113 F7
Juniper St.
Target Cl., Felt. 141 H6
Tariff Cres. SE8 133 J4
Tariff Rd. N17 60 D6
Tarleton Gdns. SE23 171 E1
Tarling Cl., Sid. 176 B3
Tarling Rd. E16 115 F6
Tarling Rd. N2 73 F2
Tarling St. E1 113 E6
Tarling St. Est. E1 113 F6
Tarn St. SE1 27 J6
Tarnbank, Enf. 43 E5
Tarnwood Pk. SE9 174 C1
Tarquin Ho. SE26 170 D4
Tarragon Cl. SE14 133 H7
Tarragon Gro. SE26 171 G6
Tarrant Pl. W1 15 J2
Tarrington Cl. SW16 168 D3
Tarry La. SE8 133 H4
Tarver Rd. SE17 35 H4
Tarver Rd. SE17 131 H5
Tarves Way SE10 134 B7
Tash Pl. N11 58 B5
Woodland Rd.
Tasker Cl., Hayes 121 F7
Tasker Ho., Bark. 117 G2
Dovehouse Mead
Tasker Rd. NW3 91 J5
Tasman Rd. SW9 151 E3
Tasman Wk. E16 116 A6
Royal Rd.
Tasmania Ter. N18 59 J6
Tasso Rd. W6 128 B6
Tatam Rd. NW10 88 C7
Tate & Lyle Jetty E16 136 B2
Tate Rd. E16 136 C1
Newland St.
Tate Rd., Sutt. 198 D5
Tatnell Rd. SE23 153 H6
Tattersall Cl. SE9 156 B5
Tatton Cres. N16 76 C7
Clapton Common
Tatum St. SE17 36 C2
Tatum St. SE17 132 A4
Tauheed Cl. N4 93 J2
Taunton Av. SW20 183 H2
Taunton Av., Houns. 143 J2
Taunton Cl., Ilf. 65 J6
Taunton Cl., Sutt. 198 D1
Taunton Dr. N2 73 F2
Taunton Dr., Enf. 43 G3
Taunton Ms. NW1 7 J6
Taunton Pl. NW1 7 J5
Taunton Pl. NW1 109 J4
Taunton Rd. SE12 155 E5
Taunton Rd., Grnf. 103 H1
Taunton Way, Stan. 69 H3
Tavern Cl., Cars. 185 H7
Tavern La. SW9 151 G2
Taverner Sq. N5 93 J4
Highbury Gra.
Taverners Cl. W11 128 B1
Addison Av.
Taverners Way E4 62/63 E1
Douglas Rd.
Tavistock Av. E17 77 H3
Tavistock Av., Grnf. 104 D2
Tavistock Cl. N16 94 B5
Crossway
Tavistock Cres. W11 108 C5
Tavistock Cres., 186 E4
Mitch.
Tavistock Gdns., Ilf. 99 H4
Tavistock Gate, Croy. 202 A1
Tavistock Gro., Croy. 188 A7
Tavistock Ms. E18 79 G4
Avon Way
Tavistock Ms. W11 108 C6
Lancaster Rd.
Tavistock Pl. E18 79 G3
Avon Way
Tavistock Pl. N14 42 B7
Chase Side
Tavistock Pl. WC1 9 J5
Tavistock Pl. WC1 110 E4
Tavistock Rd. E7 97 F4
Tavistock Rd. E15 97 F6
Tavistock Rd. E18 79 G3
Tavistock Rd. N4 76 E6
Tavistock Rd. NW10 107 F2
Tavistock Rd. W11 108 C5
Tavistock Rd., Brom. 191 F4

Tavistock Rd., Cars. 199 G1
Tavistock Rd., Croy. 202 A1
Tavistock Rd., Edg. 70 A1
Tavistock Rd., Well. 158 C1
Tavistock Rd., 120 A1
West Dr.
Tavistock Sq. WC1 9 J5
Tavistock Sq. WC1 110 D4
Tavistock St. WC2 18 B5
Tavistock St. WC2 111 E7
Tavistock Ter. N19 92 D3
Tavistock Wk., Cars. 199 G1
Tavistock Rd.
Taviton St. WC1 9 H5
Taviton St. WC1 110 D4
Tavy Cl. SE11 35 F3
Tavy Cl. SE11 131 G5
Tawney Rd. SE28 118 B7
Tawny Cl. W13 124 E1
Tawny Cl., Felt. 160 A3
Chervil Cl.
Tawny Way SE16 133 G4
Tayben Av., Twick. 144 B6
Taybridge Rd. SW11 150 A3
Tayburn Cl. E14 114 C6
Taylor Av., Rich. 146 B2
Taylor Cl. N17 60 D7
Taylor Cl., Hmptn. 161 J5
Taylor Cl., Houns. 143 J1
Taylor Cl., Orp. 207 J4
Taylor Ct. E15 96 C5
Clays La.
Taylor Rd., Mitch. 167 H7
Taylor Rd., Wall. 200 B5
Taylors Bldgs. 136/137 E4
SE18
Spray St.
Taylors Cl., Sid. 175 J4
Taylors Grn. W3 106/107 E6
Long Dr.
Taylors La. NW10 88 E7
Taylors La. SE26 170 E4
Taylors La., Barn. 40 C1
Taymount Ri. SE23 171 F2
Tayport Cl. N1 93 E7
Tayside Dr., Edg. 54 B3
Taywood Rd., Nthlt. 103 F3
Teak Cl. SE16 133 H1
Teal Cl. E16 116 A5
Fulmer Rd.
Teal Pl., Sutt. 198 B2
Gander Grn. La.
Teale St. E2 13 J1
Tealе St. E2 112 D2
Tealing Dr., Epsom 196 D4
Teasel Cl., Croy. 203 G1
Teasel Way E15 114 E3
Tebworth Rd. N17 60 C7
Teck Cl., Islw. 144 D2
Tedder Cl., Chess. 195 F5
Tedder Cl., Ruis. 84 B5
West End Rd.
Tedder Rd., S.Croy. 203 F7
Teddington Lock, 162 E4
Tedd.
Teddington Pk., 162 C5
Tedd.
Teddington Pk. Rd., 162 C4
Tedd.
Tedworth Gdns. SW3 31 J4
Tedworth Sq. SW3 31 J4
Tedworth Sq. SW3 129 J5
Tee, The W3 106 E6
Tees Av., Grnf. 104 B2
Teesdale Av., Islw. 144 D1
Teesdale Cl. E2 13 J2
Teesdale Cl. E2 112 E2
Teesdale Gdns. SE25 188 B2
Teesdale Gdns., Islw. 144 D1
Teesdale Rd. E11 79 F6
Teesdale St. E2 112 E2
Teesdale Yd. E2 13 J2
Teeswater Ct., Erith 138 D3
Middle Way
Teevan Cl., Croy. 188 D7
Teevan Rd., Croy. 188 D7
Teignmouth Cl. SW4 150 D4
Teignmouth Cl., Edg. 69 J2
Teignmouth Gdns., 104 D2
Grnf.
Teignmouth Rd. NW2 90 A5
Teignmouth Rd., 158 C2
Well.
Telcote Way, Ruis. 66 C7
Woodlands Av.
Telegraph Hill NW3 90 E3
Telegraph La., Esher 194 C6
Telegraph Ms., Ilf. 100 A1
Telegraph Pl. E14 134 B4
Telegraph Rd. SW15 147 H7
Telegraph St. EC2 20 B3
Telemann Sq. SE3 155 H3
Telephone Pl. SW6 128 C6
Lillie Rd.

Telfer Cl. W3 126 C2
Church Rd.
Telferscot Rd. SW12 168 D1
Telford Av. SW2 168 E1
Telford Cl. E17 77 H7
Telford Cl. SE19 170 C6
St. Aubyn's Rd.
Telford Cl. W3 126 C2
Church Rd.
Telford Dr., Walt. 178 C7
Telford Rd. N11 58 C6
Telford Rd. NW9 71 G6
West Hendon Bdy.
Telford Rd. SE9 175 G2
Telford Rd. W10 108 B5
Telford Rd., Sthl. 103 H7
Telford Rd., Twick. 143 G7
Telford Ter. SW1 33 F5
Telford Ter. SW1 130 C6
Telford Way W3 106 E5
Telford Way, Hayes 102 E5
Telham Rd. E6 116 D2
Tell Gro. SE22 152 C4
Tellson Av. SE18 156 A1
Telscombe Cl., Orp. 207 H2
Temeraire St. SE16 133 F2
Albion St.
Temperley Rd. SW12 150 A7
Templar Dr. SE28 118 D6
Templar Ho. NW2 90 C6
Shoot Up Hill
Templar Pl., Hmptn. 161 G7
Templar St. SE5 151 H2
Templars Av. NW11 72 C6
Templars Cres. N3 72 D2
Templars Dr., Har. 52 A6
Temple EC4 111 G7
Temple Av. EC4 19 F5
Temple Av. EC4 111 G7
Temple Av. N20 41 G7
Temple Av., Croy. 203 J2
Temple Av., Dag. 101 G1
Temple Cl. E11 78/79 E7
Wadley Rd.
Temple Cl. N3 72 C2
Cyprus Rd.
Temple Cl. SE28 137 F3
Temple Ct. E1 113 G5
Rectory Sq.
Temple Fortune Hill 72 D5
NW11
Temple Fortune La. 72 D6
NW11
Temple Fortune Par. 72 C5
NW11
Finchley Rd.
Temple Gdns. N21 59 H2
Barrowell Grn.
Temple Gdns. NW11 72 C6
Temple Gdns., Dag. 100 D3
Temple Gdns., Enf. 43 H3
Temple Gro. NW11 72 D6
Temple Gro., Enf. 43 H3
Temple La. EC4 19 F4
Temple Mead Cl., 52 E6
Stan.
Temple Mill La. E15 96 B4
Temple Pl. WC2 18 D5
Temple Pl. WC2 111 F7
Temple Rd. E6 116 B1
Temple Rd. N8 75 F4
Temple Rd. NW2 89 J4
Temple Rd. W4 126 C3
Temple Rd. W5 125 G3
Temple Rd., Croy. 202 A4
Temple Rd., Houns. 143 H4
Temple Rd., Rich. 145 J3
Temple Sheen SW14 146 C5
Temple Sheen Rd. 146 B4
SW14
Temple St. E2 112 E2
Temple Way, Sutt. 199 G3
Temple W. Ms. SE11 27 G6
Temple W. Ms. SE11 131 H3
Templecombe Rd. E9 113 F1
Templecombe Way, 184 B5
Mord.
Templehof Av. NW2 71 J7
Templeman Rd. W7 104 C5
Templemead Cl. W3 106 E6
Templeton Av. E4 62 A4
Templeton Cl. N16 94 B5
Truman's Rd.
Templeton Cl. SE19 188 A1
Templeton Pl. SW5 128 D4
Templeton Rd. N15 76 A6
Templewood W13 105 E5
Templewood Av. NW3 90 E3
Templewood Gdns. 91 E3
NW3
Tempsford Av., Borwd. 38 D4
Tempsford Cl., Enf. 43 J3
Gladbeck Way
Temsford Cl., Har. 67 J2

Name		
Tenbury Cl. E7	98	A5
Romford Rd.		
Tenbury Ct. SW2	168	D1
Tenby Av., Har.	68	E2
Tenby Cl. N15	76	C4
Hanover Rd.		
Tenby Cl., Rom.	82	E6
Tenby Gdns., Nthlt.	85	G6
Tenby Rd. E17	77	H5
Tenby Rd., Edg.	69	J1
Tenby Rd., Enf.	45	F3
Tenby Rd., Rom.	83	E6
Tenby Rd., Well.	158	D1
Tench St. E1	132	E1
Tenda Rd. SE16	132/133	E4
Roseberry St.		
Tendring Way, Rom.	82	C5
Tenham Av. SW2	168	D1
Tenison Ct. W1	**17**	**F5**
Tenison Way SE1	**26**	**E2**
Tenison Way SE1	131	F1
Tenniel Cl. W2	**14**	**C4**
Tennis Ct. La., E.Mol.	180	C3
Hampton Ct. Way		
Tennis St. SE1	**28**	**B3**
Tennis St. SE1	132	A2
Tennison Av., Borwd.	38	B5
Tennison Rd. SE25	188	C4
Tenniswood Rd., Enf.	44	C1
Tennyson Av. E11	79	G7
Tennyson Av. E12	98	B7
Tennyson Av. NW9	70	C3
Tennyson Av., N.Mal.	183	H5
Tennyson Av., Twick.	162	C1
Tennyson Cl., Enf.	45	G5
Tennyson Cl., Felt.	141	J6
Tennyson Cl., Well.	157	J1
Tennyson Rd. E10	96	B2
Tennyson Rd. E15	96	E7
Tennyson Rd. E17	77	J6
Tennyson Rd. NW6	108	C1
Tennyson Rd. NW7	55	G5
Tennyson Rd. SE20	171	G7
Tennyson Rd. SW19	167	F6
Tennyson Rd. W7	104	C7
Tennyson Rd., Houns.	143	J2
Tennyson St. SW8	150	B2
Tensing Rd., Sthl.	123	G3
Tent Peg La., Orp.	193	F5
Tent St. E1	112	E4
Tentelow La., Sthl.	123	G5
Tenter Grd. E1	**21**	**F2**
Tenter Pas. E1	**21**	**G4**
Tenterden Cl. NW4	72	A3
Tenterden Cl. SE9	174	C4
Tenterden Dr. NW4	72	A3
Tenterden Gdns. NW4	72	A3
Tenterden Gdns., Croy.	188	D7
Tenterden Gro. NW4	72	A4
Tenterden Rd. N17	60	C7
Tenterden Rd., Croy.	188	D7
Tenterden Rd., Dag.	101	F2
Tenterden St. W1	**16**	**E4**
Tenterden St. N1	110	B6
Terborch Way SE22	152	B5
East Dulwich Gro.		
Teredo St. SE16	133	G3
Terence Ct., Belv.	139	F6
Nuxley Rd.		
Teresa Rd. E17	78	A4
Teresa Wk. N10	74	B5
Connaught Gdns.		
Terling Cl. E11	97	F3
Terling Rd., Dag.	101	G2
Terling Wk. N1	111	J1
Britannia Row		
Terminus Pl. SW1	**25**	**E6**
Terminus Rd. SW1	130	B3
Terrace, The E4	62/63	E3
Chingdale Rd.		
Terrace, The N3	72	C2
Hendon La.		
Terrace, The NW6	108	D1
Terrace, The SW13	147	E2
Terrace, The, Har.	86	E1
Terrace, The,	63	G6
Wdf.Grn.		
Broadmead Rd.		
Terrace Gdns. SW13	147	F2
Terrace La., Rich.	145	H6
Terrace Rd. E9	95	F7
Terrace Rd. E13	115	G1
Terrace Rd., Walt.	178	A7
Terrapin Rd. SW17	168	B3
Terretts Pl. N1	93	H7
Upper St.		
Terrick Rd. N22	75	E1
Terrick St. W12	107	H6
Terrilands, Pnr.	67	F3
Terront Rd. N15	75	J5
Tessa Sanderson Pl.	150	B3
SW8		
Tessa Sanderson	86	A5
Way, Grnf.		
Lilian Board Way		
Testerton Wk. W11	108	A7
Tetbury Pl. N1	111	H1
Upper St.		
Tetcott Rd. SW10	**30**	**C7**
Tetcott Rd. SW10	129	F7
Tetherdown N10	74	A3
Tetty Way, Brom.	191	G2
Teversham La. SW8	151	E1
Teviot Cl., Well.	158	B1
Teviot St. E14	114	C5
Tewkesbury Av. SE23	171	E1
Tewkesbury Av., Pnr.	67	E5
Tewkesbury Cl. N15	76	A6
Tewkesbury Rd.		
Tewkesbury Cl., Loug.	48	B6
Tewkesbury Gdns.	70	B3
NW9		
Tewkesbury Rd. N15	76	A6
Tewkesbury Rd. W13	104	D7
Tewkesbury Rd.,	199	G1
Cars.		
Tewkesbury Ter. N11	58	C6
Tewson Rd. SE18	137	H5
Teynham Av., Enf.	44	A6
Teynham Grn., Brom.	191	G5
Teynton Ter. N17	75	J1
Thackeray Av. N17	76	D2
Thackeray Cl. SW19	166	A7
Thackeray Cl., Har.	85	G1
Thackeray Cl., Islw.	144	D2
Thackeray Dr., Rom.	82	A7
Thackeray Rd. E6	116	A2
Thackeray Rd. SW8	150	B2
Thackeray St. W8	**22**	**B4**
Thackrah Cl. N2	73	F2
Thakeham Cl. SE26	170	E5
Thalia Cl. SE10	134	D6
Thame Rd. SE16	133	G2
Thames Av. SW10	149	F1
Thames Av., Dag.	119	H4
Thames Av., Grnf.	104	C2
Thames Bank SW14	146	C2
Thames Circle E14	134	A4
Westferry Rd.		
Thames Cl., Hmptn.	179	H2
Thames Ct., W.Mol.	179	H2
Thames Ditton	180	D5
Island, T.Ditt.		
Thames Gateway,	119	F2
Dag.		
Thames Meadow,	179	G2
W.Mol.		
Thames Path SE1	**19**	**F6**
Thames Path SE1	111	G7
Thames Path SE7	135	J3
Thames Pl. SW15	148	A3
Thames Rd. E16	136	A1
Thames Rd. W4	126	A6
Thames Rd., Bark.	117	J3
Thames Side, Kings.T.	181	G1
Thames St. SE10	134	B6
Thames St., Hmptn.	179	H1
Thames St., Kings.T.	181	G2
Thames St., Sun.	178	B4
Thames Village W4	146	C1
Thames Wf. E16	135	F1
Thamesbank Pl. SE28	118	C6
Thamesgate Cl.,	162/163	E4
Rich.		
Locksmeade Rd.		
Thameshill Av., Rom.	83	J2
Thameside, Tedd.	163	G7
Thameside Ind. Est.	136	B2
E16		
Thameside Wk. SE28	117	J6
Thamesmead, Walt.	178	A7
Thamesmead Spine	159	H4
Rd., Belv.		
Thamesmere Dr. SE28	118	A7
Thamesvale Cl.,	143	G3
Houns.		
Thane Vil. N7	93	F3
Thane Wks. N7	93	F3
Thane Vil.		
Thanescroft Gdns.,	202	B3
Croy.		
Thanet Dr., Kes.	206	A3
Phoenix Dr.		
Thanet Pl., Croy.	201	J4
Thanet Rd., Bex.	159	G7
Thanet St. WC1	**10**	**A4**
Thanington Ct. SE9	157	H6
Thant Cl. E10	96	B3
Tharp Rd., Wall.	200	D5
Thatcham Gdns. N20	41	F7
Thatcher Cl., West Dr.	120	B2
Classon Cl.		
Thatchers Cl., Loug.	49	F2
Thatchers Way, Islw.	144	A5
Thatches Gro., Rom.	82	E4
Thavies Inn EC1	**19**	**F3**
Thaxted Av., Dag.	101	H7
Thaxted Pl. SW20	166	A7
Thaxted Rd. SE9	175	F2
Thaxted Rd., Buck.H.	48	B7
Thaxton Rd. W14	128	C6
Thayer St. W1	**16**	**C2**
Thayer St. W1	110	A5
Thayers Fm. Rd.,	189	H1
Beck.		
Theatre Sq. E15	96	D6
Salway Rd.		
Theatre St. SW11	149	J3
Theberton St. N1	111	G1
Theed St. SE1	**27**	**E2**
Theed St. SE1	131	G2
Thelma Gdns. SE3	156	A1
Thelma Gdns.,	160/161	E3
Felt.		
Hampton Rd. W.		
Thelma Gro., Tedd.	162	D6
Theobald Cres., Har.	67	H1
Theobald Rd. E17	77	J7
Theobald Rd., Croy.	201	H2
Theobald St. SE1	**28**	**B6**
Theobalds Av. N12	57	F4
Theobalds Ct. N4	93	J2
Queens Dr.		
Theobald's Rd. WC1	**18**	**C1**
Theobald's Rd. WC1	111	F5
Theodore Rd. SE13	154	C6
Therapia La., Croy.	187	E6
Therapia Rd. SE22	153	F6
Theresa Rd. W6	127	G4
Therfield Ct. N4	93	J2
Brownswood Rd.		
Thermopylae Gate	134	B4
E14		
Theseus Wk. N1	**11**	**H2**
Thesiger Rd. SE20	171	G7
Thessaly Rd. SW8	130	C7
Thetford Cl. N13	59	H6
Thetford Gdns., Dag.	100	D7
Thetford Rd., Dag.	118	D1
Thetford Rd., N.Mal.	182	D6
Thetis Ter., Rich.	126	A6
Kew Grn.		
Theydon Gro.,	63	J6
Wdf.Grn.		
Theydon Pk. Rd., Epp.	49	H1
Theydon Rd. E5	95	F2
Theydon St. E17	77	J7
Thicket Cres., Sutt.	199	F4
Thicket Gro. SE20	170	D7
Anerley Rd.		
Thicket Gro., Dag.	100	C6
Thicket Rd. SE20	170	D7
Thicket Rd., Sutt.	199	F4
Third Av. E12	98	B4
Third Av. E13	115	G3
Third Av. E17	78	A5
Third Av. W3	127	F1
Third Av. W10	108	B3
Third Av., Dag.	119	H1
Third Av., Enf.	44	C5
Third Av., Hayes	121	J1
Third Av., Rom.	82	C6
Third Av., Wem.	87	G2
Third Cl., W.Mol.	179	H4
Third Cross Rd.,	162	A2
Twick.		
Third Way, Wem.	88	B4
Thirleby Rd. SW1	**25**	**G6**
Thirleby Rd. SW1	130	C3
Thirleby Rd., Edg.	70	D1
Thirlmere Av., Grnf.	105	F3
Thirlmere Gdns.,	87	F1
Wem.		
Thirlmere Ho., Islw.	144	C5
Summerwood Rd.		
Thirlmere Ri., Brom.	173	F6
Thirlmere Rd. N10	74	B1
Thirlmere Rd. SW16	168	D4
Thirlmere Rd., Bexh.	159	J2
Thirsk Cl., Nthlt.	85	G6
Thirsk Rd. SE25	188	A4
Thirsk Rd. SW11	150	A3
Thirsk Rd., Mitch.	168	A7
Thirston Path,	88	C4
Borwd.		
Thistle Gro. SW10	**30**	**D3**
Thistle Gro. SW10	129	F5
Thistle Mead, Loug.	48	D3
Thistlebrook SE2	138	C3
Thistlebrook Ind. Est.	138	C2
SE2		
Thistlecroft Gdns.,	69	G1
Stan.		
Thistledene, T.Ditt.	180	B6
Thistledene Av., Har.	85	E3
Thistlemead, Chis.	192	E2
Thistlewaite Rd. E5	95	E3
Thistlewood Cl. N7	93	F2
Thistleworth Cl.,	124	A7
Islw.		
Thistley Cl. N12	57	H6
Summerfields Av.		
Thomas a'Beckett Cl.,	86	C4
Wem.		
Thomas Baines Rd.	149	G3
SW11		
Thomas Darby Ct.	108	B6
W11		
Thomas Dean Rd.	171	J4
SE26		
Kangley Br. Rd.		
Thomas Dinwiddy	173	H2
Rd. SE12		
Thomas Doyle St. SE1	**27**	**G5**
Thomas Doyle St. SE1	131	H3
Thomas Hardy Ho.	59	F7
N22		
Thomas La. SE6	154	A7
Thomas More St. E1	**21**	**H6**
Thomas More St. E1	112	C7
Thomas More Way N2	73	F3
Thomas Pl. W8	**22**	**A6**
Thomas Rd. E14	113	J6
Thomas St. SE18	136	E4
Thomas Wall Cl.,	198/199	E5
Sutt.		
Clarence Rd.		
Thompson Av., Rich.	146	A3
Thompson Cl., Ilf.	99	F2
High Rd.		
Thompson Rd. SE22	152	C6
Thompson Rd., Dag.	101	F3
Thompson's Av. SE5	**35**	**J7**
Thompson's Av. SE5	131	J7
Thompson's La.,	47	F1
Loug.		
Thomson Cres.,	201	G1
Croy.		
Thomson Rd., Har.	68	B3
Thorburn Sq. SE1	**37**	**H2**
Thorburn Sq. SE1	132	D4
Thorburn Way SW19	185	G1
Willow Vw.		
Thoresby St. N1	**12**	**A3**
Thoresby St. N1	111	J3
Thorkhill Gdns.,	194	D1
T.Ditt.		
Thorkhill Rd., T.Ditt.	180	E7
Thorn Av., Bushey	51	J1
Thorn Cl., Brom.	192	D6
Thorn Cl., Nthlt.	103	F3
Thorn Ho., Beck.	189	H1
Thorn Ter. SE15	153	F3
Nunhead Gro.		
Thornaby Gdns. N18	60	D6
Thornbury Av., Islw.	124	A7
Thornbury Cl. N16	94	B5
Truman's Rd.		
Thornbury Gdns.,	38	C4
Borwd.		
Thornbury Rd. SW2	150	E6
Thornbury Rd., Islw.	144	A1
Thornbury Sq. N6	92	C1
Thornby Rd. E5	95	F3
Thorncliffe Rd. SW2	150	E6
Thorncliffe Rd., Sthl.	123	F5
Thorncombe Rd.	152	B5
SE22		
Thorncroft Rd., Sutt.	198	E4
Thorncroft St. SW8	130	E7
Thorndean St. SW18	167	F2
Thorndene Av. N11	58	A1
Thorndike Av., Nthlt.	102	D1
Thorndike Cl. SW10	**30**	**C7**
Thorndike Cl. SW10	129	F7
Thorndike St. SW1	**33**	**H3**
Thorndike St. SW1	130	C4
Thorndon Cl., Orp.	193	J2
Thorndon Gdns.,	196	E4
Epsom		
Thorndon Rd., Orp.	193	J2
Thorndyke Ct., Pnr.	51	F7
Westfield Pk.		
Thorne Cl. E11	96	E4
Thorne Cl. E16	115	G6
Thorne Cl., Erith	139	J6
Thorne Pas. SW13	147	E2
Thorne Rd. SW8	130	E7
Thorne St. E16	115	F6
Thorne St. SW13	147	E3
Thorneloe Gdns.,	201	G5
Croy.		
Thornes Cl., Beck.	190	C3
Thornet Wd. Rd.,	192	D3
Brom.		
Thorney Cres. SW11	129	G7
Thorney Hedge Rd.	126	B4
W4		
Thorney St. SW1	**34**	**A1**
Thorney St. SW1	130	E4
Thorneycroft Cl.,	178	C6
Walt.		

Name	No.	Grid
Thornfield Av. NW7	72	B1
Thornfield Rd. W12	127	H2
Thornford Rd. SE13	154	C5
Thorngate Rd. W9	108	D4
Thorngrove Rd. E13	115	H1
Thornham Gro. E15	96	D5
Thornham St. SE10	134	B6
Thornhaugh Ms. WC1	**9**	**J6**
Thornhaugh St. WC1	**17**	**J1**
Thornhaugh St. WC1	110	D4
Thornhill Av. SE18	137	H7
Thornhill Av., Surb.	195	H2
Thornhill Br. Wf. N1	111	F1
Caledonian Rd.		
Thornhill Cres. N1	93	F7
Thornhill Gdns. E10	96	B2
Thornhill Gdns., Bark.	99	H7
Thornhill Gro. N1	93	F7
Lofting Rd.		
Thornhill Ho. N1	93	G7
Thornhill Rd.		
Thornhill Rd. E10	96	B2
Thornhill Rd. N1	93	G7
Thornhill Rd., Croy.	187	J7
Thornhill Rd., Surb.	195	H2
Thornhill Sq. N1	93	F7
Thornlaw Rd. SE27	169	G4
Thornley Cl. N17	60	D7
Thornley Dr., Har.	85	H2
Thornley Pl. SE10	134/135	E5
Caradoc St.		
Thornsbeach Rd. SE6	172	C1
Thornsett Pl. SE20	188	E2
Thornsett Rd. SE20	188	E2
Thornsett Rd. SW18	167	E2
Thornside, Edg.	54	A6
High St.		
Thornton Av. SW2	168	D1
Thornton Av. W4	127	E4
Thornton Av., Croy.	187	F6
Thornton Av., West Dr.	120	C3
Thornton Cl., West Dr.	120	C3
Thornton Ct. SW20	184	A5
Thornton Dene, Beck.	190	A2
Thornton Gdns. SW12	168	D1
Thornton Gro., Pnr.	51	G6
Thornton Hill SW19	166	B7
Thornton Pl. W1	**16**	**A1**
Thornton Pl. W1	109	J5
Thornton Rd. E11	96	D2
Thornton Rd., Wem.	87	G5
Thornton Rd. N18	61	F3
Thornton Rd. SW12	150	D7
Thornton Rd. SW14	146	D3
Thornton Rd. SW19	166	A6
Thornton Rd., Barn.	40	B3
Thornton Rd., Belv.	139	H4
Thornton Rd., Brom.	173	G5
Thornton Rd., Cars.	199	G1
Thornton Rd., Croy.	187	F7
Thornton Rd., Ilf.	98	E4
Thornton Rd., Th.Hth.	187	F7
Thornton Rd. E. SW19	166	A6
Thornton Rd.		
Thornton Rd. Retail Pk., Croy.	187	F6
Thornton Row, Th.Hth.	187	G5
London Rd.		
Thornton St. SW9	151	G2
Thornton Way NW11	73	E5
Thorntree Rd. SE7	136	A5
Thornville Gro., Mitch.	185	F2
Thornville St. SE8	154	A1
Thornwood Cl. E18	79	H2
Thornwood Rd. SE13	154	E5
Thorogood Gdns. E15	97	E5
Thorold Rd. N22	59	E7
Thorold Rd., Ilf.	98	E2
Thorparch Rd. SW8	150	D1
Thorpe Cl. W10	108	B6
Cambridge Gdns.		
Thorpe Cl., Orp.	207	H2
Thorpe Cres. E17	77	J2
Thorpe Hall Rd. E17	78	C1
Thorpe Rd. E6	116	C1
Thorpe Rd. E7	97	F4
Thorpe Rd. E17	78	C2
Thorpe Rd. N15	76	B6
Thorpe Rd., Bark.	99	G7
Thorpe Rd., Kings.T.	163	H7
Thorpebank Rd. W12	127	G1
Thorpedale Gdns., Ilf.	80	D4
Thorpedale Rd. N4	93	E1
Thorpewood Av. SE26	171	E2
Thorsden Way SE19	170	B4
Oaks Av.		
Thorverton Rd. NW2	90	B3
Thoydon Rd. E3	113	H2
Thrale Rd. SW16	168	C5
Thrale St. SE1	**28**	**A2**
Thrale St. SE1	131	J1
Thrasher Cl. E8	112	C1
Stean St.		
Thrawl St. E1	**21**	**G2**
Thrawl St. E1	112	C5
Threadneedle St. EC2	**20**	**C4**
Threadneedle St. EC2	112	A6
Three Barrels Wk. EC4	**20**	**A5**
Three Colt St. E14	113	J7
Three Colts Cor. E2	**13**	**H5**
Three Colts La. E2	113	E4
Three Cors., Bexh.	159	H2
Three Cups Yd. WC1	**18**	**D2**
Three Kings Rd., Mitch.	186	A3
Three Kings Yd. W1	**16**	**D5**
Three Kings Yd. W1	110	B7
Three Mill La. E3	114	C3
Three Oak La. SE1	**29**	**F3**
Threshers Pl. W11	108	B7
Thriffwood SE26	171	F3
Thrift Fm. La., Borwd.	38	B2
Thrigby Rd., Chess.	195	J6
Throckmorten Rd. E16	115	H6
Throgmorton Av. EC2	**20**	**C3**
Throgmorton Av. EC2	112	A6
Throgmorton St. EC2	**20**	**C3**
Throgmorton St. EC2	112	A6
Throwley Cl. SE2	138	C3
Throwley Rd., Sutt.	199	E5
Throwley Way, Sutt.	199	E4
Thrupp Cl., Mitch.	186	B2
Thrush Grn., Har.	67	G4
Thrush St. SE17	**35**	**J3**
Thruxton Way SE15	**37**	**G7**
Thunderer Rd., Dag.	118	E4
Thurland Rd. SE16	**29**	**H5**
Thurland Rd. SE16	132	D3
Thurlby Cl., Har.	68	D6
Gayton Rd.		
Thurlby Rd. SE27	169	G4
Thurlby Rd., Wem.	87	G6
Thurleigh Av. SW12	150	A6
Thurleigh Rd. SW12	150	A6
Thurlestone Av. N12	57	J6
Thurlestone Av., Ilf.	99	J4
Thurlestone Rd. SE27	169	G3
Thurloe Cl. SW7	**31**	**G1**
Thurloe Cl. SW7	129	H3
Thurloe Pl. SW7	**31**	**F1**
Thurloe Pl. SW7	129	G4
Thurloe Pl. Ms. SW7	**31**	**F1**
Thurloe Sq. SW7	**31**	**G1**
Thurloe Sq. SW7	129	H4
Thurloe St. SW7	**31**	**F1**
Thurloe St. SW7	129	G4
Thurlow Cl. E4	62	B6
Higham Sta. Av.		
Thurlow Gdns., Ilf.	65	G6
Thurlow Gdns., Wem.	87	G5
Thurlow Hill SE21	169	J1
Thurlow Pk. Rd. SE21	169	H1
Thurlow Rd. NW3	91	G5
Thurlow Rd. W7	124	D2
Thurlow St. SE17	**36**	**C3**
Thurlow St. SE17	132	A5
Thurlow Ter. NW5	92	A5
Thurlstone Rd., Ruis.	84	A3
Thurnby Cl., Twick.	162	B3
Thursland Rd., Sid.	176	E5
Thursley Cres., Croy.	204	D7
Thursley Gdns. SW19	166	A2
Thursley Rd. SE9	174	C3
Thurso St. SW17	167	G4
Thurstan Rd. SW20	165	H7
Thurston Rd. SE13	154	B2
Thurston Rd., Sthl.	103	F6
Thurtle Rd. E2	112	C1
Thwaite Cl., Erith	139	J6
Thyer Cl., Orp.	207	F4
Isabella Dr.		
Thyra Gro. N12	57	E6
Tibbatts Rd. E3	114	B4
Tibbenham Wk. E13	115	F2
Tibberton Sq. N1	93	J7
Popham Rd.		
Tibbets Cl. SW19	166	A1
Tibbet's Cor. SW15	148	A7
Tibbet's Cor. Underpass SW15	148	A7
West Hill		
Tibbet's Ride SW15	148	A7
Tiber Gdns. N1	111	F1
Treaty St.		
Ticehurst Cl., Orp.	176	A7
Grovelands Rd.		
Ticehurst Rd. SE23	171	H2
Tickford Cl. SE2	138	C2
Ampleforth Rd.		
Tidal Basin Rd. E16	115	F7
Tidenham Gdns., Croy.	202	B3
Tideswell Rd. SW15	147	J5
Tideswell Rd., Croy.	204	A3
Tideway Cl., Rich.	162/163	E4
Locksmeade Rd.		
Tidey St. E3	114	A5
Tidford Rd., Well.	157	J2
Tidworth Rd. E3	114	A4
Tiepigs La., Brom.	205	E2
Tiepigs La., W.Wick.	205	E2
Tierney Rd. SW2	168	E1
Tiger La., Brom.	191	H4
Tiger Way E5	94	E4
Tilbrook Rd. SE3	155	J3
Tilbury Cl. SE15	**37**	**G7**
Tilbury Rd. E6	116	C2
Tilbury Rd. E10	78	C7
Tildesley Rd. SW15	147	J6
Tile Fm. Rd., Orp.	207	G3
Tile Kiln La. N6	92	B1
Winchester Rd.		
Tile Kiln La. N13	59	J5
Tile Kiln La., Bex.	177	J2
Tile Yd. E14	113	J6
Commercial Rd.		
Tilehurst Pt. SE2	138	C2
Yarnton Way		
Tilehurst Rd. SW18	167	G1
Tilehurst Rd., Sutt.	198	B5
Tileyard Rd. N7	92	E7
Tilford Gdns. SW19	166	A2
Tilia Cl., Sutt.	198	C5
Tilia Rd. E5	94/95	E4
Clarence Rd.		
Tilia Wk. SW9	151	H4
Moorland Rd.		
Tiller Rd. E14	134	A3
Tillett Cl. NW10	88	C6
Tillett Sq. SE16	133	H2
Howland Way		
Tillett Way E2	**13**	**H3**
Tilling Rd. NW2	89	J1
Tilling Way, Wem.	87	G2
Tillingbourne Gdns. N3	72	C3
Tillingbourne Way N3	72	C3
Tillingbourne Gdns.		
Tillingham Way N12	56	D4
Tillman St. E1	112/113	E6
Bigland St.		
Tilloch St. N1	93	F7
Carnoustie Dr.		
Tillotson Rd. N9	60	C2
Tillotson Rd., Har.	51	H7
Tillotson Rd., Ilf.	80	D7
Tilney Ct. EC1	**12**	**A5**
Tilney Dr., Buck.H.	63	G2
Tilney Gdns. N1	94	A6
Tilney Rd., Dag.	101	F6
Tilney Rd., Sthl.	122	C4
Tilney St. W1	**24**	**C1**
Tilney St. W1	130	A1
Tilson Gdns. SW2	150	E7
Tilson Ho. SW2	150/151	E7
Tilson Gdns.		
Tilson Rd. N17	76	D1
Tilt Yd. App. SE9	156	C6
Tilton St. SW6	128	B6
Tiltwood, The W3	106	C7
Acacia Rd.		
Timber Cl., Chis.	192	D2
Timber Mill Way SW4	150	D3
Timber Pond Rd. SE16	133	G1
Timber St. EC1	**11**	**J5**
Timbercroft, Epsom	196	E4
Timbercroft La. SE18	137	H6
Timberdene NW4	72	A2
Timberdene Av., Ilf.	81	F1
Timberland Rd. E1	113	E6
Timberwharf Rd. N16	76	D6
Timbrell Pl. SE16	133	J1
Silver Wk.		
Time Sq. E8	94	C5
Times Sq., Sutt.	199	E5
Timothy Cl. SW4	150	C5
Elms Rd.		
Timothy Cl., Bexh.	158	E5
Timothy Ho., Erith	138/139	E2
Kale Rd.		
Timothy Rd. E3	113	J5
Timsbury Wk. SW15	165	G1
Tindal St. SW9	151	H1
Tinderbox All. SW14	146	D3
Tine Rd., Chig.	65	H5
Tinniswood Cl. N5	93	G5
Drayton Pk.		
Tinsley Rd. E1	113	F5
Tintagel Cres. SE22	152	C4
Tintagel Dr., Stan.	53	G4
Tintagel Gdns. SE22	152	C4
Oxonian St.		
Tintern Av. NW9	70	B3
Tintern Cl. SW15	148	B5
Tintern Cl. SW19	167	F7
Tintern Gdns. N14	43	E7
Tintern Path NW9	70/71	E6
Ruthin Cl.		
Tintern Rd. N22	75	J1
Tintern Rd., Cars.	199	G1
Tintern St. SW4	151	E4
Tintern Way, Har.	85	H1
Tinto Rd. E16	115	G4
Tinwell Ms., Borwd.	38	C5
Cranes Way		
Tinworth St. SE11	**34**	**B3**
Tinworth St. SE11	131	H5
Tippetts Cl., Enf.	43	J1
Tipthorpe Rd. SW11	150	A3
Tipton Dr., Croy.	202	B4
Tiptree Cl. E4	62	C3
Mapleton Rd.		
Tiptree Cres., Ilf.	80	D3
Tiptree Dr., Enf.	44	A4
Tiptree Est., Ilf.	80	D3
Tiptree Rd., Ruis.	84	B4
Tirlemont Rd., S.Croy.	201	J7
Tirrell Rd., Croy.	187	J6
Tisbury Ct. W1	110	D7
Rupert St.		
Tisbury Rd. SW16	186	E2
Tisdall Pl. SE17	**36**	**C2**
Tisdall Pl. SE17	132	A4
Titchborne Row W2	**15**	**H4**
Titchfield Rd. NW8	109	J1
Titchfield Rd., Cars.	199	G1
Titchfield Wk., Cars.	185	G1
Titchfield Rd.		
Titchwell Rd. SW18	149	G7
Tite St. SW3	**31**	**J4**
Tite St. SW3	129	J5
Tithe Barn Cl., Kings.T.	181	J1
Tithe Barn Way, Nthlt.	102	B3
Tithe Cl. NW7	71	G1
Tithe Cl., Walt.	178	B6
Tithe Fm. Av., Har.	85	G3
Tithe Fm. Cl., Har.	85	G3
Tithe Wk. NW7	71	G1
Titley Cl. E4	62	A5
Titmuss Av. SE28	118	B7
Titmuss St. W12	127	H2
Tiverton Av., Ilf.	80	D3
Tiverton Dr. SE9	175	F1
Tiverton Rd. N15	76	A6
Tiverton Rd. N18	60	B5
Tiverton Rd. NW10	108	A1
Tiverton Rd., Edg.	69	J2
Tiverton Rd., Houns.	143	J2
Tiverton Rd., Ruis.	84	A3
Tiverton Rd., Th.Hth.	187	G5
Willett Rd.		
Tiverton St. SE1	**27**	**J6**
Tiverton St. SE1	131	J3
Tiverton Way, Chess.	195	F5
Tivoli Ct. SE16	133	J2
Tivoli Gdns. SE18	136	B4
Tivoli Rd. N8	74	D5
Tivoli Rd. SE27	169	J5
Tivoli Rd., Houns.	142	E4
Toad La., Houns.	143	F4
Tobacco Quay E1	112/113	E7
Wapping La.		
Tobago St. E14	134	A2
Manilla St.		
Tobin Cl. NW3	91	H7
Toby La. E1	113	H4
Toby Way, Surb.	196	B2
Todds Wk. N7	93	F2
Andover Rd.		
Token Yd. SW15	148	B4
Montserrat Rd.		
Tokenhouse Yd. EC2	**20**	**B3**
Tokyngton Av., Wem.	88	A6
Toland Sq. SW15	147	G5
Tolcarne Dr., Pnr.	66	B3
Toley Av., Wem.	69	H7
Tollbridge Cl. W10	108	B4
Kensal Rd.		
Tollesbury Gdns., Ilf.	81	G3
Tollet St. E1	113	G4
Tollgate Dr. SE21	170	B2
Tollgate Dr., Hayes	102	D7
Delamere Rd.		
Tollgate Gdns. NW6	**6**	**A1**
Tollgate Gdns. NW6	108	E2
Tollgate Rd. E6	116	A5

Name	Page	Grid
Tollgate Rd. E16	115	J5
Tollhouse Way N19	92	C2
Tollington Pk. N4	93	F2
Tollington Pl. N4	93	F2
Tollington Rd. N7	93	F4
Tollington Way N7	92	E3
Tolmers Sq. NW1	9	G5
Tolpuddle Av. E13	115	J1
Rochester Av.		
Tolpuddle St. N1	10	E1
Tolpuddle St. N1	111	G2
Tolsford Rd. E5	95	E5
Tolson Rd., Islw.	144	D3
Tolverne Rd. SW20	183	J1
Tolworth Cl., Surb.	196	B1
Tolworth Gdns., Rom.	82	D5
Tolworth Pk. Rd., Surb.	195	J2
Tolworth Ri. N., Surb.	182	C7
Elmbridge Av.		
Tolworth Ri. S., Surb.	196	C1
Warren Dr. S.		
Tolworth Rd., Surb.	195	H2
Tolworth Twr., Surb.	196	B2
Tom Coombs Cl. SE9	156	B4
Well Hall Rd.		
Tom Cribb Rd. SE28	137	F3
Tom Gros. Cl. E15	96	D5
Maryland St.		
Tom Hood Cl. E15	96	D5
Maryland St.		
Tom Jenkinson Rd. E16	135	G1
Tom Mann Cl., Bark.	117	H1
Tom Nolan Cl. E15	114	E2
Tom Smith Cl. SE10	134/135	E6
Maze Hill		
Tom Thumbs Arch E3	114	A2
Malmesbury Rd.		
Tomahawk Gdns., Nthlt.	102	D3
Javelin Way		
Tomlins Gro. E3	114	A3
Tomlins Orchard, Bark.	177	F1
Tomlins Ter. E14	113	J5
Rhodeswell Rd.		
Tomlins Wk. N7	93	F2
Briset Way		
Tomlinson Cl. E2	13	G4
Tomlinson Cl. E2	112	C3
Tomlinson Cl. W4	126	B5
Oxford Rd. N.		
Tompion St. EC1	11	G4
Tomswood Ct., Ilf.	81	F1
Tomswood Hill, Ilf.	65	E7
Tomswood Rd., Chig.	64	D6
Tonbridge Cres., Har.	69	H4
Tonbridge Ho. SE25	188	D3
Tonbridge Rd., W.Mol.	179	E4
Tonbridge St. WC1	10	A3
Tonbridge St. WC1	110	E3
Tonbridge Wk. WC1	110/111	E3
Tonbridge St.		
Tonfield Rd., Sutt.	198	C1
Tonge Cl., Beck.	190	A5
Tonsley Hill SW18	149	E5
Tonsley Pl. SW18	149	E5
Tonsley Rd. SW18	149	E5
Tonsley St. SW18	149	E5
Tonstall Rd., Mitch.	186	A2
Tony Cannell Ms. E3	113	J3
Maplin St.		
Tooke Cl., Pnr.	66	E1
Took's Ct. EC4	19	E3
Tooley St. SE1	28	C1
Tooley St. SE1	132	A1
Toorack Rd., Har.	68	A2
Tooting Bec Gdns. SW16	168	D4
Tooting Bec Rd. SW16	168	A3
Tooting Bec Rd. SW17	168	A3
Tooting Gro. SW17	167	H5
Tooting High St. SW17	167	H6
Tootswood Rd., Brom.	190	E5
Top Ho. Ri. E4	46	C7
Parkhill Rd.		
Top Pk., Beck.	190	E5
Topaz Wk. NW2	72	A3
Marble Dr.		
Topcliffe Dr., Orp.	207	G4
Topham Sq. N17	75	J1
Topham St. EC1	11	E5
Topiary Sq., Rich.	145	J3
Topley St. SE9	156	A4
Topmast Pt. E14	134	A2
Topp Wk. NW2	89	J2
Topsfield Cl. N8	74	D5
Wolseley Rd.		
Topsfield Par. N8	74/75	E5
Tottenham La.		
Topsfield Rd. N8	74	E5
Topsham Rd. SW17	167	J3
Tor Gdns. W8	128	D2
Tor Rd., Well.	158	C1
Torbay Rd. NW6	90	C7
Torbay Rd., Har.	84	E2
Torbay St. NW1	92	B7
Hawley Rd.		
Torbitt Way, Ilf.	81	J5
Torbridge Cl., Edg.	53	H7
Torbrook Cl., Bex.	159	E6
Torcross Dr. SE23	171	F2
Torcross Rd., Ruis.	84	B3
Tormead Rd., Sutt.	198	D6
Tormount Rd. SE18	137	H6
Toronto Av. E12	98	C4
Toronto Rd. E11	96	D4
Toronto Rd., Ilf.	99	E1
Torquay Gdns., Ilf.	80	A4
Torquay St. W2	14	A2
Torr Rd. SE20	171	G7
Torre Wk., Cars.	199	H1
Torrens Rd. E15	97	F6
Torrens Rd. SW2	151	F5
Torrens Sq. E15	97	E6
Torrens St. EC1	11	F2
Torrens St. EC1	111	G2
Torres Sq. E14	134	A5
Napier Av.		
Torriano Av. NW5	92	D5
Torriano Cotts. NW5	92	C5
Torriano Av.		
Torriano Ms. NW5	92	D5
Torriano Av.		
Torridge Gdns. SE15	153	F4
Torridge Rd., Th.Hth.	187	H5
Torridon Rd. SE6	172	D1
Torridon Rd. SE13	154	D7
Torrington Av. N12	57	G5
Torrington Cl. N12	57	G4
Torrington Cl., Esher	194	B6
Torrington Dr., Har.	85	H4
Torrington Dr., Loug.	49	F4
Torrington Gdns. N11	58	C6
Torrington Gdns., Grnf.	87	F7
Torrington Gdns., Loug.	49	H4
Torrington Gro. N12	57	H5
Torrington Pk. N12	57	G5
Torrington Pl. E1	29	J2
Torrington Pl. E1	132	D1
Torrington Pl. WC1	17	H1
Torrington Rd. E18	79	G3
Torrington Rd., Dag.	101	F1
Torrington Rd., Esher	194	B6
Torrington Rd., Grnf.	105	F1
Torrington Sq. WC1	9	J6
Torrington Sq. WC1	110	D4
Torrington Sq., Croy.	188	A7
Tavistock Gro.		
Torrington Way, Mord.	184	D6
Torver Rd., Har.	68	B4
Torver Way, Orp.	207	G3
Torwood Rd. SW15	147	G5
Tothill St. SW1	25	H4
Tothill St. SW1	130	D2
Totnes Rd., Well.	138	B7
Totnes Wk. N2	73	G4
Tottan Ter. E1	113	G6
Tottenhall Rd. N13	59	G6
Tottenham Ct. Rd. W1	9	G6
Tottenham Ct. Rd. W1	110	C4
Tottenham Grn. E. N15	76	C4
Tottenham La. N8	74	E5
Tottenham Ms. W1	17	G1
Tottenham Rd. N1	94	B6
Tottenham St. W1	17	G2
Tottenham St. W1	110	C5
Totterdown St. SW17	167	J4
Totteridge Common N20	55	G2
Totteridge Grn. N20	56	D2
Totteridge La. N20	56	D2
Totteridge Village N20	56	B1
Totternhoe Cl., Har.	69	F5
Totton Rd., Th.Hth.	187	G3
Toulmin St. SE1	27	J4
Toulmin St. SE1	131	J2
Toulon St. SE5	35	J7
Toulon St. SE5	131	J7
Tournay Rd. SW6	128	C7
Toussaint Wk. SE16	29	J5
Tovil Cl. SE20	188	D2
Towcester Rd. E3	114	B4
Tower Br. E1	29	F2
Tower Br. E1	132	C1
Tower Br. SE1	29	F2
Tower Br. SE1	132	C1
Tower Br. App. E1	29	F1
Tower Br. App. E1	132	C1
Tower Br. Piazza SE1	132	C1
Horselydown La.		
Tower Br. Rd. SE1	28	D6
Tower Br. Rd. SE1	132	B3
Tower Cl. NW3	91	G5
Lyndhurst Rd.		
Tower Cl. SE20	170	E7
Tower Cl., Ilf.	65	E6
Tower Cl., Orp.	207	J2
Tower Ct. WC2	18	A4
Tower Gdns., Esher	194	D7
Tower Gdns. Rd. N17	75	J1
Tower Hamlets Rd. E7	97	F4
Tower Hamlets Rd. E17	78	A3
Tower Hill EC3	21	E6
Tower Hill EC3	112	B7
Tower Hill Ter. EC3	112	B7
Byward St.		
Tower La., Wem.	87	G3
Main Dr.		
Tower Ms. E17	78	A4
Tower Mill Rd. SE15	36	D6
Tower Pier EC3	29	E1
Tower Pier EC3	132	C1
Tower Pl. EC3	20	E6
Tower Pt., Enf.	44	A4
Tower Ri., Rich.	145	H3
Jocelyn Rd.		
Tower Rd. NW10	89	G7
Tower Rd., Belv.	139	J4
Tower Rd., Bexh.	159	H4
Tower Rd., Orp.	207	J2
Tower Rd., Twick.	162	C3
Tower Royal EC4	20	A5
Tower St. WC2	17	J4
Tower St. WC2	110	D6
Tower Ter. N22	75	F2
Mayes Rd.		
Tower Vw., Croy.	189	G7
Towers Pl., Rich.	145	H5
Eton St.		
Towers Rd., Pnr.	66	E1
Towers Rd., Sthl.	103	G4
Towfield Rd., Felt.	161	F2
Towing Path Wk. N1	10	A1
Town, The, Enf.	44	A3
Town Ct. Path N4	93	J1
Town Fm. Way, Stai.	140	A7
Town La.		
Town Fld. Way, Islw.	144	D2
Town Hall App. N16	94	B4
Milton Gro.		
Town Hall App. Rd. N15	76	C7
Town Hall Av. W4	126	D5
Town Hall Rd. SW11	149	J3
Town La., Stai.	140	A6
Town Meadow, Brent.	125	G7
Town Quay, Bark.	117	E1
Town Rd. N9	61	E2
Towncourt Cres., Orp.	193	F5
Towncourt La., Orp.	193	G6
Towney Mead, Nthlt.	103	F2
Towney Mead Ct., Nthlt.	103	F2
Towney Mead		
Townfield Rd., Hayes	121	J1
Townholm Cres. W7	124	C3
Townley Ct. E15	97	F6
Townley Rd. SE22	152	B5
Townley Rd., Bexh.	159	F5
Townley St. SE17	36	B3
Townmead Rd. SW6	149	F2
Townmead Rd., Rich.	146	B2
Townsend Av. N14	58	D4
Townsend Ind. Est. NW10	106	D2
Townsend La. NW9	70	D7
Townsend Rd. N15	76	C5
Townsend St. SE17	36	C2
Townsend St. SE17	132	A4
Townsend Yd. N6	92	B1
Townshend Cl., Sid.	176	B6
Townshend Est. NW8	7	G1
Townshend Est. NW8	109	H1
Townshend Rd. NW8	109	H1
Townshend Rd., Chis.	174	E5
Townshend Rd., Rich.	145	J4
Townshend Ter., Rich.	145	J4
Towpath Way, Croy.	188	C6
Towton Rd. SE27	169	J2
Toynbec Cl., Chis.	174/175	E4
Beechwood Ri.		
Toynbee Rd. SW20	184	B1
Toynbee St. E1	21	F2
Toynbee St. E1	112	C5
Toyne Way N6	73	J6
Gaskell Rd.		
Tracey Av. NW2	89	J5
Tracy Cl., Stan.	53	F7
Trade Cl. N13	59	G4
Trader Rd. E6	116	E6
Tradescant Rd. SW8	131	E7
Trading Est. Rd. NW10	106	C4
Trafalgar Av. N17	60	B6
Trafalgar Av. SE15	37	G4
Trafalgar Av. SE15	132	C5
Trafalgar Av., Wor.Pk.	198	A1
Trafalgar Business Cen., Bark.	117	J4
Trafalgar Cl. SE16	133	H4
Greenland Quay		
Trafalgar Gdns. E1	113	G5
Trafalgar Gdns. W8	22	B5
Trafalgar Gro. SE10	134	D6
Trafalgar Pl. E11	79	G4
Trafalgar Pl. N18	60	D5
Trafalgar Rd. SE10	134	D6
Trafalgar Rd. SW19	167	E7
Trafalgar Rd., Twick.	162	A2
Trafalgar Sq. SW1	25	J1
Trafalgar Sq. SW1	130	D1
Trafalgar Sq. WC2	25	J1
Trafalgar Sq. WC2	130	D1
Trafalgar St. SE17	36	B3
Trafalgar St. SE17	132	A5
Trafalgar Ter., Har.	86	B1
Nelson Rd.		
Trafalgar Way E14	134	C1
Trafalgar Way, Croy.	201	F2
Trafford Cl. E15	96	B5
Trafford Cl., Ilf.	65	J6
Trafford Rd., Th.Hth.	187	F5
Tralee Ct. SE16	132/133	E5
Masters Dr.		
Tramway Av. E15	96	E7
Tramway Av. N9	45	E7
Tramway Path, Mitch.	185	J5
Tranby Pl. E9	95	G5
Homerton High St.		
Tranley Ms. NW3	91	H4
Fleet Rd.		
Tranmere Rd. N9	44	C7
Tranmere Rd. SW18	167	F1
Tranmere Rd., Twick.	143	H7
Tranquil Pas. SE3	155	F2
Tranquil Vale		
Tranquil Vale SE3	155	E2
Transay Wk. N1	94	A6
Marquess Rd.		
Transept St. NW1	15	G2
Transept St. NW1	109	H5
Transmere Cl., Orp.	193	F6
Transmere Rd., Orp.	193	F6
Transom Cl. SE16	133	H4
Plough Way		
Transom Sq. E14	134	B5
Transport Av., Brent.	124	E5
Tranton Rd. SE16	29	J5
Tranton Rd. SE16	132	D3
Traps Hill, Loug.	48	C3
Traps La., N.Mal.	182	E1
Travellers Way, Houns.	102	A2
Travers Cl. E17	77	G1
Travers Rd. N7	93	G3
Treacy Cl., Bushey	51	J2
Treadgold St. W11	108	A7
Treadway St. E2	112	E2
Treaty Rd., Houns.	143	H3
Hanworth Rd.		
Treaty St. N1	111	F1
Trebeck St. W1	24	D1
Trebovir Rd. SW5	128	D5
Treby St. E3	113	J4
Trecastle Way N7	92	D4
Carleton Rd.		
Tredegar Ms. E3	113	J3
Tredegar Ter.		
Tredegar Rd. E3	113	J2
Tredegar Rd. N11	58	D7
Tredegar Sq. E3	113	J3
Tredegar Ter. E3	113	J3
Trederwen Rd. E8	112	D1
Tredown Rd. SE26	171	F5
Tredwell Cl. SW2	169	F2
Hillside Rd.		
Tredwell Cl., Brom.	192	B4
Tredwell Rd. SE27	169	H4
Tree Cl., Rich.	163	G1
Tree Rd. E16	115	J6
Treen Av. SW13	147	F3

Treeside Cl., West Dr. 120 A4
Treetops Cl. SE2 139 E5
Treetops Vw., Loug. 47 J6
High Rd.
Treeview Cl. SE19 188 B1
Treewall Gdns., Brom. 173 H4
Trefgarne Rd., Dag. 101 G2
Trefil Wk. N7 93 E4
Trefoil Ho., Erith 138/139 E2
Kale Rd.
Trefoil Rd. SW18 149 F5
Tregaron Av. N8 75 E6
Tregaron Gdns., N.Mal. 182/183 E4
Avenue Rd.
Tregarvon Rd. SW11 150 A4
Tregenna Av., Har. 85 F4
Tregenna Cl. N14 42 C5
Tregenna Ct., Har. 85 G4
Trego Rd. E9 96 A7
Tregothnan Rd. SW9 151 E3
Tregunter Rd. SW10 30 C5
Tregunter Rd. SW10 129 F6
Trehearn Rd., Ilf. 65 G7
Trehern Rd. SW14 146 D3
Treherne Ct. SW9 151 G1
Eythorne Rd.
Treherne Ct. SW17 168 A4
Trehurst St. E5 95 H5
Trelawn Rd. E10 96 C3
Trelawn Rd. SW2 151 G5
Trelawney Cl. E17 78 B4
Orford Rd.
Trelawney Est. E9 95 F6
Trelawney Rd., Ilf. 65 G7
Trellick Twr. W10 108 C4
Trellis Sq. E3 113 J3
Malmesbury Rd.
Treloar Gdns. SE19 170 A6
Hancock Rd.
Tremadoc Rd. SW4 150 D4
Tremaine Cl. SE4 154 A2
Tremaine Rd. SE20 189 E2
Trematon Pl., Tedd. 163 F7
Tremlett Gro. N19 92 C3
Tremlett Ms. N19 92 C3
Trenance Gdns., Ilf. 100 A3
Trench Yd. Ct., Mord. 184/185 E6
Green La.
Trenchard Av., Ruis. 84 B4
Trenchard Cl. NW9 70/71 E1
Fulbeck Dr.
Trenchard Cl., Stan. 52 D6
Trenchard Ct., Mord. 184/185 E6
Green La.
Trenchard St. SE10 134 D5
Trenchold St. SW8 34 A6
Trenchold St. SW8 130 E6
Trenholme Cl. SE20 171 E7
Trenholme Rd. SE20 170 E7
Trenholme Ter. SE20 170 E7
Trenmar Gdns. NW10 107 H3
Trent Av. W5 125 F3
Trent Gdns. N14 42 B6
Trent Rd. SW2 151 F5
Trent Rd., Buck.H. 63 H1
Trent Way, Wor.Pk. 197 J3
Trentbridge Cl., Ilf. 65 J6
Trentham St. SW18 166 D1
Trentwood Side, Enf. 43 F3
Treport St. SW18 149 E7
Tresco Cl., Brom. 172 E6
Tresco Gdns., Ilf. 100 A2
Tresco Rd. SE15 153 E4
Trescoe Gdns., Har. 67 E7
Tresham Cres. NW8 7 G5
Tresham Cres. NW8 109 H4
Tresham Rd., Bark. 99 J7
Tresham Wk. E9 95 F5
Churchill Wk.
Tresilian Av. N21 43 F5
Tressell Cl. N1 93 H7
Sebbon St.
Tressillian Cres. SE4 154 A3
Tressillian Rd. SE4 153 J4
Trestis Cl., Hayes 102/103 E5
Jollys La.
Treswell Rd., Dag. 119 E1
Tretawn Gdns. NW7 55 E4
Tretawn Pk. NW7 55 E4
Trevanion Rd. W14 128 B5
Treve Av., Har. 67 J7
Trevelyan Av. E12 98 C4
Trevelyan Cres., Har. 69 G7
Trevelyan Gdns. NW10 107 J1
Trevelyan Rd. E15 97 F4
Trevelyan Rd. SW17 167 H5
Treveris St. SE1 27 G2
Treverton St. W10 108 A4
Treves Cl. N21 43 F5
Treville St. SW15 147 H7
Treviso Rd. SE23 171 G2
Farren Rd.
Trevithick St. SE8 134 A5
Trevone Gdns., Pnr. 67 E6
Trevor Cl., Barn. 41 G5
Trevor Cl., Brom. 191 F7
Trevor Cl., Har. 52 C7
Kenton La.
Trevor Cl., Islw. 144 C5
Trevor Cl., Nthlt. 102 C2
Trevor Gdns., Edg. 70 D1
Trevor Gdns., Nthlt. 102 C2
Trevor Pl. SW7 23 H4
Trevor Pl. SW7 129 H2
Trevor Rd. SW19 166 B7
Trevor Rd., Edg. 70 D1
Trevor Rd., Hayes 121 H2
Trevor Rd., Wdf.Grn. 63 G7
Trevor Sq. SW7 23 J4
Trevor Sq. SW7 129 J2
Trevor St. SW7 23 H4
Trevor St. SW7 129 H2
Trevose Rd. E17 78 D1
Trevose Way, Wat. 50 C3
Trewenna Dr., Chess. 195 G5
Trewince Rd. SW20 183 J1
Trewint St. SW18 167 F2
Trewsbury Ho. SE2 138 D2
Hartslock Dr.
Trewsbury Rd. SE26 171 G5
Triandra Way, Hayes 102 D5
Triangle, The EC1 111 H4
Goswell Rd.
Triangle, The N13 59 G4
Lodge Dr.
Triangle, The, Bark. 99 F6
Tanner St.
Triangle, The, Hmptn. 179 J1
High St.
Triangle, The, Kings.T. 182 C2
Kenley Rd.
Triangle Ct. E16 116 A5
Tollgate Rd.
Triangle Pas., Barn. 41 F4
Triangle Pl. SW4 150 D4
Triangle Rd. E8 112 E1
Trident Gdns., Nthlt. 102 D3
Jetstar Way
Trident St. SE16 133 G4
Trident Way, Sthl. 122 B3
Trig La. EC4 19 J5
Trigon Rd. SW8 34 D7
Trigon Rd. SW8 131 F7
Trilby Rd. SE23 171 G2
Trim St. SE14 133 J6
Trimmer Wk., Brent. 125 H6
Trinder Gdns. N19 92/93 E1
Trinder Rd.
Trinder Rd. N19 93 E1
Trinder Rd., Barn. 39 J5
Tring Av. W5 125 J1
Tring Av., Sthl. 103 F6
Tring Av., Wem. 88 A6
Tring Cl., Ilf. 81 F5
Trinidad St. E14 113 J7
Trinity Av. N2 73 G3
Trinity Av., Enf. 44 C6
Trinity Buoy Wf. E14 115 F7
Trinity Ch. Pas. SW13 127 H6
Trinity Ch. Rd. SW13 127 H6
Trinity Ch. Sq. SE1 28 A5
Trinity Ch. Sq. SE1 131 J3
Trinity Cl. E8 94 C6
Trinity Cl. E11 97 E2
Trinity Cl. NW3 91 G4
Hampstead High St.
Trinity Cl. SE13 154 D4
Wisteria Rd.
Trinity Cl., Brom. 206 B1
Trinity Cl., Houns. 143 E4
Trinity Cotts., Rich. 145 J3
Trinity Rd.
Trinity Ct. N1 94 B7
Downham Rd.
Trinity Ct. SE7 136 A4
Charlton La.
Trinity Cres. SW17 167 J2
Trinity Gdns. E16 115 F4
Cliff Wk.
Trinity Gdns. SW9 151 F4
Trinity Gro. SE10 154 C1
Trinity Ms. SE20 189 E1
Trinity Ms. W10 108 A6
Cambridge Gdns.
Trinity Path SE26 171 F3
Trinity Pl., Bexh. 159 F4
Trinity Ri. SW2 169 G1
Trinity Rd. N2 73 G3
Trinity Rd. N22 75 E1
Trinity Rd. SW17 167 J2
Trinity Rd. SW18 149 G5
Trinity Rd. SW19 166 D6
Trinity Rd., Ilf. 81 F3
Trinity Rd., Rich. 145 J3
Trinity Rd., Sthl. 122 E1
Trinity Sq. EC3 21 E6
Trinity Sq. EC3 112 B7
Trinity St. E16 115 G5
Vincent St.
Trinity St. SE1 28 A4
Trinity St. SE1 131 J2
Trinity St., Enf. 43 J2
Trinity Wk. NW3 91 F6
Trinity Way E4 61 J6
Trinity Way W3 107 E7
Trio Pl. SE1 28 A4
Tristan Sq. SE3 155 E3
Tristram Cl. E17 78 D3
Tristram Rd., Brom. 173 F4
Triton Sq. NW1 9 F5
Triton Sq. NW1 110 C4
Tritton Av., Croy. 201 E4
Tritton Rd. SE21 170 A3
Triumph Cl., Hayes 121 F7
Triumph Ho., Bark. 118 B3
Triumph Rd. E6 116 C6
Trojan Ct. NW6 90 B7
Willesden La.
Trojan Way, Croy. 201 F3
Troon Cl. SE16 132/133 E5
Masters Dr.
Troon St. E1 113 H6
Trosley Rd., Belv. 139 G6
Trossachs Rd. SE22 152 B5
Trothy Rd. SE1 37 J1
Trott Rd. N10 57 J7
Trott St. SW11 149 H1
Trotwood, Chig. 65 G6
Troughton Rd. SE7 135 H5
Trout Rd., West Dr. 120 A1
Troutbeck Rd. SE14 153 H1
Trouville Rd. SW4 150 C6
Trowbridge Est. E9 95 J6
Osborne Rd.
Trowbridge Rd. E9 95 J6
Trowlock Av., Tedd. 163 F6
Trowlock Island, Tedd. 163 G5
Trowlock Way, Tedd. 163 G6
Troy Ct. SE18 137 E4
Troy Rd. SE19 170 A6
Troy Town SE15 152 D3
Trubshaw Rd., Sthl. 123 H3
Havelock Rd.
Truesdale Rd. E6 116 C6
Trulock Ct. N17 60 D7
Trulock Rd. N17 60 D7
Truman Cl., Edg. 54 B7
Pavilion Way
Truman's Rd. N16 94 B5
Trump St. EC2 20 A4
Trumpers Way W7 124 B3
Trumpington Rd. E7 97 F4
Trundle St. SE1 27 J3
Trundlers Way, Bushey 52 B1
Trundleys Rd. SE8 133 G5
Trundleys Ter. SE8 133 G4
Truro Gdns., Ilf. 80 B7
Truro Rd. E17 77 J4
Truro Rd. N22 59 E7
Truro St. NW5 92 A6
Truslove Rd. SE27 169 G5
Trussley Rd. W6 127 J3
Trust Wk. SE21 169 H1
Peabody Hill
Tryfan Cl., Ilf. 80 A5
Tryon St. SW3 31 J3
Tryon St. SW3 129 J5
Trystings Cl., Esher 194 D6
Tuam Rd. SE18 137 G6
Tubbenden Cl., Orp. 207 H2
Tubbenden Dr., Orp. 207 G4
Tubbenden La., Orp. 207 H3
Tubbenden La. S., Orp. 207 G5
Tubbs Rd. NW10 107 F2
Tudor Av., Hmptn. 161 G6
Tudor Av., Wor.Pk. 197 H3
Tudor Cl. N6 74 C7
Tudor Cl. NW3 91 H5
Tudor Cl. NW7 55 G6
Tudor Cl. NW9 88 C2
Tudor Cl. SW2 151 F6
Elm Pk.
Tudor Cl., Chess. 195 H5
Tudor Cl., Chig. 64 D4
Tudor Cl., Chis. 192 C1
Tudor Cl., Pnr. 66 A5
Tudor Cl., Sutt. 198 A5
Tudor Cl., Wall. 200 C7
Tudor Cl., Wdf.Grn. 63 H5
Tudor Ct. E17 77 H7
Tudor Ct., Felt. 160 C4
Tudor Ct. N., Wem. 88 A5
Tudor Ct. S., Wem. 88 A5
Tudor Cres., Enf. 43 H1
Tudor Cres., Ilf. 65 E6
Tudor Dr., Kings.T. 163 H5
Tudor Dr., Mord. 184 A6
Tudor Est. NW10 106 B2
Tudor Gdns. NW9 88 C2
Tudor Gdns. SW13 146/147 E3
Treen Av.
Tudor Gdns. W3 106 A6
Tudor Gdns., Har. 68 A2
Tudor Rd.
Tudor Gdns., Twick. 162 C1
Tudor Gdns., W.Wick. 204 C3
Tudor Gro. E9 95 F7
Tudor Gro. N20 57 H3
Church Cres.
Tudor Pl. W1 17 H3
Tudor Pl., Mitch. 167 H7
Tudor Rd. E4 62 B6
Tudor Rd. E6 115 J1
Tudor Rd. E9 113 E1
Tudor Rd. N9 45 E7
Tudor Rd. SE19 170 C7
Tudor Rd. SE25 189 E5
Tudor Rd., Bark. 117 J1
Tudor Rd., Barn. 40 D3
Tudor Rd., Beck. 190 B3
Tudor Rd., Hmptn. 161 G7
Tudor Rd., Har. 68 A2
Tudor Rd., Houns. 144 A4
Tudor Rd., Kings.T. 164 A7
Tudor Rd., Pnr. 66 C2
Tudor Rd., Sthl. 102 E7
Tudor St. EC4 19 F5
Tudor St. EC4 111 G7
Tudor Wk., Bex. 159 E6
Tudor Way N14 58 D1
Tudor Way W3 126 A2
Tudor Way, Orp. 193 G6
Tudor Well Cl., Stan. 53 E5
Tudway Rd. SE3 155 H3
Tufnell Pk. Rd. N7 92 C4
Tufnell Pk. Rd. N19 92 C4
Tufter Rd., Chig. 65 J5
Tufton Gdns., W.Mol. 179 H2
Tufton Rd. E4 62 A4
Tufton St. SW1 25 J5
Tufton St. SW1 130 D3
Tugboat St. SE28 137 H2
Tugela Rd., Croy. 188 A6
Tugela St. SE6 171 J2
Tugmutton Cl., Orp. 206/207 E4
Acorn Way
Tuilerie St. E2 13 H1
Tuilerie St. E2 112 D2
Tulip Cl. E6 116 C5
Bradley Stone Rd.
Tulip Cl., Croy. 203 G1
Tulip Cl., Hmptn. 161 F6
Partridge Rd.
Tulip Cl., Sthl. 123 J2
Chevy Rd.
Tulip Ct., Pnr. 66 C3
Tulip Gdns., Ilf. 98 E6
Tulip Way, West Dr. 120 A3
Wise La.
Tull St., Mitch. 185 J7
Tulse Cl., Beck. 190 C3
Tulse Hill SW2 151 G6
Tulse Hill Est. SW2 151 G6
Tulsemere Rd. SE27 169 J2
Tumbling Bay, Walt. 178 A6
Tummons Gdns. SE25 188 B2
Tun Yd. SW8 150 B2
Peardon St.
Tuncombe Rd. N18 60 B4
Tunis Rd. W12 127 H1
Tunley Grn. E14 113 J5
Burdett Rd.
Tunley Rd. NW10 106 E1
Tunley Rd. SW17 168 A1
Tunmarsh La. E13 115 J3
Tunnan Leys E6 116 D6
Tunnel Av. SE10 134 D2
Tunnel Gdns. N11 58 C7
Tunnel Rd. SE16 133 F2
St. Marychurch St.
Tunstall Cl., Orp. 207 H4
Tunstall Rd. SW9 151 F4
Tunstall Rd., Croy. 202 B1
Tunstall Wk., Brent. 125 H6
Tunstock Way, Belv. 139 E3
Tunworth Cl. NW9 70 C6
Tunworth Cres. SW15 147 F6
Tupelo Rd. E10 96 B2
Turenne Cl. SW18 149 F4
Turin Rd. N9 45 F7
Turin St. E2 13 H4
Turin St. E2 112 D3
Turkey Oak Cl. SE19 188 B1
Turk's Head Yd. EC1 19 G1
Turks Row SW3 32 A3
Turks Row SW3 129 J5

Name	Page	Grid
Turle Rd. N4	93	F1
Turle Rd. SW16	186	E2
Turlewray Cl. N4	93	F1
Turley Cl. E15	115	E1
Turnagain La. EC4	**19**	**G3**
Turnage Rd., Dag.	100	E1
Turnberry Cl. NW4	72	A2
Turnberry Cl. SE16	132/133	E5
Ryder Dr.		
Turnberry Ct., Wat.	50	C3
Turnberry Quay E14	134	B3
Pepper St.		
Turnberry Way, Orp.	207	G1
Turnbury Cl. SE8	118	D6
Turnchapel Ms. SW4	150	B3
Cedars Rd.		
Turner Av. N15	76	B4
Turner Av., Mitch.	185	J1
Turner Av., Twick.	161	J3
Turner Cl. NW11	72	E6
Turner Cl. SW9	151	H1
Langton Rd.		
Turner Cl., Wem.	87	G5
Turner Dr. NW11	72	E6
Turner Rd. E17	78	C3
Turner Rd., Edg.	69	J3
Turner Rd., N.Mal.	182	D7
Turner St. E1	112	E5
Turner St. E16	115	F6
Turners Meadow	189	J1
Way, Beck.		
Turners Rd. E3	113	J5
Turners Way, Croy.	201	G2
Turneville Rd. W14	128	C6
Turney Rd. SE21	152	A7
Turnham Grn. Ter.	126	E4
W4		
Turnham Rd.	126/127	E4
Ter. Ms. W4		
Turnham Rd. SE4	153	H5
Turnmill St. EC1	**11**	**F6**
Turnmill St. EC1	111	G4
Turnpike Cl. SE8	133	J7
Amersham Vale		
Turnpike Ho. EC1	**11**	**F1**
Turnpike Ho. EC1	111	H3
Turnpike La. N8	75	F4
Turnpike La., Sutt.	199	F5
Turnpike Link, Croy.	202	B2
Turnpike Way, Islw.	144	D1
Turnpin La. SE10	134	C6
Turnstone Cl. E13	115	G3
Turnstone Cl. NW9	70/71	E2
Kestrel Cl.		
Turpentine La. SW1	**32**	**E3**
Turpin Rd., Felt.	141	J6
Staines Rd.		
Turpin Way N19	92	D2
Elthorne Rd.		
Turpin Way, Wall.	200	B7
Turpington Cl.,	192	B6
Brom.		
Turpington La., Brom.	192	B7
Turpins La., Wdf.Grn.	64	C5
Turquand St. SE17	**36**	**A2**
Turret Gro. SW4	150	C3
Turton Rd., Wem.	87	H5
Turville St. E2	**13**	**F5**
Tuscan Rd. SE18	137	G5
Tuskar St. SE10	134	E5
Tustin St. SE15	133	F6
Tuttlebee La., Buck.H.	63	G2
Tweedale Cl. E15	96	C5
Tweeddale Rd., Cars.	199	G1
Tweedmouth Rd.	115	H2
E13		
Tweedy Cl., Enf.	44	C5
Tweedy Rd., Brom.	191	G1
Tweezer's All. WC2	**18**	**E5**
Twelvetrees Cres. E3	114	C4
Twentyman Cl.,	63	G5
Wdf.Grn.		
Twickenham Br., Rich.	145	F5
Twickenham Br.,	145	F5
Twick.		
Twickenham Cl.,	201	F3
Croy.		
Twickenham Gdns.,	86	D5
Grnf.		
Twickenham Gdns.,	52	B7
Har.		
Twickenham Rd. E11	96	D2
Twickenham Rd., Felt.	161	F3
Twickenham Rd.,	144	D3
Islw.		
Twickenham Rd.,	145	F4
Rich.		
Twickenham Rd.,	162	D5
Tedd.		
Twickenham Trd. Est.,	144	C6
Twick.		
Twig Folly Cl. E2	113	G2
Roman Rd.		
Twilley St. SW18	148	E7
Twine Tumps Way	118	A7
SE28		
Twine Cl., Bark.	118	B3
Thames Rd.		
Twine Ct. E1	113	F7
Twine Ter. E3	113	J4
Ropery St.		
Twineham Grn. N12	56	D4
Tillingham Way		
Twining Av., Twick.	161	J3
Twinn Rd. NW7	56	B6
Twisden Rd. NW5	92	B4
Twybridge Way NW10	88	C7
Twycross Ms.	134/135	E4
SE10		
Blackwall La.		
Twyford Abbey Rd.	105	J3
NW10		
Twyford Av. N2	73	J3
Twyford Av. W3	106	A7
Twyford Cres. W3	126	A1
Twyford Pl. WC2	**18**	**C3**
Twyford Rd., Cars.	199	G1
Twyford Rd., Har.	85	H1
Twyford Rd., Ilf.	99	F5
Twyford St. N1	111	F1
Tyas Rd. E16	115	F4
Tybenham Rd. SW19	184	D3
Tyberry Rd., Enf.	45	E3
Tyburn La., Har.	68	B7
Tyburn Way W1	**16**	**A5**
Tyburn Way W1	109	J7
Tycehurst Hill, Loug.	48	C4
Tye La., Orp.	207	F5
Tyers Est. SE1	**28**	**E3**
Tyers Est. SE1	132	B2
Tyers Gate SE1	**28**	**D3**
Tyers St. SE11	**34**	**C3**
Tyers St. SE11	131	F5
Tyers Ter. SE11	**34**	**C4**
Tyers Ter. SE11	131	F5
Tyeshurst Cl. SE2	139	E5
Tylecroft Rd. SW16	186	E2
Tylehurst Gdns., Ilf.	99	F5
Tyler Cl. E2	**13**	**F1**
Tyler Cl. E2	112	C2
Tyler St. SE10	135	E5
Tylers Cl., Loug.	48	B7
Tyler's Ct. W1	**17**	**H4**
Tylers Gate, Har.	69	H6
Tylers Path, Cars.	199	J4
Rochester Rd.		
Tylney Av. SE19	170	C5
Tylney Rd. E7	97	J4
Tylney Rd., Brom.	192	A2
Tynan Cl., Felt.	160	A1
Sandycombe Rd.		
Tyndale Ct. E14	134	B4
Tyndale La. N1	93	H7
Upper St.		
Tyndale Ter. N1	93	H7
Canonbury La.		
Tyndall Rd. E10	96	C2
Tyndall Rd., Well.	157	J3
Tyne St. E1	**21**	**G3**
Tyneham Rd. SW11	150	A2
Tynemouth Cl. E6	116/117	E6
Covelees Wall		
Tynemouth Rd. N15	76	C4
Tynemouth Rd. SE18	137	J5
Tynemouth Rd.,	168	A7
Mitch.		
Tynemouth St. SW6	149	F2
Type St. E2	113	G2
Tyrawley Rd. SW6	148	E1
Tyrell Cl., Har.	86	B4
Tyrell Ct., Cars.	199	J4
Tyrols Rd. SE23	171	G1
Wastdale Rd.		
Tyron Way, Sid.	175	H4
Tyrone Rd. E6	116	C2
Tyrrel Way NW9	71	F7
Tyrrell Av., Well.	158	A5
Tyrrell Rd. SE22	152	D4
Tyrrell Sq., Mitch.	185	H1
Tyrwhitt Rd. SE4	154	A3
Tysoe St. EC1	**11**	**E4**
Tyson Rd. SE23	153	F7
Tyssen Pas. E8	94	C6
Tyssen Rd. N16	94	C3
Tyssen St. E8	94	C6
Tyssen St. N1	**12**	**E2**
Tytherton Rd. N19	92	D3

U

Name	Page	Grid
Uamvar St. E14	114	B5
Uckfield Gro., Mitch.	186	A1
Udall St. SW1	**33**	**G2**
Udney Pk. Rd., Tedd.	162	D5
Uffington Rd. NW10	107	G1
Uffington Rd. SE27	169	G4
Ufford Cl., Har.	51	H7
Ufford Rd.		
Ufford Rd., Har.	51	H7
Ufford St. SE1	**27**	**F3**
Ufford St. SE1	131	G2
Ufton Gro. N1	94	A7
Ufton Rd. N1	94	B7
Uhura Sq. N16	94	B3
Ujima Ct. SW16	168/169	E4
Sunnyhill Rd.		
Ullathorne Rd. SW16	168	C4
Ulleswater Rd. N14	59	E4
Ullin St. E14	114	C5
St. Leonards Rd.		
Ullswater Cl. SW15	164	D4
Ullswater Cl., Brom.	173	E6
Ullswater Ct., Har.	67	G7
Oakington Av.		
Ullswater Cres. SW15	164	D4
Ullswater Rd. SE27	169	H2
Ullswater Rd. SW13	127	G3
Ulster Gdns. N13	59	J4
Ulster Pl. NW1	**8**	**D6**
Ulster Ter. NW1	**8**	**D5**
Ulundi Rd. SE3	135	E6
Ulva Rd. SW15	148	A5
Ravenna Rd.		
Ulverscroft Rd. SE22	152	C5
Ulverston Rd. E17	78	D2
Ulverstone Rd. SE27	169	H2
Ulysses Rd. NW6	90	C5
Umberston St. E1	112/113	E6
Hessel St.		
Umbria St. SW15	147	G6
Umfreville Rd. N4	75	H6
Undercliff Rd. SE13	154	A3
Underhill, Barn.	40	D5
Underhill Pas. NW1	110	B1
Camden High St.		
Underhill Rd. SE22	152	E6
Underhill St. NW1	110	B1
Camden High St.		
Underne Av. N14	58	B2
Undershaft EC3	**20**	**D4**
Undershaft EC3	112	B6
Undershaw Rd.,	173	E3
Brom.		
Underwood, Croy.	204	C5
Underwood, The SE9	174	C2
Underwood Rd. E1	**13**	**H6**
Underwood Rd. E1	112	D4
Underwood Rd. E4	62	B5
Underwood Rd.,	64	A1
Wdf.Grn.		
Underwood Row N1	**12**	**A3**
Underwood Row N1	111	J3
Underwood St. N1	**12**	**A3**
Underwood St. N1	111	J3
Undine Rd. E14	134	B4
Undine St. SW17	167	J5
Uneeda Dr., Grnf.	104	A1
Union Cl. E11	96	D4
Union Cotts. E15	96/97	E7
Welfare Rd.		
Union Ct. EC2	**20**	**D3**
Union Ct., Rich.	145	H5
Eton St.		
Union Dr. E1	113	H4
Canal Cl.		
Union Gro. SW8	150	D2
Union Pk. NW10	106	C3
Acton La.		
Union Rd. N11	58	D6
Union Rd. SW4	150	D3
Union Rd. SW8	150	D2
Union Rd., Brom.	192	A5
Union Rd., Croy.	187	J7
Union Rd., Nthlt.	103	G2
Union Rd., Wem.	87	H6
Union Sq. N1	111	J1
Union St. E15	114	C1
Union St. SE1	**27**	**H2**
Union St. SE1	131	H1
Union St., Barn.	40	B4
Union St., Kings'T.	181	G2
Union Wk. E2	**13**	**E3**
Unity Cl. NW10	89	G6
Unity Cl. SE19	169	J5
Crown Dale		
Unity Way SE18	136	A3
Unity Wf. SE1	**29**	**G3**
University Cl. NW7	55	F7
University Gdns.,	159	F7
Bex.		
University Pl., Erith	139	H7
Belmont Rd.		
University Rd. SW19	167	G6
University St. WC1	**9**	**G6**
University St. WC1	110	C4
University Way E16	136	D1
Unwin Av., Felt.	141	H5
Unwin Cl. SE15	**37**	**H6**
Unwin Cl. SE15	132	D6
Unwin Rd. SW7	**23**	**F5**
Unwin Rd., Islw.	144	B3
Upbrook Ms. W2	**14**	**D4**
Upcerne Rd. SW10	129	F7
Upchurch Cl. SE20	171	E7
Upcroft Av., Edg.	54	C5
Updale Rd., Sid.	175	J4
Upfield, Croy.	203	E2
Upfield Rd. W7	104	C4
Upgrove Manor Way	151	G7
SW2		
Trinity Ri.		
Uphall Rd., Ilf.	99	E5
Upham Pk. Rd. W4	127	E4
Uphill Dr. NW7	55	E5
Uphill Dr. NW9	70	C5
Uphill Gro. NW7	55	E4
Uphill Rd. NW7	54	E4
Upland Ms. SE22	152	D5
Upland Rd.		
Upland Rd. E13	115	F4
Sutton Rd.		
Upland Rd. SE22	152	D5
Upland Rd., Bexh.	159	F3
Upland Rd., S.Croy.	202	A5
Upland Rd., Sutt.	199	G7
Uplands, Beck.	190	A2
Uplands, The, Loug.	48	C3
Uplands, The, Ruis.	84	A1
Uplands Av. E17	77	G2
Blackhorse La.		
Uplands Business Pk.	77	G2
E17		
Uplands Cl. SW14	146	B5
Monroe Dr.		
Uplands End, Wdf.Grn.	64	B7
Uplands Pk. Rd., Enf.	43	G3
Uplands Rd. N8	75	F5
Uplands Rd., Barn.	58	A1
Uplands Rd., Rom.	82	D3
Uplands Rd., Wdf.Grn.	64	B7
Uplands Way N21	43	G5
Upney La., Bark.	99	H6
Upnor Way SE17	**37**	**E3**
Uppark Dr., Ilf.	81	F6
Upper Abbey Rd.,	139	F4
Belv.		
Upper Addison Gdns.	128	B2
W14		
Upper Bardsey Wk.	93	J6
N1		
Clephane Rd.		
Upper Belgrave St.	**24**	**C5**
SW1		
Upper Belgrave St.	130	A3
SW1		
Upper Berkeley St. W1	**15**	**J4**
Upper Berkeley St.	109	J6
W1		
Upper Beulah Hill	188	B1
SE19		
Upper Brighton Rd.,	181	G6
Surb.		
Upper Brockley Rd.	153	J2
SE4		
Upper Brook St. W1	**16**	**B6**
Upper Brook St. W1	110	A7
Upper Butts, Brent.	125	F6
Upper Caldy Wk. N1	93	J6
Clephane Rd.		
Upper Camelford	108	B6
Wk. W11		
Lancaster Rd.		
Upper Cavendish Av.	72	D3
N3		
Upper Cheyne Row	**31**	**G6**
SW3		
Upper Cheyne Row	129	H6
SW3		
Upper Clapton Rd. E5	94	E1
Upper Clarendon Wk.	108	B6
W11		
Lancaster Rd.		
Upper Dengie Wk. N1	111	J1
Popham St.		
Upper Elmers End	189	H4
Rd., Beck.		
Upper Fern Rd.,	179	F4
W.Mol.		
Upper Fosters NW4	71	J5
New Brent St.		
Upper Grn. E., Mitch.	185	J3
Upper Grn. W., Mitch.	185	J3
London Rd.		
Upper Grenfell Wk.	108	A7
W11		
Whitchurch Rd.		
Upper Grosvenor St.	**16**	**B6**
W1		
Upper Grosvenor St.	110	A7
W1		
Upper Grotto Rd.,	162	C2
Twick.		
Upper Grd. SE1	**26**	**E1**

Upper Grd. SE1	131	H1
Upper Gro. SE25	188	B4
Upper Gro. Rd., Belv.	139	F6
Upper Gulland Wk. N1	93	J6
Clephane Rd.		
Upper Ham Rd.,	163	G4
Kings.T.		
Upper Ham Rd., Rich.	163	G4
Upper Handa Wk. N1	94	A6
Clephane Rd.		
Upper Harley St.	**8**	**C5**
NW1		
Upper Harley St.	110	A4
NW1		
Upper Hawkwell Wk.	111	J1
N1		
Popham Rd.		
Upper Hitch, Wat.	51	E1
Upper Holly Hill Rd.,	139	H5
Belv.		
Upper James St. W1	**17**	**G5**
Upper John St. W1	**17**	**G5**
Upper Lismore Wk.	93	J6
N1		
Clephane Rd.		
Upper Mall W6	127	G5
Upper Marsh SE1	**26**	**D5**
Upper Marsh SE1	131	F3
Upper Montagu St.	**15**	**J1**
W1		
Upper Montagu St.	109	J5
W1		
Upper Mulgrave Rd.,	198	C7
Sutt.		
Upper N. St. E14	114	A5
Upper Palace Rd.,	180	A3
E.Mol.		
Upper Pk., Loug.	48	A4
Upper Pk. Rd. N11	58	B5
Upper Pk. Rd. NW3	91	J5
Upper Pk. Rd., Belv.	139	H4
Upper Pk. Rd., Brom.	191	H1
Upper Pk. Rd.,	164	A6
Kings.T.		
Upper Phillimore	128	D2
Gdns. W8		
Upper Ramsey Wk.	94	A6
N1		
Clephane Rd.		
Upper Rawreth Wk.	111	J1
N1		
Popham Rd.		
Upper Richmond Rd.	148	B4
SW15		
Upper Richmond Rd.	146	B4
SW14		
Upper Richmond Rd.	146	A4
W., Rich.		
Upper Rd. E13	115	G3
Upper Rd., Wall.	200	D5
Upper St. Martin's	**18**	**A5**
La. WC2		
Upper Selsdon Rd.,	202	C7
S.Croy.		
Upper Sheppey Wk.	93	J7
N1		
Clephane Rd.		
Upper Sheridan Rd.,	139	G4
Belv.		
Coleman Rd.		
Upper Shirley Rd.,	203	F2
Croy.		
Upper Sq., Islw.	144	D3
North St.		
Upper St. N1	**11**	**F1**
Upper St. N1	111	G2
Upper Sunbury Rd.,	179	E1
Hmptn.		
Upper Sutton La.,	123	G7
Houns.		
Upper Tachbrook St.	**33**	**F1**
SW1		
Upper Tachbrook St.	130	C4
SW1		
Upper Tail, Wat.	51	E3
Upper Talbot Wk.	108	B6
W11		
Lancaster Rd.		
Upper Teddington	181	F1
Rd., Kings.T.		
Upper Ter. NW3	91	H5
Upper Thames St.	**19**	**H5**
EC4		
Upper Thames St.	111	J7
EC4		
Upper Tollington Pk.	93	G1
N4		
Upper Tooting Pk.	167	J2
SW17		
Upper Tooting Rd.	167	J4
SW17		
Upper Town Rd.,	103	H4
Grnf.		
Upper Tulse Hill SW2	151	F7
Upper Vernon Rd.,	199	G5
Sutt.		
Upper Walthamstow	78	D4
Rd. E17		
Upper Wickham La.,	138	B7
Well.		
Upper Wimpole St.	**16**	**D1**
W1		
Upper Wimpole St.	110	A5
W1		
Upper Woburn Pl.	**9**	**J4**
WC1		
Upper Woburn Pl.	110	D3
WC1		
Upperton Rd., Sid.	175	J5
Upperton Rd. E. E13	115	J3
Inniskilling Rd.		
Upperton Rd. W. E13	115	J3
Uppingham Av.,	69	E1
Stan.		
Upsdell Av. N13	59	G6
Upstall St. SE5	151	H1
Upton Av. E7	97	G7
Upton Cl., Bex.	159	F6
Upton Ct. SE20	171	F7
Blean Gro.		
Upton Dene, Sutt.	198	E7
Upton Gdns., Har.	69	E5
Upton La. E7	97	G7
Upton Pk. Rd. E7	97	H7
Upton Rd. N18	60	D5
Upton Rd. SE18	137	F6
Upton Rd., Bex.	159	F6
Upton Rd., Bexh.	158	E4
Upton Rd., Houns.	143	G3
Upton Rd., Th.Hth.	188	A2
Upton Rd., Th.Hth.	159	F6
Upway N12	57	H7
Upwood Rd. SE12	155	G6
Upwood Rd. SW16	187	E1
Urlwin St. SE5	**35**	**J6**
Urlwin St. SE5	131	J6
Urlwin Wk. SW9	151	G2
Urmston Dr. SW19	166	B1
Ursula Ms. N4	93	J1
Portland Ri.		
Ursula St. SW11	149	H1
Urswick Gdns.,	100/101	E7
Dag.		
Urswick Rd.		
Urswick Rd. E9	95	F5
Urswick Rd., Dag.	100	D7
Usborne Ms. SW8	**34**	**C7**
Usborne Ms. SW8	131	F7
Usher Rd. E3	113	J2
Usk Rd. SW11	149	F4
Usk St. E2	113	G3
Utopia Village NW1	110	A1
Chalcot Rd.		
Uvedale Rd., Dag.	101	G3
Uvedale Rd., Enf.	44	A5
Uverdale Rd. SW10	129	F7
Marlborough Rd.		
Uxbridge Rd. W3	105	H7
Uxbridge Rd. W5	105	H7
Uxbridge Rd. W7	124	C1
Uxbridge Rd. W12	127	G1
Uxbridge Rd. W13	124	C1
Uxbridge Rd., Felt.	160	C2
Uxbridge Rd., Hmptn.	161	G4
Uxbridge Rd., Har.	51	J7
Uxbridge Rd., Hayes	102	C7
Uxbridge Rd.,	181	G4
Kings.T.		
Uxbridge Rd., Pnr.	51	H7
Uxbridge Rd., Sthl.	123	G1
Uxbridge Rd., Stan.	52	C6
Uxbridge Rd., Uxb.	102	B6
Uxbridge St. W8	128	D1
Uxendon Cres., Wem.	87	H1
Uxendon Hill, Wem.	87	J1

V

Valan Leas, Brom.	191	E3
Vale Av. E4	63	F1
Vale, The N10	74	A1
Vale, The N14	42	D7
Vale, The NW11	90	A3
Vale, The SW3	**31**	**E5**
Vale, The SW3	129	G6
Vale, The W3	126	D1
Vale, The, Croy.	203	G3
Vale, The, Felt.	142	B6
Vale, The, Houns.	122	E6
Vale, The, Ruis.	84	C4
Vale, The, Sun.	160	A6
Ashridge Way		
Vale, The, Wdf.Grn.	63	G7
Vale Av., Borwd.	38	B5
Vale Cl. N2	73	J3
Church Vale		
Vale Cl. W9	**6**	**C4**
Vale Cl., Orp.	206	D4
Vale Cotts. SW15	164	D4
Kingston Vale		
Vale Ct. W9	**6**	**C4**
Vale Cres. SW15	165	E3
Vale Cft., Esher	194	B7
Vale Cft., Pnr.	66	E5
Vale Dr., Barn.	40	C4
Vale End SE22	152	B4
Grove Vale		
Vale Gro. N4	75	J7
Vale Gro. W3	126	D1
The Vale		
Vale La. W3	106	A5
Vale of Health NW3	91	G3
East Heath Rd.		
Vale Par. SW15	164	D4
Kingston Vale		
Vale Ri. NW11	90	C1
Vale Rd. E7	97	H6
Vale Rd. N4	75	J7
Vale Rd., Brom.	192	D2
Vale Rd., Epsom	197	F4
Vale Rd., Mitch.	186	D3
Vale Rd., Sutt.	198	E4
Vale Rd., Wor.Pk.	197	F4
Vale Rd. N., Surb.	195	H2
Vale Rd. S., Surb.	195	H2
Vale Row N5	93	H3
Gillespie Rd.		
Vale Royal N7	92	E7
Vale St. SE27	170	A3
Vale Ter. N4	75	J6
Valence Av., Dag.	100	D3
Valence Circ., Dag.	100	D3
Valence Wd. Rd., Dag.	100	D3
Valencia Rd., Stan.	53	F4
Valentia Pl. SW9	151	G4
Brixton Sta. Rd.		
Valentine Av., Bex.	176	E2
Valentine Ct. SE23	171	G2
Valentine Pl. SE1	**27**	**G3**
Valentine Pl. SE1	131	H2
Valentine Rd. E9	95	G6
Valentine Rd., Har.	85	J3
Valentine Row SE1	**27**	**G4**
Valentine Row SE1	131	H2
Valentines Rd., Ilf.	98	E1
Valerian Way E15	115	E3
Valeswood Rd., Brom.	173	F5
Valetta Gro. E13	115	G2
Valetta Rd. W3	127	E2
Valette St. E9	95	E6
Valiant Cl., Nthlt.	102	D3
Ruislip Rd.		
Valiant Cl., Rom.	83	G2
Valiant Ho. SE7	135	J5
Valiant Path NW9	54/55	E7
Blundell Rd.		
Valiant Way E6	116	C5
Vallance Rd. E1	**13**	**J4**
Vallance Rd. E1	112	D4
Vallance Rd. E2	**13**	**J4**
Vallance Rd. E2	112	D3
Vallance Rd. N22	74	C2
Vallentin Rd. E17	78	C4
Valley Av. N12	57	G4
Valley Cl., Loug.	48	C6
Valley Cl., Pnr.	66	B2
Alandale Dr.		
Valley Dr. NW9	70	A6
Valley Flds. Cres.,	43	G2
Enf.		
Valley Gdns. SW19	167	G7
Valley Gdns., Wem.	87	J7
Valley Gro. SE7	135	J5
Valley Hill, Loug.	48	B7
Valley Link Ind. Est.,	45	H6
Enf.		
Valley Ms., Twick.	162	D2
Cross Deep		
Valley Rd. SW16	169	F4
Valley Rd., Belv.	139	H4
Valley Rd., Brom.	191	E2
Valley Side E4	62	A2
Valley Side Par. E4	62	A2
Valley Side		
Valley Vw., Barn.	40	B6
Valley Vw., Croy.	203	F2
Valleyfield Rd. SW16	169	F5
Valliere Rd. NW10	107	H3
Valliers Wd. Rd., Sid.	175	G1
Vallis Way W13	104	D5
Vallis Way, Chess.	195	G4
Valmar Rd. SE5	151	J1
Valnay St. SW17	167	J5
Valognes Av. E17	77	H1
Valonia Gdns. SW18	148	C6
Vambery Rd. SE18	137	F6
Van Dyck Av., N.Mal.	182	D7
Vanbrough Cres.,	102	C1
Nthlt.		
Vanbrugh Cl. E16	116	A5
Fulmer Rd.		
Vanbrugh Dr., Walt.	178	C7
Vanbrugh Flds. SE3	135	F7
Vanbrugh Hill SE3	135	F5
Vanbrugh Hill SE10	135	F5
Vanbrugh Pk. SE3	135	F7
Vanbrugh Pk. Rd. SE3	135	F7
Vanbrugh Pk. Rd. W.	135	F7
SE3		
Vanbrugh Rd. W4	126	D3
Vanbrugh Ter. SE3	155	F1
Vanburgh Cl., Orp.	207	H1
Vancouver Rd. SE23	171	H2
Vancouver Rd., Edg.	70	B1
Vancouver Rd., Hayes	102	B4
Vancouver Rd., Rich.	163	F4
Vanderbilt Rd. SW18	167	F1
Vanderville Gdns. N2	73	F2
Tarling Rd.		
Vandome Cl. E16	115	H6
Vandon Pas. SW1	**25**	**G5**
Vandon St. SW1	**25**	**G5**
Vandon St. SW1	130	C3
Vandy St. EC2	**12**	**D6**
Vandyke Cl. SW15	148	A7
Vandyke Cross SE9	156	B5
Vane Cl. NW3	91	G4
Vane Cl., Har.	69	J6
Vane St. SW1	**33**	**G1**
Vanessa Cl., Belv.	139	G5
Vanguard Cl. E16	115	G5
Vanguard Cl., Croy.	201	H1
Vanguard Cl., Rom.	83	H2
Vanguard St. SE8	154	A1
Vanguard Way, Wall.	200	E7
Vanneck Sq. SW15	147	G5
Vanoc Gdns., Brom.	173	G3
Vansittart Rd. E7	97	F4
Vansittart St. SE14	133	H7
Vanston Pl. SW6	128	D7
Vant Rd. SW17	167	J5
Vantage Ms. E14	134	C1
Prestons Rd.		
Varcoe Rd. SE16	133	E5
Varden St. E1	112	E6
Vardens Rd. SW11	149	G4
Vardon Cl. N3	72	B1
Claremont Pk.		
Vardon Cl. W3	106	D6
Varley Par. NW9	71	E4
Varley Rd. E16	115	H6
Varley Way, Mitch.	185	G2
Varna Rd. SW6	128	B7
Varna Rd., Hmptn.	179	H1
Varndell St. NW1	**9**	**F3**
Varndell St. NW1	110	C3
Varsity Dr., Twick.	144	B5
Varsity Row SW14	146	C2
William's La.		
Vartry Rd. N15	76	A6
Vassall Rd. SW9	131	G7
Vauban Est. SE16	**29**	**G6**
Vauban Est. SE16	132	D3
Vauban St. SE16	**29**	**G6**
Vauban St. SE16	132	C3
Vaughan Av. NW4	71	G4
Vaughan Av. W6	127	F4
Vaughan Cl.,	160/161	E6
Hmptn.		
Oak Av.		
Vaughan Gdns., Ilf.	80	C7
Vaughan Rd. E15	97	F6
Vaughan Rd. SE5	151	J3
Vaughan Rd., Har.	67	J7
Vaughan Rd., T.Ditt.	180	E7
Vaughan Rd., Well.	157	J2
Vaughan St. SE16	133	J2
Vaughan Way E1	**21**	**H6**
Vaughan Way E1	112	D7
Vaughan Williams Cl.	134	A7
SE8		
Watson's St.		
Vauxhall Br. SE1	**34**	**A4**
Vauxhall Br. SE1	130	E5
Vauxhall Br. SW1	**34**	**A4**
Vauxhall Br. SW1	130	E5
Vauxhall Br. Rd. SW1	**33**	**G1**
Vauxhall Br. Rd. SW1	130	C4
Vauxhall Gdns.,	201	J6
S.Croy.		
Vauxhall Gdns. Est.	**34**	**D4**
SE11		
Vauxhall Gro. SW8	**34**	**C5**
Vauxhall Gro. SW8	131	F6
Vauxhall St. SE11	**34**	**D4**
Vauxhall St. SE11	131	F5
Vauxhall Wk. SE11	**34**	**C3**
Vauxhall Wk. SE11	131	F5
Vawdrey Cl. E1	113	F4
Veals Mead, Mitch.	185	H1
Vectis Gdns. SW17	168	B6
Vectis Rd.		
Vectis Rd. SW17	168	B6
Veda Rd. SE13	154	A4

Velde Way SE22	152	B5
East Dulwich Gro.		
Veldene Way, Har.	85	F3
Velletri Ho. E2	113	G2
Vellum Dr., Cars.	200	A3
Venables Cl., Dag.	101	H4
Venables St. NW8	**15**	**F1**
Venables St. NW8	109	G4
Vencourt Pl. W6	127	G5
Venetia Rd. N4	75	H6
Venetia Rd. W5	125	G2
Venetian Rd. SE5	151	J2
Venn St. SW4	150	C4
Venner Rd. SE26	171	F6
Ventnor Av., Stan.	69	E1
Ventnor Dr. N20	56	E3
Ventnor Gdns., Bark.	99	H6
Ventnor Rd. SE14	133	G7
Ventnor Rd., Sutt.	199	E7
Venture Cl., Bex.	158	E7
Venue St. E14	114	C5
Venus Rd. SE18	136	C3
Vera Av. N21	43	G5
Vera Lynn Cl. E7	97	G4
Dames Rd.		
Vera Rd. SW6	148	B1
Verbena Cl. E16	115	F4
Cranberry La.		
Verbena Cl., West Dr.	120	A5
Magnolia St.		
Verbena Gdns. W6	127	G5
Verdant La. SE6	173	E1
Verdayne Av., Croy.	203	G1
Verdun Rd. SE18	138	A6
Verdun Rd. SW13	127	G6
Vere Rd., Loug.	49	F4
Vere St. W1	**16**	**D4**
Vere St. W1	110	B6
Vereker Dr., Sun.	178	A3
Vereker Rd. W14	128	B5
Verity Cl. W11	108	B6
Vermeer Gdns. SE15	153	F4
Elland Rd.		
Vermont Cl., Enf.	43	H4
Vermont Rd. SE19	170	A6
Vermont Rd. SW18	149	E6
Vermont Rd., Sutt.	198	E3
Verney Gdns., Dag.	100	E4
Verney Rd. SE16	132	D6
Verney Rd., Dag.	100	E5
Verney St. NW10	88	D3
Verney Way SE16	132	E5
Vernham Rd. SE18	137	F6
Vernon Av. E12	98	C4
Vernon Av. SW20	184	A2
Vernon Av., Wdf.Grn.	63	H7
Vernon Cl., Epsom	196	C6
Vernon Ct., Stan.	68/69	E1
Vernon Dr.		
Vernon Cres., Barn.	42	A6
Vernon Dr., Stan.	68	D1
Vernon Ms. E17	77	J4
Vernon St.		
Vernon Ms. W14	128	B4
Vernon St.		
Vernon Pl. WC1	**18**	**B2**
Vernon Pl. WC1	111	E5
Vernon Ri. WC1	**10**	**D3**
Vernon Ri. WC1	111	F3
Vernon Ri., Grnf.	86	A5
Vernon Rd. E3	113	J2
Vernon Rd. E11	97	E1
Vernon Rd. E15	97	E7
Vernon Rd. E17	77	J4
Vernon Rd. N8	75	G3
Vernon Rd. SW14	146	D3
Vernon Rd., Ilf.	99	J1
Vernon Rd., Sutt.	199	F5
Vernon Sq. WC1	**10**	**D3**
Vernon St. W14	128	B4
Vernon Yd. W11	108	C7
Portobello Rd.		
Veroan Rd., Bexh.	158	E2
Verona Dr., Surb.	195	H2
Verona Rd. E7	97	G7
Upton La.		
Veronica Gdns. SW16	186	C1
Veronica Rd. SW17	168	B3
Veronique Gdns., Ilf.	81	E5
Verran Rd. SW12	150	B7
Balham Gro.		
Versailles Rd. SE20	170	D7
Verulam Av. E17	77	J6
Verulam Bldgs. WC1	**18**	**D1**
Verulam Av., Grnf.	103	G4
Verulam St. WC1	**18**	**E1**
Verwood Dr., Barn.	41	J3
Verwood Rd., Har.	67	J2
Vesey Path E14	114	B6
East India Dock Rd.		
Vespan Rd. W12	127	G2
Vesta Rd. SE4	153	H2
Vestris Rd. SE23	171	G2

Vestry Ms. SE5	152	B1
Vestry Rd. E17	78	B4
Vestry Rd. SE5	152	B1
Vestry St. N1	**12**	**B3**
Vestry St. N1	112	A3
Vevey St. SE6	171	J2
Veysey Gdns., Dag.	101	G3
Viaduct Pl. E2	112/113	E3
Viaduct St.		
Viaduct St. E2	112	E3
Vian St. SE13	154	B3
Vibart Gdns. SW2	151	F7
Vibart Wk. N1	110/111	E1
Outram Pl.		
Vicarage Av. SE3	155	G1
Vicarage Cl., Erith	139	J6
Vicarage Cl., Nthlt.	85	F7
Vicarage Cl.,	196	E1
Wor.Pk.		
Vicarage Ct. W8	**22**	**A3**
Vicarage Ct., Felt.	141	F7
Vicarage Cres. SW11	149	G1
Vicarage Dr. SW14	146	D5
Vicarage Dr., Bark.	99	F7
Vicarage Dr., Beck.	190	A1
Vicarage Fm. Rd.,	142	E2
Houns.		
Vicarage Flds., Walt.	178	C6
Vicarage Gdns. SW14	146	C5
Vicarage Rd.		
Vicarage Gdns. W8	128	D1
Vicarage Gdns.,	185	H3
Mitch.		
Vicarage Gate W8	**22**	**A3**
Vicarage Gate W8	128	E2
Vicarage Gro. SE5	152	A1
Vicarage La. E6	116	C3
Vicarage La. E15	97	E7
Vicarage La., Chig.	65	F2
Vicarage La., Ilf.	99	G1
Vicarage Pk. SE18	137	F5
Vicarage Path N8	74	E7
Vicarage Rd. E10	96	B1
Vicarage Rd. E15	97	F7
Vicarage Rd. N17	60	D7
Vicarage Rd. NW4	71	G6
Vicarage Rd. SE18	137	F5
Vicarage Rd. SW14	146	C5
Vicarage Rd., Bex.	177	H1
Vicarage Rd., Croy.	201	G3
Vicarage Rd., Dag.	101	H6
Vicarage Rd., Kings.T.	181	G2
Vicarage Rd.,	181	F1
(Hampton Wick), Kings.T.		
Vicarage Rd., Sutt.	198	E4
Vicarage Rd., Tedd.	162	D5
Vicarage Rd., Twick.	162	B2
Vicarage Rd.	143	J6
(Whitton), Twick.		
Vicarage Rd., Wdf.Grn.	64	B7
Vicarage Way NW10	88	D3
Vicarage Way, Har.	67	G7
Vicars Br. Cl., Wem.	105	H2
Vicars Cl. E9	113	F1
Northiam St.		
Vicars Cl. E15	115	G1
Vicars Cl., Enf.	44	B2
Vicars Hill SE13	154	B4
Vicars Moor La. N21	43	G7
Vicars Oak Rd. SE19	170	B6
Vicars Rd. NW5	92	A5
Vicars Wk., Dag.	100	B3
Viceroy Cl. N2	73	H4
Market Pl.		
Viceroy Ct. NW8	**7**	**H1**
Viceroy Par. N2	73	H3
High Rd.		
Viceroy Rd. SW8	150	E1
Vickers Way, Houns.	143	E5
Victor Gro., Wem.	87	H7
Victor Rd. NW10	107	H3
Victor Rd. SE20	171	G7
Victor Rd., Har.	67	J3
Victor Rd., Tedd.	162	B4
Victor Vil. N9	60	A3
Victor Wk. NW9	70/71	E2
Booth Rd.		
Victoria Av. E6	116	A1
Victoria Av. EC2	**20**	**E2**
Victoria Av. N3	72	C1
Victoria Av., Barn.	41	G4
Victoria Av., Houns.	143	F5
Victoria Av., Surb.	181	G7
Victoria Av., Wall.	200	A3
Victoria Av., Wem.	88	B6
Victoria Av., W.Mol.	179	G3
Victoria Cl., Barn.	41	G4
Victoria Cl., W.Mol.	179	G3
Victoria Av.		
Victoria Cotts., Rich.	145	J1
Victoria Cres., Wem.	88	A6
Victoria Cres. N15	76	B5
Victoria Cres. SE19	170	B6
Victoria Cres. SW19	166	C7

Victoria Dock Rd. E16	115	G7
Victoria Dr. SW19	148	A7
Victoria Embk. EC4	**18**	**C6**
Victoria Embk. EC4	111	F7
Victoria Embk. SW1	**26**	**B3**
Victoria Embk. SW1	131	G2
Victoria Embk. WC2	**18**	**C6**
Victoria Embk. WC2	131	G2
Victoria Gdns. W11	128	D1
Victoria Gdns., Houns.	142	E1
Victoria Gro. N12	57	F5
Victoria Gro. W8	**22**	**C5**
Victoria Gro. W8	129	F3
Victoria Ind. Est.	106	E3
NW10		
Victoria La., Barn.	40	C4
Victoria La., Hayes	121	F5
Victoria Ms. NW6	108	D1
Victoria Ms. SW4	150	B4
Victoria Ri.		
Victoria Ms. SW18	167	F1
Victoria Pk. E9	95	H7
Victoria Pk. Rd. E9	113	F1
Victoria Pk. Sq. E2	113	F3
Victoria Pas. NW8	**7**	**E5**
Victoria Pl., Rich.	145	G5
Victoria Pt. E13	115	G2
Victoria Rd.		
Victoria Retail Pk.,	84	E5
Ruis.		
Victoria Ri. SW4	150	B3
Victoria Rd. E4	63	E1
Victoria Rd. E11	96	E4
Victoria Rd. E13	115	G2
Victoria Rd. E17	78	C2
Victoria Rd. E18	79	H2
Victoria Rd. N4	75	F7
Victoria Rd. N9	60	C4
Victoria Rd. N15	76	D4
Victoria Rd. N18	60	C4
Victoria Rd. N22	74	C1
Victoria Rd. NW4	71	J4
Victoria Rd. NW6	108	C1
Victoria Rd. NW7	55	F5
Victoria Rd. NW10	106	D5
Victoria Rd. SW14	146	D3
Victoria Rd. W3	106	D5
Victoria Rd. W5	105	E5
Victoria Rd. W8	**22**	**C5**
Victoria Rd. W8	129	F3
Victoria Rd., Bark.	99	E6
Victoria Rd., Barn.	41	G4
Victoria Rd., Bexh.	159	G4
Victoria Rd., Brom.	192	A5
Victoria Rd., Buck.H.	64	A2
Victoria Rd., Bushey	51	H1
Victoria Rd., Chis.	174	D5
Victoria Rd., Dag.	101	H5
Victoria Rd., Felt.	160	B1
Victoria Rd., Kings.T.	181	J2
Victoria Rd., Mitch.	167	H7
Victoria Rd., Ruis.	84	C5
Victoria Rd., Sid.	175	J3
Victoria Rd., Sthl.	123	F3
Victoria Rd., Surb.	181	G6
Victoria Rd., Sutt.	199	G5
Victoria Rd., Tedd.	162	D6
Victoria Rd., Twick.	144	D7
Victoria Sq. SW1	**24**	**E5**
Victoria Sta. SW1	**33**	**E1**
Victoria Sta. SW1	130	B4
Victoria Steps, Brent.	125	J6
Kew Br. Rd.		
Victoria St. E15	96	E7
Victoria St. SW1	**25**	**F6**
Victoria St. SW1	130	C3
Victoria St., Belv.	139	F5
Victoria Ter. N4	93	G1
Victoria Ter.	106/107	E3
NW10		
Old Oak La.		
Victoria Ter., Har.	86	B1
Victoria Vil., Rich.	145	J3
Victoria Way SE7	135	H5
Victoria Wf. E14	113	H7
Victorian Gro. N16	94	B3
Victorian Rd. N16	94	B3
Victors Dr., Hmptn.	161	E6
Victors Way, Barn.	40	C3
Victory Av., Mord.	185	F5
Victory Business Cen.,	144	C3
Islw.		
Victory Pl. E14	113	H7
Northey St.		
Victory Pl. SE17	**36**	**A1**
Victory Pl. SE17	131	J4
Victory Pl. SE19	170	B6
Westow St.		
Victory Rd. E11	79	H4
Victory Rd. SW19	167	F7
Victory Rd. Ms. SW19	167	F7
Victory Rd.		
Victory Wk. SE8	154	A1
Ship St.		

Victory Way SE16	133	H2
Victory Way, Houns.	122	C5
Victory Way, Rom.	83	H2
Vidler Cl., Chess.	195	F6
Merritt Gdns.		
Vienna Cl., Ilf.	80	B2
Coburg Gdns.		
View, The SE2	139	E5
View Cl. N6	73	J7
View Cl., Chig.	65	G5
View Cl., Har.	68	A4
View Rd. N6	73	J7
Viewfield Cl., Har.	69	H7
Viewfield Rd. SW18	148	C6
Viewfield Rd., Bex.	176	C1
Viewland Rd. SE18	137	J5
Viga Rd. N21	43	G6
Vigilant Cl. SE26	170	D4
Vignoles Rd., Rom.	83	G7
Vigo St. W1	**17**	**F6**
Vigo St. W1	110	C7
Viking Cl. E3	113	H2
Selwyn Rd.		
Viking Ct. SW6	128	D6
Viking Gdns. E6	116	B4
Jack Dash Way		
Viking Pl. E10	95	J1
Viking Rd., Sthl.	103	E7
Villa Rd. SW9	139	J3
Villa Rd. SW9	151	G3
Villa St. SE17	**36**	**C4**
Villa St. SE17	132	A5
Villacourt Rd. SE18	138	A7
Village, The SE7	135	J6
Village Arc. E4	62	D1
Station Rd.		
Village Cl. E4	62	C5
Village Cl. NW3	91	H5
Ornan Rd.		
Village Hts., Wdf.Grn.	63	F5
Village Ms. NW9	88	D2
Village Pk. Cl., Enf.	44	B6
Village Rd. N3	72	B1
Village Rd., Enf.	44	B6
Village Row, Sutt.	198	D7
Village Way NW10	88	D4
Village Way SE21	152	A6
Village Way, Beck.	190	A2
Village Way, Pnr.	67	E7
Village Way E., Har.	67	F7
Villas Rd. SE18	137	F4
Villiers Av., Surb.	181	J5
Villiers Av., Twick.	161	F1
Villiers Cl. E10	96	A2
Villiers Cl., Surb.	181	J4
Villiers Cl., Surb.	181	J4
Villiers Ct. N20	41	F7
Buckingham Av.		
Villiers Path, Surb.	181	H5
Villiers Rd. NW2	89	G6
Villiers Rd., Beck.	189	G2
Villiers Rd., Islw.	144	B2
Villiers Rd., Kings.T.	181	J3
Villiers Rd., Sthl.	123	F1
Villiers St. WC2	**18**	**A6**
Villiers St. WC2	110	E7
Vincam Cl., Twick.	143	G7
Vince St. EC1	**12**	**C4**
Vince St. EC1	112	A3
Vincent Av., Surb.	196	B1
Vincent Cl. SE16	133	H2
Vincent Cl., Barn.	40	D3
Vincent Cl., Brom.	191	H4
Vincent Cl., Ilf.	65	F6
Vincent Cl., Sid.	175	H1
Vincent Cl., West Dr.	120	D6
Vincent Gdns. NW2	89	F3
Vincent Ms. E3	114	A2
Vincent Rd. E4	62	D6
Vincent Rd. N15	75	J4
Vincent Rd. N22	75	G2
Vincent Rd. SE18	137	E4
Vincent Rd. W3	126	C3
Vincent Rd., Croy.	188	B7
Vincent Rd., Dag.	100	E7
Vincent Rd., Houns.	142	D2
Vincent Rd., Islw.	144	A1
Vincent Rd., Kings.T.	182	A3
Vincent Rd., Wem.	87	J7
Vincent Row, Hmptn.	161	J6
Vincent Sq. SW1	**33**	**G1**
Vincent Sq. SW1	130	C4
Vincent St. E16	115	F5
Vincent St. SW1	**33**	**H1**
Vincent St. SW1	130	D4
Vincent Ter. N1	**11**	**G1**
Vincent Ter. N1	111	H2
Vincents Path,	84/85	E6
Nthlt.		
Arnold Rd.		
Vine Cl., Surb.	181	J6
Vine Cl., Sutt.	199	F3
Vine Cl., West Dr.	120	D4
Vine Ct. E1	**21**	**J2**
Vine Ct., Har.	69	H6

Vine Gdns., Ilf. 99 F5
Vine Hill EC1 10 E6
Vine La. SE1 28 E2
Vine Pl. W5 125 H1
  The Common
Vine Pl., Houns. 143 H4
Vine Rd. SW13 147 F3
Vine Rd. E15 97 F7
Vine Rd., E.Mol. 179 J4
Vine Rd., Orp. 207 A6
Vine Sq. W14 128 C5
Vine St. EC3 21 F5
Vine St. W1 17 G6
Vine St., Rom. 83 J5
Vine St. Br. EC1 11 F6
Vine St. Br. EC1 111 G4
Vine Yd. SE1 28 A3
Vinegar All. E17 78 B4
Vinegar St. E1 132/133 E1
  Reardon St.
Vinegar Yd. SE1 28 D3
Viner Cl., Walt. 178 C6
Vineries, The N14 42 C6
Vineries, The, Enf. 44 B3
Vineries Bank NW7 55 H5
Vineries, The, Dag. 101 G6
  Heathway
Vineries Cl., West Dr. 120 D6
Vines Av. N3 72 E1
Viney Rd. SE13 154 B3
Vineyard, The, Rich. 145 H5
Vineyard Av. NW7 56 B7
Vineyard Cl. SE6 172 A1
Vineyard Cl., Kings.T. 181 J3
Vineyard Gro. N3 73 E1
Vineyard Hill Rd. 166 D4
  SW19
Vineyard Pas., Rich. 145 H5
  Paradise Rd.
Vineyard Path SW14 146 D3
Vineyard Rd., Felt. 160 A3
Vineyard Row, 181 F1
  Kings.T.
Vineyard Wk. EC1 11 E5
Vineyard Wk. EC1 111 G4
Vining St. SW9 151 G4
Vintry Ms. E17 78 A4
  Cleveland Pk. Cres.
Viola Av. SE2 138 B4
Viola Av., Felt. 142 C6
Viola Sq. W12 107 F7
Violet Cl. E16 115 E4
Violet Cl., Wall. 200 B1
Violet Gdns., Croy. 201 H5
Violet Hill NW8 6 C2
Violet Hill NW8 109 F2
Violet La., Croy. 201 H5
Violet Rd. E3 114 B4
Violet Rd. E17 78 A6
Violet Rd. E18 79 H2
Violet St. E2 112/113 E4
  Three Colts La.
Virgil Pl. W1 15 J2
Virgil St. SE1 26 D5
Virgil St. SE1 131 F3
Virginia Cl., N.Mal. 182 C4
  Willow Rd.
Virginia Gdns., Ilf. 81 F2
Virginia Rd. E2 13 F4
Virginia Rd. E2 112 C3
Virginia Rd., Th.Hth. 187 H1
Virginia St. E1 21 J6
Virginia St. E1 112 D7
Virginia Wk. SW2 151 F6
Viscount Cl. N11 58 B5
Viscount Dr. E6 116 C5
Viscount Gro., Nthlt. 102 D3
  Wayfarer Rd.
Viscount St. EC1 11 J6
Viscount Way, Houns. 141 H4
Vista, The SE9 156 A6
Vista, The, Sid. 175 J5
  Langdon Shaw
Vista Av., Enf. 45 G2
Vista Dr., Ilf. 80 A5
Vista Way, Har. 69 H6
Viveash Cl., Hayes 121 J3
Vivian Av. NW4 71 H5
Vivian Av., Wem. 88 A5
Vivian Cl., Wat. 50 A1
Vivian Gdns., Wat. 50 A1
Vivian Gdns., Wem. 88 A5
Vivian Rd. E3 113 H2
Vivian Sq. SE15 152/153 E3
  Scylla Rd.
Vivian Way N2 73 G5
Vivien Cl., Chess. 195 H7
Vivienne Cl., Twick. 145 F6
Voce Rd. SE18 137 G7
Voewood Cl., N.Mal. 183 F6
Volta Way, Croy. 201 F1
Voltaire Rd. SW4 150 D3
Voluntary Pl. E11 79 G6
Vorley Rd. N19 92 C2

Voss Ct. SW16 169 E6
Voss St. E2 13 J4
Voss St. E2 112 D3
Voyagers Cl. SE28 118 C6
Vulcan Cl., Wall. 201 F7
Vulcan Gate, Enf. 43 G2
Vulcan Rd. SE4 153 J2
Vulcan Sq. E14 134 A4
  Britannia Rd.
Vulcan Ter. SE4 153 J2
Vulcan Way N7 93 F6
Vyne, The, Bexh. 159 H3
Vyner Rd. W3 106 D7
Vyner St. E2 113 E1
Vyse Cl., Barn. 39 J4

W

Wadbrook St., Kings.T. 53 G7
  High St.
Wadding St. SE17 36 B2
Wadding St. SE17 132 A4
Waddington Cl., Enf. 44 B4
Waddington Rd. E15 96 D5
Waddington St. E15 96 D6
Waddington Way 169 J7
  SE19
Waddon Cl., Croy. 201 G3
Waddon Ct. Rd., 201 G4
  Croy.
Waddon Marsh Way, 201 F1
  Croy.
Waddon New Rd., 201 H3
  Croy.
Waddon Pk. Av., 201 G3
  Croy.
Waddon Rd., Croy. 201 G3
Waddon Way, Croy. 201 G6
Wades Gro. N21 43 G7
Wades Hill N21 43 G6
Wades La., Tedd. 162 D5
  High St.
Wades Ms. N21 43 G7
  Wades Hill
Wades Pl. E14 114 B7
Wadeson St. E2 113 E2
Wadeville Av., Rom. 83 F7
Wadeville Cl., Belv. 139 G6
Wadham Av. E17 62 B7
Wadham Gdns. NW3 109 H1
Wadham Gdns., Grnf. 86 A6
Wadham Rd. E17 78 B1
Wadham Rd. SW15 148 B4
Wadhurst Cl. SE20 188 E2
Wadhurst Rd. SW8 150 C1
Wadhurst Rd. W4 126 D3
Wadley Rd. E11 78 E7
Wadsworth Business 105 F7
  Cen., Grnf.
Wadsworth Cl., Enf. 45 G5
Wadsworth Cl., Grnf. 105 F7
Wadsworth Rd., Grnf. 105 E2
Wager St. E3 113 J4
Waggon Ms. N14 58 C1
  Chase Side
Waghorn Rd. E13 115 J1
Waghorn Rd., Har. 69 G3
Waghorn St. SE15 152 D3
Wagner St. SE15 133 F7
Wagstaff Gdns., Dag. 100 C7
  Ellerton Rd.
Wagtail Cl. NW9 70/71 E2
  Swan Dr.
Waights Ct., Kings.T. 181 H1
Wainfleet Av., Rom. 83 J2
Wainford Cl. SW19 166 A1
  Windlesham Gro.
Wainwright Gro., 144 A4
  Islw.
Waite Davies Rd. 155 F7
  SE12
Waite St. SE15 37 F5
Waite St. SE15 132 C6
Waithman St. EC4 19 G4
Wakefield Gdns. SE19 170 B7
Wakefield Gdns., Ilf. 80 B6
Wakefield Ms. WC1 10 B4
Wakefield Rd. N11 58 D5
Wakefield Rd. N15 76 C5
Wakefield Rd., Rich. 145 G5
Wakefield St. E6 116 A1
Wakefield St. N18 60 D5
Wakefield St. WC1 10 B5
Wakefield St. WC1 111 E3
Wakeham St. N1 94 A6
Wakehams Hill, Pnr. 67 F3
Wakehurst Rd. SW11 149 H6
Wakelin Rd. E15 114 E2
Wakeling Rd. W7 104 C5
Wakeling St. E14 113 H6
Wakeman Rd. NW10 107 J3
Wakemans Hill Av. 70 D5
  NW9
Wakering Rd., Bark. 99 F6

Wakerley Cl. E6 116 C6
  Truesdale Rd.
Wakley St. EC1 11 G3
Wakley St. EC1 111 H2
Walberswick St. SW8 131 E7
Walbrook EC4 20 B5
Walbrook EC4 112 A7
Walbrook Ho. N9 61 F1
Walbrook Wf. EC4 111 J7
  Upper Thames St.
Walburgh St. E1 112/113 E6
  Bigland St.
Walcorde Av. SE17 36 A2
Walcot Sq. SE11 45 J2
Walcot Sq. SE11 35 F1
Walcot Sq. SE11 131 G4
Walcott St. SW1 33 G1
Waldair Ct. E16 136/137 E2
  Barge Ho. Rd.
Waldair Wf. E16 136 E2
Waldeck Gro. SE27 169 H3
Waldeck Rd. N15 75 H4
Waldeck Rd. SW14 146 C3
  Lower Richmond Rd.
Waldeck Rd. W4 126 A6
Waldeck Rd. W13 105 E6
Waldeck Ter. SW14 146 C3
  Lower Richmond Rd.
Waldegrave Av., 162 C5
  Tedd.
  Waldegrave Rd.
Waldegrave Gdns., 162 C2
  Twick.
Waldegrave Pk., 162 C4
  Twick.
Waldegrave Rd. N8 75 G3
Waldegrave Rd. SE19 170 C7
Waldegrave Rd. W5 105 J6
Waldegrave Rd., 192 B4
  Brom.
Waldegrave Rd., Dag. 100 C2
Waldegrave Rd., 162 C4
  Tedd.
Waldegrave Rd., 162 C4
  Twick.
Waldegrove, Croy. 202 C3
Waldemar Av. SW6 148 B1
Waldemar Av. W13 125 F1
Waldemar Rd. SW19 166 D5
Walden Av. N13 59 J4
Walden Av., Chis. 174 C4
Walden Av., Belv. 139 F5
Walden Gdns., 187 F3
  Th.Hth.
Walden Rd. N17 76 A1
Walden Rd., Chis. 174 C6
Walden St. E1 112 E6
Walden Way NW7 56 A6
Walden Way, Ilf. 65 H7
Waldenshaw Rd. SE23 171 F1
Waldo Cl. SW4 150 C5
Waldo Pl., Mitch. 167 H7
Waldo Rd. NW10 107 G3
Waldo Rd., Brom. 192 A3
Waldram Cres. SE23 171 F1
Waldram Pk. Rd. 171 G1
  SE23
Waldram Pl. SE23 171 F1
  Waldram Cres.
Waldrist Way, Erith 139 F2
Waldron Gdns., 190 D3
  Brom.
Waldron Ms. SW3 31 F5
Waldron Rd. SW18 167 F3
Waldron Rd., Har. 86 B1
Waldronhyrst, 201 H4
  S.Croy.
Waldrons, The, Croy. 201 H4
Waldrons Path, 201 J4
  S.Croy.
Waldstock Rd. SE28 118 A7
Waleran Cl., Stan. 52 C6
  Chenduit Way
Waleran Flats SE1 132 B4
  Old Kent Rd.
Walerand Rd. SE13 154 C2
Wales Av., Cars. 199 J5
Wales Cl. SE15 132 E7
Wales Fm. Rd. W3 106 D5
Waley St. E1 113 G5
Walfield Av. N20 41 E7
Walford Rd. N16 94 B4
Walfrey Gdns., Dag. 101 E7
Walham Grn. Ct. 128/129 E7
  SW6
  Waterford Rd.
Walham Gro. SW6 128 D7
Walham Ri. SW19 166 B6
Walham Yd. SW6 128 D7
  Walham Gro.
Walkden Rd., Chis. 174 D5
Walker Cl. N11 58 C4
Walker Cl. SE18 137 F4
Walker Cl. W7 124 B1

Walker Cl., Hmptn. 161 F6
  Fearnley Cres.
Walkers Cl. E8 94 D6
Walkers Pl. SW15 148 B3
Walkers Ct. W1 17 H5
Walkerscroft Mead 169 J1
  SE21
Walkford Way SE15 37 F7
Walks, The N2 73 G3
Wall End Rd. E6 98 D7
Wall St. N1 94 A6
Wallace Cl. SE28 118 D7
  Haldane Rd.
Wallace Cres., Cars. 199 J5
Wallace Rd. N1 93 J6
Wallace Way N19 92 D2
  Giesbach Rd.
Wallbutton Rd. SE4 153 H2
Wallcote Av. NW2 90 A1
Waller Dr., Nthwd. 66 A2
Waller Rd. SE14 153 G1
Wallers Cl., Dag. 119 E1
Wallers Cl. 64 C6
  Wdf.Grn.
Wallers Hoppit, Loug. 48 B2
Wallflower St. W12 107 F7
Wallgrave Rd. SW5 30 A1
Wallgrave Rd. SW5 128 E4
Wallingford Av. W10 108 A5
Wallington Cor., Wall. 200 B4
  Manor Rd. N.
Wallington Rd., Ilf. 81 J7
Wallington Sq., Wall. 200 B6
  Woodcote Rd.
Wallis All. SE1 28 A4
Wallis Cl. SW11 149 G3
Wallis Ms. N22 75 G3
  Brampton Pk. Rd.
Wallis Rd. E9 95 J6
Wallis Rd., Sthl. 103 H6
Wallis's Cotts. SW2 150 E7
Wallman Pl. N22 75 F1
  Bounds Grn. Rd.
Wallorton Gdns. 146 D4
  SW14
Wallwood Rd. E11 78 D7
Wallwood St. E14 113 J5
Walm La. NW2 90 A5
Walmar Cl., Barn. 41 G1
Walmer Cl. E4 62 B2
Walmer Cl., Orp. 207 G4
  Tubbenden La. S.
Walmer Cl., Rom. 83 H2
Walmer Gdns. W13 124 D2
Walmer Ho. N9 44 C7
Walmer Pl. W1 15 J1
  Latimer Rd.
Walmer Rd. W10 107 J6
Walmer St. W1 15 J1
Walmer Ter. SE18 137 F4
Walmgate Rd., Grnf. 104 E1
Walmington Fold N12 56 D6
Walney Wk. N1 93 J6
  St. Paul's Rd.
Walnut Av., West Dr. 120 D3
Walnut Cl. SE8 133 J6
  Clyde St.
Walnut Cl., Cars. 199 J5
Walnut Cl., Ilf. 81 F4
  Civic Way
Walnut Ct. W5 125 H2
  Rowan Cl.
Walnut Gdns. E15 96/97 E4
  Burgess Rd.
Walnut Gro., Enf. 44 A5
Walnut Ms., Sutt. 199 F7
Walnut Rd. E10 96 A2
Walnut Tree Av., 185 H3
  Mitch.
  De'Arn Gdns.
Walnut Tree Cl. SW13 147 F1
Walnut Tree Cl., Chis. 193 F1
Walnut Tree Cotts. 166 B4
  SW19
  Church Rd.
Walnut Tree Rd. SE10 135 E5
Walnut Tree Rd. E. 125 H6
  Brent.
Walnut Tree Rd., Dag. 100 D2
Walnut Tree Rd., 123 F6
  Houns.
Walnut Tree Wk. SE11 34 E1
Walnut Tree Wk. SE11 131 G4
Walnut Way, Buck.H. 64 A3
Walnut Way, Ruis. 84 C6
Walpole Av., Rich. 145 J2
Walpole Cl. W13 125 F2
Walpole Cl., Pnr. 51 G6
Walpole Cres., Tedd. 162 C5
Walpole Gdns. W4 126 C5
Walpole Gdns., Twick. 162 B2

Walpole Ms. NW8 109 G1
Queen's Gro.
Walpole Ms. SW19 167 G6
Walpole Rd.
Walpole Pk. W5 125 F1
Walpole Pl. SE18 136/137 E4
Anglesea Rd.
Walpole Pl., Tedd. 162 C5
Walpole Rd. E6 97 J7
Walpole Rd. E17 77 H4
Walpole Rd. E18 79 F1
Walpole Rd. 75 J3
(Downhills Way) N17
Walpole Rd. 75 J2
(Lordship La.) N17
Walpole Rd. SW19 167 G6
Walpole Rd., Brom. 192 A5
Walpole Rd., Croy. 202 A2
Walpole Rd., Surb. 181 H6
Walpole Rd., Tedd. 162 C5
Walpole Rd., Twick. 162 B2
Walpole St. SW3 31 J3
Walpole St. SW3 129 J5
Walrond Av., Wem. 87 H5
Walsham Cl. N16 76 D7
Braydon Rd.
Walsham Cl. SE28 118 D7
Walsham Rd. SE14 153 G2
Walsham Rd., Felt. 142 B7
Walsingham Gdns., 197 E4
Epsom
Walsingham Pk., 193 G2
Chis.
Walsingham Pl. SW4 149 J4
Clapham Common W. Side
Walsingham Pl. SW11 150 A6
Walsingham Rd. E5 94 D3
Walsingham Rd. W13 124 D1
Walsingham Rd., Enf. 44 A4
Walsingham Rd., 185 J5
Mitch.
Walsingham Wk., 139 G6
Belv.
Walt Whitman Cl. 151 H4
SE24
Shakespeare Rd.
Walter Rodney Cl. E6 98 C6
Stevenage Rd.
Walter St. E2 113 G3
Walter St., Kings.T. 181 H1
Sopwith Way
Walter Ter. E1 113 G6
Walter Wk., Edg. 54 C6
Walters Ho. SE17 35 G6
Walters Rd. SE25 188 B4
Walters Rd., Enf. 45 F5
Walters Way SE23 153 G6
Walters Yd., Brom. 191 G2
Walterton Rd. W9 108 C4
Waltham Av. NW9 70 A6
Waltham Av., Hayes 121 F3
Waltham Dr., Edg. 70 A2
Waltham Pk. Way E17 78 A1
Waltham Rd., Cars. 185 G7
Waltham Rd., Sthl. 122 E3
Waltham Rd., 64 B6
Wdf.Grn.
Waltham Way E4 61 J3
Walthamstow Av. E4 62 A7
Walthamstow 78 C2
Business Cen. E17
Waltheof Av. N17 76 A1
Waltheof Gdns. N17 76 A1
Walton Av., Har. 85 F5
Walton Av., N.Mal. 183 F4
Walton Av., Sutt. 198 C3
Walton Cl. E5 95 G3
Orient Way
Walton Cl. NW2 89 H2
Walton Cl. SW8 34 B7
Walton Cl. SW8 131 E7
Walton Cl., Har. 68 A4
Walton Cres., Har. 85 F4
Walton Dr. NW10 88 D6
Mitchellbrook Way
Walton Dr., Har. 68 A4
Walton Gdns. W3 106 B5
Walton Gdns., Wem. 87 H2
Walton Grn., Croy. 204 C7
Walton Pl. SW3 23 J5
Walton Pl. SW3 129 J3
Walton Rd. E12 98 D4
Walton Rd. E13 115 J2
Walton Rd. N15 76 C5
Walton Rd. E.Mol. 179 G4
Walton Rd., Har. 68 A4
Walton Rd., Sid. 176 C2
Walton Rd., Walt. 178 C5
Walton Rd., W.Mol. 179 E4
Walton St. SW3 31 H1
Walton St. SW3 129 H4
Walton St., Enf. 44 A1
Walton Way W3 106 B5
Walton Way, Mitch. 186 C4

Walworth Pl. SE17 36 A4
Walworth Pl. SE17 131 J5
Walworth Rd. SE1 35 J1
Walworth Rd. SE1 131 J4
Walworth Rd. SE17 35 J1
Walworth Rd. SE17 131 J4
Walwyn Av., Brom. 192 A3
Wanborough Dr. 165 H1
SW15
Wanderer Dr., Bark. 118 B3
Wandle Bank SW19 167 G6
Wandle Bank, Croy. 200 E3
Wandle Ct., Epsom 196 C4
Wandle Ct. Gdns., 200 E4
Croy.
Wandle Rd. SW17 167 H2
Wandle Rd., Croy. 201 J3
Wandle Rd. 201 E3
(Waddon), Croy.
Wandle Rd., Mord. 185 F4
Wandle Rd., Wall. 200 B2
Wandle Side, Croy. 201 F3
Wandle Side, Wall. 200 B3
Wandle Way SW18 166 E1
Wandle Way, Mitch. 185 J5
Wandon Rd. SW6 129 E7
Wandsworth Br. SW6 149 E3
Wandsworth Br. 149 E3
SW18
Wandsworth Br. Rd. 148 E1
SW6
Wandsworth 149 H6
Common SW12
Wandsworth 149 F5
Common W. Side SW18
Wandsworth High St. 148 D5
SW18
Wandsworth Plain 148 E5
SW18
Wandsworth Rd. SW8 34 A5
Wandsworth Rd. SW8 130 D7
Wangey Rd., Rom. 82 D7
Wanless Rd. SE24 151 J3
Wanley Rd. SE5 152 A4
Wanlip Rd. E13 115 H4
Wannock Gdns., Ilf. 65 E7
Wansbeck Rd. E9 95 J7
Wansdown Pl. SW6 30 A7
Wansey St. SE17 35 J2
Wansey St. SE17 131 J4
Wansford Pk., Borwd. 38 E4
Wansford Rd., 79 J1
Wdf.Grn.
Wanstead Cl., Brom. 191 J2
Wanstead La., Ilf. 80 A6
Wanstead Pk. E11 80 A7
Wanstead Pk. Av. 98 A2
E12
Wanstead Pk. Rd., Ilf. 98 C1
Wanstead Pl. E11 79 G6
Wanstead Rd., Brom. 191 J2
Wansunt Rd., Bex. 177 J1
Wantage Rd. SE12 155 F5
Wantz Rd., Dag. 101 H4
Wapping Dock St. 132/133 E1
E1
Cinnamon St.
Wapping High St. E1 29 H2
Wapping High St. E1 132 D1
Wapping La. E1 113 E7
Wapping Wall E1 133 F1
Warbank La., Kings.T. 165 F7
Warbeck Rd. W12 127 H1
Warberry Rd. N22 75 F2
Warboys App., 164 B6
Kings.T.
Warboys Cres. E4 62 C5
Warboys Rd., 164 B6
Kings.T.
Warburton Cl. N1 94 B6
Culford Rd.
Warburton Cl., Har. 52 A6
Warburton Rd. E8 95 E1
Warburton Rd., 161 H1
Twick.
Warburton St. E8 112/113 E1
Warburton Rd.
Ward Cl., S.Croy. 202 B5
Ward Rd. E15 114 D1
Ward Rd. N19 92 C3
Wardalls Gro. SE14 133 F7
Wardell Cl. NW7 55 E7
Wardell Fld. NW9 71 E1
Warden Av., Har. 85 F1
Warden Rd. NW5 92 A6
Wardens Gro. SE1 27 J2
Wardle St. E9 95 G5
Wardley St. 148/149 E7
SW18
Garratt La.
Wardo Av. SW6 148 B1
Wardour Ms. W1 17 G4

Wardour St. W1 17 H5
Wardour St. W1 110 D7
Wardrobe Pl. EC4 19 H5
Wardrobe Ter. EC4 19 H5
Wards Rd., Ilf. 81 G7
Ware Pt. Dr. SE28 137 G2
Wareham Cl., Houns. 143 H4
Waremead Rd., Ilf. 80 E5
Warenford Way, 38 A1
Borwd.
Warfield Rd. NW10 108 A3
Warfield Rd., Felt. 141 H7
Warfield Rd., Hmptn. 179 H1
Warfield Yd. NW10 108 A3
Warfield Rd.
Wargrave Av. N15 76 C6
Wargrave Rd., Har. 85 J3
Warham Rd. N4 75 G5
Warham Rd., Har. 68 C2
Warham Rd., S.Croy. 201 J5
Warham St. SE5 35 H7
Warham St. SE5 131 H7
Waring Cl., Orp. 207 J6
Waring Dr., Orp. 207 J6
Waring Rd., Sid. 176 C6
Waring St. SE27 169 J4
Warkworth Gdns., 124 D7
Islw.
Warkworth Rd. N17 60 A7
Warland Rd. SE18 137 G7
Warley Av., Dag. 83 F7
Warley Av., Hayes 102 A5
Warley Cl. E10 95 J1
Millicent Rd.
Warley Rd. N9 61 F2
Warley Rd., Hayes 102 A6
Warley Rd., Ilf. 80 D1
Warley Rd., Wdf.Grn. 63 H7
Warley St. E2 113 G3
Warlingham Rd., 187 H4
Th.Hth.
Warlock Rd. W9 108 D4
Warlters Cl. N7 92/93 E4
Warlters Rd.
Warlters Rd. N7 93 E4
Warltersville Rd. N19 74 E7
Warmington Cl. E5 95 G3
Orient Way
Warmington Rd. 151 J6
SE24
Warmington St. E13 115 G4
Barking Rd.
Warminster Gdns. 188 D2
SE25
Warminster Rd. SE25 188 C2
Warminster Sq. SE25 188 D2
Warminster Rd.
Warminster Way, 186 B1
Mitch.
Warndon St. SE16 133 G4
Warne Pl., Sid. 158 B6
Westerham Dr.
Warneford Rd., Har. 69 G3
Warneford St. E9 113 E1
Warner Av., Sutt. 198 B2
Warner Cl. E15 97 E5
Warner Cl. NW9 71 F7
Warner Cl., Hmptn. 161 F5
Warner Cl., Hayes 121 G7
Warner Par., Hayes 121 G7
Warner Pl. E2 13 J2
Warner Pl. E2 112 D2
Warner Rd. E17 77 H4
Warner Rd. N8 74 D4
Warner Rd. SE5 151 J1
Warner Rd., Brom. 173 F7
Warner St. EC1 11 E6
Warner St. EC1 111 G4
Warner Ter. E14 114 A5
Broomfield St.
Warner Yd. EC1 10 E6
Warners Cl., Wdf.Grn. 63 G5
Warners La., Kings.T. 163 G4
Warners Path, 63 G5
Wdf.Grn.
Warnford Ind. Est., 121 H2
Hayes
Warnford Rd., Orp. 207 J5
Warnham Ct. Rd., 199 J7
Cars.
Warnham Rd. N12 57 H5
Warple Ms. W3 126/127 E2
Warple Way
Warple Way W3 126 E2
Warren, The E12 98 B4
Warren, The, Hayes 102 A6
Warren, The, Houns. 123 F7
Warren, The, Wor.Pk. 196 D4
Warren Av. E10 96 C3
Warren Av., Brom. 172 E7
Warren Av., Orp. 207 J5
Warren Av., Rich. 146 B4
Warren Av., S.Croy. 203 G7

Warren Cl. N9 45 G7
Warren Cl. SE21 151 J7
Lairdale Cl.
Warren Cl., Bexh. 159 G5
Warren Cl., Hayes 102 C5
Warren Cl., Wem. 87 G2
Warren Ct., Chig. 65 G4
Warren Cres. N9 44 C7
Warren Cutting, 164 D7
Kings.T.
Warren Dr., Grnf. 103 H4
Warren Dr., Ruis. 66 D7
Warren Dr., The E11 79 J7
Warren Dr. N., Surb. 196 B1
Warren Dr. S., Surb. 196 C1
Warren Flds., Stan. 53 F4
Valencia Rd.
Warren Footpath, 145 G6
Twick.
Warren Gdns. E15 96 D5
Ashton Rd.
Warren Gro., Borwd. 38 D4
Warren Hill, Loug. 47 J6
Warren Ho. E3 114 B3
Bromley High St.
Warren La. SE18 136 E3
Warren La., Stan. 52 D2
Warren Ms. W1 9 F6
Warren Pk., Kings.T. 164 C6
Warren Pk. Rd., Sutt. 199 G6
Warren Pl. E1 113 G6
Pitsea St.
Warren Pond Rd. E4 63 F1
Warren Ri., N.Mal. 182 D1
Warren Rd. E4 62 C2
Warren Rd. E10 96 C3
Warren Rd. E11 97 J1
Warren Rd. NW2 89 F2
Warren Rd. SW19 167 H6
Warren Rd., Bexh. 159 G5
Warren Rd., Brom. 205 G2
Warren Rd., Bushey 51 J1
Warren Rd., Croy. 202 B1
Warren Rd., Ilf. 81 G5
Warren Rd., Kings.T. 164 C6
Warren Rd., Orp. 207 J5
Warren Rd., Sid. 176 C3
Warren Rd., Twick. 143 J6
Warren St. W1 9 F6
Warren St. W1 110 C4
Warren Ter., Rom. 82 D4
Warren Wk. SE7 135 J6
Warren Way NW7 56 B6
Warren Way, 205 F2
Brom.
Warrender Rd. N19 92 C3
Warrender Way, Ruis. 66 A7
Warrens Shawe La., 54 B1
Edg.
Warriner Dr. N9 60 D3
Warriner Gdns. SW11 149 J1
Warrington Cres. W9 6 C6
Warrington Cres. W9 109 F4
Warrington Gdns. W9 6 C6
Warrington Pl. E14 134 C1
Yabsley St.
Warrington Rd., Croy. 201 H3
Warrington Rd., Dag. 100 D2
Warrington Rd., Har. 68 B5
Warrington Rd., Rich. 145 G5
Warrington Sq., Dag. 100 D2
Warrior Sq. E12 98 D4
Warsaw Cl., Ruis. 84 B6
Glebe Av.
Warsdale Dr. NW9 70 D5
Mardale Dr.
Warspite Rd. SE18 136 B3
Warton Rd. E15 96 C7
Warwall E6 116 E6
Warwick Av. W2 6 C6
Warwick Av. W2 109 F4
Warwick Av. W9 6 C6
Warwick Av. W9 109 F4
Warwick Av., Edg. 54 B3
Warwick Av., Har. 85 F4
Warwick Cl., Barn. 41 G5
Warwick Cl., Bex. 159 F7
Warwick Cl., Hmptn. 161 J7
Warwick Cl., Orp. 207 J2
Warwick Ct. SE15 152 D2
Warwick Ct. WC1 18 D2
Warwick Ct., Surb. 195 H2
Hook Rd.
Warwick Cres. W2 14 C1
Warwick Cres. W2 109 F5
Warwick Dene W5 125 H1
Warwick Dr. SW15 147 H3
Warwick Est. W2 14 B2
Warwick Est. W2 108 E5
Warwick Gdns. N4 75 J5
Warwick Gdns. W14 128 C3
Warwick Gdns., Ilf. 99 E1
Warwick Gdns., 180 C5
T.Ditt.
Warwick Gro. E5 94 E1

Name	Page	Grid
Warwick Gro., Surb.	181	J7
Warwick Ho. St. SW1	**25**	**J1**
Warwick Ho. St. SW1	130	D1
Warwick La. E4	**19**	**H4**
Warwick La. EC4	111	H6
Warwick Pas. EC4	**19**	**H3**
Warwick Pl. W5	125	G2
Warwick Rd.		
Warwick Pl. W9	**14**	**C1**
Warwick Pl. W9	109	F5
Warwick Pl. N. SW1	**33**	**F2**
Warwick Pl. N. SW1	130	C4
Warwick Rd. E4	62	A5
Warwick Rd. E11	79	H5
Warwick Rd. E12	98	B5
Warwick Rd. E15	97	F6
Warwick Rd. E17	77	J1
Warwick Rd. N11	58	D6
Warwick Rd. N18	60	B4
Warwick Rd. SE20	189	E3
Warwick Rd. SW5	128	C4
Warwick Rd. W5	125	G2
Warwick Rd. W14	128	C4
Warwick Rd., Barn.	40	E4
Warwick Rd., Borwd.	38	D3
Warwick Rd., Houns.	142	B3
Warwick Rd., Kings.T.	181	F1
Warwick Rd., N.Mal.	182	C3
Warwick Rd., Sid.	176	B5
Warwick Rd., Sutt.	199	F4
Warwick Rd., T.Ditt.	180	C5
Warwick Rd., Th.Hth.	187	G3
Warwick Rd., Twick.	162	B1
Warwick Rd., Well.	158	C3
Warwick Rd., West Dr.	120	B1
Warwick Row SW1	**25**	**E5**
Warwick Row SW1	130	B3
Warwick Sq. EC4	**19**	**H3**
Warwick Sq. SW1	**33**	**F3**
Warwick Sq. SW1	130	C5
Warwick Sq. Ms. SW1	**33**	**F2**
Warwick Sq. Ms. SW1	130	C4
Warwick St. W1	**17**	**G5**
Warwick St. W1	110	C7
Warwick Ter. SE18	137	G6
Warwick Way SW1	**33**	**F2**
Warwick Way SW1	130	C4
Warwick Yd. EC1	**12**	**A6**
Warwickshire Path SE8	133	J7
Washington Av. E12	98	B4
Washington Cl. E3	114	C6
Washington Rd. E6	97	J7
St. Stephens Rd.		
Washington Rd. E18	79	F2
Washington Rd. SW13	127	G7
Washington Rd., Kings.T.	182	A2
Washington Rd., Wor.Pk.	197	H2
Wastdale Rd. SE23	171	G1
Wat Tyler Rd. SE3	154	C2
Wat Tyler Rd. SE10	154	C2
Watchfield Ct. W4	126	C5
Watcombe Cotts., Rich.	126	A6
Watcombe Pl. SE25	188/189	E5
Albert Rd.		
Watcombe Rd. SE25	188	E5
Water Gdns., Stan.	53	E6
Water La. E15	97	E6
Water La. N9	60	E1
Water La. NW1	92	B7
Kentish Town Rd.		
Water La. SE14	133	F7
Water La., Ilf.	99	H3
Water La., Kings.T.	181	G1
Water La., Rich.	145	G5
Water La., Sid.	177	F2
Water La., Twick.	162	D1
The Embk.		
Water Lily Cl., Sthl.	123	J2
Navigator Dr.		
Water Ms. SE15	153	F4
Water Rd., Wem.	105	J1
Water St. WC2	**18**	**D5**
Water Twr. Hill, Croy.	202	A4
Water Twr. Pl. N1	111	G1
Liverpool Rd.		
Waterbank Rd. SE6	172	B3
Waterbeach Rd., Dag.	100	C6
Waterbrook La. NW4	71	J5
Watercress Pl. N1	94	B7
Hertford Rd.		
Waterdale Rd. SE2	138	A6
Waterden Rd. E15	96	A6
Waterer Ri., Wall.	200	D6
Waterfall Cl. N14	58	C3
Waterfall Cotts. SW19	167	G6
Waterfall Rd. N11	58	B4
Waterfall Rd. N14	58	C3
Waterfall Rd. SW19	167	G6
Waterfall Ter. SW17	167	H6
Waterfield Cl. SE28	138	B1
Waterfield Cl., Belv.	139	G3
Waterfield Gdns. SE25	188	B5
Waterford Rd. SW6	149	E1
Watergardens, The, Kings.T.	164	C6
Watergate EC4	**19**	**G5**
Watergate, The, Wat.	50	D2
Watergate St. SE8	134	A6
Waterhall Av. E4	62	E4
Waterhall Cl. E17	77	G1
Waterhouse Cl. E16	116	A5
Waterhouse Cl. NW3	91	G5
Lyndhurst Rd.		
Waterhouse Cl. W6	128	A4
Great Ch. La.		
Waterhouse Sq. EC1	**19**	**E2**
Waterhouse Sq. EC1	111	G5
Wateridge Cl. E14	134	A3
Westferry Rd.		
Waterloo Br. SE1	**18**	**C6**
Waterloo Br. SE1	111	F7
Waterloo Br. WC2	**18**	**C6**
Waterloo Br. WC2	111	F7
Waterloo Cl. E9	95	F5
Churchill Wk.		
Waterloo Est. E2	113	F2
Waterloo Gdns. E2	113	F2
Waterloo Gdns. N1	93	H7
Barnsbury St.		
Waterloo Pas. NW6	90	D7
Waterloo Pl. SW1	**25**	**H1**
Waterloo Pl. SW1	130	D1
Waterloo Pl., Rich.	145	H5
Sheen Rd.		
Waterloo Pl. (Kew), Rich.	126	A6
Waterloo Rd. E6	97	J7
Waterloo Rd. E7	97	F5
Wellington Rd.		
Waterloo Rd. E10	78	A7
Waterloo Rd. NW2	89	G1
Waterloo Rd. SE1	**27**	**E3**
Waterloo Rd. SE1	131	G2
Waterloo Rd., Ilf.	81	F2
Waterloo Rd., Sutt.	199	G5
Waterloo Ter. N1	93	H7
Waterlow Ct. NW11	72/73	E7
Heath Cl.		
Waterlow Rd. N19	92	C1
Waterman St. SW15	148	A3
Waterman Way E1	132	E1
Waterman's Cl., Kings.T.	163	H7
Woodside Rd.		
Watermans Wk. SE16	133	H3
Watermead La., Cars.	185	J7
Watermead Rd. SE6	172	C4
Watermead Way N17	76	E3
Watermeadow La. SW6	149	F2
Watermen's Sq. SE20	171	F7
Watermill Cl., Rich.	163	F3
Watermill La. N18	60	B5
Watermill Way SW19	185	F1
Watermill Way, Felt.	161	F2
Watermint Quay N16	76	D7
Waters Gdns., Dag.	101	G5
Waters Pl. SW15	147	J2
Danemere St.		
Waters Rd. SE6	172	E3
Waters Rd., Kings.T.	182	B2
Waters Sq., Kings.T.	182	B3
Watersedge, Epsom	196	C4
Watersfield Way, Edg.	53	G7
Waterside, Beck.	190	A1
Rectory Rd.		
Waterside Cl. E3	113	J1
Waterside Cl. SE16	**29**	**J4**
Waterside Cl., Bark.	100	A4
Waterside Cl., Nthlt.	103	F3
Waterside Cl., Surb.	195	H2
Culsac Rd.		
Waterside Dr., Walt.	178	A5
Waterside Pl. NW1	110	A1
Princess Rd.		
Waterside Pt. SW11	**31**	**H7**
Waterside Rd., SW11	129	H7
Waterside Rd., Sthl.	123	G3
Waterside Trd. Cen. W7	124	B3
Waterside Way SW17	167	F4
Watersmeet Way SE28	118	C6
Waterson St. E2	**13**	**E3**
Waterson St. E2	112	B3
Watersplash Cl., Kings.T.	181	H3
Watersplash La., Hayes	122	A4
Watersplash La., Houns.	122	B5
Waterview Ho. E14	113	H5
Waterworks La. E5	95	G2
Waterworks Rd. SW2	151	F6
Waterworks Yd., Croy.	201	J3
Surrey Rd.		
Watery La. SW20	184	C2
Watery La., Nthlt.	102	C2
Watery La., Sid.	176	B6
Wates Way, Mitch.	185	J6
Wateville Rd. N17	75	J1
Watford Cl. SW11	149	H1
Petworth St.		
Watford Rd. E16	115	G5
Watford Rd., Har.	86	D2
Watford Rd., Wem.	86	D2
Watford Way NW4	71	G4
Watford Way NW7	71	G4
Watkin Rd., Wem.	88	B3
Watkinson Rd. N7	93	F6
Watling Ct. EC4	**20**	**A4**
Watling Fm. Cl., Stan.	53	F1
Watling Gdns. NW2	90	B6
Watling St. EC4	**19**	**J4**
Watling St. EC4	111	J6
Watling St. SE15	**36**	**E6**
Watling St., Bexh.	159	H4
Watlings Cl., Croy.	189	H6
Watlington Gro. SE26	171	H5
Watney Mkt. E1	112/113	E6
Commercial Rd.		
Watney Rd. SW14	146	C3
Watney St. E1	113	E6
Watneys Rd., Mitch.	186	D5
Watson Av. E6	98	D7
Watson Av., Sutt.	198	B2
Watson Cl. N16	94	A5
Matthias Rd.		
Watson Cl. SW19	167	H6
Watson St. E13	115	H2
Watson's Ms. W1	**15**	**H2**
Watsons Rd. N22	75	F1
Watson's St. SE8	134	A7
Watsons Yd. NW2	89	F2
North Circular Rd.		
Wattisfield Rd. E5	95	F3
Watts Cl. N15	76	B5
Seaford Rd.		
Watts Gro. E3	114	B5
Watts La., Chis.	193	E1
Watts La., Tedd.	162	D5
Watts Rd., T.Ditt.	180	D7
Watts St. E1	133	E1
Watts St. SE15	152	C1
Watts Way SW7	**23**	**F5**
Wauthier Cl. N13	59	H5
Wavel Ms. N8	74	D4
Wavel Ms. NW6	90/91	E7
Acol Rd.		
Wavel Pl. SE26	170	C4
Sydenham Hill		
Wavell Dr., Sid.	157	H6
Wavendon Av. W4	126	D5
Waveney Av. SE15	153	E4
Waveney Cl. E1	**29**	**J1**
Kennet St.		
Waverley Av. E4	61	J4
Waverley Av. E17	78	D3
Waverley Av., Surb.	182	B6
Waverley Av., Sutt.	199	E2
Waverley Av., Twick.	161	F1
Waverley Av., Wem.	87	J5
Waverley Cl. E18	79	J1
Waverley Cl., Brom.	192	A5
Waverley Cl., Hayes	121	G4
Waverley Cl., W.Mol.	179	G5
Waverley Cres. SE18	137	G5
Waverley Gdns. E6	116	B5
Oliver Gdns.		
Waverley Gdns. NW10	105	J3
Waverley Gdns., Bark.	117	H2
Waverley Gdns., Ilf.	81	F2
Waverley Gdns., Nthwd.	66	A1
Waverley Gro. N3	72	B3
Waverley Ind. Est., Har.	68	A3
Waverley Pl. N4	93	H2
Adolphus Rd.		
Waverley Pl. NW8	**6**	**E1**
Waverley Pl. NW8	109	G2
Waverley Rd. E17	78	C3
Waverley Rd. E18	79	J1
Waverley Rd. N8	74	D6
Waverley Rd. N17	60	E7
Waverley Rd. SE18	137	G5
Waverley Rd. SE25	188	E4
Waverley Rd., Enf.	43	H4
Waverley Rd., Epsom	197	H5
Waverley Rd., Har.	85	F1
Waverley Rd., Sthl.	103	G7
Waverley Vil. N17	76	C2
Waverley Wk. W2	108	D5
Waverley Way, Cars.	199	H5
Waverton Ho. E3	113	J1
Waverton Rd. SW18	149	F7
Waverton St. W1	**24**	**C1**
Waverton St. W1	130	A1
Wavertree Ct. SW2	169	F1
Streatham Hill		
Wavertree Rd. E18	79	G2
Wavertree Rd. SW2	169	E1
Waxlow Cres., Sthl.	103	G6
Waxlow Rd. NW10	106	C2
Waxwell Cl., Pnr.	66	D2
Waxwell La., Pnr.	66	D2
Waxwell Ter. SE1	**26**	**D4**
Waye Av., Houns.	142	A1
Wayfarer Rd., Nthlt.	102	D4
Wayfield Link SE9	157	G6
Wayford St. SW11	149	H2
Wayland Av. E8	94	D5
Waylands Mead, Beck.	190	B1
Wayleave, The SE28	118	B7
Waylett Pl. SE27	169	H3
Waylett Pl., Wem.	87	G4
Wayman Ct. E8	94	E6
Wayne Cl., Orp.	207	J3
Wayneflete Sq. W10	108	A7
Wayneflete St. SW18	167	F2
Wayside NW11	90	B1
Wayside SW14	146	C5
Wayside, Croy.	204	B6
Field Way		
Wayside Cl. N14	42	C6
Wayside Commercial Est., Bark.	118	A1
Wayside Ct., Twick.	145	F6
Wayside Ct., Wem.	88	A3
Oakington Av.		
Wayside Gdns. SE9	174	C4
Wayside Gro.		
Wayside Gdns., Dag.	101	G5
Wayside Gro. SE9	174	C4
Wayside Ms., Ilf.	80	D5
Gaysham Av.		
Weald, The, Chis.	174	C6
Weald Cl. SE16	132/133	E5
Stevenson Cres.		
Weald Cl., Brom.	206	B2
Weald La., Har.	68	A2
Weald Ri., Har.	52	C7
Weald Sq. E5	94/95	E2
Rossington St.		
Weald Way, Rom.	83	H6
Wealdstone Rd., Sutt.	198	C2
Wealdwood Gdns., Pnr.	51	H6
Highbanks Rd.		
Weale Rd. E4	62	D3
Wear Pl. E2	112	E3
Weardale Gdns., Enf.	44	A1
Weardale Rd. SE13	154	D4
Weare St. SE13	154	B4
Weatherley Cl. E3	113	J5
Weaver Cl. E6	116/117	E7
Trader Rd.		
Weaver St. E1	**13**	**H6**
Weaver St. E1	112	D4
Weaver Wk. SE27	169	H4
Weavers Cl., Islw.	144	B4
Weavers Ter. SW6	128	D6
Weavers Way NW1	110	D1
Webb Cl. W10	107	J4
Webb Est. E5	76	D7
Webb Gdns. E13	115	G4
Kelland Rd.		
Webb Pl. NW10	107	F3
Old Oak La.		
Webb Rd. SE3	135	F6
Webb St. SE1	**28**	**D6**
Webb St. SE1	132	B3
Webber Row SE1	**27**	**F5**
Webber St. SE1	131	H2
Webber St. SE1	**27**	**F3**
Webber St. SE1	131	H2
Webbs Rd. SW11	149	J5
Webbs Rd., Hayes	102	B3
Webbscroft Rd., Dag.	101	H4
Webster Gdns. W5	125	G1
Webster Rd. E11	96	C3
Webster Rd. SE16	**29**	**J6**
Webster Rd. SE16	132	D3
Wedderburn Rd. NW3	91	G5
Wedderburn Rd., Bark.	117	H1
Wedgewood Wk. NW6	90/91	E5
Lymington Rd.		

Wedgwood Ms. W1 17 J4
Wedgwood Way SE19 169 J7
Wedlake St. W10 108 B4
Kensal Rd.
Wedmore Av., Ilf. 80 D1
Wedmore Gdns. N19 92 D2
Wedmore Ms. N19 92 D3
Wedmore St.
Wedmore Rd., Grnf. 104 A3
Wedmore St. N19 92 D3
Weech Rd. NW6 90 D4
Weedington Rd. NW5 92 A5
Weekley Sq. SW11 149 G3
Thomas Baines Rd.
Weigall Rd. SE12 155 G4
Weighhouse St. W1 16 C4
Weighhouse St. W1 110 A6
Weighton Rd. SE20 188 E2
Weighton Rd., Har. 68 A1
Weihurst Gdns., Sutt. 199 G5
Weimar St. SW15 148 B3
Weir Est. SW12 150 C7
Weir Hall Av. N18 60 A6
Weir Hall Gdns. N18 60 A5
Weir Hall Rd. N17 60 A5
Weir Hall Rd. N18 60 A5
Weir Rd. SW12 150 C7
Weir Rd. SW19 167 E3
Weir Rd., Bex. 159 H7
Weir Rd., Walt. 178 A6
Weirdale Av. N20 57 J2
Weir's Pas. NW1 9 J3
Weir's Pas. NW1 110 D3
Weirside Gdns., West Dr. 120 A1
Weiss Rd. SW15 148 A3
Welbeck Av., Brom. 173 G4
Welbeck Av., Hayes 102 B4
Welbeck Av., Sid. 176 A1
Welbeck Cl. N12 57 G5
Torrington Pk.
Welbeck Cl., Borwd. 38 A3
Welbeck Cl., Epsom 197 G7
Welbeck Cl., N.Mal. 183 F5
Welbeck Rd. E6 116 A3
Welbeck Rd., Barn. 41 G6
Welbeck Rd., Cars. 199 H1
Welbeck Rd., Har. 85 H1
Welbeck Rd., Sutt. 199 G2
Welbeck St. W1 16 D3
Welbeck St. W1 110 A5
Welbeck Wk., Cars. 199 H1
Welbeck Rd.
Welbeck Way W1 16 D3
Welbeck Way W1 110 B6
Welby St. SE5 151 H1
Welch Pl., Pnr. 66 C1
Weld Pl. N11 58 B5
Weldon Cl., Ruis. 84 B6
Weldon Dr., W.Mol. 179 F4
Welfare Rd. E15 97 E7
Welford Cl. E5 95 G3
Denton Way
Welford Pl. SW19 166 B4
Welham Rd. SW16 168 A5
Welham Rd. SW17 168 A5
Welhouse Rd., Cars. 199 H1
Well App., Barn. 39 J5
Well Cl. SW16 169 F4
Well Cl., Ruis. 84/85 E3
Parkfield Cres.
Well Cottage Cl. E11 79 J7
Well Ct. EC4 20 A4
Well Ct. SW16 169 F4
Well Gro. N20 41 F7
Well Hall Par. SE9 156 C4
Well Hall Rd.
Well Hall Rd. SE9 156 C3
Well La. SW14 146 C5
Well Pas. NW3 91 G3
Well Rd. NW3 91 G3
Well Rd., Barn. 39 J5
Well St. E9 95 F7
Well St. E15 96 E6
Well Wk. NW3 91 G4
Wellacre Rd., Har. 69 E6
Wellan Cl., Sid. 158 B5
Welland Gdns., Grnf. 104 C2
Welland Ms. E1 29 J1
Welland St. SE10 134 C6
Wellands Cl., Brom. 192 C2
Wellbrook Rd., Orp. 206 D4
Wellclose Sq. E1 21 J5
Wellclose Sq. E1 112 D7
Wellclose St. E1 21 J6
Welldon Cres., Har. 68 B6
Weller St. SE1 27 J3
Weller's Ct. N1 10 A2
Wellesley Av. W6 127 H3
Wellesley Ct. W9 6 C3
Wellesley Ct. Rd., Croy. 202 A2
Wellesley Cres., Twick. 162 B2
Wellesley Gro., Croy. 202 A2
Wellesley Pk. Ms., Enf. 43 H2
Wellesley Pl. NW1 9 H4
Wellesley Rd. E11 79 G5
Wellesley Rd. E17 78 A6
Wellesley Rd. N22 75 G2
Wellesley Rd. NW5 92 A5
Wellesley Rd. W4 126 A5
Wellesley Rd., Croy. 201 J1
Wellesley Rd., Har. 68 B5
Wellesley Rd., Ilf. 98 E2
Wellesley Rd., Sutt. 199 F6
Wellesley Rd., Twick. 162 B3
Wellesley St. E1 113 G5
Wellesley Ter. N1 12 A3
Wellesley Ter. N1 111 J3
Wellfield Av. N10 74 B3
Wellfield Rd. SW16 169 E4
Wellfield Wk. SW16 169 F5
Wellfields, Loug. 48 D3
Wellfit St. SE24 151 H3
Hinton Rd.
Wellgarth, Grnf. 86 E6
Wellgarth Rd. NW11 91 E1
Wellhouse La., Barn. 39 J4
Wellhouse Rd., Beck. 189 J4
Welling High St., Well. 158 B3
Welling Way SE9 157 G3
Welling Way, Well. 157 G3
Wellings Ho., Hayes 122 B1
Wellington Av. E4 62 A2
Wellington Av. N9 61 E3
Wellington Av. N15 76 C6
Wellington Av., Houns. 143 G5
Wellington Av., Pnr. 67 F1
Wellington Av., Sid. 158 A6
Wellington Av., Wor.Pk. 197 J4
Wellington Bldgs. SW1 32 C4
Wellington Cl. SE14 153 G1
Rutts Ter.
Wellington Cl. W11 108 D6
Ledbury Rd.
Wellington Cl., Dag. 101 J7
Wellington Cl., Wat. 51 F3
Highfield
Wellington Ct. NW8 7 E2
Wellington Ct., Stai. 140 B7
Clare Rd.
Wellington Cres., N.Mal. 182 C3
Wellington Dr., Dag. 101 J7
Wellington Gdns. SE7 135 J6
Wellington Gdns., Twick. 162 A4
Wellington Gro. SE10 134 D7
Crooms Hill
Wellington Ms. SE7 135 J6
Wellington Ms. SE22 152 D4
Peckham Rye
Wellington Pk. Est. NW2 89 G2
Wellington Pas. E11 79 G5
Wellington Rd.
Wellington Pl. N2 73 H5
Great N. Rd.
Wellington Pl. NW8 7 G2
Wellington Pl. NW8 109 H2
Wellington Rd. E6 116 C2
Wellington Rd. E7 97 F4
Wellington Rd. E10 95 H1
Wellington Rd. E11 79 G5
Wellington Rd. E17 77 H4
Wellington Rd. NW8 7 F1
Wellington Rd. NW8 109 G2
Wellington Rd. NW10 108 A3
Wellington Rd. SW19 166 D2
Wellington Rd. W5 125 F3
Wellington Rd., Belv. 139 F5
Wellington Rd., Bex. 158 D5
Wellington Rd., Brom. 191 J4
Wellington Rd., Croy. 187 H7
Wellington Rd., Enf. 44 B5
Wellington Rd., Felt. 141 H5
Wellington Rd., Hmptn. 162 A5
Wellington Rd., Har. 68 B3
Wellington Rd., Pnr. 67 F1
Wellington Rd., Twick. 162 A5
Wellington Rd. N., Houns. 143 F3
Wellington Rd. S., Houns. 143 F4
Wellington Row E2 13 G3
Wellington Row E2 112 C3
Wellington Sq. SW3 31 J3
Wellington Sq. SW3 129 J5
Wellington St. SE18 136 D4
Wellington St. WC2 18 B5
Wellington St. WC2 111 E7
Wellington St., Bark. 117 F1
Axe St.
Wellington Ter. E1 132 E1
Wellington Ter. N8 75 G3
Turnpike La.
Wellington Ter., Har. 86 A1
West St.
Wellington Way E3 114 A3
Wellmeadow Rd. SE6 155 E7
Wellmeadow Rd. SE13 154 E6
Wellmeadow Rd. W7 124 D4
Wellow Wk., Cars. 199 G1
Wells, The N14 42 D7
Wells Cl., Nthlt. 102 C3
Yeading La.
Wells Dr. NW9 88 D1
Wells Gdns., Dag. 101 H5
Wells Gdns., Ilf. 80 B7
Wells Ho. Rd. NW10 106 E5
Wells Ms. W1 17 G3
Wells Pk. Rd. SE26 170 D3
Wells Ri. NW8 109 J1
Wells Rd. W12 127 J2
Wells Rd., Brom. 192 C2
Wells Sq. WC1 10 C4
Wells St. W1 17 F2
Wells St. W1 110 C6
Wells Ter. N4 93 G2
Wells Way SE5 36 C5
Wells Way SE5 132 B6
Wells Way SW7 22 E5
Wells Way SW7 129 G3
Wells Yd. N7 93 G5
Holloway Rd.
Wellside Cl., Barn. 39 J4
Wellside Gdns. SW14 146 C5
Well La.
Wellsmoor Gdns., Brom. 192 D3
Wellsprings Cres., Wem. 88 B3
Wellstead Av. N9 45 G7
Wellstead Rd. E6 116 D2
Wellwood Rd., Ilf. 100 A1
Welsford St. SE1 37 H3
Welsford St. SE1 132 D5
Welsh Cl. E13 115 G3
Welshpool Ho. E8 112 D1
Benjamin Cl.
Welshpool St. E8 112/113 E1
Broadway Mkt.
Welshside Wk. NW9 70/71 E6
Fryent Gro.
Welstead Way W4 126/127 E5
Bath Rd.
Weltje Rd. W6 127 G4
Welton Rd. SE18 137 H7
Welwyn Av., Felt. 141 J6
Welwyn St. E2 113 F3
Globe Rd.
Wembley Commercial Cen., Wem. 87 G2
Wembley Hill Rd., Wem. 87 J5
Wembley Pk. Business Cen., Wem. 88 B3
Wembley Pk. Dr., Wem. 87 J3
Wembley Pt., Wem. 88 B7
Wembley Rd., Hmptn. 161 G7
Wembley Way, Wem. 88 B6
Wemborough Rd., Stan. 53 F7
Wembury Rd. N6 74 B7
Wemyss Rd. SE3 155 F2
Wendela Ct., Har. 86 B3
Wendell Rd. W12 127 F2
Wendle Ct. SW8 34 A6
Wendle Ct. SW8 130 E6
Wendling Rd., Sutt. 199 G1
Wendon St. E3 113 J1
Wendover SE17 36 D4
Wendover SE17 132 B5
Wendover Cl., Hayes 102/103 E4
Kingsash Dr.
Wendover Dr., N.Mal. 183 F6
Wendover Rd. NW10 107 F2
Wendover Rd. SE9 156 A3
Wendover Rd., Brom. 191 H3
Wendover Way, Well. 158 A5
Wendy Cl., Enf. 44 C6
Wendy Way, Wem. 105 H1
Wenlock Ct. N1 12 C2
Wenlock Gdns. NW4 71 G4
Rickard Cl.
Wenlock Rd. N1 11 J2
Wenlock Rd. N1 111 J2
Wenlock Rd., Edg. 54 B7
Wenlock St. N1 12 A2
Wenlock St. N1 111 J2
Wennington Rd. E3 113 G2
Wensley Av., Wdf.Grn. 63 F7
Wensley Cl. SE9 156 C6
Wensley Rd. N18 60 E6
Wensleydale Av., Ilf. 80 B2
Wensleydale Gdns., Hmptn. 161 H7
Wensleydale Pas., Hmptn. 179 G1
Wensleydale Rd., Hmptn. 161 G6
Wentland Cl. SE6 172 D2
Wentland Rd. SE6 172 D2
Wentworth Av. N3 56 D7
Wentworth Cl. N3 56 E7
Wentworth Cl. SE28 118 D6
Wentworth Cl., Brom. 205 G2
Hillside La.
Wentworth Cl., Mord. 184 D7
Wentworth Cl., Orp. 207 H5
Wentworth Cl., Surb. 195 G2
Wentworth Cres. SE15 132 D7
Wentworth Cres., Hayes 121 G3
Wentworth Dr., Pnr. 66 A5
Wentworth Gdns. N13 59 H4
Wentworth Hill, Wem. 87 J1
Wentworth Ms. E3 113 J4
Eric St.
Wentworth Pk. N3 56 D7
Wentworth Pl., Stan. 52/53 E6
Greenacres Dr.
Wentworth Rd. E12 98 A4
Wentworth Rd. NW11 72 C6
Wentworth Rd., Barn. 40 A3
Wentworth Rd., Croy. 187 G7
Wentworth Rd., Sthl. 122 C4
Wentworth St. E1 21 F3
Wentworth St. E1 112 C6
Wentworth Way, Pnr. 66 E4
Wenvoe Av., Bexh. 159 H2
Wernbrook St. SE18 137 F6
Werndee Rd. SE25 188 D4
Werneth Hall Rd., Ilf. 80 C3
Werrington St. NW1 9 G2
Werrington St. NW1 110 C2
Werter Rd. SW15 148 B4
Wesley Av. E16 135 G1
Wesley Av. NW10 106 D3
Wesley Av., Houns. 143 E2
Wesley Cl. N7 93 F2
Wesley Cl. SE17 35 H2
Wesley Cl. SE17 131 H4
Wesley Cl., Har. 85 J2
Wesley Rd. E10 78 C7
Wesley Rd. NW10 106 C1
Wesley Rd., Hayes 102 A7
Wesley Sq. W11 108 B6
Bartle Rd.
Wesley St. W1 16 C2
Wesleyan Pl. NW5 92 B4
Gordon Ho. Rd.
Wessex Av. SW19 184 D2
Wessex Cl., Ilf. 81 H6
Wessex Cl., Kings.T. 182 B1
Gloucester Rd.
Wessex Dr., Pnr. 51 E7
Wessex Gdns. NW11 90 B1
Wessex La., Grnf. 104 A2
Wessex Rd., Houns. 140 A2
Wessex St. E2 113 F3
Wessex Way NW11 90 B1
West App., Orp. 193 F5
West Arbour St. E1 113 G6
West Av. E17 78 B4
West Av. N3 56 D6
West Av. NW4 72 A5
West Av., Pnr. 67 F6
West Av., Sthl. 103 F7
West Av., Wall. 201 E5
West Av. Rd. E17 78 A4
West Bank N16 76 B7
West Bank, Bark. 116/117 E1
Highbridge Rd.
West Bank, Enf. 43 J2
West Barnes La. SW20 183 H2
West Barnes La., N.Mal. 183 H3
West Carriage Dr. W2 23 F2
West Carriage Dr. W2 109 G7
West Cen. St. WC1 18 A3
West Cen. Av. W10 107 H3
Harrow Rd.
West Chantry, Har. 67 H1
Chantry Rd.
West Cl. N9 60 C3
West Cl., Barn. 39 H5
West Cl. (Cockfosters), Barn. 42 A4
West Cl., Grnf. 103 J2
West Cl., Hmptn. 160/161 E6
Oak Av.

West Cl., Wem. 87 J1
West Common Rd., 205 G2
Brom.
West Common Rd., 205 H4
Kes.
West Cotts. NW6 90 D5
West Ct. SE18 156 C1
Prince Imperial Rd.
West Cr., Wem. 87 F2
West Cromwell Rd. 128 C4
SW5
West Cromwell Rd. 128 C4
W14
West Cross Cen., 124 D6
Brent.
West Cross Route 108 A7
W10
West Cross Route 108 A7
W11
West Cross Way, 124 E6
Brent.
West Dene, Sutt. 198 B6
Park La.
West Drayton Pk. 120 B3
Av., West Dr.
West Dr. SW16 168 C4
West Dr., Har. 52 A6
West Dr. Gdns., Har. 52 A6
West Eaton Pl. SW1 32 B1
West Eaton Pl. SW1 130 A4
West Eaton Pl. Ms. 32 B1
SW1
West Ella Rd. NW10 88 E7
West End Av. E10 78 C5
West End Av., Pnr. 66 D4
West End Ct., Pnr. 66 D4
West End Gdns., 102 C2
Nthlt.
Edward Cl.
West End La. NW6 108 D1
West End La., Barn. 40 A4
West End La., Hayes 121 F7
West End La., Pnr. 66 D3
West End Rd., Nthlt. 84 C7
West End Rd., Ruis. 84 B5
West End Rd., Sthl. 122 E1
West Gdn. Pl. W2 15 H4
West Gdns. E1 113 E7
West Gdns. SW17 167 H6
West Gate W5 105 H3
West Grn. Pl., Grnf. 104 A1
Uneeda Dr.
West Grn. Rd. N15 76 A4
West Gro. SE10 154 C1
West Gro., Wdf.Grn. 63 J6
West Halkin St. SW1 24 B5
West Halkin St. SW1 130 A3
West Hall Rd., Rich. 146 B1
West Hallowes SE9 174 A1
West Ham La. E15 96 E7
West Ham Pk. E7 97 G7
West Hampstead Ms. 90 E6
NW6
West Harding St. 19 F3
EC4
West Heath Av. 90 D1
NW11
West Heath Cl. NW3 90 D1
West Heath Dr. NW11 90 D1
West Heath Gdns. 90 D1
NW3
West Heath Rd. NW3 90 D2
West Heath Rd. SE2 138 D6
West Hendon Bdy. 71 F6
NW9
West Hill SW15 148 A1
West Hill SW18 148 D5
West Hill, Har. 86 B2
West Hill, Wem. 87 J1
West Hill Ct. N6 92 A3
West Hill Pk. N6 91 J2
Merton La.
West Hill Rd. SW18 148 D6
West Hill Way N20 56 E1
West Holme, Erith 159 J1
West Ho. Cl. SW19 166 B1
West India Av. E14 134 A1
West India Dock Rd. 113 J6
E14
West Kentish Town 92 A5
Est. NW5
West La. SE16 132 E2
West Lo. Av. W3 126 A1
West Mall W8 128 D1
Palace Gdns. Ter.
West Mead, Epsom 197 E6
West Mead, Ruis. 84 C4
West Mersea Cl. E16 135 H1
Hanameel St.
West Ms. N17 60 E6
West Ms. SW1 33 F2
West Oak, Beck. 190 D1
West Pk. SE9 174 B2
West Pk. Av., Rich. 146 A1

West Pk. Cl., Houns. 123 F6
Heston Gra. La.
West Pk. Cl., Rom. 82 D5
West Pk. Rd., Rich. 146 A1
West Pk. Rd., Sthl. 123 J1
West Parkside SE10 135 E2
West Pier E1 132/133 E1
Wapping High St.
West Pl. SW19 165 J5
West Poultry Av. EC1 19 G2
West Quarters W12 107 G6
West Quay Dr., Hayes 102 E5
West Ramp, Houns. 140 D1
West Ridge Gdns. 103 J2
Grnf.
West Rd. E15 115 F1
West Rd. N17 60 E6
West Rd. SW3 32 A4
West Rd. SW3 129 J6
West Rd. SW4 150 D5
West Rd. W5 105 H5
West Rd., Barn. 58 A1
West Rd., Felt. 141 G6
West Rd., Kings.T. 182 C1
West Rd. 82 D6
(Chadwell Heath), Rom.
West Rd., West Dr. 120 C3
West Row W10 108 B4
West Sheen Vale, 145 J4
Rich.
West Side Common 165 J5
SW19
West Smithfield EC1 19 G2
West Smithfield EC1 111 H5
West Sq. SE11 27 G6
West Sq. SE11 131 H3
West St. E2 113 E2
West St. E11 96 E3
West St. E17 78 B5
Grove Rd.
West St. WC2 17 J4
West St., Bexh. 159 F4
West St., Brent. 125 F6
West St., Brom. 191 G1
West St., Cars. 199 J3
West St., Croy. 201 J4
West St., Har. 86 A1
West St., Sutt. 198 E5
West St. La., Cars. 199 J4
West Temple Sheen 146 B4
SW14
West Tenter St. E1 21 G4
West Tenter St. E1 112 C6
West Thamesmead 137 H3
Business Pk. SE28
Nathan Way
West Twrs., Pnr. 66 D6
West Vw. NW4 71 J4
West Vw., Felt. 141 F7
West Vw., Loug. 48 C3
West Wk. W5 105 H5
West Wk., Barn. 42 A7
West Wk., Hayes 122 A1
West Warwick Pl. 33 E2
SW1
West Warwick Pl. 130 B4
SW1
West Way N18 64 D1
West Way NW10 88 D3
West Way, Croy. 203 H2
West Way, Edg. 54 B6
West Way, Houns. 143 F1
West Way, Pnr. 66 D4
West Way, W.Wick. 190 D6
West Way Gdns. 203 G2
Croy.
West Woodside, Bex. 159 E7
West World W5 105 H3
Westacott Cl. N19 92 D1
Westall Rd., Loug. 49 E3
Westbank Rd., 161 J6
Hmptn.
Westbeech Rd. N22 75 G3
Westbere Dr., Stan. 53 G4
Westbere Rd. NW2 90 B5
Westbourne Av. W3 106 D6
Westbourne Av., 198 B2
Sutt.
Westbourne Br. W2 14 C2
Westbourne Br. W2 109 F5
Westbourne Cl., 102 B4
Hayes
Westbourne Cres. W2 14 E5
Westbourne Cres. W2 109 G7
Westbourne Cres. Ms. 14 E5
W2
Westbourne Dr. SE23 171 G2
Westbourne Gdns. 14 A3
W2
Westbourne Gdns. 108 E6
W2
Westbourne Gro. W2 108 D6
Westbourne Gro. 108 C7
W11

Westbourne Gro. Ms. 108 D6
W11
Westbourne Gro.
Westbourne Gro. Ter. 14 A3
W2
Westbourne Gro. Ter. 108 C6
W2
Westbourne Pk. Ms. 14 A3
W2
Westbourne Pk. Pas. 108 D5
W2
Westbourne Pk. Vil.
Westbourne Pk. Rd. 108 D5
W2
Westbourne Pk. Rd. 108 B6
W11
Westbourne Pk. Vil. 108 B6
W2
Westbourne Pl. N9 60/61 E3
Eastbournia Av.
Westbourne Rd. N7 93 G6
Westbourne Rd. SE26 171 G6
Westbourne Rd., 138 E7
Bexh.
Westbourne Rd., 188 C6
Croy.
Westbourne St. W2 15 E5
Westbourne St. W2 109 G7
Westbourne Ter. 171 G2
SE23
Westbourne Dr.
Westbourne Ter. W2 14 D3
Westbourne Ter. W2 109 G6
Westbourne Ter. Ms. 14 C3
W2
Westbourne Ter. Ms. 109 F6
W2
Westbourne Ter. Rd. 14 C2
W2
Westbourne Ter. Rd. 109 F5
W2
Westbridge Rd. SW11 149 G1
Westbrook Av., 161 F7
Hmptn.
Westbrook Cl., Barn. 41 G3
Westbrook Cres., 41 G3
Barn.
Westbrook Rd. SE3 155 H1
Westbrook Rd., 123 F7
Houns.
Westbrook Rd., 188 A1
Th.Hth.
Westbrook Sq., Barn. 41 G3
Westbrooke Cres.
Westbrooke Cres. 158 C3
Well.
Westbrooke Rd., Sid. 175 G2
Westbrooke Rd., 158 B3
Well.
Westbury Av. N22 75 H3
Westbury Av., Esher 194 C6
Westbury Av., Sthl. 103 G4
Westbury Av., Wem. 87 H7
Westbury Cl., Ruis. 66 A7
Westbury Gro. N12 56 D6
Westbury La., Buck.H. 63 J2
Westbury Lo. Cl., 66 D3
Pnr.
Westbury Par. SW12 150 B6
Balham Hill
Westbury Pl., Brent. 125 G6
Westbury Rd. E7 97 H5
Westbury Rd. E17 78 A4
Westbury Rd. N11 58 E6
Westbury Rd. N12 56 D6
Westbury Rd. SE20 189 G1
Westbury Rd. W5 105 H6
Westbury Rd., Bark. 117 G1
Westbury Rd., Beck. 189 H3
Westbury Rd., Brom. 192 A1
Westbury Rd., 63 J2
Buck.H.
Westbury Rd., Croy. 188 A6
Westbury Rd., Felt. 160 D1
Westbury Rd., Ilf. 98 D2
Westbury Rd., N.Mal. 182 D4
Westbury Rd., Wem. 87 H7
Westbury St. SW8 150 C2
Westbury Ter. E7 97 H6
Westchester Dr. NW4 72 A3
Westcombe Av., 187 E6
Croy.
Westcombe Ct. SE3 135 F7
Westcombe Pk. Rd.
Westcombe Dr., Barn. 40 D5
Westcombe Hill SE3 135 G5
Westcombe Hill SE10 135 G5
Westcombe Rd. SE3 135 E6
SE3
Westcoombe Av. 183 F1
SW20
Westcote Rd. SW16 168 C5
Westcott Cl. N15 76 C6
Ermine Rd.

Westcott Cl., Brom. 192 B5
Ringmer Way
Westcott Cres. W7 104 B6
Westcott Rd. SE17 35 H5
Westcott Rd. SE17 131 H6
Westcourt, Sun. 178 B2
Westcroft Gdns., 184 C3
Mord.
Westcroft Rd., Cars. 200 A4
Westcroft Rd., Wall. 200 A4
Westcroft Sq. W6 127 G4
Westcroft Way NW2 90 B4
Westdale Pas. SE18 136 E6
Westdale Rd. SE18 137 E6
Westdean Av. SE12 173 H1
Westdean Cl. SW18 149 E6
Westdown Rd. E15 96 C4
Westdown Rd. SE6 154 A7
Westerdale Rd. SE10 135 G5
Westerfield Rd. N15 76 C5
Westergate Rd. SE2 138 E5
Westerham Av. N9 60 A3
Westerham Dr., Sid. 158 B6
Westerham Rd. E10 78 B7
Westerham Rd., Kes. 206 A6
Westerham Rd., 171 J5
Kes.
Westerley Cres. SE26 171 J5
Westerley Ware, 126 A6
Rich.
Kew Grn.
Western Av. NW11 72 A6
Western Av. W3 106 D5
Western Av. W5 105 J4
Western Av., Dag. 101 J6
Western Av., Grnf. 105 G3
Western Av., Nthlt. 103 F1
Western Av. 105 J3
Underpass W5
Western Av.
Huntley Dr.
Western Gdns. W5 106 A7
Western Gateway E16 115 G7
Western La. SW12 150 A7
Western Ms. W9 108 C4
Great Western Rd.
Western Pl. SE16 133 F2
Canon Beck Rd.
Western Rd. E13 115 J1
Western Rd. E17 78 C5
Western Rd. N2 73 J4
Western Rd. N22 75 F2
Western Rd. NW10 106 C4
Western Rd. SW9 151 G3
Western Rd. SW19 185 G1
Western Rd. W5 105 G1
Western Rd., Mitch. 185 G1
Western Rd., Sthl. 122 D3
Western Rd., Sutt. 198 D5
Western Ter. W6 127 G5
Chiswick Mall
Western Trd. Est. 106 C4
NW10
Western Vw., Hayes 121 J2
Station Rd.
Western Way SE28 137 G3
Western Way, Barn. 40 D6
Westernville Gdns., 81 F7
Ilf.
Westferry Circ. E14 133 J1
Westferry Rd. E14 134 A1
Westfield, Loug. 47 J3
Westfield Cl. NW9 70 C3
Westfield Cl. SW10 129 F7
Westfield Cl., Enf. 45 H3
Westfield Cl., Sutt. 198 C4
Westfield Dr., Har. 69 G4
Westfield Gdns., Har. 69 G4
Westfield La., Har. 69 G4
Westfield Pk., Pnr. 51 F7
Westfield Pk. Dr., 64 B6
Wdf.Grn.
Westfield Rd. NW7 54 D3
Westfield Rd. W13 124 D1
Westfield Rd., Beck. 189 J2
Westfield Rd., Bexh. 159 J2
Westfield Rd., Croy. 201 H2
Westfield Rd., Dag. 101 E4
Westfield Rd., Mitch. 185 G5
Westfield Rd., Sthl. 181 G5
Westfield Rd., Sutt. 198 C4
Westfield Rd., Walt. 179 E7
Westfield St. SE18 136 A3
Westfield Way E1 113 H3
Westfields SW13 147 F3
Westfields Av. SW13 147 E3
Westfields Rd. W3 106 B5
Westgate SE25 188 E4
Westgate St. E8 112 E1
Westgate Ter. SW10 30 B4
Westgate Ter. SW10 129 E5
Westglade Ct., Har. 69 G5
Westgrove La. SE10 154 C1

Westhay Gdns. SW14 146 B5
Westholm NW11 72 E4
Westholme, Orp. 193 H7
Westholme Gdns., 84 A1
 Ruis.
Westhorne Av. SE9 155 G6
Westhorne Av. SE12 155 G7
Westhorpe Gdns. 71 J3
 NW4
Westhorpe Rd. SW15 147 J3
Westhurst Dr., Chis. 175 E5
Westlake Cl. N13 59 G3
Westlake Cl., 102/103 E4
 Hayes
 Lochan Cl.
Westlake Rd., Wem. 87 G2
Westland Cl., Stai. 140 B6
Westland Dr., Brom. 205 F2
Westland Pl. N1 12 B3
Westlands Cl., Hayes 122 A4
 Granville Rd.
Westlands Ter. SW12 150 C6
 Gaskarth Rd.
Westlea Rd. W7 124 D3
Westleigh Av. SW15 147 H5
Westleigh Dr., Brom. 192 B1
Westleigh Gdns., Edg. 70 A1
Westlinks, Wem. 105 G3
 Alperton La.
Westlinton Cl. NW7 56 B6
 Frith La.
Westmead SW15 147 H6
Westmead Cor., Cars. 199 H4
 Colston Av.
Westmead Rd., Sutt. 199 G4
Westmede, Chig. 65 F6
Westmere Dr. NW7 54 D3
Westmill Ct. N4 93 J2
 Brownswood Rd.
Westminster Av., 187 H2
 Th.Hth.
Westminster Br. SE1 26 B4
Westminster Br. SE1 131 E2
Westminster Br. SW1 26 B4
Westminster Br. SW1 131 E2
Westminster Br. Rd. 26 D4
SE1
Westminster Cl., Felt. 131 G3
 SE1
Westminster Cl., Felt. 160 A1
Westminster Cl., Ilf. 81 G2
Westminster Cl., 162 D5
 Tedd.
Westminster Dr. N13 58 E5
Westminster Gdns. 63 E1
 E4
Westminster Gdns., 117 H2
 Bark.
Westminster Gdns., 81 F2
 Ilf.
Westminster Rd. N9 61 E1
Westminster Rd. W7 124 B1
Westminster Rd., 199 G2
 Sutt.
Westmoat Cl., Beck. 172 C7
Westmont Rd., Esher 194 B2
Westmoor Gdns., Enf. 45 G2
Westmoor Rd., Enf. 45 G2
Westmoor St. SE7 136 A3
Westmoreland Av., 157 H3
 Well.
Westmoreland 111 J5
 Bldgs. EC1
 Bartholomew Cl.
Westmoreland Pl. 33 E4
SW1
Westmoreland Pl. 130 B5
 SW1
Westmoreland Pl. W5 105 G5
 Mount Av.
Westmoreland Pl., 191 G3
 Brom.
Westmoreland Rd. 70 A4
 NW9
Westmoreland Rd. 36 A5
SE17
Westmoreland Rd. 132 A6
 SE17
Westmoreland Rd. 147 F1
 SW13
Westmoreland Rd., 191 E5
 Brom.
Westmoreland St. W1 16 C2
Westmoreland St. W1 110 A5
Westmoreland Ter. 32 E4
SW1
Westmoreland Ter. 130 B5
 SW1
Westmoreland Wk. 36 B5
SE17
Westmorland Cl. E12 98 A2
Westmorland Cl., 145 E6
 Twick.
Westmorland Rd. E17 78 A6

Westmorland Rd., 67 H5
 Har.
Westmorland Sq., 186/187 E5
 Mitch.
 Westmorland Way
Westmorland Ter. 171 E7
 SE20
Westmorland Way, 186 E5
 Mitch.
Westmount Rd. SE9 156 C2
Westoe Rd. N9 61 E2
Weston Av., T.Ditt. 180 B7
Weston Av., W.Mol. 179 E3
Weston Ct. N4 93 J3
 Queens Dr.
Weston Dr., Stan. 68 E1
Weston Gdns., Islw. 144 B1
Weston Grn., Dag. 101 F4
Weston Grn., T.Ditt. 194 B1
Weston Grn. Rd., 194 A1
 Esher
Weston Grn. Rd., 194 B1
 T.Ditt.
Weston Gro., Brom. 191 F1
Weston Pk. N8 75 E6
Weston Pk., Kings.T. 181 H2
 Fairfield W.
Weston Pk., T.Ditt. 194 B1
Weston Pk. Cl., T.Ditt. 194 B1
 Weston Pk.
Weston Ri. WC1 10 D2
Weston Ri. WC1 111 F2
Weston Rd. W4 126 C3
Weston Rd., Brom. 173 F7
Weston Rd., Dag. 101 E4
Weston Rd., Enf. 44 A1
Weston Rd., T.Ditt. 194 B1
Weston St. SE1 28 C5
Weston St. SE1 132 A3
Weston Wk. E8 94/95 E7
 Mare St.
Westover Hill NW3 90 D2
Westover Rd. SW18 149 F6
Westow Hill SE19 170 B6
Westow St. SE19 170 B6
Westpoint Trd. Est. 106 B4
 W3
Westpole Av., Barn. 42 A4
Westport Rd. E13 115 H4
Westport St. E1 113 G6
Westrow SW15 147 J5
Westrow Dr., Bark. 99 J6
Westrow Gdns., Ilf. 99 J2
Westside NW4 71 H2
Westvale Ms. W3 127 E1
Westview Cl. NW10 89 F5
Westview Cl. W7 104 B6
Westview Cl. W10 107 J6
Westview Cres. N9 44 B7
Westview Dr., 80 A2
 Wdf.Grn.
Westville Rd. W12 127 G2
Westville Rd., T.Ditt. 194 D1
Westward Rd. E4 61 J5
Westward Way, Har. 69 H6
Westway SW20 183 H3
Westway W2 108 D5
Westway W9 108 D5
Westway W10 108 B6
Westway W12 107 G7
Westway, Orp. 193 G5
Westway Cl. SW20 183 H3
Westways, Epsom 197 F4
Westwell Rd. SW16 168 E6
Westwell Rd. 168/169 E6
 App. SW16
 Westwell Rd.
Westwick Gdns. W14 128 A2
Westwick Gdns., 142 B2
 Houns.
Westwood Av. SE19 187 J1
Westwood Av., Har. 85 H4
Westwood Cl., Brom. 192 A3
Westwood Gdns. 147 F3
 SW13
Westwood Hill SE26 170 D5
Westwood La., Sid. 158 A5
Westwood La., Well. 157 J3
Westwood Pk. SE23 153 E7
Westwood Rd. E16 135 H1
Westwood Rd. SW13 147 F3
Westwood Rd., Ilf. 99 J1
Wetheral Dr., Stan. 69 E1
Wetherby Cl., Nthlt. 85 H6
Wetherby Gdns. SW5 30 C2
Wetherby Gdns. SW5 129 F4
Wetherby Ms. SW5 30 A3
Wetherby Pl. SW7 30 C2
Wetherby Pl. SW7 129 F4
Wetherby Rd., Enf. 43 J1
Wetherby Way, 195 H7
 Chess.
Wetherden St. E17 77 J7
Wetherell Rd. E9 113 G1

Wetherill Rd. N10 74 A1
Wexford Rd. SW12 149 J7
Wey Ct., Epsom 196 C4
Weybourne St. SW18 167 F2
Weybridge Ct. SE16 37 J4
Weybridge Pt. SW11 150 A2
Weybridge Rd., 187 G4
 Th.Hth.
Weydown Cl. SW19 166 B1
Weyhill Rd. E1 21 J3
Weylond Rd., Dag. 101 F3
Weyman Rd. SE3 155 J1
Weymouth Av. NW7 54 E5
Weymouth Av. W5 125 F3
Weymouth Cl. E6 116/117 E6
 Covelees Wall
Weymouth Ct., Sutt. 198 D7
Weymouth Ms. W1 16 D1
Weymouth Ms. W1 110 B5
Weymouth St. W1 16 C2
Weymouth St. W1 110 B5
Weymouth Ter. E2 13 G1
Weymouth Ter. E2 112 C2
Weymouth Wk., Stan. 52 D6
Whadcote St. N4 93 G2
 Seven Sisters Rd.
Whalebone Av., Rom. 83 F6
Whalebone Ct. EC2 20 C3
Whalebone Gro., Rom. 83 F6
Whalebone La. E15 96/97 E7
 West Ham La.
Whalebone La. N., 83 E5
 Rom.
Whalebone La. S., 83 F7
 Dag.
Whalebone La. S., 83 F7
 Rom.
Wharf La., Twick. 162 D1
Wharf Pl. E2 112 D1
Wharf Rd. E15 114 D1
Wharf Rd. N1 11 J2
Wharf Rd. N1 111 J2
Wharf Rd., Enf. 45 H6
Wharf St. E16 114 E5
Wharfdale Cl., E5 95 G4
 Rushmore Rd.
Wharfdale Rd. N1 10 B1
Wharfdale Rd. N1 111 E2
Wharfedale Gdns., 187 F4
 Th.Hth.
Wharfedale St. SW10 30 A4
Wharfedale St. SW10 128 E5
Wharfside Rd. E16 115 E5
Wharncliffe Dr., Sthl. 124 A1
Wharncliffe Gdns. 188 B2
 SE25
Wharncliffe Rd. 188 B2
 SE25
Wharton Cl. NW10 89 E6
Wharton Rd., Brom. 191 H1
Wharton St. WC1 10 D4
Wharton St. WC1 111 F3
Whateley Rd. SE20 171 G7
Whateley Rd. SE22 152 C5
Whatley Av. SW20 184 B3
Whatman Rd. SE23 153 G7
Wheat Sheaf Cl. E14 134 B4
Wheatfield Way, 181 H2
 Kings.T.
Wheatfields E6 116/117 E6
 Oxleas
Wheatfields, Enf. 45 H2
Wheathill Rd. SE20 188 E3
Wheatlands, Houns. 123 G6
Wheatlands Rd. 168 A3
 SW17
 Stapleton Rd.
Wheatley Cl. NW4 71 G2
Wheatley Cres., 102 A7
 Hayes
Wheatley Gdns. N9 60 B2
Wheatley Rd., Islw. 144 C3
Wheatley St. W1 16 C2
Wheatley's Ait, Sun. 178 A5
Wheatsheaf Cl., 84 E5
 Nthlt.
Wheatsheaf La. SW6 127 J7
Wheatsheaf La. SW8 34 B7
Wheatsheaf La. SW8 130 E7
Wheatsheaf Ter. SW6 128 C7
Wheatstone Cl., 185 H1
 Mitch.
Wheatstone Rd. W10 108 B5
Wheel Fm. Dr., Dag. 101 J3
Wheeler Cl., Wdf.Grn. 64 C5
 Chigwell Rd.
Wheeler Gdns. N1 110/111 E1
 Outram Pl.
Wheelers Cross, 117 G2
 Bark.
Wheelock Cl., Erith 139 H7
Wheelwright St. N7 93 F7
Whelan Way, Wall. 200 D3
Wheler St. E1 13 F6

Wheler St. E1 112 C4
Whellock Rd. W4 126 E3
Whenman Av., Bex. 177 J2
Whernside Cl. SE28 118 C7
Whetstone Cl. N20 57 G2
 Oakleigh Rd. N.
Whetstone Pk. WC2 18 C3
Whetstone Rd. SE3 155 J2
Whewell Rd. N19 93 E2
Whichcote St. SE1 26 E2
Whidborne Cl. SE8 154 A2
 Cliff Ter.
Whidborne St. WC1 10 B4
Whidborne St. WC1 111 E3
Whimbrel Cl. SE28 118 C7
Whimbrel Way, 102 D6
 Hayes
Whinchat Rd. SE28 137 G3
Whinfell Cl. SW16 168 D5
Whinyates Rd. SE9 156 B3
Whipps Cross Rd. E11 78 D5
Whiskin St. EC1 11 G4
Whiskin St. EC1 111 H3
Whisperwood Cl., 52 B7
 Har.
Whistler Gdns., Edg. 69 J2
Whistler Ms. SE15 132 C7
 Commercial Way
Whistler Ms., Dag. 100 B5
 Fitzstephen Rd.
Whistler St. N5 93 H4
Whistlers Av. SW11 129 G7
Whiston Rd. E2 13 F1
Whiston Rd. E2 112 C2
Whitakers Way, Loug. 48 C1
Whitbread Cl. N17 76 D1
Whitbread Rd. SE4 153 H4
Whitburn Rd. SE13 154 B4
Whitby Av. NW10 106 B3
Whitby Gdns. NW9 70 A3
Whitby Gdns., Sutt. 199 G2
Whitby Rd. SE18 136 C4
Whitby Rd., Har. 85 J3
Whitby Rd., Ruis. 84 B3
Whitby Rd., Sutt. 199 G2
Whitby St. E1 13 F5
Whitcher Cl. SE14 133 H6
Whitcher Pl. NW1 92 C7
 Rochester Rd.
Whitchurch Av., Edg. 53 J7
Whitchurch Cl., Edg. 53 J6
Whitchurch Gdns., 53 J6
 Edg.
Whitchurch La., Edg. 53 G7
Whitchurch Rd. W11 108 A7
Whitcomb Ct. WC2 110 D7
 Whitcomb St.
Whitcomb St. WC2 17 J6
Whitcomb St. WC2 110 D7
White Acre NW9 71 E2
New End Sq.
White Br. Av., Mitch. 185 G4
 Belgrave Wk.
White Butts Rd., Ruis. 84 D3
White Ch. La. E1 21 H3
White Ch. La. E1 112 D6
White Ch. Pas. E1 21 H3
White City Cl. W12 107 J7
White City Est. W12 107 H7
White City Rd. W12 107 H7
White Conduit St. N1 11 F1
White Craig Cl., Pnr. 51 G5
White Gdns., Dag. 101 G6
White Hart Ct. EC2 112 B6
 Bishopsgate
White Hart La. N17 60 A7
White Hart La. N22 75 G3
White Hart La. NW10 89 F6
 Church Rd.
White Hart La. SW13 147 E3
White Hart La., Rom. 83 G4
White Hart Rd. SE18 137 H4
White Hart Slip, 191 G2
 Brom.
 Market Sq.
White Hart St. SE11 35 F3
White Hart St. SE11 131 G5
White Hart Yd. SE1 28 B2
White Heron Ms., 162 C6
 Tedd.
White Horse Hill, 174 D4
 Chis.
White Horse La. E1 113 G4
White Horse Ms. SE1 27 F5
White Horse Rd. E1 113 H6
White Horse Rd. E6 116 C3
White Horse St. W1 24 D2
White Horse St. W1 130 B1
White Horse Yd. EC2 20 B3
White Ho., Dar., Stan. 53 F4
White Kennett St. E1 21 E3
White Lion Ct. EC3 20 D4

White Lion Hill EC4 19 H5
White Lion Hill EC4 111 H7
White Lion St. N1 11 E2
White Lion St. N1 111 G2
White Lo. SE19 169 H7
White Lo. Cl. N2 73 H6
White Lo. Cl., Sutt. 199 F7
White Lyon Ct. EC2 111 J4
Fann St.
White Oak Dr., Beck. 190 C2
White Oak Gdns., Sid. 157 J7
White Orchards N20 40 C7
White Orchards, Stan. 52 D5
White Post La. E9 95 J7
White Post La. SE13 154 A3
White Post St. SE15 133 F7
White Rd. E15 97 E7
White St., Sthl. 122 D2
White Swan Ms. W4 126/127 E6
Bennett St.
Whiteadder Way E14 134 B4
Whitear Wk. E15 96 D6
Whitebarn La., Dag. 119 G1
Whitebeam Av., Brom. 192 D6
Whitebeam Cl. SW9 131 F7
Clapham Rd.
Whitebeam Twr. E17 77 H3
Hillyfield
Whitebridge Cl., Felt. 141 J6
Whitechapel High St. E1 21 G3
Whitechapel High St. E1 112 C6
Whitechapel Rd. E1 21 H2
Whitechapel Rd. E1 112 D5
Whitecote Rd., Sthl. 103 H6
Whitecroft Cl., Beck. 190 D4
Whitecroft Way, Beck. 190 C5
Whitecross Pl. EC2 20 C1
Whitecross St. EC1 12 A5
Whitecross St. EC1 111 J4
Whitefield Av. NW2 71 J7
Whitefield Cl. SW15 148 B6
Whitefoot La., Brom. 172 C4
Whitefoot Ter., Brom. 173 E3
Whitefriars Av., Har. 68 B2
Whitefriars Dr., Har. 68 A2
Whitefriars St. EC4 19 F4
Whitefriars St. EC4 111 G6
Whitegate Gdns., Har. 52 C7
Whitehall SW1 26 A1
Whitehall SW1 130 E1
Whitehall Ct. SW1 26 A2
Whitehall Ct. SW1 130 E1
Whitehall Cres., Chess. 195 G5
Whitehall Gdns. E4 62 D1
Whitehall Gdns. SW1 26 A2
Whitehall Gdns. W3 126 A1
Whitehall Gdns. W4 126 B6
Whitehall La., Buck.H. 63 G2
Whitehall Pk. N19 92 C1
Whitehall Pk. Rd. W4 126 B6
Whitehall Pl. E7 97 G5
Station Rd.
Whitehall Pl. SW1 26 A2
Whitehall Pl. SW1 130 E1
Whitehall Pl., Wall. 200 B4
Bernard Rd.
Whitehall Rd. E4 62 E2
Whitehall Rd. W7 124 D2
Whitehall Rd., Brom. 192 A5
Whitehall Rd., Har. 68 B7
Whitehall Rd., Th.Hth. 187 G5
Whitehall Rd., Wdf.Grn. 62 E2
Whitehall St. N17 60 C7
Whitehaven Cl., Brom. 191 G4
Whitehaven St. NW8 7 G6
Whitehead Cl. N18 60 A5
Whitehead Cl. SW18 149 F7
Whitehead's Gro. SW3 31 H3
Whitehead's Gro. SW3 129 H5
Whitehills Rd., Loug. 48 D3
Whitehorse La. SE25 188 A4
Whitehorse Rd., Croy. 187 J7
Whitehorse Rd., Th.Hth. 188 A6
Whitehouse Av., Borwd. 38 B3
Whitehouse Way N14 58 B2
Whiteledges W13 105 F6
Whitelegg Rd. E13 115 F2
Whiteley Rd. SE19 170 A5
Whiteleys Cotts. W14 128 C4
Whiteleys Way, Felt. 161 G3
Whiteoaks La., Grnf. 104 A2
Whites Av., Ilf. 81 H6
Whites Grds. SE1 28 E4
Whites Grds. SE1 132 B2
Whites Grds. Est. SE1 28 E3
White's Row E1 21 F2
White's Row E1 112 C5
White's Sq. SW4 150 D4
Nelson's Row
Whitestile Rd., Brent. 125 F5
Whitestone La. NW3 91 F3
Heath St.
Whitestone Wk. NW3 91 F3
North End Way
Whitethorn Gdns., Croy. 203 E2
Whitethorn Gdns., Enf. 44 A5
Whitethorn St. E3 114 A4
Whitewebbs Way, Orp. 193 J1
Whitfield Pl. W1 9 F6
Whitfield Rd. E6 97 J7
Whitfield Rd. SE3 154 D1
Whitfield Rd., Bexh. 139 F7
Whitfield St. W1 17 H2
Whitfield St. W1 110 D5
Whitford Gdns., Mitch. 185 J3
Whitgift Av., S.Croy. 201 J5
Whitgift Cen., Croy. 201 J2
Whitgift St. SE11 34 C1
Whitgift St. SE11 131 F4
Whitgift St., Croy. 201 J3
Whiting Av., Bark. 99 E7
Whitings, Ilf. 81 G5
Whitings Rd., Barn. 39 J5
Whitings Way E6 116 D5
Whitland Rd., Cars. 199 G1
Whitley Cl., Stai. 140 B6
Whitley Rd. N17 76 B2
Whitlock Dr. SW19 148 B7
Whitman Rd. E3 113 H4
Whitmead Cl., S.Croy. 202 B6
Whitmore Cl. N11 58 B5
Whitmore Est. N1 112 B1
Whitmore Gdns. NW10 107 J2
Whitmore Rd. N1 112 B1
Whitmore Rd., Beck. 189 J3
Whitmore Rd., Har. 67 J7
Whitnell Way SW15 148 A5
Whitney Av., Ilf. 80 A4
Whitney Rd. E10 78 B7
Whitney Wk., Sid. 176 E6
Whitstable Cl., Beck. 189 J1
Whitstable Ho. W10 108 A6
Whitstable Pl., Croy. 201 J4
Whitta Rd. E12 98 A4
Whittaker Av., Rich. 145 G5
Hill St.
Whittaker Rd. E6 97 J7
Whittaker Rd., Sutt. 198 C3
Whittaker St. SW1 32 B2
Whittaker St. SW1 130 A4
Whittaker Way SE1 37 J2
Whittell Gdns. SE26 171 F3
Whittingstall Rd. SW6 148 C1
Whittington Av. EC3 20 D4
Whittington Ct. N2 73 J5
Whittington Ms. N12 57 F4
Fredericks Pl.
Whittington Rd. N22 58 E7
Whittington Way, Pnr. 67 E5
Whittle Cl. E17 77 H6
Whittle Cl., Sthl. 103 H6
Whittle Rd., Houns. 122 C7
Whittle Rd., Sthl. 123 H2
Post Rd.
Whittlebury Cl., Cars. 199 J7
Whittlesea Cl., Har. 51 J7
Whittlesea Path, Har. 67 J1
Whittlesea Rd., Har. 67 J1
Whittlesey St. SE1 27 E2
Whitton Av. E., Grnf. 86 B5
Whitton Av. W., Grnf. 85 J5
Whitton Av. W., Nthlt. 85 J5
Whitton Cl., Grnf. 87 E6
Whitton Dene, Houns. 143 J5
Whitton Dene, Islw. 144 A5
Whitton Dr., Grnf. 86 D6
Whitton Manor Rd., Islw. 143 J5
Whitton Rd., Houns. 143 H4
Whitton Rd., Twick. 144 C6
Whitton Wk. E3 114 A2
Whitton Waye, Houns. 143 G6
Whitwell Rd. E13 115 G3
Whitworth Pl. SE18 137 E4
Whitworth Rd. SE18 136 D7
Whitworth Rd. SE25 188 B3
Whitworth St. SE10 135 E5
Whorlton Rd. SE15 152 E3
Whymark Av. N22 75 G3
Whytecroft, Houns. 122 D7
Whyteville Rd. E7 97 H6
Wick La. E3 114 A2
Wick Rd. E9 95 G6
Wick Rd., Tedd. 163 E7
Wick Sq. E9 95 J6
Eastway
Wicker St. E1 112/113 E6
Burslem St.
Wickers Oake SE19 170 C4
Wickersley Rd. SW11 150 A2
Wicket, The, Croy. 204 A5
Wicket Rd., Grnf. 104 D3
Wickets Way, Ilf. 65 J6
Wickford St. E1 113 F4
Wickford Way E17 77 G4
Wickham Av., Croy. 203 H2
Wickham Av., Sutt. 197 J5
Wickham Chase, W.Wick. 190 D7
Wickham Cl., Enf. 45 E3
Wickham Cl., N.Mal. 183 F5
Wickham Ct. Rd., W.Wick. 204 C2
Wickham Cres., W.Wick. 204 C2
Wickham Gdns. SE4 153 J3
Wickham Ho. E1 113 G5
Wickham La. SE2 138 A5
Wickham La., Well. 138 A5
Wickham Ms. SE4 153 J2
Wickham Rd. E4 62 C7
Wickham Rd. SE4 153 J3
Wickham Rd., Beck. 190 B2
Wickham Rd., Croy. 203 G2
Wickham Rd., Har. 68 A2
Wickham St. SE11 34 C3
Wickham St. SE11 131 F5
Wickham St., Well. 157 H2
Wickham Way, Beck. 190 C4
Wickliffe Av. N3 72 B2
Wickliffe Gdns., Wem. 88 B2
Wicklow St. WC1 10 C3
Wicklow St. WC1 111 F3
Wicks Cl. SE9 174 A4
Wicksteed Ho., Brent. 125 J5
Green Dragon La.
Wickwood St. SE5 151 H2
Widdecombe Av., Har. 84 E2
Widdenham Rd. N7 93 F4
Widdin St. E15 96 D7
Wide Way, Mitch. 186 D3
Widecombe Gdns., Ilf. 80 B4
Widecombe Rd. SE9 174 B3
Widecombe Way N2 73 G5
Widegate St. E1 21 E2
Widenham Cl., Pnr. 66 C5
Bridle Rd.
Widgeon Cl. E16 115 H6
Maplin Rd.
Widley Rd. W9 108 D3
Widmore Lo. Rd., Brom. 192 A2
Widmore Rd., Brom. 191 G2
Wieland Rd., Nthwd. 50 A7
Wigan Ho. E5 94/95 E1
Warwick Gro.
Wigeon Path SE28 137 G3
Wigeon Way, Hayes 102 D6
Wiggins Mead NW9 55 F7
Wigginton Av., Wem. 88 B6
Wigham Ho., Bark. 99 F7
Wightman Rd. N4 75 G5
Wightman Rd. N8 75 G4
Wigley Rd., Felt. 160 D2
Wigmore Pl. W1 16 D3
Wigmore Pl. W1 110 B6
Wigmore Rd., Cars. 199 G2
Wigmore St. W1 16 B4
Wigmore St. W1 110 A6
Wigmore Wk., Cars. 199 G2
Wigram Rd. E11 79 J6
Wigram Sq. E17 78 C3
Wigston Cl. N18 60 B5
Wigston Rd. E13 115 H4
Wigton Gdns., Stan. 69 H1
Wigton Pl. SE11 35 F4
Wigton Rd. E17 77 J1
Wilberforce Rd. N4 93 H3
Wilberforce Rd. NW9 71 G6
Wilberforce Way SW19 166 A6
Wilbraham Pl. SW1 32 A1
Wilbraham Pl. SW1 129 J4
Wilbury Way N18 60 A5
Wilby Ms. W11 128 C1
Wilcox Cl. SW8 34 B7
Wilcox Cl. SW8 131 E7
Wilcox Cl., Borwd. 38 C1
Wilcox Pl. SW1 25 G6
Wilcox Rd. SW8 34 A7
Wilcox Rd. SW8 130 E7
Wilcox Rd., Sutt. 198 E4
Wilcox Rd., Tedd. 162 A4
Wild Ct. WC2 18 C3
Wild Ct. WC2 111 F6
Wild Goose Dr. SE14 153 F1
Wild Hatch NW11 72 D6
Wild St. WC2 18 B4
Wild St. WC2 111 E6
Wildcroft Gdns., Edg. 53 G6
Wildcroft Rd. SW15 147 J7
Wilde Cl. E8 112 D1
Wilde Pl. N13 59 H6
Medesenge Way
Wilde Pl. SW18 149 G7
Heathfield Rd.
Wilde Rd., Erith 139 H7
Wilder Cl., Ruis. 84 B1
Wilderness, The, E.Mol. 179 J5
Wilderness, The, Hmptn. 161 H4
Park Rd.
Wilderness Rd., Chis. 175 E7
Wilderton Rd. N16 76 B7
Wildfell Rd. SE6 154 B7
Wild's Rents SE1 28 D5
Wild's Rents SE1 132 B3
Wildwood Cl. SE12 155 F7
Wildwood Gro. NW3 91 F1
North End Way
Wildwood Ri. NW11 91 F1
Wildwood Rd. NW11 73 F7
Wildwood Ter. NW3 91 F1
Wilford Cl., Enf. 44 A3
Wilfred Owen Cl. SW19 167 F6
Tennyson Rd.
Wilfred St. SW1 25 F5
Wilfred St. SW1 130 C3
Wilfrid Gdns. W3 106 C5
Wilkes Rd., Brent. 125 H6
Wilkes St. E1 21 G1
Wilkes St. E1 112 C5
Wilkie Way SE22 170 D1
Lordship La.
Wilkin St. NW5 92 B6
Wilkin St. Ms. NW5 92 B6
Wilkin St.
Wilkins Cl., Hayes 121 J5
Wilkins Cl., Mitch. 185 H1
Wilkinson Rd. E16 115 J6
Wilkinson St. SW8 131 F7
Wilkinson Way W4 126 D2
Wilks Gdns., Croy. 203 H1
Wilks Pl. N1 12 E2
Will Crooks Gdns. SE9 155 J4
Willan Rd. N17 76 A2
Willan Wall E16 115 F7
Victoria Dock Rd.
Willard St. SW8 150 B3
Willcocks Cl., Chess. 195 H3
Willcott Rd. W3 126 B1
Willen Fld. Rd. NW10 106 C2
Willenhall Av., Barn. 41 F6
Willenhall Rd. SE18 136 E5
Willersley Av., Orp. 207 G3
Willersley Av., Sid. 175 J1
Willersley Cl., Sid. 175 J1
Willes Rd. NW5 92 B6
Willesden La. NW2 90 A6
Willesden La. NW6 90 A6
Willett Cl., Nthlt. 102 C3
Broomcroft Av.
Willett Cl., Orp. 193 H6
Willett Pl., Th.Hth. 187 G5
Willett Rd.
Willett Rd., Th.Hth. 187 G5
Willett Way, Orp. 193 G5
William Barefoot Dr. SE9 174 D4
William Bonney Est. SW4 150 D4
William Booth Rd. SE20 188 D1
William Carey Way, Har. 68 B7
William Cl. N2 73 G3
King St.
William Cl., Rom. 83 J1
William Cl., Sthl. 123 J2
Windmill Av.
William Dunbar Ho. NW6 108 C2
William Dyce Ms. SW16 168 D4
Babington Rd.
William Ellis Way SE16 29 J6
William IV St. WC2 18 A6

William IV St. WC2 110 E7
William Gdns. SW15 147 H5
William Guy Gdns. E3 114 B3
 Talwin St.
William Margrie Cl. 152 D2
 SE15
 Moncrieff St.
William Ms. SW1 **24** **A4**
William Morley Cl. 116 A1
 E6
William Morris Cl. 77 J3
 E17
William Morris Way 149 F3
 SW6
William Pl. E3 113 J2
 Roman Rd.
William Rd. NW1 **9** **E4**
William Rd. NW1 110 B3
William Rd. SW19 166 B7
William Rd., Sutt. 199 F5
William Saville Ho. 108 C2
 NW6
William Sq. SE16 113 H7
 Rotherhithe St.
William St. E10 78 B6
William St. N17 60 C7
William St. SW1 **24** **A4**
William St. SW1 129 J2
William St., Bark. 99 F7
William St., Cars. 199 H3
Williams Av. E17 77 J1
Williams Bldgs. E2 113 F4
Williams Cl. N8 74 D6
 Coolhurst Rd.
Williams Gro. N22 75 G1
Williams Gro., Surb. 181 F6
William's La. SW14 146 C2
Williams La., Mord. 185 F5
Williams Rd. W13 104 D7
Williams Rd., Sthl. 122 E4
Williams Ter., Croy. 201 G6
Williamson Cl. SE10 135 F4
 Lenthorp Rd.
Williamson Rd. N4 75 H6
Williamson St. N7 93 E4
Williamson Way NW7 56 B6
Willifield Way NW11 72 C5
Willingale Cl., Loug. 49 F2
 Willingale Cl.,
Willingale Cl., 64 A6
 Wdf.Grn.
Willingale Rd., Loug. 49 F3
Willingdon Rd. N22 75 H2
Willingham Cl. NW5 92 C5
 Leighton Rd.
Willingham Ter. NW5 92 C5
 Leighton Rd.
Willington Way, 182 A3
 Kings.T.
Willington Ct. E5 95 H3
 Mandeville St.
Willington Rd. SW9 150 E3
Willis Av., Sutt. 199 H6
Willis Rd. E15 115 F1
Willis Rd., Croy. 187 J7
Willis Rd., Erith 139 J4
Willis St. E14 114 B6
Willmore End SW19 184 E1
Willoughby Av., 201 F4
 Croy.
Willoughby Gro. N17 60 E7
Willoughby La. N17 61 E7
Willoughby Ms. SW4 150 B4
 Wixs La.
Willoughby Pk. Rd. 60 E7
 N17
Willoughby Pas. E14 134 A1
Willoughby Rd. N8 75 G3
Willoughby Rd. NW3 91 G4
Willoughby Rd., 181 J1
 Kings.T.
Willoughby Rd., 145 G6
 Twick.
Willoughby St. WC1 **18** **A2**
Willoughby Way SE7 135 H4
Willoughbys, The 146/147 E4
 SW14
 Upper Richmond Rd. W.
Willow Av. SW13 147 F2
Willow Av., Sid. 158 A6
Willow Bank SW6 148 B3
Willow Bank, Rich. 163 E3
Willow Br. Rd. N1 93 J6
Willow Business 185 J5
 Cen., Mitch.
Willow Cl., Bex. 159 F6
Willow Cl., Brent. 125 F6
Willow Cl., Brom. 192 C5
Willow Cl., Buck.H. 64 A3
Willow Cl., Th.Hth. 187 H6
Willow Cotts., Mitch. 186 C3
Willow Cotts., Rich. 126 A6
 Kew Grn.
Willow Ct. EC2 **12** **D5**

Willow Ct., Edg. 53 H4
Willow Dene, Pnr. 66 D2
Willow Dr., Barn. 40 B4
Willow End N20 56 D2
Willow End, Nthwd. 50 A6
Willow End, Surb. 195 H1
Willow Fm. La. SW15 147 H3
 Queens Ride
Willow Gdns., 143 G1
 Houns.
Willow Grn. NW9 70/71 E1
 Clayton Fld.
Willow Grn., Borwd. 38 D5
Willow Gro. E13 115 G2
 Libra Rd.
Willow Gro., Chis. 174 D6
Willow La., Mitch. 185 J5
Willow Mt., Croy. 202 B3
 Langton Way
Willow Pl. SW1 **33** **G1**
Willow Pl. SW1 130 C4
Willow Rd. NW3 91 G4
Willow Rd. W5 125 H2
Willow Rd., Enf. 44 B3
Willow Rd., N.Mal. 182 C4
Willow Rd., Rom. 83 E6
Willow Rd., Wall. 200 B7
Willow St. E4 46 D7
Willow St. EC2 **12** **D5**
Willow St. EC2 112 B4
Willow St., Rom. 83 J4
Willow Tree Cl. E3 113 J1
 Birdsfield La.
Willow Tree Cl. 166/167 E1
 SW18
 Cargill Rd.
Willow Tree Cl., 102 C4
 Hayes
Willow Tree La., 102 C4
 Hayes
Willow Tree Wk., 191 H1
 Brom.
Willow Vale W12 127 G1
Willow Vale, Chis. 174 E6
Willow Vw. SW19 185 G1
Willow Wk. E17 77 J5
Willow Wk. N2 73 G2
Willow Wk. N15 75 H4
Willow Wk. N21 43 F6
Willow Wk. SE1 **37** **E1**
Willow Wk. SE1 132 B4
Willow Wk., Orp. 206 E3
Willow Wk., Sutt. 198 C3
Willow Way N3 56 E7
Willow Way SE26 171 E3
Willow Way W11 128 A1
 Freston Rd.
Willow Way, Epsom 196 D6
Willow Way, Sun. 178 A4
Willow Way, Twick. 161 H2
Willow Way, Wem. 86 D3
Willow Wd. Cres. 188 B6
 SE25
Willowbrook Rd. **37** **G6**
 SE15
Willowbrook Rd. 132 C6
 SE15
Willowbrook Rd., 123 G3
 Sthl.
Willowcourt Av., Har. 69 E5
Willowdene N6 73 J7
 Denewood Rd.
Willowdene Cl., 143 J7
 Twick.
Willowfield Cl. 58/59 E3
 SE18
 Conway Rd.
Willowhayne Dr., 178 B7
 Walt.
Willowhayne Gdns., 197 J3
 Wor.Pk.
Willowmead Cl. W5 105 G5
Willows, The, Buck.H. 64 A3
Willows, The, Esher 194 B6
 Albany Cres.
Willows Av., Mord. 185 E5
Willows Cl., Pnr. 66 C2
Willowtree Way, 187 G1
 Th.Hth.
 Kensington Av.
Willrose Cres. SE2 138 C5
Wills Cres., Houns. 143 H6
Wills Gro. NW7 55 G5
Wilman Gro. E8 94 D7
Wilmar Gdns., 204 B1
 W.Wick.
Wilmcote Ho. W2 **14** **A1**
Wilmcote Ho. W2 108 E5
Wilmer Cl., Kings.T. 163 J5
Wilmer Cres., 163 J5
 Kings.T.

Wilmer Gdns. N1 112 B1
Wilmer Lea Cl. E15 96 D7
Wilmer Pl. N16 94 C2
 Stoke Newington Ch. St.
Wilmer Way N14 58 D5
Wilmington Av. W4 126 D7
Wilmington Gdns., 99 G6
 Bark.
Wilmington Sq. WC1 **11** **E4**
Wilmington St. WC1 **11** **E4**
Wilmington St. WC1 111 G3
Wilmot Cl. N2 73 F2
Wilmot Cl. SE15 132 D7
Wilmot Pl. NW1 92 C7
Wilmot Pl. W7 124 B1
 Boston Rd.
Wilmot Rd. E10 96 B2
Wilmot Rd. N17 76 A3
Wilmot Rd., Cars. 199 J5
Wilmot St. E2 112 E4
Wilmount St. SE18 136 E4
Wilna Rd. SW18 149 F7
Wilsham St. W11 128 A1
Wilshaw St. SE14 154 A1
Wilsmere Dr., Har. 52 C7
Wilsmere Dr., Nthlt. 85 E6
Wilson Av., Mitch. 167 H7
Wilson Cl., S.Croy. 202 A5
 Bartlett St.
Wilson Cl., Wem. 69 J7
Wilson Cl., West Dr. 120 A6
 Hatch La.
Wilson Dr., Wem. 69 J7
Wilson Gdns., Har. 67 J7
Wilson Gro. SE16 132 E2
Wilson Rd. E6 116 A3
Wilson Rd. SE5 152 B1
Wilson Rd., Chess. 195 J6
Wilson Rd., Ilf. 80 C7
Wilson St. E17 78 C5
Wilson St. EC2 **20** **C1**
Wilson St. EC2 112 A5
Wilson St. N21 43 G7
Wilsons Pl. E14 113 J6
 Salmon La.
Wilsons Rd. W6 128 A5
Wilstone Cl., 102/103 E4
 Hayes
 Kingsash Dr.
Wilthorne Gdns., 101 H7
 Dag.
 Acre Rd.
Wilton Av. W4 127 E5
Wilton Cl., West Dr. 120 A6
 Hatch La.
Wilton Cres. SW1 **24** **B4**
Wilton Cres. SW1 130 A2
Wilton Cres. SW19 184 C1
Wilton Gdns., W.Mol. 179 G3
Wilton Gro. SW19 184 C1
Wilton Gro., N.Mal. 183 F6
Wilton Ms. SW1 **24** **C5**
Wilton Ms. SW1 130 A3
Wilton Par., Felt. 160 A2
 Highfield Rd.
Wilton Pk. Ct. SE18 156 D1
 Prince Imperial Rd.
Wilton Pl. SW1 **24** **B4**
Wilton Pl. SW1 130 A2
Wilton Rd. N10 74 A2
Wilton Rd. SE2 138 C3
Wilton Rd. SW1 **25** **E6**
Wilton Rd. SW1 130 C3
Wilton Rd. SW19 167 H7
Wilton Rd., Barn. 41 J4
Wilton Rd., Houns. 142 D3
Wilton Rd., Ilf. 98/99 E3
 Ilford La.
Wilton Row SW1 **24** **B4**
Wilton Row SW1 130 A2
Wilton Sq. N1 112 A1
Wilton St. SW1 **24** **D5**
Wilton St. SW1 130 B3
Wilton Ter. SW1 **24** **B5**
Wilton Ter. SW1 130 A3
Wilton Vil. N1 112 A1
Wilton Way E8 94 D6
Wiltshire Cl. NW7 55 F5
Wiltshire Cl. SW3 **31** **J1**
Wiltshire Gdns. N4 75 J6
Wiltshire Gdns., 161 J1
 Twick.
Wiltshire Rd. SW9 151 G3
Wiltshire Rd., 187 G3
 Th.Hth.
Wiltshire Row N1 112 A1
Wilverley Cres., 183 E6
 N.Mal.
Wimbart Rd. SW2 151 F7
Wimbledon Br. 166 C6
 SW19
Wimbledon Common 165 G4
 SW19

Wimbledon Hill Rd. 166 B6
 SW19
Wimbledon Pk. SW19 166 C2
Wimbledon Pk. Est. 166 B1
 SW19
Wimbledon Pk. Rd. 148 C7
 SW18
Wimbledon Pk. Rd. 166 C1
 SW19
Wimbledon Pk. Side 166 A2
 SW19
Wimbledon Rd. SW17 167 F4
Wimbledon Sta. 166 C6
 SW19
 The Bdy.
Wimbolt St. E2 **13** **H3**
Wimbolt St. E2 112 D3
Wimborne Av., 102 B6
 Hayes
Wimborne Av., Sthl. 123 G4
Wimborne Cl. SE12 155 F5
Wimborne Cl., 63 H2
 Buck.H.
Wimborne Cl., 197 J1
 Wor.Pk.
Wimborne Dr. NW9 70 A3
Wimborne Dr., Pnr. 66 D7
Wimborne Gdns. W13 105 E6
Wimborne Rd. N9 60 D2
Wimborne Rd. N17 76 B2
Wimborne Way, 189 G3
 Beck.
Wimbourne Av., Orp. 193 J4
Wimbourne Ct. N1 112 A2
 Wimbourne St.
Wimbourne St. N1 **12** **B1**
Wimbourne St. N1 112 A1
Wimpole Cl., Brom. 191 J4
 Stanley Rd.
Wimpole Cl., Kings.T. 181 J2
Wimpole Ms. W1 **16** **D1**
Wimpole Ms. W1 110 B5
Wimpole Rd., 120 A1
 West Dr.
Wimpole St. W1 **16** **D3**
Wimpole St. W1 110 B6
Wimshurst Cl., Croy. 201 E1
Winans Wk. SW9 151 G2
Wincanton Cres., 85 G5
 Nthlt.
Wincanton Gdns., Ilf. 80 E2
Wincanton Rd. SW18 148 C7
Winchcomb Gdns. 156 A3
 SE9
Winchcombe Rd., 185 G7
 Cars.
Winchelsea Av., 139 F7
 Bexh.
Winchelsea Cl. SW15 148 A5
Winchelsea Rd. E7 97 G4
Winchelsea Rd. N17 76 B3
Winchelsea Rd. 106 D1
 NW10
Winchelsey Ri., 202 C6
 S.Croy.
Winchendon Rd. 128 C7
 SW6
Winchendon Rd., 162 A4
 Tedd.
Winchester Av. NW6 108 B1
Winchester Av. NW9 70 A3
Winchester Av., 123 F6
 Houns.
Winchester Cl. E6 116 B6
Winchester Cl. SE17 **35** **H2**
Winchester Cl. SE17 131 H4
Winchester Cl., Brom. 191 F3
Winchester Cl., Enf. 44 B5
Winchester Cl., 164 B7
 Kings.T.
Winchester Cl. E17 77 G1
 Billet Rd.
Winchester Dr., Pnr. 66 D5
Winchester Ho. SE18 136 A7
 Shooter's Hill Rd.
Winchester Ms. NW3 91 G7
 Winchester Rd.
Winchester Pk., Brom. 191 F3
Winchester Pl. E8 94 C5
 Kingsland High St.
Winchester Pl. N6 92 B1
Winchester Pl. W3 126 C2
 Avenue Rd.
Winchester Rd. E4 62 C7
Winchester Rd. N6 74 B7
Winchester Rd. N9 60 D1
Winchester Rd. NW3 91 G7
Winchester Rd., 158 D2
 Bexh.
Winchester Rd., 191 F3
 Brom.
Winchester Rd., Felt. 161 F3
Winchester Rd., Har. 69 H4

Name	Page	Grid
Winchester Rd., Hayes	121	H7
Winchester Rd., Ilf.	99	G3
Winchester Rd., Twick.	144	E6
Winchester Sq. SE1	**28**	**B1**
Winchester Sq. SE1	132	A1
Winchester St. SW1	**32**	**E3**
Winchester St. SW1	130	B5
Winchester St. W3	126	C1
Winchester Wk. SE1	**28**	**B1**
Winchester Wk. SE1	132	A1
Winchet Wk., Croy.	189	F6
Medway Cl.		
Winchfield Cl., Har.	69	F6
Winchfield Rd. SE26	171	H5
Winchilsea Cres., W.Mol.	179	J2
Winchmore Hill Rd. N14	58	D1
Winchmore Hill Rd. N21	58	D1
Winckley Cl., Har.	69	J5
Wincott St. SE11	**35**	**F1**
Wincott St. SE11	131	G4
Wincrofts Dr. SE9	157	G4
Windall Cl. SE19	188	D1
Windborough Rd., Cars.	200	A7
Windermere Av. N3	72	D3
Windermere Av. NW6	108	B1
Windermere Av. SW19	184	E3
Windermere Av., Har.	69	F7
Windermere Av., Ruis.	66	C7
Windermere Av., Wem.	69	F7
Windermere Cl., Orp.	206	E3
Windermere Ct. SW13	127	F6
Windermere Ct., Wem.	69	F7
Windermere Av.		
Windermere Gdns., Ilf.	80	B5
Windermere Gro., Wem.	87	F1
Windermere Av.		
Windermere Ho., Islw.	144	C5
Summerwood Rd.		
Windermere Rd. N10	74	B1
Windermere Rd. N19	92	C2
Holloway Rd.		
Windermere Rd. SW15	164	E4
Windermere Rd. SW16	186	C1
Windermere Rd. W5	125	F3
Windermere Rd., Bexh.	159	J2
Windermere Rd., Croy.	202	C1
Windermere Rd., Sthl.	103	F5
Windermere Rd., W.Wick.	204	E2
Windermere Way, West Dr.	120	C1
Providence Rd.		
Winders Rd. SW11	149	H2
Windfield Cl. SE26	171	G4
Windham Rd., Rich.	145	J3
Winding Way, Dag.	100	C3
Winding Way, Har.	86	B4
Windlass Pl. SE8	133	H4
Windlesham Gro. SW19	166	A1
Windley Cl. SE23	171	F2
Windmill All. W4	126/127	E4
Windmill Rd.		
Windmill Av., Sthl.	123	J2
Windmill Br. Ho., Croy.	202	B1
Windmill Cl. SE1	**37**	**J1**
Windmill Cl. SE13	154	C2
Windmill Cl., Surb.	195	E1
Windmill Ct. NW2	90	B6
Windmill Dr. SW4	150	C5
Windmill Dr., Kes.	205	J4
Windmill Gdns., Enf.	43	G3
Windmill Gro., Croy.	187	J7
Windmill Hill NW3	91	F3
Windmill Hill, Enf.	43	H3
Windmill La. E15	96	D6
Windmill La., Barn.	39	F6
Windmill La., Bushey	52	B1
Windmill La., Grnf.	103	J5
Windmill La., Islw.	124	B4
Windmill La., Sthl.	123	J3
Windmill La., Surb.	181	E7
Windmill Ms. W4	126/127	E4
Windmill Rd.		
Windmill Pas. W4	126	E4
Windmill Ri., Kings.T.	164	B7
Windmill Rd. N18	60	A4
Windmill Rd. SW18	149	G6
Windmill Rd. SW19	165	H1
Windmill Rd. W4	126	E4
Windmill Rd. W5	125	F4
Windmill Rd., Brent.	125	G5
Windmill Rd., Croy.	187	J7
Windmill Rd., Hmptn.	161	H5
Windmill Rd., Mitch.	186	C5
Windmill Row SE11	**35**	**E4**
Windmill Row SE11	131	G5
Windmill St. W1	**17**	**H2**
Windmill St. W1	110	D5
Windmill St., Bushey	52	B1
Windmill Wk. SE1	**27**	**F2**
Windmill Wk. SE1	131	G1
Windover Av. NW9	70	D4
Windrose Cl. SE16	133	G2
Windrush, N.Mal.	182	C3
California Rd.		
Windrush Cl. SW11	149	G4
Maysoule Rd.		
Windrush Cl. W4	146	C1
Windrush La. SE23	171	G3
Windrush Sq. SW2	151	G4
Rushcroft Rd.		
Windsock Cl. SE16	133	J4
Windsor Av. E17	77	H2
Windsor Av. SW19	185	F1
Windsor Av., Edg.	54	B4
Windsor Av., N.Mal.	182	C5
Windsor Av., Sutt.	198	B3
Windsor Av., W.Mol.	179	G3
Windsor Cen., The SE27	169	J4
Advance Rd.		
Windsor Cl. N3	72	B2
Windsor Cl. SE27	169	J4
Windsor Cl., Borwd.	38	A1
Windsor Cl., Brent.	124	E6
Windsor Cl., Chis.	175	E5
Windsor Cl., Har.	85	G3
Windsor Cl., Nthwd.	66	A2
Windsor Cl. N14	42	C7
Windsor Cl., Sun.	160	A6
Windsor Rd.		
Windsor Cres., Har.	85	G4
Windsor Cres., Wem.	88	B3
Windsor Dr., Barn.	41	J6
Windsor Gdns. W9	108	D5
Windsor Gdns., Croy.	200/201	E3
Richmond Rd.		
Windsor Gdns., Hayes	121	G3
Windsor Gro. SE27	169	J4
Windsor Pk. Rd., Hayes	121	J7
Windsor Pl. SW1	**25**	**G6**
Windsor Rd. E4	62	B4
Chivers Rd.		
Windsor Rd. E7	97	H5
Windsor Rd. E10	96	B2
Windsor Rd. E11	97	G1
Windsor Rd. N3	72	B2
Windsor Rd. N7	93	E3
Windsor Rd. N13	59	G3
Windsor Rd. N17	76	D2
Windsor Rd. NW2	89	H6
Windsor Rd. W5	105	H7
Windsor Rd., Barn.	40	B6
Windsor Rd., Bexh.	158	E4
Windsor Rd., Dag.	101	E3
Windsor Rd., Har.	68	A1
Windsor Rd., Houns.	142	B2
Windsor Rd., Ilf.	99	E4
Windsor Rd., Kings.T.	163	H7
Windsor Rd., Rich.	145	J2
Windsor Rd., Sthl.	123	F3
Windsor Rd., Sun.	160	A6
Windsor Rd., Tedd.	162	A5
Windsor Rd., Th.Hth.	187	H2
Windsor Rd., Wor.Pk.	197	G2
Windsor Ter. N1	**12**	**A3**
Windsor Ter. N1	111	J3
Windsor Wk. SE5	152	A2
Windsor Way W14	128	B4
Windsor Wf. E9	95	J5
Windsors, The Buck.H.	64	B2
Windspoint Dr. SE15	132/133	E6
Ethnard Rd.		
Windus Rd. N16	94	C1
Windus Wk. N16	94	C1
Windy Ridge, Brom.	192	B1
Windy Ridge Cl. SW19	166	A5
Wine Cl. E1	113	F7
Wine Office Ct. EC4	**19**	**F3**
Winery La., Kings.T.	181	J3
Winey Cl., Chess.	195	G6
Ashlyns Way		
Winford Ho. E3	95	J7
Winford Par., Sthl.	103	H6
Telford Rd.		
Winforton St. SE10	154	C1
Winfrith Rd. SW18	149	F7
Wingate Gdns., Croy.	186	D6
Wingate Rd. W6	127	H3
Wingate Rd., Ilf.	99	E5
Wingate Rd., Sid.	176	C5
Wingate Trd. Est. N17	60	D7
Wingfield Ms. SE15	152	D3
Wingfield St.		
Wingfield Rd. E15	96	E4
Wingfield Rd. E17	78	B5
Wingfield Rd., Kings.T.	164	A6
Wingfield St. SE15	152	D3
Wingford Rd. SW2	150	E6
Wingmore Rd. SE24	151	J3
Wingrave Rd. W6	127	J6
Wingrove Rd. SE6	173	E2
Wings Cl., Sutt.	198	D4
Winifred Gro. SW11	149	J4
Winifred Pl. N12	57	F5
High Rd.		
Winifred Rd. SW19	184	D1
Winifred Rd., Dag.	101	E2
Winifred Rd., Hmptn.	161	G4
Winifred St. E16	136	C1
Winifred Ter. E13	115	G2
Victoria Rd.		
Winifred Ter., Enf.	44	C7
Great Cambridge Rd.		
Winkfield Rd. E13	115	H2
Winkfield Rd. N22	75	G1
Winkley St. E2	112	E2
Winlaton Rd., Brom.	172	D4
Winmill Rd., Dag.	101	F3
Winn Common Rd. SE18	137	H6
Winn Rd. SE12	173	G1
Winnett St. W1	**17**	**H5**
Winnings Wk., Nthlt.	84/85	E6
Arnold Rd.		
Winnington Cl. N2	73	G6
Winnington Rd. N2	73	G6
Winnipeg Dr., Orp.	207	J6
Winnock Rd., West Dr.	120	A1
Winns Av. E17	77	J3
Winns Ms. N15	76	B4
Grove Pk. Rd.		
Winns Ter. E17	78	A2
Winsbeach E17	78	D3
Winscombe Cres. W5	105	G4
Winscombe St. N19	92	B2
Winscombe Way, Stan.	52	D5
Winsford Rd. SE6	171	J3
Winsford Ter. N18	60	A5
Winsham Gro. SW11	150	A5
Winslade Rd. SW2	151	E5
Winslade Way SE6	154	B7
Rushey Grn.		
Winsland Ms. W2	**15**	**E3**
Winsland St. W2	**15**	**E3**
Winsland St. W2	109	G6
Winsley St. W1	**17**	**G3**
Winsley St. W1	110	C6
Winslow SE17	**36**	**D4**
Winslow SE17	132	B5
Winslow Cl. NW10	88/89	E3
Neasden La. N.		
Winslow Cl., Pnr.	66	B6
Winslow Gro. E4	62	E2
Winslow Rd. W6	127	J6
Winslow Way, Felt.	160	D3
Winsor Ter. E6	116	D5
Winsor Ter. Roundabout E6	116/117	E5
Royal Docks Rd.		
Winstanley Est. SW11	149	G3
Winstanley Rd. SW11	149	G3
Winstead Gdns., Dag.	101	J5
Winston Av. NW9	70	E7
Winston Cl., Har.	52	C5
Winston Cl., Rom.	83	H4
Winston Cl., Har.	52	C5
Winston Rd. N16	94	A4
Winston Wk. W4	126	D4
Acton La.		
Winston Way, Ilf.	99	E3
Winstre Rd., Borwd.	38	A1
Winter Av. E6	116	B1
Winter Box Wk., Rich.	145	J4
Winterborne Av., Orp.	207	G3
Winterbourne Rd. SE6	171	J1
Winterbourne Rd., Dag.	100	C2
Winterbourne Rd., Th.Hth.	187	G3
Winterbrook Rd. SE24	151	J6
Winterburn Cl. N11	58	A6
Winterfold Cl. SW19	166	B2
Wintergreen Cl. E6	116	B5
Yarrow Cres.		
Winters Rd., T.Ditt.	181	E7
Winterstoke Gdns. NW7	55	G5
Winterstoke Rd. SE6	171	J1
Winterton Ho. E1	113	E6
Winterton Rd. SW2	151	E5
Winthorpe Rd. SW15	148	B4
Winthrop St. E1	112	E5
Winthrop Wk., Wem.	87	H3
Everard Way		
Winton Av. N11	58	C7
Winton Cl. N9	45	G7
Winton Gdns., Edg.	53	J7
Winton Rd., Orp.	206	E4
Winton Way SW16	169	G5
Wisbeach Rd., Croy.	188	A5
Wisdons Cl., Dag.	101	H1
Wise La. NW7	55	H6
Wise La., West Dr.	120	A4
Wise Rd. E15	114	D1
Wiseman Ct. SE19	170	B5
Wiseman Rd. E10	96	A2
Wiseton Rd. SW17	167	H1
Wishart Rd. SE3	156	A1
Wisley Rd. SW11	150	A5
Wisley Rd., Orp.	176	A7
Wisteria Cl. NW7	55	F6
Wisteria Cl., Ilf.	98	E5
Wisteria Cl., Orp.	207	E2
Wisteria Rd. SE13	154	D4
Witan St. E2	113	E3
Witham Cl., Loug.	48	B6
Witham Rd. SE20	189	F3
Witham Rd. W13	124	D1
Witham Rd., Dag.	101	G5
Witham Rd., Islw.	144	A1
Witherby Cl., Croy.	202	B5
Witherington Rd. N5	93	G5
Withers Cl., Chess.	195	F6
Coppard Gdns.		
Withers Mead NW9	71	F1
Witherston Way SE9	174	D2
Withy Mead E4	62	D3
Withycombe Rd. SW19	148	A7
Witley Cres., Croy.	204	C6
Witley Gdns., Sthl.	123	F4
Witley Rd. N19	92	C2
Holloway Rd.		
Witney Cl., Pnr.	51	F6
Witney Path SE23	171	G3
Wittenham Way E4	62	D3
Wittering Cl., Kings.T.	163	G5
Wittersham Rd., Brom.	173	F5
Wivenhoe Cl. SE15	152	E3
Wivenhoe Ct., Houns.	143	F4
Wivenhoe Rd., Bark.	118	A2
Wiverton Rd. SE26	171	F6
Wix Rd., Dag.	118	D1
Wixs La. SW4	150	B4
Woburn Cl. SE28	118	D6
Summerton Way		
Woburn Cl. SW19	167	F6
Tintern Cl.		
Woburn Ct. SE16	132/133	E5
Masters Dr.		
Woburn Pl. WC1	**9**	**J5**
Woburn Pl. WC1	110	E4
Woburn Rd., Cars.	199	H1
Woburn Rd., Croy.	201	J1
Woburn Sq. WC1	**9**	**J6**
Woburn Sq. WC1	110	D4
Woburn Wk. WC1	**9**	**J4**
Woburn Wk. WC1	110	D3
Wodehouse Av. SE5	152	C1
Woffington Cl., Kings.T.	181	F1
Woking Cl. SW15	147	F4
Woldham Pl., Brom.	191	J4
Woldham Rd., Brom.	191	J4
Wolds Dr., Orp.	206	D4
Wolfe Cl., Brom.	191	G6
Wolfe Cl., Hayes	102	B3
Ayles Rd.		
Wolfe Cres. SE7	136	A5
Wolfe Cres. SE16	133	G2
Wolferton Rd. E12	98	C4
Wolffe Gdns. E15	97	F6
Wolffram Cl. SE13	154	E5
Wolfington Rd. SE27	169	H4
Wolftencroft Cl. SW11	149	G3
Wollaston Cl. SE1	**35**	**J1**
Wolmer Cl., Edg.	54	B4
Wolmer Gdns., Edg.	54	A3
Wolseley Av. SW19	166	D2
Wolseley Gdns. W4	126	B6

Name	Grid	Ref
Wolseley Rd. E7	97	H7
Wolseley Rd. N8	74	D6
Wolseley Rd. N22	75	F1
Wolseley Rd. W4	126	C4
Wolseley Rd., Har.	68	B3
Wolseley Rd., Mitch.	186	A7
Wolseley St. SE1	29	G4
Wolseley St. SE1	132	C2
Wolsey Av. E6	116	D3
Wolsey Av. E17	77	J3
Wolsey Av., T.Ditt.	180	C5
Wolsey Cl. SW20	165	H7
Wolsey Cl., Houns.	143	J4
Wolsey Cl., Kings.T.	182	B1
Wolsey Cl., Sthl.	123	J3
Wolsey Cl., Wor.Pk.	197	G4
Wolsey Cres., Mord.	184	B7
Wolsey Dr., Kings.T.	163	H5
Wolsey Gdns., Ilf.	65	F6
Wolsey Gro., Edg.	54	D7
Wolsey Ms. NW5	92	C6
Wolsey Ms., Orp.	207	J5
Osgood Av.		
Wolsey Rd. N1	94	A5
Wolsey Rd., E.Mol.	180	A4
Wolsey Rd., Enf.	45	E2
Wolsey Rd., Hmptn.	161	H6
Wolsey St. E1	113	F5
Sidney St.		
Wolsey Way, Chess.	196	A5
Wolstonbury N12	56	D5
Wolvercote Rd. SE2	138	D2
Wolverley St. E2	112/113	E3
Bethnal Grn. Rd.		
Wolverton SE17	36	D3
Wolverton Av.,	182	A1
Kings.T.		
Wolverton Gdns. W5	105	J7
Wolverton Gdns. W6	128	A4
Wolverton Rd., Stan.	53	E6
Wolverton Way N14	42	C5
Wolves La. N13	59	G7
Wolves La. N22	59	G7
Womersley Rd. N8	75	F6
Wonford St. E3,	183	E1
Kings.T.		
Wontner Cl. N1	93	J7
Greenman St.		
Wontner Rd. SW17	167	J2
Wood Cl. E2	13	H5
Wood Cl. E2	112	D4
Wood Cl. NW9	70	D7
Wood Cl., Har.	68	A7
Wood Dr., Chis.	174	B6
Wood End Av., Har.	85	H4
Wood End Cl., Nthlt.	86	A5
Wood End Gdns.,	85	J5
Nthlt.		
Wood End La., Nthlt.	85	H6
Wood End Rd., Har.	86	A4
Wood End Way,	85	J5
Nthlt.		
Wood La. N6	74	B6
Wood La. NW9	70	E7
Wood La. W12	107	J6
Wood La., Dag.	100	C4
Wood La., Islw.	124	C7
Wood La., Stan.	52	D3
Wood La., Wdf.Grn.	63	F5
Wood Lo. Gdns.,	174	B7
Brom.		
Wood Lo. La.,	204	C3
W.Wick.		
Wood Pt. E16	115	G5
Fife Rd.		
Wood Retreat SE18	137	G7
Wood Ride, Barn.	41	G1
Wood Ride, Orp.	193	G4
Wood Ri., Pnr.	66	A5
Wood St. E16	115	H7
Ethel Rd.		
Wood St. E17	78	C3
Wood St. EC2	20	A4
Wood St. EC2	111	J6
Wood St. W4	126	E5
Wood St., Barn.	40	A4
Wood St., Kings.T.	181	G1
Wood St., Mitch.	186	A7
Wood Vale N10	74	C5
Wood Vale SE23	170	E1
Wood Vale Est. SE23	153	F6
Wood Way, Orp.	206	D2
Wood Wf. SE10	134	B6
Woodall Cl. E14	114	B7
Lawless St.		
Woodall Cl., Chess.	195	G6
Ashlyns Way		
Woodall Rd., Enf.	45	G6
Woodbank Rd.,	173	F3
Brom.		
Woodbastwick Rd.	171	G5
SE26		
Woodberry Av. N21	59	G2
Woodberry Av., Har.	67	H4
Woodberry Cl., Sun.	160	A6
Ashridge Way		
Woodberry Cres. N10	74	B3
Woodberry Down N4	75	J7
Woodberry Down Est.	75	J7
N4		
Woodberry Gdns. N12	57	F6
Woodberry Gro. N4	75	J7
Woodberry Gro. N12	57	F6
Woodberry Way E4	62	C1
Woodberry Way N12	57	F6
Woodbine Cl.,	162	A2
Twick.		
Woodbine Gro. SE20	171	E7
Woodbine La.,	197	J3
Wor.Pk.		
Woodbine Pl. E11	79	G6
Woodbine Rd., Sid.	175	H1
Woodbine Ter. E9	95	F6
Morning La.		
Woodbines Av.,	181	G3
Kings.T.		
Woodborough Rd.	147	H4
SW15		
Woodbourne Av.	168	D3
SW16		
Woodbourne Cl.	168/169	E3
SW16		
Woodbourne Av.		
Woodbourne Dr.,	194	C6
Esher		
Woodbourne Gdns.,	200	B7
Wall.		
Woodbridge Cl. N7	93	F2
Woodbridge Cl. NW2	89	G3
Woodbridge Ct.,	64	B7
Wdf.Grn.		
Woodbridge Rd.,	99	J5
Bark.		
Woodbridge St. EC1	11	G5
Woodbridge St. EC1	111	H4
Woodbrook Rd. SE2	138	A6
Woodburn Cl. NW4	72	A5
Woodbury Cl. E11	79	H4
Woodbury Cl., Croy.	202	C2
Woodbury Hill, Loug.	48	B3
Woodbury Hollow,	48	B2
Loug.		
Woodbury Pk. Rd.	104	E4
W13		
Woodbury Rd. E17	78	B4
Woodbury St. SW17	167	H5
Woodchester Sq. W2	14	A1
Woodchester Sq. W2	108	E5
Woodchurch Cl., Sid.	175	G3
Woodchurch Dr.,	174	A7
Brom.		
Woodchurch Rd. NW6	90	D7
Woodclyffe Dr., Chis.	192	D2
Woodcock Ct., Har.	69	H7
Woodcock Dell Av.,	69	G7
Har.		
Woodcock Hill, Har.	69	G7
Woodcocks E16	115	J5
Woodcombe Cres.	171	F1
SE23		
Woodcote Av. NW7	55	J6
Woodcote Av.,	187	H4
Th.Hth.		
Woodcote Av., Wall.	200	B7
Woodcote Cl., Enf.	45	F6
Woodcote Cl.,	163	J5
Kings.T.		
Woodcote Dr., Orp.	207	G1
Woodcote Ms., Loug.	47	J7
Fallow Flds.		
Woodcote Ms., Wall.	200	B6
Woodcote Pl. SE27	169	H5
Woodcote Rd. E11	79	G7
Woodcote Rd., Wall.	200	B6
Woodcroft N21	59	F1
Woodcroft SE9	174	C3
Woodcroft, Grnf.	86	D6
Woodcroft Av. NW7	55	E7
Woodcroft Av., Stan.	68	C1
Woodcroft Ms. SE8	133	H4
Croft St.		
Woodcroft Rd.,	187	H5
Th.Hth.		
Woodedge Cl. E4	63	F1
Woodend SE19	169	J6
Woodend, Sutt.	199	F2
Woodend Gdns., Enf.	42	E4
Woodend Rd. E17	78	C2
Wooder Gdns. E7	97	F4
Wooderson Cl. SE25	188	B4
Woodfall Av., Barn.	40	C5
Woodfall Rd. N4	93	G1
Woodfall St. SW3	31	J4
Woodfall St. SW3	129	J5
Woodfarrs SE5	152	A4
Woodfield Av. NW9	71	E4
Woodfield Av. SW16	168	D3
Woodfield Av. W5	105	F4
Woodfield Av., Cars.	200	A6
Woodfield Av., Wem.	87	F3
Woodfield Cl. SE19	169	J7
Woodfield Cl., Enf.	44	B4
Woodfield Cres. W5	105	F4
Woodfield Dr., Barn.	58	A1
Woodfield Gdns. W9	108	C5
Woodfield Rd.		
Woodfield Gdns.,	183	F5
N.Mal.		
Woodfield Gro. SW16	168	D3
Woodfield La. SW16	168	D3
Woodfield Pl. W9	108	C4
Woodfield Rd. W5	105	F4
Woodfield Rd. W9	108	C5
Woodfield Rd.,	142	B2
Houns.		
Woodfield Rd., T.Ditt.	194	C2
Lynwood Rd.		
Woodfield Way N11	58	D7
Woodford Av., Ilf.	80	C5
Woodford Av.,	80	B3
Wdf.Grn.		
Woodford Br. Rd., Ilf.	80	A3
Woodford Ct. W12	128	A2
Shepherds Bush Grn.		
Woodford Cres., Pnr.	66	B2
Woodford New Rd.	78	E4
E17		
Woodford New Rd.	79	E1
E18		
Woodford New Rd.,	79	E1
Wdf.Grn.		
Woodford Pl., Wem.	87	H1
Woodford Rd. E7	97	H4
Woodford Rd. E18	79	G4
Woodford Trd. Est.,	80	A3
Wdf.Grn.		
Woodgate Av., Chess.	195	G5
Woodgate Cres.	50	A6
Woodgate Dr. SW16	168	D7
Woodger Rd. W12	127	J2
Goldhawk Rd.		
Woodget Cl. E6	116	B6
Remington Rd.		
Woodgrange Av. N12	57	G6
Woodgrange Av. W5	126	A1
Woodgrange Av.,	44	D6
Enf.		
Woodgrange Av.,	69	F5
Har.		
Woodgrange Cl.,	69	G5
Har.		
Woodgrange Gdns.,	44	D6
Enf.		
Woodgrange Rd. E7	97	H4
Woodgrange Ter.,	44	D6
Enf.		
Great Cambridge Rd.		
Woodhall Av. SE21	170	C3
Woodhall Av., Pnr.	66	E2
Woodhall Dr. SE21	170	C3
Woodhall Dr., Pnr.	66	D1
Woodhall Gate, Pnr.	50	D7
Woodhall La., Wat.	50	D4
Woodhall Rd., Pnr.	50	D7
Woodham Ct. E18	79	F4
Woodham Rd. SE6	172	C3
Woodhatch Cl. E6	116	B6
Remington Rd.		
Woodhaven Gdns.,	81	F3
Ilf.		
Brandville Gdns.		
Woodhayes Rd.	165	J7
SW19		
Woodhead Dr., Orp.	207	H2
Sherlies Av.		
Woodheyes Rd. NW10	88	D5
Woodhill SE18	136	B4
Woodhill Cres., Har.	69	G6
Woodhouse Av.,	104	C2
Grnf.		
Woodhouse Cl., Grnf.	104	C2
Woodhouse Cl.,	121	H3
Hayes		
Woodhouse Eaves,	50	A5
Nthwd.		
Woodhouse Gro. E12	98	B6
Woodhouse Rd. E11	97	F3
Woodhouse Rd. N12	57	G6
Woodhurst Av., Orp.	192	E6
Woodhurst Rd. SE2	138	A5
Woodhurst Rd. W3	106	C7
Woodington Cl. SE9	156	D6
Woodison St. E3	113	H4
Woodknoll Dr., Chis.	192	C1
Woodland App., Grnf.	86	D6
Woodland Cl. NW9	70	C6
Woodland Cl. SE19	170	B6
Woodland Hill		
Woodland Cl., Epsom	197	E6
Woodland Cl.,	63	H3
Wdf.Grn.		
Woodland Cres. SE10	134	E6
Woodland Cres. SE16	133	G2
Woodland Gdns. N10	74	B5
Woodland Gdns.,	144	B2
Islw.		
Woodland Gro. SE10	134	E6
Woodland Hill SE19	170	B6
Woodland Ri. N10	74	B4
Woodland Ri., Grnf.	86	D6
Woodland Rd. E4	62	C1
Woodland Rd. N11	58	B5
Woodland Rd. SE19	170	B5
Woodland Rd., Loug.	48	B3
Woodland Rd.,	187	G4
Th.Hth.		
Woodland St. E8	94	C6
Dalston La.		
Woodland Ter. SE7	136	B4
Woodland Wk. NW3	91	H5
Woodland Wk.	134/135	E5
SE10		
Woodland Gro.		
Woodland Wk., Brom.	172	E4
Woodland Way N21	59	G2
Woodland Way NW7	55	E6
Woodland Way SE2	138	D4
Woodland Way, Croy.	203	H1
Woodland Way,	168	A7
Mitch.		
Woodland Way,	184	C4
Mord.		
Woodland Way, Orp.	193	F4
Woodland Way, Surb.	196	B2
Woodland Way,	204	B4
W.Wick.		
Woodland Way,	63	H3
Wdf.Grn.		
Woodlands NW11	72	B6
Woodlands SW20	183	J4
Woodlands, Har.	67	G4
Woodlands, The N14	58	B1
Woodlands, The SE13	154	D7
Woodlands, The SE19	169	J7
Woodlands, The,	144	C2
Islw.		
Woodlands Av. E11	97	H1
Woodlands Av. N3	57	F7
Woodlands Av. W3	126	B1
Woodlands Av.,	182	C1
N.Mal.		
Woodlands Av., Rom.	82	E6
Woodlands Av.,	84	D1
Ruis.		
Woodlands Av., Sid.	175	H1
Woodlands Av.,	197	F2
Wor.Pk.		
Woodlands Cl. NW11	72	B5
Woodlands Cl.,	38	B4
Borwd.		
Woodlands Cl., Brom.	192	C2
Woodlands Cl.,	194	C7
Esher		
Woodlands Dr., Stan.	52	C6
Woodlands Dr., Sun.	178	C2
Woodlands Gro.,	144	B2
Islw.		
Woodlands Pk., Bex.	177	J4
Woodlands Pk. Rd.	75	H5
N15		
Woodlands Pk. Rd.	134	E6
SE10		
Woodlands Rd. E11	96	E2
Woodlands Rd. E17	78	C3
Woodlands Rd. N9	61	F1
Woodlands Rd. SW13	147	F3
Woodlands Rd.,	159	E3
Bexh.		
Woodlands Rd.,	192	B2
Brom.		
Woodlands Rd., Enf.	44	A1
Woodlands Rd., Har.	68	C5
Woodlands Rd., Ilf.	99	F3
Woodlands Rd., Islw.	144	B2
Woodlands Rd., Sthl.	122	D1
Woodlands Rd., Surb.	181	G7
Woodlands St. SE13	154	D7
Woodlands Way	148	C5
SW15		
Oakhill Rd.		
Woodlawn Cl. SW15	148	C5
Woodlawn Cres.	161	H2
Twick.		
Woodlawn Dr., Felt.	160	D2
Woodlawn Rd. SW6	128	A7
Woodlea Dr., Brom.	191	E5
Woodlea Rd. N16	94	B3
Woodleigh Av. N12	57	H6
Woodleigh Gdns.	169	E3
SW16		
Woodley Cl. SW17	167	J7
Arnold Rd.		
Woodley La., Cars.	199	G3
Woodman La. E4	46	E5
Woodman Path, Ilf.	65	H6

Name	Page	Grid
Woodman St. E16	136	D1
Woodmans Gro. NW10	89	F5
Woodmans Ms. W12	107	H5
Woodmansterne Rd. SW16	168	D7
Woodmere SE9	174	C1
Woodmere Av., Croy.	189	G7
Woodmere Cl. SW11	150	A3
Lavender Hill		
Woodmere Cl., Croy.	189	G7
Woodmere Gdns., Croy.	189	G7
Woodmere Way, Beck.	190	D5
Woodnook Rd. SW16	168	B5
Woodpecker Cl. N9	44	E6
Woodpecker Cl., Bushey	51	J1
Woodpecker Cl., Har.	68	C1
Woodpecker Rd. SE14	133	H6
Woodpecker Rd. SE28	118	C7
Woodquest Av. SE24	151	J5
Woodridge Cl., Enf.	43	G1
Woodridings Av., Pnr.	67	F1
Woodridings Cl., Pnr.	51	E7
Woodriffe Rd. E11	78	D7
Woodrow SE18	136	C4
Woodrow Cl., Grnf.	87	E7
Woodrow Ct. N17	60/61	E7
Heybourne Rd.		
Woodrush Cl. SE14	133	H7
Southerngate Way		
Woodrush Way, Rom.	82	D4
Woods, The, Nthwd.	50	A5
Woods Cl. SE19	170	B6
Woodland Hill		
Woods Ms. W1	**16**	**A5**
Woods Ms. W1	110	A7
Woods Pl. SE1	**28**	**E6**
Woods Rd. SE15	152	E1
Woodseer St. E1	**21**	**G1**
Woodseer St. E1	112	C5
Woodsford SE17	**36**	**B4**
Woodsford Sq. W14	128	B2
Woodshire Rd., Dag.	101	H3
Woodside NW11	72	D5
Woodside, Buck.H.	63	J2
Woodside Av. N6	73	J5
Woodside Av. N10	73	J5
Woodside Av. N12	57	F4
Woodside Av. SE25	188	E6
Woodside Av., Chis.	175	F5
Woodside Av., Esher	180	B7
Woodside Av., Wem.	105	H1
Woodside Cl., Stan.	52	E5
Woodside Cl., Surb.	182	C7
Woodside Cl., Wem.	105	H1
Woodside Ct. N12	57	F4
Woodside Av.		
Woodside Ct. Rd., Croy.	188	D7
Woodside Cres., Sid.	175	H3
Woodside End, Wem.	105	H1
Woodside Gdns. E4	62	B5
Woodside Gdns. N17	76	B2
Woodside Gra. Rd. N12	57	E4
Woodside Grn. SE25	188	E6
Woodside Gro. N12	57	F3
Woodside La. N12	57	E3
Woodside La., Bex.	158	D6
Woodside Ms. SE22	152	C6
Heber Rd.		
Woodside Pk. SE25	188	D5
Woodside Pk. Av. E17	78	D4
Woodside Pk. Rd. N12	57	E4
Woodside Rd., Wem.	105	H1
Woodside Rd. E13	115	J4
Woodside Rd. N22	59	F7
Woodside Rd. SE25	188	E6
Woodside Rd., Brom.	192	B5
Woodside Rd., Kings.T.	163	H7
Woodside Rd., N.Mal.	182	D2
Woodside Rd., Sid.	175	H3
Woodside Rd., Sutt.	199	F3
Woodside Rd., Wdf.Grn.	63	G4
Woodside Way, Croy.	189	E6
Woodside Way, Mitch.	186	B1
Woodsome Rd. NW5	92	A3
Woodspring Rd. SW19	166	B2
Woodstead Gro., Edg.	53	H6
Woodstock Av. NW11	72	B7
Woodstock Av. W13	124	D3
Woodstock Av., Islw.	144	D5
Woodstock Av., Sthl.	103	F3
Woodstock Av., Sutt.	184	C7
Woodstock Cl., Bex.	177	F1
Woodstock Cl., Stan.	69	H2
Woodstock Cl. SE12	155	G6
Woodstock Cres. N9	44	E6
Woodstock Gdns., Beck.	190	B1
Woodstock Gdns., Ilf.	100	A2
Woodstock Gro. W12	128	A2
Woodstock La. N., Surb.	195	F2
Woodstock La. S., Chess.	195	F4
Woodstock La. S., Esher	194	E5
Woodstock Ms. W1	**16**	**C2**
Woodstock Ri., Sutt.	184	C7
Woodstock Rd. E7	97	J7
Woodstock Rd. E17	78	D2
Woodstock Rd. N4	93	G1
Woodstock Rd. NW11	72	C7
Woodstock Rd. W4	127	E3
Woodstock Rd., Cars.	200	A5
Woodstock Rd., Croy.	202	A3
Woodstock Rd., Wem.	87	J7
Woodstock St. E16	114/115	E6
Victoria Dock Rd.		
Woodstock St. W1	**16**	**D4**
Woodstock Ter. E14	114	B7
Woodstock Way, Mitch.	186	B2
Woodstone Av., Epsom	197	G5
Woodsyre SE26	170	C4
Woodthorpe Rd. SW15	147	H4
Woodtree Cl. NW4	71	J2
Ashley La.		
Woodvale Av. SE25	188	C3
Woodvale Wk. SE27	169	J5
Elder Rd.		
Woodvale Way NW11	90	A3
The Vale		
Woodview Av. E4	62	C4
Woodview Cl. N4	75	H7
Woodview Cl. SW15	164	D4
Woodview Cl., Orp.	207	F2
Crofton Rd.		
Woodville SE3	155	H1
Woodville Cl. SE12	155	G5
Woodville Cl., Tedd.	162	D4
Woodville Gdns. NW11	72	A7
Woodville Gdns. W5	105	H6
Woodville Gdns., Ilf.	80	E3
Woodville Gro., Well.	158	A3
Woodville Rd. E11	97	F1
Woodville Rd. E17	77	H4
Woodville Rd. E18	79	H2
Woodville Rd. N16	94	B5
Woodville Rd. NW6	108	C2
Woodville Rd. NW11	72	A7
Woodville Rd. W5	105	G6
Woodville Rd., Barn.	40	E3
Woodville Rd., Mord.	184	D4
Woodville Rd., Rich.	163	E3
Woodville Rd., Th.Hth.	187	J4
Woodville St. SE18	136	B4
Woodhill		
Woodward Av. NW4	71	G5
Woodward Cl., Esher	194	C6
Woodward Gdns., Dag.	100	C7
Woodward Rd.		
Woodward Gdns., Stan.	52	C7
Woodward Rd., Dag.	100	B7
Woodwarde Rd. SE22	152	B6
Woodway Cres., Har.	68	D6
Woodwell St. SW18	149	F5
Huguenot Pl.		
Woodyard Cl. NW5	92	A5
Gillies St.		
Woodyard La. SE21	152	B7
Woodyates Rd. SE12	155	G6
Wool Rd. SW20	165	H6
Woolacombe Rd. SE3	155	J1
Woolacombe Way, Hayes	121	H4
Wooler St. SE17	**36**	**B4**
Wooler St. SE17	132	A5
Woolf Cl. SE28	138	B1
Woollaston Rd. N4	75	H6
Woolmead Av. NW9	71	G7
Woolmer Gdns. N18	60	D5
Woolmer Rd. N18	60	D5
Woolmore St. E14	114	C7
Woolneigh St. SW6	148	E3
Woolstaplers Way SE16	**29**	**H6**
Woolstaplers Way SE16	132	D4
Woolston Cl. E17	77	G2
Riverhead Cl.		
Woolstone Rd. SE23	171	H2
Woolwich Ch. St. SE18	136	B3
Woolwich Common SE18	136	D6
Woolwich Ferry Pier E16	136	D2
Woolwich Foot Tunnel E16	136	D2
Woolwich Foot Tunnel SE18	136	D2
Woolwich Garrison SE18	136	C6
Woolwich High St. SE18	136	D3
Woolwich Ind. Est. SE28	137	H3
Hadden Rd.		
Woolwich Manor Way E6	116	E6
Woolwich Manor Way E16	136	E2
Woolwich New Rd. SE18	136	D5
Woolwich Rd. SE2	138	D6
Woolwich Rd. SE7	135	G5
Woolwich Rd. SE10	135	F5
Woolwich Rd., Belv.	138	D6
Woolwich Rd., Bexh.	159	G4
Wooster Gdns. E14	114	D6
Wooster Ms., Har.	67	J3
Fairfield Dr.		
Wooster Pl. SE1	**36**	**C1**
Wootton Gro. N3	72	D1
Wootton St. SE1	**27**	**F3**
Wootton St. SE1	131	G1
Worbeck Rd. SE20	189	E2
Worcester Av. N17	60	D7
Worcester Cl. NW2	89	H3
Newfield Ri.		
Worcester Cl., Croy.	203	J2
Worcester Cl., Mitch.	186	B3
Worcester Cres. NW7	54	E3
Worcester Cres., Wdf.Grn.	63	H5
Worcester Dr. W4	127	E2
Worcester Gdns. SW11	149	J5
Grandison Rd.		
Worcester Gdns., Grnf.	85	J6
Worcester Gdns., Ilf.	80	B7
Worcester Gdns., Wor.Pk.	197	E3
Worcester Ms. NW6	90/91	E6
Lymington Rd.		
Worcester Pk. Rd., Wor.Pk.	196	C3
Worcester Rd. E12	98	C4
Worcester Rd. E17	77	G2
Worcester Rd. SW19	166	C5
Worcester Rd., Sutt.	199	E6
Wordsworth Av. E12	98	B6
Wordsworth Av. E18	79	F3
Wordsworth Av., Grnf.	104	A2
Wordsworth Dr., Sutt.	197	J4
Wordsworth Rd. N16	94	B4
Wordsworth Rd. SE1	**37**	**F2**
Wordsworth Rd. SE20	171	G7
Wordsworth Rd., Hmptn.	161	F4
Wordsworth Rd., Wall.	200	C6
Wordsworth Rd., Well.	157	H1
Wordsworth Wk. NW11	72	D4
Wordsworth Way, West Dr.	120	B4
Worfield St. SW11	129	H7
Worgan St. SE11	**34**	**C3**
Worgan St. SE11	131	F5
Worgan St. SE16	133	G3
Worland Rd. E15	97	E7
World's End Est.	**30**	**E7**
World's End Est. SW10	129	G7
Worlds End La. N21	43	F5
Worlds End La., Enf.	43	F5
Worlds End La., Orp.	207	J6
World's End Pas. SW10	**30**	**E7**
Worlidge St. W6	127	J5
Worlingham Rd. SE22	152	C4
Wormholt Rd. W12	107	G7
Wormwood St. EC2	**20**	**D3**
Wormwood St. EC2	112	B6
Wornington Rd. W10	108	B5
Wornzow Rd. NW8	109	G1
Worple Av. SW19	166	A7
Worple Av., Islw.	144	D5
Worple Cl., Har.	85	F1
Worple Rd. SW19	166	B7
Worple Rd. SW20	183	J2
Worple Rd., Islw.	144	D4
Worple Rd. Ms. SW19	166	C6
Worple St. SW14	146	D3
Worple Way, Har.	85	F1
Worple Way, Rich.	145	H5
Worship St. EC2	**12**	**C4**
Worship St. EC2	112	A4
Worslade Rd. SW17	167	G4
Worsley Br. Rd. SE26	171	J4
Worsley Br. Rd. Beck.	171	J5
Worsley Rd. E11	96	E4
Worsopp Dr. SW4	150	C5
Worth Gro. SE17	**36**	**B4**
Worthfield Cl., Epsom	196	D7
Worthing Cl. E15	114/115	E2
Mitre Rd.		
Worthing Rd., Houns.	123	F6
Worthington Cl., Mitch.	186	B3
Worthington Rd., Surb.	195	J1
Worthy Down Ct. SE18	156	D1
Prince Imperial Rd.		
Wortley Rd. E6	98	A7
Wortley Rd., Croy.	187	G7
Worton Gdns., Islw.	144	A2
Worton Hall Ind. Est., Islw.	144	B4
Worton Rd., Islw.	144	B3
Worton Way, Houns.	144	A2
Worton Way, Islw.	143	J1
Wotton Rd. NW2	89	J4
Wotton Rd. SE8	133	J6
Wouldham Rd. E16	115	F6
Wragby Rd. E11	97	E3
Wrampling Pl. N9	60	D1
Wrangthorn Wk., Croy.	201	G4
Epsom Rd.		
Wray Av., Ilf.	80	D3
Wray Cres. N4	93	E2
Wrayfield Rd., Sutt.	198	A3
Wraysbury Cl., Houns.	142/143	E5
Dorney Way		
Wrekin Rd. SE18	137	F7
Wren Av. NW2	89	J5
Wren Av., Sthl.	123	F4
Wren Cl. E16	115	F6
Wren Cl. N9	61	G1
Ibbotson Av.		
Wren Cres., Bushey	51	J1
Wren Dr., West Dr.	120	A3
Wren Gdns., Dag.	100	D5
Wren Landing E14	134	A1
Cabot Sq.		
Wren Path SE28	137	G3
Wren Rd. SE5	152	A1
Wren Rd., Dag.	100	D5
Wren Rd., Sid.	176	C4
Wren St. WC1	**10**	**D5**
Wren St. WC1	111	H4
Wrentham Av. NW10	108	A2
Wrenthorpe Rd., Brom.	172	E4
Wrenwood Way, Pnr.	66	B4
Wrestlers Ct. EC3	112	B6
Camomile St.		
Wrexham Rd. E3	114	A2
Wricklemarsh Rd. SE3	155	H1
Wrigglesworth St. SE14	133	G7
Wright Rd. N1	94	B6
Burder Cl.		
Wright Rd., Houns.	122	C7
Wrights All. SW19	165	J6
Wrights Cl. SE13	154	D4
Wisteria Rd.		
Wrights Cl., Dag.	101	H3
Wrights Grn. SW4	150	D4
Nelson's Row		
Wrights La. W8	**22**	**A5**
Wrights La. W8	128	E3

Wrights Pl. NW10 88 C6
  Mitchell Way
Wrights Rd. E3 113 J2
Wrights Rd. SE25 188 B3
Wrights Row, Wall. 200 B4
Wrights Wk. SW14 146 D3
Wrigley Cl. E4 62 D5
Wrotham Rd. NW1 92 C7
  Agar Pl.
Wrotham Rd. 124/125 E1
  W13
  Mattock La.
Wrotham Rd., Barn. 40 B2
Wrotham Rd., Well. 158 C1
Wroths Path, Loug. 48 C1
Wrottesley Rd. NW10 107 G2
Wrottesley Rd. SE18 137 F6
Wroughton Rd. 149 J6
  SW11
Wroughton Ter. NW4 71 J4
Wroxall Rd., Dag. 100 C6
Wroxham Gdns. N11 58 C7
Wroxham Rd. SE28 118 D7
Wroxton Rd. SE15 153 E2
Wrythe Grn., Cars. 199 J3
  Wrythe Grn. Rd.
Wrythe Grn. Rd., 199 J3
  Cars.
Wrythe La., Cars. 199 F1
Wulfstan St. W12 107 F6
Wyatt Cl. SE16 133 J2
Wyatt Cl., Felt. 160 C1
Wyatt Cl., Hayes 102 A5
Wyatt Dr. SW13 127 J7
Wyatt Pk. Rd. SW2 169 E2
Wyatt Rd. E7 97 G6
Wyatt Rd. N5 93 J3
Wyatts La. E17 78 C3
Wybert St. NW1 9 E5
Wyborne Way NW10 88 C7
Wyburn Av., Barn. 40 C3
Wych Elm Dr., Brom. 173 F7
  London La.
Wych Elm Pas., 163 J7
  Kings.T.
Wyche Gro., S.Croy. 201 J7
Wycherley Cl. SE3 135 F7
Wycherley Cres. 40 E6
  Barn.
Wychwood Av., Edg. 53 G6
Wychwood Av., 187 J3
  Th.Hth.
Wychwood Cl., Edg. 53 G6
Wychwood Cl., Sun. 160 A6
Wychwood End N6 74 C7
Wychwood Gdns., 80 C4
  Ilf.
Wychwood Way 170 A6
  SE19
  Roman Ri.
Wyclif St. EC1 11 G4
Wycliffe Cl., Well. 157 J1
Wycliffe Rd. SW11 150 A2
Wycliffe Rd. SW19 167 E6
Wycombe Gdns. 90 D2
  NW11
Wycombe Pl. SW18 149 F6
Wycombe Rd. N17 76 D1
Wycombe Rd., Ilf. 80 C5
Wycombe Rd., Wem. 106 A1
Wydehurst Rd. 188 D7
  Croy.
Wydell Cl., Mord. 183 J6
Wydeville Manor Rd. 173 H4
  SE12
Wye Cl., Orp. 193 J7
Wye St. SW11 149 G2
Wyemead Cres. E4 62 E2
Wyevale Cl., Pnr. 66 A3
Wyfields, Ilf. 80/81 E1
  Ravensbourne Gdns.
Wyfold Ho. SE2 138 D2
  Wolvercote Rd.
Wyfold Rd. SW6 128 B7
Wyhill Wk., Dag. 101 J6
Wyke Cl., Islw. 124 B5
Wyke Gdns. W7 124 D3
Wyke Rd. E3 96 A7
Wyke Rd. SW20 183 J2
Wykeham Av., Dag. 100 C6
Wykeham Cl., 120 D5
  West Dr.
Wykeham Grn., Dag. 100 C6
Wykeham Hill, Wem. 87 J1
Wykeham Rd. N20 56 B1
Wykeham Rd. NW4 71 J5

Wykeham Rd., Har. 68 E4
Wyld Way, Wem. 88 B6
Wyldes Cl. NW11 91 F1
  Wildwood Rd.
Wyldfield Gdns. N9 60 C2
Wyleu St. SE23 153 H1
Wylie Rd., Sthl. 123 G3
Wyllen Cl. E1 113 F4
Wylo Dr., Barn. 39 G6
Wymering Rd. W9 108 D3
Wymond St. SW15 147 J3
Wynan Rd. E14 134 B5
Wynash Gdns., Cars. 199 H5
Wynaud Ct. N22 59 F6
  Palmerston Rd.
Wyncham Av., Sid. 175 H1
Wynchgate N14 58 D1
Wynchgate N21 58 E1
Wynchgate, Har. 52 B7
Wyncroft Cl., Brom. 192 C3
Wyndale Av. NW9 70 A6
Wyndcliff Rd. SE7 135 H6
Wyndcroft Cl., Enf. 43 H3
Wyndham Cl., Orp. 207 F1
Wyndham Cl., Sutt. 198 D7
Wyndham Cres. N19 92 C3
Wyndham Cres., 143 G6
  Houns.
Wyndham Est. SE5 36 A7
Wyndham Est. SE5 131 J7
Wyndham Ms. W1 15 J2
Wyndham Pl. W1 15 J2
Wyndham Pl. W1 109 J5
Wyndham Rd. E6 98 A7
Wyndham Rd. SE5 131 H7
Wyndham Rd. W13 124 E3
Wyndham Rd., 57 J1
  Barn.
Wyndham Rd., 163 J7
  Kings.T.
Wyndham St. W1 15 J1
Wyndham St. W1 109 J5
Wyndham Yd. W1 15 J2
Wyneham Rd. SE24 152 A5
Wynell Rd. SE23 171 G3
Wynford Pl., Belv. 139 G6
Wynford Rd. N1 10 C1
Wynford Rd. N1 111 F2
Wynford Way SE9 174 C3
Wynlie Gdns., Pnr. 66 B2
Wynn Br. Cl., 79 J1
  Wdf.Grn.
  Chigwell Rd.
Wynndale Rd. E18 79 H1
Wynne Rd. SW9 151 G2
Wynns Av., Sid. 158 A5
Wynnstay Gdns. W8 128 D3
Wynter St. SW11 149 F4
Wynton Gdns. SE25 188 C5
Wynton Pl. W3 106 B6
Wynyard Ter. SE11 34 D3
Wynyard Ter. SE11 131 F5
Wynyatt St. EC1 11 G4
Wyre Gro., Edg. 54 B3
Wyre Gro., Hayes 122 A4
Wyresdale Cres., 104 C3
  Grnf.
Wythburn Pl. W1 15 J4
Wythens Wk. SE9 156 E6
Wythenshawe Rd., 101 G3
  Dag.
Wythes Cl., Brom. 192 C2
Wythes Rd. E16 136 B1
Wythfield Rd. SE9 156 C6
Wyvenhoe Rd., Har. 85 J3
Wyvern Gro., Hayes 121 E7
Wyvil Est. SW8 34 A7
Wyvil Rd. SW8 34 A6
Wyvil Rd. SW8 130 E6
Wyvis St. E14 114 B5

Y

Yabsley St. E14 134 C1
Yalding Rd. SE16 29 H6
Yalding Rd. SE16 132 D3
Yale Cl., Houns. 143 F5
  Bramley Way
Yarborough Rd. 185 G1
  SW19
  Runnymede
Yardley Cl. E4 46 B5
Yardley La. E4 46 B5
Yardley St. WC1 10 E4
Yardley St. WC1 111 G3
Yarmouth Cres. N17 76 E5

Yarmouth Pl. W1 24 D2
Yarnfield Sq. SE15 152 D1
  Clayton Rd.
Yarnton Way SE2 138 D2
Yarnton Way, Erith 139 F3
Yarrow Cres. E6 116 B5
Yateley St. SE18 136 A3
Yates Ct. NW2 90 A6
Yeading Av., Har. 84 E2
Yeading Fork, Hayes 102 C5
Yeading Gdns., 102 B5
  Hayes
Yeading La., Hayes 102 B6
Yeading La., Nthlt. 102 C3
Yeames Cl. W13 104 D6
Yeate St. N1 94 A7
Yeatman Rd. N6 73 J6
Yeats Cl. NW10 88 E6
Yeats Cl. SE13 154 D2
  Eliot Pk.
Yeend Cl., W.Mol. 179 G4
Yeldham Rd. W6 128 A5
Yellow Hammer Ct. 70/71 E2
  NW9
  Eagle Dr.
Yelverton Rd. SW11 149 G2
Yenston Cl., Mord. 184 D6
Yeo St. E3 114 B5
Yeoman Cl. E6 116/117 E7
Yeoman Cl. SE27 169 H3
Yeoman Rd., Nthlt. 85 E7
Yeoman St. SE8 133 H4
Yeomans Acre, Ruis. 66 A6
Yeomans Ms., Islw. 144 B5
  Queensbridge Pk.
Yeoman's Row SW3 23 H6
Yeoman's Row SW3 129 H3
Yeomans Way, Enf. 45 F2
Yeomans Yd. E1 21 G5
Yeoveney Cl., Stai. 139 J3
Yeovil Cl., Orp. 207 H2
Yeovilton Pl., 163 G5
  Kings.T.
Yerbury Rd. N19 92 D3
Yester Dr., Chis. 174 B7
Yester Pk., Chis. 174 C7
Yester Rd., Chis. 174 C7
Yew Cl., Buck.H. 64 A2
Yew Gro. NW2 90 A4
Yew Tree Cl. N21 43 G7
Yew Tree Cl., Well. 158 A1
Yew Tree Cl., 197 E1
  Wor.Pk.
Yew Tree Gdns. 83 E5
  (Chadwell Heath), Rom.
Yew Tree Rd. W12 107 F7
Yew Tree Wk., 143 F5
  Houns.
Yew Wk., Har. 86 B1
Yewdale Cl., Brom. 173 E6
Yewfield Rd. NW10 89 F7
Yewtree Cl. N22 74 C1
Yewtree Rd., Beck. 189 J2
Yoakley Rd. N16 94 B2
Yoke Cl. N7 92/93 E6
  Ewe Cl.
Yolande Gdns. SE9 156 B5
Yonge Pk. N4 93 G3
York Av. SW14 146 C5
York Av. W7 124 B1
York Av., Sid. 175 H2
York Av., Stan. 68 E1
York Br. NW1 8 B5
York Br. NW1 110 A4
York Bldgs. WC2 18 B6
York Cl. E6 116 C6
  Boultwood Rd.
York Cl. W7 124 B1
  York Av.
York Cl., Mord. 184 E4
York Cres., Borwd. 38 D2
York Cres., Loug. 48 B3
York Gate N14 42 E7
York Gate NW1 8 B6
York Gro. SE15 153 F1
York Hill SE27 169 H3
York Hill, Loug. 48 B3
York Hill Est. SE27 169 H3
York Ho., Wem. 87 J4
York Ho. Pl. W8 22 A3
York Ms. NW5 92 B5
  Kentish Town Rd.

York Ms., Ilf. 98 D3
  York Rd.
York Par., Brent. 125 G5
York Pl. SW11 149 G3
York Pl. WC2 18 B6
York Pl., Dag. 101 J6
York Pl., Ilf. 98 D2
  York Rd.
York Ri. NW5 92 B3
York Ri., Orp. 207 H1
York Rd. E4 62 A5
York Rd. E7 97 G6
York Rd. E10 96 C3
York Rd. E17 77 G5
York Rd. N11 58 D6
York Rd. N18 60 E6
York Rd. N21 44 A7
York Rd. SE1 26 D4
York Rd. SE1 131 F2
York Rd. SW11 149 F3
York Rd. SW18 149 F3
York Rd. SW19 167 F6
York Rd. W3 106 C6
York Rd. W5 125 F3
York Rd., Barn. 41 F5
York Rd., Brent. 125 G5
York Rd., Croy. 187 G7
York Rd., Houns. 143 H3
York Rd., Ilf. 98 D3
York Rd., Kings.T. 163 J7
York Rd., Nthwd. 66 A2
York Rd., Rich. 145 J5
  Albert Rd.
York Rd., Sutt. 198 D6
York Rd., Tedd. 162 B4
York Sq. E14 113 H6
York St. W1 16 A1
York St. W1 109 J5
York St., Bark. 117 F1
  Abbey Rd.
York St., Mitch. 186 A7
York St., Twick. 162 D1
York Ter. E. NW1 8 C6
York Ter. E. NW1 110 A4
York Ter. W. NW1 8 B6
York Ter. W. NW1 110 A4
York Way N1 111 E1
York Way N7 92 D6
York Way N20 57 J3
York Way, Borwd. 38 D2
York Way, Chess. 195 H7
York Way, Felt. 161 F3
York Way, St. N1 111 E1
York Way Est. N7 92/93 E6
  York Way
Yorkland Av., Well. 157 J3
Yorkshire Cl. N16 94 B3
Yorkshire Gdns. N18 60 E5
Yorkshire Grey Pl. 91 F4
  NW3
  Heath St.
Yorkshire Grey Yd. 18 C2
  WC1
Yorkshire Rd. E14 113 H6
Yorkshire Rd., Mitch. 186 E5
Yorkton St. E2 13 H2
Yorkton St. E2 112 D2
Young Rd. E16 115 J6
Young St. W8 22 A4
Young St. W8 128 E2
Youngmans Cl., Enf. 43 J1
Young's Bldgs. EC1 12 A5
Youngs Rd., Ilf. 81 G5
Yoxley App., Ilf. 81 F6
Yoxley Dr., Ilf. 81 F6
Yukon Rd. SW12 150 B7
Yuletide Cl. NW10 88 E7
Yunus Khan Cl. E17 78 A5

Z

Zampa Rd. SE16 133 F5
Zander Ct. E2 13 J2
Zangwill Rd. SE3 156 A1
Zealand Av., 120 A7
  West Dr.
Zealand Rd. E3 113 H2
Zennor Rd. SW12 168 C1
Zenoria St. SE22 152 C4
Zermatt Rd., Th.Hth. 187 J4
Zetland St. E14 114 B5
Zion Pl., Th.Hth. 188 A4
Zion Rd., Th.Hth. 188 A4
Zoar St. SE1 27 J1
Zoffany St. N19 92 D2